OPERATION WORLD
21st Century Edition

Updated and Revised

Commendations of Operation World...

'I consider this volume essential for anyone who cares about people around the world.'
Ron Blue, president of CAM International

'Of inestimable value to those of us involved in global missions at the local church level.'
Monroe Brewer, pastor

'Every Christian should be praying for the world outside their own borders. And to do that intelligently, I know of no resource as helpful as *Operation World.*'
Ajith Fernando, National Director, Youth For Christ, Sri Lanka

'More than any other volume, *Operation World* has contributed to the local church member's knowledge of world missions.'
Jim Reapsome, former editor, Evangelical Missions Quarterly

'When I was a mobilizer for TEAM, we received a good number of applications for service where the applicant cited *Operation World* as the means God used to call them into missions.'
Mike Pocock, professor of missions, Dallas Theological Seminary

'*Operation World* is an extremely useful book for everyone who has a personal or professional interest in the missionary work of the church.'
Wade Coggins, former director of the Evangelical Fellowship of Mission Agencies

'The most powerful tool we have in communicating the development of the evangelical movement as a worldwide phenomenon.'
Dwight Gibson, North American director of the World Evangelical Fellowship

'In the best missiological tradition, *Operation World* offers ...information and motivation for prayer. If Paul the Apostle would come today I am sure he would use it!'
Samuel Escobar, Missiologist, Eastern Baptist Theological Seminary

'Has helped tens of thousands of believers develop a balanced perspective, create focused vision, fuel informed prayer, and escalate strategic involvement in global mission.'
T V Thomas, chair of the North American Council of South Asian Christians

'*Operation World,* in its Spanish and Portuguese editions, has radically changed the way Iberoamerican churches understand the world. The "great awakening" our churches are experiencing towards missions could not have been possible without *Operacion Mundo,*'
Carlos Calderon, president of the Iberoamerican Insititute of Cross-Cultural Studies

'Because of the visionary power on every page of the book, we know more than what to pray about. We have learned what to pray toward. Our prayers have been enlarged so that we pray huge, kingdom-sized prayers for entire nations.'
Steve Hawthorne, director of Waymakers

'For those interested in praying for the cause of Christ all around the world, there is no resource to be compared with this. Full of useful facts, *Operation World* is conveniently arranged and focused on the right kinds of things to help Christians understand the church around the world, and to pray faithfully, intelligently, and passionately.'
Don Carson, Professor of New Testament Studies, Trinity Evangelical Divinity School

OPERATION WORLD

21ˢᵗ Century Edition

Updated and Revised

Patrick Johnstone

and

Jason Mandryk

with

Robyn Johnstone

Authentic Lifestyle

International Research Office

WEC International

1st edition	Dorothea Mission	1974
2nd edition	STL	1978
revised	STL	1979
3rd edition	STL	1980
4th edition	STL & WEC International	1986
	reprinted 1986, 1987, 1990 (twice)	
5th edition	OM Publishing	1993
	reprinted with corrections	
	OM Publishing	1995
	reprinted 1997, 1998, 2000	
6th edition	Authentic Lifestyle	2001
	Updated and revised Edition 2005	
	reprinted 2006 (twice)	

Published by Authentic Media
9 Holdom Avenue, Milton Keynes MK1 1QR, UK
and
285 Lynnwood Avenue, Tyrone, GA 30290, USA
OM Authentic Media
Medchal Road, Jeedimetla Village, Secunderabad 500 055, A. P.
www.authenticmedia.co.uk
Authentic Media is a division of Send the Light Ltd., a company limited
by guarantee (registered charity no. 270162)

ISBN 978-1-85078-357-2
ISBN 1-85078-357-8

British Library Cataloguing in Publication Data
A catalogue record for this book is available from the British Library

Typeset by WEC International, Bulstrode, Gerrards Cross, UK
and printed in the United States of America
for the publishers by R.R. Donnelley & Sons, Harrisonburg, Virginia

• CONTENTS •

Preface	**x**
The Ethos of *Operation World*	**xii**
Prayer and world evangelization	**xiii**
How to use *Operation World*	**xv**
The *Operation World* CD	**xvii**
Explanation of the statistics and abbreviations	**xviii**
Prayer Calendar	**xxii**

REGIONS

The World - Introduction and Map	1
Africa - Introduction and Map	19
Americas, The - Introduction and Map	29
Asia - Introduction and Map	39
Europe - Introduction and Map	49
Pacific - Introduction and Map	57

COUNTRIES

1 **BOLD CAPITALS** — Continents including both maps and introductions - see REGIONS.

2 **Bold lower case** — states and territories included in the main body of the book.

3 Lower case — an alternative or commonly used name. The name used in the book follows in bold type.

4 *Lower case italics* — either a name no longer used or a territory that has been absorbed by the state which follows it in bold.

Name	**Page**		
Afghanistan	61	**Benin**	106
Albania	63	**Bermuda**	109
Algeria	66	**Bhutan**	110
American Samoa	69	**Bolivia**	111
Andorra	70	**Bosnia**	115
Angola	71	**Botswana**	117
Anguilla	74	*Bougainville* see under	
Antigua & Barbuda	75	**Papua New Guinea**	
Argentina	76	**Brazil**	119
Armenia	79	Britain see **United Kingdom**	
Aruba	82	**British Indian Ocean Territory**	124
Australia	83	**British Virgin Islands**	125
Austria	86	**Brunei**	126
Azerbaijan	89	**Bulgaria**	127
Bahamas, The	91	**Burkina Faso**	131
Bahrain	92	*Burma* now **Myanmar**	
Bangladesh	94	**Burundi**	134
Barbados	98	*Byelorussia* see **Belarus**	
Belarus	99	**Cambodia**	137
Belau see **Palau**		**Cameroon**	140
Belgium	101	**Canada**	143
Belize	104	**Canary Islands** see under **Spain**	
		Cape Verde Islands	147
		CARIBBEAN see **AMERICAS, THE**	

gratis

101584

Caroline Islands see **Micronesia**
Cayman Islands 149
Central African Republic 149
Chad 152
Channel Islands see under
    United Kingdom
Chile 155
China, People's Republic of 159
China, Hong Kong 181
China, Macau 184
China, Taiwan 186
Christmas Island see under **Australia**
Cocos (Keeling) Island
    see under Australia
Colombia 189
Comoros 193
Congo (Brazzaville) 195
Congo–DRC (Kinshasa) 197
Cook Islands 203
Costa Rica 205
Côte d'Ivoire 208
Croatia 212
Cuba 214
Cyprus 217
Czech Republic 219
Czechoslovakia now **Czech Republic**
    and **Slovakia**
Denmark 223
Djibouti 224
Dominica 226
Dominican Republic 227
East Germany see **Germany**
East Timor see **Timor Lorosae**
Eastern Samoa see **American Samoa**
Ecuador 230
Egypt 233
Eire see **Ireland**
El Salvador 236
England see **United Kingdom**
Equatorial Guinea 238
Eritrea 240
Estonia 242
Ethiopia 243
EURASIA see EUROPE and ASIA
Faeroe Islands 247
Falkland Islands 248
Fiji 249
Finland 252
France 254
French Guiana 259
French Polynesia 261
Gabon 262
Gambia, The 265
Gaza Strip see **Palestine**
Georgia 267
Germany 269
Ghana 274

Gibraltar 278
Gilbert Islands see **Kiribati**
Great Britain see **United Kingdom**
Greece 279
Greenland 282
Grenada 283
Guadeloupe 284
Guam 286
Guatemala 287
Guinea 290
Guinea-Bissau 293
Guyana 296
Haiti 298
Holland see **Netherlands**
Holy See, The (Vatican City State) 301
Honduras 302
Hong Kong see **China, Hong Kong**
Hungary 304
Iceland 307
India 309
Indonesia 338
Iran 352
Iraq 355
Ireland 359
Ireland, Northern see under
    United Kingdom
Irian Jaya now **[West] Papua** under
    Indonesia
Isle of Man see under **United Kingdom**
Israel 361
Italy 364
Ivory Coast see **Côte d'Ivoire**
Jamaica 368
Jan Mayen Islands see under **Norway**
Japan 370
Johnston Island see under **Guam**
Jordan 375
Kampuchea now **Cambodia**
Kashmir see **India** and **Pakistan**
Kazakhstan 377
Kenya 380
Kirgizia now **Kyrgyzstan**
Kiribati 384
Korea, Democratic People's
    Republic of (North) 385
Korea, Republic of (South) 386
Kosovo see under **Yugoslavia**
Kuwait 390
Kyrgyzstan 392
Laos 395
LATIN AMERICA see AMERICAS, THE
Latvia 397
Lebanon 399
Leeward Islands see **Anguilla, Antigua &**
    Barbuda, St Kitts, etc.
Lesotho 403
Liberia 405

CONTENTS   vi

Libya 408
Liechtenstein 410
Lithuania 411
Luxembourg 413
Macau see **China, Macau**
Macedonia 414
Madagascar 416
Malawi 419
Malaysia 422
Maldives 427
Mali 428
Malta 431
Malvinas, Islas see **Falkand Islands**
Marshall Islands see under **Micronesia**
Martinique 432
Mauritania 434
Mauritius 436
Mayotte see **Comoros Islands**
Mexico 438
Micronesia, Federated States of 443
MIDDLE EAST see **ASIA** and **AFRICA**
Midway Island see under **Guam**
Moldova (Moldavia) 448
Monaco 450
Mongolia 451
Montenegro see **Yugoslavia** (Serbia and
   Montenegro)
Montserrat 454
Morocco 455
Mozambique 458
Myanmar 462
Namibia 465
Nauru 468
Nepal 469
Netherlands 473
Netherlands Antilles 476
New Caledonia 478
New Guinea see **Papua New Guinea** and
   [West] Papua under **Indonesia**
New Zealand 479
Nicaragua 482
Niger 485
Nigeria 487
Niue see under **Cook Islands**
Norfolk Island see under **Australia**
NORTH AMERICA see **AMERICAS, THE**
North Korea see **Korea, Democratic**
   People's Republic of
Northern Cyprus see **Cyprus**
Northern Mariana Islands see under
   Micronesia
Norway 496
Oman 498
Pakistan 500
Palau see under **Micronesia**
Palestine 504
Panama 506

Papua New Guinea 509
Paraguay 513
Peru 516
Philippines 520
Pitcairn Island see under **Cook Islands**
Poland 526
Portugal 528
Puerto Rico 531
Qatar 532
Réunion 534
Romania 535
Russia 539
Rwanda 550
Sahara, Western see under **Morocco**
Samoa 553
San Marino 554
São Tomé & Príncipe 555
Saudi Arabia 556
Scotland see under **United Kingdom**
Senegal 558
Serbia and Montenegro see **Yugoslavia**
Seychelles 561
Sierra Leone 563
Singapore 566
Slovakia 569
Slovenia 571
Solomon Islands 572
Somalia 574
Somaliland see **Somalia**
South Africa 576
SOUTH AMERICA see **AMERICAS, THE**
South Korea see **Korea, Republic of**
Soviet Union see separate states
Spain 582
Spanish North Africa see **Spain**
Spanish Sahara see **Western Sahara**
   under **Morocco**
Sri Lanka 586
St Helena 591
St Kitts & Nevis 592
St Lucia 593
St Pierre & Miquelon 594
St Vincent 595
Sudan 596
Suriname 600
Svalbard Islands see under **Norway**
Swaziland 602
Sweden 605
Switzerland 607
Syria 610
Taiwan see **China, Taiwan**
Tajikistan 612
Tanzania 615
Thailand 618
Tibet see under **China, People's**
   Republic of
Timor Leste (Timor Lorosae) 622

Togo   624
Tokelau see under **Cook Islands**
Tonga   627
Trinidad & Tobago   629
Tunisia   631
Turkey   633
Turkmenistan   637
Turks & Caicos Islands   639
Tuvalu   640
UAE see **United Arab Emirates**
Uganda   641
UK see **United Kingdom**
Ukraine   644
Union of Soviet Socialist Republics
    see separate states
United Arab Emirates   647
United Kingdom of Great Britain
    and Northern Ireland   649
United States of America   657
Uruguay   664
US Virgin Islands see **Virgin Islands**
    of the USA
USA see **United States of America**
USSR see separate states
Uzbekistan   666
Vanuatu   670
Vatican City State see **Holy See, The**
Venezuela   671
Vietnam   675
Virgin Islands see **British Virgin Islands**
    and **Virgin Islands of the USA**
Virgin Islands of the USA   678

Wake Island see under **Guam**
Wallis and Futuna Islands   679
Wales see under **United Kingdom**
West Bank see **Palestine**
Western Sahara see under **Morocco**
Western Samoa see **Samoa**
Windward Islands see **Dominica,**
    Grenada, St Lucia, etc.
Yemen   680
Yemen, North see **Yemen**
Yemen, South (Aden) see **Yemen**
Yugoslavia   682
Zaire see **Congo-DRC**
Zambia   685
Zimbabwe   688

Note:

1. Territories without permanent inhabitants have not been listed — including Antarctica.

2. States under the occupation or jurisdiction of other states are included under the latter. For instance, the Western Sahara is under Morocco; Hong Kong is under China; Kosovo is under Yugoslavia. This is to represent the *de facto* situation and is not an expression of a political opinion.

SPECIALIZED MINISTRIES

These are included in the prayer calendar for the last three weeks of December. The following have been selected from the many ministries and specific outreaches which operate worldwide.

Name	Page
Audio Cassette Tape Ministries	693
Christian Radio	694
Christian Television	695
The *JESUS* film	696
The Internet	696
Bible Societies and Bible Translation	698
Christian Literature	699
Theological Education by Extension	700
Bible Correspondence Courses	701
Relief and Development	701
Medical Mission Work	702
Missionary Aviation	703

Maritime Ministry   704
Christian Tentmakers   705
Short-Term Workers   706
Student Ministries   706
Ministry to Children   707
Outreach to Sects or Cults   709
Urban Evangelization   710
International Cooperation   711
Operation World   712
The Lord's Return   713

APPENDICES

1 Leaders of the World's Nations   715
2 Further prayer information
    a) Publications   720
    b) Internet websites   722
    c) International prayer networks   730
3 Agencies (selected)
    a) Interdenominational Inter-mission Agencies   731
    b) Mission agency addresses and websites 733
    c) Mission agency statistics   743
4 The World's Missionary Force   747
5 Abbreviations   753
6 Definitions   755
7 *Operation World* database   760
8 Statistical Sources   763
9 Other related sources   765

INDICES

Persecution   222
Peoples   767
Places   788

• PREFACE •

We have many emotions as we prayerfully send this edition to the printers!

• **Relief** that we completed such a massive project with its global and eternal implications.

• **Worship to God** for His grace, enabling and guiding in its compilation.

• **Thankfulness** to all past and present servants of the Lord who have contributed to making Operation World into the prayer and mobilization tool that it has become.

• **Anticipation** for the thousands of users who will impact the world through their intercession and commitment to the fulfilment of the Great Commission and its specific challenges for us in the 21st Century.

Such a book cannot be produced by one person alone. It is only the tip of a pyramid made of layers of foundations and building blocks laid by others. Only a few of this "apostolic succession" of people and events can be mentioned here.

1792 **William Carey**'s vision for a lost world led to his writing the book *An Enquiry into the Obligation of Christians to Use Means for the Conversion of the Heathens*. This was the first global survey ever printed. His life and writing has inspired me.

1900 **Dr Andrew Murray**, that great man of God in South Africa, challenged a sleeping Church in his book, *The Key to the Missionary Problem*, to hold **Weeks of Prayer for the World.**

1943 **Hans von Staden** was called of God to minister in the rapidly developing urban slums of Southern Africa. The Dorothea Mission, under his leadership, developed with a passion for evangelism and a strong emphasis on prayer, faith and vision for world evangelization. This became my heritage when I joined the work in 1962.

1962 **Weeks of Prayer for the World** began, and over the years probably 100 or so of these were held in Africa and Europe. It was my early involvement in these which impelled me into making maps and gathering information that ordinary African Christians could understand and turn into intercession.

1964 The first *Operation World* was proposed by Hans von Staden, who also suggested the title. It was a little booklet, covering 30 countries with basic information and some prayer items for use in the Weeks of Prayer.

1968 **Jill Amsden** became my wife, co-worker and then mother of our three children. She was a wonderful support in every way, and ultimately became the author of a children's equivalent of *Operation World* entitled *You Can Change the World*. She wrote this while ill with cancer, and completed the text of that remarkable book just before she died in 1992. **Daphne Spraggett** prepared the book for print and then wrote a second volume. Daphne has re-worked both books to produce a combined new volume entitled *Window on the World* which is being published simultaneously with this edition.

1974 The first **global** *Operation World*. When I was challenged in 1970 to re-write it, I rashly said that any future edition would need to cover the world. I did not understand the enormity of the task! The work began, using odd moments in a busy itinerant ministry of team evangelism and Bible translation in Zimbabwe (then Rhodesia). My office was the back of a van, or church vestries in towns and cities of that land. Two cardboard boxes served as a filing cabinet. My major problems were lack of any good missiological libraries and increasing postal isolation from the outside world due to sanctions imposed on Rhodesia. This limited edition was printed by the Dorothea Mission Press.

1975 **Dr Ralph Winter** arranged for its re-publication by the William Carey Library under the title *World Handbook for the World Christian*. This was a courageous step, for other publishers turned it down as "unmarketable". We reckon now that, in all six editions and in over 14 languages, over 2 million copies had been printed by 2004.

1976 **George Verwer** of **Operation Mobilization** became involved. He pressed for a new edition which we completed in 1978. This was the first edition published by **STL** (now

Paternoster Publishing). George has ever since remained one of the most enthusiastic distributors of *Operation World*.

1977 **Dave Hicks**, then OM leader of the ship MV Logos (now President of Bethany Fellowship), used the information in *Operation World* to compile the first set of prayer cards covering 52 needy nations – a ministry which multiplied and spread around the world and in over 20 languages. This also led to a year's ministry for our family on that ship in Asia and the Pacific during 1979.

1978 **Other language editions of *Operation World*** developed out of the 1978 edition. Editions have been published in German, French, Spanish, Portuguese, Korean and one edition in another 8-10 languages. These versions have played a significant role in the burgeoning missions movement in the non-English-speaking world.

1979 **WEC International.** Jill and I were released by the Dorothea Mission and commenced our ministry as International Directors for Research in WEC. This has been a fulfilling and exciting ministry as part of the leadership of a large pioneer church planting mission with workers from all continents. These years have been a time of restructuring, rapid change, growth and advances into pioneer areas. It was in this context that the 1986 and 1993 editions of *Operation World* were written. Our WEC colleagues were patient with us and released us from some responsibilities in order that we complete these. During this time we developed our research office with its large holdings of global information, maps, databases and also tools for envisioning the Church.

1995 **Robyn Erwin** became my wife and stands with me in all the demands of public ministry and as co-worker in the writing of this present edition. **Jason Mandryk,** a WEC missionary from Canada, joined us and also became a co-author. Without them this volume would never have been completed.

1998 *The Church is Bigger than You Think* was published by Christian Focus Publications. Into that volume I could pour my heart concerns and burden in a way not possible in *Operation World*. It is a necessary companion to the latter and helped to define much of the emphasis in my public ministry to motivate and equip the body of Christ for world evangelization. A new edition of this book incorporating the new statistics and further insights is planned for late 2001.

2001 The **Sixth Edition** owes much to many and as authors we thank:

> **Our extended IRO Team** – **Terrie Jackson**'s data entry, **Lee Nicholson**'s copy editing and typesetting, **Justine Garner**'s determined pursuit of corrections to the text and to addresses of agencies, **Michael Jaffarian**'s assembling of two appendices, **Glenn Myers**' compilation of the Index, **Marko Jauhiainen**'s care for our computers, etc.

> **Maurice Manktelow** who delivered us from a programming crisis and over three years re-wrote our essential programmes and refined them at a distance of 300 km.

> **Chris Lawther, John Longridge** and **Jonathan Manktelow** who provided expert and timely advice on design, layout, typesetting and the graphs and charts.

> **Our Publishers (and team)**, especially for the gracious ministry of **Jeremy Mudditt** and **Pieter Kwant** in ensuring that the book could be printed, published and marketed.

> **The Global Mapping International Team** who have prepared the companion CD version and also **Loren Muehlius** who prepared our maps.

> **The thousands of friends, advisers and informants** who gave of their time to give us the needed information, corrections, etc.

> **The many who prayed** for us over this intense and gruelling period of preparation.

June 2001 As we send this book out for publication we pray fervently that the Lord Jesus Christ might be glorified, the Church mobilized and world evangelization furthered. To Him alone be the praise, glory and victory in the spiritual battles ahead of us.

February 2004. The first copies of the Sixth edition were sold on 8th September 2001. Three days later our world was changed forever by the devastating surprise attack of Al Qaeda terrorists on the USA. From this day history has flowed along a new channel, and we have adapted the text of many countries in recognition of this.

Many people have also sent in valuable improvements and corrections. These we have been able to include in this revision. Over 80 countries have been either corrected or updated. These revisions are indicated in the Country map box.

2004.   Patrick and Robyn hand over *Operation World* to Jason Mandryk who will lead the team for the seventh edition, God willing, later in this decade.

Patrick and Robyn Johnstone and Jason Mandryk
WEC International
Gerrards Cross,
Bucks SL9 8SZ
England
[www.operationworld.org]

• THE ETHOS OF *OPERATION WORLD* •

We have made fundamental assumptions in compiling this book. We realize that we cannot satisfy all readers, but we trust that we have been sensitive to other theological and political points of view. However, our own perspectives inevitably influence the selection of material and opinions expressed, and for these we must accept responsibility.

All views here expressed are our own and not necessarily those of the publishers or of any organization mentioned in this book. We value constructive advice for future revisions. Please obtain current email addresses at our website. We made the following decisions:

1 **Readership**. We are writing for Bible-believing Christians who want to obey the last great command of the Lord Jesus by evangelizing the world. This means primarily evangelical Christians (which broadly means Protestant, Pentecostal, Charismatic and Independent Christians), though we realize there are many outside these categories who use *Operation World*. We trust that we have been sensitive enough to enable this book to be used more widely yet without compromising our own theological position.

2 **Theology**. As evangelical believers, we took a central position in more controversial issues that perplex Evangelicals, such as church government, baptism, the sovereignty of God, the work of the Holy Spirit and social involvement. The perceptive reader will, no doubt, see an unintended bias that reflects the authors' own views.

3 **Politics**. We are Western Christians and cannot divorce ourselves completely from the society of which we are a part. We are also global Christians, so have sought as far as possible to write about each country with sensitivity as if we were of that country – even if we have had to speak to the endemic wrongs of the nation or the Church. How far does one condone perceived wrong for the sake of local sensitivities and the continuing ministry of the Lord's servants? Our aim here was for balance, but we have probably failed many times. Our desire is that the book be of global value.

4 **Time validity**. The accelerating rate of change in the world can quickly date information. We have covered relevant events to April 2001 and expect this edition to be valid through the first decade of the 21st Century. We trust that by then a new team might be in place to prepare another edition should this be God's will. Its design and handling of information is likely to be different, but with the same passion and burden.

5 **An emphasis on the Church**. Early editions were rightly criticized for over-emphasizing mission agencies and the contribution of missionaries. We sought to rectify this, but it is important to realize that it is often these very agencies that are the best communicators of prayer information, hence the system of highlighting mission initials of those whose addresses are given in Appendix 3. In these later editions we have centred our information on the body of Christ in each country.

6 **The selection of agencies mentioned** is not intended to be a mark of validation or rejection. We have sought to draw attention to some having international and interdenominational interest to a wider spectrum of English-speaking readers. Hopefully, the other language versions will give greater place to agencies based in their own language areas. There is much more information on other agencies on the CD version of the book.

7 **The burden for prayer**. Our longing is that the book will be seen as a tool for prayer. The spiritual tone and vision that expresses the heart of our heavenly Father is what should be in the forefront. All other issues *must* be secondary.

Many have requested that the contents of this book be made available on the Internet. We have consistently refused this request for the following reasons:

Security. Many opposed to the gospel would misuse the contents of the book if it were so readily available. We are investigating creative ways of using the Internet on our website [www.operationworld.org].

Cost. The income from sales of *Operation World* is used primarily to seed the production of subsequent volumes.

• PRAYER AND WORLD EVANGELIZATION •

The book in your hands weighs less than one kilogram, yet if all the desires, requests and goals expressed in it were to be implemented it would radically change the nations of this world. Wars would be ended, ethnic hatreds tamed, politicians become honest, ecological restoration begun, global warming and AIDS halted, poverty reduced. The Church of the Lord Jesus Christ would be provided with godly leaders, it would be renewed, revived, united in vision, mobilized for mission and readied for the return of its Head. Jesus would return with the world evangelized and the Church complete! That is the wish. How much of the earthly and how quickly the eternal agendas would be achieved depends on ONE activity – prayer in the name of Jesus to a loving, sovereign Father.

How can we weak, frail, puny creatures speak to our omnipotent Creator to make a difference to our world? It is a breath-taking mystery. A picture comes to my mind of a strange European custom at the launch of a ship. Some VIP is invited to "launch" a ship. The mighty ship lies on its slipway where it was constructed awaiting the VIP to break a bottle of wine on its bows and give it the name it will bear. Once done the ropes and cables restraining the ship are loosed by unseen hands and the ship majestically slides off to begin its career on water. There are similarities to intercession. The proclamation of the ship's name by the VIP is an important action, but the ship could be launched without it. It is a mystery that our loving Father has somehow limited His omnipotence to teaming up with His redeemed people so that His actions in the world are inextricably linked with prayer.

Hans von Staden, the man of God used to instigate and name *Operation World*, often quoted these words:

> When man works, man works;
> when man prays, God works.

The Publishers in designing the cover proposed using the latter half of this quote on the cover with good reason. The ministry of the children of God is not doing but praying, not strategizing, but prostrate before God seeking His will, not clever stratagems for manipulating people and events but trusting in God who moves in the hearts of even His most implacable enemies. Through prayer Nebuchadnezzar, and today's dictators get converted, Manassah and today's persecutors repent and kingdoms of Babylon and Iron Curtains are torn down. We do not engage in ministry and pray for God's blessing on it, prayer IS the ministry from which all other ministries must flow.

Psalm 2 reveals the Father's Great Commission to His Son and how the destiny of nations is tied in with their rejection of or submission to His Kingly Son. Look at the command and promises of Psalm 2:8.

> Ask of Me, and I will make the nations your heritage,
> and the ends of the earth your possession.
> You shall break them with a rod of iron,
> and dash them in pieces like a potter's vessel.

Surely this was very much in the forefront in Jesus' prayer life when He was offered the kingdoms of this world by Satan and when He approached His crucifixion. Only this gave meaning to the immense sacrifice He was to make for the redemption of the nations. He asked for them and is now receiving the reward of His sufferings as millions become part of His Church from every nation and nearly every people on earth. He will soon also mete out stern, but just judgement on those who rejected Him.

Dare we apply this command and these promises to ourselves? We can and for this we have scriptural warrant. John wrote these astonishing words to the Church in Thyatira in Revelation 2:26:

> He who conquers and keeps my works to the end,
> I will give him power over the nations,
> and he shall rule them with a rod of iron,
> as when earthen pots are broken in pieces.

John applies the more unlikely section of the Psalm 2 passage to believers. The power over the nations is not that of the Constantinian distortion of Christianity where politics and human armanents became the preferred weapons of the Church but rather that of reigning with Christ in the Heavenlies as intercessor-rulers who impact our world.

God spoke to me from Psalm 2:8 as a young Christian at university in Bristol, England. I heard for the first time of the work of the Dorothea Mission in the urban slums of Southern Africa. I *knew* that God was speaking to me that this was His will for me, but I asked the Lord for scriptural confirmation, and it was this passage which spoke to me – South Africa was, for me, one of the ends of the earth for which I could ask. I did not realize at the time that this "asking for the nations" would actually define a large part of my ministry for the next 40 years in successive editions of *Operation World*! Then when God spoke to Jill and me about moving from Africa to a new global ministry, I again felt moved emotionally that this was right for us, but wanted further objective confirmation. Again this passage leapt to my mind. It was as if God was saying, "I called you to one end of the earth, but now I am giving you all the ends!".

The following pages give something of the needs and challenges of our needy, sin-sick, doomed world. The nations are there for the asking. God is calling you and me into the ministry of intercession for them. Through these prayers much will happen – above all we could ask or expect. In this edition we have added a new feature of giving a few answers to prayers requested in earlier editions for which there has been some answer. Daniel heard God's voice in Daniel 7:27 (RSV):

> The kingdom and the dominion and the greatness
> of the kingdoms under the whole heaven shall be given
> to the people of the saints of the Most High;
> their kingdom shall be an everlasting kingdom,
> and all dominions shall serve and obey **them.**

The cost is great, for these words were preceded in verse 21-22 by:

> As I looked, this horn made war with the saints, and prevailed over them,
> until the Ancient of Days came,
> and judgement was given for the saints of the Most High,
> and the time came when the saints received the kingdom.

We have plenty of opposition in the heavenlies and from human powers and persecutors. The enemy will seek to frighten us with these and dangle allurements to distract us from the vision of a heavenly, eternal kingdom filled with people from every race, tribe, people and tongue. Yet Jesus offers you a share in his reign. We may look up to Him in agony at times, but see your true position looking down with Him exercising the authority bequeathed to you by Him in the Great Commission He has given to you and every Christian. May you become an intercessor with a world vision that prays Satan-defeating, kingdom-taking, people-reaching, captive-releasing, revival-giving, Christ-glorifying prayers.

Prayer not only changes people, situations and even the course of history, but also those who pray! It is dangerous for the enemy and also 'dangerous' for you. There is a price to pay to be a person who stands in the gap between fallen man and a righteous God. That price may mean becoming an answer to your own prayers in giving time, finances and even going out as a witness in your Jerusalem (where you now live), your Judea (your own country), your Samaria (the other ethnic groups in your own country) or even to the ends of the earth. Our prayer is that many will give their whole lives for this most noble of causes – to obey Jesus' last command in making disciples of all nations and so ready the Church and the world for the grand climax of His glorious return.

Patrick Johnstone

• HOW TO USE *OPERATION WORLD* •

This book is written for two main purposes:

1 **To inform for prayer**. The layout of this book is in the form of a prayer diary, with a section of prayer requests assigned for each day of the year. A new feature in this edition is a section, for most countries, on answers to prayer over the past decade. A two page prayer calendar is given on p. xxii in which we apportion out the year by continent and country.

2 **To mobilize for witness**. Information and relevant statistics are given to channel that witness to the least reached parts and peoples of our world. For many Christians this book is their only source of global information. Earlier editions have become an essential resource for the growing missions movement around the world — in a particular way this has been true of the non-English editions.

To enhance its usefulness, we offer some suggestions which may help you to use this book appropriately and effectively:

In private

1 **Pray through the book using the running calendar**, perhaps taking *only one or two items* which the Holy Spirit lays on your heart. Why not mark items covered in prayer and then later make note of God's answers. *Those of special significance are indicated by a highlighted prayer number - note the number at the beginning of this paragraph.*

2 **Keep the book near your television, radio or newspaper**. When news comes of major events in a far-off land, find out the spiritual dimensions and turn secular news into spiritual dynamite.

3 **Use it together with prayer letters, mission magazines and Internet websites**. Often the wider context is missing. This book will give depth and perspective.

In the family

1 **Read a small section at the meal table** and pray for the country of the day. Why not use the children's versions (*You Can Change the World* or rewritten version entitled *Window on the World*)? They are designed as a beautiful family prayer diary.

2 Use the book as a source of informative fun and quiz games.

In your church

Missions and prayer for the world should be at the heart of every fellowship. *Operation World* can help to give praise and prayer points that stimulate this.

1 **Church services.** Use prayer items in the intercessory period in worship services.

2 **Prayer meetings.** Wise use of the information in this book can stimulate more informed prayer for the world and for your mission outreach. We have also produced numerous maps and diagrams on overhead transparencies and in electronic format which may help in this. Please refer to the last pages in the book which tell how you may obtain these.

3 **Church bulletins and magazines.** Use quotes from relevant sections of the book in your church publications to gain interest and stimulate prayer. Please quote the source!

In teaching on missions

Some Bible schools have made praying through the book a core component of their course. Instructors have used it for teaching on missions — many Christians have been led into specific missionary service as a result.

For Christian Research

Operation World contains only a small proportion of the large amount of text and statistics assembled in its production. Some of this information will be available on the companion CD which may be used for the following:

1 **Powerful search tools** to locate and bring together linked information for exporting and printing.

2 **Access to the databases** from which our statistics and sources for the book were selected, by means of hot links. These include:

a) The world's denominations. Data on the number of congregations, membership, affiliated Christians and, where known, attendances for 6,355 specific denominations and records referring to a total of 30,000 or so denominations covering the period 1960-2000. Every figure is sourced, or shown as estimated or derived.

b) The religions of the world between 1900 and 2025 (projected) showing the astonishing changes in religious affiliation over that period for every country.

c) The mission agencies and missionaries of the world and statistics gathered by field and/or region (where information may be sensitive) covering the period 1980-2000. Reports show the number of missionaries to and from nearly every country of the world and information on 3,400 mission agencies, and their 16,336 mission fields.

d) Country information with a wider range of categories than we could use in the book.

3 **Graphics and maps.** All graphics and maps used in *Operation World* but in full colour together with graphics used in the book *The Church is Bigger Than You Think*. Please refer to the back of this book for more details.

For use in prayer days, conferences, concerts of prayer, prayer journeys, etc.

The original purpose of this book was to provide fuel for prayer conferences for the world. Here are a few guidelines for prayer session leaders:

1 **Be brief**. The people are gathered to *pray* and not to be impressed by the amount of information presented. Only a quarter to one-third of the time should be set aside for reporting on the need.

2 **Be personal**. We have deliberately refrained from mentioning individuals, but rather have given the overall situation in a country. Personal information on individual workers and specific situations will give focus to the prayer time.

3 **Be selective**. Too many facts will not be retained unless they are written down. Rather select those items for prayer that will burden believers long after the meeting.

4 **Be careful with statistics**. Too many figures make any report very dull! This is why the statistical sections are in a smaller type. Only choose those statistics that specifically apply to the prayer items you mention. The many figures are given so that you may have the resources you might need.

5 **Be dependent on the leading of the Holy Spirit**. The burdens imparted by Him will inspire others to pray in the Spirit and move them into God's will for their lives. This could mean commitment in intercession, financial giving, or going to a particular area or people for which prayer has been made.

Other Resources

Operation Mobilization has produced a new set of prayer cards, a global map and various other items based on the information in this edition. Order these through the address for OM Publishing at the front of this book. See Appendix 9 for more details.

Also in Appendix 9 is a range of materials that supplement or enhance the information in this book.

The ***Operation World*** CD is both a great deal more and (in a good way) less than the book, all designed to enhance your use of this invaluable prayer resource.

The "more" is more information, made more useful:

- **Do in-depth analysis of the church and missions situation** – with a tremendous amount of additional information and statistics on every country. The WEC International Research Office collects vastly more data than appears in the ***Operation World*** book. On the CD, much of this additional data has been formatted into additional reports and tables for you. If you want to go still deeper, Windows users may view the full research database (with some data altered for security reasons) utilizing the same software as was used to develop the book. You may also analyze the data using your own database manager or spreadsheet (incorporating portions of the data into your own applications), since the database is available as individual .dbf tables.

- **Quickly find all occurrences of any desired word or phrase.** Similar to a computer concordance, the CD is fully word-searchable using a Java-based search engine that works within the web browser* on both Mac and Windows.

- **Create your own customized versions of *Operation World* text.** Within generous limits, you may "copy and paste" portions of the text and graphics into other documents; reformat, print and distribute for Christian ministry use.

- **Display and print larger, full-color versions of the maps and charts.** All the maps and charts in this book have been recreated in larger, full-color formats on the CD. These, as well as additional country maps and flags of each country, can be easily printed onto paper or overhead transparency film, or incorporated into your own computer slideshow or other graphics applications.

- **Access broader information.** The CD includes additional Web links not found in the book. If you have an Internet connection, you can simply click on any link to go to the referenced websites for each country.

The "less" is less bulk, less hassle:

- **Start each day with a simple daily summary,** automatically opened when the CD starts up, giving you today's prayer requests along with background information. Click on any item in the summary to take you to the greater detail in the full ***Operation World*** text.

- **Take it with you wherever you go.** The CD can be easily shipped or carried internationally (a single CD is far smaller than the printed book). And you may even load the entire ***Operation World*** CD onto your laptop computer to travel with you.*

- **So easy to use!** If you've ever used the World Wide Web, you already know how to use the ***Operation World*** CD. The content is viewed using popular Web browser software (included on the CD).

If a copy of the CD did not accompany this book, you may order the CD alone, Product Code OPW16, published by Paternoster Lifestyle (an imprint of Paternoster Publishing), from the same organisation that sold you this book. If they are unable to supply the CD, see the ***Operation World*** website at www.operationworld.org for additional distributors, or contact Paternoster at PO Box 300, Kingstown Broadway, Carlisle, Cumbria, CA3 0QS, UK. Tel. (44) 01228 512512. Fax. (44) 01228 593388, for assistance in locating a vendor.

* Expected system requirements: PC with Windows 95 or above Macintosh PowerPC with Microsoft® Internet Explorer 4.0 or above (IE 5.5 included on CD) or Netscape Navigator 4.0 or above. Word search function requires substantial additional memory and disk space beyond minimum needed for Web browser. Copying full CD to disk will require approximately 400 MB disk space. Browser-based content and Java-based search engine are expected to work with other browsers and operating systems, but have not been tested in such environments. See www.operationworld.org for more detailed system requirements.

• EXPLANATION OF THE STATISTICS AND ABBREVIATIONS •

The purpose of this book is to inspire God's people to prayer and action to change our world. Statistics are an important support for this in providing solid factual basis for action. In this we believe we are entirely scriptural. We follow in the footsteps of Moses, Joshua, Ezekiel, Luke and John in giving meticulous and carefully compiled statistics.

This book's description of each region and country is divided into two parts:
1 The two columns of statistical background information.
2 The specific items for praise and prayer.

The statistics are included as background to the prayer information, hence the difference in type size and font as well as the background tinting.

A brief explanation of their significance is given below. A fuller explanation of the sources and how these figures were handled is given in appendices 7 and 8.

Availability, consistency and accuracy of secular, religious and Christian statistics vary enormously from country to country and among denominations. Some denominations do not even keep statistics. Inadequate sources, varying dates of publication and our further editing and compiling of the statistics all add to the margin of error. We have used the most recent and reliable information available. We therefore plead for the sympathy of the reader for any errors or discrepancies discovered. Please send any corrections for inclusion in future editions to the WEC Research Office address on p. 765 or to those given at the *Operation World* website: [www.operationworld.org].

Our prayer is that these statistics may present a reasonably balanced account of what God is doing in our world, and the extent of the unfinished task. Only in the *World Christian Encyclopedia* and in *Operation World* can such a complete body of data relating to world evangelization be found – with all their deficiencies.

On the CD version of the book (see p. xvii) is a complete set of data we gathered covering:
1 **Country data** (secular statistics on populations, economy, education, health, etc.)
2 **Religions data** with statistics covering the period 1900-2025.
3 **Denominational data** with statistics covering the period 1960-2000.
4 **Mission agency data** with non-sensitive information on bases, fields and numbers of workers. Data for sensitive countries is stored in regional and global categories.
5 **Flat file reports** may be generated from the above, giving summaries and totals.

All the information is sourced. Where estimates or derivations have been made from existing data, this is indicated. We do not have a unique peoples or languages database. These may be found respectively in the 2001 *World Christian Encyclopedia*, Volume 2 and in the WBT Ethnologue of 2001 — *Operation World* research has had significant input into both of these publications.

Below is an explanation of how each category of statistics is handled in the order and format used throughout the book.

Our statistical base date is June 2000. Most of the statistics used are compiled from data gathered between 1996 and 2001. The textual information is valid for May 2001.

GEOGRAPHY

Area. Given in square kilometres, the area does not imply approval or disapproval of the political status quo of disputed territories but is a reflection of the actual situation in May 2001. In this category are such areas as the Western Sahara (included under Morocco) and the Falkland Islands (Islas Malvinas — included as a British dependent territory).

Population. Figures given are for 2000, 2010 and 2025. These figures are not rounded but are exact quotes of estimates from the 1998 UN population database. Average annual growth rates are given in the second column, and population density in people/sq.km is given in the third column rounded to the nearest whole number.

Capitals and Cities. Statistics were derived from a number of sources. As far as possible, the conurbation figure is given and not just the population that may live within specific municipal boundaries. The figures given are often significantly higher than those officially quoted. Most world-class cities are mentioned by name, i.e. those with populations that exceed one million.

PEOPLES
The ethnic diversity is shown in a manner considered the most helpful for the reader.

1 **Major groupings of peoples** are given in larger type as a percentage of the country's total population. The larger ethnic groups within those groupings are given in absolute numbers in smaller type, and are valid for June 2000. Subsets of peoples are indented but any percentage figure is in relation to the national population.

2 **Smaller peoples** are not mentioned by name unless there is a particular challenge or point of wider interest.

3 **The total number of ethno-linguistic peoples** given in the country text is derived from our own sources where known or appropriate. Those in the regional tables (pages 20-81) are derived from the 2001 *World Christian Encyclopedia* and from the AD2000 Joshua Project List of 1997. In both sets of tallies, the totals represent the sum total of identifiable ethno-linguistic peoples within a country that fit the parameters of the respective lists. For instance, the Tamil are counted 33 times in the global totals because Tamil communities exist in at least 28 countries, likewise the Kurds 46 times (because of both country and language differences).

4 **Refugees and temporarily resident communities** are often listed but not always included in national percentages.

Language/Literacy. The highest publicized figure for **literacy** is given. Functional literacy may be much lower and an estimate is sometimes given.

Official languages. Those languages known to be recognized as such in June 2000.

All languages. This represents the total of all indigenous languages spoken within each nation. The figure is quoted from the 1998 *Ethnologue* (**SIL**) unless fuller information was available elsewhere.

Languages with Scriptures. The number of languages in which there is a full Bible (Bi), or only a New Testament (NT), or just portions (por) is given. The number of active language translation projects is indicated by w.i.p. (work in progress). Further information on translation needs is given in the points for prayer.

ECONOMY
1 **HDI — Human Development Index.** This is a composite of data about life expectancy, infant mortality, income and health and is measured on a scale from 0.20 to 0.98. We have figures

for 174 countries taken from the annual UN Human Development Report, where each country is ranked according to this total.

2 **Public debt/person** represents the total public debt and is given as a percentage of the GNP. This gives a rough guide to the health of the economy – a high percentage of over 100% is most unhealthy.

3 **Income/person** is the gross national product (GNP) in US dollars divided by the population. This is also given as a percentage of the USA figure. This gives a rough indication of living standards, but is *not* an indication of purchasing power within the country which reduces the disparities.

POLITICS
The brief comments are intended to be aids to prayer and not a full political assessment. It is hopefully not too biased by the authors' own viewpoint.

RELIGION
1 After the comments about the levels of **religious freedom,** we have sometimes included a **Persecution Index** ranking. This ranking is derived by Open Doors and published four times a year. There were 74 countries listed with significant levels of persecution. We have given the ranking of such countries as of March 2000.

2 **Religions** are listed in order of their percentage of the national population and the absolute number. We did not round the latter figure, but this does NOT indicate such a level of accuracy in counting! The growth rate given is for the period 1995-2000.

CHRISTIAN (MEGABLOC) TABLES
1 **Six ecclesiological megablocs** of Christians have been used:

Protestant	P
Independent/Indigenous	I
Anglican	A
Catholic	C
Orthodox	O
Marginal	M

PLEASE NOTE — this is very different from the classification used in previous editions, but the change was made to be more compatible with the 2001 *World Christian Encyclopedia*. Please see Appendix 6 and 7 for a fuller description of this. The **letter** after the megabloc is important, and is used frequently as an abbreviation in the text and in tables.

Use of computer databases to derive the denominational tables and ease of layout and reading made it preferable to list them in the order given above irrespective of size. See Appendix 6 for explanation on why we have used a broad definition of Christian, for instance, even including Mormons as "Christian".

STATISTICS AND ABBREVIATIONS

2 **The percentage of Christians** represents the total number of the population who are claimed to be Christian, either by individuals themselves in a government census, or by the churches to which they are affiliated. Whichever is the larger percentage is the figure used.

3 Where the official or estimated percentage is higher than that claimed by the churches, an **unaffiliated percentage and total** is added under the six megabloc statistics to reconcile the two.

4 **Double affiliation** can seriously distort totals. Where this is known to be a factor, a subtraction total is also appended to the megabloc table to allow for those who have changed religion or denomination but are counted by both. This subtraction total is also appended to the list of denominations that follows the megabloc table.

5 **Church attendance** is emphasized by those who promote saturation church planting (the DAWN movement) as a more objective way of measuring growth and commitment. At first we sought to include these figures throughout, but the inconsistency of results and the paucity of countries with such figures forced us to abandon this as a consistent practice. Any such figures are entered into the database which is on the CD version of the book.

6 **Growth rates** are given and represent average annual growth between 1995 and 2000.

7 **The denominational listings** contain a representative selection of the larger denominations with:

a) The number of Congregations (with widely differing denominational differences in what constitutes a congregation).

b) Adult baptized/confirmed Members (the figure usually used by Baptists, Pentecostals and Free Churches).

c) Affiliates represents the whole Christian community or inclusive membership, which includes children, non-member adherents, etc. This is the figure usually used by Catholic, Anglican, Lutheran and many Reformed Churches.

We have sought to cross-calculate a derivation for all three figures when only one or two are provided so that meaningful comparisons and totals can be made. We have also had to make projections to 2000 for denominations where recent statistics were not available. See a fuller explanation in Appendix 7, and all details in the CD version of *Operation World*.

TRANS-BLOC GROUPINGS TABLES

1 **Evangelical percentages** for 1960-2000 are carefully derived according to the methodology described in Appendix 7. The degree of accuracy is reduced and assessment more subjective in lands where there are large state or traditional churches to which a majority of the population belongs (e.g. Scandinavia). The denominational tables on the CD give the assigned estimates.

PLEASE NOTE that we have largely retained the definition and classification of Evangelicals as used in earlier editions of *Operation World*. The 2001 *World Christian Encyclopedia* has moved to a radically different classification from the 1980 edition and also from this book, so these figures cannot be compared any longer.

2 **Charismatic percentages** for 1990-2000 are derived as described in Appendix 6. We have not been able to estimate adequately the denominational breakdown of charismatics before 1990.

PLEASE NOTE that our estimates for Charismatics are more cautious than those of the *World Christian Encyclopedia*. All these figures must be considered broad estimates.

3 **Pentecostals** are defined by denominational type and are exclusively within the Protestant and Independent megablocs. All Pentecostals are, by definition both Charismatic and Evangelical, and therefore a sub-set of both. This is indicated by the indentation in the table.

4 **The inter-relatedness of these three transbloc groupings** is complex, but has to be faced, because it represents the real world in which we live today. See the diagrams on p.4. Evangelicals and Charismatics are found in at least five of the six megablocs, but in varying proportions. Not all Evangelicals are Charismatic nor are Charismatics necessarily Evangelical.

MISSIONARY STATISTICS

These have been compiled after considerable effort to scour the world, so included here is a fairly comprehensive totalling of the global missionary force. Each country has a total for missionaries received and sent as well as the number of agencies involved. We have sought to overcome widely differing definitions of what constitutes a missionary so that like can be compared with like. This is how we have sought to do this:

1 **All missionaries serving in other lands** whether cross-cultural or working among expatriate communities. This is the commonly used definition in North America.

2 **All missionaries serving cross-culturally**, whether at home or abroad. This is a more commonly used European and Latin American definition.

3 **All with an apostolic (missionary) calling** to evangelize and plant churches in the same or a related culture as well as in distant cultures. This is generally used in Africa and Asia.

This enables us to give more objective figures for the world's missionary numbers and compare the growing non-Western missions movement with the older Western movements. See Appendices 2, 3 and 4 for a fuller analysis.

Organizational abbreviations

Those in bold type are the 120 or more agencies for which we have given contact addresses. A fuller list of agencies with addresses is available in the electronic version of *Operation World*.

A full list of agency abbreviations used in the book is given in Appendix 3. Other abbreviations are listed in Appendix 5.

GRAPHS

These tell a fascinating story of growth and decline in the world's religions and also in Trans-bloc groupings, such as Evangelicals. Some have asked for explanations of the changes. Space unfortunately prohibits this!

RELIGION GRAPHS

The purpose of the graph is to show the growth of the missionary religions over the 20th century and extrapolation to 2010.

Non-Christian religions and ideologies are shown from the top downwards.

Major Christian traditions are shown from the bottom upwards. Where the number of Christians is very small, only the total Christian population is indicated with 'X'. Sometimes a combination of the smaller Christian megablocs are represented by 'X' alongside larger, individual megablocs.

The non-Christian religions which are too small in percentage to be of significance are left as white space at the very top of the chart. Please refer to the accompanying statistics for that country to identify them.

The letter on the graph will help identify the religion without referring constantly to this key. It is usually the **first** letter of the religion listed under the **Religion** statistcs section. Only the more significant religions are shaded and labelled. See the sample graph below:

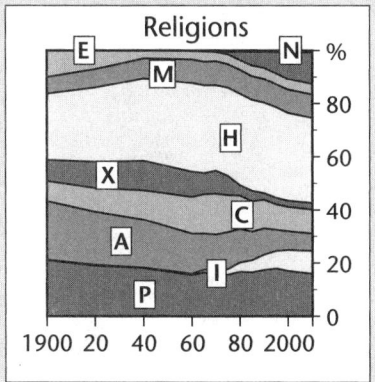

Religions

Key to the figures:

The time scale on the bottom line is 1900-2010.
2000 is the year for which the statistics in this book

are valid. 2000-2010 represents projections through that period.

The right-hand vertical scale allows the proportion of the major religious groups to be seen in comparison with each other, and as a percentage of the country's total population.

Abbreviations of non-Christian religious groupings are shown below (Christian megabloc abbreviations explained on p. xix).

> B - Buddhist
> Ch - Chinese
> E - Ethnic traditional
> H - Hindu
> J - Jewish
> M - Muslim (only for religion graph)
> N - Non-religious
> Z - Other, various combined groups
> S - *Christian marginal sects (usually M, except in religion graph)*

TRANS-BLOC GROUPINGS GRAPHS

The growth of **affiliated** Evangelicals is always given (not members, so as to compare percentages with other religions). Usually, the estimated growth of Charismatics from 1990-2000 is given.

Likewise, the growth of Pentecostals (who are by definition both Evangelical and Charismatic) is also given when their numbers warrant.

Occasionally another growing group is given for comparison — this will almost always be either the Marginal or Independent megabloc.

The **time scale** is *different* from the Religions graph and only covers 1960-2000, the period of the most dramatic change in history for these Trans-bloc groups.

The **percentage of the population** indicated varies according to countries. Note carefully the scale on the right-hand side before making comparisons. See sample graph below:

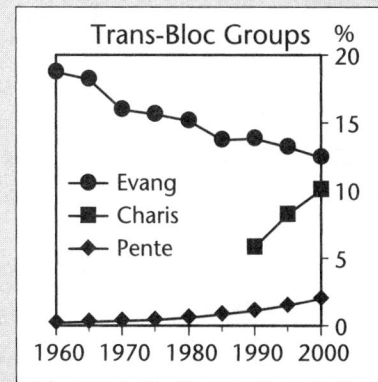

Trans-Bloc Groups

STATISTICS AND ABBREVIATIONS

• PRAYER CALENDAR •

January

1	WORLD
2	
3	
4	
5	
6	
7	
8	
9	
10	AFRICA
11	
12	
13	
14	
15	
16	
17	AMERICAS
18	
19	
20	
21	
22	
23	
24	ASIA
25	
26	
27	
28	
29	
30	EUROPE
31	

February

1	EUROPE
2	
3	
4	PACIFIC
5	
6	
7	Afghanistan
8	
9	Albania
10	Algeria
11	
11	American Samoa, Andorra
12	Angola
13	
13	Anguilla, Antigua
14	Argentina
15	
16	Armenia
17	Aruba
18	Australia
19	
20	Austria
21	
22	Azerbaijan
23	Bahamas, Bahrain
24	Bangladesh
25	
26	
27	Barbados
28	Belarus

March

1	Belgium
2	Belize
3	Benin, Bermuda
4	Bhutan
5	Bolivia
6	
7	Bosnia
8	Botswana
9	Brazil
10	
11	
12	Brit Indian Ocean Terr
12	Brit Virg Is, Brunei
13	Bulgaria
14	Burkina faso
15	Burundi
16	Cambodia
17	Cameroon
18	Canada
19	
20	Cape Verde, Cayman Islands
21	Central African Republic
22	Chad
23	Chile
24	China, PRC
25	
26	
27	
28	
29	
30-31	

April

1	
2	
3	
4	
5	
6	China, Hong Kong
7	China, Macau
8	China, Taiwan
9	
10	Colombia
11	
12	Comoros
13	Congo
14	Congo-DRC
15	
16	Cook Islands
17	Costa Rica
18	Côte d'Ivoire
19	Croatia
20	Cuba
21	Cyprus
22	Czech Republic
23	Denmark
24	Djibouti
25	Dominica
25	Dominican Rep
26	Ecuador
27	Egypt
28	
29	
30	El Salvador

May

1	Eq Guinea
2	Eritrea
3	Estonia
4	Ethiopia
5	
6	Faeroe Is, Falkland Is, Fiji
7	Finland
8	France
9	
10	
11	French Guiana, Fr Polynesia
12	Gabon
13	Gambia, The
14	Georgia
15	Germany
16	
17	
18	Ghana
19	
20	Gibraltar, Greece
21	Greenland, Grenada
21	Guadeloupe, Guam
22	Guatemala
23	Guinea
24	Guinea-Bissau
25	Guyana
26	Haiti, Holy See
27	Honduras
28	Hungary
29	
30	Iceland
31	India

June

1	India
2	
3	
4	
5	
6	
7	
8	
9	
10	
12	
13	
14	
15	
16	
17	Indonesia
18	
19	
20	
21	
22	
23	
24	
25	
26	
27	Iran
28	
29	
30	Iraq

• PRAYER CALENDAR •

July
1   Iraq
2   Ireland
3   Israel
4
5   Italy
6
7
8   Jamaica
9   Japan
10
11
12
13 Jordan
14 Kazakhstan
15
16 Kenya
17
18 Kiribati, Korea,North
19 Korea, South
20
21 Kuwait
22 Kyrgyzstan
23 Laos
24 Latvia
25 Lebanon
26 Lesotho
27 Liberia
28 Libya
29 Liechtenstein, Lithuania
30 Luxembourg
31 Macedonia

August
1   Madagascar
2   Malawi
3   Malaysia
4
5
6   Maldives
7   Mali
8   Malta
9   Martinique, Mauritania
10 Mauritius
11 Mexico
12
13 Micronesia
14 Moldova, Monaco
15 Mongolia, Montserrat
16 Morocco
17
18 Mozambique
19
20 Myanmar
21
22 Namibia, Nauru
23 Nepal
24
25 Netherlands, Neth Antilles
26 New Caledonia
27 New Zealand
28 Nicaragua
29 Niger
30 Nigeria
31

September
1   Nigeria
2
3   Norway
4   Oman
5   Pakistan
6
7
8
9   Palestine, Panama
10 Papua New Guinea
11
12 Paraguay
13 Peru
14
15 Philippines
16
17
18 Poland
19
20 Portugal
21 Puerto Rico
22 Qatar
23 Réunion
24 Romania
25
26 Russia
27
28
29
30

October
1   Rwanda
2   Samoa, San Marino
2   São Tomé
3   Saudi Arabia
4
5   Senegal
6   Seychelles
7   Sierra Leone
8   Singapore
9   Slovakia, Slovenia
10 Solomon Islands
11 Somalia
12-13 South Africa
14
15 Spain
16
17 Sri Lanka
18
19 St Helena, St Kitts
19 St Lucia, St Pierre & Miquelon
19 St Vincent
20 Sudan
21
22 Suriname
23 Swaziland
24 Sweden
25 Switzerland
26 Syria
27 Tajikistan
28 Tanzania
29
30-31 Thailand

November
1   Timor Lorosae
2   Togo
3   Tonga
3   Trinidad & Tobago
4   Tunisia
5   Turkey
6
7
8   Turkmenistan
8   Turks & Caicos Is, Tuvalu
9   Uganda
10
11 Ukraine
12
13 United Arab Emirates
14 United Kingdom
15
16
17 United States of America
18
19
20
21
22
23 Uruguay
24 Uzbekistan
25
26 Vanuatu
27 Venezuela
28
29 Vietnam
30

December
1   Virg Is (USA), Wallis &
Futuna
2   Yemen
3
4   Yugoslavia (Serbia &
5   Montenegro)
6   Zambia
7
8   Zimbabwe
9
10 Audio Cassette Tape
11 Christian Radio
12 Christian TV
13 *JESUS* Film
14 Internet
15 Bible Societies & Translation
16 Christian Literature
17 Theological Education & TEE
18 BCCs
19 Relief & Development
20 Medical Mission Work
21 Missionary Aviation
22 Maritime Ministry
23 Christian Tentmakers
24 Short-term Workers
25 Student Ministries
26 Ministry to Children
27 Outreach to Sects/Cults
28 Urban Evangelization
29 Intl Coop for World Evang
30 *OPERATION WORLD*
31 The Lord's Return

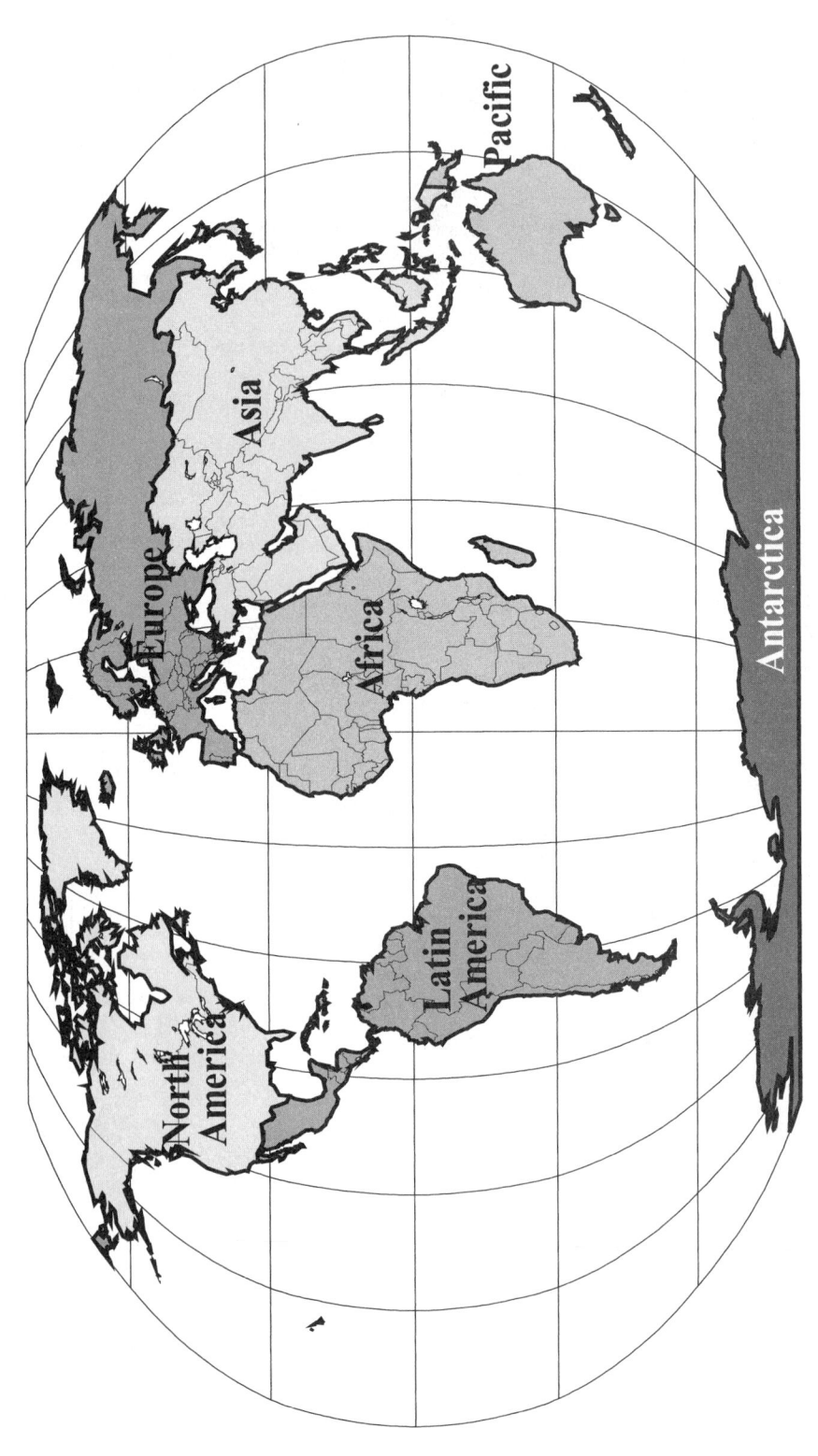

The World

JANUARY 1-9

Updated February 2004

The world's six continents - as defined by the United Nations. In this book we have followed this classification with one exception - Cyprus is included in Europe.

GEOGRAPHY

Area 135,488,200 sq.km. Antarctica, with 14 million sq.km, is not included. There are 237 states and territories described in this book.

Population	Millions	Ann.Gr.	Density
1950	2,523	+0.96%	19 per sq. km
1960	3,026	+1.81%	22 per sq. km
1970	3,702	+2.01%	27 per sq. km
1980	4,447	+1.83%	33 per sq. km
1990	5,275	+1.70%	39 per sq. km
2000	6,065	+1.39%	45 per sq. km
2010	6,808	+1.15%	50 per sq. km
2020	7,508	+0.98%	55 per sq. km
2025	7,834	+0.86%	58 per sq. km

The world's population doubled between 1960 and 2000. Global population growth peaked around 1970 and has steadily declined since then - largely through smaller family size and, increasingly, AIDS in Africa.

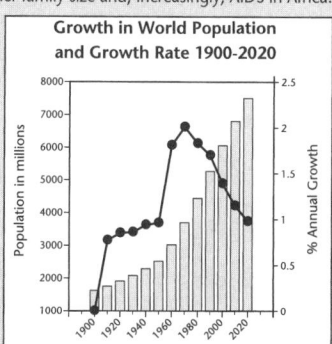

Growth in World Population and Growth Rate 1900-2020

Cities There are 482 cities of over 1 million inhabitants and 20 of over 10 million. The five largest conurbations: Tokyo/Yokohama 28 mill.; Mexico City 18.1m; São Paulo 17.7m; New York 16.6m. **Urbanites** 48%.

PEOPLES

In the World Christian Encyclopedia there are approximately 12,000 ethnolinguistic peoples within the nations of the world - transnational peoples being counted multiple times. The Joshua Project II listing (which also includes ethno-cultural peoples for which specific church planting might be needed) has 16,000 names. We have used the former classification in our summaries and the latter in our coverage of such

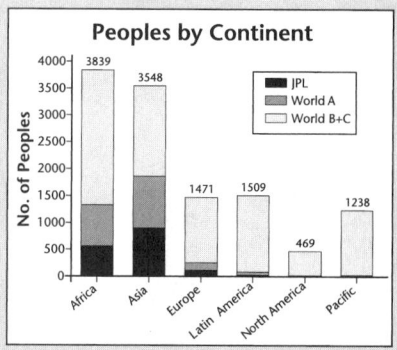

Peoples by Continent

countries as India with its complex caste system.

Languages The ministry envisaged helps define the boundary between a language and a dialect. The total numbers, therefore, vary.

The Ethnologue (with Bible translation in view) 7,148. The World Christian Encyclopedia: 13,511 and 30,000 dialects.

Largest languages (mother tongue): Chinese (Putonghua) 1,000 million; English 350 mill.; Spanish 336m; Hindi-Urdu 263m; Arabic 248m; Bengali 217m; Portuguese 184m; Japanese 128m; German 106m.

Official languages - populations in countries with: English 1,895m; Chinese 1,290m; Spanish 373m; French 289m; Arabic 242m; Portuguese 215m; Russian 207m; Turkic 130m; German 110m. Not all in these countries speak the official language. There are only 35 languages that are used as languages of instruction in the world's universities.

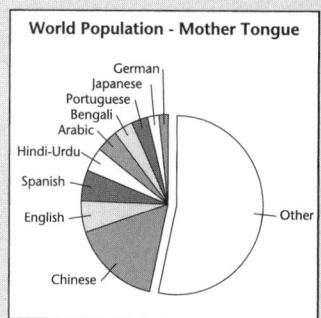

World Population - Mother Tongue

World Population - Official Language

Languages with Scriptures 383Bi 987NT 891por 672w.i.p.

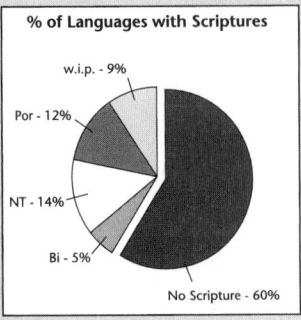

% of Languages with Scriptures

w.i.p. - 9%
Por - 12%
NT - 14%
Bi - 5%
No Scripture - 60%

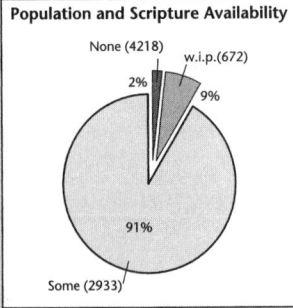

Population and Scripture Availability

None (4218) 2%
w.i.p.(672) 9%
91%
Some (2933)

ECONOMY
The global economy expanded considerably during the 1990s - the major motor for growth being the expansion of the US economy and, to a lesser extent, the EU. Japan stagnated and in 1998 the Asian 'tiger' economies suffered a sharp recession from which they are slowly recovering. Poorer countries generally became poorer and relief of crippling national debt became a global issue. Global warming, population growth and ecological degradation helped to multiply the frequency and intensity of natural disasters.

POLITICS
The collapse of European Communism and the ending of the Cold War in 1989-91 radically changed global politics. The impact of ideology waned and that of ethno-centrisms and religions increased. Various forms of democracy and market economics became more widespread. The coalescing of continental groupings of nations into economic trading blocs is counter-balanced by many nations being threatened by ethnic fragmentation. The impact of 9/11 has been a major setback for democratic freedoms.

RELIGION
The 20th Century was a time of dramatic shifts in religious profession. Religious freedom increased in former Communist-ruled nations, but decreased in the latter in the 1990s as national religions sought to marginalize or suppress all minorities. There are 66 nations and states which have significant restrictions on religious belief.

Muslim nations	42
Secular/Marxist	7
Orthodox	6
Buddhist	4
Hindu	2
Catholic	3

Religions	Population %	Adherents	*Ann.Gr.
Christian	32.54	1,973 mill.	+1.43%
Muslim	21.09	1,279 mill.	+2.17%
non-Religious	15.46	938 mill.	+0.97%
Hindu	13.52	820 mill.	+1.44%
Buddhist	6.60	400 mill.	+1.21%
Chinese	6.31	383 mill.	-1.28%
Traditional ethnic	2.90	176 mill.	+1.72%
Sikh	0.34	20.5 mill.	+1.70%
Jewish	0.24	14.2 mill.	+0.63%
Other	1.00	60.8 mill.	+1.53%
Total	**100.00**	**6,065.1 mill.**	**+1.39%**

*Only religions with a growth rate of over 1.39% are increasing faster than the world's population.

This table shows the breakdown of the world's countries by continent and the predominant religion.

	Africa	Asia	Europe	Americas	Pac.	World
Christian	31	3	47	51	32	164
Muslim	23	26	1	-	-	50
Buddhist	-	11	-	-	-	11
Non-Rel.	-	5	1	-	-	6
Hindu	1	2	-	-	-	3
Ethnic	2	-	-	-	-	2
Jewish	-	1	-	-	-	1
Total	**57**	**48**	**49**	**51**	**32**	**237**

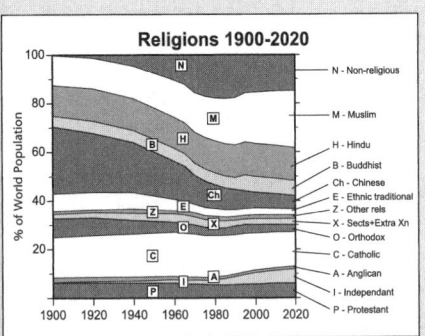

Religions 1900-2020

% of World Population
1900 1920 1940 1960 1980 2000 2020

N - Non-religious
M - Muslim
H - Hindu
B - Buddhist
Ch - Chinese
E - Ethnic traditional
Z - Other rels
X - Sects+Extra Xn
O - Orthodox
C - Catholic
A - Anglican
I - Independant
P - Protestant

Christians	Denom.	Affil.%	,000	Ann.Gr.
Protestant	8,226	5.77	349,329	+2.2%
Independent	22,356	5.00	303,289	+5.5%
Anglican	166	1.12	67,806	+2.4%
Catholic	291	15.56	943,499	+0.5%
Orthodox	549	3.48	211,246	+0.1%
Marginal	1,611	0.67	40,904	+2.7%
Unaffiliated		3.21	194.4m	n.a.
Doubly affiliated		*-2.39*	*-141.3m*	*n.a.*

The Orthodox and Catholics are declining as a percentage of the world's population, but the Protestants and Anglicans are growing slowly (mainly because of growth in the non-Western world). The Marginal megabloc (mainly JWs and Mormons) grew substantially from under one million followers in 1900 to 41 million in 2000. It is the growth of newer 'post-denominational' churches and networks that has characterized the 20ᵗʰ Century with a bewildering variety of expressions of Christianity. This Independent megabloc has grown from 7 million in 1900 to well over 300 million in 2000. Many are independent Evangelical, Pentecostal and charismatic denominations and networks. There are also a number of break-aways from all megablocs as well as indigenous, sometimes syncretistic, movements.

The following diagram illustrates this change over the 20ᵗʰ Century and projection to 2020 if present trends continue.

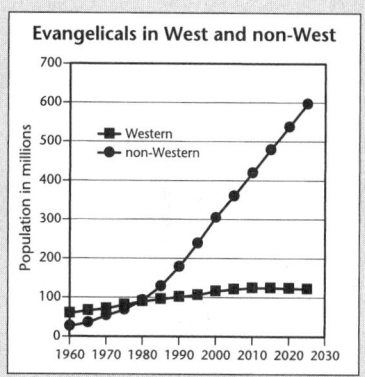

Evangelicals in West and non-West

Pentecostals sprang out of early 20ᵗʰ Century revivals. Their growth in the 20ᵗʰ Century has been spectacular — from virtually no Pentecostals in 1900 to over 115 million in 2000. Pentecostals are by definition Evangelical and also usually First Wave Charismatic.

Charismatics began to multiply within nearly all megablocs and denominations from the 1950s and 1960s (Second Wave Charismatics). Other Charismatics formed their own new networks and structures (Third Wave). It is this latter that comprises a large segment of the Independent megabloc. All Charismatics (including historic Pentecostal denominations, those in non-charismatic denominations and those in post-denominational networks) have grown from less than a million in 1900 to maybe 345 million in 2000.

This diagram shows the growth of these movements over the 20ᵗʰ Century and projection to 2030 if present trends continue.

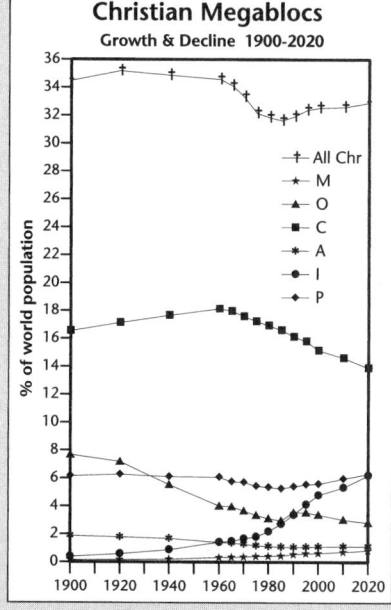

Christian Megablocs
Growth & Decline 1900-2020

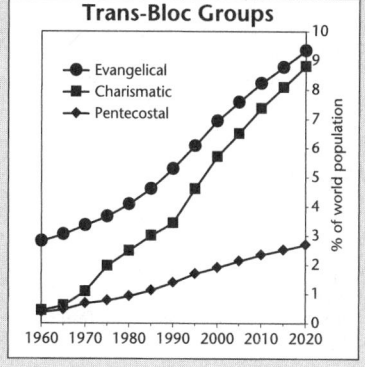

Trans-Bloc Groups

Trans-bloc Groupings pop. %		,000	Ann.Gr.
Evangelical	6.9	420,058	+4.7%
Charismatic	5.7	345,692	+3.9%
Pentecostal	1.9	115,826	+4.5%

The most dynamic growth in Christianity has been within movements that transcend the Christian megablocs and component denominations and networks. These are:

Evangelicals who emerged as a dynamic force after the revivals of the 18ᵗʰ and 19ᵗʰ Centuries and were used of God in the great expansion of Christianity in the 19ᵗʰ and 20ᵗʰ Centuries. The startling growth of non-Western (AfAsLA) Evangelicals in the latter half of the 20ᵗʰ Century is evident. Note the possible continued growth to 2025 when 83% of the world's Evangelicals could be in the non-Western world.

The following diagrams seek to illustrate this complex picture and the proportions of each of these three movements in each Christian megabloc in 2000.

Note: These following two diagrams can be found enlarged on p. 60.

Note: All Pentecostals are both Evangelical and Charismatic and are PI. Most Evangelicals are P, I or A and smaller numbers are C or O. Most Charismatics in P,I,A are Evangelicals; much less so among C. NOT all charismatics are Evangelical - their respective totals overlap.

Missionaries in the world
These represent P,I,A missionaries only; data being incomplete for other megablocs.

Mission agencies
Mission agencies: 2,932. Missionaries sent to other lands: 97,732. Cross-cultural missionaries: 143,189. Missionaries serving in homelands: 103,528. All missionaries: 201,260. For more details, see Appendix 4.

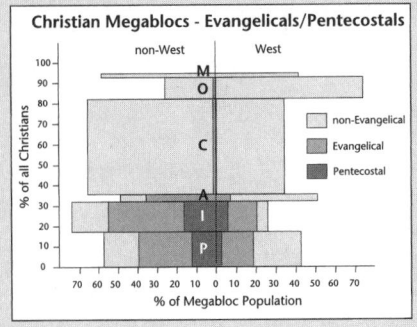

Christian Megablocs - Evangelicals/Pentecostals

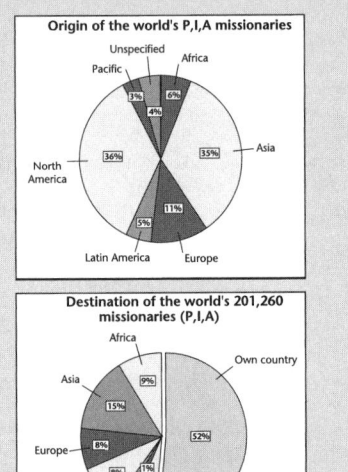

Origin of the world's P,I,A missionaries

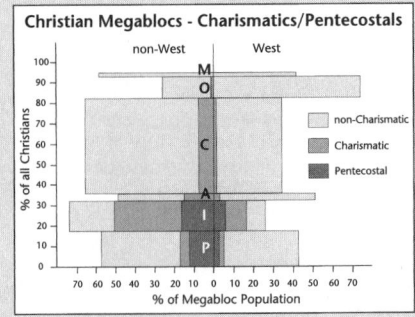

Christian Megablocs - Charismatics/Pentecostals

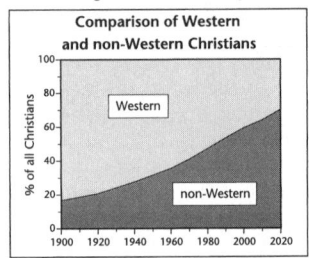

Destination of the world's 201,260 missionaries (P,I,A)

• Answers to Prayer

The visual media have eroded the faith of believers in God's sovereignty in the world. Television cameramen, like vultures, swoop on the wars, famines, disasters and tragedies of this world. The beautiful, wholesome and good is less photogenic, so what God does and what God's servants are achieving are rarely noticed. Like Elisha's servant (2 Kings 6) we need our eyes opened to see reality.

The view from a heavenly vantage point is very different! There is a titanic struggle going on in the heavenlies between the forces of the Lord Jesus and the hosts of darkness and the effects in our world are dramatic. Yet the victory has already been won on the cross. So here and in subsequent sections of the book we begin with answers to prayer — especially those from the 1990s.

1 The unprecedented harvest being won in Africa, Asia and Latin America (AfAsLA) in contrast to the stagnation in North America and the Pacific, and the decline in Europe (EuNAPa). The tables and graphs below reveal a remarkable story. The table of statistics shows the relative change of the world's population for each of the six megablocs. The graph beside the table reveals that though Chrstianity's percentage in the world population has changed little, the proportions between EuNAPa and AfAsLA have changed dramatically.

Change in megablocs as a % of world population

	1900	1960	2000	2010
P	6.2	6.1	5.6	6.0
I	0.4	1.4	4.8	5.3
A	1.9	1.4	1.1	1.1
C	16.5	18.1	15.2	14.6
O	7.7	4.0	3.4	3.0
M	0.2	0.3	0.6	0.7
All Chr	**34.5**	**34.6**	**32.5**	**32.6**

Comparison of Western and non-Western Christians

Christianity has slightly declined as a percentage of the world's population — only the Marginals with some increase and the Independent/Indigenous megabloc with major increases have gone against this trend. This conceals an astonishing shift of the centre of gravity of Christianity to the non-Western world. Note the growth in proportions of each megabloc in AfAsLA:

Christians in AfAsLA as percentage of all Christians

	1900	1960	2000
Protestant (P)	5.4	19.1	57.3
Independent (I)	2.6	3.5	74.0
Anglican (A)	3.9	9.6	48.8
Catholic (C)	26.9	40.7	65.6
Orthodox (O)	9.2	13.7	25.8
Marginal (M)	61.4	26.5	58.2
All Christians	**16.7**	**35.6**	**59.4**

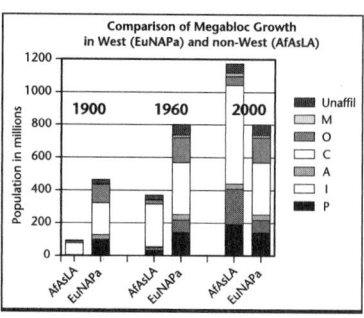

Comparison of Megabloc Growth in West (EuNAPa) and non-West (AfAsLA)

Christianity is now truly a global religion once more — a status it lost 12 centuries ago.

2 **The expansion of Evangelicals** since 1960. They numbered 84.5 million (2.8%) in 1960, but in 2000 they were 420 million (6.9%). The growth peaked around 1990 at 5.6%. The graph below shows the remarkable growth rate between 1975 and 2000. We give projected growth rates to 2025 with the likelihood that this momentum would not be maintained without a significant outpouring of the Holy Spirit.

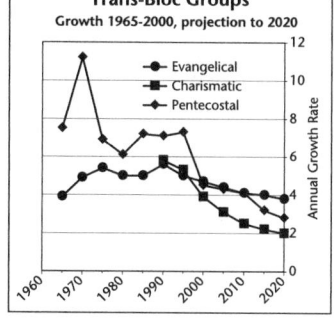

Trans-Bloc Groups
Growth 1965-2000, projection to 2020

The post-war surge of evangelical missions was an astonishing success story, but most of the subsequent growth came from a new generation of indigenous evangelical movements around the world.

3 **The spread of Pentecostalism** has been astonishing. After its birth around the beginning of the 20th Century, Pentecostal denominations grew and proliferated. The most significant growth has been since 1960 from about 11 million worldwide to 116 million in 2000 and an average growth rate of around 7%. See the graph above.

4 **The huge impact of the Charismatic movement** on almost every denomination and megabloc. These figures include First Wave Pentecostal denominations, Second Wave mainline denominations and also newer independent post-denominational networks. Figures are at best reasonable, but low, estimates. Those shown here indicate the size of this movement: 1990 — 181 million; 1995 — 261 million; 2000 — 345 million. See graph above.

5 **The strength and growth of the Church in lands that have, or have had, severe persecution** — such as Ethiopia, Sudan, China, Korea, India and a number of Muslim lands.

6 **The manifest failure of human ideologies,** which became more obvious in the 1980s and '90s.

a) **The collapse of Communism** as a global threat, and the bankruptcy of atheism has caused significant turning to Christ in answer to prayer.

b) **Fundamentalist Islam** has gained in political power and in numbers. Its ability to cause havoc in the world through subversion and terrorism was demonstrated in the infamous attack on the USA in 2001. The cause of Islamic *jihad* has polarized the Muslim world, losing credibility in the minds of many Muslims (many of whom are becoming secularized). As a result, many have become more open to the gospel and to receive Christ despite the danger. The last 20 years have been a time of more Muslims coming to Christ than ever before in history. There are the beginnings of what we believe could be a flood - demonstrating that Jesus is Lord even over Islam.

c) **The Buddhist world** has long proved a tough challenge with few major breakthroughs, but the rising tide of interest and concern for the Buddhist heartlands of Tibet and Mongolia is bearing fruit. Mongolia has opened and Tibet is increasingly surrounded — north, south and east — by an active Christian witness. Communism has been a means of preparing many Asian Buddhist cultures for the coming of the gospel.

7 **The globalization of the world missions movement.** Since 1980 there has been a surge of interest and involvement. The world missions force is now multi-cultural and multi-national.

a) **The USA still remains the largest foreign missionary-sending nation,** but South Korea has replaced the UK as the second after the USA.

b) **India's missionary movement** has grown enormously even as the foreign component has dwindled. India could now be the world's second-largest missionary-sending country, though the vast majority serve in their own country — most in a cross-cultural environment.

In Appendix 4 on p. 747 is a listing of the world's missionaries sent and received by country.

8 **The AD2000 and Beyond Movement** launched in 1989 proved to be the most global, focused movement for world evangelization that there ever has been. Its ministry came to an end in January 2001 according to its charter, but the effects will impact the 21st Century. It was a coordinating network of many of the more activist evangelical bodies around the world. Its goals were 'The gospel for every person and a church for every people.' Despite criticisms and inadequacies, much was achieved:

a) **The 10/40 Window focus** was brilliantly successful. The unusual phrase became a household phrase across the evangelical world. The most neglected part of the world basked in unaccustomed attention, thousands of congregations were mobilized for prayer and action, hundreds of agencies re-formulated strategies and recruitment of workers for the unreached significantly increased. In the authors' own agency, deployment in the 10/40 Window went up from 34% in 1984 to over 70% in 2000. The concept became almost too successful — sometimes in being applied to invalidate any mission activity outside the Window!

b) **A great increase in research into the world's peoples** — at a global level in producing the Joshua Project List (JPL) of unreached peoples and at regional/national levels with the multiplication of indigenous research efforts in Africa, Asia, Latin America, etc. The 1990s saw the most concerted attempt at analyzing the need of the world ever — of which **Operation World** itself was a part. Every JPL people was prayed for, profiled, mapped and most received some ministry visits. In many, ministry was initiated and churches planted.

c) **The Joshua Project I** was launched in 1995 to facilitate strategic planning, coordinated research and cooperative church planting during the remaining years of the 20th Century. The list of 12,000 peoples was broken down as follows:

People Category	Number in category	Approximate population	% of world's Population
Above 10,000 pop. and more than 2% evangelical or more than 5% adherents to Christianity	6,000	3,620 million	60.3
Above 10,000 pop. and less than 2% evangelical and less than 5% adherents [this constitutes the JPL]	1,600	2,350 million	39.2
Below 10,000 population [many being migrant over or cross-border minorities]	4,400	30 million	0.5
World Totals	**12,000**	**6,000 million**	**100.0**

d) **A Church for every people** — how far was the goal achieved? The challenge to national and international congregations and agencies to adopt peoples for prayer and ministry gained momentum in the 1990s. Progress was logged for the 1,583 peoples listed in the October 2000 JPL with the following results:

Joshua Project — Least Reached Peoples — Progress towards church planting 1990 — 2000

Percent of Peoples	1990	Oct. 1997	Oct. 2000	Achievement
Targeted for church planting by mid-2002	est. 66%	77%	100%	Complete
Targeted for church planting by 2000	est. 66%	77%	85%	Five-sixths
Church planting team currently on site	est. 39%	43%	68%	Two-thirds
Reported Fellowship of at least 100 believers	n.a.	4%	31%	One-third

This meant that by the end of 2000, there was a reported church planting team(s) in 1,084 of the peoples and evidence of a congregation of 100 members in 487. This, of course, does not include the possible 2,000 peoples of under 10,000 in population that remain inadequately researched and may be needing pioneer work. Praise God for these exciting initial achievements and pray that the momentum might increase in the period after 2000. There are weaknesses — inadequate mechanisms for holding those committed to their promises for adoption, insufficient verification and over-simplification of the task — but thank God for what was achieved!

e) **The gospel for every person.** The Mark 16:15 version of the Great Commission exhorts preaching the gospel to every person. The AD2000 and Beyond goal of the 'Gospel for Every Person' is in tune with this. It is harder to measure the impact of multiple means of ministry to the unconverted — personal witness, literature, Scripture translation, Christian video, cassettes, television, radio, the Internet and many other tools God has given us. We can measure potential accessibility by many of these ministries — though the *reality* may fall far short of this. However, the cumulative effects of multiple layers of ministry increase the likelihood of non-Christians hearing the gospel and the possibility of response. The AD2000 and Beyond Movement brought together major networks of specialist agencies. Here are listed some of the major thrusts of the 1990s:

i   *Scripture translation.* Through the combined ministry of the Bible Societies and Bible translation agencies, 94% of the world's population has access to a NT in their own language or soon will through existing translation projects. **WBT** has set the goal of researching the remaining languages of the earth and initiating a Bible translation programme for each one requiring it by 2020 (see p.698).

ii   *The World by Radio consortium* of Christian broadcasting agencies (see p.694) made a commitment to provide Christian radio programming for every person on earth in a language they could understand. In practical terms, it meant ensuring weekly broadcasts in 372 mega-languages. In the 1990s, 115 languages were added, leaving only 164 with no broadcasts. It is estimated that the potential audience is now 99% (assuming good radio reception, availability of radios and power and also interest in seeking the correct frequencies).

iii   *The **JESUS** film* (see p.696) has had 4.1 billion individual viewings — maybe representing 3 billion people and has yielded over 128 million enquirers. The goal of translating the script into every language spoken by 50,000 people had virtually been achieved by 2001. Well over 99% of the world's population would be able to view the film in a language they know.

iv   *Many other international ministries* such as **SAT-7** satellite TV coverage in the Middle East, **EHC**, **GRN**, etc., could also be added to these multiple layers of global coverage.

v   *Witnessing by local believers.* Ultimately this is the best and most fundamental means for sharing the gospel. Only 6.3% of the world's population lives in a culture without a witnessing church — though in large populations many would have little chance to visit one such. To this 93.7% of the population with a Church in their own culture could be added the 98% of the world's population that has a resident national or expatriate witness in their midst.

This diagram shows these layers of witness which have the potential to cover the whole world's population multiple times. Of course the actual truth is that most of these ministries reach a proportion of the potential. Praise God for the amazing tools we can use and the resourcefulness of Christian agencies in using them well.

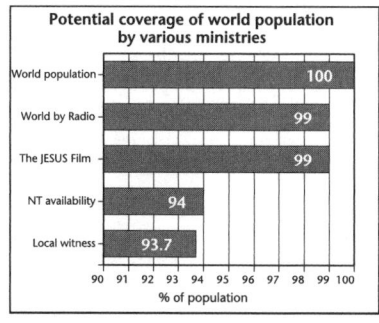

Potential coverage of world population by various ministries

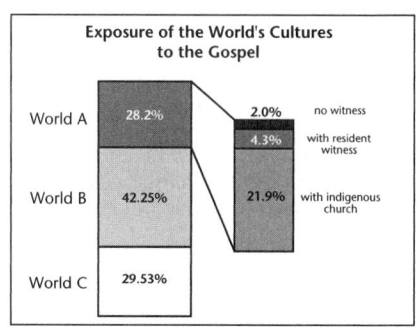

Exposure of the World's Cultures to the Gospel

The sobering fact is that even with all this activity, probably 15-25% of the world's population has not really heard the gospel in such a way as to respond to the offer of eternal salvation in Jesus Christ.

• Global Hot Spots

Here are listed some of the critical international hot spots likely to cause much grief, suffering and death in the coming decade. These need to be covered in prayer. Please see the individual regions and countries for more detail.

Note Feb 2004. These words below were written before the destruction of the Twin Towers in New York on 11 September 2001 (9/11). The whole world was changed by the Al Qaeda terror network and this launched a long and bitter global war that affects every country in the world. It has become the defining issue of the early part of the 21st Century.

1 **The future of Jerusalem**. The fundamental issue of this world-renowned city's future is possibly the biggest flash-point in the world today. The conflict between the Israelis and Palestinians has resisted major international efforts to resolve it. War between the heavily armed Israelis and surrounding Muslim states is not unlikely. This unresolved issue cripples many international efforts to reinforce peace and economic betterment.

2 **The Balkan-Central Asia** belt stretches across a region of conflict - the Balkan ethnic hatreds, Kurdish desires for nationhood, the Caucasus cauldron of wars and confrontations together with potentially vast oil wealth, the clash between the Muslim and Orthodox worlds in Central Asia and the future of revolutionary Iran, post-Taliban Afghanistan and a Pakistan crippled by Islamism.

3 **The Himalayan cultural, religious and political divide** with the growing nuclear abilities of antagonistic Pakistan, China and India.

4 **China's growing assertiveness** — with its military capability threatening East and southeast Asia as it seeks to regain Taiwan and control surrounding seas and small island archipelagos.

5 **International terrorism**. The sophistication, power and transportability of weapons of mass destruction (nuclear, chemical and biological) are a present reality, distorting world economics and vastly increasing threats to security and the need for costly countermeasures. Whole nations are held to ransom.

6 **Africa's zones of conflict**. These are partly due to unsuitable, colonially-drawn frontiers in the 19th Century. Recent conflict zones:
a) *Far West Africa* where greed and ethnic loyalties plunged Liberia, Sierra Leone and increasingly Guinea into war with unspeakable barbarities committed. An uneasy peace prevailed by 2004.
b) *The Central African* chain of interlinking wars stretching from the Indian Ocean to the Atlantic caused cumulatively over 10 million deaths in the past 20 years through famine or war. These were and are between Ethiopia and Eritrea, the genocidal wars of Rwanda and Burundi, the civil wars of Somalia, Sudan, Uganda, the two Congos and Angola. Since 2002 war-weariness, terrible economic distress and international interventions are helping to bring a measure of peace, but this area will remain tense and challenging.
c) *The unresolved issue of the Western Sahara*, now controlled by Morocco.
d) *The civil war in Algeria*.

One positive for Africa — there is peace in Southern Africa after nearly 40 years of conflict.

7 **The scarcity of water** in many parts of the world is becoming a major cause of tension and even conflict between nations. Major hydro-politics tension points:
a) *The Amu Darya/Oxus* of Central Asia.
b) *The Tigris-Euphrates* (Turkey, Syria, Iraq, Iran).
c) *The Jordan* (Israel, Syria, Jordan).
d) *The Nile* (Egypt, Sudan, Ethiopia).
e) *The nations to the north and south* of the Sahara Desert.
f) *The Amur* (Russia, China).

There are 26 nations already suffering from a severe water deficit. It is reckoned that by 2025 3 billion people will have problems accessing fresh water.

• Global Issues to Watch

Below are major trends in our world that hint at ever faster and more severe changes that bring both danger and opportunity for Christian witness. Turn these into intercession for the continued intervention of God into the lives of the world's population.

1 **The pressures on world leaders** continue to increase and so do the uncertainties and dangers. Pray for the world's leaders. Those who lead their countries are listed in Appendix 1 on p.715. Pray specifically for:

a) *Those who give just and godly leadership, many of whom are committed Christians.* They need to be upheld in prayer. They have to make difficult decisions for a majority who may not share their faith. Pray that they may continually stand firm for what is good, moral and just for the nations they rule and not give way to numerous pressure groups who would wish to gain advantage for vested interests, nor push for the relaxation of laws that forbid what the Bible names as sin.

b) *Those who face major crises.* Pray for courage to take the right decisions, however unpopular. It is easy to go for the soft or cheap option which ultimately proves hard and costly. The new millennium will provide an ever-multiplying number of these crises.

c) *Christians to be active* in their homelands to promote justice, righteousness, honest government and wise rule for the good of all. In too many cultures, Christians have either opted out of the political process and allowed the wrong ones to rule by default, or they have become part of the problem and compromised.

d) *Good rulers to be raised up.* The collapse of Communism and the spread of democratic governmental systems has not ended tyrannies, autocratic power-seekers or corrupt, greedy dictators. Pray for those who are unfit to rule their lands that they may repent and change (as did Nebuchadnezzar) or be removed (Pharoah, Belshazzar).

2 **Global warming** has become a reality through a series of knock-on effects with unknown results in the long-term — probably with the sea-level rising, flooding of lowlands, destruction of coral reefs, more cataclysmic storms, more severe climate changes, a sudden catastrophic rise in world temperature, etc. The wealthy nations with 20% of the world's population produce 80% of the greenhouse gases that contribute to global warming (the USA with 4.5% of the world's population produces 22% of the greenhouse gases).

3 **The insidious power of international crime empires**. Globalization has also globalized crime:

a) *Drug networks* linking the largest growers (Andean republics, Central Asia, the Golden Triangle of SE Asia) with the largest users (the West). Some such are the Italian/US Mafia, the Colombian drug barons, Chinese Triads, Japanese *yakuza*, Jamaican yardies, Russian mafia, etc.

b) *Money laundering* on a massive scale.

c) *Control of national economies* and politicians.

d) *Huge trading in people* — sex slaves, illegal migrants, women as captured wives, etc.

4 **The impact of older and newer diseases** has markedly increased — AIDS, malaria, tuberculosis being some of the more infamous and prominent. Africa and tropical countries will be more adversely affected.

5 **The treatment of women** continues to be a scandal in many parts of the world. Of the 1.3 billion in deep poverty, 70% are women. They work longer hours for less reward and all too often bear the greater financial burden to raise their families. Countries where female infanticide is widely practised, such as China and India, will trigger a growing smuggling of women and girls for the sex trade and for forced marriages.

6 **International migrations.** Population growth in poorer countries and the increasing gap between the richer and poorer nations is driving many to seek a better future in another land. Large scale migrations into Western Europe, North America, South Africa, Siberia, etc., will continue to grow regardless of whatever barriers are raised or legislation passed. This 'threat' could also be a great opportunity for Christian witness — most migrants coming from less-evangelized lands.

7 **Electronic communications have gone global** at a rate none could have conceived — fibre-optic cables, microwave/mobile phone networks and the ubiquitous Internet are impacting nearly every country and culture. The possibilities and dangers are enormous.

8 **Language extinctions**. Globalization threatens the world's rich language diversity.

a) *The Internet and technological revolution* has made English the global language. A disproportionate number of the world's wealthy speak English. This aids in international communication, but is a cultural juggernaut that is crushing many smaller cultures.

b) *Only 65 languages are spoken by more than 10 million people* and only 45 are used as a main teaching medium in secondary schools.

c) *Languages are dying out.* Over 50 have one speaker only, 426 are nearly extinct and some estimate that half of the 7,148 languages may be extinct in 2100. The work of Bible translators together with literacy workers is one significant ministry in preserving languages and restoring pride in their cultures.

9 **Increased persecution — especially for Christians**. The era of Constantinian Christianity is rapidly passing in which the Christian religion and politics were inextricably entwined. The Christian religion and a Christian worldview are being marginalized and levels of persecution increased.

a) *Open Doors* maintains a persecution index for the world's nations. There are 74 which persecute religious believers — especially Christians. About 400 million Christians live in these lands.

The main offenders:

i *Muslim states* — the rise of Islamism and increasing application of shari'a law and promotion of violent *jihad* are creating multiplied opportunities for persecution. In Afghanistan and Saudi Arabia the courts may sentence a national to death for becoming a Christian. In most Muslim countries relatives will sometimes murder those who come to believe in Christ. In many Muslim areas (Indonesia, Philippines, Pakistan, Egypt) there have been massacres of Christians for no other reason than that they are Christian.

ii *Marxist states* continue to make life very difficult for Christians — this is especially true in North Korea where profession of faith leads to imprisonment and death, and also in China, Vietnam and Laos where unregistered Christians have suffered severely.

iii *Hinduist extremism* has led to heightened pressure and acts of terror against Christians in India and Nepal.

iv *Buddhists* have persecuted and maltreated Christians in Bhutan and Sri Lanka.

v *Western democratic governments* — notably France, Austria and Belgium — have passed legislation against 'sects', but the failure to define 'sects' has led to unwarranted discrimination. All over the Western world, the worship of 'tolerance' has led to increased pressure on those intolerant enough to believe in absolutes and right and wrong.

c) *Networks of Christian intercessors* exist to pray for the persecuted Church. There is an annual Day of Prayer for the Persecuted Church which is coordinated globally by **WEA**. (See Appendix 2).

• The Church and the Great Commission

The whole of God's plan of redemption centres round the Church of his beloved Son. This is why he called Abraham (Genesis 12:3; Galatians 3:8). Christ died for the Church (Ephesians 2:16) and he lives as its Head (Ephesians 1:22). As part of his Body, our longing should be for its up-building and perfection (Col. 1:24). One day soon the Bride of Christ, the Church, will be complete and perfect (Ephesians 5:27; Rev. 7:9-10)!

The Church on earth is only an imperfect manifestation of the one, true and invisible Church of the Lord Jesus Christ, yet we are promised by Jesus that the gates of hell will not prevail against it. In some lands there are hundreds of thousands of congregations and in others maybe only one or two. The wheat and the tares are mixed, the divisions and weaknesses are all too plain and obvious, yet the Holy Spirit is working in and through the Church in all its diversity of doctrines, denominations, languages and personalities. It is through the Church that God wants redemption to be proclaimed to mankind. Many prayer points through the book major on the needs of the Church. Here are a few suggested items of wider application:

1 **Maintaining a clear witness to the uniqueness of Christ** in the midst of a growing religious pluralism, non-Christian religious revival, urbanization, modernity and relativism. Christians will be increasingly criticized for being "intolerant".

2 **Sustaining the centrality of the Scriptures** in today's world at a time when many Evangelicals in the West are becoming less firm in their convictions. Too often believers' thoughts, prejudices and fears are moulded more by the prevailing culture, philosophies, superstitions and religions of the society around them than by the Bible. Humanism in the West, Hinduism in India, etc., are examples. All such can rob Christians of their assurance, power and joy in the face of a hostile world, and side-track believers into focusing on secondary or irrelevant issues.

3 **The effective functioning of local congregations.** Each should be an organism, a body. Each member has gifts to contribute to the up-building of the whole, yet rarely do congregations function in this way. This emphasis on "body life" has come into prominence in the past three decades. New, innovative models of 'church' and its ministry are emerging. May every congregation be an effective body through which the Holy Spirit can work!

4 **Leadership — the key.** Pastors, ministers and elders need constant upholding in prayer. There is a worldwide lack of men and women truly called of God and deeply taught in the Scriptures to lead the churches — people willing to suffer scorn, poverty and the shame of the Cross for the sake of the Saviour who redeemed them. Those who accurately and effectively expound the Scriptures are few, especially in areas where the churches are growing rapidly. May all leaders be an example to their flocks in holy living, evangelism and missionary concern for a lost world!

5 **Spiritual depth.** This is rare in many congregations. Superficiality, an inadequate devotional life and worldliness are common. This highlights the need for effective teaching, in the mother tongue, of the Bible's content, doctrines, and applicability to life and witness.

6 **Victorious optimism** is rare where evangelical believers are a small and despised minority or in countries where there is widespread decline in commitment to the Lord. These believers are often introspective and timid, and hardly a mighty force for the pulling down of the fortifications of the devil. Believers need prayer that they may witness boldly and effectively.

7 **Young people.** In this modern age they are often lost to the Church and become worldly, even after a Christian upbringing, because of a growing generation gap and the pressures of the world around them. Every new generation needs to be evangelized afresh, or the churches soon become nominal. Young people need prayer as never before.

8 **Revival** has occurred in various parts of the world this century (see Regions), but not on the scale, nor with the effect, for which believers long in this critical and momentous time of history.

9 **Missionary vision.** An Acts 1:8 strategy is needed for every church and denomination. Amazing results have been achieved by a dedicated few. How speedily the world would be evangelized if all believers and every congregation obeyed the commands of Jesus in Acts 1, and believed His promises for enablement through the Holy Spirit! Pray for the awakening and growth of missionary concern. Pray for effective and practical missionary involvement in praying, giving and going and for the following:

a) *The speediest possible completion of the goals given in the Great Commission* by the Lord Jesus to His Church.

b) *All churches to make obedience to the Great Commission their primary ministry objective.* Only through this will the resources be available to bring the task to conclusion, or closure, in our generation.

c) *Leadership training institutions and programmes* to ensure that missions be a fundamental and core component of every course. Failure to do this has caused the centuries of neglect and marginalization of world evangelization in churches and agencies.

d) *Mission agency prayer, planning and deployment* to emphasize reaching unreached areas, peoples and cities. The Adopt-a-People Clearinghouse and the AD2000 and Beyond Movement have compiled a list of over 6,000 unreached and adoptable peoples submitted by agencies as targeted for entry. Many are those included in our World A totals, others are World B and C peoples. (See Appendix 2 for addresses of these organizations and agencies who can provide further information.)

e) *The adoption of unreached peoples* by churches, Christian groups, prayer circles and individuals. The task can be completed only as Christians take responsibility in earnest intercession until believers are won and churches planted in each people.

Note: For the vital role of the Church in God's plan for world evangelization and the history of what went right and wrong over the centuries, and what we should do about it, see *The Church is Bigger Than You Think* also written by Patrick Johnstone, and published by Christian Focus Publications. The book is due for revision using new data prepared for this edition of *Operation World*. See Appendix 9

• The Great Commission Harvesters

The Church is God's means for evangelizing the world, and from New Testament times men and women as individuals and teams have been set apart and sent out with the apostolic task of preaching the gospel beyond the reach of local congregations. Those members of the Church who move out in this way constitute the missionary force of the world.

1 **Mission agencies**. There has been a multiplication of Protestant missionary sending and support agencies over the past two centuries; this has become a worldwide phenomenon of great significance. Pray for:

a) *Effective strategies* to evangelize the world and plant churches among its diverse peoples. Lack of such can lead to misuse of resources and frustration for personnel.

b) *Adaptability* in a rapidly changing world. Few agencies are able to change structures and strategies to cope with the new and challenging demands of a changing world.

c) *Leadership* in mission agencies. These leaders need wisdom in setting clear objectives, guidance in the selection and placing of workers and ability to give them pastoral care and to maintain good relationships with secular authorities.

d) *Harmonious cooperation and fellowship between missionary-sending and missionary-receiving churches*. The growing emphasis on local church responsibility for world evangelism can lead to tensions and misunderstandings unless mutual responsibilities and relationships are clearly understood. The local churches and missionary agencies need each other. Neither can do the job alone.

e) *Effective cooperation between missionary agencies*. There is often unnecessary duplication of effort, and a lack of corporate planning together about ways to get the job done. The manner of entry of many agencies into the former Communist bloc after 1989 was a demonstration of how *not* to do it. See the Special Ministries section on p. 711.

f) *Working networks* in areas difficult to enter overtly as missionaries. The development of non-residential missionary programmes advanced quickly in the '80s. This and the tactful ministry of **Interdev**, a service agency dedicated to brokering such networks, are significant for new advances into what are often called *creative-access nations*. During the 1990s there were many new field partnerships initiated linking the churches and agencies from many nations. This needs to be developed and deepened.

2 **Missionaries**. The old type of individualistic missionary of the colonial era is no longer acceptable. Teamwork and an ability to work with, and under, leaders of other nationalities make great demands. The modern missionary must be a self-effacing spiritual giant! The missionary's personal walk with God is vital. The harsh realities of the modern world soon dispel the imagined glamour of pioneer missionary work. Pray for:

a) *Vital, supportive home fellowships of believers* who are willing to pray the missionary out to the field and keep him or her there through the years of greatest effectiveness. This is difficult to maintain with the rapid changes and turn-over in membership and in the pastoral team in most congregations.

b) *The supply of his/her financial need*. Missionary ministries are more expensive to maintain than those at home. Many live sacrificially for Christ, yet their living standards may appear sumptuous to local people, and a wise balance is needed. The problems of exchange control, export of currency, inflation, artificial exchange rates, endemic bribery, etc., are constant time-wasting frustrations.

c) *Adequate preparation for missionary work*. This is arduous and long — theological training, ministry experience, language learning and adaptation to a new land may take years before an effective ministry can be exercised. Those years can be traumatic and discouraging for both single workers and young married couples. The rising number of missionaries who fail to return for a second term of service is indicative of possible deficiencies in selection, preparation, structure and pastoral care.

d) *Cultural adjustment.* Culture shock is the subject of much humour, but is very real. Many prospective missionaries cannot make the adjustment to new foods, life styles, languages, value systems and attitudes. Some return home disillusioned and with a sense of failure; others react wrongly on the field and hinder fellowship and witness; yet others go too far in their adaptation and compromise their health and sometimes their faith. Balance and objectivity are needed.

e) **Protection from Satan's attacks.** The powers of darkness are real. In many areas Satan's kingdom has never been challenged before. Missionaries need discernment and authority to resist attacks he makes through health, the mind, opponents of the gospel and even Christian workers. Physical dangers are real — with an increase in hostage-taking, life-threatening diseases and insecurity. Missionaries need the victorious faith that will "bind the strong man and spoil his goods".

f) **Family life.** For singles, the missionary call may mean foregoing marriage for the sake of the gospel — loneliness can be a heavy burden to bear. For others, family life may be made difficult by living conditions, inadequate amenities or lack of finance, or be disrupted by long separations, many visitors and excessive workloads. Missionaries' children may be separated from their parents for long periods because of education, and can become resentful or rebellious in their teens. Pray that missionary families may be an effective witness and example of all that a Christian family should be.

g) **Commitment to God's will.** The assurance that God has guided to a particular ministry is often the only anchor to retain workers in difficult situations, misunderstandings, broken relationships and "impossible" crises. Pray that none may leave a place of calling for a negative or superficial reason, but only because of a positive leading from God.

h) **Fruitfulness.** All workers need the anointing of God on their lives, and an effective ministry that bears eternal fruit. For this they need clear objectives and time to achieve them. Too much time can be spent on survival and handling trivial interruptions, and too little on the real reason for being there. Only the Holy Spirit can give a worker that constraining love of Christ for sinners — human pity and love are inadequate.

i) **A sense of urgency.** Expulsions or enforced departure from the field could suddenly terminate a ministry. Missionaries need to work hard to train their successors and help local believers to maturity.

j) **Homecoming** for furlough, or for home ministry, which can be traumatic. Returning missionaries need the continued support of God's people for overcoming re-entry shock, establishing an effective rapport with churches at home and building an effective ministry.

• The Unfinished Task — Religious Systems

The World's Religions and the Challenge they represent. The 20th Century was one in which secularism seemed to triumph, but the 21st Century is likely to be one in which the world's religions vie with one another for the hearts and minds of humankind. The supposed 'tolerance' of the post-modern West is unlikely to extend globally to the religious systems of this world. Here follows a very brief mention of some of these religious systems and several global prayer challenges. More detail will be given in the subsequent sections of the book.

1 Christianity has become the most global of religions. There is no country without a Christian witness and only 10 without a visible congregation of indigenous believers (8 in Asia, 2 in Africa). There are 18 countries with a resident Christian population of less than 1%, and a further 22 with less than 5%. Over the 20th Century, Christianity declined slightly from 34.5% in 1900 to 32.5% in 2000. The precipitous decline of the past 30 years in Europe has been balanced by the growth in Asia and Africa. Much has been covered in the section on the Church in the previous pages.

a) **Nominalism** has become a major issue. In many countries the 'Christians' themselves need to be evangelized. Their spiritual needs cannot be ignored. Living in the after-glow of a Christian heritage does not confer eternal salvation. Many traditionally Christian populations know nothing of a personal faith, true repentance from sin and a trust in the finished work of Christ for their salvation. It is estimated that 1.2 billion (60%) are nominal and non-practising 'Christians'. Many millions more trust more in their good deeds than in God's grace for salvation. Many areas of Europe, Latin America and parts of Africa and Asia are Christianized but unconverted. Occultism and sin reign unchallenged. Pray for renewal, re-evangelization and new growth in such areas.

b) **Christo-pagans** who, while statistically counted as Christians, are practising occultists, shamanists, fetishists, etc. under a veneer of Christianity. This is particularly prevalent in Latin America among the Amerindians and Mestizo. It is also widespread in Africa where many indigenous groups are more influenced by ethnic religions than by the gospel. Europe and Asia, too, have millions of professing Christians who are just as syncretistic. Evangelizing such people and making them into disciples of the Lord Jesus is just as necessary as winning those of other religions — even if this results in accusations of proselytism.

c) **Sectarianism.** The term 'sect' is loaded and misused. Many genuine believers in Christ are persecuted or harassed because of being so described. Yet there are millions of 'Christians' who define their own church or group as the sole possessors of Truth — some such are the Mormons, Jehovah's Witnesses and many other smaller groups. They need to be freed from the teachings that have ensnared them. See the Special Ministries section on p. 709.

2 **Muslims** live largely in the great arc of territory stretching from West Africa through Central Asia, to Indonesia. Their growth in the 20th Century has been significant — from 12.3% in 1900 to 21.1% in 2000. Most of this growth has been through a higher birth rate and expansion through migration. Conversion growth has been greatest in West Africa, Indonesia and the USA. Pray for:

a) **The eyes and hearts of Muslims to be opened** to the person of the Lord Jesus Christ. Built into Islam are specific denials of truths fundamental to us who believe in Him. The barriers to faith are so numerous that it requires a deep working of the Holy Spirit — often through supernatural revelations or miracles.

b) **Muslim background believers in Christ** who are relatively few. Only in a few areas such as parts of Indonesia, Central Asia, Nigeria and Algeria have there been significant turnings to Christ. They face severe pressures and even death. Many Muslim lands have adopted *shari'a* laws which require the death penalty for apostates from Islam.

c) **Christian ministries to Muslims.** These have long been limited, but are on the increase. Yet only about 6% of all foreign missionaries are working for the blessing of Muslims, who constitute a third of all non-Christians. Pray for more to be called, equipped and led into fruitful ministry to Muslims.

d) **Outreach to Islamists.** Some estimate that 30% of Muslims would now align themselves with Islamism and its goal of world domination by force, if necessary. Pray for effective means of reaching them.

3 **The non-religious bloc** has shown the most growth in the 20th Century, with about 0.2% of the world's population in 1900 and peaking in 1980, but in 2000 representing 15.5% — mainly Europeans and Chinese. Since the collapse of Communism, there has been a rise in spirituality and slight decline in the non-religious percentage. Nevertheless Christians have generally proved ineffective in communicating the gospel in a relevant and winsome way to secular, post-modern culture. Pray for change — for Christians to become relevant, effective witnesses and for the tide of materialistic secularism to be turned.

4 **Hinduism** has made notable missionary inroads in the West through the wide acceptance of transcendental meditation, yoga, New Age thinking, sects such as Hare Krishna and Indian *gurus*. It has also become more militant and repressive of all other religious minorities in its heartlands of India and Nepal.

a) **The Indian sub-continent** has the largest concentration and variety of least-reached peoples and people groups on earth. The gospel has spread most to the poor and marginalized, while the main body of caste Hindus remains unevangelized.

b) **The need for workers able to reach caste Hindus** is great. Pray for Indian Christians and others to be called and enabled to reach them despite present restrictive laws and a rampant Hindu militancy that persecutes Christians.

c) **A de-Westernized, culturally appropriate pattern of Christian living and community** is needed. Pray for the Holy Spirit to bring the light of the gospel to influential Hindus.

d) **Since 2001 the downtrodden Dalit-Bahujan population** have become politically active in response to extremist Hinduists, and threaten to cut all links with the Hinduism that oppressed them. Up to 300 million people could choose another religion over the next decade or two.

5 **Buddhism** is the state religion of five nations in Asia, the majority in a further four, and a significant minority in yet another 11. Over half of this total are followers of the mixture of the Chinese religions, Taoism, Confucianism and Buddhism. The various religious systems are so intermingled that a clear differentiation is hard to make. There are also major new religions which are offshoots of Buddhism — Cao Dai in Vietnam, Falun Gong in China, Sokka Gokkai in Japan. Since the discrediting of Communism after 1990, Buddhism has had a measure of resurgence in East and Southeast Asia, but overall it continues its gradual decline. The Dalai Lama of Tibet has popularized Buddhism in the West. Relatively few Buddhists have come to Christ despite two or more centuries of presenting the gospel to them in such lands as Thailand, Myanmar, Sri Lanka, Tibet, etc.

6 **Ethnic religions** and the more modern varieties of spiritism continue to decline in world percentage but are showing significant increase in vitality in every continent. Many followers of world religions remain, in practice, shamanists, animists, idolaters, spiritists, ancestor worshippers, fetishists, *wiccan*, etc. Widespread fascination with the occult is an indication of the fierceness of the spiritual conflict in which we are engaged.

7 **Sikhism** is one of the more recent world religions and originated in northeast India. Many Sikhs have migrated to other countries — Canada, East Africa, Britain, Southeast Asia. Few Christians have ever sought to understand their religion and find ways of sharing the gospel. So Christians from a Sikh background remain relatively few.

8 **Jews** are declining in numbers in most countries — through low birthrates, secularization, conversions to Christ and emigration to Israel. Nearly 30% of all Jews now live in Israel. Of the 14 million Jews, some estimate that there may be about 100,000 Messianic Jews, the majority in the USA. That Jews should find salvation in Messiah Yeshua remains a key concern for Christians.

9 **Numerous other religions** remain a challenge for Christian witness — the 6 million **Baha'i** worldwide, 4 million **Jains** in India and the 3.5 million **Parsees**. Very few Jains or Parsees have ever come to faith in Christ.

• The Unfinished Task — The World's Peoples

It was only during the 1990s that a reasonably complete listing of the world's peoples and languages was developed. For the first time in history we have a reasonably clear picture of the remaining task for us to disciple the nations.

Here is a summary of our present assessment of the least reached peoples. Of the world's 12,000 ethnolinguistic peoples, about 3,000-3,600 are 'World A' peoples in which less than 50% are likely to have heard the gospel. Nearly all originate from the 10/40 Window area and most can be broadly classified in 11 major Affinity Blocs. Their affinities include culture, language use, geography, history, etc. See the map on p.17. The table below shows the number of peoples, their populations (in 1,000's) and the number of professing Christians (also in 1,000's) for all peoples (Worlds A, B, C) and for the least reached (World A).

Affinity Bloc	Peoples		Population		Christians		Area
	Total	World A	Total	World A	Total	World A	
Sub-Saharan	1,709	893	307,288	124,167	86,432	2,830	W Africa to Sudan.
Horn of African	135	83	50,890	24,944	13,360	619	Excluding Ethiopians.
Arab World	410	242	247,225	·98,351	19,405	252	North Africa and West Asia.
Indo-Iranian	141	134	127,557	100,283	113	74	E Turkey, Iran, Afghan., NE Pakistan.
Turkic/Altaic.	139	126	90,079	89,927	42	8	Turkey, C Asia, Siberia, China, Mongo- lia.
Tibeto-Burman	422	276	80,049	35,022	6,945	808	W China, Himalayas, Myanmar, etc.
South Asian	773	437	1456,468	735,576	47,066	7,068	Important caste distinctions not incl.
SE Asian	429	338	204,842	98,637	8,223	1,270	Indo-China, Thailand, S & SW China.
East Asian	73	28	151,605	146,789	3,718	2,047	Excl. Chinese, South Koreans.
Malay	938	554	245,355	123,334	25,923	1,116	Excl. Filipinos, Malagasy, Chamorro.
Jewish	175	92	14,318	2,693	549	0	Mainly N Amer., Israel, but also global.
Rest of World	6,656	354	3,090,324	82,277	1,761,224	3,908	C&E Africa, Eur, E Asia, Americas, Pacific.
World Total	**12,000**	**3,557**	**6,066,000**	**1,662,000**	**1,973,000**	**20,000**	

Over 90% of all the least-reached peoples on earth either live within the areas shown on the above map or have migrated to other parts of the world. In all the rest of the world are about 350 peoples with 82 million individuals which are in the least-reached category.

There are an estimated 20 million Christians among the World A peoples, and probably some ongoing church-planting ministry among 2,500 of the 3,500 peoples. Within these Affinity Blocs are the more closely related 160 or so people clusters into which a majority of these less-reached can be grouped. Many of these are mentioned later in the book. Here we briefly cover the 11 Affinity Blocs themselves and some of the more important people clusters:

Affinity Bloc	Some Major Unreached People clusters
Sub-Saharan	Malinke, Soninke, Fulbe, Wolof, Gur, Chadian peoples, Hausa, Songhai, Kanuri, Zerma, Pygmy.
Horn of African	Afar, Beja, Somali, Oromo, Tigre, Nubian.
Arab World	Arabian Arab, Levant Arab, North African Arab, Hassaniya Arab, Berbers, Tuareg
Indo-Iranian	Persian, Kurd, Pathan, Baluch, Brahui, Tajik, Hazara, Mazanderani.
Turkic/Altaic	Azeri, Turk, Turkmen, Uyghur, Uzbek, Bashkort, Kazakh, Kyrgyz, Tatar, Mongolian, Siberian peoples.
Tibeto-Burman	Tibetan, Bhutanese, Burmese, Gurung, Newar, etc.
South Asian	Assamese, Bengali, Bhil, Bihari, N Indian, Deccani, Gond, Marathi, Gujarati, Gypsy, Sindhi, etc.
S.E Asian	Thai, Dai, Lao, Vietnamese, Khmer, Puyi.
East Asian	Hui and Hakka Chinese, Japanese, Taiwanese, Manchurian.
Malay	Sumatran peoples, Minangkabau, Sunda, Madura, Malay, Bali, Sasak, Bugi, Philippine Muslims & Tribals.
Jewish	Sephardi (of Spanish/North African origin), Ashenkazi (European origin), Falasha (Ethiopia), etc.
Rest of World	Caucasus peoples, Bosnian, Albanian, Arctic peoples, Mexican indigenous peoples, West Irian peoples.
World Total	Approximately 160 people clusters embracing about 80% of the world's least reached peoples.

• Challenges for Prayer

1 **Many of the least-reached** are hedged in by political, religious, social and spiritual barriers, but they need cross-cultural gospel input from workers called of God. Pray that they may have a revelation of the grace and power of God for effective growing churches to be planted.

2 **Relatively few of these 3,500 peoples have no known Christians** among them, but in most they constitute a small minority — on average 1.2% of the population. They face many pressures and even persecution. Pray that these Christians may know the sustaining grace of God and power of the Holy Spirit to witness to their own people.

3 **Nearly 1,500 of these peoples have populations of less than 10,000**. For many, we do not have adequate information. This highlights the need for good national and international research teams to find out the need for these and larger peoples so that the Church may be activated to bring them the good news.

4 **Churches around the world need to gain a vision for unreached peoples**. Pray for congregations that have already adopted a people that this adoption may lead to significant progress among the adopted people. Pray that more congregations may catch such a vision.

5 **There must be disciples made from every people on earth**. This implies the need for a body of believers in every people and, more, a church that impacts every part of that people. This is a noble and achievable goal. It is also linked to the coming again of the Lord Jesus for His Church. Pray that the Church may passionately pursue this goal to conclusion and then be the generation that brings back the King!

• The Great Commission and the Unfinished Task

The Lord Jesus Christ gave His Church clear instructions in His resurrection ministry:

The evangelistic challenge in Mark 16:15.

The discipling/church planting challenge in Matthew 28:18-20.

The teaching challenge of Luke 24.

The missions challenge of John 20:21.

The global challenge of Acts 1:8.

This encompasses the task before us, and we want to see its completion as soon as possible! I believe the evidence of this book is that we have a measurable, finishable task — big though it might still be — it is impossible through human planning, effort, strategizing or sacrifice, but only in complete dependence on our God. Hence the challenge to pray!

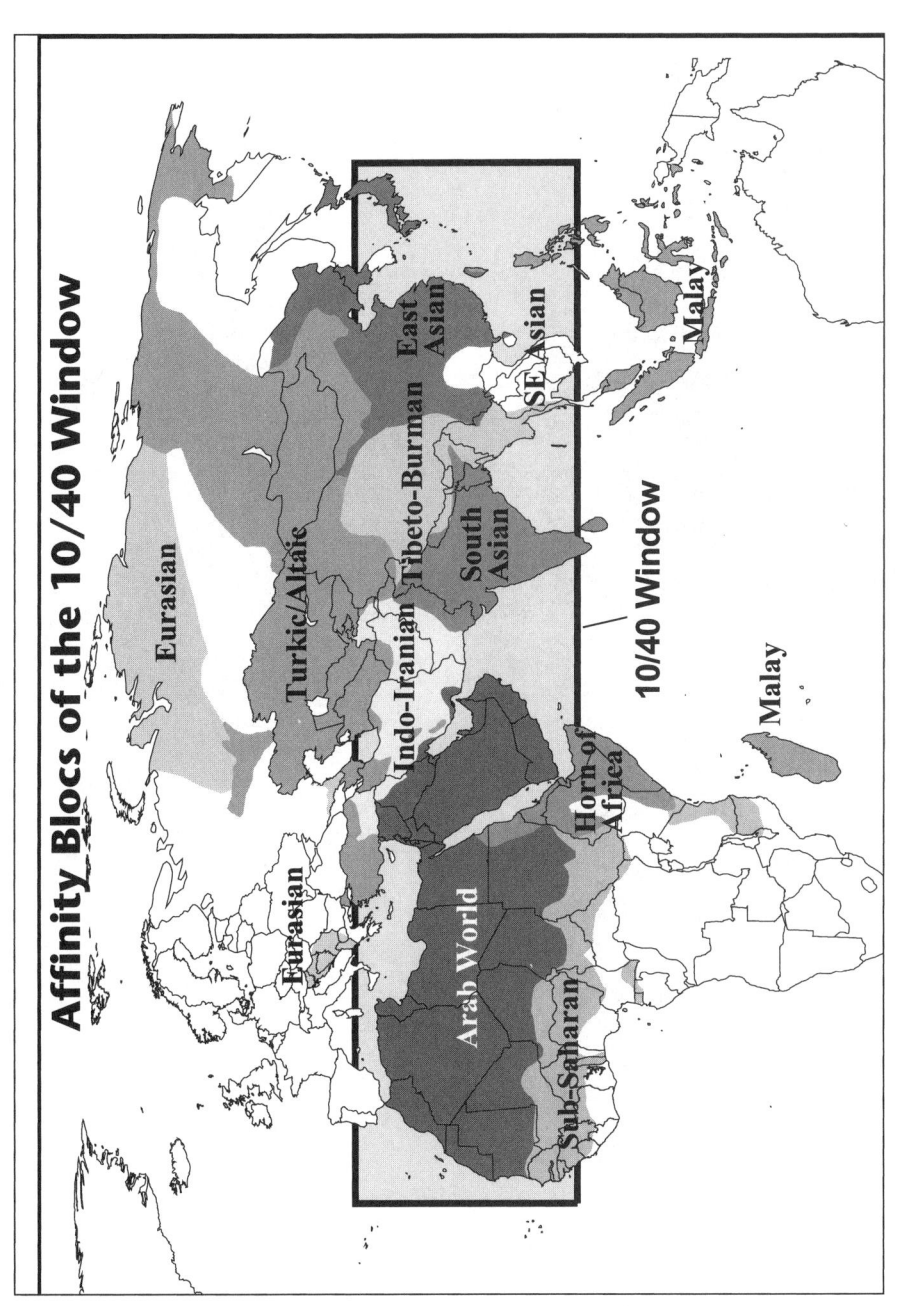

Affinity Blocs of the 10/40 Window

Eurasian

Turkic/Altaic

Indo-Iranian

Tibeto-Burman

East Asian

SE Asian

South Asian

Malay

10/40 Window

Malay

Eurasian

Arab World

Horn of Africa

Sub-Saharan

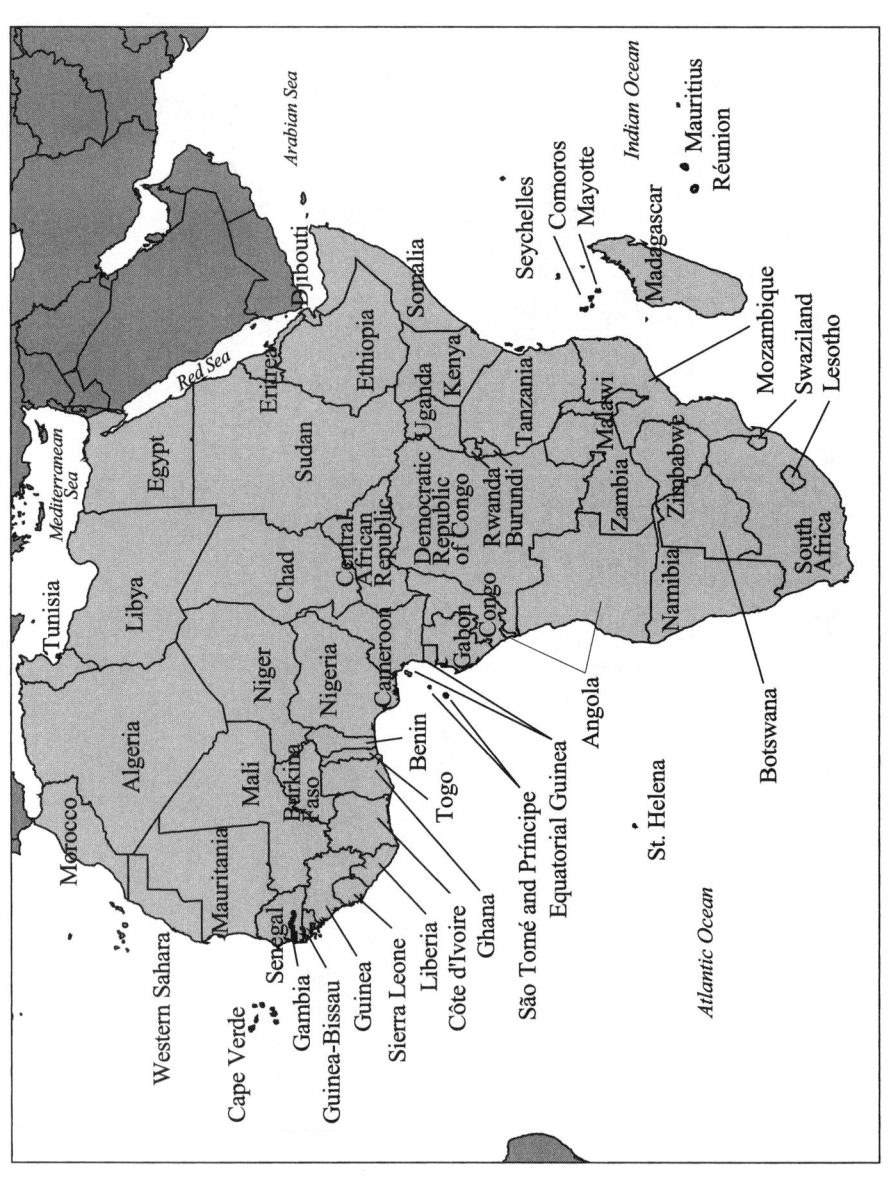

AFRICA

	Population 2000	Main Religions	non-Chr%	All Chr %	Evang-elical%	Peoples All	World A	JPL
Algeria	31.5	M	99.7	0.3	0.2	43	36	16
Angola	12.9	X	5.9	94.1	16.4	59	7	1
Benin	6.1	EXM	68.2	31.8	4.2	57	29	13
Botswana	1.6	XE	33.1	66.9	8.0	53	20	4
British Indian Ocean	0.0	na	0.0	0.0	0.0	4	0	0
Burkina Faso	11.9	MEX	81.6	18.4	8.0	79	61	24
Burundi	6.7	XE	9.9	90.1	20.0	13	3	0
Cameroon	15.1	XM	31.0	69.0	6.4	296	75	30
Cape Verde Islands	0.4	X	4.9	95.1	4.7	6	0	0
Central African Republic	3.6	XME	29.6	70.4	34.8	94	19	5
Chad	7.7	MXE	72.2	27.8	13.5	135	86	42
Comoros	0.6	M	99.2	0.8	0.1	10	6	3
Congo	2.9	X	8.7	91.3	13.8	78	2	1
Congo-DRC	51.7	X	4.7	95.3	19.4	259	4	0
Côte d'Ivoire	14.8	MXE	68.2	31.8	9.2	192	39	18
Djibouti	0.6	M	95.3	4.7	0.1	9	5	4
Egypt	68.5	M	87.0	13.0	2.5	37	21	15
Equatorial Guinea	0.5	X	4.9	95.1	3.2	22	2	2
Eritrea	3.9	MX	52.6	47.4	1.7	15	7	0
Ethiopia	62.6	XM	35.0	65.0	19.7	144	64	25
Gabon	1.2	XEM	22.1	77.9	14.2	50	2	1
Gambia, The	1.3	ME	95.9	4.1	0.3	31	19	7
Ghana	20.2	XME	36.5	63.6	14.8	107	24	12
Guinea	7.4	ME	95.3	4.7	1.0	43	32	14
Guinea-Bissau	1.2	MEX	85.7	14.3	1.1	31	23	4
Kenya	30.1	XEM	21.4	78.6	35.8	123	45	15
Lesotho	2.2	XE	28.2	71.9	8.2	12	0	0
Liberia	3.2	EXM	61.7	38.3	9.1	46	5	6
Libya	5.6	M	97.5	2.5	0.3	39	26	18
Madagascar	15.9	XEM	37.2	62.8	8.8	54	11	5
Malawi	10.9	XME	22.2	77.8	20.4	30	3	1
Mali	11.2	ME	98.2	1.8	0.8	44	39	23
Mauritania	2.7	M	99.8	0.2	0.0	25	21	4
Mauritius	1.2	HXM	67.1	32.9	7.9	23	1	1
Mayotte	0.1	M	97.1	2.9	0.0	9	7	0
Morocco	28.2	M	99.9	0.1	0.0	31	24	12
Mozambique	19.7	XEM	42.4	57.7	13.5	56	7	5
Namibia	1.7	XEN	20.1	80.0	10.3	32	11	1
Niger	10.7	M	99.6	0.4	0.1	36	24	14
Nigeria	111.5	XME	47.4	52.6	23.5	490	189	45
Réunion	0.7	XHN	15.1	84.9	5.2	16	2	0
Rwanda	7.7	XM	19.2	80.8	22.8	12	3	1
São Tomé	0.1	X	7.1	92.9	2.2	6	0	1
Senegal	9.5	M	95.2	4.8	0.1	57	38	20
Seychelles	0.1	X	3.1	96.9	5.3	9	1	0
Sierra Leone	4.9	MEX	88.3	11.7	3.2	30	15	9
Somalia	10.1	M	100.0	0.1	0.0	28	22	8
South Africa	40.4	XEN	26.5	73.5	19.3	69	2	0
St Helena	0.0	X	4.3	95.7	5.2	3	0	0
Sudan	29.5	MXE	76.8	23.2	10.3	244	165	90
Swaziland	1.0	XE	17.3	82.7	29.4	11	1	0
Tanzania	33.5	XME	48.6	51.4	17.0	162	38	16
Togo	4.6	XEM	49.3	50.7	9.0	52	11	15
Tunisia	9.6	M	99.8	0.2	0.0	24	15	4
Uganda	21.8	XM	11.4	88.7	46.3	62	5	5
Western Sahara	0.3	M	0.0	0.0	0.0	11	10	0
Zambia	9.2	XE	15.0	85.0	25.0	85	5	4
Zimbabwe	11.7	XE	28.3	71.7	25.3	41	3	1
Total (58 countries)	**784.3**		**51.6**	**48.4**	**14.8**	**3839**	**1335**	**565**

Africa

GEOGRAPHY

Area 30,212,000 sq.km; 22.3% of the surface area of the world's 238 countries. Of this, 20.6 million sq.km is in countries south of the Sahara and 9.68 mill. in the 7 nations of North Africa.

NOTE In this edition of Operation World we are including the statistics of the 7 North African, Arabic-speaking countries in Africa. The 1993 edition included North Africa with the Middle East, which is no longer handled as a single entity. Please see Asia and the Arab World subsection for further information relevant to the Arab majority of North Africa.

Comments on countries included in the map, table and text.

1 All countries included — 55.

2 Western Sahara is included with Morocco because Morocco occupies the territory.

3 The Spanish city enclaves of **Ceuta** and **Melilla** on Morocco's north coast are included together with the Canary Islands in Spain.

4 The following small island territories around Africa are included under Africa: **Cape Verde, Comores, St Helena, Mauritius, Réunion, Seychelles, British Indian Ocean Territory.**

5 Somalia still includes **Somaliland** and **Puntland**, despite their 'independence'.

Population		Ann.Gr.	Density
2000	784,315,000	+2.41%	26 per sq. km.
2010	973,181,300	+2.15%	32 per sq. km.
2025	1,298,171,000	+1.81%	43 per sq. km.

Africa's population growth rate is slowing rapidly — largely through the effects of AIDS and the return of killer diseases such as malaria and tuberculosis. Africa has 12.9% of the world's population.

Cities There are 84 cities in Africa with over one million inhabitants, 4 of these being over 10 million. Urbanites 30%.

PEOPLES

Over 3,500 ethnic groups.

African 77.9%. Almost entirely Negroid peoples of three major types — West African, Sudanic and Bantu. There are remnants of the pre-negroid peoples:

Pygmies in the rainforests of Central Africa (765,000).

Khoi-khoi (Khoisan) in Southern Africa (495,000).

Arab 17.3%. Almost all in North Africa and some in the Sahel and on the East African coast. Many mutually unintelligible dialects spoken.

Imazighen (Berber) 2.6%. The indigenous peoples of North Africa; including the Tuareg of the Sahara and Maures (mixed Arab/Berber) in West Africa.

European 1.1%. Mostly South Africa, but significant minorities in most lands.

Mixed race 0.7%. Mostly South Africa, Réunion and Mauritius.

Asian 0.4%. Predominantly Indians in Mauritius and KwaZulu-Natal in South Africa. Significant minorities in East and Central Africa.

Languages 2,110; 30.5% of the world's total. **Official languages** Arabic in North Africa (7 countries). Elsewhere French (22), English (21), Portuguese (4), Spanish (1). The increasing use of European languages in education is at the expense of local languages. In only 6 nations is an African language officially used as the main means of conducting the nation's business.

Bible translation Africa is the greatest remaining challenge for Bible translation with existing openings for missionary translators. **Languages with Scriptures** 130Bi 237NT 250por. There is work in progress in 373 and a definite need for translators in 297 more. This latter number could rise to 1,290 after careful field research.

ECONOMY

Africa's economy has stagnated for 40 years; many countries have become poorer, a few have made progress. There are many causes for decline:

1 Population growth with rapid deforestation and desertification. Most Africans are subsistence farmers.

2 Low investment in agriculture and development of viable methods of food production, distribution and sale. Food aid often distorts local marketing and diet patterns.

3 Corrupt rulers who have enriched themselves or their ethnic group. In some countries such as Nigeria and Congo-DRC the national debt probably equals the money stolen by unethical leaders.

4 Foreign debt. This has steadily grown. Many impoverished countries spend more on debt servicing than on health and education. The global movement to cancel such debts (Jubilee 2000) would only help if, as has often happened, the gains were not then transferred to off-shore banks or to benefit illegal arms dealers.

5 Natural disasters — devastating famines, both drought- and war-induced in the Sahel and Horn of Africa (Ethiopia, Somalia).

6 Disease. The terrible effects of AIDS and the return of old scourges such as prophylactic-resistant malaria, sleeping sickness, TB, etc. Whole economies in central and southern Africa are disintegrating as a result.

7 War has deeply affected 19 nations during the 1990s. Most of the world's active wars in 2000 were in Africa. Countries such as Sierra Leone,

Liberia, Congo-DRC, Burundi, Rwanda, Sudan, Eritrea and Somalia have suffered immense damage and casualties. Millions have become refugees.

The **HDI** is a measure of the quality of life of 174 nations. Of the bottom 40 in this list, 33 are in Africa. **Income/person** $660 (2% of USA). Only 1.7% of the world's GNP is generated in Africa.

POLITICS

Black Africa's isolation from the rest of the world ended in the 'Scramble for Africa' by the European colonial powers in the 19ᵗʰ Century. A century of colonial rule brought a measure of peace, education, improvement in living standards and some economic development. The negative was the legacy of inappropriate colonial borders which cut through African ethnic, economic and political networks and has subsequently been the cause of much pain, tension and war. Between 1957 and 1994 all states in Africa became independent. Only the small island territories of Réunion, Mayotte, St Helena and the British Indian Ocean Territory remain linked to Europe. Post-Cold War Africa is very different. In the past superpower rivalry led to the courting of African countries' votes in the UN.

1 Foreign interest and investment has waned.

2 There have been increased efforts to make multi-party politics and democracy work — but with limited success. In the 1990s, 49 states held multi-party elections, but only 10 led to a change of government and only 3 Presidents have stepped down voluntarily after an electoral defeat.

3 The colonially drawn frontiers that defined African countries for 40 years are under threat. Eritrea's successful independence bid from Ethiopia broke that pattern. Secessionist movements and wars have afflicted Sudan, Somalia, Ethiopia, Congo-DRC, etc. The dismemberment of the vast territories of Congo-DRC could be a result of the 9-nation Central African Great Lakes War that followed the Rwanda genocide of 1994.

4 'Ethnic cleansing' has caused tragic bloodshed, tides of refugees and even armies with many child-soldiers in Rwanda, Burundi, Congo, Liberia, Sierra Leone, Sudan and Uganda.

5 Violent Islamist movements have deeply affected the continent from Algeria in the north to South Africa. Bitter guerrilla warfare in Algeria, terrorist attacks in Kenya, *jihad* against Christians in Sudan and massacres of Christians in northern Nigeria are just some of the evidences of this.

RELIGION

Religious freedom has increased over much of Africa during the 1990s, but persecution of Christians by Muslims has also increased in Egypt, Sudan, northern Nigeria and the Comores.

Religions	Population %	Adherents	Ann.Gr.
Christian	48.37	379.4m	+2.83%
Muslim	41.32	324.1m	+2.53%
Traditional ethnic	8.74	68.6m	-0.97%
non-Religious/other	1.15	9.0m	+4.85%
Hindu	0.22	1.71m	+1.42%
Baha'i	0.19	1.47m	+2.32%
Jewish	0.01	96,400	+1.02%

Christians	Denom.	Affil.%	,000	Ann.Gr.
Protestant	1,927	12.59	98,768	+4.2%
Independent	13,137	9.99	78,360	+3.9%
Anglican	36	4.12	32,329	+5.2%
Catholic	63	15.10	118,423	+2.6%
Orthodox	54	5.96	46,727	+0.5%
Marginal	164	0.45	3,506	+6.0%
Unaffiliated		3.65	28,664	n.a.
Doubly affiliated		*-3.46*	*-27,119*	*n.a.*

Trans-bloc Groupings	pop. %	,000	Ann.Gr.
Evangelical	14.8	116,076	+4.6%
Charismatic	10.7	83,792	+4.3%
Pentecostal	5.2	41,145	+5.3%

Missionaries from African agency bases
P,I,A 12,442 in 620 agencies with 3,126 in other lands.

Missionaries to Africa
P,I,A 17,737 expatriates in 620 agencies.

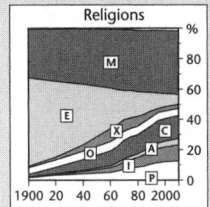
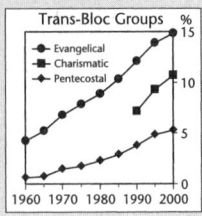

• Answers to Prayer

1 **The peaceful ending of apartheid in South Africa** and transition to multi-racial democratic government was considered impossible. The miracle occurred in answer to fervent prayer by millions of Christians in South Africa and beyond.

2 **In the 20ᵗʰ Century**, Christianity became the religion of the majority in sub-Saharan Africa. In 1900 there were 8 million Christians (10% of the population of Africa); by 2000 there were 351 million (48.4% of the population of Africa — 60% of sub-Saharan Africa).

3 **The growth of Evangelicals has been even more spectacular**. In 1900 Evangelicals were 1.6 million (1.5%), but in 2000 were 116million (14.8%).

4 **Remarkable revival movements** have blessed the Church - in East Africa in the 1940s - '60s, and more recently in Ethiopia which resulted in massive church growth.

5 **The work of evangelical missions** has been blessed by God with much fruit. Huge families of churches have come into being — through **SIM** (nearly 9m affiliated) and **AIM** (6.5m).

6 **A new sense of strongly evangelical Third Wave Pentecostal** denominations has emerged over the past 30 years. They are strong on the Scriptures and outreach, expectant of miracles, fervent in prayer and courageous against the powers of darkness. To name only a few: The Redeemed Christian Church in Nigeria with 2 million linked to them, the Deeper Life Bible Church in Nigeria has rapidly grown to 450,000 members with mission work in over 42 countries of the world, and the Zimbabwe Assemblies of God, Africa to 1.6m affiliates to become the largest denomination in the country.

7 **Countries which experienced exceptional evangelical growth** during the 1990s — Ethiopia, Nigeria, Mozambique, Zambia, Zimbabwe and Algeria (the turning of many Kabyle Berbers to Christ) being some.

8 **The impact of the gospel on the educated**. The ministry of **SU**, **IFES** and others among students has been remarkable; through this and the ministry of churches and agencies a large proportion of Africa's professionals and leaders in Anglophone countries are committed Christians. Their influence is becoming decisive in addressing corruption and social evils and in affecting the power structures of society. The democracy movement, Zambia's change of government and pressure for positive change in Malawi, Congo-DRC, South Africa, Uganda and other countries is much due to Christian involvement. May this impact grow!

9 **A vision for saturation church planting** has grown. The pioneering movement was in Ghana in the 1980s and a number of other countries have taken up this challenge — the most successful being Zimbabwe and Chad.

10 **Mission vision**. This has grown, and the number of African missionaries and agencies is steadily increasing. Notable in this respect is the maturity and variety of South African and Nigerian missions, many of the latter with a strong emphasis on Muslim and unreached people outreach. Also praiseworthy are missionary training initiatives all over Africa (AEM), South Africa (with a multiplicity of options), West Africa (Calvary Ministries and others) and East Africa (Africa Inland Church).

• Africa's Hot Spots

NOTE Feb 2004 - Post 11 September 2001 developments. There are significant changes to note and pray over:

1 **Africa's Wars.** The wars in Angola and Sierra Leone have ended with an uneasy peace arranged, but now comes the need to heal these traumatized nations. Côte d'Ivoire has slid into a war which is a northern revolt (largely Muslim and immigrant populations) against the southern peoples who happen to be largely Christian. Tortuous peace negotiations sputter on between the warring groups in Congo, CAR and Sudan.

2 **Poverty has increased** in much of the continent – especially in Zimbabwe where President Mugabe's dictatorial control through gangs of thugs has brought the country to famine conditions and economic destitution.

3 **The seriousness of the AIDS catastrophe** in Africa is beginning to receive more attention from national politicians and international bodies, but too little is being done. The vast costs of the post-9/11 security needs have crimped vital help to the most needy countries.

These warrant passionate prayer:

1 **The Great Lakes War**. This became Africa's first major international conflict. Tensions between the Hutu and Tutsi peoples in Rwanda and Burundi have led to civil wars and periodic genocidal massacres over the past four decades. The Rwanda genocide of 1994 triggered a chain reaction of war and waves of refugees affecting surrounding countries. This interlocked with the wars already being fought in Angola, Sudan and between Ethiopia and

Eritrea. The impact on Congo has been devastating for much of the country and continues to affect millions of people. Pray for:

a) **African and international peacemakers** in their arduous, thankless task and for resolution of the underlying causes of war.

b) **The warring factions** and their leaders to end their fighting and for peace to be restored.

c) **The millions of refugees** to be adequately provided for and ultimately resettled. Many NGOs are involved.

d) **Recovery** through repentance of perpetrators, justice for the offended, forgiveness given and received and the long process of reconstruction for ruined lives, families and countries.

2 **The Horn of Africa** was the scene of terrible events in the 1990s.

a) **Somalia descended into anarchy** with humiliating failures for the UN and the USA in finding solutions. Pray that the Somalis may find workable solutions to the chaos they have created.

b) **Ethiopia and Eritrea's unexpected, unnecessary war** in 1998-2000 between two largely Christian nations led to heavy casualties. An uneasy cease-fire prevailed in 2001, but lasting peace, restoration of trust and reopening of trade are needed. Eritrea has become a dictatorship.

3 **The West African debacle** of Liberia's civil wars in the last decade resulted in the immense destruction of lives, property and mass exploitation of children as soldiers. This conflict spilled over to Sierra Leone, Guinea and Côte d'Ivoire. It has drawn in West African and UN forces who have who have sought to impose a measure of peace. A whole generation has been deeply scarred.

4 **The Maghreb conflicts** — the Algerian civil war with its unending bloody massacres of civilians, and the unresolved conflict about the future of the Western Sahara occupied by Morocco since 1974.

5 **Sudan's 40-year civil war** with its Islamic *jihad* overtones in which the Muslim north is seeking to subjugate the largely Christian south and impose *shari'a* law and Islam.

6 **The tragic economic collapse of once-wealthy Zimbabwe** was provoked by the efforts of President Mugabe to retain power and eliminate all challenges to misrule and looting of the country's wealth.

• Trends to Watch

A few of the major international trends are given for prayerful attention. See under individual countries for more specific detail.

1 **AIDS in Africa** now overshadows the future of the continent — 71% of the world's AIDS cases in 1999 were in Africa. By 2000 a moderate estimate was of 25 million infected with HIV and 12.25 million orphans due to AIDS. Nearly 10% of the adult population of sub-Saharan Africa was infected. Lowered immunity has stimulated the spread of TB and other diseases. Life expectancies are dropping fast. Whole families, communities and economic structures are being decimated. Deaths by 2000 were estimated at 13.7 million; 6,000 were dying daily in 1999. Pray for:

a) **The focal areas of infection.** These are **South-Central Africa** with 20-25% of the adult population of Zimbabwe, Botswana, Lesotho, Namibia and Swaziland infected. Only 30% of Zimbabwe's 15-year old girls are expected to reach the age of 30. Malawi, South Africa and Zambia are not far behind. Other focal areas are East Africa, Congo-DRC and Abidjan in Côte d'Ivoire. Only in Uganda has the rapid spread of AIDS been reversed. Pray that the leaders of African nations might be roused from lethargy, pull their heads from the sand and take all necessary action to stem this human catastrophe.

b) **Radical changes in society** that deal with the moral, social and spiritual deficiencies that spread the disease. Widespread promiscuity even among Christians, pernicious lies ('men become sick unless they frequently have sexual intercourse'; 'sex with a virgin cures AIDS') and the stigma of confessing to having the virus all contribute to this spread.

c) **Mobilization of churches** to tackle the causes and effects of AIDS. They alone have the belief system, moral authority and local presence to be effective in ministries of prevention and care. Most churches have long ignored the issue or run away from the implications of involvement. Pray that out of this tragedy may emerge a more effective, caring, relevant, attractive Church in Africa.

d) ***Deployment of Christian agencies*** and skills to empower the Church in this new realm of ministry. For decades, this will be a key area for medical missions as national health systems crumble under the effects of low investment and the AIDS pandemic.

2 **The ongoing weaknesses of African democratic institutions**. Despotism, 'kleptocracies' (rulers that rob the national treasury), tyranny and suppression of any opposition still plague many countries. Intercede for effective and peaceful change to accountable government and riddance of despotism in Libya, Kenya, Congo-DRC, Zimbabwe, Angola, Gabon, Togo, Liberia, Equatorial Guinea and Congo-Brazzaville. Pray that Christian politicians who are transparently honest, flint-faced against corruption and nepotism may be raised up and preserved in their testimony once in power. President Moi in Kenya, a member of an evangelical church, has lost his credibility and President Chiluba of Zambia, an active Pentecostal, is in danger of the same. Pray for Christian Presidents such as Obasanjo of Nigeria, Mkapa of Tanzania and Matthieu Kérékou of Benin that they may rule without favour and in fairness as they grapple with the serious problems of their nations. The rapid spread of mobile phones and the Internet in Africa can be one means of exposing sin, corruption and abuse of power.

3 **The Muslim-Christian fault-line** stretching from Senegal across the Sahel to Ethiopia and along Africa's Indian Ocean seaboard. The potential for widened conflagrations and confrontations is high because of increasingly aggressive Islamist movements and African Christian evangelism gaining converts from within Muslim communities. Only in Sudan and Nigeria has this led to war or mass violence, but Guinea-Bissau, Côte d'Ivoire and Chad are in danger of trouble in the near future.

4 **Africa's deepening poverty** and the right means to alleviate it in the long-term. Part is locally induced — poor health care, massive corruption, greed, war. Part is of foreign origin — inappropriate aid programmes, unfair trading agreements, short-term aid in crises without long-term development, use of foreign rather than local skills and cultural mechanisms. The overall effects — distorted economies, a brain drain of African professionals, 40% of children not in school, degeneration of health care and communications.

a) ***The governments of richer trading nations*** need to implement a range of measures to ensure a fair price for African produce and realize that failure leads to raised need for aid. Dumping unwanted and inappropriate foodstuffs and medicines as aid can create more problems than it solves.

b) ***Secular and religious NGOs*** from the World Bank to the smallest Christian aid agency need a humble sensitivity to local culture and needs in the short- and long-term and avoid any appearance of neo-colonialistic control or manipulation because of the power of their money.

5 **The continued power of African traditional religions.** The low percentage of followers of the pre-Christian ethnic religions is not a true reflection of reality. Underlying both Muslim and Christian religious profession is a value system steeped in the old ways — fetishism, ancestor worship, idolatry, etc. Personal, tribal and national crises reveal this in reversion to the old ways. The terrible events in Africa which have so impacted many nations in recent years cannot be understood without realizing this. Pray for the powers of darkness to be bound in Jesus' name, and pray that Christian leaders and churches may challenge these powers and not succumb to them.

• The Church in Africa

The colonial and apartheid past is fading and a new level of confidence, dynamism, vision and maturity is evident in many parts of Africa. In many countries the Church is the only effective social organization that can bring reconciliation between ethnic groups and cope with the many economic, health and education challenges in collapsing societies. Pray that the Church of the 21st Century might rise to the challenge. Challenges to face in the new millennium:

1 **More effective discipling of new believers**. Millions have been evangelized and responded, but non-Christian customs and worldviews have invaded the Church. Syncretism is a major problem in many areas. Thorough-going repentance and renunciation of sin and the works of darkness are often lacking and many Christians are not free from the fear of witchcraft and evil spirits. The new generation, or third wave of African Christianity, takes a clear stand against these but many churches are seriously compromised.

2 **Unity in great diversity**. There are around 15,000 denominations, clusters of churches and networks in Africa. Pray:

a) *That the carnality of inter-personal relationship breakdowns*, desire for power and ethnic favouritism that lie behind many denominational splits may be crucified with Jesus on the cross.

b) *For pan-African bodies such as the* AEA (Association of Evangelicals of Africa). The role of the AEA is strategic in linking national evangelical denominations in fellowship, stimulating vision and in promoting leadership training, culturally relevant biblical theology and social action. Over 188 denominations and agencies are members and these represent a 50 million Christian constituency.

3 **Leadership training is the critical bottleneck**. There is a lack of funds for training and supporting full-time workers. Leadership is limited at every level: for village congregations, for the urban educated and for theological training. Pray for:

a) *Theological institutions.* These have multiplied for students with primary, secondary and post-secondary level. There are only two significant interdenominational graduate-level theological schools. ACTEA, Africa's accreditation body, lists in its directory over 100 seminary-level members and many more schools, over half being in 4 countries — Nigeria (130), South Africa (111), Congo-DRC (85) and Kenya (66).

b) *A relevant curriculum* that is biblical, yet Africa-oriented. Too much is geared to Western theological battles and perceptions.

c) *Harmony between staff.* Tensions among missionaries and between missionary and national staff have sometimes not been a spiritual example to the students they teach.

d) *Selection of students.* Discernment is needed to know who are anointed of the Spirit for future leadership and who apply out of baser motives of prestige, desire for education, etc.

e) *Funds.* The poverty of the Church and lack of understanding among potential donors hampers the development of Bible training institutions. The needs for buildings, libraries, student grants and travel are endless. Western churches need to give as freely for providing spiritual food to the starving Christians as they have done to provide for Africa's famines.

f) *TEE programmes,* which are vital for training lay leadership. Over 100 programmes are in operation, but some are less successful. Funding, difficulties in travel, low motivation and the failure to involve the real leaders have all been hindrances.

g) *African theologians.* There is a theological vacuum to be filled. A truly indigenous evangelical African theology has been slow to develop. A clear stand by African theologians to expound the universal and unchangeable truths of Scripture in the African context is needed which will also counteract error, African misconceptions of the gospel and the very real powers of darkness.

4 **More effective cross-cultural missions**. The missionary force is increasingly African and multi-continental and less Western. Much sensitivity and humility is required for effective ministry that reaches the unevangelized and defers to the maturity and vision of the growing African Church. The need for missionaries continues to be greater than the supply of those with the gifting and vision for:

a) *Pioneer areas.* These still abound; see below. A high degree of commitment and sacrifice will be required to reach present pioneer areas where conditions are sometimes very hard. In some cases missionaries will need to learn two to four languages before they can reach the least-reached.

b) *Church support personnel* for teaching, youth work, etc., which are needed as never before. Yet the willingness to work under African leadership and as part of the Church in Africa is essential.

c) *Specialists* for Bible translation, education, agriculture, health, radio, television, cassette ministries, Internet evangelism, etc., yet who will also make a spiritual impact through their lives.

d) *Social projects and aid ministries* which are in ever-growing demand. In many countries governments have been unable to provide basic services to their people and

Christian churches and agencies have had to take these up. Physical needs must be met, but such is the pressure that this can lead to neglect of spiritual needs that may be the ultimate cause of suffering and deprivation.

5 **The development of missions vision in the Church**. Praise God for the rapid growth and spread of African missions — in 2000 there were estimated to be nearly 13,000 African missionaries with most serving in a cross-cultural setting. Much of past and present church planting has been through humble, dedicated African missionaries. Pray for:
a) Churches to see missions as fundamental to the gospel itself, and the task of every believer — not just a white Christian!
b) Funds to be made available to train and send out missionaries. Exchange controls and poverty prevent many churches from realizing their mission vision to the full.
c) Effective cross-cultural training for missions — few Bible schools do this, but they should. Innovative training mechanisms have been set up and are growing in different parts of Africa — in West Africa through such as the Nigerian **Calvary Ministries** and **CMF**, in East Africa through the Africa Inland Church, in South Africa through various agencies.

6 **Christian research** has flourished through the enthusiastic efforts of a new generation of talented African researchers. The AD2000 and Beyond Movement was used of God to encourage a national research initiative in many African countries — especially prominent in this are Nigeria, Chad, Côte d'Ivoire, Ethiopia and Zimbabwe. Especially needing such initiative are Kenya, Tanzania and Congo-DRC.

7 **The expatriate mission force**. Honour must be given to the huge impact of dedicated missionaries who achieved so much despite the frequent neglect or even opposition of colonial rulers in the past. These missionaries educated, healed, uplifted and modernized much of Africa in what became a massive social transformation. Generations of African leaders were educated in Christian schools. Inevitably there were weaknesses — importation of Western individualism, dualism (division between spiritual and physical), structures and theological presuppositions, but the Church became rooted in Africa as a result. Praise God for both the lives of these heroes of the faith and for the emergence of the Church. The 21st Century brings new challenges:
a) Partnership. The mission force is increasingly African and multicultural. The growth and expansion of the Church means that relationships, partnering, unity in vision and sharing of resources are fundamental for progress. Pray for unity and fellowship that transcends all social and cultural barriers within mission agencies, among agencies themselves, and between the indigenous churches and agencies.
b) Health and restorative ministries. The increase of wars, disasters and economic failures has provided an enormous need for a new type of medical missions and for restorative ministries — AIDS ravaged societies, war-traumatized populations, children in crisis (abuse, child-soldiers, child prostitution, etc.).

• The Unreached of Africa

Much has been achieved; Christians are numbered in their millions, but serious challenges must be met, and the Church in Africa and world-wide must be mobilized to meet them.

PEOPLES

Much of Africa is within the 10/40 Window area. Of the world's 10 major geographical Affinity Blocs of peoples, 2fi are in Africa: the Sub-Saharan peoples, the Horn of Africa peoples and the western half of the Arab world. For more information about the Arabs, see the section on Asia — West. Then, within these 2fi blocs are clusters of peoples with more closely related cultures and situations. Here are listed most of the major ones with a few details. Most of these clusters are found in more than one country, so their global statistics are given. Please see individual countries for more information. Most are in a belt of territory stretching across the Sahel and then down Africa's east coast. Note the map showing these clusters.

1 **The Imazighen, or Berber** of North Africa. They were the original inhabitants, but were conquered by Rome; many becoming Christians. Then in the 8th Century they were conquered by the Arabs, their culture and history suppressed and most were absorbed into the conquering race. There are 20 million Imazighen in 76 distinct ethnic groups living in 17 countries. Major groups (with many sub-groups) being the Kabyle (3.5m), Shilha (10.7m), Shawiya (1.8m). Only among the Kabyle has there been a significant turning to Christ. Less than 0.3% might be considered Christian. Several partnerships of agencies concerned for them exist.

2 **The Tuareg** (Tamasheq) are related to the Berber, but have a unique culture and live in the central Sahara Desert. They number 3 million in 8 countries and comprise 16 ethnic groups. Only in Niger and Mali are there a few groups of believers. A number of agencies have formed a partnership for their evangelization.

3 **The West Atlantic cluster** with 6.4 million speaking 77 languages and dialects. Most live in Senegal, the Gambia and Guinea, Guinea-Bissau and Sierra Leone. Some, such as the Balanta, Mandyak, Serer and Papel have responded to the gospel, but among the more Muslim Wolof (3.7m), Jola (600,000), Beafada (43,000) and Nalu (23,000) response has been very small and these are still pioneer peoples.

4 **The Mande peoples** live mainly in Africa west of Nigeria, and are in a majority in Mali and Guinea. Most are Muslim. There are 17 million in the main body of Mande peoples and a further 5.5 million in scattered smaller peoples across West Africa. Jula, a Mande language, has become a major trade language for much of the western half of West Africa. In the main body of Mande only the Malian Bambara (4.3m), Kassonke (280,000), and the Sierra Leonian Kono (232,000) have a number of Christians. The most needy are the Mandingo-related (5.5m), Jula-related (1m), Soso-Yalunka (1.3m) and Wassulunke (740,000).

5 **The Soninke-Bozo peoples** — mainly of Senegal and Mali are 1.6 million with only a handful of believers. Several agencies are seeking to reach them.

6 **The Songhai-Zarma peoples** — 4.7 million living mainly in Mali and Niger and speaking 18 languages and dialects. Muslim; very few Christians.

7 **The Fulbe** (Pulaar, Fulani) number 20 million in 40 or so distinct ethnic groups speaking related dialects. They have spread from Senegal to become a major component of nearly every country of the Sahel as far east as Sudan. They are the largest nomadic-culture people in the world. More than half now live settled lifestyles and are more strongly Muslim than the nomadic or semi-nomadic Fulbe. Planting churches among them has been hard and slow with small breakthroughs in Benin, Nigeria and Chad. The Fulbe represent one of the major challenges for missions in Africa today. There are dozens of agencies with some outreach or ministry to Fulbe and several partnerships have been formed specifically to synergize ministry among them.

8 **The Volta-Gur peoples** number nearly 15 million in 165 ethnic groups. Most live in the Sahel; Côte d'Ivoire, Burkina Faso, Ghana, Benin and Togo. Among the many peoples related to the Mossi (10.3m), Grusi (3.5m), Gurma (2m) and Dogon (900,000), a significant minority are active Christians. The Senufo (3m) and Lobi (500,000) are more resistant and response is slow. Many peoples are largely unreached in Burkina Faso but few of the larger peoples remain without a witness.

9 **The Hausa** are dominant in Niger and northern Nigeria, but live in 27 countries and number 30 million. Hausa has become the major language for much of Nigeria, Niger and beyond. Many resources exist in Hausa — the Bible, the *JESUS* film, radio broadcasting, and much ministry is done in Hausa, but few have turned to Christ from Islam. Response has been greatest among the Maguzawa section of the Hausa. This large people remains one major challenge to the Church.

10 **Kanuri-Kanembu** — 5.1 million in northeast Nigeria and the Chad basin. They are the least reached cluster of peoples in the Sahel. They, and the related Teda and Daza of north Chad, have no known churches. After years of effort to reach them the fruit is meagre.

11 **The Chadian peoples**. Five intermingled clusters of Sudanic, Saharan and Chadic peoples live in the large area of central Nigeria, north Cameroon, Chad and the Darfur Province of Sudan. They speak over 400 languages and dialects and nearly half of these are without churches, the Scriptures, or much of any other form of witness. Much pioneer work in arduous conditions and among small language groups must still be undertaken. This medley of smaller peoples constitutes one of the most complex challenges for pioneer ministry in Africa today. Special mention must be made of the many peoples linked with the Maba (953,000), Fur (800,000), Tama-Mararit (353,000), Daju (322,000), Masalit (300,000) and Naba (266,000). To these must be added the Shuwa Arab nomads who may number up to 2 million.

12 **Cushitic-Horn of Africa peoples**. There are 55 million in over 140 ethnic groups living mainly in Sudan, Eritrea, Ethiopia and Somalia. Many of the peoples in Ethiopia are Christian. The challenge remains to reach the Somali (14m), Beja (2.5m) and Saho-Afar (1.5m). To these must be added the 1.8 million Nubians of the Nile Valley in Egypt and Sudan — long a Christian people until forcibly Islamized in the 17th Century but now with only a few hundred known believers. Many Christian agencies are burdened to bring the gospel to them and see a harvest — there have been many attempts.

13 **The East Coast peoples** of Kenya, Tanzania, Mozambique and Malawi. Almost all are Muslim and most are able to communicate in Swahili. Major groupings: Swahili (3.8m — including the Comorians and Zanzibarians), Makonde (2.2m), Yao (1.7m) and Zaramo (630,000).

14 **The Pygmy peoples** of the central African forests. They were the original peoples of the region but invading Bantu peoples pushed them into the more inaccessible areas. They number 765,000 in 33 ethnic groups in 8 countries. They have long been ignored, or evangelized using Bantu languages. Only in recent years have more culturally sensitive church planting efforts been made. Results have been good during the 1990s; around 17% are now Christians. **Evangelism Resources** is an agency that has championed their cause, but a number of agencies and denominations are now planting churches among them.

• Major Great Commission Challenges

1 **Islam** is the major challenge for Christianity today — both the 160 million Muslims north of the Sahara and the 157 million in sub-Saharan Africa. Islam has been steadily gaining converts from traditional religions in countries west of Ghana and all across the Sahel. More recently Muslim missionary efforts have extended to nearly every country in Africa. The use of oil-funded education, aid projects and grants and a well-orchestrated drive to give Islam a role in Africa's political life has had some success. African Christians as well as mission agencies need to make Muslims a priority for demonstrations of the love of Christ and culturally sensitive approaches must be developed for planting churches among them.

2 **Nations** with the smallest number of Evangelicals. These are priority countries with less than 0.1% Evangelicals: Mauritania, Morocco, Libya, Tunisia, Comores, Djibouti, Niger, Senegal and Somalia. These are the countries with less than 1% Evangelicals: Algeria, Gambia, Guinea, Guinea-Bissau, Mali.

3 **Cities**. Africa's urban population has rapidly risen from 130 million in 1990 to maybe 240 million in 2000. Lack of economic development and greater poverty has meant that it is the slums, shanty towns and informal settlements that have mushroomed. These cities have become focal points for dire poverty, squalor, crime, prostitution, AIDS and misery. New ways must be found to impact these cities for God and plant churches that will transform urban areas.

4 **Christian Help Ministries**:

a) **Bible distribution.** Increased poverty has reduced Bible distribution. **The Bible League** estimates 100 million Christians do not even possess a Bible. Pray for effective, self-sustaining Bible printing and distribution by the Bible Societies and others.

b) **Bible translation** remains one of the major tasks to be accomplished in Africa. Of Africa's 2,110 languages, 297 are definitely in need of Bible translation work. The major concentrations of these languages are in Nigeria, Cameroon, Chad and the Sudan.

c) **Christian radio.** Both **FEBA** in the Seychelles and **TWR** in Swaziland and South Africa have major short-wave transmitters broadcasting in most of the major languages of Africa. More use is now being made of national and local broadcasting stations who want to air Christian programmes. **TWR**, **FEBA** and **HCJB** work closely with a growing number of community Christian radio stations in Africa by providing satellite delivery of Christian programming and offering technical expertise.

LATIN AMERICA & CARIBBEAN

	Population 2000	Main Religions	non-Chr%	All Chr %	Evang-elical%	Peoples All	World A	JPL
Anguilla	0.0	X	7.5	91.5	19.9	4	0	0
Antigua and Barbuda	0.1	X	6.2	93.9	16.8	5	0	0
Argentina	37.0	X	7.9	92.9	10.8	63	1	3
Aruba	0.1	X	3.4	96.5	6.4	6	2	0
Bahamas, The	0.3	XN	7.5	92.4	30.8	8	1	0
Barbados	0.3	X	3.4	95.7	28.6	10	1	0
Belize	0.2	X	7.2	91.0	14.1	18	1	0
Bolivia	8.3	X	6.0	93.9	11.8	57	5	1
Brazil	170.1	X	11.6	91.4	12.6	223	16	1
British Virgin Islands	0.0	X	13.4	86.0	27.2	7	0	0
Cayman Islands	0.0	XEN	22.1	78.0	25.5	5	1	0
Chile	15.2	XN	11.6	89.2	16.8	24	1	1
Colombia	42.3	X	4.6	95.5	4.7	98	8	1
Costa Rica	4.0	X	5.1	94.7	12.4	21	1	0
Cuba	11.2	XNE	53.5	46.9	4.6	14	1	0
Dominica	0.1	X	3.5	94.9	13.5	9	0	0
Dominican Republic	8.5	X	6.4	95.2	7.6	13	0	0
Ecuador	12.6	X	2.7	97.4	6.1	32	4	2
El Salvador	6.3	X	2.2	97.3	21.7	14	2	0
Falkland Islands	0.0	X	6.0	94.3	22.7	5	0	0
French Guiana	0.2	XN	14.5	84.9	3.3	23	3	0
Grenada	0.1	X	3.7	97.0	18.0	9	0	0
Guadeloupe	0.5	X	5.2	94.6	5.4	6	0	0
Guatemala	11.4	X	2.6	97.5	26.0	64	1	1
Guyana	0.9	XHN	56.1	43.6	11.1	23	1	0
Haiti	8.2	X	4.9	95.5	22.2	8	1	0
Honduras	6.5	X	3.1	96.7	17.7	26	2	0
Jamaica	2.6	XE	16.0	84.1	26.3	13	1	0
Martinique	0.4	XN	8.2	91.6	5.4	8	0	0
Mexico	98.9	X	6.0	94.5	6.7	277	4	19
Montserrat	0.0	X	2.5	95.5	27.6	7	0	0
Netherlands Antilles	0.2	X	5.8	96.1	7.6	14	0	0
Nicaragua	5.1	XN	9.2	90.9	16.3	21	1	0
Panama	2.9	X	8.5	88.1	18.2	32	0	0
Paraguay	5.5	X	5.1	98.0	4.8	44	2	0
Peru	25.7	XN	9.8	90.1	8.7	110	15	0
Puerto Rico	3.9	X	3.4	97.0	27.6	11	0	0
St Kitts-Nevis	0.0	X	4.0	95.6	22.9	5	0	0
St Lucia	0.2	X	4.1	96.1	12.3	6	1	0
St Vincent	0.1	X	7.7	92.2	24.4	12	0	0
Suriname	0.4	XHM	52.3	46.9	4.1	27	4	0
Trinidad & Tobago	1.3	XHM	28.9	71.2	15.2	15	1	0
Turks & Caicos Islands	0.0	X	7.9	93.2	34.3	4	0	0
Uruguay	3.3	XNE	39.7	60.2	4.5	31	1	0
Venezuela	24.2	X	4.8	94.7	10.1	69	5	2
Virgin Is of the USA	0.1	X	3.2	96.9	25.8	8	1	0
Totals (46 countries)	**519.1**		**8.3**	**91.7**	**10.6**	**1509**	**89**	**31**

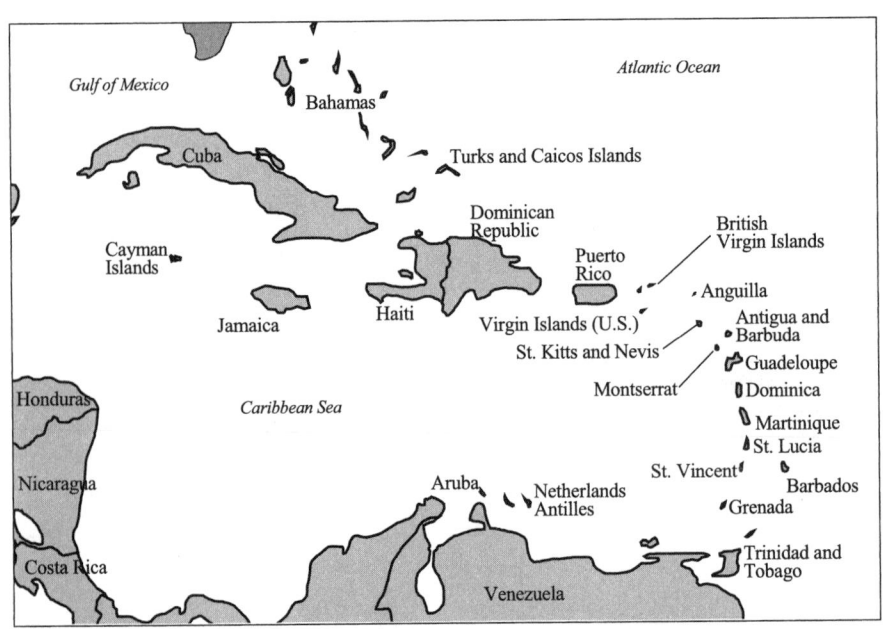

Map 1 (The Americas)

Mexico
Gulf of Mexico
See Caribbean Inset
Atlantic Ocean

Belize
Guatemala
Honduras
El Salvador
Nicaragua
Costa Rica
Panama

Guyana
Suriname
French Guiana

Venezuela

Colombia

Ecuador

Brazil

Peru

Bolivia

Paraguay

Pacific Ocean

Chile

Argentina

Uruguay

Falkland Islands

Caribbean Inset

Gulf of Mexico

Atlantic Ocean

Bahamas

Cuba

Turks and Caicos Islands

Cayman Islands

Dominican Republic

British Virgin Islands

Puerto Rico

Anguilla

Jamaica

Haiti

Virgin Islands (U.S.)

St. Kitts and Nevis

Antigua and Barbuda

Guadeloupe

Montserrat

Dominica

Martinique

St. Lucia

Honduras

Caribbean Sea

Nicaragua

Aruba

Netherlands Antilles

St. Vincent

Barbados

Grenada

Costa Rica

Trinidad and Tobago

Venezuela

NORTH AMERICA

	Population 2000	Main Religions	non-Chr%	All Chr %	Evang-elical%	Peoples All	World A	JPL
Bermuda	0.1	X	6.7	93.3	19.6	6	1	0
Canada	31.1	X	24.3	75.7	10.8	151	1	4
Greenland	0.1	X	3.4	96.6	1.6	4	0	0
St Pierre & Miquelon	0.0	X	2.3	97.7	0.4	2	0	0
United States of America	278.4	X	15.5	84.5	32.5	306	22	6
Totals (5 countries)	**309.6**		**18.4**	**81.6**	**30.3**	**469**	**24**	**10**

The Americas

JANUARY 17-23

Revised February 2004

The Americas represent two continents and 51 countries and territories. The diversities are many and large — but so too are the commonalities.

1 The indigenous Amerindian inhabitants, who were wrongly called 'Indians' by the Europeans who accidentally stumbled upon their continents in 1492.

2 The extraordinary history of European colonization — the theft, plunder and subjugation of the Americas by adventurers, explorers and settlers from Europe.

3 The tragic history of the use of African slave labour in most warmer countries.

4 The common time-frame of the ending of colonial rule — largely between 1776 and 1830 for most countries.

5 Rapidly developing inter-relatedness with trade patterns, migration of peoples from south to north and the impact of drug trafficking.

Here the statistics of North America are handled separately from the Caribbean/Latin America, but the analysis and prayer points are presented together.

North America

the USA has the potential to overwhelm its neighbours, which encourages a defensive nationalism on the part of the latter.

GEOGRAPHY

Area 21,675,600 sq.km. North America contains three of the 13 largest countries of the world: Canada (2ⁿᵈ largest); USA (4ᵗʰ) and Greenland (13ᵗʰ). Nearly 16% of the world's land surface.

Population	Ann.Gr.	Density
2000	309,631,093	+0.85%	14 per sq. km.
2010	332,050,930	+0.68%	15 per sq. km.
2025	363,611,501	+0.54%	17 per sq. km.

In 2001 this was 5.1% of the world's population.

Cities There are 71 cities or conurbations of over one million inhabitants. **Urbanites** 76%.

PEOPLES

Euro-American 64.6%. Communities from every ethnic group in Europe have settled in the Americas.
Hispanic 11.4%. Most are from Mexico, Central America and the Caribbean. Rapidly increasing.
Afro-American 11.4%. Almost entirely urban. Most are descendants of slaves imported from Africa between the 17ᵗʰ and 19ᵗʰ Centuries. A majority in Bermuda.
Asian 4.8%. The majority are immigrants from east Asia and have settled primarily on North America's Pacific Coast. An increasing component from South Asia.
Middle Eastern 4%, of which Jews are 5.9 million.
Other/mixed 2.7%.
Native Americans 1.1%. Only in Greenland are they in a majority; elsewhere often a marginalized underclass alongside a large majority that overran their continent.

All languages 245. English is the major language of communication except for French in Quebec, Canada and in St Pierre & Miquelon; Danish in Greenland. Spanish is of increasing importance.

Bible translation See below under Latin America.

ECONOMY

The world's wealthiest continent and the economic engine on which the world's economy depends for growth. The NAFTA trading bloc embraces Canada, Mexico and the USA. Visionary plans are being discussed for making all of the Americas into a single trading bloc.

POLITICS

The economic and political strength of

RELIGION

The continent with the least religious discrimination.

Religions	Population %	Adherents	Ann.Gr.
Christian	81.57	259.0 mill	+0.66%
non-Religious	12.04	31.8 mill	+1.95%
Jewish	1.83	5.9 mill	-0.07%
Muslim	1.68	4.6 mill	+2.28%
Buddhist/Eastern	0.99	2.9 mill	+3.60%
Hindu	0.49	1.3 mill	+2.70%
Traditional ethnic	0.38	1.1 mill	+1.83%
Baha'i	0.26	787,000	+0.85%
Sikh	0.18	412.000	+2.48%
Other	0.58	1.6 mill	+2.64%

Christians	Denom.	Affil.%	,000	Ann.Gr.
Protestant	793	23.11	71,568	-0.1%
Independent	2,515	21.94	67,928	+2.2%
Anglican	4	1.02	3,162	-1.0%
Catholic	9	22.81	70,616	-0.6%
Orthodox	76	2.06	6,381	+0.7%
Marginal	395	3.55	10,982	+0.6%
Unaffiliated		15.62	48,371	n.a.
Doubly affiliated		*-6.51*	*-20,157*	*n.a.*

Trans-bloc Groupings	pop. %	,000	Ann.Gr.
Evangelical	30.3	93,813	+2.0%
Charismatic	23.2	71,909	+1.6%
Pentecostal	6.9	21,479	+2.4%

Missionaries from North America
P,I,A 71,088 in 672 mission agencies of which 50,720 are in other countries.

Missionaries to North America
P,I,A 3,008 expatriates in 151 mission agencies.

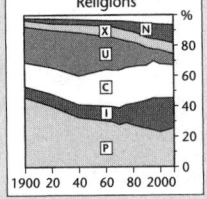

Religions

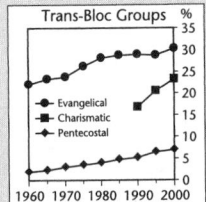

Trans-Bloc Groups

Latin America/ Caribbean

GEOGRAPHY
Area 20,537,000 sq.km. Comprising 46 countries and territories, of which 25 are islands; 15.1% of the world's land area.

Population		Ann.Gr.	Density
2000	519,131,119	+1.59%	25 per sq. km.
2010	595,023,969	+1.31%	29 per sq. km.
2025	696,641,498	+0.93%	34 per sq. km.

Latin America has 8.6% of the world's population.

Cities There are 52 cities of over one million inhabitants. Mexico City and São Paulo are two of the world's largest cities. **Urbanites** 71%.

PEOPLES
Racial intermingling is such that a breakdown of ethnic groups is only approximate. There is generally more class consciousness than colour consciousness, but there are wide differences in ethnic composition between the countries. There are 5 main components to the population:

Euro-American 40.5%. A majority in Argentina, Brazil, Costa Rica, Cuba and Uruguay, and a large minority in Chile, Paraguay, Mexico and the Andean republics. Politically dominant throughout the continent. Immigrant European minority communities have retained language and cultural distinctives in many lands, but are steadily being absorbed into the host cultures.

Mixed race 39.1%. A majority in 9 countries.
  Mestizo (in South America) and **Ladino** (in Central America) are mixed European and Amerindian. Many Amerindians become Mestizo simply by adopting Spanish as their language.
  Mulatto are of mixed European and African origin.
Amerindian 10.2%. The original inhabitants. They were decimated by European conquests and diseases in the 16th to 19th Centuries. A majority in Guatemala and Bolivia, nearly half the population in Peru and Ecuador and a large minority in Mexico and Paraguay. Politically resurgent in most of these countries.

Afro-American 9.1%. Descendants of slaves brought from Africa. A majority in most Caribbean states, but most numerous in Brazil. Many live in states with Caribbean coastlines.

Asian 1.1%. South Asians and Indonesians brought by the British and Dutch to their colonies in the region in the 19th Century; Japanese, Chinese and Korean immigration in the 20th Century. Asians are a majority in Guyana and Suriname, and a large minority in Trinidad.

Literacy over 85%. **All languages in the Americas** 1,183. **Indigenous languages with Scriptures** 25Bi 254NT 200por 249w.i.p.

ECONOMY

Rapid development since the early 1980s when democracy and free market economics took root, trade barriers were lowered and inter-state and inter-island communications improved. Growth then slowed by inadequate restructuring, vested interests, inadequate and costly communications and the big gap between the rich and poor. The Caribbean states vary between the richer (off-shore banking, tourism and impact of drug trafficking) and the poorer which are dependent on aid, advantageous trade agreements with Europe and tourism.

POLITICS
The ending of the Cold War and the eclipse of Communism reinforced the trend to more democratic government throughout Latin America. In many countries, such as Haiti, Guatemala, Peru, Venezuela, Nicaragua, etc., commitment to accountable democracy has been low with authoritarian tendencies still evident. In Cuba alone has a dictatorship survived.

RELIGION
In 1900 almost the entire Spanish-speaking population was considered Catholic. The changes since then have been dramatic — from a narrow traditionalism, with strong opposition to Protestant missionary activity, to freedom of religion and a rapid growth of Evangelicals. The Catholic Church has responded with a vigorous drive to check these losses and regain the initiative and hearts of the people. The Caribbean states' religion was largely determined by that of the pre-1800 colonizing power.

Religions	Population %	Adherents	Ann.Gr.
Christian	91.65	476.6 m	+1.52%
non-Religious	4.28	21.4 m	+2.66%
Traditional ethnic	2.73	14.7 m	+1.17%
Muslim	0.34	1.4 m	+2.88%
Jewish	0.20	1.1 m	+1.47%
Baha'i	0.18	829,000	+3.11%
Buddhist/Eastern	0.16	723,000	+1.81%
Hindu	0.13	894,000	+0.38%
Sikh	0.01	40,000	-0.70%
Other	0.33	1.9 m	+5.67%

Spiritism has grown rapidly in influence in Brazil, Cuba, Uruguay and Venezuela, and has always been strong in Haiti.

Christians	Denom.	Affil.%	,000	Ann.Gr.
Protestant	1,874	7.11	36,889	+3.7%
Independent	2,894	4.58	23,752	+4.6%
Anglican	44	0.18	928	+1.0%
Catholic	48	78.77	408,941	+0.8%
Orthodox	64	0.10	533	+0.7%
Marginal	276	1.76	9,150	+4.7%
Unaffiliated		3.30	17,106	n.a.
Doubly affiliated		*-4.00*	*-20,708*	*n.a.*

Evangelicals have grown rapidly, but not as fast as some have claimed (largely exuberant Pentecostal over-reporting).

Trans-bloc Groupings pop. %		,000	Ann.Gr.
Evangelical	10.59	54,958	+4.0%
Charismatic	16.47	85,488	+2.2%
Pentecostal	6.24	32,416	+4.3%

Missionaries from Latin America
P,I,A 10,192 from 346 agencies of which 3,827 serve in other countries.

Missionaries to Latin America
P,I,A 16,980 expatriates in 539 agencies.

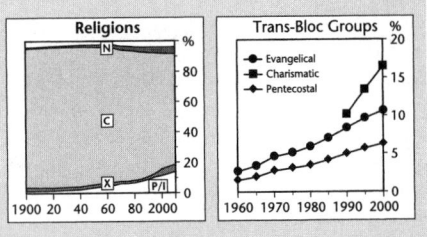

• Answers to Prayer in the Americas

1 **The growth of Evangelicals in Latin America** in the 20th Century has been spectacular. In 1900 Evangelicals numbered about 700,000, or 1% of the population (only about 200,000 of these being in Spanish-speaking countries). By 2000 they had multiplied to 55 million (over 50 million in Spanish-speaking countries). The breakthrough point for Evangelicals came with the wide implementation of congregation mobilization through national Evangelism-in-Depth programmes in the 1960s.

2 **Pentecostal Evangelicals** have demonstrated the greatest vigour and have become the largest component of Evangelicals in Latin America with over 32 million affiliates. This is 28% of the world's Pentecostals. Their greatest success has been amongst the poor. Growth has been weakened by multiplied splits, inadequate discipling of converts and often exaggerated claims of growth.

3 **The spiritual impact of North America**, and especially the USA, on the world. Praise God for:

a) *Great evangelists* who have touched the world (Finney, Moody, Billy Graham and others).

b) *Great missionary statesmen* and visionaries who helped to lay the foundations for the present global harvest.

c) *Unstinting generosity* in giving for great causes — especially missions advances.

May this influence continue, and supplant the blatant secularism propagated by the media. The Hollywood view of American life is not the whole story!

4 **The impact of the Scriptures on Catholics** has opened the hearts of millions to a personal encounter with the Lord Jesus. Many have become fervent evangelical believers, both within the Catholic Church and, increasingly, outside it.

5 **People movements are growing among the Amerindians** who have long been resistant or indifferent to the gospel. The present growth of Quechua and Aymara churches in the Andes and Mayan peoples in Central America is exciting.

6 **The divinely ordered convergence in Latin America** of greater freedom of religion, more open and accountable democracy, a series of military, natural and economic disasters which loosened the hold of traditional structures have enabled many to come to Christ. The 1990s were a time of resurgence of Christianity in Cuba despite the decades of Marxist propaganda and pressure.

7 **The Bible translation achievements of WBT/SIL and UBS** have been remarkable. The pioneer work of **WBT/SIL** in providing New Testaments in indigenous languages has sparked ingatherings of peoples into churches across the Americas. In some lands the work of translation has been virtually completed. Praise the Lord for a task well done!

8 **The missionary contributions of North Americans** in the 20th Century. Increasingly the missionary enterprise is becoming global, but even in 2001 it is still predominantly North American. They make up over 50% of missionaries in other lands and 34% of all missionaries (home and foreign).

9 **There has been rapid growth and maturation of missions vision in Latin America**. The 1987 COMIBAM conference in São Paulo, Brazil, generated continent-wide interest and sparked off numerous initiatives to reach the unreached. Major missionary-contributing nations are Brazil, Costa Rica and Argentina, but in most lands missionary sending structures are developing.

10 **The impact of the media** has been significant all over the New World. Widespread use of local, national and international radio and television networks by Christians has had a big influence. International Christian radio agencies broadcast an estimated 3,000 hrs/wk in Spanish and 320 hrs/wk in Portuguese by satellite as well as by short and medium wave. The multiplication of local television and radio stations and broadcasts further widens the opportunities for proclamation of the gospel.

• Hot Spots of the Americas

1 **The moral devastation caused by drug trafficking** is corrupting politicians, law enforcement agencies and judicial systems, filling the prisons with the small-fry and destroying the lives of millions of drug users across the two continents. The desperate poverty of the growers and the seemingly insatiable craving for drugs — especially in wealthy North America — makes for lucrative opportunities for criminal drug cartels and leftist guerrilla movements who exploit this dual need. Drug enforcement bodies and billions of US dollars have scarcely dented the problem. Colombia, Peru, Bolivia, Jamaica, Haiti and other nations have been so impacted by this that the traffickers often wield more power than the central government. Pray that this evil might be tamed, and even eliminated, and that those in authority might pursue viable and effective policies to achieve this.

2 **The unresolved issue of widespread poverty.** Economic progress has often failed to filter down to the poor. Marxist guerrilla insurrections once plagued many countries, but since 1990 these have been reduced in number. Only in Colombia is there widespread military conflict with rightist militia and leftist guerrillas controlling large areas of the country and financing their forces with drug trafficking. Low-scale insurrection continues in Peru and Mexico and an uneasy peace after years of war prevails in Nicaragua and Guatemala. Democratic government is fragile and economies are struggling in many countries. Pray for the resolution of existing conflicts and courageous government actions to alleviate the conditions that provoke uprisings.

3 **The political resurgence of indigenous Amerindian peoples**. The Guatemalan civil war was largely a protest by the repressed, marginalized Mayan peoples. The violent Peruvian revolt was likewise a movement of the Quechuas, and the quirky guerrilla movement in south Mexico is a demand for redress by marginalized Amerindian peoples. Pray that the centuries of wrongs against the indigenous peoples may be righted and their economic, cultural and political rights restored.

 Countries facing an uncertain, possibly traumatic future:

a) ***Cuba*** after the departure of President Castro will need to recover from over 4 decades of Marxism and economic isolation.
b) ***Haiti*** with its desperate poverty and appalling history of dictatorships, rigged elections and bad government.
c) ***Guyana and Suriname*** with unresolved ethnic tensions and unstable governments.
d) ***Countries struggling to survive***, such as: Nicaragua — after civil war; Honduras — natural disasters; Paraguay — dictatorships and coups.

5 **Unresolved territorial disputes** — Venezuela and Suriname's claims on Guyana; Argentina's on the Falklands (Islas Malvinas) and Guatemala's on Belize.

• Trends to Watch

1 **Increasing economic integration.** NAFTA (North American Free Trade Area) and MERCOSUR (Argentina, Brazil, Paraguay and Uruguay) are changing trading patterns. There are many with a vision for a free trade area for all the nations of the Americas. Pray for political courage to take the right decisions in this process — courage that is not moved by selfish vested interests of ethnicity, economic power, structures or big business. Pray that the results may also benefit the poor and the marginalized and improve the quality of life and human rights as well as address vital ecological concerns.

2 **Continued fragility of democratic institutions** in many countries. A culture of despotism inherited from colonialism in Latin America still prevails despite the demise of dictatorships in every country of Latin America but Cuba. Autocratic populism is a concern for countries such as Ecuador, Peru, Venezuela, Guyana and Paraguay. Pray that responsible, accountable governments may win power through unmanipulated election processes.

3 **The huge movements of population** — such as Latin Americans to North America, Nicaraguans to Costa Rica, Brazilians from the poor northeastern states to Amazonia and the inflow of Asians to the Americas — especially Chinese. All have deep demographic, political and spiritual implications.

4 **The insidious growth of HIV/AIDS infection**. The growth has been slowed in the USA and Brazil, but it is beginning to ravage a number of Caribbean nations — especially Haiti (5% of adult population) and the Bahamas (4%). The overall rates: Caribbean 2.1%, North America 0.6% and Latin America 0.5%.

5 **The rise of an anti-Christian secularism** that seeks to marginalize the Church through control of the media and legislation. Promotion of multiculturalism, pluralism and tolerance disguise an intolerant rejection of the absolutes of the Christian faith.

• The Church in the Americas

1 **During the 20th Century, the Americas proved to be the most dynamic Christian continent**. In 1900, 25.2% of Christians of all 6 megablocs lived in the Americas. By 2000 this had reached 37.3%. The growth and dynamism of Evangelicals was such that by 2000 35% of all Evangelicals, 45.5% of all charismatics and 46.5% of all Pentecostals lived in the region. May the influence of believers be such that the world of the 21st Century be blessed and the Kingdom of God extended.

2 **The Roman Catholic Church** has passed through 40 years of tumultuous change, in part spurred by the growth of Evangelicals. The traditional monolithic structure that once dominated the continent has gone forever. Many regret the misused four centuries of monopoly which bred complacency and condoned syncretism that is widespread among ordinary people. The effects of the Vatican II Council, theological diversity, emphasis on Bible reading and the charismatic movement have been enormous. Pope John Paul II has pulled the Church back from political and doctrinal extremes to a more traditional Catholicism. Various powerful movements are discernible:

a) Concern for the poor and social justice. Some priests have become revolutionaries espousing liberation theology. Over 200,000 Base Communities brought lay leadership and social involvement to the fore all over the continent, but often seek to interpret social issues exclusively in terms of class conflict. In many countries, the Church moved from being a supporter of the ruling elite to a champion of the poor.

b) The charismatic movement. This grew rapidly during the 1970s, but is not growing at the same pace now. Millions have been involved; some joined evangelical churches, but others remained within the Catholic Church.

c) Traditional Catholicism. This has re-emerged as a strong force and is leading to a further cooling of relationships with Evangelicals. Popular, and often syncretistic, Catholicism is still widespread. Pray for Catholics to come to a personal faith in Christ. Millions still strive to earn their entrance into heaven and gain temporal blessings by their pilgrimages, works and ceremonies.

3 **The challenges for Evangelicals in the 21st Century**. Pray for:

a) Wise handling of political power in Latin America. There is increased sensitivity among Evangelicals to their cultural, economic and political context and concern to influence society. With the power afforded by the vote in democratic systems, Evangelicals are thrust into political participation. Such power can divert believers from evangelism or stifle the Church's prophetic voice in a society in need of moral absolutes and ethical standards. The lure of such power has often subverted Evangelicals to seek political power for selfish ends, and brought discredit to the cause of Christ. Evangelicals are increasingly being voted into the highest offices of their respective countries.

b) Willingness to confront social and economic injustices in a biblical way. Pray that Latin Americans may develop their own biblical theology by keeping in balance a faithfulness to the gospel and social involvement. The Latin American Theological Fraternity, founded in 1969, has an important role in this.

c) *Religious freedom.* This is still an issue despite legislation 'guaranteeing' it in many Latin American countries. Discrimination against Evangelicals still occurs in such countries as Peru and Venezuela. Localized persecution of Evangelicals by Maoist guerrillas in Peru and Colombia continues.

d) *Adequate training for present and future pastors,* whether by informal TEE, church programmes or formal training. The majority of Latin and Caribbean evangelical congregations are led by pastors with little or no formal theological training. There is a strong tendency toward authoritarian leadership without sufficient checks and balances. This leads to dictatorial power, divisiveness, development of cults, moral failures and scandals.

e) *Maturity in the churches.* Evangelistic outreach gains a large following, but many churches fail to conserve the fruit. In some churches the back door is used as much as the front. Pentecostals have successfully enfranchised the poorer classes and shown zeal in evangelism, but ineffective discipling, fragmentation into thousands of denominations and exaggerated claims of growth have blunted their spiritual impact.

f) *The need for biblical standards* in morals and ethics. Immorality is a serious problem — especially in the Caribbean states where illegitimacy rates are as high as 80-85%; most claiming to be Christian. Pray for revival that transforms family life and whole communities.

g) *Denominationalism,* which is a major problem. The structure of society, encouraging powerful father-figure pastors, gives rise to partisan evangelism and divisions over personalities.

h) *The integration of Amerindian churches* into the mainstream of Christianity in their countries.

i) *Christians to face up to the challenge of cults* — both Jehovah's Witnesses and the Mormons and also spiritism from Brazil. The latter is growing at a faster rate than even the Pentecostals.

4 **The Evangelical missions movement** has had an enormous impact on the world — firstly from North America and now increasingly from Latin America. The maturing, evangelical, Latin American missions movement has expanded greatly since the 1980s. Pray for:

a) *Churches to learn the privileges and responsibilities* of supporting cross-cultural outreach within their own lands and abroad.

b) *Finance, which is a major limitation.* Lack of it will prevent the present trickle of cross-cultural missionaries from becoming a flood. High inflation in Brazil is a particularly acute problem.

c) *The development of viable and locally applicable sending structures* and training programmes that result in fruitful long-term missions involvement.

d) *The ability to relate to the international missions world* and to Western and Asian missionaries.

• The Unfinished Task in the Americas

Despite the large Christian presence and much evangelical activity, major challenges remain:

1 **There are 8 countries where Evangelicals are below 5%** of the total population:

a) *North America:* Greenland, St. Pierre & Miquelon.

b) *Latin America:* Colombia, Cuba, French Guiana Paraguay, Suriname and Uruguay.

2 **Upper and middle classes in Latin America**. These are generally less evangelized by Evangelicals, most of whom come from among the poor. Specific strategies are needed to reach these other classes.

3 **The urban poor.** In North America they usually live in the decaying hearts of major cities; in Latin America it is in huge slums that ring or even permeate the major cities — deprivation, drug abuse, unwanted street children, crime and disease are the result.

4 **Whole regions of some countries** are far less evangelized than the rest of the country, such as Quebec Province in Canada, the northeastern states and Amazonia in Brazil, and a number of Mexico's states.

5 **Students** in the universities. Only a small minority are Evangelicals, usually far smaller than the national average. **CCCI** has an extensive ministry to campuses and **IFES** has a well-established work in over 12 countries, with younger movements in others. Pray for all agencies concentrating on this strategic sector of the community. A clear, radiant, evangelical student witness in every university is a key target for prayer.

6 **Amerindian peoples**. In most of the smaller tribes there are Bible translation and church-planting ministries. However, among some tribes in Colombia, Venezuela and parts of Brazil and Mexico various factors have prevented the effective establishment of an ongoing work. These are: historic resentment at centuries of maltreatment, geographical inaccessibility, government restrictions, the assiduous activities of anti-Christian anthropologists and, increasingly, narcotics gangs who have taken over whole areas and terrorized local people to further their illegal activities. The total population of unreached is relatively small, probably not exceeding one million, but found in numerous small tribes. Amerindian leaders are actively using the international media to expose their plight and gain recognition of their cultural, political and land rights.

7 **Immigrant communities** from all over the world. Nearly every significant culture has a migrant community in the Americas. For special mention:

a) *Chinese* — nearly 3 million all over the Americas. The one million in Latin America are less reached. Their numbers are being augmented by immigrants from both Taiwan and Mainland China. The latter need specialized ministry in order to reach them.

b) *Japanese* — nearly 1.4 million with communities in the USA, Brazil and Peru.

c) *Muslims* — mainly Arabs in Latin America, rapidly increasing in numbers through immigration from the Middle East. There are also South Asian Muslims in the Anglophone countries and Javanese Muslims in Suriname. Little Christian work is being undertaken among them.

8 **The Jews** of the southern part of Latin America — one of the least evangelized major concentrations of their people in the world.

9 **The Roma (Gypsies)** — living as distinct communities in most Latin American countries and numbering around one million. They remain as marginalized in society as their relatives in Europe.

ASIA

	Population 2000	Main Religions	non-Chr%	All Chr %	Evang-elical%	Peoples All	World A	JPL
Afghanistan	22.7	M	100.0	0.0	0.0	69	65	22
Armenia	3.5	XN	15.0	85.0	8.1	24	10	2
Azerbaijan	7.7	MN	95.4	4.6	0.1	34	22	3
Bahrain	0.6	MX	89.6	10.4	3.1	13	6	3
Bangladesh	129.2	MH	99.3	0.7	0.4	60	30	21
Bhutan	2.1	BH	99.5	0.5	0.4	26	24	10
Brunei	0.3	MXBE	88.8	11.3	4.6	26	11	4
Cambodia	11.2	B	98.8	1.2	0.5	36	25	5
China, People's Rep	1262.6	NChBX	92.8	7.3	6.0	476	187	75
China, Hong Kong	7.0	ChNX	90.0	10.1	5.1	n.a.	n.a.	n.a.
China, Macau	0.4	NChBX	92.7	7.3	1.7	n.a.	n.a.	n.a.
China, Taiwan	22.4	ChNBX	93.9	6.1	2.7	29	6	3
Georgia	5.0	XMN	37.5	62.5	1.4	34	17	4
India	1013.7	HM	93.7	6.3	1.8	438	308	179
Indonesia	213.0	MX	84.0	16.0	4.0	743	284	115
Iran	67.7	M	99.7	0.3	0.0	77	65	46
Iraq	23.1	M	98.5	1.6	0.1	35	22	17
Israel	5.1	JM	97.8	2.3	0.2	52	29	11
Japan	126.7	BZ	98.4	1.6	0.4	33	18	8
Jordan	6.7	M	97.3	2.8	0.2	19	9	3
Kazakhstan	16.2	MXN	75.3	24.7	0.6	48	25	13
Korea, North	24.0	NEZ	98.3	1.7	1.5	6	3	0
Korea, South	46.8	NXBE	68.3	31.7	15.5	8	1	0
Kuwait	2.0	MX	91.8	8.2	0.6	26	8	5
Kyrgyzstan	4.7	MNX	92.2	7.8	0.6	41	24	11
Laos	5.4	BE	98.2	1.9	1.2	96	82	32
Lebanon	3.3	MXZ	68.1	31.9	0.6	18	3	2
Malaysia	22.2	MChXH	90.8	9.2	4.1	173	95	31
Maldives	0.3	M	99.9	0.1	0.0	8	5	1
Mongolia	2.7	NEB	99.3	0.7	0.5	20	18	7
Myanmar	45.6	BX	91.3	8.7	5.2	132	63	33
Nepal	23.9	HBM	98.1	1.9	1.6	117	100	43
Oman	2.5	M	97.5	2.5	0.3	25	13	8
Pakistan	156.5	M	97.7	2.3	0.4	92	80	53
Palestine Authority	3.4	MJ	98.1	1.9	0.1	20	5	0
Philippines	76.0	XM	6.8	93.2	16.7	182	91	43
Qatar	0.6	MXH	89.5	10.5	2.5	20	9	2
Saudi Arabia	21.6	M	95.5	4.5	0.9	38	18	18
Singapore	3.6	BMNXCh	85.4	14.6	7.8	46	9	3
Sri Lanka	18.8	BHMX	92.4	7.6	1.3	21	9	6
Syria	16.1	MX	94.9	5.1	0.1	27	8	8
Tajikistan	6.2	MN	98.6	1.4	0.1	40	23	8
Thailand	61.4	BM	98.4	1.6	0.7	94	52	32
Timor Lorosae	0.9	XE	10.8	89.2	2.5	21	1	0
Turkey	66.6	M	99.7	0.3	0.0	56	36	22
Turkmenistan	4.5	MN	97.3	2.7	0.0	37	21	7
United Arab Emirates	2.4	MHX	90.8	9.3	0.8	38	18	12
Uzbekistan	24.3	MN	98.7	1.3	0.3	63	35	15
Vietnam	79.8	BNXEZ	91.8	8.2	1.4	99	52	22
Yemen	18.1	M	100.0	0.1	0.0	21	11	11
Total (50 countries)	**3692.0**		**91.4**	**8.6**	**3.6**	**3548**	**1862**	**909**

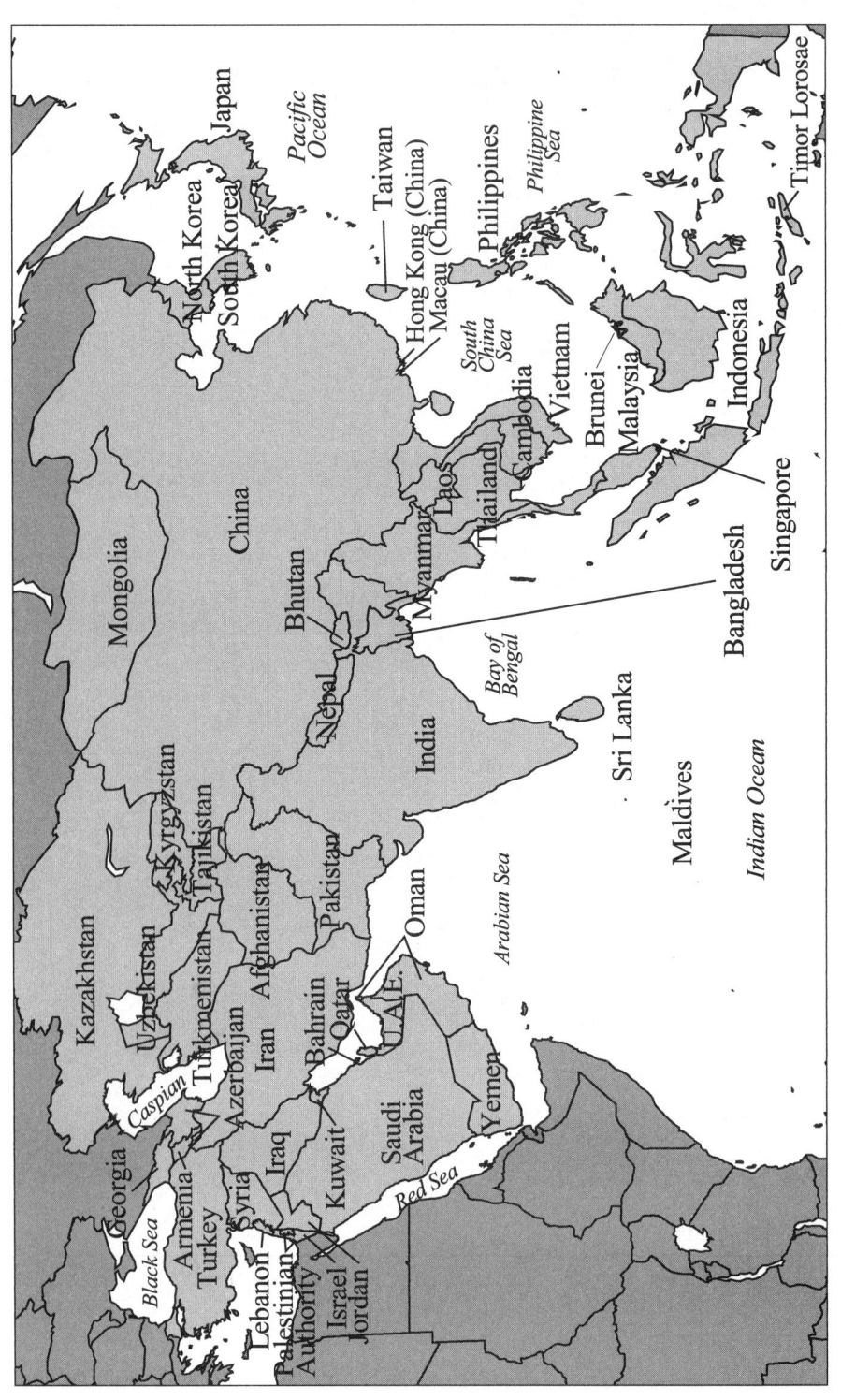

Asia

JANUARY 24-29

Updated February 2004

GEOGRAPHY
Area 31,829,200 sq.km. Approximately 23.5% of the world's surface area. Russia east of the Ural Mountains is part of Asia, but here all of the Russian Federation is included with Europe. Included here are the Trans-Caucasus states (Armenia, Azerbaijan and Georgia) as well as the West Asian/Middle East countries.

Population		Ann.Gr.	Density
2000	3,691,526,969	+1.41%	116 per sq. km.
2010	4,146,894,219	+1.12%	130 per sq. km.
2025	4,731,357,401	+0.78%	149 per sq. km.

Nearly 61% of the world's population lives in Asia.

Cities Over 195 megacities, including 14 of the world's largest conurbations — the largest being Tokyo with 34.5 million people. **Urbanites** 33%.

PEOPLES
There are around 3,550 ethno-linguistic peoples in Asia's nations. These are grouped into 28 of the world's 71 ethno-linguistic families. These can be further grouped in 9 Affinity Blocs of peoples which contain over 80% of the world's least reached peoples.

Languages About 2,240 distinct languages; 31% of the world's languages. **Languages with Scriptures** 110Bi 199NT 380w.i.p.

ECONOMY
Great extremes of wealth (Japan, Brunei, Singapore, Hong Kong, Gulf States) and poverty (Bangladesh, Nepal, parts of India, China and Indonesia). Immense differences in development from highly urbanized, industrial or post-industrial (Hong Kong, Singapore, South Korea, Japan, Taiwan) to rural subsistence economies (Bhutan, Nepal, Cambodia, Laos). The massive economic growth of Japan, South Korea, Thailand and Indonesia in the 1980s faltered in the '90s and in the Asian recession of 1997. The vast populations of India and China are seeing significant improvements in living standards as their economies grow.

POLITICS
For five centuries the European nations and those around the Atlantic Ocean were the centre of gravity of world politics. That centre has moved decisively to the newly powerful, vigorous nations of Asia and the Pacific. In 1900 all but five Asian nations were under Western control. By 2000 there were none. US military power in Asia has been steadily reduced and only in Korea and

Japan is there a permanent US military presence. The Cold War confrontation between capitalist and Marxist states was far from cold in Asia with continual military conflict somewhere in the continent for 60 years (China, Korea, Vietnam and Afghanistan being major regional wars). Over 32 Asian nations have either been ruled by or suffered from Communist warfare during this period. Asia remains the most militarized continent with four nuclear powers and others aspiring to join them. Asia has the majority of the world's most sensitive flash points.

RELIGION
The influence of religion on national and international politics is growing. This is increasingly a threat to religious freedom and ethnic harmony. Asia is the only continent where Christianity is not the largest religion and thus remains the greatest challenge for world evangelization.

Religions	Population %	Adherents	Ann.Gr.
Muslim	24.69	911.2 m	+2.05%
Hindu	22.08	815.0 m	+1.44%
non-Religious	19.16	707.1 m	+0.88%
Buddhist/other	10.70	394.8 m	+1.19%
Chinese	10.36	382.2 m	-1.29%
Christian	8.58	316.5 m	+3.66%
Traditional ethnic	2.43	89.5 m	+4.06%
Sikh	0.53	19.6 m	+1.68%
Jewish	0.13	4.6 m	+2.42%
Baha'i	0.09	3.3 m	+1.92%
Other	1.19	46.5 m	+0.73%

Christians	Denom.	Affil.%	,000	Ann.Gr.
Protestant	1,731	1.83	67,517	+4.2%
Independent	2,659	3.41	125,922	+8.7%
Anglican	33	0.02	693	+2.3%
Catholic	77	2.60	95,845	+1.0%
Orthodox	114	0.31	11,353	-0.2%
Marginal	246	0.32	11,880	+2.1%
Unaffiliated		0.71	26,243	n.a.
Doubly affiliated		*-0.60*	*-21,982*	*n.a.*

Only 3 Asian states have a Christian majority — Armenia, Georgia and the Philippines.

Trans-bloc Groupings	pop. %	,000	Ann.Gr.
Evangelical	3.6	133,171	+7.6%
Charismatic	2.4	87,378	+7.5%
Pentecostal	0.4	15,342	+5.9%

Missionaries from Asia
P,I,A 69,203 in 601 agencies; 13,607 in other countries.

Missionaries to Asia
P,I,A 29,305 expatriates in 875 agencies.

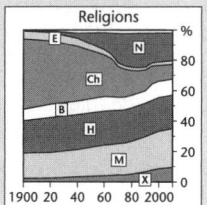

Religions

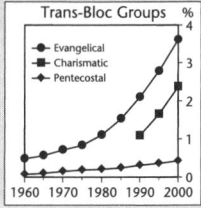

Trans-Bloc Groups
- Evangelical
- Charismatic
- Pentecostal

• Answers to Prayer in Asia

1 **The spectacular growth of the Church** in some countries of Asia observed in the 1980s has continued in the 1990s. In the 1980s the most notable countries were China, Korea and Indonesia. In the '90s it was China, India, Nepal, Central Asia and Mongolia (the latter two having virtually no indigenous Christians at all in 1990).

a) *All Christians* have increased from 22 million (2.3%) in 1900 to over 300 million (8.3%) in 2000.

b) *Protestant and Independent Christians* increased from under 4 million in 1900 to over 193 million in 2000.

c) *Catholic growth was slower* — from 11.1 million (1.2%) to 96 million (2.6%) over the same period.

d) *Asian Evangelicals*, over 130 million, have become almost as numerous as all Evangelicals in the Americas, where there are 148 million.

2 **The establishment of the Church in lands long sealed off from all overt Christian work** with hundreds of churches and thousands of believers in Mongolia, Kazakhstan, Kyrgyzstan, Uzbekistan, Turkey and footholds for the gospel gained in a number of others. There remain only 4 countries with no known, legally permitted Christian congregations: Maldives, Saudi Arabia, Afghanistan and North Korea (but in each there are known to be followers of the Lord Jesus and/or expatriate groups meeting informally).

3 **South Korea's maturing Church**. South Korea is a land of Christian superlatives — the largest Christian gatherings ever held, the world's largest congregations of Pentecostals, Presbyterians and Methodists, the largest theological seminaries and the largest non-Western missionary-sending nation! All this in a land that only opened up for the gospel just over a century ago.

4 **Indonesia** is the first largely Muslim country to have many Muslims coming to Christ. Some estimate that a fifth of the population could be Christian today, though not all of these come from a Muslim background.

5 **The increase in the number of Muslim Background Believers** (MBBs), despite or even because of, the activities of Islamist extremism. Their numbers are small, and their identities and locations here obscured, but over the 1990s there were significant increases. This has come through directed intercession, increased efforts to reach them, more sensitive cultural approaches and the widespread use of media — **SAT-7** television programmes, radio, the *JESUS* film/video, the spreading influence of the Internet, etc.

6 **Detailed and dedicated research** during the 1990s in India, China, Indonesia and SE Asia has revealed the spiritual needs and the extent of Christian outreach, or the need for it, to the various peoples in these complex, multi-cultural lands.

7 **The emergence of a mature, international missionary involvement.** The growth of commitment and involvement in cross-cultural outreach in India is praiseworthy. South Korea, the Philippines and the Chinese diaspora have become major components of the world's missionary outreach.

• Hot Spots of Asia

Listed below is a selection of the flash points of Asia that will impinge on global politics, tax the skills of world leaders, provide the stage on which the Church must perform and affect the strategies used to further world evangelization. Turn these into earnest intercession.

1 **China's re-emergence as a superpower** after 7 centuries of eclipse is possibly THE major global political factor in the first decades of the 21st Century. Its Marxist political structure, increasingly capitalist economy and potentially expansionist nationalism all combine to make for regional instability for Taiwan and the nations ringing the South China Sea. There are likely to be difficulties with Japan, Korea and the USA and also pressures on under-populated and under-developed Russian Siberia. Tibetan nationalism and Xinjiang's desired independence remain unresolved internal issues for China.

2 **The conflict between Israel and the Palestinians**. The breakdown of all international efforts to broker a viable peace deal foundered in 2001 on the deep differences between the claimants on the land and Jerusalem itself and also on the post-11 September 2001 war on terror. A resolution is unlikely and future war, humanly speaking, is inevitable. All sides have fearsome arsenals of weapons of mass destruction. Pray for all parties involved in the confrontation and world leaders attempting to defuse the situation.

3 **The agony of Afghanistan** continues after decades of invasion and wars. Although the US-led war against the Taliban and Al Qaeda allies led to the formation of a new government in 2002, the terrorist network regrouped in the lawless mountainous border regions of Afghanistan and Pakistan where they are likely to continue with impunity their efforts to plot acts of terror globally.

4 **Kashmir** is the focal point of the half-century stand-off between India and Pakistan. It has contributed to three wars and a nuclear arms race between the two nations.

5 **The Korean Peninsula** has remained one of the world's most dangerous flash points since the Korean War ceasefire in 1951. Pray for an end to the sufferings of North Koreans and a wisely managed eventual re-unification of Korea. In 2003 North Korea resumed its development of nuclear weapons.

6 **The possible disintegration of Indonesia** in the face of its ethnic and geographical diversity. The complex interplay of weak democratic government, powerful vested interests, Islamic extremism and ethnic resentments have eroded the links that held the country together. Indonesia could become a tragic global nightmare.

7 **The deep mistrust between the Persian Shi'a Muslim and the Arab Sunni Muslim worlds.** The 7 year war between Iran and Iraq in the 1980s was a chapter in the centuries-old conflict.

8 **The aftermath of the US-led invasion of Iraq** in 2003 is unclear. Differences between the rival ethnic and religious groups look irreconcilable.

9 **The festering problem of 27 million nation-less Kurds** directly impacts the lands where they form a large, restive minority — Turkey, Iraq and Iran as well as 32 other countries where they live.

• Trends to Watch

Globalization and modernization are bringing huge changes to billions of peoples. Listed here are some of the major trends. These will mould government planning, stimulate further massive demographic changes and impact Christian theology, ministry and deployment of workers and will change the responsiveness to the gospel of whole populations.

1 **The issue of water**, or lack of it, makes the international waterways a matter of life or death for the countries drained by them — the Jordan (Arabs and Israelis), the Tigris/Euphrates (Turkey, Syria, Iraq), the Oxus/Amu Darya (Central Asia), the Indus/Ganges/Brahmaputra (South Asia), the Mekong (China and Indo-China), the Amur (China and Russia). These may become the cause of bitterly fought wars, massive soil degradation, famine and millions of refugees.

2 **The tarnishing of the glitter of Asia's economic boom of the 1980s.** Japan's post-war rise as the world's economic superpower ended with stagnation in the 1990s and weak political leadership unwilling to address fundamental structural and cultural issues that caused it. The Asian economic crash of 1997 tipped Thailand, Indonesia and other countries into recession with serious long-term effects and implications for the region and the world.

3 **The massive flows of migrant labour** from poorer nations to the oil states of the Middle East, the industrial sweat-shops of India, Southeast Asia, Japan, etc., and sadly, the brothels of India, Thailand and beyond. For the Philippines, Bangladesh, Nepal, China, India, Pakistan and Myanmar, the export of people has become a major earner of foreign exchange. The long-term effects on politics, economic development, spread of disease and stability of family life will be immense.

4 **Secessionist wars have multiplied** and threatened the stability and territorial integrity of over 14 nations during the 1990s: Myanmar (6 ethnic conflicts), India (3), Indonesia (4 — Timor, Papua, Aceh, Kalimantan), China (2- Tibet, Xinjiang), Georgia (4), Thailand (Malays), Central Asian states (4), Yemen, Sri Lanka (Tamil), Iraq and Turkey (Kurds).

5 **The resurgence of non-Christian world religions** is increasingly influencing politics, restricting religious freedom, heightening inter-ethnic divisions and affecting Christian outreach and strategies.

a) ***Extreme Hindu groups*** have grown in political influence in both India and Nepal — Asia's two Hindu-majority lands. India's already complex social fabric is being torn asunder by Hinduist attacks on Muslims and Christians and forced 'conversions' of Dalits and Tribals. The Church in both lands is under renewed pressure and India's long-renowned tolerance is becoming a thing of the past.

b) ***Islam has become more militant and less tolerant*** with *shari'a* law replacing existing legislation in many Middle Eastern nations (Iran, Afghanistan, Pakistan, Brunei and the Maldives). There are strong movements to achieve the same in Malaysia and Indonesia, despite their large non-Muslim populations. The level of persecution against Christians has markedly increased. The post-11 September world has seen a rise in anti-Americanism and the Islamists are striving to portray the war on terror as an attack on Islam and the Arab World. There are 27 Asian countries with a Muslim majority.

c) ***Buddhists*** are reacting to effective Christian ministry in Sri Lanka, Myanmar and among Tibetan peoples. Korean Buddhism is experiencing rapid growth whilst earlier Christian growth has plateaued. Buddhism together with underlying ethnic religions (Taoism, Shintoism, Shamanism, etc.) is the majority religion of 13 Asian countries and is strong in those still under Communist rule.

d) ***Asia's indigenous ethnic religions***, have regained influence — Shintoism in Japan, Taoism and Confucianism in Chinese countries, shamanism in Mongolia, etc.

e) ***Extreme Orthodox Judaism*** wields a disproportionately large political influence on Israel — a factor which further complicates any efforts made for peace.

6 **The resilience of totalitarianism.** The extreme repression of the North Korean Communist regime, continued suppression of any meaningful political discussion in Vietnam, Laos, China, Myanmar, Turkmenistan, Saudi Arabia, etc., could lead to unexpected and sudden events that reverberate round the world. In only about 5-6 Asian countries is there a genuine, deep-rooted culture of democratic freedom. Democracy in Indonesia, the Philippines, Thailand and Mongolia is fragile. In many countries there is a range of authoritarian democracies where the opposition has little likelihood of replacing existing rulers through the ballot box.

7 **The Information Technology (IT) revolution** cannot but deeply affect Asia. India and China, for example, are rapidly developing satellite and fibre optic networks to take advantage of the Internet with unimaginable influence on their populations, politics and economies, and which will create multiple applications for both evil and good.

8 **The seriousness of the AIDS pandemic** is rapidly becoming apparent. There have been two major infection points — Mumbai, India and Bangkok, Thailand. Here the flourishing sex 'industry' has helped spread the scourge to poorer, surrounding lands such as Nepal, Myanmar, Cambodia and Laos where trafficking in girls and boys has been fuelled by poverty and greed. There were at least 6 million infected with AIDS in Asia, largely in the lands mentioned.

9 **The rapid increase of drug trafficking.** There are two main hubs of heroin production: Afghanistan and the Golden Triangle (where Thailand, Laos and Myanmar meet). Intricate criminal networks link the growers and users. The vast wealth generated, and the increasing local use of drugs, are further destabilizing factors for Asia.

10 **Ecological degradation** is becoming a serious issue: the drying out of the Aral Sea in Central Asia; rapid destruction of tropical forests with resultant flooding; smoke pollution; loss of coral reefs due to global warming; China's massive dam-building; and indiscriminate industrial pollution are all major problems with likely serious outcomes.

• The Church in Asia

1 **The Middle East/West Asia.**

a) ***The birthplace of the Church could become its grave*** if present emigration of Christian communities from the lands of West Asia continues. Praise God for the tenacity of Middle Eastern Christians over centuries of discrimination and times of persecution. Muslim extremists have increased the pressure to marginalize and eliminate any Christian presence in the region. Orthodox Jewish pressures on Messianic Jews are also acute. Pray that the ancient Orthodox and Catholic communities might come to new life and vigour to become an effective witness.

b) ***Protestant denominations*** are few and small. Most believers are from a nominal Christian background. Interdenominational relationships have often been strained. Pray for spiritual unity and warm fellowship at a time when Christians are under threat.

c) ***Believers from a Muslim background*** are few and often scattered. Pressures on them are usually acute — from relatives, employers and authorities. For many, emigration is the only way out of impossible situations. Pray for:

i *All who have come to Christ out of Islam.* They need fellowship, but often cannot find it with Christians from a different background. They need to study the Word and become established, but rarely have a caring network, the time or the facilities. They need courage in the face of intimidation, threats, ostracism and even physical danger.

ii *The witness of believers.* They need deliverance from fear, a commendable lifestyle, inspiration to witness wisely, and expectation of fruit from their witness.

iii *Christian homes.* These are few. Unequal marriages between Christians and Muslims are a major cause of backsliding. The Muslim world needs to see the beauty of a Christian home.

iv *Church planting.* Too few congregations of former Muslims exist.

d) ***Trained leadership for the Protestant churches*** is inadequate. There are few in training and few institutions in the Middle East that can provide it. Many of those who study in the West find good ministry opportunities there, and few return home. Pray for the development of fellowship links between indigenous Christian workers.

e) ***A missions vision needs to develop.*** Some Middle Eastern Christians work in lands closed to normal mission work — Libya, Saudi Arabia, etc.

2 **Central Asia.**

a) ***Indigenous evangelical Christians have multiplied*** to number thousands in Azerbaijan, Kyrgyzstan, Kazakhstan, Uzbekistan and even Turkey, but in every country they are under pressure from the authorities, Muslims, the Orthodox hierarchy and relatives. The foreign origin of Evangelicalism, their faith and practices are under suspicion and religious freedoms challenged. Pray for continued growth, national credibility, commendable lifestyles and mature indigenous leadership. Pray also for Russian, Ukrainian, German, Korean and expatriate believers who comprise the majority of Evangelicals in these lands.

b) ***Pressures on Christians are more severe*** in Uzbekistan, Tajikistan and especially Turkmenistan. Believers have been harassed, leaders imprisoned on trumped-up charges or exiled. In Afghanistan, under the Taliban, any indigenous believers face an automatic death sentence for apostasy from Islam.

c) ***Multi-national partnerships of expatriate believers*** have laboured hard since 1990 to help in the birth of indigenous fellowships in this region. Pray for their increase, perseverance and fruitfulness.

3 **South and East Asia.**

a) ***Areas of decline.*** For decades the church in Sri Lanka steadily declined as a percentage of the population — this has only recently been reversed. Hong Kong is losing as many Christians through emigration as it is gaining through conversion. North India has a small Christian presence, but this is nominal and in decline in many areas. Pray for a reversal to this trend.

b) ***Nominalism.*** This has become a problem in some Christian communities in Indonesia, India, Myanmar and the Philippines; yet in these same countries many denominations are growing vigorously. Pray for renewal.

c) ***Syncretism.*** Evangelical theological education in east and southeast Asia has expanded as nowhere else in the world. Theology is being indigenized and is losing some of the Western emphases, but is in danger of compromise in the areas of universalism, evolution, veneration of ancestors, etc.

d) ***Persecution.*** The collapse of Communism in other parts of the world has less affected Asia. Persecution of all believers is still acute in North Korea and persecution of unofficial Christianity in China and Vietnam remains harsh. Pressure or persecution of Christians by Muslims in Indonesia, Pakistan, Malaysia and Brunei increased during the 1990s. Buddhists in Bhutan and Sri Lanka have stepped up pressure on Christians. There is greater freedom in Hindu Nepal, but persecution of Christians continues. In India the level of persecution since the mid-1990s has markedly increased.

e) ***Missions vision.*** This has grown spectacularly during the 1980s and '90s. At first, most of this vision was for unreached ethnic groups within their own nations (especially India, the Philippines, Myanmar and Indonesia) or to their own ethnic communities in other lands (Japanese, Koreans and Chinese especially). However, this has changed and the cross-cultural foreign missionary force is growing fast. Particular areas to cover in prayer:

i *Maturity in missions* and willingness to learn from mistakes of the past and not repeat them — for example in paternalism and use of funds.

ii *Partnerships with Western missions to be mutually beneficial,* whether serving together in international agencies or through inter-agency cooperation on fields.

iii *Effective local church and denominational support for missions.* Few understand the cost, the long periods of time required for language and culture learning, the need for supportive ministries and the effort to see fruit in a pioneer field.

iv *Retention of Asian missionaries* who are serving cross-culturally. This will be a big long-term problem unless issues such as the education of missionaries' children and retirement are tackled.

• The Unfinished Task in Asia

1 **While we praise God for great strides** in the evangelization of Asia, the remaining challenge is awesome. Asians comprise:

a) ***Over 83%*** of the 4.4 billion non-Christians in the world.

b) ***Over 87% of World A*** unevangelized individuals.

c) ***The three largest non-Christian religions*** in the world and the most challenging for Christians: 832 million Muslims, 805 million Hindus, 400-900 million Buddhists (the higher figure if the Chinese, Japanese and other intermingled ethnic religions are included).

2 **Of the 55 countries of the world that are less than 10% Christian**, 44 are in Asia.

3 **The least evangelized people on earth** are predominantly Asian. The **Joshua Project List**, used at the 1997 GCOWE conference in Pretoria, had 1,739 unreached peoples listed — 1,107 of these were from Asia.

4 **The unreached peoples of Asia** can be grouped by affinities of language, race, culture, geography and history. The salient needs are briefly shown here by these Affinity Blocs. See map on p. 17.

a) ***The Arab World*** (including North Africa, but excluding African minorities). Population: 248 million with 476 peoples. While there are many Arabic-speaking Christians in Egypt and West Asia, the majority of the 20 Arab countries have very few believers. Major ministry possibilities:

i *Arab believers* need courage to use opportunities to witness, and to trust God that Muslims can be saved and become committed believers.

ii *SAT-7 television programmes* broadcast daily are being watched by millions of Arabic-speaking Muslims. In many countries satellite dishes are owned by nearly every home.

iii *Radio broadcasts* produced by CBN, **IBRA** and others are broadcast by **FEBA**-Seychelles, **TWR**-Cyprus and **HCJB**. Many young people listen and then receive tactful follow-up ministry.

iv *The JESUS film/video* has been widely used in broadcasting and through personal distribution of tapes.

v *The 4 million Arabs* in Western Europe are more accessible to Christian witness — but not necessarily more open.

vi *The Magalla Arabic magazine* with its quietly overt Christian testimony is widely distributed in Middle Eastern countries.

vii *The Internet* is proving an exciting means of witness and discipling.

viii *There are many opportunities for Christian expatriates* to serve in Arab lands and live for Jesus.

b) **The Indo-Iranian bloc**. Population: 123 million; 252 peoples. Major people clusters: Persian (62m); Pathan (32m); Kurds (20-25m); Baluch (9m). These are some of the least evangelized peoples on earth. Major opportunities for witness:

i *Expatriate Christians* — openings are few, but they do exist.

ii *Many have become refugees* as a result of war, oppression and poverty. Among the expatriate Afghans, Persians and Kurds, there are Christians and churches have been planted.

iii *Media ministries* — radio broadcasts in the various languages are increasing in number, variety of languages and quality but follow-up is difficult.

c) **The South Asian bloc** is the largest of the 8 with 1.3 billion individuals, nearly 800 ethno-linguistic peoples and thousands of ethno-cultural caste groups (see India). There are three major components — the 1,066 million Indo-Aryans, the 240 million Dravidians and 12 million Tribals (excluding NE India, see (*f*) below). In only a small minority of these has there been a significant turning to Christ, and these have mostly been from the lower classes of society. The upper castes, the ruling and middle classes remain untouched.

d) **The Turkic bloc** stretches from SE Europe to NE Siberia across most of Central Asia. Population: 156 million with 322 peoples. The Turkic peoples are the last major bloc to open up for Christian witness. Apart from Turkey, most of the Turkic peoples were under Communist rule for much of the 20th Century. Significant beginnings in church planting have only been made in Turkey since 1960, and other areas since 1990. Major opportunities for witness:

i *Expatriate Christians* have professional and business openings to serve in most areas today. There may be around 1,500 doing so today.

ii *Local believers* have significantly increased among the Turks and Central Asians but the total number of Evangelicals may not be much more than 10-12,000 or less than 0.01% of the Turkic population.

iii *Media input* has increased through Bible translation (**IBT**, **UBS**, etc.), literature, radio and the *JESUS* film.

e) **The East Asian bloc** comprising those cultures deeply impacted by the Chinese. Population: 1.42 billion. Major people clusters: Han Chinese (1,250m); Japanese (130m); Korean (76m). There is now a large dynamic Christian presence among the Koreans and most Mainland and Overseas Chinese communities. The challenges remaining are the open but reluctant Japanese, the Chinese Muslim Hui, Taiwan and a number of less-evangelized provinces in China.

f) **The Tibeto-Burman bloc** of the Himalayas, Central Asia, NE India, Myanmar and China. Population: 81.4 million in 472 peoples. Major people clusters: Burmese (48m); Tibetan (13.4m); Kuki-Chin (5.6m); Karen (4.9m). Many peoples in NE India and Myanmar have become Christian. The major challenges are:

i *The strongly Buddhist Tibetans*, most living in Chinese Tibet, Bhutan and N. Nepal. Believers are numbered in hundreds only. Ministry opportunities are limited, but workers are needed to witness to them.

ii *The long-resistant Burmese* have been hearing the gospel for two centuries, but few have turned from Buddhism to Christ. Many of the tribal peoples have.

g) **The Southeast Asian bloc** — the four nations of Indo-China, Thailand and South China. Population: 202 million in 400 peoples. Major people clusters: Dai/Thai (97m); Vietnamese (73m); Mon-Khmer (20m); Hmong/Meo (12m). Most are Buddhist or animist. There has been a varied response to the gospel. Some, such as groups among the Hmong/Montagnard peoples of Vietnam, Khasi of India, Wa of Myanmar and China, have many Christians. There are also a significant number of Christians among the Vietnamese. The special challenges are for:

i   *The Thai* where nearly 200 years of freedom to proclaim the gospel has resulted in low response, weak churches and an unchallenged, entrenched spiritism and Buddhism.

ii *The many Dai peoples of China* and SE Asia. In only a handful of the 100+ peoples are there viable, growing churches.

iii *The Laotians* where Communist rulers have been particularly harsh in repressing the Christians — most of whom are minority peoples and relatively few are ethnic Lao.

h) **The Malay peoples**. The Malay family of peoples extend westwards to Madagascar in Africa and to Polynesia in the Pacific. The more outlying Filipinos, Pacific Islanders, eastern Indonesian peoples and the Malagasy are largely Christian, but the Malay/Indonesian heartlands are largely Muslim. Christians are very few in most peoples. Of special challenge are:

i   *Sumatra, Indonesia* — one of the world's largest islands with 40 million people and only a large Christian population among the Batak and Nias peoples.

ii *Java* with 125 million people but only a significant Christian community in cosmopolitan Jakarta and among sections of the Jawa. The Sunda and Madura peoples remain unreached.

iii *The Malay of Sumatra, Kalimantan* and the Riau of Indonesia, Malaysia, Brunei and South Thailand number 86 million and remain one of the largest clusters of unreached peoples in the world.

5 Special areas of ministry need:

a) **The Parsees** are followers of the Persian Zoroaster. They favoured the Jews in the time of their exile in Daniel's day. The wise men who came to worship the infant Lord Jesus were Parsees, yet they remain one of the most secretive and unreached religious groups of today. They may number 3 — 4.5 million or more, but only 30 believers are known. Many are wealthy and influential in South Asia and the West.

b) **Children in crisis**. The 1997 economic down-turn in Asia affected the quality of life of millions of children. Child labour became even more widespread. It was reckoned in 1997 that one million or more children were forced into sex slavery in Asia. Malnutrition affects over 60% of India's children.

c) **Bible translation** presents a major challenge with 1,300 languages having a definite or likely need. Work is in progress in 271 Asian languages.

EUROPE

	Population 2000	Main Religions	non-Chr%	All Chr %	Evang-elical%	Peoples All	Peoples World A	Peoples JPL
Albania	3.1	XMN	58.5	41.5	0.3	11	4	2
Andorra	0.1	XN	6.6	93.4	0.2	10	3	0
Austria	8.2	X	10.2	89.8	0.5	35	3	1
Belarus	10.2	XN	21.3	78.7	1.5	25	6	2
Belgium	10.2	XN	32.3	67.7	0.7	25	7	2
Bosnia	4.0	MX	65.0	35.0	0.07	19	3	3
Bulgaria	8.2	XMN	19.8	80.2	2	34	6	1
Channel Islands	0.2	XN	15.1	84.9	0	5	0	0
Croatia	4.5	X	5.6	94.4	0.5	30	2	1
Cyprus	0.8	XM	25.9	74.1	0.2	9	2	1
Czech Republic	10.2	XN	46.8	53.2	1.1	25	1	0
Denmark	5.3	XN	14.2	85.9	4.8	28	2	0
Estonia	1.4	NX	61.4	38.6	5.7	23	4	0
Faeroe Islands	0.0	XN	6.0	94.0	28.5	4	0	0
Finland	5.2	XN	12.9	87.1	12.5	30	7	0
France	59.1	XNM	32.3	67.7	0.8	96	12	16
Germany	82.2	XN	30.5	69.5	2.9	78	4	5
Gibraltar	0.0	XM	11.6	88.4	1.4	6	0	0
Greece	10.6	X	4.9	95.2	0.4	30	4	1
Holy See (Vatican)	0.0	X	0.0	100.0	0	3	0	0
Hungary	10.0	XN	8.0	92.0	2.7	22	2	2
Iceland	0.3	X	4.4	95.6	3.3	9	0	0
Ireland	3.7	X	4.7	95.4	3.3	20	1	0
Isle of Man	0.1	XN	11.2	88.8	0	4	0	0
Italy	57.3	XN	22.7	77.4	0.9	59	4	2
Latvia	2.4	XN	41.8	58.3	7.6	34	8	1
Liechtenstein	0.0	XN	11.3	88.7	0.4	5	1	0
Lithuania	3.7	XN	23.8	76.2	0.4	23	7	1
Luxembourg	0.4	X	6.1	93.9	0.3	14	1	0
Macedonia	2.0	XMN	36.6	63.4	0.2	23	3	2
Malta	0.4	X	2.8	97.2	1	10	0	0
Moldova	4.4	X	4.6	95.4	3.3	31	10	2
Monaco	0.0	XN	12.3	87.7	1	14	1	0
Netherlands	15.8	XNM	44.1	55.9	4.5	45	3	7
Norway	4.5	XN	6.3	93.7	9.3	31	3	0
Poland	38.8	XN	9.7	90.3	0.2	23	4	0
Portugal	9.9	XN	5.6	94.4	3.1	29	1	0
Romania	22.3	XN	12.2	87.9	6.3	28	6	5
Russia	146.9	XNM	45.9	54.1	0.7	168	83	42
San Marino	0.0	XN	7.7	92.3	0	3	0	0
Slovakia	5.4	XN	17.1	82.9	1.5	18	1	0
Slovenia	2.0	XN	14.8	85.2	0.2	14	0	0
Spain	39.8	XN	32.2	67.8	0.4	35	3	0
Svalbard	0.0	XN	47.0	57.0	0	2	0	0
Sweden	8.9	XN	45.4	54.7	4.9	50	5	1
Switzerland	7.4	XN	13.4	86.6	4.1	38	4	1
Ukraine	50.5	XN	11.9	88.1	2.7	65	23	7
United Kingdom	58.8	XN	32.4	67.6	8.5	94	9	9
Yugoslavia	10.6	XMN	32.1	67.9	1.4	34	4	5
Total (52 countries)	**729.8**		**28.9**	**71.1**	**2.4**	**1471**	**257**	**122**

This includes all the countries of Europe and the entire Russian Federation (including all of Siberia which is technically in Asia). We have also included Cyprus in Europe since it is likely to join the EU in the lifetime of this book.

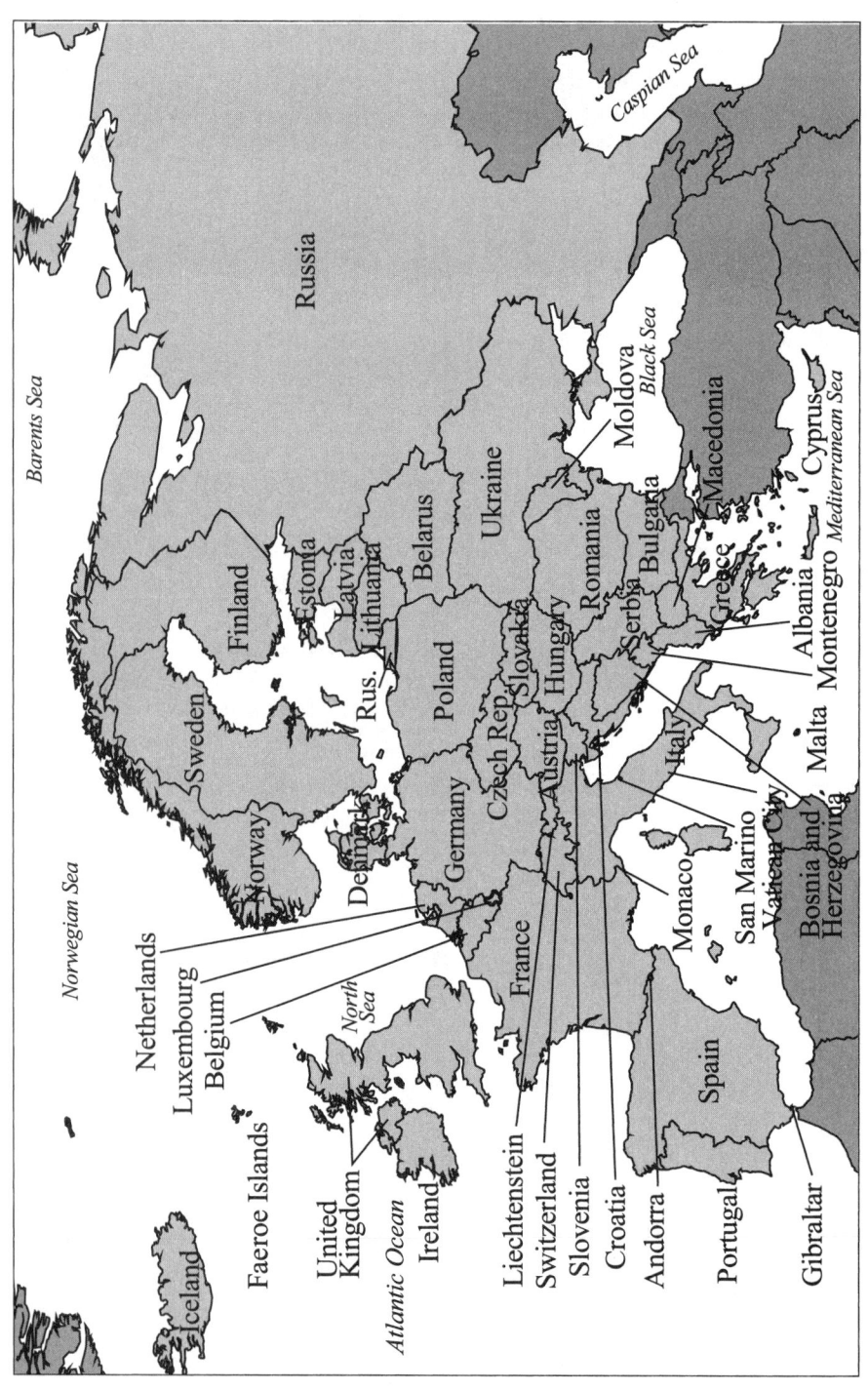

Europe

JANUARY 30-FEBRUARY 3
Revised February 2004

GEOGRAPHY
Area 22,978,500 sq.km of which 74% is in the Russian Federation. This is 17% of the earth's surface.

Population		Ann.Gr.	Density
2000	729,802,252	+0.03%	32 per sq. km.
2010	725,218,750	-0.09%	32 per sq. km.
2025	703,375,405	-0.27%	31 per sq. km.

Europe has 12% of the world's population.

Urbanites 74%. Europe is the world's most urbanized continent.

PEOPLES
Europe's ethnic diversity and long history of conflicts ultimately moulded much of the political framework of the nations of today. Major groupings of peoples:
Slavic 31.6%. Central and Eastern Europe. Majority in 12 nations.
Latin/Romance 29.4%. Southern and southwestern Europe and also Romania. Majority in 11 countries.
Germanic 24.8%. Predominantly central and northwestern Europe. Majority in 15 countries.
Finno-Ugric 2.9%. Northern Europe, Hungary and Russian Arctic. Majority in 3 countries.
Turkic 2.3%. Central Russia; many migrants to western Europe since the 1960s.
Greek 1.6%. Greece, Cyprus and Central Europe.
Celtic 1.5%. Northwestern Europe; majority in Ireland.
Roma (Gypsy) 0.9%. In nearly every country of Europe. Their numbers may be far higher than official figures show.
Other European 2.1%. Including Albanians, Basques, Baltic peoples.
Other 2.9%. Middle Eastern 12.9 m.; Asian 3.8m of which 1.2m are Chinese; Caribbean 1.6m; African 957,000. Many are refugees or migrants — mostly in southern and western Europe.

Languages indigenous to Europe 269. **Languages with Scriptures** 48Bi 13NT 52w.i.p.

ECONOMY
From 1500-1940 the world's dominant trading and industrial region. Innovative development slowed in Western Europe by reluctance to change, the costly welfare state, and restrictive practices in trade and industry. The long-term disastrous distortions of Marxist economies in central and eastern Europe has adversely affected national infrastructures, ecology and the work ethic of the people. During the last half of the 20th Century, the North American and then the east and southeast Asian economies forged ahead of those of Europe. The dominant realities of the 1990s have been the gradual recovery of most former Communist states and the strengthening and planned expansion of the EU from the 13 members in 2001 to most nations in Europe over the first decade of the 21st Century. The combined impact of affluence and a rapidly falling birthrate has made Western Europe a magnet for millions from more impoverished lands of Eastern Europe, Africa and Asia.

POLITICS
From the French Revolution in 1789 until the tearing down of the Berlin Wall in 1989, European political ideologies have had worldwide dominance. Humanism, secularism, socialism, Marxism, fascism, nazism and amoral capitalism have all contributed to such evils as global wars, colonialism and oppression. To the surprise of secular Europeans, ethnocentrism (as in the Balkans, etc.) and religion have again become important and major causes for political confrontations since 1990. Europe is going through a period of unprecedented peace but, with political and economic integration, there is also ethnic fragmentation.

RELIGION
After the Muslim invasions of the 8th Century, Christianity was virtually wiped out in the lands of the Middle East where the early Church first took root. For nearly 1,000 years the countries of the West became the last major refuge for Christianity. The encircling Muslim lands effectively prevented any missionary outreach to Africa and Asia. It was not until the Reformation in the 16th Century that the Church was revitalized to eventually become a force for world evangelization. The last 250 years have been years of worldwide advance for the gospel but, conversely, decline in Europe. Europe is the world's prodigal continent.

Religions	Population %	Adherents	Ann.Gr.
Christian	71.13	519.1m	-0.44%
non-Religious/other	22.79	166.2m	+0.88%
Muslim	5.09	37.2m	+2.05%
Jewish	0.33	2.4m	-1.20%
Buddhist/Chinese	0.27	2.0m	+3.07%
Traditional/Spiritist	0.22	1.6m	+4.91%
Hindu	0.08	603,000	+1.55%
Sikh	0.05	401,000	+2.36%
Baha'i	0.02	164,000	+5.12%

The rise of secularism was temporarily slowed by the collapse of Communism, but as greater freedom of religious belief becomes commonplace, a practical atheism or fuzzy spirituality has become the predominant belief system among Europeans with numbers far higher than the non-Religious figures above would indicate.

Christians	Denom.	Affil.%	,000	Ann.Gr.
Protestant	1,510	9.24	67,403	-0.9%
Independent	1,000	0.91	6,674	+2.2%
Anglican	33	3.54	28,805	-0.3%
Catholic	68	33.10	241,578	-0.9%
Orthodox	203	19.96	145,639	+0.0%
Marginal	356	0.64	4,655	+3.0%
Unaffiliated		4.91	35,816	n.a.
Doubly affiliated		*-1.19*	*-8,681*	*n.a.*

The rate of decline of Christians is accelerating. Many of the Christians in the percentages above have no meaningful involvement with Church life. Regular church-goers would probably be under 10% of Europe's population.

Trans-bloc Groupings pop. %		,000	Ann.Gr.
Evangelical	2.4	17,275	+1.8%
Charismatic	1.9	13,870	+1.2%
Pentecostal	0.6	4,325	+3.6%

Missionaries from Europe
P,I,A 22,897 from 413 agencies with 16,077 serving outside their own country.

Missionaries to Europe
P,I,A 16,197 expatriates in 564 agencies.

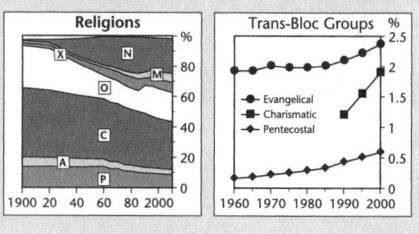

• Answers to Prayer

1 **The collapse of European Communism** and the dismantling of the Iron Curtain that had divided Europe for nearly half a century was a direct answer to the prayers of millions. The proud boasts of atheist persecutors about the imminent demise of the Church (with their active efforts!) proved hollow.

2 **Europe's decade of peace in the 1990s** — the first in two millennia without imperial tyrannies, major wars or superpower competition, the Balkan wars are the exception.

3 **The advent of religious freedom** on a scale not known in Europe's history. The persecution of Christians and all religions under Communism was unprecedented in modern times. Especially severe were the devastating purges of Stalin in the USSR (1930s) when an estimated 12 million Christians of all varieties were martyred. The down side of this new freedom is that it has not necessarily led to effective use of that freedom by the Church or to significant church growth.

4 **Signs of hope in the midst of spiritual decline:**

a) *The growth in strength and confidence of Evangelicals*. In mainline denominations, their proportion is increasing and newer evangelical and charismatic fellowships and networks are growing but from a relatively small base.

b) *The emergence of new church and worship patterns* in youth networks which are impacting many young people.

c) *Post-modernism's questioning* of past unchallenged certainties are leading many to seek spiritual solutions. There is a greater openness for dialogue on spiritual things for Christians willing to meet seekers where they are.

d) *The emergence of pan-European visions* such as *Hope for Europe*, and movements such as the European Evangelical Alliance, TEMA with its large European conferences, and others.

5 **Specific people movements to Christ in the past 10 years**.

a) *Europe's 7 million Roma* have been turning to Christ — first in France and Spain (where they are the most evangelical ethnic group), and more recently in the UK and parts of Central Europe.

b) *The Bulgarian Muslim Millet and Roma* have been responding to Christ and thousands are seeking.

c) *Albanians* — first in post-communist Albania and more recently in UN-controlled Kosovo.

6 **The impact of Christian radio and television** has been significant right across the former Soviet Union. Some of the world's most powerful radio stations, once used by Communists, are now used by Christian agencies as part of their world-wide network.

• Hot Spots of Europe

The relative peace of Europe is not universal. Of particular concern for prayer:

1 **The Balkans** with its long history of violent conflict, ethnic hatreds and convoluted politics remains a dangerous flash point and a vortex that has sucked in many nations seeking to quell the violence and lay foundations for peace and economic progress. The ending of the Yugoslav/Serbian dictatorship in 2001 still leaves many problems unsolved — the future of Montenegro, Kosovo, Bosnia and Macedonia as well as that of Serbia itself all hang in the balance. The extremists among Albanians and Serbs still wield great power and future wars are not unlikely. Pray for all local and international leaders involved in seeking to settle the multiple problems and centuries of treachery, mistrust and vendettas. Pray for genuine inter-communal forgiveness, an effective demilitarization of the area and for democratic freedoms to be instituted.

2 **The Caucasus** with its ethnic and religious diversity, history of war and repression and straddling the oil-rich but politically sensitive region where many major powers (Russia, Turkey, Iran and the West) have conflicting areas of concern, is also a hot spot. There could be decades of unrest ahead. Its peoples represent one of the most difficult challenges for evangelization with many ethnic groups still totally unreached.

3 **The political future of Russia**. A decade of a measure of democracy, associated with greed, crime, self-seeking politicians, a pervasive mafia and degeneration of the quality of life has caused many to hanker after the authoritarian certainties of Communist dictatorship. Both a new nationalistic militarism and political collapse of the Russian Federation would have tragic world-involving consequences. Pray for a new Russia to emerge which provides effective government, rapid economic betterment and respects human rights and freedoms.

4 **Areas of conflict**: needing peace — Northern Ireland, the Basque region of Spain, Chechnya in the Russian Federation.

• Trends to Watch

1 **The massive culture-change** in Europe as postmodernism and post-Christian world views predominate and control the media. Younger Europeans have moved away from the certainties of their Judeo-Christian heritage to New Age thinking, relative truth, reincarnation and the occult. Pray that Christians may be willing to adapt their lifestyle, method of communication and structures to both evangelize and welcome this generation into fellowships where they can grow and feel they belong.

2 **The political integration of Europe** has gathered pace — the ultimate form, the degree of democratic accountability and the extent of sacrifice of national sovereignty are matters for intense debate and concern. The EU has not been renowned for its transparent finances, democratic accountability and visionary leadership. Pray that the emerging Europe may not lose its spiritual heritage and that the Holy Spirit might be poured out on these nations.

3 **The ethnic fragmentation of Europe**. Even as the EU expands the vexed issue of ethnic nationalisms in the UK, France, Spain, Central Europe, Belgium, the Hungarian minorities, and the Russian federation has grown in significance. Racism has reared its ugly head in the 'ethnic cleansing' of the Balkans and the treatment of immigrants and Roma people in many countries. This is a challenge to Christians to demonstrate Christ's love and that the power of the gospel transcends culture.

4 **A steady erosion of religious freedom all over Europe**. This comes from:

a) *Secular society* which regards Christian absolutes with intolerance and as the 'unpardonable sin'. Bible-believing Christians are ridiculed, marginalized and even legislated against through the insistence of secularists on equality before the law of deviant lifestyles contrary to Scripture.

b) *Governments* who have over-reacted to extreme acts of small sectarian groups and arbitrarily black-listed a wide range of innocent religious groups in France, Austria, Belgium, Belarus, Russia and elsewhere.

c) **The Orthodox Church** which, in many countries of central and eastern Europe, has reacted vigorously to minority religious groups through pressing for discriminatory legislation, harassment and misleading propaganda against them. Evangelicals in Greece, Bulgaria, Romania, Belarus and Russia have had considerable difficulties in their ministry and witness.

5 **The increasing flow of immigrants — both legal and illegal from outside Europe.** This is a threat to cultural homogeneity and therefore resisted, but an economic necessity with Europe's ageing population. It is also an opportunity for the gospel as many come from countries where Christian witness is restricted or limited. There may now be nearly 30 million immigrants in Europe since 1945 who originated from other continents. Despite stricter controls, the rate is increasing and has become a lucrative source of income to criminal networks. Nearly 500,000 apply for asylum in Europe every year. Pray that Christians may be alerted and activated for ministry and witness to this rising tide of humanity.

6 **The growth of Muslim communities** through immigration and a higher birth rate is such that Islam has become the second religion of Europe. Muslims are successfully pressing for legislation which favours their religious beliefs in many countries. It is the majority religion of Bosnia, and would be of potential nations — Kosovo in Yugoslavia and Tatarstan, Bashkortostan, Chechnya and Dagestan in the Russian Federation. It is the single largest religious group in Albania. Pray that Christians might be alerted to the need of these people for the gospel and be equipped to meet it.

• The Church in Europe

1 **The Church in general has lost the younger generation** in both western Europe and those lands formerly under Communism. Christian profession is likely to decline dramatically over the coming two decades. Pray for continent-wide revival to reverse this trend.

2 **Liberal theology** rose to dominate theological institutions all over western Europe by the beginning of the 20th Century. Most mainline Protestant denominations were spiritually crippled by the resulting loss of confidence in the Scriptures and in the uniqueness of the gospel. Liberal theological institutions are sparsely patronized by students today and this aberration is losing influence. In contrast, evangelical institutions have done better. Pray for a return to relevant biblical theology, preaching and lifestyle in the mainline denominations. Free Church and Pentecostal Christians are only a small proportion of the total Christian community in Europe.

3 **The Church in central and eastern Europe** emerged from the long night of Communist propaganda, manipulation, oppression and often outright persecution battered but alive. Although more than a decade of relative freedom has passed, many serious hangovers from the past remain that need prayerful attention.

a) *Healing of past wounds*. Under Communism, government interference in Church life, appointment of leaders, dispensing of privileges and persecution caused division in nearly every denomination between the legal and illegal, or registered and unregistered. Those divisions are still evident. Pray for humility, confession, restoration and renewal. The division between non-Pentecostal and Pentecostal Evangelicals has hampered their witness.

b) *The overcoming of an inferiority complex among Evangelicals*. Their severe repression, denial of education and professional openings under Communism has left them marginalized and often ineffective in society. Many leaders are reluctant to adapt in the face of cultural and generational change. As a result, many congregations appear irrelevant and unable to address 21st Century needs. Evangelicals could have a vital role in restoring moral, ethical and spiritual standards in a society that has lost its way.

c) *The lack of open, appropriate evangelism*. Since outreach was banned in the past, new opportunities in the 1990s were often missed or misused. Some denominations and networks have grown, but others have stagnated. The growth of the early 1990s has tailed off. Discipling of seekers has been disappointing. Pray for Holy Spirit inspiration, innovation and faith for growth in the 21st Century.

d) *Handling relationships* with the dominant Orthodox Church in Romania, Bulgaria, Greece, Macedonia, Serbia, Belarus and Russia. Orthodox efforts to marginalize, discredit and even eliminate other religions and minority Christian ministry have led to discriminatory legislation in these countries.

e) ***Handling links with the global Church.*** After decades of isolation, the shock of relating to Christian bodies from other lands has been often traumatic to both sides. Expatriate bodies need sensitivity and wisdom and to learn from the many mistakes of the 1990s. Foreign missionaries have gained a negative image — especially when much aid, help and involvement was on a short-term basis with little cultural sensitivity, linguistic ability or spiritual discernment. Pray for long-term cooperation and mutual appreciation, with more support of local initiatives.

f) ***The training of a new generation of leaders.*** All more structured theological education was controlled or banned. In the 1990s, numerous new seminaries, Bible schools and TEE programmes sprang up across these lands. Increasingly, these are indigenously led and are maturing. Much help is needed to make them more viable and effective and have the resources to give effective training.

• The Unfinished Task in Europe

1 **Great swathes of Western Europe are truly post-Christian** with a small, 'irrelevant', committed Christian remnant, and need to be evangelized again — for example, North Germany, parts of Sweden, rural England and Wales, and much of France. Many of these areas have not had much meaningful exposure to biblical Christianity for several generations.

2 **Evangelical churches are few in much of southern Europe**, and especially southeastern Europe. About 24 nations in Europe have less than 1% Evangelicals, and of these, 11 have less than 0.2%. Look prayerfully through the list alongside the Europe map and pray for the planting of many vibrant, witnessing groups of believers in these lands.

3 **Major peoples in Europe with a Christian tradition** but very few Evangelicals. To name a few: Lithuanian, Serbian, Montenegrin, Macedonian, Greek, Basque, Belarusian, Russian, etc.

4 **Young people** are a challenge. In few countries has Christianity any meaning for youth. Christians are considered remnants of a past age that hinder progress. New Age spirituality, an eastern religious worldview and fascination with the occult have diverted millions from their Christian heritage and its absolutes. In central and eastern Europe, 25% of young people are unemployed, and drug and alcohol abuse and suicide are common. Pray for those involved in outreach and discipling ministries among youth.

5 **Unreached peoples**. Nearly 400 non-Christian peoples within Europe's countries are only partially evangelized at best. Many are immigrant or refugee peoples for whom specialized outreach is needed. Of particular challenge are:

a) ***Muslim ethnic groups*** from the Middle East, North Africa, black Africa and southeast Europe (especially Bosnians, Albanians and Turks).

b) ***Roma minorities*** — especially those of the Balkan states.

c) ***The Jewish remnant*** — decimated in many countries during the Holocaust and through emigration to Israel, but still needing to be brought to the Messiah.

d) ***The many ethnic minorities of the Russian Federation*** — in the Caucasus, Siberia, the Urals and the Arctic.

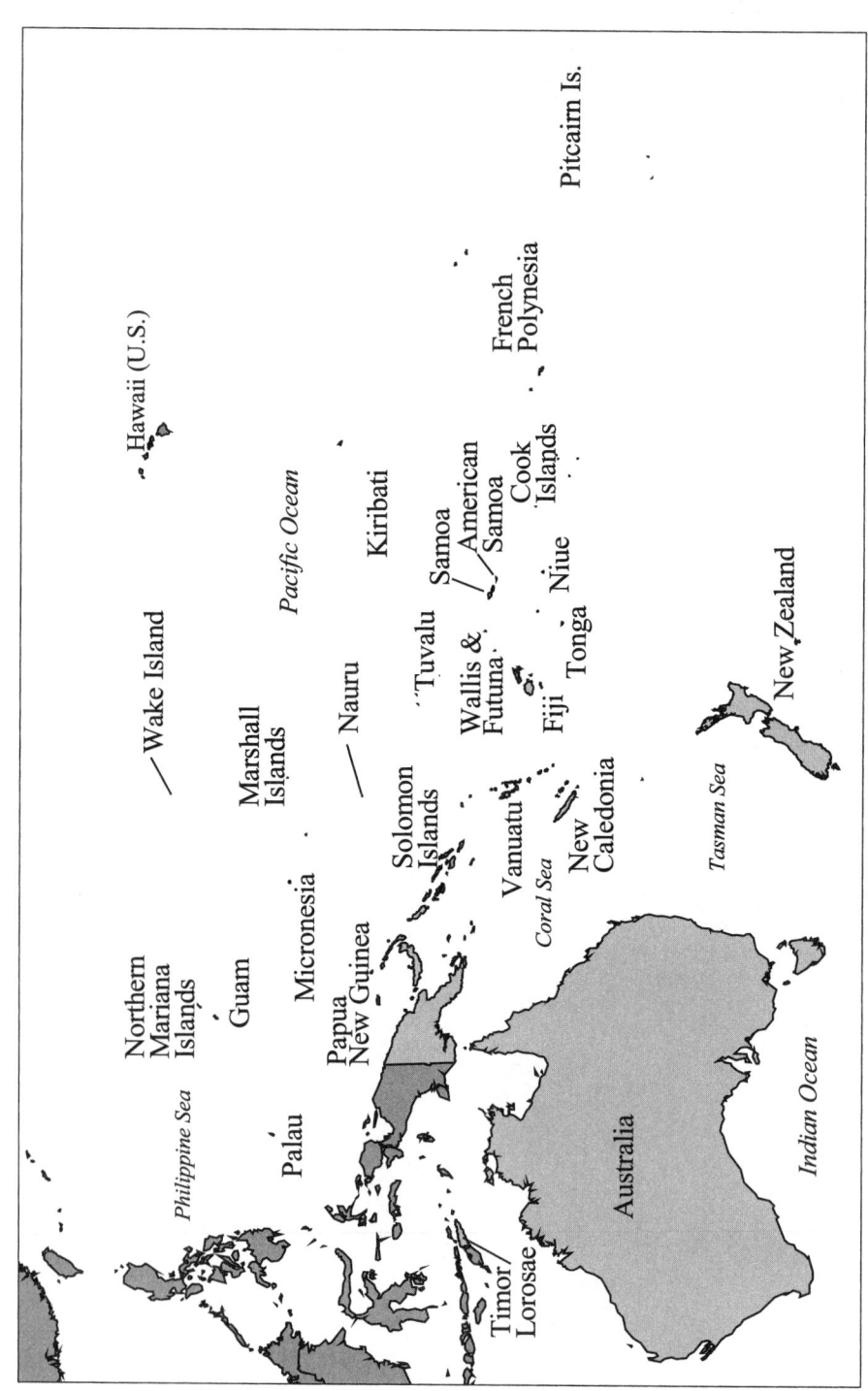

PACIFIC

	Population 2000	Main Religions	non-Chr%	All Chr %	Evang-elical%	Peoples All	World A	JPL
American Samoa	0.1	X	4.3	95.7	17.9	9	1	0
Australia	18.9	XN	32.5	67.5	12.5	132	16	3
Christmas Island	0.0	MNX	87.0	13.0	0.0	7	3	0
Cocos (Keeling) Is.	0.0	MXN	63.0	37.0	0.0	4	2	0
Cook Islands	0.0	X	2.0	98.0	12.1	7	0	0
Fiji	0.8	XHM	41.7	58.3	17.5	29	1	2
French Polynesia	0.2	XN	15.0	85.1	5.6	14	0	0
Guam	0.2	X	4.4	95.6	12.6	12	1	0
Johnston Island	0.0	X	30.0	70.0	0.0			0
Kiribati	0.1	XE	5.6	94.4	7.0	5	0	0
Marshall Islands	0.1	X	4.8	95.2	42.8	2	0	0
Micronesia, Fed. States	0.1	X	6.2	93.8	21.5	21	0	0
Midway Islands	0.0		0.0	0.0	0.0			0
Nauru	0.0	X	9.5	90.5	9.0	8	0	0
New Caledonia	0.2	XN	17.2	82.8	7.5	49	0	0
New Zealand	3.9	XN	38.3	61.7	22.1	47	0	0
Niue	0.0	X	5.1	94.9	8.5	3	0	0
Norfolk Island	0.0	XN	25.0	75.0	0.0	5	3	0
Northern Mariana Is.	0.1	XCh	9.5	90.5	10.4	9	0	0
Palau	0.0	X	3.9	96.1	21.1	4	0	0
Papua New Guinea	4.8	X	2.7	97.3	21.1	861	26	2
Pitcairn Islands	0.0	X	0.0	100.0	0.0	2	0	0
Samoa	0.2	X	3.1	96.9	4.0	7	0	0
Solomon Islands	0.4	X	3.8	96.2	34.6	75	0	0
Tokelau Islands	0.0	X	1.0	99.0	3.7	2	0	0
Tonga	0.1	X	4.8	95.2	21.6	9	0	0
Tuvalu	0.0	X	2.0	98.0	5.1	6	0	0
Vanuatu	0.2	X	8.9	91.1	31.7	122	1	0
Wallis & Futuna Islands	0.0	X	2.2	97.8	0.6	8	0	0
Totals (29 countries)	**31.3**		**26.7**	**73.3**	**15.2**	**1238**	**31**	**2**

Pacific

FEBRUARY 4-6

GEOGRAPHY
Area 8,515,800 sq.km constituting 6.3% of the world's land surface. There are 25,000 islands scattered over 88 million sq.km of ocean. This is larger than the combined areas of Africa, Asia and Europe. It comprises 1 continent (Australia), two large land-masses (New Zealand and Papua New Guinea) and 26 smaller island states and territories. The smallest territories are grouped with related states in the country section that follows: Christmas Is., Cocos Is., Norfolk Is. with Australia; Johnston Is., Midway Is., Wake Is. with Guam; Niue, Pitcairn Is. and Tokelau with Cook Islands.

Population	Ann.Gr.	Density
2000	31,277,932	+1.32%	4 per sq. km.
2010	35,194,378	+1.17%	4 per sq. km.
2025	40,832,012	+0.88%	5 per sq. km.

The Pacific has 0.5% of the world's population.

Cities There are 6 mega cities in the region — 5 in Australia, 1 in New Zealand. **Urbanites** 70%.

PEOPLES
There are 5 major groupings and 1,238 ethnolinguistic peoples:

European 68.5%. The majority in Australia and New Zealand, where most are of British descent but increasingly diverse in origin. Large French minority in New Caledonia.

Melanesian 20.7% (Melanesia means 'black islands'). The majority of indigenous inhabitants in Papua New Guinea, Solomon Islands, New Caledonia and Fiji. A significant minority in Australia. Melanesians are unique for the variety of languages spoken.

Asian 3.8%. South Asian majority in Fiji, and smaller communities in Australia and New Zealand. Chinese communities expanding in many territories throughout the region.

Polynesian 3.5% (Polynesia means 'many islands'). The majority of indigenous inhabitants of New Zealand and islands of the central Pacific. The Polynesians are one of the most remarkable seafaring races in the world.

Micronesian 1.1% (Micronesia means 'small islands'). The majority in island groups on, or north of, the equator.
Other 2.4%.

Languages 1,362. **Languages with Scriptures** 21Bi 180NT 200por 235w.i.p. There are between 159 and 600 languages in which Bible translation work may still be needed, most being spoken by a very small number of people.

ECONOMY

Australia and New Zealand are affluent 'first world' countries. All other states range from wealthy Nauru to poor Kiribati. The small populations, limited resources and the vast distances between island states hold back development of most islands. Most states have subsistence economies with few job opportunities and limited health and education facilities. These factors, and overpopulation, have caused a significant proportion of islanders to emigrate to wealthier areas.

POLITICS

All but a handful of the smaller territories are either independent or have internal self-government. There is growing interest to develop regional cooperation for protection of the island economies and cultures from abuse by Pacific Rim nations.

RELIGION

In every state and territory except Fiji the great majority of people are Christian, but nominalism and secularism have eroded commitment to the Church.

Religions	Population %	Adherents	Ann.Gr.
Christian	73.34	22,939,000	+0.74%
non-Religious/other	21.55	6,794,000	+2.91%
Hindu	1.27	396,800	+2.22%

Buddhist/Chinese	1.31	353,400	+6.16%
Muslim	1.21	379,300	+1.50%
Traditional/Spiritist	0.72	224,200	+6.34%
Jewish	0.29	91,600	+1.27%
Baha'i	0.24	74,600	+2.77%
Sikh	0.07	23,000	+2.91%

Christians	Denom.	Affil.%	,000	Ann.Gr.
Protestant	440	22.97	7,185	+1.5%
Independent	151	2.09	655	+5.5%
Anglican	16	15.63	4,889	-0.4%
Catholic	26	25.88	8,096	+0.3%
Orthodox	238	1.96	614	+1.8%
Marginal	174	2.33	730	+1.2%
Unaffiliated		11.04	3,454	n.a.
Doubly affiliated		*-8.56*	*-2,679*	*n.a.*

Mormonism grew rapidly among Polynesians in the 20th Century exposing the inadequate discipling of the Churches.

Trans-bloc Groupings	pop. %	,000	Ann.Gr.
Evangelical	15.2	4,765	+0.7%
Charismatic	10.4	1,120	+1.3%
Pentecostal	3.6	3,255	+5.3%

Missionaries from the Pacific
P,I,A 6,654 in 132 agencies of which 3,526 are in other countries.

Missionaries to the Pacific
P,I,A 4,124 expatriates in 184 agencies.

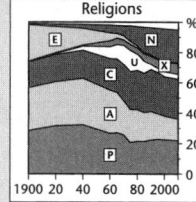

Religions

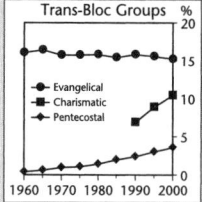

Trans-Bloc Groups

• Answers to Prayer

1 **The strength of Christianity in the Pacific.** The Pacific was one of the first areas to be evangelized in the modern Protestant missionary era. By the end of the 19th Century most of the Pacific region had become Christian through the sacrificial labours of early LMS, Methodist, Anglican and Pacific Islander missionaries. Missionary casualties were high through disease, violent death and cannibalism.

2 **Great people movements** over the past 200 years have brought whole peoples and islands to Christianity. Some of the most strongly Protestant Christian nations in the world are in this region. These people movements continue to this day in Papua New Guinea.

3 **A renewal in the 1990s of the Pacific Islander missionary vision of the 19th Century.** In recent years, New Zealand has had a good record in sending out missionaries.

• Hot Spots in the Pacific

1 **Fiji's unhappy, recent history** of coups and tension between indigenous Fijians and the large ethnic Indian population remains unresolved.

2 **Bougainville Island's** 10-year war for independence from Papua New Guinea is still not settled despite a cease-fire in 1998.

3 The Solomon Islands has endured inter-ethnic tensions and fighting since 1998 which has affected the stability and economy of the country. The underlying issues need resolution.

• Trends to Watch

1 Historic wrongs associated with the arrival of Europeans are at last beginning to be faced.

a) *The British handling* of Australia and its penal colonies.

b) *Wrongs done to the indigenous populations* — those most affected being the Australian Aborigines, New Zealand Maori and Fijians.

Christians needs to be in the forefront in doing all possible to achieve fair reconciliations, honour cultural distinctives and lay foundations for inter-ethnic harmony.

2 The struggle for survival of many isolated island communities is threatened by modernity and globalization, economic unviability, large scale unemployment, heavy dependence on aid, isolation from health, education and modern consumer goods, together with increasing costs for inter-island travel.

• The Church in the Pacific

1 The decline of Christianity is especially acute in Australia, New Zealand and New Caledonia with a rapid rise in secularism, family breakdown and indifference to spiritual things. The churches need new vision, flexibility in methods and understanding of cultural changes to communicate a relevant biblical message and become a more effective discipling community.

2 Nominalism in the Pacific Islands has increased due to inadequate teaching on true repentance, personal faith and the need for a daily walk with the Lord. This has led to a widespread misunderstanding of the true nature of the gospel, syncretistic beliefs, unmodified political power structures and, in Melanesia, a range of syncretistic cults.

3 The rapid growth of Mormonism in Polynesia, winning many nominal Protestants, is a rebuke to the traditional churches. Polynesia is rapidly becoming Mormon — especially Tonga and the two Samoas which are over 20% Mormon.

4 The relative failure to launch an effective inter-state evangelical network. The Evangelical Fellowship of the South Pacific has struggled with the low degree of cooperation among Evangelicals in many countries, lack of unifying vision, lack of finance and the high costs of travel.

5 The need to revive a missions vision. After a century of decline in missions commitment in the Islands, renewed vision has sprung up. The Deep Sea Canoe Mission was founded in 1989 to stimulate vision, identify and train missionaries and channel them overseas. The New Zealand record in sending missionaries has been good, and those of Fiji and Papua New Guinea are increasing.

6 Completing the task of world evangelization in the Pacific.

a) *Remaining unevangelized and unoccupied tribes* in New Guinea's interior — a few such still exist. Many more are only superficially evangelized.

b) *The few evangelical believers* in parts of New Caledonia, French Polynesia and on many of the nominally Christian island groups. Some areas need to be re-evangelized.

c) *The Indians of Fiji*, the largest unreached people in the Pacific. Pray for effective evangelization of these Muslims and Hindus.

d) *The Chinese* are increasing through immigration. In some islands this is for trade or low-paid labour; in Australia and New Zealand it is as professionals. Many small trading communities remain unevangelized.

e) *Bible translation*. This is a major necessity. What remains to be done is being researched, but many hundreds of smaller language groups may still need translators.

Christian Megablocs - Evangelicals/Pentecostals

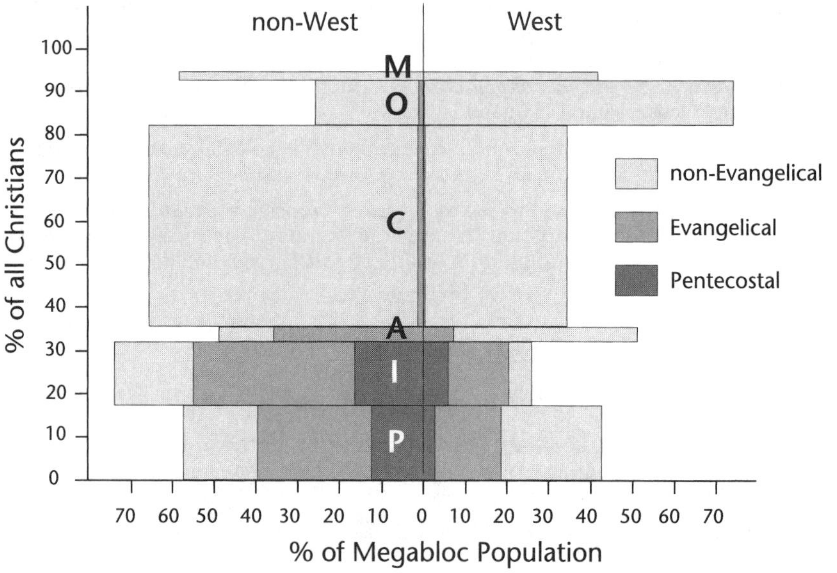

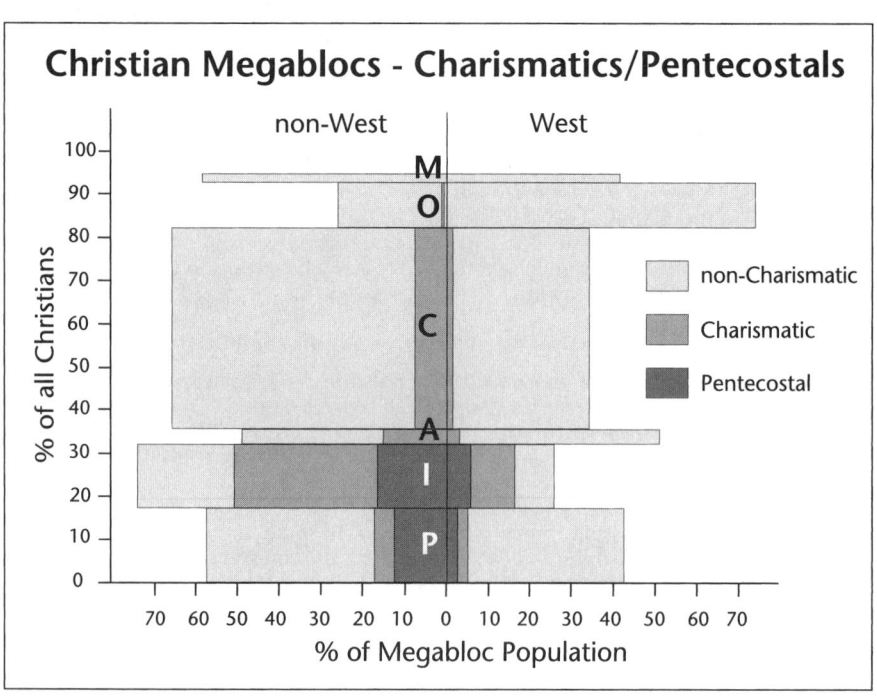

non-West
West
M
O
C
A
I
P
100
90
80
70
60
50
40
30
20
10
0
% of all Christians
70 60 50 40 30 20 10 0 10 20 30 40 50 60 70
% of Megabloc Population
non-Evangelical
Evangelical
Pentecostal

Christian Megablocs - Charismatics/Pentecostals

non-West
West
M
O
C
A
I
P
100
90
80
70
60
50
40
30
20
10
0
% of all Christians
70 60 50 40 30 20 10 0 10 20 30 40 50 60 70
% of Megabloc Population
non-Charismatic
Charismatic
Pentecostal

Afghanistan

Islamic Republic of Afghanistan

FEBRUARY 7-8
ASIA
Revised January 2004

GEOGRAPHY
Area 652,225 sq.km. Dry and mountainous, but with fertile valleys. This strategic land has been fought over by rival foreign empires for nearly three thousand years.

Population		Ann.Gr.	Density
2000	22,720,000	+2.93%	35 per sq. km.
2010	32,902,000	+2.58%	50 per sq. km.
2025	44,934,000	+1.95%	69 per sq. km.

No census or careful ethnic survey has ever been made. Figures are all estimates. Afghan refugees in 2000 numbered 1.4 million in Iran, 2.2 to 3 million in Pakistan and smaller numbers across the world after peaking in the 1990s at 6.5 million. Many refugees have returned home since 2002.
Capital Kabul 2,700,000. The civil war extensively damaged the capital. Other cities: Kandahar 420,000; Mazar-e-Sharif 270,000. **Urbanites** 22%.

PEOPLES
70 peoples.
Indo-Iranian 86.8%. Largest: Pashtun (Pathan) 9.7mill.; Tajik 4m; Hazara/Aimaq (of Turkic origin) 1.8m; Other Persian-speaking 770,000; Baluch 260,000; Nuristani peoples(11) 250,000.
Turkic-speaking 10.7%. 10 peoples. Uzbek 1.8m; Turkmen 520,000.
Other 2.5%. Brahui 240,000; Pashai 160,000.
Literacy 10-31% (much lower for women).
Official languages Pashto (used by 50% of population), Dari (Afghan Persian, 35%). **All languages** 50. **Languages with Scriptures** 2NT 3por.

ECONOMY
Shattered by 22 years of USSR occupation, civil war, Taliban misrule and the US-led invasion of 2002. The countryside was bombed and mined; half the housing, most of the complex irrigation systems and a high proportion of the livestock were destroyed. The most lucrative agricultural crop is now opium (Afghanistan is the world's largest producer) which paid for weapons for the warring factions. The rebuilding of the country is slowed by the lack of funds, lawlessness and factionalism. **HDI** n.a. **Public debt** 95% of GNP. **Income/person** $250 (0.8% of USA).

POLITICS
The monarchy was overthrown in 1973. Republican government ended in a Marxist coup in 1978. Then followed an invasion by the USSR. Ten years of war ensued culminating in the humiliating withdrawal of the Soviet forces in 1988-89. This was followed by a destructive civil war between ethnic and religious factions. The extreme Islamist (mainly) Pashtun Taliban gained control of over 90% of the country by 2001. They also provided a base and training facilities for the extreme Islamist Al Qaeda terror network which radically changed our world and its security. This provoked the US-led invasion of 2002 and the ousting of the Taliban government. A country-wide Grand Council finally approved a new constitution in January 2004 with promised elections in mid-2004.

RELIGION
The Taliban take-over of the country imposed a strict interpretation of Islam. The results devastated the economy and the lot of women in society. The 2004 constitution did not bow to Islamist demands for *shari'a* law but no law may be passed which is against the beliefs and provisions of Islam. There is little prospect of full religious freedom.

Religions	Population %	Adherents	Ann.Gr.
Muslim	97.89	22,241,015	+2.9
Parsee	1.50	340,806	+2.9
Hindu	0.35	79,521	+0.2
Traditional ethnic	0.10	22,720	+2.9
Baha'i	0.10	22,720	n.a.
Christian	0.02	3,000	n.a.
Sikh	0.02	4,544	+2.9
non-Religious	0.01	2,272	+2.9

Non-Muslim figures may be now much lower than these stated. No Christian churches are permitted. The number of Afghan Christians is estimated to be 1,000 to 3,000. Some Christian expatriate workers are allowed to serve in relief and social uplift programmes.

• Answers to Prayer

1 **The demise of the largely Pashtun Taliban in 2002.** They had swept to power with Pakistani military support, U.S. arms and Saudi money. Traditional and rural in outlook, they used Islam to legitimate their authority. A narrow interpretation of *shari'a* law outlawed playing games, use of cassette tapes, videos and TV (and much more) and tyrannized the Shi'a Muslims, women and anyone deviating from the Taliban's interpretation of the law.

• Challenges for Prayer

A

1 The post-Taliban interim government has little influence outside the capital. The north is dominated by warlords and the south and south-east by terror groups linked with Taliban and Al Qaeda. Pray that the new constitution and future national leadership may provide a more democratic, moderate and fair government for the whole country. Pray also for an end to anarchy, a discrediting of Islamic extremism, and dis-empowering of warlords and terror groups.

2 Two decades of unremitting war have brought most of the population to ruin and destitution. An estimated 1 million lost their lives, 2 million were maimed and 4 million children orphaned. The result is ecological disaster, a shattered infrastructure, over 12 million uncleared anti-personnel mines and the capital in ruins. Pray for lasting peace, effective reconstruction, an awakening to moderation and tolerance and a realization that Marxism and Islam cannot provide the solutions to heal their land.

3 Afghanistan is one of the least reached countries in the world. There are 48,000 mosques but not a single church building. Pray for the 70 unreached peoples of this land, especially:

a) ***Pashtun.*** Approximately half the Afghan population, and politically dominant, the Pashtuns on both sides of the Afghanistan-Pakistan border comprise what has been called the largest Muslim tribal society in the world — approximately 27 million people in over 30 major sub-tribes. There are few Christians among them, though urban, educated Pashtuns in exile have shown responsiveness. Pray that multitudes might be released from the strongholds of Islam, fear, prejudice and pride in pashtunwali (their tribal code of honour).

b) ***Uzbek and Turkmen*** of the north have shown some responsiveness as refugees in other lands. Pray for churches to be planted in their homelands.

c) ***Tajik*** in the north-east. They were among the last people to resist the Taliban and have gained considerable political influence. Pray for their spiritual freedom.

d) ***The Hazara***, Shi'a Muslims of Mongol descent, were severely persecuted and even massacred by the Sunni Taliban. More responsive to the gospel in recent years.

e) ***The Kuchi nomads*** in central and western regions who numbered 2.5m before the war destroyed their lifestyle. Most are Pashto- or Persian-speaking. Many fled to Pakistan.

f) ***The Aimaq*** of the west and the ***Baluch*** and ***Brahui*** of the south.

g) ***The Nuristani tribes*** in the mountains north and east of Kabul. They speak a number of mutually unintelligible languages. The major peoples are the Waigeli 40,000; Kati 100,000; Ashkun 10,000. They were forcibly converted to Islam a century ago. Some parts of Nuristan were much influenced in the 1990s by Wahhabism, a strict Islamic sect, very hostile to anything Christian.

h) ***The Sikh, Hindu and Parsee minorities*** who are mainly traders.

4 Though there is no visible church in Afghanistan, the number of Afghan believers is increasing in urban and some remote rural areas. Because of fear and suspicion, many believers find it difficult to meet in groups. Some find help and encouragement through Christian radio programmes in the main languages of Afghanistan. Pray for their protection, consistency of faith and clarity of witness whenever opportunity arises. Pray also that the churches and small fellowships of Afghan Christians that have come into being in South Asia, Europe and North America may become bold witnesses for Christ.

5 Women in the cities were severely repressed by the Taliban regime. They were banished from public life, forbidden employment, restricted to the home, denied education (girls) and health services and suffer at the hands of men, with no recourse to any justice. One in four women are widows, and many are destitute. Depression and suicide are commonplace. The new constitution guarantees that 25% of the parliamentary seats will be reserved for women. Pray that Afghan women may find political, social, economic and, above all, spiritual freedom.

6 Christian aid ministries. Since 1966 a number of Christian relief and development agencies have ministered to the blind, maimed, sick, deprived, illiterate and needy in the name and Spirit of the Lord Jesus. Pray for their protection – Islamist terror groups have targeted them. Pray for courage in the face of restrictions and harassment and that their lives might commend the gospel. Pray that professionals may respond to the many needs of the land.

7 **The need for the Scriptures.** The whole Bible is available in Iranian Persian, but differences between this and Afghan Persian makes it difficult for many to read. A translation of the Bible was made in the 19th Century but this is unavailable and its language archaic. The NT in Dari (Afghan Persian) and in a Pakistani dialect of Pashto have been well received. Translations into major dialects of Afghan Pashto are still needed. The OT is slowly progressing in Dari and Pashto; pray for their speedy completion. Translations do not exist in any indigenous minority language. Pray that these might come to fruition. Pray also for the entry and distribution of God's word in this land.

8 **The Media.** Pray that all appropriate methods of witness may be used effectively.

a) ***GRN***(LRI) has made audio recordings in 38 languages and dialects but means for effective distribution and use are, humanly-speaking, virtually non-existent in Afghanistan.

b) ***Christian radio***. This is the most strategic way to proclaim the good news at the present time and there has been a significant response. **FEBA**, with **IBRA** as partners, broadcast in Persian (4.5 hrs/wk), Dari (5), Pashto (3.25), Uzbek (1.75) and also Baluch and Turkmen. Pray for the provision of and support for more Dari- and Pashto-speaking Christians to prepare programmes and answer mail. Pray also for programming to commence in other Afghan languages.

c) ***The JESUS film*** is available in Brahui, Dari, Pashto, Tajik, Turkmen and Uzbek, but its use inside Afghanistan is difficult at the present time.

d) ***Literature.*** Discipleship and other training materials are being developed in the major languages of Afghanistan, in addition to many other types of evangelistic materials. Pray for those involved in producing, distributing and studying these materials.

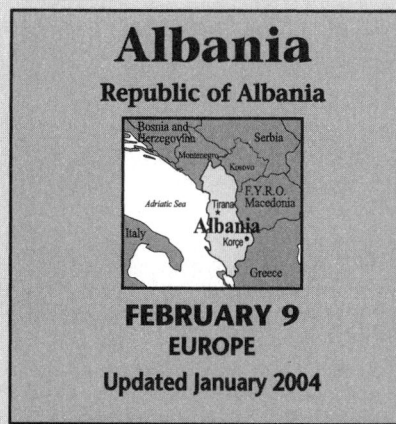

Albania
Republic of Albania

FEBRUARY 9
EUROPE
Updated January 2004

GEOGRAPHY
Area 28,748 sq.km. A mountainous Balkan state on the Adriatic Sea, adjoining Serbia, Montenegro, Kosovo, Macedonia and Greece.

Population		Ann.Gr.	Density
2000	3,113,434	–0.40%	108 per sq. km.
2010	3,346,892	+0.83%	116 per sq. km.
2025	3,819,763	+0.84%	133 per sq. km.

Over 500,000 Albanians fled or emigrated from the country in 1991-2000, reducing the above figures. A further

300,000 Kosovar refugees entered Albania in 1998-99.

Capital Tirana 275,000. Unofficially the population is nearer 1,000,000. **Urbanites** 48%.

PEOPLES

Albanian 91.5%. Tosk in south; Gheg in north.
Other 8.5%. Greek 85,000; Roma (Gypsy) 80,000+; Vlach (Arumun) 40,000; Macedonian (Pataree and Gorani Muslim) 15,000.

Literacy 92%. **Official language** Albanian. **All languages** 6. **Languages with Scriptures** 3Bi 1NT 1por 1w.i.p.

ECONOMY
The combined effects of wars, 46 years of nationalistic Marxism and the chaotic situation in the Balkans in the 1990s have ensured its continuation as one of Europe's poorest countries. Economic life is almost wholly dependent on remittances from Albanians abroad, smuggling and foreign aid. **HDI** 0.699; 100th/174. **Public debt** 24% of GNP. **Income/person** est. $670 (2.2% of USA).

POLITICS
The Communist regime imposed on the country in 1945 crumbled in 1991 soon after Dictator Enver Hoxha's death. Two multi-party elections finally resulted in a democratic government in 1992. Then ensued six years of anarchy

followed by more stability since 1998. Any unrest in Montenegro, Kosovo and Macedonia would deeply impact Albania.

RELIGION

No religion was allowed to exist in Communist Albania. The ban was lifted in 1990, but no legal provision for religious freedom was made until 1998. The very existence of Evangelicals and other faiths is often portrayed by Muslims, Orthodox and Catholics as a disturbance to social custom.

Religions	Population %	Adherents	Ann.Gr.
Christian	41.48	1,291,452	+2.7%
Muslim	38.79	1,207,701	+0.5%
non-Religious/other	19.54	608,365	−6.9%
Baha'i	0.18	5,604	+12.0%
Jewish	0.01	311	n.a.

Many reckon that the majority is atheist or secular, and cultural origins to be closer to 70% Muslim, 20% Orthodox, 10% Catholic. Superstition and folk Islam are strong. Many Muslims belong to the syncretistic Sufi Bektash movement.

Christians	Denom.	Affil.%	,000	Ann.Gr.
Protestant	9	0.15	5	+15.6%
Independent	14	0.25	8	+13.4%
Catholic	1	16.75	521	+1.5%
Orthodox	2	24.09	750	+3.5%
Marginal	2	0.24	7	+20.1%

Churches	MegaBloc	Cong.	Members	Affiliates
Orthodox Ch of A	O	270	431,138	720,000
Catholic	C	200	312,210	521,390
Greek Orthodox	O	10	18,000	30,000

Jehovah's Witnesses	M	38	1,805	7,000
Charis/Pente grps [6]	I	48	1,885	3,200
New Apostolic	I	12	1,205	2,000
Baptist Foundation	P	8	600	1,000
Christian Brethren	P	25	500	800
Word of Life	I	8	550	800
Assemblies of God	P	4	410	600
Disciples of Jesus	I	6	400	550
Evangelical (SE)	P	6	365	500
Other denoms [13]		39	2,350	3,700
Total Christians [30]		**669**	**770,942**	**1,291,000**

Trans-bloc Groupings	pop.%	,000	Ann.Gr.
Evangelical	0.3	10	+16.4%
Charismatic	4.1	127	+2.5%
Pentecostal	0.2	5	+14.0%

Missionaries from Albania
P,I,A 50 in 6 agencies.

Missionaries to Albania
P,I,A 460 in 71 agencies: USA 140, UK 77, Korea 28, Germany 20, Netherlands 19, Brazil 14.
C 250. **M** 70.

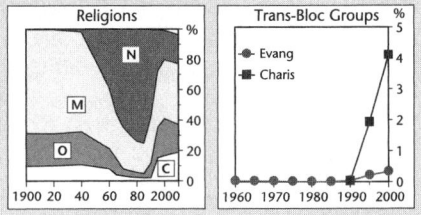

• Answers to Prayer

1 The dictator, Enver Hoxha's, proud boast of eliminating all religion in 1967 has been overturned with over 74% of the population claiming a faith in God.

2 Religious freedom was declared in the 1998 constitution despite strong efforts to limit it by the four 'traditional' communities.

3 Every town and city now has a group of evangelical believers.

4 Radio Tirana was built to propagate atheism. TWR now broadcasts from this station 80 hours weekly to eastern Europe and Asia.

• Challenges for Prayer

1 Albania's experience with Communism was economically, morally and spiritually devastating. The savagery of the repression was such that 700,000 were killed or imprisoned for long periods. A high proportion of the population was coerced into spying on neighbours. The anarchy, chaos and corruption of the 1990s is an outworking of this grim past. Pray for the peace and development of Albania and for the provision of just and fair government.

2 Religious freedom could be lost. After Communism's collapse the Muslims, Catholics (in the north) and Orthodox Christians (in the south) sought to regain past influence and limit any other religious activity. Pray that the Balkan cauldron of ethnic and religious hatreds may not erode present freedoms.

3 **Muslim countries have poured in huge amounts of aid and missionaries.** Over one million Qur'ans were distributed, 900 mosques refurbished or built between 1993 and 1995, and thousands given scholarships to study Islamic theology abroad. The government secretly joined the World Muslim League and the Organization of the Islamic Conference to the dismay of many. Most of the mosques are poorly attended and ignorance of Islam is high among professing Muslims. Pray that Albania may be spared the sorrows of extreme Islamism, and that Muslims may turn from the religion forced on the population in the 14th Century by their Turkish Ottoman conquerors.

4 **The evangelical witness in Albania has grown dramatically since 1991.** Before WWII there was one functioning evangelical congregation — in Korçe. By the end of 1992 there were over 1,000 believers gathering regularly in 19 congregations and 17 home fellowships. By 2000 there were over 55 denominations in over 130 congregations and 55 emerging groups. Over 80% of these are linked with the **Albania Encouragement Project**. The Albanian Evangelical Alliance (VUSh) links together 60% of all evangelical churches and agencies. Pray that Evangelicals may be recognized as having a wholesome role in the recovery of the country.

5 **The training of leaders** after the devastations wrought by the Communists is a major preoccupation of the Church. The Catholics and Orthodox had 136 in training for pastoral ministry in 1998. Evangelical agencies had to accelerate leadership development for the young congregations when so many expatriates were forced out of the country in the violence and anarchy of 1997. A number of agencies are involved in leadership training — Albanian Bible Institute, **YWAM** DTS, Church Multiplication International, Lightforce and others. About 75 Albanians are in full-time training and many more on TEE distance-learning programmes (ABI).

6 **Evangelical mission agencies have multiplied since 1990.** In 1995 Albania was the most heavily 'missionized' country in Europe — by both Muslims and Christians. Over 70 agencies have networked as part of the **Albania Encouragement Project** in both aid projects, literature production, evangelism and church planting. The larger groups are New Life (**CCCI**), Christar (16), Albanian Evangelical Mission (15), **YWAM** (12), **Frontiers** (11), **OM** (10), Ancient World Outreach (7), Brethren (6). Pray for:

a) **Unity.** Deep trust, coordination and close fellowship that will set high spiritual standards.

b) **Long-term vision and goals.** Many workers came in the early 1990s, but did not stay long enough to become effective. Pray for the calling of long-term workers who learn the language and culture and then contribute to the maturing of churches and the training of leaders.

c) **Wisdom in transition** from aid to development. Misuse of aid has been a serious and spiritually damaging problem.

d) **Tact and discernment** as Albanian leadership emerges.

7 The least reached-minorities:

a) **The 300,000 Bektashi** are a Sufi dervish movement not recognized as Muslims by the Sunni majority as their beliefs are more influenced by folk religion and the occult. Some have become evangelical believers.

b) **The Vlach** (related to the Romanians), Macedonians and Greeks are culturally Orthodox. Most live in the south and south-east of Albania. The Romanian Missionary Society has work among them in Gjirokaster.

c) **The Gorani and Pataree Macedonians** who are culturally Muslim. The Cham, Muslim Albanians who fled from Greece between 1920 and 1945, are a socially closed people.

d) **The Roma** speak Romany or Albanian and often live in town ghettos. Only a few Albanian-speaking Roma have become Evangelicals.

8 **The Albanian diaspora.** Over half of all Albanians live outside Albania. Their spiritual need is now greater than that of Albania itself. Pray for:

a) **Kosovar Albanians** who are 98% Muslim with very few Christians. The 1998 Kosovo War between Serbians and Albanians resulted in UN intervention and control of this province which is still legally part of Serbia and Montenegro. The massive flow of refugees resulted in many hearing the gospel for the first time. Albanian and expatriate Christians became deeply committed to their evangelization — pushing the young

Albanian Church into missions and church planting in Kosovo once the refugees returned. Pray that the Albanian Church may continue to grow in vision and maturity as a result.

b) *Albanians living in the adjoining regions* of Macedonia (nearly one million) and Montenegro (35,000) — almost all are Muslim, with very little Christian outreach to them.

c) *Albanians in the EU.* There have long been indigenous Albanian populations in Italy (350,000) and Greece (25,000), but many ethnic Albanians now live and work in Switzerland (175,000), Germany (700,000), France, Belgium and the Netherlands. Pray that these may be reached.

9 Christian help ministries:

a) *Distribution of the Scriptures is vital.* A paraphrased Bible was completed in 1992 and a further translation in 1993. Large numbers of NTs and Bibles have been distributed. Pray for their spiritual impact.

b) *Christian, Muslim and cult literature* has flooded into Albania during the 1990s. EHC has twice distributed gospel literature in every home of every village with over 3,000 responses. Christian books are being published in Albania by the indigenous Vernon Karte e Pende and Shigjeta as well as by several missions. There are several Christian bookstores. Pray that Albanians may read the right literature and benefit from it.

c) *The JESUS film* in both Gheg and Tosk is being widely and effectively used to touch the hearts of many, and through it new churches have been planted.

d) *Christian radio* programmes transmitted by TWR/ECM from Monte Carlo have impacted the country for decades. Local Christian radio stations have been started since 1998.

Algeria

Democratic and Popular Republic of Algeria

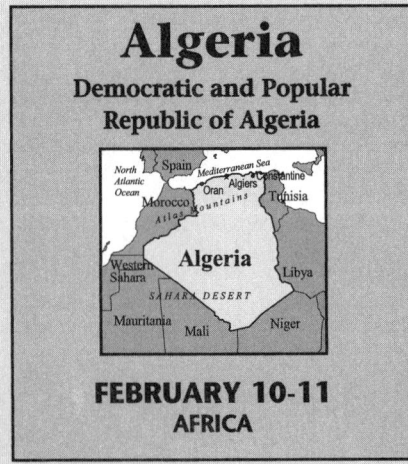

FEBRUARY 10-11
AFRICA

GEOGRAPHY
Area 2,381,741 sq.km. Agriculture is possible on the Mediterranean coast, in the Atlas mountains and at oases; 80% is desert.

Population		Ann.Gr.	Density
2000	31,471,278	+2.32%	13 per sq. km.
2010	38,303,706	+1.84%	16 per sq. km.
2025	46,610,551	+1.23%	20 per sq. km.

Over 90% live north of the Atlas Mountains. About 600,000 are nomadic or semi-nomadic in the Sahara. A further 2.5 million Algerians or those of Algerian descent live in Europe.
Capital Algiers 4,447,000. Other major cities: Oran 932,000; Constantine 664,000. **Urbanites** 56%.

PEOPLES
Arabic-speaking 77.1%. Many are Arabized Berber. Also over 3 million Bedouin.
Berber 22%+ (Tamazight-speaking Imazighen). Main groups are: Kabyle(2) 3m; Shilha(4) 1.5m; Shawiya 1,640,000; Mzab(5) 230,000; Tuareg 35,000. **Other** 0.9%. Moroccans 130,000; French 10,000; Hausa 10,000; Songhai 2,600; Xoraxai Gypsy 2,500. Refugees: 190,000 Western Saharans in four main camps around the desert oasis town of Tindouf.

Literacy 61.6%. **Official language** Arabic. Berber, French and increasingly, English are widely used and 25% speak one of the Berber languages. **All languages** 17. **Languages with Scriptures** 2Bi 2NT 5por 2w.i.p.

ECONOMY
Heavily dependent on oil exports. Economic stagnation due to widespread state ownership, a bloated bureaucracy, high population growth and political instability. **Unemployment** 22%. **HDI** 0.665; 109th/174. **Public debt** 65% of GNP. **Income/person** $1,500 (4.8% of USA).

POLITICS
French colony for 132 years. Independence in 1962 after a bitter war of liberation. A one-party socialist regime backed by the army held power for over 25 years. Economic failure and political abuses of power have provoked widespread agitation for change. Democratic elections in 1992 gave victory to an Islamic political party, but the results were annulled by the army. The ensuing civil war has caused over 100,000 deaths. Both sides were edging towards a settlement in 2000.

RELIGION

Since independence, the government has actively encouraged the development of an Islamic Arab socialist state. Proselytism is not allowed. The Catholic and the Protestant Church of Algeria are the only Christian bodies officially recognized. Muslim fundamentalists are strongly agitating for the institution of Islamic *shari'a* law. Sunni Muslims are polarized between the radicals and the secularists. The Mzab are Ibadi Muslims.

Religions	Population %	Adherents	Ann.Gr.
Muslim	96.68	30,426,432	+2.1%
non-Religious	3.02	950,433	+6.6%
Christian	0.29	91,267	-3.7%
Baha'i	0.01	3,147	+2.3%

Christians	Denom.	Affil.%	,000	Ann.Gr.
Protestant	1	0.01	3	+2.7%
Independent	3	0.21	65	+3.6%
Anglican	1	0.00	0	+0.0%
Catholic	1	0.06	20	-5.8%

Orthodox	1	0.01	2	+0.0%
Marginal	1	0.00	0	+4.5%

Churches	MegaBloc	Cong.	Members	Affiliates
Indig/secret believers	I		16,000	40,000
Indigenous Evang grps	I	50	12,500	25,000
Catholic	C	20	11,429	20,000
All Protestant groups	P	40	1,900	3,400
Jehovah's Witnesses	M	3	80	200
Other denoms [9]		6	1,371	2,040
Total Christians [25]		119	43,280	90,640

Trans-bloc Groupings	pop.%	,000	Ann.Gr.
Evangelical	0.2	68	+3.5%
Charismatic	0.2	49	+3.6%

Missionaries from Algeria
P,I,A 15, in 4 agencies.

Expatriates to Algeria
Most are based outside the country.

• Challenges for Prayer

1 **Opposition to the gospel is intense.** Over 160 years of tearful sowing by a tenacious succession of missionaries is only now bearing fruit. North Africans have long and bitter memories of "Christian" conquests, colonialism and atrocities. Pray that centuries of prejudice and misunderstandings may be taken away and hearts opened to the gospel message.

2 **Around 100,000 civilians have been murdered** in gruesome massacres during the savage civil war. No section of the nation has been spared the killings, however no evangelical Christians were killed during the war itself. Democracy had been long striven for, but seems to have failed. After years of one-party dictatorship many have looked for solutions in an Islam that would impose *shari'a* law, yet another tyranny, on the country. Pray for political, religious and spiritual freedom for the Algerian people.

3 **There is a new openness** to the West and a political drive to encourage tourism and foreign investment. Along with this will come opportunities for more missions input. Pray for wisdom in this process and for genuine partnerships to develop. There is the possibility for money and self-interest to have a very negative impact on what God is doing through His Holy Spirit.

4 **The Berber peoples** may comprise as much as 40% of the population. The Arab majority has long sought to impose their rule, culture and language, and resent Berber intransigence. Berber nationalism is becoming a significant force as they seek to reaffirm their identity and return to their cultural roots. Their forebears were once Christian, and many thousands have turned to Christ among the Kabyle — some through supernatural revelations of the Lord Jesus but mainly through personal evangelism.

a) Praise God for the protection of this movement of the Spirit from reprisals. Some Muslim leaders accuse Christians of poisoning the Kabyle with the gospel.

b) Algeria has long been plagued by clannishness and divisions. This carries over into the many new and young groups of believers. Legalism and majoring on minor issues often divide. Pray for unity and maturity amongst believers.

5 **The local church.** Small fellowships exist where Arabic is used, but most local Christians use a mixture of French and Kabyle. Believers in the cities are few in number and keep a lower profile, whilst in many Kabyle villages, Christian meetings are well-known and held openly. Pray for evangelism to succeed in the following ways:

a) The establishment of strong indigenous groups with effective leaders steeped in the Word. Training is now taking place in-country, which should help discourage the easy option to emigrate to Europe. A good leadership training programme is developing. A small TEE programme makes headway each year as groups gather in several regions of the country. Pray for the many who desire training, that more would be willing to take on leadership responsibility.

b) *The protection of Arab believers in persecution.* Believers face threats and intimidation by family, friends, employers and Muslim extremists. Fear leads to withdrawal from fellowship, compromise and backsliding. Pray for perseverance, willingness to suffer for Jesus and boldness in witness.

c) *A strengthening of Christian families.* Religious and social pressures force Christian girls into marriage to Muslims. Pray for the few Christian couples, for their strength and endurance, that they may minister to the Church. Teaching on, and modelling of, Christian family life is much needed in this Islamic culture.

d) *Musicians* for worship services and *children's workers* to be raised up.

6 **The unreached** comprise virtually the whole nation.

a) *The growing cities* — the educated elite, the middle classes, and the teeming slums.

b) *Young people* who are frustrated and disillusioned. Nearly 70% of the population is under 30; well over half of the 16-25s are unemployed. Pray for those with the expertise and a heart for young people to develop ministry especially for them, and to train local believers in this area.

c) *The Berber peoples* of the Atlas Mountains. It is mostly the Kabyles that have responded. Any overt missionary outreach to the unreached Shawiya, Shilha or other Imazighen could be considered subversive.

d) *The Tuareg.* A handful of believers is known. No continuing work in Algeria.

e) *The Mzab* oasis towns in the Sahara. No known effort has ever been made to evangelize these tight-knit communities, yet there is a handful of Christians.

7 **The active mission force.** Praise God for the witness through martyrdom of 19 Catholic clergy during the civil war. Pray that God would raise up more workers for the strengthening of the local church. Work is under way in many areas. Especially pray for:

a) *Relief work* — an urgent priority.

b) *Christian music.* Much is being written in local languages; it needs to be disseminated.

c) *Work among the children of Christians.*

d) *Protection* for those who witness in the course of their daily routine.

e) *The leadership of the Algerian church* in Europe, and for missionary calls to their homeland. There are over 1,000 Algerian Christians in Europe.

f) *The spiritual and financial support* of local missionaries and their fruitfulness in ministry.

g) *Local leadership training* — vital for the development of a strong indigenous church.

h) *The Berbers, who have the potential* to sweep across the whole of North Africa with the gospel! Pray for the resources to realize the growing vision.

8 **Bible translation** and distribution is fraught with obstacles and restrictions. **The Bible Society** has recently been allowed to re-open its work in the country. Translation work is proceeding in two Berber languages, but nothing has been done for several of the dialects. These projects need much perseverance and finance to put the translation onto cassette and video. Praise God that the translation of the whole New Testament into Kabyle in the Latin script was completed in 1997. Translation has begun into Shawiya. Work is in progress in Algerian Arabic, a language spoken by up to 25 million people — most do not understand Standard Arabic. Pray for those choosing which Bible passages to translate first, and pray that this work might brighten the spiritual climate of the nation.

9 **Christian literature** in the national languages and French is often requested but hard to supply. Pray for permission to import, print, and distribute Bibles, books, teaching materials, and audio cassettes, as well as BCCs. Postal censorship is severe, leading to confiscation of mail and interrogation of recipients; pray for deliverances in this. There is an increasing need for BCCs and other materials in Kabyle and Algerian Arabic. Pray for those responsible for literature preparation and distribution.

10 **Algerians in Europe** may number 2.5 million; many are there without proper papers. They are more accessible to the gospel in Europe, but also to Islamic preaching. Pray for the network of agencies and churches seeking to reach them (**AWM, GMU,**

WEC and others). Pray for the discipling of individuals and planting of Arabic- and Berber-speaking congregations which can then be channels for the gospel to their homeland.

11 **Christian media** are important in this internally restrictive situation. Pray for:

a) Radio. Both **AWM** and **GMU** have a comprehensive strategy preparing radio programmes, evangelistic and discipling literature, and follow-up programmes (radio, satellite TV, personal counselling, magazines and BCCs). Both Algerian Arabic and Kabyle are targeted by **World By 2000** — pray for more broadcasting hours. **AWR**-Slovakia broadcasts 7 hours/week in Arabic, **TWR**-Monaco broadcasts 9.75 hours/week in Arabic and 2.75 hours/week in Kabyle and **IBRA**-Portugal 3-5 hours/week in Arabic. Thousands have come to faith as a result of this — in 1997 more than 400 converts were baptised. Pray for the expansion and continued fruitfulness of these ministries.

b) Audio-visual. The JESUS film on video has had a wide impact in Kabyle and also in Arabic. In this oral culture, potential is great for such quality audio-visuals. Pray for effective distribution from outside the country.

c) Satellite TV programmes. Algerian Arabic and Kabyle language broadcasts began in 1999 (**CBN**). Pray for the partnership between agencies and Algerian Christians who prepare the programmes, and for follow-up to viewers' responses.

d) Use of cassettes. Music and Scripture tapes are produced and distributed in two of the national languages. Pray for open local distribution channels.

American Samoa

Territory of American Samoa

South Pacific Ocean
Pago Pago
American Samoa

FEBRUARY 11
PACIFIC

GEOGRAPHY
Area 199 sq.km. Archipelago in the Polynesian Pacific.

Population	Ann.Gr.	Density
2000	68,089	+3.71%	342 per sq. km.
2010	94,712	+3.24%	476 per sq. km.
2025	142,680	+2.54%	717 per sq. km.

Capital Pago Pago 5,973. **Urbanites** 11%. There are many Samoans living in mainland USA (75,000) and Hawaii (20,000).

PEOPLES

Polynesian 93%. Samoan 60,000; Tongan 2,500.
Caucasian 2%. Americans.

Other 5%. Mixed race, Korean, Chinese, Filipino.
Literacy 98%. **Official languages** Samoan, English.
All languages 4. **Languages with Scriptures** 3Bi.

ECONOMY
A largely traditional Polynesian economy. Main economic activities are tuna fishing and canning. Nearly half the territory's revenue is direct US federal grants. Its remoteness and devastating hurricanes limit economic development. **Public debt** 74% of GNP. **Income/person** $2,600 (13.7% of mainland USA).

POLITICS
US unincorporated territory since 1900.

RELIGION
Freedom of religion.

Religions	Population %	Adherents	Ann.Gr.
Christian	95.70	65,161	+3.6%
non-Religious/other	2.09	1,423	+6.4%
Baha'i	1.45	987	+4.4%
Buddhist	0.64	436	+6.1%
Chinese	0.12	82	+5.8%

Christians	Denom.	Affil.%	,000	Ann.Gr.
Protestant	11	48.22	33	+1.6%
Independent	6	3.16	2	+1.9%
Anglican	1	0.28	0	+4.2%
Catholic	1	13.91	9	+2.2%
Marginal	4	23.40	16	+3.7%
Unaffiliated		9.15	6	n.a.
Doubly affiliated		*-2.42*	*-2*	*n.a.*

Churches	MegaBloc	Cong.	Members	Affiliates
Congregational Chr	P	36	10,778	18,000
Latter-day Saints (Morm)	M	33	7,300	14,600
Catholic	C	8	3,788	9,470
Assemblies of God	P	20	4,474	6,800
Methodist	P	14	3,497	5,000
Seventh-day Adventist	P	8	1,100	2,200
Jehovah's Witnesses	M	3	200	580
Other denoms [16]		159	2,290	3,900
Doubly affiliated			-825	-1,650
Total Christians [23]		281	32,600	58,900

Trans-bloc Groupings	pop. %	,000	Ann.Gr.
Evangelical	17.9	12	+0.6%
Charismatic	14.3	10	+0.2%
Pentecostal	11.9	8	-0.2%

Missionaries from American Samoa
n.a.

Missionaries to American Samoa
P,I,A 10 serving with 5 agencies: USA 10.
C 30. **M** 70.

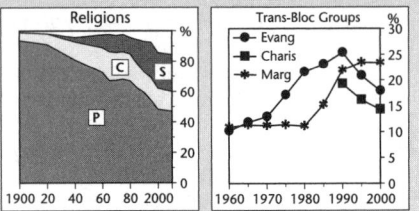

• Challenges for Prayer

1 **Samoans in this U.S. territory are relatively well-off** in comparison to independent Samoa to the west, but are adversely affected by the dominant materialistic culture and wealth of their rulers. Pray for the indigenous people that they may find their destiny in wholehearted commitment to the Lord Jesus Christ.

2 **Praise God for the evangelical ministries and churches** making an impact for the Lord. The Assemblies of God have grown through evangelism. There is also a large **YWAM** base in the islands.

3 **Spectacular Mormon growth** demonstrates the spiritual poverty of the mainline churches who have lost large numbers to this erroneous system. Pray for new spiritual life and vigour in these churches.

Andorra
Principality of Andorra

FEBRUARY 11
EUROPE

GEOGRAPHY
Area 468 sq.km. In the heart of the Pyrenean mountains between France and Spain.

Population		Ann. Gr.	Density
2000	77,985	+4.00%	167 per sq. km.
2010	108,765	+3.18%	232 per sq. km.
2025	154,335	+1.95%	330 per sq. km.

Most growth is through immigration.

Capital Andorra la Vella 23,000. **Urbanites** 63%.

PEOPLES
European 97.5%. Andorran 15,750; Spanish 34,600; Portuguese 8,450; French 5,300. **Other** 2.5%.

Literacy near 100%. **Official Language** Catalan. **All languages** 3. **Languages with Scriptures** 3Bi.

ECONOMY
A duty-free tax haven. Surrounded by EU, but not part of it. Wealthy through tourism (6 million visitors annually). Most employment derives from the tourist industry. **Public debt** 10.4% of GDP. **Income/person** $18,790 (60% of USA).

POLITICS
Self-governing co-principality since 1278; nominally ruled by the French President and Spanish bishop of Urgel. Since 1993 Andorra has had its own constitution, judiciary and foreign policy.

RELIGION
Official freedom of religion since 1993. The Catholic Church remains the established church.

Religions	Population %	Adherents	Ann. Gr.
Christian	93.44	72,869	+3.9
non-Religious	5.00	3,899	+4.0
Muslim	0.63	491	+19.1
Other	0.93	725	+13.0

Christians	Denom.	Affil.%	#	Ann. Gr.
Protestant	3	0.10	80	+0.0%
Independent	1	0.09	70	+12.9%
Anglican	1	0.05	40	+2.5%
Catholic	1	89.16	70,000	+4.1%
Marginal	3	0.77	600	+15.2%
Unaffiliated		3.26	2	n.a.

Churches	MegaBloc	Cong.	Members	Affiliates
Catholic	C	8	55,628	69,535
Jehovah's Witnesses	M	2	325	500
Christian Community	I	1	54	70
Christian Brethren	P	1	20	35
Other denominations [5]		5	128	185
Total Christians [9]		17	56,155	70,325

Trans-bloc Groupings	pop.%	#	Ann. Gr.
Evangelical	0.2	124	+10.5%
Charismatic	1.1	848	+4.7%
Pentecostal	0.1	70	+12.9%

Missionaries to Andorra
P,I,A 2 in 1 agency: USA 2.
C 8.

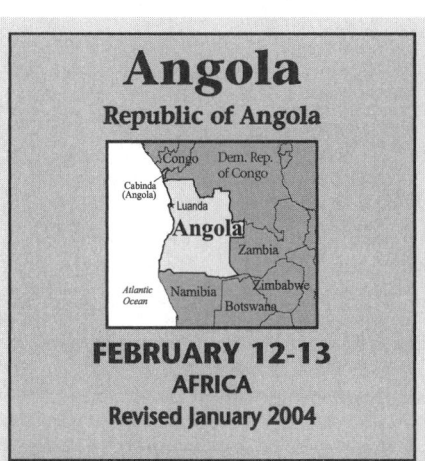

• Challenges for Prayer

1 **Materialism holds Andorra in a tight grip**. Once a smugglers' refuge, Andorra now attracts well-heeled tourists and international finance. Pray that the myth of fulfilment through materialism would be exposed for the lie that it is.

2 **The occult is a stronghold in this beautiful principality.** Most people consult mediums, seers, and astrologers for guidance and advice, usually at great financial cost. Few seek out priests of the majority Catholic Church. Ask God to break down these strongholds and to open the eyes of Andorrans and expatriates alike to see the light of the gospel.

3 **Biblical Christianity is gaining a foothold, slowly but surely.** There are now three evangelical churches when there were none a few years ago, and there are now some indigenous Andorran believers. This is a change from 5 years ago, when nearly all of the handful of Christians were expatriates. Praise God for the first-fruits of the harvest in Andorra, and ask that it may grow.

Angola
Republic of Angola

FEBRUARY 12-13
AFRICA
Revised January 2004

Population		Ann.Gr.	Density
2000	12,878,188	+3.25%	10 per sq. km.
2010	17,235,659	+2.79%	14 per sq. km.
2025	25,106,861	+2.35%	20 per sq. km.

All population figures are estimates. No effective census for 40 years because of continual war.

Capital Luanda 2,665,000 (unofficially nearly 4 million). Other major cities: Huambo 250,000; Benguela 200,000. **Urbanites** 32%. Massive overcrowding in cities because of war refugees may have raised this to 60%.

PEOPLES
Bantu 97.9%. 39 peoples, largest: Ovimbundu 4,970,000; Mbundu 2,690,000; Kongo(3) 1,866,000; Chokwe 664,000; Luvale 464,000; Ovambo(4) 438,000; Mbwela(3) 222,000; Nyemba 222,000; Lunda 178,000; Luchazi 155,000; Herero(3) 141,000; Mbunda 135,000; Nsongo 92,000; Yaka 80,000; Nyaneka 76,000.
Khoisan 0.6%. 8 peoples, largest: Kwadi 28,000; Kung 23,000; Hukwe 20,000.
Other 1.5%. Mixed race 139,000; Westerners 40,000, Pygmies 11,000.

GEOGRAPHY
Area 1,246,700 sq.km. Coastal state dominating Congo-DRC's and Zambia's trade routes to the Atlantic. Cabinda is an oil-rich coastal enclave to the north of the Congo River.

Literacy Officially 42% (but more likely 27%). **Official language** Portuguese. **All languages** 42. **Languages with Scriptures** 12Bi 3NT 13por 5w.i.p.

ECONOMY
Enormous potential — rich and well watered agricultural land, diamonds, iron. Oil and diamond wealth is being squandered and pawned to fund the civil war. The infrastructure has collapsed and the population is almost completely dependent on food aid for survival. **HDI** 0.398; 160th/174. **Public debt** 294% of GNP. **Income/person** $270 (0.8% of USA).

POLITICS
A Portuguese colony for 450 years. Independence was won in 1975 after 15 years of warfare. The Marxist-oriented MPLA gained control of the government with Cuban military assistance. This rule was contested by the UNITA nationalist movement, initially supported by the West and by South Africa, in a civil war that dragged on for over 25 years. The legacy of greed, power-seeking, revenge, mistrust and broken promises on both sides will take generations to heal. The defeat of UNITA in 2002 led to a measure of peace and hope that the country will now have a chance for recovery.

RELIGION
The first President, a Marxist, vowed to eradicate Christianity within 20 years, there have been many incidents of repression and outright persecution of Christians. The harsh realities of war and the ideological collapse of Communism in the 1990s resulted in an easing of nearly all discrimination against Christians.

Religions	Population %	Adherents	Ann.Gr.
Christian	94.07	12,114,511	+3.5%
Traditional ethnic	4.96	638,758	+1.1%
non-Religious/other	0.95	122,343	–4.5%
Baha'i	0.01	1,288	+3.3%
Buddhist	0.01	1,288	+3.3%

Christians	Denom.	Affil.%	,000	Ann.Gr.
Protestant	29	18.44	2,374	+1.8%
Independent	104	6.74	868	+4.3%
Anglican	2	0.70	90	+2.4%
Catholic	1	62.12	8,000	+4.1%

	MegaBloc			
Marginal	1	1.09	140	+6.0%
Unaffiliated		6.60	850	n.a.
Doubly affiliated		*-1.62*	*-208*	*n.a.*

Churches	MegaBloc	Cong.	Members	Affiliates
Catholic	C	260	4,571,429	8,000,000
Assemblies of God	P	431	190,000	600,000
Kimbanguist	I	165	165,017	500,000
Evangelical Congreg.	P	1,405	182,609	420,000
Christian Brethren	P	1,200	170,000	350,000
Seventh-day Adventist	P	1,667	176,000	300,000
Ev Ch of SW Ang.(AME)	P	938	75,000	170,000
United Methodist	P	400	100,000	150,000
Jehovah's Witnesses	M	343	35,000	140,000
New Apostolic	I	350	70,000	140,000
Anglican [2]	A	300	45,000	90,000
Church of God	P	113	35,000	80,000
Ev Baptist[2]	P	57	35,928	60,000
Ev Ch of S Angola(SIM)	P	194	17,483	50,000
Ev Pentecostal	P	346	25,974	40,000
Free Baptist	I	40	20,000	38,000
Baptist Convention	P	135	17,000	34,000
United Evang	P	268	20,359	34,000
Mennonite Brethren	P	27	4,000	8,000
Other denoms [116]		1,156	116,100	268,000
Doubly counted			-104,000	-208,000
Total Christians [137]		**9,800**	**5.992m**	**11.264m**

Trans-bloc Groupings	pop.%	,000	Ann.Gr.
Evangelical	16.4	2,111	+2.7%
Charismatic	16.0	2,061	+3.0%
Pentecostal	5.6	720	+1.0%

Missionaries from Angola
P,I,A 44 in 5 agencies and in 5 lands.

Missionaries to Angola
P,I,A 187 in 30 agencies and from 13 lands: Canada 37, USA 34, Brazil 26, Switzerland 19.
C 1,400. M 50.

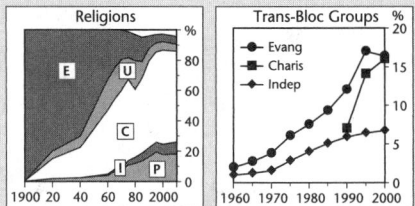

• Answers to Prayer

1 The failure of **Communism** to eradicate Christianity.

2 The growth of **biblical Christianity** in the midst of appalling suffering and deprivation.

• Challenges for Prayer

Continual war for 40 years has been devastating. The 25-year civil war became an unscrupulous battle for power using aid programmes, NGOs and the suffering civilian population as weapons of war. Anti-personnel landmines outnumber the population, and by 1999 there were 100,000 amputees. Forced recruitment of young people is widespread. A large proportion of the rural population has fled to urban areas due to widespread famine. The psychological, social and spiritual wounds are even more harmful and long-lasting. Pray for:

a) *The healing of the nation* at every level.

b) *Lasting peace and a righteous government* sensitive to the well-being of the people.

c) *Those seeking to alleviate suffering* by clearing mines, rebuilding the infrastructure, homes, hospitals, schools and churches. In many areas the destruction is over 80%. Many agencies including **WVI**, **TEAR Fund** and a consortium of churches and agencies called Church Action in Angola are involved.

2 **Luanda and other major cities** have become the home of refugee populations living in squalid despair. Many orphaned or abandoned children struggle to survive; many victims of the war aggressively beg on the streets. Pray for churches and agencies seeking to alleviate their suffering.

3 **Christians have suffered ostracism, abuse, discrimination and outright persecution** for many decades. In the first ten years after independence there was intense persecution of Christians, dozens of pastors and thousands of believers were martyred or abducted, and many churches were deliberately destroyed. Many simple Christians kept the faith and witnessed. As a result, congregations have multiplied in both the UNITA and MPLA areas during the conflict. Services are packed, and despite their desperation and destitution hundreds of thousands have trusted in the Lord Jesus Christ. Pray that this growth may continue and lead to the total evangelization of the country.

4 **The church has not emerged unscathed** and needs much prayer — specifically for:

a) *Love that transcends* tribal loyalties and the violent politics that fed on such, often dividing Christians.

b) *Forgiveness* of the perpetrators of violence and of Christians who compromised under pressure.

c) *The ending of state restrictions* and manipulation, and the emergence of true freedom of religion. Only about half of the 150 denominations have been granted registration.

d) *Christ-like, holy living* by followers of the Lord Jesus that commends the gospel to unbelievers, and a passion for outreach to their disillusioned, apathetic neighbours.

e) *Unity in the gospel.* The Angola Evangelical Alliance links 10 denominations for coordinated action, but because of war it can hardly function.

5 **The dearth of trained, godly leadership** is the most critical problem limiting church growth and maturity. The results — many leadership struggles, divisions, petty legalisms, compromise and condoned sin. Many are not free from all aspects of witchcraft. For years, little formal training could be given, but now there are seven Bible schools and four seminaries (Ecumenical, Evangelical [at Lubango, **AEF, AME, AIM**], Baptist and Catholic in Luanda). Pray for the provision of funds, buildings, libraries and, above all, godly teachers and for the effective spiritual growth and ministry of those trained.

6 The unreached and needy:

a) *Chaos has prevented a survey of needs.* This is an urgent requirement, especially for Bible translation. There is ongoing translation work in five languages, but at least 21 are without either Scriptures or translators.

b) *Specific peoples yet to be evangelized.* Most are in the dry and isolated regions of the south and southwest bordering on Zambia (the Mashi/Mbwela, Mbukushu, Ngankala) and Namibia (Herero, Kwangali, Nyaneka and the various San peoples). The main missions with involvement are **YWAM**, **SIM**(AEF) and **AME**.

7 **Young people and children** are spiritually deprived both in and outside the churches. The Marxism exclusively propagated in earlier years is no longer taught, but the negative attitudes to religion still make any Christian witness difficult in schools, and have discouraged churches from running Sunday schools and youth groups. Pray for:

a) *Primary and secondary schools* to be opened up for religious teaching and SU activities.

b) *Churches to recover a vision* for evangelizing and discipling children and young people.

c) *University students* face campus unrest and the looming inevitability of being drafted into the armed forces. Pray for the ministry of IFES with 3 groups and 1 staff worker.

8 **The life and witness of a depleted missionary force** through the years of suffering was a good testimony. Pray for continued ministry within the churches by **YWAM** (33), **MAF** (22), **AME** (20), **SIM** (15), all Baptists (13), Brethren (9) and others. Pray that a new generation of missionaries may be raised up to reconstruct the country, restore health services, strengthen the Church and evangelize unreached peoples and areas. Pray for the provision of visas and for favour in the eyes of the government. Pray also for their safety and fruitfulness in these desperate and dangerous times.

9 Media and support ministries:

a) *The Bible Society* is active and involved in development of Scriptures in nine languages, and new translations into Luchazi, Umbundu and Kongo. There is a great demand for Bibles, but deep poverty limits sales. There is no longer much hindrance to Bible importation or distribution. The Gideons are allowed to distribute NTs in hospitals, but not hotels, schools or prisons.

b) *Christian literature* is scarce and little is available in Portuguese and even less in indigenous languages.

c) *Radio broadcasts* reach the land in seven indigenous languages from **TWR** in Swaziland and also in Portuguese.

d) *The JESUS film* is available in Portuguese, Kongo, Kwangali and Kwanyama, but 20 more languages need to be tackled. Pray for the completion of these and their effective use.

e) *GRN* has made recordings in 30 languages and dialects.

Anguilla

British Dependency of Anguilla

FEBRUARY 13
LATIN AMERICA

GEOGRAPHY
Area 91 sq.km. The most northerly of the Leeward Islands.

Population	Ann. Gr.	Density
2000	8,309	+1.28%	91 per sq. km.
2010	9,361	+1.17%	103 per sq. km.
2025	10,984	+1.02%	121 per sq. km.

Capital The Valley 1,280.

PEOPLES
Afro-Caribbean 95.6%
Euro-American 3.6%
East Indian 0.8%.
Literacy 95%. **Languages** English, English Creole.

ECONOMY
Tourism is virtually the only industry.

POLITICS
A British dependent territory. There is representative internal self-government.

RELIGION
Complete freedom of religion.

Religions	Population %	Adherents	Ann.Gr.
Christian	91.51	7,604	+1.0
Spiritist	5.47	455	+7.1
non-Religious	1.23	102	+2.6
Baha'i	1.04	86	+1.9
Muslim	0.55	46	+5.5
Hindu	0.20	17	+9.9

Christians	Denom.	Affil.%	,000	Ann.Gr.
Protestant	9	49.66	4	+0.9%
Anglican	1	31.89	3	+0.0%
Catholic	1	3.73	0	+1.3%
Marginal	1	1.68	0	+5.0%
Unaffiliated		4.55	0	n.a.

Churches	MegaBloc	Cong.	Members	Affiliates
Anglican	A	5	1,060	2,650
Methodist	P	4	1,000	2,000
Seventh-day Adventist	P	3	600	720
Baptist	P	2	217	650
Ch of God of Prophecy	P	2	200	400
Catholic	C	2	124	310
Other denominations [3]		3	221	506
Total Christians [9]		21	3,422	7,236

Trans-bloc Groupings pop. %		,000	Ann. Gr.
Evangelical	19.9	2	+1.7%
Charismatic	12.0	1	+1.8%
Pentecostal	4.9	0	+2.7%

Missionaries from Anguilla
n.a.

Missionaries to Anguilla
P,I,A 4 in 2 agencies and from 2 countries.
C 2.

• Challenges for Prayer

1 **Anguilla is a remnant of a bygone era** as a little colonial outpost. Pray that this little island and its churches may not be bypassed by the Holy Spirit. There is religion, but without much vision for evangelism, committed discipleship or taking the gospel to other parts of the world.

2 **Inter-denominational cooperation has not been the best** despite the island's smallness. Pray that Christ's followers may function effectively as His body.

Antigua and Barbuda

State of Antigua and Barbuda

FEBRUARY 13

LATIN AMERICA

 GEOGRAPHY
Area 442 sq.km. Three islands; Antigua is volcanic, Barbuda coralline.

Population	Ann.Gr.	Density
2000	67,560	+0.55%	153 per sq. km.
2010	70,919	+0.47%	160 per sq. km.
2025	75,080	+0.34%	170 per sq. km.

Capital St John's 28,000. **Urbanites** 37%.

PEOPLES
Afro-Caribbean 95%.
Other 5%. Euro-American 1,600; Arab 400; South Asian 300; Amerindian 200.

Literacy 90%. **Languages** English, Creole.

ECONOMY
Officially, tourism and light industry are the mainstays. Money laundering, gun-running and drug-dealing are realities despite efforts to crack down on these lucrative sources of income. **HDI** 0.828; 38th/174. **Public debt** 95% of GNP. **Income/person** $7,330 (23.5% of USA).

POLITICS
British colony for 349 years; independence in 1981 as a constitutional monarchy.

RELIGION
Freedom of religion.

Religions	Population %	Adherents	Ann.Gr.
Christian	93.91	63,446	+0.4
Spiritist/Rastafarian	3.29	2,223	+3.1
non-Religious	1.39	939	+3.5
Baha'i	0.93	628	+2.1
Muslim	0.40	270	+0.5
Hindu	0.08	54	+15.7

Christians	Denom.	Affil.%	,000	Ann.Gr.
Protestant	17	31.07	21	+0.2%
Independent	4	1.78	1	+1.5%
Anglican	1	33.47	23	-2.0%
Catholic	1	11.55	8	-0.3%
Marginal	2	1.63	1	+4.5%
Unaffiliated		14.41	10	n.a.

Churches	MegaBloc	Cong.	Members	Affiliates
Anglican	A	8	10,186	22,613
Catholic	C	6	5,132	7,800
Moravian	P	7	2,300	5,750
Wesleyan	P	38	1,916	3,200
Methodist	P	4	1,800	3,096
Seventh-day Adventist	P	2	680	2,720
Pentecostal Assemblies	P	6	1,200	1,656

				Trans-bloc Groupings pop. %		,000	Ann.Gr.
Ch of God (Cleveland)	P	7	310	700			
Jehovah's Witnesses	M	6	412	1,030			
Ch of God of Prophecy	P	6	375	700			
Baptist	P	4	350	580			
Ch of God (Anderson)	P	5	236	520			
Other denoms [14]		23	1,530	2,780			
Total Christians [26]		123	26,500	53,300			

Trans-bloc Groupings pop. %		,000	Ann.Gr.
Evangelical	16.8	11	+1.0%
Charismatic	12.7	9	+0.7%
Pentecostal	4.3	3	+2.9%

Missionaries from Antigua and Barbuda
P,I,A 4 in 2 agencies.

Missionaries to Antigua and Barbuda
P,I,A 19 in 5 agencies and from 2 countries.
C 30.

• Challenges for Prayer

1 **Antiguans are almost all Christian in name,** with many Evangelicals among them, but they are complacent in the face of serious moral and spiritual breakdown. Pray for revival which galvanizes Christians to prayer and involvement which impacts their society.

2 **Strongholds of sin** are drug-dealing, violence, gambling, prostitution and a growing kidnapping 'industry'. Pray that these may be broken down.

3 **Oneness in fellowship and vision is a great need.** Pray for effective cooperation between the constituent congregations and agencies of the United Evangelical Association.

4 Social and spiritual needs to cover in prayer:

a) *Many refugees from Montserrat* have fled to Antigua since the 1997 volcanic eruption on their island.

b) *The small Hispanic, Lebanese, Muslim and Hindu* trading communities.

Argentina
Argentine Republic

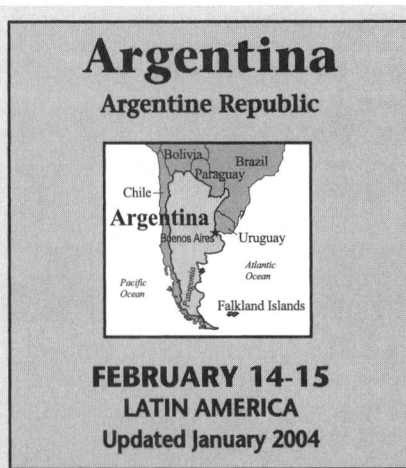

FEBRUARY 14-15
LATIN AMERICA
Updated January 2004

 GEOGRAPHY
Area 2,780,092 sq.km. Latin America's second largest country with a great range of climate, rainfall and topography. The 16,300 sq.km. Islas Malvinas (Falkland Islands) are claimed by Argentina, but remain under British rule. There is one federal district and 24 provinces.

Population		Ann.Gr.	Density
2000	37,027,297	1.27%	13 per sq. km.
2010	41,467,500	1.08%	15 per sq. km.
2025	47,150,313	0.79%	17 per sq. km.

Capital Buenos Aires City 3,500,000; conurbation 12,400,000. Other mega cities: Cordoba 1,407,000; San Justo 1,246,000; Rosario 1,228,000. **Urbanites** 88%.

PEOPLES
European 81.4%. A fusion of many nationalities, but largely Spanish, Italian and other East and West Europeans. Many minorities have retained their cultural identity.
Mestizo 10%. Many Bolivian, Chilean & Paraguayan immigrants.
Amerindian 3.7%. 18 peoples; largest: Quechua(3) 1.08m; Mapuche 54,000; Aymara 27,000; Wichi (Mataco) 28,000; Toba 20,000; Chiriguano 16,000.
Middle Eastern 4.7%. Lebanese, Syrian & Palestinian Arabs 1.1m; Jews 500,000.
Other 0.2%. Korean, 35,000; Japanese 32,000; Chinese 30,000.
Literacy 95%. **Official language** Spanish. **All languages** 23. **Languages with Scriptures** 3Bi 7NT 4por.

ECONOMY
Blessed with abundant natural resources which were squandered by inept gov-

ernments for most of the 20th Century. A decade of transformation under President Menem was dramatic. Inflation was tamed, corruption exposed and restructuring promoted, but after 2000 a serious economic collapse impoverished the country. 58% of the population live in poverty. **Unemployment** 16%. **HDI** 0.827; 39th/174. **Public debt** 23% of GNP. **Income/person** $8,060 (23.5% of USA).

POLITICS

Independent from Spain in 1816. Peronist misrule, inflation and leftist urban terrorism provoked the 1976 military takeover. Military incompetence, adventurism and a bad record on human rights led to the restoration of democratic rule in 1983, but successive governments have failed to grapple with fundamental structures and vested interests which hinder needful change to restore the economy to its former prosperity.

RELIGION

Roman Catholicism has state support, but there is freedom of religion and considerable respect for Evangelicals, though not all legal discrimination against religious minorities has ended.

Religion	Population %	Adherents	Ann.Gr.
Christian	92.91	34,402,062	+1.1%
non-Religious	3.68	1,140,441	+5.7%
Muslim	1.35	500,000	+5.1%
Jewish	1.32	488,760	+2.2%
Other	0.49	181,434	+4.7%
Traditional ethnic	0.16	59,244	– 1.5%
Buddhist	0.05	18,514	+11.0%
Baha'i	0.03	11,108	+5.5%
Hindu	0.01	3,703	+5.4%

Christians	Denom.	Affil. %	,000	Ann.Gr.
Protestant	86	6.16	2,279	+3.8%
Independent	73	4.25	1,573	+2.6%
Anglican	1	0.05	19	+0.5%
Catholic	1	91.15	33,750	+1.1%
Orthodox	9	0.43	159	+0.8%
Marginal	7	1.51	560	+3.4%
Unaffiliated		1.10	410	n.a.
Doubly affiliated		*-11.75*	*-4,350*	*n.a*

Churches	MegaBloc	Cong.	Members	Affiliates
Catholic	C	6,000	23.276m	33.75m
Assemb. of God (Swed)	P	1,300	450,000	750,000
Nat. Union of AoG (USA)	P	877	335,000	690,000
Waves of Love and Peace	I	300	275,000	340,000
Latter-day Saints (Morm)	M	844	135,000	270,000
Jehovah's Witnesses	M	1,690	120,849	250,000
New Apostolic	I	288	75,000	150,000
Baptist Convention	P	481	70,000	120,000
Christian Brethren	P	1,500	67,000	113,900
Vision do Futuro	I	300	80,000	112,000
Seventh-day Adventist	P	387	71,996	110,000
Intl Ch Foursquare G.	P	220	50,000	73,000
Church of God Assoc.	I	591	26,000	65,000
Ev Pente. Ch of Chile	I	30	36,000	61,200
Ch of God (Cleveland)	P	391	27,227	49,000
Ch of the Lord Mission	I	151	19,000	47,500
United Evang (Toba)	I	265	21,000	40,000
Ev Lutheran	P	277	19,000	31,100
Anglican	A	74	10,440	19,000
Ch of the Nazarene	P	240	10,500	19,000
Other denoms [160]		8,022	742,587	1,279,894
Pentecostal overcounting	*P*		*-283,333*	*-510,000*
Doubly affiliated			*-2,648,276*	*-3,840,000*
Total Christians [181]		24,228	22.99m	33.99m

Trans-bloc Groupings	pop.%	,000	Ann. Gr.
Evangelical	10.8	3,992	+5.7%
Charismatic	18.9	7,006	+3.1%
Pentecostal	9.4	3,468	+6.5%

Missionaries from Argentina
P,I,A 477 in 39 agencies to over 50 countries: Argentina 151, Spain 23, Uruguay 16, many in the Middle East.

Missionaries to Argentina
P,I,A 729 in 92 agencies from 22 countries: USA 405, Korea 74, UK 56, Brazil 46, Spain 38, Sweden 26. **C** 9,350. **M** 500.

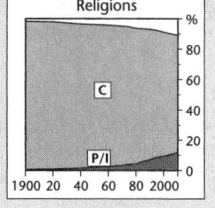
Religions

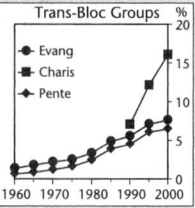
Trans-Bloc Groups

• Answers to Prayer

1 **Renewal, much prayer and large-scale evangelism** since 1983 have deeply affected the nation and touched the world through Argentinian evangelists, teachers, missionaries and leaders.

2 **Out of dictatorship and the defeat** in the Falklands/Malvinas war in 1982 have come significant changes leading to religious hunger, democratic government and a period of economic recovery.

3 **Prison ministry** has revolutionized the nation's jails. Revival began in Olmos high security prison and by 1996 half its 3,000 inmates were believers with the movement spreading to 200 other institutions. Of the 200,000+ prisoners, 10% were then reckoned to be born again.

• Challenges for Prayer

A

1 **Spiritual hunger has led to growth**. Evangelicals were under 1 million in 1980, but had increased to nearly 3m by 2000. Pray for a deepening of the work of the Holy Spirit in believers. The spiritual hunger in the nation is also winning large followings for cults and Umbanda occultism from Brazil.

2 **Renewal has impacted nearly every denomination**. Revival based on Scripture (rather than emotion) is needed, which deeply changes individuals, congregations and the nation. Godly and humble leadership, holy living and high ethical standards are in short supply. Pray that the Church might also impact every level of society for good.

3 **Spiritual warfare against the forces of darkness** has played a prominent part in Christian ministry, with decisive blows struck against bondage, witchcraft and sin. Pray for the protection and continued spiritual health of all in the forefront of the battle.

4 **Unity of believers** is essential to growth and revival. At a local level, Councils of Pastors meet for prayer in the cities and, slowly, trust is being built and cooperative ministry enhanced. At a national level, the **National Council of Christian Evangelical Churches** (*Consejo Nacional Cristiano Evangelico*) has drawn together leaders from across the evangelical spectrum. Pride and fear in the midst of massive changes in church structures and society can damage the desired unity. Pray that leaders may hear what the Spirit is saying to the Church today.

5 **Appropriate leadership** for the churches is a critical bottleneck to growth. Leaders that disciple and empower other leaders and who know both the power of the Spirit and the depths of the Word are too rare. Pray for those involved in training through seminaries, Bible schools and TEE. Pray also for students, who are hindered by finance, lack of facilities and time.

6 **Vision for the future.** In 1996, evangelical leaders committed themselves to plant a further 21,000 churches (then 14,000) and double the percentage of evangelicals in 10 years (DAWN). Pray that this may be achieved. Many rural and provincial areas have been little affected by the spiritual fervour of the cities.

7 **Amerindians** have long been marginalized, exploited and demeaned, their cultures ravaged by the majority. Only in 1996 did the peoples of the Chaco region gain official title to their lands. Over the 20th Century, Chaco peoples have become Christians through the work of **SAMS**, (Wichi, Toba, Chiriguano), Mennonites (Wichi) and **CBI** (Guarani). Pray for the maturation of the indigenous Church and for sensitivity to this on the part of the expatriates in the agencies involved. Pray also for ongoing translation programmes in six indigenous languages (**SIL, UBS, SAMS**).

8 **Specific sections of the population** with definite ministry and outreach needs:

a) *The estimated 500,000 strong Jewish community*, mostly in Buenos Aires, is the world's sixth largest. They are highly secularized and prosperous. Chosen People Ministries and 10 other agencies have ministry to Jews. There are five Messianic assemblies in Buenos Aires.

b) *The sophisticated upper class of the capital*, who have been harder to reach with the gospel.

c) *The urban poor.* Local churches are doing more to address social needs among them, but the challenge is enormous.

d) *University students,* many living below the poverty line, number 927,000 in 1700 tertiary institutions, over half being in Buenos Aires. There are few actively witnessing students. Pray for ABUA(**IFES**) groups and staff.

e) *Quechua and Aymara* from Argentina, Chile and Bolivia have flocked to Buenos Aires where they have become a labouring under-class.

f) *Chinese number 30,000* and come from both Taiwan and the mainland. Pray for CMA ministry among both groups.

9 **The missionary vision** of the Argentine Church is growing and maturing with a significant interest in Spain and North Africa. A number of Argentinians are internationally respected mission leaders. The *Red. de Cooperación Nacional: Misiones Mundiales* (COMIBAM) has a major interdenominational role in stimulating and facilitating the vision for missions. Pray that pastors and churches may gain a vision for the unreached peoples of the world and have the means to support that vision.

10 **Expatriate mission agencies** have a continuing role in Bible teaching and implanting a missions vision through partnership with national agencies and churches. Pray for the work of missionaries with **IMB-SBC** (81), **AoG** (58), **YWAM** (42), BBF (26), **CMA** (24), **LL** (22), **Brethren** (20), **GMU** (20).

11 Media ministries for prayer:

a) ***EHC*** has been involved in house-by-house distribution since 1958, and covered the country twice.

b) ***The JESUS film***. By 1999 it had been seen by a large proportion of the population, and was available in 3 indigenous languages.

c) ***GRN***. Recordings are available and have been distributed in 5 main Old World and 18 indigenous languages.

d) ***Radio and television***. FM radio stations all over the country are used by Christians for broadcasting. Both **TWR** and **HCJB** broadcast by satellite, short wave from Bonaire, and on FM from Buenos Aires with coverage for much of the day. Christian programmes on cable TV are being produced by **YWAM**.

Armenia

Republic of Armenia, Hayastan

FEBRUARY 16

ASIA

GEOGRAPHY
Area 29,800 sq.km. Landlocked, mountainous Caucasus state. Nagorno-Karabakh, a 4,400 sq.km. enclave in Azerbaijan populated by Armenians, is controlled by Armenia together with the Azeri territory in between.

Population		Ann.Gr.	Density
2000	3,519,569	-0.31%	118 per sq. km.
2010	3,697,258	+0.66%	124 per sq. km.
2025	3,946,381	+0.28%	132 per sq. km.

Capital Yerevan 1,450,000. **Urbanites** 68%.

PEOPLES
Armenians 96.6%. A distinctive Indo-European people.
Other 3.4%. Russians 80,000; Georgian 40,000; Kurds 40,000; Ukrainian 8,000; Assyrian 6,000; Greek 4,000.

Literacy 99%. **Official language** Armenian.
Languages with Scriptures 2Bi 2w.i.p.

ECONOMY
Potentially wealthy with minerals, agriculture and hydro power. Crippled by a devastating earthquake in 1988 and by wars and unrest in the Caucasus region restricting communications with the rest of the world. Agriculture and industry is being privatized and modernized, but progress is hampered by lack of finance. Under-employment and poverty are widespread. **HDI** 0.728; 87th/174. **Public debt** 24% of GNP. **Income/person** $630 (1.8% of USA).

POLITICS
Only at rare points in it's 2,500-year history has Armenia been independent. This country has been a victim of its location as a strategic buffer between the Byzantine/Turkish, Russian/USSR and Persian empires. The conflict with Azerbaijan over the status of Nagorno-Karabakh dominates the life of the country. An armed cease-fire since 1994 has left the country in an uncomfortable limbo. Internally, the government is stable and has become more democratic since 1997.

RELIGION
Religious freedom followed the collapse of Communism. The intimate link between government and the Armenian Apostolic Church during the mid-90s eroded that freedom with discriminatory legislation against minority religious groups and some persecution. Since 1997 this has moderated.

Religions	Population %	Adherents	Ann.Gr.
Christian	85.04	2,993,000	+1.4%
non-Religious/other	13.71	482,200	-6.4%
Muslim	1.20	42,235	-4.7%
Baha'i	0.04	1,408	-0.3%
Jewish	0.01	352	-0.3%

Christians	Denom.	Affil.%	,000	Ann.Gr.
Protestant	6	0.32	11	+4.9%
Independent	8	1.55	55	+11.3%
Catholic	1	4.55	160	+4.6%
Orthodox	2	78.19	2,752	+0.7%
Marginal	2	0.43	15	+24.3%

Churches	MegaBloc	Cong.	Members	Affiliates
Armenian Apostolic	O	150	1,505,495	2,740,000
Catholic	C	19	95,808	160,000
Pentecostal [4]	P	500	20,000	50,000
Jehovah's Witnesses	M	39	5,254	15,000
Russian Orthodox	O	2	6,000	12,000
Baptist	P	30	2,500	5,000
Charismatic groups [3]	I	13	2,300	4,000
Seventh-day Adventist	P	10	865	1,800
Other denoms [7]		34	3,375	5,320
Total Christians [20]		797	1,642,000	2,993,000

Trans-bloc Groupings	pop.%	,000	Ann.Gr.
Evangelical	8.1	286	+2.9%
Charismatic	3.3	117	+5.9%
Pentecostal	1.4	50	+10.8%

Missionaries from Armenia
n.a.

Missionaries to Armenia
P,I,A 35 in 13 agencies from 9 countries.
C 4. O 10. M 4.

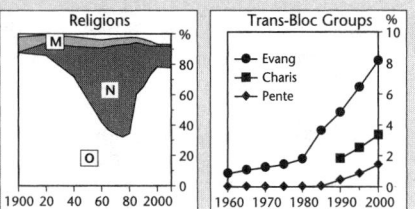

Religions

Trans-Bloc Groups
—●— Evang
—■— Charis
—◆— Pente

• # Answers to Prayer

1 The survival of the Armenian Church through the centuries, and the growth in numbers of committed believers since 1990.

2 The most significant turning of Kurds to Christ anywhere in the world has occurred among the Kurds of Armenia with about 1,000 believers from the Yezidi community.

• # Challenges for Prayer

1 Armenia needs peace and good relations with surrounding nations for survival and economic reconstruction. Centuries of bitter conflict, oppression and massacres have left a legacy of hatred and mistrust of these nations. In 1915 the Turks massacred 1.5 million Armenians because they were Christian and considered a threat. Pray for forgiveness by all and for wise rebuilding of trust and good neighbourliness by the nation's leaders.

2 The 1700 years of Armenia as a Christian nation, the world's first, was celebrated in 2001. Pray that Armenian Christians might become a source of light and blessing to surrounding nations — few have a significant indigenous church. Over the past 10 years a number of Armenians have gone to serve the Lord in Russia and Muslim lands. Pray that this movement may grow.

3 The baleful impact of 70 years of Marxism and a century of severe persecution of Armenians have left deep moral and social wounds. The pain, anger, bitterness and vengefulness need to be cleansed in the blood of Jesus. The whole education system requires transformation and the restoration of Christian values. Pray for deep repentance and revival.

4 The Armenian Apostolic Church has long been a cultural refuge in times of persecution but the old liturgy is not in modern language so is less appropriate for ordinary people. The 1988 earthquake helped to bring about a powerful revival with national repentance before the Lord and a resurgence of interest in the Scriptures. Pray for:
a) *Complete recovery from division and compromise* — two main factions had emerged which crippled the Church.
b) *Deep spiritual regeneration of the Church* and for godly leaders.
c) *An appreciation of, and fellowship with, the smaller denominations in Armenia.* Some Orthodox were supportive of discrimination and persecution of Evangelicals in the mid-1990s.

5 The Armenian Church Loving Brotherhood is the evangelical arm of the Apostolic Church which has its roots in the fifth century. The Brotherhood suffered much in past centuries and under Communism, but has been able to operate openly since the late

1980s as an autonomous body within the Apostolic Church. Their main emphases are on biblical preaching, personal witness, charitable works and publishing and distributing evangelical literature and Bibles. By 1999 they had grown to 20,000 active members and had 500 preaching points all over Armenia. Pray for this movement and its influence for good on the nation.

6 **The major growth of Evangelicals** since the earthquake and the collapse of Communism has been through the Brotherhood and Pentecostals who have had a national impact. There are also a growing number of independent charismatic congregations. The Baptists have grown but less so. Pray for continued growth and maturity for all these groups.

7 **Training for leaders is lacking**. Adequate residential training is not yet available, nor are TEE courses widely used. There is one small Pentecostal Bible School in Yerevan. Armenian Christian workers are strategically located to bless surrounding nations as Armenia is an island of Christianity in a sea of Islam.

8 **The unresolved issue of control of Nagorno-Karabakh,** nominally independent, is an open wound. Pray for the 150,000 Armenians (many are refugees from Azerbaijan) living here; some have come to faith in Christ. Refugees on both sides of the conflict (500,000 Armenians from Azerbaijan and one million Azeris from Armenia and the west of Azerbaijan) still suffer deprivation and marginalization. The international ramifications of the dispute for surrounding nations, NATO and Russia are significant. Pray for resolution.

9 **Evangelical Christianity has thrived** among the 3.5m Armenians of the diaspora, with many congregations in the Middle East, North America and elsewhere. Most Armenians have retained close links even after many generations. Since 1988 a number of Armenian churches and ministries have given generously and invested in reaching their homeland, with remarkable results. Pray for the world to be blessed through this global people.

10 **The Kurds** are mainly of the ancient Yezidi religion; some are Shi'a Muslim. The growing Kurdish church is reaching out to Kurds in Armenia, the CIS countries and elsewhere. Pray for the necessary resources for them to continue this outreach, and that the 25 million Kurdish people may be reached.

11 **Christian help ministries**. Pray for:

a) **Relief work.** The long-standing economic crisis has heightened the value of indigenous and foreign relief and aid programmes. There is real need for work-creating projects (**TEAR Fund, ELAM**, Love Armenia).

b) **Student witness** is being pioneered by **IFES** and others. Pray for acceptance from state and university authorities and development of the work.

c) **Bible distribution**. The newly completed Kurdish Kermanji NT is being distributed. **The Bible Society** has an established ministry with a well-used Bible Centre in Yerevan.

d) **The JESUS film** has been widely used in four languages.

e) **Christian Radio**. **TWR** in Albania and Cyprus broadcast in Kurmanji and Armenian. **TWR** also broadcasts from Armenia to nine Central Asian and Middle Eastern countries; 60 of the least reached mega-peoples are within range of the station.

Aruba

Caribbean Sea

Oranjestad
Aruba

Netherlands Antilles

Venezuela

FEBRUARY 17
LATIN AMERICA

 GEOGRAPHY
Area 193 sq.km. An island 28 km north of Venezuela. Dry and sandy with no fresh water and few natural resources.

Population		Ann.Gr.	Density
2000	102,747	+4.74%	532 per sq. km.
2010	154,785	+4.00%	802 per sq. km.
2025	250,376	+2.89%	1,297 per sq. km.

Capital Oranjestad 22,723. **Urbanites** 70%.

PEOPLES

Netherlands citizens 84.9%. Antillean Creole 83,500; Dutch 3,700.
Other 15.1%. Spanish-speaking (Latin American) 9,700; English-speaking 3,000; Asian 1,500.
Literacy 95%. **Official language** Dutch. **Unofficial language** Papiamento (a Spanish, Portuguese, Dutch and English Creole).

ECONOMY
Heavily dependent on tourism, transhipment facilities, oil refining and loans from the Netherlands. **Public debt/person** 48% of GNP. **Income/person** $21,000 (53% of USA).

POLITICS
Aruba withdrew from the Netherlands

Antilles in 1986. It is a self-governing part of the Kingdom of the Netherlands.

 RELIGION
Full religious freedom

.Religions	Population %	Adherents	Ann.Gr.
Christian	96.45	99,099	+4.7%
non-Religious/other	2.83	2,900	+6.6%
Muslim	0.28	288	+8.4%
Chinese	0.16	164	+7.7%
Baha'i	0.14	144	+4.7%
Jewish	0.14	144	+4.0%

Christians	Denom.	Affil.%	,000	Ann.Gr.
Protestant	11	7.2	7	+1.6%
Independent	4	1.3	1	+4.1%
Anglican	1	0.7	1	+1.3%
Catholic	1	82.1	84	+8.2%
Marginal	1	1.5	2	+3.5%
Unaffiliated		3.7	4	n.a.

Churches	MegaBloc	Cong.	Members	Affiliates
Catholic	C	37	16,860	84,300
Jehovah's Witnesses	M	8	610	1,525
Other Indep [4]	I	9	900	1,350
Dutch Reformed	P	5	778	1,300
Evangelical	P	11	470	1,300
Assemblies of God	P	6	520	1,300
Pentecostal [4]	P	17	640	1,280
Seventh-day Adventist	P	5	600	960
Baptist	P	4	350	584
Other denoms [4]		10	635	1,434
Total Christians [18]		112	22,363	95,333

Trans-bloc Groupings	pop.%	,000	Ann.Gr.
Evangelical	6.4	7	+2.9%
Charismatic	8.2	8	+5.5%
Pentecostal	2.5	3	+2.6%

Missionaries from Aruba
P,I,A 1

Missionaries to Aruba
P,I,A 2. C 5. M 2.

• Challenges for Prayer

1 **There has been growth in evangelical witness** — predominantly among the more recent arrivals. Considerable numbers have immigrated from Latin America, the Caribbean and Asia. There are nearly 40 evangelical congregations with outreach, about half in English. Inter-church rivalry has harmed overall witness. The major spiritual growth is in **AoG**- and **TEAM**-related churches, though the Methodists too have experienced a strong move of the Spirit. Pray for a greater impact on the Papiamento-speaking population.

2 **Media.** Radio Victoria (**TEAM**) and the **AoG** station broadcast to the Antilles and to the whole Caribbean in Papiamento and other languages. **TWR** broadcasts from Bonaire 14 hours a day in Spanish. Pray for enduring fruitfulness for this ministry.

Australia

Commonwealth of Australia

FEBRUARY 18-19

PACIFIC

GEOGRAPHY
Area 7,682,300 sq.km. This island continent is largely grassland and desert in the interior but better watered in the east, southeast and southwest coastal regions, where most live in highly concentrated urban areas. There are three permanently inhabited dependent territories; Norfolk Is. (35 sq.km.; 2,500 pop), Christmas Is. (135 sq.km.; 2,300 pop), Cocos Is. (14 sq.km.; 600 pop).

Population		Ann.Gr.	Density
2000	18,879,524	+1.03%	2 per sq. km.
2010	20,608,386	+0.85%	3 per sq. km.
2025	23,090,790	+0.69%	3 per sq. km.

Capital Canberra 328,370. Other major cities: Sydney 4,041,000; Melbourne 3,417,000; Brisbane 1,601,000; Perth 1,364,000; Adelaide 1,092,000. **Urbanites** 86%.

PEOPLES
Over 25.5% of Australians are foreign-born and 16.8% were born in a non-English speaking country. Figures below are approximate.
Anglo-Celtic 67.8%. Predominantly British and Irish.
Other European 20%. Migrants from nearly every ethnic group in Europe, many still retaining their cultural identity.
Asian 6%. Chinese 450,000; Vietnamese 150,000; Filipino 100,000; Indian 90,000; Malay-Indonesian 50,000; Japanese 30,000; Cambodian 25,000.
Middle Eastern 3.0%. Arabic-speaking 300,000; Turks 70,000; Iranian 25,000; Kurds 25,000.
Australian Aborigine 2%. Total 350,000, half of whom speak one of the 111 living indigenous languages. In 1780 there were 300,000 speaking 260 languages.
Other 1.2%. Pacific Islander, Latin American, African.

Literacy 99%. **Official language** English. Over 19% of the population do not use English as their first language. **All indigenous languages** 234. **Languages with Scriptures** 1Bi 8NT 26por 19w.i.p.

ECONOMY
Mixed economy based on industry, agriculture and mining. Although the economy was restructured in the '90s, the Asian recession, external debt and severe periodic droughts limited growth for a time, but by 2001 economic growth was restored. **HDI** 0.922; 7th/174. **Public debt** 23% of GNP. **Income/person** $20,090 (66% of USA).

POLITICS
A federal, parliamentary democracy formed in 1901 with 6 states and 2 federal territories. The British monarch is the constitutional head of state, represented by a governor general. A referendum was held in 2000 about becoming a republic, but it was rejected.

RELIGION
A secular state with freedom of religion. A rapid increase of those claiming no religion and the arrival of many non-Christian immigrants is making Australia a much more pluralistic society.

Religions	Population %	Adherents	Ann.Gr.
Christian	67.50	12,743,679	+0.0%
non-Religious/other	28.21	5,325,914	+3.1%
Buddhist	1.40	264,313	+6.6%
Muslim	1.33	251,098	+5.2%
Hindu	0.47	88,734	+6.5%
Jewish	0.45	84,958	+1.0%
Chinese	0.26	49,087	+1.0%
Traditional ethnic	0.25	47,199	+71.6%
Sikh	0.08	15,104	+4.5%
Baha'i	0.05	9,440	+6.8%

Christians	Denom.	Affil.%	,000	Ann.Gr.
Protestant	155	12.83	2,423	+0.0%
Independent	28	1.06	199	+10.1%
Anglican	1	20.23	3,820	-0.6%
Catholic	1	25.21	4,760	-0.2%
Orthodox	35	3.20	605	+1.8%
Marginal	56	1.30	245	+0.5%
Unaffiliated		14.88	2,809	n.a.
Doubly affiliated		*-11.21*	*-2,100*	*n.a.*

Churches	MegaBloc	Cong.	Members	Affiliates
Catholic	C	1,226	3,328,671	4,760,000
Anglican	A	3,300	687,050	3,820,000
Uniting	P	2,700	156,757	1,254,056
Greek Orthodox [2]	O	118	258,741	370,000
Baptist Union	P	930	64,000	310,000
Assemblies of God	P	997	69,820	155,000
Jehovah's Witnesses	M	770	61,723	110,000
Chr Outreach Centres	I	200	55,000	110,000
Latter-day Saints (Morm)	M	410	67,832	97,000
Lutheran	P	533	35,185	95,000
Salvation Army	P	450	24,000	75,000
Churches of Christ	P	470	45,000	71,000
Presbyterian	P	775	36,000	68,000
Coptic Orthodox	O	20	47,552	68,000
Seventh-day Adventist	P	415	50,000	57,000
Russian Orthodox	O	22	29,605	45,000
Serbian Orthodox	O	23	31,763	44,151
Chr Brethren (Open)	P	288	19,000	42,180

A

Chr Revival Crusade	I	200	21,000	28,350
Other denoms [259]		2,952	235,600	473,000
Doubly affiliated			-1,167,000	-2,100,000
Total Christians [279]		16,800	4,157,700	9,952,800

Trans-bloc Groupings pop. %	,000	AnnGr
Evangelical	12.5	2,351	-0.5%
Charismatic	10.0	1,897	+0.3%
Pentecostal	2.0	379	+8.3%

Missionaries from Australia
P,I,A 4,388 in 97 agencies and in 134 countries: PNG 260, Middle East 106, USA 83, Philippines 82, Indonesia 80, Thailand 70, India 67, Japan 50, Cambodia 34,

Nepal 32, Congo-DRC 31, Tanzania 29, Spain 27.

Missionaries to Australia
P,I,A 3,277 in 109 agencies: Australia 2,116 (928 cross-cultural), USA 337, New Zealand 173, Korea 85, UK 51.

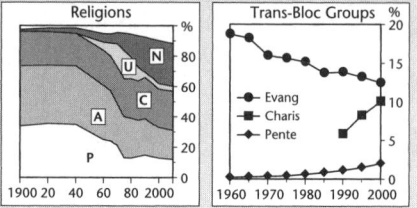

• Challenges for Prayer

1 **Secularism and a pursuit of leisure, pleasure and wealth** characterize Australia. Although 68% of Australians claim to be Christian, negative attitudes towards authority and tradition make it hard for the average man in the street to see the gospel as meaningful or the church as relevant. There is widespread interest in spirituality, but people are not turning to the churches to explore it. Pray that many might find solutions to life's problems and find their identity in a relationship with the Lord Jesus Christ.

2 **Church attendance declined steadily** from 35% in 1966 to 12% in 1990. This appears to have stabilized with about 10% of Australians in church on an average Sunday, and 18-20% in regular contact with church life. Decline continues in some of the larger and more traditional churches. There is some growth in the Salvation Army and various Pentecostal and charismatic churches though even this growth slowed in the late 1990s. In 1998 the Prime Minister, Leader of the Opposition and about a third of all parliamentarians were professing Christians. Pray for revival – something Australia has never known.

3 **Evangelicals** are strong in the Sydney Anglican diocese and a growing minority in the Melbourne diocese (30%). Several mainline churches have evangelical majorities while all of the rest have significant and active minorities. However mainline churches are in varying degrees of polarization over such issues as the ordination of women, homosexuality and traditional church structures which are leading to further divisions. The casualty rate among pastors is a concern — there are over 10,000 ex-pastors, almost the same number as presently serving pastors. Pray for a greater understanding of the postmodern world, more effective proclamation of the gospel in relevant ways and use of appropriate structures for growing the Christian community.

4 **Although some Australian churches have a good mission focus**, there is a general lack of missions vision in most churches. The relatively large number of Australian missionaries suffer from lack of support at every level. The vision for world evangelization has to be imparted to pastors during their theological training. Mission awareness courses, such as Perspectives on the World Christian Movement, are now being used in every state of Australia and the steady growth in numbers is encouraging. Students of all ages are being changed and are getting involved as goers or active senders. Pray for them and that churches may be enthused through them. Pray also for the missionary force, especially those who have gone to pioneer areas.

5 **Less reached peoples** are found both among the indigenous Aborigines, the many post-war migrants and the 6.5 million of non-British origin – both Australian-born and immigrants. Pray for those local churches with an active ministry to such cultural communities and also for the work of local congregations, **ECM** and other agencies among the European minorities.

a) ***Aboriginal tribes***. Only a few isolated groups have failed to respond to the very considerable missionary effort of past years. Most Aborigines are professing Christians, but there is a strong move to reassert their cultural identity.

b) ***Many people in working-class urban areas*** and in isolated mining and farming communities in the vast interior, northwest and north have had no vital biblical witness.

c) **Muslims** – around 255,000 from over 70 countries (40% Arabic-speaking, 20% Turkish, 9% Bosnian, 7% Indonesian/Malay), with 125,000 living in the Sydney area and 82,000 in the Melbourne area. Muslims have increased a hundred-fold since 1947, and there are now over 80 mosques in use. Small beginnings are being made to reach these peoples by the Baptist Union, Uniting Church and Stepping Stone Mission's Training Community, resulting in Arabic- and Turkish-speaking groups of believers beginning to emerge. **MECO**'s Centres of Fellowship are a significant ministry to Muslims.

d) **Chinese** – A high proportion of immigrants from SE Asia are ethnic Chinese and they may total as much as 450,000. About 20% of the Chinese are professing Christians; others are secular or adhere to the various Chinese traditional religions. There are over 130 Chinese evangelical congregations in the cities. Australia's largest Presbyterian Church is Chinese. Some of the most lively student groups in universities are of the Overseas Christian Fellowships and these are predominantly Chinese. Pray for the complete evangelization of the Buddhists and non-Christians among them.

e) **Vietnamese** – possibly 150,000, mostly refugees over the past 25 years and their offspring. There are a few Christian congregations. **AsEF** is expanding a ministry to Asian communities in each state.

f) **The diverse peoples** from the former Yugoslavia. Most still retain the use of their mother tongues: Croatian 80,000; Macedonian 70,000, Serbian 35,000; Bosnian 14,000; Albanian 10,000. They come from some of Europe's least evangelized countries, and there are very few evangelical believers among them.

g) **Jews** number 85,000; half live in Melbourne. Celebrate Messiah Australia has a fruitful ministry among Melbourne's growing Jewish community where there are many recent immigrants from Russia. **CWI** has a witness in Sydney.

h) **Southern Europeans**. Many use their original mother tongues, however many second- and third-generation settlers have assimilated into English-speaking Australian society and become estranged from their cultural roots. They neither fit into the ethnic churches of their parents nor feel at home in Anglo-Celtic churches. Pentecostal churches and the Jehovah's Witnesses have had more success. Major groups being Italians 500,000; Greeks 300,000; Polish 120,000; Maltese 80,000; Spanish 70,000. These represent minorities that, if evangelized and motivated, could make an impact for God on their native lands.

6 The 350,000 indigenous Aborigines have been demoralized in their contacts with Western culture and greed and have been frustrated about their lack of control over their lands and their heritage. Recognition of the land rights of the first Australians has become a major political issue in recent years. Reconciliation between black and white Australians is a crucial issue yet to be resolved. Some have adapted to the invading culture, but many have been marginalized, and others have retreated into the more inaccessible and inhospitable parts of the country. There are a number of areas, especially in the north and west of the country where there are strong congregations with effective outreach.

a) **Pray for the Aboriginal Evangelical Fellowship**, a key coordinating body of Aboriginal Christians, as it encourages leadership development through its training college, outreach and church planting in every Aboriginal community. Pray that believers may boldly proclaim the liberating power of the gospel in the face of hostility from political activists.

b) **Pray for the nearly 500 missionaries** in 26 denominational and interdenominational agencies working among these people (such as the Aborigine Inland Mission, United Aborigine Mission, **CMS** and **MAF**).

c) **Bible translation** is in progress in 19 of these small language groups (through the 38 **SIL** and **UBS** workers); 26 languages have a portion of the New Testament. About 13 may still need translators.

d) **The use of GRN records and cassettes** in 86 languages is a vital contribution to the task because of the great linguistic variety among the Aborigines.

7 Witness among the 630,000 students in the 36 universities and colleges is barely adequate. AFES (**IFES**) with 70 groups, Student Life (**CCCI**), and the **Navigators** and Students for Christ are significant campus ministries, but the overall impact on student bodies is not large. Pray for a greater evangelistic zeal, a larger harvest for the Kingdom, and an increased flow of missionaries to the world from these groups.

8 **Young people and children**. There has been a drastic drop in Sunday School attendance, and alternative methods must be found to reach the younger generation. The Christian school systems are growing rapidly. The Inter-Schools Christian Fellowship (SU) has a valuable ministry in secondary schools. In every State but South Australia religious instruction is conducted in schools by volunteers from the churches. Many groups, such as Youth For Christ, the Crusader Movement, God Squad and others are seeking to evangelize young people. The innovative Fusion Ministries has developed a well-researched and culturally relevant range of ministries to youth and to families based in 25 centres with 200 full-time workers across the country.

9 Christian Media

a) *Radio*. This could be more effectively utilized by Evangelicals through the national and local broadcasting networks, which are required, by law, to give a percentage of time weekly to religious broadcasts. Several explicitly Christian radio stations are attempting to obtain broadcasting licenses. Funding is a big bottleneck.

b) *Literature*. There are 300 Christian bookstores (9 of **CLC**) in Australia. Pray for literature to impact the younger generation of Christians. The evangelistic and teaching materials produced by **The Bible Society**, **SGM**, ACTS International and World Home Bible League are especially worthy of prayer support.

c) *Video*. Create International based in Perth produces Christian videos of great value in witnessing. The *JESUS* film is being used in an innovative plan to focus on ethnic minorities called "JESUS: Gift to the Nation".

Austria

Republic of Austria

FEBRUARY 20-21
EUROPE

GEOGRAPHY
Area 83,855 sq.km. Landlocked. The Alps, in the south and west; flat plains along the Danube River in the east.

Population	Ann. Gr.	Density
2000	8,210,520	0.52%	98 per sq. km.
2010	8,347,849	0.06%	100 per sq. km.
2025	8,185,725	-0.23%	98 per sq. km.

Capital Vienna 2,072,000 — over 25% of the population. **Urbanites** 65%.

PEOPLES
Indigenous 93%. German-speaking 7,635,000; Gypsy 9,200.
Immigrants and Refugees 7%. Former Yugoslavian (Albanian, Slovene, Croat, Bosnian, Serb) 240,000, Turks 100,000; Other EU 100,000; Roma (Gypsy) 40,000; Kurd 25,000; Arab 4,000; Iranian 3,000; Chinese 2,000.

Literacy 100%. **Official language** German.

ECONOMY
Predominantly industrial. Many trade and commercial links with the developing economies of Central Europe. Over 10% of the workforce is foreign. **HDI** 0.904; 16ᵗʰ/174. **Public debt** 54% of GNP. **Income/person** $26,890 (89% of USA).

POLITICS
The heart of the former Austro-Hungarian Empire until 1918. A multi-party democratic republic. A neutral buffer state between West and East from 1945 to 1990. A member of the EU. The FPÖ, a nationalist right-wing party, grew and became part of a coalition government leading to increased pressure on the large immigrant population and severe restrictions on further immigration.

RELIGION
The relationship between the state and the Catholic/Reformed Churches is defined in the constitution. Freedom of religion was restricted by new legislation in 1998 when conditions for formal recognition of newer and smaller religious groups were made more difficult. This has impacted all evangelical groups.

Religions	Population %	Adherents	Ann.Gr.
Christian	89.77	7,370,584	+0.2%
non-Religious/other	7.68	634,700	+3.7%
Muslim	2.23	183,095	+3.8%
Jewish	0.10	8,211	+8.0%

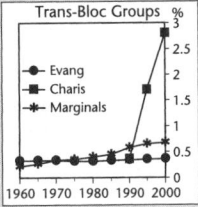

Buddhist	0.06	4,926	+25%
Baha'i	0.05	4,105	+21%
Hindu	0.03	2,463	+9.0%
Chinese religions	0.02	1,642	+0.5%

Christians	Denom.	Affil.%	,000	Ann. Gr.
Protestant	38	4.47	367	-0.7%
Independent	6	0.42	35	+0.2%
Anglican	1	0.04	3	+1.4%
Catholic	1	71.37	5,860	-1.8%
Orthodox	11	1.89	155	+3.8%
Marginal	18	0.79	65	+2.8%
Unaffiliated		10.79	885	n.a.

Churches	MegaBloc	Cong.	Members	Affiliates
Catholic	C	3,048	1,930,000	5,860,000
Lutheran	P	199	167,500	335,000
Jehovah's Witnesses	M	299	20,577	37,039
Old Catholic	I	14	8,000	23,000
Protestant Reformed	P	9	7,800	10,381
New Apostolic	I	3	5,100	10,200
Seventh-day Adventist	P	67	3,700	7,100
Latter-day Saints (Morm)	M	10	3,259	4,400
Free Christian (AoG)	P	36	2,150	3,750
Anglican	A	8	1,240	3,100
Federation of Baptist	P	18	1,101	1,982
Evangelical Free [19]	P	70	1,200	1,716

Evang Methodists	P	8	700	1,500
Other denoms [47]		272	115,749	176,424
Total Christians [78]		4,061	2,272,000	6,476,000

Trans-bloc Groupings	pop. %	,000	Ann.Gr.
Evangelical	0.4	30	+1.3%
Charismatic	2.8	230	-1.4%
Pentecostal	0.1	6	+8.%

Missionaries from Austria
P,I,A 69 in 18 agencies to 26 countries: Austria 19, Papua New Guinea 5, Sudan 4, Malawi 4.

Missionaries to Austria
P,I,A 539 in 70 agencies from 21 countries: USA 248, Germany 95, UK 48, Canada 35, Switzerland 27.
C 10.

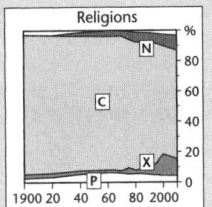

• Challenges for Prayer

1 Austria is a cultured nation famed for its music, art and beautiful scenery. Yet Austrians need a personal faith in Christ, and only a small minority have clearly heard how they may find one. Over 75% of the population is Christian in name, but with no meaningful link with any church, yet an estimated 80% have had dealings with the occult. The high suicide, abortion and alcoholism statistics indicate the spiritual need. Pray for this nation to be set free by the power of Jesus.

2 Austria is Catholic by culture, not commitment. The annual membership loss accelerated in the 1990s to 35-40,000. The number of priests has declined and the priesthood has been stained by prominent sex scandals. Twelve years of religious education during childhood 'inoculates' the population against vital personal faith in Christ and results in rejection of both the Catholic Church and any others. In 1539 over 90% of Austrians were following the Reformation; today 3% of the younger generation go to church. There is a small renewal movement in the Catholic Church. Pray that prejudice and antipathy may be broken down.

3 New legislation restricting the rights and privileges of smaller religions and churches further marginalize the many small and struggling evangelical fellowships. Especially in rural areas, those who seek the Lord are ostracized or pressured so that few dare seek for personal salvation. Pray for legal and social barriers to the gospel to be demolished.

4 The Lutheran and Reformed Churches are declining by nearly 1% annually (3,000 adherents lost every year). Formalism and tradition have little attraction for the younger generation. There are a number of Bible-believing pastors, but nominalism is even more prevalent than in the Catholic Church. Pray for ABCÖ, a group of evangelical pastors and lay leaders which seeks to deepen spiritual life and combat theological liberalism within the Lutheran Church. Pray too for a move of the Spirit of God in these churches that will make them a force for the evangelization of the land.

5 Newer evangelical/Pentecostal churches are few and small in number, but growing. During the 1980s, congregations almost doubled in number, rising from 57 to 97, and attendances tripled, but in the 1990s this growth slowed. Born-again believers in these

A churches and in the mainline denominations combined may still number less than 20,000. Pray for the multiplication of congregations where the Lord Jesus Christ is proclaimed and honoured. Pray also for the efforts of both the **Evangelical Alliance** (ÖEA) and the **Fellowship of Evangelical Congregations in Austria** (ARGEGÖ) to bring more cooperative action to the fragmented evangelical cause.

6 **Pastors for the congregations** are needed. Too few Austrians enter full-time Christian service, and even fewer go as missionaries to other lands. Too many rely on foreigners. BAÖ (Bible Training on Location), a de-centralized programme of non-formal courses based in Vienna, has 450 students receiving training. Pray for the expansion of **BAÖ** in Austria and beyond. Pray also for EBÖ, a second TEE-type programme launched in 2001. Pray for God to raise up people with a passion for the Kingdom, for holiness, and for people to be won.

7 **Less reached sections** of the population:

a) *Provinces*: Lower Austria and Burgenland in the east, Styria in the southeast and Voralberg and Tyrol in the west have fewer Evangelicals.

b) *Towns*: In 1985, there were 55 towns of over 5,000 people without an evangelical witness. There has only been a small improvement since then.

c) *Cultists*: The aggressive activities of New Age movements, Eastern cults, Jehovah's Witnesses (more numerous than evangelicals) and Mormons have gained a considerable following among younger people. Pray both for the nullification of these efforts and for the release of those ensnared.

8 **Refugees** have flooded into Austria since WWII — from Communism up to 1990 and, later, from the Yugoslav wars and economic hardships in Central Europe. Many have integrated into Austrian society. Pray that Austrian believers may reach out to these strangers in their midst.

a) *The six ethnic groups of the former Yugoslavia*. There are several evangelical congregations, but these peoples are some of the least reached of Europe.

b) *Muslim Turks, Kurds, Arabs and Iranians*. Among them only one group of believers is known.

9 **Expatriate missionaries** have declined in numbers through attrition and visa restrictions. Major agencies are **IT** (43 workers), **OM** (42), **Christian Brethren** (39), **CBI** (31), **TEAM** (28), **YWAM** (27), **GEM** (20), **ECM** (19), **CEF** (16), **AoG** (12). The majority of churches planted have been through the ministry of expatriates in winning and discipling Austrians. Progress is slow, but the spiritual need remains great. Pray for perseverance, expectation of a coming harvest and fruitfulness for these missionaries.

10 **Witness among the 222,000 students** is one of the most fruitful in the land today. Over half of these are in Vienna, where there are also 15,000 international students. Strong groups in the seven universities are growing in depth and outreach. Pray that these young Christians may have an impact on the land and its churches. Pray also for the ministries of ÖSM (**IFES**), **CCC** and **Navigators** on the campuses of Austria. Both CEF (with 18 workers) and SU have an appreciated, but limited, ministry to school-age children.

11 **Media ministries** for prayer:

a) *Literature ministries*. Scripture distribution by **The Bible Society** and the literature ministries of Austrian Bible Mission and **CLC** all need prayer. The Bible is used as a textbook in schools and supplied free to every child.

b) *The JESUS film* has been seen by about 17% of the population.

c) *Radio*. TWR broadcasts in German via the Astra satellite and over Radio Tirana in Albania.

Azerbaijan
Republic of Azerbaijan

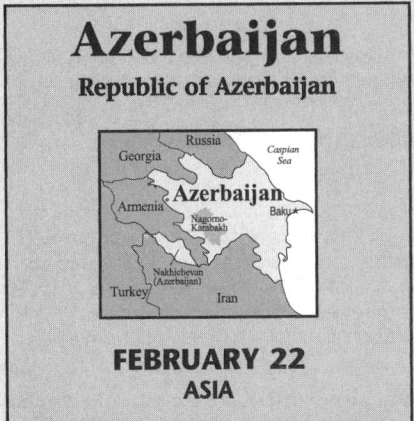

FEBRUARY 22

ASIA

GEOGRAPHY
Area 86,600 sq.km. Caucasian republic on the Caspian Sea, including a 5,632 sq.km. enclave, Nakhichevan, between Armenia and Iran, and the disputed 4,400 sq.km. region of Nagorno-Karabakh currently controlled by Armenia.

Population	Ann.Gr.	Density
2000	7,734,015	+0.45%	89 per sq. km.
2010	8,411,360	+0.91%	97 per sq. km.
2025	9,402,570	+0.57%	109 per sq. km.

Capital Baku 1,946,000. **Urbanites** 53%.

PEOPLES
Turkic 89%. Azerbaijani 6,830,000; Tatar 33,000; Turkish 20,000. One million Azeri live in other parts of the fSU, and a further 15m in Iran.
Indo-European 6.6%. Russian 230,000; Armenian 155,000; Ukrainian 30,000. In decline through emigration.
Caucasus peoples 3.4%. Lezhgi 173,000; Avar 50,000; Georgian 16,000; Tsakhur 14,000; Udi 3,000.
Indo-Iranian 1%. Tat (Jewish and Muslim) 33,000; Talysh 22,000; Kurds 14,000.

Literacy 97%. **Official language** Azerbaijani (with 20 dialects). **All languages** 16. **Languages with Scriptures** 2Bi 6NT 4por 6w.i.p.

ECONOMY
Oil-dominated economy with large reserves under the Caspian Sea. Baku was the world's original oil-boom city a century ago. The post-Communist switch to a market economy has been marred by bureaucracy, organized crime, rampant corruption, collapse of oil prices, ecological disasters and the effects of the war with Armenia. The majority of the population live in poverty. Living standards are steadily deteriorating. **HDI** 0.695; 103rd/174. **Public debt** 6% of GNP. **Income/person** $480 (1.6% of USA).

POLITICS
A long history of subjugation by Arabs, Mongols, Persians, Turks and Russians. Independent in 1991 from the USSR. It's first decade has been difficult — internal coups and war with Armenia over the largely Armenian-populated enclave of Nagorno-Karabakh in West Azerbaijan. Armenia occupies 20% of Azeri territory. Over one million Azeris have become refugees. Pan-Turkism and affinity with Turkey and the West, as well as a desire to escape Russian political manipulation, determine government policy.

RELIGION
Official religious freedom is tempered by reaction against 'Christian' Russian and Armenian hostility, and fears of Islamist extremism. Foreigners are prohibited from engaging in 'religious propaganda'. Muslims are largely either Shi'a (70%) or Sunni (30% — in the north).

Religions	Population %	Adherents	Ann.Gr.
Muslim	83.67	6,471,050	+0.7%
non-Religious	11.31	874,717	-0.7%
Christian	4.63	358,085	-0.3%
Jewish	0.37	28,616	-1.6%
Baha'i	0.02	1,547	n.a.

Christians	Denom.	Affil.%	,000	Ann.Gr.
Protestant	2	0.02	2	+2.6%
Independent	4	0.05	4	+8.7%
Catholic	1	0.10	8	-0.5%
Orthodox	3	4.46	345	+1.1%

Churches	MegaBloc	Cong.	Members	Affiliates
Armenian Apostolic	O	14	126,374	230,000
Russian Orthodox	O	9	68,182	105,000
Catholic	C	7	4,360	7,500
Word of Life	I	2	700	1,150
Seventh-day Adventist	P	5	600	900
Baptist	P	15	500	770
Other denoms [9]		6	7,807	12,450
Total Christians [15]		58	208,523	358,000

Trans-bloc Groupings	pop.%	,000	Ann.Gr.
Evangelical	0.1	11	+3.9%
Charismatic	0.1	10	+3.6%
Pentecostal	0.0	1	+10.0%

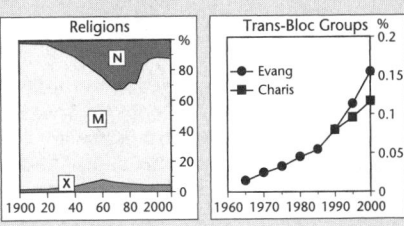

• Answers to Prayer

1 For the first time there are now **Azeri churches** and possibly 2,000 Azeri believ-ers in the country. In 1990 there were estimated to be only 40 Azeri believers in the world.

2 A decade of relative freedom for the gospel despite opposition.

• Challenges for Prayer

1 **Azerbaijan's political situation is complex and potentially dangerous.** The unresolved conflict with Armenia and the growing international confrontation between Armenia, Russia and Iran on one side and Azerbaijan, Turkey, Georgia and NATO countries on the other over the exploitation and transport of oil could lead to war. Pray for peace with a just resolution of the Nagorno-Karabakh conflict—a legacy of Stalin's border re-alignments.

2 **Christianity is associated with Russian imperialism and Armenian occu-pation** of much of Azeri territory. Post-independence openness to the gospel has been diminished by resentment, rising nationalism, legal restrictions on proselytising and the propaganda of Islamists. Pray that these hindrances may be bound in the name of Jesus and that many Azeris find peace with God.

3 **Azerbaijani believers continue to increase in number**. Many are in Baku where there are several congregations with a majority of Azeris. Pray for the maturing of upcoming Azeri leaders, their growth in ministry and for good fellowship among them. There are several small Bible schools in Baku. There needs to be better coordination of train-ing ministries. Pray for a strong Church with an effective witness to non-Christians.

4 **The majority of Christians are Russian-speaking** or from other ethnic minori-ties. Some evangelical churches have had great difficulty in obtaining official recognition and permission to find places for worship. Pray for their witness to the major-ity Muslim population that it may be with humility, sensitivity and love.

5 **Nagorno-Karabakh and its surrounding area** is almost entirely Armenian. Armenia began the expulsion of Azeris from Armenia in 1987-88, then the Armenians of Nagorno-Karabakh attempted to have its sovereignty transferred to Armenia. Due to the unstable situation created by the influx of refugees from Armenia, and the death throes of the Soviet Union, agitators were able to exploit the situation. This led to the massacre of Armenians in Sumgayit in 1989, provoking the Armenians of Nagorno-Karabakh to declare independence in 1990, culminating in warfare. Armenia wants to annex the region which is impoverished and deeply affected economically and socially by the war. Orthodox churches have been re-established but there is little known non-Orthodox evangelical wit-ness. Pray for the gospel to be proclaimed, forgiveness given and received and a Christian lifestyle to be manifested to their Muslim neighbours.

6 **Expatriate Christians** have difficulty obtaining visas, but a number are seeking to live for the Lord through secular openings and NGO projects. They are forbidden to engage in 'religious propaganda'. Pray for the calling and entry of new workers and the long-term fruitfulness of their ministries despite the restrictions.

7 **The Unreached:**

a) *Most of the Azerbaijani towns and villages* have never been evangelized.

b) In 2000 there were still *600,000 homeless and largely unemployed refugees* from Arme-nia and Nagorno-Karabakh. Pray for compassionate ministry to them.

c) *The Caucasus peoples* are almost all Muslim and unevangelized. The only exceptions are the Georgians and Udi who are traditionally Christian. Pray for the Lezhgi, Avar and Tsakhur peoples.

d) *The Indo-Iranian speaking minorities* of Tat, Talysh and Kurds are unreached.

8 Christian help ministries. Pray for the impact of:

a) *Christian literature.* The Azeri NT and Children's Bible as well as the Russian Bible are widely available for sale. There are 11 Azeri Christian titles printed and 25 in preparation. It is hard to import adequate stocks of new publications or to print them locally. Pray for obstacles and restrictions to be removed and permission to publish books to be granted. A Christian bookstore has opened in Baku.

b) Bible translation. The Azeri Bible in both N. and S. Azeri should be completed by 2002. There are 5 languages that need assessment for NT translation. Work is in progress in Avar, Jewish and Muslim Tat, Lezhgi and Tsakhur. Pray for their successful publishing and distribution.

c) Christian radio. **World by 2000** languages: Azeri (**FEBA** fl hour), Kurmanji (**TWR** fi hour) and Georgian (**HCJB**/hour) are broadcast weekly. **IBRA** Radio has enabled local recording and distributing of audio and video cassettes. Pray for local and national opportunities to broadcast Christian material regularly. A major need is a radio station to deliver medium wave signals internationally.

d) The JESUS film is available in Avar, N. Azeri, Kurmanji, Lezhgi, Russian and Talysh.

Bahamas

Commonwealth of the Bahamas

FEBRUARY 23
LATIN AMERICA

 GEOGRAPHY
Area 14,000 sq.km. An archipelago of 700 coral islands between Florida and Cuba. Forty are inhabited.

Population	Ann.Gr.	Density
2000	306,529	+1.80%	22 per sq. km.
2010	354,213	+1.34%	25 per sq. km.
2025	414,631	+0.98%	30 per sq. km.

Capital Nassau 162,179. **Urbanites** 86%.

PEOPLES

Afro-Caribbean 85%. Haitian refugees and their descendants 20,000.
Euro-American 12%.
Other 3%. Hispanic 2,000; Jews 900; S. Asians 300.
Literacy 98%. **Official language** English.

ECONOMY
Tourism and banking are very important. Drug trafficking has declined through better policing. **Unemployment** 10%. **HDI** 0.851; 31ˢᵗ/174. **Public debt** 43% of GNP. **Income/person** $11,380 (38% of USA).

POLITICS
Independent from Britain in 1973 as a parliamentary monarchy. A stable democracy since 1992.

RELIGION
Complete freedom of religion.

Religions	Population %	Adherents	Ann.Gr.
Christian	92.39	283,202	+1.7%
non-Religious/other	5.30	16,246	+3.4%
Traditional ethnic	1.55	4,751	+3.9%
Baha'i	0.40	1,226	+7.8%
Jewish	0.30	920	+1.8%
Chinese	0.06	184	+1.8%

Christians	Denom.	Affil.%	,000	Ann.Gr.
Protestant	23	54.52	167	+1.5%
Independent	12	6.20	19	+3.6%
Anglican	1	8.81	27	-0.2%
Catholic	1	15.66	48	+1.2%
Orthodox	1	0.12	0	-0.3%
Marginal	4	1.60	5	+1.2%
Unaffiliated		5.48	17	n.a.

Churches	MegaBloc	Cong.	Members	Affiliates
Baptist Union	P	211	57,000	78,400
Catholic	C	30	27,429	48,000
Anglican	A	95	11,345	27,000
Seventh-day Adventist	P	43	15,000	21,000
Methodist	P	92	7,207	16,000
Ch of God (Anderson)	P	38	3,795	11,500
Ch of God (Cleveland)	P	75	4,800	9,000
Ch of God of Prophecy	P	55	3,457	7,500
Baptist Int'l Missions	P	19	4,100	6,300
Assemblies of God	P	28	1,676	6,200
Jehovah's Witnesses	M	24	1,450	4,205
Christian Brethren	P	70	2,800	4,000
Ch of the Nazarene	P	11	1,400	2,000
Other denoms [29]		81	5,487	25,307
Total Christians [42]		872	146,946	266,412

Trans-bloc Groupings	pop.%	,000	Ann.Gr.
Evangelical	30.8	95	+1.7%
Charismatic	14.0	43	+1.8%
Pentecostal	8.5	26	+2.2%

Missionaries from Bahamas
P,I,A 2 in one agency.

Missionaries to Bahamas
P,I,A 54 in 14 agencies from 4 countries: USA 46, Canada 4.
C 120. M 20.

B

• Answers to Prayer

1 **The morally crippling impact** of the large drug trafficking trade of the 1970s and '80s has greatly diminished.

• Challenges for Prayer

1 **Materialism stimulated by tourism and drug money** has deeply affected every level of society. Nearly all Bahamians claim to be Christian, but nominalism is widespread. A 55% illegitimacy rate, widespread drug addiction and family breakdown are symptoms of spiritual need. Pray for God-glorifying changes.

2 **Among Christians, commitment is low** despite the large percentage of Evangelicals in the country. Few are willing to commit themselves to the Lord's work, and many congregations are without adequate pastoral care. Pray for revival, and for a missionary vision among believers.

Bahrain

The State of Bahrain

FEBRUARY 23
ASIA

GEOGRAPHY
Area 691 sq.km. A group of one larger and 34 smaller barren islands in the Arabian Gulf between the Qatar peninsula and Saudi Arabian mainland — linked to the latter by a causeway.

Population		Ann. Gr.	Density
2000	617,217	+2.05%	893 per sq. km.
2010	713,145	+1.35%	1,032 per sq.km.
2025	858,368	+1.11%	1,242 per sq.km.

Capital Manama 376,456. **Urbanites** 90%.

PEOPLES
Arab 65.4%. Bahraini 380,000; Other Arab (Saudi, Palestinian, Egyptian, etc.) 25,000.

Iranian 12%. Farsi, Kurds, etc.
South Asian 13%. Indian (Malayali, Tamil, Telugu, etc.) Pakistani 30,000.
Other Asian 6.4%. Filipino, Korean, etc.
European 2%. UK 7,000; USA 3,500.
Other 1.2%.

Literacy 85%. **Official language** Arabic.

ECONOMY
Diversification from oil production to oil refining, aluminium (the world's largest smelter) manufacturing and banking. Nearly half the labour force is foreign. **HDI** 0.832; 37th/174. **Public debt** 62% of GNP. **Income/person** $8,330 (27% of USA).

POLITICS
British Protectorate until 1971. Absolute monarchy between 1975 and 2001. The Amir ruled with the help of an appointed Cabinet and Consultative Council. Every attempt at political expression by the disenfranchised Shi'a majority was vigorously repressed. In 2001 the new Amir committed the country to a constitutional monarchy and democratic government to be instituted in 2003.

RELIGION
Islam is the official religion, and all Bahrainis are considered Muslim. No evangelism among them is permitted. The ruling elite are Sunni Muslims, but 61% of the population are Shi'a. Expatriate Christians are free to worship together.

Religions	Population %	Adherents	Ann. Gr.
Muslim	82.31	508,031	+2.1%
Christian	10.36	63,944	+3.4%
Hindu	6.25	38,576	-0.7%
non-Religious/other	0.69	4,259	+0.6%
Baha'i	0.22	1,358	+3.1%
Jewish	0.10	617	+2.1%
Buddhist	0.07	432	+8.6%

Christians	Denom.	Affil.%	,000	Ann.Gr.
Protestant	5	0.82	5	+3.4%
Independent	20	2.29	14	+6.2%
Anglican	1	0.49	3	+0.3%
Catholic	2	4.05	25	+1.9%
Orthodox	2	0.36	2	+0.0%
Marginal	1	0.01	0	+9.1%
Unaffiliated		2.34	15	n.a.

Churches	MegaBloc	Cong.	Members	Affiliates
Catholic	C	11	5,750	23,000
Anglican	A	10	1,796	3,000
Coptic Orthodox	O	1		800	2,000

		P	21	1,138	1,900
National Evang		P	21	1,138	1,900
Pentecostal groups [6]		I	9	450	900
Other denoms [21]			59	7,105	18,679
Total Christians [31]			111	17,039	49,479

Trans-bloc Groupings pop. %		,000	Ann.Gr.
Evangelical	3.1	19	+5.1%
Charismatic	2.4	15	+3.6%
Pentecostal	1.3	8	+4.0%

B

Missionaries from Bahrain n.a.

Expatriates to Bahrain
P,I,A 45 from 5 countries.

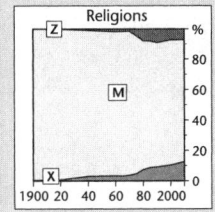

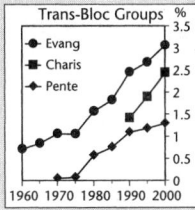

• Challenges for Prayer

1 **Bahrain is a political and spiritual key** for the whole Gulf area — more so since the Gulf War in 1991. Islam impacts life less comprehensively than in surrounding states. Pray that democratic and religious freedoms might be fully implemented.

2 **Bahrain has provided a good base** for Christian ministry for over a century. The American Mission Hospital is well known and highly regarded. Pray that this may continue and that there may be fruit from the tactful witness of believers.

3 **The largest Arab Christian community** in the Gulf states is here — most being expatriate. There are several informal networks of these believers. Pray for them and their witness.

4 **Amongst the large expatriate community**, predominantly from South and East Asia and also the West, are a considerable number of active Christians meeting formally and informally. Pray that individuals may have courage and wisdom to share their faith outside their own cultural group.

5 **The labour force of nearly 200,000** is 58% expatriate, and drawn from 45 nations. Amid the prevailing concern for material things, pray that Christians within some of these national groups may win people for Christ. The less evangelized of these expatriate communities are the Iranians, Hindus and Muslims from India and Pakistan. Nearly half the congregations and house groups are Indian.

6 Media Ministries:

a) *Christian Radio*. **FEBA** Radio broadcasts 14 hrs/week in Arabic from Seychelles and is developing a specialized simple English service. **TWR** also broadcasts from Cyprus.

b) *Christian literature*. The Christian bookstore in Manama is well visited and has a Gulf-wide distribution.

Bangladesh

People's Republic of Bangladesh

FEBRUARY 24-26

ASIA

GEOGRAPHY
Area 143,998 sq.km. Occupies the delta and floodplains of the Ganges and Brahmaputra Rivers, with high rainfall and frequent flooding.

Population	Ann.Gr.	Density
2000	129,155,152	+1.72%	897 per sq. km.
2010	151,799,126	+1.55%	1,054 per sq. km.
2025	178,751,214	+0.99%	1,241 per sq. km.

Capital Dhaka 10,979,000. Other major city: Chittagong 2,289,000. **Urbanites** 20%.

PEOPLES
All ethnic groups 61.
Bengali (Bangla) 96.9%. Muslims and Hindus have distinct cultures and dialects. Other related groups: Sylheti 7.06 mill; Hajong 36,000; Rajbangsi 15,000.
Other South Asian 2%. Urdu 907,000; Hindi 451,000; Bihari 260,000; Burmese 300,000; Arakanese (Mogh) 200,000; Rohingya (refugees from Myanmar) 200,000.
Tribal 1.1%. Over 35 groups. Most Tibeto-Burman, some Austro-Asiatic in origin. Largest: Chakma 352,000; Garo(5) 250,000; Khasi 242,000; Santal 157,000; Tripuri(3) 152,000; Tipera 100,000; Mru(Chin,10) 54,000; Oraon 31,000.
Literacy 38%. **Official language** Bangla; English often used. **All languages** 35. **Languages with Scriptures** 13Bi 8NT 3por 3w.i.p.

ECONOMY
One of the world's poorest nations, suffering from gross over-population and periodic natural disasters such as devastating floods and cyclones with enormous loss of life and property. There seems little hope that the poverty of this land will ever be substantially alleviated. Major sources of foreign exchange are aid, textiles, clothing, jute and funds sent home from Bengalis working abroad. Over 55% live below the poverty line. **Under-employment** over 50%. **HDI** 0.440; 150th/174. **Public debt** 33% of GNP. **Income/person** $360 (1% of USA).

POLITICS
For 24 years part of Pakistan. Independence in 1971 after a bitter civil war. Political instability thereafter with assassinations, 18 military coups and a nine-year military dictatorship which ended in 1991. A restored democracy has been marred by the bitter dispute between the two ambitious women who dominated the political scene during the 1990s. The prevailing corruption, cronyism, strikes and unrest have hindered political and economic progress. The opposition party has taken a stronger Islamist line with demands for *shari'a* law.

RELIGION
A secular state 1971-88. Islam declared the state religion in 1988. Officially there is religious freedom, but this is being steadily eroded by Islamist pressure and a legal system which gives no safeguards to ethnic or religious minorities. The Islamists are a strong and growing minority.

Religions	Population %	Adherents	Ann.Gr.
Muslim	85.63	110,556,810	+1.8%
Hindu	12.38	15,989,408	+1.5%
Christian	0.72	929,917	+3.2%
Buddhist	0.62	800,762	+2.0%
Traditional ethnic	0.57	736,184	+2.4%
non-Religious/other	0.08	103,324	-15.3%

Christians	Denom.	Affil.%	,000	Ann.Gr.
Protestant	24	0.17	215	+3.0%
Independent	11	0.37	476	+2.6%
Catholic	1	0.18	235	+3.0%

Included are thousands of true followers of Jesus who have not left their culturally Hindu or Muslim identities.

Churches	MegaBloc	Cong.	Members	Affiliates
Indigenous groups	I		118,000	360,000
Catholic	C	81	129,121	235,000
Bangla. Baptist Fell	P	518	16,498	40,000
Seventh-day Adventist	P	100	13,000	29,510
Bangla. Baptist Sangha	P	325	12,500	28,000
All One in Christ Fell	I	138	11,000	27,500
Garo Baptist Union	P	156	11,960	23,900
New Apostolic	I	50	10,000	20,000
Evang Christian	P	50	6,557	16,000
Assemblies of God	P	160	5,000	14,000
Ch of Bangladesh	P	43	4,755	13,600
Evang Lutheran [2]	P	126	5,028	9,000
Evang Ch of Bangla.	P	92	3,689	9,000
Presbyterian Synod	P	98	3,911	7,000
Free Baptist	I	84	2,102	7,000
Other denoms [27]		650	36,340	94,417
Total Christians [43]		2,748	389,794	930,000

Trans-bloc Groupings	pop. %	,000	Ann.Gr.
Evangelical	0.4	584	+2.8%
Charismatic	0.3	400	+2.4%
Pentecostal	0.0	16	-6.3%

Missionaries from Bangladesh
P,I,A 407 in 11 agencies in 5 countries: Bangladesh 401.

Expatriates in Bangladesh
P,I,A 428 in 65 agencies from: USA 170, Korea 46,
Canada 27, Norway 25, Finland 21, NZ 21. C 400.

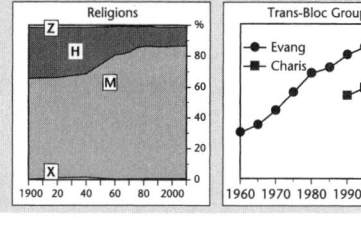

• Answers to Prayer

1 **A continued relative openness to the gospel** continues despite, or even because of, the increased Islamist propaganda and violence, disillusionment with politicians and a series of natural mega-disasters. Pray the openness may increase and yield an abundant harvest.

2 **Continued church growth** and the emergence of many new, younger church leaders during the 1990s.

3 **Indigenous and international NGOs** such as the Grameen Bank, WVI and HEED, have made a significant contribution towards reducing poverty through micro loans and self-help schemes for the very poor.

• Challenges for Prayer

1 **The downward spiral of poverty and suffering** cannot be reversed without good, honest and impartial leadership for the nation. The majority of the population is illiterate, malnourished and without adequate medical care. Pray for political stability and a government that is courageous to stand against Islamist demands for increased Islamization and against corruption. It also needs to make tough decisions to improve the quality of life for all.

2 **Discrimination against ethnic and religious minorities**, under pressure from extremist Muslim groups, has increased. Christians, Hindus and Buddhists suffer many disadvantages and there have been cases of destruction of churches and persecution of Christians for their faith. Pray for the binding of the powers of darkness operating in the religious, social and ethnic realms. Pray also that constitutional freedom for all to practise and propagate their own religions might be maintained.

3 **The churches have been growing** at twice the population rate over the past 40 years. Though still constituting officially only 0.3% of the population, they are having an increasing impact on society. Over 80% are literate. Pray specifically for:

a) *Growing churches* such as the Bangladesh Baptist Fellowship, Assemblies of God and the Bangladesh Free Baptist churches which have set bold outreach goals for the future.

b) *The Great Commission Movement*, launched in 1991, which brought together evangelical congregations with the commitment to prayer, research and cooperation in planting a church in every one of the 464 sub-districts and each of the ethnic groups of the country by the year 2000. Pray that this momentum might be maintained.

c) *The people-movement tribal churches*. Nearly all the Bawm, Pankhu, Garo and most of the Oraon, Mahili and Khasi have become Christian, and the Santal and Munda peoples have a large and growing minority of Christians. Pray that these churches may become strong, mature and full of missions vision.

d) *The churches among sections of the Hindu* population. Response has largely been among the Namasudra and Muchi castes. Pray that these Christians may be able to reach other Hindu castes still little affected by the gospel.

4 **Revival of the Church** is the greatest need. Pray that the Holy Spirit may move in these areas:

a) *Nominal Christianity*. Early people movements brought thousands of marginalized sections of society into the Church. Poverty, illiteracy and lack of trained and godly leadership have led to shallowness and nominalism.

b) *Unity*. Imported and indigenous divisions have hindered the effectiveness of witness in the past. Pray for the National Christian Fellowship of Bangladesh as it seeks to encourage evangelical unity and cooperative action in evangelism, teaching and aid programmes.

c) **Outreach**. After years of little interest, there is growing involvement in reaching out to the major non-Christian communities.

B

5 **Leadership for the churches**. God is raising up a new generation of leaders who exercise a ministry beyond their own community, yet they are few. Pray for multiplication of leaders.

a) **The College of Christian Theology**, the Christian Discipleship Centre and the Dhaka United Theological Seminary are key interdenominational residential schools. The CCT and CDC also run TEE and short-term programmes.

b) **Five denominational Bible schools and seminaries** (**AoG**, ABWE, Free Baptist, Lutheran and Church of Bangladesh).

6 **There are over 20,000 registered NGOs** which have multiplied to meet the land's deep social needs — Bangladesh may lead the world in the number, diversity and relative impact of NGOs on the life of the country. Indigenous secular NGOs such as the Grameen Bank have significantly improved the life of millions of the poor, and especially women, with self-help schemes and loans. Christian NGOs have administered aid since independence and, during the nation's frequent natural calamities, have been generous and impartial. HEED and **World Vision** seek to uphold Christian values and prepare the way for local church and mission involvement. **TEAR Fund** seconds workers and helps in funding projects. Pray for wisdom and sensitivity for all involved in implementing these programmes — that aid not be perceived as manipulative or dependency-producing.

7 **Bengali people** are by far the largest unreached people in the world with a global total of over 230 million. The majority live in Bangladesh and India, but large communities live in Britain, USA, etc. It was to the Bengali that William Carey went as a missionary. Although they revere Carey's memory, the great breakthrough has still not come after 200 years. Now could be the time for the Bengali people! Many are torn between being good Bengali and good Muslims. Pray specifically for:

a) **Muslims, who number over 110 million**. The majority follow 'folk' Islam — a blend of indigenous culture and Hinduism, overlaid by a thin blanket of Islam. Pray for:

i *Openness to the gospel* — the vast majority have never heard the true gospel.

ii *More workers* — in 1985 there were only 25 committed to their evangelization. There has been some improvement since then, but both needs and opportunities are greater.

iii *Those who have responded*. Thousands have come to trust in Jesus. Many of these continue to live in their communities. Pray for great wisdom in nurturing this movement; its leadership, worship patterns and cultural relevance without compromise of biblical truth. Pray for unity to develop and for leaders to model confession and forgiveness. Pray they would learn dependence on God in poverty, firmness under persecution from Muslim neighbours, evangelistic vision and positive relationships with the older Christian community from a different cultural background.

b) **The Hindus** who feel vulnerable as a religious minority. Their insecurity increased during the time of the Babri Mosque crisis in India when Muslims retaliated by destroying Hindu temples. Pray that this may open many to the truth of Jesus. Many thousands of followers of Jesus remain within the Hindu context and do not link up with 'foreign' Christian bodies. Of the 29 lower castes, only four are over 2% Christians, and in a further six there has been a smaller response. The upper castes have remained resistant to the gospel.

8 **The tribal peoples'** very existence is threatened by the general population explosion pushing hundreds of thousands of Bengali to invade their territory. The Chakma of the Chittagong Hill Tracts have responded with guerrilla warfare to the destruction of their villages, occupation of their land and even massacres by invading Bengali. Pray for a just settlement — the granting of limited autonomy to the region has not improved the situation much. Pray also for Christian agencies seeking to bring the tribal peoples to Christ (ABMS, BMS, **IMB-SBC**, Presbyterians and Lutherans).

9 Other unreached groups:

a) *Non-Christian tribal groups.* Some are resistant to the gospel or have not had adequate opportunity to hear: the animist Mru (work by Baptists), the Buddhist Chakma (Baptists), Mogh and Khyang (several thousand Christians).

b) *The Bihari Muslims* who, while being refused Bangladeshi citizenship, are also denied entry to India and Pakistan. They live in large refugee camps. Pray that their dilemma may bring an openness to the gospel.

c) *Rohingya Muslims.* In 1978 200,000 became refugees, and again in 1992, fleeing Myanmar government persecution. They have never been evangelized — pray for those seeking openings to reach them.

B

10 Young people are strategic but little is done to meet their spiritual needs.

a) *Over half the population is under 16*, most living in great poverty.

b) *Students number over 650,000* in 458 tertiary colleges. There are 600 Christian students in 17 groups led by two staff workers. It is not possible for them to meet on the campuses. Pray for real commitment among these believers and a vision for outreach.

11 Missions have been welcomed for their social uplift programmes — hence the emphasis on institutions and aid programmes — but too few are directly involved in evangelistic outreach and church planting. Pray for increased opportunities to fulfill their primary calling. Since 1980 limitations have been placed on missionaries, with all projects, plans and finances needing government approval and strict quotas placed on the number of missionaries allowed. Reinforcements with a vision for evangelism and discipling are needed, yet the expatriate force continues to dwindle. Pray for visas, patience with red tape, and strategic usefulness for the small missionary force in a pressurized situation. Some significant agencies are Association of Baptists for World Evangelization, Norwegian Santal Mission, Scandinavian Pentecostals, Mennonite Central Committee, **Interserve**, **IMB-SBC** and **SIM**.

12 Christian literature is in great demand because of the hunger created by:

a) *Widespread distribution* by **EHC** and ABWE, the latter with a large literature division.

b) *Bible Correspondence Courses* run by **SIM** and others; the former have a staff of 5 in Dhaka processing over 2,000 papers a month. Pray for these and all efforts to follow up contacts, and for many to be added to the churches. Pray for inspired, national writers and for efficient production of suitable evangelistic and teaching literature.

13 Distribution of Scripture portions and sales of Bibles have risen year by year. Pray specifically for:

a) *The Bible Society* and its extensive ministry of Scripture production.

b) *The wise distribution of the Scriptures* in the Bengali Muslim dialect. Many copies of the NT have been distributed since 1981. It has been well received and appreciated by Muslims, but initially met with opposition from some churches. A temporary ban on its import in 1990 enhanced sales. Praise for the publishing of the entire Bible in 2000.

c) *The translation of the Bible into tribal languages.* At least six, possibly nine, translations are needed; work is in progress in three of these.

14 Other Christian media are important since a high proportion of the population is illiterate. Pray for effective outreach through:

a) *Radio.* Christian broadcasters (**TWR**, **FEBC** and **FEBA**) transmit eight hours a week in Bengali and 88 hours in English. Pray especially for the production of suitable and sufficient programmes for the non-Christian majority.

b) *The JESUS film* has been used among Hindus and Muslims with good response. It is completed in Bangla, Sylheti, Assamese and nine tribal languages and is in preparation in five more. Pray for freedom to show the film in villages and for protection for the operators.

c) *Cassettes.* GRN have a team of recordists working on master tapes in indigenous languages; 21 languages have been recorded. Pray for the completion of the recordings in a further 13 languages and effective use of the finished product.

d) *Drama teams* are being used to communicate biblical truth to village people. A long tradition of village drama allows more freedom to raise questions and address social issues on the stage than in general society.

Barbados

St. Lucia

Barbados

Caribbean Sea

Bridgetown

North Atlantic Ocean

FEBRUARY 27

LATIN AMERICA

GEOGRAPHY
Area 430 sq.km. The most easterly of the Windward Islands.

Population	Ann.Gr.	Density
2000	270,449	+0.46%	629 per sq. km.
2010	282,304	+0.43%	657 per sq. km.
2025	296,753	+0.25%	690 per sq. km.

Capital Bridgetown 123,682. **Urbanites** 38%.

PEOPLES
Afro-Caribbean 92.5%.
Mixed 2.8%.
European-origin 3.2%.
Other 1.5%. South Asian, Chinese.

Literacy 98%. **Official language** English. Bajan is a distinctive Barbadian dialect of English.

ECONOMY
One of the more prosperous and successful island states of the Caribbean with an increasingly diverse economy based on tourism, sugar, light industry and off-shore banking. **HDI** 0.857; 29ᵗʰ/174. **Public debt** 118% of GNP. **Income/person** $8,380 (21% of USA).

POLITICS
Parliamentary government since 1647. Independent from Britain in 1966. Stable democratic rule since then.

RELIGION
Complete freedom of religion.

Religions	Population %	Adherents	Ann.Gr.
Christian	95.69	258,793	+0.4%
non-Religious/other	1.89	5,111	+2.1%
Baha'i	1.30	3,516	+2.1%
Muslim	0.75	2,028	+2.4%
Hindu	0.33	892	+3.1%
Buddhist	0.04	108	+3.4%

Christians	Denom.	Affil.%	,000	Ann.Gr.
Protestant	31	32.39	88	+0.6%
Independent	11	6.04	16	+5.8%
Anglican	1	31.80	86	-0.1%
Catholic	1	3.88	10	+1.0%
Orthodox	1	0.11	0	+0.7%
Marginal	5	3.06	8	+4.3%
Unaffiliated		18.41	50	n.a.

Churches	MegaBloc	Cong.	Members	Affiliates
Anglican	A	43	23,243	86,000
Seventh-day Adventist	P	52	13,500	17,000
Methodist	P	20	5,000	16,000
Catholic	C	6	6,402	10,500
Pente Assemblies (PAWI)	P	20	7,000	10,500
NT Ch of God (Clev)	P	44	3,400	8,000
Jehovah's Witnesses	M	24	2,500	7,300
Ch of God (Anderson)	P	18	1,800	6,000
Ch of the Nazarene	P	33	2,700	4,500
Wesleyan Holiness	P	38	3,000	4,500
Christian Brethren [3]	P	10	1,000	2,500
Ch of God of Prophecy	P	16	870	2,200
Other denoms [36]		142	14,018	33,990
Total Christians [50]		**466**	**84,433**	**208,990**

Trans-bloc Groupings	pop. %	,000	Ann.Gr.
Evangelical	28.6	77	+1.2%
Charismatic	18.6	50	+2.0%
Pentecostal	12.0	32	+2.3%

Missionaries from Barbados
P,I,A 25 in 7 agencies in 8 countries: Barbados 12, USA 3.

Missionaries to Barbados
P,I,A 39 in 6 agencies from 6 countries: USA 24, Canada 6, St. Lucia 4.

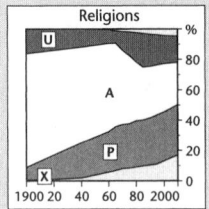

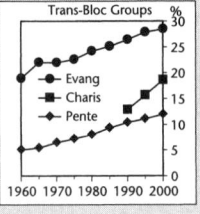

• Answers to Prayer

1 The November 1998 event 'Prayer for the Nation' led to deep repentance for the centuries-old curse of English-introduced slavery and to reconciliation between descendants on both sides. It is this tragic past which has crippled spirituality and destroyed the concept of a stable two-parent family home. In 1999 a prominent white evangelical leader publicly apologized for the sin of slavery. Pray that such moves of repentance may spiritually lift the whole nation.

• Challenges for Prayer

1 **Since settlement in 1627, Barbados has been Protestant.** Despite religious profession and a large number of Evangelicals, real commitment to the Lordship of Jesus is not the norm. Materialism, decreasing church attendance, increased violence and crime are the symptoms of spiritual malaise. Pray for the renewal of God's people and a spiritual awakening throughout the country.

B

2 **The Church needs a fresh touch from God.** There is much disunity, competition and mistrust between leaders of denominations. Pray that there might be a loving commitment to fellowship and prayer among those in Christian ministry. Pray for the Barbados Evangelical Association that seeks to provide the platform for this.

3 **External challenges to the gospel** are evident in the activity of Satanist groups and increased efforts by Muslims and Mormons to win those disillusioned with what they see of traditional Christianity. Pray for the confounding of these efforts and for Christians to demonstrate the love and power of God.

4 **Young people** need clear spiritual models and direction. The pervasive culture of immorality is almost as widespread among those who go to church as those who don't. Over 73% of all births are illegitimate and only 13% of adults are legally married. Pray that churches may offer effective programmes for children and youth. Pray also for the outreach of **CEF** to children, as well as for the ministry of IS/ISUF(**IFES**) in schools and colleges.

5 **Barbadian missions vision is limited**, with only a handful who have been or are involved in overseas ministry. Pray that churches may catch this vision and run with it.

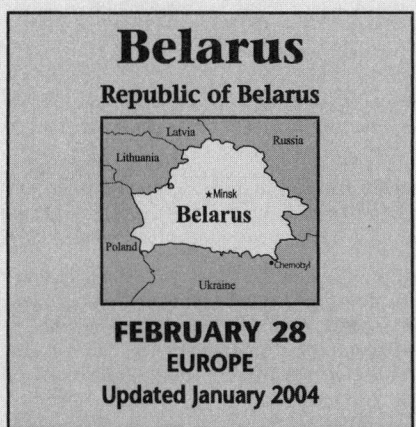

Belarus
Republic of Belarus

Belarus

FEBRUARY 28
EUROPE
Updated January 2004

GEOGRAPHY
Area 207,600 sq.km. Landlocked, fertile agricultural land with extensive forests on the North European plains. Surrounded by Russia, Ukraine, Poland, Lithuania and Latvia. Smallest of the three Slavic nations of the former USSR.

Population	Ann.Gr.	Density
2000	10,236,181	-0.30%	49 per sq. km.
2010	9,973,382	-0.22%	48 per sq. km.
2025	9,495,683	-0.39%	46 per sq. km.

Capital Minsk 1,862,000. **Urbanites** 65%.

PEOPLES
Slav 98.8%. Belarusian 7,964,000; Russian 1,351,000; Polish 417,000, Ukrainian 296,000. Jews 1.1%.
All other peoples 0.9%.

Literacy 97.9%. **Official languages** Belarusian and Russian; many are more fluent in the latter. **All indigenous languages** 2. **Languages with Scriptures** 2Bi.

ECONOMY
A strong agricultural and industrial base. The failure to change Soviet economic structures has fuelled inflation, hindered foreign investment and crippled economic development. Economic decline has been even worse than that of Russia and Ukraine. The dire consequences of the Chernobyl nuclear disaster still massively impact the Belarusian economy and health services. **HDI** 0.763; 60th/174. **Public debt** 3% of GNP. **Income/person** $2150 (6.8% of USA).

POLITICS
A separate member of the UN since WWII, but Belarus had never been an independent state until 1991. Political leadership still clings to the autocratic Communist past and has alienated many foreign powers with its xenophobia and aggressive stance. The government continues to press for Belarus to be included in the Russian Federation.

RELIGION

The religious freedom of the post-Communist era has faded. Christianity of all stripes has flourished in recent years, although the dominant Orthodox Church seeks to restrict the activities of other Christian groups. Protestant churches are refused building permits in the cities. In 2002 extremely repressive legislation was passed severely limiting religious freedom. All unregistered religious activity is being banned and very few applications for registration by minority religions approved.

Religions	Population %	Adherents	Ann.Gr.
Christian	78.70	8,055,874	+1.0%
non-Religious/other	20.20	2,067,709	-4.1%
Jewish	1.00	102,362	-1.5%
Muslim	0.10	10,236	-8.6%

Christians	Denom.	Affil.%	,000	Ann.Gr.
Protestant	17	1.58	162	+5.9%
Independent	2	0.91	93	+0.3%
Catholic	3	13.19	1,350	+0.8%
Orthodox	2	48.71	4,986	+0.8%
Marginal	1	0.08	8	+7.8%
Unaffiliated		14.23	1,457	n.a.

Note: 1999 census gives non-Religious 50%, Orthodox 40%, Catholic 7%.

Churches	MegaBloc Cong. Members Affiliates

Russian Orthodox	O	799	2,797,203	4,000,000
All Catholics [3]	C	400	808,383	1,350,000
Pentecostal — unregistered	P	462	37,000	74,000
Old Believers	I	30	37,662	58,000
Pentecostal Union	P	510	22,000	44,000
Fringe Orthodox [3]	I	23	22,727	35,000
Evang Chr Baptist Union	P	232	11,848	23,696
Seventh-day Adventist	P	60	7,000	9,100
Jehovah's Witnesses	M	24	2,402	8,000
Other denoms [15]		211	595,687	996,734
Total Christians [26]		2,751	4,341,000	6,599,000

Trans-bloc Groupings	pop.%	,000	Ann.Gr.
Evangelical	1.5	150	+5.8%
Charismatic	1.3	135	+6.2%
Pentecostal	1.2	118	+7.0%

Missionaries from Belarus
P,I,A 14 in 5 agencies.

Missionaries to Belarus
P,I,A 82 in 16 agencies from 9 countries. USA 44, Belarus 13, UK 6, Korea 4, Argentina 4. C 250. M 10.

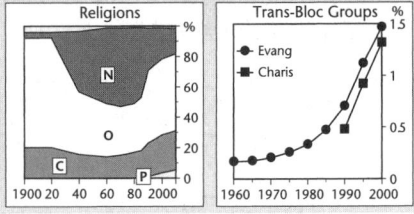

• Challenges for Prayer

1 **Belarus stumbled into an unexpected independence** and is still searching for a national identity. Progress is crippled by the lack of political and economic freedom needed for growth. Pray for true democratic and religious freedom.

2 **The cultural dominance of Poland and Russia** lasted for many centuries. Pray for a truly indigenous expression of Belarusian Christianity to be developed and then spread using all methods: church services, theological education, literature, broadcasting.

3 **The Chernobyl catastrophe** in 1986 occurred in the Ukraine, but affected Belarus most severely. The environmental, economic, and psychological impact of the nuclear fallout has since devastated the country. Twenty-five percent of the land area — much of it formerly productive agricultural land — is considered uninhabitable. Radiation-related health problems still occur at 80 times the global average. Pray that in this climate of despair God may use believers as ministers of restoration and hope.

4 **The post-Communist honeymoon with religion** is ending. While the Orthodox Church enjoys privileged status as a Slavic religious entity, other denominations are experiencing opposition from the establishment. While many call themselves Christian, there is still a great need for renewal within the large Orthodox and Catholic structures. Pray for the Holy Spirit to sweep through Belarus, bringing people to personal faith in Christ.

5 **Evangelical Christians are increasing** despite low-level persecution. Pray that the various evangelical groups — different denominations, registered and unregistered churches — might be able to work together in unity. The inability of Evangelicals to use public buildings for church meetings and the forbidding of public evangelism hampers growth. Pray for:

a) The governmental and social pressure against any evangelism by believers to be lifted.

b) The cultural bias against evangelical Christianity to be overcome by Spirit-led sharing of the gospel.

c) ***Training of the hundreds of Belarusians*** in full- or part-time ministry. Ask the Lord to raise up bold and godly leaders to guide the church in His steps.

d) ***Greater cooperation*** to replace the mistrust between many denominations.

6 **Missions**. Belarus has received far less attention from missions than her Slavic neighbors, Russia and the Ukraine. Pray that the Lord might call more people to serve long-term in this needy land. Pray that Western missionaries in Belarus might have a sensitive and humble spirit, working as servants with the local churches. Pray for a spirit of wisdom in ministering which avoids drawing negative attention from hostile authorities and the media.

7 **The less evangelized**. There are some significant non-Christian minorities:

a) ***Jews***. Nearly 50,000 Jews live in Minsk, but many are emigrating. There is a Messianic Jewish group in Minsk, but the majority still need to be reached.

b) ***Muslims***. Small communities of Azeris and Tatars exist. Diverse Muslim immigrants are moving illegally into the most contaminated regions of the country, and have little chance to hear the gospel.

8 **Christian help ministries** for prayer:

a) ***The Bible Society*** (**UBS**) has found a widespread desire for the Bible and Children's Bibles in both official languages. Thousands are being distributed, and a new Belarusian New Testament has been commissioned in cooperation with the Orthodox Church.

b) ***Christian literature*** needs to be made more available. **CLC** has a presence in the country, but more solid evangelistic and teaching material needs to be translated into Belarusian and then distributed throughout the country.

c) ***EHC*** has reached every home, with millions receiving Christian tracts.

d) ***The JESUS film*** has been seen by most of the population in Belarusian or Russian. Resources for follow-up are still too limited to help all who are touched.

e) ***TWR*** has established a local base for programme production. They are also broadcasting into the country in both major languages.

Belgium
Kingdom of Belgium

Belgium

MARCH 1
EUROPE

GEOGRAPHY
Area 30,518 sq.km. One of the Low Countries, often called *The Crossroads of Europe*.

Population		Ann.Gr.	Density
2000	10,161,164	+0.14%	333 per sq. km.
2010	10,135,688	-0.07%	332 per sq. km.
2025	9,917,861	-0.20%	325 per sq. km.

Europe's second most densely populated country; after the Netherlands.

Capital Brussels 2,450,000; capital of the EU and

HQ of NATO. Other major city: Antwerp 1.2 mill. **Urbanites** 97%.

PEOPLES
Indigenous 90%.
Flemish 54.7%. Language related to Dutch; mainly in north and west.
Walloon 32.3%. French-speaking; mainly in south and east.
German 0.7%. In districts adjoining Germany.
Jews 0.32%. Mainly in Antwerp.
Foreign 10%.
EU Citizens 5%. Italian 280,000; French 110,000; Spanish 70,000; Dutch 70,000.
Other 5%. Arabic-speaking (mainly North African) 200,000; Turkish 70,000; Kurdish 25,000; Chinese 20,000; Congolese 15,000.

Literacy 99%. **Official languages** Flemish, French and German. **All indigenous languages** 4. **Languages with Scriptures** 3Bi.

ECONOMY
Wealthy service and export-oriented economy, but unemployment relatively high at 9.6%. **HDI** 0.923; 5th/174. **Public debt** 97% of GNP. **Income/person** £26,730 (85% of USA).

POLITICS
Became a nation in 1830 as a constitutional monarchy. Fully federal constitution since

1993 to reduce tensions between the Walloons and Flemings and stave off possible national fragmentation. Political parties have been widely discredited because of scandals in the 1990s, giving a boost to extreme right-wing parties.

RELIGION
There is full freedom of religion, but official recognition given to selected main religions. Many smaller religious groupings, including most evangelical denominations, were listed as 'sects' in a 1997 government investigation and thus put under a shadow of suspicion. Efforts to rectify this are likely to be successful.

Religions	Population %	Adherents	Ann.Gr.
Christian	67.66	6,875,000	-0.7%
non-Religious/other	28.22	2,867,500	+2.2%
Muslim	3.60	365,802	+1.3%
Buddhist	0.29	29,467	+7.9%
Jewish	0.21	21,338	-3.3%
Baha'i	0.02	2,032	+15.0%

Christians	Denom.	Affil.%	,000	Ann.Gr.
Protestant	55	0.78	80	+2.6%
Independent	16	0.24	24	+5.3%
Anglican	1	0.06	6	-3.0%
Catholic	3	58.07	5,901	-1.4%
Orthodox	4	0.55	56	+0.7%
Marginal	15	0.64	65	-0.3%
Unaffiliated		7.32	743	n.a.

Churches	MegaBloc	Cong.	Members	Affiliates
Catholic [2]	C	3,962	6,060,606	8,000,000
Jehovah's Witnesses	M	377	26,408	53,000
Greek Orthodox	O	12	29,197	40,000
United Protestant	P	105	4,700	27,000

Indep Charismatic [10]	I	140	3,600	11,000
Un. of Free Evang [3]	P	110	4,000	10,000
Indep Pentecostal	I	90	3,000	8,300
Union of Pente (VVP)	P	40	3,250	6,500
Assemblies of God [2]	P	70	3,527	5,794
Ch of God (Cleveland)	P	15	2,000	3,968
Union of Evang Baptists	P	33	1,000	2,500
Other Foreign	P	18	900	2,300
All Reformed Chs [3]	P	8	135	1,800
Brethren (Exclusive, 3)	P	20	790	1,450
Brethren (Open)	P	21	850	1,130
Other denoms [69]		250	25,600	57,700
Disaffiliated Catholics			*-1,590,000*	*-2,100,000*

Total Christians [103]   5,271   6,169,562   8,232,500

Trans-bloc Groupings	pop.%	,000	Ann.Gr.
Evangelical	1.1	109	+2.8%
Charismatic	2.8	282	+0.7%
Pentecostal	0.3	26	+8.0%

Missionaries from Belgium
P,I,A 83 in 20 agencies: Belgium 28, Papua New Guinea 4, Angola 3.

Missionaries to Belgium
P,I,A 473 in 53 agencies: USA 184, UK 63, Netherlands 45, Canada 40, Germany 30, South Africa 28.

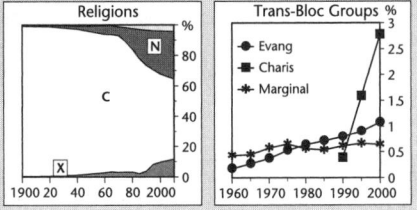

• Answers to Prayer

1 **The slow, but steady growth** of the small evangelical witness — especially among Pentecostal denominations.

2 **Flemish areas** have long had far fewer Evangelicals than the French-speaking south, but in the last 10 years have had the greater growth. Much has been through the varied and effective ministries of **BEM** and the outreach of Pentecostals.

3 **A growing mutual respect between historical Protestants and evangelical networks**. A nation-wide Protestant-evangelical body (ARPEE/CACPE) is being formed that will represent both Protestants and Evangelicals to the government.

• Challenges for Prayer

1 **Belgium is a deeply divided nation.** Its territory has straddled the cultural divide between the Latin/Romance and Germanic worlds for 2,000 years. It has also long been oppressed and fought over by surrounding nations. Though one in Catholic culture, the Walloon-Flemish rivalry and resentments colour the use of language, the economy, politics, religious life and worldviews of both communities. Pray that national leaders at every level may successfully work for the unity of the nation. The break-up of the nation could occur without this.

2 **The Protestant Church** is only now recovering from the destruction of its 600 congregations by the Spanish Inquisition in the 16th Century. Pray that the light of the gospel may shine clearly once more, overcoming fears and prejudices, and attract many.

3 **The population is culturally Catholic but rapidly secularizing.** Although 90% would be classified as Catholic, 71% have been baptized and Mass attendance has plummeted to 11% of the population. In 1998 a survey revealed 37% of Belgians were unchurched and only 57% claimed to be Catholic. The Church faces four major crises — declining commitment, waning influence, lack of students in seminaries and mass defections. The number of priests has nearly halved since 1960, and their average age is 64. The charismatic movement brought some new life, but has had little lasting influence.

B

4 **The nation was shocked in the 1990s** by the exposure of murderous paedophile rings, some with Satanist practices, that reached into the top levels of society. Christian churches were even affected. These have led to a deep distrust of political and religious leaders. There is a rapid rise in neo-paganism and the occult. Pray that these works of darkness might be bound, exposed and routed out and that many may be set free in Jesus.

5 **Protestantism** has hardly grown over the past 30 years. The growth of evangelical, and especially Pentecostal, groups and the evangelical wing of the largely liberal United Protestant Church (EPUB) has offset the dramatic decline of the latter's numbers. Major issues that need prayerful resolution:

a) ***The division between the EPUB*** and evangelical networks was heightened by the former's efforts to claim to speak at government level for all Protestants.

b) ***The strengthening of fellowship and ministry links between denominations.*** The *Evangelische Alliantie* was formed in Flanders in 1980, the *Fédération des Evangéliques* in Wallonia in 1989 and a nation-wide body in 1994. Pray also for an effective Protestant-Evangelical body to be formed. The lack of unity does not help in gaining national credibility and a better response.

6 **The lack of Belgian, and especially Flemish, Christian workers and pastors** is crippling indigeneity and growth. Only 40% of Flemish-speaking congregations have an indigenous pastor. Pray for this to change and for many Belgians to be called into ministry. Pray also for these significant Bible training institutions: Heverlee (Seminary up to doctoral level); *Institut Biblique Belge* for French-speakers in Charleroi and the **AoG** Continental Theological Seminary (French and English). There are several small part-time Flemish Bible Schools. The **AoG** run their effective ICI TEE ministry from Brussels, serving the Church all over Europe and beyond.

7 **Vision for growth.** The nation-wide DAWN surveys in Wallonia (1996) and in Flanders (1998) clearly revealed the need for church planting:

a) ***Of Flanders' 308 administrative districts***, 116 had no evangelical witness.

b) ***Of Wallonia's 281 administrative districts***, 168 had no evangelical witness in 1996. Pray for the mobilization of the Church for the unfinished task.

8 Goals for achievement by the year 2015 that need prayer:

a) ***Increase Francophone churches*** (Project Gabriel) from 415 to 1,417.

b) ***Increase Flemish churches*** from 253 to 590. Church planting in Belgium is a long and slow process — there is freedom, but it is hard to gain a hearing.

c) ***In 2000, the Flemish Pentecostal churches*** (VVP) launched the vision of planting 120 churches by 2015.

d) ***BEM's ongoing vision*** for distributing gospel packets with a personal explanation to everyone in Belgium. By 1999 over 45% had been reached. The successful Project East Flanders in 1996, Liège 1998 and West Flanders in 1999 will be repeated in other provinces. **OM Love Europe** teams and an increasing number of local churches assist in this. **BEM** plans to plant 50 churches by 2015.

9 Specific outreach challenges:

a) ***Belgium, as a nation, is spiritually one of the neediest countries in Europe.***

b) ***The provinces with the greatest need*** — Flemish Brabant and East Flanders, also the Francophone Liège, Namur and Luxembourg.

c) ***Brussels*** is a strategic city. It is 29% foreign and over 8% Muslim. Brussels is 5.9% evangelical and a further 3% historic Protestant. Many of the larger churches are of ethnic minorities — especially Congolese. The spiritual needs of the diplomatic, business and

Eurocrat communities are many. There are now growing prayer networks among and for them. The Full Gospel Businessmen's Association has had a significant impact.

d) **Antwerp** has only 40 or so evangelical congregations — a large proportion being for non-Flemish. The majority of the Jewish community of Belgium lives in the city — one missionary couple ministers among them. No church exists for the 20,000 Moroccans.

e) **North Africans** (predominantly Moroccan) have increased through legal and illegal immigration — the majority living in poorer urban areas. They are almost entirely Muslim but there are now two Arabic-speaking congregations. **AWM** and **BEM** have two couples ministering to them, but many more workers are needed. 'Good news by telephone' has proved a fruitful method of witness, and a 'Good news by radio' ministry is planned.

f) **Turks and Kurds** have proved hard to reach with the gospel. There is one small fellowship of believers.

g) **The German-speaking cantons** on the eastern border were neglected by Evangelicals until recently — there are now 2 **BEM** churches.

h) **The student population** of 135,000 in 17 universities and colleges is a major challenge. **IFES** has a ministry in 8 Flemish universities (Ichthus with 120 students involved) and in 5 French universities (GBU), but the total membership in each of the two branches is 50. Pray for the evangelistic ministry of **OM** in cooperation with these groups and in a teaching ministry in the **IFES** groups; there is one staff couple.

10 Christian media ministries — pray for their effective use:

a) **Christian literature** is produced by **SU**, Biblical Literature Fellowship (BLF, 18 workers), **OM** and the **AoG**. BLF has a large printing press and has published over 500 titles.

b) **Christian bookstores** number 17 (10 in French, 7 in Dutch) in Belgium — **BEM** with 7.

c) **Christian radio and TV**. A total of 1 hour of television and 5.5 hours of radio are produced by ERTS on Flemish TV and radio channels.

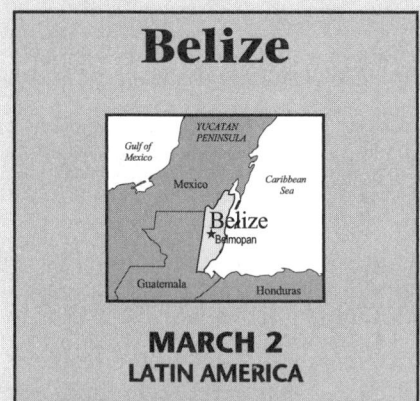

Belize

MARCH 2
LATIN AMERICA

GEOGRAPHY
Area 22,965 sq.km. Caribbean coastal enclave bordering on Guatemala and Mexico. It has the world's second-largest coral barrier reef.

Population		Ann.Gr.	Density
2000	240,709	+2.44%	10 per sq. km.
2010	294,499	+1.97%	13 per sq. km.
2025	370,035	+1.49%	16 per sq. km.

Central America's most sparsely populated country.

Capital Belmopan 6,817. Other major city: Belize City 130,000. **Urbanites** 48%.

PEOPLES
Mestizo/Ladino 43%. Predominantly Guatemalans and Hondurans, with considerable illegal immigration in the 1980s.
Afro-Caribbean 29.5%. Mainly English-speaking. Politically dominant.
Amerindian 11%. Mayans, 3 main languages: Ketchi 20,000; Mopan 6,000; Yucatec 5,600.
Garifuna (Black Carib) 6.6%. Descendants of African slaves and Arawakans.
Europeans 3.9%. Mainly German Mennonites and British.
Other 6%. East Indian 8,400; Chinese 6,000.
Literacy 70%. **Official language** English. Spanish spoken by 50% of the population. **All languages** 9. **Languages with Scriptures** 2Bi 5NT.

ECONOMY
Poorly developed infrastructure slows economic progress, yet relatively prosperous. Main sources of income: ecotourism (40% of country is set aside as national parks and reserves), US aid, agriculture. HDI 0.732; 83rd/174. **Public debt** 32% of GNP. **Income/person** $2,700 (8.5% of USA).

POLITICS
Independence from Britain in 1981 as a stable parliamentary democracy. Guatemala long laid claim to Belize, but now recognizes it as an independent state.

RELIGION

A secular state with freedom of religion.

Religions	Population %	Adherents	Ann.Gr.
Christian	90.95	218,925	+2.4%
Baha'i	2.88	6,932	+3.9%
Hindu	2.30	5,536	+6.9%
Jewish	1.08	2,600	+2.4%
Spiritist/Trad. ethnic	1.03	2,479	-2.0%
non-Religious/other	0.83	1,998	+1.6%
Muslim	0.58	1,396	+4.0%
Buddhist	0.35	842	+8.3%

Christians	Denom.	Affil.%	,000	Ann.Gr.
Protestant	25	21.96	53	+2.9%
Independent	5	2.71	7	+2.4%
Anglican	1	4.36	10	-1.8%
Catholic	1	56.89	137	+1.7%
Marginal	2	2.22	5	+3.8%
Unaffiliated		9.30	22	n.a.
Doubly affiliated		*-6.49*	*-16*	*n.a.*

Churches	MegaBloc	Cong.	Members	Affiliates
Catholic	C	50	74,021	136,939
Seventh-day Adventist	P	89	17,000	24,000
Anglican	A	26	3,571	10,500
Methodist	P	25	4,964	6,800
Ch of the Nazarene	P	40	1,800	4,000
Jehovah's Witnesses	M	31	1,380	3,450
Baptist Association	P	52	2,050	2,800
Assemblies of God	P	49	900	2,700
Ch of God in Christ	I	23	1,700	2,500
Ch of God (Cleveland)	P	26	1,100	1,800
Mennonite	P	4	540	1,600
Latter-day Saints (Morm)	M	7	1,138	1,900
Assoc of Evang Chs	P	12	1,050	1,350
Ch of God of Prophecy	P	14	351	600
Other denoms [20]		247	6,601	11,238
Doubly affiliated			*-9,235*	*-15,700*
Total Christians [34]		695	108,931	196,500

Trans-bloc Groupings	pop. %	,000	Ann.Gr.
Evangelical	14.1	34	+2.7%
Charismatic	8.9	21	+2.5%
Pentecostal	4.5	11	+3.3%

Missionaries from Belize
P,I,A 27 in 5 agencies.

Missionaries to Belize
P,I,A 123 in 31 agencies from 9 countries: USA 92, Canada 31, Belize 25, Guatemala 7.

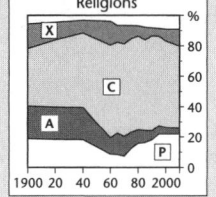

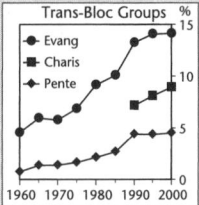

• Challenges for Prayer

1 **Belizeans are largely professing Christians**, but nominalism and syncretism are common. The Spanish-speaking immigrants with their superstitions and superficiality, the Mayans with their underlying paganism, and the Garifuna with their black magic — each need a culturally relevant and sensitive presentation of the gospel. Many settlements still need church-planting ministry, despite the five-fold increase in congregations since 1960.

2 **Evangelicals have steadily grown** from 4.6% in 1960 to 14% in 2000. There has been exceptional growth in some denominations. Challenges to be tackled:

a) *Few full-time workers*, most must work part-time due to lack of congregational support.

b) *Much evangelism* but little evidence of 'converts' in the churches, because of poor follow-up.

3 **Cultural diversity and denominational variety** make unity and common goals for Christians difficult to attain. Pray for:

a) *The Mennonites,* many of whom live in introspective communities with their own dialect of German. Belize has a higher percentage of Mennonites than any other country. Pray for revival in their communities.

b) *Effective fellowship* between Spanish- and English-speaking believers in united nationwide initiatives for the Kingdom.

4 The less-reached:

a) *The Mayan peoples* — there are a few Nazarene and Mennonite believers.

b) *The Garifuna* have had their own NT since 1983. Their strong animistic culture has only been marginally penetrated (CoN, Brethren). There are some Nazarene and Brethren believers among them.

c) *The Chinese* have increased through immigration from China, Hong Kong and Taiwan, but only a few are evangelical believers.

d) *The East Indians* are almost entirely Muslim or Hindu.

Benin
Republic of Benin

MARCH 3
AFRICA

The government has since remained stable under the elected President.

RELIGION
Complete religious freedom under the present government. The President actively encourages Christian ministry, although all religions are free to practice and propagate their faiths.

Religions	Population %	Adherents	Ann.Gr.
Traditional ethnic	47.70	2,908,059	+1.4%
Christian	31.78	1,937,486	+3.5%
Muslim	20.03	1,221,141	+4.3%
non-Religious/other	0.29	17,680	+8.0%
Baha'i	0.20	12,193	n.a.

Widespread syncretism among Muslims and nominal Christians means ethnic religions could be nearer 80%.

Christians	Denom.	Affil. %	,000	Ann.Gr.
Protestant	17	5.48	334	+10.5%
Independent	23	3.16	193	+3.5%
Catholic	1	20.74	1,264	+1.4%
Marginal	2	2.02	123	+13.7%
Unaffiliated		0.38	23	n.a.

Churches	MegaBloc	Cong.	Members	Affiliates
Catholic	C	141	706,275	1,264,232
Protestant Methodist	P	450	100,000	150,000
Assemblies of God	P	656	67,750	117,500
Christianisme Celeste	M	250	50,000	100,000
New Apostolic	I	85	17,000	51,000
Nigerian Apostolic	I	300	15,000	32,000
Jehovah's Witnesses	M	144	6,500	23,205
UEEB	P	188	7,000	20,000
Baptist	P	89	3,400	11,400
Ch of Foursquare Gospel	P	65	3,600	9,000
Un of Bapt of Prot Chs	P	44	3,300	6,600
Other denoms [32]		1,088	60,000	129,000
Total Christians [42]		3,500	1,039,000	1,914,000

Trans-bloc Groupings	pop. %	,000	Ann.Gr.
Evangelical	4.2	257	+10.3%
Charismatic	6.1	369	+6.9%
Pentecostal	2.7	164	+12.8%

GEOGRAPHY
Area 112,600 sq.km. A long, narrow country wedged between Nigeria and Togo.

Population	Ann.Gr.	Density
2000	6,096,559	+2.70%	54 per sq. km.
2010	7,902,809	+2.60%	70 per sq. km.
2025	11,109,357	+2.07%	99 per sq. km.

Capital Porto-Novo 265,276. Other major city Cotonou 709,250. **Urbanites** 43%.

PEOPLES
About 58 ethnic groups.
Southern Peoples 69.2%. Fon 1,750,000; Yoruba(10) 580,000; Aja 480,000; Ayizo 283,000; Gun 243,000; Ife 176,000; Nagot 175,000; Gen 158,000; Waci 138,000; Maxi 87,000; Tofin 76,000; Xweda 52,000.
Northern Peoples 30.2%. Bariba 425,000; Fulbe (Fulani) 339,000; Ditammari (Somba) 150,000; Boko 87,000; Burba 85,000; Pila (Yom) 74,000; Lamba 69,000; Nateni 66,000; Gurma 62,000; Tem (Kotokoli) 50,000; Lokpa 50,000.
Other 0.6%. French and other non-Africans. Migrants from Niger and Burkina Faso may number up to 4% of the population.

Literacy 37%. **Official language** French. **Trade languages** Fon in south, Dendi in north. **All languages** 51. **Languages with Scriptures** 6Bi 9NT 1por 12w.i.p.

ECONOMY
Still largely functions as a satellite economy of Nigeria. Free-market reforms after failed experiments with Marxism have helped Benin make significant economic progress in the last decade. **HDI** 0.421; 155th/174. **Public debt** 62.5% of GNP. **Income/person** $328 (1.2% of USA).

POLITICS
Independent from France in 1960. After seven coups and one Marxist regime, a multi-party democracy was formed through elections in 1991.

Missionaries from Benin
P,I,A 66 in 6 agencies to 3 countries: Benin 60.

Missionaries to Benin
P,I,A 222 in 35 agencies from 19 countries: USA 87, Nigeria 42, UK 18, Switzerland 15, Canada 14.

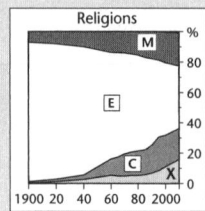

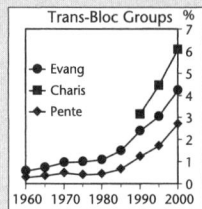

• Answers to Prayer

1 **Praise God for spiritual breakthroughs in the 1990s.** The civil government is facing up to its challenges and responsibilities, and there have been many churches planted in previously unevangelized groups. Benin, a country which was once the source of many slaves, is now beginning to experience freedom through Christ.

2 **The President is a born-again Christian** after years of flirting with communism and the occult. Often called the "pastor-president", he actively advocates Christian ministry in the country. Pray that he may not compromise his testimony, and that his eventual successor may also encourage evangelization.

3 **Church growth is occurring in all regions.** The 1990s may well be seen as the decade of breakthrough for church growth: in AoG churches in the north (Natimba, Burba, Belime, Fulbe, etc.) and south (Mina, Nago, Aja, Gun and now the Fon); UEEB/**SIM** in the north and centre (Lokpa, Bariba, Cabe, Fulbe, Boko, Ditammari and Fon, etc. and now Dassa, Dendi, and Sola); **IMB-SBC** in the south; and Evangelical Baptists in the far north (Dendi and Gurmantche). Pray for the vision to reach out to every unreached people and community, and the strategy to implement it.

• Challenges for Prayer

1 **Government corruption.** Pray that the commitment to genuine democracy might be honoured and the endemic corruption in the country tackled. Pray also that all of the leaders may work for the good of the people rather than for self-enrichment.

2 **Less-reached peoples.** No people in Benin has a Christian majority and evangelical believers are few. Benin has Africa's highest percentage of followers of traditional religions and is the least evangelized non-Muslim country in Africa south of the Sahara. Specific peoples for prayer:

a) *The Fon* are an influential, strategic people in Benin. It was from Fon animism that Voodoo developed. The Fon have a significant, but nominal, Christian minority (20%), but live in fear and superstition. However, vigorous church-planting and prayer efforts have yielded much fruit in the 1990s, with the work of several missions experiencing rapid church growth (including **AoG, SIM, SBC**). But leaders are desperately needed for the new believers, as there is only one trained worker for every 10 Fon churches.

b) *The Gbe peoples* include the Fon and 19 other related people groups, forming a complex medley of unreached and unevangelized peoples with a population of over 3 million. Among most of these peoples few indigenous evangelical churches exist.

c) *The Nagot* are located on the southeastern border with Nigeria in the region of Ketou. Until recently, the Nagot had little exposure to the gospel. However, missionary efforts are beginning to bear fruit with indigenous evangelical churches planted among them.

d) *The Idacca* (30,000+) living in south central Benin. Currently, there is no missionary work among them.

e) *The Ife* (176,000) straddle the borders of Benin and Togo and are currently experiencing rapid growth in church planting. Ife churches are reaching out to neighbouring villages that have no gospel witness and bringing them the Word of Life.

f) **Muslim peoples.** Recently **IMB-SBC** workers have started ministry among the Anii and Mokolé. Little work has been done among the more urban Dyerma, Hausa and Mossi. Islam is expanding into many central and northern peoples, but among the Fulbe (Fula) there has been a breakthrough with more than 2,000 coming to Christ (**SIM, AoG**).

g) *The one million urbanites* of the two capitals. From the 1980s to the 1990s the evangelical community grew five-fold to over 4,000, but the majority have still not been reached. Nearly a fifth of the population is Muslim, and no one is working full time specifically for their evangelization. **SIM** and a number of Nigerian missions are doing urban evangelism in several cities and **SIM** is targeting the many government workers.

h) *A Benin national research team* (**ARCEB**) is engaged in making a strategic survey of the country, its churches and peoples which could have major impact on church growth strategy. Pray for a successful conclusion and application in mobilizing the Church for the unreached.

3 **The Church in Benin needs leaders.** The recent church growth has yielded many new Christians, but has led to a shortage of trained leaders to teach the Bible and demonstrate a life of holiness. Many tribes and villages are asking for pastors or missionaries to show them a biblical Christianity to replace their often-syncretized faith. Pray for the teachers and students at the **AoG** Bible Institute (32 students), the ICI Correspondence School, the one French and seven vernacular primary level Bible Schools (200 students) run by the UEEB, and 300+ studying in a TEE programme. These vital schools need general staff and lecturers, as well as bursaries and scholarships for the students, who are usually impoverished.

4 **Missions.** Only since 1946 has the centre and north been penetrated by missions. The largest of these are **SIM** (71), EMS-Nigeria, **IMB-SBC** (20), **SIL/WBT** (19), Evangelical Baptists (8), **AoG** (4). Considering the needs of the country, the small church-planting missionary force must be increased. **SIM** runs the only evangelical mission hospital and has a ministry of rural development.

5 **Young people** are now a core element of the Benin church. Conversions through youth centres, camps and the extensive use of the *JESUS* film together with good follow-up has often resulted in churches in both towns and rural areas. Praise the Lord that there is student witness throughout the whole of Benin. There are more than 700 active members of the GREEB(**IFES**) student groups.

6 **Bible translation** is still a major need. Almost half of Benin's 51 languages are without a Bible or NT. **SIM** translation teams are working in seven languages, the AoG in seven, and SIL in four. Pray for the inter-mission linguistic centre which helps facilitate translation work by the provision of technology and resources. Other literature is also being translated and printed: TEE materials, Bible commentaries, etc. Pray that this might help the church to become biblically literate.

7 **Media opportunities** abound in the new day of freedom. Pray for:

a) *The effective use of audio recordings* in evangelism and teaching. **GRN** has recordings in 38 languages.

b) *The best use of the JESUS film* in French, Fon, Bariba, Gurma, Kabiye, Tem, and Yoruba.

c) *Radio*. After Radio ELWA (Liberia) was destroyed, Radio Parakou, a government owned station, began to broadcast gospel messages with some results. There is daily programming in Fon, Bariba and Fulfulde, and weekly broadcasts in French. There is also progress in developing a shortwave station in Benin. *Maranatha* is a full-time Christian FM station broadcasting from Cotonou.

d) *Television*. WorldReach broadcasts 30 minutes of Christian television per week.

Bermuda
Colony of Bermuda Islands

North Atlantic Ocean

Hamilton

Bermuda

MARCH 3
NORTH AMERICA

 GEOGRAPHY
Area 54 sq.km. About 360 small coral islands in the North Atlantic. The world's most northerly coral reefs.

Population	Ann.Gr.	Density
2000	64,590	+0.82%	1,196 per sq.
2010	69,443	+0.70%	1,286 per sq.
2025	75,613	+0.51%	1,400 per sq.

Capital Hamilton 17,441. **Urbanites** 100%.

 PEOPLES
About 27% of the population is foreign-born.
Afro-Caribbean 61%.
Other 39%. Mainly UK, USA, Canada and Portugal.
Literacy 98%. **Official language** English.

ECONOMY
Its superb climate and geographical position makes it a tourist paradise and a lucrative tax haven. There are over 4,500 offshore companies registered in Bermuda. **Income/person** $34,670 (111% of USA).

POLITICS
A dependent territory of the UK. A stable parliamentary democracy.

RELIGION
Freedom of religion.

Religions	Population %	Adherents	Ann.Gr.
Christian	93.34	60,288	+0.9%
non-Religious/other	4.03	2,603	-1.8%
Spiritist	2.07	1,337	+2.6%
Baha'i	0.50	323	+11.7%
Buddhist	0.03	20	-12.5%
Jewish	0.03	20	+9.6%

B

Christians	Denom.	Affil.%	,000	Ann.Gr.
Protestant	25	30.19	20	+0.7%
Independent	3	10.84	7	-0.1%
Anglican	1	37.47	24	+0.9%
Catholic	1	16.08	10	+1.3%
Marginal	4	2.63	2	+3.4%
Unaffiliated		7.13	5	n.a.
Doubly affiliated		*-11.00*	*-7*	*n.a.*

Churches	MegaBloc	Cong.	Members	Affiliates
Anglican	A	19	4,840	24,200
Catholic	C	9	7,988	10,384
African Methodist Epis	I	12	2,640	6,600
Seventh-day Adventist	P	11	3,300	4,500
Methodist	P	3	841	2,800
New Test CoG (Clev)	P	6	950	1,600
Chr Brethren	P	9	520	860
Baptist	P	4	400	812
Ch of God (Anderson)	P	3	283	650
Other denoms [26]		69	5,314	2,900
Doubly affiliated			*-3,900*	*-7,100*
Total Christians [35]		145	23,200	48,200

Trans-bloc Groupings	pop. %	,000	Ann.Gr.
Evangelical	19.6	13	+0.2%
Charismatic	20.1	13	+0.6%
Pentecostal	3.0	2	+1.1%

Missionaries from Bermuda
P,I,A 2 in Sri Lanka.

Missionaries to Bermuda
P,I,A 9 in 5 agencies. C 30. M 10.

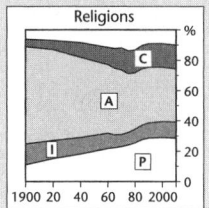
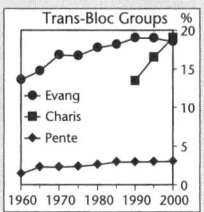

• Challenges for Prayer

1 **Bermuda is an earthly paradise,** but despite having numerous gospel-preaching churches, it is spiritually impoverished. Pray for revival that brings lifestyles in line with biblical knowledge.

2 **The impact of the churches is blunted** by lack of unity and common spiritual goals. Pray for a willingness to come together and build bridges for effective ministry in Bermuda and beyond.

3 **The world's wealthiest Black-majority territory**, but it has little missions involvement. Pray that Bermudans may make a significant impact on world evangelization.

Bhutan

Kingdom of Bhutan — Druk Yul

MARCH 4
ASIA

docile Dzongkha-dominated parliament and a slow democratization taking place. India plays a major role in its foreign affairs. The government fiercely protects its own sovereignty. Large-scale Nepali immigration over the past century and agitation for more democracy have provoked severe measures against non-Drukpa peoples since 1985.

RELIGION
Lamaistic Buddhism with a strong element of Bon, the pre-Buddhist demon-worship, is the state religion. All other religions are barely-tolerated foreign intrusions. All proselytization of Buddhists and Hindus is banned.

Religions	Population %	Adherents	Ann.Gr.
Buddhist	72.04	1,530,108	+3.1%
Hindu	23.00	488,513	+2.4%
Muslim	4.00	84,959	+0.0%
Traditional ethnic	0.50	10,620	+1.6%
Christian	0.46	9,770	+7.4%

GEOGRAPHY
Area 47,000 sq.km. A small kingdom in the eastern Himalaya mountains.

Population	Ann.Gr.	Density
2000	2,123,970	+2.83%	45 per sq. km.
2010	2,753,954	+2.58%	59 per sq. km.
2025	3,903,897	+2.21%	83 per sq. km.

The government claims a much lower figure.

Capital Thimpu 17,156. **Urbanites** 7%.

PEOPLES
Drukpa 63%. 12+ groups, related to Tibetans. The largest: Kebumtamp 310,000; Sharchagpakha 243,000; Dzongkha (Ngalops) 260,000; Sangla 131,000; Dzalakha 60,000.
Nepali 30%. Pahari 300,000; Gurung 230,000; Limbu 25,000.
Other 7%. Assamese 40,000; Lepcha 35,000; Hindi speakers 25,000 (Santali, Loba, Kirabi).

Literacy 18%. **Official language** Dzongkha. Nepali is also widely used. **All languages** 15. **Languages with Scriptures** 2Bi 2NT 2por 1w.i.p.

ECONOMY
Undeveloped subsistence economy but with development potential should the government desire it. Tourist numbers are strictly controlled. **HDI** 0.459; 145ᵗʰ/174. **Public debt** 28% of GNP. **Income/person** $390 (1.4% of USA).

POLITICS
Autocratic Buddhist monarchy with a

Christians	Denom.	Affil.%	,000	Ann.Gr.
Protestant	2	0.15	3	+58.4%
Independent	3	0.28	6	+7.2%
Catholic	1	0.03	1	+1.8%

Churches	MegaBloc	Cong.	Members	Affiliates
Indigenous house chs	I		2,045	3,200
Believers' Church (GFA)	P	80	2,000	3,000
Other Indigenous	I	21	1,062	1,700
Catholic	C	1	451	600
Other denominations [2]		9	633	1,200
Total Christians [6]		111	6,191	9,700

Trans-bloc Groupings	pop.%	,000	Ann.Gr.
Evangelical	0.4	9	+25%
Pentecostal & Charismatic	0.3	6	+22%

Missionaries from Bhutan
P,I,A 16, most in Bhutan.

Expatriates committed to Bhutan
P,I,A 63 in 14 agencies; majority Indian.

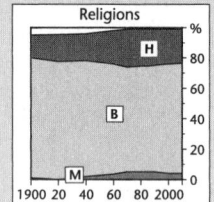

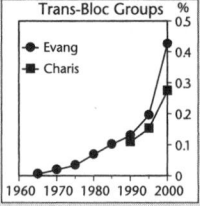

• Challenges to prayer

1 **Bhutan is one of the world's least evangelized nations**. The strongly isolationist policies of the government further reinforce the hold of Tantric Buddhism with much that is demonic and occultic. Pray for true spiritual liberation for this land of the Dragon (Druk Yul). Pray for King Wangchuk and his salvation.

2 **Bhutan was closed to all Christian witness until 1965**. There followed 25 years of slight relaxation during which Indian and other expatriates were able to witness through NGOs. Over the 1990s restrictions increased because of the success of that witness, especially among the Nepali. There are now a few legally permitted congregations with their own buildings. Pray for the growth of the Church in this land.

3 **The Drukpa majority** is strongly Buddhist, and Christians among them number only a few hundred. Most of these believers are isolated and scattered with little opportunity for fellowship, and some have suffered for their faith. Pray for the emergence of a vital witnessing fellowship in every ethnic group of the Bhutanese.

4 **The 'ethnic cleansing' of the Nepali population** has been vigorously promoted since 1990. Suppression of Nepali culture and language, beatings, destruction of homes, rape and many expulsions have created anger, fear and a large refugee problem with over 100,000 in UN refugee camps in SE Nepal. Pray for a wise, enlightened government that gives peace and freedom to all the land's peoples.

5 **Bhutanese Nepalis** have responded to the gospel and since 1970 there has been steady growth. There are little churches and house fellowships all along the southern half of the country that have been planted through several Indian agencies. Many groups have suffered harassment and persecution. Pray for them.

6 **Mission agencies** have been welcomed to operate leprosy hospitals and be involved in health, agricultural and educational programmes, but only on the condition that they do not proselytize. Since leprosy is almost eradicated, such ministries are being phased out. A few small aid projects continue. Pray for the silent witness of Christians in various aid missions (**TLM**, Interserve, Norwegian Santal Mission, etc.) and for a relaxation of restrictions on entry and witness for missionaries. Visas are difficult to obtain. Pray that more aid workers may be called by God and granted visas. **GFA** has a small training base in India near Bhutan's border.

7 **Indian believers** in India's border region are active in evangelism and literature distribution among visitors from Bhutan. Many of the Christians in Bhutan have come to the Lord by these means. Pray for conversions among the Bhutanese. Pray also that Bhutanese students in India and lands around the world may hear the gospel.

8 **Literature distribution** is possible in Bhutan in a limited way, through personal contacts and the mail. Pray for fruit from the Christian literature now spreading through the land (**EHC** and **GFA**).

Bolivia

Republic of Bolivia

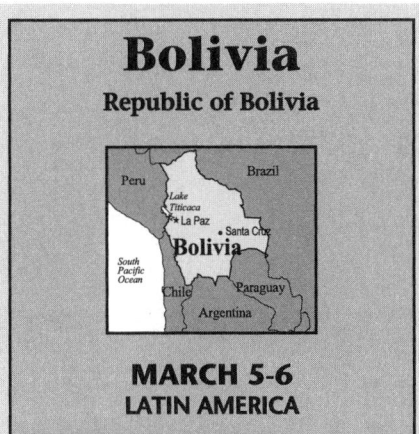

MARCH 5-6
LATIN AMERICA

GEOGRAPHY
Area 1,099,000 sq.km. Landlocked Andean state. High plateau in southwest, tropical lowlands in north and east. It is one of only two landlocked republics in the Americas.

Population		Ann.Gr.	Density
2000	8,328,665	+2.35%	8 per sq. km.
2010	10,229,354	+1.98%	9 per sq. km.
2025	13,131,183	+1.49%	12 per sq. km.

Capital La Paz (administrative) 1,458,000; Sucre (legal) 200,000. Other major citiy: Santa Cruz 1,110,000. **Urbanites** 61%.

PEOPLES
Mestizo 30.5%. Mixed race, Spanish-speaking, predominantly urban.
Amerindian 63.9%.
  Highland peoples 62%. Quechua (5 groups) 4.27m; Aymara (4 groups) 2.62m.
  Lowland peoples 1.9%. About 35 groups. A further seven have recently become extinct. Major groups: Chiquitano 34,000; Guarani(2) 36,000; Guarayu 8,000; Tsimane 9,200; Ignaciano 7,700; Trinitario 7,700; Tacana 6,200; Yuracare 3,700; Mataco 2,600; Ayoreo 2,000.
European 5.1%. Mainly of Spanish descent; they dominate the political and economic life of the country. Also Low German (Mennonites) 27,000; Greek 3,000.
Other 0.5%. Japanese 19,000; Chinese 6,000; Jews 3,300.

Literacy 77%; functional literacy less than 50%.
Official languages Spanish, Aymara, Quechua.
All languages 39. **Languages with Scriptures** 4Bi 16NT 9por 7w.i.p.

ECONOMY
Once South America's richest area, but corrupt, unstable governments, the fall in silver, tin and cotton prices on the international markets, and lack of adequate roads and railways led to decline and economic disaster in the 1980s. Reforms since 1984 have reversed the decline. Shared responsibility for ending illegal cocaine exports between the consumers and producers is bringing in foreign aid to build a more healthy agricultural industry. **HDI** 0.652; 112th/174. **Public debt** 55% of GNP. **Income/person** $830 (3% of USA).

POLITICS
Independence from Spain in 1825 after a long war for freedom. Over 200 successful coups or revolutions have held back meaningful progress. Between 1985 and 1994 successive democratic governments have stabilized the country and given cautious hope for improvement. Since 1994 there has been increasing recognition of the rights of the underprivileged indigenous peoples. The vigorous efforts to suppress coca growing is causing stress and controversy in the country.

RELIGION
The Catholic Church retains State Church status, but rapid growth of non-Catholic religious bodies has threatened this. Religious freedom and separation of Church and State is not yet fully resolved. About 60% of the population has been baptized Catholic, but are practicing animists or Christo-pagan, so statistics here must be interpreted in this light. Most of the Quechua and Aymara are in this category.

Religions	Population %	Adherents	Ann.Gr.
Christian	93.91	7,821,449	+2.3%
Baha'i	3.23	269,016	+2.8%
non-Religious/atheist	1.72	143,253	+3.1%
Traditional ethnic	0.82	68,295	+1.4%
Chinese	0.20	16,657	+2.4%
Buddhist	0.06	4,997	-0.5%
Jewish	0.04	3,331	+2.4%
Muslim	0.02	1,666	+9.7%

Christians	Denom.	Affil.%	,000	Ann.Gr.
Protestant	51	9.39	782	+5.4%
Independent	34	2.61	217	+6.3%
Anglican	1	0.01	1	+2.4%

Catholic	1	84.05	7,000	+1.5%
Orthodox	1	0.05	4	+2.1%
Marginal	2	1.80	150	+6.0%
Unaffiliated		3.50	92	n.a.
Doubly affiliated		*-7.50*	*-650*	*n.a.*

Churches	MegaBloc	Cong.	Members	Affiliates
Catholic	C	500	4,070,000	7,000,000
Evang Christian Union	P	1,100	65,000	130,000
Seventh-day Adventists	P	208	75,000	127,500
AoG of Bolivia	P	1,133	86,746	114,476
Latter-day Sts (Morm)	M	228	52,083	100,000
Jehovah's Witnesses	M	238	15,388	50,000
Baptist Union	P	190	22,000	44,000
Bolivian AoG	I	500	23,000	42,000
Friends Holiness Mission	P	300	18,000	30,060
Ekklesia Bolivia	I	5	15,000	30,000
Ch of the Nazarene	P	240	19,000	27,550
Friends Nat. Evang	P	230	17,308	27,000
Boliv. Evang Ch. of God	P	260	13,000	23,400
Evang Methodist	P	178	13,000	19,500
Reformed Ch of God	I	153	11,500	18,400
Holiness	P	257	9,000	18,000
Boliv. Evang Lutheran	P	90	5,405	18,000
Christian Brethren	P	400	12,000	17,575
Evang Pentecostal	P	123	4,800	17,000
Nat. Evang Work (NTM)	P	53	2,500	12,000
Ch of God (Cleveland)	P	50	4,500	9,900
Ch of God of Prophecy	P	147	4,500	9,900
Baptist Convention	P	39	4,015	6,705
Other denoms [68]		2,172	130,812	261,322
Doubly affiliated			*-363,372*	*-625,000*
Total Christians [91]		8,708	4,327,000	7,529,000

Trans-bloc Groupings	pop.%	,000	Ann.Gr.
Evangelical	11.8	981	+5.6%
Charismatic	9.8	817	+4.7%
Pentecostal	4.5	372	+7.8%

Missionaries from Bolivia
P,I,A 95 in 16 agencies to 9 countries: Bolivia 79.

Missionaries to Bolivia
P,I,A 1,790 in 100 agencies from 28 countries: USA 495, UK 110, Brazil 94, Korea 50, Sweden 35, Switzerland 33.

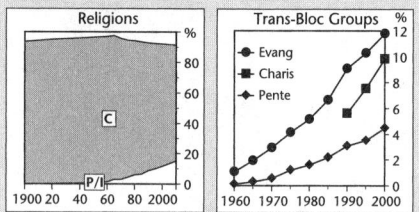

• Answers to Prayer

1 The **40 year responsiveness** of many sections of the population has continued through the 1990s, with Evangelicals increasing from 600,000 to nearly 1 million.

2 The **Aymara**, descendents of a great pre-Inca civilization, continue to turn to Christ with over 20% now evangelical believers.

3 The long-indifferent Quechua have begun to respond to the gospel in large numbers in the 1990s.

4 A significant spiritual hunger and turning to God in the Bolivian army.

• Challenges for Prayer

1 Democracy and freedom are new realities for Bolivia. The benefits are only now beginning to reach the Amerindian majority that has long been mired in poverty, exploited and politically marginalized. Pray for courage and moral integrity for the national leaders as they grapple with the economic inequalities and social ills of society, not least of the latter being the cocaine "industry". About 50% of the world's cocaine is grown in Bolivia. Pray that Bolivian Evangelicals may live holy, exemplary lives as they seek to bring change for the good of their land.

2 The growing of coca and manufacture of cocaine have become the major economic activity of many Bolivians. Poor roads and distance from markets make alternative crops far less viable. Government and international efforts to suppress the illegal industry have had limited success. Pray for believers that have compromised, and also for those who stood against the pressure — and are impoverished as a result.

3 The Catholic Church is confronted by multiple crises. Its long-held political supremacy is threatened; annual losses to other churches and religions have provoked local discrimination and pressures against non-Catholics. It has failed to develop an indigenous clergy or challenge the rampant paganism within the majority it claims to shepherd. Pray that millions of nominal and Christo-pagan "Catholics" might come to a living faith in Christ.

4 Evangelical Christians are a growing influence in society. The Association of Evangelicals (ANDEB) is a major fellowship link for them. Pray for unity and continued commitment to prayer and outreach with a vision to see their nation transformed.

5 The spiritual darkness of centuries is beginning to be broken, but Christians need to grapple in prayer with the entrenched idolatry and pagan superstitions of society, the injustices, corruption and vested interests of those with power and, above all, to strip the 'strong man' of his long-held possessions.

6 Growing churches are numerous, but so also are the needs and challenges. These include illiteracy, lack of understanding of the basics of true Christianity, apathy and widespread compromise with the social evils of fornication, family breakdown, violence and alcohol abuse. Pray for revival.

7 Leadership training at various levels is vital for the many growing churches — from jungle village tribal churches to sophisticated elite city congregations. There are over 30 Protestant seminaries and Bible schools as well as a variety of TEE institutes and BCCs. These cannot provide maturity and spiritual authority without the deep working of the Spirit of God. Men and women who know their God are needed!

8 The less reached:

a) *The upper classes* have long held exclusive control of the reins of power, but were shocked by the national disasters of the '80s. Few were evangelicals before 1985, but all is changing and many are seeking the Lord. The Ekklesia Church came out of the 1986 revival; many of its members are from this class.

b) *The rural villages* — a high proportion of the Quechua, Aymara and lowland peoples live in hard-to-access mountain or forest regions. Well over half of these villages are beyond the reach of present efforts.

c) *The 100,000 tertiary students* in the nine universities are disillusioned with traditional Catholicism, often secular, promiscuous, consumed with feelings of guilt and inadequacy and discouraged by interrupted courses and bleak future prospects. About 500 students in eight universities are linked with the CCU**(IFES)**; others are linked with the ministry of **CCCI** in several universities.

d) **The youth** are largely neglected, yet over 53% of the population is under 19. Few churches know how to meet their spiritual needs. Unemployment, urban violence and increasing drug abuse intensify the growing generation gap. Pray for the work of SU and others seeking to reach and disciple the youth.

e) **Children**. Over 80% live in extreme poverty, and 100,000 under 14 in urban areas have to work. Over 80,000 are known to be addicted to drugs. Pray for the development of childrens' ministries and for churches to see the importance of these.

9 The lowland tribes have been largely evangelized through great sacrifice and with considerable success. Praise the Lord for the work of **NTM, SIM**, WGM, UWM, South American Mission, **SIL** and others. Their ministries have been strongly attacked by anti-Christian anthropologists and commercial exploiters of these lands as "genocidal", but in answer to prayer the effects of these attacks have been reduced. Pray for the neutralizing of these assaults, the maturation of indigenous leaders, the integration of these believers into Bolivian life, the sound conversion of the second generation of Christians and the development of a healthy indigenous Christianity as part of their culture.

10 Major goals for 2000-2010:

a) **Bolivia to be 30% evangelical** by 2010.

b) **A strong Church** active in outreach and missions. The missions vision is slowly growing, some Bolivians have been sent to other lands.

c) **Strong, servant leaders** who give a good role model to others.

d) **Effective DAWN programme** accomplished with a church in every community.

11 **Foreign missions**. Early missionaries struggled long against hostility, persecution and harsh living conditions before the harvest ripened. The contribution of AEM (now **SIM**) was unique in pioneering most of the major gospel advances and ministries in the country, but the work of **AoG** and Ekklesia is also significant in new visions and advance. The missionary body now needs to concentrate more on leadership among the Quechua, Aymara and upper classes and the discipling of the youth. Major missions include **NTM** (136), **SIM** (88), **LL** (84), **GMU** (70), **AoG** (53), **WGM** (40), **Christian Brethren** (38), Mennonites (38), South American Mission (34), Swedish Free Mission (33), **IMB-SBC** (27), Swiss Indian Mission (23), Norwegian Lutherans (21), **YWAM** (21). There are six Korean missions in the country, and Koreans have founded two of the three Christian universities.

12 **Bible translation and distribution. The Bible Society** has played a major role in every aspect of Bible work and now has its own press. Over one million New Testaments have been distributed in schools. The Aymara and Quechua Bibles are in great demand but effective literacy programmes are a vital need. **SIL** has almost achieved the objective of completing the Bible translation programme for all the Amerindian languages that warrant it. There are still 7 languages in which translation work continues and 3 more need a translation survey. May God's Word become part of the life of the entire nation!

13 Christian Media

a) **TV and radio** have continued to make a big impact. A radio is a vital possession in every family. Local radio stations have an increasing listenership — Ekklesia with its commercial Christian radio, *Musoj Chaski* radio in Quechua launched by **NTM, SIM**, Pioneers, and others. International stations (**HCJB, TWR, FEBC** and others) broadcast daily in Spanish and **HCJB** especially in Quechua and Aymara. Pray for this vital medium in a country where all other media are restricted in impact by illiteracy, poverty and isolation.

b) **Christian literature** — especially tracts, teaching materials and books — is in short supply in Aymara and Quechua. **SIM** have a significant ministry in this area. There are 13 Christian bookstores.

c) **The JESUS film**, widely used with considerable impact in Spanish, Aymara, Quechua and Chiriguano, has been seen by a high proportion of the country on television, video and in the cinema.

Bosnia

Bosnia and Herzegovina

[map: Croatia, Serbia, Bosnia and Herzegovina, Sarajevo, Bosniak, Serb, Adriatic Sea, Montenegro]

MARCH 7
EUROPE

GEOGRAPHY
Area 51,129sq.km. Mountainous Balkan state bracketed by Serbia-Montenegro and Croatia.

Population	Ann.Gr.	Density
2000	3,971,813	+3.06%	78 per sq. km.
2010	4,329,808	+0.45%	85 per sq. km.
2025	4,323,818	-0.22%	85 per sq. km.

Between 1992-95 over 1.3 million Bosnians fled to other lands and a further million or more were internally displaced. By 2000 only a quarter had returned, but few to their own homes.

Capital Sarajevo 485,855. **Urbanites** 36%.

PEOPLES
Massive changes 1991-2000. Second figure is for 2000.
Slav 88%. Nearly all speaking Serbo-Croat, but a patchwork of three mutually hostile, major Slavic nationalities.
  Bosnian Muslim (or Bosniaks) 38.3-50%. Mainly in Central Bosnia.
  Croat 17.3-19%. Mainly in SW & on N border.
  Serb 30.1-20%. Mainly in the 'Serb Republic' in N & E Bosnia.
Other 12%. Vlach Gypsy 400,000; Rumelian Turk 4,000.

Literacy 86%. **Official language** Bosnian. **All languages** 2. **Languages with Scriptures** 1Bi 1NT.

ECONOMY
Bosnia was Europe's second poorest country before the Bosnian War. Its fragile agrarian economy was shattered by the war, massive population movements, wholesale destruction and disruption of communications by the de facto partition of the country. Foreign aid is virtually the only source of income. **Unemployment** 60%+. **Income/person** $1,380 (4.4% of USA, an optimistic figure).

POLITICS
Bosnia straddles the cultural divide between east and west. It became separated from Serbia in 960, and during the 500-year Turkish occupation many Bosnians became Muslim. The recent break-up of Yugoslavia led to a Croat-Muslim alliance in support of independence in March 1992, which was immediately militarily contested by the Serb minority. The tragic three-sided war between Serbs, Croats and Bosnian Muslims caused immense damage, loss of life and the partition of Bosnia. The war ended in 1995 with the country almost equally divided between Serbs in the Serb Republic and the Croat-Muslim Federation. An uneasy peace is maintained by NATO armies.

B

RELIGION
Nationalistic religions have replaced Communism as the prevailing ideology and tend to be equally tyrannical and hostile to any who 'traitorously' deviate. Religious freedom is more theory than practice.

Religions	Population %	Adherents	Ann.Gr.
Muslim	60.06	2,385,471	+6.4%
Christian	35.00	1,390,135	-1.0%
non-Religious/other	4.93	195,810	-0.9%
Jewish	0.01	397	

Christians	Denom.	Affil.%	,000	Ann.Gr.
Protestant	8	0.07	3	+9.1%
Independent	2	0.02	1	-0.1%
Catholic	1	17.15	681	+1.6%
Orthodox	1	17.73	700	-3.1%
Marginal	1	0.03	1	+5.4%

Churches	MegaBloc	Cong.	Members	Affiliates
Serbian Orthodox	O	250	482,759	700,000
Catholic	C	310	469,748	681,135
Jehovah's Witnesses	M	12	600	1,300
Seventh-day Adventist	P	20	650	1,000
Evangelical (Pente)	P	16	400	700
Ev Chr Ch of B(Luth)	P	2	350	500
Baptist in BiH	P	12	250	400
Other denoms [6]		10	541	967
Total Christians [13]		632	955,308	1,386,000

Trans-bloc Groupings	pop. %	,000	Ann.Gr.
Evangelical	0.07	5	+3.7%
Charismatic	0.54	42	+1.8%
Pentecostal	0.02	1	+8.7%

Missionaries to Bosnia
P,I,A 137 in 21 agencies from 9+ countries: USA 85, Canada 10, Korea 7. **C** 30. **M** 10.

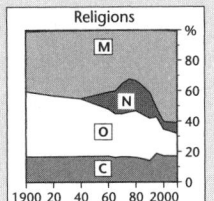

Religions chart: M, N, O, C — 1900 20 40 60 80 2000

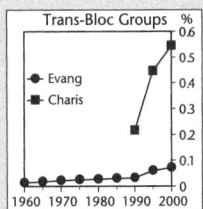

Trans-Bloc Groups chart: Evang, Charis — 1960 1970 1980 1990 2000

• Challenges for Prayer

B

1 **The Bosnian tragedy** was provoked by the political follies of the West and Serbian nationalism distorted by the megalomania of the Yugoslav Serbian leader Milosevic. The 'ethnic cleansing,' looting, destruction of 25% of all buildings (plus damage of a further 50%), and 250,000 deaths have left deep scars and an abiding hatred between communities that once lived together, spoke the same language and even intermarried. Pray for greater wisdom and foresight on the part of world and Bosnian leaders in implementing a workable peace, a just settlement and a viable future.

2 **Bosnian refugees are scattered around the world** as well as in Bosnia itself. Of the 1.3 million who fled to other lands only 400,000 had returned by 2000. Most of the internally displaced are still homeless. Pray that Muslims, Orthodox and Catholics alike might find healing for their deep psychological wounds, peace with God and with one another through faith in Christ and willingness to forgive the perpetrators of their misery. Pray for UN personnel, as well as secular and Christian NGOs who seek to help Bosnians rebuild their lives.

3 **The miniscule evangelical witness** has grown since 1991. Then there were only 2 to 3 congregations, but this had grown to 29 in 2000 with 700 people attending services. Evangelicals have gained credibility as the only ones to bridge the gulf between ethnic groups. Pray for the few believers and their witness in this war-torn land, amid a population uniquely receptive — for a while. A small Bible School with 20 students was started in 1996 in Mostar.

4 The unreached:

a) *Only a very small percentage of the population* has ever been clearly presented with the claims of Christ and the need for personal repentance and faith.

b) *The Bosniak Muslims* — from only a handful, the number of believers in Jesus has grown to 300-400, but most are unreached.

c) *The Serbs.* Over 500,000 became refugees, but they received the least aid and are bitter against the world that has ganged up on them. Pray for their eyes to be opened to the message of peace in Jesus.

d) *The largely Muslim Gypsy,* and wholly Muslim Turkish, minorities have only a few specific ministries directed to their evangelization (Vineyard, **IMB-SBC**).

e) *Student ministry.* By 2000 there were 30,000 students in Sarajevo. Hitherto no work has been done among them, but in 2000 a new ministry was begun. Pray for lasting fruit.

5 **Expatriate Christian input** is needed if sensitively provided. Pray for those engaged in aid, rehabilitation, outreach and church-planting ministries to fully identify with the people and that through them a harvest may be won. Pray for effective networking among expatriates. The largest agencies: **IMB-SBC** (30), Novi Most International (16), **Pioneers** (11), **CMA** (10), Church Resource Network (10), Team Expansion (5).

6 **Christian Media ministries** for prayer:

a) *The Federation of Bosnia and Herzegovina Bible Society* was formed in 1999 as a cooperative effort for Scripture and literature publication.

b) *TWR* broadcasts 8 hrs/wk in Serbian, Croatian and Bosnian from Monaco and Albania.

c) *The JESUS film* is available in Serbian, Bosnian and Croatian and is in preparation in Vlach.

Botswana

Republic of Botswana

MARCH 8
AFRICA

Religions	Population %	Adherents	Ann.Gr.
Christian	66.89	1,085,102	+2.6%
Traditional ethnic	31.86	516,839	+0.6%
Baha'i	0.77	12,491	+1.4%
Muslim	0.20	3,244	+3.6%
Hindu	0.14	2,271	+1.9%
non-Religious/other	0.14	2,271	+3.5%

Christians	Denom.	Affil.%	,000	Ann.Gr.
Protestant	47	12.22	198	+1.9%
Independent	154	37.17	603	+3.5%
Anglican	1	0.65	10	+4.8%
Catholic	1	3.70	60	+3.2%
Orthodox	1	0.01	0	+0.0%
Marginal	4	0.61	10	+2.5%
Unaffiliated		12.50	203	n.a.

Churches	MegaBloc	Cong.	Members	Affiliates
Spiritual Healing	I	88	35,000	70,000
Catholic	C	65	34,884	60,000
Zion Christian (ZCC)	I	14	25,000	50,000
United Cong Ch of S Af	P	61	20,000	41,000
Seventh-day Adventist	P	71	20,000	28,000
Assemblies of God	P	46	9,500	17,000
Evang Lutheran	P	46	11,565	17,000
Dutch Reformed	P	62	5,500	14,850
Apostolic Faith Mission	P	22	5,500	11,000
Anglican	A	93	3,153	10,500
Evang Luth Ch of SA	P	19	2,797	8,000
Pentecostal Holiness	P	51	4,000	6,680
Pentecostal Protestant	P	36	3,600	6,012
Lutheran Ch of Africa	P	12	2,400	6,000
Methodist Ch in Sthn Af	P	6	2,600	5,200
Holiness Union	P	6	600	3,000
Jehovah's Witnesses	M	40	1,000	2,780
Africa Evangelical	P	16	700	1,600
Baptist Mission	P	17	575	960
Other denoms [191]		2,640	237,000	515,000
Total Christians [211]		3,415	429,000	882,000

Trans-bloc Groupings	pop.%	,000	Ann.Gr.
Evangelical	8.0	129	+3.2%
Charismatic	38.2	619	+3.3%
Pentecostal	4.7	76	+3.3%

Missionaries from Botswana
P,I,A 2.

Missionaries to Botswana
P,I,A 237 in 59 agencies from 18 countries: USA 91, South Africa 37, UK 25, Canada 21, Germany 19.

GEOGRAPHY
Area 581,730 sq.km. The Kalahari Desert covers 80% of the country. Dry and prone to severe droughts.

Population	Ann.Gr.	Density
2000	1,622,220	+1.93%	3 per sq. km.
2010	1,831,933	+1.25%	3 per sq. km.
2025	2,241,857	+1.21%	4 per sq. km.

Capital Gaberone 180,000. **Urbanites** 29%.

PEOPLES
Bantu 94.8%.
Tswana 70%. Eight major tribes, most living along south-eastern border with South Africa.
Other 24.8%. Kalanga 240,000; Ndebele 30,000; Herero 25,000; Yeyi 23,000; Lozi 20,000; Pedi 16,000; Shona 15,000; Mbukushu 8,000; Subia 7,000.
San (Bushmen) 3.4%. Speaking 32 languages and dialects.
Other 1.8%. Zimbabwean, Angolan, South African and South Asian.

Literacy 86%. **Official language** English. **National language** Tswana. **All languages** 26. **Languages with Scriptures** 3Bi 1NT 2por 3w.i.p.

ECONOMY
Benign neglect in colonial times. Rapid development since independence through export of meat, diamonds, copper, nickel and gold. Earnings have been wisely used to develop country. A 20-year high rate of economic growth despite periodic droughts. **HDI** 0.609; 122nd/174. **Public debt** 10% of GNP. **Income/person** $3,310 (11% of USA).

POLITICS
Independence from Britain in 1966. Has a stable, multi-party democracy; a rarity in Africa.

RELIGION
Complete freedom of religion. After two centuries of having the gospel, the old tribal religions remain strong, and often spiritually unchallenged.

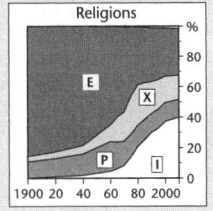

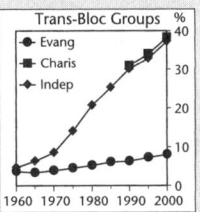

• Challenges for Prayer

1 The Tswana were the first Bantu people in Africa to respond to the gospel; several tribes turned to God in the 19th Century through the LMS from England. Other missions followed. Nominalism soon became a major problem, since each mission planted what became virtually a 'state' church for the tribe that received that group. The majority of Tswana are Christian in name but given over to immorality and drunkenness accentuated by the breakdown of family life. In some areas, over 90% of children are illegitimate. Pray for a reversal of the moral decline.

2 AIDS has become a terrible scourge. Widespread promiscuity has rapidly spread the disease to 30-35% of the population. The result — 60,000 AIDS orphans by 1999; of children under 5 who died in 2000, 64% died because of AIDS; 50% of university students HIV+ and a soaring national death rate. The social and economic life of the country will be devastated during the next decade. Pray for agencies such as BOCAIP, the Church's response to HIV/AIDS, who teach and advocate moral purity and Christian standards to prevent the spread of AIDS and also care for those affected. The ministry of many congregations is dominated by coping with AIDS deaths among their members. Pray for a radical change in the culture of the nation.

3 Protestant Churches are not maintaining their numbers. Nominalism is pervasive. Many congregations have few men. The United Congregational Church has only a few aging pastors and few candidates for the ministry. Some smaller evangelical and Pentecostal denominations are growing. Pray for revival, a new level of commitment and a recovery of vision for evangelism. Pray also for the 5 Protestant theological training institutions, among them the AoG Bible College in Gaberone, the Evangelical Lutheran Seminary and Kgolagano College.

4 Vision among Christians was stimulated by the GCOWE 1997 Conference. A fellowship network of mission agencies and churches was initiated. Pray for wisdom, godly leadership and visionary developments to impact Botswana.

5 African indigenous churches have multiplied. There are now over 150 such denominations. Their emphasis on healing (especially with the AIDS crisis), and local culture can often lead to syncretistic beliefs. Many are led by those with little education or theological training. Several basic theological courses run by the Mennonites and the Botswana Bible Training Institute are specifically geared to help these leaders. Pray for these churches and for the Scriptures to mould their development and outreach.

6 Less reached peoples

a) The 50,000 Bakgalagadi are mixed Tswana and San, but they speak Tswana. They are partially nomadic, living in the western desert. Pray for agencies such as **Word to Africa** and outreach teams from South Africa seeking to reach them.

b) The Kalanga resent the cultural dominance of the Tswana. There are few active Christians among them, but during the 1990s more were coming to Christ. The NT has been newly translated — pray for its impact.

c) The Yeyi of the Okavango Swamp have only been exposed to nominal Christianity in the medium of the Tswana language. The efforts of **Love Botswana Outreach**, **Word to Africa** and **Calvary Ministries** have begun to see a small response.

d) The Mbukushu and Subia in the north are isolated from the main flow of national life and have little opportunity to hear the gospel.

e) The Herero are mostly nominal Lutheran or belong to the fire-worshipping 'Oruuano' Church.

f) The San have suffered the complete destruction of their desert-adapted way of life due to the development of ranching, mining and tourism. There are no longer any nomadic San — all are resettled in poverty on the fringes of towns and villages. Response has been slow but several thousand San may now be Christian in about 15 congregations through the efforts of 10 agencies (Lutheran, **SIM**, Dutch Reformed, RTU, **Word to Africa** and Charles Haupt Ministries). Pray that these folk may help the San to adapt to modernity, yet retain their cultural heritage and, above all, find their true identity in Christ.

7 The last 20 years have been a time of **new evangelical penetration** for outreach, church planting and the founding of new Bible training institutions. The growing work of the Mennonites (37), **SIM** (16), **IMB-SBC** (16), Finnish Lutherans (16), Korean agencies (12), Brethren (7) and others, needs prayer. The spiritual and physical conditions are not easy. Pray for the planting of witnessing churches in which Christians exhibit true holiness and a love for the Scriptures.

B

8 **Young people** need spiritual help. Teenage pregnancies are 'normal' and offspring of single parents are likely to be HIV+ and poor. Religion is taught as an obligatory subject in schools. Pray for the ministry of **SU** in providing Christian teaching materials for the schools, and nurturing the **SU** groups meeting in 30 (out of the 73) secondary schools. Pray for more part- and full-time workers for this ministry. There is a lively **IFES** group at the University of Botswana.

9 Christian Media and support ministries for prayer:

a) *The Bible Society* oversees the translation programme. Pray for wisdom in choice of minority languages for translation projects, the most challenging being the many small San languages.

b) *Radio broadcasts and Christian TV* on the national network are supervised by the International Church Radio Council. **TWR** Swaziland broadcasts 45 minutes daily in Tswana. **Radio LBOM** is being constructed in Maun, NW Botswana. Plans are to broadcast 24 hrs/day in three languages of Botswana and neighbouring lands.

c) *Literature* for the rapidly increasing literate population is scarce and often expensive. Little variety is available in Tswana, and virtually nothing in minority languages. Pray for bookstore ministries.

d) *The JESUS film* is being used in 5 languages including Tswana, Herero, Kalanga and Afrikaans. Production is under way in Kgalagadi, Yeyi and one San language.

e) *The Flying Mission* serves the cause of Christ with 6 planes based in Maun and Gaberone.

f) *GRN* has available recordings in 26 languages — 18 of them San.

g) *Botswana Christian Prison Fellowship* (PFI) has a ministry in all the country's prisons.

Brazil
Federated Republic of Brazil

MARCH 9-11
LATIN AMERICA

GEOGRAPHY
Area 8,511,965 sq.km. One half of the land surface and population of South America. The world's fifth largest country.

Population	Ann.Gr.	Density
2000	170,115,463	+1.32%	20 per sq. km.
2010	190,875,224	+1.11%	22 per sq. km.
2025	217,929,781	+0.77%	26 per sq. km.

Capital Brasilia 1,985,000. Other major cities: São Paulo 17.7 mill.; Rio de Janeiro 10.6m; Belo Horizonte 4.2m; Porto Alegre 3.7m; Recife 3.3m; Salvador 3.2m; Fortaleza 3m; Curitiba 2.6m; Campinas 1.86m; Belem 1.63m; Manaus 1.4m; Cubatao 1.3m; Santos 1.3m; Goiania 1.1m. **Urbanites** 78%.

PEOPLES
Brazil is a 'melting pot' of nations, with much intermarriage, so percentages given below are not meant to indicate rigid categories.
European 53.5%. Portuguese 15%; Italian 11%; Spanish 10%; German 3% in origin; other 15%.
Mixed race 34.4%. Mestizo and Mulatto.
African 11%. Descendants of slaves brought from West Africa and Angola.
Asian 1%. Japanese 1,400,000; Arab 180,000; Chinese 180,000; Korean 70,000.
Amerindian 0.14%. In 1900 there were 500,000 in 230 tribes, but now there are an estimated 240,000 in 200 tribes, still decreasing through the encroachments of new settlers, loss of land and disease.

Literacy 83%. **Official language** Portuguese. **All living languages** 195. **Languages with Scriptures** 1Bi 40NT 31por 55w.i.p.

ECONOMY

Vast economic potential in the developing hinterland of the north and west. Rapid growth and industrialization in the 1960s and '70s in the south made Brazil one of the world's leading industrial and trading nations. Massive inflation in the 1980s, crippling foreign debts and gross disparity between the rich 30% and the poor 70% brought Brazil to the brink of disaster. There was economic improvement in the 1990s, but the core issues of corruption, protectionism, state ownership, regional overspending and the growing ecological crisis in Amazonia have yet to be addressed. **Unemployment** 6%. **HDI** 0.739; 79th/174. **Public debt** 11% of GNP. **Income/person** $4,400 (15% of USA).

POLITICS

Independent from Portugal in 1822 as a kingdom, it became a federal republic in 1889. Authoritarian military rule between 1964 and 1985 left a legacy of social inequality, bureaucratic inefficiency and state ownership of large parts of the economy. Multi-party democracy restored in 1985. Popular outcry at the corruption of the President forced his resignation in 1992, and democratic accountability to the people has improved since then.

RELIGION

Freedom of religion and separation of Church and state. There is still a residual bias to Catholicism in government circles.

Religions	Population %	Adherents	Ann.Gr.
Christian	91.43	155,536,568	+0.7%
Animist/Spiritist	5.00	8,505,773	+1.7%
non-Religious/other	3.01	5,125,476	+2.9%
Buddhist	0.25	425,289	+0.5%
Jewish	0.21	357,242	+2.3%
Muslim	0.10	170,115	+1.3%

Christians	Denom.	Affil.%	,000	Ann.Gr.
Protestant	116	6.63	11,274	+1.1%
Independent	216	5.80	9,859	+3.6%
Anglican	1	0.07	125	+7.5%
Catholic	1	73.18	124,500	-0.4%
Orthodox	15	0.11	188	+0.8%
Marginal	59	1.16	1,970	+3.9%
Unaffliated		4.48	7,621	n.a.

Churches	MegaBloc	Cong.	Members	Affiliates
Catholic	C	25,500	90.876m	124.50m
Assemblies of God	P	22,000	2,000,000	4,100,000

Seventh-day Adventist	P	3,378	882,352	1,500,000
Christian Cong.	I	4,500	675,000	1,350,000
Baptist Convention	P	5,765	843,638	1,200,000
Brazil for Christ	I	4,500	800,000	1,200,000
Jehovah's Witnesses	M	7,730	528,034	1,200,000
God is Love	I	5,000	600,000	1,200,000
Lutheran Confession	P	2,700	713,287	1,020,000
Catholic Apostolic	I	349	300,000	600,000
Latter-day Saints (Morm)	M	1,310	437,956	600,000
Univ Ch K'dom of God	I	1,200	300,000	600,000
Int'l Ch of Frsqr Gospel	P	2,300	212,000	500,000
National Baptist Conv	I	1,294	220,000	370,000
Presbyterian	P	1,867	280,000	370,000
Evang Congreg Chr	P	2,250	180,000	300,000
Ev Luth Church of Brazil	P	1,800	125,749	210,000
Methodist	P	2,400	120,000	200,000
Restoration Church	I	560	140,000	200,000
Episcopal	A	320	51,230	125,000
Christian Brethren	P	810	65,000	120,000
Indep Presbyterian	P	500	60,000	100,200
Conv of Evang Baptists	P	1,204	65,000	90,000
Adv Ch of the Promise	I	473	26,000	56,000
Chr Evang Alliance	P	665	13,308	35,000
Other denoms [387]			2,807,230	6,261,000

Total Christians[410]		103.282m	147.916m

Note: Both the Catholics and various Pentecostal groups claim high numbers. These have been adjusted in line with census and independent research groups. Figures given here are substantially lower than those given in the 1993 edition of *Operation World*.

Trans-bloc Groupings	pop.%	,000	Ann.Gr.
Evangelical	12.6	21,379	+4.4%
Charismatic	23.2	39,524	+2.4%
Pentecostal	7.9	13,523	+5.3%

Missionaries from Brazil
P,I,A 4,754 in 132 agencies to 100 countries: Brazil 3,440; Portugal 103; Paraguay 85; USA 68; Guinea-Bissau 66; Mozambique 63; Spain 62; UK 52; Peru 51.

Missionaries to Brazil
P,I,A 3,100 in 205 agencies from 41 countries: USA 2,060; UK 210; Germany 200; Korea 140; Canada 132.

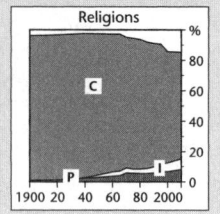

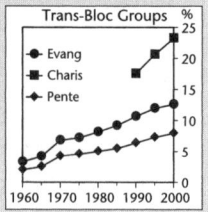

• Answers to Prayer

1 **Continued spiritual hunger** in the midst of economic uncertainty has caused many to seek after God. Evangelicals continue to grow in numbers and influence — but not at the rate many have believed in the past. Note the growth in the graph above.

2 **The state of Goias was well known for spiritism,** but massive intercession by women is breaking this power. In 1992 Evangelicals were 7% of the population, but by 1999 they had greatly increased.

3 The Brazilian missionary movement is continuing to grow and mature.

• Challenges for Prayer

1 The government continues to dodge the painful restructuring and righting the wrongs of the past. It is said Brazil is a paradise for some, purgatory for most and hell for 20%. Pray that the endemic corruption, cronyism, injustices of society and discrimination — against the poor, underprivileged children and indigenous tribal peoples — may be ended.

2 The Catholic Church is in crisis. Brazil is the world's largest Catholic country with nearly 10% of all Catholics. Annual losses of 600,000 to Evangelicals and to spiritism continue. Only 13% of Catholics are active in their commitment; nominalism and spiritism are rife among those who profess. Change must come, but the 'Base Community' movement, once two million-strong, has lost much of its cutting edge. Widespread espousal of liberation theology in the 1970s and 1980s faded with increased prosperity and democracy. Positive changes are these:

a) Vocations to the priesthood among Brazilians have increased and now only 23% of the 15,300 priests are foreign.

b) The growth of the charismatic movement continues apace with over 15 million active participants.

c) The successes of evangelical denominations have stimulated a more people-friendly, contemporary worship and ministry, and a greater growth of Evangelical Catholics as well as traditional mass attendance.

Pray that the Bible and its truths may mould the lives of Catholics.

3 Challenges facing Brazilian Evangelicals. Intercede for the following:

a) Relevance and a prophetic voice in Brazilian society. Evangelistic vision is rarely extended to a vision to bring a message of righteousness to a society ravaged by inequality, injustice, selfishness, crime, immorality and AIDS. Evangelicals have increased their political leverage, but there have been many evidences of carnality as well as moral and ethical failure among those with a high public profile. Pray that they may use their growing influence wisely and in biblical holiness and humility.

b) Spiritual depth. Success rather than holiness has spawned many unhealthy trends: an overemphasis on healing and prosperity, a 'worshipping' of large numbers with much exaggeration, a great zeal for evangelism but less concern for retaining or discipling in depth those who seek help. The result is over-evangelized but underfed converts, many petty legalisms, a growing Pentecostal nominalism, and an enormous rate of backsliding with millions of ex-Evangelicals now disillusioned with Christianity.

c) Godly servant leadership accountable to those to whom they minister. Some leaders have sought political and ecclesiastical power, fame and selfish gain. There have been too many widely-publicized scandals and moral failures.

d) Effective modelling and training for those called to Christian ministry. Only a minority of the 75,000 evangelical congregations are led by those with basic theological training. In 1992 there were 321 seminaries and institutes where over 12,000 were being trained for ministry and also 275 **AoG** Bible schools with over 12,000 students. This has greatly increased — over 7,000 were being trained in Baptist seminaries by 1999, but all forms of theological training need to be increased to provide the Church with pastoral care and biblical leadership. Too few are willing to serve where the need is greatest.

e) Unity. There are anywhere between 400 and 4,000 denominations among Evangelicals. Unresolved inter-personal relationships, jealousies and hatreds have weakened their voice. Pray for the Evangelical Association of Brazil, founded in 1991, that it may be a means of fostering lasting unity, fellowship and prayerful cooperation.

4 Goals for the new Millennium. A visionary conference sponsored by *Projeto Brasil 2010* and associated with **DAWN** was a catalyst for an unprecedented unity and cooperative commitment to national goals for prayer and action:

a) Thousands of new churches to be planted as a multi-denominational national initiative. In order that there be a church for every 1,000 urban dwellers and a church for every rural and river community, there must be 250,000 congregations by 2010.

b) ***Adoption of, and church planting among,*** the 139 Amerindian tribal groups still unreached.

c) ***A focus on the hundreds of Brazilian towns*** and municipalities with less than 1% Evangelicals. Nearly all of these are in the north-east.

d) ***Adoption of 173 unreached peoples*** in other lands.

B

5 **Spiritism is a dynamic force for evil in Brazil.** Not only is Brazil the largest Catholic country, but also the largest spiritist country in the world. It appeals to the emotions and offers physical healing; both traits make it an attractive alternative to traditional Christianity. In 1975 there were at least 14,000 spiritist centres guided by 420,000 mediums. There are seven million Brazilians practising Kardecism ('high' spiritism) and millions more practising Umbanda and Macumba ('low' spiritism with African roots). A majority of Brazilians are involved — most still claiming to be Christian. Pray both for Christians willing and spiritually equipped to minister to those bound by Satan, and for the deliverance of many.

6 **The challenge of the less evangelized peoples.** Pray for effective outreach and church planting in:

a) ***The squalid favelas.*** These slums are a highly visible blight in every major city — home to nearly 20 million poverty-stricken and needy people, and 20-25% of Rio de Janeiro and São Paulo's population. These lawless areas are rarely entered by the police and are hotbeds of crime, drugs, violence, prostitution and disease. AIDS is a major problem.

b) ***The northeast***, which is poor and underdeveloped and also has Brazil's lowest percentage of Evangelicals. About 15 million people live in the poor ***Sertão*** but only 3% are Evangelicals. There is a great exodus of poor to the Amazon and the cities of the southeast. Pray for wise Christian relief and development through an effective Brazilian and expatriate missionary presence.

c) ***The Amazon basin***, which is larger than the whole of non-Russian Europe, and is of global importance because of its oxygen-generating forests and huge biodiversity. It is also spiritually needy. The challenges for outreach are the pioneer settlements springing up along new roads through the forests and the 36,000 yet unchurched river communities accessible only by boat. **UFM**, **AoG**, Baptists, **YWAM** and others are involved with **MAF** support in some areas. Church planting is made difficult by the relative poverty, loss of key members to cities, and geographical isolation.

d) ***The cities.*** Though they have numerous churches, cities also contain ethnic minorities and the nation's elite which are far less reached. Pray that the Church may find effective means to break through into these groups.

e) ***The Japanese.*** Over 60% are Roman Catholic but only 3% Protestant. In 1992 there were 80 evangelical churches with 7,000 adult Japanese believers, with little increase since then. Pray for the witness of the Japan Holiness Church (OMSI), Japan Evangelical Mission and **UFM**. Many Brazilian Japanese have gone to Japan as low-paid labourers — the Holiness Church has sent missionaries to work amongst them.

f) ***The 180,000 Chinese*** who live largely in São Paulo, where there are 12 small evangelical congregations, but the percentage of Christians (1.7%) is low. By contrast, there are more than 42 churches for the 60,000 Koreans.

7 **The under-18s are over 50% of the population.** There is a widespread gap in ministry to children and young people both inside and beyond the churches. Pray specifically for:

a) ***Children in crisis.*** Remember before the Lord:

i *The 10 million children* who make their living from the streets. Pray for the many churches and agencies which have orphanages, homes of refuge, rehabilitation and training ministries (**YWAM**, **UFM**, **WH**, **WEC**, **AM**, etc.).

ii *The hundreds of thousands of street kids* who have no home and are subject to drug abuse, prostitution, misuse by criminal gangs and even murder by police death squads (over 1,500 murders every year).

iii *The 7 million child labourers.*

iv *The 500,000 involved in prostitution.*

v *The 540,000 already infected with the AIDS virus in 1999.*

Pray also for Christians to be active in social action to address the spiritual and economic causes.

b) ***Young people who face many pressures*** — especially in university. There are about 1,700,000 students in 851 universities. Pray for more workers to minister to them. The **CCCI** and **Navigators** are active, and the ABU(**IFES**) is having a significant impact with groups in most universities. They help students come to the Lord, build them up in the Word and encourage missionary vision. The ABU has a ministry to Christian graduates.

c) ***Appropriate ministry for children and young people*** in the churches. There is a huge gap in this area in the majority of congregations. Without this the next generation will be at best, poorly discipled and at worst, will reject their parents' faith.

8 **The indigenous Amerindians,** as elsewhere in the Americas, have had a long history of prejudice, oppression, massacres and exploitation that continues to this day. There are now protective laws for the remaining small tribal groups but they are rarely applied. The continued survival of these peoples is threatened by encroaching woodcutters, gold prospectors and ranchers. Their cultures are disintegrating through despair, disease, alcohol abuse and suicide. The six million indigenous peoples of 1500AD now number 240,000 with many reduced to small bands in inaccessible areas of the Amazon basin. Pray for:

a) ***A change in attitude on the part of Brazilians,*** and wise balance on the part of government agencies, in protecting existing cultures and their integration into national life. Tragically it is often those appointed to 'protect' them who become the chief oppressors and exploiters.

b) ***A reversal of restrictions on mission work*** among them. In 1978 the ministry of **SIL** in 41 tribes, **NTM** in 20 and **UFM** in 5 was severely curtailed. This was triggered by anti-Christian anthropologists, land-grabbers, gold-diggers and corrupt officials. Pray that this unholy alliance may be thwarted in their hindering of evangelism, church planting and Bible translation. There has been some easing of restrictions over the past decade.

c) ***Christian agencies ministering to them.*** There are nearly 1,000 national and expatriate workers in ministry among Amerindians. Pray for an increased commitment to this ministry by Brazilians — they face fewer hassles. Pray for the work of **NTM** with 251 missionaries in 17 tribes (targeting a further 22), **SIL** in 45, **UFM** in 7, **SAM** in 4, **YWAM** in 2 and various Brazilian agencies. Pray also for sensitivity in applying the gospel message in ways that are biblical yet give pride in their language and culture.

d) ***Bible translation*** — **SIL**, the Brazilian ALEM and **NTM** have made a large investment of effort, time and personnel into this ministry. Over 55 translation projects are in hand and a further 56 languages need surveys to clarify their need for translators. Over 19 languages are on the verge of extinction.

e) ***The unreached.*** About 40 small tribal groups totalling around 5,000 people have yet to be contacted with the gospel. A total of 131 are listed as still without viable congregations of evangelical believers. Pray for their complete evangelization and the preservation of the integrity of their societies.

f) ***The Yanomami*** with some 15,000 people straddle the Brazil-Venezuela border. Their land has been invaded, despoiled and poisoned by illegal gold-diggers. Over 2,000 have been killed in clashes with settlers. Many powerful bodies seek the expulsion of missionaries working among them.

g) ***The Guarani*** on the Paraguay border number 30,000 but have been deprived of their lands so frequently that they are rapidly dying out through a wave of suicides, tuberculosis and malnutrition. There are only about 300 known believers.

9 **The role of missionaries** has changed over the years. The most important ministries for missionaries today are in leadership training, preparing Brazilian missionaries and in pioneer work in the Amazon region. Missions with the largest number of workers: **YWAM** (1,068, 93% Brazilian), **NTM** (451, 58% Brazilian), **IMB-SBC** (267), SIL/**WBT** (177), Baptist Mid-Mission (177), ABWE (135), **UFM** (121), **AoG** (115, 20% Brazilian), **LL** (58), Chs of Christ/Christian Chs (57), **MAF** (53), Brethren (52), **WEC** (52, 54% Brazilian), **BMS**-UK (48), **CBI** (39), **GMU** (35). Pray for the wise and strategic deployment of the missionary force to the best advantage of the Brazilian Church.

10 **Praise God for the rapid growth** and maturing of the Brazilian missions movement. Brazil has become a major missionary-sending nation. Pray for:

a) ***The AMTB*** — an association of cross-cultural missionary agencies that links many of the 2,000 cross-cultural Brazilian missionaries serving in 92 agencies and 85 nations.

b) ***Brazilian missionaries*** — their recruitment, effective training and preparation for the field and their long-term survival and fruitfulness in cross-cultural situations.

c) ***Christian congregations*** to increase their long-term commitment to pray for, send and support missionaries. The danger is that initial enthusiasm can quickly fade, and inflation erode promised financial support. General attitudes to cross-cultural missions have changed little during the 1990s.

d) ***The Associação de Conselhos Missionários de Igrejas*** (ACMI), founded in 1990, which aims to help local churches set up viable missions structures, programmes and channelling mechanisms.

11 **Christian literature.** Brazil's most widely sold books are about magic and the occult. The evangelical community, as a whole, reads one book per person per year, though the rate of Bible reading is high — 84% of Evangelicals read it every day. Pray for change through:

a) ***Christian publishers*** such as the two large **AoG** publishing houses, JUERP (Baptist Conv), EVN (New Life, **CBI**), *Betânia* (Bethany Fellowship), *Mundo Cristão* (EUSA) and ABEB (**IFES**). Most of these operate under the umbrella of the Evangelical Literature Committee of Brazil.

b) ***Bible distribution*** which increased markedly in the '90s. **The Bible Society** has massive sales of Bibles and portions of Scripture, distributing over one million Bibles and 142 million portions or leaflets annually. The Gideons distributed 10 million NTs and a further 17.2 million copies of the leaflet 'New Life for the '90s'.

12 Christian media — for prayer:

a) ***The JESUS film*** has been widely used and over half the Brazilian population has seen it. The video version has been successful among professionals. The film is in preparation in two indigenous Amerindian languages. Pray for those who respond and for their integration into Bible study groups and churches.

b) ***Radio.*** Brazilian Evangelicals operate numerous TV stations and local and national radio stations. The wide use of these media can lead to abuse. Internationally, **TWR** Bonaire, KYFR USA, and **HCJB** Ecuador beam in 226 hours of broadcasts per week. *Projeto Luz* (700 Club) gains huge audiences across the country. Pray for lasting impact.

c) ***Cassettes.*** GRN have prepared tapes in 90 indigenous languages.

British Indian Ocean Territory

MARCH 12
AFRICA

GEOGRAPHY
Area 153 sq.km. Mainly the Chagos Archipelago in the central Indian Ocean.

Population At present approximately 2,000 US and UK military personnel.

POLITICS
The original islanders were removed to Mauritius to make way for opening up the island of Diego Garcia as a strategic US/UK military base. In 2000, the evicted islanders won a court ruling against the British government which has opened the way for their eventual return and resettlement.

See under **Mauritius**.

British Virgin Islands

Colony of British Virgin Islands

MARCH 12
LATIN AMERICA

$15,000 (54% of USA).

 POLITICS
A dependent territory of the UK, with internal democratic government.

RELIGION
There is freedom of religion.

Religions	Population %	Adherents	Ann.Gr.
Christian	86.00	18,375	+2.6%
Spiritist	8.60	1,837	+3.2%
non-Religious/other	3.80	812	+4.5%
Baha'i	0.90	192	+2.7%
Muslim	0.40	85	+6.2%
Hindu	0.30	64	+2.7%

Christians	Denom.	Affil.%	,000	Ann.Gr.
Protestant	11	42.83	9	+0.7%
Independent	8	5.62	1	+5.7%
Anglican	1	13.10	3	+1.5%
Catholic	1	3.28	0	+0.6%
Marginal	1	2.11	0	+2.9%
Unaffiliated		19.06	4	n.a.

Churches	MegaBloc	Cong.	Members	Affiliates
Methodist	P	5	2,396	4,600
Anglican	A	3	924	2,800
Seventh-day Adventist	P	4	980	1,300
Ch of the Nazarene	P	14	650	1,000
Catholic	C	10	280	700
Baptist	P	2	248	620
Ch of God (Holiness)	P	3	370	610
NT Ch of God	P	1	170	500
Jehovah's Witnesses	M	2	169	450
Other denoms [15]		14	962	1,860
Total Christians [24]		50	7,149	14,440

Trans-bloc Groupings	pop. %	,000	Ann.Gr.
Evangelical	27.2	6	+2.6%
Charismatic	11.6	2	+4.4%
Pentecostal	4.2	1	+4.8%

Missionaries from British Virgin Islands
P,I,A 2.

Missionaries to British Virgin Islands
P,I,A 2 from USA.

GEOGRAPHY
Area 153 sq.km. An archipelago of 60 coralline and volcanic islands of which 15 are inhabited. The north-easternmost of the Leeward Islands.

Population		Ann.Gr.	Density
2000	21,366	+2.74%	140 per sq. km.
2010	27,248	+2.37%	178 per sq. km.
2025	36,663	+1.81%	240 per sq. km.

Capital Road Town 3,793.

PEOPLES
Over 40% of the population were born in other countries.
Afro-Caribbean 87.5%.
Euro-American 10%.
Other 2.5%. East Indian 200.
Literacy 98%. **Official language** English.

 ECONOMY
Tourism is by far the most important economic activity. Tightened laws have curbed off-shore banking and the money-laundering mafia organizations it attracted. **Income/person**

• Challenges for Prayer

1 **The tourist trade** brings large numbers of pleasure-seeking visitors and also attracts many illegal and often less-desirable immigrants, with the resultant impact on the moral life of the island. Pray for local Christians and their witness to the tourists.

2 **This 'Paradise' is one of the most beautiful in the world,** yet sin mars many. Most of the population profess Christianity and even belong to congregations that preach holiness, yet 75% of births are out of wedlock. Pray for a Christian lifestyle that is in accordance with their confession.

3 **The motto of the Virgin Islands is 'Where there's no vision the people will perish'.** Pray that the Christians might have a vision for the lost locally and globally, which is largely absent.

Brunei
State of Brunei Darussalam

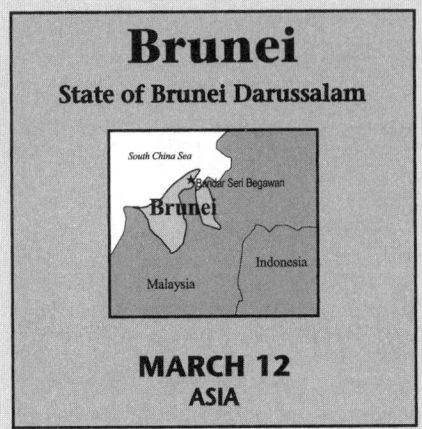

South China Sea

Bandar Seri Begawan

Brunei

Indonesia

Malaysia

MARCH 12
ASIA

GEOGRAPHY
Area 5,765 sq.km. Two small enclaves in Sarawak, East Malaysia on the island of Borneo. Tropical, 70% forest, with heavy rainfall.

Population		Ann.Gr.	Density
2000	328,080	+2.19%	57 per sq. km.
2010	384,439	+1.45%	67 per sq. km.
2025	458,972	+1.05%	80 per sq. km.

Capital Bandar Seri Begawan 99,854. **Urbanites** 58%.

PEOPLES
Malay 63.9%. Dominant in government and civil service. Many of the tribal peoples have been absorbed into the Malay population.
Chinese 15.6%. Of these, 80% are non-citizen residents. Gradual decline through emigration. Dominant in commerce.
Tribal 6%. Predominantly Iban. Also Kedayan, Kayan, Kenyah, Kiput, Murut and Tutung.
Other 14.5%. Considerable immigration of work seekers; largest: Filipino 10,600; Thai 8,600; Nepali 4,000; Anglo-Saxon 3,300; Indian 3,000; Bangladeshi 1,000.

Literacy 88%. **Official languages** Malay, English. **All languages** 16. **Languages with Scriptures** 8Bi 1NT

ECONOMY
One of the richest states in Asia. Oil is the sole source of wealth and reserves may be used up by 2020. The need for diversification is urgent. **HDI** 0.878; 25th/174. **Income/person** $25,160 (80% of USA).

POLITICS
Refused to join the Malaysian Federa-

tion in 1963. A Protectorate of Britain until full independence in 1983. The Sultan rules as an absolute monarch. No criticism of the government is allowed; all democratic structures were suspended in 1962.

RELIGION
Islam is the state religion. Constitutional guarantees for the free practice of other religions are being eroded and limitations on Christian activity are increasing.

Religions	Population %	Adherents	Ann.Gr.
Muslim	64.39	211,185	+2.0%
Christian	11.25	36,909	+4.5%
Buddhist	9.09	29,822	+1.3%
Traditional ethnic	7.60	24,934	+3.4%
Chinese	5.31	17,421	-0.3%
non-Religious/other	1.22	4,070	+4.3%
Hindu	0.84	2,756	+2.0%
Baha'i	0.30	984	+0.9%

Christians	Denom.	Affil.%	,000	Ann.Gr.
Protestant	6	1.80	6	+3.0%
Independent	10	2.53	8	+7.3%
Anglican	1	1.40	5	+0.4%
Catholic	1	1.71	6	+0.5%
Marginal	1	0.03	0	+9.0%
Unaffiliated		3.78	12	n.a.

Churches	MegaBloc	Cong.	Members	Affiliates
Catholic	C	3	3,128	5,600
Anglican	A	3	700	4,600
Tribal churches [4]	I	12	1,500	3,000
Brunei Christian Fell	I	2	850	1,700
Christian Brethren	P	2	450	810
Other denoms [11]		21	2,382	8,790
Total Christians [19]		43	9,010	24,500

Trans-bloc Groupings	pop. %	,000	Ann.Gr.
Evangelical	4.6	15	+5.1%
Pentecostal & Charismatic	2.7	9	+5.0%

Missionaries from Brunei
P,I,A 1.

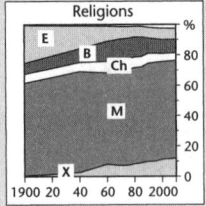

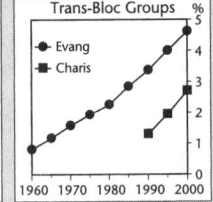

• Challenges for Prayer

1 **Muslims aim for a 'pure' Islamic state by 2020**. Islamization by offers of houses, jobs and favours and by intimidation of Christians has yielded a slow but steady trickle of converts from among the tribal and Chinese minorities. Pray for both the thwarting of these designs and the re-instatement of constitutionally guaranteed religious freedom.

2 **The king is reputed to be the world's wealthiest man.** Pray for conversions to Christ in the large royal family. Pray also for political liberalization in the country.

3 **The Christian Church is under much pressure.** No foreign Christian workers are permitted — even to visit, and all Catholic priests and nuns were expelled in 1991. No Bibles or Christian literature may be imported legally. All schools, including the 6 Christian schools must give instruction on Islam alone. There are three registered churches but many others' applications for registration are ignored, and they must meet secretly. Pray for:

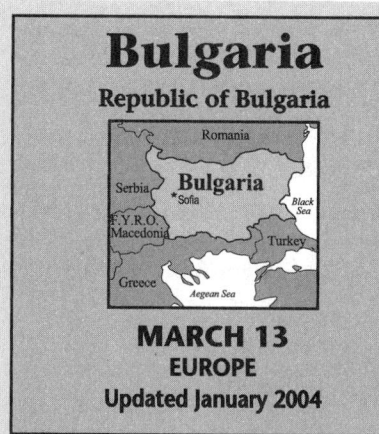

a) *Unity, courage and a wise boldness.* The pressure has increased the earnestness of many and a moving of the Holy Spirit among locals and Filipinos is reported.
b) *Provision of mature Christian leaders* and teachers of the Word.
c) *Further growth despite the restrictions.* Most of those converted are local tribals and Chinese.

4 **The unreached**

a) *The Malay majority* is Muslim with no known Christians. Witchcraft and materialism are strong.
b) *The Chinese* feel insecure and are still treated as foreigners even if born in Brunei. Most still follow the traditional religions of China or are secular. Only 15% are Christian, but fewer are committed to Christ.
c) *Tribal peoples* have either been converted to Islam and absorbed into the mainstream of national life, or have remained isolated in jungle villages. Among the latter, many Iban, Kelabit, Murut and others have come to Christ through the witness of the Anglicans, Brunei Christian Fellowship and Bethel Chapel. Pray for the evangelization of each of these communities.
d) *The expatriate workforce* continues to grow fast. The Muslim Bangladeshis, the Hindu Indians and Nepalis (the latter making up much of the Brunei army) and the Buddhist Thai are the largest and most needy spiritually.

5 **Brunei students usually complete university education in** Malaysia, Britain, Australia or other lands. Pray that they may come into contact with a vibrant Christian witness, be won for Christ, and ultimately return home as witnesses to their Saviour.

Bulgaria
Republic of Bulgaria

MARCH 13
EUROPE
Updated January 2004

Some official projections indicate decline to between 7.1 and 7.5 million by 2010.

Capital Sofia 1,188,000. **Urbanites** 53%.

PEOPLES
Slavic 86%. Bulgarian 6,830,000; Macedonian 218,000; Russian 16,000; Serbian 8,000; Czech 6,000.
Turkic 9.4%. Turks 900,000; Gagauz 12,000; Crimean Tatar 5,000.
Roma (Gypsy) 3.7%. 300,000 speaking Romani, Turkish or Bulgarian.
Other 0.9%. Armenian 13,000; Greek 10,000; Jews 3,400.

Literacy 98% (in practice nearer 90%). **Official languages** Bulgarian, Turkish. **All languages** 12. **Languages with Scriptures** 3Bi 1NT 3por 4w.i.p.

GEOGRAPHY
Area 110,912 sq.km. Balkan state adjoining Turkey, Greece, Macedonia, Serbia and Romania.

Population	Ann.Gr.	Density
2000	8,225,045	-0.65%	74 per sq. km.
2010	7,752,691	-0.59%	70 per sq. km.
2025	7,023,064	-0.72%	63 per sq. km.

ECONOMY
Poverty increased by 45 years of Communist rule which ended in 1989. Essential economic reforms were only begun in 1997 after a disastrous three-year government of former Communists in collusion with the 'mafia.' Wars in the former Yugoslavia have slowed the rate of progress since then. **Unemployment** 11.4%. **HDI** 0.758; 63rd/174. **Public debt** 79% of GNP. **Income/person** $1,170 (3.7% of USA).

POLITICS

A nation since the 5th Century, but rarely independent. Ruled by the Ottoman Empire 1396-1878; severe Communist rule 1947-1989; multi-party democracy instituted in 1990. A see-saw struggle for power since then between Democrats and Socialists (ex-Communist Party) but only since 1997 have genuine democratic reforms taken place. Bulgaria seeks entry into NATO and the EU.

RELIGION

Orthodoxy was the state religion until 1945. The Communists persecuted Christians and manipulated denominational leadership until 1989. The constitution proclaims religious freedom for all, but makes the status of the Orthodox Church one of ambiguous primacy, further reinforced between 1994-7. Since then the government has promised to end all existing religious discrimination.

Religions	Population %	Adherents	Ann.Gr.
Christian	80.24	6,599,776	+0.2%
Muslim	11.87	976,313	-0.4%
non-Religious	7.83	644,021	-7.7%
Jewish	0.05	4,113	-0.7%
Baha'i	0.01	823	n.a.

Christians	Denom.	Affil.%	,000	Ann.Gr.
Protestant	26	1.09	90	+2.6%
Independent	13	7.05	580	+5.2%
Catholic	1	1.09	90	+5.0%
Orthodox	3	70.93	5,834	-0.3%
Marginal	4	0.08	6	+7.2%

Churches	MegaBloc	Cong.	Members	Affiliates
Bulgarian Orthodox	O	3,769	4,296,296	5,800,000
Orthodox Church of B	I	325	370,370	500,000

Catholic	C	32	66,667	90,000
Pentecostal Union	P	550	25,000	57,000
Church of God	I	269	36,000	45,000
Church of God Union	I	180	23,000	31,000
Armenian Orthodox	O	11	14,599	20,000
Seventh-day Adventist	P	94	6,925	9,400
Baptist Union	P	102	5,000	7,500
Congregational	P	64	3,000	5,000
Methodist	P	36	3,200	5,000
Other denoms [36]		214	16,292	30,208
Total Christians [47]		5,646	4,866,000	6,600,000

Trans-bloc Groupings	pop.%	,000	Ann.Gr.
Evangelicals	2.0	166	+6.0%
Charismatic	1.8	150	+6.3%
Pentecostal	1.6	134	+6.7%

Update Jan 2004: Many evangelical churches have tripled in size since 1990. There were over 130,000 evangelical believers in 2003 in 1,530 churches, 75 of which were in Sofia.

Missionaries from Bulgaria
P,I,A 89 in 6 agencies: Bulgaria 77, Turkey 12.

Missionaries to Bulgaria
P,I,A 132 in 31 agencies from 11 countries: USA 59, Korea 12, Australia 9. C 10. M 51.

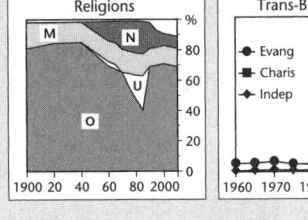

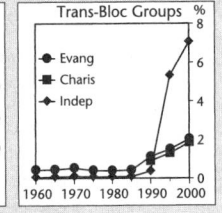

• Answers to Prayer

1 **Bulgaria's transformation** from harsh repression in the 1980s to today's relative freedom of religion and hunger for spirituality.

2 **The first major breakthrough for the gospel** in modern times in a Turkic people with possibly 10,000 Turkish Millet coming to Christ in the 1990s.

• Challenges for Prayer

1 **Religious freedom is still not fully achieved.** In the past, persecution was severe with many Christians imprisoned or killed and by manipulation through informers, infiltrators and imposters in the churches. The subversion of the Orthodox hierarchy was particularly widespread. Some leaders courageously suffered, others compromised—a fact that still breeds division, mistrust and lack of cooperation in Orthodox, Protestant and Pentecostal churches alike. Pray for repentance, reconciliation, healing and spiritual unity.

2 **Some Orthodox leaders have orchestrated a virulent media campaign** against non-Orthodox, and particularly Evangelicals. Accusations of cannibalism, extremism, links with crime and destruction of culture were levelled with no rebuttals allowed. This has led to violence by neo-Nazi gangs and governmental restriction or obstruction against non-Orthodox religious groups. Over 240 organizations have thus, in effect, been banned. This has slowed open evangelism, but it has also drawn evangelicals together. Pray for bridges of trust to be built between the major Christian bodies and an end to ongoing discrimination.

3 **The Orthodox church needs renewal and new life.** It has split into 3 denominations over leadership and political power and is trapped in a cycle of schism, corruption and compromise. This has created increased openness to consider a personal faith in Christ. There have been very few educated Bulgarians converted through evangelical Christian witness. Pray for a deep work of the Holy Spirit in the Bulgarian people.

B

4 **The growth and maturation of evangelical denominations** has been accelerated by the pressures of the 1990s. Pray for:
a) *The Evangelical Alliance,* formed in 1863, but closed by the Communists and re-formed in 1993, that it may be a united and prophetic voice for God in a divided and discouraged nation.
b) *The Alliance for Saturation Church Planting*, which seeks to coordinate evangelism and multiplication of congregations across the country.
c) *The body of Christ.* It is poised to play a significant part in the reconstruction of the country where 50% live below the poverty line, abortions far exceed the number of live births, and where hope for the future is rare.

5 Maturing the Church is a major challenge. Pray for:
a) *Training of church leadership* which was banned until 1990. Residential, TEE and informal training courses have multiplied, and a growing number of leaders released into ministry. Pray especially for the interdenominational Theological Evangelical Institute (formerly BBAL) which operates in both Sofia and Stara Zagora, also the various evangelical and Pentecostal theological schools, their staff and students, provision of finances, libraries and anointing of the Holy Spirit.
b) *The right structures to enhance growth.* The tendency is for autocratic, central leadership. Pray for a clearer vision for multiplying churches and plurality of leadership, thus avoiding personality clashes and denominational divisions. Networking and loving communication between leaders is a great need.
c) *The discernment of doctrinal error.* Every modern heresy and cult seems to have targeted the country — Mormons, Children of God, Jehovah's Witnesses, extreme "prosperity" teachings, as well as eastern cults. Christians are being swayed by every wind of doctrine.
d) *Complete religious freedom for Evangelicals.* Their ministry is hampered by constant obstructions in obtaining building sites, hiring meeting venues, negative press reports and harassment of any youth or children's ministry.
e) *The multiplicity of new indigenous agencies* that have sprung up for reaching children, prisoners, and ethnic minorities, and for providing literature, Bibles, and Christian teaching in schools and camps. There are also international agencies setting up local branches — **CEF**, **EHC**, and the Gideons among others. The need for wise coordination and adequate funding mechanisms is urgent.

6 **Cross-cultural missions vision is slowly growing.** There are now six couples serving in Turkey. Pray for a greater awareness among Christians for the ethnic minorities in Bulgaria and sensitivity to their cultures. The Pentecostal denominations have an effective church planting ministry among the Gypsies, Millet and Pomaks.

7 **Ethnic minorities have suffered severely** at times at the hands of the Bulgarian majority. There continues to be considerable discrimination and both Turks and Gypsies have formed political parties to fight for their rights. Specifically pray for:
a) *The Rumelian Turks* who deeply resented the attempts of the Communist regime to forcibly Bulgarianize them in the 1980s. Their language, religion and culture are now fully recognized. Muslim missionaries have been working hard to make them better Muslims. Barely 150 evangelical believers are known among them, and only in 1999 did specific long-term church planting ministry commence (**WEC** and others). Pray for a significant breakthrough.

b) ***The Millet*** — an oppressed Turkish-speaking mix of Turk and Gypsy, yet among them during the 1990s occurred an astonishing people movement to Christ of about 10,000 all over the country. Up to 80% of these are women and children, most coming to faith by way of dreams, visions and healings. Pray for the conversion of men — largely unemployed and bound by alcohol. Pray for the freeing of many from the occultism that underlies their nominal Muslim faith. Pray too for Christians with knowledge of Turkish as they seek to disciple the many Christian groups (**WEC**, Ichthus Fellowship and Bulgarian national groups).

c) ***The Roma (Gypsies)*** who are generally despised and at the bottom of the social order with widespread illiteracy. About 60% are Orthodox and 40% Muslim, but most are still deeply involved in the occult, crime and gambling. Between 10,000 and 20,000 have turned to the Lord, mainly through the outreach of the Pentecostals and Baptists in the Bulgarian language. Others are linked to the indigenous Turkish-speaking movement. Pray for specific outreach to them. A third of all Roma use Romani as their first language. There is now a Romani New Testament.

d) ***The Pomaks*** (250,000), Bulgarian-speaking Muslims. A specific ministry is needed to reach them. They have an identity crisis — rejected both by Bulgarians (religion) and Turks (language). Several young congregations have been planted in the south.

e) ***The Jews.*** They were not persecuted during World War II, but many have migrated to Israel. There are only 8 believers known amongst them.

8 **Foreign missions** have found it hard to retain long-term workers because of visa and other problems. There is need for long-term missionaries and tentmakers who will learn the culture and language, stay long enough for mature ministry and earn the confidence of the people through effective role-modelling. The need is less for pioneer evangelism and more for providing teaching skills and support to an evangelistically-minded church. Pray for:

a) ***The calling of workers*** to serve in this day of opportunity. Visas are difficult to obtain.

b) ***Wisdom in the use of short-term visits and ministry.*** Too much has been done (and even undone) by enthusiastic, but ill-prepared, visitors on foray ministries. All needs to be integrated into a wider, coordinated strategy that has been developed indigenously.

c) ***Sensitive use of foreign funds.*** The chronic lack of finance and poverty of those in Christian work makes every infusion of funds a potentially damaging or distorting influence to the spiritual life of churches and individuals. Employment by foreign agencies can easily take away key workers from the ministries most needed by the church. Yet how vital such financial help is!

9 **Ministry to young people is under-developed.** Few churches know how to meet their needs which are so different from their Communist-era parents. Pray for freedom to evangelize and disciple young people in schools. CCCI has an active campus ministry. IFES has established student groups in 13 cities but have a great need for Bulgarian staff to coordinate and support student outreach.

10 **Christian help ministries.** Pray for lasting fruit from:

a) ***Literature.*** New Man became the first Bulgarian Christian publisher with a vision for producing solid evangelical books, Scripture aids and teaching/evangelistic materials. There are four Christian bookstores (**CLC**, Berean Publishers). Pray for viability in the prevailing poverty. **EHC** has plans for a nation-wide literature distribution campaign. Effective cooperation between foreign and national literature agencies is needed.

b) ***Bible translation and distribution.*** Praise God for the registration of the Bulgarian Bible Society in 1993. **The Bible Society** has at last gained inter-confessional agreement for a new translation of the archaic Bulgarian Bible. Work has begun; pray for its rapid completion. Pray also for the continued impact of the Cyrillic Turkish NT and the Children's Bible. Illiteracy among the Turk and Gypsy populations is a hindrance.

c) ***Christian radio and TV.*** **TWR** has a studio producing programmes in Bulgarian and Romani (the latter being a **World by 2000** project). Studio 865 prepares TV programmes for local stations.

d) ***The JESUS film*** is available in Bulgarian, Romani, Romanian and Turkish; viewers are 25% of the population.

Burkina Faso

MARCH 14
AFRICA

GEOGRAPHY
Area 274,200 sq.km. A landlocked country of the Sahel. Prone to drought and famine.

Population	Ann.Gr.	Density
2000	11,936,823	+2.77%	44 per sq. km.
2010	15,751,319	+2.85%	57 per sq. km.
2025	23,321,336	+2.46%	85 per sq. km.

Almost 2 million Burkinabé (people of Burkina Faso) have migrated to other lands: 80% to Côte d'Ivoire, others to Niger, Mali and France.

Capital Ouagadougou 1.13 mill. **Urbanites** 14%.

PEOPLES
Over 77 distinct ethno-linguistic people groups in four major language families.
Gur-Voltaic (48 groups) 69.9%.

Oti-Volta: Moore (Mossi) 5.3m; Gurma 0.5m; Dagaari 388,000; Bulli 109,000; Gurenne (Frafra) 33,000; Kusale 16,000. The Mossi are the dominant people in Burkina Faso and comprise 45% of the population.

Grusi: Nuna 145,000; Kuruma 196,000, Lyele 130,000; Kassena 111,000; Ko 21,000; Puguli 18,000; Sisaala 7,200.

Senufo: Karaboro(2) 85,000; Nanerge 56,000; Senari 50,000; Sicijuubi (Tagba) 38,000.

Other Gur: Lobi 373,000; Red Bobo(2) 210,000; Birifor 144,000; Gouin 82,000; Tusian(2) 66,000; Turka 60,000; Yana 21,000; Doghosie 19,000; Dyan 19,000; Tiefo 14,000; Kaanba 10,000; Vige 7,700; Komono 4,000.

Mande peoples 14.8%. Bissa 422,000; Black Bobo 312,000; Samo 197,000; Marka 186,000; Jula 133,000; Bolon 14,000; Sambla 13,000; Seeku 13,000.

West Atlantic 11%. Fulbe 1,310,000.

Other African 4.1%. Dogon 250,000; Songhai 169,000; Tuareg 30,000.

Non-Africans 0.2%. Arab 12,000; Westerners 9,500.

Literacy 14%. **Official language** French, spoken by 10% of the population. **Trade languages** Moore, Jula in south. **All languages** 71. **Languages with Scriptures** 6Bi 11NT 10por 26w.i.p.

ECONOMY
One of the world's poorest countries, over 80% of the population relies on subsistence agriculture. The domestic economy is deprived of resources, and the national debt soars with attempts to Westernize. **HDI** 0.304; 171st/174. **Public debt** 44% of GNP. **Income/person** $320 (0.7% of USA).

B

POLITICS
Independent of France in 1960. Six coups since 1966. A military coup in 1987 ousted the then-leftist government, but the coup leader has since been elected twice to office. A republican democracy was formed in 1992, but most of the viable opposition to the ruling party was subsumed in a political merger in 1996.

RELIGION
Freedom of religion.

Religions	Population %	Adherents	Ann.Gr.
Muslim	50.00	5,968,412	+3.2%
Traditional ethnic	30.96	3,695,640	+2.4%
Christian	18.36	2,191,601	+2.0%
non-Religious/other	0.66	78,783	+8.6%
Baha'i	0.02	2,387	+18.1%

Christians	Denom.	Affil.%	,000	Ann.Gr.
Protestant	15	7.66	914	+2.2%
Independent	11	0.46	55	+7.5%
Catholic	1	10.21	1,219	+1.9%
Marginal	1	0.03	3	+3.0%

Churches	MegaBloc	Cong.	Members	Affiliates
Catholic	C	1,575	708,721	1,219,000
Assemblies of God	P	2,100	400,000	695,000
Chr and Miss Alliance	P	328	17,017	74,369
Evang Ch Association	P	400	26,000	65,000
Apostolic	P	115	12,500	23,000
Apostolic Mission	P	95	8,000	20,000
Baptist Convention	P	123	7,435	12,000
Evang Pentecostal Assoc	P	127	2,801	10,000
Protestant Evang	P	72	1,500	7,500
Other denoms [19]		205	28,000	65,000
Total Christians [27]		5,140	1,212,000	2,191,000

Trans-bloc Groupings	pop. %	,000	Ann.Gr.
Evangelical	8.0	949	+2.4%
Charismatic	7.2	854	+1.5%
Pentecostal	6.3	749	+1.2%

Missionaries from Burkina Faso
P,I,A 46 in 7 agencies to 6 countries: Burkina 28, Niger 7, Togo 6.

Missinaries to Burkina Faso
P,I,A 410 in 35 agencies from 23 countries: USA 164, Canada 46, UK 46, Switzerland 45, France 33. **C** 550. **M** 20.

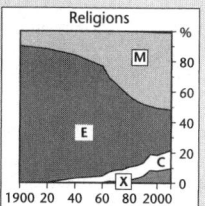
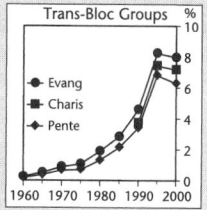

• Answers to Prayer

1 **The continuing growth of evangelical churches** during the 1990's, when membership nearly doubled. The growth spurt of the early 1990s, however, has subsequently slowed.

2 **Significant people movements** with thousands of conversions among the Mossi (**AoG**), Lyele (**IMB-SBC**), Gurma (**SIM**), Bwamu, Bobo and Samo (**CMA**), Nuna and Sissala (Canadian Pentecostals).

3 **The vibrant AoG family of churches**, with nearly 700,000 adherents and a strong missionary vision. Nearly half may have been converted from Muslim backgrounds.

• Challenges for Prayer

1 **The Unreached**. Despite church growth, increased missionary exertions and greater responsiveness, there remain 24 peoples without an effective witness; 11 of these are Muslim. A more comprehensive survey is currently being undertaken but needs more local denominational backing. Most unevangelized lie within the area of witness of existing missions. Churches and missions working in areas with unreached people often tend to favour more responsive or closely-related peoples. Pray for the recruitment and deployment of pioneer workers from Africa and the world to evangelize the unreached. Specific challenges:

a) Muslims, who are stronger in the north but continue to grow in nearly every ethnic group. Only a fraction of the missionary force in Burkina is specifically committed to ministering among Muslims: the urbanized Soninke, Jula and the rural Tuareg in the north (WH, **AoG**); Bolon in the northwest and the Kurumba with some believers in the north (**AoG**); Songhai in the northeast; Doghosie, Komono in the south.

b) The partly nomadic Fulbe who are beginning to respond through the witness of three SIM teams, and AoG workers. This outreach needs to be expanded.

c) Unreached non-Muslim peoples: the Dogon of the northeast, the Bulsa and Gurenne on Ghana's border, many Senufo sub-groups in the southwest (**CMA** and Mennonites), and the numerous small groups of the south (**WEC**).

2 **The power of the occult** has yet to be decisively challenged and broken in many peoples of Burkina Faso. Few countries in West Africa are more dominated by idolatry, fetishism and secret societies. Even in the churches occult power is wielded, hampering and polluting the message of Christ. Especially strong is that of the many Lobiri peoples in the southwest (**WEC**), Gurma (**SIM**) in the east, Gurunsi (Canadian Pentecostals, **AoG**), Senufo and Bobo (**CMA**) in the west. Pray that the power of the risen Christ might be demonstrated for the saving of many.

3 **The Catholics have grown steadily**, but the rate of growth has slowed in the 1980s and 1990s with increasing losses to Islam. Around 10% of the Mossi and most of the Dagaari are Catholic, yet the strong idolatry and fetishism within the hearts of the converts is often unchallenged.

4 **There is a serious spirit of denominationalism** in Burkina Faso. Churches usually do not cooperate unless there is some obvious benefit. There is much talk of greater kingdom collaboration but rarely does any fruit come of it. Sadly, the larger denominations often seek to hinder the growth of the smaller or younger denominations and organisations; pray that the Holy Spirit might convict the hearts of believers and build unity among them for the greater glory of God.

5 **The resources of the evangelical churches have been over-stretched** by the influx of new converts. In fact, in some areas where there has been growth, many have since backslidden and some have become Muslims. There are many needs:

a) There are too few trained leaders. Pray for Bible schools run by the major churches and missions in local languages and in French (**SIM, CMA, AoG, WEC** and Pentecostals). It often seems that pastors lack training due to paternalistic attitudes on the part of the mission.

b) Economic hardship is widespread and literacy levels are very low, though higher among believers. Pray that national believers may overcome a "poverty and dependence mentality" and begin to give sacrificially of their resources.

c) Pray for church leaders at this vital time. Their success in church growth has created a great challenge: to disciple the many new believers. Pray for mature, godly wives for these pastors and evangelists, for there are a great many men in ministry who cannot find an appropriate helpmate. Pray for Christian leaders able to stand firm against the idolatrous practices of tribal society and against the demands of non-Christian national leaders.

d) The growing AIDS crisis is not being widely faced. Nearly 7% of the adult population has HIV. **Vigilance** is a Christian organization that promotes sexual abstinence and fidelity in the fight to prevent the spread of AIDS.

e) The Church in general does not yet have a strong missions vision. This is tied up with dependency issues and the churches' parent missions. Calvary Ministries, World Outreach and others work to mobilize churches and provide cross-cultural training to those called. Pray that the Lord might stir a strong grass roots movement that places missions at the top of church agendas.

6 **Young people.** They are better educated than their parents, but local prospects for employment and advancement are poor, so they are frustrated and disillusioned. Street kids are becoming common, as few jobs are available. There are few full-time workers targeting these young people. Pray for the work of **SU** in the high schools and the expanding ministry of **CCCI** and GBUAF**(IFES)** in the high schools and Ouagadougou University. There are over 1,500 linked with the latter in cell groups around the country and one group of 60 in the university. More staff to expand the work is a great need.

7 **The massive emigration of Burkinabé** to the cities and to Côte d'Ivoire is both a challenge and an opportunity for the gospel. The social upheavals, family breakdowns and economic stagnation caused by the emigration of most of the active men in the community are severe. There are estimated to be over 1.5 million Burkinabé in Côte d'Ivoire. As many as 70% of these convert to Islam within a few months of arrival. Burkina churches have been taking up the challenge by sending pastors and missionaries to these Burkinabé abroad, especially **AoG, CMA** and **WEC**, but more are needed. Pray for an abundant harvest and effective church planting.

8 **Missionaries working in Burkina Faso** have a vital role in a land of so much physical and spiritual need. The work has been hard, and victories long in coming. But receptivity is high, and missionaries are welcome. Major missions working in the country are **SIL/WBT** (76 workers), **SIM** (54), **CMA** (36), all Mennonites (34), **AoG** (32), **IMB-SBC** (30), Apostolic Church (23), **WEC** (14). Pray for their protection and encouragement. Missionary reinforcements are needed in a wide range of ministries.

9 **VIMAB (the Burkinabé AoG) could become a success story of indigenous missions.** AoG workers from Burkina Faso are beginning to be used to reach the surrounding nations, supported by Burkinabé churches. Most of their work, both inside and out of Burkina, is among the more evangelized Mossi. Pray that these dynamic churches might truly catch a vision to reach the unreached peoples among them and in neighboring nations. Pray for their growth as a mission sending body, and for the sacrificial ministry of both the missionaries and their supporters.

10 **Christian aid and relief.** Much has been coordinated by the Federation of Evangelical Churches as well as others such as CREDO. Much has been done in alleviating suffering and staving off future disasters. Literacy centres are being set up to enable a better future for many. Wisdom is needed by both missions and Christian leaders in the administration of this help, especially in such a poor country with so many infrastructure needs. The long-term presence of aid workers lends much credibility to the Christian cause and a willingness to listen. Pray for the hearts of both Muslims and fetishists to be opened to God's Word.

11 **Bible translation** is a ministry of major significance with 3 key bodies involved; **UBS**, ANTBA (a national translation and literacy agency) and **SIL**. Only 2 indigenous languages have the whole Bible — Moore and Bambara. **SIL** has 76 workers committed to 13 language programmes. Five other missions are involved in translation work in 15 languages. Present and future translators need prayer to complete the immense task. Literacy programmes are essential for many areas so that Burkinabé may read the new translations; ANTBA is doing extensive work in this area.

12 **Media ministries.** High levels of illiteracy and poverty and the limited availability of literature in local languages enhance the importance of other media.

a) ***Radio*** is being used to broadcast the gospel in 10 languages. *Radio Evangélique Développe-ment* is possibly the only indigenously launched and operated gospel radio in Africa. Local radio is used extensively by churches in different areas.

b) ***Audio materials for evangelism and teaching*** have not been adequately used, yet they are vital for ministry. **GRN** have made recordings in over 50 languages and dialects. In 1998 alone **GRN** translated material into 21 'tail-ender' languages which previously had no translated Scriptures.

c) ***The JESUS film*** is proving a key pioneer evangelistic tool in Bambara/Jula and is available in Bissa, Bomu, Dogon, French, Gurma, Gurenne, Kassena, Moore and Soninke. Pray for the ongoing translation into 21 other Burkinabé languages.

Burundi

Republic of Burundi

MARCH 15
AFRICA

GEOGRAPHY
Area 27,834 sq.km. A mountainous, fertile country on the north shore of Lake Tanganyika, south of its 'twin' Rwanda.

Population		Ann.Gr.	Density
2000	6,695,001	+1.69%	241 per sq. km.
2010	8,496,970	+2.23%	305 per sq. km.
2025	11,568,648	+1.87%	416 per sq. km.

Large movements of refugees in and out of the country in the 1990s.

Capital Bujumbura 600,000. **Urbanites** 12%.

PEOPLES
Rundi-speaking 97%. Considerable inter-ethnic mixing.
>**Tutsi** 14%. The politically dominant minority.
>**Hutu** 82%. A further 300,000+ live as refugees in Tanzania and Congo-DRC.
>**Twa Pygmies** 1%. Despised by other groups.
Other African 2.8%. Rwandan 90,000; Congolese 40,000.
Other 0.2%. South Asian 2,500; European 2,400; Arab 1,600.

Literacy 19%. **Official languages** kiRundi, French. All speak kiRundi. **All languages** 4. **Languages with Scriptures** 2Bi.

ECONOMY
One of the world's poorest states in 1990. Mineral resources little exploited. Soil erosion is a serious problem. Ethnic strife and wars have displaced 1.7 million people, denuded much of the country, and led to international sanctions against the existing regime in 1996, reducing much of the population to destitution and dependence on aid. **HDI** 0.324; 170th/174. **Public debt** 44% of GNP. **Income/person** $250 (0.8% of USA).

POLITICS
For 400 years, Tutsi lordship over the Hutu majority has dominated the political life of Burundi. After the country's independence from Belgium in 1962, the Tutsi constitutional monarchy was replaced by a republican military regime in 1966. A succession of Tutsi-dominated governments and military regimes since then have managed to retain Tutsi domination of the army, commerce and education. The human rights record of the government has been appalling; Hutu attempts to gain power have been followed by pogroms in 1972, 1988, and 1993-95. There have been periods of some power sharing between the two ethnic groups since 1988. The Great Lakes War feeds weapons and soldiers into an ongoing civil war in Burundi that contrives to thwart international efforts to mediate a peaceful solution.

RELIGION
Freedom of religion.

Religions	Population %	Adherents	Ann.Gr.
Christian	90.06	6,029,518	+1.4%
Traditional ethnic	6.72	449,904	+1.2%
Muslim	3.00	200,850	+15.3%
Baha'i	0.08	5,356	+1.7%
Hindu	0.08	5,356	+4.4%
non-Religious/other	0.06	4,017	+1.7%

Christians	Denom.	Affil.%	,000	Ann.Gr.
Protestant	18	12.61	844	+2.2%
Independent	12	1.88	126	+23.8%
Anglican	1	7.47	500	+3.6%
Catholic	1	57.17	3,828	+1.3%
Orthodox	1	0.02	1	-2.6%
Marginal	1	0.07	4	+9.7%
Unaffiliated		10.84	725	n.a.

Churches	MegaBloc	Cong.	Members	Affiliates
Catholic	C	1,562	2,187,166	3,828,000
Church of Pentecost	P	2,773	208,000	520,000
Protestant Episcopal	A	5,669	170,000	500,000
Seventh-day Adventist	P	210	62,000	100,000
Methodist Ch Union	P	160	29,000	60,000
Eglise Vivante	I	50	35,000	70,000
Evang Episcopal	P	168	21,000	42,000
Union of Baptist	P	167	20,000	35,000
Friends (Quakers)	P	84	8,000	16,000
Brotherhood of Christ	I	20	2,000	4,000
Other denoms [26]		820	69,676	135,000
Total Christians [35]		11,633	2,810,000	5,305,000

Trans-bloc Groupings	pop. %	,000	Ann.Gr.
Evangelical	21.0	1,406	+4.4%
Charismatic	13.4	895	+4.8%
Pentecostal	9.5	639	+5.6%

Missionaries from Burundi
P,I,A 36 in 3 agencies all in Burundi.

Missionaries to Burundi
P,I,A 49 in 13 agencies from 9 countries: USA 21, Sweden 15.

B

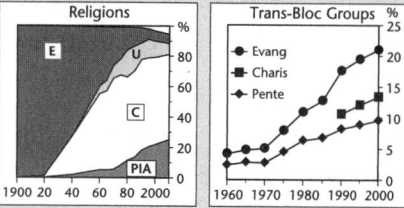

• Challenges for Prayer

1 **Pray for reconciliation** between Tutsi and Hutu and for peace to come to the land. Centuries of oppression and cycles of killings, reprisals and counter-killings have left a legacy of pain and hatred that bode ill for any resolution. All national and international attempts at mediation have failed to bring Hutu rebel factions to the negotiating table.

2 **Revival in the 1950s** brought blessing and great church growth, but a generation later the land has been physically, morally and spiritually devastated. The Church is the only institution in the land able to give the point where reconciliation could begin. Only a miracle from God in many hearts will achieve this. Pray for all the satanic enmity, bondage and guilt to be cleansed through the blood of Jesus.

3 **Both Protestant and Catholic leaders** have been prominent in opposing ethnic hatred and 'cleansing', but many Hutu and Tutsi church leaders have been killed or driven into exile. Many churches have been destroyed in the fighting. Pray for unity, wisdom, the love of Christ and courage for all who seek the good of the country and growth of the Church. Pray also that the churches many be able to rebuild the schooling system which has largely broken down; the government has asked for this, but resources are lacking.

4 **Leadership for the churches** is in short supply; persecution and closure of Bible schools cut off the supply of newly trained leaders. Pray for the full re-establishment of the Mweya Theological Institute (Friends, Free Methodists and WGM), the Pentecostal Bible School and for the effective launching of the Matana Theological College (Anglican-MAM). Pray for the restoration of full teaching programmes and adequate, godly staff in each institution and for the effective re-commencing of TEE courses.

5 **In the midst of suffering, evangelical Christians have continued to grow.** The most significant are a number of Pentecostal churches, Anglicans, Free Methodists and Eglise Vivante. Pray for the witness of believers when all around has collapsed and so many people are embittered with the ongoing genocide being perpetrated by both sides.

6 Areas of greater spiritual need:

a) *The Twa* are relatively less well evangelized. About 7% are Christian.
b) *Refugee camps in Tanzania and Congo* where spiritual life is tough and where it is difficult to maintain a clear witness. Pray for the churches in them.
c) *Displaced refugees* within Burundi.

d) *The Muslim community* which, though small, is growing because of the bad witness of the many 'Christians' involved in the killings. Over 700 Muslims perished in the 1995 killings.

B **7** **Young people and children** — special items for prayer:

a) *Children are suffering,* many are orphans, and few have the chance of schooling or employment. Very little ministry, specifically to children, remains.

b) *SU* has had a good impact in the past — pray that this ministry may be resumed.

c) *A small GBU(IFES) group* continues in the one University, but student numbers have dropped drastically. The Christians are determined not to be divided racially.

8 **Missionary involvement is small.** A former regime expelled nearly all missionaries between 1970 and 1985 and few returned thereafter because of ongoing instability. Many will be needed to work with national leaders to help in the massive reconstruction of church and national life, restoring literacy programmes and reviving theological education. Pray for the calling of the right missionary personnel and for safety, effectiveness, godly modelling and good relationships with national believers.

9 **Christian media — specific prayer targets:**

a) *Literacy programmes* — the vast majority of the population is illiterate, including many believers.

b) *Bibles* — there is such a dearth that some reckon 4 million are needed. **The Bible Society** has distributed many Bible portions that challenge readers concerning reconciliation.

c) *Radio.* **TWR** and **SU** have established a communications centre in Bujumbara, where locally-produced programmes are prepared. In 2000 a Christian station, Radio Outreach-Ivyizigiro (Hope) started broadcasting from Bujumbura to Burundi and neighbouring countries. Pray for life to be imparted through these broadcasts.

d) *The JESUS film* has been viewed by most Burundians. Pray for lasting impact.

Cambodia
Kingdom of Cambodia

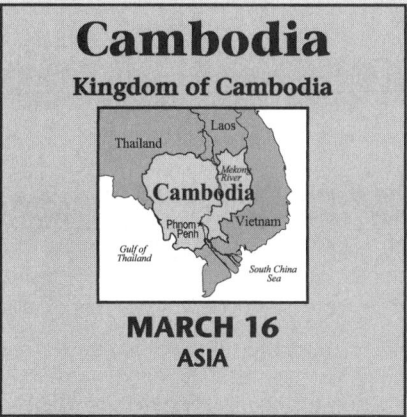

Updated January 2004

 GEOGRAPHY
Area 181,035 sq.km. Fertile, forest-covered state of south-west Indo-China on the Mekong river.

Population	Ann.Gr.	Density
2000	11,167,719	+2.27%	62 per sq. km.
2010	13,250,035	+1.67%	73 per sq. km.
2025	16,526,449	+1.23%	91 per sq. km.

Capital Phnom Penh 950,000. **Urbanites** 21%.

 **PEOPLES**

Mon-Khmer 86.5%. 16 peoples.
Khmer 83.3%.
Tribal 3.2%. Largest: Kui 212,000; Stieng 31,000; Mnong 30,000; Jarai 28,000; Tampuan 15,000; Brao 10,000; Chong 8,000; Kravet 6,000; Somray 3,000.
Malay 3.8%. Cham 41,000; Malay 10,000.
Other 9.7%. Vietnamese 620,000; Chinese 350,000; Lao 70,000; Thai 28,000.

Literacy 65%. **Official language** Khmer. **All languages** 17. **Languages with Scriptures** 2Bi 1NT 1por 2w.i.p.

 ECONOMY
Rich agricultural potential. The last 25 years of war, genocide and the power-lust and greed of subsequent governments have impoverished most of the population. The major economic activities are receiving international aid (the largest per capita receiver nation in the world) and sin (pornography, prostitution, drugs and illegal logging). **HDI** 0.514; 137th/174. **Public debt** 66% of GNP. **Income/person** $300 (1% of USA).

POLITICS
A constitutional monarchy. Powerful

kingdoms from 1st to 14th Centuries. Thereafter for 500 years a pawn in regional and global conflicts with Thai, Vietnamese, French, Japanese and US invasions or occupations. A tragic victim of the Vietnam War (1970-75) which opened the way for the extreme Marxist Khmer Rouge take-over in 1975, followed by one of the most savage slaughters in the 20th Century. Almost all former military personnel, civil servants, educated or wealthy people and their families were killed, and the nation turned into a vast labour camp. The Vietnamese army ousted the Khmer Rouge in 1978, but civil war between four contending armies raged with superpower support until 1991. International efforts to bring democracy with elections in 1993 and 1998 were hugely expensive and manipulated by the leader Hun Sen to entrench his personal power base, and crush opposition. Nevertheless, since 1998 there has been no further warfare. A member of ASEAN since 1998, the restored monarchy may not survive into a second decade.

RELIGION
Buddhism has been the national religion since the 15th Century. The Khmer Rouge sought to eradicate all religion; 90% of Buddhist monks and most Christians perished. Since 1978 there have been periods of more tolerance, but only since 1990 have Christians been allowed to worship openly. There is increasing freedom of religion for Cambodians.

Religions	Population %	Adherents	Ann.Gr.
Buddhist	82.57	9,221,186	+2.2%
Chinese	4.69	523,766	+5.6%
Traditional ethnic	4.35	485,796	+5.6%
Muslim	3.90	435,541	+4.5%
non-Religious/other	2.92	326,000	-7.0%
Christian	1.19	132,896	+4.7%
Hindu	0.26	29,036	+14.2%
Baha'i	0.12	13,401	+6.1%

Christians	Denom.	Affil.%	,000	Ann.Gr.
Protestant	13	0.20	23	+9.7%
Independent	8	0.78	87	+5.9%
Catholic	1	0.20	22	+1.6%
Marginal	2	0.01	1	+7.5%

Churches	MegaBloc	Cong.	Members	Affiliates
New Apostolic	I	200	25,000	50,000
National Churches	I	120	9,600	24,000
Catholic	R	16	11,000	22,000
Cambodia for Christ	I	68	5,000	13,000
Seventh-day Adventist	P	25	2,500	5,000
Chr Chs/Chs of Christ	P	19	3,000	4,500
Christian Alliance	P	29	1,165	4,431
Assemblies of God	P	3	719	1,200
Other denoms [14]		60	4,554	8,770

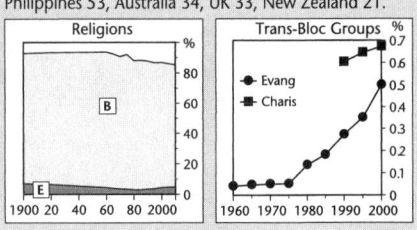

Total Christians [22]	540	62,538	133,000

Philippines 53, Australia 34, UK 33, New Zealand 21.

Trans-bloc Groupings	pop.%	,000	Ann.Gr.
Evangelical	0.5	56	+11.9%
Charismatic	0.7	75	+3.7%
Pentecostal	0.0	1	+10.6%

Missionaries from Cambodia
P,I,A 81 in 6 agencies: 78 in Cambodia.

Missionaries to Cambodia
P,I,A 402 in 55 agencies from 25 countries: USA 155,

• Answers to Prayer

1 **An open door for the gospel** in the nation despite, or even because of, the awful past.

2 **Rapid growth of indigenous church planting ministries and multiplication of churches**. In 1999 there were over 300 evangelical congregations with more than one new church starting each week. By 2004 there were 700 congregations in the EFC representing 100,000 Evangelicals.

• Challenges for Prayer

1 **The terrible genocide of 1975-79 in which nearly 2 million were killed has left deep physical and emotional scars.** There are over 30,000 who have lost limbs to landmines, and almost the entire population needs deep healing from the trauma of their losses and suffering. Pray for:

a) ***Justice*** to be seen to be done regarding those who perpetrated the crimes. The Khmer Rouge have so far shown little remorse.

b) ***Those seeking to remove mines*** and restore the country to a decent living standard. Many Christian NGOs are involved.

c) ***Those caring for the maimed***, the orphans, widows, and now AIDS victims.

d) ***A government that seeks the good of all,*** and is worthy of the trust of the people. Violence, manipulation, graft and selfishness hitherto have been the rule.

2 **The spiritual darkness of Cambodia** must be lifted by prayer. That darkness is shown by the ubiquitous spirit shrines, the strong opposition of Buddhism to any ideological rival and the moral collapse. The sex industry thrives, but a third of all prostitutes (an estimated 50,000) are children. Cambodia has the highest rate of child abandonment in SE Asia. HIV is spreading rapidly with 180,000 known to be infected in 1999 and 3,500 children born with HIV each year. Pray for the light of the gospel to so shine that the structures of society as well as individuals may be decisively changed.

3 **The Cambodian Church** has survived against all odds. Beginning in 1923, CMA missionaries laboured for 47 years before the breakthrough began. There were only 700 believers in evangelical churches in 1970, but by 1975 this had grown to 9-12,000. Only 2,000 survived the slaughter — many fled to Thai refugee camps where a great harvest was reaped for the Kingdom. During the 1990s churches spread to all 19 provinces. Pray for:

a) ***Freedom from government manipulation and interference,*** and wisdom in how to relate to the authorities.

b) ***Freedom and deep deliverance*** from past sin, hatred, suffering and abuse through faith in the precious blood of Jesus.

c) ***Children and young people*** to be effectively discipled in the churches. Few are equipped for this, yet over half the population is under 21.

d) ***Many Christian families to be raised up*** who can live for Christ as examples of his power to save and change.

e) ***A vision for the lost*** and to take the gospel to every person.

4 **Mature leadership** for the churches is the greatest challenge. The loss of so many educated people in the Khmer Rouge slaughter, and the dysfunctional society pushed many new Christians quickly into leadership before they were ready. Pray for:

a) **The Bible schools** — The Phnom Penh Bible School and the Cambodia For Christ (CFC) Ministry Training College are two key institutions.

b) **Existing pastors** — in 1999 there were 755 registered as such with the government, 200 with CFC. Pray for purity, power in the Spirit, and discernment in their ministry, and for their dependence in God rather than on foreign aid.

c) **Unity.** Only four bodies are recognized by the government with which all denominations must register — Cambodian Christian Evangelical Alliance, Evangelical Fellowship of Cambodia (EFC), Cambodian Christian Federation and the Cambodian Baptist Convention. These are increasingly working together. Pray for this to be effective and a positive impact on the country. The Cambodian Church has had many problems with divisiveness.

5 **Christian ministry to physical needs** is a major concern.

a) **Refugees** poured out of Cambodia between 1975 and 1985. About 700,000 fled to Thailand, where many came to Christ in refugee camps. Many agencies have had a remarkable ministry there (**SAO, YWAM, WVI, SBC,** Christian Outreach, **OMF, CMA** and others). Some 350,000 moved on to the USA, France, Canada and other lands, where there are now dozens of Cambodian Christian fellowships. The remaining 350,000 had returned home by 1993 to rebuild their lives. They need much help.

b) **The social needs are enormous.** The murder of most of those with skills or an education makes expatriate input essential. Rehabilitation, orphanages, reconstruction, health care, projects for agriculture, fisheries, water management and education are all ministries where Christians have significant input. Pray for:

i   *The 30 or more Christian NGOs* (World Concern, Christian Outreach, World Relief, Food for the Hungry, Harvest International Services (HIS), **SAO, OMF, CMA, WVI, AoG, YWAM,** Mennonites and Servants to Asia's Urban Poor).

ii   *Effective cooperation* among the Christian agencies.

iii   *More long-term expatriate workers* who learn the language and identify with the culture. Humanitarian ministries can fail in this and encourage only short-term involvement. Missionary visas are now being granted to such agencies as **OMF, AoG, WVI** and **CMA**.

iv   *Spiritual and physical health* of new workers and fruitfulness in ministry.

v   *This land to open fully* and remain open for all needed expatriate workers — especially pioneers, church planters and Bible teachers.

6 **The less reached.** There is a window of opportunity for the land that must be prayerfully kept open. Pray for:

a) **The Buddhist majority.** Though reviving, Buddhism has lost some of its monopolistic grip on the people.

b) **The Cham** are almost entirely Muslim. Probably 60% are deeply involved in spirit worship. They have increased rapidly in numbers. Few are Christians and there are no churches among them.

c) **The tribal peoples.** Only among the Mnong have significant numbers come to Christ. There are small, but growing churches among the Tampuan, Krung, Kravet and Jarai. Pray for an adequate survey of the need, and the calling of pioneers to reach them.

7 **Christian media ministries.** Pray specifically for:

a) **Literature.** CMA missionaries have translated a range of materials, and continue to do so. There is a real need for teaching materials, for false teachings abound. The largest church, the New Apostolic Church, is sectarian. The **UBS** and others are providing Khmer Bibles and New Testaments. A new Khmer Bible was completed in 1998. **SGM** Scripture portions are widely appreciated.

b) **The JESUS film** is being used in Khmer, Chinese and Vietnamese. Its greatest impact was through national television.

c) **Christian radio.** FEBC and CCCI have been allowed to broadcast 6 hours a week on local radio — a first! **Lutheran Hour** has also been given a similar opportunity. **FEBC** also broadcast from Manila in Khmer (12 hrs/wk) as well as in Jarai and Stieng. **TWR** have recently begun weekly broadcasts.

d) **MAF** has a plane servicing Christian work.

Cameroon

Republic of Cameroon

MARCH 17
AFRICA

Literacy 63%. **Official languages** French, English. **All languages** 279. **Languages with Scriptures** 18Bi 29NT 27por 54w.i.p.

ECONOMY
Largely based on agriculture and oil exports. Great potential for development with ample rain and minerals. Development has been slowed by decline in world prices for coffee and cocoa and widespread corruption. Unemployment is high. **HDI** 0.536; 134th/174. **Public debt** 91% of GNP. **Income/person** $620 (2% of USA).

POLITICS
A German colony between 1884 and 1919, then divided between Britain and France. Independence from France in 1960, and union with English-speaking West Cameroon in 1961 as a bilingual one-party republic. Popular pressure forced the President to accede to multi-party elections in 1992, but opposition groups have not been allowed to compete fairly in elections. There are effectively two constitutions which are manipulated by the government to retain control. Cameroon has applied for membership of the British Commonwealth. There is a simmering secessionist movement in the Anglophone West.

RELIGION
Secular state which guarantees religious freedom. Islam is strong in the north — especially among the Fulbe.

GEOGRAPHY
Area 475,442 sq.km. On the continental 'hinge' between West and Central Africa. Semi-arid in the north, grasslands in the centre, rainforest in the south.

Population		Ann.Gr.	Density
2000	15,084,969	+2.73%	32 per sq. km.
2010	19,239,891	+2.37%	40 per sq. km.
2025	26,484,402	+2.03%	56 per sq. km.

Capital Yaounde 1,446,000. Other major city: Douala 2 mill. **Urbanites** 42%.

PEOPLES
Over 280 languages, maybe 500 or more ethnic groups; Africa's most complex country. Only the larger or noteworthy are mentioned here. Major language groups:

Bantu 58.5%. In south and west 116 groups: Bamiléké(20) 2m; Ewondo 1,353,000; Fang(3) 860,000; Bassa 421,000; Mum 415,000; Nkom 232,000; Duala 215,000; Nso 200,000; Widekum 168,000; Makaa 154,000; Limbum 141,000; Ngemba 128,000; Eton 133,000; Kundu 119,000, Kaka 119,000; Bassossi 117,000.

Chadic-Hausa 16.7%. In north, 61 groups: Mafi 416,000; Masa 284,000; Tupuri 251,000; Giziga(2) 162,000; Gidar 136,000; Musgum 129,000; Kotoko 116,000; Daba 100,000; Kapsiki 90,000; Mandara 61,000.

West Atlantic 9.4%. Adamawa Fulbe 1,437,000; Mbororo Fulbe 134,000.

Bantoid 6.5%. 49 groups: Mbo 150,000; Fungom 109,000; Bete 83,000; Tigon 66,000; Ejagham 64,000.

Sudanic 6.1%. In the north, 46 groups: Gbaya 241,000; Mundang 111,000; Fali(2) 66,000; Mbum 62,000.

Arab 0.9%. Shuwa (Baggara) 147,000.

Saharan 0.7%. Kanuri 103,000.

Kwa 0.4%. Igbo 67,000.

Adamawa (Pygmy) 0.4% Baka 48,000; Bayaka 5,000.

Other 0.4%. French 33,000; British 5,000; Greek 3,000.

Religions	Population %	Adherents	Ann.Gr.
Christian	68.96	10,402,595	+3.6%
Muslim	25.00	3,771,242	+3.2%
Traditional ethnic	4.54	684,858	-6.8%
Baha'i	0.90	135,765	+4.0%
non-Religious/other	0.60	90,510	+11.0%

Christians	Denom.	Affil.%	,000	Ann.Gr.
Protestant	25	13.28	2,003	+2.2%
Independent	66	3.19	481	+4.9%
Anglican	1	0.01	1	+5.1%
Catholic	1	26.42	3,985	+2.1%
Orthodox	1	0.01	1	+0.0%
Marginal	4	0.57	86	+7.1%
Unaffiliated		25.48	3,843	n.a.

Churches	MegaBloc	Cong.	Members	Affiliates
Catholic	C	4,773	2,386,323	3,985,160
Evang Ch of Cameroon	P	1,800	335,329	560,000
Presb Ch in Cam (PCC)	P	1,040	173,653	290,000
Presb Ch of Cam (EPC)	P	1,865	167,832	240,000
Seventh-day Adventist	P	750	98,000	160,000
Baptist Convention	P	1,000	80,000	130,000
Evang Lutheran	P	389	77,844	130,000
Cameroon Baptist	I	167	55,000	110,000
Lutheran Brethren	P	1,067	53,892	106,000
Baptist Union	P	408	51,000	97,000
Presb Orthodox	I	1,018	50,898	85,000
Jehovah's Witnesses	M	520	27,000	81,000
Un of Ev Chs in Cam	P	223	26,800	67,000
Assemblies of God	P	353	32,000	65,000

x

Chr Discipleship [CMFI]	P	600	30,000	50,000
Full Gospel Mission	P	410	19,200	48,000
Other denoms [84]		2,540	213,000	418,000
Total Christians [98]		18,900	3,878,000	6,623,000

Many of these statistics are estimates; few denominations keep records.

Trans-bloc Groupings	pop. %	,000	Ann.Gr.
Evangelical	6.4	962	+4.0%
Charismatic	5.1	765	+4.5%
Pentecostal	2.0	308	+6.7

Missionaries from Cameroon
P,I,A 291 in 11 agencies to 35 countries.

Missionaries to Cameroon
P,I,A 613 in 60 agencies from 27 countries: USA 246, Germany 68, Canada 53, Switzerland 48, Nigeria 40.

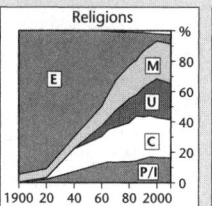

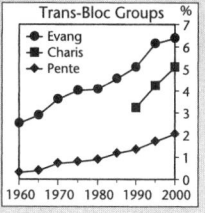

• Answers to Prayer

1 **Fast growth of Evangelicals** in the 1990s through newer churches, Cameroonian missionaries and major evangelistic efforts — Reinhard Bonnke crusades, the *JESUS* film and CBN TV coverage.

2 **Many significant leaders** in the professions, army, police and politics have been converted — giving hope for changing society.

3 **Freedom for private Christian radio and television** broadcasting, granted in 2000. This will open many doors for Christian ministry.

• Challenges for Prayer

1 **Some claim Cameroon is the most corrupt nation on earth** — and there are many 'claimants' for that title. Massive corruption in the government, administration, police, the legal system and business have debased living standards, crippled economic growth and brought despair and hopelessness to the great majority of the population. Pray that:

a) *True Christians of integrity* may be raised up to lead the nation and make the radical reforms needed to lift it from its sorry state.

b) *There may be freedom for a national consultation* that paves the way for a new era for the country.

c) *The Lord might raise up committed and God-fearing Christian leaders* to play key roles in national decision making in the public arena.

2 **The spiritual poverty** of the churches is the country's greatest tragedy. Nominal Christianity is a bigger problem in this land than in any other in Africa. The early pioneer work of Catholics, Presbyterians, Lutherans and Baptists was damaged by compromise and the arrival of liberation theology. These large churches lost spiritual life and opened their doors to millions who had no personal faith in Christ and with no one to lead them to Him. Tribalism, pagan practices, alcoholism and low moral standards are endemic. Most in these churches have no concern for the unreached of the north, nor do they have a prophetic voice to address the major ills of society. Pray for deep repentance, lasting deliverance and true revival, and a restoration of Bible reading, preaching and holiness among Christians.

3 **There is a need for godly leaders** well trained in the Scriptures. Today's spiritual disaster has its roots in a failure in theological training. Church leadership is more noted for pride, power-struggles, disunity, moral failure and misuse of funds than for holy living. Pray for the provision of born-again, godly national and expatriate staff for the 10 accredited denominational and interdenominational schools in Cameroon. Pray also for a spiritual revolution in these theological faculties and seminaries which will bring new life and biblical standards to churches so long deprived of these.

4 **Newer evangelical churches** have grown rapidly in the last 20 years after a late start due to the hostility of older churches. Pentecostal and charismatic congregations have multiplied. Pray for:

a) *Greater spiritual unity* and cooperation between charismatic and non-charismatic groups.

b) *More effective discipling* of those evangelized. The strong growth of recent years has caused a lack of trained leaders and discipling programmes. Pray for the formation of a genuinely evangelical association of churches in Cameroon.

5 Signs of hope to cover in prayer:

a) *Greater evangelical cooperation* to reach the unconverted. Specific initiatives:
  i   *Cameroon Mission 2000* for reaching the nation's unreached.
  ii *Cameroon for Christ* was launched in 1996 and involved many denominations and churches in research and evangelism of the 2,400 villages of the north. By 1999, 10,000 Christians had been trained and 1,000 villages reached with good local response.
  iii *Mission BINAM* is a network targeting the idol worshippers of W. Cameroon — especially the Bamiléké.
  iv *Christian Missionary Fellowship International* (CMFI) is a Cameroonian mission which has a remarkable ministry in prayer, missions and publishing with a global impact.

b) *The growing involvement of Cameroonians in cross-cultural missions.* Dozens of indigenous denominations and churches are sending out missionaries to the north and to neighbouring lands. The Evangelical Missionary Alliance is spreading the vision for world evangelization and the sending and supporting of workers. CMFI has sent out and supported 98 missionary couples in 35 countries.

6 Bible translation for Cameroon's 279 languages is an overwhelming task. The lack of indigenous, heart-language Scriptures is one of the contributory causes of spiritual poverty in the churches. Only 47 languages have a Bible or NT. Pray for:

a) *Existing translation and literacy projects.* Both the UBC and SIL (with 190 workers) have invested much in these. Cameroon is SIL's largest African involvement. This is bearing fruit in church life.

b) *Surveys* which are needed for a further 126 languages without the Scriptures.

c) *The indigenous Cameroon Association for Bible Translation and Literacy* with commitment to a growing number of translation projects.

d) *The calling of more indigenous and expatriate workers* for translation, literacy and support work. Lutheran Bible Translators have 10 workers committed to translation.

7 Young people are adversely affected by the national malaise. Education appears futile because of lack of employment, rampant cheating and bribery for passing exams and favouritism at all levels. Many turn to crime and prostitution. Pray for:

a) *Effective Christian discipling* in churches and by youth and children's agencies. Little is available.

b) *The ministry of SU* in schools and GBEEC(**IFES**). The latter has 3,100 members in schools, colleges and universities. There are 460,000 secondary schools and 125,000 tertiary students in the country.

8 Less reached peoples — a national survey in this complex nation is an urgent need. The Joshua Project listing has 16 peoples, all but one being targeted for church planting. The major challenges:

a) *Muslims* — a majority in 8 peoples and a significant minority in most northern peoples.
  i   *The Fulbe* have long been the proud rulers of the area. Christians among them have grown from the 10 known in 1991, but are still few. Several agencies have ministry among them (**AP**, Swiss-German **SUM**, Baptists, Lutheran Brethren).
  ii *The Kanuri and Kotoko*, about 30 believers known.
  iii *The Hausa, Fali and Mbum* — a few believers.
  iv *The Shuwa Arabs* are nomadic, moving between Chad and Cameroon. Only one or two believers known with no direct church planting yet.

b) *The many peoples of the Mandara mountains,* 30% Muslim but mostly fetishist. Some church planting agencies are seeing the beginnings of breakthroughs.

c) *The northern plains peoples* — Giziga, Mofu, Kapsiki, Gude and Gidar among whom several missionaries and churches are at work (Lutheran Brethren, Baptists, UECC).

d) *The Pygmies* have long been neglected in the southeastern forests. About 7% are at least nominally Christian. There are now specific efforts by Pygmy and cross-cultural workers to plant churches and translate the Bible (**WorldTeam**, **SIL**, CMFI).

9 **The missionary force.** The largest agencies are Vision Africa (40), Norwegian Lutheran Mission (32), North American Baptist Conference (32), European Baptist Mission (25) and **AP/SUM** (18). Pioneer missionaries are needed to reach the Muslims and northern pagan peoples, and for Bible translation ministry. Evangelical missionaries could help bring new life and vigour to the more nominal churches — but this requires skill and gifting of a high order.

10 **Support ministries** for which intercession is needed: **C**

a) *Christian literature* is a major need. CMFI run a publishing house that has already printed 3 million books and 10 million tracts. More literature workers, both expatriate and national, are needed for writing, publishing and distributing French, English and local language materials.

b) *Christian radio programmes* may be aired on local and private stations; but few workers have the skills or equipment to prepare quality material. *Sawtu Linjilla* is a studio run by the various churches and missions working in Cameroon, Chad and Central African Republic, which produces French and Fulani radio programmes, cassettes, and audio-visual materials. The aim is pre-evangelism among the northern Cameroon peoples who use Fulani as a trade language. More Christian radio and television stations and programmes are needed in Cameroon.

c) *The JESUS film* has become a major evangelistic tool. Maybe 63% of the population has viewed it. It was available in 10 languages in 1999, but 70 other language versions were in production with a further 28 needing research.

d) *EHC* launched a nation-wide literature distribution in 1996.

e) *The Swiss-based Helimission* operates a helicopter service for Christian ministries.

Canada

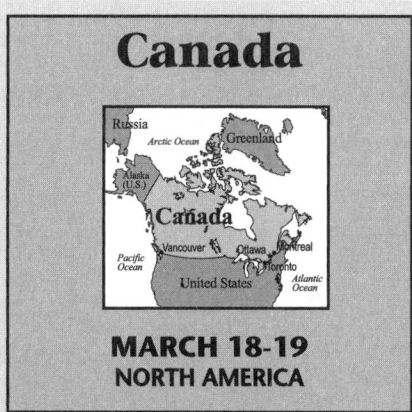

MARCH 18-19
NORTH AMERICA

GEOGRAPHY
Area 9,970,610 sq.km. The world's second largest country. Wide diversity of mountains, prairie grasslands and forests but much is sparsely populated wilderness and arctic tundra.

Population		Ann.Gr.	Density
2000	31,146,639	+1.01%	3 per sq. km.
2010	33,928,551	+0.83%	3 per sq. km.
2025	37,896,497	+0.68%	4 per sq. km.

Capital Ottawa 1,085,000. Other major cities: Toronto 4,657,000; Montreal 3.4 mill.; Vancouver 1.99m. **Urbanites** 78%.

PEOPLES
Canada is a mosaic of indigenous and immigrant nations and peoples, many of whom have retained much of their original cultures. The high degree of cultural mixing makes classifications only approximate.
British 31%. Majority in east, centre and west.
French 21%. Majority in Quebec. Although Canada is federally bilingual, with equal rights for all, there is a sizeable separatist contingent amongst Francophones.
Mixed origins 21%.
Other European 13.4%. Representing every nation in Europe. Includes many Germans, Italians, Ukrainians.
Asian 7.2%. Chinese 930,000; Indo-Pakistani 715,000; Filipino 255,000; SE Asian 190,000.
Indigenous 2.8%. Native Canadian and Métis (mixed race) 830,000 speaking 64 languages; Inuit 46,000.
Afro-Caribbean 2%. African, African-American, and Afro-Caribbean.
Arab/Middle East 1%.
Latin American 0.6%.

Literacy 99%. **Official Languages** English, French. **All indigenous languages** 76 (several are nearly extinct). **Languages with Scriptures** 6Bi 11NT 23por 12w.i.p.

ECONOMY
One of the world's leading industrial nations, and a member of the 'G8' economic powers. Over 75% of Canada's trade is with the USA, in which, along with Mexico, it is closely linked in the North American Free Trade Agreement

(NAFTA). This interdependence moderates trends towards an economic nationalism. Increasing economic links with Asia reflect new realities within the country. **HDI** 0.932; 1st/174. **Public debt** 92% of GNP. **Income/person** $19,020 (62% of USA).

POLITICS

A federal monarchy with parliamentary government. Independent of Britain in 1867. The unity of Canada is under threat due to increasing polarization between Francophone Quebec and the other, Anglophone, provinces. A Quebec referendum in 1995 voted to remain in Canada by only the narrowest of margins. Possibly as much as 20% of the country's land area is gradually being restored to Canada's indigenous peoples.

RELIGION

Freedom of religion, but rapid secularization and pluralization are taking place at every level of society.

Religions	Population %	Adherents	Ann.Gr.
Christian	75.73	23,587,350	+0.0%
non-Religious	18.27	5,690,500	+4.4%
Muslim	1.60	498,000	+8.9%
Jewish	1.20	373,760	+1.0%
Hindu	0.80	249,173	+3.7%
Sikh	0.70	218,026	+4.2%
Other	0.70	218,026	+4.2%
Buddhist/Chinese	0.70	218,000	+8.7%
Baha'i	0.20	62,293	+1.0%
Traditional ethnic	0.10	31,147	+1.0%

Christians	Denom.	Affil.%	,000	Ann.Gr.
Protestant	89	12.53	3,904	-0.4%
Independent	102	0.75	235	+2.3%
Anglican	2	2.37	738	-0.6%
Catholic	5	40.45	12,599	+0.3%
Orthodox	8	1.93	601	+0.3%
Marginal	31	1.59	496	+1.5%
Unaffiliated		16.11	5,018	n.a.

Churches	MegaBloc	Cong.	Members	Affiliates
Roman Catholic	C	5,799	8,118,421	12.340m
United Ch of Canada	P	3,780	680,000	1,800,000

Anglican [2]	A	2,900	421,714	738,000
Canadian Baptist Mins	P	1,130	131,000	259,380
Jehovah's Witnesses	M	1,400	122,000	230,580
Greek Orthodox	O	76	140,244	230,000
Pentecostal Assemblies	P	1,100	142,857	220,000
Presbyterian	P	1,100	140,000	210,000
Evang Lutheran	P	650	140,000	197,000
Latter-day Saints (Morm)	M	410	72,727	160,000
Ukrainian Catholic	C	71	128,385	128,385
Ukr Greek Orthodox	O	258	81,560	115,000
Chr and Miss Alliance	P	400	42,489	99,000
Fell of Evang Bapt	P	509	66,000	89,000
Lutheran Ch — Canada	P	338	62,222	84,000
Salvation Army	P	380	20,000	82,000
Christian Reformed	P	238	48,000	80,000
Maronite Catholic	C	132	6,667	80,000
Mennonite Brethren	P	200	30,000	48,300
Gen Conf Mennonites	P	127	24,000	40,080
Pente Assem of N'fndlnd	P	140	14,000	28,500
Assoc Gospel Chs	P	140	10,500	27,000
Ch of the Nazarene	P	185	12,300	24,000
Conv of Southern Bapts	P	137	9,000	18,000
Other Independent [31]	I	488	30,652	70,500
Other denoms [204]		5,611	611,953	1,174,000
Total Christians [260]		27,580	11.327m	18.572m

Trans-bloc Groupings	pop. %	,000	Ann.Gr.
Evangelical	10.8	3,354	+0.3%
Charismatic	10.5	3,262	+0.1%
Pentecostal	1.3	398	+1.0%

Missionaries from Canada
P,I,A 7,094 in 152 agencies to 180 countries.

Missionaries to Canada
P,I,A 453 in 56 agencies from 31 countries: Korea 159, USA 114, UK 45.

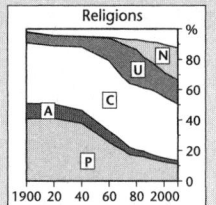

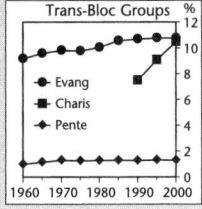

• Challenges for Prayer

1 **The Christian Church has become marginalized** in Canadian society. Many major historic denominations have suffered disastrous declines in membership. The loss of biblical roots, lack of vision for evangelism, and compromise on ethical issues have all contributed to this tragic situation. The church has allowed pluralism and secularization to undermine its foundations. Canada needs revival.

2 **Evangelical witness has generally declined** through the 20th Century.

a) *Evangelicals represented 25% of the population in 1900*, but less than 8% in 1989; this had risen, however, to 10.8% by 2000. While evangelical and charismatic denominations were the fastest growing religious groups in Canada in the 1980s and '90s, the decline of the historic denominations more than offset this growth.

b) *Canadian Evangelicals are working together more effectively* than in earlier years but are still too fragmented. Pray for effective cooperation for the Kingdom.

c) There are positive signs. The newer evangelical groups are growing, using new structures and styles. The controversial 'Toronto Blessing' nevertheless stimulated much-needed renewal for many. Pray that evangelical Christians would further unite and make a decisive impact on this spiritually needy land.

3 **Vision Canada**, nurtured under the Evangelical Fellowship of Canada, was launched by 40 denominations and agencies. The purpose: to serve the Body of Christ in evangelism so that every person in Canada will have the opportunity to see, hear and respond to the gospel by the year 2000. A formal goal of planting 10,000 new churches by 2015 was affirmed by leaders of 39 denominations in 1997. Since 1998 there has been a marked improvement in church planting activity in a wide array of denominational groups. Pray that this advance may be achieved.

4 **The large number of Bible institutes,** colleges and theological seminaries committed to a Biblical view of Scripture are fulfilling a major role in strengthening evangelical witness. They are mostly concentrated in the western Prairie provinces, and many are experiencing renewal and growth. Pray for the students and their teachers, that missions may be a central issue in their education.

5 **French Canadians are 85% Catholic in culture,** but a decreasing number of them (25%) ever attend mass. Pray for spiritual life and renewal in Catholic institutions and congregations, as Quebec has experienced four consecutive decades of secularization. Evangelicals are less than 1% of the Francophone population of the province, but have grown well from 1970-88 but more slowly to 2000. Pray for:

a) Increased receptivity amidst growing social and political change and instability. Evangelism is yielding less fruit than in the period 1975-85. For Vision Canada to be achieved, 2,300 Francophone congregations would need to be started in Quebec.

b) Quebec separatism, which is a potent political movement with unknown implications for Canada's future. Pray that the uncertainty of this may stimulate maturity and growth in the churches.

c) The small, but growing, French-speaking Protestant missionary force.

d) The growing prayer movement in Quebec that is bringing together believers from many denominations.

e) Continued growth in fruitful fellowship between denominations — there has been marked improvement since 1997.

6 **Canadian indigenous peoples** are largely Christian in name, but active evangelistic churches among them are desperately few. There are 2,400 reservations without an ongoing evangelical witness.

a) Pray for a moving of God's Spirit to overcome the shameful treatment of these people by whites in the past. The government has finally admitted the dismal failure of its policies towards indigenous peoples in the last 150 years. The church is assuming an increasing role in this reconciliation, but court cases against churches are rising over involvement in residential schools earlier in the 20th Century. Only the grace of God can enable the indigenous people to receive Christ despite serious economic and social problems, and strident anti-white, anti-Christian propaganda that draws many back into old animistic customs.

b) Pray for the growth of strong, well-led churches that are culturally appropriate. Especially pray for the development of indigenous leadership. There are many encouraging signs of growth and renewal in the native evangelical community, where a contextualized church is beginning to flourish.

c) Pray for missions seeking to evangelize and plant churches — often in the inhospitable northern parts of the country. Both denominational (Native Evangelical Fellowship of Canada, **CMA**, PAOC) and mission agencies, united as Inter-Mission Cooperative Outreach, are dedicated to this. Indigenous missions movements to evangelize their own are also developing.

d) Bible translation or revision is still needed. Revisions or translations are required in several of the 25 actively used languages. Five new translations of the New Testament or Bible have been completed in the last few years, leaving 12 works currently in progress. Pray for the translators with **SIL** and other groups. There are also an increasing number of Christian radio and TV programmes aimed at aboriginals.

e) **The hundreds of thousands of native Canadian Indians** living outside reservations are neglected and spiritually needy, especially in the cities, where poverty and substance abuse continues to afflict them.

7 **The Inuit (Eskimo) in the Arctic** are mostly Anglican in name, but the impact of the worst of Western civilization has greatly altered and harmed the Eskimo way of life. The suicide rate is four times the national average. The recent establishing of a new Inuit Territory, Nunavut, has given autonomy and hope to the local people. Likewise, since 1982, there has been evidence that the Holy Spirit is stirring, by waves of conversions and awakenings from nominalism. Helpful is the fact that the church is still often the centre of the community in these isolated northern towns. Pray that the new-found autonomy of the Inuit people would be made complete by finding freedom in Christ.

8 **Immigrant communities** have multiplied. Toronto claims to be the world's most racially diverse city. Vancouver is the world's second-largest Sikh city. Especially significant are:

a) **Asian Indians** (numbering 715,000) — 220,000 Sikhs (less than 0.1% Christian), 250,000 Hindus and 190,000 Muslims form the biggest bloc of unreached peoples in the country. **OM** and **IT** have teams ministering to them in Vancouver and Toronto.

b) **Arabic-speaking peoples**, mostly Muslim or Orthodox Christian; very little specific outreach to them has been undertaken. Most of the few believers are Lebanese or Palestinian.

c) **The Southern and Eastern European** communities with few evangelical churches.

d) **The Chinese** (930,000) who will soon number a million people with the steady influx of immigrants. There are over 100 growing churches among them in several cities. While growth is not a problem, assimilation and second-generation withdrawal from the church is. Pray also that Chinese churches would integrate well into the larger body of Christ in Canada.

9 **Missionary vision** has been great in the past, but the number of missionaries declined by 15% between 1992 and 1999. Giving to national missionaries and relief and development programmes, however, has increased in recent years. Pray for increased involvement by churches and individuals in the evangelization of the unreached in Canada and around the world. Pray for increased missionary concern in the many growing evangelical churches among the ethnic minorities; such a vision is vital for Canada, and could be strategic for the evangelization of their lands of origin. Pray also for the unifying and strategic work of the Task Force for Global Mission of the Evangelical Fellowship of Canada.

10 Specialized ministries for prayer:

a) **Christian media**. There are a number of widely appreciated religious programmes on secular radio and TV networks, particularly **Crossroads** and **It's a New Day**. US Christian programmes continue to be larger in number, but the Canadian government has now allowed Vision TV, an interfaith network, to carry more programming.

b) **Student ministries** in the 272 colleges and universities. These give wide exposure to sections of the campus community. There are three movements linked with IVCF**(IFES** — English), **GBU** (French) and Ambassadors for Christ (Chinese). There are also extensive ministries linked with **Navigators** and **CCCI**. **YFC** and **OAC** have good ministries in high schools. Pray that these and other ministries may make a deep and lasting impact on nearly 1 million tertiary students.

Cape Verde Islands

Republic of Cape Verde

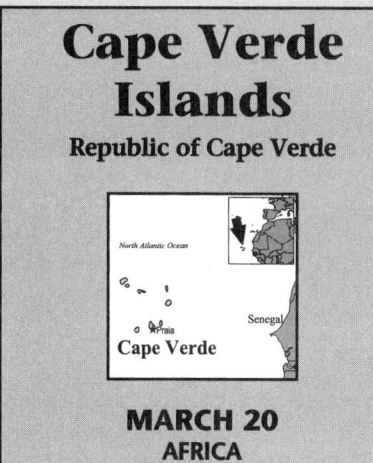

North Atlantic Ocean

Praia
Senegal

Cape Verde

MARCH 20
AFRICA

GEOGRAPHY
Area 4,033 sq.km. Fifteen dry, barren islands 600 km. off the west coast of Africa.

Population		Ann.Gr.	Density
2000	427,724	+2.37%	106 per sq. km.
2010	529,110	+2.04%	131 per sq. km.
2025	670,931	+1.42%	166 per sq. km.

Capital Praia 80,937. **Urbanites** 30%.

PEOPLES
Caboverdian Creole (mixed race) 71%.
African 28%. Mainly from Guinea-Bissau.
European 1%.

Literacy 72%, but the majority of the population has had no formal education. **Official language** Portuguese. Trade language Portuguese Creole. **All indigenous languages** 4. **Languages with Scriptures** 2Bi, 2por.

ECONOMY
Deforestation and overgrazing followed by 20 years of drought devastated the economy in the late 1980s and early 1990s. Heavily dependent on aid and remittances from Caboverdian migrants. **Unemployment** 26%. **HDI** 0.677; 106th/174. **Public debt** 48% of GNP. **Income/person** $1,010 (3.5% of USA).

POLITICS
Independent of Portugal in 1975 as a one-party socialist republic. A revised constitution in 1990 led to multi-party elections and a peaceful change of government.

RELIGION
The privileged position of the Catholic Church ended in 1975. A secular state with freedom of religion.

Religions	Population %	Adherents	Ann.Gr.
Christian	95.13	406,894	+2.0%
Muslim	2.77	11,848	+21.0%
Traditional ethnic	1.13	4,833	+6.0%
non-Religious/other	0.97	4,150	-1.6%

Christians	Denom.	Affil.%	,000	Ann.Gr.
Protestant	4	5.03	22	+5.9%
Independent	5	2.90	12	+17.2%
Catholic	1	93.99	402	+2.0%
Marginal	2	2.10	9	+8.2%
Doubly affiliated		-8.89	-38	n.a.

Churches	MegaBloc	Cong.	Members	Affiliates
Catholic	C	30	188,732	402,000
Ch of the Nazarene	P	26	3,780	10,743
Seventh-day Adventist	P	52	3,185	10,000
New Apostolic	I	22	2,500	6,000
Jehovah's Witnesses	M	30	1,720	5,000
Latter-day Saints (Morm)	M	18	2,963	4,000
God is Love Pentecostal	I	16	2,500	4,000
Universal Ch of K. of G	I	13	1,000	1,500
Other denominations [4]		12	735	1,680
Doubly affiliated			-17,840	-38,000
Total Christians [12]		219	189,275	407,000

Trans-bloc Groupings	pop. %	,000	Ann.Gr.
Evangelical	4.7	20	+5.7%
Charismatic	8.5	36	+6.9%
Pentecostal	1.4	6	+11.0%

Missionaries from Cape Verde
P,I,A 5.

Missionaries to Cape Verde
P,I,A 45 in 11 agencies from 10 countries: Brazil 25, Argentina 4, UK 3.

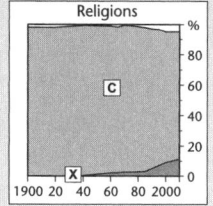

Religions %

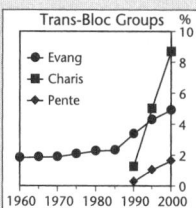

Trans-Bloc Groups %
- Evang
- Charis
- Pente

• Challenges for Prayer

1 **The political leaders must address the ecological and economic problems** confronting the nation. Scant resources were poorly managed in the past, exacerbating the Republic's poverty. Pray for stable and wise government, and for social and economic betterment.

2 **Caboverdians are Christian in name,** but in practice are more influenced by superstitions and African fetishism. Pray for true conversions among them. Christian literature is lacking in Creole, and most understand Portuguese only partially.

3 **The increasing growth of Evangelicals** has been largely though the ministries of the Nazarene Church and the more recently-arrived Pentecostal groups. Pray that more indigenous workers may be trained up for these growing groups. Pray that believers might mature and increase despite the poverty and geographical isolation.

4 **There are 350,000 Caboverdians who live in migrant communities**, the largest being in New England, USA (170,000), Portugal (37,000), Angola, Senegal, Italy, and France. Pray that many in these communities may become true disciples of Jesus and be a blessing to their homeland.

Cayman Islands

Cayman Islands
George Town

MARCH 20
CARIBBEAN

GEOGRAPHY
Area 264 sq.km. Three coral islands south of Cuba.

Population	Ann.Gr.	Density
2000	38,371	+3.70%	145 per sq. km.
2010	53,015	+3.15%	201 per sq. km.
2025	77,938	+2.33%	295 per sq. km.

Capital Georgetown 20,555.

PEOPLES
Residents come from 120+ nations, over half being foreign-born.
Afro-Caribbean 59.2%.
Euro-Caribbean 30%. American, Canadian, British.
Latin American/Hispanic 7.9%. Mainly Honduran, Cuban, Nicaraguan.
Other 2.9%. Jewish 650, various Asian groups.
Literacy 97.5%. **Official language** English.

ECONOMY
The wealthiest economy in the Caribbean. The wealth of the territory derived from banking, tourism and insurance. **Income/person** $40,000 (142% of USA).

POLITICS
A British dependent territory with representative government, most assembly members being elected.

RELIGION
Freedom of religion.

Religions	Population %	Adherents	Ann.Gr.
Christian	77.96	29,914	+3.4%
Spiritist	14.00	5,372	+3.7%
non-Religious/other	5.00	1,919	+7.9%
Jewish	1.71	656	+3.8%
Baha'i	0.88	338	+5.5%
Hindu	0.26	100	+4.6%
Muslim	0.19	73	+4.7%

Christians	Denom.	Affil.%	,000	Ann.Gr.
Protestant	16	54.99	21	+3.3%
Independent	7	9.28	4	+3.2%
Anglican	1	1.30	0	+1.2%
Catholic	1	1.56	1	+6.0%
Marginal	3	1.47	1	+6.9%
Unaffiliated		9.36	4	n.a.

Churches	MegaBloc	Cong.	Members	Affiliates
United	P	9	8,553	13,000
Seventh-day Adventist	P	8	1,400	2,400
Ch of God (Anderson)	P	5	800	1,700
Baptist	P	3	360	1,000
Ch of God Holiness	P	5	600	900
Catholic	C	2	240	600
Jehovah's Witnesses	M	1	139	324
Baptist Convention	P	1	200	320
Ch of God (Cleveland)	P	1	150	250
Other denoms [19]		36	2,850	5,800
Total Christians [28]		71	15,306	26,325

Trans-bloc Groupings	pop. %	,000	Ann.Gr.
Evangelical	25.5	10	+3.2%
Charismatic	11.8	5	+3.3%
Pentecostal	1.7	1	+2.6%

Missionaries from Cayman Islands
P,I,A 2.

Missionaries to Cayman Islands
P,I,A 17 in 5 agencies from 2 countries: USA 15.
C 4.

• Challenges for Prayer

1 **Much of the wealth** passing through the nearly 600 banks has been 'laundered' by international criminals. There is one bank for every 50 people, and a registered company for every inhabitant. The Caymans were vulnerable to manipulation by international drug traffickers but laws were tightened. Pray that the wealth of the islands may be used to extend God's Kingdom.

2 **Christianity is numerically strong**. Most of the 70+ churches are evangelical. Pray that the government and people might hold fast to Christian values. Pray that Christians may live exemplary and consistent lives in the midst of wealth and the materialistic, complacent lifestyle it brings.

3 **Over a million tourists a year visit the islands.** Pray for many to be confronted by the claims of Christ while in the pursuit of pleasure.

Central African Republic

République Centrafricaine

MARCH 21
AFRICA

GEOGRAPHY
Area 622,436 sq.km. A landlocked state in Africa's geographical centre. Variation from tropical forest in the southwest to semi-desert in the northeast.

Population	Ann.Gr.	Density
2000	3,615,266	+1.92%	6 per sq. km.
2010	4,333,276	+1.84%	7 per sq. km.
2025	5,703,795	+1.74%	9 per sq. km.

Capital Bangui 687,104. **Urbanites** 39%.

PEOPLES
Over 100 ethnic groups.
Adamawa-Ubangi 79.2%. About 60 ethnic groupings; largest: Gbaya 857,000; Banda 846,000; Mandja 531,000; Sango 350,000; Ngbaka 275,000; Mbum 228,000; Kare 93,000; Zande 72,000; Nzakara 58,000.
Sudanic 8%. Over 14 ethnic groups on northern border. Sara 235,000; Kaba 72,000; Dagba 44,000; Runga 23,000.
West Atlantic 6.5%. Mbororo Fulbe 170,000; Bagirmi Fulbe 45,000 (partly nomadic and increasing).
Bantu 3.2%. 11 groups in the SW. Mbati 65,000;

Kaka 10,000.
Semitic 1.8%. Nomadic Shuwa Arabs 65,000.
Pygmy 0.8%. Five groups: Yaka 20,000; Gundi 12,000, mainly SW forests.
Other 0.5%. Mainly French. Many refugees in 1999 from the two Congos, Chad and Sudan.

Literacy 33%. **Official languages** French and Sango (trade language used by 90% of the population). **All languages** 69. **Languages with Scriptures** 4Bi 1NT 5por 8w.i.p.

ECONOMY
Underdeveloped. Abundant natural resources, but poor communications and distance from the sea hinder development. Main income is from diamonds. Warfare in surrounding countries has further damaged the economy with the severing of trade links and influx of refugees. Over 80% of the working population are subsistence farmers. Health facilities are limited and average life-expectancy is only 49 years. **HDI** 0.378; 165th/174. **Public debt** 76% of GNP. **Income/person** $310 (1.1% of USA).

POLITICS
Formerly part of French Equatorial Africa. Independent in 1960. Periods of democracy interspersed with military regimes and Bokassa's bizarre 'Empire', 1976-79. A series of military rebellions in 1996-97 were suppressed by French troops. Frequent French interventions politically and militarily since independence have been deeply resented. Deepening economic malaise, civil wars in the Congos and Sudan and inter-ethnic tensions are ongoing, unresolved issues.

RELIGION
Freedom of religion.

Religions	Population %	Adherents	Ann.Gr.
Christian	70.38	2,544,424	+1.5%
Muslim	15.60	563,981	+4.1%
Traditional ethnic	12.80	462,754	+1.9%
non-Religious/other	0.89	32,176	+1.7%
Baha'i	0.33	11,930	+3.2%

Christians	Denom.	Affil.%	,000	Ann.Gr.
Protestant	17	24.64	891	+3.5%
Independent	38	12.27	444	+4.4%
Catholic	1	18.71	677	+1.7%
Marginal	2	0.32	11	+7.1%
Unaffiliated		14.43	521	n.a.

Churches	MegaBloc	Cong.	Members	Affiliates
Catholic	C	2,751	393,355	676,570
Union of Ev. Brethren	P	921	200,000	350,000
Elim Evangelical	P	210	80,000	140,000
AEBEC (ex BMM)	I	350	65,000	120,000
Evang Baptist	P	845	60,000	110,000
UFEB (ex BMM)	I	200	50,000	95,830
Frat Union of Baptist	P	350	50,000	95,000
Coop Evang Centrafric	I	338	45,000	90,000
Evangelical Lutheran	P	300	38,000	62,000
AEAC Apostolique	P	530	35,000	50,000
Churches of Christ	P	140	14,000	23,000
Evang Chs of the East	P	500	15,000	19,500
Evang Baptist Comm	I	72	12,000	17,000
Jehovah's Witnesses	M	68	2,700	11,259
Evang Ch of the West	I	48	6,000	11,200

Union of Baptist Chs	I	50	5,556	10,000
Other denoms [43]		760	79,000	141,000
Total Christians [59]		8,433	1,151,000	2,022,000

Trans-bloc Groupings	pop. %	,000	Ann.Gr.
Evangelical	34.8	1,257	+3.8%
Charismatic	11.8	427	+5.8%
Pentecostal	8.1	293	+6.6%

Missionaries from Central African Republic
P,I,A 49 in 6 agencies, most in CAR.

Missionaries to Central African Republic
P,I,A 192 in 29 agencies from 18 countries: USA 110, Switzerland 16, Sweden 12, Germany 12.

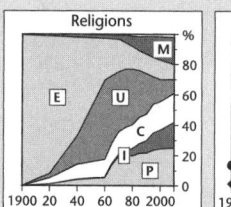

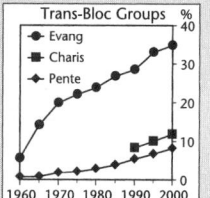

• Answers to Prayer

1 **A well-known national evangelical leader** was used of God in 1998 to broker a significant reconciliation meeting after a generation of instability, coups and violence.

2 **Many local churches** and some denominations experienced considerable growth in the 1990s.

• Challenges for Prayer

1 **Widespread evangelism since the 1960s** has yielded a massive response. The CAR has Africa's highest percentage of Evangelicals, but lack of effective discipleship of both the new and second- and third-generation Christians has created multiple problems:

a) *Evangelical nominalism and a syncretistic world-view* is fairly common, and there is little depth of commitment or mature grasp and application of truths of Scripture.

b) *Divisions in the Church* have hindered cooperative efforts. Pray against the root causes:

i *Ethnic based denominations* enhance tribalism and create barriers.

ii *Widespread breakdown* between church leaders and missionaries have caused deep heartache, multiplied splits and isolated ministries from one another. Pray for repentance, healing of past wounds and a deeper appreciation and level of trust among God's servants, both national and expatriate.

iii *Spiritual pride*, greed, misuse of funds, lack of trust, selfishness, paternalistic attitudes and rigid doctrinal views have all played their part.

2 **The unity of the Church** is a fundamental need. There is some working together within the main Baptist, Pentecostal and 'Evangelical' blocs, but this needs to be widened and deepened. Pray for:

a) *The AEC* (Alliance Evangélique Centrafricaine) and others that they might work effectively for a unified, God-glorifying witness in the country.

b) *Cooperative research* of the harvest force and harvest field in the CAR. The AD2000 Movement, AMI/**CMF** and others have made a beginning in this. Pray for its completion and application of its results to mobilize the Church for discipling, church planting and pioneer missions. There is, at present, little concern in local churches for wider outreach.

3 **Training and ministry modelling for leadership** is a great need for the Church in the CAR. The distances between towns, widespread poverty and functional illiteracy limit training possibilities. Pray for:

a) *The dozen or more Bible schools* — all are limited by lack of staff, students, funds and resources.

b) *The Bangui Evangelical Graduate School of Theology (BEST)* opened in 1977 as a result of the initiative of AEA (Association of Evangelicals of Africa). This was the first evangelical, theological degree-level school for French-speaking Africa. Pray for this institution and its spiritual impact throughout Africa. Pray for the provision of the right permanent staff and resources. There were 75 students in the Master's programme in 2000 and a further 36 women in the special women's programme. The lack of funds is a major brake on development. The Grace Evangelical Brethren also have a seminary at Bata.

c) *TEE is important in this large, underpopulated land,* but much work must be done to develop and maintain this programme all over the country.

d) *Missions vision needs to increase*, though some are gaining a vision for the Pygmies and Fulbe in the west. AMI/**CMF** runs a small Bible school with emphasis on cross-cultural missions. Pray that this may raise the profile of, and involvement in, missions. Pray that the people filling the churches might be impacted by the Lord's desire to see all peoples evangelized. Pray that those facilitating missions vision might see support and enthusiasm increase.

4 **Young people and children**. Few churches have the vision, structures and workers to disciple the up-coming generation. One exception is the Evangelical Baptist Church with 25,000 youth actively involved in a well-organized structure. Pray for:

a) *The impact of CEF and SU on children's ministry.* **CEF** commenced Bible clubs in schools in 1994. Churches are permitted to organize Bible teaching in school buildings after school hours.

b) *Secondary students*. The UJC**(IFES)** is active in 33 of the 47 institutions in the country and over 1,000 students are involved in the groups. Political unrest has hitherto frequently disrupted studies for the 3,000 university students. There is widespread lack of hope for the future with limited job opportunities.

5 **Bible translation**. Only 4 indigenous languages (the trade language, Sango, also Gbaya, Mbai and Zande) have the whole Bible. Pray for effective use of the newly revised Sango NT to be released soon and for the revision of the OT currently in progress. In 6 other languages Bible translation is now being undertaken (**The Bible Society, SIL, BMM**), but in five more there is a definite translation need. A further 49 still need to be surveyed. In 1994, the Central African Association for Bible Translation and Literacy (ACATBA) was formed. Pray for a determined effort to provide the Word of God for every language which needs it.

6 **The less reached**. Though most of the country has been at least superficially evangelized there are specific areas and peoples still to be reached.

a) *The northern lobe* is difficult to access and largely Muslim. In an area 600 by 300km there are only eight congregations. Pray specifically for the Runga (90% Muslim, 23,000) — Apostolic Church, AMI/CMF; the Kara (60% Muslim, 5,000) — **SIL**, AMI/**CMF**; and the Luto (60% Muslim, 17,000) — **BMM**, AMI/**CMF**.

b) *The Muslims have increased through immigration* (M^{bororo} Fulbe, Arabs, Sudanese, Chadians) and increasingly by conversions. Muslims now control much of the trading and transporting network. Relatively little outreach is specifically directed to them, and few Christians feel able or equipped for this. Pray specifically for:

i   The *influential urban Muslims* (Arab, Hausa).

ii The *nomadic Shuwa Arabs and Mbororo Fulbe.*

iii The *increasing Muslim minorities* among Christianized peoples. Sudanese influence, Libyan and Saudi money as well as grants to study abroad in Saudi Arabia are bringing many to Islam.

c) *The forest areas.* There is great need for adequate research but there are pockets of unreached among:

i   The *Pygmy*— some reckon they may number 200,000. They speak 5 languages (Grace Brethren).

ii *Bofi and Bokoto*, sub-groups of the Gbaya.

iii *The Langbassi*, a sub-group of the Banda.

d) *Sara peoples* along the Chad border have lower percentages of Christians.

7 **Mission agencies** have played an important role in education and health as well as in planting churches, translating the Scriptures, etc., though personnel are now much reduced in numbers. The largest are Baptist Mid-Missions (41), Grace Brethren (21), Inter-Act (12), Evangelical Lutheran Church of America (8). The great challenge is for effective partnership as equals between the national churches and missions. Pray for good relationships and cooperation for outreach and support ministries.

C 8 **Christian media and help ministries:**

a) *Christian radio* — pray for the removal of all obstacles to setting up an effective evangelical radio station in Bangui.

b) *EHC launched a nation-wide distribution of literature* — some for illiterates — in every home in 1995. Pray for the successful completion of the task.

c) *The JESUS film* has been widely shown in French, Sango, Gbaya and Zande, and is in production in other languages. Pray that good follow-up may lead to more and stronger churches.

d) *MAF* has two planes for serving the churches and missions in this large country.

e) *GRN has recordings available* in 17 languages, but this number could be increased.

Chad

Republic of Chad

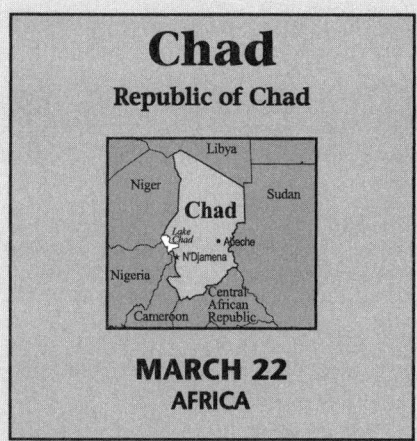

MARCH 22
AFRICA

GEOGRAPHY
Area 1,284,000 sq.km. Desert in the north, dry grassland in centre, thick bush in the south. The sea is 1000 km distant.

Population	Ann.Gr.	Density
2000	7,650,982	+2.67%	6 per sq. km.
2010	9,887,331	+2.58%	8 per sq. km.
2025	13,908,122	+2.08%	11 per sq. km.

Capital N'djamena 650,000. **Urbanites** 21%.

PEOPLES
Largely Sudanic, Chadic and Saharan, here grouped in people clusters:
Sudanic 45%. South and southwest, over 100 peoples; largest: Sara (Ngambai, Kaba, Gulai, Ngam, Majingai, etc.) 1.3mill.; Mundang 184,000; Marba 142,000; Massa 125,000; Mbai 106,000; Tupuri 104,000; Nancere 81,000; Lele 80,000; Gabri 78,000; Kado 75,000; Dai 57,000; Kera 51,000; Ngam 50,000.
Saharan 13.3%. Nine peoples in the north: Kanembu 445,000; Goran (Daza) 300,000; Kanuri 107,000;

Bideyat-Zaghawa 89,000; Teda 30,000.
Arab 11.3%. Over 11 peoples, mostly nomadic Shuwa (Baggara) Arabs.
Ouaddai-Fur 11%. 18 peoples in the east: Maba 362,000; Masalit 129,000; Tama 72,000; Daju 71,000; Mimi 46,000; Abu Charib 31,000; Masmaje 30,000; Assangori 27,000; Runga 25,000.
Guera-Naba 10%. 22 peoples in and around central mountains: Hadjerai tribes (18) 474,000; Naba 266,000.
Chari-Bagirmi 5.9%. 22 peoples: Buduma 59,000; Barma (Bagirmi) 52,000; Kotoko 25,000.
Other 2.5%. Fulbe(5) 152,000; Hausa 42,000.
Foreign 1%. African 48,000; European 1,800.

Literacy 10% (8% in French, 2% in Arabic). One of the lowest literacy levels in the world. **Official languages** French (only spoken by the educated), Arabic (spoken by about 60% of the population). **All languages** 127. **Languages with Scriptures** 9Bi 18NT 5por 28w.i.p.

ECONOMY
A subsistence economy. Lack of rainfall, severe droughts, distance from the sea, post-independence civil wars and a rudimentary road system have hindered any economic progress. Very few natural resources but for cattle. Significant oil deposits near Lake Chad and in the southwest could bring progress if wisely developed. **HDI** 0.393; 162nd/174. **Public debt** 57% of GNP. **Income/person** $160 (0.7% of USA).

POLITICS
Independent from France in 1960. The non-Muslim Southerners were politically dominant until 1978, but since 1979 northern Muslim factions have fought amongst themselves for power, with interventions by Libya, France and others. There has been a succession of military governments, interspersed with localized rebellions. A Zaghawa-dominated government pays lip service to democracy.

RELIGION

Officially a secular state with freedom of religion, but the government favours Islam. Muslims have become dominant in government, trade and the army, though barely a majority in the country.

Religions	Population %	Adherents	Ann.Gr.
Muslim	55.00	4,208,040	+3.8%
Christian	27.78	2,125,443	+1.7%
Traditional ethnic	16.00	1,224,157	+0.3%
Baha'i	1.05	80,335	+8.4%
non-Religious/other	0.17	13,000	+2.7%

Christians	Denom.	Affil.%	,000	Ann.Gr.
Protestant	12	12.92	988	+4.1%
Independent	25	2.04	156	+2.9%
Catholic	1	6.56	502	+3.0%
Marginal	1	0.03	2	+6.5%
Unaffiliated		6.23	477	n.a.

Churches	MegaBloc	Cong.	Members	Affiliates
Catholic	C	105	265,692	502,158
Evang Ch in Chad (EET)	P	1,150	147,796	437,000
Christian Brethren (ACT)	P	915	120,000	300,000
Baptist	P	415	53,892	90,000
Lutheran Brethren	P	828	24,000	70,000
New Apostolic	I	123	37,000	62,900
Apostolic	P	200	9,500	23,750

Grace Brethren (EEF)	P	130	7,000	18,500
Ch of God (Cleveland)	P	120	6,000	18,000
Evang Ch of C (ECWA)	I	100	7,000	17,000
Seventh-day Adventist	P	50	1,500	8,500
Assemblies of God	P	112	2,800	6,000
Evang Assemblies (Breth)	I	24	1,500	4,500
Other denoms [26]		472	33,965	90,000
Total Christians [39]		4,700	718,000	1,648,000

Trans-bloc Groupings	pop. %	,000	Ann.Gr.
Evangelical	13.5	1,031	+4.0%
Charismatic	2.4	187	+3.5%
Pentecostal	0.8	63	+5.3%

Missionaries from Chad
P,I,A 92 in 8 agencies to 6 countries: Chad 85.

Missionaries to Chad
P,I,A 295 in 37 agencies from 23 countries: USA 77, Germany 39, UK 35, Switzerland 30, France 23.

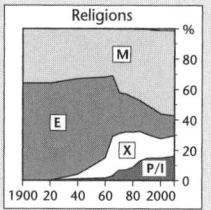

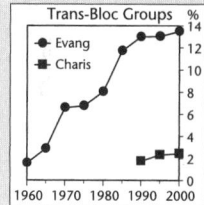

• Answers to Prayer

1 **Praise God for continued religious freedom** and for the welcome given to missionaries.

2 **The slowing of church growth has been reversed** in the 1990s with considerable church mobilization in the Chad for Christ campaign, with the vision to reach every sub-prefecture of Chad. Every year thousands of believers are mobilised for evangelism.

3 **Significant beginnings of response among Muslims** with Muslim Background Believer groups emerging.

• Challenges for Prayer

1 **A government that is impartial, honest and fully representative** of both north and south, Muslim and Christian and the many ethnic divisions, is a great need. Only then can peace come, with subsequent economic development and social uplift to one of the poorest and most illiterate countries in the world.

2 **Freedom of religion** is a precious reality, but is threatened by the polarization of the country. The population is almost equally divided between the politically dominant Muslim northerners and the increasingly marginalized Christian/ethnic religion southerners. Their cultures are so different and their history is one of northerners enslaving southerners. Although most of the schooling is in French, many in the north only read Arabic. Pray both for continued freedom of religion throughout the country and peace between the different religious and ethnic communities.

3 **Islam** has been in the ascendant for the past two decades, Muslims now controlling all the levers of power — government, trade and the armed forces. Muslim missionaries are multiplying, mosques are being built in non-Muslim areas and large sums of money are being invested in constructing two Muslim universities. Christians are ill-equipped to withstand such an onslaught and untrained in how best to witness to Muslims. Pray for:

a) *The overcoming* of the many emotional, cultural and historical barriers for southerners witnessing to Muslims.

b) *Various denominations* which have a vision for Muslim outreach. Pray for Chadian Brethren and EET national missionaries seeking to plant churches in Muslim areas. At Ba Illi is a missionary training college (EET/MEU-**AIM**) for cross-cultural workers. CERFEM is a Chadian research and resource centre which focuses the Church on the unreached.

4 **The Church**, its maturation and mobilization are key prayer targets. More specifically:

a) *Bible translation and literacy programmes*. Pray for rapid progress and for Chadian believers called to these ministries. Many Christians are illiterate and without anything of God's Word in their languages. NT projects are in progress in 28 languages, but another 68 need to be surveyed or tackled. Pray for the ministry of SIL with its large team of 50 workers, and also **The Bible Society** in furthering these.

b) *Tribalism*, syncretistic lifestyle and petty legalisms cripple many congregations. Pray for liberation from all bondages by a deep working of the Holy Spirit in every congregation.

c) *Unity among believers* is improving. Nearly every Protestant and Independent denomination is Evangelical. There are two main network fellowships to which most belong: the *Entente des Eglises et Missions au Tchad* and the Pentecostal Alliance. Pray for the improvement of strong biblical fellowship between these two groups.

d) *The Chad for Christ annual campaigns* have been used of God for mobilizing and giving basic training to thousands of believers, and sending out hundreds of teams from Entente denominations since 1993. The vision is to reach every village in the country. The real challenges are for reaching Muslim villages of the centre and north and improving the follow-up so that churches are planted. The lack of trained personnel and logistical support make this impossible at the present. Threats and violence by Muslims has increased in some areas — pray for protection, boldness and wisdom for evangelists.

5 **Training of leaders** is a major challenge — poor communications, poor churches, regional instabilities, wars and lack of finances have hindered the training of pastors and evangelists. Pray for the Shalom Higher School of Theology in N'Djamena (which serves the *Entente*), the Apostolic Bible School ESDRAS and the CoG Bible Institute. Pray also for secondary- and primary-level Bible schools in the south. Pray that the new generation of pastors may be men full of the Holy Spirit. Pray, too, for refresher courses arranged for those already in the ministry.

6 **The least evangelized.** There are more unreached peoples in Chad than in any other African country. Since 1985 the momentum of research of the peoples and their languages has increased through EET/**AIM/TEAM**, **YWAM**, **IMB-SBC**, CERFEM, **SIL** and others. The major people-cluster challenges:

a) *The Saharan peoples* are politically dominant but live in the northern deserts, Tibesti Mountains and northern shores of Lake Chad. The pioneer efforts of **TEAM** are only in the beginning stages. Only a handful of Christians are known.

b) *The Naba* are one of the largest unreached peoples in Chad and live between N'Djamena and the Guera mountains.

c) *The Guera Mountains* are the home of 19 small peoples of which only 6 have churches — the remainder are rapidly turning to Islam. The Brethren are the main denomination in this area. Evangelization and Bible translation for these peoples is urgent.

d) *The Ouaddai peoples* are Muslim and live in the eastern provinces of Biltine, Ouaddai and Salamat bordering Sudan. They are a major challenge — variety of languages, harsh living conditions, lack of roads. It is one of the least evangelized areas of Africa. French-Swiss **SUM**, **WEC** and AP have pioneered this area, but only among the Maba and Massalit has work been established with two small groups of Muslim Background Believers. Most of the 19 peoples are still completely unreached, but the Runga (**SUM**), Assangori, Tama and the Shuwa Arabs (**WEC**) are being targeted for entry.

e) *The Chari-Bagirmi*. The Barma were pioneered by **WEC**, the Lutheran Brethren and **AIM**, but only about five Christians are known. To their east, along the Chari River, live a medley of smaller peoples, some of which have been pioneered by EET-**AIM**, but much work remains to be done.

f) **The Arabs** — some urbanized but most are nomadic. Theirs is the main language of communication in the country, so it is important to evangelize them, but no permanent witness to them has been established.

g) **The nomadic Mbororo Fulbe** have begun to respond to the gospel in the south, but much more needs to be done.

h) **N'Djamena**, the only city in the country, is rapidly becoming a centre of Islamic propagation, with many Mosques but only 100 or so churches. There are only two Arabic-speaking congregations — the predominant language of the city. Many southern Christians gather in these churches, but they make little impression on the Muslim majority. French SUM has a work among the street children. Pray for missionaries working in N'Djamena and for others to be called.

7 **Ministry to young people.** Only larger urban churches have much ministry specifically for young people. Many Christian students are affiliated with *Union des Jeunes Chrétiens* (**IFES**). **CCCI**, **SU**, UBF (Korean) and independent evangelists also minister to young people and students. The great need is for suitable literature, disciplers and trainers of leaders. Four Chadian graduates serve in other lands with **IFES**.

8 **Missionary work** continues despite the upheavals of the past three decades. The main missions are working together under the EET Church in an organization called COCOAM. Present member missions: **TEAM** (32), **WEC** (22), French SUM/AP/Vision Afrique (21), **AIM** (15), MEDAF (1). Other missions include **SIL** (50), **MAF** (13, with 2 planes), EMET (10) and **IMB-SBC** (7). The need for more workers is obvious, but pray for those with a pioneer spirit and perseverance to give years to language learning, necessary to contribute much to the unreached and to developing churches. Pray also for their daily provision and safety. Pray also for the small, but growing number of Chadian missionaries involved in pioneer church planting and Bible translation.

9 **Christian media ministries:**

a) **The JESUS film**, widely used in Arabic, is also available in Fulfulde (Fulbe), Kanuri and Sango. About 30% of the population have seen the film. The Chad Arabic version has been well received, and over 37 other Chadian language versions are also being prepared.

b) **GRN** has prepared gospel messages in 298 languages and dialects and a further 30 were being recorded in 1999.

Pray that these films and recordings may be widely and effectively used.

Chile
Republic of Chile

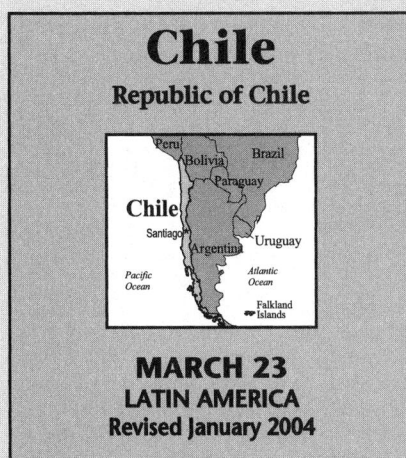

MARCH 23
LATIN AMERICA
Revised January 2004

GEOGRAPHY
Area 756,626 sq.km. A 4,200 km long country wedged between the mountains of the Andes and the Pacific Ocean and averaging only

150 km in width. Also Easter Island in the Central Pacific. Great extremes of climate from the hot northern Atacama Desert to Antarctic tundra in the south.

Population		Ann.Gr.	Density
2000	15,211,294	+1.37%	20 per sq. km.
2010	17,010,268	+1.06%	22 per sq. km.
2025	19,547,916	+0.81%	26 per sq. km.

About 40% of the population live near the capital and 85% overall in the temperate central provinces. The northern desert and wet, cold mountains in the south have few inhabitants.

Capital Santiago 5,261,000. **Urbanites** 86%.

PEOPLES
A relatively homogeneous society.
Chilean 89.7%.
Mestizo 70.7%.
European 19% (Spanish, Italian, French, German, British, etc.).
Amerindian 8%. 9 peoples. Mapuche (Auracan) about half of whom still speak Mapudungun 1,100,000; Quechua 120,000; Aymara 76,000.
Polynesian 0.2%. Rapa Nui 27,000.

Other 2.1%. European 120,000; Roma 60,000; Arab 3,000; Chinese 2,000.
Literacy 95%. **Official language** Spanish (but Mapudungun increasingly recognized). **All languages** 10. **Languages with Scriptures** 2Bi 2NT 1por 2w.i.p.

📰 ECONOMY
Mining and export of minerals, especially copper, is the most important economic activity. Much industrialization and agricultural development. Draconian implementation of free market policies by the former regime brought economic stability, a trade surplus, tamed inflation, curbed corruption and fostered growth, but at great social cost. A prospective member of NAFTA. About 30% of the population live in poverty. **Unemployment** 13%. **HDI** 0.844; 34th/174. **Public debt** 6% of GNP. **Income/person** $4,860 (15% of USA).

🏛 POLITICS
Republic independent from Spain in 1810. The socialist government elected in 1970 was ousted in a bloody military coup in 1973. The controversial Pinochet regime imposed political conformity and economic change with many cases of human rights abuse. The referendum and electoral defeats in 1988/9 opened the way for a democratic government which is cautiously attempting to heal the wounds of the past and the deep divisions in society.

🕊 RELIGION
The Catholic Church was disestablished in 1925. There is freedom of religion, but legislation to make all denominations equal under law foundered in the 1990s on Catholic objections.

Religions	Population %	Adherents	Ann.Gr.
Christian	89.16	13,562,390	+1.3%
non-Religious/other	9.55	1,452,679	+2.1%
Traditional ethnic	0.88	133,859	+1.1%
Jewish	0.22	33,465	+2.3%
Baha'i	0.12	18,254	+3.2%
Buddhist	0.04	6,085	+4.3%
Muslim	0.03	4,563	+5.6%

Christians	Denom.	Affil.%	,000	Ann.Gr.
Protestant	39	3.36	512	+3.5%
Independent	1,192	14.31	2,177	+0.4%
Anglican	1	0.08	12	+0.5%

Catholic	1	72.97	11,100	+1.1%
Orthodox	5	0.16	24	-0.7%
Marginal	3	3.85	585	+3.6%
Unaffiliated		2.97	452	n.a.
Doubly affiliated		*-8.54*	*-1,300*	*n.a.*

Churches	MegaBloc	Cong.	Members	Affiliates
Catholic	C	800	,646,707	11.10 mill.
Pentecostal Methodist	I	4,000	300,000	602,000
Latter-day Sts (Morm)	M	1,036	269,461	450,000
Evang Pentecostal	I	1,800	180,000	361,000
Pentecostal	I	340	110,000	157,300
Jehovah's Witnesses	M	645	59,519	135,000
Seventh-day Adventist	P	480	96,000	135,000
Evang Army of Chile	I	200	60,000	75,000
Chr & Miss. Alliance	P	128	18,139	70,000
Baptist Convention	P	270	35,000	47,000
Methodist	P	120	16,000	30,000
Ch of God (Cleveland)	P	231	17,301	30,000
Assemblies of God	P	194	8,944	16,000
Anglican Ch of Chile	A	46	6,000	12,500
Other denoms [1,227]		11,828	1,278,387	2,190,000
Doubly counted	I		-556,000	-1,000,000
Doubly affiliated			*-844,000*	*-1,300,000*
Total Christians [1,241]		23,197	7.990m	13.377m

Estimates for Independents/Evangelicals vary widely. Few indigenous groups keep statistics. A 2002 survey indicates 13.9% of the population is evangelical.

Trans-bloc Groupings	pop. %	,000	Ann.Gr
Evangelical	16.8	2,556	+1.7%
Charismatic	24.4	3,705	+1.2%
Pentecostal	12.2	1,850	+0.1%

Missionaries from Chile
P,I,A 233 in 16 agencies to 27 countries: Chile 170, Bolivia 7, Middle East 6.

Missionaries to Chile
P,I,A 630 in 72 agencies from 22 countries: USA 387, Paraguay 46.

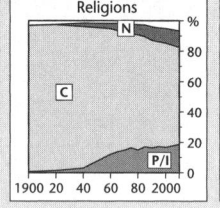
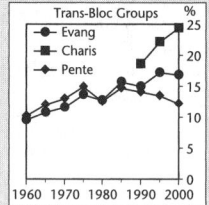

• Answers to Prayer

1 **The stabilization of democratic government,** and obtaining of equal privileges for Evangelicals with the Catholics.

2 **The steady growth of Evangelicals** this century to 16% of the population by 2000. This growth is unique. A Pentecostal revival in 1909 within the Methodist Church gave birth to a dynamic, indigenous Pentecostal movement with great evangelistic zeal. The lower classes were evangelized and churches and denominations multiplied. Pentecostal growth has catalyzed change in the Catholic Church; there is now a significant Catholic charismatic renewal movement.

• Challenges for Prayer

1 **Chile is a deeply divided nation.** The political problems of the past — violence and crimes on the part of the extreme left, then the severe repression of the subversives with the disappearance of about 1,500 people and exile of many more by the military government — continue to be live issues. The great need is for both sides to forgive and forget the past and become reconciled to each other. Christians are also divided on the issue.

2 **The Roman Catholic Church** has been deeply impacted by three major forces:

a) *Liberation theology*. The identification of many Catholic leaders with liberation theology (with its Marxist presuppositions) alienated many Chileans of the middle and upper classes from the Church and did little to win the poor who had already abandoned it because of its past identification with the ruling classes.

b) *Loss of political power* — now that there is equality of all religions before the law.

c) *The widespread distribution and use of the Bible*, the growth of the charismatic movement, and a significant exodus of Catholics to evangelical churches. About 20% of the population was born Catholic, but has left the Roman Catholic Church. Only 15% of Catholics regularly attend church.

Pray that Catholics may adapt to a new era and that many might find true liberation and peace through a personal faith in Christ.

3 **Evangelicals** are poised to exercise a pivotal role in the new millennium. The danger remains that goodwill and respect may be eroded by failures and squandered opportunities. Pray against:

a) *Disunity and fragmentation of Evangelicals*. It is estimated there are between 1,200 and 5,000 denominations, with one or two starting every week. Nowhere in the world has there been so many divisions among Pentecostals. There is a need for humility and reconciliation.

b) *Traditionalism*. A century of growth and success is increasing a gift-less Pentecostal nominalism, perpetuating dynamic methods of evangelism no longer effective and imposing dictatorial leadership patterns that stunt spiritual growth. Revival is needed.

c) *Contempt for theological education* and message preparation before services has resulted in poor teaching, legalism, the Word becoming less important than personal visions, personality cults — especially among Pentecostals — and a steady loss of Evangelicals to the Mormons and Jehovah's Witnesses. Pray for TEE (SEAN and FLET) programmes and the various theological institutions addressing this widespread need, such as the National Bible Institute of Chile with 700 students in the capital and a further 700 in the provinces.

d) *Isolationism*. Of the 16% of the population that is evangelical, 75% belong to indigenous denominations that have impacted the lower classes but have few links with global Christianity. This stunts a vision for missions, and leaves culture quirks and weaknesses unchallenged.

e) *Affluence*. Numerical growth and increasing wealth breed complacency. Only 38% of Evangelicals are regular church-goers. Pentecostal nominalism is a major problem. For the past 15 years growth has plateaued.

4 **The middle and upper classes** have been far less impacted by Evangelicals. Only 6% of Evangelicals are of these groups. Evangelical denominations from abroad have generally been more effective than Pentecostals in reaching them. Santiago has 1,150 evangelical congregations, but only 20 of them are middle/upper class. The Baptists, **CMA**, Anglicans (**SAMS**), **AoG**, CoN, **SIM** and others have made some progress in planting churches among them. Pray for every stratum of Chilean society to be reached.

5 **The Chilean Church lacks mission vision**. Its contribution for its size is very small. Pentecostal churches have shown little concern for world evangelization. The country's geographical and spiritual isolation and political upheavals have all contributed to this deficiency. The influence of COMIBAM and locally based mission agencies (**OM**, **YWAM**, **CMA**, CENCAMI, **SIM**, **WBT** and others) on the Latin American Missions movement in setting up missions training programmes have stimulated some interest in missions.

6 **Foreign missions in Chile.** The major agencies are Christian Chs/Chs of Christ (92 workers), **YWAM** (81), **IMB-SBC** (62), ABWE (40), **CMA** (39), **AoG** (35), Gospel Mission of South America (29), MTW (21), **Brethren** (20), BBF (19) and **SAMS** (15). The major task for missionaries is to serve the large Chilean Church in teaching, developing Chilean leadership and encouraging a missionary vision. Pioneer work is limited to some peoples listed below and among the upper class and the urban slum dwellers. Pray that the missionaries' contribution may prove vital for maturing the Chilean Church.

7 **Less reached peoples.**

a) *The Mapuche* (speaking Mapudungun) are the largest and most independent of Chile's indigenous peoples. A strong nationalist movement is agitating successfully for improved land rights and cultural recognition. About 70% are nominally Catholic, but the old animistic religion is still the most influential spiritual force and years of abuse, exploitation and oppression by outsiders have bred deep mistrust. The work of the Anglican Church has resulted in a strong community of 4,000 Christians. **CMA, AoG,** MttW and others have initiated work among them; **SIM** is developing Mapudungun TEE programmes. The Pentecostals have won many Mapuche migrants in the cities. Two **SIL** workers completed the New Testament into one of the dialects in 1997.

b) *Rapa Nui (Easter Islanders)* are a largely Polynesian people. The majority now live on the mainland. Their society is in disintegration and many are losing hope. Tourism, movie-making, AIDS, alcohol and emigration have all exacted their toll. Most are nominally Catholic, but there are about 50 evangelical believers in two small fellowships. One **SIL** couple is seeking to translate the NT into their language.

c) *Drug abuse* is a major problem in the cities. Pray for those seeking to bring deliverance to those affected.

d) *The Jews of Santiago.*

e) *The Roma (Gypsies)* have been neglected. Only the SdA have a church among them.

f) *The handicapped.* Little has been done to reach the deaf, blind and other handicapped.

8 **Student witness** in the 17 universities and among the 233,000 students is not strong. There are 14 GBU(**IFES**) groups and three full-time staff workers. **CCCI** (40 overseas workers) has a considerable impact on secondary schools and some universities.

9 **Christian media:**

a) *Literature* is proving a vital evangelistic and teaching tool, but too few Christians have developed a reading habit. Pray that more pastors buy study books. **CLC** is the only major book distributor in the country; pray for the 26 workers, the seven bookstores and the large wholesale distribution network. **SIM** also plans to open a literature ministry.

b) *Christian radio and TV programmes* are widely available on national, commercial and 25 Christian stations. Radio has had a big influence on the spread of the gospel in Chile. IBRA radio has continuous transmission from 10 stations. International broadcasts from **TWR**-Bonaire, **HCJB**-Ecuador and others from the USA beam in many hours of Spanish programmes.

c) *The JESUS film* is in wide use in both Spanish and Mapudungun.

China
Peoples' Republic of China

Russia
Kazakhstan
Mongolia
Kyrgyzstan
Tajikistan **China** Beijing N.Korea
Nepal S.Korea
Pakistan Bhutan
India Taiwan
Hong Kong
Macau
Myanmar Vietnam

MARCH 24 - APRIL 5
ASIA
(See p. 181 for Hong Kong, p. 184 for Macau, and p. 186 for Taiwan.)

Revised January 2004

GEOGRAPHY
Area 9,573,000 sq.km. The third largest state in the world, also containing the highest mountains and plateaus in the world. The climate varies from tropical in Hainan in the south to sub-arctic in Heilongjiang in the north. Hong Kong, Macau and Taiwan are all integral parts of China, though their statistics are not included here.

Population	Ann.Gr.	Density
2000 1,262,556,787	+0.93%	132 per sq. km.
2010 1,356,939,193	+0.69%	142 per sq. km.
2025 1,462,931,461	+0.35%	153 per sq. km.

Capital Beijing (Peking) 12,033,000. **Other major cities:** Shanghai 14.2 mill.; Tianjin 10,239,000; Guangzhou 6,389,000; Shenyang 5,681,000; Changchun 5,566,000; Harbin 5,475,000; Chengdu 5,293,000; Jinan 4,789,000; Wuhan 4,750,000; Qingdao 4,376,000. There are 80 other cities of over 1,000,000 inhabitants. **Urbanites** 32% (unofficially considerably higher).

PEOPLES
Han Chinese 91.3%. One national language: Putonghua (Mandarin) 783 mill. 15 regional mega-languages, largest (in millions): Wu 82m; Yueh (Cantonese) 59m; Jin 53m; Gan 37m; Xiang (Hunanese) 36m; Min Nan 32m; Hakka 31m; Min Dong 8.8m; Hainanese 5.1m; Huizhou 3.6m; Min Bei 2.6m. There are estimated to be 600 Han dialects, but one written language common to all.
Ethnic minorities 8.7%. There are 456 distinct ethnic groups, but 55 'nationalities' officially recognized for administrative convenience. Main groups (see China's provinces for more details):
Tai 2.2%. Over 55 peoples in the southern provinces.
Tibeto-Burman 2.1%. 249 peoples in western and southwestern provinces.

Mongolian-Altaic 1.6%. 29 peoples mainly in the northern border states of Manchuria (Jilin, Liaoning, Heilongjiang and Inner Mongolia).
Hmong-Mien 0.86%. 70 peoples in the southern border provinces.
Hui 0.84%. Chinese Muslims in all provinces, especially Ningxia and Gansu.
Turkic 0.86%. 17 peoples in northwest.
Mon-Khmer 0.05%. 23 peoples in southern provinces of Guizhou, Guangxi and Yunnan.
Other 0.29%. Korean 2.2m; Tajik(2) 43,000; Vietnamese 27,000; Russian 17,400; Austronesian(4) 17,200; Foreigners 100,000.

Literacy 81.5%. **Official language** Putonghua (Mandarin Chinese); local languages in the five Autonomous Regions. **All languages** 470. **Languages with Scriptures** 13Bi 13NT 16por 24w.i.p.

ECONOMY
The Cultural Revolution with its application of an extreme Marxist economic system was a fiasco. Since 1978, the see-saw conflict between the hardliners and pragmatists within the Communist government has been reflected in the degree of economic liberalization pursued. First agriculture and then much industry was privatized with dramatic improvements in food production, consumer goods and living standards. Massive growth in the 1980s and somewhat slower growth in the '90s have partially restored China's industrial might after two centuries of eclipse to become the 8th largest economy in the world. The greatest growth has been in Hong Kong's hinterland and more recently in most coastal cities. Fear of political liberalization, widespread corruption and unwillingness to deal with large state- and army-run industries is holding back growth. The massive increase in unemployment and widespread poverty could create serious social unrest. Unemployment is officially 4.8%, but it is estimated that the urban labour surplus is 18% and rural 30%. This means about 200 million without a meaningful income. **HDI** 0.701; 98th/174. **Public debt** 11% of GNP. **Income/person** $860 (2.7% of USA).

POLITICS
This great and ancient nation has regained its place of importance in the world after nearly two centuries of decline and humiliation at the hands of the Western powers and Japan. After the final conquest of mainland China in 1949, the Communist Party remoulded the nation along Marxist lines. The Cultural Revolution (1966-76) was the culmination of Mao's policy. It caused immeasurable suffering and economic chaos. Intellectuals and religious believers were cruelly persecuted. It is estimated that 20 million Chinese lost their lives during that time. The death of Mao Zedong in 1976 and discrediting of radical leftists in 1978 was followed by a more pragmatic leadership under Deng. He initiated a series of economic, political and cultural reforms and developed links

with other nations, but all within the limits set by Deng. The crushing of the 1989 student protest in Tienanmen Square in Beijing and also the collapse of Communism in Europe and the USSR left China diplomatically isolated as the oldest surviving Communist regime. The threatened government responded with a reversion to ideological rigidity and repression of all political, ethnic and religious dissent. Economic reform with tight political control has been government policy during the 1990s. In 1997 and 1999 Hong Kong and Macau reverted to Chinese rule. China's growing economic strength could be directed at the absorption of Taiwan, seizure of island archipelagos in the South China Sea and possibly other surrounding countries. Russia's under-populated Siberia could also come under pressure from over-populated China.

RELIGION

Elimination of all religious groups has always been the ultimate aim of the Marxist government. In the 1950s the government engineered the infiltration, subversion and control of all organized Christianity. By 1956 this had been achieved through the Three Self Patriotic Movement among Protestants, and the Catholic Patriotic Association among Catholics. During the Cultural Revolution even these puppet structures were banned, and all religious activity forced underground, giving birth to the house church movement. In 1978 restrictions were eased and the TSPM and CPA resurrected as a means of regaining governmental control of the thousands of house churches. This has been only partially successful. The collapse of Communism in Europe is perceived as due to 'religion', so strict controls are maintained over Christian and Muslim organizations and all unregistered activity repressed wherever possible. All figures are estimates.

The Communist Party claims that there are 100 million 'believers' in the five recognized religions (Buddhism, Daoism, Islam, Catholicism and Protestantism) with 85,000 registered meeting places and 300,000 religious personnel. The actual figures are probably double this.

The beliefs of the Chinese and many minorities are a blend of folk religions, Daoism and Buddhism. The Buddhists are of three major strands: Mahayana and Theravada among the Chinese and southern peoples such as the Dai, Zhuang, Manchu, etc., and Lama Buddhism among the Tibetan and Mongolian peoples of the west and north.

Islam is dominant in Xinjiang and Ningxia, and is the major religion of the Hui, Uygur, Kyrgyz, Kazak, Dongxiang, etc.

The severe suppression of the Falun Gong sect in 1999 and onwards has also greatly intensified persecution of the Christian networks outside the TSPM. **Persecution Index** 3rd in the world.

Religions	Population %	Adherents	Ann.Gr.
non-Religious/other	49.58	625,975,655	+1.0%
Chinese	28.50	359,828,684	-1.4%
Buddhist	8.38	105,802,259	+1.9%
Christian	7.25	91,535,367	+7.7%
Traditional ethnic	4.29	54,163,686	+6.4%
Muslim	2.00	25,251,136	+0.9%

Christians	Denom.	Affil.%	,000	Ann.Gr.
Protestant	5	0.05	645	+6.2%
Independent	23	7.26	91,700	+9.3%
Catholic	1	0.57	7,200	+3.7%
Marginal	21	0.16	2,000	+3.3%
Doubly affiliated		-0.79	-10,000	n.a.

Churches	MegaBloc	Cong.	Members	Affiliates
Three-Self Patriotic Movt	I	9,000	17.00m	23.00m
Born Again Movement	I	50,000	16.00m	23.00m
House Ch Networks [18]	I	150,000	18.00m	20.00m
Assembly Hall-Little Flock	I	47,619	14.29m	20.00m
Catholic	C	20,000	5,000,000	7,200,000
Catholic Patriotic Assoc	I	4,100	3,100,000	4,500,000
True Jesus	I	4,000	800,000	1,200,000
Seventh-day Adventist	P	650	250,000	350,000
Other Protestant [4]	P	700	200,000	295,000
Other denominations [22]		4,122	1,272,000	2,030,000
Doubly affiliated			-6,666,667	-10.00m
Total Christians [51]		290,000	69.241m	91.575m

Accurate Christian statistics are not available. Those listed here are only indicative of a remarkable work of the Holy Spirit. Various official and house church network leaders have given estimates which are used here. A number of China-watchers have sought to painstakingly piece together the bigger picture from every scrap of evidence available. Estimates of all Christians vary from 30 million to 150 million. Note that some TSPM figures are inclusive of non-TSPM Christians in their areas — hence the doubly affiliated estimate.

Trans-bloc Groupings	pop.%	,000	Ann.Gr.
Evangelical	6.0	76,127	+8.8%
Pentecostal & Charismatic	4.1	51,781	+8.8%

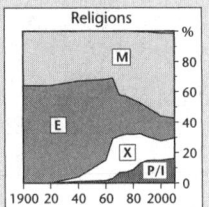

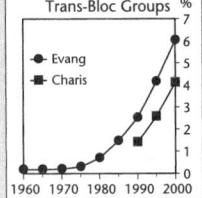

• Answers to Prayer

1 **The survival and reviving of the Church in China** was one of the decisive events of the 20th Century.

2 **The growth of the Church in China since 1977** has no parallels in history. The 1,266,000 Protestant members and 1.8 mill. affiliates in 1949 had become 17m members and maybe 26m affiliates in 2000 as well as a much larger uncounted, but estimated, 45m house church Christians. The Catholics grew from 3m to 12m over the same period.

3 **The millions of intercessors who travailed** in prayer for the long-delayed breakthrough. The cumulative impact of 150 years of global prayer for China has been enormous. Prayer is changing China.

4 **The atheist rulers of China became unwitting instruments** in the hand of our Sovereign God to prepare the way for this growth. Mao Zedong sought to destroy all religious 'superstition' but in the process cleared spiritual roadblocks for the advancement of Christianity. Deng reversed the horrors inflicted by Mao and in freeing up the economy, gave more freedom to the Christians, who made use of the opportunity.

5 **The manifest failure of Communism.** Colossal blunders and changes in Party policy over 45 years have disillusioned the people. The fall of personality-cult leaders and the failure of promises for a better future have created a vacuum which only the gospel can fill. The nepotism, corruption and factionalism of the present Communist Party are repugnant to the majority. The Church of the Lord Jesus is larger than the Communist Party of China.

6 **The faith and commitment of Christians** under what may prove to be the most harsh and widespread persecution of the Church in all history. The persecution purified and indigenized the Church and has inured it to successive waves of further repression and government efforts to weaken or destroy it.

7 **The aftermath of the Beijing massacre in Tiananmen Square in 1989.** This was a defining moment in Chinese history. The discredited leadership is still haunted by the debacle, and the result was a significant turning to God for the first time among urban intellectuals. Christians are now found in every stratum of Chinese society.

8 **The loving witness of ordinary Christians** ministering in the power of the Holy Spirit. His power has often been manifested in miracles, healings and exorcisms. The majority of these evangelists and church planters have been women — many still in their teens. In many areas 70-80% of the Christians are women.

9 **The fruitfulness of Christian radio** and the remarkable faith of those who broadcast into China for years with little visible evidence of a response — that evidence is now plain to see.

10 **The Internet is creating extraordinary new openings** for evil and for good — the latter in providing discipleship and leadership development materials.

• Challenges for Prayer
GENERAL

1 **There may only be a ten-year window of opportunity** for receptivity. Materialism with increasing wealth, the debilitating effects of spreading corruption, the moral decline and the social impact of the one-child policy all are conspiring to blunt the cutting edge of the Church. Pray that present openness in the midst of opposition may be used to the full.

2 **Communist Party members** are the elite and number some 60m. All are officially atheist, but among them are many who are secretly religious and even Christian. Pray for the collapse of the whole atheistic system and its lies so assiduously propagated in the education system, and pray for the conversion of those within the Party.

3 **Market socialism** is a convenient term to gloss over the ideological bankruptcy of the Marxism still espoused by the ruling elite. The government vainly tries to control information while promoting the Internet, and to indoctrinate a bored and disillusioned new generation that hankers after freedom. The irreconcilable conflict between crass capitalism and personal greed and the refusal to allow any political reform will lead to change. Pray that this change might be both peaceful and spiritually beneficial to the Chinese.

4 **The 'One Child' policy** is a draconian means of taming the growth of the population. Family life has been deeply impacted, shown in: a higher divorce rate, 10m abortions a year (nearly all girls), suicide (40% of the world's suicides are in China), pampered children with poor interpersonal skills and the abandonment of baby girls and older people. The rising generation will pay a heavy cost — in 2000 there were 90m marriageable unmarried men; in some areas young men outnumber young women by 30-40% — rape, abductions, female slavery, incest, prostitution and the rapid spread of AIDS could all be the result. Pray for family stability and health. Pray also for wise policies to be implemented that will stabilize the population.

5 **Economic liberalization** has made a few very wealthy and improved living standards for many, but made others worse off:
a) *The millions of unemployed* have become an impoverished under-class. Multitudes flock to cities seeking employment.
b) *The poorer inland provinces* far from the sea where there has been less development; housing, education, health etc., are at a much lower standard.
c) *The elderly* — with the one-child policy limiting family care for them.
d) *Those in the penal system* with 15-20 million incarcerated.
e) *Those with disabilities.*
Pray for a fairer and more free society to emerge.

6 **The social and health needs** in China overwhelm the available resources. Diseases are a challenge — 1.9m with tuberculosis, over 300,000 with HIV/AIDS, 10m mentally retarded through iodine-deficiency, 60m disabled, 13m blind and 520,000 registered drug addicts. Then there are the unemployed and the numerous victims of famines, floods and earthquakes due to the density of the population. Pray that Christians may find many openings to serve such in the social and caring professions and opportunities to show and speak about the love of Jesus for them.

7 **China faces environmental disasters** on many fronts — deforestation causing massive flooding, the unknown impact of the massive Three Gorges Dam on the Yangtze River, polluted rivers filled with industrial and human waste, nine of the ten most polluted cities in the world, desertification in the north and east, and the continued increase of the population. Pray for a government courageous and trusted enough to take the difficult decisions required for the long-term well-being of the nation.

THE CHURCH IN CHINA

1 **The Three Self Patriotic Movement (TSPM)** was instituted by 'patriotic' and often theologically liberal Christians with the strong encouragement of the Communist Party as the interface between the government and Church. After 13 years of oblivion it was reconstituted in 1979 to wrest the initiative from the burgeoning house church movement, and enable the government to control and manipulate the Church. The China Christian Council is the governing body for all official church-related activities. Pray for:
a) *The neutralization of all measures to impose unbiblical doctrines* on the churches, limit evangelism, and force conformity to the dictates of the atheist government. Pray also for an end to the enforced compromises in the state-controlled TSPM-related churches.
b) *Leaders who have compromised the faith* and bowed to government pressure. The restrictions laid down are: no childrens' or youth work, avoid preaching on the Lord's return and on creation, a ban on healing or exorcism, and limited evangelism. Praise God for many who quietly ignore the rules of men.
c) *The continued growth of the registered churches.* Many godly leaders quietly continue to serve the Lord in TSPM churches. The growth in congregations and members is downplayed by the authorities but is dramatic. There were 1,000 open church buildings in 1983; 7,000 churches and 20,000 official meeting points in 1988, becoming 13,000

and 35,000, respectively, by 1997. Six churches a day are being registered. There are estimated to be 500,000 baptisms in the TSPM churches every year, and adult membership in 1997 was estimated at 17 million.

d) ***Relationships between the TSPM churches and house churches.*** Most house churches regard with distaste government manipulation and control and see separation as fundamental to the survival of a spiritual Church. Some house church leaders reject all contact, others have succumbed to the increased pressures and outright persecution since 1989 to register. In 1995, an estimated 30% of Protestant Christians were linked with TSPM churches. This has probably risen to 40% in 2000. Increasingly there is overlap with many attending and ministering in both. There is also a steady drift away to house churches by new converts disillusioned with the level of compromise.

e) ***The future of the TSPM.*** Growth, despite its major flaws and weaknesses, has been astonishing. This is likely to slow as the TSPM leadership becomes entrenched in bureaucratic, corrupt ways and fails to address either the spiritual needs of ordinary Christians or the serious social problems of China. The result is likely to be fragmentation, regionalization, renewed denominationalism and massive defections to house church networks. Pray for revival and renewal to purify the TSPM and its associated churches.

2 **Leadership training is woefully deficient,** and a crisis need. It is reckoned that there is but one ordained pastor for every 7,000 TSPM members. By 1999 there were 18 official seminaries with 1,200 residential and 3,000 distance-learning students. Pray for:

a) ***Faculty*** — often selected for their political correctness rather than for their walk with God. Pray for those teaching who are Evangelical despite the prevailing liberal theology and textbooks. Pray that biblical teaching and holiness of life might be central in their lives. In 2000 the anti-Evangelical stance was strengthened.

b) ***Students.*** Many apply, but few are selected; nevertheless most are Evangelical but face a constant battle against the erosion of their faith. The number of students and ordinations has been deliberately restricted, but during 1999 a considerable expansion in facilities and enrolment was reported. Only 800 pastors were ordained 1992-95, and most of these were over 45 years of age.

c) ***Protection from interference.*** During 1999 a severe purge of evangelical faculty, textbooks and students was carried out at the national seminary in Nanjing. Support from congregations for Nanjing, the five regional and 12 provincial seminaries is very low because of the political manipulation. Libraries are usually poorly stocked.

3 **The Catholics** were divided when the Marxists set up the Catholic Patriotic Association in 1957 with its own structure and hierarchy independent of the Vatican. The majority of Catholics demurred and went 'underground', with their own bishops and illegal seminaries. The loyalist Catholics have suffered severe persecution because of their commitment to a foreign leader. More recently there has been a growing rapprochement between the two. There are over 12m Catholics in the two bodies, and over 60,000 are converted annually. Many Catholics are charismatic and ardent in their faith.

4 **The unregistered or house church networks** are the heart of the true Church in China. Intense persecution has indigenized and purified it. Prayer, revival, simple living and a christocentric theology characterize it. Twenty or more larger networks are known to exist, but their numbers are a matter of conjecture. Reasonable estimates range between 30 and 80 million, or 50% to 80% of the total Christian population. There are many challenges to pray over:

a) ***Persecution is a present reality.*** Increasing pressure since 1989 is a measure of the fear of the Communists of such a large movement they do not control. Their aim is subjugation or elimination of this threat. Since 1996 the level of persecution has increased on house churches not willing to register with the TSPM. Arrests (hundreds in 1999), heavy fines, forcible closures and destruction of church buildings (200 in 1997) have increased in some key areas. Pray for the continued commitment of believers to preach Christ and Him crucified whatever the cost and without compromise.

b) ***Ongoing evangelistic outreach.*** Witnessing Christians and itinerant preachers, though violently opposed by the authorities, have spread far and wide, but many provinces, districts and towns are still unreached. Pray that Christians may continue to be bold for Jesus and implement their missionary strategy for reaching China.

c) Challenges to face:

i *Isolation and lack of teaching* can lead to extremes in legalism, theological emphases and use of spiritual gifts.

ii *How to handle increased contacts and communications* with evangelical Christians around the world — finance is a major component for good and bad. The new quarterly magazine *Voice of China* is compiled by leaders of house church networks for distribution worldwide.

iii *How to make what has long been a strong rural movement* impact those who are urban and intellectuals. The lack of formal education of many leaders, many of which are women, hampers this. Pray that more men may be converted and that an impact for God might be made on the cities. The authorities are better able to control and restrict any Christian activity in cities, so house churches tend to be smaller and more secretive.

d) The intellectual elite is largely urban. Only since 1989 have large numbers of students and professionals come to Christ, yet the proportion that believe is far lower than in the rural areas. Networks of small, often secret, groups have emerged. Pray for the multiplication of such, for this is of inestimable importance for the future of the gospel in China.

e) Leadership for the churches. The widespread lack of Bibles, teaching materials and Bible-literate leaders has stimulated many innovative discipleship ministries in different house church networks during the 1990s. Pray for many godly men and women to be raised up.

f) The multiplication of heretical sects and doctrinal extremist groups. The lack of Bible knowledge and of mature leadership has opened the way for many exotic messianic, syncretistic and divisive groups, some of which have spread over much of China. In some areas they now constitute 5% or more of the unregistered church population. Many have exotic names such as Lightning in the East, Lingling, Shouters, Established King, Cold Water, etc. Pray that this growth might be slowed by the loving proclamation of the truth of God's Word through radio, literature and preaching.

g) Spiritual unity has been furthered by recent persecution. Leaders of various house church networks are increasingly standing together in both affirming their common biblical faith and making public statements to the authorities. Pray for continued development of trust and fellowship between different house church networks and between Bible-believing leaders of the house churches and the TSPM.

h) Missions vision. Some house church networks have long cherished and supported missions outreach to other provinces and to ethnic minorities. There is growing vision for foreign missions and some Mainland Chinese have become missionaries in other lands. Some predict China could become the greatest sending nation in the 21st Century!

THE LESS EVANGELIZED

About 7% of China's population is Christian today, but their distribution is not even. In this section are given some of the nationally significant but less evangelized sections of the population.

1 **The nearly 60 million Communist Party members** are, by definition, atheists, but ideology is a facade to cover self-seeking opportunism. Disillusionment and defection to Christianity has led to many resignations. Pray that the Holy Spirit may convict many more of their sin and need. Among them are also many secret believers.

2 **The armed forces,** who are the protectors of the Marxist state, and who jealously guard their privileged position and network of industries. There are 2.8m in uniform, but very few Christians among them.

3 **The 'lost generation',** the young people mobilized as the Cultural Revolution Red Guards. The millions involved were morally warped and exploited, losing their youth, education prospects and hopes of betterment in the madness of those years. Pray that they may find hope in Christ.

4 **Those still bound by the idolatrous superstitions** of Daoism, Buddhism and the legalism of Confucianism. These customs and philosophies are being revived, but young people are not so attracted to them. A new religion, Falun Gong, gained world publicity and shocked the authorities in 1999 with a quiet protest in Beijing — they claim 70m followers in China. Pray for the millions still bound and needing the freedom only the gospel can give.

5 Children and young people under 18 number over 500m. It is illegal to teach them religious 'superstitions'. The TSPM churches are not allowed to run Sunday Schools or youth groups — most have forgotten how or are afraid to minister to children and young people, but some are quietly doing more to disciple them. One of the great needs of China today is for teaching materials and the know-how of Christian ministry to this group.

6 University students (3m) are the key for the future. The shock of the events of 1989 have brought many to Christ, but most students are still unreached. Pray for:
a) *Christians among them* to be built up in their faith and to be fervent witnesses.
b) *The establishment of Bible study groups* on every one of the 1,054 campuses.
c) *Those who study abroad.* About 100,000 go overseas annually for study, but only about 25% return. Most go to Japan, USA, Europe and Australia. Their numbers in 1996 globally were 600,000. Among them is an unprecedented openness and a good proportion have come to the Lord.

7 Muslims number 25m, and are almost entirely linked to specific ethnic groups — the indigenous Uygur, Kazak, Uzbek, Kyrgyz, Tajik, Tatar of Xinjiang, the Salar of Qinghai, Dongxiang of Gansu and the Chinese Hui of Ningxia and scattered all over China. (See under the provinces below.) Islam is a sensitive issue in China because of a past history of Hui revolts and unrest in Xinjiang. Few ministries are targeting the Muslim peoples, and few Chinese believers feel adequately prepared for such outreach. Pray for the evangelization of these peoples and for the calling of committed workers to them.

8 Ethnic Minorities comprise 8.7% of the population, 100m people in 464 distinct non-Han ethno-linguistic groups. This chart gives an indication of the spread of the gospel among 450 of them:

Christian %	No. of Peoples	Population
Over 50%	8	596,079
20 — 50%	15	4,064,510
5 — 20%	18	1,269,260
1 — 5%	41	5,341,140
0.1 — 1%	69	43,874,550
0.01 — 0.1%	40	39,602,380
0.00%	259	5,752,507
Total	450	100,500,426

Note:
• Only 8 peoples are majority Christian. This includes the A-Hmao and the Gha-Mu (Miao peoples), Eastern Lipo and the Ayi.
• A further 15 peoples have large Christian populations including the Korean, Lisu, Wa, Nasu, Kado and Jingpo.
• Over 368 peoples have less than 1% Christian.
• Nearly 260 peoples have no known Christians at all.

Pray for:
a) *A global concern* for the evangelization of these numerous unreached peoples, and that many peoples still inaccessible to foreigners might be opened up.
b) *Greater involvement of Christian tribals* and Chinese Han Christians in reaching them. Over one hundred cross-cultural house church missionaries are known to be active among unreached minorities.
c) *The planting of indigenous churches* and discipling of leaders.

SUPPORTIVE MINISTRIES

The rapid growth of the Church and its influence on the democracy movement has heightened the ideological clash since 1989. The Communist Party and the old men that run it feel threatened by the powerful attraction of Christianity. The influence of foreign visitors, students and experts, and the pervasive impact of Christian radio programmes, videos, literature and Bibles and the explosive growth in the use of the Internet have been perceived as decisive in this. Opposition to and vigilance against all activities conducted by foreigners has increased since 1989. Pray that economic desire may overcome ideological fears and keep the door open for needed Christian input. Pray also that all who go may humbly listen, learn and adapt to the language and culture so as to maximize their long-term spiritual impact.

1 Missionaries, as such, are not welcome in China. Yet China's desire to improve trading relations with the world makes it possible for many Chinese and foreign Christians to enter as:

a) **Tourists** — over 30m visited China in 1995 and spent $US9 billion. Many Christians were among them. Pray for their ministry of bringing literature, aid, comfort and, in some cases, teaching. Pray also for safety for them and their baggage, tact and wisdom in their contacts, and guidance for travel.

b) **Students** — usually for language or cultural studies in various universities. In 2000 there were over 10,000 from 120 countries. Living conditions are often spartan and uncensored friendships with Chinese hard to maintain. Pray for Christians among them to be used of God to share Christ with those who are genuinely seeking the Lord.

c) **Foreign experts and businessmen.** China aims to recruit about 30,000 experts annually to teach English, Japanese and German as well as other subjects, and also to build up China's technology and industry. Pray that many may be radiant Christians able to impart their faith while on the job.

d) **Chinese family members who visit their ancestral homes.** These have flocked to China in their millions. Christians among them have sometimes seen astonishing results when staying with relatives.

2 **Provision of Bibles is still inadequate,** despite the large increase in the number of copies available. By 1999 it was reckoned that there were 36m Bibles in China. The famine of the Scriptures is most acute in provinces far from the 60 legal distribution points and for the house churches. Amity Foundation, founded in 1986 and sponsored by the TSPM and the **UBS**, set up a large printing operation in China, and over 22m Bibles and New Testaments had been printed by 1999 — nearly all going to TSPM congregations. House churches have now commenced their own Bible printing presses. A further 12m Bibles and NTs are estimated to have been brought in by visitors. Pray that this flow might increase and that Christians might have access to a copy of God's Word. There is a great need for study and children's Bibles. Importation of Bibles is not illegal but prevented for ideological reasons. The Bible League and **OD** are two of the largest suppliers of Bibles to the house churches.

3 **Video and audio tapes.** The increasing availability of play-back machines is making foreign-produced Scripture, song, evangelism and teaching tapes a useful means for disseminating the Truth. Pray for all involved in preparing and distributing these tapes.

a) **The JESUS film** is being widely seen on home video in 20 completed language versions (including eight Chinese dialects, Mongolian, Uygur and Zhuang). Many other language editions are in production or planned. Pray that the film may receive official recognition for public showing.

b) **Teaching tapes** that deal with the moral and ethical devastation left by Marxist thought and provide solid biblical teaching are a great need to help the many intellectuals who are coming to faith. Pray for the production of reading materials and tapes to fill this need.

c) **GRN** has produced gospel messages or tapes in 160 languages and dialects; much being done during 1999, but recordings are needed in many more.

4 **Christian literature.** There is an insatiable demand for hymn books, Bible study and other teaching materials, biographies, tracts, and apologetic materials to explain the gospel to students and intellectuals. Pray for:

a) **Literature production** in Hong Kong from where a widening range of literature is being published. Millions of copies are sent to the Mainland. Many agencies are involved in this ministry including Christian Communications Ltd., Chinese Church Support Ministries, **AO**, **OD** as well as denominational bodies. Pray for all aspects of publication and distribution.

b) **Suitable literature and books** for intellectuals are a great need. **OMF** have an extensive ministry to this group, having printed over 1.5m booklets.

c) **The Amity Foundation Press** in Nanjing has printed 10m copies of 130 book titles — many being commentaries and devotionals.

5 **The Internet** has become very popular and in 2000 there were an estimated 10m Internet users. Despite government efforts to control this medium, it is proving fertile soil for dissidents and many religious groups. Pray for its effective use for the gospel.

6 **Christian radio** has been and still is one of the most potent pre-evangelism and Christian teaching media for China today. Nearly every home now has a TV, and most a radio; less so in rural areas. Pray for:

a) *The many hundreds of hours of broadcasting* in Putonghua and other Han Chinese dialects which pour in from many Christian stations. Pray for lasting impact. **TWR** reckons their ministry has birthed 40,000 home groups, 50,000 leaders and 1m believers.

b) ***FEBC's*** use of four wave bands in Guam to minister simultaneously to young people, young Christians, church leaders and ethnic minorities. **FEBC**'s DAWN China project encourages churches to adopt specific provinces and cities for intercession.

c) *The protection of listeners.* The authorities seek to obtain addresses of letter-writers to Hong Kong. Pray also for wisdom and tact for all links with listeners.

PROVINCES OF CHINA

Nearly all of China's provinces are larger than most members of the United Nations. They warrant specific prayer. Bear in mind the following:

1 **Peoples are classified in two ways** that are mutually incompatible.

a) *The government census figures* for the, then, 55 official 'nationalities' by province. These are usually represented as percentages of the present province population.

b) *The 2001 publication, Operation China*, a survey of nearly 500 ethno-linguistic groups of China. These are grouped by language family, and peoples are listed with their national population in the province where the highest proportion lives. So, each ethnic minority is listed with its population once, even if present in multiple provinces.

2 **Religions.** Only the missionary religions are enumerated, namely Christianity, Lama Buddhism and Islam. It is assumed that the rest of the provincial population will be either atheist, secular, or of the mix of religions and philosophies prevalent in China.

3 **Christians.** The counting of Christians in China is clouded by propagandists on both sides who either want to deflate numbers (TSPM/government) or inflate them (some Christian agencies). Here we have sought to be as objective as possible using many sources to apportion national figures to each province. There is still wide margin for error but, though somewhat speculative, we believe this reflects as true a picture as we can obtain at this time.

ANHUI PROVINCE

GEOGRAPHY   Area 139,900 sq.km. One of the poorest provinces. Central China.
Population 63,400,000; 454 people/sq.km.
Capital Hefei 1.5 mill. Other major cities: Suixian 1.52m; Suzhow 1.27m; Huzhou 1.14m.

PEOPLES   Han Chinese 99.5%
Hui 0.5%. Main languages Putonghua, Huizhou.

RELIGION   Muslim 0.5%. Christian 11.6%: House churches 7.8%, TSPM 2.5%, all Catholics 1.3%.

1 Utopian Maoism was a disaster for Anhui's people. Huge numbers died in famines and flood. In their disillusionment many turned to Christ. Praise God for widespread revival, especially in the north, and blessing from there which has flowed to many parts of China.

2 Christian growth has been remarkable. From 50,000 Protestants in 1949 to 3m adults claimed by the TSPM today. The house church movement is much larger and there may be over 12m Christians of all varieties today.

3 Lack of leadership in the churches has resulted in the forming of a number of extreme or heretical groups. Some call Anhui 'the cradle of heresies.' In 1994 there were 40 pastors for 2,000 TSPM churches. Pray for the raising up of mature, godly leaders.

4 Persecution of unregistered churches became more severe in 1999 with a major drive against 'cults', harsh 're-education' programmes, closure of meetings, heavy fines and imprisonments. Pray for perseverance and purity of life and witness for believers.

BEIJING MUNICIPALITY

GEOGRAPHY   Area 23,000 sq.km. The nation's capital.
Population 13,500,000; 586 people/sq.km. 25% are work-seeking migrants from other parts of China.
PEOPLES   Han Chinese 96.5% speaking Putonghua.
Hui 2%.
Manchu 1.4%.
Mongolian 0.1%.

RELIGION   Christian 4.4%: House churches 3.7%, all Catholics 0.4%, TSPM 0.3%.

1 China is ruled from Beijing. Pray for the leaders of the nation — for wisdom, humanity, seeking of the good of the people rather than self-interest, and courage to make the long-delayed economic and political decisions essential for the future.

2 The Communist authorities keep tight control of the Christians and Christian activity, being particularly severe on unofficial ministry. Beijing is the only part of China where Protestants in registered churches are fewer in number than in 1949. There are only 8 registered churches but many small home meeting points of the TSPM. House churches were also few, but a number of secret intellectual groups came into being after 1989. House church believers numbered 150,000 in 1998, but grew rapidly to 500,000 by 2000. Pray for a further opening of the capital to the gospel.

3 There are 3 million migrants without legal residence papers. They form a vast under-class in poor ghettos. There are many street children. Pray for the evangelization of these marginalized peoples.

CHONGQING MUNICIPALITY

GEOGRAPHY   Area Approximately 120,000 sq.km. China's newest municipality carved out of the eastern fifth of Sichuan Province.
Population 31,200,000; 260 people/sq.km.
Capital Chongqing 3.9m. Other major city: Fuling 1.37m.

PEOPLES   Han Chinese 98.5%.
Other 1.5%. Hui, Tujia, Miao.

RELIGION   Chinese. Some Muslims. Christian 2.6%: House churches 1.5%, TSPM 0.7%, all Catholics 0.4%.

1 Chongqing is the industrial and trade hub for southwest China on the Yangtze River, and reputedly one of the ten most polluted cities in the world through heavy use of coal. Pray for the growth of Christian outreach in this strategic but spiritually needy city where there are only 56 approved TSPM meeting places.

2 **Many of the 800,000 people being displaced by the nearby Three Gorges Dam** will be resettled in Chongqing and Fuling. Pray for hearts opened to the gospel as they go through traumatic change.

FUJIAN PROVINCE

GEOGRAPHY **Area** 123,100 sq.km. On the coast facing Taiwan.
Population 34,300,000; 279 people/sq.km.
Capital Fuzhou 1,827,000.

PEOPLES **Han Chinese** 97.5%. Speaking 8 lan-guages, largest:
Min Nan, Min Dong, Puxian, Min Bei.
Minorities 2.5%. She 450,000; Hui 41,000; 3 Austronesian peoples 3,700.

RELIGION Buddhism and Daoism strong. Muslim 0.1%. Christian 10.7%: House churches 6.8%, TSPM 2.7%, all Catholics 1.2%.

1 **The first Protestant missionaries arrived in the early 19ᵗʰ Century.** Since the Communist Revolution the Church has grown much — especially the house church networks. The Assembly Halls (Watchman Nee) and the True Jesus Church are strong. Pray for continued growth. There have been crack-downs and church closures by the authorities in recent years.

2 **Buddhism and Daoism have revived** — over 20,000 temples have been illegally built or restored. Pray that the millions seeking the help of religion may come to Jesus.

3 The unreached in two significant groups:

a) *The 800,000 She* are a Hmong people related to the Miao, but Christians are only around 1,000 (0.12%).

b) *The 4,000 Ami, Bunun and Paiwan* are related to the mountain peoples of Taiwan where most have become Christian. Their mainland relatives have no known witness among them.

GANSU PROVINCE

GEOGRAPHY **Area** 366,500 sq.km. Large northwestern province on the edge of the Gobi Desert. China's poorest province.
Population 25,700,000; 70 people/sq.km.
Capital Lanzhou 2.17m. Other major city: Tianshui 1.4m.

PEOPLES
Han Chinese and other migrants 91.7%.
Hui 4.8%.
Mongolian 2%. Dongxiang 482,000; Bonan 11,000; Enger Yugur 5,000.
Tibetan 1.5%. Rongmahbrogpa Amdo 147,000; other Tibetan peoples(3) 142,000; Saragh Yugur 10,000.

RELIGION Muslim 6% — mainly Hui, Dongxian. Lama Buddhism 1.7%. Christian 1.9%: House churches 1.1%, TSPM 0.4%, all Catholics 0.4%.

1 **The Christian population is relatively small.** The area was pioneered by CIM(**OMF**), **CMA** and **AoG**. There were only 7,000 Protestants in 170 churches in 1949, so praise God for growth since then. Areas of weakness — too few leaders with training and the rise of a number of marginal sects. **FEBC** radio broadcasts have led many to Christ in Gansu villages.

2 The least evangelized:

a) *The Dongxian, Bonan and Enger Yugur are of mixed Mongolian background* and are strongly Muslim. No one has ever sought to evangelize these isolated peoples — probably China's least evangelized. There are no known believers.

b) *The Muslim Hui* are numerous in the cities; the city of Linxia has only a handful of believers. There is very little outreach and few Christians.

c) *Tibetans* are largely Buddhist and number 400,000. There is one Tibetan church. Four Tibetan peoples are indigenous to Gansu — the Jone and Saragh Yugur have a handful of believers, but the Zhugqu and Boyu have none.

GUANGDONG PROVINCE

GEOGRAPHY **Area** 197,100 sq.km. On southeast coast. Both Hong Kong and Macau were British and Portuguese colonial enclaves of Guangdong and though now under Chinese rule, remain Special Administrative Zones with their own autonomy.
Population 72,409,000; 367 people/sq.km.
Capital Guangzhou (Canton) 5.2m. Other major cities: Chaozhou 1.4m; Zhongshan 1.3m; Shantou 1.15m; Zhanjiang 1.08m; Shenzhen 1.04m.

PEOPLES **Han Chinese** 98.2%. Predominantly Cantonese and, in northeast, Hakka; also Dan and Shaozhou.
Ethnic minorities 1.8%. Zhuang. Indigenous Yao(2) 62,000.

RELIGION Predominantly secularism and traditional Chinese religions. Christian 1.4%: House churches 0.6%, all Catholics 0.5%, TSPM 0.3%.

1 **Guangdong was the first province evangelized by Protestants.** Robert Morrison arrived in Macau in 1807. The British seizure of Hong Kong and western opium wars against China have soured Guangdong's people to the gospel to this day. Christianity is still seen as a foreign imposition and response to the gospel is relatively limited. Pray for healing from the past and removal of all obstacles so that many may turn to Christ.

2 **Cantonese and Hakka Chinese** are often traders and entrepreneurs. This flair, plus the proximity of Hong Kong and its global links with overseas Chinese, have boosted the economy, but with much moral declension, corruption and greed. Pray for the Holy Spirit to work in individuals and society for God-pleasing change.

3 **Christians have been under severe pressure** from the police who, since 1999, have made great efforts to subjugate the house churches. Christians in Guangzhou are only about 1% of the population, and registered churches few. Pray for the brethren and their perseverance.

4 **The Biao Mien and Zaomin Yao** in the northern mountains are two distinct peoples, but in both there are only a few believers, mainly young people.

5 **Cantonese and Hakka** are two major components of the Overseas Chinese in SE Asia and other continents. The Overseas Chinese are some of the wealthiest peoples of the world and also have proved receptive to the gospel. Pray for a continued harvest among them and that they might be a blessing to Guangdong, China and the world.

GUANGXI ZHUANG AUTONOMOUS REGION

GEOGRAPHY **Area** 220,400 sq.km. The southernmost mainland coastal state; adjoining Vietnam. Subtropical. The home area of China's largest ethnic minority, the Zhuang, and the province therefore given a higher, though nominal, degree of autonomy.
Population 47,800,000; 217 people/sq.km.
Capital Nanning 1.6m. Other major cities: Guigang 1.86m; Yulin 1.45m; Qinzhou 1.35m; Liuzhou 1m.

PEOPLES **Han Chinese** 56.2%. Mainly Putonghua, Hakka, Cantonese, Pinghua and Pingdi.
Ethnic minorities 43.8%
Tai 38%; 10 peoples, largest: Zhuang(2) 15,772,000; Mulao 206,000; Nung 137,000; Tho 134,000; Maonan 52,000; E 35,000.
Hmong-Mien 5.6%. 11 peoples, largest: Iu Mien(3) 1,010,000; Biao Mien(3) 74,000; Nunu 49,000.
Other 0.2%. Jing 25,000; Palyu 12,000.

RELIGION Mainly Chinese religions and animism among the minorities. Christian 1.0%: House churches 0.4%, TSPM 0.3%, all Catholics 0.3%.

1 **The growth of Christians among the Thai-related Zhuang** and also among the Han gives cause for praise! From 7,000 Christians in 1949 there are over 10 times that membership today — about half are Zhuang. The Christian community also has a significant number of house church folk as well. Yet government regulations against Christians have been rigorously applied. Pray for ongoing growth and provision of leadership. The TSPM only had 22 registered ordained pastors for the province in 1997 for the 250 churches.

2 **The Zhuang** have responded in the last decade through a concerted prayer and ministry effort for their evangelization — radio ministry (**FEBC**), the *JESUS* film, Bible translation, etc. There are now over 46,000 Christians in 250 fellowships — mainly among the Northern Zhuang. In other Tai groups there has been a little response from the Tho, Nung, Mulao, but no witness among the E, Lakkia, Pusha and Yerong.

3 **The Yao peoples** total about 2.2m in the mountains of Guangxi. They speak hundreds of languages and dialects — six in Guangxi. Only in two of the Iu Mien peoples have little Christian groups emerged, with a maximum of 10,000 Christians (0.4%). Among the Younuo, Nunu, Changping Iu Mien, Bunuo and Biao Mien there has been no ministry or response. Pray for the evangelization of every people in Guangxi. Bible translation for most peoples has yet to begin, and the Zhuang NT is still incomplete

GUIZHOU PROVINCE

GEOGRAPHY **Area** 174,000 sq.km. Mountainous; southern inland province. Poor and underdeveloped.
Population 37,000,000; 212 people/sq.km.
Capital Guiyang 2,230,000. Other major cities: Liupanshui 2,479,000; Anshun 1,567,000.

PEOPLES
Han Chinese 67.4%.
Ethnic minorities 32.6%. Over 10 Chinese sub-groups.
Hui 0.4%.
Hmong-Mien 18.5%. 41 peoples, largest: Miao-related: Hmu(3) 2.7m; Miao(20) 1.46m; A-Hmao

387,000; Hmong(4) 276,000; Gha-Mu 108,000; Ge 103,000; Mjuniang 76,000; Ga Mong 54,000. Yao-related: Baheng(2) 46,000; Baonuo 25,000.
Tai 11%. 13 peoples, largest: Bouyei 3.18m; Dong(2) 3.08m; Shui 430,000; Yanghuang 49,000; Mulao Jia 30,000.
Sino-Tibetan 2.7%. 10 peoples, largest: Nasu (Yi) 539,000; Shuixi Nosu 235,000; Nanjingren 122,000; Guopu 17,000.

RELIGION Buddhism mixed with polytheism and animism is strong among ethnic minorities. Muslim 0.4%. Christian, mainly among Miao and minorities, 3.9%: House churches 2.2%, TSPM 1.1%, all Catholics 0.6%.

1 **Praise God for amazing growth of the Church** in some areas. Two Miao peoples, A-Hmao and Gha-Mu, are majority Christian and the Yi peoples have large Christian minorities (Guopu 18%, Lagou 33%, Wusa Nasu 24%, Tushu 8%). Most of these Christians are in the northwest. The 10,000 Christians of 1949 have probably grown to 1 — 1.5 million since then. There is a chronic shortage of educated leaders.

2 **The challenge of the unreached** is great. Success in a few ethnic groups obscures the remaining need.
a) *The more heavily populated southeast* of Guizhou has possibly only 1,000 believers in registered churches.
b) *The 20 Miao peoples* — two are Christian, two have a significant minority of believers, six have a handful of believers, but 10 have none at all.
c) *There are 39 peoples indigenous to Guizhou* with no witness whatsoever, including the 4 Yao peoples. Among the 13 Tai peoples only the Bouyei (0.16% Christian) and Cai (1.5%) have churches, most have no believers. The Hmong, Hmu, Shui are all large clusters of peoples, but with only a handful of believers. Pray for local and outside Christians to reach out to these unreached peoples.

HAINAN PROVINCE

GEOGRAPHY **Area** 34,300 sq.km. A tropical island facing Vietnam. China's southernmost and smallest province, but its largest Special Economic Zone and tourist haven.
Population 7,594,000; 221 people/sq.km.
Capital Haikou 700,000.

PEOPLES **Han Chinese** 75.7%. Mainly Hainanese, some Hakka.
Tai 24%. Li(5) 1.18m; Lingao 641,700; Cun 79,000.
Other 0.3%. Indonesian 9,000; Utsat (Malay) 7,000.

RELIGION Mixture of polytheism, Buddhism and Daoism among indigenous peoples. Christian 4.6%: House churches 3.9%, TSPM 0.5%, all Catholics 0.2%.

1 **Hainan had an economic boom in the 1980s** which led to spectacular growth as a Special Economic Zone and huge corruption, followed by an equally spectacular bust. There has been a considerable turning to God with an annual doubling by 2000 to 360,000 believers. There are numerous house churches, but there are divisions among Christian leaders. Pray for the effective witness of the Christians to an immoral society.

2 **The Li are the largest indigenous people.** They have rebelled 32 times in the past against Chinese rule. Pray that they may openly receive the King of kings — only 1,000 have done so. Among the related Lingao there are 5,000 Christians, and the Cun 200. There is nothing of God's Word, nor known recordings, nor the *JESUS* film in any of the 8 languages or dialects. Pray that these peoples may be reached.

3 **The Utsat are China's only Malay people.** They are all Muslim with no known believers or attempts to reach them.

HEBEI PROVINCE

GEOGRAPHY **Area** 202,700 sq.km. North China and almost surrounding Beijing.
Population 67,415,000; 333 people/sq.km.
Capital Shijiazhuang 1.88m. Other major cities: Handan 3.76m; Tangshan 1.63m; Pingxiang 1.52m; Xintai

1.37m; Huainan 1.27m.

PEOPLES **Han Chinese** 98.6%, speaking Putonghua.
Hui 1.4%.

RELIGION Secularism and traditional Chinese religions. Muslim 1.4%. Christian 4.0%: all Catholics 2.3%, house churches 1.2%, TSPM 0.5%.

1 **Hebei is one of the most rigidly policed provinces** and Christians have suffered much over the past two decades. Pray for both grace and greater freedom for the Christians in their strategic province.

2 **Hebei is the heart of Catholicism in China** with a large proportion of Catholics. Many remain loyal to the Vatican. These latter have suffered particularly severely since 1997. Protestant and Independent Christians have increased in numbers in some areas, but repression has hindered registration of churches.

HENAN PROVINCE

GEOGRAPHY **Area** 167,000 sq.km. North central China on the fickle Yellow River, prone to flooding and course changes with frequent loss of life.
Population 95,400,000; 571 people/sq.km.
Capital Zhengzhou 2.28m. Other major cities: Luoyang 1.57m; Puyang 1.28m.

PEOPLES **Han Chinese** 99% speaking Putonghua.
Hui 1.0%.

RELIGION Muslim 1%. Christian 10.4%: House churches 5.2%, TSPM 2.1%, marginal groups 2%, all Catholics 1.1%.

1 **Mao's disastrous policies** caused over 8 million Henanese to die of famine. Henan was declared an 'Atheistic Zone' in the 1960s, but today Communist officials complain of it as a 'Jesus Nest' suffering from 'Christianity fever'! Praise God for the spectacular growth of the Church. Revival began during the Cultural Revolution with mass conversions, miracles and vision for evangelizing China. Some counties are reported to be largely or completely Christian today.

2 **Outreach from Henan churches** has been one of the great stories of the expansion of Christianity. Church planting teams (often young women) fanned out over China, followed by discipling teachers. Dangers for this movement:
a) *Multiplication of extremes* and deviant sects because of lack of teaching or due to leadership disputes.
b) *Increased denominationalism.*
c) *Increased persecution* since 1999 with many arrests, punitive fines and destruction of some church buildings

HEILONGJIANG PROVINCE

GEOGRAPHY **Area** 463,600 sq.km. China's most northerly province, bordering on Siberia. One of the three provinces of former Manchuria. Huge natural resources, but many 'rust belt' industries.
Population 38,805,000; 84 people/sq.km.
Capital Harbin 5.48m. Other major cities: Qiqihar 1.92m; Jiamusi 1.13m.

PEOPLES **Han Chinese** 96.4%.
Manchu 2.8%.
Hui 0.4%.
Mongolian 0.4%. 3 peoples, largest: Daur 150,000.
Turkic-Altaic 0.02%. 4 peoples.
Other 0.02%. Japanese 6,000.

RELIGION Shamanism and Buddhism are prevalent among the indigenous peoples. Muslim 0.4%. Christian 5.3%: House churches 3.1%, TSPM 1.6%, all Catholics 0.6%.

1 **Rapid church growth** has occurred in both TSPM and especially in house churches. There are thousands of worshipping groups and churches, but only 24 ordained TSPM pastors. Pray for maturity and stability as well as provision of godly leadership.

2 **Most of the small indigenous Mongolian and Altaic peoples** are shamanistic. Many are resentful of the Chinese 'takeover' of their homelands. The largest, the Daur, have begun to respond to the gospel. There are about 1,000 Christians. Pray for non-Han missionaries to commit their lives to reaching these peoples. Most, such as the Hezhen, Bogol, Khakas, Kyakala, Olot and Saman, total only about 15,000 people. There is nothing of the Scriptures or other media for these peoples — except portions of the Scriptures in Hezhen.

HUBEI PROVINCE

GEOGRAPHY
Area 187,500 sq.km. Astride the Yangtze River, a province of many lakes and much agriculture.
Population 60,653,000; 323 people/sq.km.
Capital Wuhan 4.75m. Other major cities: Suizhou 1.94m; Xiantao 1.84m; Jingmen 1.5m; Echeng 1.1m; Honghu 1.1m.

PEOPLES Han Chinese 96.3%, speaking Putonghua.
Tujia 3.1%.
Miao 0.4%.

RELIGION Muslim 0.2%. Christian 1.3%: House churches 0.7%, all Catholics 0.3%, TSPM 0.3%.

1 **The Church grew considerably before 1949,** but since then growth has not matched that of many other areas The authorities have maintained a tight control — especially over the cities, so registered churches are relatively few. Pray for a shattering of the political, ideological and spiritual chains that bind the people.

2 **The house churches** are strong in some rural areas but isolation and poverty hinder expansion.

HUNAN PROVINCE

GEOGRAPHY
Area 210,500 sq.km. Central China.
Population 66,895,000; 318 people/sq.km.
Capital Changsha 1.74m. Other major cities: Changde 1.65m; Yueyang 1.24m, Leiyang 1.5m; Lianyuan 1.35m; Xiangxiang 1.15m.

PEOPLES Han Chinese 95.7%. Putonghua and Xiang are spoken.
Hmong-Mien 2%. Miao peoples: Ghao-Xong(2) 1.1m. Yao peoples: Iu Mien 168,000; Wunai 10,000.
Sino-Tibetan 1.6%: Tujia 740,000; Mozhihei 5,000.
Tai 0.7%.

RELIGION Muslim 0.1%. Christian 2.4%: House churches 1.8%, TSPM 0.3%, all Catholics 0.3%.

1 **Maoism in this, Mao's home province, is still strong.** There has long been an anti-foreign spirit which has slowed the penetration of the gospel. Hunan is possibly China's spiritually hardest Han Chinese population. Pray for the removal of the spiritual barriers.

2 **The less evangelized:**

a) *Changsha,* the capital, has relatively few Christians; most of the growth in house churches is rural and, in some areas thriving.

b) *The Tujia* are one of the larger peoples in the world without anything of the Bible, and not yet even a script. There are now about 30,000 Christians (0.3%).

c) *The Miao peoples.* The Ghao-Xong are marginally reached with 5,000 Catholics, but the Yao Iu Mien and Wunai have no known believers.

INNER MONGOLIA AUTONOMOUS REGION (NEI MONGOL)

GEOGRAPHY Area 1,177,500 sq.km. Windswept, barren grassland and desert bordering on Mongolia. The western point is 3,500km from its north-eastern point.
Population 23,928,000; 20 people/sq.km.
Capital Hohhot 1.26m. Other major cities: Baotou 1.68m; Huaide 1.1m; Chifeng 1.04m.

PEOPLES Han Chinese 84.2%, speaking Putonghua.
Mongolian 13.3%. 5 peoples, largest: Mongolian 5.8m; Buryat 100,000; Khalkha 52,000.
Manchu 1.3%.
Hui 0.9%.
Turkic-Altaic 0.2%: Evenki(2) 29,000; Oroqen 9,000.
Other 0.1% Korean.

RELIGION Most Mongolians are Lamaistic Buddhist but many of the smaller minorities are Shamanists. Christian 4.7%: House churches 2.7%, all Catholics 1.3%,TSPM 0.7%.

1 Mongolians have become a minority in their own land because of the massive immigration of Han Chinese. Yet there are more Mongolians here than in independent Mongolia to the north. Few have become Christian (some estimate 12,000 or 0.21%). Pray for:

a) *Workers* (Mongolian from the growing churches in Mongolia, or other nationalities) to be called.

b) *The New Testament* to be translated and printed in the Mongolian vertical script.

c) *Churches to be planted.* Officials claim that there is no justification for churches since no missionaries were here in the past.

d) *The binding of demonic powers* in the Lamaism and black magic practiced by Mongolians.

e) *FEBC radio broadcasts* to them.

2 House churches have multiplied across the region but almost all are Han groups. They have to keep a low profile because of the prevailing repression. Pray for continued growth, also for outreach to non-Han indigenous peoples.

3 Among the nomadic Evenki and Oroqen along the Russian border there is no permanent witness, and only a handful of Christians among the Evenki. Few have heard the gospel. Violence and alcoholism is a special problem for the Oroqen.

JIANGSU PROVINCE

GEOGRAPHY Area 102,600 sq.km. Relatively prosperous, fertile coastal province west of Shanghai.
Population 73,866,000; 720 people/sq.km.

Capital Nanjing 3.38m. Other major cities: Xuzhou 1.83m; Wuxi 1.05m.

PEOPLES Han Chinese — speaking Putonghua.

RELIGION Muslim 0.2%. Christian 7.6%: House churches 5.1%, TSPM 1.5%, all Catholics 1%.

1 Church growth has been spectacular since 1980, with over one million associated with TSPM churches and many more with burgeoning house churches. Pray that no subterfuge or attack of the enemy of souls may succeed in hindering that growth.

2 Nanjing is an important centre for Christians — one of the most prestigious TSPM seminaries and the Amity Press are located here.

JIANGXI

GEOGRAPHY Area 164,800 sq.km. South-central China.
Population 42,654,000; 259 people/sq.km.
Capital Nanchang 1.84m. Other major cities: Pingxiang 1.87m; Fuzhou 1.42m.

PEOPLES Han Chinese — speaking Putonghua and Gan.

RELIGION Christian 4.8%: House churches 3.4%, TSPM 0.9%, all Catholics 0.5%.

1 The Communist Long March began here — a march that ended with the political triumph for that ideology, but an immense disaster for China. The blight of that history still affects Jiangxi. Pray for the release of the province from all that opposes God.

2 **There are some areas where Christians have multiplied**, but many parts of the province are relatively under-evangelized.

JILIN PROVINCE

GEOGRAPHY Area 187,000 sq.km. Part of former Manchuria, bordering on North Korea and Siberia. **Population** 27,153,000; 145 people/sq.km. **Capital** Changchun 2.95m. Other major cities: Jilin 1.77m; Gongzhuling 1.33m.

PEOPLES **Han Chinese** 91.9%, speaking Putonghua. **Korean** 4.9%. **Manchu** 2.3%. **Hui** 0.5%. **Mongolian** 0.4%.

RELIGION Many Koreans practice a mix of Buddhism and Shamanism. Muslim 0.5%. Christian 5.7%: House churches 4.1%, TSPM 0.9%, all Catholics 0.7%.

1 **The Church is relatively strong** with many registered and unregistered congregations. A large minority of the Christians are Koreans. Nearly a third of the 2.1m Koreans in Liaoning, Jilin and Heilongjiang Provinces are Christian. Praise God for this.

2 **Changchun** has a much lower percentage of Christians. Pray for churches to be multiplied.

3 **The Chinese Korean Church** has an unusual role to play for North Korea. The terrible plight of their kinsfolk in that repressed land has brought many famine and political victims to them. In the event that Communism collapses, these Christians will play a vital part in the healing and re-evangelization of North Korea.

LIAONING PROVINCE

GEOGRAPHY Area 151,000 sq.km. Southernmost of the three provinces of Manchuria, bordering on the Yellow Sea and North Korea. Heavily industrialized — much of it state-controlled. **Population** 42,863,000; 284 people/sq.km. **Capital** Shenyang (Mukden) 5.68m. Other major cities: Dalian 3.15m; Anshan 1.94m; Fushun 1.7m; Taian 1.57m; Wafangdian 1.34m; Dandong 1.2m; Benxi 1.17m; Haicheng 1.16m; Fuxian 1.14m.

PEOPLES **Han Chinese** 90%, speaking Putonghua. **Manchu** 5.7%. **Korean** 2.4%. **Mongolian** 1.2%. **Hui** 0.7%. Also Xibe 180,500.

RELIGION Muslim 0.7%. Christian 5.1%: House churches 3%, all Catholics 1.1%, TSPM 1%.

1 **The Church has grown significantly** from a strong Presbyterian pre-revolution base. Over 20% of Christians in the province are Korean. A special effort began in 1997 to suppress Protestant and Catholic 'illegal' activities and compel the numerous house churches to register. Foreigners, especially Koreans, were noted to be especially active in church planting. Pray for wisdom, fortitude and evangelistic fervour for the believers.

2 **The Manchu conquered and ruled China** from 1644 to 1911, but in the process lost their culture. Of the 12.6m Manchu, only 200,000 retain a distinctly Manchu culture and their language is almost extinct. The majority live in the three provinces of former Manchuria but are also scattered across China. Most follow the range of Chinese secular and religious views, but some are still shamanist. Response to the gospel is very limited and known Christians are only 10,000 in number — less than 0.1% of the Manchu. Pray for this large unreached people.

3 **The Xibe are an Altaic-Tungus people** that have been largely assimilated into Chinese culture, but only a handful are known to be Christian.

NINGXIA HUI AUTONOMOUS REGION

GEOGRAPHY Area 66,400 sq.km. Arid steppe with a fertile strip along the Yellow River in north China. **Population** 5,410,000; 81 people/sq.km. **Capital** Yinchuan 300,000.

PEOPLES **Han Chinese** 66.5%, speaking Putonghua. **Hui** 33.4%. **Manchu** 0.1%.

RELIGION Muslim 34%. Christian 3.9%: all Catholics 1.9%, house churches 1.8%, TSPM 0.2%.

1 **The Hui** number 10.6m, but are found in every province of China. Only a minority live in their Autonomous Region. They are descendants of Muslim traders, Mongolians and Chinese. They strongly retain their culture and religion, but speak Putonghua. They are the largest Muslim ethnic group in China. After 30 years of mission outreach before 1951, very few had become Christians. There is renewed interest in reaching them. There are only about 200 scattered believers among them. Pray that in every city across China, local Christians might have a burden to reach them and the willingness to adapt their approach to be effective.

2 **There is a large-scale turning to Christianity** in the north along the Yellow River where there are many Han immigrants. The Catholic Church has seen the greatest growth. Pray for adequate leadership and good literature for these Christians — both in short supply.

QINGHAI PROVINCE

GEOGRAPHY **Area** 721,000 sq.km. A huge, high alpine desert province in West China on the Tibetan Plateau.
Population 5,098,000; 7 people/sq.km.
Capital Xining 937,000.

PEOPLES **Han Chinese** 59.9%, speaking Putonghua.
Sino-Tibetan 19.4%. 8 peoples, largest: Amdo Tibetan(2) 710,000; Golog 128,000; Khampa Tibetan 118,000; Sogwo Arig 37,000.
Hui 13.7%.
Mongolian 4.8%. 4 peoples: Tu 200,000; Oirat 91,000; Mongour 40,000; Bonan 6,000.
Turkic-Altaic 2.2%. 2 peoples: Salar 113,000; Kazakh 3,000.

RELIGION Muslim 16%. Christian 2.3%: House churches 1.4%, TSPM 0.6%, all Catholics 0.3%.

1 **This desolate region** is dotted with labour camps. Many thousands of prisoners have endured great hardship there — including many believers. Pray for all prisoners of conscience that their faith in God might grow and bless those around them.

2 **In the 1940s there were only a few hundred Christians,** mainly in Xining, but in the last 20 years growth has been significant in the few urban areas. There are only five registered TSPM churches and 40 meeting points in the province. The believers are poor but fervent in outreach — pray that this ministry might be fruitful.

3 **The unreached:**

a) *The Tibetans* are strong in their Lamaistic Buddhism. Their living conditions are harsh, and they depend on their large herds of yak. Unprecedented heavy snows in 1996 decimated these herds and made many destitute. Christian help for them gave opportunities for witness. There are now a handful of isolated believers. Pray for open hearts, bound demonic powers and for many people to be free in Jesus.

b) *The Tu and Mongour* are Lamaistic Buddhists with no known believers. They are isolated from existing outreach.

c) *The Muslim Hui* in Xining are numerous and there are a handful of Christians, but few witness to them.

d) *The Muslim Salar and Bonan* remain completely unreached.

SHAANXI PROVINCE

GEOGRAPHY **Area** 195,800 sq.km. in north-central China.
Population 36,828,000; 188 people/sq.km.
Capital Xian 3,352,000. Once the capital of China in the T'ang dynasty. Famous for the buried terracotta army.

PEOPLES **Han Chinese** 99.6%, speaking Putonghua.
Hui 0.4%.

RELIGION Muslim 0.4%. Christian 4.5%: House churches 2.7%, TSPM 1.0%, all Catholics 0.8%.

1 **Shaanxi was the birthplace of Christianity in China.** The Nestorians built their first church in Xian in 635. Terrible persecution wiped out this witness. Pray that the 21st Century may be one of triumph for the Church.

2 **The Church has grown dramatically** from 30,000 Christians in 1949 to officially 350,000 and unofficially maybe nearly 3 million today. Pray for the spiritual unity and health of Shaanxi Christians and that they may retain the fire of the Holy Spirit into the next generation.

SHANDONG PROVINCE

GEOGRAPHY **Area** 153,300 sq.km. Northern coastal province on the Shandong Peninsula in the Yellow Sea. **Population** 90,928,000; 593 people/sq.km. **Capital** Jinan 4.79m. Other major cities: Qingdao 4.38m; Zibo 3.34m; Tai'an 1.9m; Zaozhuang 2.4m; Linyi 1.61m;

Weifang 1.23m; Laiwu 1.23m; Heze 1.18m; Rizhau 1.15m; Liling 1m.

PEOPLES **Han Chinese** 99.6%, speaking Putonghua.
Hui 0.4%.

RELIGION Muslim 0.4%. Christian 3%: House churches 1.7%, TSPM 1%, all Catholics 0.3%.

1 **Shandong was the birthplace and home of Confucius,** whose philosophy and writings have deeply moulded Chinese culture to this day. Pray that the Chinese may be freed from the social demands which hinder many from commitment to Christ.

2 **Tai'an is near one of China's most 'holy' mountains,** Taishan. This is a major spiritual stronghold on which prayer should be focused.

3 **The Jesus Family,** a remarkable form of communal Christianity, began in this province. They were influential in the start of the house church movement of which they are a part today. Pray for the spiritual health of all forms of indigenous Christianity and for the centrality of Scripture in their life and teaching.

SHANGHAI MUNICIPALITY

GEOGRAPHY **Area** 6,200 sq.km. China's largest and most wealthy city (after Hong Kong) and an industrial hub for the country with a large international seaport. **Population** 14,773,000; 2,382 people/sq.km.

PEOPLES **Han Chinese** 99.6%, speaking Wu and Subei.
Other 0.4%.

RELIGION Muslim 0.4%. Christian 9.6%: House churches 5.7%, all Catholics 2.8%, TSPM 1.1%.

1 **In 1950 there was a varied and effective church life** with 256 churches, but all was destroyed in the Cultural Revolution. Even today there are but 27 churches and 80 registered meeting points of the TSPM. A large network of small house churches has developed — some estimate between 3,000 and 20,000. In a crackdown in 1999, 1,000 were forcibly closed. Pray for freedom for congregations to grow and multiply.

2 **The economic growth** has been a magnet for up to 3 million poor, rural work-seekers from all over China who eagerly take up the dangerous and menial jobs on the margins of society. Pray for the evangelization of this uprooted mass of people.

3 **For years Shanghai has been a base for Christian outreach** to the whole country. One of the major house church networks is doing just that today. Pray that the drive, wealth and sophistication of this city might be harnessed for the spread of the gospel.

SHANXI PROVINCE

GEOGRAPHY
Area 157,100 sq.km. Northeast China, west of Beijing. Not to be confused with neighbouring Shaanxi. [Shanxi = West of the Mountains; Shaanxi = West of the Mountain Passes].
Population 32,251,000; 205 people/sq.km.

Capital Taiyuan 2.76m. Other major cities: Datong 1.8m; Yangcheng 1.48m.

PEOPLES **Han Chinese** 99.7%, speaking Putonghua and Jin.
Other 0.3%: Hui, Manchu.

RELIGION Muslim 0.2%. Christian 3.4%: House churches 2.1%, TSPM 0.7%, all Catholics 0.6%.

1 **The CIM did much work here before 1949.** In 1950 there were 26,000 Protestants. This number had offically grown to 220,000 (unofficially nearly 900,000) by 1999. There are also many Catholics. There has been much repression of both registered TSPM and house churches.

2 **The Boxer Rebellion** of 1900 led to many martyrs — thousands of Chinese as well as 159 missionaries and 46 children in Shanxi alone. Pray that their blood may prove good seed for today's Church.

3 **Datong has a low percentage of Christians** and is, historically, a major Buddhist centre. Pray for the breaking down of spiritual strongholds.

C SICHUAN PROVINCE

GEOGRAPHY Area 426,000 sq.km. A large rice-growing province on the Yangtze River ringed by high mountains. The 'panda province'.
Population 87,681,000; 205 people/sq.km.
Capital Chengdu 5.3m. Other major cities: Suining 1.7m; Neijiang 1.42m; Leshan 1.44m; Zigong 1.3m; Mianyang 1.22m.

PEOPLES **Han Chinese** 95.4%, speaking Putonghua.

Sino-Tibetan 4.6%: 44 peoples, largest:
Tibetan E. Khampa 1.25m, Jiarong(5) 190,000; Rtahu Amdo 79,000, Ergong 49,000.
Yi Nosu(4) 1.83m; Suodi 190,000; Qiang(12) 183,000; Mosuo 30,000; Chrame 39,000; Bai Ma 15,000.
Hmong-Mien 0.8%. Miao(2) 667,000.

RELIGION Lamaistic Buddhist 4%. Among Tibetans, Jiarong, Mosuo, Chrame. Animist, polytheist among Nosu, Bai Ma, Qiang, Miao. Christian 1.4%: House churches 0.7%, all Catholics 0.5%, TSPM 0.2%.

1 **Sichuan had the lowest Christian percentage** of the Han-majority provinces until recently. The Catholics arrived in 1696 and LMS and CIM in 1868/81, but there had been no major breakthrough until a recent significant growth in the house churches. Pray that the spiritual mountains that ring this province might be breached, and millions turn to Christ.

2 **Chengdu** with over 5m people is a key city for the whole of western China, but there are officially only two large TSPM churches and 3,000 Protestant Christians. There may be a further 50,000 house church believers. There is a large number of ethnic minority groups in the city — especially Tibetans. Pray for this needy city and those seeking to reach it.

3 **Ethnic minorities indigenous to Sichuan** total 4m in 44 peoples, but 33 of them have no Christians and no known outreach to them. Of the 11 among whom there are some Christians, only the Chuan Miao and Shengzha Nosu have over 1% Christians. Intercede for:

a) *The major groups with no witness;* the Qiang cluster of peoples, the Tibetan groups, Suodi, Mosuo, Enshi Miao, etc. Many of these peoples, though related, speak mutually unintelligible languages.

b) *The Nosu* who are a particular challenge. They are a proud people that once dominated their area and enslaved the Han Chinese. They were only finally subdued by the central government in 1953. They are known for their violence, war-making, intimidation and polytheism. The *JESUS* film has had some impact, and there are 12,000 Christians in the largest of the 4 Nosu peoples. Pray for this spiritual stronghold to be breached.

c) *The small Christian groups* among them to become strong, effective witnesses.

d) *Ethnic minorities* in Yunnan and elsewhere with large Christian communities to become missionaries to these peoples.

e) *Bible translators.* The Bible is available for the Khampa and Amdo Tibetans, and there are portions of Scripture for the Chuan Miao and Shengzha Nosu, but no other group has anything of God's Word.

TIANJIN MUNICIPAL-ITY

GEOGRAPHY Area 11,300 sq.km. The port city of Beijing.
Population 9,883,000; 875 people/sq.km.

PEOPLES **Han Chinese** 97.8%, speaking Putonghua.
Hui 1.8%.
Other 0.4%.

RELIGION Muslim 1.8%. Christian 2.3%: All Catholics 1.7%, house churches 0.4%, TSPM 0.2%.

1 **The Church is almost as tightly controlled** as in nearby Beijing, and church growth has been more limited. Catholics have fared better. Pray for an easing of the harsh restrictions and for more church growth.

TIBET — XIZANG AUTONOMOUS REGION

GEOGRAPHY Area 1,222,000 sq.km. High, barren Tibetan plateau north of the Himalaya Mountains, much of which is uninhabited and includes Mount Qomolangma (Everest); often called the 'Roof of the World'.
Population 2,500,000; 2 people/sq.km.
Capital Lhasa 310,000.

PEOPLES Han Chinese 20%. Large-scale immigration and a large military presence.
Sino-Tibetan 80%. 24 peoples, largest: Central (Lhasa) 741,000; Gtsang 596,000; Western Khampa 205,000; Monba(2) 41,000; Deng(2) 20,000; Lhoba 12,000.

RELIGION Lama Buddhist 80%. Two factions: Yellow Hat and Red Hat. Interwoven with the pre-Buddhist Bon religion. Muslim 0.2%. Christian 0.2%, largely Catholic in southeastern corner of Tibet.

1 **Tibet is a contentious international issue.** It lost its temporary independence as a theocratic Buddhist state in 1950 when China invaded the land. The Communists have systematically sought to destroy the culture, religions and ethnic identity of the Tibetan people. Resistance to the occupiers has resulted in frequent revolts and unrest. Over one million people may have lost their lives and a further 100,000 may have been forced into exile including the spiritual and political leader of Tibetans, the Dalai Lama. Pray for a just and peaceful settlement for all concerned.

2 **Tibetan Buddhism** has a strong hold on the people. There is much demonic bondage; the pre-Buddhist Bon religion with its spirit appeasement and occultism permeates society. Blood covenants were made with the powers of darkness in past centuries — these must be renounced. There are officially still 1,780 monasteries and 46,000 Buddhist monks. Pray that present sufferings may be God's means for bringing spiritual freedom to Tibetans.

3 **After centuries of failed attempts** and limited fruit there may be about 1,000 evangelical and 2,000 Catholic Christians among the 5m Tibetans in the world. There are two secret groups of Tibetan believers in Tibet. Pray for all efforts through radio, the *JESUS* film, personal witness in Tibet and from the surrounding provinces of Gansu, Qinghai, Sichuan and elsewhere to reach them. Around 500,000 Tibetans live in exile in Nepal, India and the West, where they are a little more accessible.

4 **Political sensitivity** and tensions in Tibet make entry and travel difficult for both Chinese and foreign Christians who desire to share the love of Jesus there. Pray for open doors and freedom to proclaim the gospel.

5 **There is a growing number of Han Chinese in Tibet.** Pray for the planting of house fellowships among them — some have been started. Lhasa has become a Han Chinese city with only 30% of its inhabitants Tibetan, who are poor and marginalized.

XINJIANG UYGUR AUTONOMOUS REGION

GEOGRAPHY Area 1,646,900 sq.km. Ringed with mountains surrounding the Taklamakan Desert in northwest China.
Population 17,582,000; 11 people/sq.km. Most living on desert oases or in the mountains.
Capital Urumqi 1,635,000.

PEOPLES Turkic 60.7%. 14 peoples, largest: Uygur(7) 9.13m; Kazakh 1.15m; Kyrgyz 180,000; Uzbek 18,000.
Han Chinese 33.1%. Rapidly increasing through immigration; most living in the cities. Urumqi is 90% Han.
Hui 4.2%.
Mongolian-Tungus 1.7%. 4 peoples: Torgut 146,000; Western Xibe 42,000; Tuva 3,200.
Other 0.3%: Tajik(2) 44,000; Russian 18,000.

RELIGION Muslim 65.1%. The Turkic peoples, Tajik, Salar and Hui. Lamaistic Buddhist 1.5%, Mongolians. Christian 2.2%: House churches 1.6%, all Catholics 0.4%; TSPM 0.2%.

1 **Xinjiang's rich natural resources** and strategic location make it important for China's future. Uygur separatism, fuelled by Islamist support from the Middle East and Central Asia, has increased over the 1990s and has been met with vigorous repression. Many lives have been lost, thousands executed and many imprisoned. Pray for a satisfactory resolution for both sides. The tension has hindered any religious activity.

2 **Almost all the indigenous peoples are Muslim** and unreached. There are a few isolated believers among the Uygur and Kazakh and they are under continual pressure to return to Islam. Most are unreached, with few seeking to minister to them.

3 **There were once believers and some churches among the Uygur** in the 1930s, but in violent persecution the churches were destroyed and believers killed or scattered. There are now only a few Uygur believers, but there are nearly 500 Uygur believers in Kazakhstan — may they witness to those in Xinjiang. Pray for the completion and distribution of the New Testament and also the dissemination of the *JESUS* film in Uygur. Pray also for churches to be planted among them once more.

4 **The 360,000 Christians in Xinjiang,** almost all Han Chinese, are culturally isolated from the indigenous population. Pray that they may have a vision for and understanding of witnessing to Muslims. Most live in the capital, Urumqi. There are only about 50-60 known Christians among the non-Chinese; their numbers are growing, but they are subjected to heavy pressure by Muslims to return to Islam.

YUNNAN PROVINCE

GEOGRAPHY Area 436,200 sq.km. In China's mountainous southwest.
Population 42,030,000; 96 people/sq.km.
Capital Kunming 1.9m. Other major city: Qujing 1.1m.

PEOPLES   Han Chinese 68%.
Sino-Tibetan 20.6%. 11.6m in 154 peoples. Main groups: Yi (104 in official nationality, but not necessarily closely related), largest: Nisu(4) 1.5m; Nasu(4) 752,000; Laluo(2) 610,000; Luoluopo(3) 584,000; Nosu(2) 506,000; East and West Lipo 237,000; Poluo 233,000; Sani 130,000; Lami 100,000. Hani(11), largest: Hani 615,000; Akha 195,000; Baihong 195,000; Haoni 123,000; Kado 123,000; Woni 110,000. Other (39), largest: Lisu(3) 720,000; Lahu 544,000; Naxi 290,000; Tibetan(2) 250,000.
Tai 7%. 2.5m in 23 peoples; largest: Tai/Dai(9) 1.5m; Giay 274,000; Gelao 50,000.
Hmong-Mien 2%. 1.1m in 8 peoples: Miao (Hmong, 4) 577,000; Yao(3) 520,000.
Hui 1.4%.
Mon-Khmer 1%. 565,000 in 22 peoples, largest: Wa 300,000; Bulang 80,000; Kawa 73,000; Lawa 55,000.

RELIGION   Buddhist, animist, polytheist and ancestor worship. Muslim 1.5%. Christian 5.3%: House churches 3.2%, TSPM 2%, all Catholics 0.1%.

1 **Yunnan is, ethnically, China's most complex province.** There have been famous and dramatic workings of the Holy Spirit among some of the tribal groups earlier last century — especially among the Lisu, Miao, Wa, Jingpo and Nu. There are over 1m Christians in these minorities — 60-70% of all the Christians in Yunnan. So the Church is thriving in a few ethnic groups, but the mountainous terrain, large number of cultures and languages, and ancient hostilities all hinder the spread of the gospel. Pray that many more areas may experience like demonstrations of God's grace and power.

2 **Yunnan's indigenous ethnic minorities**, numbering 16m in 208 ethno-linguistic peoples, are an immense challenge for the Church in China and the world.
a) ***205 peoples have no witness*** and no Christians, and a further 47 have less than 1% Christians. Many are polytheists or Buddhists.
b) ***Only 23 peoples have responded in a significant way*** and are now over 10% Christian. Just 6 are majority Christian: Hkauri (31 people), Eastern Lipo (60,000 — 67% Christian), Maru (7,600 — 79%), Ayi (2,200), Rawang (540), Xiandao (130 people). The largest Christian communities are among the: Lisu (300,000); Miao (150,000); E. Nasu (120,000); Wa (75,000), Bai (50,000); Jingpo (40,000); Naluo (10,000); Lawa (10,000); Lashi (6,000); Nu (4,000). Pray for local believers to reach out to related ethnic groups still unreached, and pray also for missionaries from China and elsewhere to reach these unreached of Yunnan. The poverty of local believers and difficulties in travel slow any attempts.

3 **The Han Chinese Christians** are relatively few in number and there has not been much growth in either TSPM, house churches or the Catholics. Pray for the growth of the Church among them.

4 Special issues needing prayer:
a) ***Bible translation*** is a massive unmet need. The Bible is available for 9 languages, the NT in a further 11, and just portions in yet another 11. Translators are working in only 5 groups. The great majority of languages have nothing. Good surveys are necessary to ascertain what needs to be done. Pray for this vital ministry to be expanded in Yunnan.

b) ***AIDS*** is becoming a problem to a number of border peoples because of drug abuse and trafficking and exposure to the sex industry in Thailand and Myanmar.

c) ***FEBC broadcasts*** in Lahu, De'ang, Miao, Jingpo, Lisu, Maru, Wa and Tai. Pray for the evangelistic and teaching ministry of this medium.

ZHEJIANG PROVINCE

GEOGRAPHY Area 101,800 sq.km. Prosperous coastal province south of Shanghai. **Population** 45,152,000; 443 people/sq.km. **Capital** Hangzhou 6.39m. Other major city: Ningbo 1.2m.

PEOPLES Han Chinese 99.6%, speaking Wu and Putonghua. **Hui** 0.4%.

RELIGION Secularism and traditional Chinese religions. Muslim 0.3%. Christian 11.2%: House churches 7.7%, TSPM 3%, all Catholics 0.5%.

1 **Wenzhou is sometimes called the Jerusalem of China.** Over 30% of its population is Christian. In many rural areas there is a prominent church building in full use every kilometre. There are over 2,400 churches and 3,500 registered meeting points as well as thousands of house churches. Many of their church buildings were destroyed in 2000 in a strong effort to eliminate unregistered Christians.

2 **Zhejiang house churches** have done much to evangelize other parts of China through evangelizing migrant labourers and following contacts to their home areas. Believers are generous in supporting these mission efforts. Pray for this vision to grow.

3 **Since 1997 pressure on house churches has grown** and some buildings destroyed by the authorities. Pray for the assaults of those opposed to the gospel to fail and for the perpetrators to be converted.

China, Hong Kong

Special Administrative Region

MAP ON PAGE 167

APRIL 6
ASIA
Updated January 2004

GEOGRAPHY Area 1,092 sq.km. A mountainous peninsula and 230 islands on the coast of Guangdong Province of the People's Republic of China (PRC).

Population	Ann.Gr.	Density
2000	6,965,000	+2.49%	6,378 per sq.km
2010	7,701,000	+1.01%	7,052 per sq.km
2025	9,000,000	+0.99%	8,242 per sq.km

The 1945 population of 600,000 rapidly increased with over 1.5 mill. refugees and migrants from China. It is one of the most densely populated areas in the world.

Capital none. Major conurbations: Hong Kong Island 1.3 mill.; Kowloon 2.5m; New Territories 2.9m. **Urbanites** 100%

PEOPLES **Chinese** 97%. Yueh (Cantonese) 6,170,000; Minnan 620,000; Hakka 250,000. **Other** 3%. Filipino 137,000; English-speaking 110,000; Pakistani 70,000; Indonesian 45,000; Indian/Nepali 40,000; Japanese 18,000; South Asian 15,000.

Literacy 92%. **Official languages** Putonghua and English, but Cantonese widely used. **All languages** 7. **Languages with Scriptures** 4Bi.

ECONOMY Rapid growth through liberal economic policies to become one of the world's richest cities, based on industry, finance and international trade between China and the world. It is the world's busiest container port. It has been the powerhouse for China's rapid modernization. Post-1997 economic downturn, the bursting of the property 'bubble' and the SARS epidemic in 2003 slowed the growth of its ruthless capitalism. **HDI** 0.880; 24th/174. **Income/person** $24,800 (80% of USA).

POLITICS The British wrested Hong Kong from China in the infamous opium wars (1840-58). British rule 1842-1997. The Basic Law guarantees the maintenance of existing legal, political and economic structures for 50 years, but China is responsible for defence and foreign policy. The PRC has largely honoured this. Since 2002 there has been a growing assertiveness for more democratic government.

Religious freedom in a secular state, guaranteed by the Basic Law, has been adhered to. Relationships between HK and PRC are to be based on 'non-interference and respect', which means HK Christians are not permitted to interfere in religious affairs of the Mainland.

Religions	Population %	Adherents	Ann.Gr.
Chinese/Buddhist	66.13	4,606,000	+2.3%
non-Religious	18.25	1,271,113	+4.1%
Christian	10.05	700,000	+0.0%
Other	3.80	264,670	+3.0%
Muslim	1.50	104,000	+7.2%
Hindu	0.25	17,000	+7.2%
Jewish	0.02	1,300	-5.5%

Christians	Denom.	Affil.%	,000	Ann.Gr.
Protestant	58	4.95	345	+0.7%
Independent	29	1.17	81	+3.4%
Anglican	1	0.33	23	-0.4%
Catholic	1	3.23	225	-1.0%
Marginal	5	0.37	26	-0.6%

Churches		MegaBloc	Cong.	Members	Affiliates
Catholic	C	62	133,136	225,000	
United HK Chr Bapt Ass	P	129	56,379	70,000	
Chr and Miss Alliance	P	93	20,582	42,000	
HK Council of Ch of Chr	P	50	26,000	32,000	
Independent	I	120	15,000	25,000	
Anglican	A	40	16,000	23,000	
Latter-day Saints (Morm)	M	28	10,056	18,000	
Chinese Methodist	P	24	11,700	15,000	
Evang Luth Ch of HK	P	54	9,000	12,099	
Ling Liang WW Evang Miss	I	15	7,800	12,000
China Rhenish, HK Synod	P	19	2,224	11,700
Evangelical Free	P	47	7,572	10,000
Assemblies of God Assoc	P	41	6,000	9,000
Lutheran Ch HK Synod	P	39	5,800	8,000
Full Gospel Assembs of God	P	21	3,500	7,500
Chinese Full Gospel	P	8	4,000	7,000
Pentecostal Holiness	P	22	4,700	7,000
Tsung Tsin Mission of HK	P	21	4,192	7,000
Hong Kong Methodist	P	24	3,800	5,500
HK Evangelical	P	19	2,700	4,000
Other denoms [71]		658	101,000	149,000

| Total Christians [96] | | 1,534 | 451,683 | 700,000 |

Trans-bloc Groupings	pop.%	,000	Ann.Gr.
Evangelical	5.1	356	+1.1%
Charismatic	1.3	89	+0.7%
Pentecostal	0.8	54	+1.6%

Missionaries from Hong Kong
P,I,A 380 (300 overseas) with 41 agencies in 48 countries.

Missionaries to Hong Kong
P,I,A 654 in 100 agencies from 26 countries: USA 420, Korea 34, UK 33.

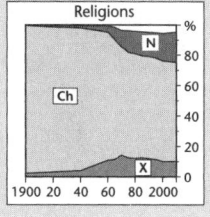

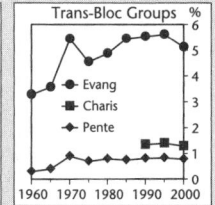

• Answers to Prayer

1 **The successful return of Hong Kong** to China and continued religious freedom thereafter.

2 **The impact of Hong Kong for the Kingdom of God has been noteworthy** — it is a hub of activity and a source of finance in outreach, discipling, media and literature ministries to the Chinese Diaspora and the Mainland. The traumatic SARS epidemic led to greater openness to the Gospel.

• Challenges for Prayer

1 **The 1997 return of Hong Kong to China** was met with a mixture of fear and euphoria — especially among Christians. Pray that God's purposes for Hong Kong may continue to be carried out, and its Christians be a blessing to the world.

2 **Will the guaranteed freedoms of Hong Kong be maintained?** Many perceive a steady, incremental erosion of press freedoms, the autonomy of the judicial system, and a government less accountable and open. Pray for wisdom and integrity for the Chief Executive and all in government leadership. They must satisfy the Communist government in Beijing and also the people who desire democratic and religious freedoms to be maintained and increased.

3 **The Christian community** is 10% of the population, but has long exerted a strong influence in running 505 of the schools, 60% of social organizations, and 25% of the hospitals. This influence could diminish if its privileged position is challenged and leaders acquiesce to negative trends, potentially exposing churches to discrimination or even persecution. Pray that the Church may be bold and uncompromising in exercising its prophetic role in society.

4 **The churches grew rapidly in the 1960s, but slowed in the 1980s** and '90s through emigration (19% of Christians) and a high drop-out rate among young adults. Christians face many pressures in Hong Kong's crowded and intense atmosphere. Some churches continue to grow vigorously — among these are denominations that have adopted a cell church structure. The number of congregations of all Protestant/Independent churches increased from 700 in 1970 to 1,200 in 2000 with 200 new churches planted 1994-99, and conversions more or less replaced Christian emigrants. Major growing groups are: **CMA**, Baptists and the independent charismatic churches.

5 **The challenges facing the Hong Kong Church:**

a) *The need for renewal and revival.* The HK Church Renewal Movement has laboured for this by encouraging prayer for revival and conversions, city-wide rallies and backing the annual **March for Jesus** events.
b) *Increasing wealth and materialism* that saps spiritual commitment.
c) *Divisions over doctrine* and the charismatic issue. Some barriers have been broken down since the GCOWE in 1995 in Korea and the 1997 hand-over with pastors praying together. Pray that churches may unite for prayer, evangelism and missions.

6 **Christian leaders** of maturity are relatively few. Three-fourths of all older leaders left HK before 1997 forcing a sudden rejuvenation of church leadership — increasing vision and dynamism as well as mistakes due to immaturity. Pray for them and for:
a) *The 27 Bible colleges and seminaries*, and for staff and students (850 in 1990).
b) *Key seminaries* such as the Alliance Seminary, the Baptist Theological Seminary and the China Graduate School of Theology.
c) *A greater missions component in leadership training* — only a few schools give this.

7 **The Church has a growing concern for missionary work abroad.** Issues for prayer:
a) *About 57% of congregations now have a missions commitment* — pray for this to develop healthily, and for other congregations to become involved.
b) *The HK Association of Christian Missions* is a focal coordinating point for 26 agencies, 14 denominations and a number of individual congregations that are channelling over 300 missionaries (180 long-term; half cross-cultural among non-Chinese) overseas.
c) *How best to serve and support the pressured, but growing Church in the PRC.* Courage, tact and wisdom is needed in this sensitive area for HK continues to be a vital conduit of ministry, help and training materials. Pray that both the HK and PRC Christians may bless each other in fellowship, ministry and outreach.

8 **The CCCOWE** (Chinese Coordinating Committee on World Evangelization) has played a vital role in linking together Christians in the 70 million Chinese diaspora for fellowship and outreach to less evangelized Chinese communities. Its headquarters is in HK. Pray for the effective mobilization of Chinese wealth and manpower for world evangelization.

9 **Hong Kong's pervasive and powerful underworld** of crime majors on the narcotics trade, the sex 'industry' and gambling and protection rackets. There are estimated to be 50 Triad Societies (the Chinese equivalent of the Mafia) with over 600,000 members. Christian ministry among criminals, drug addicts and the destitute has increased with some success (partly as a result of the work of St Stephen's Society pioneered by Jackie Pullinger).

10 **Fear for the future** has increased superstition and idolatry. In 1989 the world's largest outdoor image of Buddha was built to 'protect' HK. The spiritual powers behind these must be disarmed to bring release to:
a) *The blue-collar industrial workers*, and the wealthy financiers and businessmen.
b) *Immigrants from Mainland China.* Many are housed in squalid squatter settlements, or crowded little high-rise flats. They are disillusioned and frustrated and are also one of the most responsive sections of the population. A number of churches and missions have sought to alleviate their physical needs and meet their spiritual needs (**WVI**, **OMF**, **ECF**, **OM**, Mission to New Arrivals).

c) The South Asian population — a legacy of British rule. Most are traders (Sindhi, Panjabi, Gujarati), in the security industry (Nepali Gurkhas) or in menial jobs (Pakistanis). There are some Christians among the latter.

d) The Muslims who are largely Hui Chinese, Pakistanis, Malays, Indonesians and Middle Easterners.

11 **Student ministries have flourished.** Christians comprise 30% of university students. Most of **CCCI**'s 107 staff minister on six campuses. HKFES(**IFES**) with 48 staff workers has an extensive ministry. About 2,000 students in 11 tertiary institutions and 10,000 in 300 secondary schools are involved. Pray that these young people may decisively impact HK and beyond.

12 **The foreign mission force** has somewhat reduced during the 1990s — partly as the Chinese Church matured and partly due to the closure of ministries to the PRC based in HK. Many expatriates are involved in pioneer church planting, Bible teaching, media ministries or wider international ministries. Major agencies with ministry in Hong Kong are: **SBC** (88 workers), **YWAM** (44), **AoG** (30), SDA (30), Finnish Lutheran Mission (23), **Asian Outreach** (19), **CMA** (19), **OMS** (18), **ABWE** (16), Evangelical Free Church of America (12), Norwegian Mission Society (10), **OMF** (8).

13 **Hong Kong is a vital nerve centre for media.** Groups such as Christian Communications Ltd., The Media Evangelism Ltd., and **AO** have made significant contributions. **Literature** is written, printed, published and distributed on a massive scale (**CLC**, **EHC**, **CMA**). There are 16 Christian publishers and 57 Christian bookstores. Bibles are printed for the world, and the **Bible Society** has a key role. Hong Kong is a key location for studios preparing radio programmes (**FEBC**, **FEBA**, **TWR**, etc.). Pray that this role may be maintained in the 21ˢᵗ Century.

China, Macau

Special Administrative Region

MAP ON PAGE 167

APRIL 7
ASIA

GEOGRAPHY
Area 17 sq.km. A tiny peninsula and two islands 64 km west of Hong Kong on the coast of Guangdong Province of China.

Population	Ann.Gr.	Density
2000 445,427	+1.96%	26,202 per sq.km.
2010 524,927	+1.59%	30,878 per sq.km.
2025 644,217	+1.20%	37,895 per sq.km.

One of the most densely populated areas on earth.

Capital Macau 432,000. **Urbanites** 100%.

PEOPLES
Chinese 96%. Mainly Cantonese. Mainland migrant labour 25,000; Hong Kong 14,000.
Macanese (Eurasian) 2.7%.
Other 1.3%. Westerners 4,000; Filipino 3,000; Thai 1,500.

Literacy 90%. **Official languages** Cantonese, Portuguese.

ECONOMY
One of the richest cities in the world in the 16ᵗʰ and 17ᵗʰ Centuries. The dominant industry is now gambling and tourism. It is also an important gateway for China's special economic zones adjoining Macau. **Income/person** $17,600 (62% of USA).

POLITICS
Rented by the Portuguese in 1577. Became a Portuguese Colony in 1887, considered a Chinese Territory under Portuguese administration since 1974. Macau reverted to Chinese rule as a special autonomous region in 1999, with a high degree of economic and political autonomy. It was both Europe's first and last colonial possession in Asia.

RELIGION
Under the agreement between the colonial administration and China, there is full freedom of religion.

Religions	Population %	Adherents	Ann.Gr.
non-Religious/other	60.00	267,256	+2.0%
Chinese	19.69	87,705	+1.2%
Buddhist	13.00	57,906	+3.6%
Christian	7.31	32,561	+1.2%

Christians	Denom.	Affil.%	,000	Ann.Gr.
Protestant	14	1.13	5	+3.6%
Independent	9	0.72	3	+2.7%
Anglican	1	0.04	0	+0.0%
Catholic	1	5.18	23	+0.5%
Marginal	2	0.24	1	+5.5%

Churches	MegaBloc	Cong.	Members	Affiliates
Catholic	C	9	13,609	23,000
Independent Chs [9]	I	38	1,900	3,200
Macau Evangelical	P	12	1,200	2,000
Baptist	P	8	475	1,045
Latter-day Saints (Morm)	M	2	327	850
Other denoms [17]		25	1,269	2,403
Total Christians [30]		94	18,780	32,498

Trans-bloc Groupings	pop.%	,000	Ann.Gr.
Evangelical	1.7	8	+3.3%
Charismatic	0.8	4	+3.0%
Pentecostal	0.1	1	+7.1%

Missionaries from Macau
P,I,A 55 — all in Macau.

Missionaries to Macau
P,I,A 154 in 22 agencies from 13 countries: USA 64, Brazil 9.

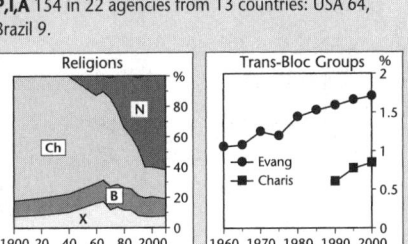

• Challenges for Prayer

1 **Macau has the dubious distinction of being the first Christian territory in Asia to become non-Christian.** In 1600 Macau was 95% Catholic. By 2000 this had been reduced to about 7.4%. The Catholic Church has suffered disastrous decline, and Protestant churches have always been small. The number of Protestant churches had grown from 33 in 1986 to 78 in 1999. Pray for the people of this territory to be changed by the Word of God.

2 **Macau was the starting point of Protestant missions to China.** There, the first Chinese convert was baptised, the first Chinese Bible translated and Robert Morrison, the first Protestant missionary to the Chinese, was buried. Yet today it is one of the least-discipled communities of Chinese in the world. The Church is small, divided, introspective and weakened by emigration and a high turn-over of leadership. Pray for local leaders to be raised up who will help the Church survive and grow and be a blessing to China and the world. The Macau Bible Institute was the first theological school, but there are now three theological institutions for training leaders.

3 **Macau was named 'City of the Name of God'** by the Portuguese, though it was a Chinese god that gave it its present name. It has truly become the 'City of Sin'. Gambling and prostitution are major money-earners which are run by ruthless Triad gangs who wage wars for control of this lucrative 'industry'. Lawlessness characterized the twilight of Portuguese rule, but the new government is seeking to change this. Pray that this city might lose its unflattering reputation and the gospel of Christ change a society so blanketed by sin.

4 **Evangelical Christians doubled in number** between 1990 and 2000. There was increasing cooperation to present a unified witness in the time leading to the hand-over to China. The major hindrances to continued growth are the lack of Christian workers, a close-knit family structure and fear of offending the local god A-Ma after which the city was named. Pray for the breaking of every chain that prevents people coming to the Lord.

5 **There are a number of missionaries from Hong Kong** and other lands, most being involved in evangelism, church planting, drug rehabilitation and Bible teaching. Major missions are Brazilian and US Baptists (**IMB-SBC**) with a total of 20 workers, **YWAM** (18), **CBI** (8) and **OMF** (5). Pray for their effectiveness in this crowded, pressurised and sinful city.

6 **The less-reached**:
a) *Many mainlanders work in Macau* — some legally, many illegally. They work long hours with rare days off, but are more open to the gospel. Pray for those seeking to reach and disciple them.
b) *Those involved in the entertainment industry.* There are a few seeking to reach them. The Macau Evangelistic Band is one such.
c) *The 12,000 Chinese refugees from Myanmar.* There is one church among them (Baptist).
d) *The Macanese are mostly nominally Catholic.* There is one very small evangelical church among them, but they are largely neglected by evangelical agencies and churches.

7 **Supportive ministries**. Much literature and over 40,000 Bibles were distributed in homes in the late 1990s (**EHC**, **UBS**). Pray for lasting impact.

China, Taiwan

C

Republic of China

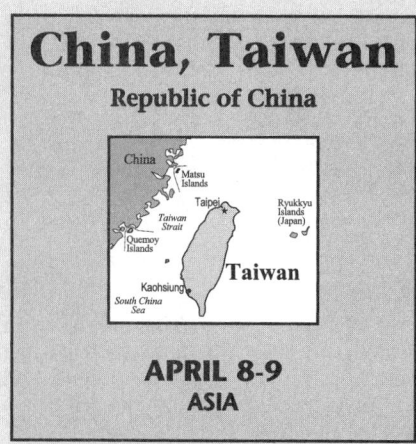

APRIL 8-9
ASIA

 GEOGRAPHY
Area 36,000 sq.km. A mountainous island 160km east of mainland China together with the Penghu archipelago and the islands of Matsu and Quemoy close to the mainland.

Population	Ann.Gr.	Density
2000	22,401,000	+0.77%	622 per sq. km.
2010	24,033,000	+0.68%	668 per sq. km.
2025	25,730,000	+0.34%	715 per sq. km.

Two million refugees from mainland China arrived 1945-1950.
Capital Taipei 7,350,000. Other major city: Kaohsiung 2,150,000. **Urbanites** 75%.

PEOPLES
Han Chinese 97.3%. Speaking 3 major languages.
Taiwanese (Hoklo, Minnan) 66.7%. Settled in Taiwan for 300 years.
Hakka 10%. Settled in Taiwan for 200 years.
Mandarin 20.6%. Refugees from mainland China 1945-50. Almost entirely urban.

Malayo-Polynesian mountain peoples 1.7%. Ten groups totalling 384,000, largest: Amis(2) 154,000; Paiwan 67,000; Tayal 54,000; Bunun 43,000; Sediq (Taroko) 33,000; Pyuma 10,000; Rukai 9,000; Yami 3,400.
Other 1%. Thai 100,000; Filipino 80,000; Westerners 25,000; Malay 11,000; Japanese 10,000.

Literacy 94%. **Official language and language of education:** Mandarin. Hoklo and Hakka are widely spoken. **All languages** 22. **Languages with Scriptures** 5Bi 6NT 3w.i.p.

ECONOMY
Rapid industrialization and economic growth to become one of the world's most dynamic export-oriented economies of the world.

Public debt none. **Income/person** $13,900 (44% of USA).

POLITICS
Under Japanese rule 1895-1945, then reverting to China. After the fall of mainland China to the Communists in 1949, Taiwan became the refuge of the Nationalist Chinese government, which claimed to represent all China. This led to international diplomatic isolation and internal political polarization between the mainlanders and many of the indigenous Taiwanese on the issue of continuing as part of greater China or as an independent nation. Taiwan was, in effect, a mainlander-dominated one-party republic until the 1987 elections. It is now a multi-party democracy. The possibility of Taiwan becoming a separate state has heightened Mainland Chinese military and diplomatic pressures on the Islanders. Taiwan remains an unresolved diplomatic 'hot potato'.

RELIGION
Secular state with freedom of religion. The great majority of the population follow the unique Chinese blend of Buddhism, Taoism and Confucianism. Buddhism has grown markedly in influence and numbers.

Religions	Population %	Adherents	Ann.Gr.
Chinese	43.21	9,679,472	-0.6%
Buddhist	25.00	5,600,250	+2.7%
non-Religious/other	25.30	5,667,500	+1.2%
Christian	6.06	1,357,501	+1.2%
Muslim	0.35	78,403	+0.2%
Traditional ethnic	0.04	9,000	-3.6%
Baha'i	0.04	8,960	+6.7%

Christians	Denom.	Affil.%	,000	Ann.Gr.
Protestant	81	1.96	438	+1.4%
Independent	33	1.67	375	+2.5%
Anglican	1	0.01	1	-1.5%
Catholic	1	1.36	304	+0.3%
Marginal	2	0.16	36	+2.9%
Unaffiliated		0.90	203	n.a.

Churches	MegaBloc	Cong.	Members	Affiliates
Catholic	C	470	167,024	304,000
Presbyterian Ch in T	P	1,220	105,000	240,000
Independent Chs	I	200	40,000	100,000
Little Flock	I	600	50,000	90,000
True Jesus Church	I	434	49,879	71,000
Local Church, The	I	33	8,000	41,000
Chinese Bapt Convention	P	128	19,463	40,000
Latter-day Saints (Morm)	M	76	17,532	27,000
Ling Leung Tang	I	35	14,000	25,000
Taiwan Holiness	P	94	11,000	22,000
China Free Methodist	P	56	5,000	17,000
Seventh-day Adventist	P	46	7,587	9,600
Zion Christian	I	25	5,000	9,000

Conservative Baptist Assoc	P	33	2,600	5,600
Christian Worship Center	I	28	4,000	5,500
Methodist Church in ROC	P	23	2,530	5,060
Fell of Chinese Covenant	P	31	3,500	5,000
Fell of Mennonite Chs	P	20	1,920	4,700
Chr & Miss Alliance	P	25	1,965	3,735
Chinese Lutheran Brethren	P	20	1,600	2,450
Other denoms [98]		972	67,000	128,000
Total Christians [118]		4,568	572,000	1,154,000

Trans-bloc Groupings	pop. %	,000	Ann.Gr.
Evangelical	2.7	604	+2.1%
Charismatic	1.1	253	+2.5%
Pentecostal	0.2	41	+2.8%

Missionaries from Taiwan
P,I,A 295 in 21 agencies to 27 countries: Taiwan 241, Hong Kong 9, Japan 9.

Missionaries to Taiwan
P,I,A 963 in 146 agencies from 26 countries: USA 463, Korea 120, Germany 33, Canada 33.

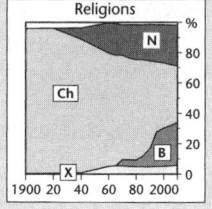

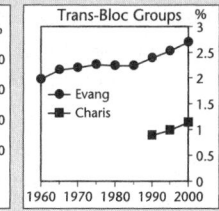

• Answers to Prayer

1 **The political survival and economic growth of Taiwan** despite diplomatic isolation in the face of Mainland China's threats and propaganda.

2 **Christian growth,** though slow, resumed in the 1990s after 30 years of stagnation and even decline in some denominations.

• Challenges for Prayer

1 **The elections in 2000** resulted in a Taiwanese majority government that openly spoke of possible independence. The great hostility of Mainland China to any change in the present ambiguous international status of the government could lead to war. Pray for wisdom and restraint for all Taiwanese, Chinese and international leaders involved.

2 **'Black gold'** is the term used for money gained through corruption fostered by many in the old regime. Pray that the new government may gain a reputation for honesty and openness.

3 **Taiwan remains the only major Han Chinese population in the world where the spiritual breakthrough has yet to come.** During the 1990s the influence of Buddhism grew markedly with a large increase in adherents (800,000 in 1983 to 4.9m in 1995). Many of their outreach techniques have been adapted from Christians. Ancestor worship is one of the major barriers to faith in Christ. Added to this is the materialism stimulated by the rapid rise of living standards. Pray that every obstacle to the reception of the gospel may be broken down.

4 **The September 1999 earthquake** left 2,400 dead, 43,000 homes destroyed and many people distressed and fearful. Pray that this and the uncertainty about the future may create a greater openness for the gospel and significant church growth. *Chinese Christian Relief Association* did much to coordinate and spearhead aid teams for the subsequent three years of rehabilitation. Pray for lasting spiritual results both among Christians and those they seek to help.

5 **The Presbyterians pioneered ministry** since 1865, but only saw significant breakthroughs among the Taiwanese in the 1930s and among the mountain people after 1940. Many other missions moved to Taiwan after the fall of the mainland to Communism, and among the 2 million mainland refugees there was a time of harvest. Between 1960 and 1990 there was stagnation. Catholics and some Protestant denominations even declined as a percentage of the national population. Only in the 1990s has some growth resumed. The major challenges to be faced by the Church are:

a) *Spiritual power* to stand against gambling, entrenched ancestor worship, rising materialism and aggressive opposition from non-Christian religions. Many Christians are still in bondage to, or in fear of, these things.

b) *Low commitment*. Too few of those converted and baptized ever become active participants in congregational life, and there is a high drop-out rate. Few Christians become soul-winners.

c) **Lack of pastors and full-time workers**. In most churches the congregation sits back expecting the pastor to do all the work.

d) **The great disparity in distribution of Christians**. The mountain peoples are largely Christian, but only 23% actively so. Nominalism is a problem. Those of **mainlander** descent are nearly 5% Christian, but the **Taiwanese** majority only 1% and the **Hakka** 0.3%. The Church needs to tackle the social and cultural barriers that hinder the progress of the gospel. The Church is perceived to be intellectual (37% of members are graduates) and not relevant to the majority.

6 **The Year 2000 Gospel Movement** (Y2GM) was formed in 1987. The vision was to: ensure church planting was initiated in every social group; renew existing churches; see 10,000 churches planted, 2 million new Christians, and 200 cross-cultural missionaries sent out, by 2000. Much was achieved, but though growth and outreach expanded, these goals were only partially realized. For the new millennium, the trans-denominational body is changing its name to the **Chinese Church Evangelistic Association**. Pray for unity, commitment and enthusiasm to see these goals accomplished.

7 **There are over 650 mountain churches** throughout the tribal areas and some in cities. Most are Presbyterian, though an increasing number are of other denominations or sectarian groups such as True Jesus and Mormons. The breakdown of tribal and family life has been hastened by alcoholism, the drift to the cities, the pervasive influence of TV, increased levels of education of young people, and inability of parents to control and raise their children in a changing society. God gave revival to the Tayal in 1973 and Amis in 1983. Pray for revival that will combat nominalism, spiritual decline and inadequate Bible teaching in these churches. Bible translation work is not yet complete — in two languages there is a definite need, and in two others a possible need, but work is in progress only in the Yami language on Orchid Island.

8 **The lack of pastors is serious,** but slowly improving. Many rural congregations in Taiwan are without pastors, the critical issue being low levels of giving in churches. There are over 33 seminaries and Bible schools, some with international acclaim, such as the China Evangelical Seminary as well as a number of TEE programmes. Pray for staff and students, and for relevant, spiritual training to be provided. There is need for good Bible teachers and effective evangelists who know their cultures and how to relate Scriptures to the root issues that hinder advance and growth.

9 **The witness among students** is important. The one million students in 141 universities and colleges are marginally more responsive. Many churches have well-used student centres. Campus Evangelical Fellowship (**IFES**) has an outreach to students with 40 full-time staff workers ministering also in secondary schools. **CCCI** also has a large campus ministry. It is now permitted to form Christian groups in some middle and high schools. Pray that this golden opportunity may be taken up and for vital, growing groups with the integration of young believers into churches.

10 **Mission vision** languished as Taiwan's diplomatic isolation increased. There has been increased interest in the 1990s. Student missions conferences have created much interest (CEF-**IFES**). The Y2GM, together with **WBT** and **OMF** have facilitated short-term mission tours. Cross-cultural training programmes have slowly increased and the number of candidates is rising, though many churches are more willing to give finances rather than their members for missions. Pray that this renewed vision might flourish.

11 **Expatriate missionary numbers** have declined, but there remain many areas of input needed — evangelism, church planting, Bible teaching, teaching English, etc. Some of the largest agencies are: **OMF** (63 workers), **YWAM** (56), **TEAM** (41), **CCCC** (39), CBI (38), **OMS** (33), **Navigators** (27), **SEND** (25), **CMA** (24), Finnish Lutheran Mission (24), **LCMS** (20), **AoG** (19).

12 **Less evangelized areas and peoples:**

a) **The Taiwanese working class** are linguistically (Hoklo/Hokkien) and culturally separated from the majority of evangelical churches which use Mandarin. They comprise 60% of the population and there are few churches or workers specifically reaching out to them.

b) **The Hakka communities** in the north-east and south-east. There is now a national group concerned for outreach: 'The World Hakka Evangelical Association'. Several missions have opened a ministry among them (**SEND**, **WEC**, **YWAM**, Presbyterians and others). There are now about 70 Hakka-speaking churches.

c) *The Muslim community* is largely Hui — originally from the Mainland and also some 11,000 Malays. There is little specific outreach to them.

d) *The Penghu Islanders* numbering 97,000. In 1964 there were 17 churches, but now two-thirds are closed. Ten thousand Vietnam Chinese have been settled on the islands.

13 Support ministries for prayer:

a) *Christian literature*. Much is now being published of both local and foreign origin. Pray for efforts by CEF(**IFES**) and others to sell Christian literature through the secular book market. **EHC** is in its fifth nation-wide distribution of evangelistic literature.

b) *Christian radio* was pioneered by the Pocket Testament League in 1951. Now much is done by the Lutherans, Baptists, **TEAM**, etc. There are also international broadcasters — both **FEBC** and **TWR** with many hours in Mandarin, and **TWR** 3.5 hrs/wk in Hakka.

c) *Christian film and video*. Most of the population have video recorders. Increasing numbers of agencies are producing good video material. The *JESUS* film has been widely used on television and film. Pray for life-changing impact.

Colombia
Republic of Colombia

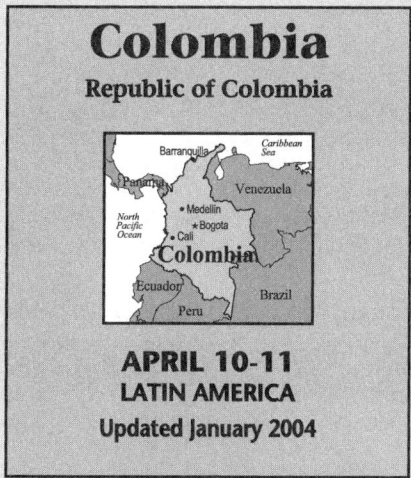

APRIL 10-11
LATIN AMERICA
Updated January 2004

GEOGRAPHY
Area 1,141,748 sq.km. Northwest corner of South America. The 4th largest country in the continent. Mountains in west, plains and forests in east.

Population		Ann.Gr.	Density
2000	42,321,361	+1.89%	37 per sq. km.
2010	49,665,304	+1.53%	43 per sq. km.
2025	59,757,874	+1.10%	52 per sq. km.

Capital Santa Fé de Bogotá 6,834,000. Other major cities: Medellín 3,831,000; Cali 2,950,000; Barranquilla 1,750,000. **Urbanites** 70%.

PEOPLES
Spanish-speaking 98.6%. Estimated composition: Mestizo (Eurindian) 57.6%; European 20%; Mulatto (Eurafrican) 14%; African 4%; Zombo (Afro-Indian) 3%.

Indigenous Amerindian 0.8% (50% of population in 1850). Still speaking 65 languages in 12 language families. Largest: Guajiro 120,000; Paez 58,000; Guahibo 22,000; Catio (Embera) 22,000.
Other 0.6%. Gypsy (3) 79,000; Arab 39,000; English-speaking 13,000; Chinese 9,000.

Literacy 70%. **Official Language** Spanish. **All languages** 77. **Languages with Scripture** 1Bi 31NT 21por 26w.i.p.

ECONOMY
Coffee and oil are the main export commodities, along with cocaine. Colombia supplies 75% of the world's cocaine. The gap between rich and poor is wide. **HDI** 0.768; 57th/174. **Public debt** 18% of GNP. **Income/person** $2,140 (7% of USA).

POLITICS
Independent of Spain in 1819 as part of Grand Colombia. A separate state in 1831. Polarization between Conservatives and Liberals has given 170 years of partisan politics, dictatorships, and civil wars. Those unrepresented by the two contending parties turned to support a variety of violent Marxist guerrilla groups. Some of the latter have aligned themselves with drug cartels who have their own terror groups, leading to a pandemic of assassinations and kidnappings. Right-wing paramilitary groups have also formed to combat the guerrillas and wage terror wars of their own. The constitution of 1991 and elections of the 1990s were aimed at ending the cycle of violence, but it was only the election of President Uribe in 2002 that has led to a more successful effort to defeat the insurgents.

RELIGION
After years of persecution of and discrimination against religious minorities, the privileged position of the Roman Catholic Church

was ended in the 1991 Constitution, which accords greater freedom to ethnic and religious minorities.

Religions	Population %	Adherents	Ann.Gr.
Christian	95.45	40,395,739	+1.7%
non-Religious	2.72	1,151,141	+6.6%
Other	0.82	347,035	+12.5%
Traditional ethnic	0.70	296,250	-0.8%
Baha'i	0.15	63,482	+6.5%
Muslim	0.11	46,553	+3.8%
Hindu	0.02	8,464	+17.0%
Jewish	0.02	8,464	-15.2%
Chinese	0.01	4,232	+1.9%

Christians	Denom.	Affil.%	,000	Ann.Gr.
Protestant	86	2.76	1,168	+6.7%
Independent	76	2.64	1,119	+8.0%
Anglican	1	0.01	4	+1.6%
Catholic	1	89.79	38,000	+1.4%
Orthodox	1	0.02	7	+0.3%
Marginal	7	1.18	498	+11.2%
Doubly affiliated		-0.95	-400	n.a.

Note: No survey of churches has been carried out for many years. Some of the statistics below are estimates.

Churches	MegaBloc	Cong.	Members	Affiliates
Catholic	C	2,700	20.106m	38.00m
Seventh-day Adventist	P	698	154,329	360,000
Jehovah's Witnesses	M	1,480	102,873	260,000
Pan-American Mission	I	470	30,000	150,000
Latter-day Saints (Morm)	M	248	86,826	145,000
NT House Churches	I	2,000	60,000	130,000
Int'l Charismatic Miss	I	1	43,333	130,000

Assemblies of God	P	523	23,243	112,294
Christian Crusade	P	250	25,000	100,000
Assoc of Interamer. Chs	P	145	30,000	90,000
Foursquare Gospel	P	1,300	40,000	75,000
Chr and Miss Alliance	P	217	22,672	72,305
Carib Assoc of Ev Chs	P	620	26,286	46,000
Colombian Bapt Conv	P	121	14,201	40,000
Assoc of Ev Chs of EC	P	120	5,200	13,000
Other denoms [158]		6,191	418,276	981,827
Doubly affiliated			-211,640	-400,000
Total Christians [173]		17,084	20.976m	40.395m

Trans-bloc Groupings	pop.%	,000	Ann.Gr.
Evangelical	4.7	1,972	+7.7%
Charismatic	17.2	7,267	+2.7%
Pentecostal	2.7	1,162	+5.6%

Missionaries from Colombia
P,I,A 286 in 33 agencies to 28 countries: Colombia 200, USA 20, Spain 12.

Missionaries to Colombia
P,I,A 820 in 84 agencies from 28 countries: USA 595, Canada 52, Australia 27.

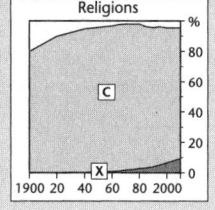

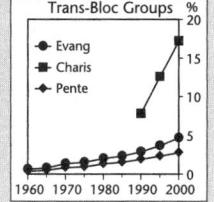

• Answers to Prayer

1 **The Church is growing rapidly** in a climate of crime, lawlessness, terror, and murder. From a tiny minority in 1960 (0.6% of the population), Evangelicals grew to nearly 5% in 2000, and Charismatics now number an estimated 17% of the population. This growth is all the more miraculous considering that Christians are often targets of drug cartels, guerrillas, paramilitaries, and others. As sin increases in Colombia, God's grace increases all the more.

2 **God is reaching the lowest and most desperate.** Bellavista Prison is a maximum security prison in Medellin that was often called "hell on earth" where the murder rate often topped one per day. Through prayer and the bold witness of some anointed believers the prison has seen a remarkable turning of the most hardened criminals to Christ. Large numbers of the inmates are now believers, and round the clock prayer chains often function. The spirit of murder has all but disappeared, and the brutal conditions improved. Now, a Bible Institute has formed in the prison, training inmates for ministry once they are released.

• Challenges for Prayer

1 **Colombia retains its reputation for being one of the most violent countries in the world.** Leftist guerrilla movements, right-wing paramiitary groups and the drug-trafficking barons control many areas of the country. Corruption, blackmail, kidnapping, assassination and revenge murders continue to brutalize society, with the abandonment of moral values and ethical standards. Pray for the political, legal and spiritual leaders of the nation — for their safety and for courage to stand up for the right. Pray that Christians may remain untainted by the evils of their society and become God's instruments for moral, social and spiritual change. Pray that the endemic fear and anger of normal Colombians may lead them to personal faith in the Lord Jesus Christ as Saviour.

2 Satan's hold on Colombia must be broken by prayer. Christ's lordship must be proclaimed over the spirits of violence, revenge, lawlessness and corruption, and occult practices that have brought the nation so low. The web that links drug barons, politicians, guerrillas, paramilitaries and Satanist groups conspires to make war upon the saints, and prevent the spread of the gospel. This usually occurs through intimidation, but often through outright destruction and murder. In 1999, over 35 pastors were killed and 300 churches forcibly closed.

3 The 1991 Constitution has brought a glimmer of hope with the opening up of the democratic process to those previously unrepresented, reforming the judicial system damaged by the violence of the drug wars, and granting greater religious freedom. Colombians are tired of violence, but all efforts to bring about peace and seek a lasting solution have failed. Evangelicals are encouraged by the freedom, opportunity and official representation that the new constitution has brought, but also fear that it may cause them to lose their cutting edge. Pray that peace may prevail, and that Evangelicals may continue their bold witness even as religious freedom increases.

4 The Roman Catholic Church has seen the changing socio-political scene radically affect its role and influence. The majority of the church is strongly traditional, but widely nominal — most Catholics never go to Mass. Pray that the dis-establishment of the Catholic Church may open the way for renewal. There is a strong charismatic element in the Church. There are also many Catholics working with the poor and speaking out against the violence, and they are likewise targets for those who hate the work of God.

5 Evangelical growth has been significant. In 1933 there were only 15,000 Evangelicals. In 2000, there were almost 2 million Protestant Evangelicals. Aggressive local, city-wide and national evangelistic outreaches have resulted in large increases in congregations and believers. In some cities church growth is occurring twenty-fold in a decade! The work of Evangelicals among the poor and disenfranchised has been a good testimony to all. But evangelical success can often make leaders targets for violence, as growing churches are seen as a threat to whatever group controls an area. Many church leaders have been martyred because of this, and many others have fled the country. Pray for solutions in:

a) The leadership crisis, which has worsened with the growth of the churches and the continued murders of leaders. There are too few deeply taught in the Word, and there have been too few examples of how to humbly lead without resorting to autocratic and humanistic methods. There are more than 20 theological training institutions, most of them packed with students, but they are desperate for qualified teachers.

b) The disunity crisis. Divisions within the Body of Christ have been a discredit to the name of the Lord and a poor witness to the government and people. Many denominations have been split over fleshly quarrels, but the first fruits of genuine unity are appearing. An Ibero-American Unity Congress in 1999 in Colombia demonstrated this, as an anointing of unity characterized the Congress. CEDECOL, the Evangelical Confederation of Colombia, is a body that links over 50 evangelical denominations and coordinates inter-church action. As Evangelicals address the great human needs in Colombia, God is knitting them together in spirit and purpose. Pray for decisive works of healing and spiritual unity.

6 Missionaries live under great stress and the constant threat of kidnapping and murder. These tragedies are all too common, often forcing withdrawal from areas controlled by leftists or drug barons. Pray for courage and faithfulness to their calling. Internal mission/church relationships have been a source of tension, division and grief in the past, but seem to be improving. Great humility and sensitivity is required in the complex ecclesiastical scene in order to have a viable, fruitful ministry. Major mission agencies: **SIL/WBT** (193), **NTM** (103), **YWAM** (77), **IMB-SBC** (42), **Brethren** (38), **AoG** (37), **TEAM** (26), **CMA** (24), **OMS** (19), ABWE (16) and **LAM** (15).

7 Colombian missionary vision still needs stimulation. Several Amerindian peoples are closed to foreigners, and too few Colombians have committed themselves to evangelize them. Pray for *Agua Viva*, a project to train Colombians to reach the Indian tribes of their own and neighboring countries. A small but growing number of Colombians have gone to other lands, but church support is limited. The Spanish edition of *Operation World* is published in Colombia. Pray for the ongoing ministry of the COMIBAM committee in inspiring Christians to be involved in mission.

8 Unreached peoples. Pray specifically for:

a) ***Less evangelized cities***. Medellín, renowned for its hardness to the gospel, is the nation's crime and narcotics capital. The city of Cali is also a special challenge for the gospel. But cooperating Evangelicals are seeing significant fruit with increased church growth as they hold prayer vigils and proclaim together Christ's lordship over these cities.

b) ***The tens of thousands of gamines***, or street urchins, of the cities. **YWAM**, **WEC** and **LAM** have ministries to them involving rescue and career training.

c) ***The urban middle class***, shrinking and crippled by political and economic crises of past years. Possibly the least responsive segment of society, they are turning to the occult in growing numbers.

d) ***The Syrian-Lebanese Muslim community***, which numbers around 15,000.

e) ***Amerindian peoples*** closed to evangelical church planters. Possibly 25-35 are in this category, including the Chami, Inga, Coreguaje, Cuiba, Desano, Epena, Huitoto, Saliba and Tucano. Almost half the indigenous tribes have not yet been reached with the gospel.

f) ***Student work*** has been slow and hard. Marxist ideology once dominated the campuses, now a post-modern approach of individualism and apathy hinders interest in serving others or seeking God. Pray for Christian students to be creative in serving and in proclaiming the gospel.

g) ***Over 1 million internally displaced refugees***, 70% of whom are women and children, victims of the faceless endemic violence. They are rootless and traumatized by the wars between the various factions, but are also open to the gospel of peace.

9 **Work among Amerindians** has been a constant struggle although the 1991 Constitution granted wide autonomy to tribes in the rain forests. Poor travel and living conditions, indifference of the people, opposition of officials and anthropologists, inter-mission rivalry and, recently, narcotics terrorists who force the Amerindians to grow cocaine and marijuana, all add to the difficulties of witness there. Despite this, there has been some response with people movements to Christ. Pray for:

a) ***Strong, viable, well-led churches***, able to cope with drug traffickers and modernization.

b) ***Church-planting ministries*** of: **NTM** (48 workers in 9 peoples); South American Mission in three northeastern peoples; **CMA** in two peoples; etc.

c) ***Bible translation***. **SIL** has 145 workers committed to 33 translation projects; a number of NTs are nearing completion. Due to the dangers, most translators live in Bogota and their language helpers commute to them — this is not conducive to translating well or quickly.

10 Support ministries:

a) ***Literature*** is an area that is increasingly important but still under-utilized, both for evangelism and for teaching believers. **CLC** has four bookstores, a wide distribution network for literature, and a growing productivity as a publisher of locally-produced Spanish titles. ***Desafío***, a **WEC** broadsheet, is used for evangelism by 50% of evangelical churches. The **Colombian Bible Society** is cooperating with various organizations to distribute Christian literature amongst the poorest and children, and has overseen large-scale distributions of hundreds of thousands of pieces of literature.

b) ***Christian radio***. Evangelicals have little access to national radio and none to TV networks. However, six evangelical broadcasters — including **HCJB** (Ecuador), **TWR** (Bonaire), and High Adventure (USA) — broadcast 686 hr/wk in Spanish. **HCJB** also broadcasts 1/2 hr/wk in the Inga Quechua language.

c) ***The JESUS film*** is available in Spanish and is being translated into 4 other languages. It is being used by 11 missions/denominations in evangelism. A large proportion of Colombians have seen this film.

Comoro Islands
Federal Islamic Republic of the Comores

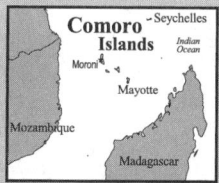

Comoro Islands — Seychelles, Indian Ocean, Moroni, Mayotte, Mozambique, Madagascar

APRIL 12
AFRICA

 GEOGRAPHY
Area 1,862 sq.km. Poor agricultural land but rich marine life in the surrounding seas. Four larger volcanic islands between Madagascar and Mozambique. The Comores declared itself independent from France in 1975, but one island voted to remain a French overseas territory. The Comores still claims Mayotte as part of its territory.

Population		Ann.Gr.	Density
2000	592,749	+2.81%	318 per sq. km.
2010	766,305	+2.49%	412 per sq. km.
2025	989,515	+1.31%	531 per sq. km.

Capital Moroni 31,187. **Urbanites** 31%.

 PEOPLES
Comorian 96.7%. Mixed Arab, African and Malagasy ancestry.
Minorities 3.3%. Makua 12,000; Malagasy 8,000; Réunionese 800; Arab 500.

Literacy 57%. **Official languages** Arabic, French. Three dialects of Comorian Swahili are widely spoken. **Languages with Scriptures** 2Bi 1NT 1por.

ECONOMY
Underdeveloped, poor and overpopu-lated. The major exports being perfumes and spices (vanilla, cloves), but the collapse of world prices for these commodities has depressed the economy. Only about 7,000 are in paid employment. **HDI** 0.506; 139th/174. **Public debt** 87% of GNP. **Income/person** $450 (1.2% of USA).

POLITICS
A one-party state until 1990, when multi-party democratic government was instituted. There have been 19 coups and attempted coups since independence, some involving foreign mercenaries and French military intervention. The two islands, Nzwani and Mwali declared themselves independent in 1997 and despite a successful military coup in 1999, abrogation of the constitution and declaration of a looser federal structure has not unified the country.

C

RELIGION
All open witness is forbidden in this Islamic state.

Religions	Population %	Adherents	Ann.Gr.
Muslim	98.07	581,309	+2.8%
non-Religious/other	1.09	6,450	+1.3%
Christian	0.84	4,979	+3.1%

Christians	Denom.	Affil.%	,000	Ann.Gr.
Protestant	4	0.14	1	+2.5%
Independent	3	0.07	0	+0.5%
Catholic	1	0.63	4	+1.8%
Marginal	1	0.00	0	+5.0%

Churches		MegaBloc	Cong.	Members	Affiliates
Catholic		C	3	2,181	3,750
Malagasy Protestant		P	2	365	730
Indigenous Comorians		I	2	100	300
Jehovah's Witnesses		M	1	10	20
Other denoms [5]			2	190	200
Total Christians [9]			10	2,846	5,000

Trans-bloc Groupings	pop.%	,000	Ann.Gr.
Evangelical	0.1	1	+1.6%
Pentecostal & Charismatic	0.1	1	+1.7%

• Challenges for Prayer

1 **Almost the entire population is Muslim.** There are 780 mosques but no official Comoran churches. They were almost completely unevangelized before 1973. Although Muslim, most are deeply involved in occult practices and spirit possession. Yet many young people are disillusioned with life in Islamic society which offers so little hope. Even today, open Christian witness is forbidden, so intercede for the opening of this land for God's Word.

2 **The quiet witness of Christian medical and veterinary workers** in the Republic and on Mayotte has won credit and public honour as well as opportunities to share the Lord Jesus with the people. Pray for continued and increased opportunities for witness and that such may bear fruit.

3 **Comoran believers** have gradually increased in number — mainly on Njazidja and Nzwani (Anjouan). They have suffered periods of harassment and persecution, and are deprived of many social and civil privileges. They need earnest prayer that they stand firm in the faith. Pray that leaders may be raised up for the several groups of believers.

4 The majority of Christians are Catholic Réunionese, Malagasy and French and some Protestant Malagasy. Pray for their tactful witness — there are severe penalties for openly distributing Bibles and Christian literature or seeking to proselytize Muslims.

Mayotte
Departmental Collectivity of Mayotte

GEOGRAPHY
Area 373 sq.km. One larger island Grande Terre and one smaller Petite Terre.

Population		Ann.Gr.	Density
2000	101,621	2.46%	272 per sq. km
2010	129,559	2.46%	347 per sq. km
2025	186,507	2.46%	500 per sq. km

Actual population in 2000 may be nearer to 145,000.

Capital Dzaoudzi 7,600. Capital designate: Mamoudzou 25,000. **Urbanites** 60%.

PEOPLES
Comorian 95.1%. shiMaore 85,000; shiBushi 42,600; Other Comorian 13,000.
Other 4.9%. French 3,000; Malagasy 1,000; Réunionese 200.

Literacy 32%. **Official languages** French; shiMaore (the local Swahili dialect) and shiBushi (a Malagasy dialect).

ECONOMY
Limited natural resources or exportable commodities, yet more prosperous than the rest of the Comores through French aid and military base. Over-population and illegal immigration from other islands hinder progress.

POLITICS
French rule is challenged by the Comoran government, but neither the local people nor the French administration have shown much enthusiasm for change, nor for welcoming back the two rebel islands of the Comores to French rule. The islanders voted to become a French Departmental Collectivity in 2000.

RELIGION
Almost all Comorans, most Africans and some Malagasy are Sunni Muslim, but mosque attendance is low.

Religions	Population %	Adherents	Ann.Gr.
Muslim	96.50	98,064	+2.4%
Christian	2.90	2,947	+3.2%
non-Religious/other	0.60	610	+6.3%

Christians	Denom.	Affil.%	,000	Ann.Gr.
Protestant	1	0.17	0	+2.4%
Independent	1	0.04	0	+15.0%
Catholic	1	1.97	2	+3.3%
Marginal	1	0.15	0	+6.1%
Unaffiliated		0.57	0	n.a.

Churches		MegaBloc	Cong.	Members	Affiliates
Catholic		C	4	1,198	2,000
Malagasy & other Prot		P	2	85	170
Other denominations [2]			1	89	188
Total Christians [4]			7	1,372	2,358

Trans-bloc Groupings	pop.%	,000	Ann.Gr.
Evangelical	0.1	0	+8.5%
Pentecostal & Charismatic	0.2	0	+3.6%

• Challenges for Prayer

1 The Muslim majority. Although there is religious freedom and direct evangelism is permitted, outreach has concentrated on the Maore and response has been slow. Pray for the barriers to come down and hearts to be opened. Pray for new initiatives planned for the unreached shiBushi speakers.

2 The change in political status in 2000 will result in massive French investment and will challenge traditional values and society. Pray that this may become a window of opportunity for the gospel, too.

3 The only organized Protestant churches in the Comores are two evangelical groups among the Malagasy on Grand Comore and Mayotte, Assemblies of God on Mayotte, and isolated Christians elsewhere. Pray for the right church-planting strategy to be applied enabling the relatively few mature Maore believers to easily integrate while retaining their cultural ties with the majority.

4 Expatriate workers — pray for their witness on Mayotte and other islands, and for an increase in their number.

5 **Support ministries** for prayer:

a) *Bible translation* continues in two languages. **AIM** workers also run a literacy programme to encourage the reading of the shiMaore NT which was completed in 1995.

b) *Radio* — **FEBA** broadcasts to the islands 10 hours/week in French and 3 in Swahili.

c) *The JESUS film* has been dubbed in shiMaore. Pray for the strategic use of this film on all four islands.

Congo

Republic of Congo [Brazzaville]

APRIL 13
AFRICA

GEOGRAPHY
Area 342,000 sq.km. Northwest of Democratic Republic of Congo (Congo-Zaire) with which it is often confused. Over 60% of the country is covered with tropical rainforest. Grasslands and bush in the north.

Population	Ann.Gr.	Density
2000	2,943,464	+2.83%	9 per sq. km.
2010	3,858,198	+2.74%	11 per sq. km.
2025	5,689,140	+2.48%	17 per sq. km.

Capital Brazzaville 1,234,000. **Other major city:** Pointe Noire 700,000. **Urbanites** 41%.

PEOPLES
Over 80 ethnic groups.
Bantu 96%. Over 55 peoples, largest: Kongo(9) 1.3 mill.; Teke(7) 454,000; Lingala 300,000; Mboshi(6) 280,000; Mbete(6) 75,000; Bangi 63,000.
Pygmy 1.5%. 5 groups: Yaka 32,000; Monzombo 8,500.
Adamawa-Ubangi 1%. 7 peoples: Ngbaka 10,000; Mbanza 10,000.
Other 1.5%. French 20,000; Hausa 10,000.

Literacy 63%. **Official language** French. **Trade languages** Lingala, Munukutuba (Kongo Creole). **All languages** 60. **Languages with Scriptures** 5Bi 3NT 10por 14w.i.p.

ECONOMY
Interior underdeveloped due to limited transportation. Rich oil and mineral deposits. Over-dependence on oil and the fall in world prices, as well as massive embezzlement of gov-

ernment funds and seven years of civil unrest and war, have reduced government spending and living standards. **HDI** 0.533; 135th/174. **Public debt** 257% of GNP. **Income/person** $670 (2.3% of USA).

POLITICS
Independent from France in 1960. A Marxist-Leninist People's Republic 1968-1991. Constitutional reform and elections in 1992 led to the ousting of President Sassou. This led to civil war and the ultimate return to power of Sassou. The capital and much of the south has been severely damaged. The involvement of foreign forces — Rwandan, Angolan, French and Congo-Zairois — has further complicated the situation.

RELIGION
During the Marxist period, the youth were heavily indoctrinated against religion, 18 denominations were banned and some missions expelled. All restrictions were removed and freedom of religion declared in 1992.

Religions	Population %	Adherents	Ann.Gr.
Christian	91.27	2,686,500	+3.5%
Traditional ethnic	4.83	142,169	-4.6%
non-Religious/other	2.16	63,578	+0.1%
Muslim	1.30	38,265	+2.8%
Baha'i	0.44	12,951	+2.1%

Christians	Denom.	Affil.%	,000	Ann.Gr.
Protestant	8	10.86	320	+1.0%
Independent	50	14.00	412	+4.8%
Catholic	1	49.31	1,451	+2.9%
Orthodox	1	0.01	0	+0.0%
Marginal	2	0.58	17	+8.1%
Unaffiliated		16.51	485	n.a.

Churches	MegaBloc	Cong.	Members	Affiliates
Catholic	C	280	843,816	1,451,364
Evangelical	P	1,800	110,000	250,000
Kimbanguist	I		89,820	150,000
New Apostolic	I	155	31,000	50,000
Salvation Army	P	154	14,000	25,000
Jehovah's Witnesses	M	96	3,850	15,000
Evang Ch of C (Likouala)	P	59	6,500	14,000
Baptist	P	108	3,904	13,000
Assemblies of God	P	70	8,500	13,000
Evang. Chr Community		10	3,500	7,000
C&MA	P	25	800	3,700
Latter-day Saints (Morm)	M	6	1,111	2,000
Other denoms [50]		156	97,241	206,600
Total Christians [62]		**2,919**	**1,214,042**	**2,201,000**

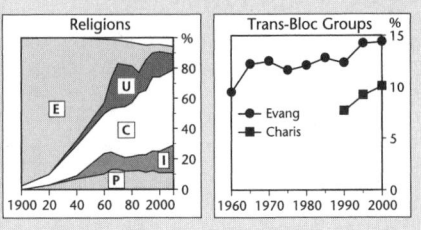

Trans-bloc Groupings pop.%	,000	Ann.Gr.
Evangelical	13.8	407	+2.5%
Charismatic	9.5	280	+4.1%
Pentecostal	0.4	13	+5.0%

Missionaries from Congo
P,I,A 30 in 4 agencies; 20 in Congo.

Missionaries to Congo
P,I,A est. 150 in 24 agencies from 19 countries: Sweden est. 60, USA 45.

• Challenges for Prayer

1 **The Congo needs peace and a government that seeks the welfare of the people**. Two decades of Communist dictatorship followed by a fragile, failing democracy and civil war have devastated the land. Six members of a team of nine church leaders seeking to mediate in 1998 were martyred. Pray for national reconciliation, the repentance and conversion of those who wreaked violence in the years of fighting, and the resettlement of the 300,000+ refugees of the civil war.

2 **Revival and restoration is the Church's need**. The massive disruption of ministry, the destruction of many churches and the flight of thousands of Christians from the cities during the war years brought discouragement, a questioning of God's presence and a feeling of abandonment. Many Christians have compromised their faith. Pray for new life, vision and trust in God. Pray also for committed Christians to be appointed to positions of national leadership.

3 **Church leadership**. Many church leaders have left the country. There had been developing cooperation between leaders of evangelical and charismatic churches just before the civil war in an attempt to heal some serious divisions within the denominations which have hindered the gospel. Pray that these hard experiences may bring about a deeper walk with God, greater unity and a passion for Christ to be formed in the lives of Congolese.

4 **Leadership training**. Pray for the full restoration of the ministry of the three Bible schools. **UWM** had a four year residential school as well as a TEE programme. **CMA** have re-launched the Bible School in Brazzaville and the **Master Life** discipleship programme in both cities has continued and grown.

5 **Young people** were denied any ministry during the Marxist days, and in subsequent years few churches developed ministries to children or youth. The GBUSC(**IFES**) had 100 meeting in 3 groups in Brazzaville and was pioneering groups elsewhere. Pray for this ministry as it becomes re-established.

6 **Mission work thrived until 1968**, but nearly all expatriates were then expelled. Some returned in the 1990s, but the civil war further complicated the full resumption of their work. Pray for the return of those best able to help the churches recover, recommence abandoned ministries and once more tackle the evangelization of every part of the country. The largest missions are the Swedish and Norwegian Mission Covenant Church working with the Evangelical Church (12), Salvation Army (8), **AoG** (8), **UWM** (6), and Global Outreach (6). A small Congo missions vision is being re-launched and there are now about 30 missionaries — 10 serving in other lands.

7 **The less reached**. The great harvest of the 1920s-60s did not reach all areas. Many of the central and northern areas are thinly populated and little evangelized. More research is needed.
a) Parts of the large group of *Teke peoples* in the centre and north are unreached.
b) *The Pygmy tribes* are semi-nomadic jungle groups who are hard to reach. Their numbers are unknown, but may be over 50,000. **UWM** started work among them in 1991 and has planted a number of churches.
c) *Other tribes* — Punu, Nzebi, Pol, Tsaangi, Pande — are believed to be unreached, but there is little information to clarify this.

Bible translation is an ongoing challenge. The Bible is available in Kongo, Lingala, Njebi, Ngbaka and Punu. **SIL** has had significant input with 19 workers involved in 5 of them and is seeking to involve and train many more Congolese in Bible translation. There is need for surveys of 33 languages for translation purposes. Pray for the completion and use of the NT in Munukutuba. Pray also that churches might catch the vision for mother-tongue Scripture use.

9 The *JESUS* film has been widely used in 4 languages, and much of the population has seen it. A further 8 languages are in production, and 4 more are to be researched.

Congo-DRC
Democratic Republic of Congo
(Formerly Zaire)

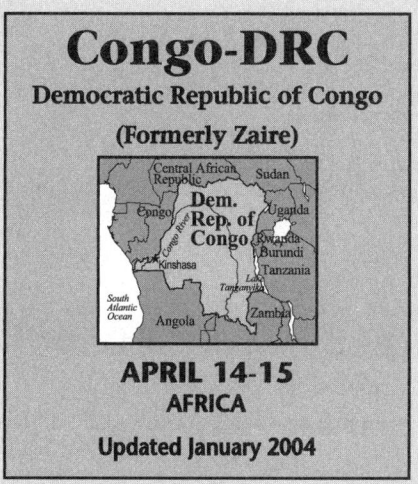

APRIL 14-15
AFRICA
Updated January 2004

GEOGRAPHY
Area 2,344,858 sq.km. Congo contains most of the Congo River system and much of the vast Central African rainforest.

Population		Ann.Gr.	Density
2000	51,654,496	+2.61%	22 per sq.km
2010	69,389,334	+2.98%	30 per sq.km
2025	104,787,601	+2.58%	45 per sq.km

Large areas are sparsely populated.

Capital Kinshasa 5,950,000. Other major cities: Lubumbashi 1,050,000; Mbuji-Mayi 1,050,000. **Urbanites** 29%.

PEOPLES
An estimated 450 ethnic and linguistic groups; numerous sub-groups.
Bantu 82.4%. Over 300 ethnic groups speaking over 150 languages in centre and south. Largest: Luba(2) 8mill.; Kongo and Kituba 7.9m; Lingala 1.9m; Tetela 1.1m; Songe 1.0m; Swahili 1.0m; Shi 980,000; Nkundu 910,000; Nandi 900,000; Yombe 780,000; Chokwe 750,000; Ngala 735,000; Lega(2) 700,000; Mongo 675,000; Phende 630,000; Haavu 595,000; Tabwa 590,000; Lala-Bisa 540,000; Banyamulenge (Tutsi living in Congo) 500,000.
Sudanic 13%. Possibly 100 peoples speaking more than 50 languages in north. Largest: Ngbaka 1.27m; Mangbetu 910,000; Lugbara 840,000; Lendu 800,000; Azande 730,000.

Nilotic 1.5%. 4 peoples in north-east. Largest: Alur 750,000.
Pygmy 0.9%. Over 450,000 in 12 peoples scattered through the country's forested regions.
Other 2.2%. Refugees from Rwanda, Burundi and Angola, Westerners, South Asians (140,000).

Literacy officially 77%. Greatly reduced by the collapse of the education system. **Official languages** French, English. **Trade languages** Lingala/Bangala in north and northwest, Swahili in east and south, Luba in centre and Kongo/Tuba in west. **All languages** 221. **Languages with Scriptures** 27Bi 10NT 40por 27w.i.p.

ECONOMY
Vast mineral resources and agricultural potential. Post-independence chaos, widespread maladministration and corruption enriched the powerful elite but impoverished the nation. The road system hardly functions and continues to deteriorate. Trade has been reduced to a trickle and profitable agricultural estates have reverted to forest. Africa's potentially most wealthy nation can no longer feed its own people, and is dependent on foreign aid. Former President Mobutu's dictatorial misrule was dedicated to plundering the nation's resources for his personal enrichment and that of the sycophants around him. This and the current wars have virtually destroyed the formal economy and the functions of state, with devastating effects on the population. **HDI** 0.479; 141st/174. **Public debt** 166% of GNP. **Income/person** $110 (0.4% of USA).

POLITICS
For centuries, Congo has suffered the depredations of Arab slavers, Western exploitation and, in recent years, exploitation by Africans. For 60 years a Belgian colony. Precipitate granting of independence to an unprepared people led to years of violence, anarchy and secessionist wars, culminating in Mobutu's military coup in 1965. Under his dictatorship, supported and condoned by the West, opposition was suppressed. Corruption spread through the whole country with Mobutu and his cronies at the apex. The Great Lakes War in Rwanda and Burundi spilled over into eastern Zaire and the area of the Banyamulenge (Tutsi) with their resentment at being denied citizenship rights in Congo. This led to Kabila's coming to power in 1997 with Rwandan and

Ugandan support. Kabila's rule was erratic and autocratic, leading to further war, invasions from Uganda and Rwanda and, ultimately, in his own murder. Kabila's regime was shored up by massive military aid from Angola, Zimbabwe, Namibia and others. Kabila was assassinated in 2001 and his son appointed in his place. The country was effectively partitioned between the Kabila faction and its allies in the west, and three or more armies in the east. For years all efforts to obtain a cease-fire and eventual peace foundered on the greed, intransigence and pride of the various nations and factions involved. Since 2002 there has been a slow wind-down of fighting, withdrawal of foreign troops and a gradual restoration of economic life.

RELIGION

In 1972 the President decreed that only six organized religions were permitted to operate and own property: Catholic; one Protestant Church (ECC), Kimbanguist Church, Orthodox, Muslims and Jews. The authenticity programme of the government between 1971 and 1978 placed controls and limitations on Christian institutions and activities. Economic disasters forced change and from 1980 onwards there has been religious freedom and a return to Christian control of a large proportion of the education and health services.

Religions	Population %	Adherents	Ann.Gr.
Christian	95.29	49,221,569	+2.7%
Traditional ethnic	2.44	1,260,370	+1.3%
Muslim	1.10	568,199	+0.8%
non-Religious/other	0.56	289,265	+1.2%
Baha'i	0.43	222,114	-0.4%
Hindu	0.18	92,978	+5.1%

Christians	Denom.	Affil.%	,000	Ann.Gr.
Protestant	102	23.77	12,280	+2.7%
Independent	106	22.17	11,450	+2.8%
Anglican	1	0.72	370	+3.6%
Catholic	1	44.53	23,000	+0.0%
Orthodox	1	0.01	5	-3.6%
Marginal	2	0.79	406	+0.7%
Unaffiliated		10.84	5,588	n.a.
Doubly affiliated		-7.55	-3,900	n.a.

Churches	MegaBloc	Cong.	Members	Affiliates
Catholic	C	14,858	13.372m	23.00m
Kimbanguist	I	14,000	3,500,000	6,500,000
New Apostolic	I	1,800	530,000	1,450,000
ECC-Presbyterian	P	525	1,001,000	1,250,000
ECC-United Methodist	P	3,750	450,000	900,000
ECC-Disciples of Christ	P	1,506	378,947	720,000
Seventh-day Adventist	P	1,200	350,000	550,000
ECC-Pentecostal ZEM	P	1,667	250,000	500,000
ECC-Baptist-River	P	229	216,538	450,000
ECC-Baptist-West	P	600	252,000	420,000
Jehovah's Witnesses	M	2,618	113,245	400,000
Anglican	A	1,000	110,000	370,000
ECC-CECCA (WEC-rel)	P	1,800	120,000	330,000
ECC-AoG,USA [2]	P	1,603	160,000	290,681
ECC-CECA (AIM-rel)	P	1,950	100,000	210,000
ECC-Evang Covenant	P	940	120,000	200,000
ECC-CMA	P	589	99,557	177,319
ECC-Baptist-Kivu	P	280	97,250	160,000
ECC-Evang Free (Ubangi)	P	1,226	114,000	160,000
ECC-Mennonite Brethren	P	400	90,000	160,000
ECC-Mennonite	P	950	100,000	140,000
ECC-Free Methodist	P	950	57,000	130,000
ECC-Ev Ch of Lubongo	P	1,054	74,850	125,000
Ch of God (Cleveland)	P	398	54,369	80,000
Other denoms [190]		21,914	3,192,757	8,860,000
Doubly affiliated			-1,950,500	-3,900,000
Total Christians [215]		77,807	22.954m	43.633m

Trans-bloc Groupings	pop.%	,000	Ann.Gr.
Evangelical	19.4	10,031	+2.7%
Charismatic	15.8	8,162	+2.1%
Pentecostal	7.9	4,098	+2.9%

Missionaries from Congo (DRC)
P,I,A estimated 445 in 39 agencies — figures much lower by 2001. About 44 outside Congo.

Missionaries to Congo (DRC)
P,I,A estimated 650 in 76 agencies from 26 countries: USA 400, UK 80, Australia 29, Nigeria 21. C 5,000.

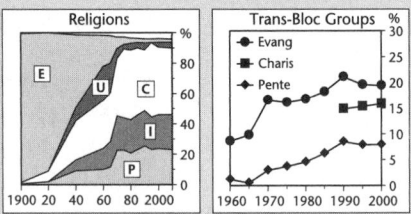

• Answers to Prayer

1 **The Church has gained in stature** as the only viable national structure to endure in the general social, political and economic collapse of the country.

2 **The turning to Christ** in the 20th Century (see graph)! The number of Christians has grown from 1.4% of the population in 1900 to over 90% professing Christianity today. Though much of this would be nominal, there have been revivals in some areas before and after independence.

3 **The many prepared to pay the price for this harvest.** Thousands of Christians and hundreds of Catholic and Protestant missionaries were martyred in the Simba Rebellion of 1964. Serving the Lord in Congo is still fraught with perils.

4 There has been a large increase in commitment to prayer, stimulated by the nation's calamities, involving millions. The result is full churches and a hunger for God.

5 The long-despised and neglected Pygmy people have turned to Christ in large numbers in some areas and during the 1990s there developed a growing self-identity and an indigenous church movement among them.

• Challenges for Prayer

1 Congo's war embroiled the military forces of seven nations and provoked the rise of local inter-ethnic conflicts and warlords. Rwanda hunted down Hutu genocidists, Uganda exploited the wealth of the north-east, Sudan sought to harm Uganda, Angola aimed to liquidate UNITA rebel bases in Congo and Zimbabwe's army was used to enrich its generals and politicians. Pray earnestly for:

a) *Peace*. Much of the country became a war zone. Nearly three million are estimated to have lost their lives through war, violence, starvation and virtual collapse of the health system. A tide of 1 to 3 million Rwandan, Burundian and Congolese refugees and rebels flowed across the land and spilled over into neighbouring countries. Pray that international efforts to broker a cease-fire and peace agreement may fully succeed despite the entrenched vested interests that profit from the conflict.

b) *The binding of the demonic powers* and the human sin that has brought such havoc and suffering through tribalism, extreme cruelty, greed and corruption — yet in a land that has such a large number of professing Christians.

c) *The establishment of an effective national government* which has the support of the people and which will rule with honesty, justice and respectful concern for the interests of the governed.

d) *Economic recovery* and wise use of finances to pay government officials, the military and police, teachers and medical workers and to rebuild the shattered national infrastructure. Without this, corruption as a way of life cannot end.

2 National and international repentance and reconciliation is essential:

a) *Arabs and Belgium's King Leopold II* enslaved and looted the country in the 19th Century. The latter's private empire in Congo probably halved the population and in 30 years led to the death of 10 million people before the Belgian government took over in 1908.

b) *Belgian colonial rule and international mining companies* exploited Congo's resources but neglected the people — most of the improvements came through extensive Protestant and Catholic efforts.

c) *Interventions by foreign powers* and, latterly, African countries often with selfish motives. The condoning of the evils of Mobutu's regime by the West is, in large part, the cause of the present chaos.

d) *Inter-ethnic hostility* has led to warfare, killings and many fleeing for their lives in Shaba in the south and the Great Lakes in the east and in the north-east during the 1990s and into the new millennium.
The evils of the past need to be admitted and put right for there to be a viable future for the Congo.

3 The Christian Church remains the only viable national social structure to survive and retain some credibility. Its role in rebuilding the nation is crucial. Most of the hospitals, clinics and schools now operate with Christian initiative. The Catholics continue to invest much into these institutions. Pray for the raising up of Christian leaders of spiritual maturity and moral integrity for both the denominations and for secular and political positions. There were many Christian leaders who compromised and lowered their standards during the manipulative dictatorship of Mobutu.

4 The Church of Christ in Congo (ECC) came into being through both government edict and pressure from some church leaders, though most evangelical leaders are now in favour of their membership in the ECC. There have been positive benefits: the divisiveness of tribalism has been diminished, unnecessary competition reduced, administration rationalized and cooperation in training schemes and media increased. However, in the new Congo, restructuring, change and renewal are imperative to face the daunting challenges of the new century. Pray for:

a) ***Biblical leadership patterns***. Centralization of leadership has sometimes harmed local congregational life and initiative, stimulated hierarchical structures, power-seeking, pride of position and misuse of funds, and compromised the Church's prophetic role. Changes must come — but may they not be at the expense of unity, fellowship and cooperation.

b) ***Commitment to the authority of Scripture***. Evangelical, liberal and even syncretistic indigenous churches were brought under the same umbrella. In early years the evangelical majority was marginalized, but this has gradually changed with strong evangelical leaders exercising a wholesome influence. Pray that spirituality and vision might increasingly characterize this composite body of 16 million Christians.

c) ***Nominal Christians*** to find new life in Christ. Nominalism has become a major problem. Large numbers have no clear grasp of repentance and faith in Christ nor of salvation by grace and not works. Much of this is due to inadequate preaching of the gospel, satisfaction with a superficial response and failure to follow-up those touched by the preaching. Animistic thought patterns, fear of witchcraft and syncretism are also major problems. Pray that believers may recognize their inheritance in Christ and confront the forces of darkness in the power of the Spirit.

d) ***Freedom to evangelize every part of Congo***. Colonial comity agreements and the formation of the ECC imposed rigid geographical boundaries on any outreach activity. This stifled zeal, left many areas devoid of an evangelical witness and hindered cross-cultural outreach. Some freedom has come — especially in the towns and cities. Pray that every part of the country may be adequately evangelized.

5 **Vision for the future.** The work of the Holy Spirit in some areas has led to increased love for God's Word, prayer movements, mobilization of youth and a new indigenous hymnody. Pray that this may result in vision for outreach and that conditions may improve to allow this. ECC leaders have bold goals for 2010 — training in evangelism and outreach, extensive use of river boats for outreach, etc.

6 **Leadership training** at every level must be a priority.

a) ***Lay leadership*** was neglected for years, and TEE programmes were few and localized. A change came with the launch of the Portable Bible Schools movement which began in 1987. Two-month intensive training courses for lay leaders and sending them out as church planters to unchurched villages has led to many new churches being planted. Pray for this vision to be implemented throughout the country.

b) ***Bible schools abound***. There are large numbers of primary local-language and trade-language Bible schools, and a smaller number of French ones. They often function with slender resources and provide training not always adequately directed towards preparation for the ministry goals envisaged. Pray that spiritual, material and teaching content may be constantly improved.

c) ***The higher-level institutions*** need prayer support. Some important ones are: *Institut Supérieur de Théologie* in Kinshasa, the *Institut Supérieur Théologique de Bunia* as well as several denominational schools. These are strategic for the provision of a new generation of well-educated pastors and leaders. Pray that such evangelical institutions may mature theologically and be able to stand firmly for the truth of the gospel in the face of doctrinal challenges. Pray too for imaginative and appropriate means to maintain themselves financially and so avoid over-dependence on foreign support.

7 **Sectors of society needing the gospel:**

a) ***Rural villages***. The shocking realization that villages with a resident Protestant pastor had been reduced from 50% of the total (in 1960) to 15% in 1985 has provoked a re-evaluation of church planting. At that stage, 18 million people lived in villages without a functioning church. The Portable Bible Schools movement helped to change this, with 25,000 lay church planters trained for church planting in the 60,000 pastor-less villages. Many new churches were planted by the 25 ECC communities involved, but there remains much to be done.

b) ***Young people***. Ministries to them are limited by lack of funding, skills and the difficulty of travel. Pray for:

i *The school system* — in many areas it is in a state of near-collapse. This, and lack of employment, has blighted the future for a whole generation of young people. Pray that the churches may use the immense opportunities for the gospel in the large number of church-run schools and that godly teachers may be raised up.

ii University students. Both **CCCI** and GBU(**IFES**) have ministry in 8 cities. The GBU is the largest in Francophone Africa.

iii Street children. They have multiplied in Kinshasa — many because of broken homes, AIDS or being wrongly accused of witchcraft.

c) The Kimbanguist Church — one of the largest indigenous African bodies with 6 — 8 million followers. This messianic, millenarian body has gained a measure of international recognition and some sections are moving to a more biblical faith. There remain significant problems in their theology and practice at a popular level where Kimbangu, the founder, is revered as the Holy Spirit or seen as a visible image of Christ. Pray for the enlightenment of this Church through biblical truth, and pray for wisdom for those called to minister to them.

d) Those affected by the AIDS pandemic. The official figures give 1.1 million as infected with 680,000 orphaned. The likely figure is far higher because of huge movements of refugees, warring armies, and lack of medical facilities. Over 20% of Kinshasa's population is infected, and all over the country the death rate is rising. Pray that churches may rise to the challenge of living and preaching biblical morality before and in marriage and may give appropriate help to the victims. **EHC** has developed effective Christian literature to address this crisis.

e) The intellectuals and the wealthy elite, predominantly in Kinshasa. Many were enriched through links with Mobutu. Few have meaningful contact with the gospel or the real world of suffering on their doorsteps.

f) The vast swamplands north-east of Kinshasa, which are sparsely populated and underevangelized. Many other similar pockets of neglect exist. Pray for more concerted research in locating these areas, and for church planting to be initiated.

g) The Swahili-speaking Muslim communities (500,000) in eastern towns, Kinshasa and along the eastern border. There is little outreach to them. There is a considerable missionary effort by Muslims to spread Islam.

h) The peoples who have been less responsive, and have a high proportion of non-Christians: Hunde 200,000; Bira(2) 160,000; Lega(2) 700,000; Kuba 28,000; Nyanga 45,000.

8 **The Pygmy peoples** have long been despised and humiliated by Congolese and largely neglected by indigenous denominations, yet about 30% are nominally Christian. As a result of the activities of expatriate agencies (Baptists, the **EHC** 'Every Tree Campaign') and indigenous bodies such as **Evangelism Resources** and *Mission Évangélique du Pygmée en Afrique*, this work has grown and spread with many coming to Christ. Pray for the maturing of this movement, provision of adequate, spiritual leadership and the emergence of a truly indigenous Pygmy Church.

9 **Missionary involvement has been drastically reduced** because of war and the breakdown of the communications network. Nearly all mission agencies are, to a great measure, highly integrated into their daughter indigenous movements and churches. A new generation of expatriate workers is needed to supplement what is lacking — especially in discipleship and leadership training, specialized and media ministries. Pray for their:

a) Wise deployment and the most effective use of their gifts.

b) Harmonious and effective partnering between nationals and expatriates.

c) Safety. Lawlessness and violence have increased as the economic situation has declined. There have been several evacuations of missionaries from whole regions since 1991 — a salutary reminder of the importance of the Church standing on its own feet. Pray that workers have peace in the midst of such uncertainties.

d) Provision of supplies and wisdom in their use when so much needs to be done.

e) Development of the right strategies for mission agencies with particular emphasis on moving the Church towards maturity and concern for the unreached. Major mission agencies with commitment of personnel: **CCCI** (159), **WBT** (60), CCCC (48), Brethren (42), **CMS** (38), Evangelical Free Church (35), **AIM** (31), United Methodists (25), SdA (22), **AoG** (17), **CMA** (16), CBI (14), **UFM** (13), **BMS** (10), **WEC** (5). **Note**: Actual deployment is much lower due to the war. Many are based outside of Congo (DRC).

10 **Christian help ministries** will be essential for some time to come because of the large-scale looting, destruction and impoverishment of the 1990s. The government nationalization of hospitals and schools in the 1970s was a disaster. Churches and missions are struggling to restore them but the demands in funding and personnel are staggering. Pray specifically for:

a) *Health Services*. There are a number of major and smaller hospitals run by different communities/missions such as **BMS**, ABFMS and **CMA**. One such is the inter-community/mission hospital at Nyankunde in the north-east (**AIM**, **Brethren**, **AoG**, **UFM**, **WEC** and others are involved in this ministry). Expatriate personnel are in constant demand.

b) *Education*. Many of the better schools are church-run. The Catholics have made an enormous effort in this field. Protestants are under much pressure to do the same, but resources are limited, and committed Christian staff hard to find and retain. Pray that the educational system may also produce fine Christian leaders for the future.

c) *Transportation*. The war, looting and other dangers have resulted in a breakdown in surface transportation and in restrictions to the 7 agencies (including **MAF**) with flying programmes. Pray for resumption of abandoned flight routes where appropriate, safety in flying over trackless forests, provision of fuel, finance and personnel.

11 **Bible translation** is a major unfinished task. The profusion of languages led to an emphasis on trade-language evangelism which limited gospel penetration and stunted the development of indigenous Christian lifestyles, music and worship.

a) *At least 30 and possibly 147 languages* are in need of translation programmes by Congolese and/or expatriate believers.

b) *Research into the needs for translation is still required*. **SIL** is involved in 17 translation projects mostly in an advisory or consultancy capacity.

12 **Christian media.** All ministries have been cut back or even crippled by Congo's woes. Pray for the resumption or growth of:

a) *Christian literature publishing and distribution*. There is a famine of contextually appropriate and helpful literature. Distribution and poverty are enormous problems. **EHC** has had a wide impact — by 1997 4.5 million pieces of evangelistic literature prompted 1.9 million enquiries.

b) *The JESUS film* has been viewed by much of the population in many areas. It is available in 19 languages, and a further 56 are in production.

c) *GRN* has messages available in 286 languages and dialects — a valuable resource in this land of many languages.

d) *Christian radio's* importance has been enhanced as communication systems broke down. There are significant radio ministries based in Bunia, Bukavu, Kindu, Katanga, Goma and the much-appreciated *Sango Malamu* with a massive following in the Kinshasa area. **TWR** have broadcasts in French and Lingala from Swaziland.

Cook Islands

South Pacific Ocean

Cook Islands

★ Avarua

APRIL 16
PACIFIC

Updated January 2004

The Cook Islands, Niue, Tokelau and Pitcairn are all officially, or unofficially in the case of the latter, related to New Zealand. None are independent states. All have seen a large part of their populations move to New Zealand or Australia.

 GEOGRAPHY
Area 236 sq.km. Over 100 coral atolls and volcanic islands 3,500 km northeast of New Zealand, 15 of which are inhabited.

Population		Ann.Gr.	Density
2000	19,522	+0.65%	83 per sq. km.
2010	20,968	+0.74%	89 per sq. km.
2025	23,736	+0.88%	101 per sq. km.

Capital Avarua 11,675. **Urbanites** 60%.

PEOPLES
Polynesian 81.6%.
Euronesian 15.4%.
European 2.4%.
Other 0.6%.

Literacy 92%. **Official languages** English, Cook Island Maori. **All languages** 5. **Languages with Scriptures** 1Bi 1NT 1w.i.p.

 POLITICS
Self-governing democracy in free association with New Zealand.

RELIGION
Freedom of religion.

Religions	Population %	Adherents	Ann.Gr.
Christian	98.00	19,132	+0.6%
Baha'i	1.00	195	+5.2%
non-Religious/other	1.00	195	+5.2%

Christians	Denom.	Affil.%	,000	Ann.Gr.
Protestant	5	66.00	13	-0.4%
Independent	1	0.77	0	+0.0%
Anglican	1	0.51	0	-9.0%
Catholic	1	18.70	4	+1.3%
Marginal	2	8.71	2	+4.9%
Unaffiliated		3.31	1	n.a.

Churches	MegaBloc	Cong.	Members	Affiliates
Cook Islands Christian	P	76	8,000	10,800
Catholic	C	16	1,825	3,650
Seventh-day Adventist	P	15	700	1,400
Latter-day Saints (Morm)	M	10	719	1,200
Assemblies of God	P	2	290	580
Jehovah's Witnesses	M	5	170	500
Other denominations [4]		5	187	355
Total Christians [10]		129	11,891	18,485

Trans-bloc Groupings	pop. %	,000	Ann.Gr.
Evangelical	12.1	2	+0.0%
Charismatic	5.3	1	+0.6%
Pentecostal	3.3	1	+0.9%

Missionaries from the Cook Islands
P,I,A 7 in 2 agencies — 6 in other lands.

Missionaries to the Cook Islands
P,I,A 4 in 3 agencies.
C 9.

Niue

 **GEOGRAPHY**
Area 258 sq.km. The world's largest coral island.

Population		Ann.Gr.	Density
2000	1,876	-1.86%	7 per sq. km.
2010	1,621	-1.32%	6 per sq. km.
2025	1,442	-0.51%	6 per sq. km.

Capital Alofi 1,100.

 PEOPLES
Polynesian 90%. Niueans 1,700.
Other 10%. Samoans, Tongans, Europeans.

Literacy 99%. **Official languages** Niuean, English. **Languages with Scriptures** 2Bi.

 ECONOMY
Aid, remittances from Niueans abroad, Internet earnings and a growing tourist industry.

 POLITICS
Self governing democracy in free association with New Zealand.

 RELIGION
Freedom of religion

Religions	Population %	Adherents	Ann.Gr.
Christian	94.88	1,780	-1.9%
non-Religious/other	4.05	76	-1.5%
Baha'i	1.07	20	-1.0%

Christians	Denom.	Affil.%	,000	Ann.Gr.
Protestant	2	59.17	1	-35.5%
Independent	2	6.40	0	+18.3%
Anglican	1	2.13	0	+0.0%
Catholic	1	4.80	0	-1.1%
Marginal	2	21.32	0	-0.5%
Unaffiliated		1.06	0	n.a.

Churches	MegaBloc	Cong.	Members	Affiliates
Niue Christian	P	16	262	1,050
Latter-day Saints (Morm)	M	7	117	260
Jehovah's Witnesses	M	1	55	140
Catholic	C	1	41	90
Other denominations [4]		4	112	220
Total Christians [8]		29	587	1,760

Trans-bloc Groupings	pop. %	,000	Ann.Gr.
Evangelical	8.5	0	+1.9%
Pentecostal & Charismatic	8.1	0	+9.2%

Pitcairn Island

Pitcairn is one of the smallest (4.7 sq.km and 49 people) and most isolated territories in the world. It is Britain's last colonial possession in the Pacific; but administered from New Zealand. It is famous for its settlement by mutineers from the British ship, the Bounty, in 1790. All are Seventh-day Adventists. Its economy is dependent on the sale of postage stamps. A serious charge of child abuse led to a New Zealand court case in 2003 and threatens the viability and even continuance of this tiny community.

Tokelau Islands

POLITICS
An external territory of New Zealand.

RELIGION
Freedom of religion.

Religions	Population %	Adherents	Ann.Gr.
Christian	99.00	1,485	+0.0%
Baha'i	1.00	15	+0.0%

Christians	Denom.	Affil.%	,000	Ann.Gr.
Protestant	2	65.33	1	+0.3%
Catholic	1	32.00	0	-0.8%
Marginal	1	0.33	0	+0.0%
Unaffiliated		1.30	0	n.a.

Churches	MegaBloc	Cong.	Members	Affiliates
Congregational	P	6	380	950
Catholic	C	2	240	480
Other denominations [2]		2	18	35
Total Christians [4]		10	638	1,465

Trans-bloc Groupings	pop.%	,000	Ann.Gr.
Evangelical	3.7	0	+0.0%
Charismatic	0.9	0	+0.0%

GEOGRAPHY
Area 12 sq.km. Three infertile coral atolls 480 km north of Samoa.

Population	Ann.Gr.	Density
2000	1,500	+0.00%	125 per sq. km.
2010	1,500	+0.00%	125 per sq. km.
2025	1,500	+0.00%	125 per sq. km.

PEOPLES
Polynesian 98%. **Other** 2%.

Literacy 99%. **Official language** Tokelauan (close to Samoan).

ECONOMY
Dependent on aid, remittances from Tokelauans abroad and sale of postage stamps.

• Challenges for Prayer

1 **Christian influence has been strong for 150 years.** The integration of secular and religious leadership created what are virtually theocratic states. Church attendance is high, but few have assurance of salvation.

2 **Many smaller islands have no known evangelical witness**. There are Evangelicals in several **AoG** churches and small groups within the older churches. Pray for a new infusion of spiritual life.

3 **Niue has become valuable cyber-territory for web sites** because of its '.nu' address. It has become a money magnet for Japanese telephone pornography, internet gambling and Russian money launderers. Pray against these global evils, the neutralization of their corrupting influence and for God to judge their criminal perpetrators.

4 **Migration to New Zealand for employment** has given another means of bringing new life into the islands. Eighty per cent of Niueans, 70% of Tokelauans and over 60% of Cook Islanders now live in New Zealand. Pray for the Island churches in Auckland and other New Zealand cities. Blessing there will affect the islands.

Costa Rica
Republic of Costa Rica

APRIL 17
LATIN AMERICA

GEOGRAPHY
Area 51,100 sq.km. Rich agricultural land straddling the Central American isthmus.

Population	Ann.Gr.	Density
2000	4,023,422	+2.51%	79 per sq. km.
2010	4,856,685	+1.75%	95 per sq. km.
2025	5,928,508	+1.18%	116 per sq. km.

Capital San José 1,063,000. **Urbanites** 44%.

PEOPLES
Spanish-speaking 94.8%. Caucasian 3.2 million; Mestizo 300,000.
English-speaking 2.5%. Afro-Caribbean 120,000.
Amerindian 0.7%. Eight peoples, only four still use their indigenous languages: Bribri 7,700; Cabecar 10,700; Guaymi 1,900; Maleku 500.
Other 2%. Chinese(4) 66,000; Europeans 23,000.
Refugees More than 600,000 Nicaraguans resident or working in Costa Rica.

Literacy 93%. **Official language** Spanish. English and Mekitelyu spoken on Caribbean coast. **All languages** 10. **Languages with Scriptures** 2Bi 5NT 6por.

ECONOMY
Decline between 1979-88, some recovery since then but 20% still live in deep poverty.

Main exports are bananas, coffee and textiles. Tourism is also important. A leading country for ecological conservation. **Unemployment** 6.2%. **HDI** 0.801; 45th/174. **Public debt** 30.6% of GNP. **Income/person** $2,640 (8.5% of USA).

POLITICS
Independent of Spain in 1821. A long history of stable, multi-party democratic government. Costa Rica has exercised a stabilizing influence in the conflicts of surrounding lands.

RELIGION
Roman Catholicism is the official state religion and all limitations on the free exercise of other religions are illegal, but in practice other religions are not yet equal before the law.

Religions	Population %	Adherents	Ann.Gr.
Christian	94.70	3,810,181	+2.4%
Chinese	2.24	90,125	+5.9%
non-Religious/other	1.73	69,605	+3.5%
Traditional ethnic	0.83	33,394	+6.1%
Baha'i	0.29	11,668	+2.5%
Jewish	0.11	4,426	+4.5%
Buddhist	0.10	4,023	+2.5%

Christians	Denom.	Affil.%	,000	Ann.Gr.
Protestant	70	9.73	392	+12.4%
Independent	65	3.51	141	+6.3%
Anglican	1	0.03	1	-4.1%
Catholic	1	73.99	2,977	+1.2%
Marginal	10	2.60	105	+4.0%
Unaffiliated		7.31	294	n.a.
Doubly affiliated		*-2.47*	*-100*	*n.a.*

Churches	MegaBloc	Cong.	Members	Affiliates
Catholic	C	250	1,575,132	2,977,000
Assemblies of God	P	224	30,300	85,000
Seventh-day Adventist	P	90	31,350	62,700
Jehovah's Witnesses	M	232	20,000	52,600
Ch of God (Cleveland)	P	450	19,302	38,000
Latter-day Saints (Morm)	M	132	22,449	33,000
Assoc of Bible Chs	P	134	8,772	18,000
Baptist Bible Fell	P	30	5,169	15,000
Foursquare Gospel	P	77	4,776	12,000
Evang Assoc of C Amer	P	69	5,923	11,850

Pentecostal Holiness	P	76	5,800	11,700
Methodist	P	70	6,300	11,500
Churches of Christ [3]	P	56	5,600	11,200
Council of Nat'l Ev Chs	I	41	4,100	8,200
Baptist Convention	P	45	3.545	6,000
Ch of the Nazarene	P	33	2,006	4,000
Other denominations [130]		1,611	132,303	258,000
Doubly affiliated			-52,910	-100,000
Total Christians [148]		3,895	1,825,000	3,516,000

Trans-bloc Groupings	pop.%	,000	Ann.Gr.
Evangelical	12.4	500	+10.3%
Charismatic	18.6	750	+6.0%
Pentecostal	7.0	281	+13.2%

Missionaries from Costa Rica
P,I,A 331 in 32 agencies to 27 countries: Costa Rica 120, Middle East 30, USA 20, Mali 18.

Missionaries to Costa Rica
P,I,A 433 in 73 agencies from 20 countries: USA 342, Canada 20.

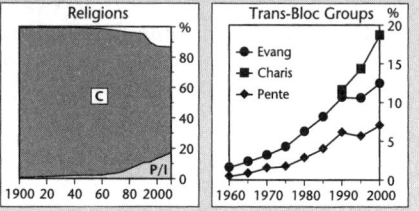

• Answers to Prayer

1 **Between 1970 and 1988 there was dramatic growth of Evangelicals** from 3% to 11%. After problems, growth has resumed — some reckon 16% to be Evangelicals. From this revival was birthed one of Latin America's most effective foreign missions advance.

• Challenges for Prayer

1 **The tragic and sudden halt to evangelical church growth** in 1988 led to a decade of little progress. There are now numerous unattached Evangelicals (6% of the population) and many more ex-Evangelicals who have returned to the Catholic Church, turned to sects or given up on Christianity. The causes need to be turned into prayer fuel.

a) ***Denominational rivalry and acrimonious divisions*** disillusioned many. Pray for love, humility and oneness in the Spirit to characterize the leadership in churches.

b) ***Inflexible sub-cultures and petty legalisms*** discouraged many new Christians and seekers. Pray for revival.

c) ***Secularism, materialism, post-modern and New Age mindsets*** are sapping the vitality of urban congregations.

d) ***The moral failure of evangelical leaders*** — both internationally known US televangelists and Costa Rican pastors. The challenge is to restore both holy living and credibility to the cause of Christ.

2 **The Roman Catholic Church** has been deeply impacted by charismatic renewal. Many came to a living, personal faith in Christ. On the one hand, attendance at mass and the number of indigenous seminarians and priests has increased. On the other hand large numbers left the Church for evangelical groups. Pray that charismatic Catholics may be able to inject greater spirituality through their 're-evangelization' programme. The great majority of Costa Ricans remain very nominal in their faith and in spiritual need — immorality, alcoholism and spiritist practices are widespread.

3 The signs of hope are:

a) ***Increased cooperative efforts for outreach and mission*** despite lingering hesitations on the part of some Evangelicals. The Costa Rican Evangelical Alliance, representing the majority of denominations has initiated a programme 'Costa Rica Century XXI' for promoting the development of churches at every level. Pray for a cutting edge to this vision, and for the leaders of this ambitious programme.

b) ***Improved leadership training***. There are 26 Bible schools and seminaries and an extensive TEE programme. IMDELA (Missiological Institute of the Americas) has opened a residential and extension programme in missions. Pray that there might be a new generation of godly, effective leaders for the churches that will commend the gospel.

4 Special evangelistic challenges:

a) ***Students*** have proved less responsive to the gospel, and drug addiction has become a serious problem. Christian student leadership has been weak in the past. There is a growing national student movement linked with ECU(**IFES**), *Alfa y Omega* (**CCCI**), Maranatha (a Pentecostal student work) and others.

b) ***All Amerindian tribes*** are being evangelized but most are either nominally Catholic or animist. There is, however, a vocal, syncretistic, indigenous church among the Cabécar, and evangelical missionary input to the Boruca, Bribri, Guaymi and Maleku. Pray that truly indigenous churches using their mother tongues may be established.

c) ***Chinese*** have increased in numbers, many immigrating from Taiwan and mainland China. Some have become Catholic, and there are now a few Evangelicals in three small groups. The Chinese Christian Mission started a work among them in 1985. Pray that cultural and spiritual barriers to faith may be broken down and churches multiply among them.

d) ***The Mekitelyu Afro-Caribbean*** community on the Caribbean coast is nominally Protestant, but few people have a vital, life-affecting faith in Christ. Pray for ongoing evangelistic campaigns and that these may result in Mekitelyu-speaking congregations.

e) ***Muslim immigrants*** are few, but increasing. Mainly Arab, Iranian and South Asian.

5 **The Federation of Evangelical Missions of Costa Rica** has become a shining example of God's grace in envisioning the Church for world evangelization. **Alcance 2000** was a vision to mobilize 12,000 prayer warriors, target 50 unreached peoples around the world and send out 500 cross-cultural missionaries. Over eight years the number of Costa Rican missionaries doubled to more than 260 in 1997. Pray for the growth and maturity of this movement.

6 **Missions.** The largest agencies are **LAM** (81), **IMB-SBC** (36), **AoG** (31), **YWAM** (28), **CoN** (26), **CRWM** (19), **CAM** (19). The stability of the country has made this a good base for many regional and global ministries. Pray for cooperation and close fellowship between agencies, as there is a frustrating duplication of effort and a dominance of North Americans in many supportive agencies. Visas are becoming more difficult to obtain.

7 **Christian help ministries:**

a) ***Radio and TV.*** There are four Christian radio and two TV stations; other secular stations air Christian programmes. Pray that efforts to restrict this ministry may fail. Also pray that broadcasts may lead to conversion among the unsaved and growth among the Christians.

b) ***LAM's 'Christ for the City' vision.*** This has resulted in short-term team ministry abroad, and in child care clinics and outreach to shanty towns at home.

c) ***The Bible Society.*** Demand for Scriptures is strong and growing. Pray that no opposition may succeed in preventing the distribution of Scriptures.

d) ***The Spanish Language Institute*** where many missionaries learn Spanish. Pray for staff and missionary students.

Côte d'Ivoire
Republic of Côte d'Ivoire

APRIL 18
AFRICA
Updated January 2004

GEOGRAPHY
Area 320,763 sq.km. On the West African coast between Ghana and Liberia. Rain forest in the south and savannah/highlands in the north.

Population	Ann.Gr.	Density
2000	14,785,832	+1.79%	46 per sq. km.
2010	18,200,343	+2.07%	57 per sq. km.
2025	23,345,116	+1.37%	73 per sq. km.

There has been a massive influx from surrounding lands, especially Burkina Faso and Mali over recent years.

Capital Yamoussoukro 166,800. Other major city: Abidjan 3,850,000. **Urbanites** 42.5%.

PEOPLES
Akan 31%. 18 groups: Baoulé 2.93 million; the dominant people today. Lagoon peoples (14) 735,000; Agni 790,000.
Gur 13%. 37 groups: Senufo (32 dialects) 1.2m; Kulango 293,000; Lobi 287,000.
Mande 12%. 9 groups: Jula 841,000; Malinke 758,000; Bambara 264,000; Mahou 192,000; Taguana 182,500; Koyaka 160,500.
Kru 9%. 24 groups: Bété 591,000; Guéré 368,000; Dida(2) 216,000; Wobe 180,000.
South Mande 7%. 9 groups: Yakuba 875,000; Gouro 414,700.
Foreign Africans 27%. Burkinabé 2.39m (of which Mossi 1.06m); Malian 848,600; Guinean 246,800; Ghanaian 142,000.
Other 1%. Lebanese 50,000; French 19,400.

Literacy 42.4%. **Official language** French, used by a high proportion of the population. Jula a trade language in the north and Abidjan. **All languages** 75. **Languages with Scriptures** 4Bi 21NT 21por 23w.i.p.

ECONOMY
One of the world's largest producers of cocoa, coffee and palm oil. Post-independence boom produced both massive immigration of job-seekers from surrounding lands and a high level of corruption. A political coup in December 1999

caused a sharp downturn in the economy as capital inflows dropped. Many businesses have since left the country. Civil servants have received no cost of living salary raise in over 18 years. The economic stability of the country has been essential for the whole region, but this is threatened by political unrest. **HDI** 0.422; 154th/173. **Public debt** 100% of GNP. **Income/person** $710 (2.2% of USA).

POLITICS
Independent from France in 1960. Formerly a one-party presidential government under Houphouet-Boigny, who died in 1993. His elected successor was deposed and fled the country during a coup at Christmas 1999. The military-led transitional government oversaw a new constitution and elections in 2000. These were characterized by politicized ethnic and religious tensions, as indigenous Ivorians seek to prevent political takeover by the growing immigrant – and largely Muslim – peoples from Burkina Faso and Mali. Civil war broke out in 2002 with an attempted Islamist-supported coup followed by an uneasy cease-fire and attempts at negotiating a settlement.

RELIGION
Religious freedom. The government remains sympathetic to missions. Traditional religions are generally stronger in the centre and west. Islam (Sunni) is strong in the northwest and Abidjan. Both Islam and Christianity are highly syncretized with African traditional beliefs, making these three religions impossible to precisely enumerate. Islamism has steadily gained in influence.

Religions	Population %	Adherents	Ann.Gr.
Muslim	38.60	5,707,331	+3.3%
Christian	31.78	4,698,937	+3.7%
Traditional ethnic	29.07	4,298,241	-1.7%
non-Religious	0.25	36,965	+1.8%
Baha'i	0.20	29,572	+1.8%
Hindu	0.10	14,786	+1.8%

Christians	Denom.	Affil.%	,000	Ann.Gr.
Protestant	35	8.69	1,284	+14.5%
Independent	148	7.62	1,126	+2.6%
Catholic	1	14.20	2,100	+2.3%
Orthodox	1	0.20	29	+3.9%
Marginal	2	0.17	25	+8.7%
Unaffiliated		0.90	133	n.a.

Churches	Megabloc	Cong.	Members	Affiliates
Catholic	C	225	1,220,930	2,100,000
Assemblies of God	P	800	300,000	500,000
Prot Ch of Central CI	P	1,617	116,671	330,000
Eglise Harriste		330	66,007	200,000
Union Eg Ev du S.O. (UFM)	P	1,136	50,000	166,500
Protestant Methodist	P	943	68,868	146,000
Ashes of Purification	I	808	80,838	135,000
Les Eglises "Reveille" [4]	I	500	50,000	75,000
Oeuvre Missionnaire	I	600	30,000	60,000
All. of Ev Chs (AEECI)	P	210	20,000	35,000
Orthodox	O		17,365	29,000
Seventh-day Adventist	P	37	6,243	20,602

Jehovah's Witnesses	M	184	6,800	19,448	
Baptist Convention	P	191	10,000	15,000	
Northern Baptist	P	260	5,200	13,000	
Other denoms [169]		982	294,140	719,601	
Total Christians [187]		8,823	2,343,062	4,564,151	

Trans-bloc Groupings	**pop.%**	**,000**	**Ann.Gr.**
Evangelical	9.2	1,363	+14.3%
Charismatic	6.0	883	+17.0%
Pentecostal	4.5	663	+21.7%

Missionaries from Côte d'Ivoire
P,I,A 57 in 11 agencies to 11 countries: C.I. 33, Togo 6, Mali 4, Niger 4.

Missionaries to Côte d'Ivoire
P,I,A 1,109 in 73 agencies from 31 countries: USA 490, Liberia 177, UK 70, Canada 45, Ghana 31, Nigeria 24.

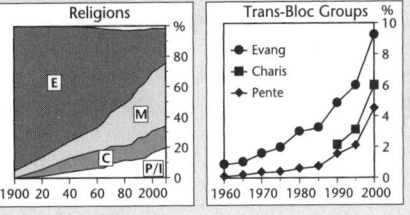

• Answers to Prayer

1 **The rapid growth that has taken place in evangelical churches.** Believers have almost doubled since 1990. Recent research has shown that there are more than 700 Protestant/Independent churches in Abidjan, a massive increase from 1990.

2 **Denominations are beginning to work together more.** This has largely come as a response to the nation's troubles — such as the interdenominational prayer concerts in several cities. Events like the *March for Jesus* and the visits of **OM/YWAM** ships have brought together thousands from many denominations.

• Challenges for Prayer

NOTE Jan 2004: The civil war of 2002 has further polarized the country, with some killings of Christians, burning of churches and limitation of Christian witness in the centre and north. Pray for peace, equitable government and the discrediting of the violent policies of the Islamists.

1 **The Catholic Church has made a deep impact** through an extensive educational system. Many Ivoirians are nominally Catholic as a result. Catholics are a large minority in the south and among the upper and middle classes. The lack is a personal relationship with the Saviour. A charismatic movement is well established in the Catholic Church.

2 **Spiritism is still strong in Côte d'Ivoire,** despite apparent numerical decline. There are 4000 evangelical churches, but 5000 sacred fetish groves. Many Christians are still affected by the power of spiritism and fetishes, compromising both their witness and their own life in Christ. Pray that all who have not fully left behind their spiritist past might be completely delivered by the power of Jesus. Pray that believers might withstand temptation to revert to old practices.

3 **Pray for unity and cooperation among Evangelicals.** If the country is to be effectively evangelized and the church to mature, then denominational differences and competition must be set aside in favour of partnerships and teamwork.
a) *The Federation of Evangelical Churches*, although it has existed for 36 years, has little to show for its efforts. Pray for a new generation of leadership that will know how to make cooperative ventures work and to bring them to pass.
b) *National strategy must be developed.* Côte d'Ivoire is the only remaining African nation with a sizeable Evangelical population that has not launched a country-wide church planting effort in the style of the **DAWN/AD2000** "National Initiatives" seen elsewhere. Pray for the birth of a national saturation evangelism programme as well as for more partnerships which target specific unreached peoples.
c) *Pray for revival* among pastors, church leaders, and members. Amidst the tremendous growth, pastors have begun to prefer a role of power, instead of one of servant-leader. Pray that this may be replaced with humility and continued burden for the lost and that the Church might develop "missionary eyes and hearts" for unreached peoples.

4 The level of Bible knowledge and discipleship is low, partly a result of rapid church growth. Many churches accept the 'prosperity' gospel, and open air campaigns sometimes focus more upon miracles and healings rather than the One who is their source. However, this trend has been counterbalanced by the growth of Bible Institutes, Study Centres, and Correspondence Courses in which thousands of students are now enrolled. Pray that students at the new **CMA** theological school may grow in the mastery of the Word. Pray for the **AoG**'s new training institute, opening soon in Abidjan. Pray also for the Navigators and other ministries that focus on the much needed area of discipleship.

5 Evangelical agencies had a late and slow start compared to other West African lands. **CMA** arrived in 1930 and focused on the Baoulé in the centre of the country. Mission Biblique began in 1927 amongst the Yacouba and Guéré in the southwest, later joined by **UFM**, and **WEC** began in 1934 among the Gouro and Gban (Gagou). The **AoG**, which started only in the 1950s, however, now has churches all over the country and has surpassed all of the other denominations in terms of growth and outreach.

6 Major missions include: AICA (177), CCCI (126), **WBT/SIL** (87), NTM (104), CBI (80), **CMA** (80), **WEC** (61), **SBC** (33), Free Will Baptists (28), **SIM** (23), CCCC (19), CMF (14). Though numbers seem high, many of these serve in international ministries based in the country or in missionary children's schools (**CBI**, **NTM** and **WEC**). There is still a great need for new long-term missionaries in pioneer evangelism, church planting and a wide range of supportive ministries. Pray for missionaries' safety. As robberies, carjacking and kidnapping increase, Christian workers and their families make tempting targets.

7 There are now several African mission agencies, some of which are denominational. They work mainly in Côte d'Ivoire but increasingly, beyond, targeting the remaining unreached peoples. Main areas for prayer:

a) Research. A small band of local researchers is committed to collecting information on the lost and helping churches build vision for cross-cultural church planting, within the country and in the sub-region. A West African researchers seminar was held in 1999 and has since developed into a regional network. Pray that their hard work may bear fruit.

b) Missionary training. **Calvary Ministries** has established a missions training institute in Abidjan to serve Francophone West Africa. It is the first such institute for this region. The great challenge is to prepare missionaries for Muslim outreach. Pray that the training may be of high quality, and be matched by students of the same.

c) Sending. Congregations are usually supportive of indigenous missionaries, but leadership often feels threatened and financially strained. Many of this new missionary generation live by faith on very little support. Pray that God might supply all of their needs and that their churches might support them in every possible way.

8 Peoples that are both unreached and unoccupied by missions or churches include the Muslim Soninke, Bambara, Wassulunke, Fulbe from several countries and the largely traditional Bisa — all peoples with their majorities in Burkina Faso, Mali or Ghana. There are also the Wolof from Senegal, Tuaregs from Mali, Hausa from Niger and Nigeria, and Lebanese and North African Muslims.

9 Peoples needing pioneer mission work with no major church planting breakthrough include:

a) The strongly Muslim peoples of the northwest: Malinke, Fulbe and Jula-speaking peoples, where only a handful have been won through the ministry of **SIM**, **WEC** and **CBI**. The Malinke/Fulbe group make up nearly 2 million people and are 99.9% non-Christian. More than 85 churches with 4000 members exist in Malinke territory, but they are composed almost exclusively of people who come from outside the region. Among the Mahou the Norwegian Lutherans have seen several congregations planted.

b) Marginally occupied peoples. For example: in the Free Will Baptist area in the northeast (Birifor, Téén); in the **WEC** area in the centre (Mona, Wan, Yaouré, Kouya, Mahou); in the **MB-UFM** area in the southwest (Toura, Dida, Bété).

c) The multiplicity of small language groups in the south. There are so many that present evangelistic, church planting and Bible translation ministries may not cover the need. Pray that this may be adequately researched and every group thoroughly evangelized. **NTM** has targeted the Glaro and Krumen in the southwest.

10 **The large influx of foreigners** presents unusual opportunities for evangelizing those who are separated from the strong ties of their tribal cultures. While their presence in Côte d'Ivoire is the source of much strife, it is also a timely evangelistic opportunity. Nearly 30% of the population is foreign, and the majority of foreigners are Muslim.

11 **Islam spread and grew rapidly during the 20th Century** — from 5% in 1900 to near 40% today. Interest by Christian Ivoirians in ministry to Muslims is growing, but the level of participation remains very low compared to actual needs. Tribal groups in the north and pockets of tribes all over the country are becoming Muslim. Urban concentrations of Muslims are high, and so are conversion rates among new immigrants to the cities. Pray that Christians may be zealous to win non-Muslims while they can, and also show more concern for the Muslims themselves. Pray for the healing of the north-south ethnic divide created by the politicians which is making outreach to Muslims even harder than before. Pray that Christians may learn how to show real love to their Islamic neighbours.

12 **Demographic sectors of society needing the gospel:**

a) Abidjan's exploding population, which doubles every 7-10 years, is the strategic key for evangelization of Côte d' Ivoire, Mali and Burkina Faso. Every people of these latter two lands has a significant community in the city, but most are neglected by the Church. There are 100 church-planting missionaries in Abidjan representing 13 churches/missions, but this is not adequate. Over 1.5 million Muslims, roughly half of the city, are scarcely touched with the gospel, and only around 10 missionaries and a few Ivoirians are seeking to reach them (**SIM, CMA, MTW**).

b) AIDS is now a major problem in the country, with 14-16% of Abidjan's population already infected with the HIV virus — few churches or ministries have faced up to this challenge. The country will soon need to care for an estimated 500,000 AIDS orphans.

c) Young people are responsive, and wherever churches minister specifically to them, there has been fruit. Liberty to teach Scripture in public schools is an exciting but underused opportunity through lack of qualified personnel. **SU** is making a vital contribution in school evangelism and discipleship. The **IFES** Francophone Africa HQ is in Abidjan, and there is a strong **GBU/IFES** group in the university. **CCC** is also well established with full-time Ivoirian staff reaching students.

13 **Literature.** Pray for the bookstores and depots of various missions, including **The Bible Society**, *Maison de la Bible*, **CLC**, *CDM*, and others. Pray for the inter-mission/church Evangelical Publication Centre (*CPE*) and other publishers, that they might find the means to print books locally at a suitable quality. Currently, many books are printed in Asia or elsewhere. Well-intentioned efforts by outside ministries to sell their literature at subsidized prices keep African authors from publishing more relevant Christian works because they cannot compete with these lower-priced books. Also needing prayer: lack of qualified staff (especially French-speaking), financial pressures and lack of good distribution outlets and marketing strategies.

14 **Bible translation** is one of the most pressing and demanding ministries for Christian workers. A considerable number of national and expatriate workers are involved in 21 translation and 20 literacy programmes linked with **UBS** and various church/mission groups. **SIL**'s contribution in a number of projects is especially significant — many being among the superficially-Christianized people of the south. Pray for newly-translated Scriptures to take root in the hearts of the people, especially since some have a negative view of their own language and want to learn to read only in French. Pray for a wider distribution of the Bibles and New Testaments already translated.

15 **Christian Media**

a) A Christian radio station in Abidjan is an answer to prayer. Radio *"Frequence Vie"* became operational in 1998, after waiting 6 years to receive its licence from the government and broadcasts in French and Jula. **SIM**'s plan is to eventually turn it over completely to the national churches, who don't yet have the financial means for this. Pray, too, for government permission for *"Frequence Vie"* to broadcast in other languages and set up relay stations throughout the country.

b) **TWR has a recording studio** for producing daily messages that are broadcast from its short-wave station in Johannesburg. Pray for the Bambara, Baoulé, Jula and Songhai as they tune in to **TWR**'s messages in their languages. **TWR** is also producing a programme on development that is being transmitted from 42 stations across West Africa.

c) **AEA's film studio, based in Abidjan**, has started full production and will be used to produce culturally relevant programmes on video for transmission by national television stations across West Africa.

d) **The JESUS film** is in use in the Baoulé, Bété, Guére, Gouro, Senufo-Cebaara, and Yakuba languages. Dubbing projects are planned for Agni, Attie, Kulango, and Lobi. Jula is a key language, but the project has been blocked for several years for one reason or another; pray for a breakthrough.

e) **GRN** *recordings* have been prepared in 49 languages.

f) **Ivoirian Christian music** has grown rapidly and seen the production of many quality tapes and videos. Pray that the messages of the songs remain biblically sound.

Croatia
Republic of Croatia

APRIL 19
EUROPE

GEOGRAPHY
Area 56,438 sq.km. Crescent-shaped country between the Danube River and Adriatic Sea. The land is almost bisected by Bosnia.

Population		Ann.Gr.	Density
2000	4,472,600	-0.09%	79 per sq. km.
2010	4,402,743	-0.17%	78 per sq. km.
2025	4,193,413	-0.40%	74 per sq. km.

Capital Zagreb 1,060,000. **Urbanites** 54%.

PEOPLES
Slavic 94.5%. Croat 3,887,000; Serb 220,000 (600,000 in 1990); Bosnian 120,000.
Romance 3.1%. Istrian 166,000; Italian 14,000; Friulian 11,000.
Other 2.4%. Gypsy(4) 131,000; German 80,000; Hungarian 20,000.

Literacy 97%. **Official language** Croatian; closely related to Serbian but written in Latin, rather than Cyrillic, script.

ECONOMY
A slow recovery from long-term Communist mismanagement and the four-year war with Serbia. Once fairly prosperous through industry and tourism on the popular Adriatic coast. Purchase of weapons, massive destruction and population movements have crippled development. **Unemployment** 19%. **HDI** 0.773; 55th/174. **Public debt** 22% of GNP. **Income/person** $3,800 (13% of USA).

POLITICS
Over 1600 years of Great Power rivalries lie behind the division between the related Croat and Serb peoples. Their mutual hatred dominated the politics of the former Yugoslavia and was one of the causes of the Balkan wars of the 1990s. Croatia lost much land to Serbia in 1991-1995, but regained it all through diplomacy and war 1995-98. A multi-party democracy, but it has been tainted by dictatorial nationalism.

RELIGION
Freedom of religion, but there is a blurred boundary between the state and the favoured Catholic church. Yet, the Catholic leadership has been at the forefront of reconciliation and justice issues.

Religions	Population %	Adherents	Ann.Gr.
Christian	94.43	4,223,476	-0.1%
Muslim	3.00	134,178	-0.1%
non-Religious/other	2.52	112,710	+1.6%
Jewish	0.05	2,236	-3.7%

Christians	Denom.	Affil.%	,000	Ann.Gr.
Protestant	11	0.89	40	+1.7%
Independent	2	0.25	11	+3.0%
Catholic	1	87.20	3,900	+2.2%
Orthodox	1	5.59	250	-18.6%
Marginal	2	0.26	12	+5.7
Unaffiliated		0.24	11	n.a.

Churches	MegaBloc	Cong.	Members	Affiliates
Catholic	C	1,445	2,689,655	3,900,000
Serbian Orthodox	O	100	172,414	250,000
Jehovah's Witnesses	M	94	5,800	11,368
Slovak Ev Chr (Luth)	P	16	7,692	11,000
Ev Ch of Croatia (Luth)	P	25	4,500	9,000
Baptist	P	41	3,000	5,000
Evangelical (Pente)	P	36	1,500	3,200
Other denoms [19]		155	11,000	23,000
Total Christians [30]		1,912	2,895,000	4,212,000

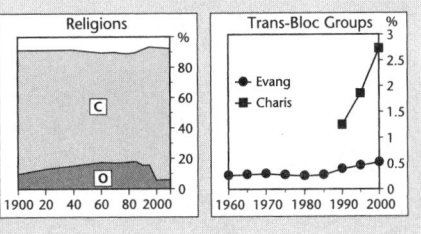

Trans-bloc Groupings	pop.%	,000	Ann.Gr.
Evangelical	0.5	23	+2.0%
Charismatic	2.7	122	+2.2%
Pentecostal	0.1	4	+2.1%

Missionaries from Croatia
P,I,A 20 in 6 agencies; 19 in Croatia.

Missionaries to Croatia
P,I,A 117 in 26 agencies from 15 countries: USA 51,
Germany 9, Korea 8.

• Challenges for Prayer

1 **The deep impact of historic and recent hatred** between Croat, Serb and Bosnian on every aspect of national life could continue to hamper the affected nations for generations to come. Only through Christ can true reconciliation be achieved.

2 **The link between ethnicity and religion** for Orthodox Serbs, Muslim Bosnians and Catholic Croats has stifled any spiritual breakthroughs. The Balkan Wars since 1991 have helped some of those who have suffered most to be more open to change. Pray for the breaking of all satanic bondages and cultural blindnesses that prevent people from repentance and personal faith in Christ.

3 **Evangelical Christians** have emerged as one of the only trans-ethnic bodies that have ministered to refugees of all communities. Hundreds of Bosnians, Croats and Serbs have been won to Christ and brought to fellowshipping together. The compassionate ministry of both foreign and indigenous church/mission agencies such as the Baptists, the Lutherans and AGAPE (the social arm of the Evangelical Church) in dispensing aid, giving trauma therapy and loving those who have suffered, has won much credit for the gospel. Pray for these ongoing outreaches and their lasting spiritual impact.

4 **Evangelical churches** have always been few in number and stronger amongst minorities, but there has been growth during the 1990s among the Croat majority. In many areas, such as Istria, Dalmatia and Zagorjé in the west and on the coast, there are very few churches. Pray for effective church planting in every part of Croatia.

5 **Leadership training**. The impact of the Evangelical Theological Seminary in Osijek has been great. From small beginnings in 1972 (under Communism) it has grown into an international, interdenominational school impacting much of Central Europe as well as Croatia. Many fruitful ministries have had their birth within it. Pray for the continued spiritual fruitfulness and theological health of faculty, students and graduates — now serving in 27 countries.

6 **Foreign mission agencies** have increased personnel in Croatia, most missionaries being involved in ministry to the refugees and traumatized, or in church-support. Pray for a healthy, wholesome partnership with the Croatian Church. Main mission-sending agencies are **CCCI** (28), **OM** (10), **GEM** (6), **AoG** (5) and International Needs (5).

7 **Specialist ministries** for prayer:

a) *Students* — there is a growing witness since 1992 among the 80,000 tertiary students through STEP(**IFES**) with 120 involved in five cities.

b) *Izvori Publishing House* of the Evangelical Church publishes literature and 3 Christian magazines. It also has a radio ministry, *Izvori-Vjere*, broadcasting over 52 stations in Croatia and Bosnia. Pray for the healthy development of literature and radio ministries.

c) *The JESUS film* is available in Croatian, Italian and Venetian (for Istria), but has not yet been widely used.

Cuba

Republic of Cuba

APRIL 20
LATIN AMERICA

 GEOGRAPHY
Area 465,468 sq.km. The largest island in the Caribbean.

Population		Ann.Gr.	Density
2000	11,200,684	+0.43%	101 per sq. km.
2010	11,516,190	+0.25%	104 per sq. km.
2025	11,798,235	+0.09%	106 per sq. km.

Capital Havana 2,077,000. **Urbanites** 76%.

 **PEOPLES**
Hispanic 99%. Mulatto 51%, White 37%, Black 11%.
Other 1%. Indo-Pakistani 34,000; Chinese 20,000; Arabs 10,000; US Military at Guantánamo Military Base 7,000.

Literacy 96%. **Official language** Spanish.

 **ECONOMY**
Production of sugar and nickel ore have been the mainstays of the economy. Repressive centralized socialist planning, a US trade embargo and the collapse of Cuba's Communist bloc trade and aid after 1989 have impoverished an already poor country. Rationing, hunger and lack of many essentials are deeply affecting the country, yet there have been great advances in literacy, education and health, and a reduction in infant mortality. Tourism has increased in recent years. **HDI** 0.765; 58th/174. **Public debt** 77% of GNP. **Income/person** $1,170 (5% of USA).

 POLITICS
Independent from Spain in 1898. Castro's revolution brought Communism to power in 1959. After 30 years of vigorously exporting revolution to Latin America and Africa, Cuba remains one of the last protagonists of Communism. The police state is diplomatically isolated and politically paranoid, but with no viable alternative government, the old dictatorship continues.

 RELIGION
Strict control of all church activities and repression of religious freedom in earlier years of Communist rule, but since 1990 the degree of pressure has lessened. The 1992 constitution declared Cuba 'secular' and discrimination against Christians, illegal. In practice, periodic harrassment of Catholics and Evangelicals continues.

Religions	Population %	Adherents	Ann.Gr.
Christian	46.88	5,250,881	+0.0%
non-Religious/other	35.47	3,972,883	+1.0%
Spiritist	17.00	1,904,116	+0.4%
Hindu	0.21	23,521	+1.4%
Chinese	0.19	21,281	+0.4%
Other	0.10	11,201	+0.4%
Muslim	0.08	8,961	+0.4%
Buddhist	0.05	5,600	+0.4%
Baha'i	0.01	1,120	+0.4%
Jewish	0.01	1,000	n.a.

Christians	Denom.	Affil. %	,000	Ann.Gr.
Protestant	33	3.40	341	+5.3%
Independent	16	1.66	185	+8.9%
Anglican	1	0.03	4	-0.3%
Catholic	1	38.82	4,348	-0.7%
Orthodox	1	0.01	1	+0.0%
Marginal	1	1.61	180	+4.0%
Unaffiliated		1.35	151	n.a.

Churches	MegaBloc	Cong.	Members	Affiliates
Catholic	C	252	2,787,000	4,367,900
Jehovah's Witnesses	M	1,252	85,714	180,000
Assemblies of God	P	325	39,028	86,028
Evang Pentecostal	I	233	42,000	80,000
Evang Conv of C (WT)	P	320	35,000	58,000
Methodist Ch of C	P	435	13,043	45,000
Seventh-day Adventist	P	184	21,278	44,000
Bapt Conv of Eastern C	P	357	20,000	33,400
Bapt Conv of Western C	P	160	16,000	30,000
Christian Pentecostal	I	130	13,000	30,000
Presbyterian Reformed	P	80	6,000	16,000
Pentecostal Holiness	P	86	6,000	11,000
Ch of God (Cleveland)	P	25	2,371	8,000
Freewill Baptist Conv	P	12	2,100	4,200
Episcopal	A	25	1,300	3,600
Other denoms [39]		2,418	67,201	122,530
Total Christians [54]		6,294	3,157,000	5,100,000

Trans-bloc Groupings	pop. %	,000	Ann.Gr.
Evangelical	4.6	521	+6.5%
Charismatic	5.6	632	+3.0%
Pentecostal	2.7	301	+6.5%

Missionaries from Cuba
P,I,A 28 in 5 agencies; 22 in Cuba.

Expatriates with ministry to Cuba
P,I,A 21 in 10 agencies.

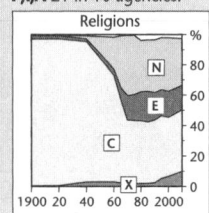

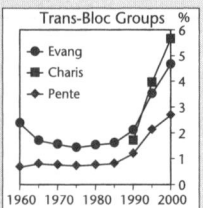

• Answers to Prayer

1 **The void created by Communism** is being filled by Christianity, Communism's arch-rival. During the '90s there has been rapid church growth despite ongoing hostility and frequent acts of harassment against Christians. Many congregations are filled with young people despite 40 years of Marxist propaganda.

2 **The greater freedom to print Bibles** in Cuba or import from abroad.

3 **Evangelicals** were allowed to convene 19 public rallies in 1999. The largest in Havana, which Castro himself attended, drew 100,000 Christians. Castro's own son is an active believer in the Methodist Church.

• Challenges to Prayer

1 **A peaceful transition from dictatorship to democracy**. Fidel Castro clings to power with his battle-cry 'Socialism or Death', but Christians proclaim 'Cuba for Christ'. May the latter be true.

2 **The healing of the wounds** inflicted by Marxism:

a) An estimated 50,000+ lost their lives and 500,000 were imprisoned for ideological reasons. Much anger and bitterness will need to be cleansed from hearts by the blood of Jesus.

b) Over one million Cubans have become ideological or economic refugees — many in Florida, USA. Both the USA and Cuba have used refugees as another weapon of war.

c) Economic hardship is widespread; survival is only possible in the illegal 'black' economy and through deceit. Many have turned to crime, drug-running and prostitution in their need. This moral rot must be excised from society if future generations are to be spared.

d) Divisions among Christians. The government has given support and favour to the more ecumenical Cuban Council of Churches (CCC) and the 22 denominations associated with it. The 32 other denominations have had a more difficult time.

3 **Cubans were highly secularized before 1959** with 61% regular church-goers. The further loss of influence of the Catholic Church after 1959 was catastrophic. Nominal adherence to Catholicism dropped from 85% in 1957 to 38.5% in 1983, and the number of priests from 725 to 200. Since the Pope's visit in 1998, the Catholic Church has revived and church attendance has increased. Pray that millions might come to personal faith in Christ.

4 **The Protestant churches were decimated** by several waves of emigration to the USA, a move encouraged by the authorities. Recovery and growth was slow, but out of the furnace of persecution high-quality leadership and committed membership arose that witnessed fervently. Since 1989 growth has become spectacular with churches springing up in every corner of Cuba. Evangelicals now outnumber church-going Catholics. The 1,250 evangelical congregations in 1990 has increased to possibly 4,500 congregations and a further 10,000 house groups in 54 denominations. A high proportion of the new Christians are young people. Pray that this growth may continue whatever the political situation.

5 **Persecution of Christians has been severe**, Catholics suffering even more than Protestants. For decades Christians were subject to arbitrary arrest, imprisonment, discrimination, and any church activities were restricted or arbitrarily banned. All open witness, evangelism and literature production and distribution was made almost impossible. That persecution has diminished but not ceased, but the capriciousness of its application breeds insecurity. Applications for registering or repairing churches are routinely ignored. Discipleship is still costly but many are prepared to pay the price and shine for Jesus. Pray for continued courage and fortitude for believers, and for complete religious freedom.

6 **Leadership for the churches** is a pressing need. Many had to flee or were expelled in the years following the revolution. Praise God for those who stood firm for Jesus and who have become mighty for God in the school of suffering. There are now a dozen evangelical and two Catholic Bible schools or seminaries. Student numbers are limited by lack of teaching materials, theologically trained faculty, and the widespread poverty. Pray that the number of formally and informally trained leaders might be multiplied. Pray also for visionary leadership for the churches that enables them to cope with the massive changes soon to come. Freedom can also be dangerous.

7 The less reached:

a) *The unchurched majority*. Church attendance was once the lowest for any country in the Western hemisphere. This has risen in the 1990s, but 80% of the population still has no meaningful contact with a church.

b) *Spiritism* has been actively supported by the government as 'cultural'. Afro-Caribbean religions under a thin veneer of Catholicism have huge followings. There may be more than 3 million devotees of Santaria and other cults such as Mayombe and Zarabanda which resemble Haitian voodoo. Pray that Christians may exercise love, understanding and spiritual power to see many delivered from this satanic bondage.

c) *The Chinese, Indians and Arabs* have been largely assimilated into the Hispanic majority, but still retain much of their old culture. Little is being done to specifically reach them.

8 Foreign missions have been restricted to tactful support and occasional pastoral visits from outside the country. A few were permitted to remain in a low-profile teaching ministry. Pray that missions may plan wisely for the day that Cuba is free once more. The Cuban Church will need humble, helping ministries rather than high-publicity, foreign-generated programmes and aid.

9 There are about one million Cuban refugees living in the USA. These were mainly from the white middle and upper classes but more recently from all sections of society. It is estimated that 80% are Catholic and 10% are Protestant. Pray that freedom may come to their land again and permit their return, but also that God might enable them to understand, adapt and be a blessing to, a very different country from the one they left.

10 Christian help ministries for prayer:

a) *Bible distribution* — the famine for God's Word has not ended despite a dramatic increase of copies available. Praise God that after 25 years of closure, the Cuban Bible Society reopened in 1990. Nearly one million copies of the Scriptures have been printed in Cuba on the Bible Society press, and a further 150,000 copies annually are imported legally. Yet a large consignment was destroyed by the authorities in 1999 as 'subversive'. The Catholics were permitted to import 100,000 Bibles in 1998. It is still difficult for many in non-CCC churches to obtain Bibles.

b) *Christian literature* has been scarcely obtainable for years. More can now be imported, but permission for local printing is difficult to obtain. There are few resources for pastors and preachers. Pray that this hunger might be satisfied.

c) *Christian radio* has been a source of strength and encouragement to many. There is no lack of choice with about 2,800 hours of international Christian broadcasting in Spanish every week from Latin America! The main providers are **TWR**, **FEBC** and **HCJB**. Local broadcasting is still not permitted.

d) *The JESUS film* is available in Spanish and widely used when possible. Pray for its impact on a population with scant knowledge of the gospel.

Cyprus

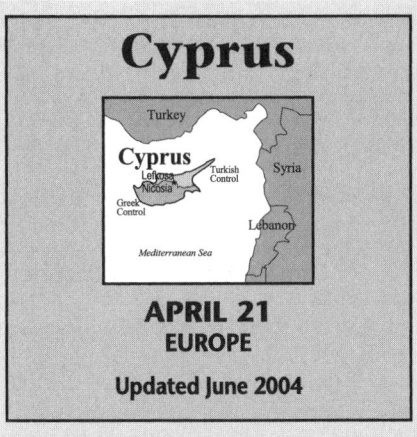

APRIL 21
EUROPE

Updated June 2004

The country has been divided as a result of the Turkish invasion of 1974 and occupation of the north. The Greek and Turkish populations have been separated: the North calling itself the Turkish Republic of Northern Cyprus (TRNC) and the South claiming the whole island as the Republic of Cyprus (ROC). The ROC is internationally recognized as the legal government of the whole island, and only Turkey recognizes the TRNC. Below, some statistics apply to the whole island and some to the two entities. By the end of 2002, serious talks had begun seeking a settlement with a possible loose federal structure so that the whole of Cyprus could enter the EU in 2004. This did not happen.

GEOGRAPHY
Area 9,251 sq.km. Strategic island in NE Mediterranean Sea. ROC in the south is 64% of the island, TRNC in the north is 36%.

Population	Ann.Gr.	Density
2000	785,551	+1.09%	85 per sq. km.
2010	843,015	+0.62%	91 per sq. km.
2025	900,281	+0.33%	97 per sq. km.

There are also 35,000 Turkish military in TRNC and 12,000 Greeks in ROC.

RELIGION
The Christians are almost all in ROC and Muslims in TRNC. There is freedom of religion in the ROC and TRNC, but proselytism by minority groups is carefully monitored.

Religions	Population %	Adherents	Ann.Gr.
Christian	74.14	582,015	+1.2%
Muslim	23.00	180,677	+0.6%
non-Religious/other	2.90	22,771	+2.3%
Jewish	0.02	160	+1.3%

Christians	Denom.	Affil.%	,000	Ann.Gr.
Protestant	13	0.21	2	+0.8%
Independent	15	0.18	1	+7.9%
Anglican	1	0.42	3	-0.6%
Catholic	3	1.30	10	+0.4%
Orthodox	3	67.78	532	+0.2%
Marginal	3	0.45	4	+1.1%
Unaffiliated		3.80	30	n.a.

Churches	MegaBloc	Cong.	Members	Affiliates
Greek Orthodox	O	379	189,286	530,000
Catholic [3]	C	12	4,500	10,200
Jehovah's Witnesses	M	21	1,900	3,400
Anglican	A	7	1,320	3,300
Armenian Apostolic	O	1	1,264	2,300
Charis. Chs/Gps [13]	I	14	700	1,000
Armenian Evangelical	P	2	140	350
Ch of God of Prophecy	P	4	220	330
Apostolic Ch of J.C.	I	2	200	300
Greek Evangelical	P	2	120	200
Christian Brethren	P	1	60	110
Other denoms [11]		13	585	1000
Total Christians [36]		459	200,300	552,500

Trans-bloc Groupings pop. %		,000	Ann.Gr.
Evangelical	0.2	1	-1.6%
Charismatic	0.2	1	-1.2%
Pentecostal	0.1	1	-1.1%

Missionaries from Cyprus
P,I,A 3 — all in Cyprus.

Missionaries to Cyprus
P,I,A 120 in 27 agencies; almost all based in Cyprus for wider ministry in the Middle East.

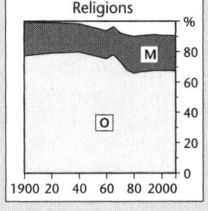
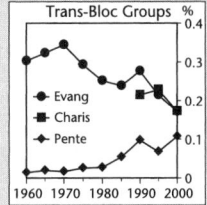

Republic of Cyprus

GEOGRAPHY
Area 5,896 sq.km. The southern, less fertile two-thirds of the island.
Population 600,500. Over 180,000 refugees from the North after the Turkish invasion in 1974.
Capital (divided) Lefkosia (Nicosia) 190,000.
Urbanites 69%.

PEOPLES
Cypriot 95.2%. Greek 562,000; Maronite 6,000; Armenian 2,700; Turk 500; Assyrian 200.
Foreign 4.8%. Arab 12,000; Russian 8,000; British 6,000; Asian 3,000.
Literacy 95%. **Official languages** Greek, Turkish; English widely used. **All languages** 5.

ECONOMY
Prostrated by the effects of the Turkish seizure of the north and a third of the population being made refugees. Rapid recovery and development of light industry and tourism. One sixth of the world's merchant ships are registered in Cyprus. **Unemployment** 2%. **HDI** 0.870; 26th/174. **Income/ person** $13,700 (48% of USA).

POLITICS
Ruled by 11 foreign empires over 3 millennia. After years of unrest by the Greek majority demanding union with Greece, independence from Britain was gained in 1960. Subsequent communal conflicts culminated in the 1974 abortive coup (supported by Greece) and subsequent Turkish invasion and partition of the island. As a result, 230,000 people became refugees. All efforts to achieve a settlement have foundered on the mistrust between the communities and intransigence of the politicians. Cyprus is in the process of joining the EU.

RELIGION
Christians 94.2%; non-Religious/other 4.8%; Muslim 1%.

• Challenges for Prayer

1 The 40-year conflict between the two communities has gone on too long. Entrenched intransigence and bitterness defy a peaceful resolution. Pray that both sides may recognize and admit past wrongs and find a satisfactory way to bring harmony and trust into their relationship, and even allow entry into the EU as a single entity.

2 The Orthodox Church has long been a refuge and guarantor of Greek Cypriot survival. The boundary between politics, culture and Church is blurred. Church attendance is high at 48%, but traditionalism is also strong. Pray for Holy Spirit renewal movements to bring many to a warm personal faith in Christ.

3 Evangelical churches among Greeks are few — the major ones being the Greek Evangelical and the Church of God of Prophecy. Negative propaganda against Evangelicals holds many back from considering joining one. Pray that the barriers of history, theology, prejudice and fear may be removed and significant church growth begin. Few workers and ministries are focused on the majority.

4 Ethnic minority Evangelicals have grown in variety and number of fellowships with significant life and outreach from the English-speaking, Russian, Filipino, Armenian, Sri Lankan and Iranian communities. Pray for the witness to their own communities and to the indigenous population.

5 The Logos bookstore (CLC) is a vital centre for books, tracts, and BCCs. Logos is also the core of a range of Christian education ministries that are a boost to the evangelical witness. Pray for the effective use and distribution of literature and also for the nation-wide **EHC** tract distribution.

6 Cyprus is a major base for Christian organizations ministering to the surrounding Middle Eastern states. All but a handful of expatriate Christian workers are involved in these rather than in local outreach. Pray specifically for:

a) *A number of missions* that have HQs or regional centres in Cyprus (**MECO**, **CCCI**, **YWAM**, **Interserve**, etc.).

b) *Arabic literature* which is both printed and stocked for distribution throughout the Middle East (MECOLIT, **SGM**). **The Bible Society** has distributed many Greek NTs throughout the ROC.

c) *SAT7 which is based in Cyprus*. This key, innovative Christian Satellite TV ministry is impacting the whole of the Arab world with its daily programmes which have a wide audience and good response.

d) *Christian radio* programmes that are broadcast by three Christian agencies over Cyprus Radio in Arabic and Armenian, but not in Greek or Turkish. **Channel 7** is a commercial Christian radio station in the ROC broadcasting in both Greek and English.

e) *The Logos School of English Education*, started in 1973, has 160 students from all over the Middle East. It has a strong Christian testimony.

7 There are two large British military bases. Pray for the witness of Ministry to Military Garrisons and chaplains. Pray that a clear witness may be given by Christian service personnel to the Cypriots. Pray also for opportunities to share the gospel with the multi-national UN Peace-keeping Force.

Turkish Republic of Northern Cyprus

GEOGRAPHY
Area 3,355 sq. km. The northern third and 55% of the coastline of the island.
Population 185,045 augmented by 45,000 Turkish Cypriot refugees in 1974 and 114,000 Turkish immigrants, but also losses of 54,000 Turkish Cypriots through emigration.
Capital (divided) Lefkosa (Nikosia) 40,000.

PEOPLES
Cypriot 99.4%. Turk 182,600; Greek 850; Maronite 420.
Other 0.6%.
Literacy 90%. **Official language** Turkish.

ECONOMY
Depressed and stagnating since 1974 because of economic and political isolation. Heavily dependent on Turkish subsidies and shares in Turkish high inflation figures. High unemployment. Standard of living much lower than ROC.

POLITICS
A democratic government set up after the 1974 partition, but diplomatic isolation followed the declaration of the separate state of TRNC in 1983 which Turkey alone recognizes and acts as its only lifeline.

RELIGION
A secular republic with two established religions — Islam (98%) and Christianity (0.7%).

• Challenges for Prayer

1 **Almost the entire population is Muslim,** but also very secularized. About 10% are regular mosque-goers. Pray that the historic prejudice against Christianity may be broken down. There is little known focused outreach to them.

2 **A small group of about 20 Turkish believers** has come into being. Pray for them, for their outreach and growth in numbers.

Czech Republic

APRIL 22
EUROPE

PEOPLES
Slavic 96.3%. Czech 9,492,000; Slovak 314,000; Polish 59,000.
Other 3.7%. Gypsy 300,000; German 50,000; Chinese 3,000; Jewish 3,000.
Literacy 99%. **Official Language** Czech. **All Languages** 8. **Languages with Scriptures** 4Bi 2NT 3w.i.p.

ECONOMY
Diverse industrialized society, but suffering from uneven implementation of market capitalism. Despite much foreign investment, significant recession since 1997. Many key industries are near bankruptcy, yet the country has the potential to be a successful market economy. **HDI** 0.833; 36ᵗʰ/174. **Public debt** 22.7% of GNP. **Income/person** $4,740 (16.5% of USA).

GEOGRAPHY
Area 78,864 sq.km. Landlocked central European state.

Population		Ann.Gr.	Density
2000	10,244,177	-0.16%	130 per sq. km.
2010	10,066,401	-0.21%	128 per sq. km.
2025	9,512,292	-0.48%	121 per sq. km.

Capital Prague 1,200,000. **Urbanites** 76%.

POLITICS
The bloodless "velvet revolution" against Communist rule in 1989 was followed by rapid democratization and the "velvet divorce" from Slovakia in 1993. Multi-party presidential democracy, aspiring to EU membership in the near future.

RELIGION
Eventful religious history. The churches suffered, especially under Communist regime, but

neither has the subsequent freedom proved easy. Now a secular state with religious freedom, but the influence of the Church is fading rapidly.

Religions	Population %	Affiliates	Ann.Gr.
Christian	53.22	5,451,951	-3.0%
non-Religious	45.02	4,611,928	+3.7%
Other	1.50	153,663	+8.3%
Muslim	0.20	20,488	+5.8%
Baha'i	0.03	3,073	+8.3%
Jewish	0.02	2,049	-0.2%
Buddhist	0.01	1,024	-0.2%

Christians	Denom.	Affil. %	,000	Ann.Gr.
Protestant	22	2.56	258	-1.0%
Independent	11	1.74	179	-0.1%
Anglican	1	0.01	1	+0.0%
Catholic	2	34.28	3,512	-3.0%
Orthodox	1	0.34	35	-8.0%
Marginal	8	0.33	34	+2.0%
Unaffiliated		13.96	1,430	n.a.

Churches	MegaBloc	Cong.	Members	Affiliates
Roman Catholic	C	2,917	3,500,000	3,500,000
Hussite	I	340	118,881	170,000
Evang Ch of Czech Breth	P	264	150,371	150,371
Silesian Evang (Luth)	P	34	27,000	48,000
Orthodox	O	36	20,000	35,000
Jehovah's Witnesses	M	289	17,500	28,000
Seventh-day Adventist	P	178	8,000	15,200
Uniate Catholic	C	13	8,770	12,200

Congregational	P	167	4,500	8,325
Moravian Ch of Brethren	P	25	2,400	4,800
Chr Fellowship Prague	I	64	2,400	4,800
Pentecostal	P	31	2,000	4,400
Slovak Evangelical	P	3	4,200	4,200
Evangelical Free	P	8	1,640	4,100
Baptist Union	P	24	2,500	4,000
Church of the Brethren	P	56	2,000	4,000
Other denoms [29]		139	12,139	22,038
Total Christians [45]		4,588	3,884,301	4,019,434

Trans-bloc Groupings	pop. %	,000	Ann.Gr.
Evangelical	1.1	108	-0.8%
Charismatic	0.6	66	-0.6%
Pentecostal	0.1	13	+3.5%

Missionaries from Czech Republic
P,I,A 24 in 6 agencies to 10 countries.

Missionaries to Czech Republic
P,I,A 232 in 45 agencies from 14 countries: USA 164, Germany 15, United Kingdom 15, Korea 9.

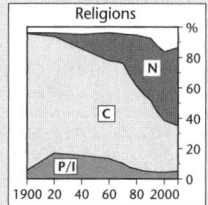

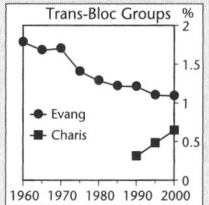

• Challenges for Prayer

1 **Though Communism is a fading memory**, the transition to another social paradigm has not been easy. The entry of market capitalism has left its trademark — wealth and hedonism for a few, but increased economic stress for many. The great moral vacuum formed by decades of Communism has not been filled. The resultant moral decline in the past decade has been accompanied by an increase in crime, substance abuse, prostitution and family breakdown. Pray that this negative spiral might be cut short by the intervention of God into this godless society.

2 **The Catholic Church outnumbers all other denominations** nearly 7 to 1, and yet is in serious decline. It had a brief opportunity to re-establish its influence after 1989, but failed due to internal dissension and insufficient action. The Church is now making conciliatory gestures towards other Christian groups and a renewal movement is active, but the leadership is old (average priest's age is 69), and the laity is aging and decreasing rapidly. Pray for God's Spirit to sweep through the Catholic Church and awaken these millions to the living reality of Christ.

3 **Czech Protestants are experiencing life without persecution** for only the second time since 1620. The Protestant churches have an important place in the history and culture of the nation. Pray that this may also become true spiritually. Pray for Evangelicals both within the larger Protestant denominations and the smaller, younger groups, such as the Baptists, Pentecostals and numerous independent congregations. Almost all evangelical churches are experiencing at least modest growth, and several are seeing this accompanied by charismatic renewal.

4 **Christian leaders** with the precious combination of spirituality and adequate biblical training are few, but on the increase. For many years, little training was permitted — especially in biblical theology. After a decade of freedom, only now is significant fruit being seen. Pray for the Protestant theological training institutes, especially the ones with a strong evangelical emphasis — Baptist, Reformed, and interdenominational Bible schools in Olomouc and the Evangelical Theological Seminary in Prague, run by the Brethren. The latter also has a training programme for government social workers, which could prove significant in transforming Czech society. TEE programmes could also prove vital for the training of capable leaders throughout the country. Foreign missionaries have not done enough to foster growth in Christian education. Pray for an improvement in this area.

5 **The recent religious freedom** has been a double-edged sword. Believers are free to minister and evangelize, but openness has taken the cutting edge off of the Church. There are more denominations and missions working in the Czech Republic than ever, but also more divisions. The influx of foreign workers in the 1990's has proved to be very helpful in some cases, and harmful in others. Pray that all those working for the evangelization of Czechs would do so with a unity of purpose and synergy of action. The Evangelical Alliance works to coordinate the efforts of member churches. Pray for the indigenous churches to mature into sending churches, fulfilling their vision of supporting missionaries both at home and abroad.

6 **Freedom of religion** means complete freedom, even to believe lies, or not to believe at all. Most mainstream Christian groups do little by way of outreach, despite general interest in spiritual things. Marginal religious groups are much more active in this area. Pray that God might awaken Czechs to their deep spiritual needs and mobilize believers to leave their spiritual ghettos and demonstrate the love of Christ to hungry hearts.

7 **Young people** are searching for life-satisfying answers, but are often cynical and apathetic about organized religion. **CEF** is working among children, **SU** in the primary schools, and **IFES** has groups in several universities. Pray for fruitful ministry for these agencies. Religious education in schools is permitted. Pray that teachers with spiritual zeal may minister life in the classrooms. Summer camps (in Czech, German, and English) are also proving helpful in evangelizing and discipling young people.

8 **Christian literature** is increasing in its distribution and its scope. **The Bible Society** continues to sell large numbers of Bibles and New Testaments. The Navrat Domu and Nova Nadeje Publishing Houses, as well as several others, are publishing more and more Christian materials in Czech. **EHC** has reached about half of Czech homes with Christian literature. Pray that the impact of the written page may remould the people and build the Church. Pray also that outside groups who come to distribute literature might work in cooperation with national groups.

9 **Christian radio and television** programmes have much potential and are open to evangelical influence. Pray that the vision and funding might come in to kick-start a national Christian broadcasting movement. There are 21 hours of Christian radio each week from **TWR** and **HCJB**, in Czech, Slovak, German and Polish. The *JESUS* film has been translated into these languages as well, and has enjoyed a wide viewership. Pray for God to use Christian radio, TV and film to both reach unbelievers and train up Christians in all truth.

PERSECUTION INDEX
February 2004

Every year, Open Doors publishes an index which grades countries according to the levels of persecution of religious believers, and Christians especially. (Open Doors World Watch List [www.opendoors.org/content/wwlist.htm])

The countries are listed in decreasing order of levels of persecution according to the Open Doors scale in columns 4 and 5.

Note that this list contains the information for the years 2003 and 2004.

No.	Country	Jan 2004	Jan 2003	Trend	No.	Country	Jan 2004	Jan 2003	Trend
1	North Korea	82,5	82,5	0	28	Tunisia	38,5	40,0	0
2	Saudi Arabia	70,5	77,0	better	29	Russian Fed (Musl.)1	37,5	40,0	0
3	Laos	69,5	70,0	0	30	Mexico (South)2	36,5	37,5	0
4	Vietnam (Highlands)	68,0	70,0	0	31	Tajikistan	36,0	35,0	0
5	Iran	63,0	59,0	worse	32	Iraq	35,5	44,5	better
6	Turkmenistan	62,0	62,0	0	33	India	35,5	32,0	worse
7	Maldives	60,5	60,5	0	34	Sri Lanka	35,0	31,0	worse
8	Bhutan	59,5	60,0	0	35	Djibouti	34,0	33,5	0
9	Myanmar (Burma)	58,5	57,5	0	36	Indonesia	33,5	33,0	0
10	China	57,5	56,5	0	37	Algeria	33,5	32,5	0
11	Somalia	57,0	58,5	0	38	Nepal	33,5	31,0	worse
12	Pakistan	53,5	61,0	better	39	Turkey	32,5	34,5	0
13	Afghanistan	53,5	56,0	0	40	Mauritania	31,5	31,5	0
14	Comoros	52,0	50,5	0	41	United Arab Emirates	30,5	30,5	0
15	Sudan	50,5	52,5	0	42	Kurdistan	28,0	32,5	better
16	Uzbekistan	49,0	48,5	0	43	Oman	27,0	28,5	0
17	Yemen	46,5	48,0	0	44	Kuwait	26,5	26,5	0
18	Eritrea	46,5	34,5	worse	45	Belarus	26,0	24,0	0
19	Egypt	46,0	46,0	0	46	Jordan	25,5	23,5	0
20	Azerbaijan	45,0	47,0	0	47	Bangladesh	25,5	22,5	worse
21	Nigeria (North)	43,0	45,5	better	48	Syria	24,5	26,0	0
22	Libya	43,0	42,5	0	49	Bahrain	22,5	23,0	0
23	Morocco	42,5	40,5	0	50	Malaysia	22,5	23,0	0
24	Cuba	41,0	42,5	0					
25	Brunei	40,5	42,0	0		*1 Muslim republics of the Russian Federation: Chechnya,*			
26	Colombia (Conflict Areas)	39,0	43,5	0		*Kabardino Balkarya, Dagestan and Tatarstan*			
27	Qatar	39,0	39,0	0		*2 Southern Mexican state of Chiapas*			

Denmark

The Kingdom of Denmark

APRIL 23
EUROPE

national Church and is supported out of a state-levied church tax.

Religions	Population %	Adherents	Ann.Gr.
Christian	85.85	4,544,246	-0.6%
non-Religious/other	11.00	582,256	+6.9%
Muslim	3.02	159,856	+7.8%
Jewish	0.13	6,881	+0.3%

Christians	Denom.	Affil.%	,000	Ann.Gr.
Protestant	39	78.25	4,142	-5.0%
Independent	3	0.02	1	+0.5%
Anglican	1	0.06	3	-5.6%
Catholic	1	0.64	34	+0.9%
Orthodox	2	0.01	1	+0.7%
Marginal	12	0.57	30	-1.6%
Unaffiliated		7.63	404	n.a.
Doubly affiliated		-1.31	-70	n.a.

D

Churches	MegaBloc	Cong.	Members	Affiliates
Lutheran	P	2,300	1,000,000	4,100,000
Catholic	C	54	18,000	34,000
Jehovah's Witnesses	M	222	15,071	22,000
Baptist Union	P	48	5,386	8,000
Pentecostal Mvt.	P	52	5,000	8,000
Latter-day Saints (Morm)	M	26	3,397	5,300
Apostolic	P	42	2,600	3,200
Danish Covenant	P	29	2,000	3,000
Methodist	P	20	1,450	2,300
Salvation Army	P	36	1,400	1,600
Other denoms [48]		244	11,230	23,000
Doubly affiliated			-52,000	-70,000
Total Christians [58]		3,073	1,014,000	4,140,000

Trans-bloc Groupings	pop.%	,000	Ann.Gr.
Evangelical	4.8	252	-6.0%
Charismatic	1.5	77	-4.2%
Pentecostal	0.2	12	-1.4%

Missionaries from Denmark
P,I,A 475 in 28 agencies to 59 countries: Tanzania 75, Ethiopia 64, Nigeria 34.

Missionaries to Denmark
P,I,A 75 in 22 agencies from 8 countries.

GEOGRAPHY
Area 43,092 sq.km. The most southerly of the Scandinavian countries. See separate entries for Faeroe Islands and Greenland, which are autonomous regions of Denmark.

Population	Ann.Gr.	Density
2000	5,293,239	+0.26%	123 per sq. km.
2010	5,327,432	+0.00%	124 per sq. km.
2025	5,238,499	-0.17%	122 per sq. km.

Capital Copenhagen 1,326,000. **Urbanites** 85%.

PEOPLES
Danish citizens 95%. Danish 5.2 mill.; Faeorese 6,000; Greenlanders 3,000.
Foreign 5%. Nordic, EU citizens 80,000; former Yugoslavia 35,000; Turk 40,000; Somali 15,000; Iraqi 10,000; Iranian 7,000.

Literacy 99%. **Official language** Danish. **All languages** 8. **Languages with Scriptures** 4Bi.

ECONOMY
Based on services, agriculture and light industry. Strongly export-oriented. **HDI** 0.905; 15th/174. **Public debt** 62% of GNP. **Income/person** $31,900 (111% of USA).

POLITICS
Stable parliamentary democracy with a constitutional monarchy. A cautious member of the European Union with a history of exercising its European right of veto.

RELIGION
There is complete religious freedom, though the Lutheran Church is recognized as the

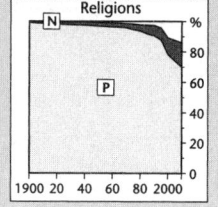

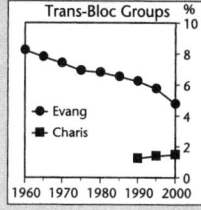

• Challenges for Prayer

1 **Denmark needs a fresh visitation from God.** Ninety percent of the population are members of the Lutheran Peoples Church. Church attendance varies between 1% and 4% in most parishes, yet many Danes still hold to their Christian identity (50% regularly pray). Pray that the Spirit may make Christ real to Danish Christians who have turned to secular or New Age thinking.

2 **Much of the Lutheran Church is formal,** and the fresh winds of the Holy Spirit must blow through this institution. A number evangelical pastors are committed to renewal of the Church. Pray for wisdom for all who seek to transform the Church and make it relevant to secular Danes.

3 **The evangelical witness needs strengthening** in every level of Danish life. Pray for the evangelizing work of such groups as the Lutheran home missions movement, **IFES** student groups, and other evangelical groups from both the Lutheran and Free Churches, that they may impact every level of Danish society.

4 **Old non-missionary, liberal theologies are devastating for the Church** by failing to equip them to be effective missionaries in a secular realm. Pray for theological and missiological renewal in all seminaries and Bible schools which will encourage a vibrant missions vision. Pray also for leaders to be raised up who are able to communicate with the Danish post-modern youth culture.

5 **Young people** have been particularly affected by the prevailing secularism and post-modernism of society, and have become more responsive to spiritual challenges. While there is a new enthusiasm towards the person of Jesus, many seek answers in new religious movements. Pray that the Church may be able to approach such young people with an effective message.

6 **There has been a steady decline** in the number of overseas missionaries. Pray for more to be called and that Danish mission agencies may contribute effectively in the globalized missionary movement.

7 **The 'New Danes'**, guest workers and refugees, need to hear the gospel. Pray that Danish Christians may be motivated to share their faith with them. A number of agencies and churches have outreach to some of these ethnic minority communities, and there are believers within some of them. Muslim groups, such as the Turks, Arabs, Iranians, Albanians, Somalis, etc., present a special challenge.

8 **Literature and Media.** The Danish Bible Society has produced a high quality CD for children and young people for widespread distribution to help them discover the Bible and its teachings. The *JESUS* film is available in Danish, as is much Christian literature and radio. Pray that distribution might be adequate in all media.

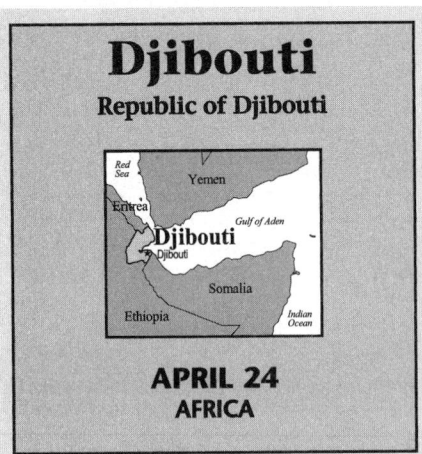

Djibouti
Republic of Djibouti

APRIL 24
AFRICA

Population		Ann.Gr.	Density
2000	637,634	+1.20%	27 per sq. km.
2010	785,170	+2.07%	34 per sq. km.
2025	1,026,235	+1.61%	44 per sq. km.

Capital Djibouti 354,548. **Urbanites** 83%.

PEOPLES
Somali 61.7%. In three major clans in southern half of the country: Issa 213,000; Gadaboursi 96,000; Issaq 85,000. Many are recent refugees from Somalia.
Afar (Danakil) 20%. In northern half.
Arab 6%. Mostly Yemeni, some Omani and Saudi.
Other 4%. French 20,000; Greek 1,600.
Refugees 8.3%. Ethiopians 50,000; Somalis.

Literacy 46%, far lower in practice. **Official languages** French and Arabic. **Trade languages** Somali, Afar. **All languages** 4. **Languages with Scriptures** 2Bi 1NT.

GEOGRAPHY
Area 23,200 sq.km. A hot, dry, desert enclave between Ethiopia, Eritrea and Somalia. Some have called it 'Hell's waiting room.'

ECONOMY
Lack of water, industry and natural resources make the country's viability dependent on French aid and the large military base. Half the GNP is derived from the French presence. The port

of Djibouti and rail link to landlocked Ethiopia is its only major economic asset. **Unemployment** over 50%. **HDI** 0.412; 157th/174. **Public debt** 52% of GNP. **Income/person** $790 (2.5% of USA).

POLITICS
The French took control of the area in 1884 because of its strategic location, but the boundaries straddled a centuries-old conflict zone between the Afars and the Somalis. This ancient conflict is still alive, and has affected political life since independence in 1977. Civil war raged between them in 1991-94, with the Somalis becoming dominant in the capital and government. There were multi-party elections in 1999. Only the large French military presence prevented Djibouti from being dragged into the war between neighbouring Eritrea and Ethiopia and clan wars in Somalia.

RELIGION
Islam has been declared the state religion, but conformity is not enforced and other religions are accorded considerable freedom.

Religions	Population %	Adherents	Ann.Gr.
Muslim	93.90	598,738	+1.2%
Christian	4.67	30,000	+1.5%
non-Religious/other	1.32	8,417	+1.5%
Baha'i	0.09	574	-0.9%
Hindu	0.02	128	+1.3%

Christians	Denom.	Affil.%	,000	Ann.Gr.
Protestant	3	0.07	0	+8.1%
Independent	1	0.03	0	+10.0%
Catholic	1	1.40	9	+2.2%
Orthodox	2	3.17	20	+1.0%

Churches	MegaBloc	Cong	Members	Affiliates
Ethiopian Orthodox	O	20	11,976	20,000
Catholic	C	7	4,890	8,900
Ethiopian Protestants	P	5	150	300
Reformed	P		50	100
Other denominations [3]		4	259	480
Total Christians [7]		36	17,325	30,000

Trans-bloc Groupings	pop.%	,000	Ann.Gr.
Evangelical	0.1	1	+5.8%
Charismatic	0.1	1	+2.6%

Missionaries to Djibouti
P,I,A 31 in 6 agencies. C 53.

• Challenges for Prayer

1 **Djibouti, Africa's third smallest state**, is a haven of calm in a stormy region. It is also a key base for Christian witness. Pray that present freedoms may not be eroded by the politics of the Horn of Africa nor by the Islamist voice which gets louder as the economic situation declines.

2 **The only legally recognized Protestant witness** is that of the French Protestant Church, which began in 1960. The FPC has given hospitality to Ethiopian, Malagasy and local believer groups and mission agencies entering the country. It also sponsors a number of social projects among refugees and the poor. The FPC and other bodies have formed a Council of Churches and Missions. Pray for continued effective cooperation and unity among Christians.

3 **Ministry specifically to the Afars and the Somalis** commenced in 1975 with the arrival of the **RSTI** with 15 workers in 2000. The US Mennonites, Baptists and Life International have joined them in this outreach. Mission work is a tough challenge in this hot, dry but often humid land, and working conditions are extreme. Pray for their ministries in education, public health, literature, Bible translation, literacy and youth work. Through these, opportunities to witness abound — pray that contacts may lead to disciples for Jesus. Pray for the calling of other long-term workers. Pray also for the long-awaited spiritual breakthroughs; every advance has been strongly contested by the enemy of souls.

4 **Ethiopian refugees are often destitute**. Many are Orthodox Christian. There are also five lively evangelical congregations among them, many with a strong desire to witness. Pray that they may be both relevant and effective in that witness.

5 **The few Somali and Afar believers are often isolated** and suffer many pressures from relatives. Most of them are jobless and some are illiterate. Pray for effective use of literacy programmes and the Scriptures in Somali and Afar. The Somali believers are meeting regularly for Bible study together. Pray that from these believers, leaders for congregations may be raised up.

APRIL 24 · DJIBOUTI

6 The less evangelized peoples of Djibouti need prayer:

a) *The Afars' main territory* is in Ethiopia and Eritrea where there is little witness at present. A minority are nomadic. There is no known church among them.

b) *The Somalis are a small branch of the larger population* in Somalia and Ethiopia. The Somalis in Djibouti are a key for the evangelization of their kinsmen across the border (**SIM**).

c) *Arabs, both local and Yemeni,* need a specific approach directed to their spiritual needs.

d) *The ethnic minorities* — Greek, French and Indians, have little exposure to vibrant Christian witness.

D

7 Christian support ministries:

a) *Bible translation and distribution.* The Afar NT is published and the OT is nearing completion (**RSTI/UBS**). There is a key project to record both Afar Scripture songs and the entire NT on tape; a vital means of communicating God's Word in a largely illiterate population. **RSTI** also runs a Christian bookstore.

b) *Radio broadcasts* by **FEBA** are a key ministry in Afar and Somali (3.5 hours/week). **TWR** also broadcasts in Arabic and Somali.

c) *The JESUS film* has been widely used in Somali; the Afar version is nearing completion. Pray for long-term impact.

Dominica
Commonwealth of Dominica

APRIL 25
LATIN AMERICA

GEOGRAPHY
Area 750 sq.km. A hurricane-prone, rugged, mountainous island between the French islands of Guadeloupe and Martinique and ruled by France until 1759. This has determined much of its religious and cultural development.

Population	Ann.Gr.	Density
2000	70,714	-0.06%	94 per sq. km.
2010	71,045	+0.08%	95 per sq. km.
2025	73,442	+0.29%	98 per sq. km.

A high rate of emigration to USA, Canada and UK. There are probably more expatriate Dominicans than indigenous.
Capital Roseau 9,133. **Urbanites** 30%.

PEOPLES
Afro-Caribbean 96.3%.
Amerindian 2.4%. Caribs 1,700, the descendents of the original inhabitants, but considerably intermarried with the Afro-Caribbean people.

Other 1.3%. Euro-American 400, East Indian 300, Syrian 200, Chinese 150.
Literacy 90% (but functionally nearer 75%).
Official language English.

ECONOMY
Dependence on export of bananas to the EU. Threatened by the ending of its protected market, diversification of the economy is being attempted. Eco-tourism in Dominica's beautiful interior is increasing, but the huge costs for constructing an international airport are controversial.
HDI 0.776; 53rd/174. **Public debt** 38% of GNP.
Income/person $3,090 (10% of USA).

POLITICS
Dominica had the British Caribbean's first Black-majority government for a period in the 19th Century. Independent in 1978 as a democratic republic.

RELIGION
Freedom of religion

Religions	Population %	Adherents	Ann.Gr.
Christian	94.90	67,108	-0.1%
Spiritist	2.70	1,909	+0.7%
Baha'i	1.70	1,202	+1.2%
Chinese/Buddhist	0.20	160	n.a.
Hindu	0.20	141	n.a.
Muslim	0.20	140	n.a.
non-Religious/other	0.10	71	+0.0%

Christians	Denom.	Affil.%	,000	Ann.Gr.
Protestant	12	18.95	13	+2.7%
Independent	6	3.51	2	+1.0%
Anglican	1	0.57	0	+0.0%
Catholic	1	79.62	56	-0.3%
Marginal	1	1.56	1	+5.8%
Doubly affiliated		*-9.31*	*-7*	*n.a.*

Churches	MegaBloc	Cong.	Members	Affiliates
Catholic	C	18	29,788	56,300
Seventh-day Adventist	P	20	4,228	5,400
Methodist [2]	P	4	1,100	2,200
All Baptist [4]	P	26	921	2,000
Other Pentecostal [4]	I	14	877	1,465
Christian Union	P	16	900	1,300
Ch of God of Prophecy	P	6	520	1,300
Jehovah's Witnesses	M	8	354	1,100
Gospel Mission Chs	I	15	560	900
Ch of God (Cleveland)	P	3	200	500
Anglican	A	3	267	400
Other denoms [3]		7	488	820
Doubly affiliated			-3,300	-6,600
Total Christians [22]		140	37,003	67,285

Trans-bloc Groupings	pop.%	,000	Ann.Gr.
Evangelical	13.5	10	+2.2%
Charismatic	8.3	6	+1.7%
Pentecostal	4.6	3	+2.5%

Missionaries from Dominica
P,I,A 4, all in Dominica.

Missionaries to Dominica
P,I,A 30 in 11 agencies from 2 countries: Korea 17, USA 9.

D

• Challenges for Prayer

1 Historically Dominica has been and remains predominantly Catholic, but Evangelical Christians have increased from 2% in 1970 to over 13% in 2000. The Association of Evangelicals has been providing good leadership. There has been interest in a saturation church-planting programme. Pray for continued growth in the gospel witness.

2 The challenges faced by the churches. Pray about these:

a) *Due to the economic situation*, many pastors have to work at a second job to support themselves. Pastoral 'burn-out' is a problem.

b) *Almost the entire population is God-fearing* and open to spiritual things, yet there is much complacency and moral laxness. Over 75% of children are born out of wedlock despite their parents' profession of Christianity. Formerly, slave owners forbade their slaves from marrying which caused a distortion of moral, and Scriptural, principles. Pray for this curse of slavery to be broken, a right understanding of Scriptural principles to be gained, and a spirit of repentance be given to all.

3 The Carib Indians live on an isolated reservation on the northeast coast of Dominica. They are the last of the indigenous peoples in the Caribbean to survive the arrival of colonialism and subsequent waves of immigrants. Most are nominally Christian, but few have a living faith in Christ. Pray that these socially deprived people may find their true identity and fulfilment in Him.

Dominican Republic

Dominican Republic

APRIL 25
LATIN AMERICA

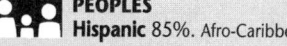 **GEOGRAPHY**
Area 48,443 sq.km. The eastern two-thirds of the island of Hispaniola, shared with Haiti.

Population		Ann.Gr.	Density
2000	8,495,338	+1.66%	175 per sq. km.
2010	9,708,026	+1.25%	200 per sq. km.
2025	11,164,412	+0.78%	230 per sq. km.

A large Haitian illegal immigrant and migrant labour population of over one million.

Capital Santo Domingo 3,601,000. The first European-founded city in the Americas. **Urbanites** 56%.

PEOPLES
Hispanic 85%. Afro-Caribbean 7,136,000; Euro-American 1,360,000.
Haitian 14%. Speaking French Creole; about half are Dominican-born.
Other 1%. Jamaican 25,000; Chinese 9,000; Lebanese 3,200; Japanese 1,700.

Literacy 82%. **Official language** Spanish. **All languages** 3. **Languages with Scriptures** 2Bi.

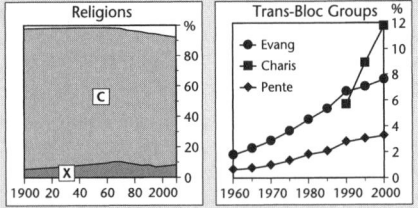

ECONOMY
Growth in the early 1970s has been replaced by devastating decline prompted by world recessions, a bloated bureaucracy and a corrupt government spending freely on costly prestige projects. Although the '90s have seen some improvement through light industry and tourism, 40% live in deep poverty and unemployment is still near 28%. **HDI** 0.726; 88th/174. **Public debt** 28% of GNP. **Income/person** $1,600 (6% of USA).

POLITICS
Independence achieved four times — twice from Spain (1821/65), once from Haiti (1844) and once from the USA (1924)! Thirty years of repressive dictatorship ended in 1961, but instability and civil war prevailed until 1966. Subsequent democratic governments have proved manipulative and corrupt, leaving the poor and the oppressed Haitian under-class disenfranchised.

RELIGION
Catholicism is the state religion and the Church jealously guards its privileged political and economic clout. There is freedom of religion in basic rights for non-Catholics.

Religions	Population %	Adherents	Ann.Gr.
Christian	95.15	8,083,314	+1.6%
non-Religious/other	2.47	209,835	+4.0%
Spiritist	2.18	185,198	+3.4%
Buddhist	0.10	8,495	+3.8%
Baha'i	0.07	5,947	+1.7%
Muslim	0.02	1,699	+1.7%
Jewish	0.01	850	+1.7%

Christians	Denom.	Affil. %	,000	Ann.Gr.
Protestant	30	5.79	491	+2.4%
Independent	36	1.65	140	+8.2%
Anglican	1	0.05	4	+0.6%
Catholic	1	88.55	7,522	+1.0%
Marginal	2	1.54	131	+4.4%
Unaffiliated		0.87	74	n.a.
Doubly affiliated		-3.30	-280	n.a.

Churches	MegaBloc	Cong.	Members	Affiliates
Catholic	C	300	3,917,867	7,522,000
Seventh-day Adventist	P	417	111,455	170,000
Jehovah's Witnesses	M	342	22,906	71,000
Ch of God of Prophecy	P	322	23,716	65,000
Assemblies of God	P	751	42,593	59,643
Ch of God (Cleveland)	P	367	24,245	55,000
Dominican Evangelical	P	180	6,803	20,000
Chr Assembly of God	I	120	9,500	18,000
Moravian	P	37	5,200	15,000
Ch of the Nazarene	P	130	6,000	14,000
Free Methodist	P	115	6,000	12,000
Christian Bible	P	50	5,000	11,000
Salvation Army	P	40	4,000	10,000
Christian Brethren	P	120	5,000	10,000
Christian Reformed	P	90	3,000	10,000
Evang Temple Assoc	P	30	2,000	5,000
Episcopal	A	30	2,767	4,400
Baptist Convention	P	23	1,417	3,200
Other denoms [52]		1,223	106,165	213,483
Doubly affiliated			-140,000	-280,000
Total Christians [70]		4,687	4,165,634	8,009,236

Trans-bloc Groupings	pop.%	,000	Ann.Gr.
Evangelical	7.6	644	+3.2%
Charismatic	11.8	999	+2.1%
Pentecostal	3.2	276	+3.4%

Missionaries from Dominican Republic
P,I,A 72 in 9 agencies to 8 countries: Dominican Rep. 55.

Missionaries to Dominican Republic
P,I,A 283 in 50 agencies from 11 countries: USA 244, Korea 13, Brazil 8.

• Answers to Prayer

1 **Evangelical growth** came relatively late, but took off in the 1970s and continued through the '90s as Evangelicals strove to multiply churches and take the gospel to 1 million Dominicans by 2000. During the '90s the number of evangelical churches increased from about 2,000 to 3,200.

• Challenges for Prayer

Columbus' importation of sugar cane has been the source of 500 years of wealth and misery. It was one factor in the genocide of the one million indigenous Arawak Taino people, the importation of slaves in the past and also the present exploitation of Haitian labour. Another factor is EU distortion of the world sugar market by exporting under-priced, subsidized beet sugar. Pray for more fair and considerate treatment of the poor by both the Dominican government and richer nations in their trade policies.

2 **Religious freedom** is not yet an issue completely resolved for non-Catholics. The 1954 Concordat limits that freedom in taxation and government institutions. CODUE, one of the two evangelical umbrella networks, seeks to coordinate activities to ensure equality for all in the sight of the law. This has led to greater unity among Evangelicals than hitherto.

3 **The major challenges** confronting Christians are:

a) *Retention of those converted*. There has been growth in many denominations, especially Pentecostals, **CMA** and the several Church of God groups, but only a small proportion of those who respond through evangelism become members.

b) *Development of Christian ethics* for Christian involvement in a society where corruption, crime and promiscuity are rampant.

c) *Cultivation of a missions vision* despite pervasive poverty. There are over 70 Dominican evangelical missionaries, of which 30 are cross-cultural.

4 **Leadership for the churches** is a constant challenge. Emigration of the gifted and moneyed to Puerto Rico and the USA is a loss the growing churches can ill afford. Pray for vision, commitment and stickability for all called to Christian work. Pray also for those willing to serve in the poorer, rural areas. Pray that the seven or more accredited, theological training schools and the National Evangelical University may provide spiritual, mature and stable leaders for the future.

5 **The large Haitian under-class** has been the most responsive of all. The Nazarene and Christian Reformed congregations have multiplied. Haitians are immigrants, or descendants of immigrants, who are often despised by Hispanics yet needed as sugar-cane and manual workers. They face discrimination from Dominicans — even Christians, and the question of their emancipation is a major unresolved issue that must be faced by both government and people. Pray for church leaders and their congregations to be good witnesses in this tense and inequitable situation.

6 **The less evangelized** for prayer:

a) *The unchurched majority* is nominally Christian but occultism is widespread, pervasive and strong. Maybe more than 4,000 villages have no evangelical witness.

b) *The middle and upper classes* have relatively fewer Evangelicals. **CMA** have majored on reaching them.

c) *Youth*. There are 30 universities and colleges with 150,000 students, but the need to work to pay for tuition, lack of job prospects and purpose in life, cripple initiative. Pray for the UJC(**IFES**) with its university (5) and school (3) groups and its need for more staff to extend the ministry. **CCCI** has a large contingent of workers in campus ministry.

d) *The Chinese*, who have only two congregations of believers among them.

Ecuador

Republic of Ecuador

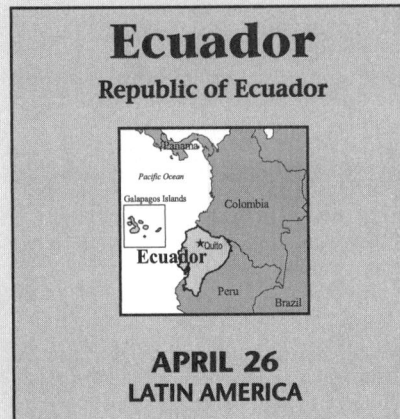

APRIL 26
LATIN AMERICA

 **GEOGRAPHY**
Area 269,178 sq.km. Amazon jungle in the east, high Andean Sierra in the centre, fertile coastal plain on Pacific Coast. Also the Galapagos Is. 1,000 km to west.

Population	Ann.Gr.	Density
2000	12,646,068	+1.99%	47 per sq. km.
2010	14,898,509	+1.55%	55 per sq. km.
2025	17,796,101	+1.03%	66 per sq. km.

Capital Quito 1.6 mill. Other major city: Guayaquil 2.15m. **Urbanites** 62%.

PEOPLES
Spanish-speaking 59%. Non-Amerindian; much racial mixing: Mestizo 4.8m; Euro-American 1.4m; Afro-American 800,000.
Amerindian 40%.
  Quichua (Quechua in surrounding nations) 39%. Spanish-speaking 3.35m. Nine other main groups, the largest: Chimborazo 1.34m; Otavalo 533,000; Canari 64,000; Calderon 37,000; Saraguro 32,000; Salasaca 15,000.
  Lowland tribes 1% (60,000+). 11 groups, the largest: Shuar(2) 49,000; Cayapa 6,700; Waorani 1,000.
Other 1%. English-speaking 80,000; German 40,000; Chinese 14,000; Norwegian 13,000; Arab 2,200.

Literacy 90%. **Official language** Spanish. **All Languages** 22. **Languages with Scriptures** 3Bi 9NT 4por 6w.i.p.

ECONOMY
The main export commodities are oil, flowers, shrimp and bananas. Ecuador is the world's largest exporter of bananas. Oil exploitation has enriched a few, but the poor have become even poorer, and the ecology and Amazon forests degraded. Failure to curb inflation, widespread corruption, the war with Peru and a series of natural disasters together with a low oil price brought the country to the brink of bankruptcy in 1999 and a default in paying off international debts. **HDI** 0.747; 72ⁿᵈ/174. **Public debt**

71% of GNP. **Income/person** $1,500 (5% of USA).

POLITICS
Independent from Spain in 1830. Political stability has been rare, the average government lasting two years. The broadening of democracy is bringing some political voice to the long-oppressed Quichua. Political upheavals continued during the 1990s over the need for painful economic reforms and half-hearted efforts to reform an inadequate constitution. The 1995 war with Peru over a disputed border area was a costly setback, but that issue has now been resolved.

RELIGION
The culture has been strongly moulded by Catholicism, so though there is freedom of religion, rural populations have not been so receptive to change.

Religions	Population %	Adherents	Ann.Gr.
Christian	97.36	12,312,212	+2.0%
non-Religious/other	1.90	245,275	+3.1%
Traditional ethnic	0.40	50,584	-0.4%
Chinese/Buddhist	0.16	20,234	+0.8%
Baha'i	0.15	18,969	+2.0%
Muslim	0.02	2,529	+17.2%
Jewish	0.01	1,265	+2.0%

Christians	Denom.	Affil.%	,000	Ann.Gr.
Protestant	49	4.81	609	+6.3%
Independent	71	1.40	178	+7.8%
Anglican	1	0.01	2	+2.4%
Catholic	1	82.24	10,400	+0.9%
Orthodox	1	0.02	2	+2.2%
Marginal	3	2.61	330	+6.0%
Unaffiliated		8.64	1,092	n.a.
Doubly affiliated		*-2.37*	*-300*	*n.a.*

Churches	MegaBloc	Cong.	Members	Affiliates
Catholic	C	960	5.714m	10.40m
Assoc of Indian Ev [4]	P	500	75,000	180,000
Latter-day Saints (Morm)	M	200	111,801	180,000
Jehovah's Witnesses	M	526	40,037	150,000
Chr and Miss Alliance	P	119	20,036	60,713
Foursquare Evangelical	P	190	45,000	60,000
Seventh-day Adventist	P	76	28,840	55,000
Baptist Convention	P	220	31,446	50,000
Assemblies of God	P	180	15,000	45,000
Ch of God (Cleveland)	P	140	23,000	45,000
Ch of the Nazarene	P	240	19,000	35,000
Assoc of Inter-Am Evang	P	40	4,000	10,000
Evangelical Covenant	P	60	7,500	10,000
Assoc of Missionary Chs	P	80	1,400	5,000
Other denoms [109]		1,506	108,000	235,000
Doubly affiliated			*-164,835*	*-300,000*
Total Christians [126]		5,037	6.079m	11.220m

Trans-bloc Groupings pop. %		,000	Ann.Gr.
Evangelical	6.1	776	+6.9%
Charismatic	5.2	652	+4.8%
Pentecostal	2.2	278	+6.1%

Missionaries from Ecuador
P,I,A 117 in 20 agencies to 9 countries: Ecuador 78, Bolivia 12.

Missionaries to Ecuador
P,I,A 924 in 88 agencies from 29 countries: USA 540, Brazil 68, Bolivia 34, Germany 33, UK 31, Norway 30.

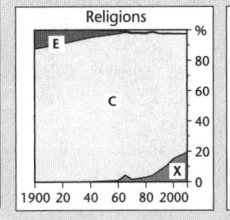

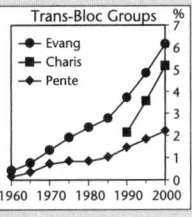

• Answers to Prayer

1 The impact of the gospel on sections of the Quichua is a modern-day miracle. In 1967 there were only 120 believers among 3 million people; now there are some areas with 45-50% Evangelicals. The most notable work has been the 100-year ministry of **GMU** with now nearly 200,000 linked with the churches planted through them.

E

2 HCJB Radio, launched in 1931, was the first of the great Christian mission radio broadcasters. Today this ministry is known around the world and both Ecuador and the world are blessed as a result.

• Challenges for Prayer

1 The country urgently needs an honest government that gives stability and peace, yet has the courage to tackle the serious economic and social problems that have held back real progress, and confront the vested interests of the entrenched, privileged elite. Pray for those in authority.

2 The Catholic Church has seen its privileged position eroded and a recent rapid increase of evangelical and marginal groups. There have been sporadic, local incidents of mob violence, burning of churches and intimidation against Evangelicals. Pray for for continued freedom of religion, harmony between denominations and an increase in spiritual life among Catholics.

3 Political uncertainty, war and a series of natural and economic disasters over the past 20 years have broken down old feudal structures of State and Church and made Ecuadorians more receptive to the gospel. Pray that this openness may lead to a great spiritual harvest in every part of the country and level of society.

4 Ecuador's Evangelicals. Ecuador had Latin America's lowest percentage of Evangelicals in 1960, but this has increased from 0.43% (19,000) to 6.1% (776,000) in 2000. This growth has been largely in the burgeoning cities and among the Quichua. Pray for unity that transcends class, culture, personalities and denominational labels so that the Body of Christ may exert a decisive influence on the life of the nation in the 21st Century. The Evangelical Confraternity is a fellowship linking most Evangelicals in vision and in speaking out on issues of social concern.

5 Specific challenges for the Church:

a) *Vision and growth to be maintained* — some churches have lost their evangelistic zeal.
b) *Cultural sensitivity* for Spanish-speaking Christians in ministry to the Amerindian evangelical Christian majority.
c) *Integration of Quichua and Lowland Indians* into the political, economic and spiritual life of the country, while preserving their cultural integrity.
d) *Improved availability and quality of pastoral training.* syncretistic beliefs, losses to cults and evangelical nominalism are otherwise inevitable. Bible schools and seminaries are increasing in number, but insufficiently to meet the need. TEE programmes are proving an effective supplement in training lay and pastoral teachers.
e) *More effective and appropriate ministry to children* and young people. Without this the next generation will be lost to the Church.
f) *A maturing of the developing missions vision.* Many congregations do not understand either the need or the commitment required.

6 **Pioneer work among the small jungle tribes** attracted worldwide attention in 1956 when one **MAF**, one **GMU** and three Brethren missionaries were killed by the primitive Waorani (Auca). Nearly all these tribes now have churches and the Scriptures through the work of Brethren and SIL/**WBT** missionaries among the Waorani and Colorado, **GMU** and **HCJB** among the Shuar, the Quichua churches among the Zaparo, and others. Pray for:

a) *The neutralization of intense anti-missionary propaganda* from humanistic anthropologists, leftist agitators, traders and jungle exploiters. At times opposition has curtailed Christian ministry and Bible translation work.

b) *The efforts by Indian believers* to preserve their lands from irresponsible oil exploration.

c) *The maturing of the jungle churches* to cope with modernity and the onslaught of the Spanish and Quichua cultures.

7 **Bible translation and distribution.** Ecuador is one of the first countries entered by **WBT**. They were involved in 12 of the NT translation projects before they were obliged to withdraw. Pray for the completion of translation programmes in progress, and for the two or three languages where translation work may yet be needed. Pray for the effective use of the Bibles and New Testaments now available. **The Bible Society** has a pivotal role in promoting and distributing the Scriptures in this nation.

8 **Missions.** The largest groups are **HCJB Radio** (242 missionaries), **IMB-SBC** (65), **CMA** (89), **AoG** (41), **GMU** (69), Norwegian Santal Mission (23), **OMS** (33), **Brethren** (33). There are many opportunities for missionary recruits in supportive ministries, church planting and pioneer work in the groups mentioned below. Pray for good church-mission relationships. There is the ever present danger of administrative and financial paternalism creeping in and stifling Ecuadorian initiatives and making Evangelical Christianity the 'gringo' (US) religion.

9 The less-evangelized:

a) *The slum-dwellers* of Quito and Guayaquil. Over 60% of the latter's population lives in slums built on a polluted marsh. Few Christian workers have a vision for these deprived people.

b) *The upper and middle classes* who have been relatively unresponsive (**CMA**, **OMS** and others).

c) *University and school students*. There are over eight agencies involved in campus ministries among the 220,000 students, including **CCCI**, **IFES**, **YFC**, **LAM** and four denominational groups. The work is small, but an impact is being made on the university campuses. The Latin American Christian University was opened in Quito in 1996.

d) *The Saraguro and Salasaca Quichua* among whom **OMS** ministers have been less responsive.

e) *The 6,000 people living on the distant and barren Galapagos Islands,* which had only one evangelical church with two members and six adherents in 1992.

f) *The provinces* of Carchi (130,000 people with 8 churches) and Loja (361,000 people with only 9 churches). **SIM** is ministering in Loja, which is still the least reached province having less than 20 churches for 424,000 people. *Operacíon Esperanza* is an umbrella organization linking **IMB-SBC**, **SIM** and WMPL in commitment to reaching Lujo.

g) *The Chinese with one young church* in their community.

10 Christian media.

a) *Radio.* **HCJB** transmits over 900 hours weekly in 12 languages on short wave, FM and by satellite (together with **TWR**) to Ecuador, Latin America and the world. **HCJB** also has an extensive range of supportive ministries — including follow-up, education, pastoral training and medicine (two teaching hospitals and clinics). Pray also for the two Quichua and one Shuar Christian radio stations, under local leadership but started by **GMU**, broadcasting to these indigenous groups. Both the Evangelical Covenant Church and Lutheran Church also run radio stations.

b) *Back to the Bible* in Spanish has become a mainstay for evangelical broadcasters producing local programmes.

c) *The JESUS film* in Spanish has been widely aired on television as well as projected as a film. It is also available in Chimborazo, Shuar and Calderon.

Egypt
Arab Republic of Egypt

APRIL 27-29
AFRICA

Revised January 2004

E

GEOGRAPHY
Area 997,739 sq.km. Mostly desert, only 3% is arable land — along the banks and delta of the Nile River and around the Western Desert oases.

Population		Ann.Gr.	Density
2000	68,469,695	+1.91%	69 per sq. km.
2010	80,063,292	+1.44%	80 per sq. km.
2025	95,615,454	+1.11%	96 per sq. km.

In fertile areas 2,230 people per sq.km!

Capital Cairo 16,000,000. Other major city: Alexandria 5,000,000. **Urbanites** 43%.

PEOPLES
Arab 92%. Egyptian, speaking Arabic but descendants of the ancient Coptic-speaking people of Biblical times. Bedouin 1.4 mill.; Sudanese ca. 500,000.
Nubians 2.4%. Arabic-speaking 1.35m; Nobiin 230,000; Kenusi-Dongola 120,000.
Berber 2%. Mostly Arabic-speaking. Zenati 5,000 at the Siwa Oasis.
Gypsy 2%. Most now Arabic-speaking. Halebi 1,000,000; Ghagar 257,000.
Other 0.4%. Westerners 250,000; Beja 77,000; Turks 32,000; Armenians 14,000.
Refugees Black Sudanese may number 1.5m or more. Also Ethiopians, Palestinians, Eritreans, etc.

Literacy 61% (functional literacy is 35-40%). **Official language** Arabic. **All languages** 11. **Languages with Scriptures** 3Bi 1NT 2por.

ECONOMY
Limited agricultural land being lost to expanding cities and high population density keep a third of the population below the poverty line. Vast new irrigation schemes in the Western Desert and Sinai are being developed. Liberalization of the economy in the 1990s has brought considerable advancement. Main source of income: tourism, oil, Suez Canal dues, US aid and remittances from expatriate Egyptians. **HDI** 0.616; 120th/174. **Public debt** 45% of GNP. **Income/person** $1,080 (4% of USA).

POLITICS
President Sadat's diplomacy (1970-81) won back control of the valuable Suez Canal and Sinai oilfields from Israel as an outcome of the 1973 Yom Kippur War. The peace treaty with Israel led to political isolation from other Arab states for some years, but the continued failure to find a lasting solution to the Palestine issue has brought disillusionment. Extreme Islamist groups exploited economic problems to mount a terror campaign against the government, Christians and foreign tourists. Vigorous and harsh suppression between 1992 and 2000 marginalized and discredited the Islamist movements. The economic and political cost was high. Multi-party democratic government is more theoretical than real, but the country is relatively stable politically.

RELIGION
Islam is the state religion; until recently the large Christian minority was left in relative peace. Archaic discriminatory laws and the rise of Islamism has resulted in the authorities turning a blind eye to a culture of police brutality and to Islamist violence and terror against Christians. International pressure since 1998 has provoked governmental efforts to rebuild its image. **Persecution Index** 14th in the world.

Religions	Population %	Adherents	Ann.Gr.
Muslim	86.52	59,239,980	+2.1%
Christian	12.98	8,887,366	+0.5%
non-Religious/other	0.50	342,348	+3.6%

The official figure for Christians is 6%, but Christians claim up to 20%. The truth is probably in between.

Christians	Denom.	Affil.%	,000	Ann.Gr.
Protestant	23	0.82	560	+1.3%
Independent	7	0.03	23	+2.0%
Anglican	1	0.00	3	+0.8%
Catholic	7	0.41	280	+2.2%
Orthodox	6	11.72	8,026	+0.4%
Marginal	4	0.00	2	+2.5%

Churches	MegaBloc	Cong.	Members	Affiliates
Coptic Orthodox	O	1,700	4,600,000	8,000,000
Evangelical Ch of EP	P	330	50,000	300,000
Catholic [7]	C	202	162,000	280,000
Assemblies of God	P	145	75,000	110,000
Free Methodist	P	120	20,000	45,000
Christian Brethren	P	200	15,000	25,000
Armenian Orthodox	O	4	8,442	13,000
Greek Orthodox	O	22	2,800	12,180
Pentecostal Ch of God	P	32	3,775	9,438
Church of Grace	I	27	2,600	3,800
Ch of God (Anderson)	P	15	1,500	3,000
Pentecostal Holiness	P	12	1,400	2,338
Ch of God of Prophecy	P	19	1,100	2,090
Other denoms [30]		475	50,700	88,000
Total Christians [49]		3,300	4,994,400	8,894,000

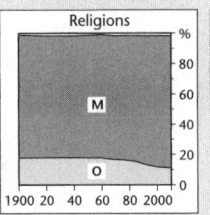

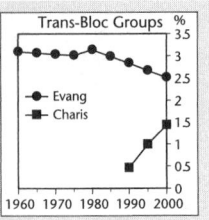

• Answers to Prayer

1 **The Church has come through nearly 2,000 years of discrimination** and times of severe persecution, yet has retained its strong spiritual character. It has earned its name as 'The Church of the Martyrs.' The last decade has been hard for Christians, but there is much life and vigour among both the Orthodox and Protestant churches.

2 **The innovative use of media** through literature (Magalla), television (**SAT-7**) and **The Bible Society** have multiplied the effectiveness of proclaiming the gospel.

• Challenges for Prayer

1 **For over 1,000 years Egypt was a majority-Christian country** — even after the Arab Muslim conquest in 640AD. Egypt gave to the Christian world some of its greatest theologians and the monastic movement. Coptic Christians are more authentic Egyptians than those who follow the religion of their Arab conquerors. Every effort has been made to expunge Egypt's great Christian heritage from the historic records, downplay the size of the Church and marginalize its contribution to society. Pray that in a rediscovery of this heritage many might turn to Christ.

2 **'Islam is the solution' has been the popular slogan** pushing for a more Islamic state as the answer to Egypt's economic and social problems. Acts of terrorism, economic sabotage and intolerance have brought discredit to Islam itself. Pray that many might investigate the claims of the gospel and the faith of their forefathers.

3 **The government has to perform a balancing act** between the vociferous and often violent Islamists, the silent majorities and minorities in Egypt, and criticisms from the outside world. Pray for fair and humane laws that are impartially applied by the courts and police for the good of the whole population.

4 **The Coptic Church is by far the largest body of Christians** in the Middle East and is a strategic key for the evangelization of the area. Pray for:

a) *The leadership of the Church*. They need a close walk with God and wisdom in handling the Muslim authorities, Islamist persecution and the questioning world.

b) *The spiritual enlivenment of the Church* in the midst of mounting pressures and communal tensions. There are many nominal Christians.

c) *The biblically-based renewal movement* in the Coptic Church which has steadily gained momentum since 1930. It has a strong emphasis on Bible study and a warm personal faith and many have become fervent witnesses for the Lord. Pray for the growth and effectiveness of this movement of the Spirit.

d) *Christians are numerous in business*, the professions and health services. Pray that their lives and witness may exalt Christ.

5 **The Protestant churches sprang from the Orthodox minority**, and for some decades had not seen significant growth. This is changing: there has been a growing renewal movement since 1973 and many young people are now coming to the Lord and a new generation of bold leaders is emerging. Several Pentecostal and evangelical denominations are growing significantly. Pray that, despite the difficulties, Muslims may be reached and welcomed into the churches. Few Christians would risk witnessing to a Muslim because of the possible consequences. Many churches have extensive social and medical programmes to help the very poor.

6 **Persecution of Christians steadily increased** in intensity during the 1980s and '90s. Harassment, severe application of ancient discriminatory laws, destruction of churches and financial incentives for Christians to adopt Islam have all been extensively used to break the morale of Christians. In some areas, especially in Upper Egypt, Muslims have even sought to displace local Christian communities to 'purify' their society. Pray for:

a) *Christians to stand firm in their faith* and live exemplary lives before their oppressors and in the face of police brutality. In the last few years over 1,300 people have died at the hands of Islamists, many of whom were Christians.

b) *Christians who waver.* It is reckoned that between 12,000 and 15,000 annually are coerced or enticed to become Muslims. There are cases of young girls being kidnapped, violated and forced to marry Muslims.

c) *Muslim-background believers* who are steadily increasing in number. Conversion is not illegal, but some are imprisoned for 'despising Islam' or 'inciting intercommunal strife'. Some have had to flee for their lives.

d) *The ending of discriminatory laws and the exclusion* of Christians from government posts and positions of influence.

7 **There is a dearth of volunteers for pastoral and missionary service**. Many evangelical churches have no pastor. Pray for many to give themselves for the Lord's work. Pray also for those in theological training at the Coptic Evangelical Church Seminary (which had 40 students preparing for the ministry in 1999), the **AoG** and the Free Methodist Bible schools.

8 **Unreached peoples.** Few Muslims have ever heard a Christian testify. Pray that Christians may take opportunities to witness by their words and Christ-like lives. Specific prayer targets:

a) *The urban population* — many are uprooted peasants in squalid slums; a high proportion are nominally Christian.

b) *The fellahin* (peasants) in the rural villages of the Nile Valley.

c) *The Nubians of Upper Egypt*. For centuries a Christian kingdom, but eventually under pressure, Nubians became Muslim in the 17th Century. Today there are only a handful of Christians, but Nubians are fairly open to the gospel. Only a minority still speak the two main Nubian dialects, but they are culturally distinct. Pray for a re-discovery of their Christian roots, and for many to come to Christ.

d) *The desert dwellers* — Bedouin, Siwa Berber and others have had little contact with the gospel.

e) *Arab visitors to Egypt* from many 'closed' Muslim lands. They come especially during Ramadan to avoid the rigours of the Muslim month of fasting!

9 **The Southern Sudanese have fled to Egypt** in their millions from the long civil war in Sudan. Many are destitute, or survive on the fringes of society. Many are professing Christians. Pray for the spiritual health of these displaced, suffering people, and for adequate Christian and social ministry to them.

10 **The missionary vision of the Egyptian church is growing**, but it is limited by lack of vision, training opportunities, experience and funds. Missionaries from Egypt would be more acceptable than Western missionaries in many Muslim lands. Pray that the many Egyptian Christians in the West and Middle Eastern oil states may catch the vision to support such a thrust. Pray for:

a) *A group drawn from several Arab nations* which is seeking to initiate indigenous church planting movements across the region.

b) *A new partnership* focused on new and effective ways of reaching the majority population.

c) *The further development of training courses* focusing on mission within Egypt and beyond.

11 **Openings for low-profile Christian service** by professionally qualified expatriates are now more numerous than for many years. There are also possibilities for ministry in expatriate community churches. Pray for qualified and experienced labourers! The spiritual battles are intense and frustrations numerous.

12 **Christian media** has proved the most potent means of witness to the majority of Egyptians. Pray for:

a) *Scripture distribution*. This has increased in the late 1990s. Effective marketing by the Bible Society at the Cairo International Bookfair every January has been remarkably successful. Video and audio cassettes have been especially popular. The Bible League has successfully used Scripture distribution for planting many small Bible study groups.

b) **W*idely distributed Christian literature*.** There are over 30 Christian bookstores. The need is for more local Christian authors to write evangelistic and teaching materials.

c) **Magalla, a mass-circulation magazine** with a Christian slant. Over 60,000 copies are sold of every issue in 16 Middle Eastern lands. Pray for the magazine's continued publication despite opposition, and for its effectiveness in breaking down misconceptions about the gospel. Pray for all engaged in its publication. Pray also for the European edition *Kitabi* and its use among the 8 million Arab speakers living in Europe as well as the numerous Arab tourists.

d) **The JESUS film** in Arabic which has been widely seen on video, satellite TV and film, and has begun to change perceptions of the gospel.

e) **Satellite television.** **SAT-7** broadcasts high quality children's and youth, as well as adult, programmes every evening. A large, loyal audience is being built among Christians and non-Christians. Over 10 million Egyptians have access to uncensored satellite programmes.

f) **Christian radio.** This is a potent tool. Pray for the various Arabic language studios where programmes are prepared, and for Christian broadcasters and listeners. There are nearly 200 hours of Arabic programming monthly by **FEBA**, **TWR**, IBRA and others.

g) **Videos.** A large church in Cairo has distributed video cassette tapes of special evangelistic rallies (Luis Palau, Billy Graham, etc.) to over 500 churches. In many cases this has significantly increased vision and outreach.

El Salvador

Republic of El Salvador

APRIL 30

LATIN AMERICA

GEOGRAPHY
Area 21,041 sq.km on the Pacific Coast of South America. The smallest and most densely populated Spanish-speaking mainland state in the Americas. Sub-tropical; susceptible to earthquakes.

Population		Ann.Gr.	Density
2000	6,276,023	+2.06%	298 per sq. km.
2010	7,440,647	+1.59%	354 per sq. km.
2025	9,062,331	+1.21%	431 per sq. km.

Capital San Salvador 1,950,000. **Urbanites** 55%.

PEOPLES
Spanish-speaking 99.4%. Ladino (Mestizo) 5,590,000; Amerindian(3) 610,000; Euro-American 70,000.

Amerindian-speaking 0.2%. Kekchi 13,000; the Lenca, Pipil and Pocomam now speak Spanish. **Other** 0.4%. North American 10,000; Chinese 2,000. **Literacy** 74%. **Official language** Spanish. **All languages** 4.

ECONOMY
Centuries of exploitation of the majority followed by 12 years of civil war held back development of this impoverished nation. There was some improvement during the 1990s, but 80% still live in deep poverty. The two large earthquakes of 2000 and 2001 were further setbacks. Coffee and light industry are the main economic activities. **HDI** 0.674; 107th/174. **Public debt** 23% of GNP. **Income/person** $1,700 (6% of USA).

POLITICS
Independent from Spain in 1821 as part of a united Central America, and as a separate nation in 1838. All power remained in the hands of wealthy plantation owners allied with the military. A long series of corrupt dictatorships and gross inequalities between the rich and poor provoked armed leftist insurrection in 1981. 75,000 were killed in fighting, cross-fire or by right-wing death squads. The ending of the Cold War, revulsion over human rights abuses and international pressure forced through a peace accord in 1992. Democratic government has slowly become more established with both main contestants in the civil war having similar representational strength in the Legislative Assembly.

RELIGION
The constitution recognizes the legal status of the Catholic Church, but there is freedom of religion for other denominations and faiths. The Catholic Church opposed oppression and human rights abuses during the war.

Religions	Population %	Adherents	Ann.Gr.
Christian	97.31	6,107,198	+2.0%
non-Religious/other	2.00	125,520	+2.1%
Baha'i	0.60	37,656	+5.8%
Traditional ethnic	0.05	3,138	-7.1%
Buddhist	0.03	1,883	+2.1%
Jewish	0.01	628	+2.1%

Christians	Denom.	Affil.%	,000	Ann.Gr.
Protestant	43	17.27	1,084	+5.0%
Independent	20	8.13	510	+4.3%
Anglican	1	0.01	0	+1.0%
Catholic	1	74.89	4,700	+0.7%
Marginal	2	2.60	163	+4.1%
Unaffiliated		2.39	150	n.a.
Doubly affiliated		-7.97	-500	n.a.

Churches	MegaBloc	Cong.	Members	Affiliates
Catholic	C	300	2,582,400	4,700,000
Assemblies of God	P	1,307	91,300	200,000
Prince of Peace	I	1,000	90,000	200,000
Seventh-day Adventist	P	261	80,000	170,000
Apos Ch of Apos & Proph	I	533	80,000	130,000
Ch of God (Cleveland)	P	659	38,046	85,000
Latter-day Saints (Morm)	M	200	58,000	82,940
Jehovah's Witnesses	M	474	27,990	80,000

Baptist Convention	P	153	45,330	75,000
United Pentecostal	P	930	32,000	74,000
Lutheran Salv Synod	P	130	11,000	68,000
Elim	P	111	18,800	47,000
Central American	P	153	20,000	38,000
Baptist Association	P	73	9,500	17,000
Ch of God (Anderson)	P	120	4,400	11,000
Ch of the Nazarene	P	44	6,000	9,000
Other denoms [53]		2,722	234,200	470,000
Doubly affiliated			-225,200	-500,000
Total Christians [69]		9,170	3,204,000	5,957,000

Trans-bloc Groupings	pop. %	,000	Ann.Gr.
Evangelical	21.7	1,365	+5.2%
Charismatic	27.6	1,729	+3.5%
Pentecostal	16.9	1,058	+4.2%

Missionaries from El Salvador
P,I,A 218 in 18 agencies to 15 countries: El Salvador 74, Ecuador 21, Honduras 16.

Missionaries to El Salvador
P,I,A 137 in 33 agencies from 12 countries: USA 80.

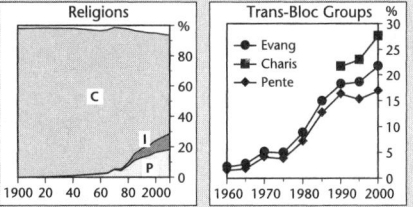

• Answers to Prayer

1 **Peace and democratic change** have developed against all expectations since 1992.

2 **The astonishing five-fold increase of Evangelicals** during the war continued in the 1990s but at a slower rate. Evangelicals were but 2.3% of the population in 1960; in 2000 they were over 22%.

• Challenges for Prayer

1 **Recovery from the social and psychological wounds** of centuries of oppression and 12 years of civil war is a priority. The web of violence, hate, suspicion, atrocities and murder will take time to unravel. At the height of the war 20% of the population fled the country and the US poured in $6 billion to shore up the government. Overall, more than 75,000 were killed. Pray for repentance, reconciliation and a fair society based on respect for human rights.

2 **The growth of Evangelicals in the midst of travail has been a modern-day miracle,** but now the need is for consolidation of the work. There is a growing number of ex-Evangelicals that underscores this need. Pray for effective discipling and motivation of believers for service, witness and missions.

3 **Goals for the first decade of the millennium.** The Salvadorean Evangelical Confraternity representing over 50 denominations set the goal of multiplying congregations from 3,400 in 1987 to 12,000 in 2000. This goal was not quite achieved, but probably reached 9,000. Pray for increased unity, renewed vision and multiplied effective outreach that this nation might belong to Jesus — El Salvador is Spanish for 'the Saviour'.

4 **Leadership for the churches** must be multiplied. The war, lack of finance, and insufficient staff have crippled what training was available. Pray for the Bible schools, seminaries and TEE programmes. Pray for the provision of all material needs for staff and students in this time of economic stress. It is in this ministry that more missionary input is needed. Many mission agencies are heavily committed to health, social betterment and educational ministries.

5 **Missions vision has grown.** The ministry of COMISAL (the national expression of COMIBAM) and indigenous missions such as MIES, AMIGA, EDEHM are expressions of this. An estimated 140 missionaries are serving in other lands. Pray that this involvement might increase and be fruitful.

6 **Sections of society which are of special challenge:**

a) *The Amerindian population* still retains many of their cultural values and traits even though they have largely lost their languages. Their treatment in the 20ᵗʰ Century has been horrific. Pray for effective ministries to begin and for culturally-sensitive church planting among them.

b) *Over 350,000 children were abandoned* during the war. Orphanages, counselling, education and job opportunities for these scarred young people is important.

c) *The 77,000 university students* are the country's future leaders. **IFES** has a ministry among them.

7 **The impact of Christian institutions and media** is wide-ranging. There are 3 Christian universities, 73 Christian schools, one TV station and 25 radio stations. Pray that the overall impact may bring about spiritual uplift in every area of national life.

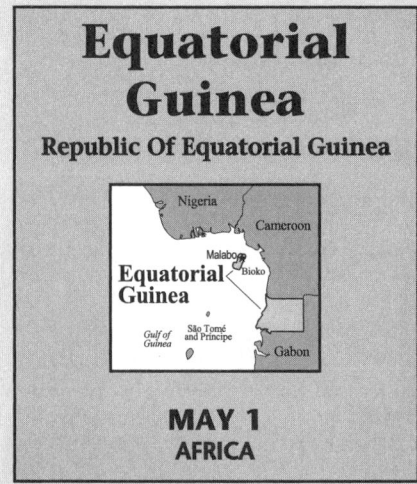

Equatorial Guinea

Republic Of Equatorial Guinea

MAY 1

AFRICA

GEOGRAPHY
Area 28,051 sq.km. A small enclave, Rio Muni, on the African mainland and several islands in the Gulf of Guinea, including Bioko (2,000 sq. km) and Pegalu (Annobon, 10 sq. km).

Population	Ann.Gr.	Density
2000	452,661	+2.53%	16 per sq. km.
2010	575,328	+2.40%	21 per sq. km.
2025	794,724	+2.01%	28 per sq. km.

The former ruler caused the deaths of about 60,000 people and the flight or expulsion of a further 140,000 between 1969 and 1978.

Capital Malabo 63,000. **Urbanites** 29%.

PEOPLES
Bantu 95.9%. Over 11 ethnic groups.
Mainland: Fang 375,000, politically dominant; Seke 11,000; Ngumba 9,000; Ngumbi 6,000; Batanga (Puku) 9,000; Benga 3,200.
Islands: Bubi 43,000.
Spanish-speaking 2.6%. Mixed race 11,000.
Creole 1.5%. Bioko 4,500; Pagalu 2,700.
Literacy 62%. **Official languages** Spanish and French. **All languages** 12. **Languages with Scriptures** 1Bi 1NT 3por 2w.i.p.

ECONOMY
Prosperous until independence, but in total collapse by 1979. Exploitation of the forests and offshore oil have been more for the benefit of the ruling elite while the vast majority live in grinding poverty. Corruption is a serious problem. During the 1990s there were improvements in the economy as commerce revived. **HDI** 0.549; 131ˢᵗ/174. **Public debt** 102% of GNP. **Income/person** theoretically $530 (1.9% of USA).

POLITICS
Independence from Spain in 1968. A coup in 1969 brought Macias Nguema to power. This atheist dictator turned his country into a slave-labour camp with Soviet Bloc assistance. A military coup in 1979 resulted in a one-party presidential government economically linked with the

neighbouring Francophone states. Western pressure for multi-party politics resulted in cosmetic changes. All dissent is suppressed and the government reacts defensively to any criticism.

RELIGION
In colonial times almost the entire population was baptized as Catholics. The savage persecution of the 1970s with the repression of religions has been followed by limited religious freedom.

Religions	Population %	Adherents	Ann.Gr.
Christian	95.12	430,571	+2.5%
Traditional ethnic	2.90	13,127	+2.2%
non-Religious/other	1.00	4,527	+2.5%
Muslim	0.60	2,716	+6.3%
Baha'i	0.38	1,720	+4.2%

Christians	Denom.	Affil.%	,000	Ann.Gr.
Protestant	7	3.19	14	+2.9%
Independent	15	3.63	16	+6.0%
Catholic	1	83.95	380	+0.8%
Marginal	2	1.18	5	+11.6%
Unaffiliated		4.58	21	n.a.
Doubly affiliated		*-1.41*	*-6*	*n.a.*

Churches	MegaBloc	Cong.	Members	Affiliates
Catholic	C	81	255,034	380,000
Council of Evangelical	P	90	4,800	8,400
New Apostolic	I	19	4,790	8,000

Jehovah Witnesses	M	11	645	3,200
Assemblies of God	P	14	540	2,240
Dove Evangelical Centre	I	9	900	1,980
Crusade	P	44	720	1,800
Seventh-day Adventist	P	4	681	1,100
Other Indigenous [7]	I	11	450	900
Baptist Convention	P	9	90	225
Other denoms [11]		162	3,600	8,400
Doubly affiliated			*-2,100*	*-6,400*
Total Christians [26]		454	270,200	410,000

Trans-bloc Groupings	pop. %	,000	Ann.Gr.
Evangelical	3.2	15	+6.4%
Charismatic	2.3	11	+6.8%
Pentecostal	1.4	6	+7.6%

Missionaries from Equatorial Guinea
P,I,A 7 in 2 agencies; all in Equatorial Guinea.

Missionaries to Equatorial Guinea
P,I,A 75 in 24 agencies from 19 countries: USA 18, Argentina 10, Nigeria 7.

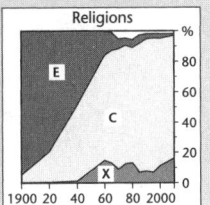

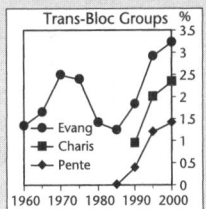

• Challenges for Prayer

1 The population was traumatized and the economy ravished by the bizarre dictatorship of the 1970s. The subsequent government led to some improvements, but the levels of corruption and injustice remained high and the government seeks to control all aspects of national life. Pray for change and a government that seeks the good of the people.

2 The persecuted Church did not emerge unscathed. Church leaders were forced to compromise or suffer. Tragically, many Protestant church leaders fell into sin and displayed more interest in power politics than in the spiritual nurture of their flocks. Pray for men of God, fearless for the truth, to be raised up to lead the churches back to a living relationship with God. Pray for both repentance and revival.

3 Since 1980 there has been increasing religious freedom and a number of newer Pentecostal, charismatic and evangelical denominations have started and grown. (AoG, Baptists, Deeper Life, etc.). Pray for purity of life and fervency in evangelism in the churches despite the prevailing poverty, corruption and despair. Pray also for full liberty for the gospel.

4 Facilities for training a new generation of leaders have increased in the 1990s. There were 3 institutions in operation in 1999 (Reformed, WEC, AoG) with 155 students. YWAM runs short-term Discipleship Training Schools. Pray that graduates may be used of the Spirit to bring spiritual life to the churches and the nation.

5 Missionaries have increased in numbers, but all need wisdom and humility in the convoluted political and untidy spiritual situation in the churches and in relating to indigenous leadership. The main agencies are: AoG (13), WEC (12) and YWAM (10).

6 The less evangelized:

a) Some areas of the mainland have few congregations with spiritual life.

b) *The Ngumba, Yaka, Batanga and Benga* have no known congregations within their cultures.

c) *Annobon Island is so isolated* and economically impoverished that it is almost impossible to reach, and is scarcely touched with the gospel.

7 The Bible Society finally gained registration in 1999 and distributes Scriptures. A NT in Bubi has just been completed. Pray for adequate distribution networks and free importation of Scriptures. The Fang NT is being translated by Pioneer Bible Translators — pray for its completion.

E

Eritrea
State of Eritrea

MAY 2
AFRICA
Updated January 2004

GEOGRAPHY
Area 121,100 sq.km. Arid, mountainous, temperate plateau and hot desert lowlands along the Red Sea Coast.

Population	Ann.Gr.	Density
2000	3,850,388	+3.86%	32 per sq km
2010	4,909,569	+2.40%	40 per sq km
2025	6,680,653	+1.83%	55 per sq km

Capital Asmara 460,000. **Urbanites** 16%.

PEOPLES
Nine indigenous peoples.
Semitic 78.2%. Tigrinya 1.8mill.; Tigre 1.2m; Rashaida Arab 12,000.
Cushitic 16.9%. Saho 180,000; Bilen 161,000; Afar 160,000; Beja (Beni Amer, Hedareb) 150,000.
Sudanic 4.9%. Kunama 107,000; Nara 80,000.

Literacy 20%. **Official language** none. Tigrinya, Arabic and English most widely used. **All languages** 11. **Languages with Scriptures** 5Bi 1NT 1por 1w.i.p.

ECONOMY
Devastated by 30 years of war, periodic drought and lack of infrastructure for development. Much potential for mineral extraction and light industry with a highly motivated population in a strategic location. **HDI** 0.346; 167th/174. **Public debt** 9% of GNP. **Income/person** $230 (0.7% of USA).

POLITICS
Italian colony 1890-1941. UN-arranged federation with Ethiopia in 1951. The war for Eritrean independence began in 1961. All three liberation movements were avowedly Marxist, but since the ending of Ethiopian rule, ideology was laid aside in the effort to rebuild the nation. Reconstruction of the country was seriously disrupted by the 1998-2000 border war with Ethiopia. In 2001 President Afwerki shut down all private media, arrested journalists and opposition leaders, isolating the country from the outside world.

RELIGION
Freedom of religion until 2001. Then all Christian denominations were shut down except for the Orthodox, Catholic and Lutheran Churches. The level of persecution of evangelical Christians has become severe. **Persecution index** 56th in the world.

Religions	Population %	Adherents	Ann.Gr.
Muslim	47.97	1,847,031	+3.5%
Christian	47.43	1,826,239	+4.2%
non-Religious/other	4.00	154,016	+4.9%
Traditional ethnic	0.60	23,102	-4.2%

Christians	Denom.	Affil.%	,000	Ann.Gr.
Protestant	10	1.35	52	+7.7%
Independent	3	0.16	6	+14.9%
Catholic	1	3.77	145	+2.9%
Orthodox	1	40.98	1,578	+4.4%
Marginal	1	0.04	2	+9.9%
Unaffiliated		1.13	65	n.a.

Churches	MegaBloc	Cong.	Members	Affiliates
Eritrean Orthodox	O	800	933,728	1,578,000
Catholic (Latin/Coptic)	C	110	84,302	145,000
Ev Ch of Eritrea (Luth)	P	52	7,343	21,000
Lutheran Ch in Eritrea	P	21	3,700	8,500
Full Gospel	P	20	1,600	5,500
Faith Church of Christ	P	16	1,000	5,000
Assemblies of God	P	20	2,000	4,000
Kale Heywet (SIM)	P	15	1,400	3,700
Jehovah's Witnesses	M	19	941	1,600
Other denominations [7]		53	4,752	10,200
Total Christians [16]		1,126	1,040,800	1,782,500

Trans-bloc Groupings pop. %	,000	Ann.Gr.
Evangelical	1.7	67	+7.9%
Charismatic	1.4	55	+7.3%
Pentecostal	0.2	10	+16.4%

Missionaries from Eritrea
P,I,A 24 in 2 agencies; 23 in Eritrea.

Missionaries to Eritrea
P,I,A 33 in 10 agencies from 4 countries.

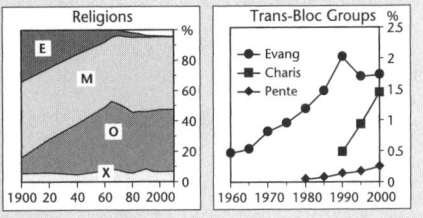

• Challenges for Prayer

1 **Peace and national recovery** has been delayed by conflicts with Ethiopia and Yemen. The Ethiopian war caused the death of 70,000+ Eritreans and Ethiopians in fierce trench warfare. The two presidents are both Tigrinya and were once friends. Pray for humility, willingness to compromise on the part of the leaders, and a just peace to end hostilities that neither country can afford.

2 **Freedom of religion has been lost.** Fear of Islamist extremism and Christian evangelicalism virtually ended international NGO projects and aid and the entry of expatriate Christian workers. The ministries of evangelical denominations have been ravaged by government hostility. Pray for a restoration of religious freedom and for harmony between the ethnic and religious communities.

3 **Christians are largely Orthodox** and almost entirely among the Tigrinya, with some Bilen and Kunama. Evangelicals are fewer. Christians of all denominations were refined and drawn together in fellowship during the hardships of war and Marxist propaganda. There is a significant biblical revival movement, *Medhanie Alam*, in the Orthodox Church, but they too have been severely persecuted since 2001. Pray that Christians may be fervent for Jesus and make a significant impact on their nation and beyond.

4 **Evangelical churches have grown markedly**, but success stirred up opposition and their banning in 2001. There is some nominalism in the Lutheran Church. The Kale Heywet Church (SIM-related) planted 11 new churches in the 5 years before 2001 and sent 21 evangelists to non-Christian and nominally Christian areas of the country. The Full Gospel Church, with AoG help, started a School of Leadership Training in Asmara, but these ministries are hampered by the present persecution. Pray for the maturing and expansion of the evangelical witness despite opposition. Hundreds of Christians have been imprisoned and tortured.

5 **The return of Christian missionaries** to serve the Church is an urgent need to supplement the handful of missionaries now in the land. Pray for a re-opened door to this land.

6 **The less-reached.** Pray specifically for:

a) *The Tigre, who are almost entirely Muslim*, and the only Eritrean or Ethiopian Semitic people which is not Orthodox. They are related to the Tigrinya, but culturally distant from them. The Bible is available, but there are few Christians.

b) *The Jabarti who are a Muslim minority* among the Tigrinya.

c) *The Afar and related Saho peoples* in the southeast with a handful of Christians and no known churches. Many are nomadic.

d) *The Beja and Nara peoples of the northwest with no known witness.* Many are nomadic.

e) *The Arab Rashiada who migrated* from Saudi Arabia in the 19th Century.

7 **Specialist Christian ministries**

a) *Students.* The **IFES** student witness has thrived since its inception in 1995. Pray for conversions and growth through them.

b) *Radio.* Both **FEBA** Seychelles (15 minutes 3 times/week) and **TWR** Swaziland (4 hours/week) broadcast in Tigrinya. There is nothing for Tigre or other languages yet.

c) *The JESUS film* has had limited use, but is available in five languages and is in preparation in three others. Pray for the effective use of this medium.

Estonia

Republic of Estonia

integrate with the Nordic nations and is a front-runner for early entry into the EU.

 RELIGION
Severe persecution of all faiths under the Soviet occupation 1940-1988. Freedom of religion since independence was regained in 1988.

Religions	Population %	Adherents	Ann.Gr.
non-Religious/other	60.41	843,400	+0.6%
Christian	38.63	539,336	-3.8%
Muslim	0.70	9,773	+10.5%
Jewish	0.26	3,630	-4.0%

Christians	Denom.	Affil.%	,000	Ann.Gr.
Protestant	9	14.12	197	-1.1%
Independent	12	0.83	12	+3.0%
Anglican	1	0.24	3	+22.8%
Catholic	1	0.27	4	+1.1%
Orthodox	4	3.51	49	-9.0%
Marginal	2	0.66	9	+4.3%
Unaffiliated		19.00	266	n.a.

MAY 3
EUROPE

GEOGRAPHY
Area 45,215 sq.km. Northernmost of the three Baltic states. Separated from Finland to the north by the Gulf of Finland.

Population	Ann.Gr.	Density
2000	1,396,158	-1.24%	31 per sq. km.
2010	1,260,920	-1.01%	28 per sq. km.
2025	1,131,222	-0.67%	25 per sq. km.

Capital Tallinn 435,000. **Urbanites** 69%.

PEOPLES
Finno-Ugric 65%. Estonian 892,000. Finnish 16,000.
Slavic 33.3%. Russian 405,000; Ukrainian 38,000; Belarusian 22,000.
Other 1.7%. Jews 3,500; Tatar 3,500.
Literacy 99%. **Official language** Estonian; Russian is also common. **All indigenous languages** 5. **Languages with Scriptures** 4Bi.

ECONOMY
Aggressive reforms from a Communist command economy to a capitalist free market society have made Estonia more prosperous than any other region of the former USSR, but not without pain to those on fixed incomes. **HDI** 0.773; 54th/174. **Public debt/person** 4% of GNP. **Income/person** $2,860 (10% of USA).

POLITICS
Long dominated by surrounding nations. Independent 1918-1940. The Soviet invasion in 1940 and subsequent deportation and murder of a large minority of Estonians is still a cause of deep resentment against Russia. Became independent during 1988-91 as a multi-party democracy. Estonia has single-mindedly sought to

Churches	MegaBloc	Cong.	Members	Affiliates
Lutheran	P	168	56,000	160,000
Estonian Orthodox	O	52	16,807	40,000
Evang Chr/Baptist Union	P	85	6,125	18,559
Jehovah's Witnesses	M	16	4,100	8,000
Christian Pentecostal	P	45	3,200	7,000
New Apostolic	I	14	3,000	4,410
Catholic	C	18	1,876	3,700
Methodist	P	19	1,850	3,200
Union of Chr Free Congr	P	6	1,100	3,146
Seventh-day Adventist	P	18	1,876	3,000
Other denoms [19]		126	13,178	23,000
Total Christians [29]		567	109,112	274,000

Trans-bloc Groupings pop. %		,000	Ann.Gr.
Evangelical	5.7	79	+0.8%
Charismatic	2.3	32	+4.2%
Pentecostal	1.6	22	+6.4%

Missionaries from Estonia
P,I,A 16 in 7 agencies to 3 countries.

Missionaries to Estonia
P,I,A 95 in 17 agencies from 9 countries: USA 44, Finland 36.

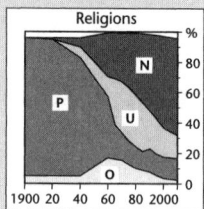

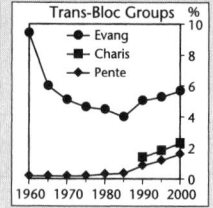

• Answers to Prayer

1 **Praise God for religious freedom!** Christians can freely evangelise, and many denominations are pressing forward in this vital task.

• Challenges for Prayer

1 **The introduction of capitalism has brought wealth** — accompanied by a moral slide. In Estonia's growing economy, luxury co-exists with severe poverty. Western-style materialism is found everywhere, and crime and divorce has skyrocketed since 1991. Pray for the Holy Spirit to create a hunger and thirst after God and His righteousness.

2 **Estonia's attempts to preserve national identity** have alienated the large Russian minority. The Russians are not popular because of 50 years of oppression and because of the $4 billion clean-up bill left by their military forces. Pray that Estonia's government may act with wisdom and discretion in establishing an identity for all of its people.

3 **The Church is now free**. Pray that it may not become 'soft' now that persecution has ended. Nominalism is widespread in an aging Lutheran state church. Younger churches (Pentecostals, charismatics, Baptists) are growing more rapidly than others.

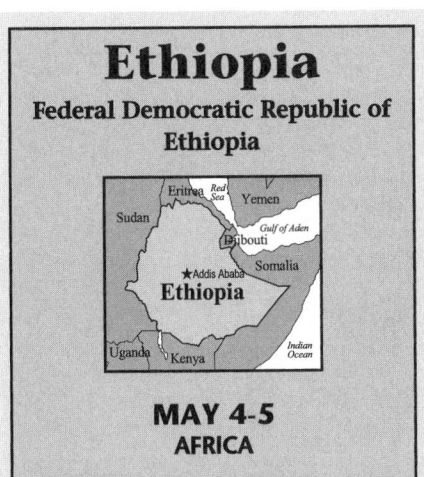

E

4 **Estonia is in need of evangelism** in much the same manner as the rest of Europe. Most people notionally recognize Christianity's principles, but have little desire to commit themselves to Christ. Pray that God might strip away their secular materialism and empower the Church to reveal the living Christ to them.

5 **Leadership training is a priority with church leaders**. Lutheran, Baptist, Methodist and Pentecostal seminaries or Bible schools now exist, training pastors and lay leaders alike. Denominations in the Estonian Evangelical Alliance all agree on the necessity of cooperation in reaching Estonia's less evangelized and are preparing believers for this goal.

6 **The contribution of foreign Christian agencies** has been significant. Finland, with its proximity, wealth, closely related culture, language and spiritual heritage has a unique role to play. Pray that all such may prove a blessing to Estonia.

7 **The Estonian Bible** revision was completed in 1996. **IFES** continues to grow. Christian radio, television, and printed media are all flourishing ministries. Pray that these may all contribute to moulding Estonia's post-Communist culture.

Ethiopia
Federal Democratic Republic of
Ethiopia

Ethiopia

MAY 4-5
AFRICA

Population		Ann.Gr.	Density
2000	62,564,875	+2.48%	57 per sq. km.
2010	79,943,539	+2.55%	72 per sq. km.
2025	115,382,091	+2.31%	104 per sq. km.

Capital Addis Ababa 2,650,000. **Urbanites** 11.5%.

PEOPLES
Semitic Origin 45%. 8 peoples, including: Amhara 17.7 mill. (North and Central Highlands); Tigray 6.09m (North and also Eritrea); Gurage 2.73m (6 major dialects, South Highlands); Adare/Harari 125,000 (3 groups); Arab 231,000. A few thousand Black Jews (Falasha) remaining — mainly Christians; over 70,000 airlifted to Israel.
Cushitic 42.2%. 25 peoples, the largest: Oromo 18.2m in a dozen tribal divisions in Central and southern Ethiopia; Somali 2.38m in east; Sidamo 1.85m; Hadiyya 945,000; Afar 857,000; Agew 720,000; Gedeo 670,000; Kambaata 638,000; Konso 138,000; Gawwada 77,000.
Omotic 11.3%. Over 25 peoples in south and southwest; largest: Wolaytta 1.6m; Gamo-Kullo 682,000; Keffa 651,000; Goffa 223,000; Bench(Gimira) 181,000; Yemsa 170,000; Aari 162,000; Basketo 67,000; Hamer-Banna 50,000.
Nilo-Sudanic 1.2%. Over 20 peoples in south and

GEOGRAPHY
Area 1,106,000 sq.km. Fertile mountain plateau surrounded by the drought-prone lowlands and deserts of the Red Sea coast, and borders on Eritrea, Somalia, Kenya and Sudan. Landlocked since the secession of Eritrea.

---

west. Largest: Me'en 74,000; Gumuz 50,000; Bertha 50,000; Anuak 45,000; Nuer 40,000; Komo 38,000; Murle 9,000.

Literacy 36%. **National working language** Amharic; 65% of population are able to speak it. Regional languages are important. **All languages** 86. **Languages with Scriptures** 6Bi 12NT 4por 20w.i.p. (6-OT, 14NT).

ECONOMY
The main export is coffee — believed to have originated in Ethiopia. The government has initiated wide-ranging reforms and is developing the communications network. This follows decades of underdevelopment due to wars and famine. Periodic droughts and the 1998-2000 war with Eritrea have slowed economic development. **Unemployment** over 35%. **HDI** 0.298; 172nd/174. **Public debt** 157% of GNP. **Income/person** $100 (0.4% of USA).

POLITICS
Probably one of the oldest nations known with a long written history. Amhara-dominated Empire 1896-1974, with Italian occupation 1936-41. The revolution of 1974 overthrew the Emperor Haile Selassie and imposed doctrinaire Marxist ideology on the country with collectivization, nationalization and repression of all dissent and of religion. Regional uprisings together with severe droughts and man-aided famines ultimately led to the collapse of Mengistu's Marxist regime in 1991. The Tigray-led government ended Amhara domination and federalized the country with a devolution of power to 10 regions largely ethnically defined. Though there is greater democratic freedom, there are limitations. The war with Eritrea has tended to unite the country despite the enormous cost in lives and finance.

RELIGION
North Ethiopia was one of the first Christian nations — from the 4th Century. The Ethiopian Orthodox Church became the State Church from 1270 until the 1974 revolution. The Marxist regime persecuted Christians, especially Evangelicals, with many church buildings destroyed and congregations scattered. Since 1991 there has been unprecedented freedom for worship and witness. The government seeks to deal even-handedly with the Ethiopian Orthodox Church and the increasingly active and growing Muslim minority. **Persecution index** 44th in the world.

Religions	Population %	Adherents	Ann.Gr.
Christian	65.02	40,679,682	+2.8%
Muslim	31.00	19,395,111	+3.1%
Traditional ethnic	2.98	1,864,433	-7.1%
non-Religious/other	1.00	625,649	+2.5%

Christians	Denom.	Affil.%	,000	Ann.Gr.
Protestant	31	18.59	11,629	+6.7%
Independent	7	0.18	116	+13.6%
Anglican	1	0.00	1	+0.0%
Catholic	1	0.67	420	+4.7%
Orthodox	3	57.54	36,000	+0.3%
Marginal	2	0.03	19	+8.9%
Unaffiliated		0.10	93	n.a.
Doubly affiliated		*-12.10*	*-7,600*	*n.a.*

Churches	MegaBloc	Cong.	Members	Affiliates
Ethiopian Orthodox	O	20,000	21.302m	36.00m
Kale Heywet Ch (SIM)	P	4,500	3,500,000	5,000,000
Mekane Yesu (Luth)	P	4,400	2,300,000	3,400,000
United Pentecostal	P	7,143	800,000	1,200,000
Full Gosp-Mulu Wengel	P	900	240,000	600,000
Heywet Birhane (AoG)	P	979	350,000	600,000
Catholic (Coptic&Rom)	C	200	248,521	420,000
Seventh-day Adventist	P	800	128,000	280,000
Meserete Kristos	P	350	114,000	160,000
Sefer Genet (FFM)	P	347	52,000	110,000
Chs of Christ	P	510	55,000	100,000
Birhane Wengel	P	95	19,000	60,000
Emmanuel Baptist	P	50	15,000	35,000
Other denoms [33]		825	88,700	221,000
Doubly affiliated			*-3,454,500*	*-7,600,000*
Total Christians [46]		41,000	25.80m	40.586m

Trans-bloc Groupings	pop. %	,000	Ann.Gr.
Evangelical	19.7	12,321	+6.4%
Charismatic	10.0	6,237	+8.3%
Pentecostal	4.1	2,556	+6.4%

Missionaries from Ethiopia
P,I,A 482+ in 11 agencies to 7 countries: Ethiopia 463.

Missionaries to Ethiopia
P,I,A 669 in 60 agencies from 23 countries: USA 253, Finland 82, Denmark 64, Sweden 60, Norway 52, Germany 41, UK 40.

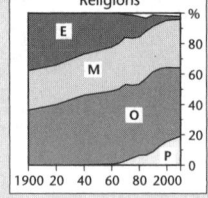

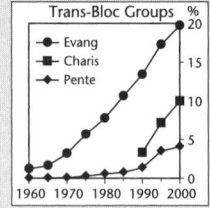

• Answers to Prayer

1 **Praise God for the thrilling growth** of the Protestant churches since 1936. Two great waves of violent persecution under the Italians in 1936-41 and the Communists in 1974-1990 refined and purified the church, but there were many martyrs. Vision, sacrificial evangelism and courageous witness have characterized Evangelicals of all denominations. There have been great seasons of harvest with millions coming to Christ, the greatest being since the failure and collapse of Communism. Protestants were fewer than 200,000 — 0.8% of the population — in 1960, but by 2000 this had become nearly 12 million and 19.7% of the population.

2 **Growth of Protestants continued** in the 1990s with numbers almost doubling to 11 million and to nearly 18% of the population.

3 **The unity between believers forged in the severe Marxist persecution** has continued and dynamic plans for outreach, pioneer evangelism and mission endeavour for the period 2000-2020 are being implemented.

4 **Increased distribution and use of the Bible** for reading and preaching has brought revival to sections of the Orthodox Church. In 1997 it was estimated there were 20,000 active, born-again Christians associated with this move of the Holy Spirit. Many have moved on to start new churches or join existing evangelical churches.

• Challenges for Prayer

E

1 **Ethiopia's political leaders confront crises on many fronts**:

a) *Hostilities with Eritrea have crippled efforts* to revive and modernize the country.

b) *Ethnic fragmentation remains a real possibility.* The central government is predominantly Tigrayan in composition and other larger ethnic groups — Amhara, Oromo, Somali and Afar — are restive.

c) *Pray for wisdom, humility, courage* and a seeking after God among those in leadership and for peace and the right climate to bring about change for the better. Repression, famines, wars and deep poverty have traumatized many.

2 **The Ethiopian Orthodox Church** is going through immense change. Centuries of isolation from the rest of the Christian world as a Christian island in a sea of Islam helped form its unique culture, theology and traditions.

a) *It has had to adjust to the loss of political privilege* under Communism, which has only been partially restored since 1990. Syncretism and the occult are widespread among the millions of nominal Orthodox.

b) *The rapid spread of the use of Scriptures* and growth of Protestant denominations has led to both millions of defections and the emergence of strong evangelical and charismatic networks in the Orthodox Church.

Pray for a deep work of the Holy Spirit to bring this ancient Church to its biblical heritage and to new life.

3 **Massive growth in Protestant and Independent churches** has created a great expectation for further harvest. Pray for:

a) *Continued revival and growth* not to be quenched by carnality, division and power-seeking in leadership. A characteristic of the recent move of the Spirit has been widespread mobilization of ordinary believers and multiplication of cell churches.

b) *Effective means for generating income* to support men and women in the service of the Lord, develop the structures and facilities needed and fund social programmes essential in the prevailing deep poverty.

c) *Preservation of the cooperation and unity among leaders* which was forged in suffering. Vigilance is needed to heal past broken relationships and prevent future fleshly discord. Pray especially for the Evangelical Churches Fellowship (ECFE) which represents the majority of Evangelicals in the country.

d) *The continued growth of missions vision.* A big commitment to missions by various evangelical denominations was cut back in 1976 due to persecution. Out of this suffering emerged a national vision and a united strategy for evangelizing Ethiopia. The 20 year integrated strategy included prayer and people-mobilization, survey training and sending out missionary evangelists to every province and people with few Evangelicals and then to other lands. By 2000 much had been achieved. Pray for the successful accomplishment of the complete vision by 2015. KHC is spearheading outreach to India and Pakistan.

4 **Leadership training** was severely restricted under Communism. Much has developed since 1991. Pray for the following:

a) *Post-graduate training* at the Ethiopian Graduate School in Addis Ababa. This was jointly established by the KHC and Mekane Yesu Churches. Pray for the provision of theologians and teachers that are both godly and steeped in the Scriptures.

b) *The degree-level training* — the Evangelical Theological College (KHC and **SIM**), Mekane Yesu Theological Seminary, the **AoG** Bible College with 100 students, Trinity College and the Orthodox St. Paul's Seminary.

c) *The numerous Bible Schools* run by denominations all over the country such as the 187 Amharic Bible schools (KHC) and Mekane Yesu with many more.

d) *The network of evening and short-term Bible schools* and TEE programmes around the country where many thousands of local leaders and evangelists are trained.

5 **The Muslim advance.** Muslims strengthened their position under Marxism, and have launched a massive campaign for the Islamization of Ethiopia by penetrating Christian areas with the offer of bribes and a mosque-building programme — many were reported to have been built during the time that many Christian churches were being closed. Their numbers are growing significantly, with converts out of both animism and the Orthodox Church. Ethiopia is strategically vital for both Islam and Christianity. Pray for a definite prayer mobilization that will lead to breakthroughs among Muslim peoples and also frustration of these Islamic stratagems. Converts out of Islam are numbered only in hundreds.

6 **The less evangelized.** The survey initiated by the ECFE has highlighted the remaining pioneer task. Of the 90 peoples listed for Ethiopia, 60 were found to still be under-evangelized. Ethiopian Christians entered 20 of them in 1995 planting 61 churches, in 1996 a further 20 were reached with 6,000 coming to Christ. The remaining 20 were entered by 2000. Though a toe-hold has been won, breakthroughs are needed in the following areas:

a) *The predominantly Orthodox Amhara and Tigray regions* in the north have few evangelical churches. Pray for infusion of spiritual life to these nominally Christian areas.

b) *The largely Muslim Somali (Dire Dawa), Harari and Afar regions* in the east. Indigenous Christians are few and there are no churches. The political, military and religious tensions are numerous and any form of Christian outreach is difficult. Many Somalis live in refugee camps in the desert. Pray for the many barriers to be removed.

c) *Many sections of Oromia* — especially in the east and south are strongly Muslim and uneasy with Tigray dominance in the capital. Kale Heywet missionary evangelists are reaching out to the Muslim Aari and Borana Oromo. Inter-tribal warfare has hindered growth among the Eastern Guji Oromo among whom some churches have been planted. Pray for the planting of live churches in every part of the Oromo people.

d) *The numerous peoples of the southwest* bordering on Sudan are isolated, some being nomadic. Nearly all are now either targeted or entered. Pray for healthy churches to be planted through pioneering work among the Aari, Bench, Bodi (5,000), Bumi (40,000), Hamer-Banna, Daasenach, Dime (15,000), Ebore (5,000), Karo (5,000), Me'en, Mali (39,000), Mursi (5,000), Tarra (15,000), Tsamai (20,000) and Wata (5,000).

e) *Sudanese refugees* from the vicious fighting in the south of that land. Many are housed in large camps. There are over 100,000 refugees in 4 camps on the border. Pray for all ministering to these unfortunate people. There are groups of believers among a number of the ethnic groups in these camps.

7 **Young people** need purpose and hope in life. Pray for **SU** ministry among young people and for its expansion among teenagers, and for EVASUE (**IFES**) ministry already established in 19 colleges with a strong evangelistic vision. There is need for more workers.

8 **Foreign mission workers** were reduced in numbers during the Marxist revolution, but are now free to minister, though their number is smaller than before. Pray that the missionary force may be wisely and sensitively deployed to best serve the maturing church. The major ministry needs are in leadership training, working together with Ethiopian missionaries in pioneer outreach to unevangelized peoples, Bible translation and technical and aid ministries. The largest agencies are: Norwegian Lutheran Mission (150 workers), Finnish Lutherans (55), Danish Lutheran Mission (54), **SIL** (50), **SIM** (39), **SBC** (25), German Lutherans (22), Swedish Pentecostal Mission (22), Finnish Pentecostal Mission (18).

9 **Bible translation** is a major task to be accomplished. There are 23 translation projects in progress sponsored and assisted by various organizations including Mekane Yesu Church, KHC, **SIM**, **The Bible Society**, **SIL** and Word for the World. Training courses for national translators are regularly given. There is growing interest on the part of the churches in translation, literacy and use of local language Scriptures. A national **Forum of Bible Translators** has recently been established. Praise God for the completion during the 1990s of the NT in Aari, Afar, Bench, Burji, Gumuz, Hadiyya, Kambaata, Kaficho Komso, Murle and Sidamo. Major projects needing prayer for completion are: the Bible in Afar, Anuak, West Gurage, Uduk and Wolaytta; the NT in Basketto, Daasenach, East Gurage, Hamer-Banna, Koorete, Majang, Male, Mursi and Suri. There are 10-15 languages with a definite translation need and a further 24 yet to be surveyed. Pray for guidance in assessing needs and for resources to start work in those requiring their own translation (**SIL**). Pray for more nationals to become involved.

10 Christian help ministries.

a) *Literature*. Intensive literacy campaigns have created many new readers. Reading materials are increasing in various languages. The challenges include the relatively small reading community, management and logistics of distribution. Pray especially for the production of reading materials for youth.

b) *Aviation*. **MAF** was required to leave the country in 1998. An Ethiopian, a former MAF pilot, continues to operate 2 aircraft as *Abyssinian Flight Services*. Pray for this ministry to the Church in a land with only a rudimentary road system and where planes are vital for ministry.

c) *AIDS has spread rapidly* with 3 million affected by the virus by 1998 — 10.6% of the adult population. There are 1.2 million AIDS orphans. Christians are working in areas of prevention, counselling, home care and orphan ministry.

d) *Radio*. FEBA broadcasts 11.5 hours/weeks in Amharic, 6.5 hours/week in Oromo and Tigray; there are plans to resume broadcasting in Afar. Pray for the preparation and impact of these programmes. Pray also for the return of the Lutheran station in Addis Ababa, Radio Voice of the Gospel, seized by the Communists after the revolution.

Faeroe Islands

Faeroe Islands

MAY 6
EUROPE

GEOGRAPHY
Area 1,399 sq.km. Archipelago of 18 rugged islands between Iceland and Scotland, 17 of which are inhabited.

Population	Ann.Gr.	Density
2000	42,749	-0.85%	31 per sq. km.
2010	39,703	-0.70%	28 per sq. km.
2025	36,604	-0.46%	26 per sq. km.

Latest statistics indicate a growing population of 46,000 in 2000.
Capital Torshavn 16,000. **Urbanites** 35%.

PEOPLES
Faeroese 97%. **Danish** 3%.
Literacy 99%. **Official languages** Faeroese, which is of the Scandinavian family; Danish. Both have Bibles.

ECONOMY

The fishing industry has long been the mainstay of the economy, but there is much growth in fish farming which has led to a booming economy. There are probably oil reserves which will attract foreign investment.

POLITICS
Parliamentary democracy, a self-governing region of Denmark. The Faeroese government has decided in favour of increasing autonomy from Denmark, a move which many feel is risky.

RELIGION
Complete freedom of religion, although the Lutheran Church is recognized as the national church and is supported by a state-levied tax.

Religions	Population %	Adherents	Ann.Gr.
Christian	93.96	40,167	-0.9%
non-Religious/other	5.84	2,497	+0.1%
Baha'i	0.20	85	+1.2%

Christians	Denom.	Affil.%	,000	Ann.Gr.
Protestant	8	92.62	40	-0.9%
Independent	5	0.94	0	+2.8%
Catholic	1	0.16	0	+0.0%
Marginal	1	0.25	0	-3.7%

Churches	MegaBloc	Cong.	Members	Affiliates
Lutheran	P	51	21,948	33,800
Christian Brethren	P	24	2,885	4,500
Pentecostal	P	8	570	878
House Churches [5]	I	8	240	400
Other Evangelical [3]	P	3	100	150

Jehovah's Witnesses	M	4	75	107
Other denoms [3]		3	191	335
Total Christians [15]		101	26,000	40,170

Trans-bloc Groupings pop. %		,000	Ann.Gr.
Evangelical	28.5	12	-0.6%
Charismatic	7.2	3	+1.0%
Pentecostal	3.0	1	+3.4%

Missionaries from Faeroes
P,I,A 68 in 11 agencies in 21 countries: Greenland 8.

Missionaries to Faeroes
P,I,A n.a. C 6. M 4.

• Challenges For Prayer

1 **Wisdom in government is needed** as the Islands decide on a more independent future. Pray that God would give the leaders wisdom to oversee increasing autonomy from Denmark, as well as the courage to make strong decisions in managing the shrinking fishing industry and potentially booming oil industry — both of these industries have great environmental and social repercussions.

2 **The Faeroes need revival**. From the largely nominal state Lutheran Church to the charismatic house churches, local Christian leaders all agree that these islands need a fresh move of the Holy Spirit. The Lutheran Church especially has declined. Only a small minority of church members regularly attend. Yet there are strong evangelical movements within its membership, such as the pietist Home Mission with 35 prayer houses and 3,000 members and a growing overseas missions commitment. Pray for the Spirit to make the Faeroes truly Christian and not just in name only.

3 **Evangelicals are many — over 28% of the population**, in contrast to the mother country, Denmark. In particular the Brethren churches have made a significant impact, both at home and abroad as missionaries. The Faeroe Islands send out a proportionally large number of missionaries (see above statistics); pray that this may continue. There are also growing charismatic and Pentecostal groups, but almost all Christian growth is hampered by a lack of trained, godly leaders, secularization and the nominal religiosity of Faeroese society.

Falkland Islands

Islas Malvinas

MAY 6
LATIN AMERICA

GEOGRAPHY
Area 12,173 sq.km. 200 islands in three groups: Falkland, South Georgia, South Sandwich Islands in the South Atlantic. The latter island groups have no permanent population and have been a separate UK dependency since 1985. The Falklands are 600 km east of Patagonia in Argentina.

Population		Ann.Gr.	Density
2000	2,255	+0.54%	0 per sq. km.
2010	2,364	+0.45%	0 per sq. km.
2025	2,496	+0.32%	0 per sq. km.

A further 1,000 or so British military personnel and contractors are based on the islands.
Capital Port Stanley 1,700.

PEOPLES
British 97%.
Other 3%.
Literacy 99%. **Official language** English.

ECONOMY
A forgotten, sheep-ranching colony until the 1982 war. Development, construction, exploitation of fisheries, and tourism have brought sudden wealth to the islanders. **Income/person** $29,400 (103% of USA).

Catholic	1	26.16	1 +0.7%
Marginal	1	1.33	0 +6.7%
Unaffiliated		0.73	0 n.a.

Churches	MegaBloc	Cong.	Members	Affiliates
Ch of England in F.	A	18	175	860
Catholic	C	1	236	590
United Free	P	5	120	530
Other denoms [4]		4	88	130
Total Christians [7]		28	619	2,110

Trans-bloc Groupings	pop. %	,000	Ann.Gr.
Evangelical	22.7	1	+0.4%
Charismatic	4.4	0	-1.0%

Missionaries from Falklands
n.a.

Missionaries to Falklands
P,I,A 7 in 2 agencies from the UK.

POLITICS
Self-governing British Overseas Territory. Argentinian claims on the islands as the Islas Malvinas led to the 1982 War of the South Atlantic. A gradual unfreezing of relationships between British and Argentinians has produced some economic agreements but without tackling the core issue of sovereignty.

RELIGION
Freedom of religion.

Religions	Population %	Adherents	Ann.Gr.
Christian	94.30	2,126	+0.4%
Other	3.40	77	+0.5%
non-Religious/other	2.00	45	+6.4%
Baha'i	0.30	7	+11.8%

Christians	Denom.	Affil.%	,000	Ann.Gr.
Protestant	4	27.94	1	-0.2%
Anglican	1	38.14	1	+0.1%

• Challenges for Prayer

1 The traumatic Argentinian invasion, and Argentina's subsequent defeat by British forces in 1982, decisively affected the economic, political and spiritual life of the once-complacent Falkland Islanders, or 'Kelpies'. Pray for a wise and fair settlement of the long-standing sovereignty issue that hampers the diplomatic and economic life of the whole region.

2 There are only three significant Protestant denominations among the Islanders (Anglican, Tabernacle United Free Church and Baptist) with a few actively witnessing Christians. Pray for believers in their witness to fellow-islanders and to the oilmen and fishermen of many nationalities who work in the seas around the islands.

3 The British forces based on these bleak, windswept Islands face a lonely, thankless task. Pray for believers in the forces as they witness to their comrades and for the work of Mission to Military Garrisons to bear fruit.

Fiji
Sovereign Democratic Republic of Fiji

MAY 6
PACIFIC

GEOGRAPHY
Area 18,274 sq.km. Two larger and 110 smaller inhabited islands, both volcanic and coralline.

Population		Ann.Gr.	Density
2000	816,905	+1.25%	45 per sq. km.
2010	936,229	+1.34%	51 per sq. km.
2025	1,104,141	+1.01%	60 per sq. km.

Capital Suva 200,000. **Urbanites** 12%.

PEOPLES
There has been intense ethnic tension between the indigenous Fijians and immigrant Indians.
Melanesian 50.8%. Fijian 415,000, speaking six related main languages and 30 dialects.
Indian 43.7%. Mainly descendants of indentured labour imported by the British between 1879 and 1916, and also subsequent Gujarati and Sikh immigrants.
  Indo-Aryan 31.5%. Hindi 211,000; Bihari 25,000; Bengali 17,000; Panjabi 7,000.
  Dravidian 12.2%. Tamil 65,000; Telugu 7,000.
Polynesian 1.7%. Rotuman 10,000 on Rotuma Island. Also immigrant Samoans and Tongans.
Other 3.8%. Euro-Polynesian 9,000; Chinese 8,000; European 3,000; I-Kiribati 2,300.

Literacy 92%. **Official language** English; Hindustani and Bau Fijian commonly used. **All languages** 10. **Languages with Scriptures** 4Bi 1NT 1por.

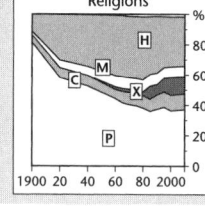 **ECONOMY**
Major export earnings are from tourism and sugar. The Indian community dominates nearly all commercial activities, but has no long-term security, not being permitted to own land. Many Indian professionals have emigrated since 1987 — a brain-drain the country could ill afford. **HDI** 0.763; 61st/174. **Public debt** 6.2% of GNP. **Income/person** $2,470 (8% of USA).

POLITICS
British rule 1874-1970. Post-independence calm, inter-racial balance and relative harmony were interrupted by two military coups in 1987. The aim was to prevent political power going to a democratically elected part-Indian government. Expulsion from the Commonwealth and a discriminatory constitution followed. Political isolation and economic decline stimulated a reversion to democratic rule, an ending of most racial discrimination, return to the Commonwealth and a multi-racial government in 1997. A further coup and intra-military conflict in 2000 again threatened inter-racial harmony and economic growth. The political situation remained volatile in 2001.

RELIGION
The 1987-1999 period was marked by emphasis on Christian traditions and strong Sunday-observance regulations.

Religions	Population %	Adherents	Ann.Gr.
Christian	58.32	476,419	+1.4%
Hindu	33.00	269,579	+0.9%
Muslim	7.00	57,183	+1.2%
non-Religious/other	0.80	6,535	+.2%
Sikh	0.55	4,493	+0.2%
Baha'i	0.30	2,451	+1.3%
Chinese	0.02	163	-6.7%
Jewish	0.01	82	+1.3%

Christians	Denom.Affil.%	,000	Ann.Gr.
Protestant	13	36.31	297	+0.3%
Independent	13	4.86	40	+5.1%
Anglican	1	1.10	9	+1.6%
Catholic	1	10.28	84	+1.3%
Marginal	3	2.01	16	+2.1%
Unaffiliated		3.76	31	n.a.

Churches	MegaBloc	Cong.	Members	Affiliates
Methodist	P	1,160	43,956	200,000
Catholic	C	34	43,750	84,000
Assemblies of God	P	268	18,231	52,231
Seventh-day Adventist	P	160	18,801	29,000
Chr. Miss Fll'ship (EHC)	I	221	13,287	19,000
Latter-day Saints (Morm)	M	22	6,145	11,000
Anglican	A	52	3,940	9,000
Jehovah's Witnesses	M	31	2,009	5,000
United Pentecostal	P	128	4,476	4,700
Chr. Outreach Centre	I	12	2,098	3,000
Church of God (Clev)	P	19	1,800	3,000
Chr Brethren	P	20	898	1,500
Other denoms [22]		117	14,600	24,000
Total Christians [34]		2,244	174,000	446,000

Trans-bloc Groupings	pop. %	,000	Ann.Gr.
Evangelical	17.5	143	+2.9%
Charismatic	12.8	105	+3.1%
Pentecostal	8.6	70	+3.7%

Missionaries from Fiji
P,I,A 91 in 7 agencies to 16 countries: Australia 15, New Zealand 12.

Missionaries to Fiji
P,I,A 143 in 34 agencies from 18 countries: USA 36, New Zealand 33, Korea 28.

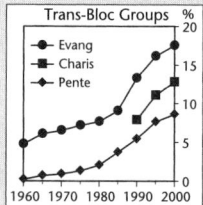

• Answers to Prayer

1 Give praise that the ten years of racial discord and discrimination by Christian Fijians against mainly non-Christian Indians has ended with the unanimous approval of the 1999 Constitution. Pray on for inter-racial respect and harmony in the future.

• Challenges for Prayer

1 **The legacy of British colonial greed has had a long-term impact on Fiji.** These effects:

a) *The resentment of the indigenous Fijians* against the importation of Indian indentured labour from 1870 onwards. The results were manifest in the high crime rate among Fijians and the 1987 coup and following discrimination against the Indians.

b) *The discrediting of Christianity in the eyes of the Indians* and the present ingrained attitudes of fear, mistrust, minority complex and insecurity.

c) *The close link between Fijian nationalism and politicized Christianity.* The coup split the dominant Methodist Church.

Pray for a spirit of repentance, healing of past wounds, a fair society, and a new freedom for the true gospel.

2 **Fijians embraced Christianity over a century ago**, but this was often cultural rather than spiritual. Legalism, nominalism and failure to confront the ongoing worship of ancestral spirit gods are widespread. Alcoholism and broken homes are major social evils. Fiji has a higher percentage of Methodists than any other nation — but there has been a considerable exodus of Fijians from the Methodist Church to other denominations. Pray for a deep work of the Holy Spirit to deal with compromise and ethnic hatred and to bring revival.

3 **Newer churches with a more strongly evangelical message are growing**, but so too are Mormons and Jehovah's Witnesses. Also within the Methodist, Anglican and Catholic churches are vigorous evangelical and charismatic movements. However, there is a need for all islands to have exposure to genuine, lived-out Christianity. Pray for agencies involved in church planting and evangelism. The small boat ministry of **YWAM** and **UBS** is unique in taking evangelistic teams and Christian literature from island to island, many of which are very isolated.

4 **Less reached peoples**. The Indians of Fiji form the largest non-Christian community in the Pacific. Only 6% of them claim to be Christian. Indian majority churches are often weakened by a spirit of receiving rather than giving, a lack of stable leadership, and emigration of their most gifted leaders. Pray specifically for:

a) *The Hindus*, who have been patchily evangelized. Yet during the past four decades there has been a steady trickle of converts to Christianity. The Methodists, **AoG**, Baptists and Pentecostals all have numbers of Indian Christians. **WEC** and **Pioneers** have church-planting ministries committed to ministry among them.

b) *The Sikhs and Panjabis* have retained more of their culture and language, but there has been little specific outreach to them.

c) *The 59,000 Muslim community* is tightly knit and very resistant to the gospel. Little is being done to reach them, and the few converted to Christ have suffered considerable persecution. There are several Fijian villages that have become Muslim.

d) **The Chinese** — mostly Cantonese in origin. There has been more recent immigration from mainland China and Hong Kong. Many speak English. There had been no ministry specifically directed to reach them until 1992 (**WEC**).

5 **Fiji is both a commercial and spiritual hub** for the many small nations of the Pacific. Pray therefore for the spiritual revival and health of the Church, more specifically in:

a) *Leadership training* for the churches. Significant institutions are the Methodist Theological College, the **AoG** Bible School (100 students), Ambassadors for Christ Bible School (11 students), the Baptist Christian Leadership College in Nasinu, the Catholic Pacific Regional Seminary. The EHC Bible and Missionary Training School and the South Pacific Missionary Training Centre were set up specifically to train workers for cross-cultural work.

b) *Ministry to young people*. Fiji has serious sociological problems amongst their youth, yet there is a responsiveness that needs to be met. Pray for those specifically ministering to young people in Fiji and the Pacific — **CEF** (4 workers amongst children), **YFC**, **SU**, and **YWAM** amongst youth, and also Pacific Students for Christ (**IFES**) and **CCCI** among students. The University of the Pacific in Fiji has students from every island territory and is strategic for impacting many islands where there is much nominal Christianity.

c) *Evangelical networks*. There are two umbrella organizations for Evangelicals — the Evangelical Alliance and the Evangelical Fellowship of Fiji. The latter relates to the Evangelical Fellowship of the South Pacific, founded in 1989, which has become a catalyst for co-operation in youth work, women's networks and missions. Pray for a deep unity among believers that transcends denomination, distance and ethnicity.

d) *Mission vision*. Over 300 Fijians have served as long-term missionaries over the last 130 years. The initial enthusiasm waned but is now being revived. **YWAM, WEC, Pioneers** and CMF have been prominent in channelling Fijians to mission fields around the world. The EFSP has launched the **Deep Sea Canoe Mission** as a cooperative effort to foster missions vision, identify and train workers. Pray for existing and greater future

Fijian missionary investment.

6 **Christian help ministries** in Fiji have Pacific-wide outreach. Pray for:

a) *The Bible Society* of the South Pacific based in Fiji. Pray for their endeavours in undertaking surveys of translation needs (much needed in Fiji's dialects now), translation work, printing and distribution of God's Word throughout the Pacific. Translation and revision work in Fijian and Fiji Hindi are important projects. There is also a lack of good Christian literature in these two languages.

b) *EHC* has been so successful in Fiji that after 3 nation-wide distributions, 6% of the population responded, over 2,000 Christ groups started, and a denomination formed with a strong missions vision.

c) *The JESUS film* has been extensively used in English, Fijian and Hindi.

d) *Specialized agencies* include: **WVI**, committed to wholistic development, Christian Women Communication International with their KYB programmes, Bible distribution of Gideons International, the prisoner rehabilitation ministry of Prison Fellowship and the Nurses Christian Fellowship. All need prayer.

F

Finland
Republic of Finland

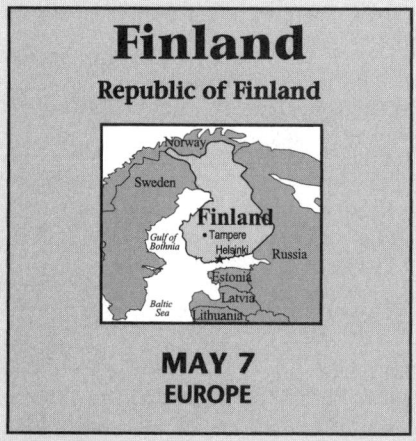

Norway
Sweden
Finland
Gulf of Bothnia • Tampere
Helsinki *Russia*
Estonia
Latvia
Baltic Sea *Lithuania*

MAY 7
EUROPE

GEOGRAPHY
Area 338,145 sq.km. This northern country is 70% forest, 10% lake, 8% arable land.

Population	Ann.Gr.	Density
2000	5,175,743	+0.26%	15 per sq. km.
2010	5,235,338	+0.07%	15 per sq. km.
2025	5,253,863	-0.05%	16 per sq. km.

Capital Helsinki 1,175,000. **Urbanites** 66%.

PEOPLES
Finno-Ugric 92.5%. Finns 4,782,000; Lapp (Same) 5,700 in Arctic, with 2,000 speaking 3 Same dialects.
Germanic 5.7%. Swedish-speaking 295,000, largely in SW and on Åland Islands in Gulf of Bothnia.
Other 1.8%. Russians 25,000; Turks 1,000; also Somalis, Romanians, and others.

Literacy 100%. **Official languages** Finnish, Swedish. **All languages** 10. **Languages with Scriptures** 4Bi 1NT 4 por.

ECONOMY
Specialized, export-oriented economy

based on wood products and, increasingly, high-tech industry. Serious recession in the early 1990s has since ended. **HDI** 0.913; 13th/174. **Public debt** 67.1% of GNP. **Income/person** $24,790 (78.7% of USA).

POLITICS
Ruled by Sweden for 700 years, then by Russia for a further 100. Independent in 1917. Member of EU.

RELIGION
Freedom of religion, but Evangelical Lutheran and Finnish (Greek) Orthodox churches have special recognition.

Religions	Population %	Adherents	Ann.Gr.
Christian	87.09	4,507,555	+0.1%
non-Religious	12.60	652,144	+1.1%
Muslim	0.18	9,316	+2.7%
Other	0.09	4,658	+5.4%
Jewish	0.02	1,035	-7.5%
Baha'i	0.01	518	+0.3%
Hindu	0.01	518	+0.3%

Christians	Denom.	Affil.%	,000	Ann.Gr.
Protestant	37	87.60	4,534	+0.1%
Independent	2	0.02	1	+0.7%
Catholic	1	0.13	7	+5.0%
Orthodox	3	1.02	53	-0.4%
Marginal	8	0.71	37	+1.2%
Doubly affiliated		-2.40	-124	n.a.

Churches	MegaBloc	Cong.	Members	Affiliates
Evang Lutheran	P	1,377	1,721,400	4,406,800
Finnish Pentecostal	P	210	49,000	70,070
Finnish Orthodox	O	115	36,364	52,000
Jehovah's Witnesses	M	320	21,000	31,000
Evangelical Free	P	98	12,600	16,380
Seventh-day Adventist	P	67	5,752	7,700
Siiloan Pentecostal	P	1	2,840	7,100
Catholic	C	11	4,738	6,776
Maranatha Pentecostal	P	26	2,550	6,375
Free Pentecostal Revival	P	34	2,400	4,800
Latter-day Saints (Morm)	M	36	3,400	4,600

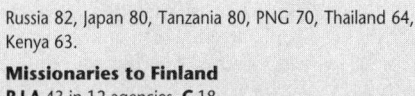

Baptist (Swedish)	P	21	1,400	1,670	Russia 82, Japan 80, Tanzania 80, PNG 70, Thailand 64,
Methodist	P	23	1,278	1,650	Kenya 63.
Ch of Sweden (Lutheran)	P	3	1,034	1,500	
Salvation Army	P	45	1,200	1,300	**Missionaries to Finland**
Other denoms [38]		237	7,600	11,500	**P,I,A** 43 in 12 agencies. **C** 18.
Doubly affiliated			*-47,300*	*-121,000*	

Total Christians [53]		2,624	1,827,300	4,510,000
Trans-bloc Groupings pop. %			**,000**	**Ann.Gr.**
Evangelical		12.5	648	+0.2%
Charismatic		6.3	325	+0.2%
Pentecostal		1.8	92	+0.7%

Missionaries from Finland

P,I,A 1,494 in 35 agencies to 84 countries: Ethiopia 82,

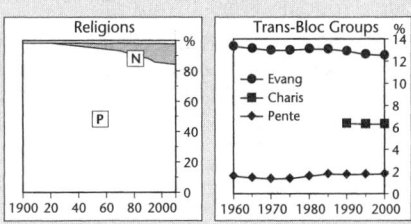

• Answers to Prayer

F

1 **The collapse of Communism** in the USSR gave unprecedented opportunities to Finns for evangelism and for the encouragement of Christians in Estonia (their ethnic cousins) and Russia. Estonia's church growth in the 1990s was due in large part to Finnish Christians. But the early boom is over. Now there is a need for long-term workers to help disciple the new churches. Finns also enjoy a strategic role to the Finno-Ugric people of the former USSR, assisting in evangelism and discipleship.

• Challenges for Prayer

1 **Secular humanism has a strong influence** with its attendant negative attitudes — two-thirds of Finns see life as gloomy and devoid of hope, and 5 out of 6 believe that the ordinary person's lot is continually declining. Unemployment and the national debt are major concerns and spiritual pluralism is becoming widespread. The last revival occurred during the 1960s. A growing interest in spiritual things could lead to another revival, but in the meantime the fastest growing religious groups are Muslims, Jehovah's Witnesses and Mormons.

2 **The Lutheran Church is much more evangelical** than most national churches in Europe — partly a heritage of the revival movements of the past that have influenced its spirituality. This body is an umbrella for a large number of autonomous fellowships, revival and prayer groups and missions. It is in these that most committed Lutherans find their fellowship and platform for evangelism. Perhaps as many as 20% of Lutherans have connections to these groups, but adherents decrease as attendance dwindles (2% of the population). Ageing congregations indicate a future intensification of this problem. The Church needs a renewal of both spirit and structure to combat passivity and nominalism. Pray that deep and lasting revival might come to the entire Lutheran church.

3 **The Free Churches, both Pentecostal and non-Pentecostal,** are relatively small but spiritually vigorous and growing. Charismatic renewal has had a marked impact. Pray for greater unity and cooperation in evangelism and missions among these various bodies, and between the Free Churches and Lutherans.

4 **A new paradigm for the Church is required** if it is truly to grow in Finland. The church planting targets set by DAWN show that there is still life and vision, but the structure of the church is in a state of change. The old forms and traditions do not address the needs of many Finns. Specific issues:

a) *The many rootless believers who "church-hop"* and lack any real commitment to a fellowship. Pray that the Spirit would convict them to integrate more fully into His body.

b) *The widespread growth of house groups.* Some of these groups are planted by established churches, some are not. Pray that all might see themselves in a wider context as part of the whole body of Christ, and contribute accordingly.

c) *The development of a national Christian vision and strategy.* Pray for wisdom and discernment for national church leaders in dealing with the wide variety of groups and backgrounds.

5 **Young people's ministries have great potential**. A high proportion of Finnish young people attend confirmation camps. This is an opportunity for them to come to a living faith in Christ. Pray that the leaders might display a godly example of the walk of faith. Pray also for the campus ministries of the Evangelical Lutheran Student Mission (**IFES**, in 12 cities), EYL and **CCCI**. Many students in Finland do not reside on campuses, so organizing the groups is much more difficult.

6 **A vision for missions is not growing** as it should. Churches need to catch a missions vision and become more involved in the sending process rather than relying totally on agencies. Many workers are hampered by a lack of support. New models of missionary sending need to be developed that counter the depersonalization of the support process. Various missions have sent out Finns in summer or short-term teams all over the world; many are now in full-time ministry.

7 **Less reached peoples.** Many refugees and asylum-seekers have come to Finland from Central and Eastern Europe and an increasing number from Asia and Africa. Many are Muslims, and few have ever heard the gospel before. Some fellowships are providing international meetings for these people, and there are some ethnic fellowships, such as the small Chinese church in Helsinki. Pray that these immigrants might have the chance to encounter Jesus in a real and attractive way.

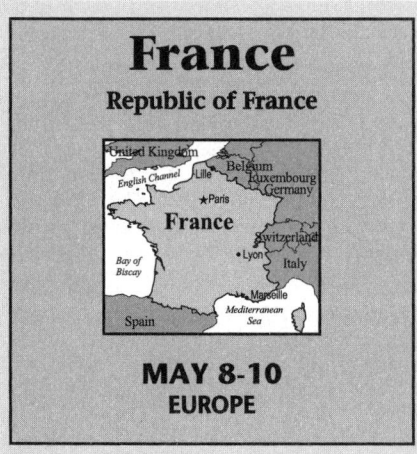

France

Republic of France

MAY 8-10

EUROPE

GEOGRAPHY
Area 543,965 sq.km. The largest country in Western Europe.

Population	Ann.Gr.	Density
2000	59,079,709	+0.36%	109/sq. km.
2010	60,596,993	+0.22%	111/sq. km.
2025	61,661,804	+0.05%	113/sq. km.

Capital Paris 10.7 mill. Other major cities: Marseille 1.4m; Lyon 1.33m; Lille 1m. **Urbanites** 73%.

PEOPLES
Indigenous and immigrant ethnic minority figures are approximate due to naturalization, assimilation, illegal immigration and intense anti-foreign propaganda obscuring the issue.
Indigenous 84%.
French 72.3%.
Regional minorities 9.4%. Breton 1.9m (26% speak Breton as first language); Occitan 1.6m; Alsatian

1.5m; Provençal 800,000 (30%); Flemish 750,000 (15%); Basque 730,000 (11% — 3 dialects); Corsican 341,000 (80%); Catalan 260,000.
Other 2.3%. Jewish 750,000; West Indian Antillean 280,000; Roma (Gypsy) 280,000 (4 languages); Réunionese 12,000.
International minorities 16%, of which 37% were foreign-born. Many illegal immigrants.
North African/Middle Eastern 9%. North African 3.7m, of which over 1.2m are Berber (Kabyle, Shawiya, Riff, etc.); Lebanese/Arab 180,000; Turk 180,000; Kurd 50,000.
European 5%. Portuguese 750,000; Italian 523,000; German 560,000; Spanish 413,000; Armenian 250,000; Polish 143,000; Russian 100,000; Yugoslav 100,000.
Asian 1.3%. Vietnamese 300,000; Chinese 180,000; Lao/Hmong 100,000; Cambodian 80,000; Tamil 30,000.
African 0.7%. Representing every Francophone nation and most West African ethnic groups — Malinke, Soninke, Fulbe, Wolof, Tuareg, etc.

Literacy 99%. **Official language** French. Regional languages in decline. French is the first language of 120 million people worldwide. **All languages** 25. **Languages with Scriptures** 12Bi 3NT 11por.

ECONOMY
Stability and growth leading to a high standard of living. The fifth largest economy in the world with a strong industrial and agricultural base. The service industry is now 70% of the economy. Danger signs: bloated bureaucracy, heavy state involvement in industry and commerce and an overgenerous social welfare system resulting in high taxation (54% of all income) and persistent unemployment (11%). **HDI** 0.918; 11th/174. **Public debt** 42% of GNP. **Income/person** $26,270 (92% of USA).

POLITICS

Democratic republic with strong executive presidency. A core member of the EU, but torn between being a good European state and retaining its own unique identity and culture.

RELIGION

Secular state with freedom of religion, but with a long history of severe persecution of dissenters and reformers before the 1789 Revolution. Rising concern in the 1990s about the activities of 'sects' led to the formulation in 2000 of legislation to limit the activities of any group labeled as a 'sect'.

Religions	Population %	Adherents	Ann.Gr.
Christian	67.72	40,008,779	-0.1%
non-Religious	19.76	11,674,150	+0.7%
Muslim	10.00	5,907,971	+2.5%
Jewish	1.18	697,141	+0.2%
Buddhist/Chinese	1.02	602,613	+4.6%
Other	0.30	177,239	+0.4%
Baha'i	0.02	11,816	+0.4%

Christians	Denom.	Affil.%	,000	Ann.Gr.
Protestant	99	1.58	935	+2.1%
Independent	45	0.38	222	+3.5%
Anglican	1	0.03	20	+0.0%
Catholic	1	67.71	40,000	-1.8%
Orthodox	13	0.79	467	-0.9%
Marginal	21	0.62	369	+0.0%
Doubly affiliated		-3.39	-2,000	n.a.

Churches	MegaBloc	Cong.	Members	Affiliates
Catholic	C	34,000	10.00m	40.00m
Reformed	P	350	50,000	300,000
Armenian Apostolic	O	110	88,000	220,000
Augsburg Conf (Luth)	P	331	125,749	210,000
Jehovah's Witnesses	M	1,626	118,079	200,000
Assemblies of God	P	620	42,000	160,000
Gypsy Evangelical Miss	I	62	32,000	100,000
Greek Orthodox	O	27	45,000	59,850
Evangelical Lutheran	P	41	4,000	40,000
Old Catholic [2]	P	6	25,000	38,000
Latter-day Saints (Morm)	M	175	23,602	38,000

Ref Ch of Alsace & Lorr	P	65	1,350	33,000
Other Indep [12]	I	206	16,500	26,400
Breth Assemb (Darby)	P	111	12,200	23,400
Full Gospel Federation	P	45	11,000	18,000
Seventh-day Adventist	P	115	9,602	14,000
Fed of Baptist Chs.	P	114	6,533	14,000
Ethnic [22]	I	89	8,000	12,000
Indep Reformed	P	70	1,860	10,600
Evang Assemb (Breth)	P	128	4,500	7,000
Assoc of Ev Mennonites	P	30	2,000	3,000
Chr & Miss Alliance	P	20	806	2,297
Assoc of Evang Baptists	P	20	1,317	2,200
Alliance of Indep Evang	P	33	900	2,070
France-Mission	P	50	1,400	2,000
Salvation Army	P	42	1,000	1,400
Union of Chrischona	P	20	930	1,330
Ch of the Nazarene	P	10	600	1,100
Other denoms [124]		1,745	196,200	473,300
Doubly affiliated			-1,481,500	-2,000,000
Total Christians [185]		40,261	9.349m	40.013m

Trans-bloc Groupings	pop. %	,000	Ann.Gr.
Evangelical	0.8	488	+5.7%
Charismatic	1.6	953	+1.5%
Pentecostal	0.5	307	+7.9%

Missionaries from France
P,I,A approx. 600 in 56 agencies to 55 countries: France 293, Burkina Faso 33, Togo 23, Chad 23, Cameroon 21.

Missionaries to France
P,I,A 1,519 in 155 agencies from 40 countries: USA 738, UK 230, Canada 74, Switzerland 70, Germany 64, Korea 34.

F

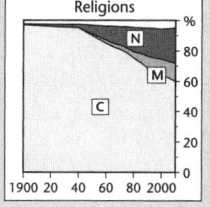

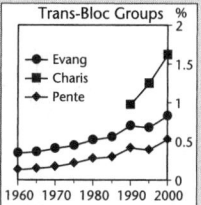

• Answers to Prayer

1 **Evangelical Christianity has grown** over the past 40 years despite the massive secularization of society, indifference and decline in church involvement. In 1940 the evangelical Protestant community in France numbered 60,000; in 1960 they were 100,000; in 1980 Evangelicals reached 277,000 and in 2000 they were 488,000.

2 **The Roma (Gypsy) minority** is now the most evangelical people in France. A people movement since 1960 has brought 25% of the population to personal faith in Christ — most in the Gypsy Evangelical Misson (links to **AoG**).

• Challenges for Prayer

1 **There are major spiritual strongholds** that hinder acceptance of the gospel:

a) *The brutal persecutions of the Huguenots* (French Protestants) in the 16th and 17th Centuries is a dark stain on the soul of France. Many were slaughtered and 200,000 fled to other lands — to their enrichment and France's impoverishment. Yet Calvin, the great reformer and theologian, produced the only authentically French theological expression of Christianity. The loss of its biblical Christian population was a contributing factor leading to the explosion of the French Revolution.

b) *The French Revolution in 1789-1801* was one of the defining moments of world history. While some good came from this upheaval, it also spawned much violence, desires for world domination, the deification of humanism and ultimately the ideologies that distorted world history for 200 years and only ended with the collapse of European Communism in 1989. The effects of that cataclysm still deeply affect French attitudes to themselves, other nations and to Christianity itself.

c) *The insensitivity of the Anglophone nations*, especially England and the USA. Evangelical Christianity is seen as an Anglo-Saxon imposition on France together with the cultural, linguistic and economic 'imperialisms' perceived to be eroding the French way of life.

d) *The surprisingly widespread involvement with occult practices*. The 50,000 full-time practitioners of these black arts outnumber the 35,000 known Christian workers. Every level of society is involved, with its inevitable spiritual impact.

2 **France is at a crossroads.** Like the national comic hero, Asterix, there is a brave fight against globalization, the need for radical reforms of the bloated welfare state, and state involvement in industry. The government needs courage to take painful decisions which are right for the country but resisted by those with vested interests.

3 **France remains historically and culturally Catholic**, but there has been a massive numerical decline in both Catholic and mainline Protestant churches. The non-religious have risen to 20% of the population and non-practicing 'Christians' have risen from 10% in 1970 to 50% in 2000. Regular church attendance has plummeted to 6 — 8% of the population. Great swathes of French society have no meaningful contact with a Christian church and have a profound ignorance of, and indifference to, the gospel. Without a dramatic change, Christianity is doomed to marginalized insignificance — pray for such a change!

4 **The Catholic Church** has lost much of its influence in society. Baptisms have declined from 75% of all children in 1970 to 20% in 1999. Many Catholics reject papal infallibility and rigid rules on contraception. Tensions exist between conservative traditionalists, liberals, modernists, radicals and charismatics. The latter group is where there is most life, and they have helped many to see the truths of God's Word and the need for a living, personal faith. Pray that more people may discover these.

5 **Protestants** were accepted at the Reformation, and at one stage some estimate that 48% of the French population had embraced the new teaching. Persecution in the 17th and 18th Centuries and humanism and nominalism in the 19th and 20th Centuries have reduced this to 1.6% in 2000. Protestantism is a respected moral force less tainted by the 'guilt' of the Catholic Church, but is spiritually too compromised by liberal theology, universalism and tolerance to exploit that advantage. Protestants are more numerous in Alsace and the south but nominalism and decline are too common. Yet there are staunch evangelical believers in most Reformed and Lutheran congregations. Pray for a restoration to the faith and commitment of their martyr forebears.

6 **Evangelical Christians are few**, scattered and split up among more than 130 Protestant denominations and nearly 3,000 congregations. Growth has been steady, doubling the number of Evangelicals between 1965 and 1990. Over 1,000 evangelical churches have been planted in the past 20 years. The Pentecostals, and the **AoG** in particular, have grown the fastest, tripling their membership over the same period. However, much of that growth has been among Roma, Antilleans and other migrants (the latter two forming a high proportion of most Parisian evangelical congregations). Pray for:

a) *An impact to be made on the core French population*. To most French people, the evangelical message is still seen as an alien ideology rather than a home-grown faith. Public over-reaction to extremist suicidal sects led to many evangelical groups and agencies being labelled 'sects' by a government commission in 1999. Evangelicals are described as 'extreme emanations from the Reformed Church'. This has made all forms of outreach more difficult.

b) **Unity among true believers.** The diversity and fragmentation of the evangelical witness hinder cooperative effort. The **FEF** (*Fédération Évangélique de France*) and the **AEF** (*Alliance Évangélique de France*) have become important for cooperation. The *Fédération Protestante* links together a wider spectrum of Reformed Protestant and Pentecostal denominations and is important in giving a larger common platform to Protestants.

c) **Revival.** Few Christians are delivered from spiritual bondages; fear of witnessing, indifference, marriage with unbelievers, and church divisions are the baleful results.

d) **Vision.** Many factors, such as dysfunctionality, insecurity and loneliness have created a search for truth and those who live it and proclaim it, which local Christians need to grasp. **France Mission** has promoted the goal, now being more widely embraced, to ensure the planting of one church for every 10,000 people by 2010. This will mean doubling the number of congregations in the country.

7 **The unreached sectors of French society are many,** such as:

a) **The nearly 50 million French** people who have no *real* link with a Christian church.

b) **The many large cities** with few evangelical churches — Nancy has 3 and Nantes, 8.

c) **Of the 38,000 communes,** around 35,000 have no resident evangelical witness. Many rural communes are quite traditional and resistant to change.

d) **The Basques** in the southwest who are virtually without an evangelical witness in their language.

e) **The Loire Valley, Brittany, Picardy, Limousin, Champagne-Ardennes and Calais** which are particularly lacking in evangelical congregations.

f) **The island of Corsica.** Birthplace of Napoleon, it is renowned for its violence. In the population of 260,000, there are 12 small groups with 250 evangelical believers.

8 **The unreached minorities:**

a) **The large Portuguese, Spanish and Italian communities** are more receptive than in their native lands. They have generally not adapted well to French society, but there are few believers who evangelize them in their own languages. There are only seven Portuguese or Spanish congregations for over one million people.

b) **The Jewish community,** fourth largest in the world and the largest in Europe with 320,000 in Paris alone and a further 100,000 in Marseille. Eighteen workers in five missions labour among them (**MT, GMU, CWI, JFJ** and the French TMPI). There are about 600 believers among them and three known assemblies of Messianic Jews.

c) **North Africans** are almost entirely Muslim, few ever having heard the gospel. The majority live in large low-cost housing areas in larger cities. The growing hostility and racism of French 'Christians' have both antagonized them and provoked a strong, well-organized Muslim movement that complicates Christian outreach to them. Pray for French and international churches and agencies seeking to break down barriers through friendship evangelism, radio, film, BCCs and literature. Agencies involved: **AWM, CCCI, WEC, SIM, SBC, UFM, IMI** and **IFES**.

d) **The Berbers** form a large minority among the North Africans and possibly make up the majority of Algerians. Kabyle believers have been increasing in number and are active in reaching out to their own people in France and North Africa and producing videos, tapes, radio programmes and literature in Kabyle. The *JESUS* film on video is being used widely in various Berber languages.

e) **Black Africans** have come in large numbers as students, refugees and work-seekers from Muslim areas of Francophone Africa. There is little specific outreach to the Bambara, Wolof, Malinke, Soninke and others. Pray for effective church-planting strategies and the committed workers to implement them.

f) **The large number of Indo-Chinese** refugees of the 1970s and '80s from France's former colonies is gradually being absorbed into French life. A small minority have become active Christians — some integrated into French churches, others in their own ethnic churches mainly planted through the ministry of **CMA**. There are 11 Hmong-Lao groups, seven Chinese (one through **COCM**), three Cambodian and two Vietnamese congregations, but the few pastors and missionaries can hardly cover the many scattered communities.

g) **The growing Turkish, Iranian and Afghan** communities need to be evangelized.

9 **Islam is now the second religion of France**. Its growth has been largely through immigration and a higher birth rate, but there are an estimated 150,000 French Muslims — mostly through marriage to a Muslim. There are deep divisions within French Islam between fundamentalists and secularists, which is exacerbated by the civil war in Algeria. There is also a large under-class of young people that is becoming a seed-bed for crime, violence and Islamism. Most Muslims are urban. There are less than 100 Christian workers seeking to reach them, but there are nearly 2,000 known Muslim-background believers with 15 groups meeting.

10 **There are over 12 residential Evangelical Bible Schools and Seminaries**, both denominational and interdenominational, with around 250 students. Notable among the latter are the European Bible Institute in Lamorlaye, *Institut Biblique de Nogent*, and the Vaux Evangelical Seminary. There are also denominational seminaries for the Baptists, Pentecostals and the Aix-en-Provence Seminary for Reformed Church students. Pray for:

a) *Full-time workers to be called for ministry* in France. There are only about 3,000 full-time Protestant workers (about one-third being foreign), and few of these are successful pioneer church planters — most of the latter being expatriates.

b) *A deep work of the Holy Spirit* to equip those trained with both the theological understanding and spiritual maturity to make an impact for eternity. There is a serious lack of basic Bible knowledge. Most, even educated believers, are content with a minimum of understanding.

c) *The blessing of the whole Francophone world* through French and foreign students who graduate. A high proportion of students are from other lands.

11 **French Evangelicals, though few, have sent out over 300 missionaries** into 55 lands. General missions interest in Protestant churches is low and support small. The largest agencies are: **YWAM** (68 workers), **AoG** (52), *Mission Baptiste Europeéne* (18), **WBT** (18), **OM** (13), **SIM** (11), *Cooperation Evangélique dans le Monde* (11). Pray for the vision for world evangelization to be embraced by the churches. Pray also for the impact of the French edition of *Operation World*, entitled *Flashes sur le Monde*.

12 **French and foreign missions have a vital servant role to play in evangelism and church planting**. There are not enough full-time French Christian workers to begin to meet the need. Missionaries find it hard to adapt and win acceptance, and church-planting has had limited effectiveness when foreign patterns are imported. Increasingly missions are finding a useful church-planting ministry with indigenous structures (**SBC**, France Mission, *Eau Vive*, **BCU**, **ECM**, **WT**, **TEAM**, **UFM**, **GEM**, **GMU**, **WEC**, etc.). Fruit is hard-won, discouragements many, and the missionary dropout rate high. Pray for good identification with French culture, perseverance, effectiveness, provision of adequate financial support and spiritual power.

13 **Youth ministries** are vital in a nation where dysfunctional families are 'normal', moral absolutes absent and where many young people are bored, frustrated and confused. Pray specifically for:

a) *Children's ministry* — **CEF** ministers through Good News Clubs and Christmas clubs in homes. From their Paris base, French literature for children is exported across the world.

b) *Young people are more receptive to the gospel*. Many groups and missions have specialized in this ministry — Youth for Christ, **YWAM**, **CCCI**, Young Life, *Eau Vive*, **ECM**, **TEAM** through camps, clubs, coffee bars and ministry in secondary schools; Teen Challenge among drug addicts; **SU** in schools and through Bible reading notes. Pray for many young people to be saved and integrated into good evangelical churches — the latter step usually being much harder than the former!

c) *There are 68 universities and over 2 million students in tertiary education* — 300,000 of these are foreign students. Ministry to these students has national and worldwide implications! Witness in this highly secular and post-Christian environment is hard. Student protests have increased during the 1990s — rebels without a worthy cause. The evangelical witness has been slow to develop, but now there are 2,000 students linked with the 55 GBU(**IFES**) groups. Less than half the universities have a GBU group, and most are very small and predominantly made up of overseas students. **CCCI** and **Navigators** also have a growing ministry on campuses. Students are more open than ever, searching for reality in an ideological vacuum.

14 **Christian Help Ministries for prayer:**

a) The Bible Society published the *Good News Bible* in French in 1982. Pray for the impact of God's Word. Only 5% of the population owns a Bible and 80% has never even handled one. The resources of the Bible Society are heavily committed to providing Scriptures for other Francophone lands. A new French study Bible was published in 2000.

b) Literature is a valuable tool for evangelism and discipleship. Literature campaigns by CMM (**EHC**), **CCCI**, and **OM** have been useful to sow the seed widely. Pray for Christian publishing houses and bookstores (80) of which 11 are run by **CLC**.

c) Radio and TV evangelism became a new tool when local broadcasting licences were more easily obtained. Pray that Christians may cooperate to make effective use of these media. An association to promote this was started in 1982. *Radio Évangile* (French branch of **TWR**) is involved in training French believers for local broadcasting. The latter also has a significant ministry via **TWR** Monte Carlo and by means of satellite and FM (8 hours/month). **HCJB** broadcasts a further 12 hrs/mo to France from Ecuador. **AWM's Radio School of the Bible**, primarily for North Africans, is aired on 3 French stations.

F

French Guiana
Department of French Guiana

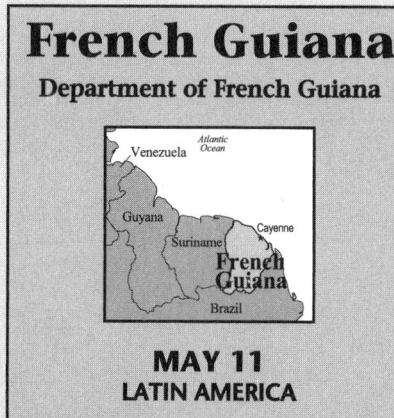

Venezuela — Atlantic Ocean
Guyana
Suriname — Cayenne
French Guiana
Brazil

MAY 11
LATIN AMERICA

GEOGRAPHY
Area 86,504 sq.km. Sparsely inhabited jungle territory in northeast South America. Great diversity of flora and fauna with over 400,000 species known.

Population	Ann.Gr.	Density
2000	181,313	+4.32%	2 per sq. km.
2010	264,502	+3.69%	3 per sq. km.
2025	416,191	+2.76%	5 per sq. km.

Capital Cayenne 67,000. **Urbanites** 73%.

PEOPLES
Afro-Caribbean 70%. Creole 86,000; Haitian 25,000; Maron 8,000; Antillean 7,000.
European 11%. Mainly French.
Asian 8%. Chinese 5,000; Laotian Hmong 2,000; Javanese 1,200; Lebanese 1,000.
Brazilian 8%.
Amerindian 3%. Speaking six languages.

Literacy 83%. **Official language** French. Guiana

Creole widely spoken. **All languages** 10. **Languages with Scriptures** 2Bi 3NT 2por 2w.i.p.

ECONOMY
Partially developed coastal strip, and undeveloped jungle hinterland. Heavily subsidized by France. Main exports — gold, shrimp and forest products. The Kourou satellite launching site is the major source of income and is bringing rapid development. **Unemployment** 24%. **Income/person** $10,580 (37% of USA).

POLITICS
Overseas Department of France. For years infamous as a French penal colony. There is little desire or incentive for independence.

RELIGION
Freedom of religion but secular in outlook.

Religions	Population %	Adherents	Ann.Gr.
Christian	84.93	153,989	+3.8%
non-Religious/other	9.47	17,170	+8.4%
Traditional ethnic	2.00	3,626	+4.3%
Muslim	1.90	3,445	+9.4%
Baha'i	0.90	1,632	+6.8%
Chinese	0.80	1,451	-0.2%

Christians	Denom.	Affil.%	,000	Ann.Gr.
Protestant	15	4.91	9	+2.8%
Independent	4	1.21	2	+1.8%
Anglican	1	0.06	0	+2.0%
Catholic	1	67.84	123	+2.6%
Marginal	2	3.95	7	+9.3%
Unaffiliated		6.96	13	n.a.

Churches	MegaBloc	Cong.	Members	Affiliates
Catholic	C	30	65,079	123,000
Jehovah's Witnesses	M	45	2,226	7,000
Seventh-day Adventist	P	6	1,414	2,600
Assemblies of God	P	2	900	1,800

New Apostolic	I	4	800	1,120
Evangelical Reformed	P	4	500	1,000
Baptist Convention	P	6	450	900
Christian Brethren [3]	P	10	400	700
Streams of Power	I	2	350	600
Chr and Miss Alliance	P	4	168	576
Church of the Nazarene	P	1	250	400
Independent	I	1	160	272
Salvation Army	P	1	160	267
Other denominations [8]		14	779	1,127
Total Christians [23]		130	73,600	141,400

Trans-bloc Groupings pop. %		,000	Ann.Gr.
Evangelical	3.3	6	+1.6%
Charismatic	4.5	8	+2.4%
Pentecostal	1.7	3	+2.3%

Missionaries from French Guiana
P,I,A 4 in 2 agencies.

Missionaries to French Guiana
P,I,A 17 in 8 agencies from 6 countries.

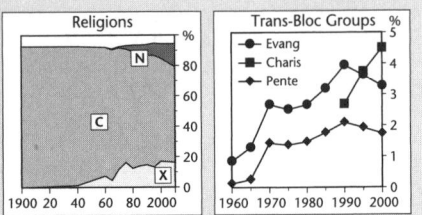

F • Challenges for Prayer

1 The penal colony image is only now wearing off, yet the economic, moral and spiritual effects remain. Of the 70,000 prisoners who were incarcerated here between 1852 and 1939, 90% died in Guiana. Only a handful of the Guianese Creole speakers are active Christians. Almost 80% of births are illegitimate, and indifference to spiritual things is widespread. Pray for the **WT** thrust to this specific people group. A translation of the New Testament for them is definitely needed.

2 The most responsive peoples are the Haitians, Antilleans, Hmong and Brazilians, and it is among these peoples that the **AoG**, Baptists, (**SBC**, **CMA**) and Brethren are growing. Pray for men and women to be called into the ministry and for the young churches to mature in understanding and vision.

3 The least reached peoples:

a) The Amerindian tribes — never has any permanent work been established among the inland tribes, but Christians of these tribes in Suriname and Brazil have made evangelistic forays. Pray for the Arawak (200), Wayana (200), Palikur (800), Oyapi (500) and Emerillon (200).

b) The nominally Catholic Caribs (1,900).

c) The inland settlements of largely animistic Maron set up by escaped slaves.

d) The Chinese. There has been a small outreach by Suriname Chinese Christians.

e) The French and European communities linked with the space programme — few are active Christians.

French Polynesia

Territory of French Polynesia

French Polynesia

South Pacific Ocean

MAY 11
PACIFIC

testing nuclear weapons provoked international opposition and fuelled the Tahitian independence movement.

RELIGION
There is complete religious freedom, but society is increasingly materialistic and secular.

Religions	Population %	Adherents	Ann.Gr.
Christian	85.05	199,919	+0.0%
non-Religious/other	13.80	32,438	+21.0%
Chinese/Buddhist	0.60	1,410	+1.8%
Traditional ethnic	0.30	705	-3.9%
Baha'i	0.25	588	+6.5%

Christians	Denom.	Affil.%	,000	Ann.Gr.
Protestant	5	45.65	107	+0.8%
Independent	11	0.89	2	+3.1%
Catholic	1	34.03	80	-2.1%
Marginal	3	12.12	28	+1.9%
Unaffiliated		5.55	13	n.a.
Doubly affiliated		*-13.19*	*-31*	*n.a.*

F

GEOGRAPHY
Area 3,521 sq.km. Five island archipelagos and 118 islands — (Society, Tuamotu, Marquesas, Austral and Gambier) in south-central Pacific. Tahiti is the largest island at 1,042 sq.km. and is where over 80% live.

Population	Ann.Gr.	Density
2000	235,061	+1.78%	67 per sq. km.
2010	272,750	+1.42%	77 per sq. km.
2025	324,439	+1.08%	92 per sq. km.

Capital Papeete 139,000. **Urbanites** 60%.

PEOPLES
Polynesian 68.5%. Speaking 7 distinct languages, largest: Tahitian 100,000; Tuamotuan 18,000; Tubuaian 10,000; Marquesan(2) 10,000; Mangarevan 2,000.
Mixed Race 15.1%. Polynesian, European, Chinese.
European 11.6%. Administrators, military, etc.
Chinese 3%. Mainly traders.
Other 1.8%.

Literacy 95%. **Official languages** French and Tahitian. **All languages** 9. **Languages with Scriptures** 3Bi 1NT 2por.

ECONOMY
Tourism, aid and the French military are the main sources of income, but the wealth generated has not benefited all. The suspension, then ending, of nuclear testing is having a big effect on the economy. **Unemployment** 15% (unofficially nearer 50%). **Income/person** $14,910 (47.5% of USA).

POLITICS
French colony in 1880, Overseas Territory in 1957, increased autonomy since 1977 but with representation in the Senate and Assembly in Paris. The controversial use of Mururoa Atoll for

Churches	MegaBloc	Cong.	Members	Affiliates
Evang Ch of Polynesia	P	81	32,000	96,000
Catholic	C	85	41,667	80,000
Latter-day Saints (Morm)	M	46	9,317	15,000
Seventh-day Adventist	P	29	4,111	10,000
Sanito (Ref. Mormons)	M	42	4,250	8,500
Jehovah's Witnesses	M	34	1,874	5,000
Other Reformed [6]	I	13	600	1,500
Assemblies of God (Fr)	P	6	509	850
Other Charismatic [3]	I	3	294	500
Assemblies of God (US)	P	7	105	175
Other denominations [5]		3	159	365
Doubly affiliated			*-16,402*	*-31,000*
Total Christians [22]		349	78,484	186,890

Trans-bloc Groupings	pop. %	,000	Ann.Gr.
Evangelical	5.6	13	+0.9%
Charismatic	13.5	32	-1.5%
Pentecostal	0.4	1	+3.8%

Missionaries from French Polynesia
P,I,A 6 in 2 agencies.

Missionaries to French Polynesia
P,I,A 30 in 6 agencies from 8 countries: France 9.

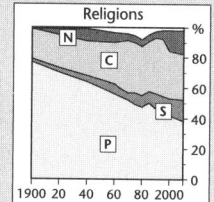

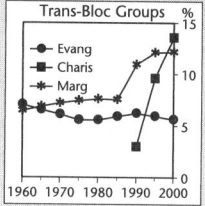

• Challenges for Prayer

1 **Tahiti is a paradise gone tragically wrong**. Once a Christian nation that sent missionaries all over the Pacific, Tahiti is now being debased by promiscuity (over 60%

illegitimate births), prostitution, alcoholism, drug abuse and the breakdown of family life. Young people are frustrated and seeking answers in their confusion, but where are the fervent messengers of the gospel? No longer do Tahitian missionaries leave for other lands as they once did.

2 **Those with a vital personal faith are now rare**. As a result, there is a reversion to the bondage of pagan occultism and a multiplication of syncretistic and foreign sects, especially two forms of Mormonism. Pray for a spiritual revolution to take place among the many nominal Catholic and Protestant Christians. Those who migrate from rural areas to Papeete are usually lost to the Church.

3 **Nearly half the population belong to the LMS-planted ECP**. Liberal theology is predominant and evangelical believers are few. The ECP is in serious decline, its credibility is low because of well-publicized misuse of funds and court cases. Splits and defections have reduced its percentage and influence. Pray for a moving of the Spirit of God to bring this church back to its first love, as in the early 19th Century.

4 **The evangelical witness is very small** and largely confined to two Assemblies of God and some charismatic groups. About a third of Catholics are charismatic and are also influential. Evangelical agencies found elsewhere in the Anglophone Pacific have neglected the Francophone territories. In contrast two varieties of Mormonism have thrived for over 150 years in these islands. There is no Evangelical Fellowship — a great need.

5 **The less-evangelized** — almost all adhere to a form of Christianity, but many are without a clear gospel witness:
a) *The outer island groups* are largely Catholic with little evangelical presence. The Marquesans, Mangarevans and Tuamotuans cannot easily understand the related Tahitian, and have little of the Bible in their languages.
b) *The Chinese* are 4% Protestant and 4% Catholic and largely secular.
c) *The French community* lives a life apart, having minimal contact with any church.

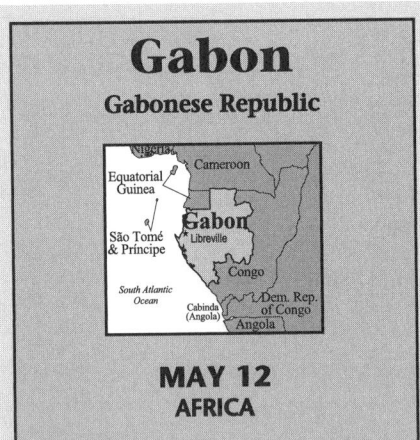

Gabon
Gabonese Republic

MAY 12
AFRICA

GEOGRAPHY
Area 267,667 sq.km. Coastal Central African state on the equator — 77% being dense tropical rain forest.

Population		Ann.Gr.	Density
2000	1,226,127	+2.62%	5 per sq. km.
2010	1,506,584	+1.97%	6 per sq. km.
2025	1,981,233	+1.75%	7 per sq. km.

Capital Libreville 469,000. **Urbanites** 75%.

PEOPLES
Indigenous 84.5%. About 65 ethnic groups.
Bantu 83.3%. Major groupings of peoples: Fang(2) 340,000; Eshira-Punu(7) 210,000; Njebi(4) 143,000; Kota-Teke(10) 142,000; Mberi(3) 120,000.
Pygmy 1.2%.
Other African 12.5%. Mostly immigrants from neighbouring countries and West Africa, drawn by economic opportunities.
Other 3.0%. French 33,000; Lebanese 1,000.
Literacy 63%. **Official Language** French. **Languages with Scriptures** 3Bi 2NT 7por 3w.i.p.

ECONOMY
One of Africa's wealthier countries, rich in natural resources, Gabon imports food and exports wood, oil and minerals. Climate and geography hamper the development needed to harness the country's full potential. **HDI** 0.607; 124th/174. **Public debt** 87% of GNP. **Income/person** $3,950 (14% of USA).

POLITICS
The President is autocratic, wanting to move the country further towards democracy, but demanding to be in control of the process. Elections in 1998-1999 determined that the president of many years remained in charge, despite accusations of vote tampering.

Freedom of religion, but a presidential decree restricted Evangelicals from ministering in interior provinces. This has not been withdrawn, but nor has it been enforced. The Catholic Church has been dominant, but its influence is waning. Traditional beliefs remain strong. The President became a Muslim in 1973, and Islam is growing in Gabon.

Religions	Population %	Adherents	Ann.Gr.
Christian	77.93	955,521	+2.9%
Traditional ethnic	13.48	165,282	-0.7%
Muslim	6.50	79,698	+5.7%
non-Religious/other	2.00	24,523	+7.3%
Baha'i	0.09	1,104	+0.5%

Christians	Denom.	Affil.%	,000	Ann.Gr.
Protestant	11	9.83	120	+4.6%
Independent	16	7.56	93	+13.7%
Catholic	1	54.24	665	+1.1%
Marginal	10	4.02	49	+0.1%
Unaffiliated		2.28	28	n.a.

Churches	MegaBloc	Cong.	Members	Affiliates
Catholic	C	70	437,500	665,000
CMA (EACMG)	P	189	21,269	50,000
Bethany	I	29	12,000	30,000

Evangelical Ch of G	P	68	10,000	25,000
Pentecostal Ch of G	P	46	6,000	15,000
Nazareth	I	19	3,500	8,000
Jehovah's Witnesses	M	45	2,226	7,500
Deeper Life Bible	I	30	2,750	6,000
Seventh-day Adventist	P	11	1,864	4,000
New Apostolic	I	36	1,250	3,000
Other denoms [28]		379	43,500	113,900
Total Christians [38]		922	541,859	927,400

Trans-bloc Groupings	pop. %	,000	Ann.Gr.
Evangelical	14.2	174	+9.1%
Charismatic	17.6	215	+7.5%
Pentecostal	5.0	61	+16.5%

Missionaries from Gabon
P,I,A 27 in 4 agencies; most in Gabon.

Missionaries to Gabon
P,I,A 105 in 15 agencies from 11 countries: USA 42, Nigeria 17, Canada 14.

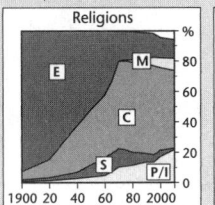

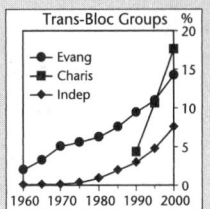

G

• Answers to Prayer

1 **The 1990s have been a time of God's moving in Gabon**. The Church has grown rapidly through the ministries of the **CMA**, Pentecostal Church (**AoG**) and newer indigenous African Pentecostal churches. Evangelicals, long an insignificant minority, have grown from 2% (10,000) in 1960 to 9.4% (87,000) in 1990 and then to 14.2% (174,000) in 2000.

2 **Peoples of the interior**, long unreached and even out of bounds for evangelical missionaries, have opened up for the gospel. In 1998 the **CMA** launched *Operation Village for Jesus* to take the gospel to all 14 peoples still totally unreached and develop the pioneering work among 44 other peoples. The results were encouraging: 11 of the unreached peoples had a witness by 2000.

3 **Libreville**, the sophisticated, cosmopolitan capital had only 16 evangelical congregations in 1990. There are now 125, some very large.

• Challenges for Prayer

1 **Gabon is a spiritual battlefield**. The conversion of the President and many government leaders to Islam, the pervasive influence of indigenous secret societies which all government leaders had to join, endemic alcoholism and widespread ignorance of the gospel are all indicators of this. While the vast majority claim to be Christian, Gabonese still fall back on their traditional religions in times of need. Pray that these influences may be broken down.

2 **Muslims have multiplied over the past 20 years** — initially by immigration of Hausa, Fulani and other West African Muslims, and more recently by conversions among Gabonese men. The West African Muslim immigrants make up much of the merchant class and thus have significant influence in the country. There are moves by the national Church to partner with missions to reach the Muslims of Gabon based on models successfully used in Côte d'Ivoire and Guinea, but this plan is only in its initial phases.

3 **The Catholic Church retains its old political influence**, and the majority of the population were baptized Catholic, but a large number still follow the old animist ways.

The Catholic Church's growth peaked decades ago, but with steady losses to Islam, other churches and sects in recent years. Pray that the many nominal Christians may see and embrace the pure gospel.

4 **The first major Protestant denomination was the fruit of French missionary work,** but the legacy of liberal theology has been a stagnant, nominal daughter church with a leadership more concerned with social issues than evangelism. Ask God's Spirit to revive this Church and make it again a force for evangelism.

5 **The evangelical witness was long limited to the CMA** (EACMG) and several smaller indigenous denominations, mainly Pentecostal. Pray for the calling and entry of church planting and specialized ministry agencies to work together in discipling the peoples of Gabon. Some missions have targeted Gabon for several years with little result. The only large grouping of evangelical missionaries are the 50 **CMA** workers. The recent rapid growth of Evangelicals now needs to become a true discipling movement that will bring holiness, obedience and love.

6 **There is a dearth of indigenous church leaders in Gabon**. Gabonese Christians need teaching and pastoring to mature, but the first step is to train national pastors and leaders for this. Opportunities for trainers are many. Pray that God might raise up those equipped for the task. There are two small Bible schools with 40 students, along with hundreds of TEE students.

7 **Vision for the future**. Evangelical churches are committed to evangelizing the whole country.
a) *A national survey of Gabon's peoples* and prefectures was carried out in the 1990s.
b) *Plans were laid* to act on its findings by planting churches in every people, and in every one of the 46 prefecture capitals.
c) *The CMA's implementation* through *Operation Village for Jesus* (1999-2000) and *Operation Barnabas* (2000-2001) has been very successful. Pray for continued progress.
d) *The vision is that by 2025 Evangelicals be 20% of the country's population* and every Gabonese person have the chance to hear the gospel.
e) *Pray that missions vision* among leaders become part of the life of congregations and stir them to action.

8 Less reached peoples:
a) *The 58 unevangelized peoples of the interior*. The national survey revealed 14 peoples to be totally unreached and 44 with only an initial penetration of the gospel. The **CMA** programmes and work of other evangelical denominations is rapidly changing this. Since 1999, 11 of the 14 unreached peoples have begun to hear the gospel. Pray that every people may soon have a growing, indigenous church and also the Scriptures in their own languages.
b) *The east and northeast regions were long closed for Evangelicals*. They are the least developed and least evangelized areas of Gabon. Born-again Christians are very few among the peoples of the area — notably the Kota, Mbede, Mahongwe, Mbangwe, Tsangi, Teke, and others. Since 1995, 20 towns have been opened up by CMA and others.
c) *The Fang are the dominant people* (28% of the population) and largely Protestant or Catholic. They are a profoundly religious people, but most of their fervency is dissipated in syncretistic ancestral worship.
d) *The Babinga,* or Pygmies, live in the virgin forest and are despised by other peoples. The CMA and Deeper Life are working among them, and are seeing much responsiveness and many conversions.

9 Help ministries requiring intercession:
a) *Bible translation* has been a neglected ministry, and a comprehensive linguistic survey is required. There may be as many as 22 languages which need the Scriptures. **CMA** are working on New Testament translations in three languages. **SIL** entered Gabon in 1998 for translation ministry.
b) *The JESUS film* in French is shown widely, and is in production for 3 more languages. It has been a key tool for opening up ministry to unreached peoples in 1998-2001.
c) *GRN* has made recordings available in 25 languages.

d) **Both national radio and TV** are wide open avenues for evangelism and Bible teaching, but are neglected. *Radio Evangile Gabon*, is being planned by a coordinating committee of 5 denominational leaders. Pray for its swift and effective implementation.

e) **Literature.** Tens of thousands of tracts are being printed and shipped to Gabon, along with 400,000 copies of the Gospel of John. Pray they might be distributed to the right people and that those reading them would be challenged.

f) **Bongolo Hospital** ministers to both the physical and spiritual needs of the thousands who visit every year. Nearly 1,000 people every year are coming to Christ through the hospital's work. Pray for continued grace in this area, and that all who visit would receive healing of body and soul.

The Gambia
Republic of The Gambia

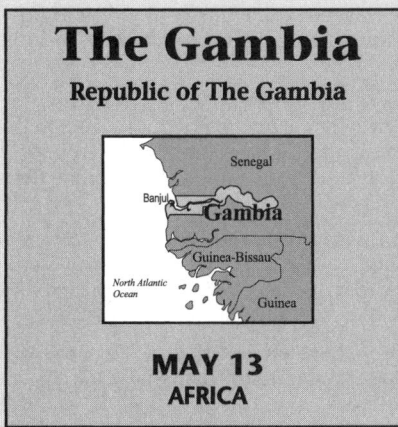

Senegal
Banjul
Gambia
Guinea-Bissau
North Atlantic Ocean
Guinea

MAY 13
AFRICA

GEOGRAPHY
Area 10,689 sq.km. A narrow 400 km-long riverine enclave that virtually divides Senegal's Casamance from the rest of the country.

Population	Ann.Gr.	Density
2000	1,305,363	+3.28%	122 per sq. km.
2010	1,651,481	+2.21%	155 per sq. km.
2025	2,150,833	+1.58%	201 per sq. km.

Capital Banjul 270,540. **Urbanites** 37%. Half the population lives in the greater Banjul area.

PEOPLES
Over 25 ethnic groups which are very intermingled.
Mande 44%. Mandinka (Mandingo) 445,000; Soninke 100,000.
West African 54%. Fulbe(3) 211,000; Wolof 164,000; Jola 120,000; Tukulor 75,000; Serer 32,000; Manjako 21,000.
Other 2%. Maure 17,000; Aku (English-speaking Creole) 10,400; Nigerians, Sierra Leoneans, etc.

Literacy 38%. **Official language** English. **Trade languages** Mandinka, Wolof. **All languages** 20. **Languages with Scriptures** 3Bi 3NT 3por 6w.i.p.

ECONOMY
Subsistence agriculture and dependent on groundnut cultivation, tourism, foreign aid and extensive smuggling over the porous border with

Senegal. **HDI** 0.391; 163rd/174. **Public debt** 106% of GNP. **Income/person** $320 (1.1% of USA).

POLITICS
Independent from Britain in 1965. Senegalese intervention to quell the 1981 coup resulted in abortive efforts to create a Senegambian confederacy which finally collapsed in 1989. A military coup in 1994 and military government was later transformed into a civilian democracy. Elections are due in 2001.

G

RELIGION
Relative religious freedom with easy-going tolerance between communities despite the large Muslim majority.

Religions	Population %	Adherents	Ann.Gr.
Muslim	88.80	1,159,162	+3.4%
Traditional ethnic	6.70	87,459	+1.8%
Christian	4.10	53,520	+3.9%
Baha'i	0.40	5,221	-1.2%

Christians	Denom.	Affil.%	,000	Ann.Gr.
Protestant	7	0.44	6	+5.9%
Independent	10	0.49	6	+1.4%
Anglican	1	0.23	3	+1.0%
Catholic	1	2.60	34	+4.6%
Marginal	1	0.02	0	+15.5%
Unaffiliated		0.32	4	n.a.

Churches	MegaBloc	Cong.	Members	Affiliates
Catholic	C	15	17,000	34,000
Anglican	A	6	850	3,000
Methodist	P	7	1,429	2,600
Church of Pentecost	P	17	1,000	1,400
Seventh-day Adventist	P	2	458	850
Baptist Convention	P	2	150	300
Jehovah's Witnesses	M	3	132	290
Evang Church of the G	P	9	110	280
Other denoms [12]		45	4,600	6,675
Total Christians [20]		106	25,800	49,400

Trans-bloc Groupings	pop. %	,000	Ann.Gr.
Evangelical	0.3	4	+8.1%
Charismatic	0.2	3	+8.0%
Pentecostal	0.1	2	+10.8%

Missionaries from The Gambia
P,I,A 5 in 2 agencies.

Missionaries to The Gambia
P,I,A 134 in 20 agencies from 16 countries: USA 49, Korea 15, UK 13, Nigeria 13, Germany 12.

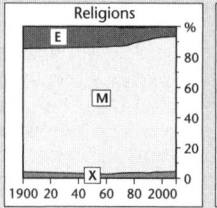

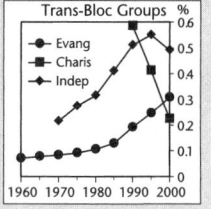

• Challenges for Prayer

1 **Islam is dominant, yet the land remains open for the gospel**. Little effort has ever been directed at reaching the Muslim majority and converts from Islam have been few — but their numbers are increasing. The Mandinka, made famous by Alex Haley's book 'Roots', are a key people. Pray for continued freedom to witness and for openness of heart for Muslims to receive the truth.

2 **Islam is gradually gaining ground** with the last few pockets of uncommitted animist peoples now becoming Muslim. Saudi Arabia has given much financial aid to the country with Islamic 'strings' attached. There is little Christian witness in the up-river towns and villages, though this is increasing. Pray for significant numbers of Muslim families from all ethnic groups to be drawn to Christ, and thus reverse this trend.

3 **There was much nominalism in the mainline denominations** and evangelical believers were few. This is changing as some leaders seek to bring renewal to the Church and many nominal Christians are coming to new life in Christ. Pray for increased momentum and zeal for growth.

4 **Missionary work in the Gambia was pioneered by the Anglicans and Methodists**. Much of their work was confined to the Aku (Creole-speaking descendants of freed slaves in Banjul). Catholics and Methodists have impacted the Jola and both have Manjako congregations. Many newer Nigerian, Ghanaian and Liberian ministries have begun, but most are working more amongst the nominally Christian groups and expatriates than the indigenous Muslim peoples. Pray that all churches may see results among the Muslim majority.

5 **Ministries specifically concentrating on the non-Christian majority are few**. **WEC** and the ECG Church have planted congregations with converts from Muslim backgrounds. There are also effective medical, agricultural, educational, literacy and rural development programmes. Other significant ministries include the **ABWE** and **IMB-SBC**. Pray for sensitivity and wisdom in these ministries, and also for visas for new missionaries. Pray too that God might raise up of Gambian believers to take on the roles long borne by missionaries.

6 **Young people have flocked to Banjul's suburban areas seeking work**. Ministry among them was pioneered by GAMFES(**IFES**) in 1996. **SU** and **YFC** have thriving ministries in the Banjul area. Most youth work is in the capital and outlying areas (**SU**, **IMB-SBC**, **WEC**, **YFC** and Korean missionaries), though **WEC** also has ministry inland.

7 **Specialized Christian ministries:**

a) *Prison evangelism* has been particularly fruitful. Pray both for conversions and for the integration of converts into their communities and churches on their release.

b) *The JESUS film* has been shown all over the country in several languages. Pray for the disarming of misconceptions about the person of Jesus through this ministry.

c) *Christian radio*. Chronological Bible teaching, *The Righteous Way*, has been recorded in two languages (Wolof, Mandinka) and is broadcast on national radio. Recordings in Fulbe and Jola are being made.

d) *Christian television programmes*. Abiding Word Ministries, the Gambia Christian Council, **YFC** and others have gained wide acceptance for the gospel through their appreciated weekly TV programmes. Pray for lasting fruit.

e) *GRN* has provided the gospel message on tape in 16 languages of the Gambia.

Georgia

Sak'art'velo

MAY 14

ASIA

Updated January 2004

GEOGRAPHY
Area 69,700 sq.km. Black Sea state between the Caucasus Mountains and Turkey. Formerly called the fruitbasket of the USSR.

Population		Ann.Gr.	Density
2000	4,967,561	-1.10%	71 per sq. km.
2010	5,010,697	+0.17%	72 per sq. km.
2025	5,178,116	+0.14%	74 per sq. km.

Capital T'bilisi 1,450,000. **Urbanites** 56%.

PEOPLES
Indo-European 94.2.%
Caucasian 82.5%. Georgian 3,030,000; Mingrelian 500,000; Armenian 467,000; Abkhazian 100,000.
Iranian 2.7%. Ossetian 100,000; Kurds 33,000.
Slav 7.0%. Russian 312,000; Ukrainian 35,000
Other 2.0%. Greek 100,000.
Turkic/Altaic 5.6%. Azerbaijani 278,000.
Other 0.2%. Jews 14,500; Assyrian 7,000.

Literacy 98%. **Official language** Georgian. **All indigenous languages** 10. **Languages with Scriptures** 1Bi 1NT 1por 2w.i.p.

ECONOMY
Productive soil and good climate for fruit, tea, cotton, wine, tourism; the supplier of 90% of the former USSR's tea and citrus fruit. Much potential for hydro-electric power and mining. Civil strife, separatist wars as well as corrupt and inept officials brought the country to destitution. Dependent on remittances from the 500,000 Georgians working abroad. The 2004 revolution and an oil pipeline for Caspian oil give hope that economic recovery is possible. **HDI** 0.729; 85th/174. **Public debt** 25.1% of GNP. **Income/person** $860 (2.7% of USA).

POLITICS
Centuries of domination by surrounding empires. Annexed by Russia in 1801. Briefly independent 1920-21 before conquest by Bolsheviks. Independent in 1991, but the first president became dictatorial and was the main cause of four conflicts in the early 1990s — two between ethnic Georgians and secessionist wars by the Abkhazian and South Ossetian minorities, the latter two aided by the Russian military. The Ossetians and Abkhazians have *de facto* independence. The Chechen war has further destabilized the country. Shevardnadze, the subsequent president, survived assassination attempts and continual interference by Russia which still maintains military bases in the country. The 2004 'Rose' Revolution has since displaced the old government with younger leaders committed to democracy and economic reform.

RELIGION
Over the centuries the Georgian Orthodox Church was the one stable factor preserving Georgian culture and nationalism. "Christian" Georgia and neighbouring Armenia are surrounded by Muslim ethnic groups. Since independence, some Orthodox leaders have sought to deny non-Orthodox Christians the opportunity to build churches and to evangelize openly. **Persecution index** 77th in the world.

Religions	Population %	Adherents	Ann.Gr.
Christian	62.47	3,103,235	-0.4%
Muslim	20.00	993,512	-1.1%
non-Religious	17.11	849,950	-5.0%
Jewish	0.30	14,903	-13.9%
Other	0.12	5,961	+7.3%

Christians	Denom.	Affil.%	,000	Ann.Gr.
Protestant	4	0.53	26	+5.1%
Independent	10	0.25	12	+4.7%
Catholic	2	0.91	45	-2.1%
Orthodox	4	57.06	2,835	-0.9%
Marginal	1	0.72	36	+12.5%
Unaffiliated		3.00	149	n.a.

Churches	MegaBloc	Cong.	Members	Affiliates
Georgian Orthodox	O	520	1,100,000	2,400,000
Armenian Apostolic	O	30	230,769	330,000
Russian Orthodox	O	35	69,930	100,000
Jehovah's Witnesses	M	132	14,085	36,000
Catholic , Latin Rite	C	9	18,182	28,000
Catholic , Eastern Rite	C	11	11,039	17,000
UECB, Evang Chr & Bapt	P	49	5,200	12,000
Pentecostal (AoG)	P	80	5,000	12,000
Other Pentecostal [3]	I	25	3,000	5,000
Syrian Orthodox	O	2	2,814	4,700
Lutheran	P	8	800	1,600
Other denoms [8]		28	3,948	8,200
Total Christians [21]		929	1,464,767	2,954,500

Trans-bloc Groupings	pop. %	,000	Ann.Gr.
Evangelical	1.4	70	+2.3%
Charismatic	0.4	21	+7.9%
Pentecostal	0.3	17	+7.6%

Missionaries from Georgia
P,I,A 11 in 2 agencies; Central Asia 10.
Missionaries to Georgia
P,I,A estimated 24 in 6 agencies.

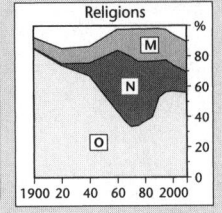

Religions

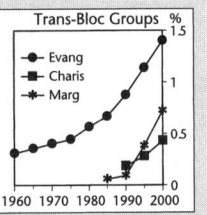

Trans-Bloc Groups %

• Answers to Prayer

1 **Since independence in 1991**, interest in spiritual things and the Christian faith in particular has increased greatly. The former Department of Atheism at the national university is now a theological faculty. Christian groups of all expressions are experiencing growth in this nation.

• Challenges for Prayer

1 **Georgia's independence**, gained with such hope has been soured by a series of inter-ethnic wars aided and abetted by Russian efforts to undermine and control the country. The lot of most Georgians is harsh due to massive unemployment and profound economic setbacks. Pray for peace, an ending of Russian interference, economic stabilization and ethnic harmony so that the nation might gain the opportunity to recover. Pray that the new government elected in 2004 may bring about needful change.

2 **The Georgian Orthodox Church** has a history stretching back to AD 150. Communist repression, infiltration and subversion brought both martyrdom and compromise. By 1970 only 80 congregations were still functioning. Stalin, the USSR's most cruel ruler, was a Georgian. Since Communism's collapse and Georgian independence, many have returned to the Church of their ancestors with even the former President being baptized. Pray that this return to their spiritual roots might be accompanied by spiritual life — for most it is more an expression of nationalism.

3 **The small Protestant Church** struggled for survival under Communism. Since independence there has been sustained hostility and opposition from factions in the Orthodox Church. Evangelical ministries have been repressed, their work maligned as sectarian. They have had problems in acquiring buildings and the necessary permits for holding meetings. There have been incidents of meetings broken up, sometimes violently, materials confiscated and some churches destroyed. Pray for religious freedom and an acceptance of the validity of diversity of beliefs which this implies.

4 **Baptists and Pentecostals** form the major component of the evangelical witness. They have experienced some growth since the late 1980s. There are major issues that hinder witness:

a) *Poverty of the people*. Village unemployment/underemployment is nearly 100%. Few congregations have the resources for supporting pastors, refurbishing and building churches or for outreach. Most meetings are in homes.

b) *Disunity*. The deep divide between the Baptists and Pentecostals hinders united witness and this issue is only now beginning to be addressed.

5 **The spiritual need of ethnic minorities**. Georgian believers are best placed to reach the ethnic minorities but need sensitivity and encouragement in doing so. There is some outreach to Muslims. Lack of resources and expectations of foreign funds hold back local initiatives. Pray for these believers and for a burden for these peoples:

a) *Muslim Abkhazians and Ossetians* who are a minority within their ethnic groups but need to be reached. The majority are Orthodox Christians. Both peoples have been embroiled with the Georgian government in bitter wars of secession. The New Testament is being translated for both peoples.

b) *Jews.* There is no known witness to them. They face a rising tide of anti-Semitism in a country which has historically been a haven for them.

c) *The Chechens and Kish*. Over 10,000 impoverished Chechens have taken refuge in the Pankisi Canyon which adjoins Chechnya in northeast Georgia where the related Kish live. The Russian military have made incursions and bombings in their attempts to quell the Chechen resistance. Pray that the limited aid programmes to assist these desperate people may be stepped up. Christian aid is being given to some by World Concern. There are no known Christians or churches.

d) ***Azerbaijanis*** who are Muslim. There are few Azeri Christians in Georgia.

e) ***The Muslim Mingrel*** (500,000) ***and Laz*** (2,000) peoples related to Georgians.

6 Christian help ministries for prayer:

a) ***Literature distribution.*** **EHC** plans a national literature campaign reaching every home, and the Georgian Bible Society is distributing Christian materials to refugees.

b) ***The Georgian Bible*** in current use was translated 900 years ago. Two new translations have recently been completed, as well as a Children's Bible. **The Bible Society** projects are a welcome success in inter-confessional ministry; they also produce a Bible magazine and run a Bible shop.

c) ***Christian radio programmes*** prepared in Georgia are broadcast by **HCJB** in Ecuador. Two hours a week is a decrease in broadcast time from the early 1990s, despite the programmes being very well received and popular. A local studio where Georgian language programmes can be produced is being planned.

d) ***The JESUS film*** has been completed in Georgian, Russian, and Ossetian, and is in production in Abkaz, Georgian Jewish, and Svan.

Germany
Federal Republic of Germany

MAY 15-17
EUROPE

GEOGRAPHY
Area 357,042 sq.km. Strategically placed in the centre of Europe and of the expanding EU.

Population		Ann.Gr.	Density
2000	82,220,490	+0.14%	230 per sq. km.
2010	82,032,281	-0.08%	230 per sq. km.
2025	80,238,159	-0.19%	225 per sq. km.

Large influx of ethnic German and other immigrants from Central and Eastern Europe after the fall of Communism in 1989/1991.

Capital Berlin 4,150,000. Other major cities: Essen/Ruhr 6.05 mill.; München (Munich) 2.9m; Stuttgart 2.65m; Hamburg 2.55m; Frankfurt 1.95m; Köln (Cologne)/Bonn 1.85m; Mannheim 1.6m; Düsseldorf 1.33m; Nurnberg 1.05m; Hanover 1.03m. **Urbanites** 82%.

PEOPLES
Indigenous 91.1%. German 74.9m;

Danes 60,000; Sorb and Wend 50,000; Frisian(2) 25,000.
European Union (as of 2000) 2.5%. Italian 620,000; Greek 363,000; Austrian 185,000; Portuguese 132,000; Spanish 131,000; British 114,000; Dutch 112,000; French 105,000.
Other Western 3%. Albanian (Kosovo, Albania) 719,000; Polish 283,000; Croat 208,000; Bosnian 190,000; American 110,000; Romanian 89,000.
Other 3.4%. Turk 1,610,000; Kurd (mainly Turkish) 500,000; Arab 290,000; Iranian 115,000; Afghan 70,000, Tamil 50,000; Pakistani 38,000.

Literacy almost 100%. **Official language** German. There are 110 million German-speakers worldwide. **All languages** 20. **Languages with Scriptures** 6Bi 3NT 5por.

ECONOMY
Dramatic post-war recovery to become one of the world's strongest economies, with huge balance-of-payments surpluses. One of the world's largest industrial economies with a third of the output of the whole EU. In the 1990s, the hugely expensive repair and rebuilding of the crippled East German economy, rigid labour laws and high social security costs hampered progress and increased unemployment — especially in former East Germany. **HDI** 0.906; 14th/174. **Public debt** 33% of GNP. **Income/person** $28,280 (90% of USA).

POLITICS
The collapse of Hitler's Reich in 1945 was followed by 45 years of partition between the democratic and capitalist Federal Republic (FRG) and the Communist 'Democratic' Republic (GDR). The collapse of Communism at the end of the 1980s led to a rapid reunification of the two states in 1990 — in reality a takeover by the FRG that proved socially and economically painful to all. A core member of the EU and plays a dominant role in European affairs.

RELIGION

Religious freedom. A close cooperation between the government and the RC Church and Protestant Established Churches (EKD) in religious education, media, etc. All denominations with 'public law status' can levy taxes on their members which are collected by the government on their behalf. High Christian numbers below are often for those who have not opted out of this taxation system. There is growing hostility to anything overtly Christian.

Religions	Population %	Adherents	Ann.Gr.
Christian	69.47	57,118,574	-1.0%
non-Religious/other	26.59	21,862,429	+2.8%
Muslim	3.70	3,042,158	+5.1%
Jewish	0.12	98,665	+6.1%
Buddhist	0.05	41,110	+20.3%
Baha'i	0.04	32,888	+6.1%
Hindu	0.03	24,666	+8.6%

Christians	Denom.	Affil.%	,000	Ann.Gr.
Protestant	152	34.05	27,995	-1.4%
Independent	69	0.66	542	+0.5%
Anglican	1	0.03	27	+0.8%
Catholic	1	32.84	27,000	-0.6%
Orthodox	16	1.32	1,088	+6.8%
Marginal	45	0.57	467	-0.4%
Unaffiliated		1.82	1,500	n.a.
Doubly affiliated		*-1.82*	*-1,500*	*n.a.*

Churches	MegaBloc	Cong.	Members	Adherents
Catholic	C	13,300	21.094m	27.00m
EKD (Luth/Ref)	P	18,200	20.938m	26.80m
New Apostolic	I	700	280,000	390,000
Greek Orthodox	O	60	265,734	380,000
Baptist/Menn, fSU [6]	P	340	150,000	312,000

Jehovah's Witnesses	M	2,114	167,497	270,000
Serbian Orthodox	O	14	100,000	200,000
Fell of Evang Free	P	900	87,000	122,000
Methodist	P	650	39,000	80,000
Christian Brethren [2]	P	290	30,000	56,000
Free Evangelical Congs	P	400	32,000	53,440
Seventh-day Adventist	P	577	35,475	53,000
Russian Orthodox	O	82	32,895	50,000
Other Charis Fells [20]	I	156	30,000	50,000
Evangelical Free	P	400	31,750	47,000
Latter-day Saints (Morm)	M	185	17,568	39,000
Indep Lutheran	P	295	27,273	39,000
Armenian Apostolic	O	6	17,500	35,000
Moravian Brethren	P	32	16,000	25,000
Other denoms [240]		3,824	529,000	1,117,000
Doubly affiliated			*-937,500*	*-1,200,000*
Total Christians [284]		42,525	42.982m	55.919m

Trans-bloc Groupings	pop. %	,000	Ann.Gr.
Evangelical	2.9	2,396	+2.1%
Charismatic	1.0	824	+0.3%
Pentecostal	0.2	177	+3.9%

Missionaries from Germany
P,I,A approx. 4,090 in about 133 agencies with about 3,000 in 150 countries.

Missionaries to Germany
P,I,A 1,531 in 150 agencies from 40 countries: USA 778, Korea 351, Canada 112.

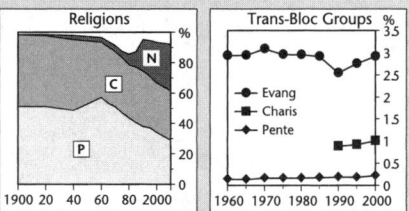

• Answers to Prayer

1 **The removal of the Berlin Wall in 1989, reunification of Germany in 1991** and Berlin once more becoming its capital, are symbols of a new Germany that has begun to lay its tragic past behind it.

2 **Increased enthusiasm among young people** for spiritual things and the growth of evangelical/charismatic churches give rise to hopes that Germany's rapid spiritual decline might be slowing.

• Challenges for Prayer

1 **Germany's wealth, power and strategic location** in the EU and Europe could be of inestimable value for the Kingdom of God. For this, a strong, courageous leadership based on Christian values is needed. Sadly, scandals have eroded the credibility of politicians and of the whole political process. Pray for leaders to be raised up who are willing to tackle unresolved issues — the economy, the remaining disparities between East and West since reunification, and Germany's place in an expanding EU.

2 **There are numerous signs of spiritual ill-health** in the nation. Humanism and destructive criticism of the Bible in the 19th Century enfeebled churches, and opened the way to compromise and a pagan Nazi tyranny in the 20th. Post-war affluence in the FRG and the corrosive and catastrophic impact of Marxist ideology in the GDR accelerated the secularization and de-Christianization of society. The Church is widely perceived as irrelevant and marginalized. Although 70% of the people claim to be Christian, only 45% believe in a personal God, and a mere 8% worship regularly. There is increased open hostility to anything Christian. The occult, alcoholism, Satanism and a New Age worldview are on the rise. There is also a disturbing increase of neo-Nazi extreme rightist movements promoting violence against Jews and foreigners in the former GDR. Pray that the spiritual blindness of most of the nation may be removed and these trends reversed.

3 **The post-war exodus from organized Christianity** accelerated during the last decades of the 20ᵗʰ Century. This is worst in the old GDR where 80% are unchurched. By 2000 only 5% of the Protestant EKD membership and 18% of the Catholics were active participants in church life. Overall only 3% of German men are actively involved. During the 1990s between 300,000 and 600,000 people annually opted out of paying church tax with serious impact on the income of the main Churches. The majority of churches have lost their identity, purpose and income. Germany needs a change as radical as Luther's Reformation nearly 500 years ago. Ask God for this.

4 **The EKD is a federation of Lutheran, Reformed and combined United Lutheran/Reformed State Churches**, but is deeply divided on political, moral and theological lines. The growing number of empty churches and church buildings falling into disrepair is a tragedy. Bible-believing pastors and evangelical/pietistic groups and congregations are more concentrated in Baden-Württemberg, Siegerland and south Saxony. Conservative evangelical bishops in the EKD are few and it is increasingly difficult for evangelical pastors to minister in congregations. Pray that there may be a return to reliance on the Bible and application of its truths in the churches.

5 **The Free Churches** have a high proportion of Evangelicals but only represent 1.5% of the nation's population. Some denominations are stagnating or declining, but others are growing. Between 1988 and 1993 there were 800 new Free churches planted, and between 1992 and 1995 a further 228. During the 1990s many western Free churches planted congregations in the east. Pray for an increase in vision, innovative outreach and effective church planting that reaches every area and population segment of the nation.

6 **German Evangelicals** in all denominations are less than 2.5 million, but are slowly growing in numbers. There are encouragements:
a) *The Pietist movement* continues to be an influential force within the EKD (especially in Württemberg in the south and in rural areas). The many evangelical fellowships of the **Gnadau Union** within the EKD represent 300,000 Christians and over 63 agencies and institutions.
b) *The Evangelical Alliance* has become a rallying point for over 1.3 million Evangelicals for cooperative projects, national prayer initiatives, evangelism, social action and missions involvement. A long-standing hostility between mainstream Evangelicals and Pentecostalism and latterly, charismatics, is beginning to be addressed. Pray for unity among God's people and that this may release rivers of life to the lost.
c) *Between 1980 and 1995 over 1,000 new independent congregations* were started — many of them charismatic in flavour, all strongly biblical. That increase continues and now represents nearly 100,000 believers.
d) *The influx of ethnic Germans from Central and Eastern Europe* over the past 20 years has led to a large increase of Mennonite and Baptist congregations catering for their spiritual health. There are over 370 such congregations with more than 300,000 believers associated with them. Increasingly they are becoming missions-minded, but are culturally isolated from the main stream of Evangelicals.

7 **Theological education** has proved a major cause of decline in the Protestant Church with high levels of scholarship but spiritually destructive teachings. The 13 universities that award theological degrees necessary for acceptance into the EKD ministry have been monopolized by liberal, neo-orthodox and other non-biblical theologians for decades and Evangelicals have been marginalized. Pray for more professors who openly proclaim the Truth to be welcomed to teach in these institutions. In the mid-1990s there were 12,000 Protestants and 10,000 Catholics in these faculties, but these numbers are in rapid decline. Pray for evangelical students in these spiritual morgues. Pray for those who seek to help them stand true to Scripture through pre-university courses and hostels that run parallel courses in the university cities.

8 **Missionary vision has long been limited**, with proportionately one of the lowest missionary-sending figures for any country with such a large Protestant community. The total number of missionaries has remained constant for some years, but the proportion of Evangelicals has risen sharply to 80% of the total. Pray for a further increase. Pray for the **Association of Evangelical Missions** (**AEM**) with 65 members and representing 2,240 missionaries — a catalytic and vital stimulant for training, promoting and sending missionaries. In 1998 the **Association of Pentecostal and Charismatic Missions** was formed — with 19 agencies and 135 missionaries. Several unique missions are the **DMG** (German Missionary Fellowship) with 278 missionaries serving with 47 international missions and the *Vereinigte Deutsche Missionshilfe* (VDM) with 111 missionaries, but with no foreign fields of their own. Other significant German missions: *Christliche Fachkräfte Int.* (160), Liebenzell (156), Wiedenest (153), *Christoffel-Blindenmission* (32). Other major missions: **YWAM** (204), **OM** (186), **WBT** (153), **WEC** (147), Alliance Mission (128), Marburger Mission (73), **Frontiers** (54). Pray also for Christians in the ex-GDR to regain a missions impetus after the years of restriction and stifling of the vision.

9 **Young people's** ministry is vital for the future of the Church. Over 55% of active Christians are now over 50 years of age. Significant outreach events and programmes such as Christival, ProChrist, March for Jesus, etc., have given a sense of cohesion and purpose to many young people. Pray for relevant and effective ways to impact the youth in a new way. Pray for the ministries of:

a) *SMD(IFES)* with about 50 groups in the 163 universities, and 1,000 groups in the 6,100 secondary schools. They also have a camping programme.
b) *CCCI* with 116 staff workers in six universities and in churches. **CCCI** has wider input into churches by means of programmes for growth and prayer campaigns.
c) *Navigators* with 33 staff in university witness.
d) *Wort und Wissen*, a significant ministry preparing students for university life by giving them good Christian foundations.
e) *YMCA*, an evangelical association and Germany's largest Christian youth organization with 260,000 members.
f) *CEF*, which has 40 staff workers committed to children's ministry. They run an effective telephone ministry for children in many cities.

10 Specific less-evangelized sections of the German population:

a) *The 'Ossies'* (former East Germans) are 80% unchurched and still affected by the years of Marxist propaganda and lies, though there is a solid core of believers who stood firm for Christ.
b) *Whole areas of Germany*, while superficially Christianized over a thousand years ago, have never really been evangelized. Despite the influence of the Reformation many are almost devoid of a live evangelical witness — the northern plains, Bavaria, the Eifel area on the Belgian border, etc.
c) *Many cities* have become extremely secular and spiritually needy. Pray especially for the city of Berlin — so long a symbol of the Cold War but now less than 50% are linked with a church.

11 **Foreigners.** The flood of immigrants, guest workers, international students and economic and political refugees since 1989 has overwhelmed the German administration and voluntary agencies. The economic woes of the former Communist countries has worsened the problem. There are many illegal immigrants and a highly-organized criminal network involved in promoting their entry from all over the world. The vast majority have never heard the gospel. There has been a violent backlash against this inflow — especially in the ex-GDR, and these foreigners have often become bitter and resentful over their mishandling. Pray that opportunities to show love and concern and to share Christ may not be lost thereby. Pray also for:

a) *The AFA* (*Arbeitsgemeinschaft für Ausländer*), a fellowship of mission groups seeking to evangelize through a wide variety of ethnic ministries. A number of local congregations also seek to reach these groups.
b) *Greater involvement in outreach by German Christians*. Some German congregations are notable exceptions to this, but in the main, most missions outreach is by foreigners (US, Swiss and others). The response to this challenge for ministry to immigrants could determine the future health and size of Protestantism in Germany.

*c) **International students**, who number over 60,000. SMD, YMCA and a number of local congregations have ministry to some.

*d) **Muslims**, whose numbers have grown, largely through immigration and a high birth rate, to over 3 million from over 40 nations today. There are also about 12,000 ethnic German Muslims — mainly Germans who married Muslims. Islamic organizations have intensified their activities and there are now over 2,200 mosques or prayer houses.

*e) **Specific peoples for prayer:**
  i *Turks,* with over 10 agencies seeking to reach them (including *Orientdienst,* **WEC, OM, CBI**). There are no more than 80 believers among them in all Western Europe.
  ii *Kurds,* with a consortium of agencies seeking to reach them and prepare Scriptures, radio programmes and Christian literature for them.
  iii *Iranians,* with several Christian groups and localized outreach attempts.
  iv *North African Arabs and Berbers* — little outreach.
  v *Albanian and Bosnian Muslims* from former Yugoslavia — no outreach.
  vi *Southern Europeans* — so many inadequately used opportunities among the nominally Catholic Italians, Spaniards and Portuguese and the Orthodox Greeks. Large areas in their homelands are devoid of an evangelical witness.
  vii *Central Europeans* — many nominally Orthodox Romanians, Bulgarians, Ukrainians and Catholics from Poland and the Baltic states need special ministry. The **Mission for SE Europe** gives out millions of pieces of Christian literature annually.
  viii *Roma (Gypsies) from Central Europe* — many have fled discrimination and persecution in Romania, Bulgaria, Czech Republic, Slovakia, etc., and are destitute.
  ix *Jews* suffered severely in the Holocaust — 564,000 in 1925 became 27,000 in 1945. Their numbers rapidly increased in the 1990s with immigration from the fSU. There are now 100,000 and about 1,000 have come to faith in Messiah Jesus.

12 Christian media for prayer:

*a) **Christian literature** and publishing has grown enormously over the past 30 years. Many have been blessed, and literature has played a major part in the evangelical resurgence. Pray for writers, publishers and distributors of books. Pray for the impact of more than 150 evangelical magazines with a total circulation of 50 million. Pray for the impact of the German edition of **Operation World**, *Gebet für die Welt*.

*b) **Every Home for Christ** has a massive, ongoing, nation-wide distribution of Christian tracts — over 450 million distributed with 200,000 responses.

*c) **Christian radio and television:**
  i *The German partner of* **TWR**, *Evangeliums-Rundfunk,* has made an impressive impact on the German-speaking world, doubling listeners between 1996-98. They claim a daily listenership of nearly 200,000 (and 4 million less frequently) on satellite, cable and medium wave and a total of 85 hours broadcast weekly.
  ii *HCJB* broadcasts 14 hours/week.
  iii *There is a 24-hour Christian radio station* that is oriented to young people.
  iv *Christian TV* is increasing with the launch of the 24-hour inter-church/agency Bible Channel in 2001 by satellite.

*d) **Internet evangelism** has great potential, but needs to be better developed and made both accessible and relevant in content (CINA-Wetzlar).

Ghana

Republic of Ghana

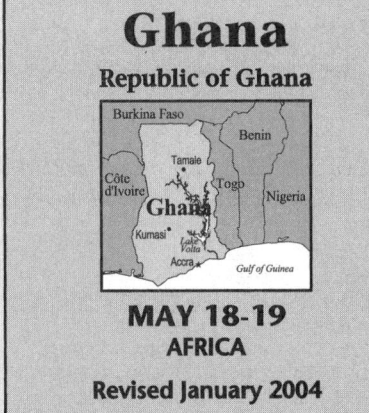

MAY 18-19
AFRICA

Revised January 2004

GEOGRAPHY
Area 238,533 sq.km. Grasslands in north, farmland and forest in south. Centre dominated by the 520 km-long Lake Volta, Africa's largest man-made lake.

Population		Ann.Gr.	Density
2000	20,212,495	+2.75%	85 per sq. km.
2010	26,366,959	+2.65%	111 per sq. km.
2025	36,876,215	+2.02%	155 per sq. km.

Most of the population live in the southern provinces. The Census 2000 population: 18,845,265.

Capital Accra 2,250,000. Other main cities: Kumasi 992,000; Sekondi-Takoradi 400,000; Tamale 270,000. **Urbanites** 37%.

PEOPLES
About 100 ethnic groups.

Kwa 71.1%. Five major groups in centre and south.
Akan 48.1%. 26 groups; largest: Ashanti 2,890,000; Fante 2,447,000; Brong (Abron) 765,000; Akyem 623,000; Akwapim 481,000; Nzema 416,000; Kwahu 403,000; Wasa 249,000; Anyi 179,000; Ahanta 135,000. Most speak dialects of Twi.
Ewe(3) 11.5%. 2,333,000 in southeast.
Ga-Adangme(3) 7.3%. 1,476,000 around Accra.
Guang(14) 3.4%. Gua(4) 280,000; Gonja 194,000; Awutu 168,000.
Central Togo(14) 0.8%. A medley of small peoples on the eastern border.
Gur 25.4%. 34 peoples in 3 major sub-groups in north. Larger groups: Dagomba 766,000; Gurenne (Frafra) 728,000; Dagaaba 616,000; Konkomba 480,000; Kusasi 373,000; Mamprusi 350,000; Sisaala(3) 324,000; Mossi 324,000; Bulsa 191,000; Gurunsi (Nankana) 169,000; Wala 144,000; Kasena 113,000; Bimoba 102,000; Birifor 87,000; Nafaanra 80,000; Kotokoli Kulango 76,000; Dega (Mo) 25,000.
Mande 1.1%. Largest of 5 peoples: Busansi 173,000; Jula-Malinke 115,000; Ligbi 13,000.
Other 2.4%. Fulbe 100,000; Westerners 50,000; refugees.

Literacy 70%. **Official language** English. **All languages** 72. **Languages with Scriptures** 8Bi 20NT 9por 17w.i.p.

ECONOMY
Main exports are cocoa, gold and timber — all susceptible to market fluctuations. Earlier government overspending, mismanagement and corruption reduced this once-prosperous land to poverty, thereby greatly reducing living standards. Since 1984 there has been a slow, but steady improvement through greater government discipline. **HDI** 0.544; 133rd/174. **Public debt** 75% of GNP. **Income/person** $400 (1.4% of USA).

POLITICS
Independent from Britain in 1957. Nkrumah's 'socialist' experiment was a disaster from which the nation is taking years to recover. There have been five military regimes and three short-lived civilian governments since Nkrumah's overthrow in 1966. The revolutionary military government of Rawlings eventually opened up the way for multi-party elections in 1992, and again in 1996 but as a presidential democracy with autocratic leanings. In 2000 there was a successful democratic election and change of government.

RELIGION
Secular state with religious freedom since 1992 following a period of some restrictions. Increasing tensions between Christians, Muslims and Traditionalists have brought in some limitations.

Religions	Population %	Adherents	Ann.Gr.
Christian	63.55	12,845,041	+2.4%
Muslim	21.00	4,244,624	+4.8%
Traditional ethnic	15.25	3,082,405	+1.6%
Baha'i	0.10	20,212	+2.7%
non-Religious/other	0.10	20,212	+2.7%

Census 2000: Christian 69%, Muslim 15.9%, Trad. 8.6%

Christians	Denom.	Affil.%	,000	Ann.Gr.
Protestant	59	13.02	2,631	+3.7%
Independent	1,123	19.27	3,894	+4.5%
Anglican	1	1.24	250	+3.6%
Catholic	1	10.39	2,100	+1.6%
Marginal	13	1.48	298	+5.7%
Unaffliated		18.15	3,672	n.a.

Churches		MegaBloc	Cong.	Members	Affiliates
Catholic	C		240	1,110,000	2,100,000
Ch of Pentecost	I		4,000	600,000	1,000,000
Presbyterian Ch of G	P		1,900	180,000	520,000
New Apostolic	I		1,333	266,700	480,000
Methodist	P		2,600	238,100	450,000
Seventh-day Adventist	P		607	208,348	400,000
Apostolic	I		1,800	260,000	380,000
Anglican	A		490	125,000	250,000
Assemblies of God	P		750	125,000	200,000
Jehovah's Witnesses	M		988	61,176	200,000
African Faith Tabernacle	I		1,100	128,000	160,000
Evang Presbyterian	P		748	41,968	143,107
Ghana Baptist Conv	P		942	80,000	130,000

Army of the Cross of Chr	I	1,022	46,000	125,000
Apostles Revelation Soc	I	285	50,000	110,000
Musama Disco	I	1,000	55,000	110,000
Chs of Christ	P	570	40,000	88,000
African Meth Epis Zion	I	150	27,000	55,000
Christ Apostolic	I	650	44,200	52,156
Evang Lutheran	P	350	22,000	32,000
Ch of God (Cleveland)	P	116	10,278	25,000
Salvation Army	P	95	13,000	22,000
Evang Church of G	P	116	3,748	10,481
Good News Churches	P	200	3,000	9,000
Ch of God (Anderson)	P	43	3,000	6,600
Chr Ch/Chs of Chr	P	75	3,000	3,000
Other denoms [1,173]		8,872	1,217,000	2,112,000
Total Christians [1,199]		31,042	4,963,000	9,174,000

Trans-bloc Groupings pop. %	**,000**	**Ann.Gr.**
Evangelical	14.8	2,994	+6.2%
Charismatic	13.0	2,626	+5.7%
Pentecostal	10.4	2,108	+6.2%

Missionaries from Ghana
P,I,A approx. 750 in 60 agencies to 32 countries, of which 144 are abroad.

Missionaries to Ghana
P,I,A 400 in 70 agencies from 23 countries: USA 228, UK 41, Nigeria 36, Germany 27, Korea 25.

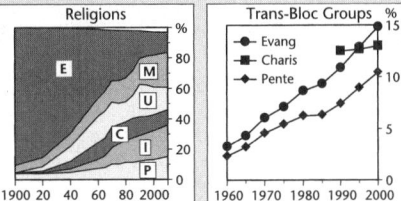

• Answers to Prayer

1 **There has been a spiritual upsurge in Ghana**. The leavening work of literature, Scripture Union **(SU)** in the schools, the New Life for All Campaign of the 1980s and the evangelistic zeal of many churches and agencies — as well as economic hardship — have brought thousands to new life and invigorated many traditional Presbyterian and Methodist churches. Numerous evangelical, charismatic and Pentecostal groups and fellowships have sprung up all over the south. In some of these denominations there has been rapid growth, but the overall growth of Christians as a percentage of society has not increased much.

2 **The National Survey orchestrated by the Ghana Evangelism Committee** (GEC) has helped to bring renewal, vision, church-planting goals and a halting of decline in many denominations.

3 **During the 1990s there was a big increase in evangelism** among the animistic and Muslim northern peoples — both in the north and among migrants to the centre and south.

4 **Only five languages had the Bible in 1965**. By 2000, 43 had the Bible, New Testament or a New Testament translation in progress (GILLBT-**SIL**, **UBS**).

• Challenges for Prayer

1 **The rocky first decades after independence** were not good soil for developing stable, fair, democratic institutions. Pray for those in government that they may subject themselves to God rather than human ideologies or demonic influences and seek the best for the diverse peoples and religious groups of Ghana. Since 1995 there have been both tribal wars and inter-religious violence.

2 **For years, Christianity has had a large following** in the more developed south. Over 64% of Ghanaians call themselves Christian, but only 40% have any link with a church and only 12% are regular church attenders. African traditional worldviews and practices have gone hand-in-hand with the claim of being Christian. The deadness and formality of many older churches have stimulated rapid growth of the African Independent Churches, which offer excitement, involvement and miracles, but not always salvation by faith. The number of these denominations may be in the thousands! Pray that the true gospel may shine into the hearts of those who call themselves Christian but who are not born from above. Pray that a decisive break may be made from all fetishism and occult bondages, and true liberty in Jesus be found.

3 **Vision for the 1990s.** A nation-wide survey 1985-89 conducted by the GEC was studied in regional and national conferences involving most denominational leaders. The results revealed the spiritual need of Ghana.

a) ***Nominal Christians*** numbered seven million.

b) ***Of the 26,000 towns and villages***, 15,000 had no congregations of Christians.

c) ***In the less evangelised north*** there were three million individuals in 40-50 peoples who were unreached or, at best, partially reached.

d) ***In the heavily evangelized south*** lived two million northerners (18% of the population) that were unreached.

e) ***The five million adherents of Islam*** and traditional religions needed to be reached.

4 **Vision for the 21ˢᵗ Century**. The 1989 GEC national conference set goals for the '90s but they were only partially achieved. These are a continuing prayer challenge:

a) ***To increase congregations*** from 22,600 to 53,000. By 2000 there were probably 30-35,000 churches.

b) ***To plant 2,000 new churches*** for northern peoples in the East and West Upper regions, the Northern region and for northerners in the South. That goal has yet to be attained, but at least eight churches and agencies are actively and vigorously planting and multiplying churches in each of these regions.

c) ***An active, witnessing church*** for every village, town, urban neighbourhood and ethnic community. This goal is only partially achieved, and 70% of Ghana's villages still have no church.

Pray that these goals might be achieved by 2010.

5 **Mature Christian leaders are in short supply** in this time of rapid growth, economic stress and doctrinal confusion. There are two diploma-awarding schools — Christian Service College (CSC) in Kumasi started by **WEC** and Maranatha Bible College (**SIM**). Trinity College awards degrees predominantly for mainline churches. There are over 30 other accredited denominational and inter-denominational Bible schools as well as a range of TEE and lay training programmes run by different denominations and agencies.

6 **The missions vision of the Ghanaian church has grown**, with agencies and workers increasing in numbers. Gradually the reluctance of more sophisticated southern Christians to go to the 'backward' north is being overcome. There are a number of significant movements worthy of prayer:

a) ***Training for missions*** is given by both CSC and Maranatha as well as Africa Christian Mission at their Amedzofe base.

b) ***Christian Outreach Fellowship*** with 24 missionaries has planted nearly 60 churches for other denominations among the Kasena, Mamprusi, Sisaala and Gonja in the Volta Region.

c) ***The Church of Pentecost*** has sent church planters to many countries in West Africa and in Europe.

7 **Young people are in the forefront of the move of the Spirit**. Praise God for the impact of **SU** on the secondary schools; GHAFES(**IFES**), **Navigators** and **CCCI** on the universities and colleges; and **CEF** with 30 workers among young children. Pray that the influence of converted young people may be decisive in church, mission and national affairs. May many hear God's call into full-time service. Very few churches have an effective programme for young people or children — youth under 15 comprise only 30% of the church-going population but 45% of the total population.

8 **Missionary personnel** to serve as Bible teachers, translators, media experts and pioneer evangelists are still needed in this day of opportunity. A key area for prayer is that there might be healthy, helpful partnerships between indigenous church leaders and missionaries. Pray for missions serving the Lord in this land; the largest: GILLBT/**SIL** (69), **SIM** (34), **IMB-SBC** (30), **WEC** (25).

9 **The less evangelized peoples of Ghana** have, generally, never been so receptive as now. Ghanaian and expatriate workers are needed for the reaping. Of the more than 35 peoples of the north, only one is even nominally Christian — the Dagaari who are 60% Catholic, and the Sisaala, Kulango, Mossi, Konkomba, Nankana, etc., are over 10% Christian. In most, less than 2% are Christian of any variety, though few have no Christians. Churches have often been small, weak, largely illiterate with many leaders having basic training only. Pray specifically for:

a) **The traditional peoples of the Upper East and West regions** adjoining Burkina Faso. Pray for greater church growth among the Sisaala (**SIM**), Kasena, Mamprusi, Nankana and Bulsa (**SIM**) with 20 churches and Frafra (**SIM, AoG, WEC**). Response is slow among the Bimoba, Kusasi and Tampulma (**AoG**). Some smaller groups are unoccupied by Christian workers.

b) **The traditional peoples of the Northern region** are a complex medley of small groups that are scarcely touched by the gospel; over 30 peoples are resident in the region, but there are viable evangelical churches in only 6-7 of these. ECG/**WEC** is planting churches in this area. Response is growing among the Birifor and Konkomba but, though targeted by ECG/**WEC**, there are not adequate labourers for the Nawuri, Nchumburu and others. The 1995 war between the Konkomba and eastern peoples and the more structured and dominant Gonja and allied Dagomba, Nanumba and others caused much destruction of life and property and has left a legacy of bitterness and division which hampers Christian ministry — especially to the Muslim groups.

c) **The Islamized peoples of the North** have responded only minimally to the gospel, and more input is needed. Examples include the dominant Gonja with only 300 believers (**WEC**), the Dagomba (**AoG, SIM, IMB-SBC, WEC**) with 1% Christian, the Kotokoli with 0.2% Christian and the Wali (Baptist Mid-Missions). Converts to Christ have often suffered verbal and physical persecution, and are often thrown out of their homes and villages. There is a new openness among the Dagomba in the **SIM** areas with new churches being planted. The 100,000 Fulbe are scattered throughout the north — there are now 3 small fellowships with 50 believers.

10 **Less evangelized sectors of society.**

a) **The cities** — which have grown by absorbing many ethnic groups. The 2.5 million northerners in southern cities easily turn to Islam; little has been done by Christians to reach them until recently. Pray that both Ghanaian and expatriate workers may be used of God to increase the number of northern-language congregations in the southern cities.

b) **Southern traditionalists are especially strong** in the Volta Region and among the numerous Ewe people and their sea and river-fishing colonies all over Ghana. The 20,000 *trokosi* (women enslaved by fetish priests) gained international attention in the 1990s and pressure to end this wicked system has yielded fruit. Pray for the liberation of all in bondage to the fetish system. The Ghanaian Volta Evangelistic Association has significant outreach in the area.

c) **Islam has grown significantly** through Muslim men marrying non-Muslim women, and through migration to cities. Now 63% of Muslims live in the non-Muslim southern seven provinces. Confrontations and violence between Muslims and Christians have escalated. Pray for peace, a lessening of animosities and for the Lord Jesus to be so lifted up as to attract Muslims to Himself. A number of Muslim imams have turned to Christ — one factor provoking Muslim ire against Christians.

d) **Abandoned, homeless street children** have increased during Ghana's economic stresses of recent years and now number over 45,000. Few have taken up the challenge to minister to them.

11 **Christian Help Ministries for prayer:**

a) **Bible translation** has made great strides over the past 20 years, GILLBT/**SIL** and The Bible Society are presently working on 17 language projects. There are still definite NT translation needs for 10 languages, and research required for a further 18. An increased use of Bible cassettes is bearing fruit — especially in illiterate Muslim peoples such as the Ligbi.

b) **Literacy programmes** have often been too slow, too late and too limited to make good use of newly translated Scriptures. Pray for many programmes now under way that they may inspire both young and old with zeal for reading. Pray also for:

i   *Use of Bible cassettes* in over 17 languages where literacy is low. This has proved effective, but needs to be increased.

ii *The Bible League's church planting literacy project* which has been successfully used to help plant churches in some areas.

c) **Literature.** A chronic shortage exists due to lack of foreign exchange and printing materials. Pray for the importation and economic distribution of Bibles (**UBS**) and Christian literature by agencies such as Book Aid in the UK and Challenge Enterprises, an indigenous organization backed by **SIM** which handles 90% of all Christian literature in Ghana. There are 13 Christian bookstores in Ghana. Africa Christian Press publishes a range of good Christian books for distribution throughout Africa. Problems in running an economically viable, indigenous publishing ministry are enormous. Bible Correspondence Courses have been most successful (**SIM**, ICI/**AoG**).

d) ***Christian films*** (**SIM**) are used with great effect. The five mobile 'cinevans' of Challenge Enterprises have a total audience of over 1.5 million annually and over a period of 14 years an estimated / million have responded to an invitation to come to Christ. The *JESUS* film is being widely used in 20 languages and a high proportion of the population has seen it. A further 19 language versions are in preparation.

e) ***GRN*** has increased its range of gospel cassettes to cover 67 languages.

Gibraltar

British Overseas Territory of Gibraltar

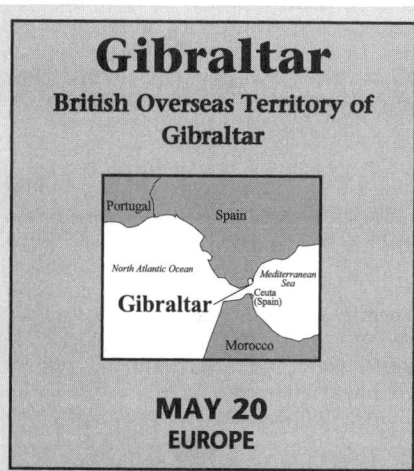

Portugal
Spain
North Atlantic Ocean
Mediterranean Sea
Gibraltar
Ceuta (Spain)
Morocco

MAY 20
EUROPE

GEOGRAPHY
Area 6.5 sq.km. A strategically placed rocky peninsula on the south coast of Spain.

Population	Ann.Gr.	Density
2000	25,082	-0.70%	4,180 per sq.
2010	23,454	-0.66%	3,909 per sq.
2025	21,393	-0.59%	3,566 per sq.

PEOPLES
Indigenous 76.4%. Gibraltarian of Italian, Maltese, British, Jewish, Spanish and Portuguese descent.
Other 23.6%. British 3,800; Moroccan 1,800 (many thousands more come for temporary work); Spanish 1,000; South Asian 500.

Literacy 90%. **Official languages** English and Spanish.

ECONOMY
The closing of the British naval dockyard and the reopening of the border with Spain has provoked radical changes. By 1990, there was an economic boom based on financial services and tourism. There are 27,000 registered companies.

Income/person $13,500 (43% of USA).

POLITICS
A British colony since its capture in 1704. It was an important British military base until 1991. The local population has steadfastly resisted Spanish pleas, pressures and blockades to restore the Rock (Gibraltar) to Spain. Its future will likely be resolved within the context of the EU.

RELIGION
There is full religious freedom.

Religions	Population %	Adherents	Ann.Gr.
Christian	88.40	22,172	-0.8%
Muslim	8.50	2,132	+0.5%
Jewish	2.00	502	+0.3%
Hindu	0.60	150	-6.3%
non-Religious/other	0.50	125	-0.8%

Christians	Denom.	Affil.%	,000	Ann.Gr.
Protestant	4	0.77	0	-4.2%
Independent	3	1.52	0	+5.8%
Anglican	1	7.58	2	-1.0%
Catholic	1	84.52	21	-1.6%
Marginal	3	1.00	0	-2.8%
Unaffiliated		5.77	1	n.a.
Doubly affiliated		*-12.76*	*-3*	*n.a.*

Churches	MegaBloc	Cong.	Members	Affiliates
Catholic	C	5	13,168	21,200
Ch of England	A	3	600	1,900
Jehovah's Witnesses	M	2	113	200
Filadelfia	I	1	100	180
Other denoms [11]		11	260	444
Doubly affiliated			*-2,000*	*-3,200*
Total Christians [15]		22	12,241	20,700

Trans-bloc Groupings	pop. %	,000	Ann.Gr.
Evangelical	1.4	0	-1.1%
Charismatic	2.2	1	+0.7%
Pentecostal	0.7	0	+7.2%

• Challenges for Prayer

1 **The majority of the population is Catholic.** There is a minority of other mainline denominations (Anglican, Presbyterian and Methodist). The evangelical witness is small with only 4 English and Spanish-speaking congregations (Brethren, Filadelphia Pentecostal [Roma], charismatic). Pray for revival and for God to inspire them with a new zeal for witnessing. The scarcity of churches in nearby North Africa and southern Spain make Gibraltar's Christians strategically placed for the gospel.

2 **Specific outreach challenges** — to the 6 million tourists, the 7,000+ Moroccan workers (with one small Arabic-speaking fellowship), the Jewish community and the South Asian-origin Hindus.

Greece
Hellenic Republic

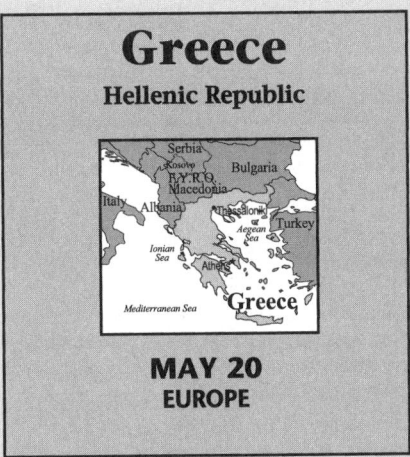

MAY 20
EUROPE

GEOGRAPHY
Area 131,957 sq.km. Southernmost part of Balkan Peninsula in SE Europe and 150 inhabited islands in the Ionian, Aegean and Mediterranean Seas. The islands constitute 20% of the land area.

Population	Ann.Gr.	Density
2000	10,644,744	+0.29%	81 per sq. km.
2010	10,554,397	-0.18%	80 per sq. km.
2025	9,862,572	-0.56%	75 per sq. km.

Capital Athens 3,150,000. Other major city: Thessaloniki 998,000. **Urbanites** 66%.

PEOPLES
Greek 90.8%. The descendants of the ancient Greeks whose civilization so enriched the world. Including: Pontian Greeks (fSU) 200,000; US/foreign Greeks 105,000; Cypriots 15,000.
Indigenous minorities 4%. Many being absorbed into Greek society: Slavic 150,000; Turk 140,000; Roma (Gypsy) 200,000+; Vlach 60,000; Albanian 25,000.
Immigrants and refugees 5.2%. Albanians 400-500,000; Middle Eastern (Arabs, Iranians, etc.) 50,000; British/US 50,000; German 19,000; Armenian 10,000.

Literacy 95.2%. **Official language** Greek. **All languages** 14. **Languages with Scriptures** 6Bi 2NT 2por.

ECONOMY
EU membership has boosted tourism, industry and modernization. Greece has the largest fleet of merchant ships in the EU. Efforts to join the euro-currency is bringing some fiscal discipline to the economy. **HDI** 0.867; 27th/174. **Public debt** 15% of GNP. **Income/person** $11,640 (37% of USA).

POLITICS
Nearly four centuries of Turkish rule ended with independence in 1827. The last 50 years have been punctuated by two civil wars, two military dictatorships, and tensions with neighbouring Turkey over the political status of Cyprus. A republic with a parliamentary democracy. The instability and ethnic hatreds of the post-Communist Balkan countries has unsettled Greece. Shared earthquake experiences with Turkey have significantly reduced tensions between these NATO members.

RELIGION
The Orthodox Church is recognized and legally protected by the state as the dominant and established religion. The constitution of 1975 removed some of the discriminatory legislation against non-Orthodox bodies, but old laws remain which are used to hinder non-Orthodox activities and persecute Protestants. Greece regularly loses cases when such are taken to the European Court of Justice, thus gradually lessening restrictions on religious minorities. **Persecution index** 62nd in the world.

Religions	Population %	Adherents	Ann.Gr.
Christian	95.15	10,128,474	+0.3%
non-Religious/other	3.30	351,277	+1.6%
Muslim	1.50	159,671	-2.2%
Jewish	0.05	5,322	+0.3%

G

Christians	Denom.	Affil.%	,000	Ann.Gr.
Protestant	17	0.47	50	+7.0%
Independent	25	0.02	2	+3.9%
Anglican	1	0.03	4	+0.5%
Catholic	4	0.61	65	+1.6%
Orthodox	8	87.86	9,352	+0.2%
Marginal	2	0.41	43	-0.4%
Unaffiliated		6.49	691	n.a.
Doubly affiliated		*-0.75*	*-80*	*n.a.*

Churches	MegaBloc	Cong.	Members	Affiliates
Ch of Greece (Orth)	O	28,893	6,600,000	9,100,000
Authent Old Calend Orth	O	184	108,500	217,000
Catholic [4]	C	95	47,445	65,000
Jehovah's Witnesses	M	425	27,327	43,000
Free Apostolic	P	140	10,000	30,000
Armenian Apostolic	O	15	6,757	15,000
Free Evang Chs of G.	P	63	4,000	5,500
Greek Evangelical	P	32	2,000	5,000
Assemblies of God	P	14	445	620
Other denoms [46]		187	18,300	36,000
Doubly affiliated			*-57,143*	*-80,000*
Total Christians [58]		30,048	6,767,600	9,437,000

Trans-bloc Groupings	pop. %	,000	Ann.Gr.
Evangelical	0.4	48	+7.6%
Charismatic	0.4	40	+9.0%
Pentecostal	0.3	36	+9.7%

Missionaries from Greece
P,I,A 36 in 15 agencies; 30 in Greece.

Missionaries to Greece
P,I,A 150 in 38 agencies from 12 countries: USA 82, UK 15, Korea 14. M 60.

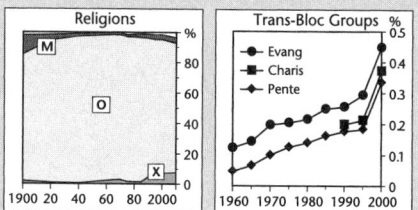

• Answers to Prayer

1 **Increasing religious freedoms** being gained despite ongoing opposition.

2 **After centuries of confrontation between Greece and Turkey**, the unexpected lowering of tensions since the Istanbul earthquake of 1999 opens up real possibilities for resolution of such intractable problems as the division of Cyprus.

• Challenges for Prayer

1 **Greece was the first European country to be evangelized** (Acts 16:10), but Christianity is now more cultural than spiritual, with only 2% of the population in church on an average Sunday. Evangelical church members number only around 15,000. The Macedonian call is just as valid today.

2 **The Orthodox Church** was a focal rallying point in the dark years of Turkish and German occupations. Orthodoxy became part of the Greek identity and made Greeks often xenophobic. All other expressions of Christianity are seen as a threat to the state and the culture. Greeks have a high regard for Orthodox institutions but are little involved in church activities. There is a godly, committed minority with a personal faith, but the great majority are in ignorance of the message of the gospel and are most unreceptive to any non-Orthodox witness. Pray for the breaking down of prejudice, blindness and fear and for biblical renewal in Orthodoxy.

3 **Discrimination, harassment and persecution** of minorities still happens — especially those who 'proselytize' — Evangelicals, Pentecostals, Mormons and Jehovah's Witnesses. Pray for cultural and legal equality for the non-Orthodox that is consistent with Greece's membership of the EU and for the constitution to be changed to grant full religious freedom.

4 **Greek Evangelicals are few,** socially marginalized and mainly concentrated in the Athens, Thessaloniki and Katerini areas. Pray for:
a) *Courage to witness* in a society that generally despises, and occasionally persecutes, them. The media often portray Evangelicals as disloyal, dishonest and a security threat. Jehovah's Witnesses have been far more successful.
b) *Unity in the Spirit.* There have been a number of debilitating divisions. The Pan-Hellenic Evangelical Alliance is increasingly recognized as the mouthpiece of Evangelicals and is becoming more pro-active in challenging official discrimination.

c) **Greater growth** after small gains during the past 40 years.

d) **Vision for multiplying congregations** in many centres as yet without an evangelical witness.

5 **Widespread evangelism with effective follow-up discipling is the need.** Specific programmes and visions for prayer:

a) **EHC's** goal to reach every home with gospel literature. Around 2.5 million gospel booklets had been distributed by 1997, but response has been limited.

b) **The OM Love Europe** and **Hellenic Ministries'** (**HM**) summer evangelistic campaigns.

c) **The Thessaloniki Evangelistic Team's** year-round evangelism and summer outreaches.

Above all, pray for the development of a nation-wide vision for prayer, outreach and church planting.

6 **Theological training** has been a lack. There are two training institutes, **GEM** with 30 students and **AoG** with 25. A seminary to provide advanced training is a real need.

7 **Many Greeks have never heard a clear presentation of the gospel**. More specifically, pray for:

a) **The 150 islands**. The majority of the Dodecanese, the Cyclades, the Ionian Islands and others are without evangelical congregations. Corfu and Crete are among the only exceptions. **HM** use their yacht *The Morning Star* for evangelizing these isolated communities.

b) **University students**. There is a strong work of **CCCI** and **IFES** among them in Thessaloniki and Athens, but most of the 270,000 students in tertiary education have little exposure to the gospel.

c) **Albanians**, who have flooded into Greece during the 1990s seeking seasonal employment, many of them illegally. Involvement in smuggling and criminal activities means high numbers end up in prisons. Pray for more Christians to minister to this underclass in society.

d) **Immigrant communities in the Athens area**. There are several outreaches and small Christian groups among the Arabs, Ethiopians and others, but few of the present opportunities are fully used. Greece is a key base for ministry to the Arab world.

e) **Indigenous ethnic minorities in the north**. They are officially ignored, and their cultural identity denied — a reflection of centuries-old Balkan conflicts. Pray for a change in Greek attitudes and fears and for effective outreach to the Albanians and Vlach and to the Muslim Turks, Roma (Gypsies) and Bulgarian-speaking Pomaks.

f) **The 200,000 drug addicts**. Pan-Hellenic Mercy Mission and others have a year-round ministry to them.

8 **Foreign missions** have not found Greece an easy field because of strong nationalism, visa restrictions and the high degree of cultural adaptation required. Major ministries are: **GEM** (14 workers), **HM** (13 expats, 6 nationals), **CCCI** (13), **AoG** (10), **WEC** (7). Greece's EU membership facilitates the residence of missionaries from other member states. Pray for labourers and for their adaptation, ministry and fruitfulness in often discouraging circumstances.

9 **Literature has been a fruitful form of evangelism**. There is little variety in Christian literature available. Pray for the seed-sowing work of the Greek Bible Society and the Gideons in disseminating the Scriptures, and **SU** in producing good Bible reading aids which are used by both Orthodox and Evangelicals. Pray also for the tract distribution ministry of **EHC** and East Europe Mission; tracts *are* read.

10 **Christian Radio and TV**. Some evangelical programmes have been aired — including the *JESUS* film. The legalization of private radio stations allowed both Pentecostals and Evangelicals to start FM stations. The latter in Athens was forcibly, but illegally, closed in 1999. It has since been allowed to continue its ministry. Pray for the best use of these media and for effective impact.

11 **The large Greek diaspora** totals nearly 5 million in 88 countries: USA 2 million; Germany 500,000; Australia 272,000; Britain 220,000; Canada 132,000; Italy 100,000; South Africa 72,000. It is both a challenge for evangelism (there are evangelical Greek churches in Australia and USA), and a good source of Christian workers for Greece itself.

Greenland

Kalallit Nunaat

MAY 21

NORTH AMERICA

GEOGRAPHY
Area 2,175,600 sq.km. Land area is 85% glacial ice cap. The world's largest island and with the lowest population density of any country.

Population	Ann.Gr.	Density
2000	56,156	+0.13%	0.03 per sq. km.
2010	57,200	+0.20%	0.03 per sq. km.
2025	59,634	+0.32%	0.03 per sq. km.

Capital Nuuk 13,000. **Urbanites** 82%.

PEOPLES
Greenland Inuit 87%.
Danes 11.5%.
US Military 1%.
Other 0.5%.

Literacy 99%. **Official Languages** Inuktitut (Greenlandic), which has 3 distinct dialects; Danish. **Languages with Scripture** 2Bi.

ECONOMY
Based on fishing and mining.
Income/person $15,500 (55% of USA).

POLITICS
Overseas administrative division of Denmark with internal self-government since 1979.

RELIGION
Freedom of religion since 1953, before which the Lutheran Church was the state church.

Religions	Population %	Adherents	Ann.Gr.
Christian	96.56	54,224	+0.2%
non-Religious/other	2.20	1,235	+2.0%
Traditional ethnic	0.74	416	-9.2%
Baha'i	0.50	281	+1.4%

Christians	Denom.	Affil.%	,000	Ann.Gr.
Protestant	7	61.92	35	-3.1%
Independent	1	0.11	0	+3.3%
Catholic	1	0.18	0	+0.0%
Marginal	1	0.53	0	+0.0%
Unaffiliated		33.82	19	n.a.

Churches	MegaBloc	Cong.	Members	Affiliates
Lutheran	P	91	25,185	34,000
Jehovah's Witnesses	M	7	158	300
Pentecostal	P	7	150	300
Evangelical (NTM)	P	3	59	100
Other denominations [6]		9	319	530
Total Christians [10]		117	25,870	35,230

Trans-bloc Groupings pop. %		,000	Ann.Gr.
Evangelical	1.6	1	-0.1%
Charismatic	0.7	0	+1.3%
Pentecostal	0.5	0	+1.3%

Missionaries from Greenland
P,I,A 3 in 2 agencies.

Missionaries to Greenland
P,I,A 34 in 9 agencies from 9 countries: Faeroe Islands 11.

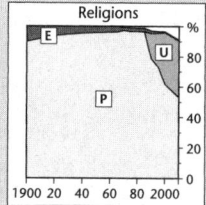
Religions

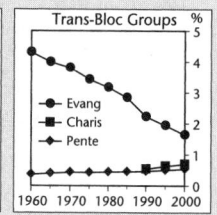
Trans-Bloc Groups

• Challenges for Prayer

1 **Greenland has been Christianized, but not converted**. Nearly every settlement has its Lutheran church building — but many are empty of biblical theology, people, or life. Pray for renewal, and new life for Dane and Greenlander alike. The Evangelical population is very low.

2 **The culture of the Greenlanders,** so finely tuned to their inhospitable environment, has been devastated by modernity. The dire results have been widespread immorality, alcoholism, apathy, mental illness and suicide. With self-government, Greenland's culture has revived. Pray that the retranslated Bible may be read, then remould the people and bring to birth a truly Greenlandic Church.

3 **Only in the 1950s was an evangelical witness established.** Through the ministry of Scandinavian Pentecostal (6 workers) and Free Church (2) missionaries, and also Faeroese Brethren (5), and more recently, **NTM** (11). Churches have been planted, including 7 Pentecostal congregations. Travel conditions are harsh and the communities along the coasts isolated. There are still 60 settlements without an evangelical gospel witness. Pray that these may have a chance to hear the gospel in the near future.

4 **More training of indigenous believers is needed** — there are only four evangelical Greenlandic pastors in the whole country. **YWAM**, in cooperation with the Pentecostal Church and **CCCI**, facilitated the translation of the *JESUS* film into the Greenlandic language, which premiered in May 1998 and was shown on national television in 2000. The film and the 2,400 videos have been shown and distributed all over the country with significant impact.

Grenada

Saint Vincent

Caribbean Sea — Grenada
Saint George's — North Atlantic Ocean

MAY 21
LATIN AMERICA

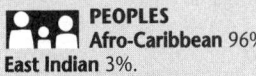 **GEOGRAPHY**
Area 345 sq.km. One larger island north of Trinidad and some of the Grenadine islets south of St. Vincent. The most southerly of the Windward Islands in the West Indies.

Population		Ann.Gr.	Density
2000	93,717	+0.34%	272 per sq. km.
2010	97,453	+0.41%	282 per sq. km.
2025	104,647	+0.51%	303 per sq. km.

Capital St. George's 27,000. **Urbanites** 34%.

PEOPLES
Afro-Caribbean 96%.
East Indian 3%.
Euro-American/Other 1%.

Literacy 85%, functional literacy nearer 35-40%.
Official language English.

ECONOMY
Major economic activities are tourism and agriculture (spices, cocoa, bananas). Gradual recovery from the disastrous post-independence flirtation with Marxism. A free market economy today, growing at around 6% annually. **Unemployment** 20%. **HDI** 0.777; 52nd/174. **Public debt** 35% of GNP. **Income/person** $2,900 (10% of USA).

POLITICS
French rule 1650-1783, when ceded to Britain. Independent in 1974 as a parliamentary monarchy. Independence has proved stormy with bizarre dictatorships, repression and two increas-

ingly Marxist coups; the last of which provoked the US invasion of 1983 and restoration of democratic government. A stable constitutional monarchy with a parliamentary democratic form of government since then.

 RELIGION
There is complete freedom of religion.

G

Religions	Population %	Adherents	Ann.Gr.
Christian	97.00	90,905	+0.3%
Rastafarian/Spiritist	1.30	1,218	+1.9%
Hindu	0.70	656	+1.8%
non-Religious	0.50	469	-4.8%
Muslim	0.30	281	+4.1%
Baha'i	0.20	187	+0.3%

Christians	Denom.	Affil.%	,000	Ann.Gr.
Protestant	23	24.94	23	+1.6%
Independent	4	4.85	5	+2.0%
Anglican	1	11.74	11	-0.7%
Catholic	1	56.55	53	-0.3%
Marginal	5	2.35	2	+2.3%
Unaffiliated		2.17	2	n.a.
Doubly affiliated		*-5.60*	*-5*	*n.a.*

Churches	MegaBloc	Cong.	Members	Affiliates
Catholic	C	20	29,121	53,000
Anglican	A	25	3,846	11,000
Seventh-day Adventist	P	29	8,627	10,500
Pentecostal Assemblies	P	22	1,600	2,600
New Test. Ch of God	P	13	900	1,800
Methodist	P	10	962	1,750
Jehovah's Witnesses	M	8	631	1,300
Foursquare Gospel	P	4	700	1,000
Presbyterian	P	9	620	876
Baptist Convention	P	5	344	700
Open Bible Std	P	4	400	700
Evang Ch of W Indies	P	9	350	650
Christian Brethren	P	8	200	340
Church of God (And)	P	4	150	210
Other denoms [20]		62	3,800	7,700
Doubly affiliated			*-2,800*	*-5,250*
Total Christians [34]		233	49,500	88,900

Trans-bloc Groupings pop. %		,000	Ann.Gr.
Evangelical	18.0	17	+1.4%
Charismatic	13.2	12	+1.5%
Pentecostal	11.1	10	+1.8%

Missionaries from Grenada
P,I,A 3 in 2 agencies.

Missionaries to Grenada
P,I,A 22 in 9 agencies. C 20.

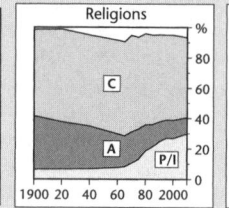

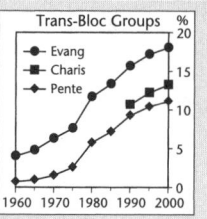

• Answers to Prayer

1 The traumatic events of 1974-1984 still have reverberations two decades later, but praise God for stability and the healing of many of the pains and divisions of society.

• Challenges for Prayer

1 Much of the population is nominally Catholic because of the earlier French legacy, but Evangelicals have steadily grown in numbers and influence since independence. The major problems to be faced:

a) *Lack of unity and suspicion between denominations* which result in little cooperation in outreach and missions. Pray for a closer fellowship and common vision to increase.

b) *Widespread nominalism* even in evangelical congregations. The illegitimacy rate is 82% and there is little known of a stable two-parent family — in part a tragic legacy of the slave culture of earlier centuries.

2 Pray that Grenadian churches might begin to assume more responsibility and initiative in evangelism and church planting.

3 Missionary vision is lacking. Pray for the **YWAM** team which is seeking to train and send out West Indian missionaries to unreached peoples elsewhere in the world.

Guadeloupe
Department of Guadeloupe

MAY 21
LATIN AMERICA

GEOGRAPHY
Area 1,780 sq.km. One larger island and five smaller island dependencies: Marie Galante, Iles des Saintes, La Désirade, St Martin and St Barthélemy. St Martin is shared with the Netherlands.

Population	Ann.Gr.	Density
2000	455,687	+1.44%	256 per sq. km.
2010	509,648	+1.05%	286 per sq. km.
2025	569,216	+0.57%	320 per sq. km.

Capital Basse-Terre 14,000. **Urbanites** 99.4%.

PEOPLES
Afro-Caribbean (black and mixed race) 89%.
Asian Caribbean 8%.
French 2%.
Asian 1%. Mainly Tamil and Syrian Arab.

Literacy 90%. **Official language** French. The French Creole Patois is widely spoken.

ECONOMY
Agriculture, tourism and light industry supplemented by large subsidies from France help maintain a reasonable living standard. Imports are 11 times the value of exports. The ending of the EU banana subsidies is forcing economic diversification. **Unemployment** 28%. **Public debt** 5% of GNP. **Income/person** $10,700 (38% of USA).

POLITICS
French colony since 1635. Overseas Department of France since 1946. Local demands for more autonomy are moderated by the high dependency on French economic aid.

RELIGION
Religious freedom, but with a strong secularist tendency.

Religions	Population %	Adherents	Ann.Gr.
Christian	94.60	431,080	+1.2%
non-Religious/other	4.10	18,683	+8.7%
Hindu	0.50	2,278	+1.4%
Baha'i	0.40	1,823	+1.4%
Muslim	0.40	1,823	+1.4%

Christians	Denom.	Affil.%	,000	Ann.Gr.
Protestant	9	7.22	33	+2.7%
Independent	6	0.55	2	+5.0%
Catholic	1	89.97	410	+1.0%
Marginal	1	3.62	16	-5.5%
Unaffiliated		2.03	9	n.a.
Doubly affiliated		*-8.78*	*-40*	*n.a.*

Churches	MegaBloc	Cong.	Members	Affiliates
Catholic	C	43	234,286	410,000
Jehovah's Witnesses	M	103	7,675	16,500
Seventh-day Adventist	P	51	10,170	16,000
Evangelical Church (WT)	P	24	3,500	9,000
Assemblies of God	P	12	1,500	3,300
Baptist Convention	P	11	811	1,354
Church of God (Cleve)	P	5	794	1,300

Evangelical Reformed	P	14	550	1,000
Other denominations [9]		43	1,832	3,400
Doubly affiliated			-22,900	-40,000
Total Christians [17]		306	238,300	421,900

Trans-bloc Groupings pop. %	,000	Ann.Gr.
Evangelical	5.4	25	+2.6%
Charismatic	7.7	35	+1.4%
Pentecostal	1.3	6	+3.2%

Missionaries from Guadeloupe
P,I,A 2.

Missionaries to Guadeloupe
P,I,A 19 in 3 agencies.

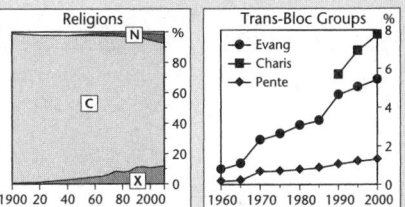

• Challenges for Prayer

1 **The grim legacy of the cruelty of slavery** has left its mark in the lack of meaningful marriage relationships and widespread occultism in the Afro-Caribbean majority. Yet it is among these that there is the greatest spiritual interest. Pray that the gospel may transform and uplift these peoples.

2 **Catholicism** is a cultural veneer for most. The rapid growth of both evangelical groups and sects highlight the spiritual emptiness. Pray for the Holy Spirit to convict of sin and bring many to true repentance.

3 **Areas and peoples less reached** with the gospel:

a) **The outlying dependencies are less evangelized** — St Barthélemy, St Martin and Marie Galante. Several missionaries of the Association of Evangelical Churches work on these islands. Both the Evangelical Church and the Church of God have planted churches on St Martin.
b) **Those of South Asian descent** number over 12,000. Most have become nominally Catholic, while retaining many of their Hindu beliefs. Little direct outreach has been aimed at this community.
c) **The French** are largely from France, but serving in the military or civil service. Few show any spiritual interest.

4 **There were hardly any born-again believers before 1946.** The work of **WT** and **AoG** has been used of God to plant a network of churches. The vital witness of believers, radio and TV evangelism and Christian literature have all played their part.

5 **Leadership training** for the growing churches is provided locally through the Evangelical Church's TEE programme with 200 students and the School of Discipleship in Guadeloupe. Pray that Christian workers may be called for service at home and in the Francophone lands around the world.

6 **Specialist Christian ministries** for prayer:

a) **Students.** The GBU(**IFES**), with a strong evangelistic and missionary focus, is very active in the schools and university, where secular-humanist values are propagated.
b) **Literature.** The Evangelical Church has a Christian bookstore on Guadeloupe. **EHC** has reached every home five times with Christian literature.

Guam

US Territory of Guam

Northern Mariana Islands

Pacific Ocean

Agana Guam

MAY 21
PACIFIC

 POLITICS
Spanish rule 1565-1898. US Territory since then. A self-governing, unincorporated territory of the USA. Guamanians are US citizens.

RELIGION
Freedom of religion.

Religions	Population %	Adherents	Ann.Gr.
Christian	95.57	160,133	+2.1%
Buddhist/Chinese	1.75	2,932	-2.4%
non-Religious/other	1.48	2,480	+6.1%
Baha'i	0.90	1,508	+3.3%
Traditional ethnic	0.30	503	-3.6%

Christians	Denom.	Affil.%	,000	Ann.Gr.
Protestant	31	11.92	20	-1.5%
Independent	2	1.01	2	+5.1%
Anglican	1	0.54	1	+1.7%
Catholic	1	77.29	130	+2.1%
Marginal	2	1.97	3	+0.5%
Unaffiliated		2.84	5	n.a.

Churches	MegaBloc	Cong.	Members	Affiliates
Catholic	C	25	74,000	129,500
United Pentecostal	P	54	4,200	7,800
Jehovah's Witnesses	M	11	619	1,900
Korean Presby. [3]	P	6	1,000	1,700
Latter-day Saints (Morm)	M	3	838	1,400
Assemblies of God	P	5	900	1,260
Seventh-day Adventist	P	6	771	1,200
Baptist Convention	P	3	340	850
Other denoms [27]		52	4,800	9,762
Total Christians [37]		**165**	**87,500**	**155,400**

Trans-bloc Groupings pop. %		,000	Ann.Gr.
Evangelical	12.6	21	-0.2%
Charismatic	13.7	23	+0.8%
Pentecostal	6.1	10	-0.3%

Missionaries from Guam
P,I,A 1 overseas.

Missionaries to Guam
P,I,A 189 in 18 agencies from 6 countries: USA 162, Korea 16.

GEOGRAPHY
Area 541 sq.km. Most southerly and largest island of the Marianas Archipelago, 6,000 km. west of Hawaii. Also included here are the three tiny US Territories of Johnston Island (2.8 sq.km, 1,300 km from Hawaii), Midway (5.2 sq.km, 2,350 km), and Wake Island (6.5 sq.km, 3,700 km).

Population	Ann.Gr.	Density
2000	167,556	+2.09%	310 per sq. km.
2010	193,836	+1.32%	358 per sq. km.
2025	227,634	+1.02%	421 per sq. km.

There are estimated to be a further 26,000 illegal immigrants. Also included here: Johnston Island, population: 1,700; Midway 13; Wake 300.

Capital Agana 2,200. **Urbanites** 45%.

PEOPLES
Micronesian 42.4%. Chamorro 63,000; Other islanders 8,200 — mainly Chuuk, Palau and Pohnpei.
Asian 29.5%. Filipino 38,000; Korean 5,000; Japanese 3,000; Chinese 2,500.
US Mainland 16.7%.
Mixed race 9.7%.
Other 1.7%.

Literacy 96%. **Official languages** English and Chamorro.

ECONOMY
One third of the island is used for US military bases. Nearly 45% of Guamanians are employed by the government or military. Tourism is increasingly important. **Income/person** $19,600 (67% of continental USA).

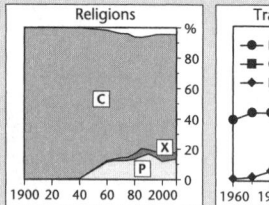

Religions

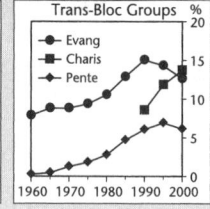

Trans-Bloc Groups %
- Evang
- Charis
- Pente

• Challenges for Prayer

1 **The Chamorro have had a long history of oppression** and, more recently, cultural disorientation with the influx of U.S. culture. The majority are Catholic, though other denominations are growing significantly. Pray for the emergence of a true Chamorro Christian culture and witness.

2 **Most Protestant congregations are multi-cultural.** Pray for a harvest among indigenous and immigrant peoples. Immigrant communities have responded well to the gospel. There are four thriving Korean Presbyterian congregations, one Chinese, and also churches in each of the Micronesian immigrant ethnic groups. The Micronesians with their protected and nominal Christian background have found adaptation difficult, and need prayer for spiritual renewal and social assimilation.

3 **The major thrust of missions** has moved from military ministries to the indigenous and migrant peoples in church planting, Bible teaching and development. Major missions are **TWR** (37 workers) Korean Presbyterians (8), Liebenzell (8), CRWM (5), **AoG** (3). There are two Bible Colleges (**AoG** and Liebenzell/CRWM), also a ministry to young people (Teen Challenge, **YWAM**), and to children (**CEF**). Youth problems are multiplying with an estimated 100 youth gangs prone to violence.

4 **The Prison Fellowship of Guam** has developed a ministry to prisoners which is also penetrating the indigenous population in a significant way. It has fostered a cooperative unity among evangelical churches which is sadly lacking. Pray for resources to develop adequate after-care programmes for converted prisoners.

5 **Christian radio.** Both **TWR** and High Adventure Ministries have powerful broadcasting stations for reaching central, south and east Asia and Siberia. **TWR's** station, KTWR, airs 264 hours of programmes in 21 languages each week. Over 80% of these hours are to China. **TWR** also broadcasts on KTWG in six Guamanian and Marianas languages. Pray for this ministry and the 52 missionaries and staff engaged in it.

Guatemala
Republic of Guatemala

MAY 22
LATIN AMERICA

GEOGRAPHY
Area 108,889 sq.km. A land of mountains, volcanoes and lakes. Mexico's southern neighbour.

Population		Ann.Gr.	Density
2000	11,385,295	+2.68%	105 per sq. km.
2010	14,631,050	+2.47%	134 per sq. km.
2025	19,816,134	+1.80%	182 per sq. km.

Capital Guatemala City 1,925,000. **Urbanites** 40%.

PEOPLES
Spanish-speaking Latinos 43%. Mixed European and Indian.
Amerindian 54%. Maya — 19 ethnic groups speaking 49 languages (40% as their first language). Largest:

Quiche(9) 1,490,000; Cakchiquel(10) 709,000; Mam(7) 442,000; Kekchi 418,000; Pocomam(3) 242,000; Kanjobal(2) 134,000; Ixil(3) 90,000; Pocomchi(2) 80,000; Achi 63,000; Tzutujil 45,000.
Afro-Caribbean 2%. Blacks on Caribbean coast. Other 1%. Garifuna 25,000; Chinese 20,000.

Literacy 56%, but in practice nearer 30%. **Official language** Spanish; not used by 40% of population as their primary language. **All languages** 42. **Languages with Scriptures** 8Bi 21NT 13por 17w.i.p.

ECONOMY
Agriculture provides 25% of the country's GDP, but two-thirds of its exports — mainly coffee, sugar and bananas. Just 2% of the population owns 80% of the land, marginalizing and oppressing the largely Maya majority. Nearly 80% of the population live below the poverty line. Since the 1996 peace accord, economic growth and living standards have improved. 1998's Hurricane 'Mitch' was a severe setback. **HDI** 0.624; 117th/174. **Public debt** 17% of GNP. **Income/person** $1,470 (5% of USA).

POLITICS
Independent from Spain in 1821, and from the Federation of Central American States in 1838, but controlled by a few plantation owners through a series of dictatorships and military governments. The poor, particularly the Mayans, suffered years of indignity and deprivation which exploded in 1960 into 36 years of guerrilla war with around 200,000 deaths, mainly at the hands of the US-armed military. The human-rights record during those years was appalling with over 40,000 'disappearances', widespread torture and displace-

ment of one million internal and 250,000 international refugees. The 1996 peace agreement has ended warfare but has not been fully implemented by the authorities. There remains a culture of violence in the country and cynicism about the government. The 2000 elections were won by those who supported the former repressive regimes.

![] RELIGION

Official separation of Church and state for over 100 years has given great freedom for Evangelicals and increased their influence at the expense of the hitherto dominant Catholic Church. Over 25% of those classified in the census as Catholics are basically Christo-pagan with Mayan gods becoming Catholic 'saints'.

Religions	Population %	Adherents	Ann.Gr.
Christian	97.52	11,102,940	+2.8%
non-Religious/other	1.90	216,321	+6.9%
Traditional ethnic	0.30	34,156	-19.3%
Baha'i	0.20	22,771	+2.7%
Buddhist	0.06	6,831	+6.5%
Chinese	0.02	2,277	-5.3%

Christians	Denom.	Affil.%	,000	Ann.Gr.
Protestant	38	18.57	2,114	+3.8%
Independent	27	8.19	933	+7.2%
Anglican	1	0.02	2	+2.4%
Catholics	1	61.48	7,000	+2.3%
Marginal	3	2.15	245	+4.9%
Unaffiliated		7.11	809	n.a.

Churches	MegaBloc	Cong.	Members	Affiliates
Catholic	C	250	3,783,784	7,000,000
Ch of God of the Full Gosp	P	2,200	160,000	300,000
Assemblies of God	P	1,782	98,570	254,000

Prince of Peace Ev. Ass	P	1,510	108,000	220,000
Calvary Chr. Ministries	P	769	100,000	190,000
Latter-day Saints (Morm)	M	541	100,000	190,000
Elim Christian Mission	P	1,200	70,000	150,000
Seventh-day Adventist	P	329	84,601	150,000
Evang Ch of Cent Amer	P	1,408	105,000	150,000
Christian Brethren	P	850	43,000	90,000
Ch of the Nazarene	P	811	47,000	90,000
Lluvias de Gracia	I	128	30,757	62,000
Baptist Convention	P	215	30,000	60,000
Jehovah's Witnesses	M	271	20,323	55,000
Nat'l Evang Presby.	P	300	12,000	26,000
Chr & Miss Alliance	P	43	6,514	10,000
Other denominations [55]		10,446	632,000	1,297,000
Total Christians [71]	23,053		5,432,000	10,294,000

Trans-bloc Groupings	pop. %	,000	Ann.Gr.
Evangelical	26.0	2,963	+4.9%
Charismatic	20.8	2,372	+4.8%
Pentecostal	17.9	2,041	+4.9%

Missionaries from Guatemala

P,I,A 255 in 31 agencies to 17 countries: Guatemala 149, Spain 29, USA 22, Mexico 13.

Missionaries to Guatemala

P,I,A 671 in 73 agencies from 18 countries: USA 572, Canada 27, Korea 18.

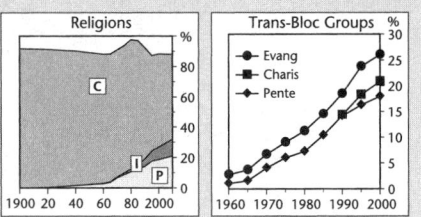

• Answers to Prayer

1 **The signing of the peace accord to end 36 years of war.** Evangelical and Catholic Christians played a significant role in achieving this.

2 **Continued growth in the Evangelical percentage** of the population from 3% (96,000) in 1960 to 25% (2,900,000) in a 2001 survey. The contributing factors being the devastating 1976 earthquake, the violence and pain of war, the effective witness of believers and the large, dedicated force of missionaries.

3 **The growing appreciation of the authorities for the contribution of Evangelicals** to the solution of the social problems — such as street children, substance abuse, homelessness and illiteracy.

• Challenges for Prayer

1 **Recognition of the wrongs committed against the indigenous population** over 500 years, and reconciliation after a generation of war with atrocities on both sides has to be faced and carried through to closure of the past. The part played by the USA in arming the oppressors and turning a blind eye to human rights abuses has only been partially acknowledged. There must be a recognition of the multi-cultural character of the country. Christians have an essential role in this. Pray especially for evangelical leaders from both Mayan and Spanish-speaking communities as they work toward the healing of the nation.

2 **The Catholic Church has declined in influence and numbers**. Defection to Evangelicals and to a revived Mayan religion has been massive. Espousal of liberation theology by some priests and the efforts to discipline the large charismatic renewal movement have further hastened the decline with many charismatics starting new churches or joining evangelical denominations. Pray for new life to permeate the Church, and that charismatics may be rooted in Scripture rather than subjective experience.

3 **Widespread evangelism is by many means** — city crusades, nation-wide efforts, 20 Christian high schools, two Christian television channels, many local Christian radio stations, numerous Christian magazines and newspapers as well as the fervent personal witness of individual Christians. Pray that the fruit may be conserved, the believers matured, and the new generation won for Christ. Shallow professions of faith and an increased rate of backsliding are becoming common as Evangelicals become more 'popular'.

4 **Vision for advance was stimulated by national and international conferences** over the past 20 years. There are now over 17,000 evangelical congregations. Pray that:
a) *Guatemala become the first country* with over 50% Evangelicals within the next 20 years.
b) *Every community might have an evangelical congregation*. There is one town, Almolonga, that is reckoned to be 60% Evangelical.
c) *PLAN 1000 DIAS of COICOM* is the major cooperative thrust of evangelical churches in 2000-2002.

Pray that unity among evangelical leaders might continue to improve and be maintained — an aim of the Evangelical Alliance of Guatemala.

5 **Leadership training is well provided for with six seminaries** (notably the Central American Theological Seminary founded by **CAMI** and now under Guatemalan leadership with 1,700 graduates in 26 countries), numerous denominational Bible schools (including 27 of **AoG**) and over six TEE programmes. TEE was pioneered here by Presbyterians in the 1960s and has now spread worldwide. Pray for humble and effective leaders who will rise above the pettiness, divisions and carnality now all too common in the Body of Christ. Pray also for effective ways of training leaders for rural churches.

6 **Mayan culture has had a re-birth** with the recovery of their ancient civilization (science, mathematics and writings) which emerged during the war. For some, this has led to a resurrection of the old, long-submerged Mayan religion, but to others a blossoming of indigenous Christianity with the many new translations of the Bible in their languages. Churches among the Mam, Quiche, Kekchi and others have grown rapidly and there has been outreach to every tribe. Notable in this have been the Presbyterians, **CAMI**, **CoN**, **UWM** and the Mennonites. Pray for these churches to become mature, effectively-led and a vital contribution to the Church in the nation.

7 **Bible Translation**. **SIL** has made a significant contribution to 38 Amerindian peoples in providing New Testaments for many of them. Work is in progress in a further 17. SIL has made the decision to hand over all remaining translation projects to national believers. Pray for the successful completion and effective use of these translations.

8 **The less reached**:
a) *Amerindian peoples with fewer active believers* — the Pocomam, Pocomchi, Ixil, Jacaltec, Chorti and Upsantec have shown less response to the gospel yet there are active, growing churches among them.
b) *Garifuna (Black Carib)* who are descendants of Africans and Carib Amerindians. The *JESUS* film has been dubbed in their language, and the whole Bible is in preparation.
c) *The Chinese* — there is only one small fellowship of believers known.
d) *Students are a ripe field*; both **CCCI** and GEU(**IFES**) have campus ministries. The GEU has a strong evangelistic ministry and also a weekly radio outreach.
e) *Children in crisis* — 27% of the under-5's are underweight; there are 56,000 war orphans and over 5,000 street children in the capital. The latter have been severely traumatized and persecuted. Pray for local and international ministries seeking to help them.

9 The Guatemalan missionary movement began in 1982 with a vision for the world. In 1984 the *Agencia Misionera Evangélica* (AME) was founded and since then other denominational and international missions have been launched. There are at least three missionary training centres. CONEMM (the National Commission of Mission to the World) coordinates the national missions effort. More than 100 cross-cultural missionaries have been sent out over the last 15 years, and the momentum is building up.

10 Foreign missions have lavished attention on the land. The hard battles in faith of the pioneers sowed today's harvest. Special note must be made of the Presbyterians, AoG, ICFG, CAMI, Brethren and Nazarene pioneers. Much of foreign input is being phased out, but still there are key areas where mission input is important.

11 Christian media:

a) *The JESUS film* has been widely used by many churches. It is available in 9 languages and is in preparation in a further 26.

b) *Christian TV/Radio* programmes are widely available on national and local stations. TWR and HCJB cooperate in using satellite broadcasting to Guatemala.

c) *Audio cassettes* are vital for the many illiterates. GRN has recorded 42 out of the 52 languages. Scripture tapes produced by SIL and others are a key contribution to teaching.

G

Guinea

Republic of Guinea

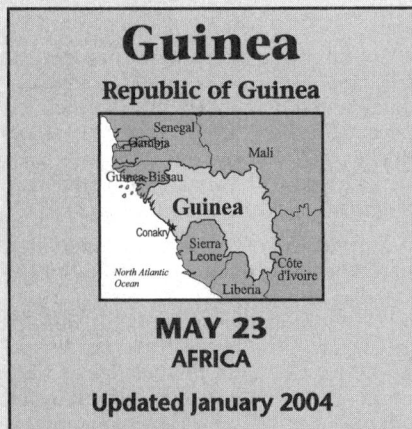

Guinea

MAY 23

AFRICA

Updated January 2004

GEOGRAPHY
Area 245,857 sq.km on Africa's west coast; between Guinea-Bissau and Sierra Leone.

Population		Ann.Gr.	Density
2000	7,430,346	+0.76%	30 per sq. km.
2010	9,427,100	+2.37%	38 per sq. km.
2025	12,496,941	+1.64%	51 per sq. km.

There are also over 600,000 refugees from Liberia and Sierra Leone.

Capital Conakry 1,425,000. **Urbanites** 27%.

PEOPLES
About 40 ethnic groups.
Mande 46%. Largest: Malinke 2,050,000; Susu 905,500; Konyanke 150,000; Yalunka 92,000; Kuranko 62,400; Manya 44,000; Lele 27,500; Mandéni 25,000; Jakanke 22,000; Mikifore 11,000.
West Atlantic 43%. Fulbe(3) 2,810,000; Kissi 316,500; Wassulunke 76,000; Baga(5) 50,000; Landoma

16,000; Konyagui 10,500; Bassari 10,000.
Mande-Fu 11%. Kpelle 380,000; Toma 150,000; Kono 97,000; Mano 71,000.
Other 0.04%. European, Lebanese, etc.

Literacy 36%. **Official language** French. **Major vernacular languages** Fulbe, Malinke, Susu, Kissi, Guerze and Toma. **All languages** 30. **Languages with Scriptures** 1Bi 9NT 2por 7w.i.p.

ECONOMY
Potentially the richest state of former French West Africa with abundant land, fertile soil, water and minerals. Reduced to subsistence and destitution by the folly and corruption of successive regimes. The IMF is establishing some development and recovery plans. **Unemployment** 65%. **HDI** 0.398; 161ˢᵗ/174. **Public debt** 78% of GNP. **Income/person** $560 (2% of USA).

POLITICS
French colony until independence in 1958. President Sékou Touré led the country into a disastrous flirtation with Marxism which virtually destroyed it. The repressive regime was swept away in a military coup in 1984. President Conté has metamorphosed from military coup leader to President of a multi-party democracy, though the validity of the democratic process in successive elections was dubious. A new constitution was introduced in 1991. Though re-elected in 2003, Conté's health is failing.

RELIGION
The former government leaders espoused Marxist rhetoric and a pro-Islamic stance. Christians, especially Catholics, suffered considerably at the hands of the authorities. There is now religious liberty for Christian witness and missionary activity. In recent years, Muslim intolerance has increased.

Religions	Population %	Adherents	Ann.Gr.
Muslim	85.41	6,346,259	+1.0%
Traditional ethnic	9.67	718,514	-3.1%
Christian	4.72	350,712	+4.9%
non-Religious/other	0.20	14,861	+6.7%

Christians	Denom.	Affil.%	,000	Ann.Gr.
Protestant	17	0.96	71	+6.2%
Independent	6	0.25	19	+11.4%
Anglican	1	0.02	1	-0.7%
Catholic	1	1.75	130	+3.4%
Marginal	1	0.04	3	+11.9%
Unaffiliated		1.70	127	n.a.

Churches	MegaBloc	Cong.	Members	Affiliates
Catholic	C	40	75,581	130,000
Evangelical Protestant (EPEG)	P	618	12,400	64,800
New Apostolic	I	50	4,000	12,000
Shekinah	I	50	2,000	5,000
Jehovah's Witnesses	M	25	1,000	3,000
Anglican	A	8	519	1,400
Free Pentecostal	P	3	600	1,200
Lutheran — Missouri Syn	P	40	303	1,000

Seventh-day Adventist	P	3	434	1,000
Eglise Baptiste Oeuvre	I	11	330	1,000
Other denoms [16]		62	1,970	3,843
Total Christians [26]		910	99,137	224,243

Trans-bloc Groupings	pop.%	,000	Ann.Gr.
Evangelical	1.0	77	+7.0%
Charismatic	0.5	38	+8.4%
Pentecostal	0.0	3	+9.9%

Missionaries from Guinea
P,I,A 27 in 3 agencies — 24 in Guinea.

Missionaries to Guinea
P,I,A 320 in 32 agencies from 19 countries. USA 153, Switzerland 35, Côte d'Ivoire 32, Canada 25.

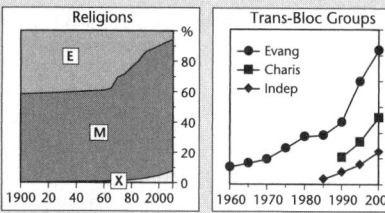

• Answers to Prayer

1 Praise God for the major improvements in the country since 1984:

a) Political and economic liberalization, but pray for stability, political leaders who place national interests above their own, and wisdom regarding IMF development plans.

b) Complete religious freedom, a reaction to the Marxist-Muslim years of terror which has made Muslims more receptive to Christianity. The liberty is being progressively eroded, however, especially in major towns outside the forest region.

c) The presence of more than 20 evangelical missions and the intensification of evangelism to the unreached — out of 30 main people groups, only 10 have no church planting effort, and of these, only the Wassulunke and Manya are larger than 30,000. The increase in work among the Muslim peoples is particularly encouraging.

2 Mission awareness has grown in the last few years. There is a growing expectancy among believers for an abundant harvest, and increased activity toward this end. The Kissi and Toma are now sending Christian workers to other tribes; the first missionary training course for Guineans was held in 1998. Pray that this increase of missions vision may continue and spread to other tribes.

• Challenges for Prayer

1 The Christian population is still a small minority, and concentrated in Conakry and the southeast forests. It is almost entirely Kissi, Kpelle and Toma in composition. The Evangelical Protestant Church (EPEG) — affiliated with the **CMA**, the **AoG**, and Shekinah churches have all more than doubled in the last decade. But outward growth has not been accompanied by revival. Pray that the Holy Spirit might transform individuals, families and tribes, making them models for a truly African Christian lifestyle.

2 Leadership training for pastors and laymen is a great need. Guinea has three Bible Schools, two run by the EPEG/**CMA**, and one by the **AoG**. Four leadership training schools for laymen have been set up for the Kissi, Toma, and Kpelle churches by the Evangelical Church in collaboration with the **CMA** and **AME**. **PAOC** continue with an ICI TEE programme, as the Evangelical Church/**CMA** begin one of their own. Despite all of this, there is still an overall lack of leaders in most areas, and further church growth intensifies this problem. Ask God to raise up more godly national leaders, who are in turn able to train others.

3 **Guinea is one of the least evangelized countries in Black Africa.** Despite the increase in missionary activity, most peoples are still a pioneer challenge, mostly Muslims with strong animistic elements. The three dominant peoples are all strongly Muslim. The believers from these groups are often unable to break free of their Muslim contexts to live openly as Christians. Pray for their courage and boldness. While the numbers of converts from these groups has grown to a steady trickle, much prayer is required before a major breakthrough is seen. Pray especially for these:

a) *Malinke.* **SIM** have them as their primary focus in Guinea; radio ministry in the past has provided a solid foundation for evangelism. **CMA** and the EPEG also have an outreach to the Malinke. The first Malinke Church with a Malinke pastor has been planted, and other groups meet in villages.

b) *Fulbe or Futa Jalon,* who are strongly Muslim and known as the custodians of Islam throughout West Africa. Many groups are recognizing their great spiritual need and strategic role in the region. Through the work of **CRWM, CMA, Calvary Ministries, WEC, SBC, AoG** and the Swiss AME/Mission Philafricaine, there are a small but growing number of believers. It is hard for new believers to break free from the societal and spiritual bonds of Islam. Radio broadcasts, Bible portions, and mission workers all help to reach the Fulbe. In recent years, three Fulbe churches with 100 believers have been planted.

c) *Susu.* Apart from the eight rather nominal Anglican congregations on offshore islands and in Conakry, there are a few believers through the witness of **CMA, Calvary Ministries, WEC,** Open Bible Standard Mission, the Nigerian Shekinah Mission and the **IMB-SBC.** The **CMA** has established a Susu church in Conakry, and the city is targeted for a cell church movement. There are also Susu believers in the southern interior. Three new Susu churches have been planted in recent years with over 100 believers, but the breakthrough has yet to come.

4 **Young peoples' ministry is vital in Guinea,** since 50% of the population is 16 or younger. **CCC, IFES,** and **YWAM** all have ministry in the country. Christian student groups operate all three universities, several colleges, and are expanding into several high schools. **Calvary Ministries** runs a youth centre in Conakry and **WEC** plans to open one there. Pray for the Spirit to draw these younger Guineans to Christ.

5 **There are still 18 peoples without missionaries.** They comprise about 5% of the population. Their smaller numbers often means they are the last to be evangelized.

a) *The Muslim Wassulunke* (76,000), of Fulbe origin. Living in eastern Guinea, they are closed to outside influence. Pray that God might open their society and hearts to the gospel. There is one tiny church with a missionary pastor among them.

b) *The Manya* live amongst the more Christianized Toma, but they have generally been neglected in outreach. A **GRN** team has made cassettes for their language — these will be primary tools for reaching them. A Toma pastor has been sent to reach them.

c) *The Mandéni, Tukulor, Jakanke, Fulacunda, and several Baga subgroups* have hardly any believers and no missionaries. **NTM** has sent a missionary family to the Jakanke; these and several other groups need specific outreach. Pray for Christians from related groups to share Jesus with them.

d) *The more than 600,000 refugees* from civil strife in Liberia and Sierra Leone. They are proving to be responsive to the gospel and missionary work (EPEG/**CMA**), but a holistic approach is obviously vital to these destitute people. Their integration into already existing churches in their areas is also a challenge.

6 **Missions.** For years the only Protestant missionaries were **CMA** (1919-1952). In 1967 all Catholic and most Protestant missionaries were expelled. Only 11 **CMA** missionaries were permitted to remain. Since 1981, EPEG/**CMA** have welcomed new evangelical agencies. Most work in close cooperation as members of the *Association des Eglises et Missions Evangéliques en Guinée.* Pray for close fellowship between missions and also with the national churches. Pray also for courage, stamina and great faith for the growing missionary force in a land of rugged living conditions and poor communications, and also for more new missionary pioneers to be called. Pray that the Lord may call more missionaries, in particular to the Muslim groups in the country. Also pray that Guinean believers may catch the vision of evangelizing the unreached in their own nation. Major missions are **NTM** (60), **CMA** (34), **AME** (21), **PBT** (20), **SIM** (20), **CRWM** (13), **IMB-SBC** (12), **AoG** (11), **Calvary Ministries** and **WEC** (9), MERN (8), and **YWAM** (7).

7 **Help ministries:**

a) **Cassette ministry** is important in this multi-lingual land. **GRI** has made recordings in 21 languages, but several old recordings must be redone. This was being done by a Sierra Leone team and is continuing under a Guinean committee.

b) **Literature is a challenge**. There are three Christian bookstores, but literacy training is needed to make use of both Christian literature and the Bible. The reading room concept has been fruitfully implemented by the **CMA, IMB-SBC, MERN, SIM, Calvary Ministries** and **WEC** as a neutral location where both converts and seekers can come to study, learn and fellowship.

c) **Bible translation** is going to be one of the major missionary tasks for years to come. Nine languages have New Testaments, including Fulbe, Susu, Kissi, Kpelle and Toma. Eleven other languages may need translation teams. Translation or revision work is in progress in eleven languages.

d) **The JESUS film** also has great potential in evangelizing Guinea. Perhaps half of the country has seen the film, as it has been translated into 10 languages, and is in production for six more. Pray for a lasting impact through this film.

G

Guinea-Bissau
Republic of Guinea-Bissau

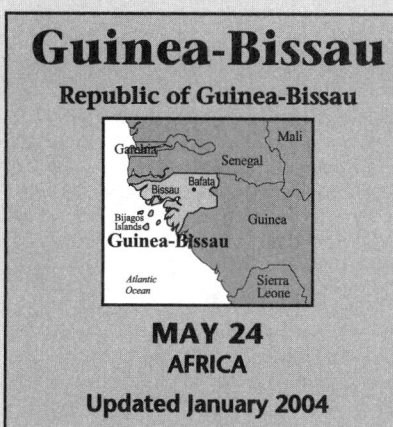

MAY 24
AFRICA
Updated January 2004

GEOGRAPHY
Area 36,125 sq.km. Coastal state wedged between Senegal and Guinea.

Population	Ann.Gr.	Density
2000	1,213,111	+2.24%	34 per sq. km.
2010	1,480,638	+1.93%	41 per sq. km.
2025	1,946,020	+1.82%	54 per sq. km.

Capital Bissau 223,000. **Urbanites** 30%.

PEOPLES
Over 27 ethnic groups.
West Atlantic (15 groups) 56.5%. Balanta 300,000; Manjako 113,000; Papel 109,000; Mankanya 43,000; Beafada 39,000; Bijago 24,500; Jola/Felupe 17,000, Nalu 10,800.
Fulbe (5 groups) 25.4%. 308,000.
Mande (5 groups) 14.9%. Mandingo (Maninka or Mandinga) 166,500; Sarakole 5,500; Susu 4,000.
Other 3.2%. Creole, Cape Verdians, Guineans, Europeans.

Literacy 25%. **Official language** Portuguese. **National language** Portuguese Creole, spoken by as many as 60% of the population. **All languages** 27. **Languages with Scriptures** 2Bi 5NT 3por 6 w.i.p.

ECONOMY
Little developed in colonial times, devastated by the long war of independence, and inhibited by subsequent socialist policies. One of the world's poorest countries, but in the past decade there has been a notable increase in commerce in the country. The main exports are fish, cashew nuts and tropical hardwoods. **HDI** 0.343; 168th/174. **Public debt** 317% of GNP. **Income/person** $250 (0.9% of USA).

POLITICS
Independent of Portugal in 1974. One-party revolutionary government until 1994, when multi-party elections took place. In 1998 a military uprising occurred against the President, which led to a new government being elected in 2000, but this did not settle the underlying national differences. A further coup in 2003 opened up the way for new elections in mid-2004.

RELIGION
Under Portuguese rule the Catholic Church functioned almost as an arm of the colonial government, and Evangelicals were forbidden or discriminated against. Since independence, the measure of freedom for Christian activities has steadily increased. Until 1990 only one Protestant mission (WEC) was allowed in the country, but since then several more have entered. There is currently freedom of religion for all groups, despite some low-level persecution of converts. There is significant syncretism between Islam or Catholicism and African traditional religions, such that it is often difficult to give accurate figures.

Religions	Population %	Adherents	Ann.Gr.
Muslim	43.00	521,638	+2.7%
Traditional ethnic	41.00	497,376	+1.6%
Christian	14.32	173,717	+2.7%
non-Religious/other	1.68	20,380	+3.2%

Christians	Denom.	Affil.%	,000	Ann.Gr.
Protestant	4	0.90	11	+1.9%
Independent	7	0.08	1	+14.9%
Catholic	1	11.71	142	+2.5%
Marginal	2	0.07	1	+17.9%
Unaffiliated		1.56	19	n.a.

Churches	MegaBloc	Cong.	Members	Affiliates
Catholic	C	30	85,030	142,000
Evangelical Ch of GB	P	105	6,000	9,500
Assemblies of God	P	6	200	680
Seventh-day Adventist	P	2	313	650
New Apostolic	M	5	300	500
Jehovah's Witnesses	M	1	111	300
Other denominations [8]		18	500	1,000
Total Christians [14]		**167**	**92,500**	**154,700**

Trans-bloc Groupings	pop. %	,000	Ann.Gr.
Evangelical	1.1	13	+2.6%
Charismatic	0.7	8	+2.8%
Pentecostal	0.1	1	-4.3%

Missionaries from Guinea-Bissau
P,I,A 16 in 3 agencies to 3 countries.

Missionaries to Guinea-Bissau
P,I,A 150 in 28 agencies from 20 countries: Brazil 67, USA 17, Nigeria 13, UK 11.

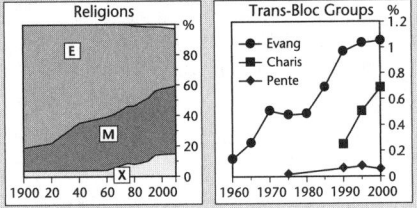

• Answers to Prayer

1 **Praise the Lord for the present receptivity to the gospel.** Unlike some neighbouring countries, Guinea-Bissau enjoys religious freedom and is open to evangelism. During the civil war of 1998-99 evangelical Christians played an important part in distributing food in Bissau and in the south. They also assisted with transport when people were fleeing Bissau. Evangelical and Catholic leaders joined together in attempting to bring reconciliation between the warring factions. The Church is therefore viewed with a good deal of respect by the government. Pray that the Church might continue to give a lead in showing practical love and compassion and in encouraging peace and reconciliation.

2 **Praise the Lord that He used the civil strife** for redemptive purposes. Due to the recent war, the majority of Christians in Bissau were forced to flee to the interior. There they took the opportunity to evangelize and preach the Bible. Many people believed and many churches were planted as a result. Pray that these new Christians might receive good teaching and be built up in their faith.

• Challenges for Prayer

1 **Leadership in the evangelical churches** is mature, with a real vision for evangelism and missions. There are still, however, many churches in the interior without any pastor. If they do have a pastor, he is often responsible for as many as 10 other congregations as well. Pray for others to be called to the ministry. Pray also for the Bible Institute, run by the Evangelical Church to train indigenous pastors. Ask the Lord for more national teachers, and that the costs of the Institute and support for the students would be increasingly met by national believers.

2 **Praise the Lord for an increase in the number of missionaries** in the country, but there are still few actually concentrating on reaching the unevangelized. **WEC** has 38 workers committed to Guinea-Bissau, working at 8 centres among 9 peoples. Also involved are **AoG** (12), Kairos (11) and **YWAM** (8, mostly short-term). Pray for reinforcements and for the health and safety of those already on the field. Not only are living conditions tough, but they are involved in a spiritual battle.

3 **The national church is strongest among the Balanta and Papel**, then the Bijago and Manjako peoples. There are a small number of Christians among the other animist and Muslim peoples. Pray that the national church might catch a missions vision, and receive the courage and gifts to be able to reach out to these groups with the gospel.

4 **The unreached for whom prayer is needed:**

a) *The Muslim Fulbe and Mandingo.* These are large dominant peoples in many West African countries with a rich history and much influence. They are largely responsible for bringing Islam to Guinea-Bissau; may they become so for the spread of the good news. The Mandingos tend to be more closed to the gospel than the Fulbe, so that while there are now some Fulbe fellowships in Bafata and the north east, there are only a handful of scattered Mandingo believers.

b) *Smaller Muslim peoples.* The Beafada, Susu, Nalu, Sarakole, Jakanka, Pajadinka and Bad-yara have had very little, if any, work concentrated on them using their language and culture. Pray for ministry among them, and that fruit might be forthcoming.

c) *Traditional religion peoples.* Praise the Lord that there are Christians from amongst the Felupe, Bayote, Mankanya and Mansoanka. Pray that these Christians might see their responsibility to reach out to their own. Pray also for the gospel to reach the other small, and often overlooked, peoples.

5 **There is one Christian bookshop in the capital** owned by a national believer. In an oral and largely illiterate society, books are not seen as a priority especially when they are expensive. Pray for the owner of the bookshop to have wisdom in choosing the right materials to stock. Pray also that national authors would write books appropriate and beneficial to Guinea-Bissau Christians.

G

6 **The publishing of the whole Bible in Portuguese Creole** in 1999 was an important point in the history of the Church in Guinea-Bissau. There are also New Testaments in Papel, Bijago, Fulbe and Mandingo, but they are not widely used. Pray for wisdom and vision in knowing how best to make use of these translations in oral societies. Pray for the continued translation work of the Balanta and Manjako NT.

7 **Church primary schools** have been established by the Evangelical Churches together with some missions (**WEC**, Kairos and **YWAM**). These meet a real need where the state schools are not coping. Pray that these schools may not only provide good education, but also be places where the gospel is taught and children receive Christ.

8 Media ministry:

a) *A Christian radio programme* is broadcast every week on the national radio. Pray for the producers to be able to improve its quality and for continued permission to broadcast. Pray for a Fulbe Christian radio station which is being prepared in the Bafata area.

b) *The cassette ministry has great potential* in a largely oral society. The Creole NT has recently been recorded by **The Bible Society** and Horizons. Pray that it will be well used.

c) *The JESUS film is now available* in Creole, Fulbe and Mandingo, and is being used widely in evangelism. Pray that it might be used wisely and bear much fruit.

Guyana
Cooperative Republic of Guyana

MAY 25
LATIN AMERICA

 **POLITICS**
Dutch rule 1750-1814, then British rule to independence in 1966. Both main political parties were Marxist in orientation but remain bitterly divided on racial lines. The Afro-Guyanese PM Party held power until ousted in an election in 1992. It was replaced by a largely Indo-Guyanese government which continued to slowly liberalize the economy despite its leader's continued allegiance to Marxism. Racial tension and confrontations continue. Venezuela to the west and Suriname to the east both lay claim to large parts of Guyana, which hinders economic development.

RELIGION
Atheism promoted until 1985, with considerable tensions between the government and the main churches. A secular state with full religious freedom since then.

Religions	Population %	Adherents	Ann.Gr.
Christian	43.57	375,283	+0.3%
Hindu	33.00	284,240	+0.1%
non-Religious/other	10.00	86,133	+5.3%
Muslim	8.70	74,936	+1.0%
Spiritist/Animist	4.10	35,315	+0.3%
Baha'i	0.40	3,445	+3.5%
Buddhist/Chinese	0.23	1,981	+1.6%

Christians	Denom.	Affil.%	,000	Ann.Gr.
Protestant	37	18.93	163	+0.7%
Independent	26	8.88	76	+7.3%
Anglican	1	7.89	68	-1.4%
Catholic	1	10.22	88	+0.2%
Orthodox	1	0.93	8	-0.5%
Marginal	10	1.74	15	+0.9%
Unaffiliated		0.66	6	n.a.
Doubly affiliated		*-5.68*	*-49*	*n.a.*

Churches	MegaBloc	Cong.	Members	Affiliates
Catholic	C	30	46,561	88,000
Anglican	A	160	17,000	68,000
Seventh-day Adventist	P	114	35,635	60,000
Full Gospel Fellowship	I	150	14,000	40,000
Assemblies of God	P	72	10,087	21,443
N T Church of God	P	51	5,419	12,500
Lutheran	P	50	5,500	11,000
Methodist (MCCA)	P	44	3,500	10,500
Ethiopian Orthodox	O	30	5,400	8,000
Jehovah's Witnesses	M	36	2,073	8,000
Presbytery of Guyana	P	25	3,250	5,600
Ch of the Nazarene	P	45	3,600	5,000
Guyana Congr Union	P	46	2,300	4,752
Baptist Coop Conv	P	31	2,229	4,000
Christian Brethren	P	34	2,600	4,000
Presby Ch of Guyana	P	44	2,000	3,000
Wesleyan	P	34	1,900	3,000
New Apostolic	I	6	778	1,400
Other denoms [60]		872	30,000	60,400
Doubly affiliated			*-23,333*	*-49,000*
Total Christians [78]		1,874	170,500	369,600

GEOGRAPHY
Area 215,000 sq.km. On north coast of South America. A developed coastal strip with underdeveloped, forested interior.

Population		Ann.Gr.	Density
2000	861,334	+0.75%	4 per sq. km.
2010	922,942	+0.74%	4 per sq. km.
2025	1,044,669	+0.83%	5 per sq. km.

About 90% live on the coast.
Capital Georgetown 300,000. **Urbanites** 36%.

PEOPLES
Colonial importation of labour for the sugar industry has created the present racial diversity and political tensions.
South Asian 49.4%. Predominantly rural farmers from the Indian sub-continent.
African/Eurafrican 42.7%. Dominant in government, civil service and in urban areas.
Amerindian 6.8%. The majority live in the sparsely inhabited interior. Main groups:
  Carib 3.7%. 5 tribes, largest: Akwaio 3,400; Patamona 3,400; Macushi 1,400; Waiwai 1,000; Carib 520; Arecuna 500.
  Arawak 1.4%. 4 tribes, largest: Arawak 4,800; Wapishana 3,700.
  Other 1.7%.
European/Asian 1.1%. Portuguese 6,000; Chinese 5,000; British 2,000.

Literacy 98.6%. **Official languages** English; Creole used by 90% of the population. **All languages** 13. **Languages with Scriptures** 1Bi 2NT 4por 6w.i.p.

ECONOMY
Mainstays are sugar, rice, forest products and minerals. A 20-year flirtation with Marxist economics impoverished the country despite its potential. Living standards plummeted, foreign investment dried up and many of the better-educated left the country. Since 1992 there has been a gradual, but steady improvement. **HDI** 0.701; 99th/174. **Public debt** 199% of GNP. **Income/person** $800 (2.5% of USA).

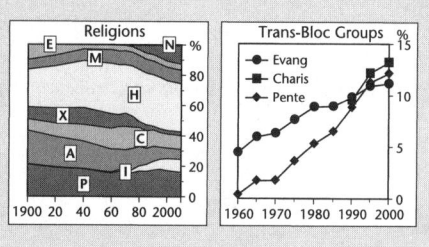

Trans-bloc Groupings pop.%	,000	Ann.Gr.
Evangelical	11.1	96	+5.5%
Charismatic	13.2	114	+4.6%
Pentecostal	12.1	104	+5.0%

Missionaries from Guyana
P,I,A 21 in 6 agencies; Guyana 18.

Missionaries to Guyana
P,I,A 87 in 22 agencies from 10 countries: USA 66, Canada 7.

• Answers to Prayer

1 **Complete religious freedom** since the waning of atheistic rhetoric in the 1980s.

2 **Increased responsiveness** to the gospel among rural Indo-Guyanans.

3 **Christian leaders** and Christians are having greater unity and unprecedented influence at every level of society.

• Challenges for Prayer

1 **Guyana's integrity as a state is threatened** by the vociferous demands from Venezuela and Suriname on 70% of its land area and by inter-racial tensions internally. A new constitution is being prepared that is aimed at protecting human rights and promoting communal harmony. Pray that with this both the present and future governments may roll back decades of societal polarization and bring about a society that is fair to all its citizens and gives hope for the future.

2 **There is a vital, vibrant, growing evangelical witness** and Evangelicals are found in all levels of society. Pentecostal, charismatic and evangelical denominations and fellowships have multiplied — notably the indigenous Full Gospel Fellowship, as well as the **AoG** and Baptists. Many of these have multi-racial congregations — the only bridge in a divided society. Pray for all believers to demonstrate the power of the gospel in their unity, ethical rectitude and divine boldness.

3 **Most of the Afro-Guyanans** are Christian, but nominalism in many denominations is widespread, stable two-parent families rare (a legacy of the time of slavery) and syncretistic and deviant beliefs common (Obeah spiritism and witchcraft, Rastafarianism and foreign sects). Pray for life-changing renewal and revival to touch every denomination.

4 **The Indo-Guyanan** community is about 65% Hindu, 18% Muslim and 15% Christian. Pray specifically for:

a) *The many Hindu rural communities* and for their evangelization.

b) *The nearly 90,000 Muslims* — divided between the Urdu-speaking older generation and the younger generation with ties to the Arab world and Islamist revivalism. A few have become Christians — some are now Christian leaders in Guyana.

5 **The Amerindian peoples** are largely Christianized and predominantly Catholic but many are now becoming Pentecostals through the ministry of **AoG**, Church of God and the Full Gospel Fellowship. The Wesleyan Church ministers among the Patamona and Akwaio, but results have been meagre. The **UFM** work in the south among the Waiwai, Macushi and Wapishana has resulted in a growing, missionary-minded church. The Scriptures are being translated in Wapishana and Machusi by **UFM** workers and in Arawak, Akwaio and Carib by **SIL** translators. Pray for the development of mature churches and leadership that can retain their cultural identity and still survive the impact of modernity. Drug-resistant malaria has become a serious problem — pray for the protection of Christian workers and the people.

6 **Ministry among young people** is vital for the development of family life and stability in society. Hopes for the future and for employment are low. AIDS is a growing menace with 3.1% of 15-49 year-olds infected. **IFES** has an extensive ministry with 8 full-time staff and 200 groups with some 40,000 young people at primary, secondary and tertiary levels.

7 **Christian missions** have deeply impacted society for good. Missionary numbers have increased again with the ending of restrictions. The majority are involved in church planting, Bible translation, leadership training and specialist media ministries. Major missions: **IMB-SBC** (11 workers), **UFM** (10), **BMM** (8), **YWAM** (5).

8 **Christian Media Ministries** for prayer:

a) *CLC* has a key Christian bookstore.
b) *EHC* has done two nation-wide distributions of Christian literature. A third is planned.
c) *The JESUS film* is extensively used in English and Hindi, but is needed in Creole.

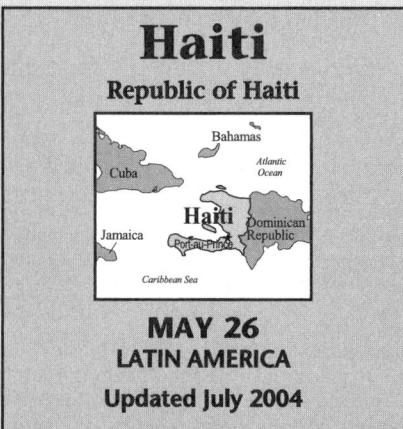

Haiti

Republic of Haiti

MAY 26
LATIN AMERICA
Updated July 2004

GEOGRAPHY
Area 27,400 sq.km. Western third of the island of Hispaniola; shared with the Dominican Republic.

Population		Ann.Gr.	Density
2000	8,222,025	+1.69%	300 per sq. km.
2010	9,669,191	+1.62%	353 per sq. km.
2025	11,988,232	+1.37%	438 per sq. km.

One of the most densely populated countries in the Americas. Many Haitians have fled or emigrated to the USA.

Capital Port-au-Prince 1,700,000. **Urbanites** 37%.

PEOPLES
Afro-Caribbean 90%.
Mulatto (Eurafrican) 9.9%.
Euro-American 0.1%.

Literacy 48%. Functional literacy may be as low as 20%. **Official language** French (10% speak it). **Common language** Haitian Creole.

ECONOMY
The poorest state in the Western hemisphere, aggravated by over-population, soil erosion, pollution, drought and famine. The rapid rise of drug abuse and spread of AIDS has further harmed the country. The lack of a viable govern-ment since 1994 has worsened the situation. The major sources of income are remittances from expatriate Haitians and foreign aid. Many Haitians are becoming economic refugees. **Unemployment** 50-70%; 75% live in abject poverty. **HDI** 0.430; 152nd/174. **Public debt** 31% of GNP. **Income/person** $310 (1.2% of USA).

POLITICS
A slave revolt against the French in 1804 created the first black republic in the world. A troubled history of bloodshed and dictatorships since then. The deposing of the Duvaliers in 1986 ended a particularly brutal dictatorship. A succession of coups and military governments aborted all attempts at introducing democracy. The coup in 1991, in response to increasing anarchy, led to the US intervention in 1994. The elected President Aristide subsequently subverted the democratic process to retain power. He was ousted in February 2004 by rebels and US intervention. The country remains unsettled with an interim government and a UN-led peace-keeping force.

RELIGION
The Roman Catholic Church's role as the State Church ended in 1987. An estimated 75% of Catholics are also actively involved in Voodoo, a development of West African spiritism and witchcraft. In 2003 Voodoo was declared a national religion. There is freedom of religion.

Religions	Population %	Adherents	Ann.Gr.
Christian	95.50	7,852,034	+1.6%
Spiritist/Voodoo	2.50	205,551	+2.5%
non-Religious/other	1.80	147,996	+4.1%
Baha'i	0.20	16,444	+1.7%

Christians	Denom.	Affil.%	,000	Ann.Gr.
Protestant	29	20.80	1,709	+3.0%
Independent	237	4.06	334	+4.6%
Anglican	1	1.28	105	+0.4%
Catholic	1	75.41	6,200	+0.3%
Marginal	2	0.81	67	+8.2%
Unaffiliated		7.14	587	n.a.
Doubly affiliated		*-14.00*	*-1,150*	*n.a.*

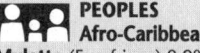

Churches	MegaBloc	Cong.	Members	Affiliates
Catholic	C	240	3,604,651	6,200,000
Seventh-day Adventist	P	306	213,938	400,000
Baptist Convention	P	453	84,600	300,000
Ch of the Nazarene	P	480	78,000	260,000
NT Church of God	P	307	70,000	140,000
Episcopal	A	367	31,532	105,000
Ev Bapt Ch of S. Haiti	P	407	39,862	100,577
Cons Baptist Mission	P	325	17,646	70,000
Jehovah's Witnesses	M	250	14,817	60,000
Faith Holiness Miss	P	280	15,000	55,000
Ch of God of Prophecy	P	310	22,000	45,000
Assemblies of God	P	220	30,000	42,000
United Pentecostal	P	429	30,000	40,000
Evang Baptist Miss	P	420	19,000	38,000
Chr Methodist Episc.	P	169	22,000	36,740
Free Methodist	P	58	15,000	32,000
Church of God (And)	P	160	10,329	22,000
Evangelical Ch of Haiti	P	20	3,000	12,000
Evangelical Lutheran	P	120	3,500	12,000
Other denoms [250]		3,114	203,500	444,500
Doubly affiliated			-668,600	-1,150,000
Total Christians [269]		8,545	3,862,000	7,265,000

Trans-bloc Groupings	pop. %	,000	Ann.Gr.
Evangelical	22.2	1,827	+3.1%
Charismatic	7.6	626	+3.7%
Pentecostal	5.8	477	+3.5%

Missionaries from Haiti
P,I,A 19 in 7 agencies to 6 countries; Haiti 13.

Missionaries to Haiti
P,I,A 449 in 76 agencies from 13 countries: USA 373, Canada 32, France 21.

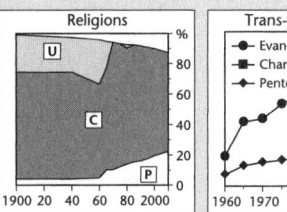

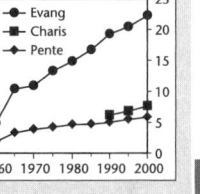

• Answers to Prayer

1 **Evangelical Christians** have increasingly and openly stood against voodooism and the Satanic dedication of the country in 1791 by the slaves plotting revolt against the French. Satan was seen to be opposed to the Christian religion of their oppressors. Vision Haiti in 1997, with a widely supported prayer and fasting movement, has been seen by many as a turning point in the ending of this curse.

• Challenges for Prayer

1 **Haiti needs to be freed from the bondages of its past.** The Spanish genocide against the indigenous Arawakans, the cruel slavery instituted and maintained by the Spanish and then the French are a tragic background. The tyrannies, cruelties and use of voodoo as a means of control by the black elite have fostered a spirit of evil which permeates every level of society. More recent interventions — especially by the USA — have not improved the lot of the people. Pray that:
a) *The powerful spirits that underly voodooism* might be bound in the name of Jesus and that this demonic system no longer be seen as Haiti's 'cultural heritage'.
b) *This nation might find true liberty* and social change through the power of the gospel.

2 **Haiti needs godly leaders** that put first the good of the nation and the addressing of its massive problems. Two centuries of misrule, tyranny and recent flawed democratic attempts have brought hopelessness and despair. The population, crime, poverty, and chaos grow unchecked. Many have looked for hope in drugs or sailing a leaky boat to surrounding lands. Pray that men and women may be raised up who will reverse these trends and bring justice, as well as economic and spiritual betterment to Haiti.

3 **The Catholic Church** is in crisis with its credibility lost and voodooism unchallenged. It is heavily dependent on foreign funds and priests. There is little sign of any effective renewal movements.

4 **The steady growth of Protestant churches** in the difficult economic and spiritual climate is cause for praise. Over 22% of the population is Evangelical (some would reckon this is nearer 30%). This has been the result of widespread evangelism, deep commitment to social development and the evident power of Jesus over Satan. Yet there are areas for concern:
a) *The rural poor* have responded more than the urban elite. Illiteracy, marginalization in society and lack of adequate teaching have all prevented Evangelicals from impacting the structures of society.

b) **Church-mission relationships** have often been poor and this has diverted energies from the real battle. The manifest poverty of the people and relative affluence of missionaries are barriers to fellowship.

c) **The fragmentation of denominations** on issues of personality, charismatic growth and liberation theology have confused and divided Christians. The Protestant Federation (formed in 1986) and the Council of Evangelical Churches are giving Protestant Christians a platform for speaking with one voice to the government, and for cooperation in social, evangelistic and prayer initiatives.

5 **Leadership training** is too limited because of the poverty of the churches. A rigid traditionalism of imported theologies and systems is widespread. Many pastors have had little training, some being barely literate. Pray for the 20 or so Bible schools/seminaries and the many TEE programmes that seek to meet the need. Pray for Haitian leaders to be men of faith and spiritual authority who are not diverted by material inducements.

6 **Desperate physical and social needs** have attracted a wide range of Christian community development agencies such as **WVI**, **TEAR Fund**, World Concern, the Mennonites and many others. Sensitivity and wisdom are needed to preserve the indigeneity, integrity and independence of the churches and their leaders. Pray that every expression of Christian concern in these medical, agricultural, social and literacy programmes may draw folk to the Saviour, and provide long-term benefit that is self-sustaining.

7 **The less evangelized** sections of the population:

a) **The Mulatto elite** are wealthy, French-orientated and isolated from the majority. Few have realized the need for a personal faith.

b) **The youth.** Some are frustrated by a perceived passivity of the Church, though some churches have vigorous youth programmes with many seeking the Lord. There are 28 GBEUH(**IFES**) groups on university campuses — pray that they might bear effective witness.

c) **Refugees** have fled by boat in their thousands — to USA, Cuba, Bahamas and elsewhere. Their destitution and need have made them spiritually receptive. A number of missions (**WT**, **OMS**, **CoN**, Free Methodist and others) have sought to minister to them in Florida and the Bahamas. There are large Haitian communities in cities such as Toronto, Canada (70,000).

8 **Missions** continue to play a significant, but increasingly supportive role. The political unrest, confrontation with the USA, and also threats and violence against missionaries have forced many to leave. Pray for these servants of the Lord, their witness and example in times of stress, and that they may contribute to the maturing of the church. The larger missions are: Baptists (8 agencies — 48 missionaries), **UFM** (41), Church of Christ (29), Mennonites (22), **OMS** (17), **WT** (15), **YWAM** (12), Wesleyan Church (11), **CoN** (8).

9 **Christian Ministries**:

a) **The Bible Society** published the Creole Bible in 1986. This has had a significant impact on the understanding and application of God's Word. Pray that the Church may be transformed and revived. Pray also for effective literacy programmes to be maintained.

b) **Christian broadcasting** is an effective tool. A high proportion of the population listens to *Radio Lumière*'s five stations in the south and centre (Evangelical Baptist Church of South Haiti [**WT**]) and 4VEH in the north [**OMS**]. **TWR** broadcasts innovative programmes to Haitian children. Pray for wisdom and safety for staff and producers in the tense political conditions where a wrong word could have dire consequences.

c) **The JESUS film** has been widely shown in French and Creole. Pray for its long-term impact in a largely illiterate society.

Holy See

Vatican City State

Italy
Rome
Holy See
(Vatican City State)
Mediterranean Sea

MAY 26
EUROPE

Population		Ann.Gr.	Density
2000	750	+0.00%	150 per sq. km.
2010	750	+0.00%	150 per sq. km.
2025	750	+0.00%	150 per sq. km.

Almost entirely comprised of members of the global Catholic hierarchy.

POLITICS
The Pope is the Head of State as well as leader of the world's 1.1 billion Catholics.

RELIGION

Religions	Population %	Adherents	Ann.Gr.
Christian	100.00	750	+0.0%

Christians	Denom.	Affil. %	,000	Ann.Gr.
Catholic	1	100.00	1	+0.0%

Churches	MegaBloc	Cong.	Members	Affiliates
Catholic	C	65	750	750

Trans-bloc Groupings	pop.%	,000	Ann.Gr.
Charismatic	30.0	0	+0.0%

GEOGRAPHY
Area 0.5 sq.km. The world's smallest state; an enclave in the heart of the city of Rome, the last remaining vestige of the once-considerable papal domains in central Italy.

H

• Challenges for Prayer

1 **The Pope** is the head of the largest religious body on earth. He exercises an enormous influence within and beyond the Roman Catholic Church. Pray that elections to this position may be of the right man for the time and bring about the radical changes required.

2 **The Roman Catholic Church is going through a time of turmoil and change**. There are many doctrines and emphases that divide this increasingly diverse body — the place of the Bible, ecumenism, the celibacy of the priesthood, the position of women. Pray that the increasing use of the Bible may mould lives, doctrines and structures and affect the 1.1 billion Catholics in the world.

3 **The loss of credibility and serious decline in vocations** (of priests, monks and nuns) will force many changes on the Church of the 21st Century.

4 **Spiritual renewal.** Catholic charismatic renewal has had an impact far beyond the 100 million or so who are, or have been, involved. A large proportion of the Catholic missionary force is charismatic. The Evangelical Catholic movement has been gaining in influence and numbers with its more biblical interpretation of faith. Pray that millions of nominal Catholics may come to a warm, living faith in the Lord Jesus. Pray that they may be a bridge to like-minded Christians in other denominations and not lose their spiritual dynamism by being absorbed and neutralized by the system.

Honduras
Republic of Honduras

MAY 27
LATIN AMERICA

GEOGRAPHY
Area 112,088 sq.km. A mountainous land with rainforests and fertile coastal plains on the Caribbean and Pacific coasts.

Population	Ann.Gr.	Density
2000	6,485,445	+2.78%	58 per sq. km.
2010	8,202,633	+2.23%	73 per sq. km.
2025	10,656,044	+1.56%	95 per sq. km.

Capital Tegucigalpa 813,900. **Urbanites** 43%.

PEOPLES
Spanish-culture 89.7%.
Mestizo(Ladino) 5,668,000; Afro-American 130,000; White 120,000.
Amerindians 8.1%. Eight peoples whose languages are rapidly disappearing. Largest: Non-tribal (mainly Lenca origin) 266,000; Lenca 76,000; Garifuna (Black Carib) 39,000; Miskito 19,000; Chorti 12,000; Sumo 1,000.
English-speaking 1.2%. Afro-Caribbean 65,000; US/British 8,000.
Other 1%. Arab 50,000; Chinese 5,000; Armenian 1,300; Turk 1,100.

Literacy 73%. **Official language** Spanish. **Other languages** English on the northern coast. **All languages** 9. **Languages with Scriptures** 2Bi 3NT 1w.i.p.

ECONOMY
The broken terrain and unequal distribution of land and wealth have hindered development. Insensitive exploitation by multinationals and corruption of politicians have also helped to keep Honduras poor. The devastating super-hurricane 'Mitch' in 1998 was a major setback with 60% of the country's infrastructure destroyed. Many decades will be needed to recover from it. Unemployment 40%. **HDI** 0.641; 114th/174. **Public debt** 88% of GNP. **Income/person** $660 (2.3% of USA).

POLITICS
Independent from Spain in 1821 but 134 revolutions by 1932. Military rule for much of the 20th Century. Democratic civilian government since 1984 has been hampered by the power and autonomy of the military and US preoccupation in the 1980s with civil wars in neighbouring El Salvador and Nicaragua. Only in recent years have the human rights abuses of the military been curbed.

RELIGION
The Roman Catholic Church is officially recognized, but there is separation of Church and State with religious freedom.

Religions	Population %	Adherents	Ann.Gr.
Christian	96.70	6,271,425	+2.7%
non-Religious/other	1.70	110,253	+8.4%
Spiritist	1.00	64,854	+7.5%
Baha'i	0.40	25,942	+2.8%
Muslim	0.16	10,377	+2.8%
Buddhist/Chinese	0.03	1,946	+2.8%
Jewish	0.01	649	+2.8%

Christians	Denom.	Affil.%	,000	Ann.Gr.
Protestant	51	13.67	886	+5.9%
Independent	57	4.77	309	+8.1%
Anglican	1	0.09	6	+2.1%
Catholic	1	81.72	5,300	+1.0%
Orthodox	4	0.10	7	-0.6%
Marginal	5	2.15	139	+9.3%
Doubly affiliated		*-5.80*	*-376*	*n.a.*

Churches	MegaBloc	Cong.	Members	Affiliates
Catholic	C	835	2,760,417	5,300,000
Seventh-day Adventist	P	115	70,807	165,000
Assemblies of God	P	800	79,740	136,460
Latter-day Saints (Morm)	M	293	60,000	100,000
Christian Brethren	P	230	35,000	75,000
Ch of God (Cleveland)	P	735	39,187	70,000
Príncipe de Paz	I	300	25,000	70,000
Central American	P	400	14,000	40,000
Jehovah's Witnesses	M	163	12,002	36,800
Baptist Convention	P	189	14,847	36,000
Foursquare Gospel	P	132	14,000	36,000
Bible Baptist	P	50	9,000	22,500
Ch of God of Prophecy	P	189	10,714	20,000
Bapt Assoc of Mosquit.	P	90	4,500	15,000
Amor Viviente	I	60	7,800	14,196
Conservative Baptist	P	145	5,500	13,000
Moravian	P	145	5,200	10,400
Friends (Quaker)	P	80	2,400	7,000
Other denoms [101]		4,049	174,000	480,000
Doubly affiliated			*-195,800*	*-376,000*
Total Christians [119]		9,000	3,148,000	6,271,000

Trans-bloc Groupings	pop.%	,000	Ann.Gr.
Evangelical	17.7	1,151	+6.5%
Charismatic	10.5	678	+6.9%
Pentecostal	9.3	603	+7.2%

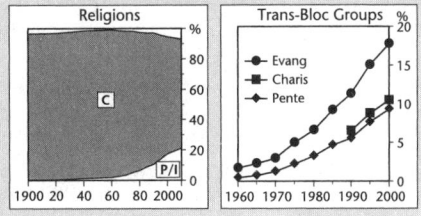

Missionaries from Honduras
P,I,A 133 in 20 agencies to 18 countries: Honduras 63, USA 35.

Missionaries to Honduras
P,I,A 435 in 69 agencies from 14 countries: USA 377, El Salvador 16.

• Answers to Prayer

1 The 40-year growth of Evangelicals took off with the successful Evangelism in Depth programme of 1963. In 1960 Evangelicals numbered 32,000 and were 1.7% of the population. They are now 1,250,000 and nearly 20%. Some believe the figure even higher.

2 The indigenous peoples of the eastern rainforests — the Miskito, Garifuna, Sumo and Tol have won significant concessions to preserve their endangered habitat and cultures in the face of logging companies and agri-business. For years they have been a voiceless, legally disadvantaged, underclass.

• Challenges for Prayer

1 The government is seeking to establish genuine democratic rule, but is hampered by a culture of crime, institutional violence with the military and vigilante death squads closely linked, and also by a corrupt judicial system that protects the privileged and is open to 'influence'. Pray that God-fearing, moral leaders may be raised up for the country. An election was due in 2001.

2 Hurricane 'Mitch' killed 11,000 people and left millions destitute. Many towns, villages and churches were devastated. Many national and international aid organizations helped in the immediate aftermath, but there is need for much input for decades to allow long-term recovery and self-sustaining, income-generating projects and industries to be established. Pray for all involved (World Relief, **TEAR Fund**, **WVI**, Lutheran World Relief, etc.).

3 The Roman Catholic Church has suffered from limited funds and personnel. Over 80% of the latter are foreign. Nominalism, pagan practices and immorality have been widespread, together with a large loss of adherents to other churches. Only about 20% of Catholics are actively involved in the Church. There is a considerable level of agreement between Catholics and Evangelicals in communal and social issues.

4 The growing numbers and influence of Evangelicals is praiseworthy, but the fragmentation of their witness into numerous denominations and the jealousies and isolationism this brings, is a hindrance — often the result of the exclusivistic views of the missionaries. Pray for the *Confraternidad Evangélica* (founded in 1990) and its members as they seek to address the need for fellowship and cooperation. Much must be done to tackle the social and economic crisis in the post-'Mitch' years.

5 Leadership training is now the vital need to supply the growing number of congregations. There are a number of seminaries and Bible schools, but many of the denominational Bible schools are in deep trouble (costs, staffing, cooperation). This enhances the importance of the networks of TEE programmes run by various denominations. Pray that the trainers may both give Biblical knowledge and be models for spiritual ministry.

6 The Amerindian peoples have been partially assimilated into Spanish culture. Among the Lenca the ministry of **WGM** and **CAMI** has borne much fruit. The peoples of the eastern forests (Miskito, Garifuna, Sumo and Tol) have retained more of their cultural identity. In recent years many have come to Christ. MOPAWI (Mosquitia Pawisa) is an indigenous body founded on Christian principles which is dedicated to the development of local cultures, community projects and to pressing for full equality under the law. Pray for the healthy development of churches among them and for all forms of exploitation to end.

7 **Missions vision** is developing. FEMEH (an interdenominational evangelical missions clearing house) sponsored a national missions convention in 1998. There are several small indigenous mission agencies. **YWAM** provides some cross-cultural training. Lack of trust and cooperation hinder the development of this vision.

8 **The less reached:**

a) **The street children.** Poverty has led to many living on the streets without a home. In 1998 there were reckoned to be 8,000 in the capital, but this number has grown since 'Mitch'. These unfortunate children face being abused, exploited for sex (30% are HIV+) and most suffer from severe malnutrition. Pray for:

  i   *The several agencies* seeking to meet their physical and spiritual needs,
  ii *Honduran churches* to own this challenge, and
  iii *The basic causes* of poverty, injustice and moral breakdown to be addressed and mitigated.

b) **The minority Arab and Chinese communities**, among whom there is little specific outreach.

9 **Missions continue to play an important partnering role** in leadership training, specialized ministries and in community projects that alleviate suffering and poverty. Pray for humble sensitivity and effective endorsement of Honduran leadership and initiatives in the exercising of their ministry. The largest agencies are: **IMB-SBC** (42), **WGM** (33), **AoG** (26), **CWRM** (24), **CAMI** (20), **Brethren** (15), **SAMS** (15), BIM (10) and **CoGWM** (10).

H **10** **Specialist Christian ministries.** Pray for:

a) **Student outreach** by both **CCCI** and **IFES** — the latter with 20 campus groups.
b) **Christian literature** — **Hosanna** and **Vida**'s bookstores are an important resources for Christian growth.
c) **Radio** — national radio gives time to several evangelical churches (**WGM**, **CAMI**) and there are 41 evangelical radio stations and 2 TV channels.

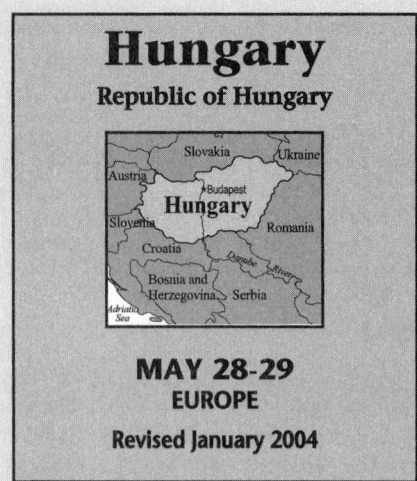

Hungary

Republic of Hungary

MAY 28-29
EUROPE
Revised January 2004

GEOGRAPHY
Area 93,030 sq.km. A landlocked, central European state on the River Danube.

Population	Ann.Gr.	Density
2000	10,035,568	-0.38%	108 per sq. km.
2010	9,626,550	-0.43%	103 per sq. km.
2025	8,900,388	-0.59%	96 per sq. km.

Capital Budapest 1,812,000. **Urbanites** 64%.

PEOPLES
Magyar (Hungarian) 88.8%. About a third of all Hungarians live in other lands; Romania 2 mill.; Slovakia 600,000; Yugoslavia 450,000; USA 450,000; Ukraine 170,000; and many in other nations.
Minorities 11.2%. Rom (Gypsy) 380,000; Ruthenian 280,000; German 170,000; Jews 80,000; Romanian 38,000; Slovak 30,000; Polish 21,000; Croat 20,000; Serb 20,000.

Literacy 99%. **Official language** Hungarian. **Languages with Scriptures** 6Bi 1NT 2por 2w.i.p.

ECONOMY
The first Communist bloc state to begin privatizing its economy, and to record positive economic growth. Poor in natural resources but with a developed industrial base and productive agricultural land. Following a painful period of adjustment, the economy grew well after 1998 with an improved standard of living. **HDI** 0.795; 47th/174. **Public debt** 33% of GNP. **Income/person** $4,340 (14.3% of USA).

POLITICS
Hungary lost 60% of its land area at the break-up of the Austro-Hungarian Empire in 1918,

leaving large Hungarian minorities in surrounding lands. During World War II the Russian army occupied the land and imposed Communism, only leaving in 1991. The Hungarian uprising of 1956 brought terrible revenge from the Russians; 80,000 were killed, wounded or deported, and 200,000 fled to the West. The first Communist bloc state to abandon Marxism and institute a multi-party democracy in 1990. The first freely elected government stabilized the country. Hungary joined NATO in 1999 and the EU in 2004.

RELIGION

In 1600, Hungary was 90% Protestant. Many reverted to Catholicism during the Counter Reformation and in the periods of discrimination that followed. The Communists enforced strict controls on all Christians from 1948-1988 through discrimination, intimidation and infiltration. In 2000, the 1,000th year of Hungary's conversion to Christianity was celebrated. There has been freedom of religion since 1990.

Religions	Population %	Adherents	Ann.Gr.
Christian	92.01	9,233,726	-0.6%
non-Religious/other	7.09	711,522	+2.6%
Jewish	0.80	80,285	-0.4%
Muslim	0.10	10,036	+4.2%

Christians	Denom.	Affil.%	,000	Ann.Gr.
Protestant	14	20.70	2,078	-2.2%
Independent	30	0.85	85	+22.5%
Catholic	1	60.29	6,050	-0.7%
Orthodox	4	0.27	27	-1.4%
Marginal	5	0.47	48	+16.1%
Unaffiliated		9.43	946	n.a.

Churches	MegaBloc	Cong.	Members	Affiliates
Catholic	C	2,000	4,548,872	6,050,000
Reformed	P	1,210	400,000	1,600,000
Evangelical Lutheran	P	398	107,500	430,000
Jehovah's Witnesses	M	280	20,690	40,000
Faith Church	I	305	20,000	40,000
Baptist	P	333	11,118	22,236
Romanian Orthodox	O	18	10,526	16,000
Fell of Ev Pentecostals	I	126	5,042	11,200
Seventh-day Adventist	P	106	4,471	10,000
Comm of Ev Brethren	I	80	4,000	6,800
Congregation of God	I	46	2,000	4,000
Other denoms [39]		586	31,042	57,300
Total Christians [50]		**5,488**	**5,165,300**	**8,287,500**

Trans-bloc Groupings	pop.%	,000	Ann.Gr.
Evangelical	2.7	273	+6.0%
Charismatic	1.7	172	+6.4%
Pentecostal	0.6	61	+15.1%

Missionaries from Hungary
P,I,A 122 in 13 agencies to 16 countries: Hungary 99.

Missionaries to Hungary
P,I,A 489 in 67 agencies from 18 countries: USA 317, Canada 30, Korea 26, UK 20.

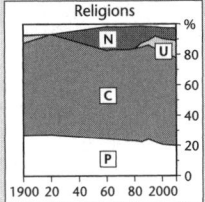

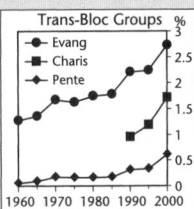

• Answers to Prayer

1 **Hungary's peaceful transition** from Communist dictatorship to parliamentary democracy and preservation from conflicts in the Balkans.

2 **The advent of religious freedom**, new opportunities for Christian ministry in public places and in the media, as well as encouraging signs of renewal. There are now Christian schools all over the country.

• Challenges for Prayer

1 **Hungarians are groping for life solutions** amidst uncertainty and rapid changes in society. There has been an increase in stress and many fall prey to alcoholism, suicide, burgeoning cults and the occult. Opportunities to minister exist in church and public schools, hospitals, prison, and in almost every element of society. Pray that the Church might truly be a relevant witness to Hungarian society, displaying both compassion for the lost and confidence in the Saviour.

2 **Suspicion, mistrust and division**, legacies of Marxism, still affect attitudes and, more sadly, the Church. This has been particularly noticeable in tensions between the emerging and the traditional churches in Hungary. Pray for a deep work of the Holy Spirit bringing repentance, reconciliation and renewal within and between all denominations. Pray for acceptance, trust and unity to truly characterize the Church.

3 **The 1990's was a time of responsiveness and growth**, but it was not on a scale for which Christians had hoped because the Church was ill-prepared to respond to the opportunities. Hungary had revivals in 1939 and 1946-50 which touched the Protestant Churches by which God providentially prepared the Church for coming persecution. There are strong charismatic and renewal movements in the Catholic Church and in the Baptist, and Reformed and other denominations. There is a Bible Union within the Reformed Church. There are several growing independent charismatic congregations and also a developing intercessors movement, including one in the national parliament. But this renewal and growth has not occurred evenly across the country, nor through all denominations. Pray that reconciliation of the nation to God, spiritual renewal, restoration and revival might flourish, affecting the whole of society.

4 **The need for evangelists is great**. The Church in general needs to mature in its ability to evangelize and overcome feelings of inferiority that restrain boldness in witness. There are many towns and cities where the number of nominal Christians is high and there are people with only a cursory contact with the good news. There is still resistance to the gospel in much of Hungary — pray for Spirit-led, creative forms of witness. There is, however, not a single town in the country without an evangelical congregation. Pray that God might raise up many workers, as well as enthusiastic support for them from the national believers.

5 **The denominations have a leadership crisis.** Pray for:

a) *Leaders of high morals and fresh vision*. There are many evangelistic challenges as yet unmet, many eyes scrutinizing the conduct of Christian leaders, and many leaders cautious because of the past. Pray that God might anoint and inspire those already in leadership.

b) *The release and empowerment of lay leaders*. Most pastors are overworked and spread too thinly. There is a flourishing Reformed Elders Association and a growing involvement of the laity in church planting and evangelism in most denominations. Pray that the Church might mature in its giving so as to support nationals involved in both local and foreign Christian work.

c) *Leadership training*. Seminaries formerly closed by the Communists are open again and Bible schools are full and growing in number. There are four Christian universities providing education in theology, humanities and law with several thousand students enrolled. There is an increasing focus on missions and evangelism. Pray also for the Protestant Institute for Mission Studies, the Pentecostal Bible School, the **AoG** ICI TEE programme in Hungarian and for teaching seminars run by the East Europe Bible Mission and others. Hungary is becoming a centre for Bible training for Central Europe with several English-medium schools (Central European Bible School, Word of Life). Increasing numbers of churches are implementing lay training and education programmes. Pray that they might bear much fruit.

6 **Ministry to young people**, one of the most receptive groups to the gospel in Hungary. Pray especially for:

a) *Teaching religious knowledge in schools*, in several hundred Christian schools and also public schools that invite this input. Pray for the provision of high quality evangelist-teachers to take up these opportunities.

b) *Children and youth programmes in churches*. The Communists prohibited children's programmes outside the churches, but this is finally being redressed by denominational youth associations such as **YMCA**, AWANA, **CEF,** Dunamisz and others. Large-scale youth conventions are proving attractive. Foreign mission groups have contributed much in this area of ministry.

c) *University students* who are open to most spiritual influences, both false and true. Nationally-led international ministries such as **CCCI**, MEKDsz(**IFES**) and Youth for Christ all reach out to these students, accounting for over 150 workers.

d) *Summer outreach programmes*, by many Hungarian churches as well as those jointly run by **The Bible League** and **OM**, which train scores of young people from various denominations to participate in evangelism and follow-up work.

7 The less-reached:

a) *The Jews*. Before the Holocaust there were 800,000. Now their numbers are down to 80,000. There are several Messianic Jewish communities. Pray for a reconciliation between Christians and Jews.

b) ***The Roma (Gypsy) community*** which has not seen the same spiritual breakthrough as in Spain, France and Romania, but there are several new Protestant and charismatic fellowships among them. A number of agencies are attempting to meet their social and spiritual needs.

c) ***As many as 200,000 refugees from former Yugoslavia***, uprooted from their homes and finding it difficult to settle in a foreign country.

d) ***Hungarians abroad*** — there is concern about discrimination against Hungarians in Serb-controlled Vojvodina and in Romanian Transylvania and southern Slovakia. Pray for reconciliation between these minorities and the various national majorities, and pray for Hungarian Christians to reach out to their own people who live in these lands.

8 **Expatriate missions increased numerically** in the 1990s, but have since levelled off. Pray for sensitivity and a true servant attitude in seeking to help the Hungarian Church. The main ministries required of expatriates are in leadership training and mentoring, equipping the laity and imparting missionary vision. There is still little understanding of missions in churches, but the great potential is beginning to be realized. The largest agencies are: **CCCI** (142 workers), **ABWE** (28), **YWAM** (27), **OM** (24), **OMS** (17), **CBI** (15).

9 **Christian help ministries:**

a) ***Scripture distribution.*** The Hungarian Bible Society was revitalized in 1989. Pray for its ministry in distributing the Bible.

b) ***Christian literature*** is in great demand. In the 1990s the publication of Christian books has increased — even by secular publishers. Many new Christian publishing companies have been founded. Literature ministry is actively used by many congregations. **CLC** has two bookstores in Hungary. The Hungarian Literature Mission is a major source of evangelistic materials.

c) ***The JESUS film.*** This is one of the best-selling videos in Hungarian.

d) ***Christian radio.*** In addition to several hours a week broadcast in Hungarian by **TWR** and **IBRA**, there are increasing local opportunities for Christian programmes on television and radio. The Hungarian Gospel Radio Foundation, the Reformed and Lutheran churches all have their own radio programmes. There is a vision for a 24-hour Christian radio station in Budapest. **IT** have set up a music recording studio to serve Central Europe.

Iceland
Republic of Iceland

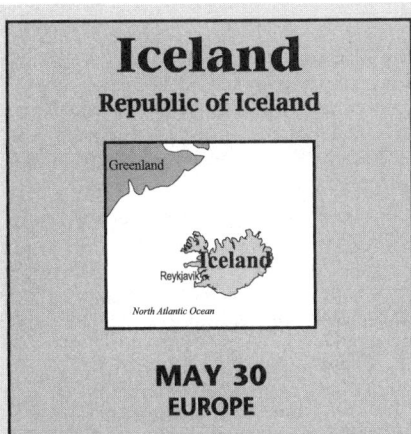

North Atlantic Ocean

MAY 30
EUROPE

GEOGRAPHY
Area 103,000 sq.km. A volcanic island in the North Atlantic; mountainous, largely barren with many large glaciers.

Population		Ann.Gr.	Density
2000	280,969	+0.92%	3 per sq. km.
2010	303,644	+0.73%	3 per sq. km.
2025	328,356	+0.44%	3 per sq. km.

Capital Reykjavik 105,487. **Urbanites** 92%.

PEOPLES
Icelandic 95.9%.
Other 4.1% (mostly European). Danish 2,250; Swedish 1,500.

Literacy 100%. **Official language** Icelandic. **All languages** 2. **Languages with Scriptures** 1Bi.

ECONOMY
The fishing industry has been the largest income source, but conservation measures limit this. Enormous potential in hydro and thermal power resources, allowing for cheap aluminium processing. **Unemployment** 3.9%. **HDI** 0.919; 9th/174. **Public debt** 45.5% of GNP. **Income/person** $27,580 (87.9% of USA).

POLITICS
The world's oldest parliament, established in 930. Under Norwegian and Danish rule 1262-1944. Parliamentary republic, and a member of NATO.

RELIGION
The Lutheran Church is still recognized as the State Church, but there is religious freedom.

Religions	Population %	Adherents	Ann.Gr.
Christian	95.61	268,634	+0.6%
non-Religious	2.14	6,013	+5.8%
Other	1.78	5,000	+12.8%
Baha'i	0.15	421	+0.9%
Buddhist	0.15	421	+11.7%
Traditional Norse	0.13	365	+14.2%
Muslim	0.04	112	n.a.

Christians	Denom.	Affil. %	,000	Ann.Gr.
Protestant	16	93.76	263	+0.6%
Catholic	1	1.38	4	+8.8%
Marginal	3	0.47	1	+4.0%

Churches	MegaBloc	Cong.	Members	Affiliates
National Church (Luth)	P	284	174,281	249,222
Evang Luth Free [2]	P	1	5,958	8,520
Catholic	C	4	2,771	3,880

Trans-bloc Groupings	pop.%	,000	Ann.Gr.
Evangelical	3.3	9	+2.3%
Charismatic	1.8	5	+4.0%
Pentecostal	1.1	3	+5.7%

Missionaries from Iceland
P,I,A 31 in 7 agencies to 7 countries.

Missionaries to Iceland
P,I,A 16 in 8 agencies from 4 countries.

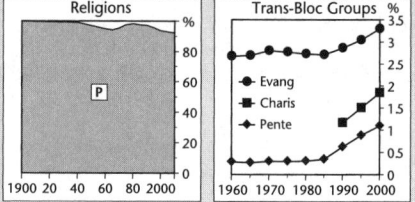

• Answers to Prayer

1 **Missions vision is small, but growing,** despite Iceland's geographical and cultural isolation. **YWAM**'s influence over the past years, and the 1996 formation of the Icelandic Mission Movement are positive factors. The evangelical/Pentecostal churches are encouraging short term missions (about 80 have gone in the past 3 years). Joint outreaches with other churches in North Atlantic/Scandanavian countries are being developed. Pray that the believing Church becomes ever more an outward-looking missionary Church.

• Challenges for Prayer

1 **The majority of Icelanders are only nominally Christian.** As modern society drifts away from faith, the rates of suicide, substance abuse, and crime have all increased. Most Icelanders have had some involvement with New Age ideologies, the occult, and other such practices. Some of the more isolated areas are spiritual wastelands, with almost no active Christianity at all. Ask the Lord to arrest this spiritual slide and awaken Icelanders to their spiritual needs.

2 **The Lutheran and smaller, but similar, Free Churches** are often compromised by liberal theology and practice; many are opposed to the preaching of the true gospel. A few pastors and congregations remain faithful, and in some cases congregations are growing. Pray that they might prosper in the Lord. Only a fraction of members actually attend church. Pray for a surge of new vigour and fervour in the congregations, the leadership and the Theological Faculty where all pastors are trained.

3 **Evangelical believers** number only about 9,000. **YWAM** ceased operations after their work within the Lutheran Church saw little fruit. But the growing Pentecostal and charismatic churches are displaying admirable unity and cooperation. They are at the forefront of a move to plant an evangelical congregation within two hours' drive of every person. Since 1996 the Pentecostals together with **World Horizons** have run a 3 month Bible school and the ex-**YWAM** training centre has become a residential Christian training community. These programmes are having a strong positive impact upon the life of the Church in general. Pray that the living faith and unity of Evangelicals might open the hearts of many to the good news.

4 **KSF(IFES) work among the 3,000 university students** is proving fruitful, and there are many encouraging signs in the evangelical youth movements. Pray that those who love the Lord may maintain a glowing testimony where indifference is so widespread.

5 **The Bible Society published a new Bible version in 1999.** Pray for the Gideons and their Bible distribution ministry. Pray also that the Word of God might filter into every element of society.

6 **Christian Radio.** Radio Lindin, which reaches about 90% of the population, has been a blessing to believers and has been used to bring some unbelievers to faith.

India
Republic of India

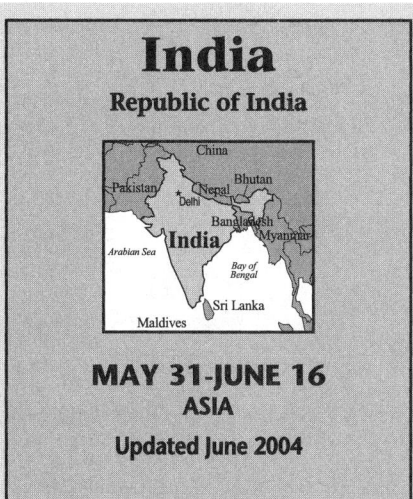

MAY 31-JUNE 16
ASIA
Updated June 2004

GEOGRAPHY
Area 3,166,000 sq.km. A further 121,000 sq.km. of Kashmir is administered by Pakistan and China. Geographically and politically India dominates south Asia and the Indian Ocean. There are 29 Union States and 6 Union Territories. Note: more detailed statistics given under individual states.

Population		Ann.Gr.	Density
2000	1,013,661,777	+1.66%	320 per sq. km.
2010	1,152,163,518	+1.16%	364 per sq. km.
2025	1,330,448,707	+0.90%	420 per sq. km.

Capital Delhi 11.3 million. Other cities: 31 over one million; nearly 400 over 100,000. Largest city: Mumbai (Bombay) 17.55 million. **Urbanites** 40% in 2001.

PEOPLES
The racial, ethnic, religious and linguistic diversity together with the caste system complicates any analysis of the population. A 1991 survey identified 4,635 distinct people groups. More detail is given under the individual states. People Groups based on culture and caste rather than language are the more important for under-standing India's complexity. The arrival of the Indo-Aryans in India three millennia ago led to the marginalization of the original inhabitants (many of the tribal peoples of today), subjugation of much of the Dravidian population and the emergence of multiple mixed race groups (now backward castes). The caste system established Brahmin control over the majority. Fundamental to Hinduism, it pervades all religious and social structures in India. Caste discrimination is forbidden by the constitution, but is socially important for over 80% of the population. There are an estimated 6,400 castes. Each functions as a separate group because of the social barriers that separate them.

Castes
Forward castes (FC) 15.4%. Brahmin (the pre-eminent priestly caste) 33.7m; Rajput 40m; Mahratta (many also OBC) 28.5m; Kayastha 12.3m; Jat (also OBC) 12m; Nayar 6.2m; Bhumihar Brahmin 4.1m; Arora 3.8m; Samon 3.7m; Vania 1.2m.
Backward castes (OBC) or Barhujan 56.6%. Yadava 31.6m; Kurmi 25.7m; Ahir 25.4m; Shaikh (Mus) 24.3m; Teli 23m; Kunbi 19.6m; Vanniyar 18.1m; Lingayat 17.8m; Nai 14.7m; Garia 13.1m; Pathan (Mus) 12.4m; Viswakarma 12.3m; Koiri 10.6m; Vakkaliga 9.9m; Telaga 9.1m; Mappila (Mus) 8.9m; Gujar 8.5m; Barhai 8.4m; Kamma 7.1m; Sonar 7.1m; Ilavar 6.9m; Kapu 6.6m; Chotra Bansi 6.4m; Kalwar 6.0m; Kuruba 5.7m.
Scheduled castes or Dalit (SC) 18.1%. Generally deprived, often landless, and exploited. Also known in past as outcastes, untouchables, Harijan. Chamar 47.3m; Mahisyada 11.4m; Pasi 7.2m; Madiga 7.1m; Mala 5.4m; Dhobi 5.3m; Dusadh 5.2m; Mahar 4.3m; Namasudra 4.1m; Rajbanshi 4.1m; Bahna 3.5m; Bhambi 3.4m; Bagdi 3.5m; Balmiki 3.3m; Pod 2.8m; Bhangi 2.3m; Dom 1.9m.
Tribal or Adivasi (ST) (580) 9.5%. Gond 10.5m; Bhil 10.1m; Santal 5.9m; Koli (Kori) 3.5m; Banjara (Lambada) 3.1m; Bhil Mina 2.9m; Oraon 2.6m; Naikda 2.2m; Munda 1.9m; Bhuiya 1.6m; Khond 1.4m; Naga 1.2m; Koli Mahadev 1.1m; Boro (Bodo) 1.1m; Tipera 1.0m; Khasi 940,000; Rabari 919,000.
Other 0.4% (not considered part of the caste system). Syrian (Christian) 2.5m. Refugees: Iranians 60,000; Afghans 50,000.

Races and Languages

Indo-Aryan 75.3%. 94 main languages, mainly north and central India. Hindi, Marathi, Bengali, Urdu, Gujarati, Oriya, Panjabi, Sindhi, Rajasthani/Mawari, Assamese, Nepali, Kashmiri, Badaga, Konkani, etc. **Dravidian** 22.5%; 23 main languages, mainly south India. Telugu, Tamil, Malayalam, Kannada, Oraon. **Austro-Asiatic** 1.13%. 16 main languages scattered over central, south and northeast India. Bhil, Gond, Santal Kui, Munda, etc. **Sino-Tibetan** 0.97%. 80 main languages. Tibetan, Manipuri, Naga, Tripuri, Garo, Mizo, Kuki-Chin, etc. **Other** 0.1%. Arabic, etc.

Literacy 62% (44% in 1981). Functional literacy much lower. No longer the world's least literate country. **Official languages** Hindi (language of Union, 66% speak it); English (legislative and judicial language and language of wider communication, 19% speak it). **Scheduled languages** 18. **All languages** 1,652 (1971 census). The SIL Ethnologue lists 407 living languages.

Language	Sub-languages	Population	Peo. Gr.
Hindi	49	407.9m	800+
Bengali	5	84.2m	159
Telugu	3	79.8m	355
Marathi	2	75.5m	170
Tamil	4	64.1m	247
Urdu	2	52.5m	163
Gujarati	4	49.2m	199
Kannada	3	39.6m	174
Malayalam	3	36.4m	129
Oriya	6	33.9m	200
Panjabi	5	28.1m	84
Assamese	2	15.9m	38
Sindhi	3	2.5m	9
Nepali	2	2.5m	24
Konkani	3	2.1m	55
Manipuri	2	1.5m	1
Kashmiri	3	68,000	47
Sanskrit	2	59,000	1

Languages with Scriptures 53Bi 42NT 40por 68w.i.p.

ECONOMY

Predominantly agricultural with 64% of the labour force, but rapid industrialization and urbanization is taking place. India is now a nuclear power and has a space industry. It is one of the world leaders in computer software production. Economic growth accelerated in the 1990s but has been offset by high birth rate, illiteracy, prejudice, widespread corruption and bureaucratic inefficiency. The 250 million middle class would benefit most from the market reforms and liberalization being instituted. Over 600 million live in deep poverty, and 300 million live below the bread-line. India's widespread use of English gives the country a major advantage as its economy opens up to the world. **HDI** 0.545; 132nd/174. **Public debt** 22% of GNP. **Income/person** $370 (1.2% of USA).

POLITICS

Independent from Britain in 1947. The world's largest functioning democracy. The RSS and the VHP (Hindu extreme nationalist movements) have grown in strength and influence with their nationalist Hindutva ideology, and with effective populist propaganda have infiltrated most of the power structures in India. On the strength of this, the Hindu nationalist BJP party has gained political power, but cannot tame the fascist-inspired forces that facilitated this. Many fear the undermining of democracy and the emergence of an intolerant Hindu dictatorship.

RELIGION

India's constitution provides for full religious freedom of worship and witness for all religions. The rise of Hindutva extremism resulted in a hate campaign against Muslims in the early 1990s and against Christians in the late 1990s as being followers of 'foreign' religions. Anti-conversion legislation and the imposition of legal restrictions on Christian activities have been strongly demanded and increasingly granted. Some states have enacted such legislation and condoned a rising wave of violence and even murder of Christian workers. Many are concerned at the erosion of guaranteed religious freedoms. In the present climate of persecution, for Christians, statistics below are not given in full, but are representative of what God is doing. **Persecution index** 29th in the world.

Religions	Population %	Adherents	Ann.Gr.
Hindu/other	79.83	792,075,313	+1.6%
Muslim	12.50	126,707,722	+2.1%
Christian	2.40	25 million*	n.a.
Sikh	1.92	19,462,306	+1.7%
Traditional ethnic	1.40	14,191,265	+1.0%
Buddhist	0.80	8,109,294	+3.0%
Jain	0.35	3,500,000	+2.0%
non-Religious	0.55	5,575,000	+1.7%
Baha'i	0.23	2,331,422	+3.1%
Parsee	0.02	150,000	+2.2%

*The religion figures for 2000 are largely derived from the 1991 census which, for many reasons, seriously under-enumerated Christians at 2.34%. Official 1991 census figures are used in the coverage of the individual states.

Christians	Denom.	% of Chris.	Ann.Gr.
Protestant	309	39.0	+4.5%
Independent	1,700	27.6	+6.8%
Catholic	3	29.2	+1.1%
Orthodox	6	3.8	+1.2%
Marginal	15	0.4	+7.7%

Note: The percentage figure given is of the total number of Christians only.

Churches		MegaBloc	Cong.	Members	Affiliates
Catholic		C	17,178	6.424m	11.50m
Ch of South India (CSI)		P	15,765	1,387,324	2,955,000
Council of Bapt Ch of NEI		P	5,400	760,000	2,000,000
Malankara Orth Syrian		O	1,346	1,143,713	1,910,000

United Ev Luth Chs in I	P	13,000	608,108	1,350,000
Ch of North India (CNI)	P	4,382	714,286	1,300,000
Samavesam of Telu. Bapt	P	893	475,639	1,110,000
Mar Thoma Syrian	I	1,547	508,982	850,000
Assemblies of God [2]	P	3,600	350,000	800,000
Presby Ch of NE I [4]	P	2,896	389,385	797,932
Indian Pente Ch of God	I	4,000	320,000	750,000
Seventh-day Adventist	P	1,056	289,417	445,000
Chr Assemblies of India	P	1,900	130,000	433,000
Evang Church of India	P	1,152	363,390	431,000
Believers Church (GFA)	I	5,000	100,000	400,000
Baptist Conv of N Circars	P	280	185,400	371,000
Indian Evang Team	I	2,893	200,000	340,000
Baptist Convention	P	2,700	165,000	330,000
Mennonite S. S.	P	2,000	80,000	310,000
Salvation Army	P	2,300	230,000	300,000
9 Garo Baptist Assocs	P	2,100	185,000	270,000
Assemblies -Jeh Shammah	I	760	80,000	250,000
United Pentecostal [2]	P	2,100	140,000	220,000
Ch of God (Cleveland)	P	1,020	95,000	190,000
Baptist U of Mizoram	P	391	70,000	180,000
Chs of Christ [6]	P	3,700	75,000	160,000
New Life Fellowship	I	1,500	80,000	160,000
N Bank Baptist Assoc	P	800	60,000	110,000
St Thomas Evangelical	I	700	65,868	110,000

Denoms listed here [39]   122,000   15.870m   30.620m

There are a further 2,000 or so smaller, mostly indigenous denominations or networks with over 200,000 churches not listed or enumerated here.

Trans-bloc Groupings pop.%		,000	Ann.Gr.
Evangelical	1.8	18,458	+5.3%
Charismatic	1.2	12,541	+4.9%
Pentecostal	0.4	3,891	+7.5%

Missionaries from India
P,I,A over 44,000 in 440 agencies of which 60% are working cross-culturally in India, 440 in foreign countries.

Expatriates to India
P,I,A approx. 1,000 in 184 agencies. **C** 5,000.

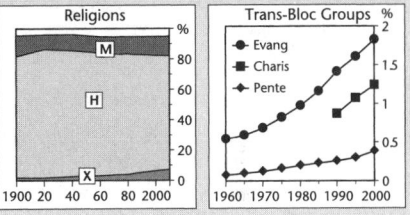

NOTE Jan 2004: Significant developments since September 2001

1 **Increased tensions in Kashmir** between nuclear-armed Pakistan and India almost led to war in 2002 . The Muslim Al Qaeda terror network is deeply implicated in the conflict.

2 **The Dalit reaction to Hindu extremism** has led to many renouncing Hinduism and adopting another religion such as Buddhism or Christianity. The rate of defections has increased rapidly since 2001 and up to 300 million could take this step over the next 20-30 years.

3 **Hindu extremism has increased** with further persecution of Christians. Draconian anti-conversion legislation was rushed through the Tamil Nadu parliament in 2002. Other states are following.

• Answers to Prayer

NOTE: **June 2004**. The unexpected defeat of the BJP-led government and return to power of the more secular Congress Party and allies in the 2004 elections was a major political upheaval and answer to prayer. The new government has promised to maintain the constitutional rights of ethnic and religious minorities. This also led to the outgoing defeated state government of Tamil Nadu rescinding the 2002 anti-conversion legislation (see below).

1 **Praise God for Christianity's two millennia in India** since the arrival of the Apostle Thomas. In the past 20 years the Christian presence representing all the world's main Christian traditions is at last beginning to be visible as an indigenous component of the mainstream of Indian life.

2 **The 200 years since William Carey,** the great Baptist pioneer, have been remarkable. The Holy Spirit has used countless thousands of Indian and expatriate workers to affect India for good in education, health, challenging social wrongs, and to plant over 300,000 churches. There have been periodic revivals in the Panjab and in South India, in Nagaland in 1976 and Mizoram in the 1980s.

3 **Praise for continued freedom for Indian Christians to proclaim the gospel** despite efforts to limit this through intimidation and persecution.

4 **Persecution in the 1990s** has refined the Church, focused its vision and brought a greater unity of purpose than ever before. It has pushed the person of Jesus and the existence of the Church to centre stage, and has also not shown extremist Hinduism in a favourable light.

5 **Praise for the flowering of Indian Christian leadership** — with world-renowned Christian apologists, theologians, preachers, writers and mission leaders during the last two decades.

6 **The dynamic growth surge of Indian mission agencies and church-based mission initiatives from south and northeast India** and elsewhere. From small beginnings in the 1960s the movement has burgeoned and matured to over 44,000 workers in nearly 500 agencies with over half in cross-cultural fields in India and beyond.

7 **The increase in effective grass-roots research during the 1990s.** A Research Teams Network has linked the efforts of **IMA**, CONS, **GFA**, The Bible League, CGAI, **YWAM** and others to analyse each state, city, people and ministry. Never before has there been such clarity about the bounds of the unfinished task! Pray for the ongoing research programme and its effectiveness in helping churches to obey the Great Commission.

• Challenges for Prayer

1 **India has more (and larger) people groups with no Christians, churches or workers than any other part of the world.** Pray that the Church world-wide might rise to complete this task.

2 **The leaders of the nation and its constituent states need prayer:**

a) *That they might continue to uphold the constitution by maintaining religious freedom* and protecting religious and ethnic minorities. Some state governments have had a bad record for abuse of human rights and discrimination against Christians, Muslims and Dalits. The Internet is rapidly becoming a powerful means of exposing corruption and forcing governments to be more accountable to the people.

b) *That they may resist growing pressures* to pass discriminatory 'anti-conversion' laws, legalize and favour extremist Hindu organizations, restrict foreign funds and buildings for minorities, and limit press freedoms for those who protest.

c) *That they may be more committed to tackle the serious ills of society* — in a culture of corruption at every level of government, find ways to free up the economy to reduce poverty, improve the national infrastructure, deal with widespread use of child labour, female infanticide, the rapid spread of AIDS and serious environmental degradation.

3 **Hinduism is the world's third largest religious system.** At its widest, a Hindu is one who lives in or identifies with India and its culture. As a religion, it is a pluralistic network of religious beliefs and systems ranging from the philosophical (self-realization), to Vedic (rituals and good works) to village Hinduism (idolatry, occultism, animism). It absorbs elements of any religion it encounters, and is widely perceived as a religion of tolerance and peace. Its global influence is significant through such movements as Hare Krishna, New Age, etc. Many concepts of Hinduism have become part of 21st century post-modern culture — yoga, gurus, karma, reincarnation and transcendental meditation. How can we pray?

a) *Hinduism has emotional appeal,* yet in their search after fulfilment and purpose Hindus still long for a true communion with the Creator that only Jesus can give. Pray that Christians may so demonstrate true spirituality and Christ-likeness that many will find their desires met in Him.

b) *The Hindu caste system* is a major unresolved issue. Constitutional equality and the legal banning of discrimination together with affirmative action favouring the underprivileged in education and government jobs have only partly addressed the problems. The rising demands by Dalits for their constitutional rights and a share in the land and wealth of the country, and by tribals for protection of their ancestral lands are often met by obstruction, intimidation and repression. Pray that:

i *the government may handle wisely the realities of casteism* and the impoverishment of a large percentage of the population.

ii *the Christian response may be both biblical and Christ-like.* Over 70% of all Christians are of Dalit and tribal communities, and the average Hindu associates the gospel with the underclasses of their society.

iii *the churches* in their outreach may be sensitive to the caste networks and facilitate people movements to Christ but in their fellowship may work towards the elimination of the dividing walls of society.

c) *Hindutva extremism* has become a major issue and casts a baleful shadow over India.

Militant Hindus of the RSS, VHP and others under the umbrella of the Sangh Parivar have worked for years to infiltrate their members into every influential part of society, and have now gained a measure of political power and patronage. They are attempting to re-write history, institutionalize discrimination against religious and ethnic minorities and control the media. The Hindutva ideology of "India is Hindu only" has been shamelessly used to gain political power. A rapid increase in intimidation and violence against Muslims and then Christians was evident in the 1990s, stigmatizing them as 'foreign'. Their model is more European fascism than ancient Hinduism. Pray that:

i *the worst of the instigators* of communal violence may repent of their evil and find forgiveness in Christ.

ii *the lies, bigotry, barrenness and destructiveness of this extremism* to India's social cohesion and unity might be exposed and lead many to consider the claims of Christ. The martyrdom of Graham Staines and his two sons in 1999, and ensuing publicity, caused widespread embarrassment to most Hindus.

iii *Christians might be united* and courageous in the face of widespread and localized persecution. The number of attacks on Christians has rapidly increased — from 1964-1996 there were 38 recorded incidents. In the subsequent three years there were over 300. By 2001 there was, on average, an incident every 36 hours. Though these are still relatively few in a country of India's size, they have a deep effect on Christians.

iv *The 're-conversion' programme by Hindu extremists* might prove an expensive failure, and that Dalit and Tribal Christians may stand firm in Christ whatever the cost.

v *Christians may show the love* and forgiveness of Christ to their persecutors.

4 The Church in India is, at the same time, both vital and growing, and nominal and in decline.

a) *Much of organized Christianity is based on people movements* over the past 400 years and in many denominations Western forms, liberal theology, universalism and a growing nominalism has dried up the rivers of the Spirit to the millions of non-Christians around them. Many congregations have no first-generation Christians from a non-Christian background. Disputes over personalities, power and property have led to many divisions, court cases, a widespread disillusionment and a steady loss of young people to secularism and nominal Hinduism. Pray that present pressures and the work of the Holy Spirit might bring new life to traditional streams of Christianity.

b) *The need for change in the Church* has never been greater. Pray for:

i *Unity.* The All India Christian Council was formed in 1998 to protect and serve Christians from all denominations. Over 2,000 denominations and associations are participating in the AICC. There is greater unity than ever known before, because of the more hostile national environment. The past has been characterised by a spirit of divisiveness. Pray for this unity to mature and develop and to be made visible to the watching world. There also needs to be a greater cooperation and accountability between local churches and sending agencies.

ii *Indigeneity in music, worship and culture* — for too long churches have appeared foreign.

iii *Greater reliance on Indian-style cell/house churches* rather than on Western-style buildings

iv *More effective discipling* of the many being touched or stirred by multiple evangelistic programmes. Pray for a greater integrity of life, earnestness and commitment to the Lord among those evangelizing.

v *More effective outreach* through personal evangelism rather than mass rallies.

vi *More relevance to impact the mainstream of national life.* The Church is seen to be linked to the marginalized, deprived sections of society. Business, politics, arts, culture, the middle and upper classes have been neglected.

c) *Biblical Christianity is thriving:*

i *Evangelical pastors* in mainline denominations are increasing.

ii *A multiplicity of dynamic, newer Pentecostal and charismatic* fellowships have sprung up and spread to many areas.

iii *The number of evangelical denominations has increased* and congregations multiplied. There are several key networks linking many denominations — the **Pentecostal Fellowship of India** (linking all major Pentecostal denominations), the Baptist Evangelical Alliance and the Evangelical Fellowship of India (linking over 100 denominations and agencies). These have been used of God in maturing, stabilizing and mobilizing believers through prayer, conventions, pastors' retreats, coordinating training, literature production, mission and outreach.

iv *The Charismatic movement in the Catholic Church* began in 1972 and has spread to nearly every Catholic church. It has had a profound impact, brought many to new life, and stimulated outreach.

d) **The growth of the Church** during the 1990s was significant but hard to measure. Many networks for intercession for the evangelization of the country, involving millions of Christians, have flourished, such as the **Arpana Prayer Network** (in 100 cities linking thousands of Christian women) and **Quiet Corner Ministries.** Millions have become responsive through widely heard radio programmes, massive distributions of Christian literature, extensive use of Christian videos, films and cassettes. Many have come into the Kingdom through multiple efforts to start new congregations. Pray that no attack of the enemy from outside or inside the Church may stunt this growth.

5 **The training of Christian workers** is fundamental for the health and growth of the Church. Poor discipling and lack of teaching have made nominalism, syncretism and losses to Hinduism a problem for Catholics, Protestants and Independents. There are about 100,000 full-time workers in India; about half are pastoring local churches. There is, on average, one pastor for every six congregations. Pray for:

a) **Degree-level seminaries**, of which there are over 40. A minority are theologically evangelical. Several for special mention — **Union Biblical Seminary** in Pune, with 225 students from 50 evangelical denominations and agencies, **Asia Biblical Seminary** in Tiruvalla, Kerala with 400 students from 31 denominations, **Hindustan Bible Institute**, etc. Pray for a stream of warm-hearted workers, anointed by the Spirit, to move out from these institutions to India and beyond.

b) **Bible schools** which now number over 300, having doubled in 10 years. Evangelical institutions are full. Bible schools need to change from merely teaching theology to giving practical skills in church planting.

c) **Training centres for indigenous workers**, largely for church planters are playing a significant role (FMPB, IEM, etc.). GFA has set up 50 such, with 5,000 in a 3-year programme in 2000.

d) **New, creative ways for multiplying leaders must be sought** and, in some cases, are being attempted. Many residential institutions are locked into a Western maintenance model which leads to minimal impact on the non-Christian majority and cannot produce the hundreds of thousands of workers needed now.

e) **The House/Cell Church Movement** is rapidly spreading in many parts of the country. One such is Operation Agapé in the north and **AoG** in the south. It is proving culturally appropriate, affordable, biblically authentic and very effective.

6 The growth of the number, size and maturity of Indian cross-cultural outreach agencies is remarkable. In 1973 there were 420 missionaries; in 1983 — 3,017; in 1993 — 12,000 in 200 agencies. By 2000 this had risen to 44,000 in 440+ Protestant/independent agencies. During the 1990s significant progress was made in upgrading training, improving the quality of ministry, planning strategically, setting goals, initializing research and partnering with others. Pray for:

a) **Indian mission agency networking structures** play a key role in furthering cooperation, goal-setting and fellowship; major ones being the **India Missions Association** (132 evangelical agencies representing 21,000 missionaries), **CONS**, North India Harvest Network.

b) **The Asian Theological Association-India and the Indian Institute of Missiology** accredit, facilitate and network missions training. There are over 100 schools providing such; almost all started since 1980; **IET** started 27.

c) **The mission agencies themselves**, for their leadership to be strategic, for provision of pastoral care and support to their workers, for fruitfulness in ministry and for spiritual unity. The largest agencies: **GFA** (10,795), **CCCI** (2,604), **IET** (1,876), **Brethren** (1,140), **OM** (1,000), Mizo Presbyterians (800), New Life (690), **IEM** (470), **EHC** (450), **FMPB** (400). There are 45 Pentecostal missions with over 4,000 workers.

d) **Indian missionaries serving in other lands** — around 440. Costs for them are much higher. Pray for provision of their finances, etc.

e) **OM graduates**. The impact of **OM** on implanting missions vision has been significant. The Association of OM Graduates links together 12,000 full-time Christian workers. Many of these lead some of the most effective agencies in India today.

f) **Indian missionaries serving in India** face heightened and organized opposition and even persecution. A number of those serving in literature distribution, showing evangelistic films, and in discipling young Christians have been martyred in recent years.

g) **A *widening of ministry* to *other needy sections of the population*.** Hitherto half the cross-cultural missionaries have gone to tribal groups and many of the rest to the downtrodden, marginalized or needy sections of the population. Few are working among the urban middle class, the higher castes, etc. — this needs to be increased, but most existing workers feel inadequately prepared for this challenge.

h) ***Better and closer relationships between local churches and sending agencies.*** Many missions are supported by multi-congregational informal prayer networks. There needs to be more accountability between workers and churches.

i) ***Expatriates serving in India*** who now number only around 1,000. Tentmaking is one way of entry for new workers, and there are many roles that could be filled by expatriates in support of existing Indian ministries and pioneering contacts in sections of the population not easily reached by indigenous workers. Many international advocates are needed to adopt peoples and areas and raise prayer for barriers to be broken down.

7 **The least evangelized areas of India** — no other part of the world has such a concentration of unevangelized people. Pray for:

a) ***The North India Ganges plains*** with their teeming millions in the Hindi-speaking heartland. In the 5 states of Haryana, Himachal Pradesh, Delhi, Rajasthan and Uttar Pradesh with 360 million people, live 650,000 Christians, but active committed believers may be no more than 120,000. Christians in India are unequally spread — 70% in the south, 25% in the northeast and only 5% in the more populated north and west.

b) ***The great cities*** cities with their growth and mix of wealth and abject poverty. Chennai (12% Christian) and Mumbai (5%) are in contrast to Kolkata, Delhi, Varanasi, etc., where Christian witness is small. Twenty-six percent of the urban population live in slums, many being newcomers to the cities. There are 41 million Indians without a home.

8 **The least reached mega people groups of India** which are resident in many different states.

a) ***The Brahmin*** are the highest and priestly caste in the Hindu world. They number 40 million but there may be only 18,000 who openly profess Christianity.

b) ***Other Forward Castes*** — the Rajput (40m), Mahratta (28m), Jat (12m), Bhumihar (4m), Arora (3.8m), Samon (3.7m), etc., may have no more than 5,000 Christians. The forward castes have a very negative view of Christian workers — Dalit, simple, cowardly, followers of the colonialists, rejectors of Indian culture and touting Western ideas. There is little effective ministry among them. These people groups will need a different and more sensitive, loving approach and adequate preparation of workers if the barriers to faith in Christ are to be breached.

c) ***Many Backward Caste peoples***, such as the Yadava (31.5m), Kurmi (25.7m), Ahir (25.4m), Gujar (8.5m), Sonar (7.1m) have no known Christians at worst, or a few thousand at best.

d) ***Dalit groups*** have responded more, such as the 47m Chamar, with 500,000 Christians, but the 5.5m Dhobi and 7.2m Pasi have shown little response.

e) ***There are still numerous tribal peoples*** un- or under-evangelized.

i   *The Banjara* (Lambadi) are the people from whom the world's Roma (Gypsy) have come. Mahars have turned to Buddhism in large numbers, but are one of the most responsive groups in Maharashtra and Madhya Pradesh. The Banjara number 4.8 million, but only 1% are Christian.

ii   *The 10 million Bhil and 10.5 million Gond* are slower in committing their lives to Christ despite years of outreach.

f) ***The Sindhi*** — 36 million equally divided between Muslims (in Pakistan) and Hindu (in India). There are 300 Christians among them in India, and about double that globally.

g) ***There are 205 people groups*** with populations over 10,000 that are still unreached.

9 **Specific communities requiring specialized ministry:**

a) ***The increasingly affluent 250 million of the middle classes*** have virtually no meaningful contact with Christianity and they are the key sector of society in the 21st Century.

b) ***Students*** numbering over 10 million in 250 universities and 10,000 colleges. A high proportion use addictive drugs. Pray for the nation-wide ministries of **YFC**, **ICCC**, **Inter-**

collegiate Pentecostal Fellowship and the **Union of Evangelical Students of India** (UESI/**IFES**). The latter has groups and staff workers in most campuses, winning new Christians annually. Pray for a clear, vibrant witness to the thousands of non-Christian students. Pray for their growth and integration into local churches. There are no UESI staff workers in Kashmir or Himachal Pradesh.

c) *Young people* — the statistics are solemn: 100 million school drop-outs, 50% living below the poverty line, 24% severely malnourished. Many live in a moral and spiritual vacuum. Most churches do not have the resources or know-how to minister to them. **YFC**, Blessing Youth Ministry, **CEF**, **SU**, **CCCI** and others reach out to some.

d) *Children in crisis* — no country can rival India's need. Of India's nearly 400m under 18, 70m+ are child labourers, 10m are bonded labourers (a form of slavery to pay off family debts), 13m are homeless, 2m are street children without families. There is widespread child abuse, and there is a deficit of 40m girls because of female foeticide — over 20,000 ultrasound clinics thrive on this illegal practice. There are 575,000 child prostitutes and there is a massive trade in Bangladeshi and Nepali girls sold into prostitution. Pray that these desperate needs may be addressed through loving Christian ministries.

e) *Leprosy sufferers* number 1.5m, 63% of the world's total. Christian agencies, in particular **TLM** and their 2,000 workers in 50 centres, minister to them.

f) *The blind.* India's 10m blind represent over a quarter of the world's total. Few have learned the Braille script, nor are there many materials in Braille in Indian languages. The **Torch Trust for the Blind** is committed to producing the whole Bible in Braille in the 12 major languages of India. At present there are some books in nine languages, but none have the whole Bible. Other agencies with ministry to blind people are **Mission to the Blind** and **India Fellowship for Physically Handicapped**. **Compass Braille** is an agency specializing in producing Braille Scriptures in Indian languages by means of computer.

g) *AIDS has spread rapidly* and is worst in Mumbai (3% of population), Maharashtra and Karnataka (2.4%), Tamil Nadu (1.8%) and NE India. Many fear that by 2000 there will be 10m carrying the virus, or 1% of the population of India. By 2020 there could be 200m carrying HIV — if present trends continue unchecked. This could become a catastrophe for India and only now are the authorities and Christian churches and agencies beginning to address the need for effective preventive and care ministries and also the need to minister to drug addicts — a major source of infection. A massive mobilization is needed.

10 Minority religious communities:

a) *Muslims* may number 140 million making India the second largest Muslim country in the world. Once the rulers of much of India for over 600 years, but now a pressured minority, they are one of the world's most accessible Muslim communities. Sixty million speak Urdu/Dekkani and 80 million, other languages. Only a few hundred Christian workers are involved with them, but there is a rising interest and concern for Muslims. Several agencies are committed to ministry among them.

b) *The Sikh community* world-wide numbers around 24 million, but there is little understanding of Sikhism among Christians to be able to dialogue and bring them to a knowledge of Christ. In recent years many Sikhs have turned to Christ in Vancouver, Canada (72 churches) and more recently in Haryana state.

c) *Buddhist Tibetans* number about 130,000, of which 90,000 are refugees from China. Only 40-50 believers are known. Dharamsala in Himachal Pradesh is the present HQ of the Dalai Lama. Pray for him and his followers.

d) *The 3,500,000 Jains and 150,000 Parsees* with their wealth, isolation from others, and their unique religions are extremely hard to reach, yet are very influential in society, industry and business.

11 Help Ministries play a vital part in the evangelization of millions who have no meaningful contacts with Christian churches. Pray for:

a) *The Bible Society* with its long and remarkable ministry and key role in distributing over 100 million portions of Scripture or Bibles annually. Other organizations are also supplying and distributing Scriptures — such as **World Home Bible League**, **Bibles for the World**, International Bible Society and **Bharatiya Bible League**. **The Bible League** has done much in research of India's states for all Christian agencies, as well as in effective Bible distribution and outreach to 70 unreached people groups.

b) **Bible translation** is a major challenge.

i   *A new effort* as great as that of William Carey 200 years ago should be mounted, or at the present rate of translation it will take 100 years to cover the languages of India!

ii   *Indian missions* are beginning to rise to the challenge of the 203 languages that still may require attention — 30 with a definite need. Over 100 languages spoken by more than 10,000 are without Scriptures.

iii   *The* **United Bible Society** has 74 translation projects in hand.

iv   *Various Indian agencies* are involved in Scripture translation projects — Indian Bible Translators (40), **IEM** (12), **FMPB**, **GFA**, ORBIT (2).

v   *The Indian Institute of Cross-Cultural Communication* is one agency which provides training in linguistics for many agencies and helps to monitor progress in over 35 projects.

vi   *There is a great need for modern*, culturally appropriate translations in Urdu and many other languages.

c) **Literature distribution.** The prodigious growth of the writing, publishing and distributing of Christian literature has been a major factor in breaking down opposition to the gospel. **EHC** teams are in the process of giving literature out to most homes in India. By 2000, 500 million pieces of literature had been distributed with 6 million responses and the formation of 16,000 Christ Group fellowships. It is estimated that 300 million or more have been exposed to the gospel through teams distributing Scriptures. **SGM** dispatches around 5 million Scripture portions to India annually in 39 languages. **GFA** produces and distributes 50 million pieces of literature annually.

d) **Christian publishing/bookstores.** Publishers must contend with lack of local writersand high costs in a poor land, but many locally-produced books have been printed and sold in large numbers. The **Evangelical Literature Fellowship of India** is a major networking body for 23 agencies. Pray for the **Gospel Literature Service** in Mumbai (publishing books, tracts, etc.), the **Evangelical Literature Service** (CLC) with HQ in Chennai (40 full-time workers, 10 stores, 150 book titles in print), and **OM Books** (publishing and nation-wide distribution). *Athmeeya Yatra* of GFA has become one of the largest producers of literature in India. The **Christian Booksellers Association** was formed in 2000.

e) **Bible Correspondence Courses** sent out from over 70 centres. These have proved fruitful. The centre linked with **TEAM** has courses in 22 languages. The **ICI** (**AoG**) sends out courses in 11 languages, with two million having completed at least one course.

f) **Cassette ministry** is significant with over half the population functionally illiterate. **GRN** has increased their language recording range to 394 with at least 171 others targeted. **World Cassette Outreach**, **People India** and **Hosanna** as well as the Bible Society have large programmes for making audio-Scriptures available in all possible languages.

g) **Christian medical work.** The **Christian Medical Association** has oversight of 430 institutions with both Indian and expatriate medical workers. The **Emmanuel Hospitals Association** has responsibility for 22 hospitals originally started by foreign missions. Pray that the witness going out from these hospitals may lead many to the Saviour. Pray for the **Evangelical Medical Fellowship of India** and **Evangelical Nurses Fellowship** with groups in many hospitals. All over India the proportion of Christian medical workers is high; pray that non-Christians may be won to Jesus through them.

h) **Christian films and video** are important:

i   *A 200 hour TV series on the life of Christ* had 70 million viewers until restrictions limited this. From this was developed *Karanamaidu*, the Indian film on Jesus, available in 21 main languages. Over 300 film teams are showing this film to powerful effect to 2-3 million annually.

ii   *The* **JESUS** *film* is available in 55 languages; 100,000 view it daily as 500 film teams move around the country. These teams need wisdom and protection in today's India.

i) **Christian radio and TV** have won an enormous following among Christians and non-Christians. Pray for:

i   *Programme producers* — the pressure is great to make quality programmes and find talented, committed, native speakers. Some agencies involved: India Gospel Outreach, HBI, **GFA**, **WEC-RW**, Back to the Bible.

ii   *Broadcasters* — the major agencies: **TWR** (Irkutsk, Russia, Sri Lanka), **FEBA** (Seychelles) and **FEBC** (Manila) broadcast between them 200 hours/week in over 42 languages on both SW and MW frequencies, and increasingly on national and local radio too.

iii   *The global inter-agency vision* **World by Radio** (see p. 694) has gathered momentum for

India: 5 languages have adequate programming, 17 need an increase in hours, 4 have an "urgent" and 14 a "probable" need for programming.

iv *The massive growth of the use of satellite TV* and 75,000 Indian cable operators means TV is replacing radio. Pray that Christian agencies may adapt and exploit the possibilities of this expensive medium.

v *Internet evangelism* is becoming important as India rapidly 'wires-up'. There were 1.4 million Internet users in 1999, but this is increasingly massively.

12 **Indians in other lands** number 22 million. There are large numbers who have emigrated to the Americas (USA 2.1m; Canada 715,000; Trinidad 517,000; Suriname 140,000), Europe (UK 1m), Africa (South Africa 1.1m; Mauritius 763,000; Kenya 210,000; Malawi 30,000), Pacific (Fiji 357,000; Australia 90,000), Asia (Malaysia 1.6m; Sri Lanka Tamil 3.2m; Myanmar 750,000; Singapore 271,000). A further one million are migrant workers in the Middle East. In some of these communities many have become Christians (probably 250,000) — as in South Africa, USA and Mauritius; in others there has been relatively little response. Pray that expatriate Indian Christians may be called as witnesses to their land of origin. Visas are easier for them to obtain.

STATES OF INDIA

Most of these states are far larger than the majority of nations covered in this book, yet limitations of space allow only a brief description of each below. In December 2000, three new states were created — Jharkhand from South Bihar, Chhattisgarh from south-east Madya Pradesh and Uttaranchal from Uttar Pradesh. These are still handled as single units below because many issues were yet to be clarified as this book went to print. All specifics about ministries and agencies have been restricted for security reasons. Many of the Indian agencies already mentioned are active in outreaches and ministries alluded to below.

ANDHRA PRADESH

GEOGRAPHY Area 275,000 sq.km. India's fifth largest state, in the south-east.
Population 79,710,000; 290 people/sq.km.

Capital Hyderabad 6.4m. Other major cities: Visakhapatanam 1.2m; Vijayawada 1,175,000.

PEOPLES 500. Major groups in their categories:
FC Brahmin 3.6m; Bania/Vaisya 3m; Sonar 1.1m.
OBC Telaga/Munnur/Mutrasi 9.8m; Ahir/Yadau/ Gowli 7.2m; Kapu/Kunbi/Reddi 6.7m; Deccani Muslim 5.1m; Dhobi/Agasa 3.3m; Viswakarma 2.3m; Andhra Coastal Muslim 1.7m; Boya 1.6m; Kalal/Idiga 1.5m; Nai 1.4m; Rayalseema Muslim 1.3m; Adi Andhra 1.0m.
SC/Dalit (60). Madiga 6m; Mala 5.1m; Adi Andhra 1.1m; Mala Sale 125,000; Arunthathiar 122,000.
ST (34): Banjara 2.1m; Koya 584,000; Yenadi 511,000; Yerukala 496,000; Gond 271,000; Konda Dhora 214,000; Jatapu 133,000; Savara 126,000.

Languages Telugu 85%; Urdu 8.3%; Hindi 2.8%; Tamil 1.1%.

RELIGION Hindu 89.1%; Muslim 8.9%; Christian 1.9%; Other 0.1%.

1 The official percentage of Christians declined from 4.2% in 1971 to 1.8% in 1991 — the only state in India to show this. Yet in this state has occurred strong church growth with millions of new Christians. There are 66,000 churches and many denominations, but nominalism has increased and Hindu efforts to 'reconvert' Dalits to Hinduism have been successful — with 30% losses in some areas. Pray for new life, revival and effective faith-sharing among and by Christians.

2 Hyderabad is the key centre for Islam in South India. Nearly 40% of the city is Muslim, and the hub of the 11 million south Indian Deccani Muslims. Islam in the state grew from 8.2% in 1971 to 8.9% in 1991. Although 150 Christian organizations are based in the city, very few Christian workers have ever focused on their spiritual need and Christians from this community are correspondingly few. Pray that this may be changed.

3 Christian outreach continues with numerous people coming to Christ. There are churches in every district, and there is steady growth among many of the tribal groups. There is a vigorous saturation church planting movement promoted by evangelical churches. The challenges:
a) *Overall growth* of the Christians to be resumed.
b) *The evangelization of the forward castes*.
c) *Relatively few* of the 26,600 villages have churches.
d) *Of the 33 tribal groups*, 16 are still unreached. There are significant breakthroughs only among the Savara, Koya, Konda and Chenchu (many Indian agencies, also Christian Outreach Uplifting New Tribes), though Indian missions have commenced work in 12 other tribes.
e) *Of the 3,522 pincode areas* 50% still had no workers resident in 1998

ARUNACHAL PRADESH

GEOGRAPHY Area 84,000 sq.km. Mountainous north-eastern frontier state bordering Bhutan, China and Myanmar. The state was inaugurated in 1987 and largely closed to outsiders, and even Indians until 1995.
Population 1,070,000; 13 people/sq.km.

Capital Itanagar.

PEOPLES Over 30 speaking 22 languages.
ST Nissi 81,000; Adi Galong 71,000; Wancho 58,100; Bangni 53,600; Tagin 45,800; Adi Minyong 34,000; Adi 41,100; Monpa 36,700; Nocte 33,300; Tanu 28,200; Ahom 21,600.

RELIGION Hindu 37%; Ethnic religions 35.6%; Buddhist 13%; Christian 13%; Muslim 1.4%.

1 The Church has grown dramatically from 0.8% of the population in 1971 to 13% today. Much of the pioneer work was done by Indian missionaries from Nagaland and N.E. India. Almost 90% of the nearly 1,000 churches are Baptists, but independent and other churches are increasing in number. There are numerous churches among the Adi, Nissi and Tangsa and, more recently, the Apatani and Nocte. Praise God for this, but pray for greater cooperation between them.

2 **Persecution was severe** in the 1970s and '80s. Heavy-handed efforts to Hinduize the indigenous Doino-Polo religion, hinder evangelism and stop church growth have broken down and pressures diminished but anti-Christian legislation has not been withdrawn. Pray that constitutionally guaranteed religious freedom may be granted to Christians.

3 **The unfinished task**. Arunachal Christians have the vision that every people in the state be reached. Some prayer targets:

a) *The Buddhist peoples of the west* adjoining Bhutan have had little opportunity to hear the gospel. There are no churches and only a handful of believers.

b) *The animist peoples* of the centre and west — the Miri, Sulung, Tangam, Tagin, Mishmi and Wanchoo.

c) *The newcomer peoples* — the Deori, Chakma and Hajong.

4 **Radio ministry** in Adi is having an impact (GFA).

ASSAM

GEOGRAPHY **Area** 78,400 sq.km. Noted for the tropical forests (60% of state) and the Brahmaputra River. Main exports: tea, oil and forest products.

Population 26,866,000; 342 people/sq.km. Large-scale immigration from Bangladesh and Nepal.

Capital Dispur.

PEOPLES People groups 60+.
FC 10.1% Brahmin 1.4m; Bania 1.3m.

OBC (9) 69.7%. Bengali Muslims (9) 5.8m; Assamese Muslims 2.5m; Tea Garden coolie (of origin) 5.8m, most are of tribal and Dalit origin from Bihar, Orissa, MP.

SC (15) 7.4%. Namasudra 626,000; Kaibartta/Jalia 665,000.

ST (22) 12.8%. Bodo 1.6m; Kachari 350,000; Miri 515,000; Rabha 399,000; Tiwa/Lalung 211,000; Arleng/Karbi 83,000; Dimasa 56,600; Deori 34,800; Barman 30,000.

RELIGION Hindu 65%; Muslim 31%; Christian 3.1%; Buddhist 0.3%; Other 0.6%.

1 **Assam is the major spiritual challenge in N.E. India.** After two centuries of Christian work, professing Christians are a marginalized and shrinking percentage of the population (6.4% in 1961, 3% in 2000). Pray for a reversal of this trend and for revival, vision and impact on society to characterize the many lukewarm traditional congregations. Major denominations are Baptist (4), Lutheran (2), CNI and Catholic.

2 **The Evangelical witness** is confined to several Baptist associations and some newer independent and charismatic groups and Indian (mainly Mizo and Naga) mission agencies. Through them there is continuing growth among the tribal peoples with a significant minority of their populations now Christian. Lack of evangelists, church planters, Bible teachers and translators and lack of cooperation between the newer and older Christian bodies blunts further growth.

3 **The less evangelized** for which prayer is needed:

a) *The 15 million Assamese* are mostly Hindu and there are only around 1,000 active Christians among them; Christians are only 0.07% of the population. They are one of the least evangelized major Hindu peoples in India.

b) *Bengalis* are largely Muslim and comprise 80% of all Muslims. Many have immigrated from poor, overpopulated Bangladesh with considerable hostility generated among Assamese. Muslims are a majority in 6 of Assam's 23 districts. There is virtually no Christian witness to or among the 8 million Muslims and only a few Bengali Christians are known.

c) *Assam tea estate workers* number 6 million. Many are migrant Santal, Munda, Kharia, Orang and other tribal minorities from other states. Only 3% are Christian. They are open to the gospel, but few are there to share it.

d) *Evangelization of the tribal peoples is incomplete*. The Rajbongsi, Deori, Mising, Mikir and Kachari are all less than 5% Christian.

e) *Of Assam's 564 pincode areas*, 58% had no resident Christian workers in 1998.

BIHAR & JHARKHAND

GEOGRAPHY **Area** 99,000 sq.km. Ganges alluvial plain. Jharkhand 75,000 sq.km. Wooded mineral-bearing hills to the south of Bihar.

Population BI: 75,834,000; 766 people/sq.km. JH: 27,500,000; 366 people/sq.km. Largely agricultural.

Capitals BI: Patna 2,100,000; JH: Ranchi 615,000. Other major city: Jamshedpur 1,000,000.

PEOPLES 261.
FC Brahmin/Bhumihar 7.2m; Rajput (Hindu) 4.3m.

OBC Bihari Muslim 16.6m; Ahir/Yadav 11.1m; Koiri/Kushwaha 4.9m; Kurmi 4.28m;Teli 2.9m; Ansari (Muslim) 2.7m; Kahar 1.8m; Tanti/Tatwa 1.7m; Dhanuk 1.7m; Kandu/Kanu 1.6m.
SC (22) Chamar 4.7m; Dosadh 4.2m; Musahar 2m; Bhuiya 1.3m; Dhobi 822,000; Pasi 680,000.
ST (31) Santal/Hor 3.1m; Oraon 1.6m; Munda 1.3m; Ho 800,000; Kharwar 322,000; Lohara 245,000; Kharia 211,000; Bhumij 203,000; Bedia 173,000; Gond 144,000; Mahli/Mhali 137,000; Malto 118,000.

Languages 75. Hindi 44%; Hindi dialects (Bhojpuri, Maithili, Magahi) 33%; Tribal languages 10%; Urdu 9%; Bengali 2.5%.

RELIGION Hindu 77%; Muslim 14.5%; Ethnic religions 5%; Christian 1% (unofficially 1.5-2%). Both Buddhism and Jainism were founded in Bihar, but few adherents remain today.

1 **Bihar has had a disastrous post-independence history.** It has become a byword for corruption, mafia-style politics, a breakdown of law and order, communal tensions, oppression of minorities and underdevelopment. In 1950 it was India's third richest state; it is now one of its poorest. The formation of Jharkhand has had economic and spiritual implications for the politically dominant but economically poorer north. Pray for a resumption of true democratic government and the raising up of righteous leaders who will restore the fortunes of the two states.

2 **North Bihar is one of the least evangelized mega-populations in the world.** It has been long known as a graveyard of missions. Years of effort have yielded little fruit among the Hindu and Muslim people of the plains.

a) *The 14 million forward caste Hindus* have had exposure to the gospel, but the message has not been socially acceptable. Only 3,000 call themselves Christian (0.03% of total).

b) *The 33 million of the backward castes* are marginally more evangelized; about 0.5% are Christian in 42 of the castes, but in at least 36 others there are no known Christians.

c) *The 15 million Muslims* are unreached and increasing as a percentage of the population. No ongoing effort is being made to reach them, and only a handful of converts to Christ are known. As a community they are insecure and subject to Hindu mob violence.

d) *The 14 million Dalit* are 0.7% Christian, but only three of the 30 castes have more than 1% Christian. People movements earlier in the 20th Century fizzled out. Pray that these abused, despised, illiterate peoples in grinding poverty might find liberty in Christ.

3 **Christian churches are in great need.** Lethargy, nominalism, and lack of outreach are commonplace. Through the impact of pioneer Lutheran, Catholic and Anglican missionaries, today 75% of all Christians are tribal and 24% are from Dalit and backward castes, almost all of whom live in Jharkhand. They have huge social and psychological barriers to overcome in order to witness to the politically powerful, but spiritually needy, middle and higher caste peoples. Pray that there may be revival and a miraculous change.

4 **Significant investment of personnel** has begun to bear fruit through the ministries of such agencies as **FMPB**, GEMS, Vishwa Vani, **GFA** and IMS:

a) *Excellent research and analysis* which has highlighted the needs.

b) *A renewed focus on prayer*, holistic evangelism and church planting — 500 new churches formed in the first six years.

c) *The Bihar Outreach Network (BORN)* was formed in 1992 and a number of churches and agencies are working together.

d) *Goals set for training and mobilizing new workers* — Indian mission agencies have increased from 40 to 60, major ones being Gospel Echoing Missionary Society, **GFA** (with 3 training centres and 400 workers), **FMPB**, **AoG**, **IET**, etc., and over 10 new Bible schools have been launched.

e) Outreach challenges:

i *50 unreached language groups* — only 40 known believers among the 12 million Magahi speakers; 10 tribal groups with no effective witness.

ii *Of the 200 larger people groups,* 20 are reached, 100 are being reached and 80 are yet untouched by sustained outreach.

iii *Of Bihar's 1,853 pincode areas,* 81% have no resident Christian workers.

DELHI

GEOGRAPHY Area 1,483 sq.km. The National Capital Territory.

Population 11,300,000; 7,619 people/sq.km. India's capital city and centre of power, wealth and industry. A trend-setting city with significant communities from nearly every ethnic and caste group in India.

PEOPLES

FC 32.5%, **OBC** 48.4%; **SC**(39) 19.1%.

RELIGION

Hindu 84%; Muslim 14.5%; Christian 0.9%.

1 **Delhi** is a city in crisis — with 500,000 immigrants annually; over half of the population living in slums, massive pollution and related diseases and a crime wave. Pray that in this turmoil many might seek after the Lord Jesus Christ.

2 **Christians number around 100,000** but only 15-20,000 are regular church-goers. About 150 denominations and agencies have a base in the city, and there are 400 congregations. Pray for revival, new life and effective outreach by those who claim to be followers of Christ. Major denominations are: Pentecostal (60+ churches), CNI (21), ECI (17), Methodist (12), Baptist (11), Delhi Bible Fellowship (8) and others. Many churches are successfully moving to a cell church mode of operation.

3 **Many India-wide Christian organizations** have headquarters in Delhi — notably Evangelical Fellowship of India, All India Prayer Fellowship, Emmanuel Hospital Association, **IET**, **TWR**-India. Pray that blessing may flow from Delhi to the whole country.

4 Specific outreach challenges for prayer:

a) *The millions of slum-dwellers* need far more input in holistic ministry and discipling programmes. Mode of Deliverance Mission and **GFA** have a successful ministry among them.

b) *Ethnic communities* among whom churches are being planted — Muslim and Hindu Bengali (2m), Nepali (50,000 — 12 churches), etc. There are new believers among the Balmiki, Sindhi, Panjabi and middle class Hindi. **IET** has planted 16 churches in 9 people groups.

c) *Refugee communities* — Tibetans, Iranians, Afghans among whom little churches are being planted.

GOA

GEOGRAPHY Area 3,700 sq.km. Portuguese colony 1510-1961. Full statehood in 1987.

Population 1,370,000; 319 people/sq.km.

PEOPLES/LANGUAGES

Konkani 60%, Marathi 25%; Gujarati 7%; Kannada 3.2%.

RELIGION Hindu 64.5%; Christian 31.2% (almost entirely Catholic); Muslim 4%; Other 0.3%.

1 **Traditional Catholicism** is the legacy of Portuguese rule. Hindu beliefs and customs are interwoven with Christianity. Goa is a centre for drug trafficking and child prostitution. New life in Christ and a clear understanding of biblical Christianity are both needs. There is a strong Catholic charismatic presence, but Protestants are only around 1,000 in number and churches very few.

2 **Workers** able to communicate in Konkani are a great need. There are few labourers to reach nominal Catholics, Hindus or Muslims.

3 **Christian literature** in Konkani is also a great need. The Goanese Konkani NT is being re-translated; the old being little understood today.

GUJARAT

GEOGRAPHY Area 196,000 sq.km. Coastal state adjoining Pakistan. Desert in NW, fertile in SW; wealth through oil, industry and agriculture. Much devastation caused in the 2001 earthquake.

Population 50,100,000; 250 people/sq.km.

Capital Ahmadabad 4,100,000. Other major cities: Surat 2,200,000; Vadodara 1,200,000.

PEOPLES
FC 14.5%. Rajput (Hindu) 2.2m; Brahmin 1.8m; Bania 1.7m.

OBC 63.2%. Kunbi 6.3m; Koli 6.2m; Gujarati Muslims 4.5m; Mahratta-Kunbi 3.8m; Bhar-

wad/ Dhangar 1.2m; Sindhi Hindu 1.1m.

SC (31) 7.4%. Mahyavanshi 1.5m; Chamar 983,000; Bhangi 800,000; Dhodia 664,000; Meghwal 197,000.

ST (28) 14.9%. Bhil 3m; Dubla 579,000; Rathawa 477,000; Kokna 400,000; Gamit 349,000; Dhanka 217,000; Varli 199,000; Koli Dhor 106,000; Koli Mahadev 76,000; Patelia 103,000.

Languages Gujarati 91%; Hindi 2.9%; Sindhi 1.7%; Marathi 1.4%; Urdu 1.3% (Tribals 14%).

RELIGION Hindu 89.5%; Muslim 8.7%; Jain 1.2%; Christian 0.5% (Catholic 0.13%; Protestant 0.37%).

1 **Gujarat is a focal point in India for the persecution of Christians.** Hindu extremist groups, with the support of the local BJP government, the police and the administration, have pursued a long-term strategy of intimidation, slander and harassment of Muslims and Christians in Dalit and tribal groups. In 1998 there were 34 churches destroyed or damaged. 'Freedom of religion' legislation is being pushed with strong 'anti-conversion' clauses, yet at the same time many tribal Christians are being openly coerced into embracing Hinduism. Pray for a government that will promote inter-communal harmony and true freedom of religion. Gujarat was Gandhi's birthplace — may the peace and tolerance he promoted become reality here.

2 **The Christian Church** is predominantly Catholic, Church of North India and Methodist. Many other smaller evangelical denominations are also present (**CMA**, Salvation Army, **TEAM**, Brethren, Believers Church and Pentecostal). Generally, nominalism, compromise with Hinduism, divisions and lack of outreach have sapped Christian spiritual life. Present hostility has stirred new life and even revival in some areas. Pray for a Holy Spirit dynamization of these churches.

3 **There is significant church growth in five districts.** The impact of Methodist Church outreach, Salvation Army and new Indian missionary efforts among tribals contrasts the earlier decline in the state, with rapid church growth in the south-eastern Dangs district. Many Bhil, Kukna, Gamit, Chaudhri, Garasia, Koli, Dhodia and others have come to Christ — slightly increasing the percentage of Christians in the state. Pray that this turning to God may continue unchecked by external opposition or internal failures.

4 **The unreached.** While some tribal peoples are responding to the gospel, much need remains. Pray out labourers for:

a) **Saurashtra**, the western peninsula in the Arabian Sea, which has 12 million people but only 0.07% are Christian. This was the worst-affected by the 2001 earthquake.

b) **Muslims** number 4.3 million and are the largest and least reached segment of the population. There are 76 distinct people groups among them — mostly in the west, north and in Ahmadabad and Baruch District in the east.

c) **Unreached caste groups**. The Dalit groups — Bhangi, Nadia and Pasi — are urbanized and becoming responsive with over 3% Christian.

d) **The 20 tribal peoples** with little outreach — the larger being the Dubla, Dhanka and Rathawa.

e) **The Parsees** (11,000 of India's 150,000 are in Gujarat) — well-educated, wealthy people of Persian origin who follow the Zoroastrian religion. There are only 30 known believers in the whole world among the 4.5 million Parsees. Pray for the beginnings of ministry among them and also for the translation of the Bible into their language.

f) **The Jain religion** is an offshoot of Hinduism with a strong emphasis on moral purity and non-violence. Gujarat has 580,000 Jains of India's total of 3.5-4.8 million. Ahmadabad is a major Jain centre with over 100 temples. Jains are often wealthy and control much trade and industry in the state. Little has ever been done to evangelize them.

5 **Aid projects.** The devastating earthquake of 2001 in Gujarat led to widespread loss of life and property. Many Christian agencies responded to the government's plea for help with a large investment of personnel, time and aid (**WVI**, AICC and many others).

6 **Large Gujarati communities** have grown up in east and central Africa and in Britain. Most have become wealthy traders but, although surrounded by Christians, there has been little success in evangelism.

HARYANA

GEOGRAPHY Area 44,200 sq.km. Between Delhi and Panjab in India's northwest.

Population 20,000,000; 450 people/sq.km.

Capital Chandigarh 850,000 (shared with Panjab and is a Union Territory). Other major city: Faridabad 618,000.

PEOPLES 310.
FC 29%. Arora 1.7m; Brahmin 1.5m; Rajput (Hindu) 1.3m; Bania 633,000.

OBC (42) 63.6%. Jat (Hindu) 3.1m; Muslims of Haryana 1.1m; Jat (Sikh) 656,000; Gujar 607,000; Teli 596,000; Ahir/Yadav 574,000; Dhanuk 434,000; Lohar 400,000.
SC (44) 7.4%. Chamar 2.1m; Balmiki/Chuhra/Bhangi 769,000.

Languages Hindi (Haryanvi) 65%; Panjabi 7%; Urdu 1.6%.

RELIGION Hindu 89.3%; Sikh 6.2%; Muslim 4.1%; Jain 0.27%; Christian 0.08% (Catholic 0.02%; Protestant 0.06%).

1 **Haryana is one of India's least evangelized states.** In 1991 only 15,700 identified themselves as Christian. There were only 500 churches and prayer cells in 44% of the state's 449 pincode areas in 1998. The Church is weak and under pressure from Hinduists. Pray for a spiritual awakening.

2 **The unreached** — only 15 of the 92 people groups are known to have any congregations of believers. Indian agencies are pioneering work among the 8 million Jat, the 3.8 million Dalit (**FMBP**, RSP, Indian Inland Mission), and the Sikhs (Indian Inland Mission). Pray for a response. Pray also for the unreached Muslims and Jains. There is nothing of the Bible translated into the local language, Haryanvi.

3 **Christian ministry.** There were a total of 265 Christian workers in Haryana in 1998. There are now 15 Christian training institutions in the state — pray for the equipping and sustenance of many new workers.

HIMACHAL PRADESH

GEOGRAPHY Area 55,700 sq.km. Mountainous Himalayan state bordering on Kashmir and Tibet.

Population 6,147,000; 110 people/sq.km.

Capital Shimla 115,000.

PEOPLES
FC 35.2%. Rajput(Hindu) 1.1m; Brahmin 710,000; Arora 320,000.
OBC (23) 35.3%. Kanet 923,000; Ghirath 391,000; Rathia 341,000.

SC (58) 25.3%. Koli 440,000; Chamar 416,000; Lohar 165,000; Pahari Muslim 114,000; Julaha 108,000.
ST (8) 4.2%. Gaddi 112,000; Kanaura 70,000; Gujjar 41,000.

Languages Hindi 89%, most actually speak Pahari, a group of languages close to Panjabi; Panjabi 6.3%; Kanauri 1.2%; Nepali 0.9%; Dogri 0.7%; Tibetan/ Bhotia 0.5%.

RELIGION Hindu 95.9%; Muslim 1.7%; Buddhist 1.2%; Sikh 1.1%; Christian 0.09%.

1 **Himachal Pradesh** has long been India's least evangelized state. It is the 'Land of the Gods' and a centre for Hindu pilgrimages. Every mountain is named after a god and there is much devotion to idols. Pray that many may be freed from bondages and find liberty in Jesus.

2 **There has been significant growth in the Church.** In 1991 known Christians numbered 4,435 in only 90 churches. Between 1992 and 1998 over 1,200 were baptised and 150 churches were planted. Pray for the vision of Himachal Outreach Network and for unity, faith and vision among leaders and churches to increase. There are nearly 300 Christian workers. Pray for their multiplication, safety in difficult travel conditions and fruitfulness. GFA and IGO run training schools for new workers.

3 **The challenges of the unreached.** Every people group is, at best, marginally evangelized. Of the 92 people groups, only 15 have congregations of believers. Pray specifically for:

a) *The Kullu Valley* — there are now several congregations (IEM). The Kullu Pahari NT is being translated.

b) *Unevangelized districts.* Kinnaur had no churches in 1995, but there were four by 1998. Bilaspur and Hamipur are the least evangelized. By 2000 there were 77 churches in the Kinnaur district.

c) *Lahul and Spiti District* is largely culturally Tibetan. About 5,000 Tibetan refugees have settled in Dharamsala, the Dalai Lama's headquarters. IET has seen some fruit among them. Much international aid flows into efforts to retain Tibetan identity, culture and language, now being lost in Tibet. Pray for the gospel to reach the 100,000 Tibetan refugees in India.

d) *Of 430 pincode areas*, 89% had no resident Christian worker in 1998.

JAMMU & KASHMIR

GEOGRAPHY **Area** 222,000 sq.km. The disputed state has been dismembered — Pakistan seizing 83,000 sq.km. in 1947 and China 38,000 sq.km. of Himalayan Ladakh in 1950.

Population 9,400,000 in Indian-controlled areas; 92 people/sq.km.

Capital Srinagar 800,000.

PEOPLES 240.
   Main groups Kashmiri Muslim 6.8m; Kashmiri Hindu 3m; Mangrik 926,000; Brahmin/Pandit

716,000; Dogra (Hindu) 655,000; Rajput (Hindu) 515,000; Rajput (Muslim) 108,000; Dogra (Muslim) 100,000.

SC (17) 9.3%. Megh 292,000; Chamar 180,000; Dom/Dum 147,000.

ST (6) 7%. Gujjar 578,000; Gaddi 20,900 (not legally a tribe).

Tibetan-related 1.5%. Balti 33,000; Brukpa 10,000; Changpa 12,000; Zanskar 10,000; Ladakhi 8,000.

RELIGION Muslim 64.2%; Hindu 32.2%; Sikh 2.2%; Buddhist 1.2%; Christian 0.16%

1 **Kashmir has become an international tragedy.** Political short-sightedness, lack of courage, and national pride have kept it in a state of war for six decades. Pakistan has fought four wars (direct or by proxy) over this divided state. The result has been polarization, Islamic militancy, 30,000 deaths and 800,000 refugees. India's democratic values, unity and territorial integrity have been threatened and Pakistan and Kashmir's economies crippled. Pray for wisdom, statesmanship, fairness to the Muslim majority and justice to the refugees to be shown by the political leaders involved, and pray for the restoration of peace.

2 **Kashmir is spiritually poverty-stricken.** In 1990 there were but 12,000 Christians in 45 churches, many of which were nominal and either low-caste or immigrant in origin. Evangelical believers were a few thousand, but in the '90s their numbers doubled and churches increased to 167 in 1998. Pray for increased effectiveness in reaching a war-weary and disillusioned population.

3 **Outreach has always been limited**, and few Christian workers have been indigenous to the state. There were just 115 Christian workers in 1998. The majority of the workers are in Jammu and not in the dangerous, war-torn Muslim-majority Kashmir. Yet there is progress for the gospel through such agencies as HEM(KEF), IET, GFA and others. Pray for new workers to be called so that there is a Christian worker in every pincode area.

4 **Unreached peoples.** All are in this category. Pray for:

a) *Kashmiri Muslims* who have become more militant for their faith. There are a number of smaller Muslim peoples such as the Baltis and Gujars who are unreached. Less than 100 Christians have come from the Muslim community, and in the Muslim uprising of the late '80s some of these were martyred and churches destroyed. Several agencies are working among them. Pray that Islamist extremism may cause Muslims to seek an alternative way in Jesus.

b) *Tibetan Buddhists* from the groups named above in the mountainous north and northeast who have been only marginally evangelized. The Moravians have a small work in

Ladakh with three churches and only 150 believers and a school with 1,000 students. The *JESUS* film is now being used in the area.

c) **The high-caste Brahmin Pandits** of Kashmir were one million in 1900, but since the 1940s Muslim hostility, terror and violence has reduced them to 50,000 today and only 3,000 in their Kashmir Valley home area. Many are still refugees. Only about 15 believers are known among them.

5 **Christian radio** — **TWR** broadcast five times a week in Kashmiri.

KARNATAKA

GEOGRAPHY   Area 192,000 sq.km. South-western coastal state.

Population 53,500,000; 278 people/sq.km.

Capital Bangalore 5,400,000.

PEOPLES   224 (174 speaking Kannada). **Main groups** (143) Lingayat 7m; Vakkaliga 6.1m; Dekkani (Mus) 5.7m; Bedar 2.3m; Brahmin 2.3m; Mahratta 1.7m; Kalal 1.3m; Viswakarma 1.2m; Gangakula 1.2m; Ahir/Yadav/Gowli 1.0m; Dhangar 1m.

SC (100) 16.4%. Adi Karnataka 2.7m; Adi Andhra 1.1m; Adi Dravida 830,000; Holaya 590,000; Chamar 518,000; Madiga 502,000. **ST** (32) 4.3%. Kuruba 3.3m; Banjara 866,000; Marathi 98,800; Gondaru 89,000.

Languages 19. Kannada 66%, many dialects; Urdu 9.5%, most speaking Deccani, distantly related to Urdu; Telugu 8.1%; Marathi 3.8%; Konkani 1.8%; Hindi 1.8%; Malayalam 1.6%.

RELIGION   Hindu 85.4%; Muslim 11.6%; Christian 2.1% (Catholic 1.4%, Protestant 0.7%); Jain 0.8%.

1 **Karnataka** is South India's most spiritually needy state. The Christian communities are inward looking and culturally isolated — the more wealthy multi-language churches of Bangalore and the south, and the more Catholic coastal districts. Pray for a breakdown of all barriers for witness and for the gospel. Hinduists are pressurizing Christian schools to teach Hinduism. Yet of late response to evangelism is encouraging despite the opposition.

2 **Bangalore** is India's 'Silicon City' and is also the Indian headquarters for many Christian churches, Indian missions (**IEM**, Quiet Corner) and international agencies (**The Bible Society**, Language Recordings India [**GRN**], **SGM**, **EHC**, Asia Graduate School of Theology, International Correspondence School of **AoG**, India Bible League, **FEBA**, etc.) and theological institutions. The Methodists and CSI are strong in the area. Pray that Bangalore's privileged Christian community may be revived.

3 **The less evangelized** — almost all of Karnataka's peoples are unreached. The Karnataka Mission network was launched in 1996. Pray specifically for:

a) **The Lingayats**, predominantly in the north, prominent in society and politics, but staunchly Hindu; very few believers. Over 12 agencies are committed to cooperate for their evangelization.

b) **The Adi Karnataka** are the original inhabitants — only 41 believers in 3 churches.

c) **The Devadasis** are girls forced into temple prostitution. There are 50,000+ in the state.

d) **The Banjara** have begun to respond through S. India Gospel Outreach and others. There are now congregations developing in 300 settlements.

Of Karnataka's 2,479 pincode areas, 80% had no resident Christian worker in 1998.

KERALA

GEOGRAPHY   Area 39,000 sq.km. India's most south-westerly state.

Population 33,000,000; 870 people/sq.km. India's most prosperous and densely populated state.

Capital Trivandrum 1,050,000. Other major cities: Cochin 1,250,000; Calicut 1,075,000.

PEOPLES   194. **Main groups** Malabar/Mappila Muslims 8.5m; Viswakarma 1m; Brahmin 604,000; Nair/Nayar 597,000; Tamil Muslim 501,000; Ilavan

459,000; Nadar/Channan 158,000. **SC** (68) 9.9%: Pulayan 1m; Cheruman 380,000; Paraiyan 351,000; Kuravan 294,000; Thandan 264,000; Kanakkam 185,000; Vettuvan 145,000. **ST** (37) 1.1%: Paniyan 74,000; Malayarayan 35,000; Alambadi Kurichchan 30,000.

Languages Malayali (Malayalam) 96%; Tamil 2.3%.

RELIGION   Hindu 57.7%; Muslim 23%; Christian 19.3% (Syrian Orthodox 6.7%, Catholic 8.9%, Protestant/Independent 4.4%).

1 **The Syrian Christians,** with links to the Syrian Jacobite Church, are direct descendants of those evangelized by the Apostle Thomas. They form the majority of Kerala's Christians and are members of Orthodox, Catholic and Protestant denominations. They have high social status but have become little more than a caste within Hindu society, and few have broken out to become vital witnesses to those of other cultures. There are, therefore, few converts out of non-Christian backgrounds in the churches. Pray that Ephesians 2:13-17 may be true for these Christians.

2 **Kerala has numerous Protestant denominations and evangelistic agencies.** Moves of the Spirit over the last 100 years brought multitudes of both nominal Syrian Christians and low-caste Hindus to faith in Christ. Over the past 40 years, the Christian percentage of the population has declined, largely through migration all over India and the world, but Kerala is still the state with the largest population of Christians. There are strong and growing mainline, Brethren and Pentecostal congregations. Casteism within the churches is an unmentioned reality. A revived Church in Kerala would have a deep impact on all of India due to the level of education, wealth and dynamism of many Christians, and their dispersal all over India and beyond. There are 1.4m people from Kerala in the Gulf countries.

3 **Unreached peoples.** Since the mid-1990s there has been a surge of interest in missions and many Kerala young people are going out with a vision for the unreached religious, caste and tribal groups in their state and beyond. Yet social barriers are very high, and believers need to be liberated from the spirit of caste both to evangelize other social groups and welcome converts as brethren in their fellowships.
a) *Of the 35 small tribal groups* only three or four have significant Christian groups and ten others a handful of believers. Most are Hindus, animists or demon worshippers. Only seven have over 10,000 people. Kerala Christians need to catch a vision to reach them — praise God a few have.
b) *The Malabar Muslims, or Mappila,* are numerous in the north of Kerala and number 7 million. The ministry of several agencies has led to several thousand known conversions and also groups of believers, but resistance to the gospel is high and new Christians have suffered much. Pray for those involved in this arduous and costly ministry.
c) *Of the higher castes and 41 Dalit groups of Hindus*, there have been people movements to Christianity from among only six or seven of the latter.
d) *Christian work is unevenly distributed*. Only 58% of pincode areas had a resident Christian worker in 1998.

4 **Christian media** have done much to generate missions interest and also TV and radio programmes to the wider population have generated a wide response (**GFA**).

MADHYA PRADESH & CHATTISGARH

GEOGRAPHY Area MP: 297,000 sq.km.; CH: 143,000 sq.km. The latter formed in December 2000. The two states are handled together as a single unit here. Poor and underdeveloped.

Population MP: 62.3m; CH: 17.6m

Capital Bhopal 2m+. Other major cities: Indore 1.2m; Jabalpur 1m.

PEOPLES 342.
Main groups Brahmin 4.6m; Ahir/Yadav 4.6m; Rajput(Hindu) 4.5m; Teli 3.6m; Hindi Belt Muslim 3.1m; Kurmi 2.3m; Kachhi 2.1m; Lodha 1.9m; Mali 1.5m; Bania 1.3m; Pathan(Mus) 1.1m; Bhoi/Kewat 1m; Nai 1m.
SC (49) 14.6%. Chamar 6.3m; Balai 1.2m; Mahar 938,000; Koli 623,000; Nau Buddh 511,000; Bhangi 370,000; Basor 366,000; Ganda 340,000; Bagri 244,000; Kumhar 199,000; Arakh 182,000.

ST (45) 23.3%, the largest concentration of tribal peoples in India and the world with 16m (11m in MP, 7m in CH). Many districts are predominantly tribal. Largest: Gond 8.6m; Bhil 4.3m; Panika 1.2m; Kawar 918,000; Sahariya 428,000; Baiga 408,000; Halba 388,000; Mina 310,000; Bharia Bhumia 252,000; Kol 202,000; Bhattra 192,000; Binjhia 151,000; Oraon 146,000; Bhaina 133,000; Saur 121,000; Korku 110,000; Savara 105,000.

Languages Hindi 80%; Gondi 10%; Marathi 2.3%; Urdu 2.2%; Oriya 1.1%.

RELIGION Hindu 92.4% (most of the Dalit groups and tribes are actually animists); Muslim 5.2%; Jain 0.85%; Christian 0.70%; Sikh 0.27%; Buddhist 0.14%.

1 This state was one of the last to open up for missions with slow response to the gospel until recently. It is strongly Hindu with stern laws limiting conversions to Christianity. Sixty percent of Christians are Catholic; many are Church of North India, Lutheran or Mennonite, and most are Dalit or tribal in origin. Pray for the ending of opposition to the gospel in high places and for the frustration of extremist Hindu efforts to 'reconvert' Christians — thousands of tribal peoples have been forced to renounce Christianity. The whole state is a pioneer mission field, but is becoming more responsive.

2 Christians declined in census statistics from 0.92% in 1981 to 0.64% in 1991, but there is much encouragement at the grass-roots. Christian institutions, especially Catholic, have had a positive impact. A state-wide saturation church planting network has seen churches increased from 500 in 1993 to 3,000 in 2000. Bible schools have increased from 4 to 15 in the same period with many new workers sent out in pioneer work. The vision of the Madhya Pradesh Harvest network is to place workers in every pincode area — in 1998 75% of the 1,601 had no workers resident, but by 2000 this had come down to 50%.

3 The challenge of the unreached:

a) The tribal peoples are a majority in the southern four districts, especially Bastar, and a large minority in the two states. There is now a burgeoning house church movement in many tribes through the labours of various agencies. However, all represent a tough pioneer challenge. Most practice a Hindu-influenced animism. Witchcraft, Saktism (worship of female energy) and Saivism (worship of Shiva) abound.

b) The 10.5 million Gond are the largest tribe in India, most in MP/CH. Only 2% are Christian, but this is lower in MP. Over 30 mission agencies minister to them and churches are multiplying despite local and state-wide opposition.

c) Bhopal, the state capital of MP and industrial centre was the scene of the world's worst ever industrial disaster — an exploding chemical plant in 1984 killed 20,000 and maimed or afflicted a further 500,000 people. The grim after-effects are still evident. The city is ringed by 300 slum areas — Christians are beginning to reach out to them. Nearly 23% is Muslim, but there is no significant ministry among them.

MAHARASHTRA

GEOGRAPHY Area 308,000 sq.km. India's most urbanized and industrialized state.

Population 95,000,000; 308 people/sq.km.

Capital Mumbai (Bombay) 17.55m; India's commercial, economic and industrial heart. Other major cities: Pune 3.35m; Nagpur 2.05m; Nashik 1.08m.

PEOPLES 339.
  Main groups: Mahratta 24.1m; Kunbi 5.9m; Deccani (Mus) 5.6m; Shaikh Muslim 5.4m; Brahmin 4.1m; Konkani Muslim 3.4m; Mali 2.6m; Lingayat 2.4m; Mahratta-Kunbi 2.2m; Bania 1.8m; Teli 1.3m; Ahir/Yadav 1.2m; Muslim of Khandesh 1m; Pathan (Mus) 1m; Sayyid

(Mus) 1m; Sonar 1m.
  SC (59) 11.1%. Nau Buddh 6.7m; Mahar 2.9m; Matang 2m; Chamar 1.6m; Bhangi 283,000; Vaddar 279,000.
  Tribes (48) 9.3%. Gond 3.6m; Bhil 1.6m; Koli Mahadev 1.3m; Varli 829,000; Kokna 584,000; Thakur 579,000; Halba 381,000; Andh 341,000; Gowari 340,000; Kathodi 296,000; Korku 182,000; Kolowar 176,000; Gamit 175,000; Pardhan 149,000; Pardhi 147,000.

Languages Marathi 73.6%; Urdu 6.9%; Hindi 6.7%; Gujarati 2.7%; Khandeshi 1.7%; Telugu 1.5%; Kannada 1.5%.

RELIGION Hindu 80.4%; Muslim 10%; Buddhist 6.2%; Jain 1.6%; Christian 1.2% (Catholic 1%, Protestant 0.2%).

1 The government was controlled by Hinduists that raised inter-communal tensions through discrimination against Muslims, Buddhists and Christians. Anti-conversion legislation and vigorous 're-conversion' of Dalit and tribal peoples to Hinduism were promoted. Pray that the state government may be impartial and also for grace and courage for Christians who are pressurized.

2 Mumbai has great influence through its economic clout. It generates 1/3 of the GDP; it is home of India's stock exchange and the film making industry ('Bollywood'). It also has a reputation for crime, Asia's largest slum (Dharavi with one million in 170 hectares), 100,000 street children, child prostitution and an alarming rise in AIDS (200,000 sufferers in

1996). It has the second highest Christian population (5%) of the mega-cities of India. There are many Catholics and a growing number of Protestant denominations and churches. Pray that the Christians may be 'salt and light' in their city. Mumbai New Life Fellowship has won many non-Christians through a massive Scripture distribution campaign, planted 1,500 churches and now has the vision to plant a church in every village of the state.

3 **The Christian Church** needs prayer. Christians are few in smaller cities and rural areas. Many are nominal; 40% do not go to church. Quarrelling, court cases and bitterness have crippled the witness of older churches. Since the early 1980s new waves of outreach have turned the tide — **Love Maharashtra**, the **CONS** saturation church planting vision and a multiplication of agencies and workers have led to many new peoples, districts and villages being reached. In the late '90s many new churches have been started. Pray that revival, growth and outreach may be normal in the life of the churches.

4 **Unreached areas and peoples.** Pray for the 150 or more Indian agencies and churches reaching out to many of the less-evangelized peoples. A few meriting special mention: Maharashtra Village Mission, **IEM**, **IET**, **GFA**, **FMPB**, **Love Maharashtra**.
a) *Many Hindu caste groups*, **Muslims** and the **Mahar** (many of whom became Buddhist in the 20th Century) have little opportunity to hear the gospel. There are very few Christians among them.
b) *Tribal groups* such as the Gond, Bhil, Korku and Kolam, and many other smaller groups, have begun to respond to the gospel but progress has been slow. In the 1990s, however, the increase in effort and response was significant. Many people groups are still without viable congregations.
c) *The 1.5 million Jains and 150,000 Parsees* in their wealthy, cocooned religious communities remain unevangelized.
d) *Of the state's 2,018 pincode areas*, 73% had no resident Christian workers in 1998.

MANIPUR

GEOGRAPHY **Area** 22,300 sq.km. On eastern border with Myanmar.
Population 2,526,000; 100 people/sq.km.
Capital Imphal.

PEOPLES
Main groups Meithei 1.3 mill.; Meitei Pangal/ Manipuri 350,000; Muslims 236,000; Assamese Muslims 97,000.
SC 2%. Dalit (7) 2%.
ST (37) 34.4%. Chin-related (9 groups, Kuki, Thado, Paite, etc.) 375,000; Naga-related (5 groups, Tangkhul, Mao) 325,000; Mizo (2) 61,000.

RELIGION Hindu 57.7%; Christian 34.1% (Protestant 31% Catholic 3.1%); Muslim 7.3%; Other 0.9%.

1 **Nearly all the Naga, Kuki-Chin and Mizo** have become Christians in the 20th Century. Baptists (21 denominations) and Presbyterians predominate. Sadly, during the 1990s civil wars broke out between Naga, Kuki, Paite and also action against the government. These denominational and ethnic conflicts severely hamper outreach by Christians to Muslims and Hindus. Pray for full reconciliation, ethnic harmony and a humble, sanctified cooperation among all who claim to follow Christ. There are hundreds of Manipur missionaries serving cross-culturally today.

2 **The challenges:**
a) *The Meitei* have been Hindu for three centuries. They invented the game of polo. A strong nationalism and independence has made them more open to the gospel. There are over 10,000 Christians in nearly 100 churches. Growth has slowed because of recent hostilities. The Bible and the *JESUS* film are available for them.
b) *Muslims and other immigrant groups* are largely unreached. There are some churches among the Nepalis, but most are still Hindu.
c) *Drug addiction and AIDS* have become a major issue — of 60,000 drug addicts, 40,000 are HIV+, but government and NGO efforts are beginning to reduce the incidence.

MEGHALAYA

GEOGRAPHY Area 22,400 sq.km. Mountainous state on Bangladesh's northern border. It has the world's highest rainfall — 12 metres annually.
Population 2,175,000; 97 people/sq.km.
Capital Shillong 260,000.

PEOPLES 78.
SC (16) 0.5%.
ST (15) 85.5%. Khasi (2) 1.1m; Garo 779,000; Hajong 40,000.
Other groups Bengali Muslims 54,000; Shaikh Muslims 49,000.

RELIGION Christian 64.6%; Hindu 14.7%; Muslim 4%; Animist/Other 16.7%.

1 **Meghalaya has become a Christian state;** the Khasis are mainly Presbyterian and Catholic; the Garo, Baptist. There are now 40 other denominations and an increasing number of growing independent and charismatic fellowships. The Catholic Church is also growing fast. Many missionaries have been recruited, but few from the Presbyterians or Baptists where traditionalism is becoming a problem. Pray for revival in the older denominations.

2 **The challenges for the Church:**

a) *The youth are drifting away from the Church* — there is much drug abuse and many youth drop-outs.

b) *Some smaller tribes,* the Hajong, Rabha Koch and Mikir are still entrenched in animistic ways. The **Hindu** and **Muslim** minorities are little touched by the gospel and their numbers are increasing by immigration from Bangladesh and other states.

c) *Shillong* has the highest concentration of non-Christians with half the population Hindu, Muslim, animist, etc. Yet there are over 150 congregations and fellowships in the city.

MIZORAM

GEOGRAPHY Area 21,000 sq.km. Almost an enclave between Bangladesh and Myanmar.
Population 860,000; 41 people/sq.km.
Capital Aizawl 182,000.
PEOPLES 54.

SC (15) 0.1%.
ST (17) 94.8%. Mizo/Lushai 555,000; Poi 71,000; Chakma 68,000; Ralte 62,000; Pawi 44,900; Kuki 40,500.
Other groups (15) 5.1%. Bengali, Nepali (4) 6,000.

RELIGION
Christian 85%; Buddhist 8%; Hindu 7%.

1 **Mizoram is one of the most active Christian states in the world.** Most are Presbyterian and Baptist, but there are now 60 other denominations and numerous independent congregations. Awakenings and revivals in recent years have dynamized the Church and transformed society. It is now the most literate and well-educated state in India. Mizo missionaries in India and beyond number over 2,000 — one of the highest sending statistics in the world.

2 **The challenges** to be tackled by the Christians:

a) *Divisions within denominations* and inter-ethnic tensions are a discredit to the unity expected of believers.

b) *Serious societal problems* — increased corruption, youth delinquency, abuse of drugs and alcohol.

c) *The largely Buddhist Chakma and Reang tribal refugees* from Tripura need to be evangelized.

NAGALAND

GEOGRAPHY Area 16,600 sq.km. Mountainous state bordering on Assam, Arunachal Pradesh and Myanmar.
Population 1,550,000; 93 people/sq.km.
Capital Kohima 63,000.

PEOPLES 50.
Tribes (22) 87.7%. Naga (16) 1.3m; Chin 40,000.
Other groups 12.3%. Assamese Muslim 220,000; Bengali Muslim 14,000, etc.

RELIGIONS Christian 87.5% (60%+ Baptist); Hindu 10.1%; Muslim 1.7%.

1 Nagaland is unique — with the highest percentage of Baptists of any state in the world. Over 100,000 Naga Christians gathered to celebrate 125 years of Christianity in 1997. Revivals in 1956, 1966 and 1972 brought new life, fervour and a surge of evangelistic and missions outreach and thousands of Nagas have served the Lord in other parts of India and beyond. Pray that the inrush of technology, materialism and casual familiarity with the gospel may not damage spiritual life and fervour.

2 The effectiveness of Christian witness is compromised by inter-ethnic feuding, a long Naga independence guerrilla war, the insidious effects of corruption, denominational fragmentation (there are 21 Baptist groupings and a growing number of newer, independent churches) and growing nominalism. Pray for a return of these Christians to their first love, and pray that churches may adapt to be relevant to the younger generation.

3 Christian leadership. Few Christian areas in the world have such a high density of theological colleges — there are at least eight. Few Nagas in training ever consider a missionary career. Pray for students to become effective pastors and missionaries. Pray also for a better coordination and growth of the already significant Naga missionary movement.

4 Bible translation. The many highly educated theologians ensure that the two million Nagas are well served with Bible translations. The 20 tribes speak 36 languages with 124 distinct dialects, but have 12 full Bibles and 11 NTs, with translation work ongoing in 6! Pray that these skills may be used to translate the Bible into many other Indian languages.

ORISSA

GEOGRAPHY Area 155,700 sq.km. Eastern coastal state prone to cyclones. The 1999 super cyclone killed 8,000 and ruined the livelihoods of 10 million people.

Population 37,500,000; 241 people/sq.km.

Capital Bhubaneshwar 500,000. Other major cities: Cuttack 500,000.

PEOPLES 279.
  Main groups Ahir/Yadav 2.5m; Brahmin 2.2m; Mahishya 2m; Gauda 1.2m; Khandait 1.2m; Teli 980,000.
SC (94) 16.2%. Pan 1.2m; Kandra 455,000.
ST (60) 22.2%. Kui 1.4m; Gond 868,000; Munda 517,000; Parja 385,000; Kisan 329,000; Oraon 310,000.

Languages 68. Oriya 83%; Hindi 2.4%; Telugu 2.1%; Santal 2.1%; Kui 2.0%.

RELIGION Hindu 94.7% (many animistic tribal peoples included); Christian 2.1% (Catholic 0.8%, Protestant 1.3%); Muslim 1.8%; Other 1.4%.

1 Persecution of Christians increased during the 1990s. Orissa shares with Gujarat the worst record for Hindu extremist violence. Many churches have been destroyed and Christian workers attacked, some molested and killed. The martyrdom of Graham Staines and his sons in 1999 caused a horrified reaction locally, nationally and globally. Discriminating legislation was further tightened in 2000 making any baptism dependent on permission from government officials. Many denominations and agencies are being intimidated in the north. Pray that this persecution may refine the Church, focus the vision and multiply new believers.

2 Church growth has increased in the 1990s with a multiplication of workers and new believers despite harsh state 'anti-conversion' laws. Growth has been patchy — Christians are 62% tribal, 25% Dalit, and most live in Sundergarh District in the north and Kandhamal and Gajapati Districts in the south. Pray for Indian agencies seeking to augment this growth — significant agencies being **FMPB, IEM, IET, EHC**, BYM, **GFA** and many others.

3 Tribal peoples of Orissa are the most responsive to the gospel, as are their brethren in adjoining south Bihar. The Oraon (40% Christian), Kharia (37%), Munda (40%), Savara (17%) Kisan (9%), Khond (9%) and Kol (5%) have significant numbers of Christians. Their illiteracy, economic deprivation and political marginalization slow what could be a large movement to Christ. Numerous denominations and agencies work among them. There is an exciting development of missions vision among these believers. **GFA**'s two training schools are full with 700 trainees and 200 interns.

4 **The unfinished challenge:**

a) *The forward (high) castes,* such as the Brahmin and Korono, have never been confronted with the claims of Christ.

b) *There are many areas with very few Christians.* The six eastern and 13 western districts are less than 1% Christian. Of the 1,111 pincode areas, 56% had no resident Christian workers in 1998.

c) *The tribals.* Of the 62 groups, 20 are less than 0.1% Christian and 42 are less than 1% Christian. Pray specifically for a breakthrough among the Bhathudi, Bhuiya, Bhumiji, Gond, Kolho, Paraja, Santal, Siyal and Koya.

5 **The ministry of the Bible.** A good new Oriya Bible was published in 1998. Yet illiteracy is high — 51% of the population, 70% of the Dalit and tribes, and 89% of women cannot read. Pray for effective use of Scripture cassettes and other audio-visual means of communicating the gospel.

6 **Radio broadcasts** have been getting encouraging response from Hindus during the 1990s. **TWR** and **FEBA** have highly effective follow-up ministry.

PANJAB

GEOGRAPHY
Area 50,400 sq.km. North-western India; one of the most productive agricultural regions of the country.
Population 24,100,000; 478 people/sq.km.
Capital Chandigarh in Haryana; largest cities: Ludhiana 1.5m; Amritsar 800,000.
PEOPLES People groups 96.
Main groups Jat(Sikh) 8.3m; Jat(Hindu) 1.5m;
Tarkhan 930,000; Brahmin 609,000; Mahtam 548,000; Saini 538,000; Kamboh 436,000; Rajput (Sikh) 429,000; Rajput (Hindu) 428,000.
SC (51) 28.3%. Mazhabi Sikh 1.8m; Chamar 1.8m; Adi Dharmi 768,000; Chuhra/Balmiki/Bhangi 790,000.
Languages Panjabi 92%; Hindi 7.3%.
RELIGION Sikh 63.6%; Hindu 34%; Christian 1.1% (Catholic 0.18%, Protestant 0.92%); Muslim 1%.

1 **The Panjab is the home state of the Sikhs,** and the only state where they are in the majority. Their famed Golden Temple is in Amritsar. A violent guerrilla war waged by Sikh extremists seeking independence led to 25,000 deaths, including Prime Minister Indira Gandhi, and much economic disruption. Praise God that peace came in 1992. This was followed by rapid economic progress, healing of inter-communal wounds and unprecedented openness for the gospel.

2 **The Sikh religion** with its unique doctrines and culture has spread to many parts of India and beyond. There are 25 million Sikhs in the world. Little specific Christian study of and dialogue with Sikhs has ever really been undertaken. Pray that this potentially responsive people might come to Christ. The Mazhabi Sikhs are the most open at present, but the Jat Sikhs are becoming so. India National Inland Mission has missionaries committed to Sikh ministry and over 40 churches and groups have been started.

3 **Most of the Christian community originated in the 19ᵗʰ Century in mass movements** from depressed Chamar and Chuhra castes. Christians were under-privileged, generally nominal, discouraged and in decline. During the 1990s there has been a wave of new outreach by many agencies and newer churches. The number of churches has doubled and church attenders tripled. There are now over 65 denominations. Operation Agape is a significant agency planting churches. Praise God for this and pray for a revived, effective, dynamic Church in the Panjab.

4 **Many churches are cooperating** for saturation church planting in **Reach Panjab 2000.** Some of the goals:

a) *Strong churches in each of Panjab's 12 districts* — the weakest being Sangrur, Bathinda, Rupnagar and Faridkot.

b) *Christian workers based in every one of the 491 pincode areas* — only 53% had them in 1998. During 1999 pincode areas without a church were reduced from 220 to 100, but by 2000 all were occupied. Pray for churches to be planted.

c) *Every people group to have a church* — 20 of the 25 largest do, but the forward castes are little touched.

5 The Ludhiana Christian Medical College and Hospital has a world-wide reputation for Christian care and witness. Pray for this witness to be maintained and to be fruitful.

RAJASTHAN

GEOGRAPHY Area 342,000 sq.km. An arid state abutting on Pakistan.

Population 53,300,000; 155 people/sq.km.

Capital Jaipur **2,050,000.**

PEOPLES 226.
Main groups Bania/Vaisya 4.9m; Rajasthani Muslim 4.8m; Brahmin 4.7m; Jat(Hindu) 3.9m; Gujar 2.2m; Shaikh Muslim 2.1m; Kumhar 1.7m; Mali 1.6m.

SC (65) 17%. Chamar 3.3m; Meghwal 1.5m; Balai 760,000; Bairwa 705,000; Thori 571,000; Bhangi 422,000.
ST (12) 12%. Mina 3.4m; Bhil/Bhilala 3m; Garasia 195,000; Sahariya 67,000.

Languages Hindi 90%, using the related Rajasthani or Mawari language; Urdu 2.2%; Panjabi 2.1%; Sindhi 0.8%.

RELIGION Hindu 89%; Muslim 7.5%; Jain 1.8%; Sikh 1.5%; Christian 0.12% (Catholic 0.07%, Protestant 0.05%).

1 Christians are a tiny minority within minority Dalit and tribal groups. There were officially 50,000 Christians in 1991, but that number has grown considerably, especially among the Bhil in the south — the majority of Christians living in the southern four districts. Noteworthy church planting ministries being those of Rajasthan Bible Institute (500 churches in 30 years), Emmanuel (50 churches and 45 schools). Pray for the continued increased in workers and churches despite anti-conversion laws and rising opposition.

2 Unreached peoples:

a) The Bhil (IEM), Mina (Indian Inland Mission, Pentecostals), Garasia (**IEM**) and others are Hindu/animist and only now beginning to respond to the gospel.

b) The Meo are Muslim; no Christians are known.

c) Higher-caste Hindus, especially the Rajputs, the Jats and Marwari, have shown no response to the gospel (INIM).

d) Jaipur, the capital, with two million people has around 10,000 Christians, many being from south India, and many rather nominal. In the 1990s the number of churches increased from five to 10-15.

3 Vision for the future emerged from a key Harvest Consultation in 1998:

a) A church in all 1404 pincode areas by 2010; only about 20% had workers resident in 1995.

b) EHC is distributing literature to every home for the third time — with increased response.

SIKKIM

GEOGRAPHY Area 7,100 sq.km. Himalayan state sandwiched between Nepal and Bhutan, and for long a buffer state between Tibet (China) and India. Annexed by India in 1975.

Population 510,000; 72 people/sq.km. Large-scale immigration of Nepalis.

Capital Gangtok.

PEOPLES
Nepali 75%: Khambu 121,000; Khas 78,000; Brahmin 59,000; Jogi 53,000; Tamang 46,000; Gurung 30,000.
Indigenous/Tibetan 20%: Lepcha 44,000; Sikkim Bhotia 92,000; Tibetan 18,000.
Indian groups 5%.
Languages Nepali is now the de facto state language.

RELIGION Hindu 64%; Buddhist 25%; Christian 10%; Muslim 0.9%.

1 Since 1994 Sikkim has had fewer restrictions on religious freedom than ever before. Despite past limitations and times of persecution, Christians have grown among the Lepcha and Nepalis. In 1999 there were 300 churches and Christians numbered nearly 30,000 (7,000 in 1981). The main church is the Evangelical Presbyterian Church and there are a number of free and Pentecostal churches. Much greater cooperation and fellowship between them came out of the 1997 Sikkim Congress on Evangelism. Pray that this unity might be maintained and outreach enhanced.

2 **New vision for the evangelization of Sikkim** is resulting in increased outreach, training of new workers (Sikkim Bible Institute and **GFA**) and an increase in the number of Sikkimese and Indian agencies and workers. The need is:

a) *To reach the northern part of Sikkim* which is largely Buddhist. There are very few Christians among the Bhotia and Tibetans.

b) *To reach neighbouring, but closed, Bhutan and Tibet.*

3 *The Lepcha and Bhotia* are the indigenous peoples of Sikkim and are largely Buddhist. They have been culturally and politically marginalized. The Lepcha continue to be responsive to the gospel. Pray that they may find their identity and motivation by following Jesus. The *JESUS* film was released in Lepcha in 1999.

TAMIL NADU

GEOGRAPHY Area 130,000 sq.km. India's most south-easterly state and close to Sri Lanka. Well-watered with a strong agricultural economy.

Population 65.3m; 502 people/sq.km.

Capital Chennai (formerly Madras) 6m. Other major cities: Coimbatore 1.2m; Madurai 1.1m.

PEOPLES 400+.
Main groups Vanniyan 9.4m; Tamil Muslim 3.7m; Ahir/Tadava/Golla 2.9m; Maravan 2.6m; Viswakarma/Kammalan 2.4m; Shaikh(Muslim) 2.3m; Nadar/ Channan 2.2m; Brahmin 2.2m; Ilavan 2m; Vellalan 1.6m; Kaikolan/Sengunthar 1.5m; Boya/ Gangavar/Vaddar 1.5m;

Nair/Nayar 1.2m; Kallan 1.2m; Telaga 1.1m.
SC (95) 19.2%. Adi Dravida 5.7m; Pallan 2.4m; Paraiyan 2.1m; Chakkliyan 1.1m; Arunthathiyan 567,000.
ST (53) 1.03%. Yenadi 823,000; Kuruba 683,000; Malayali 276,000; Irular 149,000; Konda Reddi 43,000; Kattunayakan 26,000; Kuruman 21,000.

Languages Tamil 86.7%, one of the oldest literary languages of India; Telugu (largely Chennai) 7.1%; Kannada 2.2%; Urdu 1.9%; Malayalam 1.2%.

RELIGION Hindu 88.6%; Christian 5.7%; Muslim 5.5%; Other 0.2%.The state passed the most draconian anti-conversion laws in India in 2003.

1 **The strong anti-conversion law** of 2003 was hastily passed at the instigation of Hinduists. They have shocked the Christian population, and are proving a model for similar legislation in other states. Pray for the overturning of this unconstitutional and blatantly discriminatory legislation.

2 **Christians have significantly grown in numbers** over the past 20 years — more than official statistics would imply. There are over 4 million in 60,000 churches. The Assemblies of God and indigenous evangelical, Pentecostal and charismatic groups have shown the greatest growth. Chennai has a Christian population of about 12% with over 2,000 congregations. A greater unity among believers across the denominational spectrum gives hope for future growth. Training opportunities have multiplied with hundreds of Bible Schools started. The areas of concern:

a) *Ethnic communalism and caste identity* which hinders Christian maturity and unity.

b) *Christian leaders* to have integrity in administration, finances and morality.

c) *The vision* for prayer, evangelism and outreach to all of India to be maintained and increase. One third of Indian missions and numerous interdenominational agencies are based in the state.

3 **The less evangelized** — despite the large Christian presence and numerous agencies, large segments of the population remain unreached:

a) *The majority of Christians are in Chennai* and the southern districts. Five central and northern districts are less than 2% Christian. There are 29 districts in the state.

b) *Few of the major people groups* listed above have more than a few hundred known believers — especially the Brahmin, Viswakarma, Ahir and Kaikolan.

c) *The Tamil-speaking Muslims*, the Labbai, have few Christians or Christian workers.

d) *The tribals*. At least 10 tribal groups are without churches. There are only 300 Christians among the Tamil-speaking Malayali. The snake- and rat-catching Irular are now 1% Christian and there is a breakthrough among the Badaga with an increase in Christians, churches and workers (Nakubetta Bible Fellowship).

4 **The outreach needs:**

a) *Of the 3,311 pincode areas*, 57% had no Christian workers in 1998.

b) *The Assemblies of God* began in 1973 with 7 members; they had 800 churches in the state in 2000. Pray for this ministry to flourish.

TRIPURA

GEOGRAPHY

Area 10,500 sq.km. Almost an enclave within eastern Bangladesh.

Population 3,590,000; 342 people/sq.km. Ongoing illegal immigration from Bangladesh.

Capital Argatala.

PEOPLES People groups The destabilizing effects of Bengali immigration distort the statistics. Bengalis have now become a majority and may be 69% of the population.
Main groups 52.6%, mainly various Bengali people groups: Bengali Muslims 276,000; Jogi/Nath 261,000; Kayastha 257,000; Namasudra 208,000; Brahmin 149,000; Bania 100,000.
SC (31) 16.4%: Kaibartta 83,000; Mahishya 80,000; Dhobi 55,000.
ST (23) 31%: Tripura 502,000; Tuikuk/Riang 143,000; Jamatia 82,800; Chakma 53,900; Halam 51,300; Mag 31,000.

RELIGION Hindu 85.3% — including Tripuri animists as 'Hindu'; Muslim 7.1% (Bengali); Buddhist 4.6% (Chakma); Christian 3% (tribal peoples).

1 **The indigenous peoples** are now a minority in their own state. Massive Bengali immigration has occurred over the past 40 years, and Bengalis have taken political and economic control marginalizing the indigenous peoples. This led to a violent backlash in 1980, with ongoing guerrilla activity against the migrants by the marginalized local peoples. There has come an unprecedented openness to the gospel. A large people movement has been taking place since 1970 in all indigenous peoples. Six tribes are now Christian, and at least seven are rapidly becoming so. There are Christians in every indigenous ethnic group, and their numbers exceed official figures.

2 **Christians have been persecuted** both by animists and by extremist Hindu groups. Nearly all Christians are members of one of the 440 churches in the 12 Baptist Associations. Pray that Christians may thrive and maintain their witness to non-Christians in spite of communal violence.

3 **The less evangelized** will remain so without a multiplication of workers from within and outside Tripura. Pray for:
a) *The Bengali majority* of two million which is unresponsive due to the tribal peoples turning to Christ. Little ministry is directed to their evangelization, and there are only about 100 Christians among them.
b) *The Buddhist Chakma* are slowly responding to the gospel. Over 40,000 Chakma from Bangladesh have taken refuge in Tripura.
c) *The Tripura* have become more open, and there are now some 30 Baptist churches among them. Most are animists, but coercion and bribery has been used to convert them to Hinduism.

UTTAR PRADESH & UTTARANCHAL

GEOGRAPHY Area UP: 231,000 sq.km. India's strategic heartland in the Ganges Valley, yet poor and under-developed. UA: 63,000 sq.km. to the north; abutting on the Himalayas.

Population UP: 167,271,000; 689 people/sq.km. India's most populous state. UA: 8m; 127 people/sq.km.

Capital Lucknow 2.45m. Other major cities: Kanpur 2.45m; Varanasi 1.28m; Meerut 1.2m; Agra 1.15m; Allahabad 1.1m.

PEOPLES 225.
Main groups Muslims(7+) 32.2m; Brahmin 16.2m; Ahir/Yadav 13.2m; Rajput (Hindu) 12.1m; Shaikh (Muslim) 7.1m; Kurmi 5.8m; Pathan (Mus) 4.8m; Bania 6.5m; Kahar 4.5m; Ansari (Muslim) 4.4m; Bania/Vaisya 4.1m; Lodha 3.8; Gadaria 3.7m; Jat (Hindu) 3.2m; Kumhar 2.7m; Kachhi 2.6m; Teli (Hindu) 2.6m; Badhai/Barhai 2.1m; Murao 2.1m; Bhoi/Kewat 1.8m; Lohar 1.7m.
SC (64) 21%: Chamar 16.9m; Pasi 4m; Koli 2m; Dhobi 1.6m; Bhangi/Balmiki 1.1m; Silpkar 824,000; Dhanuk 399,000; Kol 341,000.
ST (5) 0.2%: Tharu 150,000; Jaunsari 107,000; Bhoksa 50,000; Bhotia 41,000.

Languages Hindi 90%, a complex of related languages (Hindi, Bhojpuri, Awadhi, Braj, Bundeli, Charwali, Kumaoni, etc.); Urdu 9%; Panjabi 0.5%.

RELIGION Hindu 81.7%; Muslim 17.3%; Sikh 0.4%; Christian 0.14% (Catholic 0.04% Protestant 0.08%); Jain 0.13%.

1 **Uttar Pradesh is the home of Hinduism, Buddhism and Jainism,** but has given no home to the gospel. Millions of pilgrims visit Varanasi, the holy city of Hinduism on the Ganges River, but few find the Living Water that only Jesus can give. Pray that there might be a major mobilization of prayer on this key state, and that God may give the workers who will turn the tide for the gospel.

2 **The Christian Church** has long been a tiny, stagnant minority community of 230,000; 80-90% nominal and most from the Dalit Chamar and Dom groups. In 1995 there were less than 500 workers committed to the unreached. Intimidation and threats have led to a steady stream of reversions to Hinduism. Only in the past 15 years has the evangelical witness shown vitality, but their numbers are few. Pray for new life in dead and dying churches. Pray for a more indigenous expression of Christianity — both the buildings, liturgy and culture of many Christians is foreign in look.

3 **The small signs of hope** — pray these little flames will grow and spread state-wide.

a) The North India Harvest Network has brought together some in the small evangelical witness to pray, research, equip and mobilize Christians during the 1990s with increased, coordinated outreach.

b) The Presbyterians have grown among the Balmiki and now have 140,000 members.

c) Various agencies have focused on UP with increased response — Indian agencies and Pentecostal groups are being used by God. The actual number of believers may now be double the official figure.

4 **The awesome immensity of the unfinished task** should drive us to prayer:

a) The Brahmin, Ahir, Rajput and other castes in the list above despise Christianity because of its links with the Dalit. Among these 150 groups and 132 million people, there may be no more than several thousand Christians.

b) Muslims are a large minority of 29 million and have frequently been victims of Hindu mob violence. The destruction of the Babri mosque in Ayodhya in December 1992 provoked nation-wide rioting and destruction and seriously damaged India's social fabric. Several Christian agencies are seeking to reach Muslims, but results are yet meagre.

c) Students. They are a challenge! UESI/**IFES** has 12 student groups for the 26 universities and 570 colleges. Pray for these and for the two staff workers.

d) The Garhwalis (1,800,000) are largely unresponsive. However, the New Testament was recently completed through the work of **IEM** and Agape and there are now over 100 believers among them. Christian broadcasting has begun in Garhwali.

e) UP's 2,067 pincode areas — 84% had no resident Christian worker in 1998. Pray for the 15 Bible schools and for more workers to harvest the lost.

WEST BENGAL

GEOGRAPHY **Area** 88,800 sq.km. Bordering on Bangladesh (once East Bengal).

Population 81,700,000; 920 people/sq.km. There are an estimated 5 million illegal immigrants from Bangladesh — mostly Muslim.

Capital Kolkata (Calcutta) 12,800,000. Other major cities: Asansol 1,175,000.

PEOPLES 203.
Main groups Bengali Muslims 22m; Shaikh (Mus) 20.2m; Mahishya 5m; Ahir/Yadav/Sadgope/ Sadgaola 4.7m; Brahmin 4.2m; Bagdi 3.8m; Rajbansi 3.5m; Kayastha 2.6m; Tati/Tatwa 1.4m; Jogi/Nath 1.4m.

SC (63) 24%. Bagdi 2.8m; Namasudra 2.6m; Pod/Paundra 2.4m; Chamar 1.1m; Bauri 1.1m; Kaibartta/Jalia 439,400; Bhangi 396,000 Sunri 391,000; Dhobi 390,000.

ST (38) 5.9%. Santal 2.6m; Oraon 678,000; Bhumij 360,000; Munda 341,000; Kori 150,000; Mahali/Mhali 95,000; Lodha 61,000; Savara/Sawara 58,000.

Languages Bengali 85.8%; Hindi 5.3%; Santali 2.6%; Urdu 2.1%; Nepali 1.3%.

RELIGION Hindu 75.1%; Muslim 23.4%; Christian 0.6% (Catholic 250,000; Protestant 200,000).

1 **The Bengalis** number 230 million with 200 communities in India, South Asia and the world. They are the largest unreached ethnic group in the world. William Carey's pioneer work 200 years ago was among them. Carey, and his successors, achieved much in Bible translation, blessing the Bengali culture, bringing social and economic benefits, but few Bengalis are committed Christians today. The barriers: pride of culture, demonic powers, a spirit of independence, little adaptation of the Christian gospel to local culture and, in recent years, obstruction from the long-reigning Marxist state government. Pray that every barrier to Bengalis believing in Jesus may be removed.

2 **Christians are few;** 90% come from poor and marginalized communities and probably 95% of the 480,000 'Christians' are nominal. Yet there are indications of better things to come:
a) *The Reach Bengal Movement,* started in 1991, led to new prayer networks, vital research and a greater level of cooperation in what had been a very divided Church.
b) *Prayer has yielded an increased response* with significant key conversions and a new vision in some denominations to plant new congregations where there are none.
c) *There are now 150 denominations and agencies* in the state of which only a few are fully committed to unreached areas and peoples, but progress is being made. Twelve new people groups now have churches planted among them since 1994.
d) *The visionary goal* of placing a Christian worker in every state pincode area: of the 1,357 areas, 74% are without a resident witness.

3 **Kolkata** is a large industrial and trading city, but Marxist rule has hindered growth and investment. It is dedicated to Kali, the Hindu goddess of destruction. It has the lowest urban standard of living in the world with vast slums and a million or more living on the streets. The huge social needs have been highlighted by the ministry of Mother Theresa and addressed by many others less publicized yet the spiritual needs remain unmet.
a) *There are 200 churches* in the city but only 25% are Bengali-speaking. Pray for a multiplication of congregations alive in the Spirit.
b) *Mission Kolkata 2000* launched in 1994 has mobilized hundreds of Christians for massive literature distribution and church planting. Pray for lasting fruit.
c) *Non-Bengali* immigrants are 42% of the population, many of these such as the Bhojpuri, Gujarati, Oriya, Panjabi and Mawari have no Christian witness among them. Pray for workers and churches in each.

4 **The least evangelized.** All the listed caste groups and most of the tribes listed above are still effectively without a significant, vital church-planting movement.

THE SIX UNION TERRITORIES

Specific mention is made here of two of the more unique Union Territories. The other four are similar to the state of which they are enclaves: **Chandigarh** (capital of Panjab and Haryana 800,000); **Dadra** and **Nagar Havali** (Gujarat 170,000); **Daman** and **Diu** (Gujarat 123,000) and **Pondicherry** (Tamil Nadu 990,000).

1 **Andaman and Nicobar Islands** comprise 350,000 inhabitants on 38 islands in the Bay of Bengal. Over 25% of the population of mainland immigrants and indigenous Nicobari (45,000) are Christian. The unreached are the four isolated negrito peoples (only 500 people, but all mission work is forbidden among them. Ten **GFA** missionaries are now seeking to reach these and other communities.). Also the Hindu (64%) and Muslim (8.6%) Bengali, Hindi, Malayali, Telugu and Tamil immigrants, as well as Oraon, Munda and Khama from Bihar need to be reached.

2 **Lakshadweep**. Twelve coral atolls and 36 islands in the Arabian Sea. Its 32 sq.km is home to 62,000 people. Over 95% of the population is ardently Muslim, the rest are Hindu (4%) and Christian (0.7%) immigrants from the mainland. No long-term ministry to these Malayali-speaking Muslims has ever been permitted or attempted.

Indonesia

Republic of Indonesia

JUNE 17-26

ASIA

Updated January 2004

GEOGRAPHY

Area 1,919,317 sq.km. The Republic's 17,000 islands (4,000 inhabited) stretch 6,400 km of land over 9.5 million sq.km of the Indian/Pacific Oceans, with 27 provinces, 2 special regions and the capital district.

Population		Ann.Gr.	Density
2000	212,991,926	+1.44%	111 per sq. km.
2010	239,026,778	+1.09%	125 per sq. km.
2025	274,627,097	+0.84%	143 per sq. km.

The world's 4th most populous nation. Population density varies from Java's 951 people/sq.km to West Papua's (formerly Irian Jaya) 5/sq.km.

Capital Jakarta 12.2 mill. Other major cities: Surabaya 2.85m; Bandung 2.8m; Medan 2.05m; Palembang 1.5m; Semarang 1.48m; Makassar (Ujung Pandang) 1.23m; Tanjungkarang 1,025,000. **Urbanites** 39%.

PEOPLES

Major peoples — using preferred Indonesian spelling. See under regions below for more detail.

Indo-Malay 94%. Jawa 90 mill.; Sunda 35m; Madura 3.5m; Minangkabau 7.5m; Batak 6.5m; Banjar 5m; Bali 3.9m; Bugi 3.8m; Aceh 3m; Dayak 2.9m; Makassar 2.2m; Deli 2m; Riau 2m; Sasak 2m; Toraja 1.3m.

Chinese 4%. Many are becoming integrated into the Indonesian majority. Only 20% still consistently use Chinese dialects. Scattered throughout the nation. Mainly urban.

Papua peoples 1.2%. In West Timor, Alor, Halmahera and Papua.

Other 0.8%. Arab, Indian, European, mixed race.

Literacy 83.8%; rising steadily. **Official language** Indonesian (Bahasa Indonesia). Its increasing use is both unifying the nation and lessening the importance of smaller languages to the younger generation. **All languages** 726; 18 spoken by more than one million speakers; 247 spoken in Papua. **Languages with Scriptures** 20Bi 38NT 77por.

ECONOMY

Increasingly diversified economy based on oil, gas, forest products, agriculture and textiles, with large reserves of many minerals. Steady economic improvement of 30 years came to a stunning halt in the Asian economic crisis which began in 1997. The large devaluation of the local currency led to inflation and a reduction in living standards. In 1996 11% of the population lived below the poverty line, but by 2000 it was 48%. Economic recovery is hampered by endemic corruption, the continuing strength of anti-democratic forces, the increase of Islamist violence and failure to restructure banking and debt. These hold back the inflow of international aid and finance. Environmental damage has been immense with widespread deforestation in Sumatra, Kalimantan and elsewhere. Inflation was reduced to 5% by 2000. HDI 0.681; 105th/174. Public debt (2000) 99% of GNP. Income/person $450 (1.4% of USA).

POLITICS

Colonial rule by Portuguese (1511-1605), Dutch (1605-1942, 1945-9), British (1807-1815) and Japanese (1942-45). The populist President Sukarno ruled for 22 years until deposed by General Suharto after the abortive Communist coup in 1965. President Suharto sought to bring economic growth while crushing political dissent. The economic crisis in 1997 was the spark that led to Suharto's downfall, following large demonstrations against the corruption and nepotism of the regime. The transition to a popularly elected government in 1999 has been traumatic. The government has been strongly opposed by an alliance of powerful extremists in both the military and Islamic parties. Both groups manipulate ethnic and religious differences to protect or strengthen their economic and political power base and discredit the democratic movement. The appalling human rights record of the government and army threatens Indonesia with possible disintegration. There are strong secessionist movements; the most serious being in Aceh (Sumatra) where thousands have perished in 10 years of bitter fighting, East Timor (Timor Lorosae) where independence and then devastation resulted in 1999, and West Papua.

RELIGION

Monotheism and communal peace are the basis for the stated government ideology of Pancasila. All citizens must choose between Islam, Hinduism, Buddhism or Christianity (Protestant or Catholic). The numerical and political strength of Islam has been used since 1990 to give it preferential treatment, limit Christian expansion, and reduce Christian influence in public life. There are some restrictions imposed on evangelism and many Christians seek to avoid antagonizing the Muslim majority. **Persecution index** 28th in the world.

Religions	Population %	Adherents	Ann.Gr.
Muslim	80.30	171,032,517	+1.3%
Christian	16.00	34,078,708	+2.0%
Hindu	1.90	4,046,847	+1.4%
Traditional ethnic	1.00	2,129,919	+1.4%
Chinese	0.50	1,064,960	-0.5%
Buddhist	0.30	638,976	+1.4%

Religious statistics are a sensitive political issue. Official and unofficial figures often differ widely. Muslims are officially 87%, but actually far less. Approximately 30% of Indonesian Muslims are 'high identity and high practice' Muslims. Another 35% are considered 'high identity but low practice' with the remaining 35% considered 'low identity and low practice' Muslims. Many in this latter group, though enumerated as Muslims in census figures, would either be followers of the Jawa mystical religion, Kebatinan, which predates Islam, or animists who have (to a greater or lesser extent) accepted some of the outward aspects of Islam. Islam is strongest in Sumatra, West and East Jawa, and in many coastal areas in the east of the country.

Animism is not officially recognized by the government but is strong among some peoples in Papua, Sumba and inland Sumatra, Kalimantan, Sulawesi, etc. The folk Islam followed by many Indonesian Muslims is strongly influenced by animism. Nation-wide it is a dominant spiritual force.

Christians	Denom.	Affil.%	,000	Ann.Gr.
Protestant	230	7.05	15,021	+3.0%
Independent	21	1.58	3,358	+1.9%
Anglican	1	0.00	3	+0.6%
Catholic	1	2.72	5,800	+1.4%
Marginal	10	0.11	236	+1.8%
Unaffiliated		4.54	9,661	n.a.

Churches		MegaBloc	Cong.	Members	Affiliates
Catholic		C	8,000	3,200,000	5,800,000
HKPB- Batak (Luth)		P	2,400	1,350,000	2,700,000
GPdI (Pentecostal)		I	1,700	850,000	1,420,000
GMIT- W Timor (Ref)		P	1,500	700,000	850,000
GBI- Bethel (CoG)		P	1,320	380,000	700,000
GMIM- Minahasa (Ref)		P	700	256,000	640,000
GBI- Jakarta (Ref)		P	2,800	280,000	630,000
GKI- I-J (Ref)		P	1,100	300,000	600,000
GKII- (CMA)		P	2,206	193,010	560,689
Assoc of Chr Foundations		I	1,588	270,000	550,000
GPIB- W Indon (Ref)		P	223	190,000	500,000
GPM- Maluku (Ref)		P	796	317,467	453,978

Toraja Church (Ref)	P	710	200,000	400,000
BNKP- Nias (Luth)	P	578	160,000	360,000
HKI- Sumatra (Luth)	I	630	133,000	350,000
GIdI (Evangelical)	P	675	180,000	350,000
Pentecostal Ch of God	I	187	140,000	310,800
Seventh-day Adventist	P	1,089	173,128	289,124
GKE- Kalimantan (Ref)	P	960	104,000	260,000
GKPI- N.Sumatra (Luth)	P	940	171,544	255,601
GB- Tabernacle	I	667	100,000	250,000
GBKP- Karo Batak (Ref)	P	646	100,000	250,000
GKJ- Java (Ref)	P	250	132,000	220,000
GKPS- Simalungun (Luth)	P	500	86,000	190,417
S.A.GKI- Jakarta (Ref) [4]	P	170	80,000	190,000
GKST- Sulawesi (Ref)	P	360	60,000	180,000
GKS- Sumba (Ref)	P	75	68,000	180,000
Baptist Chs of I	P	832	82,229	160,000
GUP (Pentecostal)	P	327	72,000	160,000
GKJW- East Java (Ref)	P	118	97,442	153,000
Assemblies of God	P	1,200	60,000	150,000
GMIH- Halmahera (Ref)	P	328	57,342	150,000
PGGB- I J (Baptist)	P	206	74,581	150,000
GMIST- Sanghir-T (Ref)	P	355	80,000	130,000
GBIS- Full Gospel	I	440	63,000	105,000
Ev Alliance- Ir. Jaya [2]	P	350	45,000	85,000
GTdI CoG Prophecy	P	200	12,190	82,000
GMI- (Methodist)	P	235	39,500	79,000
GITJ- Java (Ref)	P	74	47,000	69,000
Gereja Kristen Rahmani	P	278	25,000	50,000
Other denoms [220]		10,051	1,641,23	3,454,099
Total Christians [264]		47,764	12.571m	24.418m

Trans-bloc Groupings	pop.%	,000	Ann.Gr.
Evangelical	4.0	8,583	+4.0%
Charismatic	2.7	5,835	+1.9%
Pentecostal	2.4	5,043	+1.6%

Missionaries from Indonesia
P,I,A an est. 3,000 of which over 70 are in 22 foreign countries.

Expatriates in Indonesia
P,I,A an est. 1,000+ in over 100 agencies.

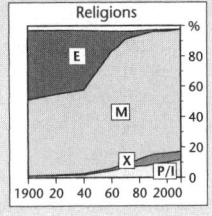

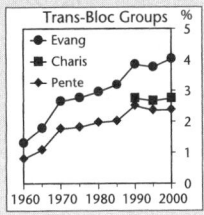

NOTE Jan 2004: Significant developments since September 2001:

1 **The 11 September Twin Towers atrocity** in the USA exposed the nature of the world-wide terrorist network. Islamic Jihad in Indonesia had close ties with this network and were responsible for many serious terror campaigns in Maluku, Sulawesi, West Irian and Jawa against Christian populations and also for the Bali terrorist bomb in October 2002.

2 **Despite the replacement of the President** elected in 1999 by Megawati Sukarnoputri, the government has had difficulty in controlling elements in government, army and society that support Islamist aims. The Bali incident shocked the world and also the government. Pray for the neutralization of the efforts by Islamists to impose their tyranny. New elections were due in April 2004.

• Answers to Prayer

Praise God for the thrilling growth of the Church over the past 40 years. During this period, Evangelicals have grown from 1.3 million (1.3% of the population) to 11.5 million (5.4%). Specific details:

1 **The Communist coup of 1965** and its bloody aftermath, in which maybe 500,000 Communist sympathizers perished, also led other sympathizers to become Christians.

2 **Fierce Muslim reprisals on the Communists offended many** — especially in Java. Many nominal Muslims turned to Christ.

3 **The harsh extremism and violence of Islamists has repelled many moderate Muslims** and the legalisms of Islam, such as forbidding the eating of pork, has made Christianity attractive to animists.

4 **The government mandate that each citizen adhere** to one of five recognized religions impelled many animists to consider the claims of the gospel.

5 **The lives of committed Christians and their vibrant witness** have made an impact on a society influenced by the power of the occult.

6 **Outpourings of the Holy Spirit brought revival** in the 1960s in West Timor, in the '70s in East and Central Java, and in the '80s and '90s in some major cities.

7 **Great people movements to Christ have occurred in many animistic peoples**, among three of the 8 Jawa sub-groups and also among Indonesians of Chinese descent. Over 50% of the latter are now Christian.

8 **The multiplication of evangelistic prayer meetings** has been accompanied by the rapid growth of Pentecostal and charismatic denominations and fellowships.

9 **Rising levels of persecution in the 1990s has fuelled greater unity** among Christians, the growth of a National Prayer Movement and commitment to cross-cultural outreach in Indonesia and beyond.

• Challenges for Prayer

1 **The democratic government elected in 1999 faces a daunting task.** Its first years were characterized by vacillation and powerlessness in the face of extremist demands from the minority Islamists and manipulation by the powerful old guard of the former regime. Pray that the President, Vice President and the government may be courageous, decisive and fair in bringing betterment to the whole nation. The old culture of corruption, cronyism and nepotism must be rooted out and the serious economic and regional issues addressed.

2 **A spiritual conflict rages for Indonesia.** Ancient and powerful occult powers seek to deny the power of the gospel, while modern Muslim stratagems to eliminate the influence of Christians have the ultimate goal of removing the presence of the gospel. Pray specifically for the binding of these powers and for continued growth of the Church in the midst of intense opposition and growing persecution.

3 **The creeping Islamization of Indonesia** is eroding the long-prevailing communal tolerance and religious freedom. The former regime began to actively promote this process during the 1990s. Muslims were favoured in appointments in government, military and academic institutions. A massive mosque-building programme, together with transmigration of Muslims to Christian-majority areas was undertaken. Christians have become marginalized, increasingly persecuted and restricted in church meetings and evangelism. The Islamists' stated aim is the complete elimination of Christianity in the country. There has been an orchestrated Islamic *jihad* against Christians — with over 600 churches destroyed by mobs. Some Christian-majority areas, such as Timor Lorosae (East Timor) and Ambon, have been subjected to outright military attacks and killings. Pray for:

a) *The frustration of these plans*, discrediting of Muslim extremism and a re-examination by many Muslims of their own religion in the light of Scripture. Pray that Muslims may seek true relationship with God through Christ.

b) *The nation's leaders*, that they not bow to Muslim extremist pressure, which could polarize the nation with disastrous results.

c) *Christians to respond with tact*, love and also firmness, and in all ways commend the gospel. Pray that fear of witnessing might be replaced by courage to share about Jesus.

d) ***Heartfelt repentance*** among all Christians for the ways they have damaged their witness by attitudes and actions of enmity and reprisals towards Muslims.

e) ***The 65+ million nominal and syncretistic Muslims***, that their eyes be opened to the truth in Jesus, and come to Him.

4 **The enemy's counter-attack within the Church** is no less severe. While praising God for Christian growth, pray also for the overcoming of these weaknesses:

a) ***Too much sensational publicity*** which exalts man or the miraculous (as with the revival in West Timor) or which provokes the attention of those who would oppose the ongoing work of the Spirit.

b) ***Too few teachers and disciplers*** for those seeking the Lord. Many traditional churches cannot adequately disciple new believers, and new seekers often do no more than increase the population of nominal Christians.

c) ***The growth of error.*** Inadequate teaching has led to a multiplicity of errors, growth of liberal theologies, syncretistic Christianity loaded with occultism and animistic thought patterns and the controversy over 'prosperity' theology in some charismatic city churches.

d) ***Nominalism*** which has blighted the Church in areas that have been Christian for centuries: Manado in North Sulawesi, North Sumatra, West Timor and Maluku. Many denominations are spiritually lifeless and riddled with carnality, internal politics, divisions and active practice of indigenous occultism. These bodies need renewal and revival with many having a true conversion experience.

5 **The need for spiritual leaders of maturity** in the churches has never been greater. The pastor has heightened importance in Indonesian church life because the majority of Christians follow the Reformed and Lutheran traditions from the Netherlands and Germany. These strongly differentiate between clergy and laity. Yet rapid growth of the Church has far outstripped the supply of full-time workers. Pray for:

a) ***The development of effective lay leadership.*** Only a third of Reformed/Lutheran congregations have a pastor. Trained lay leadership is therefore essential.

b) ***Continuing training and discipleship*** for church leaders in general and pastors in particular. Many pastors have had inadequate training and need to be retrained and fired with new zeal. Some even need to be born of the Spirit.

c) ***Effective teaching and discipling*** in primary and secondary level Bible schools. Many of these are evangelical and often provide pastors for rural congregations.

d) ***The 40 degree-level seminaries***, about half being influenced by liberal theology. Pray for evangelical faculty members. Pray also for the writing and publishing of more evangelical theological works in Indonesian. Pray for an increase in the number of evangelical pastors in the large and influential regional Lutheran and Reformed churches.

e) ***The 18 evangelical seminaries relating to the Asian Theological Association.*** All are bulging with students and potential. Pray for an outflow of life through graduates from these institutions to churches and to the mission fields of Indonesia and beyond.

f) ***The spiritual quality and commitment of current pastors and spiritual leaders*** to be high. This is even more vital than discipling and recruiting new pastors and spiritual leaders. Pray especially that current developing leaders might have a willingness to go to the harder areas of the country for Jesus' sake.

6 **A vision for the evangelization of Indonesia** has grown as the opposition has increased. A conference in Jakarta in 1988 united ecumenical, Pentecostal and evangelical Protestants in a common vision. From 1996 onwards national and regional consultations have focused on unreached Indonesian peoples. About 130 million individuals in over 300 peoples are in this category. Excellent research was done by the National Research Network and there has been a significant increase in Indonesian agencies placing workers among these peoples. Pray that Christians may fully use present freedoms to tactfully but boldly reach out to them. Pray for the attainment of these visions:

a) ***A viable witnessing church for every people group in the country.*** Indonesia contains 130 people groups larger than 10,000 people which have a Christian population of under 1%. There are another 200+ unreached people groups of less than 10,000 people. Pray that the Indonesian Church may take the lead as expatriate workers partner with them.

b) ***A church in every village.*** Of 76,000 villages in the country, 50,000 have no church.

c) ***A unified Indonesian prayer movement***, with a prayer group in every neighbourhood linked into prayer networks in every city and province.

7 **Development of a missionary vision.** The history and background of Indonesian Christianity is unique. Indonesians are able to make a significant contribution to world evangelization. Pray for:

a) *Churches* to be gripped by the challenge of unreached peoples in their own country and in other lands of Asia and Africa. The financial and manpower resources are there.

b) *The sending out of Christians* — individuals, teams and communities — as migrants to unevangelized areas; going out with a vision for church planting. Christians will need to be set free from tribalism, denominationalism and local loyalties.

c) *Indonesian missionary agencies* are increasing in number. Many are denominationally based. Most are involved in evangelistic and church-planting ministries within Indonesia, and a few have workers outside the country. Some Indonesians are also serving with international missions (**YWAM, OM, OMF**/CCM, **CLC, WEC** and others).

8 **The Transmigration Scheme** is one of the world's largest planned resettlements of people ever organized. Vast areas of virgin territory in Sumatra, Kalimantan, Sulawesi and Papua have been opened up for migrants from overpopulated Java and Bali. Over 8 million were relocated between 1969 and 1998. These new settlements have been hard on the newcomers; with harsh conditions, poor soils and inefficient financing and communications. Yet among these migrants there is an openness to the gospel, and Christian groups have thrived despite the preferential selection of Muslims. Pray that these Christians may be lights for the Lord in areas never before evangelized — especially Sumatra and Sulawesi. There are also large numbers of migrants to the cities. Urban areas are rapidly becoming multi-cultural centres where people are more open to the gospel.

9 **Young people** are a vital mission field. Present ministry in churches and by interdenominational agencies are inadequate. Pray for:

a) *Students in universities.* They number 1.5 million in over 800 universities and colleges. There are a further 1.8 million in tertiary and teacher training colleges. It is estimated that 30% of faculty and students are Christian. A number of specialized agencies have extensive ministry on campuses (**Navigators**, **IFES**, **CCCI** and others). Yet many campuses still lack an organized Christian witness. A new feature is a growing number of Islamic universities. A significant minority of Indonesians study overseas — pray that they may be reached in other lands.

b) *School children.* In primary education there are 26 million and in secondary over l0 million. **CEF** has 28 workers among children and teaching others in ministry to them.

10 **The work of missions has been blessed of God** despite the obstacles of geography, bureaucracy and the spirit world. Praise God for the fruitful ministry of Dutch and German missions before World War II and many other international missions since then. Stand with these brothers and sisters in the battle for:

a) *Visas.* Tightening of restrictions on the entry, residence and ministry of missionaries makes entry more difficult. Pray that those whom the Lord calls may obtain visas.

b) *Innovative ministry alternatives* for those seeking to live out a committed Christian life and witness in Indonesia — as business professionals, teachers, students, etc. Pray for effective cooperation among those focused on incarnating the gospel among unreached peoples. Pray also for the calling of new workers from within and outside Indonesia.

c) *Missionaries who are serving in animistic areas* of West Kalimantan and Papua, where the young churches are developing to maturity. Church/mission relationships are an area that must be covered in prayer.

d) *The great lack of missionaries* in Sumatra, Nusa Tenggara and Sulawesi to be filled. Pray that no island may remain unserved by national or international gospel workers.

e) *The wide variety of international mission organizations* working in Indonesia. Major ministries include teaching, theological training, assisting in the training of Indonesian missionaries, development work and supporting Indonesian media ministries such as literature and radio. Pray for more Asian missionaries to come to Indonesia.

11 Supportive ministries:

a) *Bible translation.* The Bible Society and other groups are involved in over 100 translation projects across the country. The rapid reduction in expatriate visas has severely hampered the progress on many translations. Pray for their speedy completion. Pray also for the Indonesian Bible translation agency, *Kartidaya*, and for the calling of many

Indonesian translators. **NTM** have a number of translator teams in the country. Indonesia is one of the major unmet Bible translation challenges in the world today, despite the increasing use of Indonesian, having 155 languages with a definite need and a further 360 with a possible need.

b) ***Literature.*** There is an insatiable appetite for good Christian literature, but too little is widely available at a price people can afford. Transportation costs can equal the cost of production. Numerous Indonesian organizations and international missions have extensive printing and publishing ministries. Most are primarily focused on providing books and other resources for Christians and churches. Some are focused on outreach and evangelistic follow-up. The economic crisis since 1997 has severely affected these ministries. Pray for the provision of literature to meet the need, especially that which is locally written — indigenous authors are few. Too often the materials are merely translations of English books which are less appropriate to the Indonesian situation.

c) ***Missionary flying.*** This is a boon to Christian workers in this huge, rugged island nation, but it is costly and dangerous. Indonesia is **MAF**-US's greatest global effort with 28 aircraft (including 4 float planes and one helicopter) operating from 11 bases throughout the islands. In some areas of Kalimantan, Sulawesi and Papua missionary work would be impossible without it. **NTM**, **WT** and SdAs also have flying programmes. Pray for the staff and for safety of the planes. Pray also for efforts made to fulfil government requirements in training Indonesian pilots.

d) ***The use of traditional art forms***, such as Wayang shadow puppets. This is a powerful but little-used means of communicating the gospel.

e) ***The JESUS film*** was completed in Indonesian and a further 20 languages by 2000. Another 90 language versions are in preparation. Pray for the liberty to show the film all over the country, and pray for film teams — their safety, travel, effective links with local churches and good follow-through.

f) ***Practical ministries.*** Development programmes, preventative medical programmes and literacy all provide opportunities for sharing the gospel (**WV** and World Relief Commission).

g) ***Christian radio.*** There is continuing development of local language broadcasting in Java, Sumatra and Sulawesi. Pray especially for programmes that are being produced for less-reached peoples on these islands. There are Christian programmes in Indonesian that are broadcast on the national network. International broadcasters transmit 75 hrs/wk in Indonesian (**TWR**, **FEBC**), and 4 hrs/wk in 15 other languages, most with few Christians. At least 10 languages with over 1 million speakers have no broadcasts. Funding and personnel for appropriate follow-up with listeners who respond is a crucial need.

h) ***Audio ministry.*** Over 440 languages and dialects are now recorded; the goal of **GRN** is 560. The widespread use of Indonesian has made many insensitive to the need for the gospel in the heart language of the people — pray for better use of this medium.

Indonesia

The Islands of Indonesia

Each major island or island archipelago is so unique and complex that some of the more significant are handled separately — from west to east. The map on the previous page will help locate them.

SUMATRA

GEOGRAPHY Area 473,000 sq.km. The world's 5th largest island. A vast potential storehouse of minerals and agricultural produce; but much is untamed jungle, swamp and volcanic mountains, with poor surface communications.

Population 40,477,000 in nine provinces: Bengkulu; Jambi; Lampung; Riau; Bangka-Belitung; North, South and West Sumatra; and the special autonomous district of Aceh. People/sq.km.: 85.

PEOPLES Major peoples: Aceh, Batak, Minangkabau, Deli, Riau, Lampung and many Melayu (Malay) sub-groups.

RELIGIONS Official figures (1985): Muslim 85.9%; Christian 10.7% (Protestant 9.2%, Catholic 1.5%); Buddhist 2.2%; Hindu 0.5%; Other (including animist) 0.7%.

1 **Sumatra is the largest unevangelized island on earth.** Most of its peoples are staunchly Muslim. If it were a nation, only 9 other nations would have more unreached peoples. Sumatra is the home of 52 known unreached people groups consisting of 25 million people. Of the 52, 48 have no indigenous churches and 34 of them have no known gospel workers.

2 **Christians are strong among formerly animist peoples** — the only areas where the Dutch colonial administration allowed mission work. These are:

a) ***Bataks*** speaking seven languages and totalling 6.5 million. The Toba, Dairi, Karo and Simalungun are probably 75% Christian — Lutherans, Methodists, Reformed and Pentecostals, with some residual animism. Most of the Angkola and Mandailing are Muslim with only a small minority of Christians. The Batak are a dynamic people who have migrated all over Indonesia and who are prominent in the armed forces, police and in business, yet their ethnic pride and strong adherence to old customs combines with frequent enmity with Sumatran Muslim peoples to hinder Bataks' effectiveness as cross-cultural witnesses.

b) ***The Nias*** (530,000) and ***Mentawai*** (55,000) living on islands off Sumatra's west coast. Nearly all are Lutherans, but sadly nominalism and animistic practices are widespread. Some Muslim groups are actively involved in seeking to convert them. A new and more intelligible Bible translation is being prepared for publication in Nias. Pray for a new obedience to its contents.

c) ***The Chinese,*** mostly in the cities and industrial areas with large numbers of professing Christians; although many still follow traditional religions and Buddhism. There is much Christian activity and evangelism being done within these communities by younger and more vigorous denominations and agencies.

Pray that these Christians may be revived and break out of their ethnic cocoons to become effective witnesses to the non-Christian peoples around them.

3 **The Muslim majority has had little exposure to the gospel.** There were never more than a few dozen foreign missionaries committed to reach them (**WEC**, IMF, Methodists, Baptists), but few remain. Some recent and encouraging progress has been made in the number of Indonesian and international Christians living among these groups, who have a heart to reach out in love and witness.

4 **The unreached:**

a) ***The 3 million Aceh*** people of northern Sumatra are strongly Muslim and have been influential in spreading Islam to other Indonesian peoples. There are less than 50 Aceh believers with most living outside the area. The New Testament was published in 1992. Unrest and violence associated with an independence movement has plagued the province for over 300 years.

b) ***The less strongly Muslim peoples of North Sumatra.*** There are very few, if any, Christians among the Tamiang (900,000), Gayo (200,000) and Simeulue (130,000), but more among the Angkola and Mandailing Batak. There is only a limited outreach to these peoples.

c) ***The Minangkabau of West Sumatra*** (7.5m) and related groups such as the Rejang (500,000) and Kerinci (400,000). The Minangkabau are one of the best educated and most successful groups in Indonesia. Their matrilineal inheritance pattern has led to many migrating throughout the country — especially the men. There may be only 200 Christians (mostly in Java). The NT was legally published with permission from the national government in 1997 but all known copies were promptly confiscated and burned by West Sumatran authorities.

d) ***The Malay-related peoples of Eastern and Southern Sumatra,*** including the Deli (2m), Melayu Riau (2m), and Jambi (800,000). There are few Christians, and though not many are reaching out to them, there has been a recent increase in outreach.

e) ***The Muslim peoples of Central and South Sumatra,*** all of whom are without a congregation of believers. There is an outreach to the Batin (70,000), Bengkulu (50,000), Enim (70,000), Kaur (50,000), Lematang (150,000), Lembak (160,000), Ogan (300,000) and Semendo (105,000); but, as yet, there are no more than a handful of Christians.

f) ***The peoples of Lampung in the south.*** The indigenous peoples are increasingly marginalized and oppressed by newcomers from both Sumatra and Java. No churches are known among the indigenous Komering (800,000), Lampung Abung (500,000), Lampung Peminggir (500,000) or Lampung Pubian (410,000). There are churches among the many Java transmigrants in the area, and some ministry among the Komering.

JAVA

GEOGRAPHY Area 132,200 sq.km. Fertile, volcanic soil. Several active volcanoes. There are six provinces.

Population 125,414,000; 60% of Indonesia's population. People/sq.km. 948. Economically,
culturally and politically dominant in Indonesia.

PEOPLES Major peoples: Jawa, Sunda, Madura.

RELIGIONS Orthodox Sunni Muslim approximately 52%; statistical/animistic Muslim 40%; Christian 4% (Protestant 2.6%, Catholic 1.4%); Buddhist 0.8%; Hindu 0.2%.

1 Praise God for the receptivity to the gospel of the Jawa people and Indonesians of Chinese descent. In spite of economic woes, socio-political upheaval, military oppression, and religious persecution, the church on Java has continued to grow in excess of 5% a year since 1992. Approximately 45% of the Chinese descent Indonesians and 4% of the Jawa profess to be Christian. Pray that no effort of the enemy may hinder a continued harvest.

2 There is much spiritual and numerical growth in the churches among the urban Jawa and Indonesians of Chinese descent. In many non-urban areas, however, Christians worship and witness with increasing risk. Syncretism among the Jawa and materialism among the Indonesians of Chinese descent are perennial snares. Many persecuted Ambon Christians have fled to Java. They, together with Minahasa, Batak, Dayak, Toraja, Maluku and Timor Christians, find refuge in the megacities of Bandung, Jakarta, Semarang and Surabaya. Pray that the heightened pressures from Muslim extremists will create a greater commitment to the Lord and increase the spread of the gospel to unreached peoples throughout the islands.

3 As never before, traditional Protestant, Evangelical and Pentecostal churches have united in prayer, mutual support and information-sharing throughout the cities of Java. A spiritual, moral and missions awakening has occurred in numerous urban churches, many of which hold services in temporary facilities. The cell church movement is rapidly expanding in most urban areas. This is a time of harvest! Pray for greater momentum in reaching out to the largely unevangelized small towns and rural villages.

4 Jakarta and Surabaya are key cities for the evangelization of Indonesia. Almost every ethnic group has a presence there. The capital of Jakarta is now over 13% Christian, with over 1,000 registered churches and thousands of cell groups. A spiritual movement in Jakarta and Surabaya is having a spiritual impact on the whole country.

5 **The major unreached people groups,** however, have been tragically resistant and neglected:

a) *The unreached Jawa ethnic sub-groups* with less than 1% Christians include: Banten (500,000), concentrated in the northwestern part of the island; Banyumasan (6.6m), located along the south central coast; Osing (350,000), living on the extreme eastern tip; Pasisir Kulon (2.5m) and Pasisir Lor (19m) populating the north central coastline. All of these are staunchly Muslim, with very small numbers of believers, despite the significant response to the gospel and millions of Jawa believers in the other three Jawa sub-groups.

b) *The* **35** *million Sunda* live in West Java. They profess Islam, but are highly influenced by underlying animism and traditional Sunda beliefs. Christian Sunda number about 12,000, but some are nominal and culturally isolated from the Muslim majority. The largest Christian body of believers, the Pasundan Church, was began many years ago as primarily Sunda; but now is a mixture of ethnic groups, and historically has been focused on co-existence rather than outreach. There is a dearth of workers, suitable literature and adequate airing of radio programmes. Pray that the increasing interest in the gospel may result in an abundant harvest.

c) *The Madura* are concentrated in East Java, although Madura food peddlers are found throughout Indonesia. In the province of East Java, Madura peoples live both on Java and on two smaller adjacent islands just to the north: Madura and Bawean. They are a needy cluster of people which has rejected the few serious attempts to bring them the good news. They are comprised of the Bawean (60,000); the Madura (13.5m) and the Pendalunga (6.5m) — the latter being the offspring of Jawa-Madura intermarriages since 1671. The Madura peoples have a reputation for anger and violence. Pray that Christians may overcome their fear and hatred to embody Christ's love to them.

d) *The Jawa Tengger* people living on the slopes of Mt. Bromo in East Java continue to resist Islamic inroads. Instead they are experiencing a Hindu resurgence through cooperative efforts with Balinese Hindu religious workers. However, several Tengger Christian groups have emerged in the area. Over the last 15 years an embryonic Tengger church and leadership has developed. Pray for its long-term viability

BALI

GEOGRAPHY **Area** 5,632.86 sq.km. Fertile, volcanic soil. Several active volcanoes.
Population 3,165,000. People/sq.km. 561.

PEOPLES   Major peoples: Bali.

RELIGIONS Hindu 92.7%; Muslim 5.6%; Christian 0.9% (Protestant 0.5%, Catholic 0.4%); Buddhist 0.8%.

1 **A unique blend of Hinduism dominates the spiritual landscape of Bali.** One million Bali people live on the neighbouring islands of Sumatra, Sulawesi and Lombok. These Bali migrants tend to be more open to the gospel. There are 49,000 Hindu temples on Bali. Protestant churches number about 85, Catholic churches 33. City churches tend to have 50% Bali members. The Bali need the liberating power of the gospel.

2 **Bali Christians are few.** The cost of discipleship is high, and converts to Christ often face ostracism, persecution and financial loss when they break with their family's and community's way of life. Pray for the witness of Christians, which has great impact in leading others to make a decision.

3 **Effective cooperation in ministry** among Bali believers is a need.

4 **The Bali Bible** was published in 1990. Its use is limited because most do not understand its 'high caste' language. The *JESUS* film is also in this language. Pray for effective communication of God's Word to all Bali peoples. Both **TWR** and **FEBC** broadcast in Bali.

WEST LESSER SUNDA ISLANDS (NUSA TENGGARA BARAT)

GEOGRAPHY Area 20,177 sq.km. The islands of Lombok and Sumbawa.

Population 3,086,000. People/sq.km. 197.

PEOPLES Major peoples: Sasak, Sumbawa, Bima.

RELIGIONS Muslim 96%; Hindu 3.3%; Buddhist 0.5%; Christian 0.2% (Protestant 0.1%, Catholic 0.1%).

1 **These staunchly Muslim islands** are some of the least evangelized in Indonesia. The 20,000 Protestants are mainly immigrant peoples in the towns (Jawa, Timor, Chinese Indonesians). Riots in Lombok in January 2000 drove most of these few Christians off the island. Most of the church buildings were totally destroyed, as were many homes of believers.

2 **Unreached peoples:**

a) *Despite ongoing efforts for the past 10+ years to reach them, the three major indigenous people groups remain unreached.* They are: the Muslim Sasak (2m) on Lombok; the Sumbawa (400,000) and Bima (600,000) on Sumbawa Island. There are only 20 known believers among the Sasak, 100 among the Bima and 20 among the Sumbawa. All three groups are strongly Muslim, but still adhere to animistic beliefs.

b) *The Hindu Bali people* — 100,000 on Lombok.

3 **Two small churches,** founded by **CMA** in the 1940s in the area of Bima, have approximately 100 believers but struggle to survive, as many young people convert to Islam in order to get married.

4 **Scriptures** are being translated into the Sasak and Bima languages

EAST LESSER SUNDA ISLANDS (NUSA TENGGARA TIMOR)

GEOGRAPHY Area 47,876 sq.km. The islands of Sumba, Flores, Lomblin, Alor and West Timor.

Population 3,908,000. People/sq.km. 80.

PEOPLES Major peoples: Timor, Manggarai, Solar, Lio, Rote, Sikka, Sumba.

RELIGIONS Christian 82.8% (Catholic 51.2%, Protestant 31.6%); Muslim 8.5%; Hindu 0.2%; Traditional ethnic 8.5%.

1 **Flores is 90% Catholic** but is steeped in pagan and idolatrous rituals sometimes involving snake worship. Born-again Christians are very few, and largely Timor people. No language of Flores has any Scriptures. The Manggarai (500,000), Lamaholot-Solar (300,000); Ende-Lio (230,000), Sikka (180,000); and Ngada (70,000) need to be evangelized in their own cultural settings and languages. Muslim minorities among the Solor (140,000) and Manggarai (30,000) are totally unreached.

2 **Sumba,** an island long known for its animism and resistance to the gospel, saw a movement of the Spirit in the late 1980s, with Protestants doubling from 75,000 to 160,000 in five years. Pray that this movement may impact all seven language groups on the island.

3 **West Timor:**

a) *There was a great outpouring of the Spirit* in 1965-8 which resulted in renewal within the Church and thousands of conversions from occultism and Islam. About 20% of the Timor were converted. Timor Christians serve the Lord as missionaries on four continents.

b) *The wide-scale killing and destruction* which followed East Timor's (Timor Lorosae) vote to become independent of Indonesia resulted in a number of refugee camps holding thousands of destitute people in West Timor. Several Christian groups, both from churches in Timor and from other parts of Indonesia, have attempted to minister physically and spiritually in the camps. Violence and intimidation continue at the hands of the militia who ruined East Timor in 1999. Pray for an end to the suffering, freedom to return home and salvation for these refugees.

c) **Sawu people** on Sawu Island and West Timor (100,000) are 80% animist in practice; the rest being nominally Christian, but few have a personal faith. Black magic is widespread.

d) **The Ambenu Timor and Belu Tetun** in West Timor are largely nominal Catholics and few are Evangelicals.

4 **The lack of Scriptures** for the languages of the two Lesser Sunda Provinces is a major reason for nominalism, unchallenged witchcraft, and lack of progress for the gospel. Only three of the 65 languages have a NT, though work is in progress in 10 of them. A major prayer request is for an adequate survey of translation needs and provision of translation teams for those languages requiring a New Testament.

KALIMANTAN

GEOGRAPHY Area 539,000 sq.km. The Indonesian three-quarters of the island of Borneo; shared with Malaysia. An island of tropical rainforest and rivers, but few roads and four provinces.

Population 11,473,000 in four provinces — West, Central, East and South Kalimantan. People/sq.km: 21.

PEOPLES Major peoples: Malay, Dayak, Banjar.

RELIGIONS Muslim 72.8%; Christian 19.3% (Catholic 9.8%, Protestant 9.5%); Traditional ethnic 3.5%; Hindu 2.5; Buddhist 1.9%.

1 **The indigenous Dayak peoples** number 3.1 million and speak a range of nearly 80 languages and numerous dialects. Church growth has been high, with large people movements into the churches; but often without a clear break from the spirit world.

a) **The CMA work in East Kalimantan** has resulted in a strong church among the Kenyah and Kayan peoples as well as outreach to other ethnic groups.

b) **In Central Kalimantan,** many of the 410,000 Ngaju, 105,000 M'anyan, and 100,000 Dohoi are linked with the Reformed Church, founded through the work of the Rhenish and Basel Missions. Sadly, few are evangelical in theology.

c) **West Kalimantan** has been a major field for **CMA**, **CBI**, **WT**, Go Ye Fellowship, **WEC** and **NTM**. Growing churches have emerged, and over 30% of the population is Christian. Some Dayak sub-groups, such as the Iban in the interior, have been more difficult to win; and many of the Dayak who profess Christianity need a personal encounter with Jesus.

2 **Leadership training** is a major need for the churches, but illiteracy, poverty, difficulties in travel and lack of indigenous Scriptures have all slowed development. There are a number of Bible schools. Pray for churches to mature and have a vision for outreach.

3 **The unreached:**

a) **The large Banjar Malay population** of 5 million along the eastern and southern coasts, and up the rivers, is strongly Muslim. In recent years, a few individuals, churches and groups have begun to pray for and reach out to them, but only a handful have believed. These believers have suffered such intense persecution, nearly all now live in hiding. Pray for whole families to come to Christ and also to remain as witnesses in their communities.

b) **Transmigrants, who number over 1 million.** These are Jawa (nominally Muslim), Bali (Hindu), Bugis and Madura (strongly Muslim). They live in transmigrant settlements and oil-boom towns in the east. Only among the Jawa are there growing churches, but they have little vision for outreach to other groups. In the late 1990s, Dayak resentment of the high-handedness of Madura transmigrants in West Kalimantan boiled over into violence with hundreds of massacres and thousands of Madura becoming refugees. Pray that local nominal Christians may overcome their anger, as well as the cultural and religious barriers, and reach out in love to transmigrant groups.

c) **The animist peoples of the interior** present a challenge. The complexities of reaching isolated tribal groups are immense — survey work is hard and living conditions difficult. Pray for more pioneers willing to reach out to these hard-to-access but receptive peoples.

d) **The Chinese-descent Indonesians,** 25% of the population in West Kalimantan, have proved less responsive to the gospel than elsewhere, though many are nominally Christian. Pray for the witness of Chinese Christians and churches on the coast, in Pontianak and up the Kapuas River.

SULAWESI

GEOGRAPHY Area 191,800 sq.km. A large, orchid-shaped mountainous island, 1,300 km from north to south. Also many satellite islands. Formerly called Celebes.

Population 15,020,000 in five provinces. People/sq.km: 78.

PEOPLES Major peoples: Bugi, Makassar, Minahasa, Gorontalo, Toraja, Sanghir.

RELIGIONS Muslim 75.3%; Christian 16.4% (Protestant 16%, Catholic 0.4%); Traditional ethnic 6%; Hindu 2%; Buddhist 0.3%.

• Challenges for Prayer

1 **Sulawesi is a patchwork** of ethnic groups and of varied response to the missionary religions of Islam and Christianity. Generally, nearly all the coastal peoples are Muslim. Christians are a majority on the two north-eastern peninsulas and in the central highlands. The main Christian ethnic groups are:

a) *The seven Minahasa peoples of Manado* (850,000) who are located on the north-east tip of Sulawesi. They have been Protestant for over 300 years. They are among the wealthiest and best-educated peoples of Indonesia, but materialism, nominalism, poor church attendance and occultism are rife. There is little concern for the evangelization of the Muslim and animist majority of the island.

b) *The Sanghir and Talaud islanders* (210,000) to the north of Manado.

c) *The Toraja* (1.6 million with eight languages and 30 dialects) are mostly adherents of one of the four Reformed Churches. Few have a personal experience with the Lord. Tradition, especially a morbid preoccupation with death, still grips many.

All these peoples need revival. Pray also for lasting fruit through the ministry of younger evangelical, Pentecostal and charismatic denominations and agencies.

2 **Less-reached peoples** are numerous, but in most of the larger groups there are small Christian minorities. Pray specifically for:

a) *The Bugis* (3.8m) and *Makassar* (2.2m) of South Sulawesi with colonies all around the coast. Trading is their major occupation. By Indonesian standards Islam is more orthodox among them. There are about 3,000 Bugi and 500 Makassar Christians, the latter being one of the few significant orthodox Muslim groups responding in any numbers to the gospel at the current time.

b) *The Muslim Gorontalo* (1m), numerous smaller Muslim-animist peoples scattered around the north, and the Bungku-Mori Toraja of the southeast, where animistic practices are more prevalent. There are small churches indigenous to these peoples, but response is slow and many areas are untouched.

3 **Bible translation** is an enormous unfinished task. Researchers spent years surveying the complex linguistic situation and are participating in most of the ongoing 18 NT translation projects, together with Indonesian translators. Pray that nothing may hinder the publication of these NTs. There are only four indigenous languages with a Bible and 16 with a NT. There are 28 languages with a definite unmet need for translators and a further 83 which will possibly need their own translations.

4 **Pray for peace and calm** in Central Sulawesi following violent confrontations between religions. Pray that the translation and church planting projects there may continue.

MALUKU

GEOGRAPHY Area 77,871 sq.km. A medley of over 1,000 small islands scattered over Indonesia's eastern seas. Two provinces: Maluku, North Maluku.

Population 3,168,000. People/sq.km. 40.

PEOPLES There are 128 1anguage groups.

RELIGIONS Muslim 59%; Christian 40.5% (Protestant 35.3%, Catholic 5.2%); Hindu 0.14%; Buddhist 0.05%; Other 0.4%.

1 **A terrible period of violence followed by 'ethnic cleansing'** of Christians by Muslims has afflicted these islands. In the 1990s tension developed between the growing Muslim communities and indigenous Christians. Propaganda, lies and subterfuge from outside Maluku provoked an eruption of violence and warfare along religious and ethnic lines. A tragic cycle of revenge led to both Muslim and some Christian atrocities. Enormous destruction of property resulted, including over 400 churches and some mosques. Many thousands of Islamist *jihad* fighters were recruited and brought to Maluku. The powerlessness of the central government to control the situation and the superior arms of the Islamists (with much help from sections of the army) swayed the balance of the conflict against the Christians. The conflict displaced most of the Christian population of the islands of Ambon, Seram, Temate, Tidore, parts of Halmahera, etc. By the end of 2000 there were over 500,000 refugees and maybe 6,000 killed. Pray for an end to the conflict, communal harmony to be restored and the deep wounds to be healed. Without these, the effects of this period could reverberate for generations.

2 **The Maluku Protestant Church,** founded in 1605, is Asia's oldest Protestant denomination. Nominalism has crippled the witness of the Church, while the Muslim population has grown through both immigration from other areas and conversion of Maluku peoples. Other denominations have entered Maluku, but they have made little headway against the inertia of nominalism or the rise of Islam. Pray that the present severe suffering may bring nominal Christians to new life and revive the churches. Pray also that the Christian community might be able to see its own need for repentance rather than seeing only the wrongs done against them. Pray that they may reach out in forgiving love and have a zeal to evangelize.

3 **The less evangelized for prayer:**

a) *Muslim peoples.* These include the Ambon Melayu (50,000), the Temate (62,000), Tidore (46,000), the seafaring Bajau (90,000), the Makian of Halmahera Island, and numerous other smaller peoples.

b) *Many island communities in South Maluku* are nominally Christian, but little evidence of faith remains. Pray for effective means for reaching them.

4 **Bible translation** is a great challenge. There are 117 languages in active use but only one has a NT yet, in spite of the fact that many of these peoples are 'Christian'. Translation teams are involved in 23 languages, 38 more have a definite need for their own translation, and a further 92 will possibly need teams. Pray for the continuation of translation work which, along with other ministries, has been disrupted by violence.

[WEST] PAPUA (IRIAN JAYA)

GEOGRAPHY Area 422,000 sq.km. Formerly Irian Jaya. The western half of the world's second largest island, New Guinea (see Papua New Guinea for the eastern half). The island is known for having a wild beauty, as well as some of the most inhospitable terrain on earth.

Population 2,133,000. People/sq.km. 5.

PEOPLES Major peoples: Only the Dani of the central highlands have a population over 100,000. Over 247 languages are spoken.

POLITICS In modern times, ruled by Netherlands until 1963, when annexed by Indonesia. Recently, there have been renewed demands for greater autonomy or independence.

RELIGIONS Christian 73.4% (Protestant 54.1%; Catholic 19.3%); Muslim 16.4%; Traditional ethnic 10.1%; Buddhist 0.08%.

• Answers to Prayer

1 **Praise God** for the people movements that have brought stone-age peoples to faith in Christ among most of the 275 tribes. These include peoples on the north coast in the 19th Century (Reformed Church), in the more densely populated highlands (**Pioneers, CMA, WT, UFM, ABMS, NTM** and others), in the Bird's Head (**TEAM**), and the southern swamps (**TEAM, WT**). Over 90% of the indigenous population is officially reckoned as Christian.

• Challenges for Prayer

1 **The future of West Papua is threatened** by massive government-initiated immigration and by Islamist extremism. The suppression of any indigenous political movement and even of Christianity itself is the aim. The government is planning to divide the island into three provinces, two of which would have a Muslim majority. Pray both for the restraint of violence, and for the preservation and growth of the indigenous Church.

2 **Strong, Bible-centred, maturely led Papuan churches** are the great need as modernization, education and the outside world impact these isolated cultures. Christians must face up to the challenges of tribalism, syncretism and separatist politics which sap the spiritual energies of some churches. Sadly, inter-village fighting has once more become a problem in some Christianized areas.

3 **The Dani peoples** total 300,000. Many turned to the Lord in great people movements over the last few decades of the 20th Century. At one stage there were 280 Dani missionaries evangelizing other areas. That vision has dimmed. Pray for renewal of life and vision for the Dani churches. There is a strong independence movement among the Dani.

4 **Missionary numbers are on the increase again** — both expatriate and indigenous Indonesians and Papuans. Most work in the towns and coastal areas and serve in a wide range of ministries. More are needed who can pioneer unreached rural areas and transmigrant communities. **NTM** has opened up a number of pioneer areas in recent years.

5 **Christian aviation** is essential in this land with few roads. **MAF**-US has planes at five bases. **WT**-Tariku and JAARS also have extensive flying programmes in some of the most rigorous conditions in the world. Pray for safety; there have been some bad accidents. Pray for more to be called for this ministry and also for its funding. Indonesia's post-1997 economic crisis has raised flying costs and deeply affected inland economies dependent on it.

6 **The less-reached.** Only in the last few years have virtually all the ethnic groups been located and contacted. Indigenous peoples still requiring pioneer evangelism and church-planting are:
a) *Small peoples east of Cenderawasih Bay* on New Guinea's 'shoulder'.
b) *Peoples in the northern foothills* of the Eastern Highlands.
c) *Peoples in the southern foothills* of the main range of mountains bisecting the island.
d) *The Baliem Dani* of the Highlands who have not been as responsive as the rest of the Western Dani.
e) *There are 14 known areas* with a total population of around 20,000 where no Christians have penetrated. Pray that national churches and agencies may reach them.

7 **The transmigrants** number nearly one million. They often had gained land and privileges at the expense of the indigenous Papuans. The Papuan independence movement has brought uncertainty and threats of violence. Pray that this may open hearts to those who bring them news of Jesus. Major church planting challenges:
a) *The Muslim Minangkabau* and *Makassar* in the coastal urban areas.
b) *Many ethnic enclaves* scattered over Papua. Recent arrivals are Ambonese refugees.

8 **Bible translation** for the many small language groups is an immense task. There are 27 languages with a NT, 23 have Bible portions finished, and 39 with work in progress. There are 54 with a definite need and 130 others with a possible need for a NT translation. Pray for:
a) *The completion, publication and effective use* of the NTs in the process of being translated or printed.
b) *Cooperation between churches and agencies* to have portions of Scripture translated into every vernacular still used as a primary language.
c) *Mother-tongue speakers* with the skills, gifts, spiritual insight and motivation to tackle the arduous task of translation.
d) *The use of audio cassettes* for Scriptures and Christian messages on tape. **GRN** have made recordings in over 200 languages.

Iran
Islamic Republic of Iran

JUNE 27-29
ASIA

GEOGRAPHY
Area 1,648,196 sq.km. Situated between the Caspian Sea in north and Arabian Sea/Persian Gulf in south. A central desert ringed by mountains.

Population	Ann.Gr.	Density
2000	67,702,199	+1.67%	41 per sq. km.
2010	76,931,899	+1.58%	47 per sq. km.
2025	94,462,501	+1.17%	57 per sq. km.

Capital Tehran 11 mill. Other major cities: Mashhad 2.15m; Isfahan 1.63m; Tabriz 1.28m; Shiraz 1.13m; Qom 880,000. **Urbanites** 61%.

PEOPLES
Over 70 ethnic groups, some being small nomadic groups.
Indo-Iranian 71.8%. Persian (Farsi, Dari, Tajik) 30mill.; Kurd (6) 5m; Luri 4,946,000; Gilaki 3,659,000; Mazanderani 2,946,000; Bakhtiari 1,154,000; Baluch 623,000; Takistani 306,000; Tat 137,000; Mamsani 127,000; Talysh 112,000.
Turkic 22%. Azeri (Azari) 11,224,000; Turkmen 1,003,000; Qashqai 962,000; Khorasani 773,000; Hazara (speaking Dari) 687,000; Teymur 206,000; Shahseven 100,000.
Semitic 3%. Arab (mainly southwest and Iraq border) 2m; Jews 20,000.
Christian minorities 0.2%. Armenian and Assyrian. Reduced from 1.5% in 1975 due to emigration.
Other 3%. Gypsy (Nawar and Ghorbati) 1,470,000; Brahui 16,000.
Refugees. At one time 4.5m Afghans, Iraqi Kurds, Shi'a Arabs and Tajiks were refugees in Iran. Maybe up to 1.5m remain, but now they are somewhat integrated into Iran.

Literacy 72%. **Official language** Persian (Farsi; Dari and Tajik are major dialects); spoken by 83% of Iranians. **All languages** 69. **Languages with Scriptures** 3Bi 2NT 4por 12w.i.p.

ECONOMY
Oil provided 75% of export earnings in 1995 and carpets, 11%. Material progress under the Shah was reversed by the bigotry of the religious leaders, national paranoia and the flight of the business and technology elite. Inefficiency, corruption, war with Iraq and economic sanctions imposed by the West brought Iran to the brink of disaster in the 1980s. There has been a slow improvement since 1990 and the lot of the rural poor has greatly improved. Rapid population growth outstrips the means to feed and employ all. **Unemployment** may be 30%. **HDI** 0.715; 95th/174. **Public debt** 7.6% of GNP. **Income/person** $1,000 (5.6% of USA, in 1982 it was 18%).

POLITICS
The Shah was deposed in the Shi'ite Muslim Revolution, and a theocratic Islamic Republic declared in 1979. Regional loyalties and anarchy brought the country close to civil war and ruin. The Iraqi invasion of 1980 led to 8 years of bitter war and over 1 million Iranian dead. Since 1990 democratic elections have increased the influence of more moderate politicians and the 2000 election was decisively won by the reformers. Yet the conservative leadership retains overriding powers which keep Iran as a theocratic police state with scant regard for human rights. Iran is extensively re-arming, engaged in diplomatic activity to regain regional superpower status in the Middle East, and vying with Turkey for influence in the Muslim Central Asian States.

RELIGION
Shi'a Islam is the state religion and 93% of Iranians follow this. Sunni Islam is respected and is largely followed by the Turkoman, Kurd and Baluch populations. All other deviations or defections from Islam are severely handled. Constitutionally the rights of Jews, Zoroastrians and Christians are guaranteed, but closely monitored. All Christian proselytism is forbidden. **Persecution index** 9th in the world.

Religions	Population %	Adherents	Ann.Gr.
Muslim	99.02	67,038,717	+1.7%
Baha'i	0.52	352,051	+0.2%
Christian	0.33	220,000	-0.6%
Other	0.10	67,702	+1.7%
Jewish	0.03	25,000	-4.0%

Christians	Denom.	Affil.%	,000	Ann.Gr.
Protestant	9	0.01	7	+3.9%
Independent	1	0.01	8	+1.4%
Anglican	1	0.00	1	+0.0%
Catholic	1	0.01	7	-7.3%
Orthodox	4	0.18	121	-4.3%
Marginal	3	0.00	0	+5.1%
Unaffiliated		0.12	75	n.a.

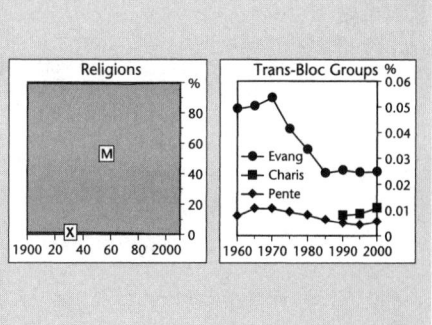

Churches	MegaBloc	Cong.	Members	Affiliates
Armenian Orthodox	O	63	72,368	110,000
Ch of the East (Nestor)	O	8	7,692	11,000
Catholic	C	17	4,000	7,000
Evangelical (Presbyterian)	P	9	1,703	3,100
Assemblies of God	P	12	1,400	3,000
Episcopal	A	3	480	1,200
Other denoms [12]		16	6,000	9,000
Total Christians [18]		129	94,000	145,000

Trans-bloc Groupings	pop.%	,000	Ann.Gr.
Evangelical	0.0	17	+2.0%
Charismatic	0.0	7	+4.3%
Pentecostal	0.0	4	+7.5%

• Answers to Prayer

1 **The Islamic Revolution** promised so much but has delivered little. The theocratic tyranny of the ayatollahs has proved more cruel and corrupt than the system it replaced in 1979. Twenty years of anti-Western, anti-Christian propaganda has opened many Muslims to seek for alternatives to Islam. Iranians are more open to the gospel than ever before.

2 **There may have been only 500 Muslim-background believers** (MBBs) in 1979, but that number has multiplied in 20 years. Estimates range from 4,000 to 20,000 with half in Iran itself. Some claim that there are thousands of secret believers, but persecution of 'apostates' from Islam is too severe to uncover the true situation.

3 **For the first time in history evangelical MBBs** outnumber those from the minority Christian communities.

• Challenges for Prayer

1 **The Islamic revolution has lost its glitter**. The legacy of bloodshed, cruelty, injustice, extremism and economic deprivation has discredited the conservative religious leaders and the Islam they promote. These leaders react with repression, restrictions and abuse of human rights because they control the police and army and manipulate the justice system. Pray for political change and a government that is truly accountable to their people and which respects human rights.

2 **Iranians battle daily to survive in economic recession**, political tyranny and, above all, the demonic system underlying it all. Pray that these shackles may be shattered and many Iranians find true liberty in believing in the Risen Lord Jesus. Pray that this land may open up again for the proclamation of the gospel.

3 **Discrimination in jobs, housing and education is a daily reality** to all Jews and Christians, but so is open and severe persecution for followers of the Baha'i religion, for all who use the Persian language for worship or witness and for all MBBs. **The Bible Society**, all Christian bookstores, conferences, camps, printing of literature and church newsletters, and production of videos are banned. Pray for true religious freedom to come to Iran.

4 **The majority of the wider Christian community** is from the traditionally Christian Armenian and Assyrian communities which are isolated cultural and language islands in a Muslim sea. Their existence has been tolerated, but fear, job discrimination, uncertainty, arbitrary arrests, interrogations, enforcement of Islamic dress for women, and Islamic religious education for children have provoked the emigration of a large proportion of these communities. Pray for a work of the Holy Spirit in these churches that the lives of Christians might radiate the glory of Jesus.

5 **Protestant Churches were generally small and struggling before the revolution**. The traumatic changes and suffering that followed gave them a brief period of renewal, outreach, literature distribution and many converts. Barriers between Presbyterians, Anglicans and Pentecostals were broken down. The 1990s were a time of severe persecution. Spies infiltrated congregations, and church buildings were seized or closed. Seven Christian leaders were martyred and others have had to flee for their lives. Pray for:

a) ***Courage and fortitude under persecution*** such that their enemies are won for Christ.

b) ***Wisdom, boldness and protection for all in leadership.***

c) ***Adequate income for Christians*** who are increasingly impoverished. Emigration is a solution, both for pressured Christians and the Muslim persecutors, but their vital witness in needy Iran is lost. Pray that believers may break through this economic pressure and resist the temptation to leave.

d) ***Supernatural deliverances and fruitfulness*** for all MBBs. Many are forced to meet together secretly or are unable to gather with other believers. Any underground church meetings are actively sought out and worshippers punished.

e) ***Churches outside Tehran which have suffered*** more. In cities such as Shiraz and Isfahan the witness has been decimated. Pray for new light to shine in every city of the land. There are 178 towns and cities but just a handful of local churches. Pray for leaders with vision and courage for planting new groups to be raised up.

6 **The Iranian Diaspora is nearly 5 million**. Most have found refuge in USA, Canada, Western Europe, Turkey, Gulf States and other lands where they can be evangelized. Pray for:

a) ***Several networks*** of over 70 Iranian diaspora churches, their growth in grace, unity (often a challenge) and preparation for return to minister one day in Iran.

b) ***The ministry of Iranian Christians International,*** **ELAM** (Elam Ministries, UK) and Persian World Outreach, each with a significant contribution to coordinating fellowship, some support for the persecuted in Iran and literature and Bible ministries.

c) ***Training of Iranian Christian workers*** — most are trained at **ELAM's** residential college in the UK, a few at NEST in Lebanon and a number are involved in non-residential courses in Iran and California. There are hundreds also studying via correspondence courses.

d) ***The many significant Iranian communities*** which have no church or witness — notably the Gulf States with over 60,000 Iranians.

7 **Missions are not free to minister in the land** but some tentmaking opportunities arise and tourism is actively encouraged. Pray for both Iranians and expatriates working among Iranians in Europe, North America and Australia. Pray that the door to Iran and its unevangelized millions may open once more. Pray also that agencies around the world may pray, plan and network together with Iranian believers in preparation for that day.

8 **The spiritual needs of religious minorities:**

a) ***The Zoroastrians or Parsees*** are followers of the ancient Persian religion and are prominent in the Bible — Cyrus and the three wise men being examples. They have their own distinct language derived from Persian. Communities of Parsees live in many South Asian, Middle Eastern and Western countries. Only 30 believers are known worldwide. Parsee numbers are probably much higher than those given officially. There may be up to two million in Iran — all totally unreached.

b) ***The Baha'i,*** a syncretistic religion that has spread worldwide since the 19th Century, are the most severely persecuted religious minority in Iran. They were outlawed, deprived of public service jobs and many maltreated or imprisoned. Very little Christian love and witness has been shared with the Baha'i in Iran or among the 6 million worldwide. Pray that in their extremity they may find refuge in the Lord Jesus.

c) ***The Persian-speaking Jews*** are descendants of those exiled to Babylon 2,700 years ago. Due to pressure and harassment they are declining through emigration. A number have become active, witnessing Christians.

9 **Unreached peoples** — all the peoples are unreached. Iran contains some of the largest totally unreached peoples in the world; only in eight of the 70 ethnic groups are there known groups of believers. Pray specifically for:

a) ***The partly nomadic*** Iranic Luri and Bakhtiari and the Turkic Qashqai who live in the Zagros Mountains. Only now are the first attempts being made to reach them and only a handful of believers are known. Pray down the barriers that these major peoples might hear the gospel. Many are illiterate.

b) ***The various Kurdish peoples*** of NW and NE Iran. They have lived through political, economic and ecological disasters in the 20th Century that have impoverished them, but their greatest poverty is lack of a knowledge of the gospel.

c) ***The Turkic Azeri, Khorasani Turks and Turkmen in the north.*** They are closely related, but scarcely have had any positive contacts with Christianity. Pray for workers to be able to reach them, the Scriptures to be translated and for churches to be planted among them. The Azeri Bible is in preparation (**ELAM**).

d) ***The peoples of the southeast*** — the Baluch and Brahui. They are restive and unhappy with Iranian rule. There are no known believers.

e) ***The Gypsy communities*** with nearly 1.5 million people but with no Christians nor workers committed to seek ways to reach them.

10 **Christian Help ministries** are of special value for the Iran of today — often being the only means of reaching the majority of the population.

a) ***Bibles are in very short supply***. The Bible Society and all Christian literature distribution outlets closed in 1988 and banned supplies have dwindled away even for Christians, but a steady trickle of Bibles continues to enter the country. Some reckon that 10 million Bibles would be gladly received were there opportunity. A new translation of the Persian NT was published in 2001; the Bible is to be completed in 2006 (**ELAM**). Pray for innovative and effective ways of distributing God's Word and for a deep impact to be made through it. Pray also for translation teams to be raised up for the many large and smaller languages without the Scriptures.

b) ***Christian literature***, when available, is much sought after. Pray for the impact of literature already distributed and that all the harsh banning of Christian literature ministries may be ended. Much has to be done from outside Iran to publish and distribute literature — Eternal Life Agape Ministries and **ELAM** are major components in this ministry.

c) ***Christian radio*** has become a key ministry. Millions listen despite government restrictions and thousands of response letters are received. Radio Voice of Christ, **IBRA**, **ELAM** and others prepare daily programmes in Persian and Azeri. **TWR** and **FEBA** cooperate in providing 2.5 hours of broadcasting daily in Persian. ELAM envisions preparing programmes also in Gilaki and Turkmen.

d) ***Christian TV, video and film ministries***. There is a large black market for banned secular and religious tapes and over seven million have access through illegal satellite dishes. Both Christian Persian-language films (ELAM) and the *JESUS* film have been shown a number of times. The *JESUS* film was available in 12 Iranian languages in 2000 with a further five in production. Pray for ongoing impact through these ministries.

Iraq
Republic of Iraq

JUNE 30-JULY 1
ASIA
Updated July 2004

GEOGRAPHY
Area 438,317 sq.km. Fertile plains of the Tigris and Euphrates, high mountains to the north and Syrian desert in southwest. Site of the ancient Sumerian, Assyrian and Babylonian empires.

Population	Ann.Gr.	Density
2000	23,114,884	+2.84%	53 per sq. km.
2010	30,338,663	+2.63%	69 per sq. km.
2025	41,013,588	+1.72%	94 per sq. km.

Capital Baghdad 5,600,000. Other major cities: Basra 1,300,000; Mosul 1,700,000; Kirkuk 730,000; and in Kurdish Autonomous Region (KAR): Irbil 840,000; Sulaymaniyah 640,000.

PEOPLES
The Sunni Arab minority long dominated other ethnic groups; all claim higher statistics for their own group for political gain [bracketed figure].
Arabs 70.2% [77.1%]. Shi'a Arab (in South) 11 mill.; Sunni Arab (in Centre) 5m; Bedouin 110,000; Madan (Marsh Arabs) 50,000.
Kurds 19% [23.7%]. 9 groups, largest: Sorani 2.24m; Kurmanji 1.7m; Central Kurds 527,000; Yazidi 100,000; Luri 80,000.
Turkic 6.1% [10.8%], in centre and north. Turkmen 1,260,000; Azeri 148,000; Turks 26,000.
Christian minorities 2.5% [5%]. Assyrian 500,000; Armenian 90,000.
Other 2.2%. Persian 290,000; Gypsy 167,000; Circassian 20,000.

Literacy 58%. **Official languages** Arabic; Kurdish in the KAR. **All languages** 23. **Languages with Scriptures** 3Bi 2NT 1por 4w.i.p.

ECONOMY

Oil-based economy — since Genesis 11! Profits were squandered on building a powerful army. War with Iran halted economic development. The Gulf Wars and 13 years of UN sanctions further devastated the economy and impoverished the ordinary people. Iraq has the world's third-largest known oil reserves. The control and fair distribution of that wealth is the key issue that will dominate the politics of the next few years. National reconstruction after 45 years of tyranny will take many years. **HDI** 0.586; 125th/174. **Public debt** 174% of GNP. **Income/person** $540 (2% of USA). It was $6,600 in 1980.

POLITICS

Created as a political entity by the victorious Allies after World War I. Independent as a monarchy in 1932. Monarchy overthrown in a revolution in 1958. The Baathist military regime, with its secularist pan-Arab socialism, became a dictatorship under Saddam Hussein. A massive military machine was built with the connivance of Arab countries and Western powers greedy for petrodollars. It was used to protect the dictatorship, repress the Kurds and Shi'a, launch a war against Iran (1980-88) and invade Kuwait in 1990. Although evicted from Kuwait in the 1991 Gulf War, Iraq was not totally defeated. Sophisticated propaganda, ruthless suppression of dissent and evasion of UN sanctions enabled the regime to survive until the US-led invasion of 2003. The whole country was occupied, but the lethal mix of long-standing ethnic and religious hatreds, the fears of the Sunni Arab supporters of Saddam of losing their privileged position and involvement of international Islamist terror groups led to intense guerrilla counter-attacks. This hampered the formation of a people-friendly government and economic reconstruction. Power was transferred to a national government in June 2004, but intercommunal tensions could make the country ungovernable.

RELIGION

Pan-Arab socialism rather than Islam was the ideology of the Baathist regime. The Shi'a Muslims were persecuted under Saddam and Christians tolerated. Since the demise of the dictatorship, Islamist groups have stepped up persecution of Christians. The Transitional Government's draft constitution proposes freedom of religious practice for non-Muslims and equal rights to women.

Religions	Population %	Adherents	Ann.Gr.
Muslim	96.85	22,386,765	+2.9%
Christian	1.55	358,281	-0.9%
Other	1.10	254,264	+2.8%
non-Religious	0.50	115,574	+6.5%

Christians	Denom.	Affil.%	,000	Ann.Gr.
Protestant	5	0.03	6	+3.4%
Independent	6	0.01	2	+0.9%
Anglican	1	0.00	0	+0.0%
Catholic	4	1.04	240	-0.2%
Orthodox	6	0.47	108	-2.7%
Marginal	1	0.00	0	+5.0%

Churches	MegaBloc	Cong.	Members	Affiliates
Catholic	C	31	129,730	240,000
Assyrian Ch of the East	O	66	32,967	60,000
Syrian Orthodox	O	29	14,371	24,000
Armenian Apostolic	O	10	9,341	17,000
Arab Evang	P	35	2,400	5,328
Other denoms [15]		48	5,756	10,482
Total Christians [20]		219	194,565	356,810

Trans-bloc Groupings	pop.%	,000	Ann.Gr.
Evangelical	0.1	22	+0.0%
Charismatic	0.0	10	-0.9%
Pentecostal	0.0	0	-3.7%

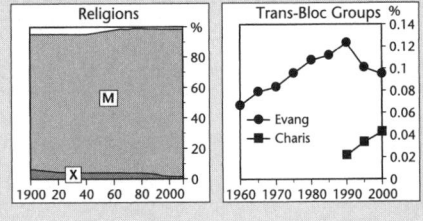

• Answers to Prayer

1 **The ending of one of the most brutal dictatorships of the latter part of the 20th Century** and the later capture of Saddam himself. Millions died in wars launched by Saddam and an estimated 200,000 Iraqis were 'eliminated' in acts of genocide, torture and mass murder. Hardly a family remains unscathed.

2 **The Christian community has suffered** more than the general population and in its pain nearly every denomination has experienced some renewal, revival and hunger for God's Word.

3 **A genuine Kurdish Church is now a reality.** There are more than five known congregations of Kurdish believers and a scattered sprinkling of Christians in the KAR.

4 **Inter-ethnic fellowship among Christians** has increased since 2003 despite the raised levels of persecution from some Muslims and deep mistrust between Christians in the past.

• Challenges for Prayer

1 **The future of Iraq is uncertain.** The war to rid the country and world of the dictatorship was won, but too little preparation was made to win the peace. Pray for:

a) *The establishment of a national government* that fairly balances the conflicting expectations of the various religious and ethnic communities, and provides an environment that promotes accountability to the people, economic growth and religious freedom. Without this the future is bleak. Anarchy, civil war, fragmentation of the country and further suffering for the people—especially Christians—could follow.

b) *Healing after decades of suffering.* Nearly every person bears scars of traumatic experiences. Only the gospel can provide a full solution; pray that this may be freely proclaimed.

c) *For true freedom of religion and from persecution.* Islamists vociferously demand exclusive rights for Muslims with full implementation of *shari'a* law. Many Christian families have been threatened, maltreated and even driven from their homes since the fall of Saddam. Many Christians fear for the future.

2 **The US-led invasion of 2003** was more directed to dealing with a post-9/11 threat from terrorism and alleged weapons of mass destruction and only secondarily to the betterment of the Iraqi people. Pray that:

a) *Western powers might be humbly repentant* for the decades of wrong political policies that created the problems of Iraq. The British carved out a politically unviable state in 1920 and failed to honour a pledge to the Kurds for an independent Kurdish state after World War I. Western countries protected and armed Saddam in the 1980s because he opposed unpopular revolutionary Iran.

b) *That US policy for and in Iraq* might be wise, sensitive and conducive to stability in Iraq and the Middle East, and, ultimately, not bring discredit to Christianity and the gospel. Pray also that this land may be opened up for Christian ministry to both body and soul.

3 **The Christian community is largely Assyrian** with some Armenians. The Assyrians are descendants of the Nestorian or Ancient Church of the East which now comprises two denominations. The Nestorian Church became one of the greatest missionary denominations of history, winning 6% of all of Asia's population 1,000 years ago. It is reduced to less than 2 million in the world today through persecution, compromise and harassment. About one third of all Christians left Iraq in the 1990s. This rate of emigration has continued since the country's liberation in 2003. Pray for a restoration of their biblical heritage, present revival beginnings to spread and a vision for outreach in the new Iraq.

4 **Most Assyrians are members of the Catholic-linked Chaldean Church** and some became Evangelicals through the activity of foreign missionaries over the past 150 years. Pray for revival and growth in this Church. Only recently has there been an openness to reach out to the Muslim majority. There are a growing number of Kurdish and Arab believers. Emigration is a major problem; pray for Christians willing to remain as lights in the darkness in spite of dire threats and persecution from Muslim extremists.

5 **The few Evangelicals mainly live in the cities.** They were persecuted in the 1960s and '70s and numbers declined. God gave revivals in the 1980s and house groups multiplied—from one in Baghdad to over 300 for a time. There are around 70 evangelical congregations in Iraq, but conversions are doing little more than replace those who are emigrating. Pray for these believers, their walk with the Lord and their witness to non-Christians. A small but growing number of Muslim-background Arabs and Kurds are seeking the Lord, both in Iraq and among Iraqi refugees in Jordan and elsewhere.

6 **Leadership for the churches is a desperate need.** Many good leaders have had to flee. Some Iraqis are in training in Jordan, Lebanon and elsewhere. Pray that many may return to Iraq and be used of God to build up the Body of Christ and inspire believers for effective witness.

7 **All peoples are unreached** apart from Assyrian and Armenian groups. Pray for:

a) *The Shi'a Arabs of Basra and the south.* The exceptional brutality of the government suppression of the Shi'ite revolt in 1991 brought death to many of their leaders, mass murders, imprisonment to many and devastation to their land and communities. As the majority population, various Shi'a Muslim clerics have considerable followings and are using all means to capture the reins of power and some to also impose *shari'a* law and eliminate all Christians. There is no known direct witness to them.

b) **The Sunni Arabs gained most from the former dictatorship,** but as they see their influence eclipsed, they are the source of a high proportion of the violent incidents against the occupying US, British and international forces in the country. Few have heard the gospel.

c) **The Madan or Marsh Arabs** are probably descended from the ancient Sumerians. The Iraq-Iran War and 1991 Shi'ite revolt reduced their population from 200,000 to 50,000. Their home habitat was largely destroyed by Saddam and many have been displaced to Basra and other parts of Iraq. There is no known outreach to them.

d) **The Bedouin, Persians and Gypsies** are all totally unreached.

8 **The Kurdish Autonomous Region** emerged after the Gulf War with UN protection. It provided a homeland for many Kurds and Turkoman. The plight of the Kurds (see Turkey, Syria and Iran for more information) has caught the attention of the world. They have fought for survival and a national identity for 70 years. The period 1985-91 was particularly bloody and cruel. Iraqi atrocities included the razing of 3,800 villages and towns (including 61 Christian Assyrian villages), destruction of the local economy, mining of fields, deportation of 500,000 to distant camps, and killing of up to 250,000. In the aftermath of the Gulf War in 1991 almost the entire Kurdish population became refugees. The KAR has its own democratic government administration, but was crippled by disunity and occasional fighting between the two main parties. The future status of the KAR in the new Iraq has yet to be decided. Pray for:

a) **A just settlement of Kurdish desires for freedom and security,** and of the national sensitivities of Turkey, Syria and Iran, as well as the Arab populations of Iraq. The Kurdish military contribution to the defeat of Saddam extended their area of influence to the oil city of Kirkuk and beyond. The whole Kurdish question remains a major hot-spot in world politics.

b) **Economic betterment.** Through NGOs much has been achieved - at a cost. Insecurity, death threats, difficulty in entering and leaving and the political divisions have all made ministry perilous and hard to maintain. Pray for safety and fruitfulness for all those involved in these NGOs and that the love and witness of Christians might touch the hearts of many.

c) **The Church.** Assyrian Christians have suffered much persecution, destruction of villages and intimidation first by Saddam and then by the Kurds. Assyrian Christians in the KAR have been reduced by emigration to 45,000.

d) **The growing number of Kurdish believers** has also suffered intimidation and several have been martyred, but the small fellowships are growing with new converts being added. Pray that a vibrant, united Kurdish Church might impact every part of Northern Iraq.

e) **The unevangelized in the KAR:**
   i   *The Yezidi* are a syncretistic offshoot of both Zoroastrianism and Islam. They speak Kurdish and are known as 'devil worshippers'. There are very few believers.
   ii *The Turkoman* are a distinct Turkic people numbering between 1 and 2.5 million, but 'claimed' by the Kurds as Kurds. There are no known believers.

9 **Christian support ministries:**

a) **The Bible Society** has been actively involved in Iraq since 1985 and has coordinated massive imports of Scriptures from Lebanon and Jordan and overseen the printing of hundreds of thousands of NTs. Pray that this ministry may be established in Iraq again. Pray also for the distribution of the recently completed Sorani NT. A Kurmanji version suitable for the KAR is needed.

b) **Christian literature is in great demand.** Much is imported. There is a need for commentaries, study books and Bibles and for means of literature distribution in Iraq.

c) **The JESUS film** is available in 10 languages and has been shown on national TV several times.

d) **Christian radio and satellite TV** broadcasts are an important means available for evangelism. Pray for the Arabic broadcasts of TWR (Monaco and Cyprus) and FEBA (Seychelles) as part of the 'World By 2000' programme. Many Iraqis have enrolled in Bible correspondence courses as a result. TWR daily airs 15-minute programmes in Sorani and less often in Kurmanji Kurdish; there is also a local radio station in the KAR run by Christians broadcasting 8 hours/day.

Ireland
Eire

JULY 2
EUROPE

Updated January 2004

GEOGRAPHY
Area 70,285 sq.km. Comprises 80% of the island of Ireland. Northern Ireland is a constituent part of the United Kingdom.

Population		Ann.Gr.	Density
2000	3,730,239	+0.66%	53 per sq.km.
2010	4,016,447	+0.76%	57 per sq.km.
2025	4,403,843	+0.48%	63 per sq.km.

Millions of Irish have emigrated all over the English-speaking world — especially to the USA and the UK. **Capital** Dublin 1,000,000. **Urbanites** 58%.

PEOPLES
Irish 94.2%. Predominantly of Celtic origin. **Other** 5.8%. UK citizens 140,000; Itinerants 24,000; increasing numbers of EU, Central European and non-Western workers.

Literacy 99%. **Official languages** Irish, English. Irish spoken as first language by 5%, used by 13% and spoken by 43% of the population.

ECONOMY
High-tech industries have replaced dairy farming and tourism as most important. EU membership in 1973 has transformed the economy, now with one of Europe's most successful growth rates. **HDI** 0.900; 20th/174. **Public debt** 73% of GNP. **Income/person** $17,110 (56.7% of USA).

POLITICS
Ireland was under British rule for over 700 years. In 1921 Ireland was partitioned between the 26 counties that were Catholic and Celtic, and the 6 counties in Northern Ireland that were predominantly Protestant Scots Anglo-Saxon. The south became independent in 1922 and then a parliamentary republic in 1949. Partition affected the political life of both parts. Of Northern Ireland's 1.6 million population, approximately 41% are Catholic and look to having closer links with the south, while 54% are mainly Protestant and determined to maintain their links with the UK. Thirty years of violence in Northern Ireland now appear to be nearing an end thanks to a peace agreement between the Irish and British governments and the political parties of Northern Ireland.

RELIGION
There is freedom of religion. The Catholic Church has no official link with the state, though it has a strong, but waning, influence on all aspects of national life.

Religions	Population %	Adherents	Ann.Gr.
Christian	95.35	3,556,783	+0.5%
non-Religious/other	4.00	149,209	+3.5%
Muslim	0.50	18,651	+39.4%
Hindu	0.08	2,984	+22.5%
Jewish	0.05	1,865	+1.3%

Christians	Denom.	Affil.%	,000	Ann.Gr.
Protestant	35	0.69	26	+0.1%
Independent	7	0.25	9	+2.4%
Anglican	1	2.43	91	-0.3%
Catholic	1	87.26	3,255	-0.2%
Orthodox	3	0.01	1	+0.0%
Marginal	5	0.29	11	+0.1%
Unaffiliated		4.42	164	n.a.

Churches	MegaBloc	Cong.	Members	Affiliates
Catholic	C	2,198	2,656,000	3,254,900
Ch of Ireland	A	487	55,000	90,600
Presbyterian Ch in I	P	107	7,105	12,290
Jehovah's Witnesses	M	113	4,582	8,000
Methodist	P	62	1,568	4,360
New Churches	I	110	1,600	3,400
Latter-day Saints (Morm)	M	10	1,631	2,300
Christian Brethren	P	28	1,250	1,800
Assemblies of God	P	12	700	1,325
Other Pentecostal [8]	P	13	530	1,200
Baptist Union	P	16	470	1,034
Other denoms [34]		173	7,000	10,500
Total Christians [52]		3,329	2,737,000	3,392,000

Trans-bloc Groupings	pop.%	,000	Ann.Gr.
Evangelical	0.9	35	+n.a.
Charismatic	6.6	246	-0.1%
Pentecostal	0.2	9	+4.4%

Claims of 90,000 or so Evangelical Catholics need confirmation, and so these are omitted from the figures here. Some believe that the evangelical population is nearer 14,000. Many also claim the charismatic figure is too high—most being Catholic charismatics; active charismatics have declined in number.

Missionaries from Ireland
P,I,A 99 in 17 agencies to 27 countries. C 3,884.

Missionaries to Ireland
P,I,A 304 in 45 agencies from 12 countries: USA 200, UK 58, Canada 25.

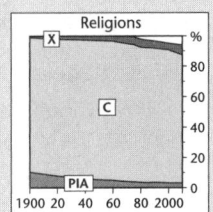

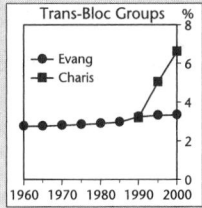

• Answers to Prayer

1 **A significant work of the Holy Spirit has gained momentum over the past 30 years.** There are hundreds of evangelical fellowships multiplying and growing across the Republic. Most are Pentecostal or charismatic in orientation. There are few towns without such groups today.

2 **Effective inter-governmental cooperation** began in the late 1990s bringing cautious hope for a lasting peace and democratic solutions to the problems of Northern Ireland.

• Challenges for Prayer

1 **Ireland's ancient Celtic Church and its missionaries** took the gospel to many nations in Europe one and a half millennia ago. Then followed centuries of suffering, oppression, violence and bloodshed at the hands of the Vikings and the British. Sadly the long conflict has, in the eyes of the world, been portrayed as religious in origin. Pray that:
a) The wounds and divisions in Irish society might be healed and the whole of Ireland be at peace.
b) All Christians might work toward communal reconciliation.
c) Ireland's ancient spiritual heritage might be restored for the blessing of the world.

2 **The Catholic Church** was for centuries the preserver and defender of the Irish. Active involvement in the Church has always been high though now declining quite fast. The Church has been blighted by high-profile scandals in the priesthood in the 1990s. The number of priests has halved since 1970, vocations have dropped dramatically and young people generally are turning away from the Church. Charismatic renewal and revival movements have in the past helped many to come into a personal experience of salvation and to a love of the Scriptures. Pray that increasing numbers of Catholics may turn from the dead works of religion to a living faith in Christ.

3 **Church attendances in non-Catholic denominations** have declined from 10% in 1900 to 3.4% of the population in 2000 through emigration, nominalism and the Catholic Church's policy on mixed marriages. Even the term 'Protestant' has a political connotation. Yet the Church of Ireland (Anglican), the Presbyterian Church, the Methodists and the Baptists have seen growth where there has been good evangelical leadership, and some new churches are being planted. Pray that these Christians may be led by the Holy Spirit for effectiveness and relevance in an increasingly secular and affluent society.

4 **Evangelicals have grown most** in both Pentecostal denominations and in more informal networks of fellowships across the country. These together with Evangelicals among Anglicans and Protestants are about 0.9% of the population — the lowest percentage of any country in the English-speaking world. Pray that these groups may be Bible-centred, preserved from division and promote unity with the wider body of Christ. Pray also for good Bible-trained leadership to be raised up. There are two Bible training centres — the Irish Bible Institute launched in 2000 as a merger of two Bible colleges and the ICI-based ministry of the **AoG**.

5 **Young people.** Ireland is a young country, with half its population under 28 years old. Their spiritual need is underlined by the dramatic rise in suicides, unwed mothers and marriage breakdowns. They are responsive to the gospel. Christian camps are run by **Scripture Union** (with some 2-3,000 children per year), **CEF**, BCM International, the Faith Mission and others. **IFES**-Ireland has an island-wide ministry in 25 colleges and universities. There is an increasing openness in Dublin to presenting the gospel by street drama and sketchboard. As this new spiritual openness is also being tapped by many cults, pray that more of Ireland's young people may come to know Jesus, who is the Truth.

6 Significant ministry challenges:
a) The Irish-speaking minority, who live mainly in the rural West, are more traditional, and born-again Christians are few.

b) **Muslims are mostly of Arabic origin.** The Islamic movement has published a major part of the Qur'an in Irish and there are now seven mosques in the Republic. Pray that God would bring Muslims to know Jesus.

c) **The 'Itinerants'** (Gypsies or Irish 'Traveller') are growing in number and little has been done to specifically reach them. They are of Rom and Celtic origin.

d) **Migrant workers** from Europe, the Middle East and Africa need specific ministry. There are African and Albanian congregations of Evangelicals in Dublin.

7 **Foreign missionaries** are working in nearly all of the 26 counties. **GEM**, with 33 workers, has been instrumental in establishing Bible churches in the greater Dublin area with a strong indigenous membership. Other significant missions include **YWAM** (37), **Brethren** (34), Global Outreach (24), **UFM** (17), **AoG** (10) and **ECM** (10). Pray for their harmonious integration into the unique Irish scene, and for fruitfulness in ministry.

8 **Ireland has long been one of the great missionary-sending countries of the world** — from the early Celtic Church onwards. Many Catholic and Protestant missionaries have gone to the ends of the earth. Catholic numbers are falling from the high of 7,085 foreign missionaries in 1965 to 3,884 in 1994. Pray for the release, training and funding of more Irish missionaries and leaders by evangelical churches and fellowships.

Israel
State of Israel

JULY 3-4
ASIA

GEOGRAPHY
Area 20,700 sq.km. A further 7,540 sq.km. of the West Bank, Gaza and the Golan Heights have been controlled by Israel since 1967.

Population	Ann.Gr.	Density
2000	5,121,683	+2.55%	247 per sq. km.
2010	6,017,886	+1.40%	291 per sq. km.
2025	6,926,755	+0.80%	335 per sq. km.

This includes Israelis in East Jerusalem and the Golan Heights. By including Israelis living in West Bank settlements in the section on the Palestine Authority (p. 504), no political statement is intended — it is simply to indicate the geo-political realities of 2001 for readers to better understand.

Capital Jerusalem 670,000; but not recognized internationally. Other major city: Tel Aviv conurbation 2.7 mill. **Urbanites** 91%.

PEOPLES
Jews 80.7%. *'Aliyah'* are immigrants from 102 countries numbering 2.8m since 1947. The largest component now Russian-Ukrainian (1m.), other compo-

nents being: Askenazim (European), Sephardim (Middle Eastern), Ethiopian (Falasha), Kochin (South Asian).
Arabs 15.6%. Israeli Arab 800,000 (including 60-150,000 Bedouin).
Other 3.7%. Druze 99,000; Adygey (Circassian) 3,500; Greek 3,000; Samaritan 600.
Migrant Labour may be 300,000 mainly Romanian, Chinese, Filipino, African. About half are in the country illegally.

Literacy 98%. **Official languages** Hebrew, Arabic. Numerous immigrant languages from all over the world are spoken. **Languages with Scriptures** 7Bi 2por 1w.i.p.

ECONOMY
Modern, sophisticated industrial state. Heavy defence expenditure, cost of absorbing new immigrants and the growing crisis of lack of water are all brakes on further growth. **Unemployment** 8.6%. **HDI** 0.883, 23rd/174. **Public debt** 27% of GNP. **Income/person** $16,180 (51% of USA).

POLITICS
The founding of Israel in 1948 ended 1,900 years of exile for the Jews. Five wars, in 1948, 1956, 1967, 1973 and 1982-85 with surrounding states have kept the country on a war footing. Military setbacks in Lebanon then withdrawal in 2000, and the rising pressure of Palestinians in civil unrest, the intifada and acts of terrorism by Islamist groups (Hamas and Hizbollah) have sapped Israeli stamina. Israeli society is deeply divided on the peace process, the future of Jewish settlements in Arab lands, the future of Jerusalem and of the Golan Heights. Holding the balance of power in successive coalition governments, the ultra-orthodox Jewish Haredi minority further polarizes society. Strenuous efforts by the USA, UN and others to engineer a peace deal have met with only limited success in a few areas of contention but all had collapsed in early 2001 in the violence of renewed *intifada*. Many fear another

Arab-Israeli war is likely.

RELIGION

All religions are free to minister within their own communities. Jews who believe in Messiah Jesus are denied legal standing as a religious body. The Haredi (extreme Orthodox Jews) hold the nation to ransom by push their agenda through their small parties thus holding the balance of power in coalition governments. This results in marginalizing Reformed and Conservative Jews, applying constant pressure to limit freedom of religion with anti-conversion laws and persecuting Messianic Jews. Many of them refuse to participate in the military but expect large grants of government money to finance their institutions. **Persecution Index** 65th in the world.

Religions	Population %	Adherents	Ann.Gr.
Jewish	80.65	4,130,637	+2.4%
Muslim	14.60	747,766	+2.7%
Other	2.50	128,042	+5.2%
Christian	2.25	115,238	+2.8%

The Jewish population is approximately 25% religious and 75% secular/humanistic.

Christians	Denom.	Affil. %	,000	Ann.Gr.
Protestant	58	0.09	5	+4.3%
Independent	2	0.12	6	+2.8%
Anglican	1	0.01	0	-2.0%
Catholic	3	1.56	80	-0.9%
Orthodox	5	0.45	23	-0.5%
Marginal	2	0.02	1	+9.0%

Churches	MegaBloc	Cong.	Members	Affiliates
Catholic (5 rites) [3]	C	56	47,337	80,000
Greek Orthodox	O	11	12,500	22,000
Messianic Assemblies	I	60	3,300	5,800
Assoc of Baptist Chs	P	13	1,000	1,800
Jehovah's Witnesses	M	5	240	800
Seventh-day Adventist	P	9	420	650
Episcopal	A	2	300	450
Coptic Orthodox	O	2	220	300
Assemblies of God	P	5	80	200
Christian Brethren [3]	P	3	125	200
Other denoms [58]		29	1,685	3,208
Total Christians [72]		**197**	**67,227**	**115,000**

Trans-bloc Groupings	pop.%	,000	Ann.Gr.
Evangelical	0.2	11	+2.5%
Pentecostal & Charismatic	0.2	9	+1.1%

Missionaries from Israel
P,I,A 30 in 7 agencies to 5 countries: Israel 24.

Missionaries to Israel
P,I,A 338 in 64 agencies from 23 countries: USA 135, UK 67, Germany 30, Finland 28.

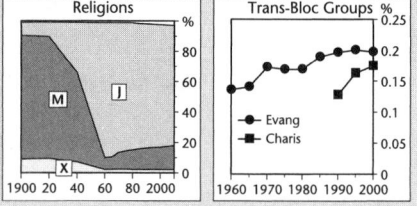

• Answers to Prayer

1 **The increase in the number of born-again believers** among Jews. Messianic Jews have increased from 250 in 1967 to possibly 7,000 in 2000, and are beginning to be recognized by many as an acceptable part of Israeli society. There has also been a steady increase in the number of Arab believers and new churches in the last 20 years.

2 **Globally there has been a significant response among the 15 million Jews**; around 132,000 are linked with Messianic congregations and a further 200,000 with Gentile churches. Most of these believers are in North America, and also in Russia-Ukraine and the UK.

• Challenges for Prayer

1 **The return of Jews to Israel** accelerated after the collapse of Communism in East Europe and Ethiopia. Although many see this as a fulfilment of prophecy (Ezekiel 20:32-34; 36:16-24), most have returned to their ancient land in unbelief. Pray for the nation's spiritual restoration through Messiah Jesus (Romans 11:25-31).

2 **The intense half-century of conflict between Arabs and Israelis** urgently needs resolution. Both sides lay claim to the land. Pray for a just, lasting and adequately guaranteed settlement.

3 **Animosity against Christianity is a barrier to be overcome in Jewish minds.** 'Christian' nations are seen to be destroyers of the Jewish nation whether by persecution (as in the Holocaust) or by proselytization. Pray that the gospel may be understood as a fulfilment of their Jewish heritage and that a widespread turning to their Messiah might come. Pray also that all attempts to limit freedom of religion and to deny the Jewish identity of Messianic believers may fail.

4 **The Christian Church in Israel is fragmented** and declining in numbers through emigration. It comprises about 80% Arab, 15% expatriate (Egyptian, Ethiopian Greek, Russian, Armenian, Italian, etc.) and 5% Jewish background. There are Catholics (five rites), Orthodox (nine traditions), and Protestants (17 denominations and over 100 mission agencies). Pray for spiritual unity that transcends history, ethnic conflict, national origins, eschatology and secondary areas of theology. Pray that many more Jews and Muslims might meet with the Risen Lord Jesus as true Messiah and Prophet.

5 **Israeli Evangelicals** are largely Messianic Jews, and Arabs who are Israeli citizens. There are about 11,000 evangelical believers in Israel of which 3,000 are Russian-origin and 500 Amharic-speaking. There are over 70 Hebrew-speaking congregations and 53 house churches. In addition to this are another 30 Russian-speaking groups and 6 Amharic-speaking (Ethiopian) congregations. Israeli-born Messianic Jews are nearly 1,000. There are about 3,500 Arab believers in 50 churches. Pray for:

a) ***Boldness in witness*** despite difficulties. The *Haredi* regard them as subversive and a threat to Judaism so malign and occasionally harass them.

b) ***Full legal rights of immigration*** and social acceptance in the face of national, social and family pressures. Atheist Jews are welcomed, but not Jewish Christians since a ruling in 1989 denied them entry under the Law of Return.

c) ***Clarity of teaching and understanding about their Jewishness***. There needs to be a cultural identity without compromise of New Testament truth.

d) ***Effective leadership*** — There is a need for growth in maturity of pastoral leadership, depth and anointing in the preaching of the Word and a rising above feelings of jealousy, pride and inferiority. The latter are fuelled by the pressures of pioneering in a hostile spiritual environment. Pray for breakthroughs in these areas.

e) ***Unity***. There have been the beginnings of meaningful fellowship between the various groups and between Hebrew- and Arabic-speaking believers in recent years. The inter-congregational Fellowship of Hebrew-speaking Congregations is becoming a point of fellowship, and the **National Evangelism Committee** for outreach, but meaningful working together is limited.

f) ***Arab Evangelicals*** are more numerous in Baptist, Assemblies of God, Brethren and Anglican congregations. There are only a few dozen Muslim-background believers known. Fellowship with Hebrew-speaking Evangelicals is limited and needs to be greatly increased.

6 Major outreach challenges:

a) ***The ultra-Orthodox Haredi*** are only 10% of the population, yet have more political leverage than the 83% who are secular Jews. They are culturally isolated, pursuing their own agenda, and also very legalistic. Pray that many of these modern Pharisees may become like Nicodemus.

b) ***The Russian and Ukrainian Jews*** are now the largest component of the population and are half of the former Jewish population of the USSR. They have changed Israel and are more receptive to the gospel.

c) ***The Ethiopian Jews*** (Falasha) have become a disillusioned, largely impoverished underclass since their immigration to Israel a decade ago. There are about 500 Christians among them, but they are enduring considerable persecution.

d) ***The Arabs*** — 97% are Muslim. Few are actively seeking to reach them. There is an urgent need for a new initiative in evangelism and house church planting in the Muslim community.

e) ***The Druze community*** (99,000) in Israel as well as the West Bank and the Golan Heights.

f) ***Guest workers***. There are a total of about 1,500 evangelical Christians among them. There is outreach to Mainland Chinese with hundreds of baptisms, and several evangelical churches among Romanians.

7 **The Protestant missionary force** is estimated at around 1,000, but many Christians have entered as individuals to serve the Lord. Some of the larger agencies are **IMB-SBC** (50), CMJ (34), Finnish Lutherans (24), Church of Scotland (12), **CWI** (10) and AoG (6). Years of seed-sowing and breaking down of long-held prejudices against Christianity are now bearing fruit, but missionary work can be frustrating and discouraging. Many come with exotic ideas about Israel and unrealistic visions, and find little fulfilment or identification with local believers. Pray that all called of God may find viable ministries, effective means of contact with non-Christians and sweet fellowship with local believers. Friendship evangelism, literature distribution and encouragement of believers are the major means of service.

8 **The Jews of the dispersion** (those outside Israel) are declining in numbers through a lower birth rate, mixed marriages, secularism, emigration to Israel and conversions to other religions. There are now an estimated 9 million outside Israel. The largest concentrations are in the USA (5.6m), former USSR (1m), France (600,000); Canada (360,000); Britain (300,000); and Argentina (230,000). There are 2 million Jews in New York. In the USA there is much openness, elsewhere less so. Pray for the ministry of **JFJ**, **MT**, **CWI**, **CMJ**, etc. The work involves long hours of loving, patient ministry to individuals and families. Pray for a greater sensitivity on the part of Gentile churches towards problems of Jewish survival and for the Jewish remnant within the Church. Little is being done for Jews in France and Argentina.

9 Supportive ministries:

a) *Literature* is of great importance for the spread of the gospel due to the multiplicity of languages and paucity of Christians who witness. Pray for **The Bible Society**, the two Christian publishing houses, the production of an increasing selection of Hebrew and Arabic Christian literature, and the nine Christian bookshops. There are 3 Messianic Jewish periodicals, some having a readership beyond the Messianic Jewish community. Too few believers are engaged in distribution. Pray that Jews may read the NT and find the Living Word. Many homes have a NT.

b) *Student work* is in its infancy. There are five groups with about 200 believers of Arab and Jewish background linked with **IFES**. Leadership is the key prayer target.

c) *The JESUS film* has been shown on prime-time TV in both Israel and the Palestine Authority in Arabic or Hebrew, and video tapes have been distributed to over 100,000 homes.

d) *Radio*. **TWR** broadcasts 5 hrs/week in Hebrew.

Italy
Italian Republic

JULY 5-7
EUROPE
Updated January 2004

GEOGRAPHY
Area 301,000 sq.km. A long, mountainous peninsula that dominates the central Mediterranean Sea. Also two large islands, Sardinia and Sicily.

Population	Ann.Gr.	Density
2000	57,297,886	-0.01%	190 per sq. km.
2010	55,781,181	-0.35%	185 per sq. km.
2025	51,269,528	-0.63%	170 per sq. km.

Over 4 million expatriate Italians. Also up to fi million illegal immigrants.

Capital Rome 3.8mill. Other major cities: Milan 3.8m; Naples 3.1m; Turin 2.2m; Palermo 1.2m;

Genoa 900,000. **Urbanites** 67%.

PEOPLES

Indigenous 94.7%
Italian 93.5%. Deep cultural differences between the north and south and with a wide variety of regional cultures, dialects and languages. Main regional groups: Lombard 9m; Neapolitan/Calabrian 7.7m; Sicilian 5.1m; Piedmontese 4.3m; Venetian 4.5m; Ligurian 1.6m; Sardinian(4) 1.7m; Friulian/Ladin 1.2m. **Other** 1.2%. Albanian 350,000; Tyrolese (German) 280,000; Romani(3) 35,000; Greek 20,000. (These are minority communities which have been in Italy for centuries.)
Non-indigenous peoples 5.3%
European 1.2%. Albanian 130,000; French 120,000; Greek 120,000; Slovenian 100,000; Romanian 60,000; etc. (Immigrants since WWII.)
Other 4.1%. Moroccan 150,000; Filipino 62,000; Ecuadorian 62,000; Chinese 50,000.

Literacy 98%. **Official language** Italian, but vigorous use of nine regional languages akin to Italian. **All languages** 33. **Languages with Scriptures** 7Bi 3NT 14por.

ECONOMY
Highly industrialized, Italy is the world's 7th largest economy. Very affluent in the north, but much poorer in the south. The private sector has resisted the controls of the highly centralized and cumbersome economic structures, but these are being changed through privatization. The black

(illegal) economy and the inherited inefficiency of public administration reduce the country's competitiveness in world markets. **HDI** 0.900; 19th/174. **Public debt** 125% of GNP. **Income/person** $20,170 (64% of USA).

POLITICS

United as a single state in 1870. Republican democracy since 1946. Weak and unstable succession of 60 governments since World War II, but with an underlying social stability. A member of the EU. The political paralysis, widespread corruption, economic differences between north and south, unchecked crimes of the Mafia and its control of much economic activity, and the total discrediting of Italy's politicians and political parties came to a head in 1992. Some improvements enabled Italy to join the Euro-currency in 1998. The election of Berlusconi as Prime Minister and massive political and business scandals since then have further damaged Italy's credibility in handling its endemic corruption.

RELIGION

Roman Catholicism ceased to be the state religion in 1984. All religions have equal freedom before the law but not in practice.

Religions	Population %	Adherents	Ann.Gr.
Christian	77.35	44,319,915	-0.4%
non-Religious/other	20.04	11,482,496	+1.1%
Muslim	2.40	1,375,149	+2.7%
Buddhist	0.09	51,568	+8.4%
Jewish	0.06	34,379	+3.7%
Baha'i	0.03	17,189	+8.4%
Hindu	0.03	15,000	n.a.

Christians	Denom.	Affil.%	,000	Ann.Gr.
Protestant	111	0.60	343	+2.7%
Independent	50	0.28	159	+5.6%
Anglican	1	0.02	12	+0.9%
Catholic	1	80.28	46,000	-0.4%
Orthodox	7	0.11	63	-1.2%

Marginal	4	0.74	424	+1.2%
Doubly affiliated		-4.68	-2,682	n.a.

Churches	MegaBloc	Cong.	Members	Affiliates
Catholic	C	25,900	34.586m	46.00m
Jehovah's Witnesses	M	3,031	228,566	400,000
Assemblies of God	P	1,090	70,000	160,000
Pentecostal Chs Fed.	I	300	35,000	47,000
Waldensian & Methodist	P	172	17,000	27,846
Evang Chr Brethren	P	255	13,000	24,000
Latter-day Saints (Morm)	M	121	11,377	19,000
Evangelical Baptist Union	P	113	5,000	15,000
Christian Adventist	P	95	5,577	14,000
Apostolic	P	90	3,800	10,000
Pente Christian Congs	I	60	5,400	10,000
Comm of Free Evang	P	24	2,200	3,000
Church of the Nazarene	P	10	600	1,100
Other denoms [162]		1,105	117,000	270,000
Doubly affiliated			-2,000,000	-2,682,000
Total Christians [175]		32,366	33.898m	45.401m

Trans-bloc Groupings	pop.%	,000	Ann.Gr.
Evangelical	0.9	512	+3.4%
Charismatic	3.8	2,181	+0.4%
Pentecostal	0.5	313	+4.7%

Missionaries from Italy
P,I,A 217 in 19 agencies to 18 countries: Italy 165, Albania 12.

Missionaries to Italy
P,I,A 549 in 94 agencies from 29 countries: USA 286, UK 56, Germany 36, Switzerland 31, Korea 23.

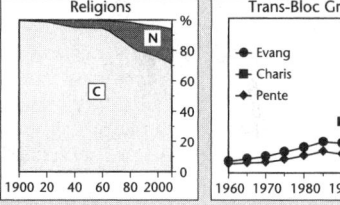

• Answers to Prayer

1 **After years of little growth in evangelical churches**, there is an increase in the number of believers in Calabria, Sicily and Campania/Naples.

2 **Emerging cooperation between churches** to reach Italy and beyond.

• Challenges for Prayer

1 **This great and gifted nation has decisively affected Western and world culture** in legal systems (Roman law), language (Latin), culture (Renaissance art, music), and innovation (clothes, cars), yet is in deep spiritual need. After the fourth century collapse of the Western Roman Empire, the Roman Catholic Church became a political as well as a spiritual power, deeply impacting the politics of Europe, the Muslim World (the Crusades) and Italy itself. The Church's temporal power, though reduced since 1870, was in conflict with its spiritual responsibilities — destabilizing, dividing and impoverishing Italy in the process. Most Italians are Catholic in culture, but deeply cynical about the Church. Pray for the removal of the multiple barriers that conceal a true understanding of the gospel.

2 **The Roman Catholic Church shows ambivalent signs of persistent crisis and renewed power**. On the one hand, it has lost over 10 million to New Age thinking, cults, the occult and materialistic secularism. Church attendance is decreasing, as are the number of priests. Yet Catholic traditions and mindset continue to permeate every aspect of national and personal life. The Catholic charismatic movement is growing, though its allegiance to the Church weakens its potential for inner renewal. Pray for millions of Italians to turn from dead tradition to the living Lord Jesus.

3 **The unresponsiveness of Italians.** Four decades of religious freedom have been met with indifference. Occultism is widespread, and there are reckoned to be 100,000 full-time consulting magicians — nearly three times the number of Catholic priests. Satanism is strong in the north, Turin being one of the global centres of its activities, which include praying for the removal of all evangelical missionaries from the country. The strong pre-Christian pagan powers have never been fully routed in 2,000 years.

4 **Protestantism** has had an 800-year history in Italy. The world's oldest Protestant denomination, the Waldensian Church, began in north Italy, but was subjected to terrible persecution for centuries. Italian Catholic bishops officially apologized for this in 1997. The Waldensian Church is now in federal union with the Methodists and some Baptists but is influenced by deadening liberal theology. The Protestant witness is weak and divided, especially between the growing Pentecostal majority and non-Pentecostal minority. New churches are often begun through bitter splits rather than strategic church planting. Most congregations are small, introspective and largely ignorant of the biblical challenge to missions and the few large congregations in the south are committed to 'prosperity' teaching. Pray for revival that breaks down barriers of individualism, mistrust and doctrinal extremes and leads to cooperative outreach.

5 **Signs of hope for the Church.** Despite the limited response and discouraging spiritual climate, water these in prayer:

a) *Increased, but limited, cooperation* — with the formation of the Evangelical Alliance, and many small independent churches combining in several federations for closer working together.

b) *A Christian magazine, Comunicazioni Cristiane,* has done much to bridge the divisions within Italian Evangelicalism by giving a common platform for sharing news and vision for missions and for Italy.

c) *The evangelistic efforts of the 1990s* — the multiplication of Pentecostal churches, the AoG Decade of Harvest, *Italia per Cristo,* tent evangelism by **Christ is the Answer** and the **Brethren**, and **YWAM**'s two outreach bases.

d) *The birth in 1998 of Italy's first interdenominational evangelical missionary movement* AMEN (Agenzia Missionaria Evangelo per le Nazioni). The challenge of Albania after 1990 has become a major focus for Italian churches.

e) *Vision for the future*. A saturation church-planting strategy was launched in the 1997 DAWN Conference — the aim: one church for every 5,000 people by 2010. This means increasing churches from 2,100 in 1997 to 11,860 by 2010.

6 **The infamous Sicilian Mafia and Neapolitan Camorra** have infiltrated every level of society. Legal and judicial attempts to destroy the power of these criminal organizations are fraught with difficulty. Government leaders and Church authorities, even in the Vatican itself, have been subverted, and the attitudes of the general population poisoned by this evil system. Murder and extortion are commonplace — the latter netting an estimated US$23 billion annually. This money, and that gained from the lucrative global trade in drugs, is used to buy politicians, influence and even industries. Pray for those courageous few who risk their lives to fight the corruption and usher in a new and more effective government system. Pray for Italian society to be freed from this bondage and to be transformed by the power of the gospel.

7 **The dearth of mature Italian Christian leaders** in Protestant churches at both the national and pastoral level is crippling the advance of the gospel. Internal conflicts and scandals due to pride, money and power-seeking have harmed the witness. Pastors speak against papal domination in the Catholic Church, but often are papal in authority too! Pray for humility, brokenness and unity among the Lord's servants. Pray that the increasing emphasis on preaching inner holiness, family unity and the life of the local congregation may bear fruit in lives. Pray also for the five denominational and two interdenominational Bible schools and seminaries and for an increase in student numbers. The **AoG** Bible schools have 45 students, and the IBE (**GEM**) in Rome a smaller number. **YWAM** runs a six-month Discipleship Training School. **IFED** runs courses at seminary level for training mature leadership and attracts some of Italy's brightest servants of God with 60 students in 2001.

8 **The most unreached sectors of the population:**

a) *Only 1,500 of Italy's 33,500 communities* have an established evangelical witness.

b) *The northeastern Veneto Region* with the cities of Venice, Padova and Vicenza has 4,437,000 people, but maybe no more than 38 churches and 2,000 evangelical Christians — mainly **AoG**, **Brethren** and three congregations related to **ECM**.

c) *Sardinia*, a Mediterranean island with a limited autonomy, has 1,660,000 people with their own language and culture. There are only about 14-15 evangelical churches, and a few Christian workers. Suspicion of outsiders, fear, vendettas, the occult and the activities of JWs all make any evangelistic outreach difficult.

d) *The wealthy, materialistic northern cities* of Milan, Turin, Bologna and Venice have few churches. Many cities and towns have no evangelical witness at all. The northern provinces of Umbria, Trentino, Lombardy, Emilia-Romagna have less than 0.1% Evangelicals.

e) *The 1,600,000 students in 48 universities* are a needy mission field. There are only around 100 students linked to the GBU(**IFES**) in eight cities, and a few others with **CCC**. Occasional outreaches by **OM** and **YWAM** teams reach others. The second largest student body (117,000 in Milan) has no evangelical campus group.

f) *An estimated 400,000 heroin addicts*, with a high incidence of HIV+ infection, pose a demanding challenge only beginning to be met by Evangelicals (Betel, in 5 centres; Teen Challenge 2; **AoG** 1).

9 Unreached minorities:

a) *The minorities in the northeast.* The **Friulians**, **Ladins**, **Slovenes** and **South Tyrolean Germans** all have their own distinctive cultures and languages, but little direct effort is being made to reach these staunchly traditional Catholics with the message of new life in Jesus.

b) *The Greek and Croatian minorities* in the south.

c) *Albanians.* The long-established Calabrian and Sicilian Albanians speak their own archaic dialects — but little specific long-term outreach has been made. Most are Orthodox or Catholic.

d) *Muslims.* They have grown rapidly through legal and illegal immigration to possibly over one million, 70% of whom are North African. The Muslim mosque in Rome is Europe's largest. There is little specific outreach to them. There is an Arabic Christian radio broadcast on 9 stations in Italy.

e) *Africans* from all over Africa, especially Eritrea, who have immigrated seeking work or fleeing war and famine. **SIM** has a small ministry to them and there is a lively group of five Eritrean churches. There are growing African-led churches among them.

f) *Italy's long coastline has become a funnel for millions of illegal immigrants* into the EU — many crossing the Adriatic Sea from Albania — a major source of criminal revenue. Pray for all seeking to alleviate the stress of people entangled in this web of crime and minister to their spiritual needs.

10 **The need for expatriate missionaries is great** but the casualty rate has been unacceptably high in the past, with only 10% on average returning for a second term. Pressures from spiritual forces and entrenched opposition to the gospel expose any personal inadequacies in a missionary. Pray out to the harvest field those with spiritual stamina, emotional maturity, cultural adaptability and God-given faith. Some significant groups (and number of expatriates) in the country are **Brethren** (59), **TEAM** (34), CBIM (25), **YWAM** (25), **ECM** (24), **CLC** (22), **UFM** (19), **AoG** (18), **SBC** (18), **CCCI** (14), **GMU** (13), **WEC** (9) and **GEM** (7). All mission groups, especially the interdenominational, have had traumatic histories. Ministries most needed are in discipleship and planting balanced, Bible-based churches.

11 **Literature and Bible distribution** have not had a wide impact due to the reluctance of Italians to read. There are about 14 Christian organizations with bookshops, including **CLC** with 22 full-time workers and 9 bookstores, and **The Bible Society** with

Italy's largest Bible and literature centre. **EHC** has given out 62 million pieces of literature, visiting every home in the process. Pray for a hunger for God's Word and a desire for wholesome Christian literature.

12 **Christian radio and TV** has become a fruitful ministry since government controls on local broadcasting were relaxed. There are now hundreds of TV and radio stations and optic-fibre cable networks. Many international radio agencies (**TWR**), churches and agencies (**Back to the Bible, ECM, GMV** and **WT**) use both cable and local FM radio. **TWR** reaches 1.5 million daily; **Back to the Bible** is one of the largest media ministries in Italy. The *JESUS* film has been seen by nearly 10% of the population — mainly through TV. Pray for good cooperation, fruitful follow-up and effective church planting through these ministries.

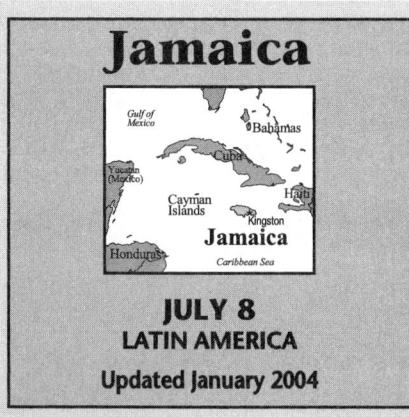

Jamaica

JULY 8
LATIN AMERICA
Updated January 2004

GEOGRAPHY
Area 10,991 sq.km. The third largest island in the Caribbean.

Population		Ann.Gr.	Density
2000	2,582,577	+0.87%	235 per sq. km.
2010	2,815,869	+0.86%	256 per sq. km.
2025	3,244,840	+0.99%	295 per sq. km.

Jamaicans have emigrated in large numbers to North America (750,000, including the US Secretary of State) and UK (ca. 500,000).

Capital Kingston 882,000. **Urbanites** 50%.

PEOPLES
Afro-Caribbean 93.7%.
Asian/Afro-Asian 5%. East Indian 46,000; Chinese 33,000; Lebanese 2,000.
Euro-American 1.3%. English-speaking 16,000; Spanish-speaking 8,000; Portuguese 5,000.
Literacy 85%. **Official language** English; 99% of the population speak Jamaican Creole.

ECONOMY
The mining of bauxite, production of sugar and bananas, and tourism are the main foreign currency earners. A 30-year decline continues — caused by the high crime rate, lower income from exports, hurricanes and heavy debt servicing. These have driven away would-be tourists and investors. Nearly 48% of government income is used to service debt. **HDI** 0.734; 82nd/174. **Public debt** 74% of the GNP. **Income/person** $1,556 (5% of USA).

POLITICS
Spanish rule in 1509, then British from 1655 until independence in 1962 as a parliamentary democracy. Partisan political parties allied to street gangs led to violence in the 1970s and empowered those who continue to perpetuate the violence.

RELIGION
There is freedom of religion.

Religions	Population %	Adherents	Ann.Gr.
Christian	84.10	2,171,947	+0.7%
Rastafarian/Spiritist	10.00	258,258	+1.9%
non-Religious/other	5.00	129,130	+1.7%
Baha'i	0.30	7,748	+4.6%
Chinese/Buddhist	0.30	7,748	+0.9%
Muslim	0.20	5,165	+0.9%
Jewish	0.10	2,583	+0.9%

Christians	Denom.	Affil.%	,000	Ann.Gr.
Protestant	52	38.65	998	+1.6%
Independent	105	8.64	223	+1.2%
Anglican	1	4.14	107	+0.4%
Catholic	1	10.38	268	+0.6%
Orthodox	1	0.12	3	-1.3%
Marginal	9	1.46	38	+2.1%
Unaffiliated		20.71	535	n.a.

Churches	MegaBloc	Cong.	Members	Affiliates
Catholic	C	125	155,814	268,000
Seventh-day Adventist	P	541	159,506	235,000
N T Church of God	P	354	80,799	140,000
Jamaica Baptist Union	P	305	47,000	120,000
Anglican	A	285	53,500	107,000
Ch of God of Prophecy	P	290	27,000	60,000
Methodist	P	180	19,000	52,000
United	P	200	18,000	48,000
Ch of God (Anderson)	P	106	15,000	45,000
Moravian	P	61	6,500	35,000
United Pentecostal	P	250	20,000	34,000
African Meth Epis Zion	I	307	12,605	30,000
Jehovah's Witnesses	M	188	11,030	30,000
Christian Brethren	P	84	6,000	19,000
Assemblies of God	P	76	5,211	12,055
Ch of Foursquare Gospel	P	40	6,200	10,000
Assoc Gospel Assemblies	P	88	4,600	9,000
Latter-day Saints (Morm)	M	27	2,395	4,000
Other denoms [153]		2,012	192,000	379,000
Total Christians [170]		5,519	842,000	1,637,000

Trans-bloc Groupings pop.%	,000	Ann.Gr.
Evangelical 26.3	680	+2.2%
Charismatic 19.4	501	+2.4%
Pentecostal 14.7	381	+2.9%

Missionaries from Jamaica
P,I,A 66 in 14 agencies to 10 countries: Jamaica 42.

Missionaries to Jamaica
P,I,A 194 in 41 agencies from 13 countries: USA 148, UK 19, Canada 12.

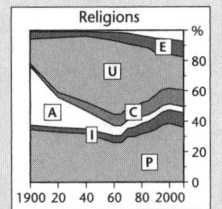

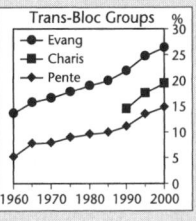

• Challenges for Prayer

1 **The country has sunk into a morass of social and economic problems** that appear insoluble. It has one of the world's highest homicide rates in the world. Violence in society is made worse by the powerful drug cartels and their distribution networks in both Jamaica and North America. Over 37% of cocaine-carrying 'mules' arrested entering the USA arrive from Jamaica. Half the male population are drug-abusers. Pray that government and church leaders may have the courage, moral integrity and determination to turn the country back from sin and to God.

2 **Christianity is numerically strong** but spiritually weak. A third of the population goes to church, but the violence, moral collapse in society and the internal divisions and compromise with sin among Christians, cripples initiative and hinders witness. By 2004 it was evident that there was a considerable fall in progress in Christian commitment and church attendance.

3 **The spiritual temperature of Jamaica** affects that of the whole Caribbean. Pray that the Jamaica Association of Evangelicals may be a model of unity and cooperation to weak and struggling associations in other countries. Pray also that the 15 Bible schools and seminaries in Jamaica, which serve the whole Caribbean, may be powerhouses of spiritual life and missions vision.

4 **Young people. OAC** has reached over one million — mainly in evangelistic outreach to school assemblies. **CEF** wants to multiply children's clubs. **IFES** and **SU** have a combined ministry in producing Bible reading materials and in witness in two universities, 20 colleges and 160 high school groups. Pray that these ministries may result in fellowships that are biblical, evangelistic and courageous. In many schools, 10% of the students belong to these groups. Pray that the nine staff workers and the many Christian teachers may see a radical moral and spiritual uplift among children so that the next generation fares better.

5 **The less evangelized** who need prayer:

a) *The very poor* have little exposure to the gospel, most churches serving the better-off. The 'barrel' children are the impoverished and often bitter, delinquent under-class whose parents have emigrated and occasionally send sustenance to them. A few Catholic and evangelical aid agencies seek to help the poor.

b) *The Rastafarians* began as a protest movement that espoused spiritism, Black Power and Black consciousness ideas and worshipped the Ethiopian Emperor (Ras Tafari). They are well known for their left-wing politics, dreadlocks, reggae music and use of *ganja* (marijuana). They have considerable influence in Jamaica and have spread to Europe and North America. They need the Saviour.

6 **There is little missions vision in the churches.** Jamaica's illustrious past contribution to the evangelization of West Africa is forgotten. Pray for the agencies NEST (Networking, Equipping, Sending Team) and the Jamaican International Missionary Fellowship, in their promotion of missions in churches and the schools. Pray also for the School of Missionary Training and missionaries sent out into cross-cultural work. Pray for Caribbean churches to once again catch a vision for world evangelization.

7 Christian help ministries — many serving the whole Caribbean.

a) *The Bible Society*, based in Kingston, is a channel for Scriptures to most of the mini-states of the region. Creole Bible cassettes are proving popular.

b) *Literature*. CLC has a notable ministry through 5 bookstores and the region-wide distribution of the *Caribbean Challenge* magazine. The seven staff are too few to adequately handle the ministry. Pray that more spiritual and teaching literature may be bought and used by Christian leaders.

c) *The JESUS film* has been viewed by almost the entire population in English and/or Creole.

Japan
Nihon

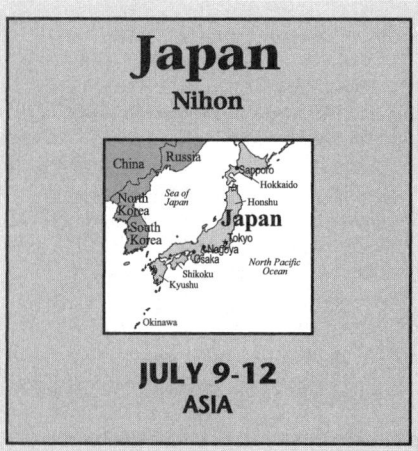

JULY 9-12
ASIA

GEOGRAPHY
Area 377,801 sq.km. A 3,000 km arc of four large islands (Honshu, Hokkaido, Shikoku, Kyushu) and 3,000 small islands in NW Pacific. Mountainous; only 13% can be cultivated.

Population		Ann.Gr.	Density
2000	126,714,220	+0.20%	335 per sq. km.
2010	127,315,474	-0.02%	339 per sq. km.
2025	121,150,001	-0.45%	321 per sq. km.

Capital Tokyo 34.5 million. There are plans to move the capital to a less earthquake-prone site. Other major cities: Osaka 17.75m; Nagoya 5.1m; Sapporo 2.2m; Fukuoka 1.95m; Hiroshima 1.7m; Kitakyushu 1.53m; Sendai 1.3m; Okayama 1.1m. **Urbanites** 78%.

PEOPLES
Indigenous 98.8%.
Japanese 98.6%. Sub-groups: Okinawan 802,000; South American Japanese returnees 233,000; Ryukyuan 148,000.
Ainu 0.2%. The aboriginal inhabitants who have largely lost their original languages.
Foreign 1.2%. Korean 675,000; Chinese 252,000; Filipino 75,000.
Illegal immigrants Possibly 500,000 Pakistani, Iranian, Bangladeshi, Filipino, Thai, Malaysian and others.

Literacy 100%. **Official language** Japanese. **All languages** 15 (including 11 Okinawan-Ryukyuan dialects). **Languages with Scriptures** 2Bi 1por.

ECONOMY
The world's most powerful export-oriented economy despite lack of natural resources and oil. High savings and low interest rates stimulated a massive global capital investment boom based on high property values. The 1989 property crash pushed the world into recession and forced changes on Japan's protectionist policy towards industry, the financial world and trading patterns. Unemployment and instability have increased, but Japan still has an enormous trade surplus with the world. The low birthrate and rapidly ageing population are beginning to put a brake on future growth. By 2001 the economy was in recession and unemployment rising. **HDI** 0.924; 4ᵗʰ/174. **Public debt** 50% of GNP. **Income/person** $38,160 (121% of USA).

POLITICS
Constitutional monarchy with a parliamentary democracy. The 45 years of stability and economic expansion since WWII have turned Japan into an economic superpower. Rising nationalism and willingness to exert political power in the Pacific causes unease among neighbours. Numerous scandals, corruption and shoddy factional politics discredit the present political system and delay the implementation of essential reforms.

RELIGION
Freedom of religion is guaranteed to all by the constitution, but the rising power of nationalistic Shintoism partly associated with the new emperor is tarnishing that freedom. Over 80% of Japanese claim no personal religion, but most follow the demands of idolatrous and ancestor-venerating Buddhism, and rituals of polytheistic Shintoism. Many also follow some of the hundreds of newer religious movements that are off-shoots of these. The main ones: Soka Gakkai 17m, Risshokosekai 5.5m, Seicho no Ie 3.7m. So figures below cannot adequately show the multiple religious loyalties of the Japanese, which could be Buddhist 85%, Shinto 90%!

Religions	Population %	Adherents	Ann.Gr.
Buddhist/Shinto	69.61	88,206,000	+0.2%
New Religions	24.43	30,956,284	+0.4%
non-Religious/other	4.27	5,410,697	-1.1%
Christian	1.56	1,976,742	+0.1%
Muslim	0.12	152,057	+6.1%
Baha'i	0.01	15,000	-10.8%

Christians	Denom.	Affil.%	,000	Ann.Gr.
Protestant	146	0.42	538	+0.8%
Independent	36	0.22	281	+0.9%
Anglican	1	0.05	62	+1.6%
Catholic	1	0.36	457	+0.5%

Churches	MegaBloc	Cong.	Members	Affiliates
Orthodox	2	0.02	26	-0.2%
Marginal	9	0.61	776	+0.1%
Disaffiliated		*-0.12*	*-152*	*n.a.*
Catholic	C	977	319,720	457,200
Jehovah's Witnesses	M	4,489	282,803	350,000
Unification (Moonies)	M		240,000	300,000
United Ch of Christ	P	1,694	138,058	205,244
Spirit of Jesus	I	614	73,653	123,000
Latter-day Saints (Morm)	M	349	96,000	120,000
Holy Catholic (Angl)	A	309	36,679	62,000
Orig Gos Tabernacle Mvt	I	865	22,500	45,000
Independent	I	739	32,435	43,000
Baptist Convention	P	333	15,957	33,191
Evang Lutheran	P	154	10,649	32,267
Seventh-day Adventist	P	114	14,314	20,000
Assemblies of God	P	215	13,688	19,234
Japan Holiness	P	179	13,046	16,000
J. Gospel Ch of Christ	P	183	9,387	13,000
Immanuel General Miss	P	198	7,401	12,952
Christian Brethren	P	161	7,261	10,000
J Christian Alliance	P	198	7,304	9,860
Ch of the Nazarene	P	75	5,835	8,500
Korean speaking [15]	P	110	5,500	8,250
Reformed Ch in Japan	P	144	3,900	7,215
Holy Ecclesia of Jesus	I	104	5,893	7,190
English speaking [10]	P	164	4,667	7,000
Japanese Alliance Ch	P	42	3,286	6,200
Baptist Union	P	80	4,791	6,000
Other denoms [154]		3,104	138,000	217,000
Doubly affiliated			*-100,000*	*-162,000*
Total Christians [202]		15,594	1,413,000	1,977,000

Trans-bloc Groupings	pop.%	,000	Ann.Gr.
Evangelical	0.4	495	+0.7%
Charismatic	0.3	331	+1.0%
Pentecostal	0.0	54	+3.4%

Missionaries from Japan
P,I,A 397 in 52 agencies of which 218 are overseas in 45 countries: Philippines 23, Brazil 16.

Missionaries to Japan
P,I,A 3,500 in 245 agencies from 33 countries: USA 1,477, Korea 546, Norway 87, Germany 87, Finland 80, UK 76, Canada 74, Australia 50. [Other sources give 2,362 foreign missionaries serving in Japan.]

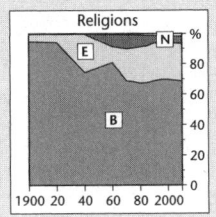

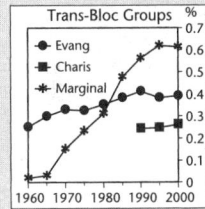

• Answers to Prayer

1 **A new openness after very little real church growth for over a century** — provoked by Japan's series of disasters in the 1990s. The Kobe earthquake, and the threat of others in the Tokyo area, the failure of the ruling class, economic meltdown, increasing rebelliousness of young people and the rise of anti-social and violent cults have all provoked soul-searching and even a questioning of Japanese value systems.

2 **A rising prayer burden for revival** coupled with some efforts to bring reconciliation in the deep divide between Pentecostals/charismatics and other Evangelicals. There has been a gradual increase in the growth of churches and conversions during the 1990s. The Church Information Service in Japan counted 7,814 churches with 270,000 worshippers in their 2000 survey.

• Challenges for Prayer

1 **Japan is in crisis economically and politically** because of a failure of the leadership. The nation drifts like a rudderless ship. Massive economic reforms, a shaking up of society's structures which favour self-seeking interest groups (political parties, *yakuza* mafia gangs, bankers, etc.) and a new opening up to the world will need leaders with courage to tackle these in the 21st Century. Pray for such.

2 **Japan is a mixture of openness and unresponsiveness**. The powers associated with idolatry in temples and ancestor worship in homes have never been decisively challenged. More specifically:

a) *Resurgence of a nationalistic Shintoism* that is hostile to anything un-Japanese. Pray for Christians to stand firm in Jesus and not compromise their faith under pressure as did many Christians during World War II. There are subtle attempts to reinstate past evils such as emperor worship and militarism.

b) *Social life*. The sincere, polite, hard-working Japanese are too busy to give heed to the gospel and understand little of what is right or wrong or of the meaning of sin because they do not know the Creator God. Most see the value of religion, 20% have a definite religion, but only 10% believe in the existence of a personal God. Pray for the Holy Spirit to bring revelation of God and then a conviction of sin to the nation.

c) **New religions.** The growth of Soka Gakkai and other religions in the 1950s and '60s. Fear to witness and compromise are major issues for believers. An average of 100 new religions are started each year — based on the occult, worship of extra-terrestrial aliens and so on. Pray for the removal of a spirit of delusion.

d) **The youth are turning away from the values and work ethic** of their parents, and turning to materialistic pleasures, drugs and possessions rather than to the living God. Pray that present economic shocks, instability and fears for the future may shake many out of complacency.

e) **The minimal impact** made by the average Japanese Christian on the centres of power in the land. The lack of radiant witnesses for Jesus in the industrial, commercial and political realms is cause for concern. Nevertheless, Christianity exerts a moral and social influence and attraction far beyond its relatively small presence.

3 **The Church in Japan experienced good growth** between 1945 and 1960, but both Catholic and Protestant percentages have only marginally increased since then, with conversions only just exceeding backslidings. The decisive breakthrough has yet to come, so pray for:

a) **The United Church** — the name given to the union of all Protestant churches formed under duress during World War II. Almost all churches in the union compromised with Shinto and emperor worship, resulting in total loss of spiritual life. After the war, many denominational groups pulled out to form their own denominations. Many see the key to future blessing and growth is repentance by the whole Christian Church in Japan for this black period in its history.

b) **The growing evangelical witness.** In 1950 Evangelicals were 40% of Protestants and Independents, but by 2000 they were over 60%. Yet the denominational fragmentation, theological divides and lack of nation-wide cooperation have hampered progress and increased attrition rates. The Japan Evangelical Association is one major coordinating body for many denominations and has sponsored 4 national congresses on Evangelism (1974, 1982, 1991, 2000) and other large evangelistic efforts.

c) **Quasi-Christian groups** such as the Moonies, Jehovah's Witnesses and Mormons have grown far faster than Evangelicals or Catholics and become the largest and most visible 'Christian' presence in many areas. Yet they remain ensnared in the enemy's power and still need spiritual release and freedom. Nearly one million Japanese are linked to these deviant groups. Little literature or specific ministry is directed to bringing the gospel to them. There are three agencies committed to helping JWs to faith in Christ.

4 Specific weaknesses in the churches:

a) **Lack of biblical teaching.** Christians need complete renewal of their minds. The pervasive influence of the demonic world, philosophies and superstitions must be replaced by a vibrant theology and a head and heart knowledge of God's greatness and holiness. Pray for new leaders, writers and evangelists to communicate God's Truth in the 21st Century.

b) **The minority complex.** Christians are a tiny minority in a society where consensus is important. Too few families come to faith, and individuals feel exposed.

c) **Non-active membership and backsliding.** Church attendance is low, having decreased since 1995; only 33% of Protestants attend services weekly. Often Christians are influenced by the Buddhist/Shinto religions which have no regular attendance requirements, and this thinking is carried over into Christian activities.

d) **The lack of breadwinning men in the churches.** The drive for success and desire to satisfy the demands of employers make it hard for men to openly identify with and become active in a church. Women are in the great majority in most congregations.

e) **Too few viable, active congregations.** At least 70% of all churches have an average attendance of less than 30. Too much is expected of the pastor. Pray for pastors willing to activate lay people to engage in persistent, innovative outreach to non-Christians.

f) **Lack of understanding about evil spirits** in spite of their heavy presence through idolatry, fortune telling and occultic new religions. Many evangelical pastors and theologians deny their existence in Japan.

5 **Bible training for Christian workers** is provided by nearly 100 denominational and interdenominational seminaries and Bible Schools in which around 3,000 are in full-time training. The great hope for the future of the Church is the high quality of many of Japan's pastors and church leaders. May their numbers be mightily increased! Pray for more men and couples to be called into pastoral and missionary work and to come for training. About 70% of pastors are over 50 years of age. Fewer and fewer young men feel the call into pastoral ministry.

6 **The missions vision of Japanese Christians is noteworthy.** Nearly 500 missionaries have been or are serving overseas. There are now 47 agencies with over 210 serving in 48 lands around the world. However, churches generally have little vision for missions or understanding of the problems of cross-cultural missions and missionaries. There are two small Missionary Training Centres backed by some Japanese churches and missions. The launching of the Tokyo Christian University is beginning to play a major role in training future missionaries to serve around the world. The Japanese Overseas Missions Association has a membership of 16 Japanese agencies. One of the big hindrances for long-term Japanese missionary service is the difficulty of re-integrating children of missionaries into Japan when they return.

7 Missions.

a) ***First-term missionaries.*** Japan is easy for missionaries to enter, but then the difficulties begin! The difficulty of the language and script, the complexities of the culture, the bewildering strands of a web society, and the pervading influence of the demonic world are all barriers to adaptation and communication. Acculturation takes years, and many missionaries are still in that tearful stage. The high cost of living is a challenge for foreign missionaries. Pray for them.

b) ***Missionary agencies*** are often small and cooperation between them is too limited. JEMA is a coordinating body for 43 mission organizations representing over 1,200 missionaries. Most are involved in church planting and evangelism, but few have found the key to growth. Pray for leaders, for the right strategies, and for Spirit-anointed ministries. The profusion of agencies and nationalities defies listing here. Largest missions: **IMB-SBC** (166), Korean Missionary Fellowship (135), **TEAM** (117), **OMF** (112), **YWAM** (105), **SEND** (57), **AoG** (46), JCCC/**CCCI** (43), BIM (40), **MTW** (40), **JCL/JEB** (38), LCMS (31), SdA (31), BBF (26), Life Ministries (25), **WEC** (19), **CMA** (16) and **OMS** (15). The growing contribution of Korean missionaries is remarkable in the light of historic animosities — they need special prayer cover that they might adapt well and have effective ministries.

c) ***Opportunities for missionary service.*** These are many, the most needful being evangelism, church planting and teaching. Long-term missionaries are the greater need because of the years needed to acquire the language and understand the culture. The Japanese Education Ministry hires 2,000 English teachers annually for assisting in high schools; this and private tuition give good contacts for tentmaking missionaries. Conducting weddings for the one-third of Japanese couples desiring a 'Christian' wedding gives missionaries and pastors unique evangelistic opportunities at unconverted gatherings.

8 The less-evangelized areas and peoples of Japan:

a) ***Of the 672 cities, there are still 9 without a church,*** unchanged in 10 years. A further 77 have but one.

b) ***Of the 2,568 towns of 15,000-30,000 people, 1,733 are without churches.***

c) ***Numerous rural areas are scarcely touched with the gospel.*** The Japanese Church has little vision for reaching out to the many towns with minimal or no Christian presence.

d) ***The ruling elite have been little influenced.*** Pray for the Emperor cocooned in tradition and committed, by his position, to Shintoism. Pray for politicians, bankers and industrialists who have such global impact through their leadership — or lack of it.

e) ***Koreans, descendants of those forcibly brought to Japan*** between 1903 and 1945, are usually denied full citizenship rights, and are still classed as resident aliens even into their third and fourth generations. They are despised and poorly paid. The Korean community is sharply divided in their allegiance to either North or South Korea. Korean missionaries have planted over 300 churches in this community, but the percentage of Christians among them is lower than that of South Korea.

f) ***Chinese,*** 60,000 residents, are largely involved in business in larger cities. The great majority are non-religious or follow the Chinese traditional religions. There are 14 churches among them with 1,100 Christians. There may be over 70,000 illegals living as a hidden underclass. There are 90,000 Chinese students in Japan, 50,000 from Mainland China — a fruitful field for ministry and the **AoG** saw 1,500 conversions among them in the 1990s.

g) The Ainu, ethnically unrelated to the Japanese, first settled in north Japan. They have been partly assimilated into Japanese culture, but a resurgence of Ainu culture may require a specific Christian outreach to them.

h) Extremist groups. Cults such as Aum Shinrikyo and their attempts at mass murder, and leftist groups such as the Japanese Red Army have become infamous globally. There are possibly 1,000 right wing extremist groups with 120,000 members. All these point to a deep unmet spiritual need.

i) Exploited women. The *yakuza* criminal network has an active role in importing 200,000 foreign women who become sex-slaves. There are an estimated 100,000 Thai and also many Filipina women involved. Pray both for this evil system to be halted and these tragically exploited women liberated at every level.

j) Muslims have increased through legal and illegal immigration of Bangladeshis, Iranians, Pakistanis and others. Some Japanese have also become Muslims — largely through marriage. Little is being done to reach them.

9 **Young people are becoming a 'rare' breed** due to the low birth rate. They are more materialistic, individualistic and often more violent — to the distress of the older generation. The 18-23 year-olds are the most responsive to the gospel. Student witness is one of the most strategic for the future of the Church. There are 1,243 universities and colleges with 3,080,000 students, but in only 183 of the colleges are there KGK(**IFES**) groups with a total of 1,300 students involved; 60% of these are seekers. Japan **CCCI** (68 workers), **YWAM** and **Navigators** (65) also minister on these campuses. Apathy towards religion and scepticism of established religion are widespread, and few make a commitment to Christ, despite the respect for the teachings of Christianity.

10 **Christian literature** — in no other country of the world is literature more appropriate for evangelism. A highly literate, reading, commuting society offers an excellent market for publishing and distributing high-quality Christian literature. Pray for:

a) More Christian writers of evangelistic and apologetic literature who can communicate with non-Christian enquirers.

b) Understanding of the Scriptures. Over 5 million Bibles are sold annually, and 43% of the under-30s possess a copy, due largely to the efforts of the Gideons, but few read them, or understand them if they do read.

c) Christian bookstores which number over 110, with several large networks including Word of Life (**TEAM** 150 workers, 20 stores) and **CLC** with 12 stores and a bookmobile ministry.

d) Evangelistic literature. New Life League is the largest producer of literature in Asia. Excellent tracts are printed in large quantities and distributed widely. **EHC** distributed 180 million pieces in four national house-to-house distributions between 1953-2000.

11 **Christian radio and TV** are useful tools for reaching the electronically-minded Japanese. Pray for:

a) Christian TV programmes on VHF channels. Dr. Paul Yonggi Cho, Pacific Broadcasting Association Lifeline and Harvest Time are notable examples of ministries with an extensive audience. Satellite and cable TV and radio broadcasting present new challenges for Christian broadcasters. Pray that these may be used widely.

b) The many Christian radio programmes aired in Japan (Pacific Broadcasting Association, **TEAM**, **FEBC**, Japan Mission, Lutheran Hour and others).

c) Foreign short-wave Christian radio stations. FEBC-Korea, **TWR**-Guam, **HCJB**-Ecuador and others broadcast a total of 60 hours/week in Japanese. Millions of young people belong to short-wave listeners' clubs and listen to these broadcasts.

d) The JESUS film on video — a new version has received high acclaim. Over 70% of homes have a VCR. Pray for an effective video distribution plan and for Christians to be trained in the effective use of the *JESUS* video. Video evangelism is proving a key method of outreach — a wider range of videos needs to be produced.

e) The growing use of the Internet presents exciting new possibilities for outreach, but few have yet exploited its potential.

Jordan

Hashemite Kingdom of Jordan

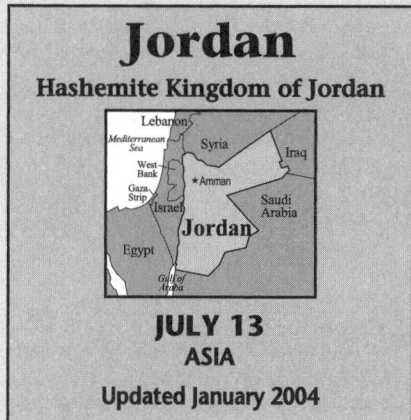

JULY 13

ASIA

Updated January 2004

powers. Turmoil in the Middle East has profoundly affected life due to loss of land, influx of refugees and economic disruption. Jordan relinquished its claim to the West Bank area, but over half its present population is Palestinian with Jordanian citizenship. The government resists pressure for greater Islamization. Future relationships with Israel are an important political issue.

RELIGION
Islam is the state religion, but the constitution prohibits discrimination and promotes the free exercise of religious belief and worship, while prohibiting the proselytism of Muslims. **Persecution index** 69th in the world.

Religions	Population %	Adherents	Ann.Gr.
Muslim	96.19	6,415,239	+3.2%
Christian	2.75	183,407	+0.8%
non-Religious/other	1.00	66,693	+1.1%
Baha'i	0.03	2,000	+3.1%
Other	0.03	2,000	+11.8%

Christians	Denom.	Affil.%	,000	Ann.Gr.
Protestant	17	0.18	12	+3.5%
Independent	2	0.04	3	+21.4%
Anglican	1	0.11	7	+0.8%
Catholic	3	1.14	76	+1.7%
Orthodox	3	1.28	86	-0.5%

Churches	MegaBloc	Cong.	Members	Affiliates
Greek Orthodox	O	29	44,693	80,000
Catholic [3]	C	66	43,429	76,000
Episcopal	A	20	4,311	7,200
Syrian Orthodox	O	1	880	4,400
Assemblies of God	P	8	430	2,600
Evang Lutheran	P	6	1,198	2,000
Jordan Baptist Conv	P	12	1,000	1,820
Evang Church of CMA	P	8	398	1,000
Free Evangelical	P	14	360	600
Ch of the Nazarene	P	7	350	500
Other denoms [15]		53	4,800	7,700
Total Christians [27]		224	102,000	184,000

Trans-bloc Groupings	pop.%	,000	Ann.Gr.
Evangelical	0.2	12	+7.9%
Charismatic	0.1	8	+6.9%
Pentecostal	0.0	3	+7.2%

GEOGRAPHY
Area 89,206 sq.km. Agriculture and population is concentrated on the eastern bank of the River Jordan. Most of the country is desert.

Population	Ann.Gr.	Density
2000	6,669,341	+3.07%	75 per sq. km.
2010	8,797,930	+2.69%	99 per sq. km.
2025	12,062,895	+1.85%	135 per sq. km.

Capital Amman 1,575,000. **Urbanites** 79%.

PEOPLES
With the massive transit of Palestinians, Iraqis and Kuwaitis through Jordan in the past decades, no precise figures exist.
Arab 97.1%. Palestinian, East Bank Jordanian.
Jordanian Minorities 1%. Adygei (Circassian), Armenian, Kurd, Turkomen, Chechen.
Non-Jordanians 1.9%. Egyptian, Greek, Western, Pakistani, other Arab.

Literacy 86%. **Official langauge** Arabic. **All languages** 8. **Languages with Scriptures** 2Bi 1NT 2por 1w.i.p.

ECONOMY
The geo-politics of the past 60 years have hindered economic development. Over a quarter of families live in poverty. Main income sources: tourism, phosphates, chemicals and fruit. Tourism and trade seriously interrupted by the resumption of the Palestinian *intifada* in 2001 and the upheavals in Iraq in 2003-4. **Unemployment** 30% in 2003. **HDI** 0.715; 94th/174. **Public debt** $104% of GNP. **Income/person** $1,520 (4.8% of USA).

POLITICS
Part of Turkish empire until 1918. Independent from Britain in 1946. Constitutional monarchy with King Abdullah having executive

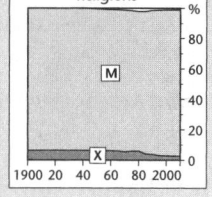

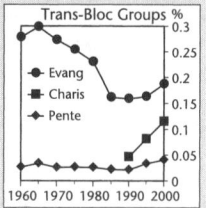

• Challenges for Prayer

1 **The passing of the throne** from King Hussein, the quintessential Arab moderate, to his son Abdullah in 1999 was a smooth transition, but difficulties lie ahead. The hundreds of thousands of immigrants from Palestine, Iraq and Kuwait have intensified economic and political stress. Pray for the peace of this land and for the King and government. Pray for the preservation of religious freedom amidst the rising extremism of some Muslims. This nation is a centre for many Christian activities and ministries, and much Christian work in the Middle East would suffer were a setback to occur in Jordan.

2 **The Christian community has suffered a numerical freefall** in the past decades, due to lower birth rates, high rate of emigration, influx of Muslim refugees and the rise of politicized Islam. From 1970-2000 Jordan's Christian population dropped by fi from 5.5 to 2.75% of the population. Still, Christians are found in all walks of life and often in positions of great influence. Both the Catholic and Orthodox Christians are an important component of Jordanian society. Pray that Christians may be salt and light in Jordanian society, and may find ways to witness to nominal Christians as well as non-Christians.

3 **Evangelical churches are experiencing encouraging growth,** more than doubling in the 1990s. There are over 40 churches and several more house groups where the 12,000 evangelicals meet. Most conversions are from the nominal Christian community, but recently more Muslims are discovering Jesus, the Lamb of God. The relationships between the traditional and evangelical churches and Muslim background believers are guarded. Pray that all Jordanian believers might work together to make Jesus Christ known.

4 **The constant loss of leadership potential** through emigration is a drain on the body of believers. Lay leadership is virtually non-existent, and only 20% of churches have a full-time pastor. But through several agencies, TEE courses and the Jordan Evangelical School of Theology, more Arab leaders are being trained for service in Jordan, Iraq and the wider Arab world. Youth work and Christian camp ministries by Manara and others have been fruitful in recent years; a strategic ministry considering that 50% of Jordan's population is younger than 15. Pray for more Jordanian believers to be called to full-time work.

5 **Foreign missionaries** have limited ministry opportunities because of the sensitive religious and political situation. Twenty or more agencies are involved in a wide range of activities, often supporting and enhancing the national church. Jordan also hosts a language school wherein many learn Arabic for their service in the Arab world. Pray that these expatriates' lives may commend the Lord Jesus and gain witness opportunities. Pray that the Jordanian church might experience growth in mission vision.

6 **The unreached** comprise the vast majority of the population. There is great openness to the gospel; 35% of Jordanians are interested in learning more about Jesus. Pray that every Jordanian may have opportunity to hear the gospel. Pray especially for:

a) The Muslim majority. Many have still not heard the clear gospel. Pray for a sensitive witness to Muslims. There have been several successful methods: literature, media ministry, friendship evangelism, development programmes, home meetings and camps. Pray for the protection of converts amidst persecution. Pray also for the legal right to convert from Islam.

b) The millions of Palestinians who are now a majority in Jordan. Many have been integrated into Jordanian life, others suffer from disillusionment, bitterness and frustration which only the Man of Calvary can heal.

c) Iraqi refugees. Since the Gulf War, hundreds of thousands of Iraqis have fled their country to Jordan. Christian work among them (**CMA** and several other churches, **WVI**, **TEAR Fund**) is experiencing a very good response. Iraqi Christians are benefiting from the training and resources available to them in Jordan.

d) The 200,000 Bedouin. Many are still nomadic, and many others are in the army or reachable in cities and hospitals. Believers are very few.

e) People of many nationalities present in Jordan. Saudi and Gulf Arabs visit for the summer. Sri Lankans, Filipinos and Egyptians come to work. Agygei and Chechens form proud minorities. Pray that they all may encounter the gospel while in Jordan.

7 **In recent years there has been increasing interest in outreach to the majority community** and the development of house churches. Pray that believers may catch a vision for a church in the home — a key for the expansion of the Church.

8 **The ministry of media.** Jordan's circumstances enhance the importance of radio, television, videos, films and literature. Arabic programmes from **FEBA**-Seychelles (18 hours/week), **TWR**-Cyprus (10.2 hours/week) and High Adventure have had a significant effect. Satellite television is having a large impact — **SAT-7** programmes are being viewed across the country. The *JESUS* film is available in Adygey, Colloquial Egyptian and Standard Arabic. Pray for long-term fruit.

9 **Literature** in Arabic is becoming more widely available. There are three Christian bookstores in Amman. They are the focal point of a successful Bible and Christian literature ministry in which **The Bible Society**, Carmel Mission, Agape and Manara are actively involved.

Kazakhstan

Republic of Kazakhstan

JULY 14-15

ASIA

GEOGRAPHY
Area 2,717,300 sq.km. Dominating Central Asia and trade routes between east and west. Much of the country is semi-desert.

Population	Ann.Gr.	Density
2000	16,222,563	-0.35%	6 per sq. km.
2010	16,492,359	+0.43%	6 per sq. km.
2025	17,698,360	+0.40%	7 per sq. km.

Capital Astana 300,000. **Other major city**: Almaty 1,200,000. **Urbanites** 56 %.

PEOPLES
At least 65 groups, 43 with populations over 1,000. The Kazakh diaspora is more than 4 million. Since 1999 there has been a massive emigration of Europeans and an influx of Kazakhs.
Turkic/Altaic 60.4%. Kazakh 8,667,000; Uzbek 403,000; Tatar(2) 271,000; Uighur 228,000; Turkish(3) 88,000; Azeri 85,000.
Indo-European 38.4%. Many emigrating.
  Slav 34.7%. Russian 4,861,000; Ukrainian 593,000; Belarusian 122,000; Polish 51,000.
  Other 3.7%. German 383,000; Kurdish 36,000; Chechen 35,000; Tajik 28,000.
All others 1.2%. Korean 109,000; Dungan 41,000.

Literacy 97.5%. **Official language** Kazakh. **All languages** 6. **Languages with Scriptures** 2Bi 2NT 2por 1w.i.p.

ECONOMY
Enormous oil and mineral reserves, large grain producer. The move to a market economy has been hesitant. The socio-economic network has unravelled, forcing wage delays, service cutbacks and rising unemployment. Ecological disasters, such as the salt and toxic waste in the shrinking Aral Sea and radioactive fallout from USSR nuclear testing, have resulted in economic strain. **HDI** 0.740; 76th/174. **Public debt** 132% of GNP. **Income/person** $1,350 (4.3 % of USA).

POLITICS
Declared independence after collapse of the USSR in 1991. The short-term failure of democratic capitalism led to an authoritarian backlash at which time the president strengthened his position. The current regime pursues a policy of market liberalization and moderate secularism and aims to strengthen Kazakh influence at all levels of government.

K

RELIGION
Under Communism all religion was suppressed. Even now, in an era of greater tolerance with religious freedom constitutionally guaranteed, religions not considered 'traditional' suffer some opposition and restrictions. Proposed changes to deny legal standing to newer groups were withdrawn after local and international protest. Some Muslim groups are pushing for greater Islamization, which is unlikely to happen under current conditions. Many religious statistics are estimates. **Persecution index** 75th in the world.

Religions	Population %	Adherents	Ann.Gr.
Muslim	60.50	9,814,651	+1.6%
Christian	24.66	4,000,484	-0.8%
non-Religious/other	14.27	2,314,960	-6.1%
Buddhist	0.50	81,113	-0.3%
Jewish	0.04	6,489	-8.1%
Shamanist	0.03	4,867	-0.3%

Christians	Denom.	Affil.%	,000	Ann.Gr.
Protestant	21	0.83	135	+4.1%
Independent	4	0.01	2	+14.9%
Catholic	2	0.33	53	-1.9%
Orthodox	4	7.59	1,232	-3.0%
Marginal	1	0.20	33	+3.6%
Unaffiliated		15.70	2,545	n.a.

Churches	MegaBloc	Cong.	Members	Affiliates
Russian Orthodox	O	210	839,161	1,200,000
Ukrainian Uniate	C	23	34,965	50,000
Ev Chr & Baptist	P	242	11,613	46,450
Lutheran	P	16	23,952	40,000
Pentecostal grps [6]	P	160	8,000	20,000
Armenian Apostolic	O	7	7,143	11,000
Korean Presbyterian	P	20	4,000	10,000
Seventh-day Adventist	P	39	3,149	6,300
Unregistered Baptists	P	30	1,000	5,000
Korean Baptist	P	11	1,600	4,000
Catholic	C	5	2,300	3,290
Mennonite	P	5	500	1,665
Other denoms [15]		44	28,416	57,650
Total Christians [32]		812	965,800	1,455,300

Trans-bloc Groupings	pop.%	,000	Ann.Gr.
Evangelical	0.6	105	+6.4%
Charismatic	0.2	36	+12.9%
Pentecostal	0.1	20	+19.8%

Religions chart (1900–2000) and Trans-Bloc Groups chart (1960–2000, Evang / Prot).

• Answers to Prayer

1 **The Kazakh Church is young**, but alive and growing strong. Where there were virtually no Kazakh believers in 1990, in 2000 there were more than 6,000! They meet in over 40 Kazakh-speaking congregations. The Church is especially growing among young people. Pray that this numerical growth may continue, but also that the Church may mature quickly.

2 **The Silk Road 2000** event in Almaty was a major breakthrough for the Christian community. Inspired by the prayer journey of Korean believers, the stadium event hosted 20,000 people from Central Asia, and was supplemented by various workshops and seminars encouraging indigenous Christianity. Repentance and reconciliation between the diverse Christian groups was a central feature to the event. Pray that there might be much long-term fruit for the Kingdom in Kazakhstan and Central Asia.

K • Challenges for Prayer

1 **The revival of Kazakh identity.** The government's deliberate promotion of Kazakh language and culture has created some social strain, and has had only limited success. About 40% of Kazakhs cannot speak their own language, and less than half the schools teach in Kazakh. Nevertheless, there is a good measure of social harmony considering the ethnic diversity of the nation. Pray that government leaders may wisely develop their nation's cultural identity, and that political and religious extremism and oppression might be avoided. Pray that the peace and tolerance which enables ministry might continue.

2 **Kazakhs have been nominally Sunni Muslims** since 1043, but theirs is a folk Islam strongly influenced by animistic practices. An Islamist movement is being fuelled by Muslim missionaries and money from Iran, Turkey and Arab countries. There were 60 mosques in 1991; nine years later there were 5,000. Christianity is still viewed as the religion of the Russian oppressors. Pray that long-held prejudices and spiritual bondages might be broken and religious tyranny avoided.

3 **Russians and Ukrainians** — most claim to be Orthodox. Many are emigrating back to their homelands. The Orthodox Church has increasingly aligned itself with the Muslims in seeking to remove the measure of religious freedom gained at independence. Pray that these attempts may be foiled and that small renewal movements in the Orthodox Church may grow.

4 **Unreached minorities.** Kazakhstan's cultural and religious diversity may make this land the most open and strategic for evangelizing Central Asian non-Christian peoples. Some Uzbeks and Uighurs in Kazakhstan are turning to Christ — pray for the Church to take root among them. Pray for all the peoples listed in the statistics section. Christianity is still largely an urban phenomenon, but the Baptists are deliberately recruiting for rural ministry. Pray that the gospel might be shared — in the listeners' language — in the many towns and villages of this vast land.

5 **While the Christian population decreased** during the 1990s, there has been a significant growth of interest from non-Eurasians as well as indigenous peoples. Korean churches have grown exponentially, as have most charismatic, Pentecostal and some Baptist groups. The challenges:

a) Coping with the mass exodus of emigrating Christians. The majority of Evangelicals under Communism were German; most have emigrated to Germany. Many Russians and Ukrainians have also left.

b) A desperate need for young, trained leadership. There are now many local Bible Colleges and discipleship training programmes (**SGA** and others). Pray that they may raise up a generation of leaders who can meet the challenges of the 21st Century.

c) Preaching of sound doctrine, holy living, and missions vision. The significant Slavic Christian population needs to develop a concern for the evangelization of the numerous Muslim ethnic groups. There is a great need for disciplers and Bible teachers in all churches and among every ethnicity.

d) Flexibility to adapt from the days of persecution and German-Russian cultural Christianity, the latter inappropriate for today's young people and Kazakhstan's culture. Some Baptist and Pentecostal congregations are traditional and legalistic.

6 **The expatriate Christian community** has been transformed from a patchwork of mostly short-term Anglo- and Russophones to a diverse but unified partnership, many of whom speak Kazakh and are committed long-term. Pray that the ministry of the Kazakh Partnership may deepen the level of cooperation between all those ministering here. There are many humanitarian and holistic mission opportunities in this troubled land; almost all efforts to assist are very well received. The needs are many: evangelism, discipling, Bible training, Christian publishing, TESOL, business, career training and basic humanitarian aid. The serious social and psychological impact of widespread substance abuse and abortions requires effective pastoral and rehabilitation ministries. Pray for many to be called to serve in this country with so many needs. Pray also that Western ministries might have humility in how they serve the indigenous church.

7 **Christian media ministries for prayer:**

K

a) Literature. The Central Asian Baptist Mission and Light in the East focus on producing evangelistic, apologetic and teaching literature in Central Asian languages. Hundreds of thousands of copies of a children's storybook Bible have been distributed, and even approved of for education in some regions. Still, there is a need for help in all areas of literature.

b) Bible. There is a great demand for Bibles, both among the Kazakhs and the Russian Orthodox. Thousands of Bibles and portions have been distributed, but only a fraction of them in Kazakh. The NT in Kazakh is now complete and also available on cassette; the Kazakh OT is being translated. Also in preparation is a Russian language Bible which is culturally sensitive to Central Asian Muslims. Pray for the wide and wise distribution of all biblical materials, and for ongoing translation projects.

c) The JESUS film is available in Kazakh, Russian, Ukrainian, Uighur and several other languages. A large proportion of the population have seen the film.

d) Radio. Kazakh broadcasts are still few. **FEBC**-Saipan and **TWR**-Monaco transmit, respectively, four and five 15-minute programmes weekly. There are also Christian broadcasts in other languages, although Russian predominates. Pray for new, quality programmes in Kazakh.

Kenya
Republic of Kenya

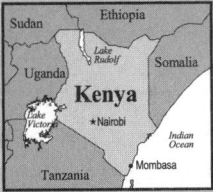

JULY 16-17
AFRICA
Revised January 2004

endemic corruption is gradually ruining the infra-structure, devastating whole industries and drying up the flow of tourists and foreign finance. A large landless, poor underclass is becoming increasingly restive and violent. HIV/AIDs is widespread and the death rate climbing with 14% of those aged 15-49 infected. **HDI** 0.519; 136th/174. **Public debt** 53% of GNP. **Income/person** $340 (1.1% of USA).

POLITICS
Independent from Britain in 1963. Virtually a one-party state for much of the time since then. President Moi's Kipsigis-favouring government has successfully held foreign creditors at bay, subverted any opposition and marginalized the major ethnic groups — the Kikuyu, Luo and Luyia. Kenya's future is not good unless there is meaningful change.A new government was elected in 2003 replacing Moi's corrupt rule.

GEOGRAPHY
Area 582,646 sq.km. Most people live in the fertile plateaus of the south and west. Much of the north and east is desert. Only 9.5% of the land is cultivated.

Population		Ann.Gr.	Density
2000	30,080,372	+2.02%	52 per sq. km.
2010	35,204,705	+1.53%	60 per sq. km.
2025	41,755,990	+1.01%	72 per sq. km.

High growth rate rapidly slowing due to impact of AIDS.

Capital Nairobi 2.3 million. Other major city: Mombasa 600,000. **Urbanites** 21%.

PEOPLES
122 ethno-linguistic groups.
Bantu 68.2%. 49 peoples, largest: Kikuyu 6.8mill; Luyia(5) 4m; Kamba 3.9m; Gusii 2.19m; Meru 1.9m; Mijikenda(9) 1.43m; Taita(3) 330,000; Embu 316,000; Kuria 209,000.
Nilotic 26%. 21 peoples, largest: Luo 4.8m; Kipsigis 990,000; Turkana 584,000; Nandi 550,000; Maasai 522,000; Teso 279,000; Tugen 274,000; Pokot 263,000; Elgeyo 233,000; Samburu 170,000; Sabaot 158,000; Marakwet 90,000.
Cushitic 3.2%. 17 peoples, largest: Somali 580,000; Boran(5) 364,000; Oromo(2) 80,000; Rendille(2) 49,000.
Khoisan 0.3%. 12 peoples.
South Asian 0.7%. Mainly Gujarati, Panjabi and Cutchi.
Other 1.6%. British, etc. 90,000; Arab 89,000.

Literacy 78%. **Official languages** English, Swahili. **All languages** 61. **Languages with Scriptures** 16Bi 6NT 9por 17w.i.p.

ECONOMY
Predominantly agricultural, light industries, and a major tourist industry. Post-independence stability aided good growth until 1976. Recession, foreign debt and mismanagement have eroded this. The venal elite has little interest other than in retaining power and amassing wealth. The

RELIGION
There is full freedom of religion and much of the population professes to be Christian — including many in leadership. Islamic extremists in Kenya have supported terrorism and apply intense pressure for constitutional amendments that favour Islam.

Religions	Population %	Adherents	Ann.Gr.
Christian	78.64	23,655,205	+2.0%
Traditional ethnic	11.50	3,459,243	+1.0%
Muslim	8.00	2,406,430	+3.9%
Baha'i	1.10	330,884	+2.0%
Hindu	0.34	102,273	-2.2%
Jain	0.20	60,161	+0.1%
non-Religious/other	0.15	45,121	+10.6%
Sikh	0.07	21,056	-0.7%

There has been no nation-wide analysis of religions or a denominational survey since 1972, so many figures are approximate. Some claim Muslims to be 15%.

Christians	Denom.	Affil.%	,000	Ann.Gr.
Protestant	71	28.66	8,622	+2.2%
Independent	341	22.88	6,882	+2.8%
Anglican	1	8.98	2,700	+5.2%
Catholic	1	22.61	6,800	+1.4%
Orthodox	2	1.94	584	+1.4%
Marginal	13	0.21	64	+2.4%
Unaffiliated		3.77	1,134	n.a.
Doubly affiliated		*-10.41*	*-3,130*	*n.a.*

Churches	MegaBloc	Cong.	Members	Affiliates
Catholic	C	600	3,597,884	6,800,000
Ch of the Prov of K	A	3,600	1,646,341	2,700,000
Africa Inland Ch (AIC)	P	5,435	1,250,000	2,100,000
Presbyterian	P	1,020	800,000	1,600,000
Pentecostal Assemblies	P	4,023	233,333	700,000
Seventh-day Adventist	P	2,135	483,049	700,000
Assemblies of God	P	1,400	380,000	600,000
African Orthodox	O	540	232,000	580,000
African Indep Pente	I	456	228,000	570,000
Baptist Convention	P	2,610	244,400	415,480
Full Gospel	P	2,714	190,000	380,000

Salvation Army	P 1,800	180,000	346,000
Methodist	P 2,000	150,000	230,000
African Brotherhood	I 991	99,099	220,000
Ch of God in East Afr	P 550	124,000	220,000
African Gospel	P 1,214	85,000	160,000
Friends (Quaker)	P 1,833	55,000	110,000
Other denoms [412]	39,664	3,184,000	7,222,000
Doubly affiliated		-1,422,727	-3,130,000
Total Christians [429]	72,585	11.739m	22.523m

Trans-bloc Groupings	**pop.%**	**,000**	**Ann.Gr.**
Evangelical	35.8	10,767	+2.8%
Charismatic	17.1	5,137	+2.6%
Pentecostal	13.6	4,089	+3.1%

Missionaries from Kenya
P,I,A 673 in 53 agencies to 17 countries: Kenya 608, Tanzania 22, Uganda 21. (Statistics are incomplete.)

Missionaries to Kenya
P,I,A 2,274 in 175 agencies from 30 countries: USA 1,332, UK 243, Germany 141, Korea 117, Canada 102.

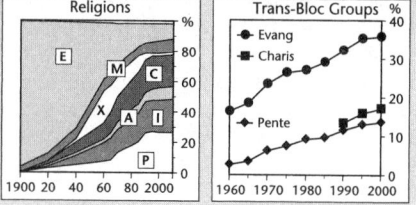

• Answers to Prayer

1 **Kenya's continued key role as a solid base** for Christian ministry to Africa and the world.

2 **Kenya has 36%, or 13 million, Evangelicals** — Africa's second highest percentage and nearly equal to all Evangelicals in Europe.

3 **The growth of a missions vision** in Kenya's churches — an outworking of GCOWE 1997 in South Africa and the 1998 National Consultation in 1998. The latter launched *Finish the Task 2000* for reaching 22 of the country's remaining unreached peoples. All of these 22 were targeted and half were engaged by 2000.

• Challenges for Prayer

1 **Praise God for the great freedom to preach the gospel** since independence, for the receptivity of the people and for the exciting growth of the Church. Over four-fifths of the population claim to be Christian, and Christians are found in every level of society. Pray that Christians may bring truth and moral uplift to the nation as it edges to the brink of political disaster with possible economic collapse and inter-ethnic conflict. Pray also for peaceful change and a democratic government, responsive to the deep needs of the people.

2 **The rising level of human rights abuses,** suppression of dissent, ethnic discrimination, and corruption needs to be challenged. Some Christian leaders have sought to speak out against these, which has led to confrontations with the government. The National Council of Christian Churches and the Evangelical Fellowship of Kenya are internally divided on how to handle these issues. Pray that all Christians in national and church leadership may both live exemplary lives and also speak out as one against wrongs in a society that claims to be largely Christian.

3 **The Protestant and indigenous churches have grown fast,** and the proportion of Evangelicals is high. The East African Revival (1948-1960) made a deep and lasting impression on the Anglican, Presbyterian and Methodist Churches. The fires of revival were quenched by legalism, divisions, materialism and personality clashes. Subsequent growth of evangelical and Pentecostal churches (international and indigenous) has been dramatic. One of the largest is the **Africa Inland Church**, the daughter body birthed out of the large missionary input of **AIM**. Few countries in Africa have been more extensively evangelized.

4 **Rapid growth** has brought its problems:

a) Nominalism has become a major issue, with a large number of nominal Evangelicals too. Nairobi is 80% 'Christian', but only 12% of the population goes to church. Pray for a revival to be given again.

b) Tribalism and tribal customs have caused endless divisions and a multiplicity of independent churches, some theologically orthodox, others little removed from the old ethnic religions. Pray for unity based on biblical truth that transcends culture and personalities.

c) **The lack of trained leaders** for the 70,000 or more Protestant/indigenous congregations gives cause for concern. There are over 60 institutions, with around 2,000 students, where workers are trained for Christian ministry. The Scott Theological College (AIC-**AIM**), St. Paul's United Theological College (Anglican, Presbyterian, Methodist) and Nairobi International School of Theology (NIST-CCCI) are influential institutions. The **Nairobi Evangelical Graduate School of Theology** (with around 100 students from 18 countries), the Pan African Christian College and Daystar University College serve all of Anglophone Africa. There are also numerous TEE programmes. Pray for these, and for lives to be set on fire for God through them. Pray for more graduates to be fully and adequately supported by their congregations — a need in all denominations.

5 **Missions vision** has continued to grow in Kenya's churches. Over 500 Kenyans are serving cross-culturally within Kenya or abroad. Pray for:

a) **The 'Finish the Task 2000' vision** launched in 1998 — that churches may be mobilized and workers called, equipped and sent to the unreached.

b) **The African Centre for Missions** started in 1998 by major denominations, AEA and others, to research and publicize the needs.

c) **Bible schools and seminaries** to make the Great Commission the bedrock on which their teaching is built.

d) **Efforts by the AIC, Anglicans, Baptists** and various indigenous missions to undertake missions outreach.

6 **Foreign missions have had a long and successful involvement in Kenya.** Almost all national ministries are now operating under Kenyan leadership, whether in pioneer outreach, Bible teaching or in service ministries. Many agencies have supportive, global or regional ministries located in Kenya, which partially accounts for the high missionary population. Some major agencies: **AIM** (250 workers), **CCCI** (154), Christian Churches/Chs of Christ (118), **IMB-SBC** (103), **YWAM** (89), **WGM** (85), SDA (73), **SIM** (49), Baptist Bible Fellowship (48), Finnish Lutheran Mission (47), **AoG** (38), **CMS** (35), **PAoC** (34), Norwegian Lutheran Mission (28), **CBI** (23), **IMI** (23), Korean Presbyterian (23+), Finnish Free Mission (21), **BCMS** (12).

7 **Major sectors of the population** needing specialized ministry:

a) **Young people.** Over half the population is under 15. Youth ministries are vital. **SU** has made a deep impact on secondary schools. FOCUS(**IFES**) has lively groups in universities and colleges where over 10% of the 50,000 students are active believers. Pray for the integration of Christian students into local churches; this is not easy, but their contribution is essential. **CEF** has 30 fill-time workers committed to children's ministry.

b) **HIV/AIDS sufferers.** This disease has become a silent disaster most refuse to recognize. Churches shy away from dealing with the desperate moral and social crisis of this national calamity. There were over 730,000 orphans, and 2,100,000 (14% of the population) infected in 2000. Pray that Christians may lead in ministry in this area.

c) **The large numbers of city slum dwellers** — including over 60,000 children living on Nairobi's streets.

d) **Muslims.** Islam has long been more passive and marginalized in Kenya than elsewhere in Africa, but this is changing. The coast and NW have been Muslim for centuries, but now Muslims are being more active in education, mosque-building and giving rewards for conversions of Christians. Pray for those seeking to witness to them.

8 **Less evangelized peoples** — about 9% of Kenya's population belongs to peoples only marginally impacted by the gospel. Both Kenya's churches and expatriate agencies are seeking to adopt and enter nearly all of these peoples. Pray for:

a) **The largely pastoralist animistic peoples of the north and west** who have begun to respond to the gospel — the Turkana (13% Christian), Sabaot (2%), Pokot (9%), Rendille (3%), Samburu (9%), Daasenach (0.1%), through the ministry of AIC/**AIM**, Anglicans and many others. Give praise for this and pray for the establishment of well-led, culturally appropriate churches. The well-known Maasai are now over 20% Christian.

b) **The largely Muslim Oromo-related peoples** of the northeast — the Borana and related Gabbra and Njemps (Chamus), also the Garreh-Ajuran Oromo, Orma, Malakote and Munyoyaya. Only among the Njemps (12 congregations) and the Borana are there churches (42 congregations and 6,000 Christians). Among them also live the Boni,

Dahalo, Sanye and Dorobo who are descended from the Khoisan (Bushmen) and are small, largely hunter-gatherer peoples. There are very few Christians among these nominally Muslim peoples.

c) *The nine Mijikenda peoples of the coastal hills*. The beliefs of the Giriama, Duruma, Chonyi and Pokomo are mixed traditional and Muslim, but they also have a large minority of Christians. The Digo, Segeju, Upper Pokomo and Bajun are more strongly Muslim and Christians are few. Pray for those seeking to reach them.

d) *The coastal Swahili and Arab population* which is strongly Muslim. Most are unreached, but Southern Baptist missionaries have seen church multiplication in the largely Muslim city of Mombasa, with over 10,000 baptisms since 1985, many of them from a Muslim background.

e) *The Somali in the northeast and cities*. The five clans of Somalis are all Muslim. A number of Christian workers (AIC/**AIM**), **SIM**, **CBIM**, Baptists, Sheepfold Ministries and Mennonites) are reaching these people and there is a steady trickle of new Christians. There are three small groups and less than 100 believers.

f) *The Asian community* is Muslim, Hindu, Jain, Parsee and Sikh. Their main languages are Cutchi, Gujarati and Panjabi. They are prominent in trading and private industries, but feel insecure and threatened as scapegoats in Kenya's declining economy. Some have become Christians through the ministry of **IMI** and Sheepfold Ministries. There are now 7 or more congregations, Fellowship Bible Church is one of the strongest. ASCKEN is a partnership of Asian, African and international ministries seeking to reach all of East Africa's Asian population.

9 **Bibles and Bible translation.** Most languages have part of God's Word, and 12 indigenous languages have the whole Bible. Pray for:

a) *The valued catalytic ministry of the Bible Society* (**UBS**) in translation, revision, publishing and distributing the Scriptures.

b) *SIL* with 129 workers, together with the related but indigenous BTL have 13 active language projects. **SIL** also serves many churches and agencies in all of East Africa.

c) *Living Bibles International*, which has translation projects in seven of Kenya's languages.

10 **Supportive Ministries:**

a) *Aid programmes* through many agencies such as **TEAR Fund**, **WVI**, etc., have played a significant part in opening the way for the gospel in arid and famine-stricken areas. Pray for those involved in a hard and difficult ministry.

b) *MAF*, with 76 workers, has a well-developed ministry, flying to many parts of East Africa and northeast Congo from their base in Nairobi. Without this ministry, much Christian work would come to a halt. **AIM-Air** also has an extensive flying programme in the region.

c) *GRN* has recordings available in 174 languages.

d) *The JESUS film* has been widely shown and in 2000 was in circulation in 20 languages with a further 16 in the process of being done.

e) *Christian radio*. There are many Christian programmes aired on the national radio and TV networks, and a Christian radio station may be established. **FEBA**-Seychelles broadcasts ten hours/week in Swahili and has an estimated audience of 650,000. **TWR**-Swaziland has a further 9 hours in Swahili and 20 hours in English. Both **FEBA** and **TWR** have studios and offices in Nairobi.

11 **Nairobi is a key hub for ministry in Africa and beyond.** Many international Christian organizations have their continental offices based there. The Ecumenical AACC (All Africa Conference of Churches), the **AEA** (Association of Evangelicals of Africa) and PACLA are a few of these. **AEA** has played a key role in promoting evangelical unity and ministries in theology, training, literature and fellowship. Pray for this work and its extension through Africa.

Kiribati
Republic of Kiribati

JULY 18
PACIFIC

K

 GEOGRAPHY
Area 849 sq.km. Three archipelagos — Gilbert, Rawaki (Phoenix) and Line, with 33 coral atolls scattered across 2,000,000 sq.km of the Pacific Ocean and 4,600 km from east to west.

Population	Ann.Gr.	Density
2000	83,387	+1.43%	98 per sq. km.
2010	96,191	+1.44%	113 per sq. km.
2025	119,324	+1.45%	141 per sq. km.

Capital Bairiki 2,500. **Urbanites** 36%.

PEOPLES
Indigenous 98.9%. I-Kiribati 81,000; Euro-Polynesian 1,300.
Other 1.1%. Tuvaluan 400, European 200.

Literacy 90%. **Official languages** Kiribati, English. **All languages** 2. **Languages with Scripture** 2Bi.

ECONOMY
Dependent on copra, fish and remittances sent from I-Kiribati abroad. Subsistence economy, with living standards well below that of other island states. The lack of commercial viability and large distances between islands make improvements difficult to achieve. **Public debt** 24% of GNP. **Income/person** $920 (2.9% of USA).

POLITICS
Independent from Britain in 1979 as a democratic republic.

RELIGION
Freedom of religion.

Religions	Population %	Adherents	Ann.Gr.
Christian	94.40	78,717	+1.4%
Baha'i	5.20	4,336	+2.2%
non-Religious/other	0.40	334	+7.5%

Christians	Denom.	Affil.%	,000	Ann.Gr.
Protestant	5	39.60	33	+0.5%
Independent	2	1.01	1	+4.8%
Anglican	1	0.18	0	+0.0%
Catholic	1	50.37	42	-0.2%
Marginal	2	8.69	7	+7.6%
Unaffiliated		1.75	1	n.a.
Doubly affiliated		-7.20	-6	n.a.

Churches	MegaBloc	Cong.	Members	Affiliates
Catholic	C	23	22,700	42,000
Kiribati Protestant	P	131	10,000	28,000
Latter-day Saints (Morm)	M	20	4,192	7,000
Ch of God (Cleveland)	P	25	1,366	2,100
Seventh-day Adventist	P	16	1,124	1,900
Assemblies of God	P	11	200	950
Other denoms [5]		9	727	1,310
Doubly affiliated			-3,000	-6,000
Total Christians [11]		235	37,000	77,000

Trans-bloc Groupings	pop.%	,000	Ann.Gr.
Evangelical	7.0	6	+7.3%
Charismatic	7.0	6	+7.6%
Pentecostal	4.4	4	+12.2%

Missionaries from Kiribati
n.a.

Missionaries to Kiribati
P,I,A 6 in 3 agencies.

• Challenges for Prayer

1 The once strong Congregational Church (Kiribati Protestant) is losing members and pastors to other Protestant groups and also to Catholics, Baha'i and Mormons. The theological college in Tarawa is not evangelical. Pray for a return to biblical preaching and for New Testament Christianity to counteract nominalism and the underlying power of the occult.

2 Evangelical Christians are steadily growing in numbers — largely through the witness of the Church of God with rapidly growing congregations, 33 pastors and a Bible School with 79 students in 1992. The AoG also has a growing presence. Pray that every island may have a clear, resident gospel witness.

3 The more needy:
a) I-Kiribati migrate for work on Nauru and as seamen on foreign ships. Many return home with AIDS and with drug problems.
b) Migrant communities moving eastwards to populate the isolated Line and Phoenix Islands.

Korea, North

Democratic People's Republic of Korea

Russia
China
North Korea
Pyongyang
Sea of Japan
South Korea
Yellow Sea
Japan

JULY 18

ASIA

North Korea invaded the South in 1950 and war dragged on until 1953. The large North Korean armed forces continue to threaten a second invasion. The fortified border between the Koreas is one of the most impenetrable in the world. One of the most repressive regimes in the world, completely dedicated to cultivating their interpretation of Stalinist ideology. Hope for reunification of the Koreas ebbs and flows with political developments — spirits are higher since the 2000 summit.

RELIGION
All religions have been harshly repressed. Many thousands of Christians have been murdered since the Korean War — in 1953 there were about 300,000 Christians, reduced to a few thousand today. The true number of Christians is of course unknown, so the figures given are estimates. **Persecution index** 16th in the world.

Religions	Population %	Adherents	Ann.Gr.
non-Religious	64.31	15,460,000	+0.9%
Traditional ethnic	16.00	3,846,000	+1.8%
Chondogyo	13.50	3,245,000	+1.3%
Buddhist	4.50	1,082,000	+10.1%
Christian	1.69	406,000	+11.3%

Christians	Denom.	Affil.%	,000	Ann.Gr.
Protestant	1	0.06	15	+2.1%
Independent	n.a.	1.46	350	+14.2%
Catholic	1	0.17	40	-2.3%

Churches	MegaBloc	Cong.	Members	Affiliates
Secret believers	I		5,000	280,000	350,000
Catholic Association	C	1	27,972	40,000
Korean Christian Fed	P	2	12,000	15,000
Total Christians		5,003	319,972	405,000

Trans-bloc Groupings	pop.%	,000	Ann.Gr.
Evangelical	1.5	355	+14.0%
Charismatic	0.6	140	+14.2%

GEOGRAPHY
Area 122,370 sq.km. The larger part of the Korean peninsula, but climate more rigorous than in the south.

Population	Ann.Gr.	Density
2000	24,039,193	+1.57%	196 per sq. km.
2010	26,451,118	+0.78%	216 per sq. km.
2025	29,387,635	+0.71%	240 per sq. km.

Capital Pyongyang 3,450,000. **Urbanites** 61%.

PEOPLES
Korean 99.3%.
Chinese 0.7%.

Literacy 99%. **Language** Korean. **Languages with Scriptures** 1Bi.

ECONOMY
Heavily industrialized, this centralized socialist economy is in freefall due to the heavy costs of militarization, attempts to become a nuclear power and the ending of aid from China and the former USSR. Huge black market. Increasingly severe famine has gripped the country for years, with no end in sight. **Public debt** 49.4% of GNP. **Income/person** $970 (2.8% of USA).

POLITICS
Occupied by Japan 1910-45. On Russian insistence, Korea was partitioned after World War II. A Communist regime was installed in 1948.

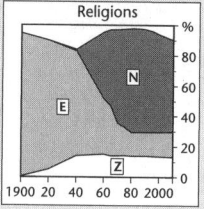

Religions
%
80
60
40
20
0
N
E
Z
1900 20 40 60 80 2000

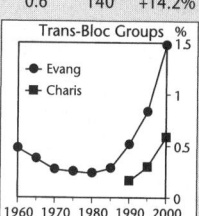

Trans-Bloc Groups %
1.5
Evang
Charis
1
0.5
0
1960 1970 1980 1990 2000

K

• Challenges for Prayer

1 **The leader of North Korea has deified his deceased father** Kim Il Sung by adulatory propaganda, erection of statues and government enforced policies. Pray that the Holy Spirit might convict him and his cadre to cease their idolatry and worship the true God.

2 **The Church in North Korea was the birthplace of Korean revival —** Pyongyang was known as the "Jerusalem of the East". But most Christians fled to the south during the Korean War or were martyred, and churches were bulldozed. Little is known about today's underground church; only that it has survived amidst great suffering. There are three propaganda 'show' churches in the capital, but over 100,000 Christians are interned in labour camps. Pray for physical and spiritual safety for North Korean believers, that they hang on to their Saviour in what is possibly the most difficult country to be a Christian.

3 **The majority have never heard the name of Jesus.** The knowledge of God has been obliterated for most by an Orwellian nightmare of repression, demands for total conformity, and isolation from the outside world. Pray that the God-shaped hole may be filled within the long-suffering Korean people. The turning to God could be dramatic when the state collapses.

4 **As many as 3 million died of starvation from 1994-2000**, yet the government stockpiles rations for the military and refuses assistance on any but the strictest of terms. Floods caused by deforestation continue to devastate crops and reports of cannibalism are leaking out of the country. Some Christian agencies have been able to offer aid, but never with permission to share the gospel. Pray for aid to reach the needy population, and for wisdom on the part of foreign governments and NGOs in handling this tragic and delicate situation.

5 Present means of witness are limited:

a) ***Radio.*** Many South Korean Christian broadcasts as well as those of **TWR**-Guam and **FEBC**-South Korea (19 programmes) reach far into North Korea, but most radios are pre-tuned to government stations, and few can hear these gospel broadcasts.

b) ***Korean Christians from China and elsewhere*** who are able to visit and gain opportunities to witness. Korea is open to Chinese businessmen, and their easy access to the country could be strategic for the gospel.

c) ***South Korean Christians who have prayed and prepared*** for years for the time when the land opens for the gospel. Pray that this may soon happen.

d) ***A group of foreign NGOs has received permission*** to establish an independent church in an area where they run agricultural training programmes.

6 **Over 100,000 North Koreans have fled to China in the last three years.** There are about 200,000 ethnic Korean Christians living in Chinese provinces which share a border with Korea. Many try to shelter the escapees and share the gospel with them in hidden "Bethlehem Centres" but Chinese are punished severely if caught harbouring escapees, and any Koreans who are sent back face almost certain death. Despite this, converted Korean escapees often return to be a witness to Jesus at extreme risk to their own lives. Pray that the Lord might protect both the sheltering hosts and the escapees from harm, and use them to reap a great harvest among these disillusioned and desperate people.

Korea, South

Republic of Korea

JULY 19-20
ASIA

GEOGRAPHY
Area 99,067 sq.km. Southern half of Korean peninsula. Forested mountain ranges; 22% arable.

Population		Ann.Gr.	Density
2000	46,843,989	+0.83%	473 per sq. km.
2010	49,975,564	+0.58%	504 per sq. km.
2025	52,532,789	+0.25%	530 per sq. km.

Capital Seoul 10,400,000. Other major cities: Pusan 3.9 mill.; Inchon 2.9m; Taegu 2.65m; Taejon 1.48m; Kwangju 1.38m; Ulsan 1.15m. **Urbanites** 85%.

PEOPLES
One of the world's most homogeneous nations.
Korean 99.8%. An ancient and cultured nation.
Other 0.2%. Chinese 100,000; US Military. Illegal migrant workers may be 250,000.
Literacy 100%. **Official language** Korean.

ECONOMY
Few natural resources. Rapid industrialization since 1953 has transformed the poor, devastated nation into the 11th largest economy in the world. A wide range of sophisticated, export-oriented industries. The Asian financial crisis of 1997-99 exposed the weaknesses in the banking

system and the *chaebol* conglomerate companies. Some restructuring and improvements were made, but these may prove inadequate in the long-term. **HDI** 0.852; 30th/174. **Public debt** 8% of GNP. **Income/person** $10,550 (34% of USA).

POLITICS

A 2,000-year history of frequent invasions and interference from surrounding nations. The Japanese occupation (1910-1945), the Russian-engineered division of Korea (1945-48) and the devastating Korean War (1950-53) have moulded the attitudes and politics of Koreans. Strong military-civilian governments held power from 1950 until 1988, when public unrest led to constitutional change and a more open multi-party democracy. The first civilian president in 32 years was elected in 1992. Economic disasters and political shenanigans in North Korea make some form of reunification inevitable.

RELIGION

There is complete religious freedom. The distinction between religious beliefs and unbelief is imprecise, so there are widely varying published figures.

Religions	Population %	Adherents	Ann.Gr.
non-Religious	35.02	16,404,765	+0.4%
Christian	31.67	14,835,500	+1.9%
Buddhist	23.89	11,191,029	+1.0%
Indigenous religions	8.00	3,747,519	-1.5%
Other	0.80	374,752	+1.1%
Chinese	0.47	220,167	+0.8%
Baha'i	0.08	37,475	+3.6%
Muslim	0.07	32,791	+4.0%

Christians	Denom.	Affil.%	,000	Ann.Gr.
Protestant	151	36.19	16,954	+4.5%
Independent	18	1.15	539	+3.8%
Anglican	1	0.16	75	+4.6%
Catholic	1	8.12	3,805	+2.1%
Marginal	59	3.75	1,757	+1.0%
Doubly affiliated		*-17.70*	*-8,291*	*n.a.*

The large number of doubly affiliated is due to widespread dual membership, denominational divisions and unrecorded transferral of membership, especially within Protestant and Independent bodies.

Churches	MegaBloc	Cong.	Members	Affiliates
Catholic	C	980	2,125,665	3,804,940
Presby.- HapDong	P	6,494	918,306	2,295,766
Presby.- TongHap	P	6,270	1,103,983	2,207,966
Korean Methodist [4]	P	4,752	656,486	1,365,490
Korea Assembly of God	P	1,178	513,953	1,130,696

Pres.- HapDong BoSu [4]	P	3,172	630,000	1,097,000
Korean Baptist Conv	P	2,245	270,000	650,000
Presb.- HapDong JeongTong	P	1,695	183,482	610,818
Jesus Korean Holiness	P	953	193,373	505,946
Korea Evangelical (I)	P	2,041	400,000	501,793
Presby.- KoShin	P	1,416	176,832	442,080
Unification (Moonies)	M	407	132,132	440,000
Presby.- YeJang	P	425	185,000	345,325
Presby.- KiJang	P	1,448	141,750	321,773
Jesus Assemb of God	I	270	120,836	302,090
Seventh-day Adventist	P	628	147,080	190,000
Presby.- YeJang Hap Bo	P	293	109,700	187,500
Presby.- HoHun [3]	P	976	145,000	182,000
Jehovah's Witnesses	M	1,502	87,179	130,000
Latter-day Saints (Morm)	M	150	47,170	75,000
Episcopal	A	88	15,000	75,000
Jesus Korean Meth.	P	330	26,224	75,000
Gospel Baptist Conv	P	155	37,500	75,000
Full Gosp Intl Gen Mtg	P	95	30,000	75,000
Ch of the Nazarene	P	210	40,000	55,000
Ch of God (Clev)	P	117	20,601	36,000
Korea Evangelical (II)	I	35	4,505	10,000
Other denoms [196]		17,496	2,896,000	5,429,000
Doubly affiliated			*-4,000,000*	*-8,291,000*
Total Christians [231]		55,822	7.359m	14.839m

Trans-bloc Groupings	pop.%	,000	Ann.Gr.
Evangelical	15.5	7,269	+3.9%
Charismatic	3.4	1,596	-1.3%
Pentecostal	3.7	1,742	+0.2%

Missionaries from South Korea
P,I,A an est'd 12,000 in 166 agencies of which an est'd 10,646 are serving in 156 other countries: Japan 546, Philippines 528, Russia 316.

Note: The KWMC estimated 8,206 missionaries in 2000, but many Korean missionaries serve in missions not part of that survey. There are also many Korean missionaries sent by denominational agencies but serving with international agencies, resulting in duplication.

Missionaries to South Korea
P,I,A 411 in 46 agencies from 12 countries: USA 373. **C** 900.

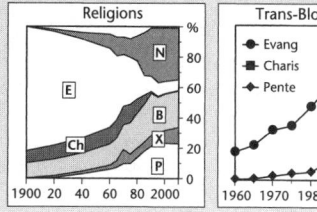

K

• Answers to Prayer

1 **Praise God for the unique Korean Church.** It was founded on sound indigenous principles, blessed with a succession of revivals, refined by persecution and is now one of the foremost in the world for missions vision. Its presence is highly visible; every level of society has been impacted and growth has been remarkable. Korea could become the first majority Protestant/evangelical country in Asia.

2 **Passionate Korean praying and commitment** has made possible these superlatives:

a) *The first Protestant church was planted in 1884.* By 1984 there were over 30,000 churches, and by 2000 over 60,000.

b) *Of the 11 largest mega-congregations in the world,* 10 are in the one city of Seoul. Here also are the largest Pentecostal, Presbyterian and Methodist congregations in the world and the second-largest Baptist.

c) *The world's largest theological colleges,* Christian baptismal services since Pentecost, and some of the largest evangelistic and Christian gatherings in history.

3 **Korean missionary numbers** have rapidly increased. The goal of 10,000 missionaries serving in other lands by 2000 was almost achieved. Korea has now 10,646 — the second-highest number of serving missionaries and only exceeded by the USA.

• Challenges for Prayer

1 **The Asian recession of 1997** with its reverberations in politics, industry, the economy and the churches was a severe shock. Materialism and pride were punctured, and though there has been some recovery, the needed restructuring and democratic checks and balances have not gone far enough. Pray that the country's political, industrial and religious leaders may face up to the need, and courageously tackle the changes needed. During the crisis many churches humbled themselves before God in repentance and revived earnestness.

2 **The looming crisis of possible economic and political disaster in North Korea** will have an enormous impact on the South. Pray that political and Christian leaders may be ready for it and make wise decisions that will be best for the healing of all Korea.

3 **The Korean Church grew strong** through early morning prayer meetings, prayer mountains for seeking God, church-based Bible study, evangelism programmes, fellowship in home meetings and at Sunday meals. Pray that this heritage may not be lost, and that revival might be rekindled.

4 **The Korean Church has major spiritual challenges** to both admit and address if its credibility before the world and effectiveness in ministry is to be restored:

a) *Spiritual pride.* There has long been a widespread belief that success and prosperity are an indication of God's blessing. There is often a pride in statistical growth, impressive organization and buildings, with exaggerated claims made. It is a temptation for leaders to seek success, wealth and degrees more than lifting up the Cross.

b) *Division.* Nearly every denomination has suffered major schisms. There was one Presbyterian denomination at the end of the Japanese occupation, but there are now nearly 100. Strong denominationalism, domineering leadership patterns and personality clashes have been at the root of this and accentuated doctrinal, ecumenical and regional disagreements. Some are actively working to remedy this. Pray for humility, reconciliation and a new spirit of cooperation to be evident in every part of the Church.

c) *Patterns of leadership.* Leadership is often too authoritarian. The high status of pastors hinders a biblical servant leadership and promotes division, formality, legalism and a stifling of expectation of personal guidance from God for 'ordinary' Christians.

d) *Inadequate discipling.* A significant number of Christians come from a background steeped in Buddhist concepts and structured by Confucian ethics. The Spirit and the Word must bring them into the full liberty of grace in the gospel.

e) *Neglect of ethical teaching* has meant little application of biblical truth to social issues. Christians have often condoned low ethical standards, bribery and corrupt practices and have neglected social wrongs. Catholics have taken a stronger stance on these and often gained more credibility than Protestants.

5 **Theological training in Korea is unique.** In no other country of the world where there is a large, growing Church is there such a surfeit of people trained for pastoral work. There are possibly 280 theological institutions in Korea. In the top accredited Presbyterian seminaries are over 16,000 students. Right across the English-speaking world are thousands more Koreans studying for Christian ministry. For many who graduate there are few openings in desirable city congregations — yet the poorer rural congregations have many! Pray that the best of these men and women may humbly commit themselves to less prominent rural pastorates and bless the world through cross-cultural missions.

6 **Young people** are more world-conscious than ever before. Pray for:

a) *University students*, who number over 2.5 million on 994 campuses. Many are involved in 15 Christian student organizations such as **CCCI** (845 staff on 90 campuses), Navigators (with over 120 staff) and Universities Bible Fellowship (UBF) with 10-20,000 students involved. Also of significance are IVCF(**IFES**) with 89 staff, Joy Mission, **YWAM**, ESF, SFC — each with 1-5,000 students involved.

b) *SU* which has a vital role to play in producing Bible study materials. Pray that young people may find the delight of personal Bible study.

c) *CEF* which has 120 workers committed to children's ministry.

7 **The missions vision of the Korean Church** has grown rapidly and matured. An increasing number of cross-cultural missionaries is being sent all over the world by over 160 Korean and international agencies (sometimes in both!). The larger Korean agencies are: UBF (751), HapDong Presbyterian (730), TongHap Presbyterian (492), Methodist (447), Holiness (290), GMF (266), Baptist (214), **CCCI** (193), KoSin Presbyterian (186), KaeHyuk Presbyterian (181), Full Gospel Mission Association (177), Tyrannus Mission (145), Korea Harbor Mission (122), and Paul Mission (89). There are also large contingents in international agencies such as: **YWAM** (658), **OM** (212), **OMF** (74), **WEC** (67) and **WBT** (52).

a) *Mobilization of young people for missions* has gained momentum. *Mission Korea* is a large biennial nation-wide mission movement of various agencies (IVCF[**IFES**], Joy Mission, **YWAM**, GMF, GP, **OMF** and others). Thousands of young people have been recruited for short-term involvement by UBF, **CCC**, **OM**, **YWAM**, Joy Mission, etc. Pray that these young people may be at the forefront of missions — either in going or in supporting those who go.

b) *Preparation and orientation for missions have developed fast*. Many institutions have been founded. To mention a few: The Centre for World Mission (Presbyterian Tong-Hap), Global Missionary Training Center, Kosin MTI, the Missionary Training Institute (Presbyterian HapDong), the Global Professionals' Training Institute (for tentmakers). Pray for effective preparation for Korean missionary trainees.

c) *Cultural adaptation* is hard for Koreans who come from a mono-cultural and mono-lingual nation. The enthusiasm and rugged dynamism of Koreans are valuable assets in pressing through to fruitfulness.

d) *Korean missionaries* serving overseas need prayer — for their adaptation to other missions and missionaries, for effective cooperation, for pastoral care and for adequate education for their children.

8 **The less-evangelized sections of the population** which need special approaches in ministry:

a) *Shamanism* is resurgent, though few openly claim to be followers of this ancient Korean religion. There are about 600,000 shamanist practitioners — mainly women.

b) *Buddhists* are probably over a quarter of the population. There are a number of indigenous religions such as Chondokyo (one million followers) and pseudo-Christian sects with Buddhist/shamanist ideas (1-2 million followers).

c) *Korean Muslims*. These are growing in number as a result of Islamic missionary efforts among Koreans working in Saudi Arabia. There are about 40,000 Korean Muslims and 60% of them live in Seoul. A Korean Islamic University is being planned. There is no specific outreach to them, and also a lack of knowledge of how to reach them.

d) *The Chinese*. There were 7 congregations with 800 members in 2000. They were then 1.4% Protestant.

e) *The 250,000+ illegal migrants* — often working in appalling conditions and for long hours.

9 **The Korean Diaspora.** Emigration and extensive business interests have multiplied Korean communities around the world. In nearly all, thriving churches have sprung up (over 3,000 in USA alone), and they too are becoming a major factor for sending missionaries.

10 **Missions in Korea** have a valuable servant role in giving fresh perspective to biblical teaching, personal holiness and student work. A number of mission agencies have made a major impact in church planting, including **SBC** (79 workers), several Presbyterian agencies (25), Baptist Bible Fellowship (19), SdA (19) and **OMS** (8). **OMF** loans workers to minister within established churches. **OMS** missionaries planted the largest denomination in Asia originating from a faith mission.

11 **Christian literature** plays a vital role. The Bible in Korean has gone through several translations and has become a treasured part of the culture. The very active Korean Bible Society has a national and global ministry of Bible printing — making Korea one of the world's major Bible production centres — printing 4.7 million Bibles/NTs for 103 countries as well as 4 million Korean Bibles/NTs in 1995. The range of theological and devotional books is rapidly increasing, and there are many Christian bookstores including Tyrannus Press, Word of Life Press (**TEAM**), Voice (**CMA**) and **CLC** (with 12 stores) and various publishers (IVCF[**IFES**], MB, Torch and **CLC** with 400 titles published). Pray that this ministry may help to form a strong, Bible-literate Church.

Kuwait

State of Kuwait

JULY 21

ASIA

Updated January 2004

GEOGRAPHY
Area 17,818 sq.km. An oil-rich wedge of desert between Iraq and Saudi Arabia at the northwest end of the Arabian Gulf.

Population		Ann.Gr.	Density
2000	1,971,634	+3.14%	111 per sq. km.
2010	2,419,713	+1.85%	136 per sq. km.
2025	2,974,454	+1.12%	167 per sq. km.

The fluctuating expatriate community dramatically affects the size and composition of the population.

Capital Kuwait 1,300,000. **Urbanites** 97%.

PEOPLES

Arab 68%.
Kuwaiti 37%.
Foreign Arab 24.6% (Egyptian, Syrian, Lebanese, Palestinian).
Bidoun 6.4%. Stateless Arab refugees.
Non-Arab 32%. Filipino, Pakistani, Indian (incl. Malayali 132,000), Iranian, Western, several others.

Literacy 79%. **Official language** Arabic. **All languages** 3. **Languages with Scriptures** 1Bi 1por 1w.i.p.

ECONOMY
The massive capital and petroleum reserves of this oil rich state were seriously damaged by the Iraqi invasion and Gulf War in

1990-91, but due to generous aid/loans, the oil is again being pumped out to the permitted OPEC limits. Warning signs: the budget deficit is ballooning, and 83% of the workforce is foreign. **HDI** 0.833; 35th/174. **Public debt** n/a. **Income/person** $20,470 (65% of USA).

POLITICS
Former British protectorate; became independent in 1961. Constitutional monarchy, but with the Amir and his family exercising quasi-autocratic control. Stuttering democratic progress since 1986. The 1990s were marked by politicized xenophobia due to the Iraqi invasion, suspicions of Kuwaiti-based Iraqi collaborators, and increasing Islamist agitation. Kuwait became a key base for the US-led invasion of Iraq in 2003.

RELIGION
Sunni Islam is the state religion with a large Shi'a minority. Immigrant religious minorities are permitted some worship facilities. Diverse Christian community in a relatively liberal Islamic regime. Proselytizing Muslims is forbidden. **Persecution index** 20th in the world.

Religions	Population %	Adherents	Ann.Gr.
Muslim	87.43	1,723,800	+2.7%
Christian	8.17	161,082	+8.7%
Hindu	2.50	49,291	+5.8%
non-Religious/other	1.10	21,688	-3.1%
Baha'i	0.50	9,858	+14.2%
Buddhist	0.30	5,915	-2.6%

Christians	Denom.	Affil.%	,000	Ann.Gr.
Protestant	30	0.46	9	+12.5%
Independent	15	0.25	5	+14.9%
Anglican	1	0.01	0	+0.0%
Catholic	2	3.91	77	+8.1%
Orthodox	5	3.54	70	+10.9%

Churches	MegaBloc	Cong.	Members	Affiliates
Catholic	C	8	46,584	75,000
Coptic Orthodox	O	6	31,579	60,000
National Evang [15]	P	3	1,250	5,000
Independent [15]	I	28	2,778	5,000
Armenian Apostolic	O	1	2,564	4,000
Greek Orthodox	O	1	2,244	3,500
Syrian Orthodox	O	2	1,366	2,200
Mar Thoma Syrian	P	2	1,242	2,000

K

					Trans-bloc Groupings	pop.%	,000	Ann.Gr.
Melkite Greek Catholic	C	1	1,111	2,000	Evangelical	0.6	12	+13.6%
Pentecostal Churches	P	6	974	1,500	Charismatic	0.5	10	+12.1%
Other denoms [16]		11	689	1,231	Pentecostal	0.2	4	+13.1%
Total Christians [54]		69	92,381	161,431				

• Challenges for Prayer

1 **Since the Iraqi occupation, Kuwait has returned to stability and affluence.** Materialism is rampant and public morals declining, but restrictions on Christianity still remain. Pray that the Kuwaiti leaders and people might become open to the Christian faith and not merely to godless Western values. Only a few hundred Kuwaitis are known to be believers.

2 **Expatriate ethnic minorities.** The Kuwaitis grudgingly accept foreigners to do most of their work for them. Few expatriates are permanent residents — most are on short-term work contracts, and many have to leave their families in their homeland. Possibly more than a million people are in Kuwait on this basis, despite the widespread poor treatment of the foreign labour force.

a) *The Palestinians and, to a lesser degree, the Egyptians*, have a history of exemplary service in Kuwait, yet were discriminated against by those who see them as collaborators with Saddam Hussein during the Gulf War. Most of the Christians among them are nominal. Pray that their low spiritual standards and poor treatment at the government's hands may be nullified by a work of the Holy Spirit, and that true believers may find many opportunities to share their faith in a meaningful way.

b) *Asians* are predominantly from South Asia and the Philippines, and are largely contract labourers or domestic servants. Increasing numbers live and work in difficult circumstances with incidents of violence and rape perpetrated upon the women. Pray for God's grace upon both the believers and the unsaved in these ethnic minorities.

c) *Middle Easterners*. Most of the several ethnic groups represented are unreached, particularly the Iranians and the *Bidoun*, stateless Arabs adrift in the Middle East. Ask the Lord to shine His light of salvation upon them.

Islamic sources claimed in 2003 that in one week 22 US citizens were converted to Islam, in one year 2,450 Europeans and since 1977, 22,000 foreigners have done the same.

3 **Expatriate Christians** gained recognition for their prayer and relief aid during and after the Iraqi occupation. There are eight sites where churches publicly meet in Kuwait, two of which are Catholic. The National Evangelical Church has become an umbrella for 35 Christian communities, which meet on a former hospital compound. The majority of these are Indian, with some Arab. Main services are held in English, Arabic, Urdu and Malayali. Pray that believers may be granted full freedom of worship and witness and that their lives might commend the Lord Jesus as Saviour.

4 **Many Kuwaitis travel to other lands** as tourists, businessmen, and students, and a number have come to know Christ. Fear of reprisal often prevents them from returning home. Pray for wisdom and boldness for the converts, and a burden to reach their own people.

5 **Christian literature** is a strategic ministry to Kuwait. The **UBS**, a private book importer and the Catholic-run Bible Resource Centre all contribute to making the Scriptures available to all in Kuwait. They primarily serve the various Christian communities in Kuwait, but sales are remarkably high for such a small group!

6 **Christian media** are important means of communicating the gospel in the restrictive situation in Kuwait. Pray for:

a) *Radio broadcasts* — with coverage by **FEBA**-Seychelles (21 hrs/wk) and **TWR**-Cyprus (10 hrs/wk). Pray for a wide audience and a lasting response.

b) *Christian video and cassette tape ministries* — for effective distribution and follow-through. The *JESUS* film on video has been widely and quietly disseminated.

c) *Satellite broadcasting* is a potent means for Christian programming, but relevant and meaningful Arabic programmes are few. **SAT-7** and The Bible Channel are making an impact.

Kyrgyzstan
Kyrgyz Republic

Kazakhstan
Bishkek
Kyrgyzstan
Uzbekistan
Tajikistan
China
Afghanistan

JULY 22
ASIA

GEOGRAPHY
Area 198,500 sq.km. Central Asian state in Tien Shan mountain range bordering on China, Kazakhstan, Tajikistan and Uzbekistan.

Population	Ann.Gr.	Density
2000	4,699,337	+0.55%	24 per sq. km.
2010	5,188,282	+1.09%	26 per sq. km.
2025	6,096,197	+1.11%	31 per sq. km.

Capital Bishkek 950,000. Other major city: Osh 600,000. **Urbanites** 35%.

PEOPLES
Over 80 ethnic groups from all over the fSU.
Turkic/Altaic 78.4%. Kyrgyz 3.6 mill.; Uzbek 676,000; Tatar 60,000; Uighur 55,000; Kazakh 42,000.
Indo-European 18.6%.
Slav 16%. Decrease from 24.3% in 1989 through emigration. Russian 660,000; Ukrainian 80,000.
Other 2.6%. Tajik 45,000; German 40,000; Kurd 15,000.
Other 3%. Dungan (Chinese Muslim) 40,000; Korean 20,000; Jews 6,000.

Literacy 97%. **Official languages** Kyrgyz, Russian. **All languages** 3. **Languages with Scriptures** 1Bi 1NT.

ECONOMY
Poorest and smallest of the Central Asian Republics of the fSU. Great potential for mining of minerals, hydro-electricity, dairy products, vegetables, and for tourism. The collapse of the fSU transportation and marketing structures has hindered development, as has criminal control of trade and businesses. The economy contracted by 50% between 1990 and 1995, but there has since been marginal improvement. **HDI** 0.702; 97th/174. **Public debt** 33% of GNP. **Income/person** $480 (1.5% of USA).

POLITICS
Independent of Russia in 1991. President Askar Akaev instituted free market reforms

and a measure of democracy. Economic hardships, criminal control of the economy and attempted invasions by Islamic militants from Tajikistan into the Fergana Valley in the south has led to some limitations of democratic freedoms in 1999.

RELIGION
A secular state with a high degree of religious freedom despite Muslim and Orthodox pressures to restrict this. Islamism is perceived by the government to be a threat. **Persecution index** 83rd in the world.

Religions	Population %	Adherents	Ann.Gr.
Muslim	78.08	3,669,242	+1.1%
non-Religious	13.60	639,110	-1.6%
Christian	7.83	367,958	-1.3%
Buddhist	0.35	16,448	+3.7%
Jewish	0.12	5,639	-1.0%
Baha'i	0.02	940	+15.5%

Christians	Denom.	Affil.%	,000	Ann.Gr.
Protestant	26	0.48	23	+6.2%
Independent	13	0.50	24	+7.2%
Catholic	1	0.26	12	-4.4%
Orthodox	3	5.34	251	-2.5%
Marginal	1	0.05	3	+11.8%
Unaffiliated		1.20	56	n.a.

Churches	MegaBloc	Cong.	Members	Affiliates
Russian Orthodox	O	40	162,338	250,000
Catholic	C	3	8,392	12,000
Ch of Jesus Christ	I	18	5,000	9,000
Baptist [5]	P	50	3,800	6,500
Pentecostal	P	25	3,000	5,500
Jehovah's Witnesses	M	35	1,400	2,520
Other Protestant [4]	P	25	1,250	2,500
Other Independent [8]	I	20	1,200	2,040
Lutheran	P	18	1,300	1,950
Presbyterian [3]	P	6	650	700
Other denoms [18]		58	10,862	19,000
Total Christians [44]		298	199,000	312,000

Trans-bloc Groupings	pop.%	,000	Ann.Gr.
Evangelical	0.6	27	+12.6%
Charismatic	0.4	18	+15.1%
Pentecostal	0.1	6	+4.9%

Missionaries from Kyrgyzstan
P,I,A 3 in 2 agencies; 2 in Kyrgyzstan.

Expatriates to Kyrgyzstan
P,I,A approximately 138 from 12 countries.

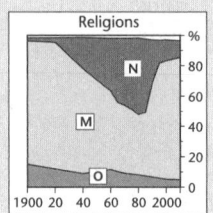

Religions

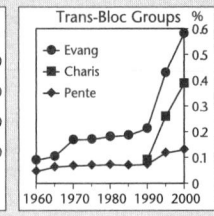

Trans-Bloc Groups %
Evang
Charis
Pente

• Answers to Prayer

1 **Continued religious freedom** despite opposition to this.

2 **The growth of the Kyrgyz Church** from about 20 believers in 1990 to over 3,200 in 2000.

• Challenges for Prayer

1 **The Kyrgyz have an unprecedented opportunity to believe in the Lord Jesus Christ.** Pray that the present harvest may continue. Pray down the barriers to faith.

a) *History.* For centuries foreigners have ruled the Kyrgyz and imposed their religions — Turkic armies in the 17th Century brought Islam, and the Russians in the 19th brought Orthodoxy, then in the 20th imposed Communism.

b) *Restored Islam.* The Kyrgyz are culturally Muslim, but practice and understanding of Islam is low. The Kyrgyz of the north are more influenced by Russian culture, but those in the south are more traditional. The 33 mosques in the country under Communism have multiplied to 120 buildings and 2,000+ prayer houses. Pakistani, Turkish and Saudi Arabian missionaries seek to strengthen Islamic institutions and commitment. A Kyrgyz becoming a Christian is seen as betrayal of ethnic identity and family cohesion.

c) *Spiritism — the actual religion of the Kyrgyz.* The ubiquitous shrines are more visible than mosques. Fear of the 'evil eye', use of amulets, the occult, shaman priests and demonization are widespread.

2 **The government** needs the courage, the resources and even miracles to transform the economy and develop trade links for Kyrgyzstan's potential to be realized. Pray for this and for the political stability, economic, social and religious freedoms the people need.

3 **Christianity** was almost entirely the religion of many of the non-indigenous Orthodox Russians and Ukrainians, Catholic Ukrainians and Protestant Germans before 1990. Most of the Germans and many of the others have emigrated. There is much nominalism among the Orthodox and, to a lesser extent, among the Catholics and Lutherans. The Baptists, Pentecostals, Adventists and newer post-1990 denominations have grown, with an increasing Kyrgyz component. The most spectacular growth has been in the charismatic, multi-cultural Church of Jesus Christ and in one district in the south where over 100 believers were baptized in 1999-2000. Pray for:

a) *Unity among Christians.* The Kyrgyz Partnership has begun to function well, bridging the earlier differences between Baptists, Pentecostals and Charismatics and between Protestant groups of different ethnic origins (Korean, Western, etc.). Pray that the levels of fellowship and cooperation may continue to deepen. The wide gulf between the Orthodox and non-Orthodox continues to be a problem.

b) *Continued growth and multiplication of churches.* There were only 45 Protestant/independent congregations in 1990; 10 years later there were over 200.

c) *The maturing and growth of Kyrgyz-speaking congregations* — over 55 in 2000. The growth rate of believers increased in 1994 to 40% a year reaching 55% a year by 2000. Effective Kyrgyz Christian leaders have come to the fore. There is a growing missionary concern both for the Kyrgyz and beyond.

d) *Leadership training.* There are now five Bible schools in Bishkek.

e) *Wisdom in outreach.* Culturally relevant and appropriate means need to be found and used. Muslims and Orthodox react strongly against high-profile outreach. Many Kyrgyz are held back from faith through fear of alienation from families and negative propaganda.

4 **The economic situation** affects, and depresses, everyone. The elderly and handicapped suffer the most. Health services are grim, but being improved by training programmes provided by expatriates. Corruption and the underground economy is everywhere. Pray that Christians might find honest employment and use legal ways of making money. Many are being helped to start micro-enterprises of their own. Major social evils to be tackled by Christians — a high rate of alcoholism, massive international drug trafficking, and a growing under-class of slum dwellers in Bishkek. Pray that churches might become viable and gain permission to register officially with the appropriate government agencies, thereby improving their legitimacy in Kyrgyz society.

5 **The less evangelized for prayer:**

a) *The rural and semi-nomadic pastoralist Kyrgyz* live in mountain villages. Few have heard of Christ.

b) *The Fergana Valley* in the south is shared with Tajikistan and Uzbekistan. The Tajik and large Uzbek minorities (over 600,000) are mostly unreached. It is the scene of seasonal Islamist terrorist activity with periodic armed incursions from surrounding lands. There are some Christian outreaches to them, but as yet no church in the Batken region.

c) *The Dungan* are descendants of Chinese Muslim refugees. In 2000 a significant multi-agency effort to reach them began.

6 **Expatriate Christians** number several hundred from Asia, the Americas and Europe. Most are tentmakers and need to keep a tactful profile. Pray for their safety and spiritual effectiveness in an area where the enemy of souls has not been challenged for 1,400 years. Pray for wisdom for those workers as they partner in ministry with nationals.

7 **Christian support ministries** are varied. There are many possibilities in literature, electronic media, medical, community development and business. Pray specifically for:

a) *Bible translation, publishing and distribution*. The New Testament was published in 1992 and 1997 (**IBT**), the same time as a Kyrgyz version of the Qur'an. Many have compared the two and are favourably impressed with the Bible message. **IBT**, **UBS** and Linguaserve are working together to produce the first full Bible by 2006.

b) *Christian literature* is a great challenge. There are two main Christian publishers — Beam of Hope and Linguaserve. **CLC** has a key bookstore in Bishkek. There is still little available in Kyrgyz and evangelistic, apologetic and teaching materials are needed. Pray for economic self-sufficiency; more indigenous authors and greater variety of titles for this ministry.

c) *The JESUS film* has been widely used in Russian and in Kyrgyz on TV and in film showings.

d) *Christian radio*. Programmes are aired by **TWR**-Armenia (1.75 hrs/wk) and **FEBC**-Saipan (one hour) in Kyrgyz, as well as in other Central Asian languages.

Laos
Lao People's Democratic Republic

JULY 23
ASIA

GEOGRAPHY
Area 236,800 sq.km. Narrow land-locked country mainly between Thailand and Vietnam. Mountainous and 55% forested.

Population	Ann.Gr.	Density
2000	5,433,036	+2.62%	23 per sq. km.
2010	6,964,623	+2.49%	29 per sq. km.
2025	9,652,526	+1.97%	41 per sq. km.

Capital Vientiane 286,000. **Urbanites** 22%.

PEOPLES
A complex mix of 138 groups, compounded by government classifications based on altitude of home environment.
Lao-Tai 58.9%. Lao 2.3 mill.; Tai(15) 454,500; Phutai 154,400; Lu 134,400; Phuan 112,800.
Mon-Khmer 30.8%. Khmu(6) 627,800; So 120,000; Katang 107,400; Mangkong 104,000; Viet 89,000; Bru 75,200; Suay 51,200.
Hmong-Mien 7.1%. Hmong Daw (White Miao) 191,000; Hmong Hjua (Blue Miao) 163,800.
Sino-Tibetan 2.7%. Akha(12) 74,300; Phunoi 40,100.
Other 0.5%. Chinese, Caucasians.

Literacy 57%. **Official language** Lao. **All languages** 92, also many dialects. **Languages with Scripture** 10Bi 8NT 11por 16 w.i.p.

ECONOMY
Subsistence agricultural economy with a growing tourist trade. The Vietnam war and its aftermath combined to make Laos the poor relation of Southeast Asia. The economy is slowly opening up to market forces, but not enough to counteract high inflation, a weak currency, and profit-skimming by those in power. **HDI** 0.491; 140th/174. **Public debt** 117% of GNP. **Income/person** $400 (1.3% of USA).

POLITICS
Independent from France in 1954. Lao and Vietnamese Communist forces were in complete control by 1975. There is a history of anti-government guerrilla activity in the northwest which has increased since 1998. The government leans heavily on Vietnam for policy direction, but indications are that many Laotians desire otherwise. The Communist leaders are still in full political control despite economic liberalisation.

RELIGION
Communist persecution of Christians was especially harsh between 1975 and 1978. Restrictions eased after that time, though the churches are still seen as potentially subversive, and are watched. Buddhism is regaining some of its old influence, but is heavily syncretized with animism. In the late 1990s persecution significantly increased and the government is intent on the complete elimination of any Christian presence in the country. **Persecution Index** 18th in the world.

Religions	Population %	Adherents	Ann.Gr.
Buddhist	61.05	3,316,868	+3.1%
Traditional ethnic	31.20	1,695,107	+1.8%
non-Religious/other	4.20	228,188	+1.2%
Christian	1.85	100,511	+5.9%
Muslim	1.10	59,763	+4.6%
Chinese	0.50	27,165	-2.6%
Baha'i	0.10	5,433	+2.6%

Christians	Denom.	Affil.%	,000	Ann.Gr.
Protestant	6	0.82	45	+8.1%
Independent	1	0.37	20	+10.8%
Catholics	1	0.66	36	+1.8%

Churches	MegaBloc	Cong.	Members	Affiliates
Lao Evangelical	P	550	22,000	44,000
Catholic	C	25	20,930	36,000
Indigenous groups	I	500	10,000	20,000
Seventh-day Adventist	P	1	192	400
Other denoms [4]		4	190	420
Total Christians [8]		1,080	53,312	100,820

Trans-bloc Groupings	pop.%	,000	Ann.Gr.
Evangelical	1.2	63	+8.8%
Charismatic	0.3	19	+9.4%

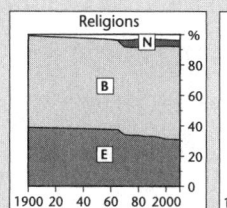

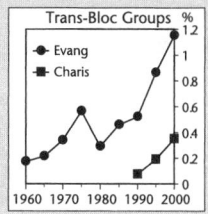

• Answers to Prayer

1 **The church has grown** despite restrictions and persecution. After the Communist takeover, two-thirds of believers fled the country, but there have been reports of people movements and whole villages turning to Christ. Many unreached people groups are being evangelized. Much of this is due to the initiative of indigenous believers. Amongst the Khmu tribe there has been a considerable turning to Christ!

• Challenges for Prayer

1 **Much of Laos is still unevangelized.** After years of hard work missionaries saw significant breakthroughs among the Hmong and Khmu, but since 1975 little could be done by expatriates. Christianity has not moved easily across the diverse ethno-linguistic boundaries, leaving many groups completely unreached. Pray that the entire country may be made open for the gospel to be proclaimed.

2 **The Church has suffered much since the Communist takeover.** Christianity has been labelled "a lying religion which violates Lao custom" and declared the number one enemy of the state. The church in Ventiane has been infiltrated by government spies, and persecution and incarceration of believers has intensified in the last few years. In 2000 there were 24 confirmed cases of imprisonment of some its leaders. Yet the church grows and spreads. Pray for:
a) Perseverance and grace for those suffering from the government's heavy hand.
b) Increased freedom for evangelism, church planting and building — presently forbidden. Many churches have been forcibly closed and believers now meet quietly in homes in many areas. Some ethnic minority Christians have been compelled to relocate in other areas.
c) A vision and burden for evangelizing the many ethnic minorities.
d) An effective unity among the leaders of evangelical churches and house groups in Laos.

3 **Leaders for the churches.** Over 90% of all trained leaders left Laos in 1975. Today, leaving the country for training is difficult and dangerous. Recently over 200 Laotians were trained in church planting and leadership based on a house church model. Pray that these methods, supplemented by TEE and radio, might equip leaders thoroughly for their ministry. A Catholic seminary opened in 1998 to train Laotian priests. Pray that permission might be granted soon for the establishment of an evangelical Bible school.

4 **Christian work** is not officially permitted, but a number of expatriate believers are helping in areas from agricultural development to removing undetonated American bombs dropped during the Vietnam war, the opportunities are many, but the government vacillates between the great need of Laos and its desire for self-sufficiency. Pray for a reopened door for Bible translators, pioneer church planters and Bible teachers — the spiritual ministries of greatest need. Pray also for wisdom for expatriates in their activities, decisions, and their relating to Lao Christian leaders.

5 **Unreached peoples:**
a) The Lao — the nation's dominant people, are described as gentle and peace-loving, but the anti-Christian government, and the passive nature of the Lao, are major obstacles to their evangelization. There are maybe 3-4,000 Christians among them, and they could be a key to bringing the gospel to the rest of Laos.
b) The Tai tribes speaking 15 languages. There are 200 Christians out of the fi million people.
c) The mountain dwelling Hmong are known for their resistance, sometimes violent, to Communism and government control. Almost all Hmong Christians fled Laos in 1975, and about a quarter of all the diaspora are believers today. Although the proportion of Christians is lower among them in Laos, the Hmong are the most responsive peoples in the country.
d) The northern peoples, many of whom have responded to the gospel in China and Thailand. Political conditions have never allowed missionary work; pray that this may change.

e) **The small southern tribes** were being evangelized for the first time from 1957-1963, but war prevented the planting of churches among most of them. They are deeply enmeshed in the fear of spirits; pray that they might find freedom through Jesus.

f) **The Vietnamese and Chinese** have only been marginally evangelized.

6 Christian Help ministries.

a) **Media ministries** are proving to be effective in evangelism, including literature, cassettes and radio. Pray that many may come into the Kingdom.

b) **Bible and literature distribution.** The **UBS** and the Bible League distribute Bibles, and from 1997 to 2000 over 200,000 pieces of literature were hand-carried into Laos. **AsiaLink** is an agency deeply committed to literature ministry for Laotians. Pray for the free and widespread distribution of all Christian literature.

c) **Bible translation.** The local linguistic situation is highly complex. A number of organizations are seeking to address this need. There are 21 languages for which there is a definite need for translation teams and possibly a further 17 languages will need them. Pray for the effective use of all available tools in speeding up the process of making God's Word available.

d) **GRN** which has prepared audio-messages in 92 languages and dialects of Laos. This is a vital ministry in a nation where literacy is relatively low.

e) **Christian Radio. FEBC** broadcasts 20 hours weekly in Lao, Hmong, Khmu, Lahu and Mien. Believers are being arrested for listening to Christian radio such that some churches are recommending people do not listen. Pray for the safety of those listening and for this spiritual pressure to lift.

f) **The JESUS film** is available in Lao and Hmong, and is being produced in several more languages.

Latvia
Republic of Latvia

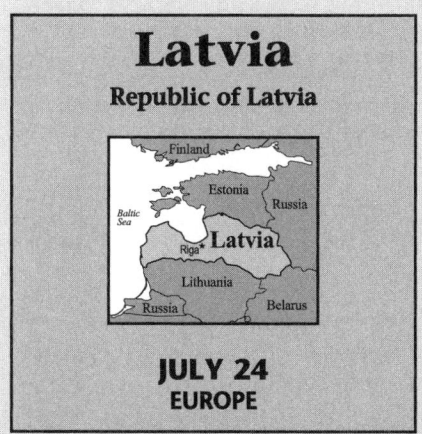

JULY 24
EUROPE

GEOGRAPHY
Area 64,610 sq.km. A fertile plain with 3,000 lakes and indented by the Gulf of Riga. The central of the three Baltic republics.

Population	Ann.Gr.	Density
2000	2,356,508	-1.46%	36 per sq. km.
2010	2,137,362	-0.85%	33 per sq. km.
2025	1,936,009	-0.64%	30 per sq. km.

Capital Riga 826,508. **Urbanites** 69%.

PEOPLES
Indo-European 98.5%.
Baltic 58%. Latvian 1,333,000; Lithuanian 35,500.

Slav 39.6%. Russian 717,000; Belarusian 92,000; Ukrainian 68,500; Polish 54,000.
Other 0.9%. Gypsy 8,000.
All other 1.5%. Jews 6,000; Tatar 5,000.
Literacy 99.5%. **Official language** Latvian (Lettish). **All languages** 5. **Languages with Scriptures** 2Bi 1NT 1por.

L

ECONOMY
Slowly recovering from the mismanagement of the Soviet regime. A lack of natural resources has forced Latvia to develop an industrialized economy. Latvia aims to become a regional high-tech centre. **HDI** 0.744; 74ᵗʰ/174. **Public debt** 5.4% of GNP. **Income/person** $2,430 (7.7% of USA).

POLITICS
Has been ruled by the Germans, Danes, Poles, Swedes and Russians since the Middle Ages. Its brief independence from Russia (1917-1940) was ended by Stalin's reconquest. Stalin liquidated a fifth of the population, deported many more and forcibly settled Russians in their place. This history still influences modern politics, as do the stirrings of ultra-right wing groups. Independent in 1991 as a multi-party democracy. Stringent citizen qualifications disenfranchise most of the Russian settlers, many of whom are leaving the country.

RELIGION
Christian beginnings go back to the 13ᵗʰ Century. Latvians were early supporters of Luther, and much of the population converted to

Lutheranism. The churches were harshly perse-cuted under both the Nazis and the Communists. Religious freedom since 1988 has caused many to return to the Church, but has also opened the door to sects.

Religions	Population %	Adherents	Ann.Gr.
Christian	58.25	1,372,666	+0.5%
non-Religious	40.32	950,144	-3.9%
Other	0.80	18,852	+1.2%
Muslim	0.38	8,955	-1.5%
Jewish	0.25	5,891	-7.9%

Christians	Denom.	Affil.%	,000	Ann.Gr.
Protestant	5	19.43	458	+1.3%
Independent	12	3.01	71	-1.0%
Catholic	1	19.94	470	-1.2%
Orthodox	5	4.39	104	-7.5%
Marginal	2	0.18	4	+6.4%
Unaffiliated		11.30	266	n.a.

Churches	MegaBloc	Cong.	Members	Affiliates
Catholic	C	241	281,437	470,000
Lutheran	P	301	160,000	400,000
Russian Orthodox	O	110	65,000	100,000
Old Believers	I	65	32,500	65,000

Baptist	P	81	6,259	40,000
Pentecostal	P	53	5,500	10,000
Seventh-day Adventist	P	44	3,868	6,962
Independent [9]	I	25	1,250	2,500
Other denoms [9]		38	7,000	12,000
Total Christians [25]		958	563,000	1,107,000

Trans-bloc Groupings	pop.%	,000	Ann.Gr.
Evangelical	7.6	179	+1.2%
Charismatic	1.6	38	+1.4%
Pentecostal	0.4	10	+2.1%

Missionaries from Latvia
P,I,A 39 in 4 agencies to 3 countries: Latvia 35.

Missionaries to Latvia
P,I,A 72 in 15 agencies from 8 countries: USA 46, Canada 10.

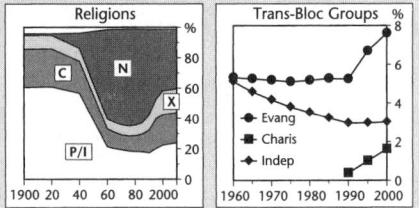

• Challenges for Prayer

1 **A sobering reality has replaced the elation of independence.** The economy is in serious need of a boost, and the gap between rich and poor is rapidly widening. The partial disintegration of society has left a moral vacuum — economic growth takes priority over the needs of the elderly and children who rely on the state for care. Yet, although many Latvians view the future pessimistically, most feel that the Church is a trustworthy institu-tion and God needs to be a part of Latvia's future. Pray that both leaders and citizens may recognize the truth of this and personally respond to it.

2 **Solutions for the vexing ethnic question** are needed. The anxious Slav commu-nity comprises 40% of the population, yet they are finding themselves marginalized because of present reactions to past Soviet wrongs. Many are leaving the country. Latvians need to re-establish their national identity, culture and language and successfully integrate the many ethnic minorities who live among them. Pray for the government as the nation's leaders wrestle with these issues.

3 **The post-independence religious bubble has burst.** The spiritual urgency of the early 1990s has largely lapsed into general spiritual apathy. While religious freedom exists, only about 2% of the population regularly attends church. Although the smaller evangelical denominations continue to grow, the Lutheran and Catholic churches still struggle with nominalism and a lack of teaching and pastors. Continue to pray for healthy growth in the churches and harmony between believers of different ethnicities.

4 **Leadership training is important,** as great hunger exists in the churches for bib-lical teaching and training. There is also a need to equip believers to recognize false teaching. In addition to the Bible seminaries (Lutheran, Baptist and Catholic) and the The-ological Faculty in Riga University, **YWAM** and the Baptists have established training centres. The Lutheran Church has a one-year training programme for lay leaders and there are 2 Russian-language Bible schools. Financial support is often a problem for students. Pray that students at all these institutions may be trained into godly, committed leaders.

5 **Youth ministries are again beginning to take off.** IFES is working in Latvia, and SU camps are ministering not only to Latvian youth, but to young people from across Eastern Europe. Among Latvian youth, 80% believe in God, but few have been introduced to Christ. Pray for more workers with the vision to reach young people.

6 **Literature.** A new Latvian translation of the Bible has been sponsored by the King of Sweden. **The Bible Society** has been very active, using their ecumenical platform to cooperate with many denominations. Some Christian books are now being translated into Latvian and a few are also being written by Latvian Christian authors. Pray that the ministry of literature may be fruitful in every segment of the population.

7 **Media.**

a) *Radio.* There are several diverse radio ministries evolving. These include:
i *Focus Radio* which translates English scripts with a training emphasis into Latvian.
ii *The Baptists,* who broadcast in English two days a week.
iii *The All Latvian Lutheran Hour* (LLH) and other Christian programmes which are broadcast on national and local radio as well as live broadcasts of services on TV.
iv *Over 20 hours* a week can be received in Russian.
v *Christian Radio* which has broadcast 24 hrs/day in Latvian since 1993.
b) *TV.* The Lutheran Church broadcasts a series of Christian films and talk shows, which are tied into church programmes.
c) *The JESUS film,* in Latvian and Russian, has been viewed by an estimated 90% of the population, in film and on national television.

Lebanon
Republic of Lebanon

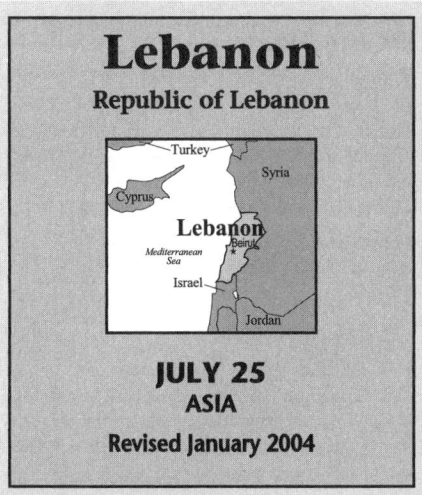

JULY 25
ASIA
Revised January 2004

GEOGRAPHY
Area 10,230 sq.km. A fertile, mountainous state in the East Mediterranean. An enclave between Israel and Syria. The site of ancient Phoenicia.

Population		Ann.Gr.	Density
2000	3,281,787	+1.75%	321 per sq. km.
2010	3,722,943	+1.16%	364 per sq. km.
2025	4,399,649	+1.07%	430 per sq. km.

During the civil war 900,000 emigrated and 170,000 were killed.
Capital Beirut 2,050,000. Over 60% live in the Beirut area. **Urbanites** 87%.

PEOPLES
Arabs 91.5%.
  Lebanese 67%.
  Other Arab 24%. Syrian 400,000 — 1,000,000

(many temporary workers); Palestinian 300,000; Egyptian 50,000.
Other 8.5%. Armenian 180,000; Persian 50,000; Kurd 20,000; Assyrian 16,000.
Literacy 92%. **Official language** Arabic; French and English are widely used. **All languages** 4. **Languages with Scriptures** 2Bi 2por.

ECONOMY
Lebanon was the commercial hub of the Middle East until the civil war reduced Beirut to rubble and ruined its profitable trading, banking and tourist industries. Recovery began in 1992 but has been slowed by both Israeli occupation of the south and successions of retaliatory bombings until 2000. Beirut is being rebuilt, but the cost is reckoned at $US25 billion. Commercial confidence is returning but there remains much poverty and destitution. Debt servicing consumes 45% of the GNP. **HDI** 0.749; 69th/174. **Public debt** 140% of government budget. **Income/person** $3,350 (11% of USA).

POLITICS
French-mandated territory 1919-1945. Independent in 1943 as a republic, with a constitution based on a delicate balance related to the size of the 18 recognized religious communities. The influx of 300,000 Palestinian refugees between 1948 and 1976 upset the status quo, precipitating the 1975-1990 civil war — with deep involvement of many Middle Eastern and Western forces, too. The Palestinians seized south Lebanon only to have their power broken by Israeli invasion and occupation (1982-85). Shi'a Muslim and Druze militia improved their political leverage at the expense of the Christians in the subsequent years of bitter fighting and hostage-taking. The Syrians manipulated for their own ends the complex medley of warring factions. The Syrian army imposed a measure of peace in 1990 and opened

L

the way for the Taif agreement of 1990/91 and a new Lebanese government. Lebanon has since had a measure of peace, but only a nominal internal independence with the Syrian army controlling 90% and Israel 10% of the country. It is hoped the total Israeli withdrawal in 2000 will also be followed by the Syrians who control all security, foreign policy, political leadership and the media. Real progress is also hampered by the constant need to balance the country's religious factions and their rights at every level.

RELIGION

Freedom of religion; the only Arab state that is not officially Muslim. The distribution of power according to the size of each community was frozen at 1932 levels. The rapid increase in size of the Muslim population, and especially of the under-represented Shi'a, is one of the basic reasons for recent conflicts. The Shi'a are 36% of the population and Sunni 23%. There are 18 recognized religious communities: four Muslim, Druze, Jewish and 12 Christian. All figures used here are estimates. (The last religious census was in 1932, when Christians were 53.7% of the population.)

Religions	Population %	Adherents	Ann.Gr.
Muslim	59.76	1,961,196	+3.5%
Christian	31.93	1,047,875	-1.1%
Druze	7.00	229,725	+1.5%
non-Religious/other	1.30	42,663	+1.8%
Jewish	0.01	328	+1.7%

Christians	Denom.	Affil.%	,000	Ann.Gr.
Protestant	23	0.54	18	+3.7%
Independent	1	0.15	5	+1.2%
Anglican	1	0.01	0	-2.0%
Catholic	6	22.00	722	-0.9%
Orthodox	6	8.96	294	-2.1%
Marginal	5	0.23	7	-1.4%
Unaffiliated		0.04	1	n.a.

Churches	MegaBloc	Cong.	Members	Affiliates
Maronite Patriarchate	C	542	370,130	570,000
Greek Orthodox	O	270	89,385	160,000
Armenian Apostolic	O	223	67,039	120,000
Melchite Cath Patriarch.	C	198	61,622	114,000
Armenian Cath Patriarch.	C	11	5,587	10,000
Latin-rite Catholic	C	9	5,587	10,000
Syrian Orthodox	O	5	5,389	9,000
Chaldean Catholic	C	2	5,028	9,000
Syrian Cath Patriarchate	C	4	5,028	9,000
Jehovah's Witnesses	M	70	3,529	6,500
Church of the East	O	3	2,571	4,500
Baptist Convention	P	22	1,300	4,500
National Evang Union	P	4	1,800	2,800
Ch of God (Anderson)	P	15	1,300	2,000
Un of Evang Armenian	P	23	1,000	2,000
Nat Evang Synod (Presb)	P	13	1,000	1,600
Seventh-day Adventist	P	5	472	1,100
Nat Ev Chr Alliance	P	4	329	844
Christian Brethren [2]	P	5	350	460
Assemblies of God	P	3	180	260
Other denoms [21]		81	4,600	9,000
Total Christians [42]		1,512	633,200	1,047,000

Trans-bloc Groupings	pop.%	,000	Ann.Gr.
Evangelical	0.6	19	+3.4%
Charismatic	2.1	67	-0.2%
Pentecostal	0.0	1	+2.8%

Missionaries from Lebanon
P,I,A 51 in 7 agencies to 8 countries: Lebanon 32.

Expatriates in Lebanon
P,I,A 112 in 26 agencies from 12 countries: USA 38, UK 35.

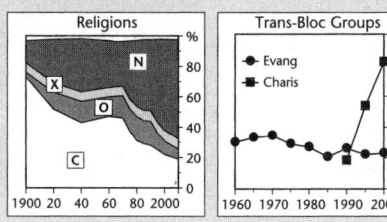

• Answers to Prayer

1 The eventual ending of the civil war in 1990.

2 The remarkable openness to spiritual things in the 1990s in the Muslim, Druze and Christian communities.

3 Lebanon is still the only land in the Middle East where anyone is legally free to change their religious affiliation. Believers from most other Arab countries can more freely come to Lebanon for training. Pray that religious freedom might be maintained.

• Challenges for Prayer

1 Lebanon's tragic history over the past 50 years with communal wars, foreign interventions and hostage-taking made world headlines. Its once-wealthy economy was destroyed, its middle class decimated and its delicate social balances disturbed. The war is over but not its effects. Pray specifically for:

a) *The government and its leaders*. According to common practice, the President must be a Maronite Christian, the Prime Minister a Sunni Muslim, and the Speaker a Shi'a Muslim. They need to set an example in harmonious working together for the good of all Lebanese.

b) *Full political freedom* to be gained and religious freedom protected.

c) *The healing of the deep hurts* in communities, families and individuals. Over 80% of the population was displaced at one time or another during the war. All have lost loved ones, many lost homes and jobs.

d) *A willingness to forgive* those who caused the suffering. Pray above all, that a work of the Holy Spirit might make world headlines instead!

e) *The rebuilding of the South* after 22 years of military occupation — for spiritual, as well as physical renewal to take place.

2 **The Christian community** has been deeply traumatized. They have lost their political and economic dominance and a major part of their population through emigration. Their population percentage has dropped from 62% in 1970 to under 32% in 2000. Pray that many may come to personal faith and deep commitment to the Lord Jesus, and thus be a blessing to the nation and the world. The Charismatic movement has had a widespread impact across the denominational spectrum. Pray also for the reversal of the trend of Lebanese young people to emigrate.

3 **The Orthodox and Catholic Churches are many and varied**. All have a long history of struggle for survival. In the midst of traditionalism and deadness are also significant renewal movements — notably in the Maronite and Eastern Orthodox Churches. Church attendance, especially among the Maronites, is at an all-time high. Pray for new life to infuse these ancient communities.

4 **The Protestant Church has struggled to grow** due to centuries of suspicion of Western Christianity and because the many small denominations communicate a message of fragmentation and divisiveness. More Armenians than Arabs have responded. Conversions have barely replaced losses through emigration. Pray for the ministry of the Baptists, **CMA**, and the Church of God — churches that are growing, but relatively few of the new converts are from a non-Christian background. Pray for the further development of fellowship and cooperation between Evangelicals — long neglected, but stimulated by a working together in providing aid to refugees resulting from fighting between Hezbollah Shi'a Muslims and the Israelis in the late 1990s. The Council of Evangelical Churches in Syria and Lebanon was the catalyst for this. Cooperation between Evangelicals is being promoted through the Lebanon Evangelical Society (LES) and the Evangelical Ministers' Fellowship.

5 **Trained leadership in evangelical churches is at a premium.** The decline in the number of residential missionaries, emigration of national leaders, and lack of workers have left many congregations in the region without effective pastoral care. Praise God, this is being reversed. Lebanon has a number of residential evangelical Bible schools — the Arab Baptist Theological Seminary (60 students), Mediterranean Bible College (Church of God), Christian Alliance Institute of Theology (**CMA** — 12 students) and the Near East School of Theology (20 students). Pray for staff, supply of needs and students in these times of renewed possibilities. Pray that increasing cooperation between these colleges would result in significant advances for the Kingdom.

6 **Lebanon has long been one of the key centres for Christian ministries to the whole Middle East**. Much of this outreach was interrupted but it is regaining momentum once more. Pray that Lebanese believers may regain a vision for others and for other lands — the war has introverted many and made them sorry for themselves and for what they lost. Pray specifically for these ministries:

a) *The Bible Society*, which has a vital role in distributing many Bibles within Lebanon and to surrounding nations. The ministry has expanded to meet the increased demand for Bibles and NTs in all communities. Book fairs have been highly successful for Bible distribution. Many in Orthodox and Catholic churches are reading and studying the Scriptures.

b) *Christian schools and orphanages*. These are much appreciated, having had a long and fruitful ministry, and have gained in credibility since the war. Many children from all communities hear the gospel and some come to Christ (LES, Lebanon Baptist Society and others). Many Lebanese political and societal leaders have been to an evangelical school.

c) **Young people**, who are often struggling in the post-war apathy, sense of loss, lack of job opportunities and gloom about the future. Drug abuse is a serious problem. Pray for relevant and effective ministry to them (YFC Lebanon, Grain du Blé, **YWAM**, local churches). More needs to be done for student ministry (**CCCI** and **IFES**).

d) **Christian literature** production which has been severely disrupted. Much of this ministry has been transferred to Cyprus, Europe and elsewhere. Pray for the Evangelical Carmel Mission, **OM**, **MECOLit**, Clarion Publishing House, the Baptist Publishing Center and others, who are publishing and distributing literature for Lebanon and the Arab world.

e) **Radio**. International broadcasters include **FEBA**-Seychelles (10 hours/week), **TWR**-Cyprus (9) and **IBRA** (36) by satellite and from Moscow. There are also many local FM stations that broadcast Christian programmes.

f) **Christian TV**. Television has become the primary source of information and entertainment. There are 10 local TV stations in Lebanon — some Christian. **SAT-7** has had a deep impact by satellite and is also re-broadcast by the Catholic TV station *Télélumière*. SAT-7's main studios for the Middle East are now in Beirut.

7 **Expatriate Christian workers** are returning to Lebanon after years of minimal presence because of widespread violence and hostage-taking. Pray for more to be called and enabled to identify with and serve the Church and all Lebanese. There are many areas where the love of Christ may be demonstrated — reconstruction, rehabilitation, young people, drug rehabilitation as well as discipleship and church development ministries (**CMA**, **MECO**, **AoG**, **IMB-SBC**, **WVI**, **WEC**, **YWAM**, **OM**-Love Lebanon and others).

8 **The unreached.** Though legal, the social consequences of personal conversion to Christ are immense. Yet the number coming to the Lord has increased in recent years. So pray for:

a) **The Shi'a Muslims** who have been the more radical of the religious groupings. They live mainly in the south on the Israel border, in the Bekaa Valley and in West Beirut. The Hezbollah faction in South Lebanon is supported by Iran, violently opposed to anything Western and any peace settlement with Israel. Pray that they may discover the emptiness of a religion without Christ — as a number have done!

b) **The Sunni** who are mainly in the northeast, and the cities of Beirut, Tripoli and Sidon.

c) **The Druze** and their well-organized, close-knit community. Their heartland is the mountain area east of Beirut. They have a secretive religion which came out of Islam. Its tenets are only taught to the 15% who are fully committed. In the last few years a multi-agency partnership has seen several hundred come to Christ — may authentic Druze churches result.

d) **The Palestinians** — a tragic, stateless people. No full peace or harmony is possible without a lasting solution to their situation — especially for those in refugee camps. There are Christians among them, some evangelical, but the majority are Muslim and unreached.

e) **The poor and disadvantaged**. The majority of the very poor are Muslim (Lebanese and Palestinian). The blind, deaf and disabled are often neglected by society in general. Pray for believers and various agencies seeking to minister to them.

Pray that Lebanese believers may regain a vision to reach out to these five groups.

Lesotho
Kingdom of Lesotho

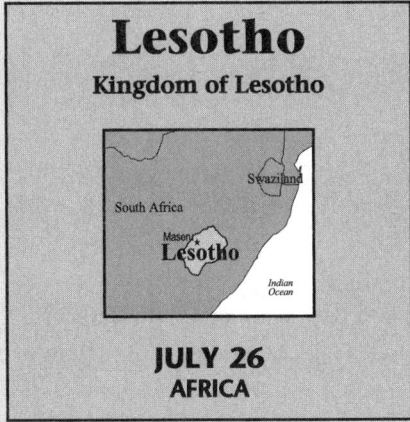

JULY 26
AFRICA

GEOGRAPHY
Area 30,355 sq.km. A mountainous country completely surrounded by South Africa. Only 11% is arable.

Population	Ann.Gr.	Density
2000	2,152,553	+2.24%	71 per sq. km.
2010	2,609,785	+1.95%	86 per sq. km.
2025	3,506,420	+1.84%	116 per sq. km.

It is the only country in the world with its entire area above 1,000 metres in altitude.

Capital Maseru 120,000. **Urbanites** 21%.

PEOPLES
Bantu 99.7%. Sotho 1.77mill.; Zulu 294,000; Xhosa 2,100.
Other 0.3%. European, Asian.

Literacy 71%. **Official languages** Sotho, English. **All languages** 4. **Languages with Scriptures** 3Bi.

ECONOMY
The mountainous topography, poor communications and lack of agricultural land, together with over-population have kept the country poor and hastened soil erosion. Over 35% of wage-earners work as migrant labour in South Africa. Major income sources: export of water from the controversial Highland Dams Project, some diamond mining. The South African invasion of 1998, to settle a political crisis, resulted in much destruction in the capital and its nascent industries and further impoverishment of the country. **HDI** 0.582; 127th/174. Public debt 46% of GNP. **Income/person** $860 (2% of USA).

POLITICS
A British protectorate in 1865. Independence in 1966 but a geographical hostage due to its size and isolation as an enclave within South Africa. A tragic, post-independence history of instability, dictatorial regimes and polarized politics culminating in the 'preventive intervention' or invasion of South African forces in 1998, which has further destabilized the little country.

RELIGION
Freedom of religion. The dominance of the Catholic Church and its control of much of the education system has been a contributory factor to political instability.

Religions	Population %	Adherents	Ann.Gr.
Christian	71.85	1,546,609	+1.2%
Traditional ethnic	27.00	581,189	+5.5%
Baha'i	1.10	23,678	+2.2%
non-Religious/other	0.04	861	+17.5%
Muslim	0.01	215	+2.2%

Christians	Denom.	Affil. %	,000	Ann.Gr.
Protestant	24	12.61	271	+0.9%
Independent	222	13.59	293	+1.8%
Anglican	1	5.02	108	+0.8%
Catholic	1	36.05	776	+1.3%
Marginal	1	0.28	6	+2.7%
Unaffiliated		4.30	93	n.a.

Churches	MegaBloc	Cong.	Members	Affiliates
Catholic	C	380	481,988	776,000
Other Indigenous [210]	I	5,190	155,689	260,000
Lesotho Evangelical	P	565	68,690	215,000
Anglican	A	431	64,671	108,000
African Methodist Epis	I	67	10,000	16,000
Methodist	P	10	5,750	11,500
Assemblies of God	P	48	4,500	9,500
Dutch Ref Ch in Afr	P	12	3,200	9,000
Full Gospel Ch of God	P	44	3,000	6,529
Jehovah's Witnesses	M	57	2,573	6,000
Seventh-day Adventist	P	20	3,466	5,788
Mahon Mission	P	22	2,700	5,400
Apostolic Faith Mission	P	25	1,250	2,000
Chs of Christ	P	8	180	378
Other denoms [27]		144	10,400	23,000
Total Christians [250]		7,023	818,000	1,454,000

Trans-bloc Groupings	pop.%	,000	Ann.Gr.
Evangelical	8.2	177	+1.9%
Charismatic	12.9	278	+1.8%
Pentecostal	1.6	34	+3.6%

Missionaries from Lesotho
P,I,A 48 in 9 agencies: Lesotho 46.

Missionaries to Lesotho
P,I,A 117 in 32 agencies from 13 countries: South Africa 44, USA 41.

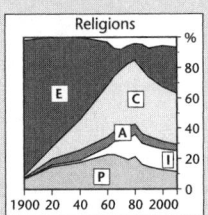

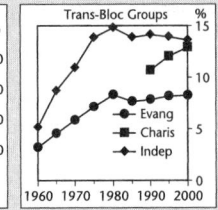

• Challenges for Prayer

1 **The people of Lesotho** are prisoners of their geographical position, the divisions and powerlessness of their politicians and lack of resources. The 1998 South African invasion has left the population angry and frustrated. Pray that God-fearing, honest leaders may be raised up for the good of all.

2 **The Sotho have been largely Christian for generations** but traditionalism and nominalism are widespread in both the Catholic Church and the Lesotho Evangelical Church. The latter is the fruit of the great pioneering work of French missionaries of the Paris Missionary Society. The rapid increase in the number of newer churches with evangelistic zeal has challenged the mainline Churches to become more spiritually vital and relevant. Pray for a humble harmony between the different denominations in place of considerable antagonism. Pray also for this land to be changed by the power of the Holy Spirit.

3 **The newer, evangelical, Pentecostal and charismatic denominations** and agencies have seen growth (**AIM**, **YWAM**, **IMB-SBC**, and various South African groups). Special items for prayer:

a) Bible teaching. There are four residential Bible schools, including the Apostolic Church Mobile School and the *Jesu Evangeli Centre* ministry with potential to provide this.

b) Leadership. The mainline, Catholic and Pentecostal churches in Lesotho have been under local leadership for many years, but a new level of leadership is emerging in the charismatic churches that is cooperating to win the nation for Christ.

c) A nation-wide prayer movement has brought a new dynamism to the witness of believers, but this vision needs to be maintained.

d) Empowering of women in Christian leadership — the absence of many men and the lower proportion of committed Christians among them makes this essential for the survival of congregations.

4 Areas of special challenge in ministry:

a) AIDS has become a terrible reality and the incidence of HIV has risen to 24% of the adult population. Churches have neither the resources nor the vision to tackle the disaster.

b) The Sephiri, a secret society to which many churchgoers from most denominations belong. Witchcraft and ancestor worship are taught and practised along with Christian ritual. Pray for both the exposure of this demonic delusion and for its followers to come to a living faith.

c) The more syncretistic, indigenous churches. Many of these groups with their robes, uniforms and ceremonies have little understanding of the Truth and need to be sensitively helped to a more biblical theology.

d) The mountain population of 600,000, most nominally Christian, but having little contact with the life-giving gospel. Various evangelical agencies have initiated outreach to them. Major agencies are **AIM**, Joy to the World, **YWAM**, Fill the Gap Ministries, the Full Gospel Church, Zoe Bible Church and Global Evangelism Ministries. Many villages are only accessible on horseback, others by **MAF** plane.

5 **Migrant labourers in South Africa.** Lack of work opportunities in Lesotho forces 37% of the men to seek employment in the mines and on the farms of South Africa. **AEF** has a fruitful evangelistic ministry in the mine compounds. Pray for lasting conversions and effective discipling follow-through.

6 Christian support ministries:

a) MAF has a unique and vital role in this land of high mountains and few roads. **MAF** planes operate on 26 landing strips — many in difficult terrain. They provide support for Christian workers and a flying doctor service. Pray for these pilots, their families/support teams and for their safety.

b) The JESUS film is being widely used in English and Sotho and is effective in planting new churches.

c) Christian radio — **TWR** Swaziland broadcasts daily in both English and Sotho.

Liberia

Republic of Liberia

JULY 27
AFRICA
Updated February 2004

Income/person $490 (1.6% of USA).

GEOGRAPHY
Area 99,067 sq.km. Heavily forested coastal state adjoining Sierra Leone, Guinea and Côte d'Ivoire.

Population		Ann.Gr.	Density
2000	3,154,001	+8.58%	32 per sq. km.
2010	4,443,705	+3.32%	45 per sq. km.
2025	6,617,526	+2.49%	67 per sq. km.

Over the 24 years of violence since 1980 an estimated 300,000 people have lost their lives and a large proportion of the population became refugees in and beyond Liberia.

Capital Monrovia 1,300,000. About half the population are civil war refugees. **Urbanites** 45%.

PEOPLES
There are 16 major ethnic groups divided in three language families. These figures include refugees in surrounding lands.
Mande 47.2%. 11 groups, largest: Kpelle 690,000; Mano 252,000; Loma 200,000; Gio 147,000; Vai 126,000; Bandi 100,000; Mandingo 60,000.
Kru 41.3%. Over 25 groups, largest: Bassa 492,000; Grebo(8) 387,000; Kru (Klao) 261,000; Krahn(3) 140,000.
West Atlantic 7.9%. Kissi 143,000; Gola 140,000.
Other 3.6%. Americo-Liberian 87,000; Lebanese 30,000.
Refugees. Many Sierra Leoneans.

Literacy 38% (64% in 1990). **Official language** English. **All languages** 34. **Languages with Scriptures** 1Bi 12NT 5por 8w.i.p.

ECONOMY
Well-watered, abundant natural resources of iron, diamonds, rubber, timber, etc. Not over-populated, but the country has been made destitute by decades of institutionalized corruption by an elite (up to 1980) and ensuing chaos and civil wars. Much of the capital, road system and most of the buildings have been destroyed and much farmland reverted to forest. Recovery will take decades — even with an upright government. **Unemployment** 95%. **Public debt** 95% of GNP.

POLITICS
In 1847 Liberia became Black Africa's first independent state. The dominance of the Liberians of American origin ended in the coup of 1980. The military government became increasingly unstable. Massive corruption and repression of the Mano and Gio peoples provoked the 1989 revolution led by Charles Taylor. The war engulfed the country in an orgy of inter-tribal killings and, ultimately, three armies contending for power. The West African States (ECOWAS) military intervention proved a disaster which prolonged the civil war until 1996 which resulted in Taylor gaining power first by military action and then in a flawed election in 1997. Taylor's misrule spread war and suffering to Sierra Leone and then Côte d'Ivoire. A second civil war to oust Taylor started in 1997 and ended with his exile in 2003. The various victorious rebel factions continue to use violence and jockey for power and lucrative government posts. There is no clear and acceptable solution to Liberia's political future even with international and UN interventions.

RELIGION
Liberia was founded as a Christian state. There continues to be freedom of religion in theory, but in practice there is pressure on Christians to conform to occult secret societies. Religious and denominational figures are mostly estimates due to massive numbers fleeing the civil war.

Religions	Population %	Adherents	Ann.Gr.
Traditional ethnic	48.37	1,525,590	+7.8%
Christian	38.33	1,208,929	+8.6%
Muslim	13.00	410,020	+11.3%
Baha'i	0.30	9,462	n.a.

Christians	Denom.	Affil.%	,000	Ann.Gr.
Protestant	39	13.91	439	+8.0%
Independent	144	6.90	218	+6.6%
Anglican	1	0.87	28	+4.6%
Catholic	1	3.49	110	+2.6%
Marginal	1	0.12	4	+1.2%
Unaffiliated		13.04	411	n.a.

Churches	MegaBloc	Cong.	Members	Affiliates
Baptist Convention	P	229	60,000	110,000
Catholic	C	70	68,323	110,000
United Methodist	P	1,058	55,000	110,000
Assemblies of God	P	350	22,000	48,000
Lutheran [2]	P	109	17,500	35,000
African Chr Fell. Intl	I	200	15,000	30,000
Seventh-day Adventist	P	35	14,564	28,000
Episcopal	A	177	17,857	27,500
United Lib. Inland (ULIC)	P	64	7,000	18,000
United Pentecostal	P	70	10,000	15,000
Mid-Liberia Baptist	P	60	3,000	6,000
Open Bible Standard	P	30	2,200	4,500
Presbyterian	P	12	1,200	3,000
Other denoms [172]		2,028	124,764	253,000
Total Christians [186]		**4,492**	**418,000**	**798,000**

Trans-bloc Groupings pop.%	,000	Ann.Gr.
Evangelical	9.1	288	+9.1%
Charismatic	4.7	147	+6.8%
Pentecostal	3.1	98	+3.9%

Missionaries from Liberia
P,I,A est. 30+. Unknown because of political situation.

Missionaries to Liberia
P,I,A Approximately 172 assigned to Liberia, many not resident in 2000, or ministering from outside the country.

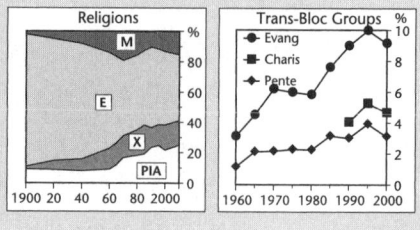

• Answers to Prayer

1 **The ending of the civil war** in 2003 and some hope of recovery.

• Challenges for Prayer

1 **The civil wars were a tragedy for Liberia**, the country was devastated and the people traumatized. It was also a blight that poisoned much of West Africa, especially Sierra Leone, Guinea and Côte d'Ivoire. Its roots lay in deep ethnic hatreds, greed, lust for power and in a compromised Christianity that gave Satan opportunity. Pray specifically for:

a) *A government and leadership* that rejects oppression, institutional violence and the endemic culture of extortion and corruption.

b) *A reconciliation between the ethnic groups* which were involved in fighting, atrocities and massacres — especially the Mandingo and Krahn on one side and the Mano and Gio on the other.

c) *A healing* of the terrible physical, psychological and spiritual wounds of the war — 65% of the population have been, and many are still, refugees. Almost the entire population have either been victims or perpetrators of unspeakable crimes.

d) *The rescue of the children of war*. Little children were forced to become soldiers. Over 50,000 were killed in the fighting. Even after the ending of the second civil war in 2003, disarmament is not occurring and many children still have weapons. All 1,400,000 children under 17 have been traumatized, lost their education and many orphaned. Hunger, violence, homelessness and drug abuse are widespread. Pray for churches and agencies seeking to repair the damage, restore family life and bring them the gospel.

2 **For decades Christians compromised with evil** on an alarming scale. Freemasonry imported by the early settlers fused with indigenous tribal secret societies to become a pervasive influence that corrupted and compromised politics and nearly every denomination, whether mainline, evangelical or Pentecostal. During the war, Christians who refused to compromise were persecuted in some areas. Stagnation, failure of the gospel to advance in Liberia's hinterland, lack of concern for the lost, and spiritual impotence so widespread in the churches are due to condoned sin, witchcraft, alcoholism and polygamy among 'Christians'. Pray for the binding of these spiritual forces, and for a new day of freedom and power in the Holy Spirit for the Church.

3 **There are signs of hope**. The agony of the nation has driven Christians to new prayer and earnestness for the gospel. Christians have had miraculous deliverances, soldiers have repented of horrible crimes, new leaders with vision have been raised up and there have been localized revivals in the midst of sorrow. Since the war ended over 150 churches have been started. The Association of Evangelicals has regrouped and begun to lay plans for future reconstruction and evangelization. Pray that out of the fires may come a purified, Church that can bring reconciliation between ethnic groups, a blessing to the many needing spiritual help and can resume the incomplete evangelization of the country.

4 **There are serious challenges** facing the church:

a) *Repair of church buildings* and reactivation of institutions closed. Looting and destruction spared few.

b) ***False teachings have multiplied*** due to many Christian leaders lost or fleeing for their lives. Pray for firmer doctrinal and spiritual standards to be laid.

c) ***African independent churches***. These are often syncretistic, but open for sensitive teaching. **CRWM** has had a ministry to them, helping them to a more biblical faith.

5 **Ministry to individuals, families and to Liberian society** — impoverished, embittered and demoralized through what they have suffered — is essential. This has to be largely a Liberian initiative. Pray for CURE (Christians United to Rehabilitate Ex-combatants) and ACCESS giving help to resettle displaced farmers. Foreign aid agencies poured in help and supplies, but unwittingly became prolongers of the war — the combatants stole the food, vehicles and aid intended for their victims. Most foreign agencies had to withdraw much of their ministry. Pray for wisdom for **WVI**, World Relief, **TEAR Fund**, **YWAM** and many others who are seeking to give assistance.

6 **Ministry to young people and children** has been halted by war and a whole generation of children needs to be evangelized. Pray for the ministry of **SU**, **YFC** and the churches, to children and young people. **IFES** is rebuilding its ministry to students.

7 **Trained spiritual leaders are few in number**. Many have had to flee or been killed; most Bible training was brought to a halt or struggles to survive with limited resources and personnel. Some refugees studied theology in the West or elsewhere in Africa and are returning with wider vision. Others have planted thriving churches among the Liberian diaspora. Bible schools and seminaries are slowly opening and rebuilding — the Baptist Seminary, Africa Bible College and ACFI Bible School among them. Pray for the raising up of a new generation of leaders who preach the whole gospel without compromise, competitiveness or jealousies.

8 **Islam's rapid expansion has slowed**. Muslim Mandingo support for the previous, largely Krahn, regime, their cruelty to Christians in areas where they were in the majority, and their relative wealth provoked a cruel response from other tribes. Many Mandingo were killed or fled to Guinea, and up to 1,000 mosques were destroyed or damaged. Liberia was to have been a major centre for Islamic growth in West Africa — one of the factors that provoked the war. Pray for the winning of many Muslims to Christ.

9 **Less-reached peoples.** Of all Liberia's indigenous peoples, only three are majority Christian, despite considerable exposure to the gospel. Most still follow traditional religions; some are Muslim. There are 16 peoples in which there is not yet a viable, growing, indigenous church-planting movement. Pray for:

a) ***Muslim groups***: the Vai (**CRWM**) in the west with about 500 Christians and Mende and Manya (**SIM**) of the northern borders are largely Muslim with few active Christians.

b) ***Traditional peoples*** with growing Muslim influence: the Dewoin (8,000) near Monrovia and the Gola and Gbandi in the north. Both are turning to Islam, but have small Christian communities (**SIM**).

c) ***Peoples with strong fetish powers*** and where a victorious gospel power-encounter must yet come: Krahn in northeast (9% Christian, **AoG**, **IMB-SBC**), Grebo in east (**AoG**, **NTM**) and Kpelle with relatively few committed Christians.

10 **Missionaries have had a long, hard, uphill struggle** to plant churches in the interior — disease, language diversity, entrenched fetishism and now the disruption of war since 1989 have all hampered the work. About 10 Protestant and Catholic missionaries have lost their lives in the conflict. All had to leave the country in 1996, a few have returned to minister in Monrovia and among the large refugee communities in surrounding lands. Pray for wisdom about the return of expatriates to assist in rebuilding the work so painstakingly established in the past and also to help the Liberian church complete the evangelization of every people. The largest missions before the war were: **SIM**, United Methodists, **NTM**, Baptist Mid-Missions, Lutheran Bible Translators, North American Lutherans, **IMB-SBC** and **CRWM**. National mission leadership is making progress in researching the nation's current status in terms of evangelization, and in missions advocacy among churches.

11 **Christian Help Ministries** for prayer:

a) ***Bible translation*** and distribution ministries were gravely disrupted. **The Bible Society** has recommenced operations but many of the seven Lutheran Bible Translators' projects have been delayed. There are still 11 languages with a definite translation need.

b) **Christian literature.** Many pastors and Christians have lost all they owned, and there is a great lack of Bibles, New Testaments and Christian literature but few available bookstores. **EHC** plans a new nation-wide literature distribution.

c) **The JESUS film** has been viewed by the majority of the population and has had converting impact on Muslims. It is available in four languages and a further 11 are in the production stage.

d) **GRN** has now a Liberian base and their tape recordings are being used in 42 languages and dialects.

e) **Christian radio.** Until its destruction in 1990 and again in 1996, **SIM**'s Radio ELWA was Africa's best known **station**, with 270 hours/week broadcasting in 44 languages. Praise God for the years of seed-sowing and discipling ministry. In February 2000 ELWA was once more resurrected — six hours daily English broadcasting but there are plans for 16 languages to be broadcast. Pray for their realization, provision of equipment and funds, and also peace and safety to permit resumption of the ministry.

Libya

Socialist People's Libyan Arab Jamahiriya

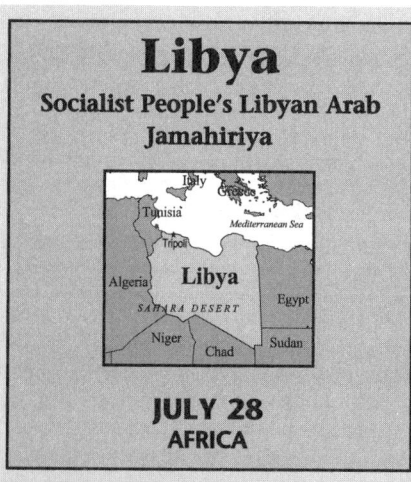

JULY 28
AFRICA

GEOGRAPHY
Area 1,775,500 sq.km. Mostly Saharan desert; only a coastal Mediterranean strip of 2% of its land area is arable.

Population	Ann.Gr.	Density
2000	5,604,722	+2.45%	3 per sq. km.
2010	6,981,828	+2.09%	4 per sq. km.
2025	8,646,769	+1.31%	5 per sq. km.

Capital Tripoli 1,300,000. **Urbanites** 86%.

PEOPLES
Population is a confused issue as foreign workers compose anywhere from 3 to 35% of Libya's total. All figures are estimates.
Indigenous 75%.
Arab 63.1%. Including 750,000 Bedouin in 5 groups.
Berber 9.4%. About half are Arabized. 8 groups, largest: Nefusi 173,000; Jalo 36,700; Zuara; 33,600; Jofra 23,000; Ghadames 10,000.
Other 2.5%. Black African 100,000; Teda 20,000; Zaghawa 8,600. Mainly in southern oases.
Expatriate 25%. Many labourers from surrounding lands. Predominantly Egyptian, Sudanese, North African and Chadean. Also Korean, European, Filipino, Pakistani and Bangladeshi.

Literacy 76%. **Official language** Arabic. **All languages** 11. **Languages with Scriptures** 2NT 1por.

ECONOMY
Transformed by discovery of oil in 1959. Oil wealth has financed revolutionary movements and the promotion of Islam in many nations, while accounting for almost all exports. Qaddafi's fickle and dictatorial government has made development patchy. US-led sanctions have hampered the economy. Widespread subsidies and free handouts limit political opposition, but unemployment among the younger generation is surprisingly high. Almost 75% of food is imported. Goods are expensive and not affordable to the majority of the population. **HDI** 0.756; 65th/174. **Public debt** 7.9% of GDP. **Income/person** $6,510 (18% of USA).

POLITICS
Ruled by Italy 1911-1943. Full independence in 1951 as a monarchy. The military coup of 1969 led to a revolutionary republic under the leadership of Muammar Qaddafi. While three groups of secret police spy on the population and each other, reports of civil strife and insurrection occasionally leak out. Executions of alleged spies in the late 1990s reveal government insecurity. Years of UN-imposed sanctions, due to Libya's involvement in terrorism, ended in 2000. Qaddafi has seemingly abandoned Arab nationalism for a pan-African polemic.

RELIGION
Sunni Islam is the state religion, but secularizing influences are strong. The government sees Islamist ideology, and related support trickling in to the country, as a threat. No form of Christian witness to Libyan citizens is allowed, and congregations of expatriates are strictly monitored. There is a state-imposed limit of one church per denomination per city. All figures below are approximations. **Persecution index** 12th in the world.

Religions	Population %	Adherents	Ann.Gr.
Muslim	96.50	5,408,557	+2.4%
Christian	3.00	168,142	+3.9%
Buddhist	0.30	16,814	+2.4%
non-Religious/other	0.20	11,209	-5.5%

Christians	Denom.	Affil.%	,000	Ann.Gr.
Protestant	5	0.12	7	+1.8%
Independent	3	0.01	0	+8.5%
Catholic	1	0.71	40	+0.0%
Orthodox	4	1.58	89	+5.2%
Unaffiliated		0.58	33	n.a.

Churches	MegaBloc	Cong.	Members	Affiliates
Coptic Orthodox	O	14	34,000	85,000
Catholic	C	2	27,972	40,000

Coptic Evangelical	P	6	2,200	4,400
Greek Orthodox	O	3	511	1,700
Other denoms [11]		99	3,100	4,600
Total Christians [15]		124	67,800	136,000

Trans-bloc Groupings	pop.%	,000	Ann.Gr.
Evangelical	0.3	18	+4.6%
Pentecostal & Charismatic	0.2	13	+4.0%

•Challenges for Prayer

1 **No open evangelism is possible.** The last missionary outpost was closed in 1960. The entire indigenous population is unreached. Despite the increasing freedom for expatriates granted by the state, Libyans are off limits for evangelism. Approaches to them are potentially dangerous to both parties. A number of expatriate workers are seeking to reach Libyans, but are hindered by the elaborate secret police networks. There is a shared sense of despair and hopelessness. Pray for the calling of more Arab Christians and tent-makers to specifically reach Libyans in a sensitive and effective manner. Pray for this tightly-shut land to open to the gospel.

2 **Personal freedom is restricted.** Political and economic sanctions of the past, as well as policies pursued by the government, continue to have long-term effects. Intercede for greater freedom for the people of Libya, and for greater openness in Libya to Christian workers from other lands. Pray that Christians might see past the Western media's caricature of Libyans as fanatical Islamists and recognise the Libyans' need for the Saviour. Pray for many to be called to serve in Libya.

3 **The Christian community** is large, but foreign. There are no more than a handful of Libyan believers, all facing many obstacles to fellowship, including fear of infiltrators. Christians among the expatriate population are largely nominal; few find opportunity for public worship, and most congregations lack pastoral care. There are some active Protestant, Catholic and Coptic Orthodox congregations, and several informal groups of believers of various nationalities from Asia, Africa, and Europe. Pray for the unhindered growth of a Christian witness among expatriates and for outreach to every national grouping among them. There was a crackdown on home meetings in 2000.

4 **Alternative means for reaching Libyans with the gospel:**

a) Broadcasting. Radio and satellite television provide two of the very few ways to evangelize Libyans. Three different radio stations broadcast programmes to Libya: **IBRA** — over Radio Moscow, **FEBA**-Seychelles, **TWR**-Monaco. With the proliferation of satellite dishes (perhaps 50% of households) **SAT-7** and other Christian satellite television broadcasts are of increasing importance. But face to face follow-up is virtually impossible, despite signs of responsiveness. Pray for creative programmes with impact, the means to disciple seekers and protection for those who respond.

b) Literature and audio and video cassettes. These may enter only by creative channels. Few Libyans have ever seen a Bible. There are no Scriptures in Libyan Arabic. Pray that work on this may start so that Libyans can read the gospel in their heart language. Pray for the circulation of Christian tapes in spite of the barriers. Pray that the recent distribution of the *JESUS* film might yield eternal fruit. Pray for the conversion of censors and that materials may find their way safely through customs and the postal system.

c) Libyans overseas. Political refugees, diplomats, students and businessmen could be introduced to Christ by believers in other lands — pray for homes and hearts to be opened for such ministry. There are growing numbers of seekers, but even while abroad, Libyans are watched closely by security forces.

d) Internet access is strictly limited in Libya, but becoming inevitably more available. Pray that Libyans may be drawn to Christian websites and attracted to the gospel.

Liechtenstein
Principality of Liechtenstein

JULY 29
EUROPE

GEOGRAPHY
Area 160 sq.km. Mountainous enclave on the Rhine between Switzerland and Austria.

Population	Ann.Gr.	Density
2000	32,843	+1.30%	205 per sq. km.
2010	36,668	+1.04%	229 per sq. km.
2025	41,252	+0.66%	258 per sq. km.

Capital Vaduz 5,017. **Urbanites** 45%.

PEOPLES
Germanic 87.5%. Liechtensteiner 20,500; Swiss 4,860; Austrian 2,270; German 1,120. **Other** 12.5%. Italian, Turkish, etc.
Literacy 100% **Official language** German.

ECONOMY
Wealthy through a diversified industrial economy and promoting free enterprise including manufacturing, banking and tourism. Nearly 30% of state revenue comes from some 75,000 companies registered in Liechtenstein whose

POLITICS
Constitutional principality in customs and monetary union with Switzerland.

RELIGION
Freedom of religion is guaranteed. The Catholic Church is effectively the state church, but disestablishment may come soon.

Religions	Population %	Adherents	Ann.Gr.
Christian	88.74	29,145	+0.9%
non-Religious/other	7.83	2,570	+4.0%
Muslim	3.43	1,127	+7.9%

Christians	Denom.	Affil.%	,000	Ann.Gr.
Protestant	4	8.57	3	+1.9%
Independent	4	0.14	0	+4.4%
Catholic	1	79.16	26	+0.8%
Orthodox	1	0.68	0	+2.2%
Marginal	1	0.19	0	-6.3%

Churches	MegaBloc	Cong.	Members	Affiliates
Catholic	C	10	19,697	26,000
Reformed	P	2	1,048	1,750
Evang Lutheran	P	4	758	1,000
Orthodox	O	1	172	223
Other denoms [6]		6	116	173
Total Christians [10]		23	21,791	29,146

Trans-bloc Groupings	pop.%	,000	Ann.Gr.
Evangelical	0.4	0	+3.2%
Charismatic	0.6	0	+1.6%
Pentecostal	0.2	0	+6.0%

Missionaries from Liechtenstein
None known.

Missionaries to Liechtenstein
None known.

• Challenges for Prayer

1 **Liechtenstein has changed** from a feudal backwater in the 1930s to a leading banking and industrial centre today. Almost the entire indigenous population is Catholic. The majority of expatriates are nominal Christians and a growing minority are Muslims. Few in this country have ever been confronted with the necessity of a personal faith in Christ. Church attendance is only a small proportion of those who claim to be Protestant. Pray that through increased contact with outsiders, many might encounter the risen Christ.

2 **The first and only evangelical fellowship of believers** was started in 1985 after an evangelistic campaign launched by British, Norwegian and Swiss believers. Pray for the health and growth of this work.

Lithuania

Republic of Lithuania

JULY 29
EUROPE
Updated February 2004

 GEOGRAPHY
Area 65,301 sq.km. The southernmost of the three Baltic states. A flat, arable land with many forests and lakes.

Population	Ann.Gr.	Density
2000	3,670,269	-0.30%	56 per sq. km.
2010	3,565,746	-0.26%	55 per sq. km.
2025	3,398,950	-0.39%	52 per sq. km.

Capital Vilnius 573,200. **Urbanites** 70 %.

PEOPLES
Baltic 71.6%. Lithuanian 2,630,000.
Slavic 27.6%. Russian 300,000; Polish 250,000; Belarusian 55,000; Ukrainian 37,000.
Other 0.8 %. Jews 6,000; Tatars 6,000.
Literacy 98%. **Official** language Lithuanian. **All languages** 3. **Languages with Scripture** 1Bi 1por.

ECONOMY
Industrial and agricultural economy whose transition from a Soviet to a Western model has been hampered by the decline of its primary trading partner, Russia. Positive signs of progress. **HDI** 0.761; 62nd/174. **Public debt** 12.5% of GNP. **Income/person** $2,260 (7.2% of USA).

POLITICS
Once a powerful duchy controlling much of West Russia, Belarus and Ukraine. Strong links with Poland. Independent from Russia 1917-1940; occupied by the Soviets 1940-1990. Independent in 1990 as a multi-party democracy, but still struggling with the legacy of 50 years of Communist misrule. Government relationships are improving with dissatisfied Polish and Russian minorities. Became a member of the EU in 2004.

RELIGION
Last European nation to be Christianized. Due to strong Polish influence, Catholicism was politically dominant until the Soviet occupation when all faiths were repressed. Religious freedom, but preference shown to Catholics and 8 other traditional religious groups who have constitutional rights that are denied to non-traditional groups, which includes all evangelical churches.

Religions	Population %	Adherents	Ann.Gr.
Christian	76.19	2,796,378	-0.5%
non-Religious/other	23.55	864,000	+0.6%
Muslim	0.14	5,138	-0.3%
Jewish	0.12	4,404	-10.0%

Christians	Denom.	Affil.%	,000	Ann.Gr.
Protestant	9	1.29	47	+0.9%
Independent	8	1.77	65	-4.4%
Catholic	1	68.14	2,501	-0.5%
Orthodox	1	4.90	180	+1.2%
Marginal	2	0.09	3	+8.6%

Churches	MegaBloc	Cong.	Members	Affiliates
Catholic	C	688	1,497,605	2,501,000
Russian Orthodox	O	31	116,883	180,000
Old Believers	I	27	12,500	50,000
Lutheran	P	55	12,000	30,000
Reformed	P	11	2,200	11,000
New Apostolic	I	25	2,545	5,600
Word of Faith	I	56	2,800	4,000
Jehovah's Witnesses	M	18	2,200	3,000
Pentecostal Chs	P	38	1,800	2,500
Seventh-day Adventist	P	21	997	2,000
Baptist Union	P	8	500	750
Other denoms [11]		38	4,740	7,142
Total Christians [22]		1,016	1,657,000	2,797,000

Trans-bloc Groupings	pop.%	,000	Ann.Gr.
Evangelical	0.4	14	+1.7%
Charismatic	2.9	105	-0.4%
Pentecostal	0.1	2	+2.1%

Missionaries from Lithuania
P,I,A 17 in 6 agencies: 15 in Lithuania.
Missionaries to Lithuania
P,I,A 62 in 15 agencies from 6 countries: USA 43, Canada 12.

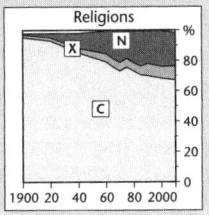

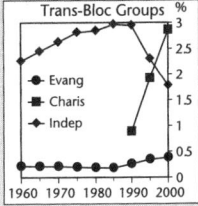

L

• Answers to Prayer

1 **Religious freedom** in the post-Soviet era has stimulated the growth of the Church, in particular newer groups of charismatics and Pentecostals. Relationships between denominations are better than in most former Soviet states.

• Challenges for Prayer

1 **The Catholic Church** plays a key role in Lithuanian society, but it has not yet recovered from years of isolation and persecution, and is unprepared for the challenges of the 21ˢᵗ Century. Vatican II reforms and renewal movements are sometimes opposed. Only 14% of Catholics attend church weekly. Younger leadership is pushing for change. There are strong Franciscan, charismatic and evangelical-style networks which are experiencing growth, especially among young people.

2 **The Protestant church faces many challenges.** Among them are:

a) *The traditional denominations* (Lutheran, Reformed and Orthodox) are largely associated with the shrinking ethnic minorities, just struggling to maintain their numbers.

b) *The Baptists, Pentecostals and Adventists* are the most established evangelical groups in Lithuania, but are struggling to come out of a Soviet-era time warp. The hyper-conservatism and defensiveness which enabled them to survive the lean years are now barriers to their growth. Pray that the leadership might see the need for forward progress under the Spirit's guidance.

c) *The newer Pentecostal and charismatic churches* have grown significantly, partly due to ambitious evangelism and outreach. However, in some cases, much of this growth was financed and directed by Western churches, who brought their cultural baggage with them. Pray that a genuinely indigenous expression of Lithuanian Christianity might develop in partnership with, and not under the patronage of, the West.

d) *Low level discrimination* against evangelical groups exists. Traditional denominations are favoured in terms of land purchasing, zoning, taxation policies, financial support from the state and official registration. Pray that the government might be just and treat all genuine Christian groups with equality.

e) *How Evangelicals can effectively work together.* There is not yet an Evangelical Alliance.

3 **There is a lack of trained leaders** due to the rapid growth of the newer churches and the difficulties of the established denominations. Religious freedom has facilitated the entry of cults and theological error. Solid biblical foundations need to be laid locally. Those leaders who train abroad often do not return, and several who do find themselves out of touch with their home situations. The Catholics have 3 seminaries and 5 faculties in universities; the Lutherans have one. The Pentecostals founded a pastoral, mission-oriented training institute, Vilnius College. Word of Faith and other charismatic groups operate training centres. Another encouraging development is Lithuania Christian College, an inter-denominational Christian liberal arts college. Pray that these institutions may be used to train godly, well-educated and visionary leaders for the nation.

4 **Ethnic minorities** with few Evangelicals. The Russian and Polish communities, the shrinking Jewish community and the Muslim Tatar community all need prayer.

5 **Expatriate missions.** There are about 25 missionaries ministering long-term in the country, plus 30-60 Western faculty and staff of the Lithuania Christian College. **YWAM** has a ministry to families through Bible studies, clubs and camps and launched their first Discipleship Training School (DTS) in 2000. Pray for more missionaries to be called to serve in this land, and to serve with commitment and sensitivity.

6 **Specialized ministries** need prayer. These include:

a) *Radio.* **TWR** broadcasts 30 min/day. More programmes in Lithuanian are needed.

b) *Christian literature.* A growing but still very small ministry. Two modern Lithuanian versions of the Bible and 12 other biblical titles have been made available recently. Word of Faith has published about 60 books in Lithuanian and produces a bi-monthly newspaper. There are now 7 Christian publishing organizations.

c) *Student ministries.* LKSB(**IFES**) operate in 4 universities. **CCCI** began ministry in 1993. **Youth at the Crossroads** has a key ministry in schools bringing Christian ethics to bear on sex education. **SU** camps have been running since 1997.

Luxembourg

Grand Duchy of Luxembourg

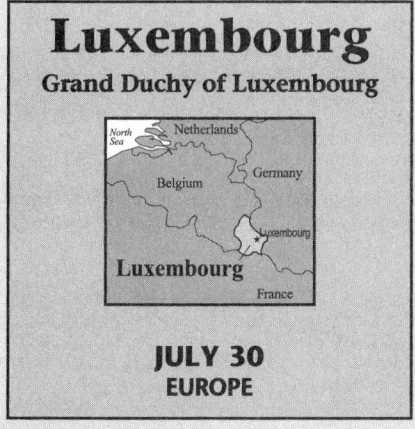

JULY 30
EUROPE

GEOGRAPHY
Area 2,586 sq.km. The smallest of the Benelux, or Low Countries, and smallest member of the European Community.

Population		Ann.Gr.	Density
2000	430,615	+1.14%	167 per sq. km.
2010	456,615	+0.41%	177 per sq. km.
2025	463,356	-0.04%	179 per sq. km.

Capital Luxembourg 76,446. **Urbanites** 88%.

PEOPLES
Luxembourgers 69.8%
Expatriates 30.2%. Portuguese 58,000; Italian 25,500; French 15,400; Belgian 11,300; German 10,900; etc.

Literacy 100%. **Official language** Lëtzebuergesch (a Franco-German dialect) is the national language; French and German the languages of education and the newspapers; and French is used in official communications.

ECONOMY
Diversified industrial economy, with banking and finance very important. **HDI** 0.902; 17th/174. **Public debt** 3.7% of GNP. **Income/person** $42,800 (144% of USA).

POLITICS
Parliamentary monarchy in economic union with Belgium and Netherlands. A member of EU, and headquarters of many EU institutions.

RELIGION
Freedom of religion. The Catholic Church is effectively the state church.

Religions	Population %	Adherents	Ann.Gr.
Christian	93.90	404,347	+1.1%
non-Religious/other	4.50	19,738	+1.6%
Muslim	1.10	4,737	+3.1%
Baha'i	0.30	1,292	+1.1%
Jewish	0.20	861	+1.1%

Christians	Denom.	Affil.%	,000	Ann.Gr.
Protestant	24	1.76	8	+0.1%
Anglican	1	0.05	0	+0.0%
Catholic	1	94.75	408	+1.1%
Orthodox	2	0.35	2	+0.0%
Marginal	3	0.89	4	+2.8%
Doubly affiliated		*-3.90*	*-17*	*n.a.*

Churches	MegaBloc	Cong.	Members	Affiliates
Catholic	C	328	321,260	408,000
Ev Prot Ch of Lux (Ref)	P	4	250	3,500
Jehovah's Witnesses	M	33	1,917	3,340
Protestant Ch of L (Luth)	P	5	1,500	1,950
Orthodox [2]	O	2	1,128	1,500
Assemblies of God	P	2	122	175
Free Evangelical	P	3	100	167
Other denoms [23]		23	1,671	2,500
Doubly affiliated			*-10,000*	*-16,766*
Total Christians [31]		401	318,000	404,000

Trans-bloc Groupings	pop.%	,000	Ann.Gr.
Evangelical	0.3	1	+0.7%
Pentecostal & Charismatic	2.1	9	+1.0%

Missionaries from Luxembourg
P,I,A 4 in 4 agencies to 3 countries.

Missionaries to Luxembourg
P,I,A 17 in 5 agencies from 5 countries.

L

• Challenges for Prayer

1 **The land is Catholic by tradition and culture** — revolutionary changes in the Church elsewhere have largely passed it by, and few have clearly heard the gospel in their own language. While the vast majority profess Catholicism, only a shrinking fraction actively practice their faith. Many Catholics dabble in Buddhism and the New Age. A confusing mixture of religions and secularism are serious challenges to the gospel. Most Luxembourgers are hesitant to leave their religious practices even if they no longer believe in them. Pray that they might encounter the living Christ who transforms all who meet Him.

2 **Protestants are a small minority**, and a high proportion of them are foreigners. Jehovah's Witnesses have had more success among the nationals than Evangelicals, and other cults are making their presence felt. There are several small evangelical congregations from different traditions, but there is still a great need for more Bible-teaching, Christ-centred churches, and for workers to labour in these churches. Pray that the Lord of the harvest may send out more workers to this field, and sustain those already there.

3 **Foreigners** are a major challenge for evangelization. There are some services and ministries in several other languages, but the vast majority of foreigners are in Luxembourg for employment, business or EU affairs, and show little interest in spiritual things. Pray for both vision and strategy for reaching each group, and for receptive hearts.

4 **Growth in evangelistic endeavour is slow.** A few isolated evangelistic efforts by **OM**, **AoG**, **BMW** summer camps, and others have sown the seed.

5 **The Lëtzebuergesch language** is spoken by the majority as their heart language. Most are fluent in French and German, but to have the Bible in Lëtzebuergesch could be the key to opening many hearts to the light of the gospel — the Gospel of Mark and the Psalms are now translated. There are two Christian bookstores in the country.

Macedonia
Republic of Macedonia

JULY 31
EUROPE

GEOGRAPHY
Area 25,713 sq.km. Landlocked state between Yugoslavia, Bulgaria, Greece and Albania.

Population	Ann.Gr.	Density
2000	2,023,580	+0.60%	79 per sq. km.
2010	2,142,050	+0.54%	83 per sq. km.
2025	2,257,977	+0.29%	88 per sq. km.

Capital Skopje 700,000. **Urbanites** 59%.

PEOPLES
Ethnic populations are a sensitive, politicized issue. Many think that the minority populations are larger than the government admits.
Slavic 65.6%. Macedonian 1.15 mill.; Bosnian 55,000; Serb 38,000.
Albanian 22.9% (possibly now up to 30%).
Roma (Gypsy) 7.5% (possibly 9.5%).
Turk 4%.

Literacy 89%. **Official language** Macedonian, one of the southern Slavonic languages. **All languages** 8. **Languages with Scripture** 3Bi 2NT 2por 1w.i.p.

ECONOMY
One of the poorest regions of former Yugoslavia. The private sector has been growing recently. Heavily reliant on agriculture, mining and manufacturing. **Unemployment** close to 40%. **HDI** 0.746; 73rd/174. **Public debt** 57% of GNP. **Income/person** $1,100 (3.5% of USA).

POLITICS
Macedonia is subject to territorial claims by its neighbours, who contested its 1992 proclamation of independence. Politics in this multi-party democracy are fragmented along ethnic and nationalist lines. Ethnic tension grows, despite the restraint shown by both Macedonians and the large and restive Albanian minority — a large proportion of which only became residents since 1944. The Kosovo crisis (see Yugoslavia) in 1999 caused the arrival of thousands more ethnic Albanians. In 2001 there was some fighting between Kosovan Albanian guerrillas and Macedonian forces.

RELIGION
Historically, the Orthodox Church has had a strong influence. A harsh policy aimed at restricting religious groups (apart from Orthodox, Catholics and Muslims) was overturned in court in 1999, but some restrictions remain.

Religions	Population %	Adherents	Ann.Gr.
Christian	63.43	1,283,557	+0.1%
Muslim	25.00	505,895	+2.7%
non-Religious/other	11.52	233,116	-0.8%

Christians	Denom.	Affil.%	,000	Ann.Gr.
Protestant	6	0.20	4	+1.7%
Independent	5	0.03	1	+5.6%
Catholic	1	0.99	20	+0.5%
Orthodox	3	62.07	1,256	+0.1%
Marginal	1	0.13	3	+24.1%

Churches	MegaBloc	Cong.	Members	Affiliates
Macedonian Orthodox	O	1,100	843,537	1,240,000
Catholic	C	26	13,000	20,000
Other Orthodox [2]	O	13	11,000	16,000
Methodist	P	13	1,300	1,500
Evangelical	P	12	403	1,136
Seventh-day Adventist	P	10	411	633
Congregational	P	3	180	400
Pente & charis [4]	I	12	165	400
Church of God	P	4	118	180
Baptist	P	4	110	160
Other denoms [3]		15	1,173	2,940
Total Christians [17]		1,212	872,000	1,283,000

M

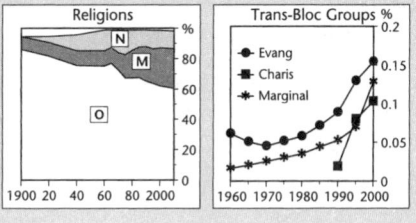

Trans-bloc Groupings	pop.%	,000	Ann.Gr.
Evangelical	0.2	3	+4.2%
Charismatic	0.1	2	+4.1%
Pentecostal	0.1	1	+4.2%

Missionaries from Macedonia
P,I,A 18 in 1 agency.

Missionaries to Macedonia
P,I,A 47 in 10 agencies from 4 countries: USA 42.

• Challenges for Prayer

1 **Macedonia's ethnic diversity dominates its political and social existence.** Macedonian pluralism resembles segregation more than harmony. Finding a balance between the demands of the respective ethnic minorities, especially the large Albanian population, is a challenge for the authorities. Pray for the government to sensitively seek peace and justice for all. Pray also for God's anointing upon President Trajkovski, who is a believer and has served as a lay preacher in the Methodist Church.

2 **The Macedonian Orthodox Church** claims to be shepherd to the majority of the population, but their 1,100 churches remain largely empty. There are only 150 priests. Spiritually weak and steeped in tradition, the Orthodox Church often actively opposes evangelical or evangelistic ministry. Pray for new life to touch this Church and all those who belong to it.

3 **The evangelical witness is small, but growing.** The Methodist, Baptist, Congregational and Evangelical Churches are growing, and vigorous new pentecostal and charismatic churches are springing up around the country. Pray for unity among believers and active vision for outreach. The opportunities are there, as the Kosovo crisis has made people more open to Jesus — largely through the aid and relief work of Christian groups.

4 **The ethnic minorities** are numerous, and all in need of ministry.

a) *Albanians, who claim to number one-third of Macedonia's population,* are rapidly increasing through both a higher birth rate and thousands of refugees who fled persecution in Kosovo. Tensions between the restive Albanian population, with their demands for increasing political influence, and the majority of Macedonians could lead to long-term problems. Though nearly all are Muslim, with only a few known Christians among them, they are open to the loving witness of evangelical believers.

b) *The large Roma population* may number 200,000. Skopje is the largest Roma city in the world. There are several believers among them, and three Roma churches.

c) *The Turkish community* live mainly in the western city of Debar (84% Muslim). There is only one small evangelical Christian house church among them.

d) *The Torbish* (Macedonian-speaking Muslims) number 16,000. No ministry among this group exists.

5 **Foreign missions** are finding Macedonia to be one of Europe's neediest lands, and one of the more difficult to access. **Worldshare**, **IMB-SBC**, **Pioneers**, **Frontiers** and **Partners International** are actively conducting ministry alongside indigenous ministry organizations. Two training/discipleship schools have been started in Macedonia; pray that they might nurture godly, anointed leadership for the young church in this nation. Pray also for the ministry of SEAM(**IFES**); many of the new converts are young people.

6 **Media and literature** are important ministries in Macedonia.

a) *The Bible Society* was formed in 1998, and is overseeing the distribution of two new Macedonian translations of the Bible, one done by **SGA.**

b) *A Christian Cultural Centre* in Skopje includes a Christian bookstore, although only a few books have been translated into Macedonian. Pray for more Christian material in Macedonian to be developed and distributed — **PI** has a vision for this.

c) *Radio.* Christian broadcasts from **TWR** can be heard in Albanian (2 hrs/wk) and Macedonian (3 hrs/wk).

d) *The JESUS film* has been widely viewed on television and film. It is available in Albanian, Macedonian, Roma and Turkish.

Madagascar

Republic of Madagascar

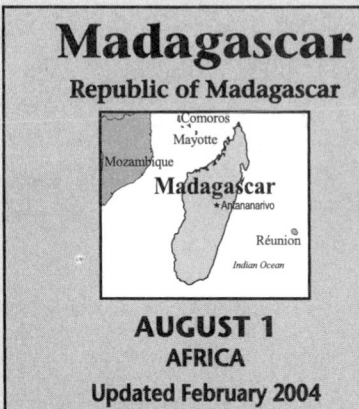

AUGUST 1
AFRICA
Updated February 2004

fact still resented by the lowlander peoples. Annexed by France in 1896; independent in 1960. A coup in 1972 led to experimentation with Marxism which was a disaster for the country. Popular protest and demands for change were violently suppressed before constitutional change was conceded. Multi-party elections in 1993 gave overwhelming victory to the democratic opposition. Corruption and lack of progress led to a change of government three years later. The former president was returned to power having dispensed with Marxism, but with minimal popular support. The 2001 presidential elections were rigged and after a 7-month stand-off and vocal public support, the corrupt former government was removed from office and President Ravalomanana took office in 2002.

GEOGRAPHY
Area 587,041 sq.km. The world's 4th largest island — 1,600 km long in the Indian Ocean 600 km off the coast of Mozambique in Africa.

Population	Ann.Gr.	Density
2000	15,941,727	+3.01%	27 per sq. km.
2010	20,691,738	+2.56%	35 per sq. km.
2025	28,963,663	+2.05%	49 per sq. km.

Capital Antananarivo 1,425,000. **Urbanites** 25%.

PEOPLES
Malagasy 98.6%. 18 main ethnic groups of mixed Indonesian, African and Arab origin speaking numerous regional forms of an Indonesian-related language. There are also the hunter-gatherer Kimoso 17,000 and Mikea 1,700.
Other 1.4%. Chinese 60,000; Réunionese 45,000; Comorian 20,000; Arab 20,000; Gujarati 18,000; French 16,000.

Literacy 46% — in decline; functional literacy even lower. **Official languages** Standard Malagasy, French. **All languages** 6. **Languages with Scriptures** 2Bi 1NT 1por.

ECONOMY
Subsistence agricultural economy, yet not producing enough rice to feed all. Slash-and-burn farming has destroyed vast areas of forest and caused bad erosion. Poor communications hinder development. Centralized socialist experiments proved a costly failure. Malaria and malnutrition have become major problems because of the economic slump. A slow economic recovery is under way. Eco-tourism has great potential — if the country's rich bio-diversity is not destroyed. **HDI** 0.453; 147th/174. **Public debt** 108% of GNP. **Income/person** $250 (0.8% of USA).

POLITICS
The highland Merina people gained control of the whole island in the 19th Century — a

RELIGION
There is now religious freedom, but the power of the old Malagasy folk religion remains pervasive. The four mainline churches have great influence and through the National Council of Churches pressure the government to restrict visas for missionaries associated with evangelical groups. The new President is an active Christian.

Religions	Population %	Adherents	Ann.Gr.
Christian	47.63	7,593,045	+3.3%
Traditional ethnic	44.77	7,137,111	+2.2%
Muslim	7.00	1,115,921	+6.2%
non-Religious/other	0.41	65,361	+6.5%
Baha'i	0.12	19,130	+6.8%
Chinese/Buddhist	0.07	11,159	+0.3%

Christians	Denom.	Affil.%	,000	Ann.Gr.
Protestant	28	27.58	4,397	+4.3%
Independent	18	2.45	391	+4.9%
Anglican	1	1.76	280	+4.0%
Catholic	1	20.70	3,300	+2.6%
Orthodox	1	0.00	1	+0.0%
Marginal	2	0.22	36	+8.0%
Doubly affiliated		-5.08	-810	n.a.

Churches	MegaBloc	Cong.	Members	Affiliates
Catholic	C	320	1,750,000	3,300,000
Ch of Jesus Christ	P	4,500	1,200,000	2,500,000
Lutheran	P	7,212	375,000	1,500,000
Episcopal	A	1,100	100,719	280,000
Ev Indigenous Mission	I	350	52,500	105,000
FTMA	I	120	50,000	100,000
Seventh-day Adventist	P	255	53,871	75,000
Pente Ch Jesus Saves	P	146	29,279	65,000
United Pentecostal	P	400	27,000	40,000
Jehovah's Witnesses	M	225	10,441	35,000
Free Evangelical	P	186	14,865	33,000
Assemblies of God	P	115	10,000	21,000
Bible Baptist	P	50	1,652	5,500
Other denoms [38]		1,739	157,500	345,000
Doubly affiliated			-400,000	-810,000
Total Christians [51]		16,718	3,433,000	7,595,000

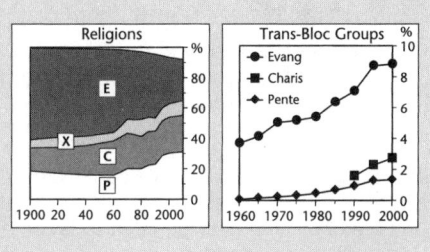

Trans-bloc Groupings	pop.%	,000	Ann.Gr.
Evangelical	8.8	1,404	+3.9%
Charismatic	2.7	433	+5.2%
Pentecostal	1.3	211	+3.7%

Missionaries from Madagascar
P,I,A 96 in 11 agencies to 10 countries: Madagascar 74, Cameroon 6.

Missionaries to Madagascar
P,I,A 222 in 33 agencies from 15 countries: USA 63, Norway 46, South Africa 38, UK 22.

• Answers to Prayer

1 **Church growth increased in the 1990s** in the midst of political and natural disasters. The Lutheran Church gained 300,000 new converts in 1995. Pentecostal and charismatic congregations have multiplied. A number of churches, including CEIM and METM, have been showing remarkable growth numerically and spiritually.

2 **Complete freedom of religion** after years of Marxist rhetoric. There is a deep spiritual hunger and now is the time of harvest.

3 **The election of a Christian President in 2002.** Pray that political and denominational leaders may use their power with humility and wisdom.

• Challenges for Prayer

1 **The Protestant Church has had a glorious history** of faith despite persecution from heathen rulers and harassment from the French Catholic colonial authorities. It grew from 5,000 in 1861 to one million in 1900. There have been significant revival movements within the larger churches in 1895, 1941, 1948, and during the 1980s. Springing from the revival movements have been the indigenous lay movements of 'shepherds', which operate within the mainline Protestant Federation Churches from 50 centres across the island. Their emphasis on healing and exorcism has led to conversions and full churches in some areas. May this movement continue to grow and be rooted in Scripture.

2 **Spiritual deadness rather than revival characterizes many congregations.** Compromise with the old beliefs, veneration of ancestral spirits, and witchcraft are widespread and even increasing among those who claim to be Christians. The forms of worship remain, but many have little understanding of the biblical message of salvation. The Christian community is 80% Christianized, but not really evangelized. Pray that the power of Jesus might be manifested, and that many may trust Him completely.

3 **Evangelical believers** are predominantly found in the revival movements in the mainline churches — especially sections of the Lutheran Church, and in the Pentecostal and Baptist Churches — most of which are of indigenous origin. Pray for unity among true believers and also for effective evangelism through them. The need for practical training for outreach is great.

4 **Theological training is the greatest source of weakness for the Church.** There are seven seminaries and ten Bible schools, but some are theologically liberal and easily accommodate astrology and heathen customs. Pray that such schools may return to the biblical theology for which their forebears laid down their lives. The Assemblies of God, Baptists, METM (with AIM involvement) and the Jesus Saves Pentecostal Church have evangelical Bible colleges. Pray for the provision of well-trained, Spirit-led leaders who are able to apply biblical truth to the Malagasy worldview.

5 **Young people** are the key for the future in the rapidly-growing population. **SU** has 15 full-time workers in school and camp ministries, and UGBM(**IFES**) has 5 staff workers with 2,000 members in 120 groups. These have had impact in the capital, but little is done in other parts of the country. **YWAM** and **YFC** also have increasing ministry. Pray for them and for the mobilization of young people for evangelism. **CEF** have a growing work among children.

6 Less-reached areas and peoples:

a) Over 5,000 villages and 5 million people live in the less-evangelized north and south. The main problem is inaccessibility. Churches and Christians are few. The ministry of **MAF** and Helimission in providing a ministry life-line is vital for advancing the gospel. Malagasy evangelists travel for days to reach such villages — pray for health, bicycles, finance and faith for them.

b) Malagasy traditionalists are in the great majority among, for example, the Sakalava in the west, and the Betsimisaraka, Mahafaly, Bara, Antambahoaka and Tankarana. Over 80% of the southern population is still non-Christian. The Mahafaly on the SW tip of the island are asking for spiritual help. Shaman healers and witchcraft abound. Demonization is a major problem.

c) Muslims are growing in numbers among the Sakalava on the west coast, the Antemoro in the east and the Antankarana in the north. International and national Muslim efforts to strengthen and spread Islam by extensive mosque-building, offers of education and teaching have gathered momentum. Folk Islam is the norm. Pray that the present spiritual vacuum might be filled by the gospel. Specific outreach to Muslims is limited. The Lutheran Church has a vigorous outreach to them with the **Shalom** programme and **AIM** has started a ministry among the Sakalava and Bara.

d) Ethnic minorities. Pray for the Muslim Comorians and Gujarati traders with few known believers among them; **AIM** seeks workers to initiate ministry to them.

7 The Protestant mission force has been small, but visa restrictions are a big limitation for increasing their numbers. The big challenge is for more pioneers, willing to go to areas where health and living conditions are difficult. Long-term commitment to, and love for, the people, their language and their culture is needed — many short-term outreaches have not been wisely planned. Many expatriates are committed to ministry with and for existing indigenous denominations — in Bible teaching, literature and holistic service. Largest mission agencies: Norwegian Lutherans (46 workers), **YWAM** (27), SdA (24), **AIM** (18), **CCCI** (17), **MAF** (14), Evangelical Lutherans, USA (14), **AoG** (8), **CBI** (4).

8 Christian support ministries — pray for eternal fruit!

a) Bibles. The Protestant Malagasy Bible has been available since 1836. It has a treasured place in the culture of the Merina but is hard for other dialects to understand. Pray that its message may enter hearts. **The Bible Society** (**UBS**) has a widely recognized ministry and a vigorous distribution programme, but lack of foreign exchange limits importation and printing of the Scriptures. A new, much more readable inter-confessional Malagasy Bible is being translated. All Christian literature is in short supply. There are few good, spiritual books in Malagasy. The Lutherans and Catholics have large printing presses.

b) Christian radio. Christian programmes are regularly aired on national and on a multiplying number of local FM stations in the larger urban centres — but all lack consistent quality, organization or leadership. *Avotra*, a local ministry, has a radio station in Nosy Be with some ministry to Muslims. **HCJB** and the Islands Mission have helped to set up a number of the FM stations. Both **TWR**-Swaziland and **FEBA**-Seychelles broadcast a total of 9 hours in Malagasy and 7 hours in French weekly. Poverty and lack of batteries in rural areas limit audiences.

c) The JESUS film, in both Malagasy and French, is being widely used, but needs to be available in dialects other than Merina.

Malawi

Republic of Malawi

Map labels: Zambia, Tanzania, Malawi, Lake Nyasa, Lilongwe, Mozambique, Zimbabwe, Indian Ocean

AUGUST 2
AFRICA
Updated February 2004

 GEOGRAPHY
Area 118,484 sq.km. Central African state extending along Lake Malawi and its outflow river, the Shire. Landlocked and virtually an enclave within Mozambique.

Population	Ann.Gr.	Density
2000	10,925,238	+2.47%	92 per sq. km.
2010	13,912,265	+2.49%	117 per sq. km.
2025	19,958,349	+2.29%	168 per sq. km.

Population could decline through AIDS deaths.

Capitals Lilongwe (ministerial and financial) 480,000; Blantyre (commercial and judicial) 500,000. **Urbanites** 11%.

PEOPLES
Over 22 Bantu peoples:
Maravi 81%. Chewa 5.7 mill.; Nyanja 1.3m; Tumbuka 940,000; Tonga 170,000.
Southern peoples 16%. Yao 1m; Sena(3) 270,000; Lomwe 250,000; Ngoni (being absorbed into Chewa) 75,000.
Northern peoples 1.6%. Ngonde 85,000; Lambya 45,000; Nyakusa 25,000.
Other 1.4%. South Asian 30,000; English-speaking 17,000. Also Mozambicans, Zambians, etc.

Literacy 56% (functionally half this). **Official languages** Chewa and English. **All languages** 15. **Languages with Scriptures** 8Bi 3por 3w.i.p.

ECONOMY
Well-watered and fertile but impoverished by overpopulation, geography (civil wars in Mozambique), falling world prices for tobacco, tea and sugar, poor communications to the outside world and AIDS. Heavily dependent on international aid and on rainfall — there have been famine conditions since 1997 and a severe economic downturn. Many Malawians work in other lands. **HDI** 0.399; 159th/174. **Public debt** 97% of GNP. **Income/person** $210 (0.67% of USA).

POLITICS
Independent from Britain in 1964. Dr. Hastings Banda ruled for 30 years as a colourful but ruthless dictator. Economic stability was gained at the expense of political freedom. Internal and international pressure against increasing corruption led to multi-party elections in 1993. The rule of Muslim President Bakili Muluzi led to improvements in human rights and democracy. New elections are due in 2004 in which Muluzi is constitutionally barred from running for a third term.

RELIGION
Freedom of religion, but some suspect a favouring of the Muslim minority.

Religions	Population %	Adherents	Ann.Gr.
Christian	79.98	8,738,005	+2.8%
Muslim	13.00	1,420,281	+2.9%
Traditional ethnic	6.20	677,365	-2.6%
non-Religious/other	0.60	65,551	+17.7%
Baha'i	0.20	21,850	+2.5%
Hindu	0.02	2,185	-5.5%

Christians	Denom.	Affil.%	,000	Ann.Gr.
Protestant	46	28.36	3,099	+5.7%
Independent	280	18.33	2,002	+7.0%
Anglican	1	1.83	200	+1.6%
Catholic	1	22.88	2,500	+1.2%
Orthodox	1	0.01	1	+0.0%
Marginal	1	0.92	100	+6.7%
Unaffiliated		7.65	836	n.a.

Churches	MegaBloc	Cong.	Members	Affiliates
Catholic	C	2,000	1,302,083	2,500,000
African Indep [230+]	I	9,572	765,766	1,700,000
CCAP (Presbyterian)	P	503	595,000	1,364,000
Seventh-day Adventist	P	557	165,911	300,000
Assemblies of God	P	1,450	120,000	250,000
Anglican	A	360	80,000	200,000
Zambezi Evangelical	P	550	80,000	190,000
African Baptist Assembly	P	800	65,000	162,500
Living Waters	I	575	70,000	120,000
Church of Christ	P	2,350	50,898	85,000
Baptist Convention	P	600	45,000	80,000
Other Charismatic	I	250	45,000	70,000
Evangelical Baptist	P	310	21,000	46,620
Ch of the Nazarene	P	160	20,000	37,000
Apostolic Faith Mission	P	167	15,000	32,000
Pentecostal Ch of M.	P	340	14,000	30,000
Ch of God (Cleveland)	P	286	13,475	30,000
Chr Chs/Chs of Christ	P	280	20,000	29,000
Africa Evangelical	P	40	9,700	22,000
Lutheran Ch of C Afr	P	180	13,000	20,000
Family Calvary	I	50	10,000	18,000
Free Methodist	P	200	10,000	16,000
Christian Brethren	P	120	8,000	16,000
Foursquare Gospel	P	150	11,000	16,000
Ch of God of Prophecy	P	50	7,000	14,000
Agape	I	30	6,000	12,600
New Life Churches	I	100	5,714	12,000
Deeper Life Christian	I	15	1,350	3,240
Other denoms [36]		3,000	214,000	526,000
Total Christians [330]		24,840	3,790,000	7,900,000

 **M**

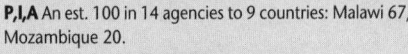

Trans-bloc Groupings	pop.%	,000	Ann.Gr.
Evangelical	20.4	2,228	+10.5%
Charismatic	16.1	1,763	+13.0%
Pentecostal	6.4	699	+26.6%

Missionaries from Malawi

P,I,A An est. 100 in 14 agencies to 9 countries: Malawi 67, Mozambique 20.

Missionaries to Malawi

P,I,A 436 in 68 agencies from 20 countries: USA 200, UK 50, South Africa 42, Zimbabwe 29.

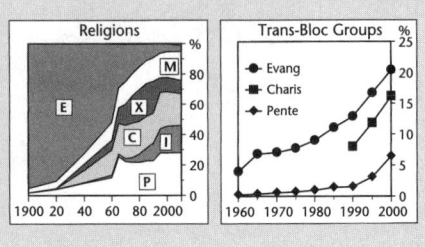

• Answers to Prayer

1 **The courage and outspokenness of Catholic and Protestant leaders** were a major factor in ending the dictatorship through democratic change.

2 **Malawi continues to be spiritually the most receptive country in central Africa.** Years of evangelical outreach (**AE, DM**, Global Field Evangelism, CFAN evangelistic campaigns), burgeoning youth outreach (**SU, IFES**), New Life For All programmes in the churches, multiplied house meetings and prayer movements have all contributed to the blessing. Since 1996 there has been a move of the Spirit at every level of the Anglican Church. The Anglican youth organization *One In Christ Youth* has had denomination-wide evangelistic impact. The gospel has penetrated into nearly every section of society, and in places there have been local revivals. Newer charismatic, Pentecostal and evangelical denominations have grown rapidly.

• Challenges for Prayer

1 **Malawi has remained relatively peaceful** since independence in a region of devastating wars and turmoil. Yet these wars have exacted a terrible economic toll in under-development. Raised expectations of democratic government have not been realized. Pray that the nation may be led by leaders of integrity and that the new democracy may lead to the improved well-being of the people.

2 **The growth of Islam** is a major challenge. Over 90% of the Yao are Muslim and constitute the bulk of Muslims in Malawi. The majority of the Asians are also Muslim. The *Qur'an* has been translated into Chewa. Islam has become more visible and confident and Muslim aid projects have increased. Malawi is now the Southern African base for the Africa Muslim Agency. Expansion of Islam to other peoples is not extensive yet but is taking place. Pray for good relations between Christians and Muslims and for an effective ministry to bring Muslims to a personal relationship with Christ. Since 9-11 there has been increasing Islamist agitation and isolated acts of violence against Christians.

3 **AIDS is a terrible, but under-reported scourge.** Life expectancy has been cut to 43, officially 16% (and perhaps over 30%) of all 14- to 49-year-olds are infected, but 60% of new infections in the 14-25 age group are girls. There are up to 400,000 AIDS orphans. The viability of families, villages, the economy and even the state are threatened. Pray that churches might be better equipped and envisioned to face AIDS with effective ministries. **SU** has launched an effective **Aid for AIDS** prevention campaign in primary schools.

4 **The CCAP is the largest Protestant denomination** and the direct fruit of the vision of the 19th Century explorer, David Livingstone. It is a union of the churches planted by the South African Dutch Reformed Church, the Church of Scotland and the Free Church of Scotland. Pray for revival as nominalism and formalism predominate, yet there are also strong evangelical leaders and congregations. Pray that second- and third-generation Christians may come to personal faith, and for many to be called into full-time ministry.

5 **The major issues to be tackled by the churches are:**

a) *Maintaining effective ministry* in the midst of deep poverty and the growing AIDS crisis.

b) *Training new workers* for spiritually weak rural churches — few can afford the training or the subsequent support. TEE courses are run by the Brethren and Baptists.

c) **Effective theological education.** There are 13 Protestant and two Roman Catholic seminaries or Bible schools. Pray that the CCAP theological faculty at Zomba might take a more strongly evangelical stand. Pray for many to be called into the ministry, and for the provision of funds to enable them to complete their studies.

d) **Unity.** Pray for more cooperation between the Evangelical Association of Malawi (**EAM**), the Christian Council (CCM) and the CHAPEL network of Pentecostals and charismatics. Pray that the Malawi National Initiative for Mission and Evangelism may unite the churches in effective evangelism and outreach.

e) **A good survey of Malawi** to analyze the unfinished task.

6 **Student ministries have flourished** (Life Ministries-**CCCI** and SCOM-**IFES**). There are over 500 SCOM high school groups and a further 25 in the universities and colleges with over a fifth of the 120,000 tertiary students involved. Students are open to the gospel — and to error. Pray for godly leadership for these groups and ultimately for the Church and nation as a result.

7 **The least evangelized.** Pray that both Malawian and expatriate workers may effectively share the love of Christ with:

a) **The Yao,** who remain the biggest challenge in Malawi. More orthodox Islamic practices are increasingly replacing the prevalent folk Islam. In earlier decades the Anglicans, CCAP, Catholics and Baptists won about 3% of the Yao, but these have become a separate people in the process. Current attempts are being made by a partnership of evangelical missions: **IMB-SBC**, **SIM**, **BiC**, **AoG**, Deeper Life and others, but very few have come to Christ in the past few decades and there is not yet an indigenous Yao Church.

b) **The Ngonde and Lambya** in the far north, who are less well evangelized, though there are some churches among them.

c) **The Sena and Lomwe** of the Shire valley in the south with relatively few Christians. The majority of these peoples live in neighbouring Mozambique where response to the gospel has mushroomed since peace came to that land.

d) **The Gujarati and Tamil,** the main groups of Asians. Only sporadic attempts are made to evangelize these Hindu and Muslim peoples.

8 **Expatriate missionaries** are primarily engaged in supporting existing denominations and agencies in training, outreach and Christian institutions. Pray for a deep heart identification with Malawian believers and fruitful ministries in this day of opportunity. The largest agencies: **CCCI** (62 workers), all Presbyterians (54), **IMB-SBC** (41), SdA (36), **CoN** (17), Churches of Christ (17), **AoG** (14), Anglicans (14), PAoC (10), **SIM** (6).

9 Christian help ministries for prayer:

a) **Bible translation.** The completion of the whole Bible in Lomwe, Ngonde, Sena and Yao are the major challenges. Several other languages are without a New Testament and may need translations.

b) **The Bible Society.** There are big demands for Scriptures for local use and for the large refugee community — but limited funds to meet them. Many rural Christians have no Bibles. The Bible on cassette is a developing ministry.

c) **Literature.** This is much sought after, but expensive. **CLAIM** is a joint publishing and distribution venture involving 14 denominations and agencies with 37 outlets and 200 agencies, as well as programmes to train workers. Pray for the adequate supply of quality reading material for the literate, growing, but poor Church.

d) **Christian radio.** The national broadcasting network regularly airs Christian programmes. The Baptist Media Centre is a key resource for many churches and agencies in preparing materials, tapes and programmes. **TWR**-Swaziland broadcasts in Chewa-Nyanja (13 hrs/wk), Lomwe (2), Tumbuka (1.5) and, together with **FEBA**, Yao (2). The African Bible College in Lilongwe and **TWR** in Blantyre have local FM radio stations.

Malaysia

AUGUST 3-5
ASIA
Updated February 2004

GEOGRAPHY

Area 330,434 sq.km. Two distinct parts: Peninsular (West) Malaysia on the Kra peninsula of mainland Asia (PM), and East Malaysia (EM) consisting of the territories of Sarawak and Sabah on the northern third of the island of Borneo. Well-watered; tropical rain forest.

Population	Ann.Gr.	Density
2000	22,244,062	+2.04%	67 per sq. km.
2010	25,919,134	+1.38%	78 per sq. km.
2025	30,968,453	+1.15%	94 per sq. km.

PM 81.5%, Sabah 9.9%, Sarawak 9.6%.

Capital Kuala Lumpur 2,150,000. **Urbanites** 57%. Chinese and Indians are largely urban.

PEOPLES

The Malay population is increasing at the expense of the Chinese and Indian populations. **Indigenous peoples** (Bumiputera) 57.7%.
   Malay 49.5%. Predominantly rural but dominating politics, civil service, armed forces and police.
   Tribal peoples 8.2%. A majority in Sarawak, and largest segment of Sabah's population. Over 130 languages spoken.
Non-indigenous 35.8%.
   Chinese 25.4%. Speaking over nine major dialects; majority Hokkien, Cantonese, Hakka and Teochew. Influential in commerce and business in PM and EM.
   Indian 7.2%. Tamil 1.2 mill.; Malayali 100,000; Telugu 67,000; Panjabi 66,000; etc. Mainly urban or poor estate workers. Almost all in PM.
   Other 3.2%. Indonesian, Filipino, British, Thai, Burmese, Sri Lankan, Pakistani.
Other migrants 6.5%. Mainly Indonesian, also many Filipino in Sabah; Bangladeshi, Thai, Myanmar, etc., in PM. Some estimate there may be as many as 1.7 million migrants — most illegal.

Literacy 84%. **Official language** Malay (Bahasa Malay). **All languages** 137. **Languages with Scriptures** 15Bi 9NT 16por 12w.i.p.

ECONOMY

Vigorous growth since independence — especially during the 1990s. Large-scale indus-

trialization together with logging, oil, mining and agriculture have transformed the country. Many immigrants from Sumatra, Philippines and other nations have been attracted by the wealth and now comprise 10% of the work force. The Asian recession of 1998 slowed growth. **HDI** 0.768; 56th/174. **Public debt** 17% of GNP. **Income/person** $4,530 (15% of USA).

POLITICS

Independent from Britain in 1957 as the Federation of Malaya. In 1963, Sabah and Sarawak joined to form Malaysia, a federation of 13 states with a constitutional monarchy. Recent years have been dominated by the efforts of the politically powerful Malays to extend their influence over the non-Malay half of the population in educational, economic and religious life. The growing power of fundamentalist Muslim political parties and affirmative action policies which favour the Bumiputera has further polarized the country, with consequent inter-ethnic and inter-religious tensions.

RELIGION

Sunni Islam is the official and favoured religion in PM, and there is continual pressure to apply the same in EM, where Islam is a minority. In the 1980s, limitations on religious freedom were introduced. In 1999 the government relaxed some restrictions, such as on places of worship, the issue of missionary visas, public meetings and publications. It is illegal to proselytize Muslims, but considerable effort is expended to induce animistic tribal people and Chinese to become Muslim. **Persecution index** 47th in world.

Religions	Population %	Adherents	Ann.Gr.
Muslim	58.00	12,901,556	+2.6%
Buddhist/Chinese	21.59	4,802,493	+0.7%
Christian	9.21	2,048,678	+2.2%
Hindu	5.00	1,112,203	+0.1%
non-Religious/other	4.50	1,000,983	+7.6%
Traditional ethnic	1.20	266,929	-5.9%
Baha'i	0.40	88,976	+2.0%
Sikh	0.10	22,244	+0.1%

Christians	Denom.	Affil.%	,000	Ann.Gr.
Protestant	46	3.00	668	+3.3%
Independent	15	1.21	269	+5.6%
Anglican	1	0.81	180	+1.4%
Catholic	1	2.86	636	-0.3%
Orthodox	1	0.01	2	+0.8%
Marginal	7	0.03	7	+5.6%
Unaffiliated		1.29	287	n.a.

Churches	MegaBloc	Cong.	Members	Affiliates
Catholic	C	147	336,508	636,000
Independent [10]	I	911	108,888	230,000
Methodist	P	1,150	90,000	210,000
Anglican	A	350	104,651	180,000
Ev Ch of Borneo SIB	P	601	62,738	150,000
Seventh-day Adventist	P	232	39,421	70,000
Basel Christian	P	115	26,374	48,000
Assemblies of God	P	201	27,820	37,000

Chr Brethren	P	140	5,500	11,000
Lutheran Ch in M & S	P	35	3,378	7,500
Jehovah's Witnesses	M	46	2,046	4,600
Elim Pentecostal	P	4	400	720
Other denoms [50]		1,086	94,500	176,400
Total Christians [71]		5,018	902,000	1,761,000

Trans-bloc Groupings	pop.%	,000	Ann.Gr.
Evangelical	4.1	908	+3.8%
Charismatic	2.3	510	+4.0%
Pentecostal	0.4	93	+5.4%

Missionaries from Malaysia
P,I,A 394 in 25 agencies to 37 countries: Malaysia 270, on ships 21.

Missionaries to Malaysia
P,I,A 285 in 54 agencies from 21 countries: USA 122, Korea 51, Philippines 25.

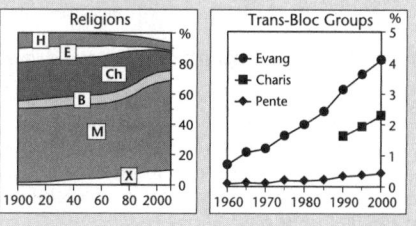

MALAYSIA, GENERAL

• Answers to Prayer

1 **Continued growth in size and maturity of the Church** despite the restriction on propagation of Christian faith to Muslims. Evangelical churches are playing a significant role in hosting and contributing to international conferences.

2 **Visionary goals set in 1992 (DAWN)** have been largely achieved:
a) *The number of evangelical churches* has grown from 2,500 to over 4,000.
b) *Over 110 Bahasa Malay congregations* by 1999 — the goal was 200 for 2000.
c) *A growing prayer movement with spiritual renewal* and a greater sense of unity among churches.

• Challenges for Prayer

1 **Muslims have been politically and socially divided** because of the vociferous Islamist minority which has pressed for radical Islamic reforms and imposition of *shari'a* law. Severe penalties for infringements by Muslims or for their apostasy have been instituted in 4 of the 13 states. Muslims, and thereby almost all Malays, have been denied the privilege of receiving the gospel. Pray both for:
a) *The Malays, now socially and legally* isolated from the Truth. It is illegal to witness to a Muslim.
b) *The rejection of proposed national legislation* to impose an apostasy law so that everyone, including Malays, may have opportunity to hear the gospel.

2 **Islamization** has brought concern to those of other faiths who comprise nearly half the population. Any attempt to impose Islamization may threaten religious freedom. In 2002 Terengganu State made the *shari'a* criminal code into law. Pray that Christians may respond and act constructively and their faith be strengthened at this time. Pray also for:
a) *The constitutional provision of religious freedom to be upheld* and that Christians may not be intimidated by threats but rather be bold to stand for their constitutional rights and for their heavenly right to proclaim the gospel.
b) *Unity among Christians* in the midst of Islamic resurgence. **The Christian Federation** brings together Evangelicals and Protestants, Catholic and mainline denominations for representation to the government. The **National Evangelical Christian Fellowship** (NECF) Malaysia is a more closely knit body to unite traditional Evangelicals, Pentecostals and Charismatics for nation-wide outreach, spiritual conferences and advocacy of missions vision.
c) *Courageous Christian leaders* who are prepared, at considerable personal risk, to reason with or confront the authorities over manifest inconsistencies and injustices in the treatment of former and non-Muslims.

3 **The Church continues to grow**, but faces real challenges:

a) *Lack of Christian workers.* Many smaller churches have no trained pastor. There are over 16 Bible colleges and seminaries. Too few are responding to God's call to service.

b) *Their marginalization* creates anxiety, a ghetto mentality and desire to withdraw from being the witnesses Christians should be. There is a high emigration of professionals and Bible school graduates.

c) *The need to re-think attitudes* and effective service to non-Christian neighbours.

4 **Since Malay became the official national language**, Christians have been pushed into a series of crises. Pray for solutions to:

a) *The need for Christian literature in the Malay language.* Writers are few and the market is still small, yet all the younger generation are being educated in this medium. Christian literature is widely available in English. There are 24 Christian bookstores and an active Bible Society.

b) *The restriction of the public use of the Indonesian Bible.* A government directive was issued to forbid the use and sale of the Bible in the related Indonesian language. This commonly uses terminology claimed exclusively by Muslims, so Indonesian Christian literature is not allowed to be sold publicly. Pray for a full resolution to this issue. Since 2002 other Christian books in Malay and local languages have been banned.

c) *The language used in church services.* Adaptation to Malay would be wise, but churches are cautious in its use for fear of any adverse implications.

5 **Ministry to young people** has been very fruitful with many Indian, Chinese and East Malaysians coming to Christ through agencies such as **YFC**, **CCCI**, **Navigators**, **SU**, FES(**IFES**) and others in schools and universities. It has become increasingly difficult to have any ministry within the schools in PM, even those founded by Christians, which makes outreach and discipling more difficult.

6 **Malaysians studying overseas.** The limited opportunities for higher education for non-Malays has forced large numbers of Malaysian Chinese and Indians to study overseas or in local private colleges. Many have come to Christ in such situations, where they often become the most enthusiastic Christian group on campus. Pray that they may retain that enthusiasm when they return home.

7 **Expatriate Christian workers** have declined in numbers because of increased visa problems. Their presence is still valued and various ministries depend on their input. Pray for the issue of necessary visas and extensions. Pray also for effective ministry within the limitations that exist.

M **8** **The missions vision** of the Church in Malaysia has continued to increase and over 800 serve with 26 agencies in countries round the world. NECF is seeking to stimulate this vision and enable local congregations to be effective sending churches. Major agencies being **OM**, **YWAM**, **OMF**, **WBT**, **WEC** and **Navigators**.

PENINSULAR MALAYSIA

GEOGRAPHY **Area** 132,000 sq.km.; 40% of Malaysia; the south-easternmost point of mainland Asia.
Population 17,973,000.

PEOPLES
Malay 56%.
Chinese 33%.
Indian 10.2%.
Orang Asli (original indigenous peoples) 0.7%.
Mon-Khmer (18 peoples) largest: Semai (Senoi 28,000; Temier 18,000; Kensiu 4,300).
Proto-Malay (5 peoples) largest: Jakun 15,000, Temuan 15,000.

RELIGION Muslim 60%; Chinese religions/Buddhist 26%; Hindu 8%; Christian 4%; Non-religious 2%.

• Challenges for Prayer

1 **The Church is growing amongst all non-Muslim ethnic groups** — about 10% of the Orang Asli, 10% of Indians and 7% of Chinese are Christian (about a third being Catholic). Yet the continual external pressure from Islam at every level, the pressure from non-Christian families to compromise and the lure of materialism have harmed real commitment. Many young people come to the Lord, but the rate of backsliding after entering employment is high. Pray for a deep work of the Holy Spirit in reviving and emboldening the believers.

2 **Worship and witness patterns** may have to be modified to survive and grow under pressure. Greater cooperation, sharing of resources between denominations and a more vital household worship style must be explored — cell churches have grown well during the 1990s. Pray for Holy Spirit guidance for the leaders and the emergence of a strong, relevant Church that impacts the majority population.

3 **The less-evangelized**. The Malaysian Church has the resources and the understanding of the local scene in PM to reach the less-reached, but also needs the courage and commitment. Pray especially for:

a) *The Malays*. The legal and social barriers are high, but for Christians to share their faith is possible. There are some Malay believers in house groups and multi-ethnic churches, but there are no viable congregations of ethnic Malays. Malays can be reached more easily abroad and in nearby Singapore.

b) *The Chinese* — although there are a significant minority of Christians, there are specific areas of need. Materialism and traditional religions are still strong. Presbyterian, Pentecostal and charismatic denominations are growing, but mostly among the urban middle-class English-speaking Chinese. There are no churches using Hainanese (200,000 people), and the Hakka, Teochew and Kwongsai are little better served. Rural and small-town Chinese are patchily evangelized and only half the 450 Chinese villages have a church.

c) *The Orang Asli* who are considered by the Malays to be Muslim even though they dislike Islam and its restrictions and remain committed to their traditional ways. In spite of Muslim offers of bribes, and obstructions for any Christian witness to them, probably 10% are now Christians. Only the Semai and Temuan have a viable church-planting movement, though there are some believers in most of the 19 peoples. Methodists, Brethren, Pentecostals and Lutherans have all planted churches among them, but the big challenge is to see an indigenous church-planting movement that is culturally their own. Only two languages have NTs and work is in progress in two more; a further 15 may need translation teams.

d) *Indians*. There are many Tamil Christians, but few among the estate labourers. Other Indian ethnic minorities are less reached — the 66,000 Panjabis (mostly Sikh) with less than 100 known believers, and the Telugus. Indian Muslims number some 50,000; there has been no specific outreach to them. The Tamil Bible Institute (**AsEF**) is training Christian workers to reach Indian communities with the gospel. A Tamil Pastor's Fellowship was formed in 1996.

e) *The socially marginalized*. Drug addiction is a major problem — especially among the Malay youth. Pray for effective Christian ministry to addicts and also for prison ministries.

f) *Minangkabau, Acehnese, Malays*, etc., from Sumatra, Indonesia, have come in their hundreds of thousands seeking work. Very few have ever heard the gospel. Some outreach in Indonesian/Malay goes on, and a few have responded. A high proportion of Bahasa Malay congregations are ethnically Indonesian.

SABAH (formerly North Borneo)

GEOGRAPHY **Area** 74,000 sq.km. Rich in natural resources.
Population 2,200,000. Augmented by more than one million immigrants from the Philippines and Indonesia.

PEOPLES — all figures approximate.
Indigenous peoples 28%. Of 38 peoples, the largest: Kadazan-Dusun(20) 500,000; Murut(13)

75,000; Bisaya 20,000; Bajau 5,000.
Other Malaysian 29%. Chinese 440,000; Malay 200,000.
Migrant peoples 43%.
Indonesian 30%. Javanese, Banjar, Bugis, Wolio; mainly Muslim.
Filipino 14%. Tausugg, Bajau, Sama, Molbog, Ilanun, Mapun; almost all Muslim.

RELIGIONS
Muslim est. 55%; Christian 33%; Traditional ethnic 5%; Other 7%.

• Challenges for Prayer

1 The State government had a bad record for corruption and plundering the forests. Pray for leadership that encourages honesty, inter-ethnic harmony and ecological sensitivity.

2 Rapid church growth is taking place among the Chinese, Kadazan, Tagal and Murut peoples through the work of the Basel Mission, Anglicans and **SIB**. The **SIB** has over 300 congregations in Sabah. The Charismatic movement has deeply affected nearly every denomination. Some 27% of the Chinese and the majority of the indigenous peoples are now Christian. Nominalism, the drift to the cities of tribal peoples and serious lack of full-time workers are unresolved problems for the churches. The Sabah Council of Churches is a catalyst for fellowship, links with the government, evangelism, conferences and Bible translation. The loss of nearly all missionary visas is a challenge for local Christians to evangelize the unreached in Sabah.

3 Less-reached peoples:

a) *The Muslim peoples* are almost untouched. Pray for specific outreach to:
   i *The Filipino-related peoples*, many being refugees from the Muslim uprising in Mindanao, Philippines.
   ii *The Indonesians*, most being illegal immigrants from Sulawesi and Java. Little is being done to reach them.
   iii *The local Malay and Muslim tribal peoples*, notably the Bisaya and Bajau.
b) *Some tribal groups*, still only partially evangelized, though there have been large people movements among them. Few languages have the New Testament. There are only 6 teams working in 14 languages, but there are virtually no foreign personnel left. Pray for the calling of local Christians for translation work — both to complete the 13 existing NT projects and to start on the 20 languages which must still be surveyed.

SARAWAK

GEOGRAPHY **Area** 124,500 sq.km. Forested — but massive over-exploitation in progress. **Population** 2,135,000.

PEOPLES — all figures approximate. **Indigenous** 50%. Over 46 groups, largest: Iban (Sea Dayak) 390,000; Dayak 110,000; Melanau 38,000; Kedayan 26,000; Kayan(3) 10,000; Kenyah(5) 9,000; Punan 3,000.

Other Malaysian 45%. Chinese, Malay. **Other immigrants** 5%.

RELIGIONS Christian est. 38%; Muslim 27%; Traditional ethnic 26%; Other 9%.

M

• Challenges for Prayer

1 Sarawak has experienced a series of thrilling movements of the Spirit over the last 60 years. Through the work of the Evangelical Church of Borneo (SIB/**OMF**) and others, people movements and revivals have taken place in many of the smaller tribes. The SIB has over 260 congregations, five Bible schools and a work in more than 10 peoples, with a vigorous outreach to towns and unreached peoples. Praise God for this, and pray for a retention of the spirit of revival in the up-and-coming generation. A number of the coastal churches among the Chinese are more nominal, others are flourishing. Nearly half the Chinese now profess to be Christians.

2 The Church is under pressure through materialism in the towns and severe pressure from Muslims in some rural areas. Pray that believers may not only stand firm in their faith, but become more bold in their witness. Pray that leadership in the churches may be able to handle the complexities of national politics and the nurture of churches scattered over a land with many transport difficulties outside the towns.

3 Growth is being held back by the lack of new workers. Nearly half the SIB congregations have no pastor, and many of the existing pastors are obliged to work part-time because of lack of finance. The sending out of supported pioneer workers is therefore limited. Pray for the calling and support of many more young people.

Maldives

Republic of Maldives

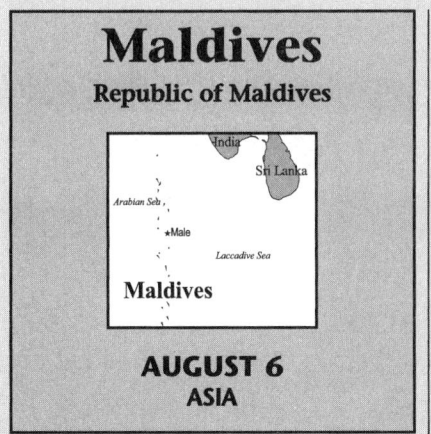

AUGUST 6

ASIA

PEOPLES
Indigenous 93%. Maldivians of Dravidian origin.
Foreign 7%. Indian, Sri Lankan, Pakistani, Bangladeshi and some Westerners, mainly in temporary employment.
Literacy 93%. **Official language** Dhivehi of Sanskrit origin.

ECONOMY
Fishing and tourism are the significant foreign exchange earners. Lack of fertile soil and fresh water and the high population density keep the people at subsistence level. **HDI** 0.716; 93rd/174. **Public debt** 51% of GNP. **Income/person** $1,180 (4% of USA).

POLITICS
Long tradition of isolated independence. The nominal British protectorate terminated in 1965. A non-party republic since 1968.

GEOGRAPHY
Area 298 sq.km. 1,200 coral islands in 19 administrative groups 600 km southwest of Sri Lanka in the Indian Ocean. Only 202 islands are inhabited. These have an average size of less than 1 sq.km and all are between one and two metres above sea level.

RELIGION
Islam is the only recognized religion. The open practice of all other religions is forbidden. Islam is strongly promoted for national unity and preservation of the government's power.

Population	Ann.Gr.	Density
2000	286,223	+2.82%	960 per sq.km.
2010	373,116	+2.63%	1,252 per sq.km.
2025	501,456	+1.57%	1,683 per sq.km.

Capital Male 70,000. **Urbanites** 27%.

Religions	Population %	Adherents	Ann.Gr.
Muslim	99.41	284,534	+2.8%
Buddhist	0.45	1,288	+1.9%
Christian	0.10	286	+7.5%
non-Religious/other	0.03	86	+11.5%
Hindu	0.01	29	+3.0%

• Challenges for Prayer

1 **Global warming** threatens the survival of the Islands through rising sea levels that could flood and destroy them. Coral mining and a recent rise in sea temperature resulting from el Niño has killed much of the coral that is the foundation of these islands. Pray that this doomsday challenge may cause many to seek the caring God who sent Jesus.

2 **The Maldivians** are still among the least evangelized on earth. No Christian mission work has ever been permitted nor Christian literature allowed. Yet by various means some Maldivians came to faith in Christ during the 1990s. A severe crack-down by the authorities in 1998 resulted in the imprisonment and torture of 50 Maldivians suspected of being Christian and the expulsion of 19 Christian expatriates from several nations. International prayer and protest levered the release of the Maldivians from prison later in the year. Pray that they may not become discouraged but live for Jesus despite the spiritual pressures under which they live.

3 **Maldivian believers** are now physically free but carefully watched. They have suffered ostracism, loss of jobs and they cannot openly meet together or read the Scriptures. Pray that their faith may be strengthened and their lives radiate the beauty of Jesus to others. Pray also that the high-handedness of the authorities may provoke many to question the dictatorial imposition of what they should believe.

4 **Other means of witness** — pray for lasting fruit through:

a) ***Witness to Maldivians in other lands*** — many travel as sailors, students, seeking medical care, etc. Also, there are Maldivian communities in Sri Lankan and Indian coastal cities.
b) ***The Scriptures*** which are being translated into Dhivehi — pray that this may be completed soon. Pray also for ways to import Scriptures and Christian literature — there is

a rigid censorship being applied. Only small portions of scripture are currently available. Pray for the progress of the translation effort and for ways that the people may have free access to the Word in their heart language.

c) Christian Radio — **FEBA** broadcast 30 minutes weekly in Dhivehi despite government efforts to prevent this.

5 **Minicoy** is part of the Indian-ruled Lakshadweep Islands to the north of the Maldives, but its population is Maldivian. Pray for an open door for the gospel.

Mali
Republic of Mali

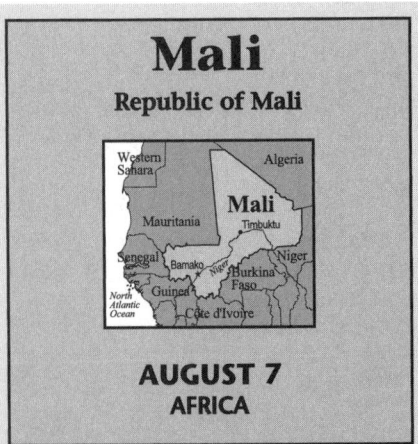

AUGUST 7
AFRICA

 GEOGRAPHY
Area 1,240,192 sq.km. Landlocked state. Dry southern grasslands merge into the Sahara Desert. The Niger River runs through the southern part of the country.

Population	Ann.Gr.	Density
2000	11,233,821	+2.47%	9 per sq. km.
2010	14,558,463	+2.69%	12 per sq. km.
2025	21,295,460	+2.37%	17 per sq. km.

Capital Bamako 1,500,000. **Urbanites** 26%.

PEOPLES
34 ethnic groups.
West African peoples 93.5%. Major linguistic groups:
Mande 55.7%. Bambara 3.7mill.; Soninke (Sarakule) 900,000; Malinke 578,000; Maninka 257,000; Kasonke 154,000; Bozo 154,000; Gana 96,500; Duun 90,000; Jula (Dioula) 64,500; Fulanke 64,500; Wassalunke 52,500.
Gur 18.4%. Senufo 643,000; Dogon 545,500; Minianka 456,000; Bobo (Bomu/Bwa) 393,000.
West Atlantic 12.1%. Fulbe (Fula) 1,325,000; Tukulor 173,500.
Nilo-Saharan 7.3%. Songhai 771,000; Idaksahak 38,700.
Berber 3.7%. Tuareg (speaking two Tamacheq languages) 418,000, 60% of whom are Bella, the former slaves of the Tukulor.
Arab 1.2%. Maure (Moor) 136,500.

Other 1.6%. French 6,000.
Literacy 31%. **Official language** French. Trade languages Bambara, Fulbe, Songhai. **All languages** 32. **Languages with Scriptures** 4Bi 5NT 5por 15w.i.p.

ECONOMY
Subsistence agricultural economy frequently devastated by drought, famine, desertification and locust plagues. The scarcity of natural resources is mitigated by the presence of large gold deposits. **HDI** 0.375; 166ᵗʰ/174. **Public debt/person** 101% of GNP. b $240 (0.8% of USA).

POLITICS
The modern successor to the great Malian empire of 1230-1400AD. Independent from France in 1960. Popular protests ousted a military dictatorship in 1991. Elections and a multi-party democracy ensued. The Tuareg in the northeast revolted against the central government in 1991 and gained a degree of autonomy in a subsequent pact in 1995.

RELIGION
A secular state with freedom of religion despite the large Muslim majority. Islam is strong in the north and centre and slowly growing in the south where traditional religions are stronger. These are strongest among the Dogon, Bobo, and Senufo/Minianka.

Religions	Population %	Adherents	Ann.Gr.
Muslim	87.00	9,773,424	+2.7%
Traditional ethnic	10.98	1,233,474	+0.7%
Christian	1.92	215,689	+2.5%
non-Religious/other	0.10	11,234	+2.5%

Christians	Denom.	Affil.%	,000	Ann.Gr.
Protestant	18	0.81	91	+3.3%
Independent	3	0.00	0	+8.5%
Catholic	1	0.98	110	+0.0%
Marginal	1	0.01	1	+17.1%
Unaffiliated		0.12	13	n.a.

Churches		MegaBloc	Cong.	Members	Affiliates
Catholic	C	40	61,453	110,000
Christian Evangelical	P	422	16,112	56,000
Evang Protestant	P	375	19,504	27,500
Assemblies of God (Fr)	P	20	601	2,000
Evangelical Free	P	22	410	1,000

Seventh-day Adventist	P	2	512	960
Jehovah's Witnesses	M	8	208	667
Norwegian Prot Mission	P	20	240	600
Alliance Mission	P	18	271	570
Seventh Day Baptist	P	2	307	512
Assemblies of God (USA)	P	17	125	350
Other denoms [12]		45	536	1,380
Total Christians [23]		991	100,300	202,000

Trans-bloc Groupings	pop.%	,000	Ann.Gr.
Evangelical	0.8	91	+3.2%
Charismatic	0.2	19	+2.9%
Pentecostal	0.0	2	+4.2%

Missionaries from Mali
P,I,A 95 in 7 agencies: 93 in Mali.

Missionaries to Mali
P,I,A 421 in 44 agencies from 27 countries: USA 215, Germany 35, Norway 33.

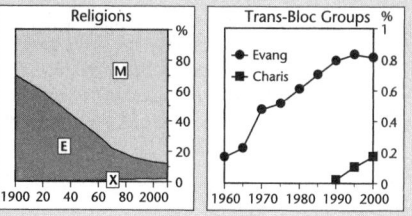

• Answers to Prayer

1 The progress of the gospel in the 1980s was praiseworthy:

a) *The Church* experienced accelerated growth — outstripping national population growth. The negative is the relative stagnation in the 1990s.

b) *The number of missions and missionaries*, both national and expatriate, more than doubled.

c) *Islam has proved a disappointment to many*, resulting in a greater openness to Christianity. There have been several large, localized people movements to Christ — among the Bambara (**GMU** area) and Bobo (**CMA** area).

d) *Inter-Mission Partnerships* have been formed for the evangelization of seven of the largest or most strategic peoples in Mali: the Bozo, Fulbe, Malinke, Soninke and Tuareg.

e) *God has used economic migration* to spread the Christians, and by extension, the gospel.

• Challenges for Prayer

1 Missions have multiplied, and few areas of the country are untargetted, but the north has a much lower concentration of Christian work. For years there were only four Protestant missions — **GMU** in the centre among the Bambara, **CMA** in the east among the Dogon, Bobo, Minianka and Senufo, **UWM** in the west among the Malinke and Evangelical Baptists in the north among the Tuareg and Songhai. Only in the more receptive **GMU** and **CMA** areas have strong churches emerged. In the 1980s, over 20 missions began work in Mali, but it is still a pioneer country — less than 2% are Christians. Pray for more missionaries to be sent out with the gifts needed to complete the evangelization of Mali — numbers did not increase in the 1990s.

M

2 The ecological crisis of the Sahel has brought much help from Christian missions and aid organizations which is reducing prejudice to the gospel. Pray for the many agencies actively involved in relief; local development to conserve soil, vegetation and water; digging wells; and medical outreach. Even so, there are only 903 medical dispensaries of any kind in Mali in contrast to 1,001 *Qur'anic* schools. Pray that these ministries might bear much fruit in the form of a mature, witnessing church.

3 Both Protestants and Catholics have grown slowly but steadily in the last two decades with significant numbers of converts from a Muslim background. Evangelicals are strong only among the Bambara (0.9%), Bobo (2.9%), Dogon (3.2%), and Senufo/Minianka (3.8%), with groups of believers in 19 other peoples. Material poverty limits funds for training and supporting pastors so Bible schools in the country are struggling. Pray for the rapid growth of believers in maturity and numbers in this day of opportunity. Pray for a decisive breakthrough among the more Muslim peoples.

4 Peoples where pioneer work has been established, but for which prayer is requested:

a) *The Bambara are a key people* for the evangelization of the country. **GMU, CMA, IMB-SBC** and **AoG** all work among the Bambara with believers in most denominations. There have been small victories in evangelism, but no major breakthroughs. Pray for the spiritual and numerical growth of the church amongst this strategic people.

b) ***The Fulbe*** are scattered throughout Mali, but with high concentrations in the south, centre, and northwest. Several groups of believers are being discipled by **CRWM/WEC**, Pioneers and Norwegian Lutherans.

c) ***The Fulanke and Kasonke***, though ethnically Fulbe, speak Malinke, and the Wassulunke speak Bambara, highlighting the need for distinct church-planting strategies. Of these, only the Kasonke are being reached (Norwegian Lutherans).

d) ***Peoples with virtually no Christians*** and no established workers: Maure, Jalunke, Kagoro, Tukulor, Wolof, etc.

e) ***Peoples where the work is in its beginning stages***: Bozo, Gana, Duun, Maninka, Marka, Jotoni and Soninke. Several agencies are ministering to these peoples, but in most there are only a few believers.

f) ***The Northern peoples*** are more strongly Muslim, yet hard pioneering work has resulted in some scattered congregations and believers among the desert Tuareg and the riverine Songhai (Ev. Baptists). The Tuareg work was gravely impaired by their insurrection in the early 1990s. The Idaksahak are a distinct Muslim people living among the Tuareg who appear responsive but for whom there are few workers. A rough draft of a Tamacheq NT was completed in 1999; pray for its wise use.

g) ***The Dogon*** have long held to their traditional religion, but many are now looking for alternatives. Many are turning to Islam. While the Dogon are more evangelized than most groups in Mali through the ministry of **CMA** (with 200 churches), this is an unprecedented opportunity for the gospel that must not be missed.

5 **Of the 34 ethnic groups, only four are more than 1% evangelical.** All peoples are in desperate need of the good news. There are 11 groups with no known evangelical believers. Among them are the Jula, Maure, and Tukulor. Pray also for the smaller (therefore often neglected) groups with 25,000 people or less and with no known believers (Duun, Mossi, Wolof, Banka, Jotoni, Pana, Samoa). Ask God to reveal the right approach so that these people might be reached with the gospel.

6 **Bamako, the capital and only major city in the country**, has 50 small churches and 100 expatriate missionaries but only a handful are involved in urban church planting. Many suburbs are still without a meaningful witness. Pray that this strategic centre may be effectively evangelized.

7 **Christian specialist and support ministries** for prayer:

a) ***Bible translation***. At least 12 languages may need translation or evaluation teams, and work is in progress in 15. Twenty-five of the **SIL** workers are involved in translation projects in 10 languages.

b) ***Cassette tapes***. With such low literacy rates, these are a vital, and greatly appreciated, evangelistic and teaching tool. **GRN** has made recordings in 37 dialects and languages.

c) ***Christian programmes on Radio Mali***. These have had a wide audience. There are 23 denomination-based radio stations and about 60 other Christian programmes are regularly broadcast on private stations. Pray that many might believe and be encouraged through this ministry.

d) ***Literature***. GMU has a literature ministry in the capital and **CMA** in Koutiala. A booktable ministry in Kayes has provided Christian literature in several languages for over 10 years. Pray for literacy programmes and the production of suitable reading materials in the various indigenous languages, as well as for Bambara Christian literature.

e) ***The JESUS film*** has been a major instrument for opening up whole areas in the south for church planting. It is available in 11 languages with four more in production. Pray for the wise and effective use of this precious resource.

f) ***MAF and Sahel Aviation Service's flying and supportive ministries***, a boon to the body of Christ. Pray for safety and effectiveness and for spiritual life to flow through these ministries. They also provide communications to isolated areas.

g) ***Student ministry***. GBEEM(**IFES**) began in Mali in 1980, and by 1999 had over 300 members in 21 groups.

h) ***Bible correspondence courses*** are beginning to be used in the southern part of the country, and TEE classes are helping to train Christian leaders.

Malta

Republic of Malta

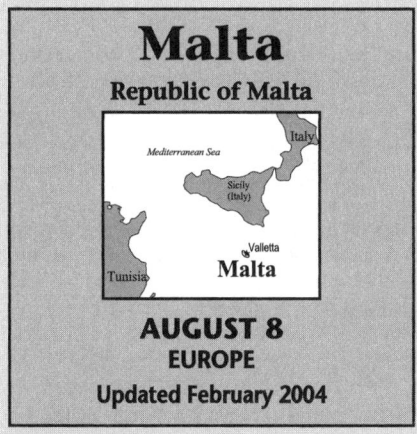

Mediterranean Sea
Italy
Sicily (Italy)
Valletta
Tunisia
Malta

AUGUST 8
EUROPE
Updated February 2004

GEOGRAPHY
Area 316 sq.km. Three small but strategic islands in the central Mediterranean. Dry limestone hills with no rivers.

Population		Ann.Gr.	Density
2000	388,544	+0.71%	1,230 per sq.
2010	412,587	+0.54%	1,306 per sq.
2025	429,847	+0.14%	1,360 per sq.

Capital Valetta 9,128. **Urbanites** 90%.

PEOPLES
Maltese 95.3%. Descendants of Phoenicians, Greeks, Romans, Arabs and others.
Other 4.7%. British 5,500; Arab 2,500; Other EU 2,000.

Literacy 96%. **Official languages** Maltese, English. Maltese is related to Arabic with a strong Italian influence.

ECONOMY
Based on tourism, ship building/repairing and light industry. Rapidly becoming a major container-port hub. **HDI** 0.850; 32nd/174. **Public debt** 44% of GNP. **Income/person** $9,330 (30% of USA).

POLITICS
Independent from Britain in 1964. Parliamentary republic since 1974. Power alternates between evenly matched socialists, who favour non-alignment and links with N. Africa, and nationalists who favour links with Europe. Malta joined the EU in 2004.

RELIGION
The Catholic Church is the State Church. Discriminatory legislation against other religions and denominations was eased in 1989 and 1990. Legally, there is religious freedom.

Religions	Population %	Adherents	Ann.Gr.
Christian	97.20	377,665	+0.6%
non-Religious/other	1.70	6,605	+6.8%
Muslim	1.10	4,274	+7.3%

Christians	Denom.	Affil. %	,000	Ann.Gr.
Protestant	7	0.17	1	+5.1%
Anglican	1	0.28	1	-0.9%
Catholic	1	88.02	342	-0.3%
Marginal	1	0.23	1	+1.1%
Unaffiliated		8.50	33	n.a.

Churches		MegaBloc	Cong.	Members	Affiliates
Catholic		C	80	213,750	342,000
Church of England		A	2	180	1,100
Jehovah's Witnesses		M	7	532	900
Chr Evangelical (AoG)		P	3	70	180
Bible Baptist		P	1	60	100
Evang Baptist		P	2	70	90
Other denoms [4]			7	160	277
Total Christians [10]			102	214,800	344,600

Trans-bloc Groupings	pop.%	,000	Ann.Gr.
Evangelical	1.0	4	+0.5%
Charismatic	4.5	17	-0.1%
Pentecostal	0.1	0	+12.6%

Missionaries from Malta
P,I,A None known.

Missionaries to Malta
P,I,A 14 in 5 agencies from 3 countries.

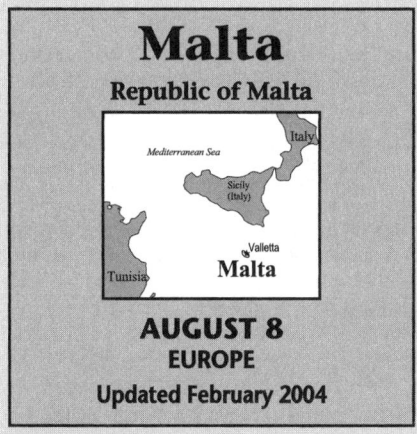

• Challenges for Prayer

1 **Malta was the first nation in Europe to embrace Christianity** — after the Apostle Paul's shipwreck on the island. It has been staunchly Catholic for many centuries with high church attendance. Despite continuing devotion to religion, few Maltese have been confronted with the need for a personal faith in the living Lord Jesus. Pray for a removal of the barriers of spiritual blindness and fear that hold many from commitment to Him.

2 **Catholic charismatic groups** have grown and spread all over the islands. They have considerable evangelistic zeal. Pray that leaders of the groups may centre their ministry on the Bible and resist pressures to compromise basic scriptural truth.

3 **A Protestant evangelical witness among Maltese did not exist until after independence in 1964.** This was not permitted by the British rulers. Praise God for steady, albeit slow, growth since then. There are over 500 associated with the 11 or so congregations. Pray for:

a) *The two Baptist groups and the AoG* and their expanding witness to Maltese, and tourists. Though official opposition to Protestant activities has largely gone, social pressures on seekers and new converts can be intense. For many, to be Maltese is to be Catholic. Pray for multitudes to come to living faith in Christ.

b) *The older, English-speaking denominations* which have long catered to the needs of the expatriate community. There is much nominalism, and little effective outreach to the indigenous population.

4 **Many Maltese have emigrated to other lands** such as Australia (150,000), Britain (36,000), Italy (25,000) and Canada (20,000) where a number have come to the Lord. Pray that some of these may return to their homeland with the gospel.

5 **North Africans** have close links with Malta — especially unevangelized Libya and also Tunisia. Pray for the many travellers, tourists and businessmen who come to Malta from these lands. Pray that there may be effective literature and personal outreach to them and that Malta may play a key role in the rebuilding of the North African Church.

6 **Christian support ministries** for prayer:

a) *The Maltese Bible Society* published the first one-volume Maltese Bible in 1980. Widespread publicity and controversy were stirred by this edition. A Catholic version was published in 1985. The **Gideons** have distributed Maltese, Arabic and English New Testaments widely in hotels, schools and institutions. Pray that many may read the Word with inner enlightenment and outward change.

b) *Christian literature* is limited in quantity and variety. Pray that evangelical titles may increase in number, and for the provision of those gifted in writing or translating. Pray for an effective publishing and distribution structure to be established.

c) *The JESUS film* has now been dubbed in Maltese — the first full-length film ever to have this.

d) *Christian radio.* In 2000 **Christian Light Radio** gained a licence for 24 hours/day FM broadcasting.

M

Martinique

Department of Martinique

Dominica

North Atlantic Ocean

Fort-de-France

Martinique

Caribbean Sea

St. Lucia

AUGUST 9
LATIN AMERICA

GEOGRAPHY
Area 1,091 sq.km. A volcanic island — the most northerly of the Windward Islands, and 100km north of its sister island, Guadeloupe.

Population	Ann.Gr.	Density
2000	395,362	+0.86%	362 per sq. km.
2010	420,797	+0.57%	386 per sq. km.
2025	450,094	+0.38%	413 per sq. km.

Capital Fort-de-France 100,000.

PEOPLES
Afro-Caribbean (black and mixed) 94%.
Asian-Caribbean 2.3%. Mainly Tamil 7,000; also Chinese, Vietnamese.
French 2.7%. Including local land-owning Beke.
Other 1%. Syrian 500.
Literacy 93%. **Official language** French. A French Creole Patois is widely spoken.

ECONOMY
Based on sugar, bananas, manufacture of rum and tourism. Heavily dependent on French aid. **Unemployment** 27%. **Public debt** 4% of GNP. **Income/person** $10,000 (32% of USA).

POLITICS
A French possession since 1635. An overseas department of France since 1946. The land-owning Martinique French *Beke* still control much of the economy; more so than in Guadeloupe.

RELIGION

There is freedom of religion.

Religions	Population %	Adherents	Ann.Gr.
Christian	91.60	362,152	+0.4%
non-Religious/other	7.10	28,000	+7.9%
Baha'i	0.50	1,977	+3.0%
Muslim	0.50	1,977	+5.5%
Hindu	0.30	1,186	+0.9%

Christians	Denom.	Affil.%	,000	Ann.Gr.
Protestant	13	9.53	38	+2.1%
Independent	5	0.35	1	+7.4%
Catholic	1	83.47	330	-1.2%
Marginal	1	2.28	9	+0.5%
Unaffiliated		6.09	24	n.a.
Doubly affiliated		*-10.12*	*-40*	*n.a.*

Churches	MegaBloc	Cong.	Members	Affiliates
Catholic	C	47	188,571	330,000
Seventh-day Adventist	P	59	12,353	20,000
Jehovah's Witnesses	M	47	4,031	9,000
Miss Chrétienne Evang.	P	29	4,336	6,200
Assembly of God	P	25	2,100	4,200
Christian Brethren	P	16	820	1,300
Other Independent [4]	I	13	650	1,300
Ch of God (Cleveland)	P	5	520	1,200
Indep Baptist	P	10	570	850
Baptist Convention	P	4	340	500
French Reformed	P	1	170	300
Ch of the Nazarene	P	6	180	250
New Apostolic	I	1	40	64

Other denominations [5]	33	1,780	2,890
Doubly affiliated		*-23,000*	*-40,000*
Total Christians [21]	296	193,600	338,000

Trans-bloc Groupings	pop.%	,000	Ann.Gr.
Evangelical	5.4	21	+1.6%
Charismatic	2.4	10	+2.5%
Pentecostal	1.4	6	+2.7%

Missionaries from Martinique
P,I,A 5 in 3 agencies.

Missionaries to Martinique
P,I,A 4 in 2 agencies.

• Challenges for Prayer

1 **Martinique has periodically suffered from major volcanic eruptions and earthquakes** — in 1902 Mt. Pelée erupted killing 30,000. Pray that the population of this beautiful isle may see their basic instability and be shaken out of their carelessness to see the things of God.

2 **The churches.** There are growing numbers of evangelical congregations among the Baptist (**SBC**), Assemblies of God and *Mission Chrétienne Evangélique.* Pray for the grounding of these churches in the Word, and the calling of young people into full-time service. Many Christians come from dysfunctional families and a background of immorality and drug abuse.

3 **Christian literature.** CLC operates a well-used bookstore which sells and lends books and tapes. Over 3,000 French Bibles are sold annually through the store. Pray that more local churches may see the value of Christian literature for spiritual growth and for evangelism.

4 **There are 300,000 Guadeloupans and Martiniquans living in France,** where they are known as Antilleans. They comprise a large minority in many Parisian evangelical churches. Pray for the witness of these believers. **WT** has established three churches amongst Antilleans in the Paris area.

M

Mauritania

Islamic Republic of Mauritania

AUGUST 9
AFRICA

GEOGRAPHY
Area 1,030,700 sq.km. Entirely desert apart from the north bank of the Senegal river on its southern border.

Population		Ann.Gr.	Density
2000	2,669,547	+2.77%	3 per sq. km.
2010	3,455,905	+2.53%	3 per sq. km.
2025	4,766,399	+1.95%	5 per sq. km.

In 1970, 70% were nomadic, but drought and urbanization have reduced this to less than 20% today.

Capital Nouakchott 735,000. **Urbanites** 54%.

PEOPLES
Numbers are estimates as ethnicity is a sensitive political issue, and not always clearly distinguished.

Arabic (Hassaniya-speaking) 70%. White Moors (Bidan) of Arab and Berber origin 1.1 mill. Black Moors (Haratine) 745,000, descended from slaves of the White Moors. There remains considerable discrimination by the dominant White Moors against other groups.

Black African 28.8%. Fulbe/Tukulor (Pulaar) 400,000; Wolof 200,000; Soninke 75,000; Bambara 30,000. Most are settled farmers in the south and despised by Moors.

Other 1.2%. French 13,000; other expatriates.

Literacy 38%. **Official Language** Arabic; the Hassaniya dialect is used. **All Languages** 8. **Languages with Scriptures** 1Bi 3NT 3w.i.p.

ECONOMY
One of the world's poorest countries. Continuing drought in the 1970s and 1980s devastated the country and sparked inter-ethnic violence over severely limited water and arable land. Much income from exported fish and iron ore is lost to corruption. **HDI** 0.447; 149th/174. **Public debt** 186% of GNP. **Income/person** $470 (1.4% of USA)

POLITICS
Independent from France in 1960. A long succession of military coups that are a continuation of Moorish tribal warfare. Slavery was not officially abolished until 1980; there are still accusations of hidden pockets of slavery in the interior. The military junta transformed itself into a multi-party democracy in 1992, but the parliament is competely dominated by the ruling party. International relations have improved since then. The dictator-turned-president was again victorious in elections in 1998, although their validity has been questioned. Diplomatic ties with Israel have resulted in internal and external opposition to the government in 2000.

RELIGION
Officially an Islamic Republic, with *shari'a* law, but the latter is intermittently applied. There is no freedom for conversion to another religion and the sentence for apostacy is death — although this sentence has not been carried out in recent years. Proselytism is illegal, but there is some freedom of religion and conscience within Islamic expression.

Religions	Population %	Adherents	Ann.Gr.
Muslim	99.84	2,665,276	+2.8%
Christian	0.16	4,271	-2.7%

Christians	Denom.	Affil. %	,000	Ann.Gr.
Protestant	4	0.02	0	+4.0%
Catholic	1	0.14	4	-2.9%
Marginal	1	0.0	0	+3.0%

Most of the Christians are expatriates.

Churches	MegaBloc	Cong.	Members	Affiliates
Catholic	C	5	2,123	3,800
Evang. fellowships [2]	P	5	175	250
Other denominations [3]		2	180	200
Total Christians [6]		12	2,478	4,250

Trans-bloc Groupings	pop.%	,000	Ann.Gr.
Evangelical	0.0	0	+3.5%
Charismatic	0.0	0	+3.2%
Pentecostal	0.0	0	+4.0%

• Challenges for Prayer

1 **Islam has been entrenched for 1,000 years** with little challenge. Many are the barriers to change — low literacy, no Scriptures completed in Hassaniya Arabic, only a few local radio broadcasts from Senegal, and laws that forbid Mauritanians from hearing the gospel or converting to Christ. The government takes great pains to keep Christianity away from the people. The strong man must be bound and his captives released for a truly Mauritanian Church to become a reality.

2 **Mauritania is one of the world's poorest countries.** One third of children are malnourished, and when there is enough food, it is often too expensive for the poor to afford. While the government's obedience to World Bank economic liberalization has brought financial growth, it has also plunged many of the working poor into even greater poverty. Pray for wisdom and discernment on the part of the government, and that the hungry and poor may have the gospel proclaimed to them.

3 **There are some expatriate Christians** in Mauritania. Mainly Westerners and Koreans, they are involved in technical or professional work linked to NGOs or the fishing industry as well as a transient population of black Africans from other lands. Discouragement is easy because of the harsh climate (with sandstorms 200 days a year), the heat, and hostility to anything Christian. Expatriates suspected of trying to proselytize Mauritanians are subject to harassment, interrogation, brief imprisonment and even expulsion. Fellowship opportunities are limited, so ask God that their lives might demonstrate clearly the love of Christ. Pray also that the Lord might grant them wisdom, protection, and empowering.

4 **All Mauritanian peoples are unreached,** in that there are no peoples with an indigenous church under indigenous leadership. There are a handful of believers worldwide, but individuals showing interest in Chrisianity in the past have been imprisoned or tortured. Pray for freedom of religion in Mauritania. Pray also for seekers and believers, that the Lord might minster to them despite the lack of opportunities to hear and grow in the gospel.

5 **Mauritanians in other lands present an opportunity.** Mauritanian traders and herdsmen have spread over many countries in West Africa, including Mali, Senegal, Gambia, Guinea, Guinea-Bissau and Côte d'Ivoire. Pray that these scattered people may be evangelized by all means. WEC has a work among them in Senegal. Ask the Lord to encourage and to increase the various Hassaniya speaking believers scattered through West Africa.

6 **Unreached minorities:**

a) *The restive Haratine*, who are Moors by culture and language but also the former slave class of Moorish society. Debate continues as to whether there are still Harantine slaves owned by White Moors.

b) *The African peoples of the Senegal River Valley* — the Tukulor, Fulbe, Soninke, Bambara and Wolof. These peoples have suffered much persecution at the hands of the Moor-dominated government, yet many previously exiled are now returning to their homeland. Their generation is more open to Christ due to the compassion shown by Christian agencies during their exile.

c) *The nomads* of the desert are descended from Berber and Arab Bedouin tribes. They are even less accessible due to their nomadic ways.

7 **Other ministries:**

a) *Bible translation*. Outside Mauritania efforts are underway to translate the Bible into Hassanyia Arabic. The Fulbe NT has recently been completed.

b) *The JESUS film* has much strategic potential, but copies are rare and distributing/ showing the film is very difficult. Nevertheless, it is available in the main languages.

c) *Radio broadcasts*, immune to closed borders, have not yet become a reality in Hassaniya Arabic. There is some programming in the Fulbe and Bambara languages.

Mauritius
Republic of Mauritius

Mozambique
Madagascar
Mauritius
Port Louis
Réunion
Indian Ocean

AUGUST 10
AFRICA

divisions. The Hindu Indian bloc is in the majority, but this is resented by the other groups.

RELIGION
Freedom of religion compromised by strong tendency for Indianization and, by implication, Hinduism at the expense of Muslims and Christians. All religious and missionary activity directed to evangelizing Hindus or Muslims is regarded with disfavour. **Persecution index** 72nd in the world.

Religions	Population %	Adherents	Ann.Gr.
Hindu	49.44	571,773	+0.9%
Christian	32.86	380,025	+0.5%
Muslim	16.30	188,509	+0.8%
non-Religious/other	0.60	6,939	+9.3%
Baha'i	0.50	5,782	+0.8%
Buddhist/Chinese	0.30	3,469	+0.0%

Christians	Denom.	Affil.%	,000	Ann.Gr.
Protestant	9	6.90	80	+4.3%
Independent	11	0.91	10	+11.9%
Anglican	1	0.61	7	+8.8%
Catholic	2	24.16	279	-0.4%
Marginal	2	0.29	3	+6.9%

Churches	MegaBloc	Cong.	Members	Affiliates
Catholic	C	50	150,838	279,050
Assemblies of God	P	110	25,000	59,000
Ch of God (Cleveland)	P	46	10,350	15,000
Anglican	A	25	4,545	7,000
Indep/Charismatic [9]	I	28	2,500	5,500
Jehovah's Witnesses	M	17	1,317	3,200
Seventh-day Adventist	P	25	1,542	3,083
Voice of Deliverance	I	82	1,650	2,500
Christian Church	I	6	1,300	2,500
Presbyterian	P	6	662	1,000
Evangelical Ch of M.	P	6	460	700
Other denoms [8]		17	710	1,480
Total Christians [27]		416	200,900	380,000

Trans-bloc Groupings	pop.%	,000	Ann.Gr.
Evangelical	7.9	91	+5.2%
Charismatic	10.9	126	+3.5%
Pentecostal	6.7	77	+4.6%

Missionaries from Mauritius
P,I,A 9 in 5 agencies to 6 countries.

Missionaries to Mauritius
P,I,A 23 in 8 agencies from 5 countries: South Africa 14, Canada 6.

GEOGRAPHY
Area 2,040 sq.km. One larger and three smaller islands east of Madagascar in the western Indian Ocean. One of these, Rodrigues Island, is 500 km to the east of the others. Mauritius also claims Diego Garcia and the Chagos archipelago, which comprise the British Indian Ocean Territory.

Population	Ann.Gr.	Density
2000	1,156,498	+0.79%	567 per sq. km.
2010	1,254,018	+0.80%	615 per sq. km.
2025	1,377,463	+0.52%	675 per sq. km.

Capital Port Louis 145,584. **Urbanites** 44%.

PEOPLES
No indigenous peoples; all immigrants.
Indian 66%. Bhojpuri 336,000; Urdu-speakers 69,000; Tamil 31,000; Panjabi 26,000.
Creole 27.5%. Mixed African and European.
Chinese 3%. Majority are Hakka.
European 3%. Largely French, controlling sugar plantations and big business.
Other 0.5%. African immigrants.

Literacy 83%. **Official Language** English. **All Languages** 5. **Languages with Scriptures** 4Bi 1por 1w.i.p.

ECONOMY
The once-dominant sugar and textile industries are being eclipsed by highly successful diversification and industrialization. Tourism, offshore banking and the use of Mauritius as a tax haven have become the main revenue generators. One of the most successful African economies. **Unemployment** 7.1%. **HDI** 0.764; 59th/174. **Public debt** 26% of GNP. **Income/person** $3,870 (12.3% of USA).

POLITICS
A French colony between 1715 and 1810, and then British until independence in 1968. The only African parliamentary democracy to have uninterrupted stability since 1960. Party politics are dominated by ethnic and religious

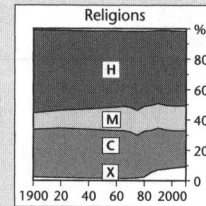

Religions %
H
M
C
X
80
60
40
20
0
1900 20 40 60 80 2000

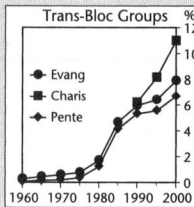

Trans-Bloc Groups %
12
10
8
6
4
2
0
◆ Evang
■ Charis
◆ Pente
1960 1970 1980 1990 2000

• Challenges for Prayer

1 **Evangelism is a challenge** in this complex, multi-ethnic and multi-religious society. Pray for much wisdom and discernment. The Hindu-ization of government and culture, as well as strong ancestral and ethnic ties make it difficult for Indians to become believers. Nevertheless, large numbers of Hindus are coming to Jesus through the bold witness of evangelical/Pentecostal churches.

2 **Most older churches are in gradual decline,** and are traditional and nominal. Many Catholics are affected by the infiltration of Hindu beliefs and practices into the Church. The charismatic movement has made a big impact on Catholics, with many coming to personal faith in Christ. Many of those impacted have now formed their own independent groups. However, the Catholic Church is experiencing a move back to Bible reading, and they run several active ministries on the island.

3 **Among Evangelicals, growth has been most rapid** within the Pentecostal and charismatic groups. Other evangelicals and independent house groups are also experiencing more modest growth, but not without opposition. Subtle discrimination when applying for official permits, as well as more open hostility towards those who share the gospel is common. In this hyper-ecumenical atmosphere, proselytisers are painted as imperialistic and intolerant. The Church has often suffered from internal division, but the formation in 1995 of the Fellowship of Christian Churches in Mauritius was a major step forward in promoting Christian unity. Pray that Evangelicals might be united in their presentation of the gospel to non-Christians.

4 **The training of leaders** is of prime importance. The **AoG** School of Ministry offers programmes ranging from correspondence through to degree-level courses. TEE is being utilised by most denominations and there are several correspondence schools, one being the Emmaus BCC. The most exciting development is the birth of the Mauritian Bible Training Institute, an evangelical Bible school. MBTI, sponsored by **SIM**, has around 50-60 students with several satellite campuses. Praise the Lord for the development of Bible training, but pray also that Mauritius might receive more teachers of the Word who are well-trained models of godliness.

5 **There is a great openness among young people.** They are less bound by ethnic loyalties, but many are held back from open commitment by family pressures or liberal church leaders. Opportunities for ministry in schools and campuses are limited (the university is non-residential), but **YFC, IFES** and **SU** are seeking creative ways to reach students.

6 **Missionary work in Mauritius is limited** due to the difficulty of obtaining long-term visas and lack of appropriately trained personnel. Evangelical missions with personnel present: Presbyterians, **AoG, SBC, SIM** (2 each). Missionaries sent out from Mauritius are limited due to isolation and lack of missions vision. Pray that Mauritian believers may become more active in supporting world evangelization. Five Mauritians are serving overseas, 4 with **WEC**.

7 **Specific unreached minorities:**

a) *Muslims*. The number of converts is insignificant compared to their population size, and there are only two Christians actively working among them.

b) *Rodrigues Islanders* (35,000) are poor, isolated, and 97% Catholic. The Anglicans and several Pentecostal denominations have started churches on the island.

c) *Speakers of major Indian languages*, Bhojpuri, Hindi and Urdu, all representing large unreached groups in India. The *JESUS* film and literature distribution are being used to reach them.

d) *The Chinese community*. Most Chinese have become Catholic. Evangelical believers number only around 600 in four or five congregations. Pray for the removal of the combined barriers of demonic powers and the drive for wealth that keep many from a full commitment to Christ.

e) *The Chagos Islanders* were evacuated to Mauritius from the British Indian Ocean Territories 1,700 km to the northeast in 1966-70, but have won the right to return. Almost all are Catholics. Pray for the return, resettlement and continued opportunities of these 5,000 Chagossians to hear and respond to the gospel.

8 Help ministries:

a) *The Bible Society* has a vital role in distributing Scriptures in all the island territories of the Indian Ocean — Seychelles, Réunion, Comores and others.

b) *Christian bookshops* have grown from two in 1990 to nine in 2000. Despite this, Christian literature is not getting into the hands of unbelievers. Pray for the provision and distribution of appropriate Christian literature.

c) *Scripture Union* distributes daily Bible reading materials and also coordinates various short-term outreaches.

d) *Christian radio broadcasts* from **FEBA**-Seychelles are beamed to Mauritius — almost 2 hours/week in French. The Catholics, Baptists and the SdA are all allotted time on the government station. An inter-church committee has been formed to produce programmes in Creole.

e) *The JESUS film* is available in Bhojpuri, Creole, French, Panjabi, Tamil, and Urdu.

Mexico
United Mexican States

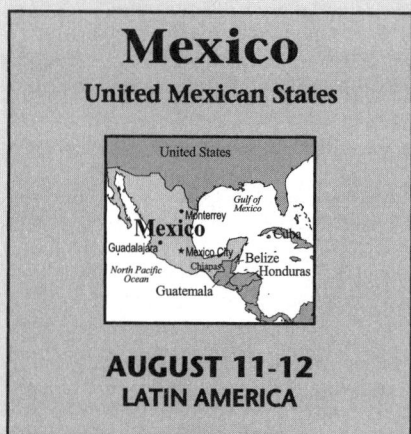

AUGUST 11-12
LATIN AMERICA

GEOGRAPHY
Area 1,958,201 sq.km. Latin America's fourth largest country. Wide range of topography and rainfall ranging from arid northern plateau, central volcanic plateau and the southern mountains and rain forests. Only 10% of the country is arable.

Population		Ann.Gr.	Density
2000	98,881,289	+1.64%	50 per sq. km.
2010	112,890,609	+1.24%	58 per sq. km.
2025	130,196,156	+0.82%	66 per sq. km.

Capital Mexico City 22.5 mill. Other major cities: (Metropolitan Area) Guadalajara 4.05m; Monterrey 3.55m; Puebla 1.83m; Leon 1.4m; Toluca 1.28m; Ciudad Juarez 1.25m; Tijuana 1.25m; Torreon 1.05m. **Urbanites** 72%.

PEOPLES
Figures below are approximate, but are an attempt to show the present cultural situation.

Mestizo (Spanish/Amerindian) 61.1%. Many are Amerindian, but now speak Spanish and are culturally Mestizo.

Amerindian 28%.
Spanish-speaking 20.5%, but still culturally Amerindian.
Amerindian-speaking 7.5%. Major groupings: Nahuatl (Aztec, 27) 1,564,000; Maya (Tzotzil, Yucatec, etc., 25 peoples) 1.3m; Zapoteco(60) 740,000; Otomi(15) 700,000; Mixteco(41) 445,000.
Euro-American 9%. Largely of Spanish origin; also some of American, German, Italian, Russian and Basque origin.
Afro-American 0.5%.
Other 1.4%. Arab 630,000; US citizens 600,000; Gypsy 63,000; Japanese 43,000; Chinese 38,000.

Literacy 89%. Functional literacy is much lower. **Official language** Spanish, the world's largest Spanish-speaking nation. **All languages** 298. **Languages with Scriptures** 5Bi 98NT 44por 76w.i.p.

ECONOMY
Oil, rapidly developing industry, tourism and agricultural products are all important. Membership of the North American Free Trade Agreement (NAFTA) is transforming the economy and changing the old-style protection of sectional interests of the elite, archaic land-tenure systems, unfairness of economic structures and institutionalized corruption, into one that is more modern and market-oriented. The poverty-stricken lower third of the population has yet to feel much benefit. The insidious evil of the drug trade continues to infect and corrupt society. **HDI** 0.786; 50th/174. **Public debt** 24% of GNP. **Income/person** $3,700 (12% of USA).

POLITICS
The sophisticated Aztec Empire in central Mexico was destroyed by the Spanish and smallpox in the early 16th Century. Independent from Spain in 1821. Much of its northern territories were lost to the USA in the 19th Century. The 1910-17 Revolution resulted in a one-party federal democracy with power centralized in the President and the Institutional Revolutionary Party (PRI).

Dominance was maintained by manipulation of power groups, electoral fraud and corruption, but the need for political and economic reform on joining NAFTA hastened the PRI's decline. Its control on the country only ended in the 2000 election of an opposition candidate as President. There are several small guerrilla movements in the south that promote land and culture rights for the native Mexican population (Amerindians) that cause embarrassment to the government.

RELIGION
Secular state with freedom of conscience and practice of religion. The 130-year break between the Mexican government and the Vatican ended with official relations being restored in 1992, and many restrictions on the Catholic Church being removed. Constitutional changes in 1992 also grant fairer treatment for religious minorities.

Religions	Population %	Adherents	Ann.Gr.
Christian	94.26	93,205,503	+1.7%
non-Religious/other	3.60	3,559,726	+1.6%
Traditional ethnic	1.79	1,769,975	-1.2%
Muslim	0.26	257,091	+2.4%
Jewish	0.05	49,441	-5.0%
Baha'i	0.04	39,553	+7.7%

A large proportion of the Amerindian population, though baptized as Catholic, still adhere to their pre-Conquest religions in practice.

Christians	Denom.	Affil.%	,000	Ann.Gr.
Protestant	285	6.20	6,128	+5.4%
Independent	18	1.81	1,794	+3.3%
Anglican	1	0.02	23	+2.5%
Catholic	1	89.50	88,498	+1.4%
Orthodox	3	0.05	50	+0.0%
Marginal	53	2.29	2,266	+4.5%
Doubly affiliated		*-5.62*	*-5,553*	*n.a.*

Churches	MegaBloc	Cong.	Members	Affiliates
Catholic	C	5,321	46.824m	88.498m
Jehovah's Witnesses	M	13,000	526,478	1,500,000
Nat'l Presbyterian	P	5,000	700,000	1,350,000
Seventh-day Adventist	P	1,545	477,813	820,000
Union of Indep Evang	I	1,333	400,000	800,000
Latter-day Saints (Morm)	M	1,300	370,000	740,000
Assemblies of God	P	4,009	200,000	480,000
Methodist	P	440	160,000	360,000
Ch of God (Cleveland)	P	1,158	105,736	260,000
Ch of God in Rep of M	I	917	110,000	220,000
National Baptist Conv	P	1,257	82,906	160,000
Indep Pentecostal Mov't.	I	2,667	80,000	145,600
Nat'l Chr Ch of AoG	I	1,222	55,000	110,000
Ch of the Nazarene	P	598	49,000	70,000
Ch of God of Prophecy	P	460	21,362	45,000
Foursquare Gospel	P	250	5,500	11,000
Other denoms [349]		28,167	1,697,000	3,188,700
Doubly affiliated			*-2,938,000*	*-5,553,000*
Total Christians [365]		68,644	48.927m	93.205m

Trans-bloc Groupings	pop.%	,000	Ann.Gr.
Evangelical	6.7	6,579	+4.7%
Charismatic	12.4	12,264	+2.5%
Pentecostal	2.7	2,695	+5.5%

Missionaries from Mexico
P,I,A 649+ in 56 agencies to 44 countries: Mexico 557, USA 89, Spain 37.

Missionaries to Mexico
P,I,A 2,140 in 190 agencies from 29 countries: USA 1,790, Canada 110, Korea 63, UK 29, Brazil 27.

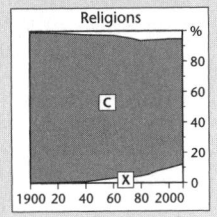

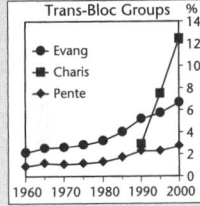

• Answers to Prayer

1 The peaceful democratic change of government in 2000 with expectation for positive change.

2 The steady growth of Evangelicals along with the lowering of legal and social barriers for ministry. Evangelicals in 1960 were 2.1% (800,000), but by 2000 were over 7% (7 million). Some claim that Evangelicals are now 15-20% of the population, however this is unlikely.

• Challenges for Prayer

1 This dynamic, growing nation is searching for an identity in its Hispanic and Indian roots. This has led to a fierce nationalism and demonstrations of independence from its large northern neighbour, the USA, along with its commitment to close economic ties in NAFTA. This is often expressed in anti-Protestant populist propaganda. Pray that Mexicans may find their true identity in a personal faith in Christ.

2 The election of a new government in 2000 ended 83 years of unbroken PRI control of the country. Hopes have been raised for economic, political and social reforms that address long-ignored issues such as the impoverished rural poor, the marginalized native Americans, the exploited slum-dwellers, and the massive drug trade. Pray that the government have the courage to deal with centuries of institutionalized graft and privilege, and bring about the changes that benefit all sections of society.

3 **For 300 years the Catholic Church dominated Mexico.** Between 1850 and 1910, revolutionary movements stripped it of much of its privilege and power, while retaining its cultural influence. During the 1990s the Church regained some of its denied privileges. The Church is in crisis — on one hand, a growing minority are regularly reading the Bible and this is seen as a threat to the traditional authority of the Catholic hierarchy, and on the other hand, nominalism and the rejection of Catholicism by young people is on the increase. Most Mexicans are culturally Catholic but still bound by sin, narrow traditionalism and syncretistic religious practices, and only 10% are regular churchgoers. Pray that the power of the ancient gods and spirit-world may be broken in the Spanish-speaking majority and, more especially, in the Christo-pagan Amerindian groups.

4 **Persecution of Evangelicals** has been a growing feature in Mexico.

a) *At a national level the media regularly, in vitriolic terms, portray Evangelicals as anti-Mexican* spies and destroyers of the culture. The exponential growth of Evangelicals has disturbed the conservative wing of the Catholic Church. Pray that evangelical growth may stimulate reform and renewal rather than persecution!

b) *At a local level*, and especially in the poor Amerindian-majority southern states of Chiapas and Oaxaca, there have been numerous incidents of mob violence, crop-burnings, destruction of churches and homes, enforced expulsions of whole evangelical communities from their villages, harassment of evangelistic outreach and arrests of believers on trumped-up charges. Pray that the believers may demonstrate the meekness and love of their Saviour when maltreated. Pray also for the full implementation of religious freedom at both national and local levels.

5 **Evangelicals have grown** — even under the pressures. Growth has been in both international denominations (especially Pentecostals and Adventists) and also in vigorous newer indigenous movements. Pray that the momentum might be maintained.

a) *The highest concentrations* are in the southern states of Chiapas (19%), Tabasco (17.5%), Campeche (15.4%) and Quintana Roo (14%), which are also where a high proportion of Amerindian peoples live.

b) *Evangelicals have a higher profile* after some notable conversions of entertainers. An in-depth infrastructure of Christian bookstores, music and leadership training is strengthening that growth. Yet most growth has been among Spanish-speaking populations of the lower classes, the northern border with the USA and in the Caribbean coastal states, also among the rural Amerindians, and latterly among the Amerindians of the south-east. Wealthier Mexicans and the central and Pacific states have been more lightly influenced.

6 **The specific challenges for Evangelicals:**

a) *Unity.* The Evangelical Fraternity of Mexico (CONEMEX) is working to strengthen unity, deal with the government and sponsor important events. A Pentecostal fellowship has been formed to bring together millions of Pentecostal Christians. There needs to be a more effective strategic partnership among mission agencies.

b) *Discipleship* and biblical commitment which impacts family life is a great need. The Mexican parallel of *Promise Keepers* has had considerable impact on the commitment of menfolk. Commitment needs to extend to giving — few pastors or missionaries are adequately supported.

c) *Leadership training* is the key to the future health of the Church. There are well over 100 Bible schools and seminaries training thousands of future leaders at all levels; from indigenous primary-level language to degree-awarding schools, as well as numerous TEE programmes. Pray that spiritual depth and evangelistic vision, as well as sound teaching, may be imparted to the students. Doctrinal shallowness, error and also moral and personal relationship breakdowns have impaired the growth of the Church. Pray also for the provision of godly pastors for poor rural and urban slum congregations.

d) **Develop missions vision.** Sending of missionaries by the Mexican Church has developed rapidly. An increasing number of congregations are sending and supporting missionaries. COMIMEX has provided a nation-wide umbrella with which most national agencies are linked. COMIMEX operates through nine departments — Adopt-A-People, Barnabas (cross-cultural preparation), missions education, research, publicity, music, prayer, missiology and church missions committees. Significant international agencies have been birthed in Mexico — such as PMI, with its involvement in the Muslim world. There are now over 500 Mexican evangelical missionaries in 70 agencies, 250 of which are serving abroad in 50 other lands.

7 **Ministry to young people is vital.** Over 50% of the population is under 20 years of age. This staggering challenge is only being partially met.

a) **University Students.** There are 3.8 million in over 9,500 campuses. Outreach is yielding exciting results. Pray for the wide-ranging ministries of **CCC** (on campuses and among churches), for **IFES**, and for outreach to high school students.

b) **Teenagers.** Few churches have targeted them; most programmes are geared for adults.

c) **Street children**, especially in Mexico City. There may be up to 600,000 who sleep rough and desperately need love and help.

d) **Christian camping.** Christian Camping International runs nearly 200 camps around the country. Many other agencies and denominations have such ministry too. Pray for this well-used and fruitful ministry.

8 **Foreign missionaries'** legal position was for years ambiguous and restrictive, but religious visas can now be obtained. The great majority are US citizens, so they need sensitivity and tact in their cultural adaptation to overcome the perceived disadvantages of their origin and wealth. Missionaries from outside North America are less than 20% of the total, but face fewer cultural and historical negatives. Openings are many for missionaries in children's and youth work, evangelism and church planting, and especially in leadership training. The largest agencies are **SIL** (235), **NTM** (102), **IMB-SBC** (101), **YWAM** (89), **LAM** (82), BBF (69), **CAMI** (60), **MTW** (48), SdA (45), BIM (44), **Brethren** (44), **OM** (37), **WEC** (28), **CCCI** (28), **CMA** (26), **Bethany Fellowship** (21), **OMS** (20), **CRWM** (18), **CoN** (17), **TEAM** (17), Action Int. Ministries (14). Pray that their ministries may assist the Church to be what God desires.

9 **Sections of the population and peoples with few committed Christians:**

a) **Evangelicals** are only between 1 and 2% in the central states of Zacatecas, Jalisco, Aguascalientes, Guanajuato, Colima, Michoacán and Querétaro, and between 2 and 4% in the states of Baja California Sur, Sonora, Sinaloa, Durango, Nayarit and Mexico.

b) **Indian peoples are largely Catholic in name but pagan in practice.** The old pantheon of gods and spirits have been given Catholic names. It has been researched by COMIMEX that of 296 people groups, 26 are without a viable Christian witness, 104 have a church that still needs help from the outside to finish preaching the gospel in their group, and a further 12 are inadequately researched. Vital discipleship and church-planting ministries must be expanded to build on the impressive Scripture translation programme of SIL. Pray for the expanding work of several mostly new national and international organizations like NTM in five tribes as well as for the extensive work of the Assemblies of God, Baptists, Presbyterians and others.

c) **The many conservative Catholic and animistic towns, cities and groups** where evangelical witness is limited and introverted, need to be reached.

d) **The wealthy elite.** There is a strong atheist-agnostic current among them reinforced by an education system designed to dilute the influence of the Church.

10 **Mexico City** is a major challenge! Its growth rate has slowed because of its air pollution and inadequate infrastructure. The Metropolitan Area is still one of the world's largest urban agglomerations. Only about 1.9% of the population is actively involved in one of the 2,300 or so evangelical congregations. Pray for:

a) **The 1,000 or so neighbourhoods** without an evangelical congregation — especially needy are the upper-class areas.

b) **The slum-dwellers.** Of the 18 million poor, over 7 million live in squalid housing as squatters in desperate economic conditions. Christian ministry to them is fraught with difficulty and challenge. Few are prepared to commit themselves to it.

c) ***The million Indians*** representing nearly every language of Mexico. Very little is being done to cater for their spiritual needs.

11 **Bible translation and distribution.** Despite centuries of social and cultural pressure, use of indigenous languages is vigorous and varied.

a) ***Translation****.* The role of **SIL** since 1936 has been remarkable, with involvement in translation programmes in 126 languages. There are at present 235 workers committed to 76 translation projects. There are 16 languages with a definite translation need and a further 32 where the need has yet to be clarified. The translation of the Yucateco Maya Bible (**UBS**) was completed in 1991. Pray for the achievement of New Testament and Bible translation goals despite virulent and scurrilous propaganda and agitation for the expulsion of all **SIL** workers by anthropologists, political factions, and even some Catholic leaders. The great need is to tie in translation work to church-planting and church-based literacy programmes.

b) ***Printing and distribution****.* The Bible Society has played an important role in production and distribution of Spanish and indigenous Scriptures in Mexico and for the whole region, as has the Bible League. Pray that the dissemination and reading of the Scriptures may transform individuals, congregations and the nation.

12 Christian support ministries for prayer:

a) ***Christian radio****.* Christian broadcasting was denied Evangelicals in Mexico in 1980, but constitutional changes in 1992 have made it possible for some programmes to be aired locally. There are numerous international broadcasts beamed towards the country with a total weekly input of 1,000 hours.

b) ***The JESUS film*** has been extensively used as a film and on TV. Viewers are now equivalent to over half the population. The film is in use in 54 Mexican languages and being prepared in a further 6. Pray for effective strategies for its use in large cities and for multiplying congregations.

c) ***Cassette recordings****.* **GRN** have messages available in 240 languages and dialects. It is a vital tool in the complex linguistic situation. Pray for recordists, new recordings, wide distribution and eternal fruit.

d) ***MAF*** has a key role in the mountainous and inaccessible regions of the southern part of the country.

e) ***Christian literature****. Prisma* magazine, published since 1969, has been used in evangelism and edifying believers. There is a growing number of Christian magazines and Mexican-authored books. Pray for a literate, well-taught Church to be the result.

M **13** **Migrant Mexican labour in California and other US border states** has long been a feature of national life. Their numbers are unknown, but may be as many as six to eight million (many illegals). There are many opportunities for them to hear the gospel. Pray for evangelistic and church-planting work in Spanish by **CAMI**, **GMU** and many denominational workers in these areas.

MICRONESIA

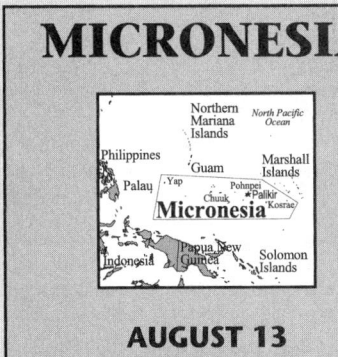

The former US-administered UN Trust Territory is retained here as a single entity because of the small populations and commonalities between the four constituent States.

 GEOGRAPHY
Area 1,950 sq.km. The 2,000 islands of the Caroline, Marshall and Mariana archipelagos lie in seven million sq.km. of the North Pacific. Only 100 are inhabited.

 POLITICS
For centuries, a strategic global pawn. Ruled by Spain 1710-1897, Germany 1897-1914, and Japan 1914-1945 before the USA took over the administration as a UN Trust Territory. Four republics in free association with the USA have emerged since 1978.

RELIGION
During Spanish rule, all islanders were forcibly Catholicized, but the underlying pre-Christian customs and animistic religion remain influential. In each republic there is, theoretically, freedom of religion, but some islands show hostility to variant newer denominations and religions.

Federated States of Micronesia

 **GEOGRAPHY**
Area 702 sq.km. Over 600 coralline islands in four main groups: Chuuk, Pohnpei, Yap and Kosrae.

Population	Ann.Gr.	Density
2000	118,689	+2.05%	169 per sq. km.
2010	144,265	+1.94%	206 per sq. km.
2025	189,609	+1.79%	270 per sq. km.

Chuuk 50.5%; Pohnpei 32%; Yap 10.5%; Kosrae 7% of population.

Capital Palikir 8,000. **Urbanites** 26%.

 PEOPLES
Micronesian 91.3%. Chuuk (5 dialects) 52,000; Pohnpeian(4) 29,000; Kosraean 8,000; Yapese 6,000; Mortlockese 5,500; Carolinian 5,000; Ulithian 4,000; Woleaian 2,000.
Polynesian 2%. Kapingamarangian 1,600; Nukuoro 1,000 on two atolls south of Chuuk.
Other 6.7%. Japanese 3,500; Chinese 2,000; Filipino 1,000.

Literacy 94%. **Official language** English. **All languages** 17. **Languages with Scriptures** 3Bi 4NT 1w.i.p.

ECONOMY
Predominantly subsistence farming and fishing. Over 90% of government income is from US aid. **Public debt** 56% of GNP. **Income/person** $2,040 (6% of USA).

 POLITICS
A federal republic with four constituent states. Independence in 1991, but in free association with the USA; the latter administering defence and foreign policy.

RELIGION
Separation of church and state, with religious freedom. Yap is predominantly Catholic; Pohnpei, Chuuk and Kosrae predominantly Protestant.

Religions	Population %	Adherents	Ann.Gr.
Christian	93.80	111,330	+1.9%
Traditional ethnic	3.00	3,561	+5.8%
Baha'i	1.60	1,899	+4.8%
non-Religious/other	0.90	1,068	+4.5%
Chinese/Buddhist	0.70	831	-5.0%

Christians	Denom.	Affil.%	,000	Ann.Gr.
Protestant	11	44.75	53	+0.0%
Independent	3	0.39	0	+3.9%
Catholic	1	48.02	57	+2.7%
Marginal	2	3.37	4	+0.6%
Unaffiliated		4.18	5	n.a.
Doubly affiliated		*-6.91*	*-8*	*n.a.*

Churches	MegaBloc	Cong.	Members	Affiliates
Catholic	C	30	33,140	57,000
Liebenzell	P	154	9,250	18,500
United Ch of Pohnpei	P	21	6,364	14,000
Prot Ch of Chuuk	P	22	6,500	13,000
Latter-day Saints (Morm)	M	29	1,737	2,900
Jehovah's Witnesses	M	6	172	1,100
Assemblies of God	P	5	400	700
Church of the Nazarene	P	3	250	550
Other denoms [9]		31	3,600	6,820
Doubly affiliated			*-4,000*	*-8,200*
Total Christians [17]		300	57,000	106,000

M

Trans-bloc Groupings	pop.%	,000	Ann.Gr.
Evangelical	21.5	25	+0.9%
Charismatic	5.7	7	+2.9%
Pentecostal	1.4	2	+4.6%

Missionaries from F.S.M.
P,I,A 10 in 5 agencies — 5 in other countries.
Missionaries to F.S.M.
P,I,A 54 in 14 agencies from 6 countries: USA 40, Germany 8. C 20.

• Challenges for Prayer

1 **Christianity is often a veneer over an animistic worldview.** Magic is widely used and this, with Western consumerism encouraged by US aid, deadens initiative and spiritual fervour. Pray for a revelation of the power and love of Jesus to these island peoples.

2 **A large proportion of the population is Protestant** — the result of a century of ministry by US Congregationals and the German Liebenzell Mission, but nominalism is widespread. Pray for revival.

3 **Bible translation and distribution.** The lack of Scriptures in Carolinian, Kapingamarani and the smaller languages, lack of the Old Testament in all but the Chuuk language, and the limited reading of the Bible and misunderstanding of its contents hold back the spiritual development of the largely Christian population, and lay them open for Western cults. Pray for the Scriptures to dynamically impact the population.

Marshall Islands
Republic of the Marshall Islands

M

GEOGRAPHY
Area 181 sq.km. There are 34 atolls with 1,156 islands, spread over nearly 2 million sq.km of Pacific.

Population	Ann.Gr.	Density
2000	64,220	+3.26%	355 per sq. km.
2010	86,434	+2.93%	478 per sq. km.
2025	127,147	+2.44%	702 per sq. km.

High density on Majuro. Many islands are sparsely inhabited.
Capital Dalap-Uliga-Darrit (on Majuro) 30,000.
Urbanites 65%.

PEOPLES
Micronesian 96%. Marshallese (two dialects).
Other 4%. Pacific Islanders 1,100; US Citizens 600; Filipinos 400.

Literacy 93%. **Official languages** Marshallese and English. **All languages** 2. **Languages with Scriptures** 2Bi.

ECONOMY
US aid is 70% of GNP, causing a dependency culture which inhibits initiative to develop potential for agriculture, fisheries and tourism. Foreign fleets plunder the fish stocks. Unemployment is high. Almost all food is imported. **Public debt** 145% of GNP. **Income/person** $1,600 (6% of USA).

POLITICS
An independent republic since 1986 in free association with the USA.

RELIGION
Freedom of religion; the churches run an extensive schooling system.

Religions	Population %	Adherents	Ann.Gr.
Christian	95.20	61,137	+3.0%
non-Religious/other	2.00	1,284	+31.4%
Baha'i	1.80	1,156	+4.4%
Traditional ethnic	1.00	642	-4.8%

Christians	Denom.	Affil.%	,000	Ann.Gr.
Protestant	5	78.64	50	+5.1%
Independent	4	7.94	5	+1.2%
Catholic	1	6.07	4	-0.5%
Marginal	2	6.38	4	+2.8%
Unaffiliated		5.51		n.a.
Doubly affiliated		*-6.07*	*-6*	*n.a.*

Churches	MegaBloc	Cong.	Members	Affiliates
United Church of Christ	P	88	7,200	24,000
Assemblies of God	P	72	4,000	22,000
Reformed Cong	I	18	1,100	4,100
Catholic	C	10	2,267	3,900
Latter-day Saints (Morm)	M	17	1,856	3,100
Jehovah's Witnesses	M	4	205	1,000
Other denoms [6]		18	2,191	5,500
Doubly affiliated			*-3,000*	*-6,000*
Total Christians [12]		227	15,800	57,600

Trans-bloc Groupings	pop.%	,000	Ann.Gr.
Evangelical	42.8	27	+7.3%
Charismatic	38.6	25	+8.3%
Pentecostal	38.0	24	+8.7%

Missionaries from Marshall Islands
n.a.
Missionaries to Marshall Islands
P,I,A 17 in 4 agencies: USA 15. C 42.

• Challenges for Prayer

1 The traumatic history of occupation, exploitation, war and the impact of US nuclear bomb testing has had a devastating effect on the Marshallese. Traditional society and culture has broken down, with attendant problems of sexual promiscuity, drugs, drunkenness, suicides and a very high birth rate. The people are confused, uprooted and insecure and many suffer the effects of nuclear radiation with genetic disorders and high rates of cancer. Pray for wise, visionary leadership for the nation that will break the spirit of dependency, and make the country economically viable.

2 The great majority of Marshallese are Protestant and nearly one third Evangelical. The churches have a big involvement at every level in society, but without adequately impacting the life, world-view and spirituality of the people. The United Church of Christ has become the de facto State Church and is losing out in numbers and spirituality. The **Assemblies of God** have had a big influence winning many to Christ in earlier decades. Pray for a life- and culture-changing revival.

3 The need for godly leadership in the churches is great. The United Church has a small theological college and the **AoG** run the Calvary Bible Institute. Pray for the spiritual depth and vitality of these institutions.

Northern Marianas
Commonwealth of the Northern Mariana Islands

GEOGRAPHY
Area 477 sq.km. A chain of 14 volcanic and coralline islands 650 km north of Guam. The southernmost islands, Saipan, Tinian and Rota, are the largest and most important economically.

Population		Ann.Gr.	Density
2000	78,356	+5.89%	164 per sq. km.
2010	131,073	+5.08%	275 per sq. km.
2025	245,191	+3.86%	514 per sq. km.

There are over 28,000 legal migrant workers and their families in the country at any one time. There are also many illegals.

Capital Saipan 48,000. **Urbanites** 65%.

PEOPLES
Pacific Islanders 32%. Chamorro 18,000; Carolinian 3,000; Other Micronesian 5,000. The Chamorro are also indigenous to nearby Guam.
Asians 64%. Mostly on contract, few long-term, many illegal immigrants. Filipino 35,000; Chinese 6,000; Korean 5,000; Japanese 1,600.
Other 4%. US mainlanders.

Literacy 96% (indigenous). **Official language** English. Chamorro widely spoken, also some Carolinian. **All languages** 3. **Languages with Scriptures** 1Bi 1por.

ECONOMY
Tourism, especially from Japan, and US aid are the main sources of national income. More prosperous than the other three Micronesian States. **Income/person** $9,700 (34% of USA) — including migrant labour.

POLITICS
A Commonwealth Territory of the USA since 1977. The population was granted US citizenship in 1990.

RELIGION
Freedom of religion. Almost the entire indigenous population was baptized in the Catholic Church.

Religions	Population %	Adherents	Ann.Gr.
Christian	90.50	70,912	+5.6%
Chinese/Buddhist	7.10	5,563	+7.8%
non-Religious/other	2.00	1,567	+12.2%
Baha'i	0.40	313	+8.7%

Christians	Denom.	Affil.%	,000	Ann.Gr.
Protestant	12	13.30	10	+3.6%
Independent	2	1.79	1	+2.1%
Catholic	1	79.13	62	+6.2%
Marginal	2	1.28	1	+6.0%
Unaffiliated		2.03	1	n.a.
Doubly affiliated		*-7.02*	*-6*	*n.a.*

M

Churches	MegaBloc	Cong.	Members	Affiliates
Catholic	C	11	34,444	62,000
Filipino Baptist	P	2	1,300	2,200
United Church of Christ	P	10	1,200	2,200
Korean	P	7	1,200	2,000
Assemblies of God	P	5	400	1,260
Iglesia ni Kristo	I	1	600	950
General Baptist	P	5	300	666
Jehovah's Witnesses	M	4	205	600
Seventh-day Adventist	P	1	123	400
Other denoms [8]		15	1,370	2,548
Doubly affiliated			*-2,750*	*-5,500*
Total Christians [17]		61	38,000	69,000

Trans-bloc Groupings	pop.%	,000	Ann.Gr.
Evangelical	10.4	8	+4.8%
Charismatic	7.4	6	+6.5%
Pentecostal	1.6	1	+9.5%

Missionaries from Northern Marianas
n.a.

Missionaries to Northern Marianas
P,I,A 92 in 16 agencies from 10 countries: Korea 23, USA 15. C 34. M 25.

• Challenges for Prayer

1 **The indigenous Chamorro would claim to be Catholic**, but the majority are non-churchgoers and animism and folk religion predominate. Pray that the light of the gospel may shine on this people. Evangelical outreach is only recent. Pray for the ministry of the Baptist and Assemblies of God churches and of the World Outreach and **YWAM** teams.

2 **The Asian population is diverse.** In 1991 there were seven thriving Korean congregations, three Chinese and several Filipino — all with vigorous outreach to their compatriots. However, many of the Asians are culturally isolated and unreached — especially the Japanese and Chinese (both from Mainland China and Taiwan). Many of the Filipinos are involved in the tourist industry; prostitution is a problem.

3 **Over one million Japanese tourists** visit the islands annually — many specifically to worship at Shinto and Buddhist shrines. Pray that they may be reached.

4 **Christian media ministries** for prayer:

a) ***Bible translation.*** Pray for the completion of the Chamorro NT and for translation to commence in the two Carolinian languages.

b) ***Radio.*** **FEBC** has two broadcast services — internationally on short wave to Russia, Central Asia, China, India and South East Asia (115 hrs/wk), and a local service to the islands in five languages. Pray for deep and lasting impact. Pray for the spiritual and physical protection of both workers and valuable facilities. Saipan is in an area prone to typhoons.

M

Palau

Republic of Palau (Belau)

 GEOGRAPHY
Area 488 sq.km. Sixteen inhabited volcanic and coralline islands.

Population	Ann.Gr.	Density
2000	19,426	+2.43%	40 per sq. km.
2010	24,391	+2.26%	50 per sq. km.
2025	33,228	+2.00%	68 per sq. km.

Capital Koror 12,300. **Urbanites** 60%.

 PEOPLES
Micronesian 80%. Three languages: Palavan 15,000; Sonsorol 600.
Other 20%. Filipino 3,000; Chinese 600; Japanese, US Mainlander, Korean.

Literacy 98%. **Official language** Palauan; English used widely. **All languages** 4. **Languages with Scriptures** 1Bi 1NT.

 ECONOMY
Subsistence agriculture, fishing and some tourism. The government is the main employer and relies heavily on US aid.

 POLITICS
The compact of free association with the USA, signed in 1982, was only implemented after repeated and violently contested referenda had failed to ratify the new constitution.

 RELIGION

Religions	Population %	Adherents	Ann.Gr.
Christian	96.10	18,668	+2.4%
non-Religious/Other	1.80	350	+7.7%
Chinese/Buddhist	1.20	233	+6.3%
Baha'i	0.90	175	+4.9%

Christians	Denom.	Affil.%	,000	Ann.Gr.
Protestant	3	30.19	6	+2.1%
Independent	3	1.84	0	+7.3%
Catholic	1	46.33	9	+2.4%
Marginal	3	12.35	2	+2.4%
Unaffiliated		5.40	1	n.a.

Churches	MegaBloc	Cong.	Members	Affiliates
Catholic	C	18	3,600	9,000
Evangelical Ch in Belau	P	18	2,200	3,500
Seventh-day Adventist	P	2	1,100	2,200
Modekngei	M		640	1,600
Latter-day Saints (Morm)	M	5	150	500
Jehovah's Witnesses	M	1	73	300

Assemblies of God	P	2	24	164
Other denoms [3]		4	185	358
Total Christians [10]		50	7,800	17,600

Trans-bloc Groupings	pop.%	,000	Ann.Gr.
Evangelical	21.5	4	+2.4%
Charismatic	3.1	1	+5.6%
Pentecostal	0.8	0	+4.9%

Missionaries from Palau
P,I,A 6 with YWAM in the Pacific.

Missionaries to Palau
P,I,A 11 in 5 agencies from 3 countries: Philippines 5, Korea 4. C 5. M 15.

• Challenges for Prayer

1 **Christianity is generally professed, but nominalism is widespread**; the most ardent Catholics being the Filipinos. Many older people are followers of the Modekngei movement, a religion unique to Palau which is a mixture of Christianity and magic. The old animistic religion is also regaining influence. Yet there are beginnings of spiritual awakening. Pray for the revival of the Evangelical church — the fruit of the work of the Liebenzell Mission. The **AoG** have a small but growing work.

2 **Hindrances to the gospel** need to be removed. Closed cultures and strong traditionalism make many villages and outlying islands unwilling for change. The debilitating effects of US aid, material comforts and enormous consumption of beer make discipleship and commitment rare. The whole Bible is not yet available in Palauan, so theological depth is lacking. Outreach to smaller unevangelized island communities is complicated by their geographic isolation.

3 **Missionary vision** for both less-evangelized Micronesian islands, and beyond, is being stimulated by the **YWAM** base in Palau.

4 **Christian radio.** High Adventure and the Seventh-day Adventists have significant radio stations broadcasting to East Asia; the former broadcasting 63 hrs/wk in 5 languages.

Moldova
Republic of Moldova

AUGUST 14
EUROPE

GEOGRAPHY
Area 33,700 sq.km. Landlocked republic between the Ukraine and Romania.

Population	Ann.Gr.	Density
2000	4,380,492	+0.02%	130 per sq. km.
2010	4,424,179	+0.17%	131 per sq. km.
2025	4,546,842	+0.13%	135 per sq. km.

Capital Chisinau 850,000. **Urbanites** 47%.

PEOPLES
Indo-European 94.5%. Much inter-marriage.
Latin 62.4%. Moldavian/Romanian 2,700,000.
Slav 29.6%. Ukrainian 613,000; Russian 569,000; Bulgarian 90,000.
Other 2.5%. Roma (Gypsy, 3 groups) 105,000
Turkic/Altaic 3.2%. Gagauz 138,000.
All other 2.3%. Jews 60,000.

Literacy 97%. **Official language** Moldovan Romanian. **All languages** 5. **Languages with Scriptures** 2Bi 2por 2w.i.p.

ECONOMY
Rich but under-used agricultural land. The poorest country in Europe due to unresolved internal political problems, lack of industry and trade, and economic dependence on Russia. Painful adherence to strict IMF measures has brought scant economic improvement. **Unemployment** is around 80%. **HDI** 0.683; 104th/174. **Public debt** 39.8% of GNP. **Income/person** $460 (1.5% of USA).

POLITICS
The USSR's seizure of Bessarabia from Romania in 1940 and its subsequent grotesque dismemberment are the root causes of present conflicts. The north and south of Bessarabia were annexed to Ukraine and the east bank of the Dniester detached from Ukraine to form the Moldovan republic. Independence declared in 1990, and a multi-party republic formed. Transnistria (Trans-Dniester), a Russian army-controlled enclave, aggressively insists on independence. This remains a canker with no foreseeable political solution. Gagauz aspirations for independence appear to have been assuaged with granting of autonomy.

RELIGION
The Orthodox Church has regained strong political influence and is not afraid to wield it against those it sees as a threat. Although religious freedom exists, the Bessarabian Church remains subordinated to the Romanian Orthodox Patriarchy and is not recognized. A current law forbids 'abusive proselytism'. A more restrictive law is being debated in parliament.

Religions	Population %	Adherents	Ann.Gr.
Christian	95.39	4,178,551	+0.5%
Non-Religious	3.31	144,944	-9.3%
Jewish	1.10	48,185	-3.3%
Muslim	0.20	8,761	+0.0%

Christians	Denom.	Affil.%	,000	Ann.Gr.
Protestant	10	3.22	141	+8.1%
Independent	5	0.06	3	+24.1%
Catholic	2	5.78	253	+0.6%
Orthodox	7	70.26	3,078	+1.7%
Marginal	1	0.89	39	+8.8%
Unaffiliated		15.18	664	n.a.

Churches	MegaBloc	Cong.	Members	Affiliates
Romanian Orthodox	O	680	1,608,392	2,300,000
Russian Orthodox	O	230	489,510	700,000
Roman Catholic	C	83	103,593	173,000
Eastern Rite Catholic	C	38	47,904	80,000
Bulgarian Orthodox	O	17	39,610	61,000
Pentecostal	P	200	28,000	60,000
Baptist Union	P	308	20,000	50,000
Jehovah's Witnesses	M	128	15,580	39,139
Seventh-day Adventist	P	116	10,022	25,000
Old Believers	O	15	6,494	10,000
Other denoms [15]		29	9,230	19,502
Total Christians [25]		1,844	2,378,000	3,517,600

Trans-bloc Groupings	pop.%	,000	Ann.Gr.
Evangelical	3.3	146	+9.1%
Charismatic	1.7	73	+13.8%
Pentecostal	1.4	60	+14.9%

Missionaries from Moldova
P,I,A 23 in 3 agencies to 2 countries: Russia 12.

Missionaries to Moldova
P,I,A 50 in 17 agencies.

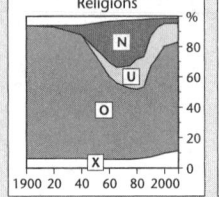

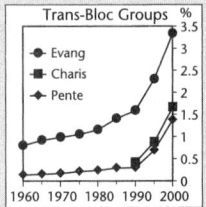

• Answers to Prayer

1 **This land is now fertile ground for the gospel**, and Protestant churches are growing and multiplying. Moldovan-flavoured renewal is occurring, and vision for evangelism and missions is increasing.

• Challenges for Prayer

1 **A peaceful and prosperous Moldovan future remains uncertain and tenuous.** The intransigence of the Transnistrian region separatists and the inability of the country to overcome economic difficulties undermine stability. About 80% of men are unemployed and 60% of men have a serious alcohol problem. The Communists regained control of the parliament in the 2001 elections. Pray that the terrible Stalinist and Communist legacies may be overcome and that present liberty might be preserved.

2 **The influence of the Orthodox Church** makes evangelical work difficult. Preaching and planting churches in traditionally Orthodox villages is especially opposed, frequently with violence. Ask God for special favour upon those who minister at the risk of their own safety. It is also difficult to obtain permission to purchase buildings or land for church purposes. Pray that the Holy Spirit would deepen the spiritual life of many from the Orthodox faith.

3 **Evangelical Christians** have multiplied, but materially they lack so much — meeting places, discipleship materials and funds. Many are very poor. Pray that God may provide their needs. There are over 4,000 believers and possibly as many as 10,000 among the predominantly Orthodox Gagauz Turks, among whom revival is reported. The strong conservatism of the Communist era remains, and suspicion and resentment hinders unity between Protestant groups. **OM** is seeking to minister to all groups. Pray that believers may develop a broader, dynamic view of the body of Christ.

4 **Training for pastors and education for Christians** is still the greatest need. **SGA** successfully launched the part-time Moldovan Mission School in 1994 — many churches have been planted by its graduates already! Both the Baptists and the Pentecostals have theological schools, there is an independent evangelical Bible School in the capital, and the Brethren are involved in Bible teaching. Pray that all these schools may raise up godly, mature leaders. Pray for the provision of resources for both students and schools alike.

5 **The less reached for prayer:**

a) *1,000 or more villages* have no evangelical witness. Many in villages are deeply involved in the occult.

M

b) *The Gypsy population* is large and virtually unreached.
c) *The Muslim minorities.* Gagauz believers have a vision to reach Muslims both in Moldova and in Eurasia. Pray for them as they mobilize for missions.
d) *The youth of Moldova* are victims the Soviet infrastructure's collapse and the freedoms and bondages that followed. Committed ministry to young people is needed — pray for more workers. There is some work already among university students and **SGA** helps run youth camps. **IFES** has had a team in Moldova since 1986.

6 **Christian help ministries for prayer:**

a) *Bible and Christian literature.* The Gagauz New Testament was completed in 2000. **SGA** distributes Bible study aids in Russian, and gospels and tracts are being distributed throughout the country in Russian and Romanian.
b) *Radio.* **TWR** broadcasts out from Moldova to many Eastern European countries. Moldovans can tune in to 19.5 hours a week in eight languages. There is also a local Christian radio station, *Micul Samaratan*, which has wide appeal.
c) *The JESUS film* is available in Romanian, Ukrainian, Russian and Bulgarian and has been widely viewed.
d) *Short-term missions.* Various groups send as many as 60 short-term teams a year to erect church buildings and assist local congregations. Pray that these Western guests to Moldova will have an effect for the long-term good of the Moldovan church.

Monaco

Principality of Monaco

GEOGRAPHY
Area 2 sq.km. The second smallest state in the world. On France's south coast.

Population	Ann.Gr.	Density
2000	33,597	+1.10%	16,799 per sq.
2010	36,867	+0.88%	18,434 per sq.
2025	40,692	+0.55%	20,346 per sq.

Capital Monte Carlo 33,597. **Urbanites** 100%.

PEOPLES
Monégasque 16%. Speaking Ligurian and French.
French 36%.
Italian 16%.
Other 32%. British 1,400; Swiss 700; Belgian 700; German 600. Many French and Italian daily commuter workers.

Literacy 99%. **Official language** French.

ECONOMY
A byword, among the very rich, for gambling and as a tax haven, though gambling only generates 5% of the national income. Tourism and light industry are the most important economically. **Income/person** $25,000 (88% of USA).

POLITICS
Independent city-state with a constitutional monarchy under French protection.

RELIGION
Roman Catholicism is the state religion, but there is freedom of religion though proselytism is strongly discouraged.

Religions	Population %	Adherents	Ann.Gr.
Christian	87.66	29,451	+0.7%
non-Religious	9.94	3,340	+4.7%
Jewish	1.70	571	+1.1%
Muslim	0.50	168	+3.3%
Other	0.20	67	n.a.

Christians	Denom.	Affil.%	,000	Ann.Gr.
Protestant	3	2.98	1	-0.4%
Independent	2	0.15	0	+4.0%
Anglican	1	0.95	0	-0.6%
Catholic	1	83.34	28	+0.7%
Orthodox	1	0.24	0	-1.2%

Churches	MegaBloc	Cong.	Members	Affiliates
Catholic	C	6	20,741	28,000
Other denominations [7]		5	357	1,450
Total Christians [8]		11	21,098	29,450

Trans-bloc Groupings	pop.%	,000	Ann.Gr.
Evangelical	1.0	0	+1.1%
Charismatic	1.5	1	+1.0%

Missionaries to Monaco
P,I,A 21 in 2 agencies: USA 20.

M

• Challenges for Prayer

1 **Monaco is culturally Catholic** and among the Monégasque, almost all are Catholic. There are no known Monégasque groups of evangelical believers.

2 **The expatriate community** is 84% of the population. There are three officially recognized congregations which serve the expatriate community — Anglican, French Reformed and the strongly evangelical English-speaking Monaco Christian Fellowship. Pray that committed believers in all three might impact the whole of society.

3 **Christian radio.** Trans World Radio's ministry from Monaco is widely respected. Powerful medium- and short-wave transmitters broadcast in 17 European and 3 North African languages. Pray for:
a) **Spiritual impact** on the materialistic and indifferent cultures of Europe and the resistant and polarized Islamic North Africa.
b) **Effective use of modern technology** — satellite broadcasting, more powerful transmitters, and the means of funding. **TWR** broadcasts 3fi hours weekly in French by Astra Satellite to Monaco itself.
c) **The network of studios** producing programmes for transmission from Monaco to the Muslim world (e.g. **GMU** and **AWM** for North Africa) and Europe (German **TWR**, etc.). The staff needs prayer, as do the listeners.
d) **The difficult but key follow-up ministries**, which are often the only follow-up links that new believers can enjoy.

Mongolia
Mongol Uls

Russia
Kazakhstan
Ulaanbaatar ★
Mongolia
China

AUGUST 15
ASIA

GEOGRAPHY
Area 1,565,000 sq.km. Grassland, forests in north, three major mountain ranges and the great Gobi Desert in the east and south. Subject to climatic extremes.

Population		Ann.Gr.	Density
2000	2,662,020	+1.66%	2 per sq. km.
2010	3,083,289	+1.45%	2 per sq. km.
2025	3,708,989	+1.06%	2 per sq. km.

Approximately 40% are nomadic pastoralists.

Capital Ulaanbaatar (Ulan Bator) 774,000. Other cities: Darkhan 85,000, Erdenet 80,000. **Urbanites** 62%.

PEOPLES
Mongolian 90%. Seven distinct dialects. Halh (Khalkha) 2,130,000; Oirat 210,000; Buryat 52,000.
Turkic 6.6%. Kazakh 182,000; Uriankhai (Tuvinian) 34,000 in far west.
Other 3.4%. Chinese, Russian, Evenki, Korean, Westerners.

Literacy 87%. **Official language** Halh Mongolian. **All languages** 12. **Languages with Scriptures** 2Bi 1NT 7w.i.p.

ECONOMY
A pastoral agricultural economy with 90% of exports being livestock and animal products but severely limited by Mongolia's distance from the sea and poor roads and infrastructure. There were devastating snowfalls, extensive fires and famines in the 1990s with great losses of livestock which impoverished many. Nearly a third of the population lives in extreme poverty. Changing from a USSR-dependent, centrally planned economy to a market economy has been traumatic. **HDI** 0.618; 119th/174. **Public debt** 64% of GNP. **Income/person** $390 (1.2% of USA).

POLITICS
Unified as nation in 1203 which, under Genghis Khan, became the greatest land empire ever known stretching from China and Korea to Central Europe. Under foreign domination between 1368 and 1911. Autonomous from Chinese and Manchu domination in 1911. A Russian-supported revolution in 1921 installed a Communist government. Marxism was renounced in 1990 and a multi-party democracy instituted. The People's Revolutionary Party was elected in 2000 with a massive majority.

RELIGION
The Constitution honours Buddhism, Shamanism and Islam as Mongolia's main religions but grants certain religious freedoms to all people. Restrictions apply to 'foreign' religions in cases where they are perceived as a possible threat to national security. **Persecution index** 59th in the world.

Religions	Population %	Adherents	Ann.Gr.
non-Religious/other	41.59	1,107,134	+1.3%
Shamanist	31.20	830,550	+1.6%
Buddhist	22.50	598,955	+2.0%
Muslim	4.00	106,481	+2.7%
Christian	0.71	18,000	+15.2%

Christians	Denom.	Affil.%	,000	Ann.Gr.
Protestant	15	0.41	11	+15.0%
Independent	7	0.15	4	+20.2%
Catholic	1	0.03	1	+2.9%
Orthodox	1	0.01	0	+0.9%
Marginal	2	0.11	3	+19.5%

Churches	MegaBloc	Cong.	Members	Affiliates
Mongolian Prot grps [10]	P	120	2,500	7,100
Charismatic groups [6]	I	12	1,850	3,100
Latter-day Saints (Morm)	M	15	1,000	2,000
Assemblies of God	P	5	350	1,680
Lutheran	P	3	200	1,054
Catholic	C	3	139	700
Other denoms [14]		34	1,600	2,800
Total Christians [34]		192	7,600	18,000

Trans-bloc Groupings	pop.%	,000	Ann.Gr.
Evangelical	0.5	15	+16.3%
Charismatic	0.4	9	+17.7%
Pentecostal	0.1	2	+22.9%

Missionaries from Mongolia
P,I,A 54 in 5 agencies: 51 in Mongolia.

Missionaries to Mongolia
P,I,A 362 in 55 agencies from 22 countries: USA 80, Korea 62.

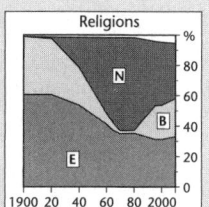

Religions
1900 20 40 60 80 2000

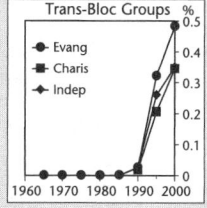

Trans-Bloc Groups
- Evang
- Charis
- Indep
1960 1970 1980 1990 2000

M

• Answers to Prayer

1 **Mongolia was once one of the most closed countries in the world**, but is now relatively open, despite restrictions, with around 400 expatriate Christian workers.

2 **In 1989 there may have been only 4 Mongolian Christians.** By 2000 there was an average of 4,000-5,000 gathering on any given Sunday, with a worshipping community of 8,000-10,000 in over 60 churches and about 100 other informal groups around the country.

• Challenges for Prayer

1 **The daunting economic situation** is a major challenge for the government and deeply affects every aspect of life — much unemployment, poverty, 200,000 malnourished children, etc. Corruption and failure to develop the economy to benefit all led to the rejection of the previous government. Pray that the leaders of Mongolia might rule with fairness and wisdom.

2 **Lamaistic Buddhism** has revived, monasteries have multiplied and many Buddhist sites and images have been restored. Underlying all are the pre-existing shamanism, astrology and occultic powers. Probably over half the population now practice Buddhism and/or Shamanism. Pray that Mongolians might find complete liberation and have transformed lives through following the Lord Jesus Christ.

3 **The Church in Mongolia** is a reality for the first time in modern history. In the Middle Ages there were Mongolian Nestorian Christians. There are now many churches in the capital and small congregations in almost every one of Mongolia's 22 provincial centres. Yet there are challenges:

a) *Great interest in the gospel has often been with misconceptions about missionaries and mixed motives* — material benefits, escape overseas from poverty. Turn-over in attendance has been high leading to some inflated claims about the number of Christians. Many are 'Christians' only for a year or two. Pray for effective discipleship and Christ-like living among believers.

b) *Age-imbalanced congregations* — most are comprised of youth with a few old folk, but the churches need to reach more working-age people, especially men.

c) *Christianity is still too foreign* and has not really become culturally Mongolian yet biblically centred. Pray for a better contextualization of biblical truths to fit Mongolian culture.

d) *Persecution of Christians occurs* — mainly through discrimination and bureaucratic difficulties created in registering churches and also from within families.

e) *Rural churches* have little support or teaching due to a lack of finances and their distance from the capital where most of the training and resources exist. An effective nomadic church concept has yet to emerge.

f) *Spiritual unity*. Out of the 1990s Mongolian Partnership has emerged the Mongolia Evangelical Fellowship, a coalition of 45 church groupings. Pray that this Fellowship may truly serve to bring all the churches together.

4 **The multiplication of other religions and sects is a concern.** Groups such as the Mormons, Jehovah's Witnesses and Baha'i are very active and are forming groups in the capital and in other parts of the country. Pray that evangelical groups may do more strategic networking in order to reach the whole country more effectively.

5 **Mongolian church leaders** are increasing in number and many are being trained at the Union Bible Training Center (100 students in 2001 from 45 congregations). Several other Bible training centres are run by local churches. There are over 600 involved in TEE courses. The Mongolian Mission Center is a discipleship and mission training school equipping Mongolians for ministry within and outside of Mongolia. Pray for the right models of leadership and appropriate support structures to develop, and that these men and women might lay good foundations.

6 **The expatriate Christian workforce has grown.** Most are members of non-religious aid agencies which are not permitted to engage in religious activities. Joint Christian Services is one such umbrella body, coordinating the work of 16 agencies. At present, many are concentrated in the capital. Pray that more expatriate and indigenous Christians might move out to work in rural areas. Pray for spiritual unity, stickability, effective identification with Mongolian culture and close, humble relationships of trust with Mongolian leaders.

7 **The desperate economic plight** of the nation has led to suffering, exploitation and social upheaval. There has been a breakdown of family life and social values. Crime, alcoholism and promiscuity are widespread, and the problem of street children is increasing. Most agencies are involved in health, relief, education and literature programmes. Pray for integrity in implementation and for maximum long-term benefit to the people and the emerging Church.

8 The less evangelized for prayer:
a) ***Nomads*** and some of the sparsely inhabited provinces.
b) ***The Kazakh*** are a majority in the far-western province of Bayan-Olgiy. Almost all are Muslim. There are now a few Christians and several Christian workers among them.
c) ***Ethnic minorities***. There is one church among the Chinese. The Russians are nominally Orthodox with a few attending one of the three Orthodox congregations. There is no known witness among the Uriankhai or Evenki.
d) ***Students***. Various student ministries such as **CCCI**, **IFES**, UBF and others are working to reach college students through camps, seminars and student discipleship groups.

9 Specific Christian support ministries for prayer:
a) ***Bible translation*** has been a rather divisive and controversial issue. There are three translations of the NT which are in use. One translation of the whole Bible was published in 2000 and another translation of the whole Bible (Bible Society of Mongolia) was to be published in 2001. The two main translations use different terms for God. Pray that the churches and agencies may come to a whole-hearted agreement on a culturally appropriate biblical terminology and that God's Word may have an impact on lives and Mongolian culture.
b) ***Christian literature***. Good discipleship and follow-up literature is needed. Several agencies are working on supplying this, but importation of supplies is often difficult.
c) ***The JESUS film*** is available in most indigenous languages and has been widely used on television and film-showings around the country. Many have been moved by it.
d) ***MAF*** was granted permission in 1999 to commence flying operations in a joint venture as *Blue Sky Aviation* and the first plane arrived in 2000. Pray that this may increase effectiveness for ministry to outlying parts of this vast country.
e) ***Christian radio and television***. **FEBC** was registered in 2001 and is operating a Christian radio station in the capital. A TV station, a joint venture between a Christian organization and a Mongolian company, has been airing some Christian programmes which includes testimonies of Mongolian believers.

Montserrat

British Overseas Territory of Montserrat

AUGUST 15
LATIN AMERICA

GEOGRAPHY
Area 102 sq.km. — since increased by lava flows from Mt. Soufrière which erupted 1995-2001+. One of the Leeward Islands in the Caribbean.

Population	Ann.Gr.	Density
2000	3,700	-19.23%	36 per sq. km.
2010	4,100	+0.50%	40 per sq. km.
2025	4,070	-0.27%	40 per sq. km.

Over 80% of the population evacuated in 1995/7 to Antigua, Guadeloupe, UK and elsewhere. Some have since returned. Only the northern third of the island is habitable. Many will never return.

Capital Plymouth, uninhabited — evacuated in 1997.

PEOPLES
Afro-Caribbean 97%. **Euro-American** 2%. **Other** 1%.

Literacy 97%. **Official language** English.

ECONOMY
Tourism, off-shore banking and manufacture of electronic parts were the main sources of income before the massive disruption of the volcanic eruption which was still active in 2001.

POLITICS
Dependent territory of the U.K.

RELIGION
All figures are estimates because of the major population movements.

Religions	Population %	Adherents	Ann.Gr.
Christian	95.50	3,534	-19.3%
non-Religious/other	2.50	93	-18.6%
Baha'i	2.00	74	-18.4%

Christians	Denom.	Affil.%	,000	Ann.Gr.
Protestant	5	42.70	2	-19.7%
Independent	2	4.05	0	-18.0%
Anglican	1	27.03	1	-20.8%
Catholic	1	8.11	0	-27.7%
Marginal	1	0.57	0	-23.8%
Unaffiliated		13.04	0	n.a.

Churches	MegaBloc	Cong.	Members	Affiliates
Anglican	A	2	500	1,000
Pentecostal Assemblies	P	2	250	450
Catholic	C	1	186	300
Methodist	P	1	160	250
Ch of God of Prophecy	P	3	100	160
Baptist Convention	P	1	70	120
Other denoms [5]		5	430	771
Total Christians [11]		15	1,696	3,051

Trans-bloc Groupings	pop.%	,000	Ann.Gr.
Evangelical	27.6	1	-17.4%
Charismatic	21.6	1	-16.6%
Pentecostal	20.5	1	-16.4%

Missionaries from Montserrat
P,I,A 1 in British Virgin Islands.

Missionaries to Montserrat
P,I,A None.

• Challenges for Prayer

1 **The massive devastation of the volcanic eruption to the island**, its economy and social life has deeply affected the people. Many are nominal Christians. Pray for the shock of these events to cause many to find a living faith in Christ.

2 **Church life** was seriously disrupted. Pray for the long task of rebuilding congregations, community life, property and outreach.

Morocco

Kingdom of Morocco

AUGUST 16-17
AFRICA

GEOGRAPHY
Area 458,730 sq.km. North-west corner of Africa. Fertile coastal areas in the north, barren Atlas mountains inland and Sahara Desert to south and south-east. A further 252,000 sq.km. of former Spanish Sahara claimed and occupied by Morocco in 1975.

Population		Ann.Gr.	Density
2000	28,220,843	+1.78%	62 per sq. km.
2010	32,682,965	+1.37%	71 per sq. km.
2025	38,529,890	+1.03%	84 per sq. km.

Capital Rabat 1,675,000. Other major cities: Casablanca 3,350,000; Rabat 1,675,000; Fes 900,000; Marrakech 870,000. **Urbanites** 51%.

PEOPLES
The indigenous Berber were gradually conquered and subdued by the Muslim Arabs after 684AD.
Arabic-speaking 65%. Moroccan Arab 16 mill.; Jebala 1.8m; Algerian 200,000; Hassaniya 45,000.
Berber (Imazighen) 34%. Many dialects; 3 main languages: Tashilhayt (Ishilhayn, S. Shilha, Souss) 2.4m; Tamazight (C. Shilha) 2m; Tarifit (Rif) 1.3m.
Other 1%. French 80,000; Spanish 20,000; Jewish 15,000.
Literacy officially 44% (actually nearer 30%). **Official language** Arabic. French and English widely used. **All languages** 11. **Languages with Scriptures** 2Bi 3NT 1por.

ECONOMY
Agriculture, tourism and especially phosphate mining are important foreign exchange earners. Morocco and the Western Sahara have 70% of the world's phosphate reserves. The cost of the Sahara war has deeply affected the economy. Widespread poverty and high unemployment (50% for youth). Severe droughts in the 1980s and '90s. Millions of Moroccans seek work elsewhere — especially Europe. Significant oil deposits were discovered in 2000. **HDI** 0.582; 126th/174. **Public debt** 54% of GNP. **Income/person** $1,260 (4% of USA).

POLITICS
Independent in 1956 from French and Spanish rule. A limited democracy with an executive monarchy under King Hassan until his death in 1999. His successor, King Mohammed VI, instituted liberalizing changes which are opposed by hitherto-suppressed Islamists. The dominant political issue since the 'Green March' of 1975 has been the occupation of the Western Sahara and the subsequent warfare with the Saharawi and tension between the UN and Morocco about its future.

RELIGION
Sunni Islam is the state religion. The government is committed to the preservation of Islam as the religion of all Moroccans. Under the present constitution, a Moroccan church of former Muslims cannot be recognized. Other religious groups are tolerated so long as their ministry is confined to expatriate communities. **Persecution Index** 10th in the world.

Religions	Population %	Adherents	Ann.Gr.
Muslim	99.85	28,178,512	+1.8%
Christian	0.10	28,221	-0.1%
Jewish	0.05	14,110	+1.8%

Over 95% of the Christians are not Moroccan in origin.

Christians	Denom.	Affil.%	,000	Ann.Gr.
Protestant	11	0.01	2	+1.1%
Independent	1	0.00	1	+4.1%
Anglican	1	0.00	0	+0.0%
Catholic	1	0.08	23	-0.5%
Orthodox	3	0.00	1	-2.6%

Churches	MegaBloc	Cong.	Members	Affiliates
Catholic	C	46	12,849	23,000
Evang Reformed	P	6	170	1,600
Other denoms [17]		40	1,672	3,174
Total Christians [19]		92	14,691	27,774

Trans-bloc Groupings	pop.%	,000	Ann.Gr.
Evangelical	0.0	4	+0.9%
Charismatic	0.0	1	+1.2%

M

• Challenges for Prayer

1 **Islam** was brought by invading Arab armies in the 7th Century. The once-strong North African, and largely Berber, Church was blotted out. Pride in Morocco's glorious past as a centre of civilization and Islamic learning, and prejudice against the truths of Scripture are barriers to the acceptance of the gospel. Probably no more than 5% of the population have had personal contact with the gospel. Pray that this nation may become open for the messengers of the gospel.

2 **There are great expectations for change** through the new King's efforts to encourage more democracy and improve the economy as well as the lot of the underprivileged. Drought, Islamist activism and the culture of corruption in the bureaucracy all could sabotage this. Pray for the King and those in government; for peace and stability.

3 **Praise God for a widespread and growing interest in the gospel,** though every advance is contested by the enemy of souls. Pray specifically for protection of enquirers and national believers from informers, compromise and from internal dissension. Pray also for greater freedom for, and recognition of, Christians. The constitution guarantees freedom of religion — but this does not extend to freedom to leave Islam. Pray for all who have taken this step and for boldness in witness.

4 **A Moroccan Church is emerging** — but at great cost. It is estimated that by 2000 there were 500 believers and some seekers in about 20 small groups meeting for fellowship. Many believers are isolated from regular fellowship. Pray for:

a) *Deep trust and fellowship* to be established between believers so that they can meet together despite the risks and that a strong, indigenous, economically self-sufficient, Moroccan Church might develop.

b) *Grace, fortitude and deliverance from fear* when pressured or harassed by family, police and the authorities. Over the years some believers have been questioned, intimidated, confined to psychiatric wards, temporarily detained and occasionally imprisoned by the police who maintain an active surveillance of anything Christian. The most acute persecution still comes from the families of believers.

c) *Those* discipling *individual believers* despite the climate of suspicion, fear and isolation and the lack of Scriptures and teaching materials.

d) *Provision of leadership* and training opportunities for believers. New leadership training programmes are being developed. Pray that there may be God-given, Spirit-gifted leadership for every group of believers.

e) *An increase in the number of Christian marriages and families*, which then provide the basis for strong, vibrant house churches.

f) *Official recognition* of the existence of Moroccan believers and their identity as genuine Moroccans.

g) *The planting of churches* in every town and city.

5 **Specific unreached peoples:**

a) *The Berber peoples* were nominally Christian until Islam came. Arabization is being resisted by some who have a Berber heritage, and there is a revival of Berber culture and script. The government ban on using the Berber languages has ceased. Literacy in these languages has been very low because of earlier insistence on the sole use of Arabic. There are some believers in each of the three major Berber peoples. Pray that there may soon be groups meeting together using the indigenous languages. The Tashilhayt NT was published in 1998.

b) *The Maghreb Jews* once numbered 250,000. Most emigrated to Israel in 1948. Today only 15,000 remain as a respected minority. There is no known outreach to them at this time.

c) *The nomadic desert tribes* of the south and east, who have little contact with the gospel.

6 **Missionary work, as such, is no longer openly permitted,** and former mission centres were closed in the late 1960s. Christian workers are able to take up various types of employment, share their faith and encourage believers. Give thanks for those who are living in this country — may their lives radiate the life of Jesus, and may they have a tactful boldness and faith for a harvest despite surveillance, pressure and discouragements. Pray for more to be able to master Arabic and the Berber languages. Pray also for the way to open for Christians to enter this land.

7 **Bible and Christian literature ministries:**

a) *In theory, Bibles may be legally imported*, but Arabic versions have been seized. Pray for effective importation and distribution of Scriptures in Arabic and Berber languages. The bilingual French-Arabic NT is popular.

b) *Bible translation* continues in the three main Berber languages in both Arabic and Berber scripts as well as in Moroccan Arabic. Pray for the translators and for a felicitous and accurate choice of words. Much is being done to record and distribute parts of the Scriptures in Tarifit.

c) **BCCs** in combination with Christian broadcasting have been successful but the authorities have sought to hinder and discredit the ministry. Pray that postal services may function without interference en route — sadly, a frequently occurrence. Over the years 250,000 have started as BCC students.

d) **Various literature agencies** — most are based in France or Spain. They are working to write, print and distribute Arabic and Berber literature for North Africa.

8 **Christian electronic media ministries** are making a potent impact:

a) **Satellite TV** has spread rapidly and is very popular in both urban and rural areas. SAT-7 has made a big impact with 25% of Arab World responses from Morocco. Pray for good reception of programmes and for impact on the lives and worldview of Moroccans.

b) **Christian radio** has been effective to bring the gospel to many — especially young people. Pray for:

i *Programmes.* The three Berber languages are a challenge — pray for these to be increased in number and variety, and for indigenous Christian music, songs, poetry and theology to be developed.

ii *Increased hours on the air* at appropriate times and intervals. **TWR** broadcasts 12 hrs/wk in Arabic and 3 hrs/wk in Tamazight. The ideal would be 24 hours a day!

iii *Strategic use of Christian radio* for effective church planting with good follow-up that does not expose contacts to risk, but leads to long-term discipling

c) **The JESUS film** is being distributed on video cassettes in Arabic and the 3 major Berber languages — especially in ports as Moroccans travel to and from Europe. A large number of the population has seen the video.

d) **There is a great effort** being made to record the Scriptures in Moroccan Arabic on cassette tape.

9 **Moroccans have migrated in large numbers** in search of employment — many illegally and dangerously. Over 3,000 have drowned in crossing the Straits of Gibraltar to Spain between 1994 and 1999. There are significant numbers of Moroccans in Europe: in France (approx. 1.5 mill.); The Netherlands (240,000); Belgium (150,000); Spain (113,000 legal and possibly 700,000 illegal); Germany (100,000); and Britain (50,000). Others reside in the Spanish North African enclave cities of Ceuta and Mellila. Pray for the various agencies seeking to reach them in these lands — some being **GMU, AWM, YWAM, OM, PMI** and **WEC**.

Western Sahara

M

GEOGRAPHY
Area 252,000 sq.km. Almost entirely desert, but has huge phosphate deposits and one of the world's richest sea fishing areas.
Population An estimated 200,000.
Capital Laayoune.

PEOPLES
Arab-Berber Moroccan 'settlers' 135,000; Saharawi indigenous 65,000; a further 190,000 refugees in 4 main camps near Tindouf, Algeria. There are also up to 100,000 Moroccan military personnel.
Literacy 95%. **Official language** Hassaniya Arabic.

ECONOMY
Great potential for development despite lack of water. The Moroccan occupation is costly and limits investment and development.

POLITICS
Ruled by Spain until 1975 and then occupied by Morocco. 16 years of Saharawi-Moroccan warfare ensued. A UN-brokered cease-fire of 1991 has not yielded the promised referendum on the future status of the area. Morocco is fully intent on holding on to it. Over 70% of the territory is controlled by Morocco behind a 1,500 km berm (earth wall) and 30% by Polisario, the Saharawi liberation movement. The Saharawi Arab Democratic Republic is recognized by 70 governments.

RELIGION
100% Muslim. Polisario is moderate and secular in orientation.

• Challenges for Prayer

1 **A peaceful and fair resolution to more than 25 years of conflict** and a return of the Saharawi to their homeland is the need. Pray for this.

2 **Until recently there were no known Christians**. There are several who now believe. Some low-key work is in progress. There are openings for ministry through relief and development to the refugees. The *JESUS* film is available and the Hassaniya NT is in preparation. Pray for those who are, and could be, serving among them.

Mozambique
Republic of Mozambique

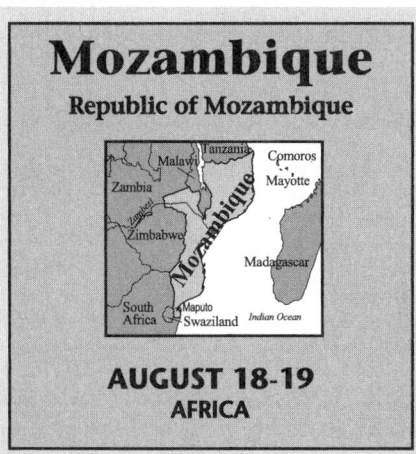

AUGUST 18-19
AFRICA

GEOGRAPHY
Area 799,380 sq.km. The Zambezi and 24 other rivers divide the 2,800 km-long land and make north-south travel difficult.

Population		Ann.Gr.	Density
2000	19,680,456	+2.51%	25 per sq. km.
2010	23,116,593	+1.50%	29 per sq. km.
2025	30,611,842	+1.96%	38 per sq. km.

At the height of the war in 1992 nearly 40% of the population were refugees — internally 4 million and in surrounding lands 1.8m. Deaths in the war mounted to more than one million. The high incidence of AIDS is likely to reduce projected population growth.

Capital Maputo 2.2m. Other major cities: Beira 700,000; Nampula 600,000. **Urbanites** 28%.

PEOPLES

Bantu peoples 97.7%.
Northern peoples 54.3%. Makhuwa(5) 6.8 mill.; Lomwe 2m; Chwabo 730,000; Makonde(2) 600,000; Yao 450,000; Swahili (and related Mwani, Makwe, Koti and Nathembo) 150,000.
Central peoples 19.2%. Sena-Podzo 1.1m; Shona (Ndau, Tewe, Manyika, Tavara) 1,030,000; Nyungwe 700,000; Marenje 500,000; Maravi (Nyanja, Chewa) 450,000.
Southern peoples 24.2%. Tsonga-Changana 1.9m; Tswa 1.1m; Chopi-Tonga 800,000; Ronga 600,000; Swazi-Zulu 140,000.
Other 2.3%. Euro-African 300,000; Portuguese 60,000; South Asian 25,000.

Literacy 40% (official); 20% (functional). **Official language** Portuguese — spoken as first language by 6.8%; understood by 30%. **All languages** 39. **Languages with Scriptures** 9Bi 5NT 9por 12w.i.p.

ECONOMY
One of the world's poorest countries — the result of centuries of colonial neglect, application of Marxist economic theories and 30 years of intense guerrilla warfare. Climatic extremes of flooding and droughts have further impoverished the population. Fertile agricultural land and large mineral wealth were under-utilized, and most rural areas became a depopulated no-man's-land. Road and rail links are few and barely usable. Heavily dependent on foreign aid. After peace came in 1995 improvements were excellent — until the setback caused by the massive damage of the cyclone in 2000. **HDI** 0.341; 169th/174. **Public debt** 225% of GNP. **Income/person** $140 (0.5% of USA).

POLITICS
A Portuguese colony for 470 years. Independent in 1975 as a Marxist-Leninist state after a long and bitter war for independence. The anti-government movement, Renamo, subsequently spread rural devastation to most of the country in an exceptionally brutal guerrilla war. The war and international pressure encouraged the Frelimo government to end the flirtation with Marxism in 1988 and to institute a multi-party democracy and a market economy in 1990. A peace accord in 1992 was fully implemented in 1995. A functioning democracy and now (surprisingly) a member of the British Commonwealth.

RELIGION
Government policy between 1975 and 1982 was the exclusive propagation of Marxism, 'all-out war on the churches' and 'destruction of religious superstitions.' Since 1988 there has been religious freedom.

Religions	Population %	Adherents	Ann.Gr.
Christian	57.65	11,345,783	+4.0%
Traditional ethnic	22.00	4,329,700	-0.9%
Muslim	18.10	3,562,163	+3.0%
non-Religious/other	2.20	432,970	-0.1%
Hindu	0.05	9,840	+2.5%

M

Christians	Denom.	Affil.%	,000	Ann.Gr.
Protestant	48	8.34	1,641	+8.1%
Independent	506	22.41	4,410	+12.3%
Anglican	1	0.51	100	+3.3%
Catholic	1	20.83	4,100	+8.2%
Orthodox	1	0.00	1	+1.5%
Marginal	1	0.53	105	+1.8%
Unaffiliated		5.03	989	n.a.

Churches	MegaBloc	Cong.	Members	Affiliates
Catholic	C	290	2,500,000	4,100,000
Indigenous/Indep. [100]	I	6,280	565,217	1,300,000
Assemblies of God	P	880	150,000	295,000
United Baptist	P	1,206	70,478	250,000
Evang Assemblies of God	P	873	96,000	240,000
Seventh-day Adventist	P	821	144,568	240,000
Assemblies of God, African	I	360	90,000	220,000
Jehovah's Witnesses	M	691	31,000	104,922
Anglican	A	206	34,965	100,000
Presbyterian	P	750	42,918	100,000
Ch of the Nazarene	P	450	45,000	85,000
New Alliance (Brethren)	I	200	20,000	50,000
United Methodist	P	1,000	17,000	45,000
Baptist Convention	P	52	18,572	40,000
Full Gospel Ch of God	P	120	10,182	30,000
Reformed Ch in M	P	130	14,000	28,000
Free Methodist	P	200	10,000	17,000
Church of God (Anderson)	P	150	7,000	14,000
Evangelical	P	16	800	2,000
Other denoms [443]		10,870	1,533,600	3,095,000
Total Christians [561]		25,545	5.401m	10.356m

Trans-bloc Groupings	pop.%	,000	Ann.Gr.
Evangelical	13.5	2,650	+10.6 %
Charismatic	8.4	1,647	+10.7%
Pentecostal	4.5	884	+10.5%

Missionaries from Mozambique
P,I,A 32 in 8 agencies: Mozambique 27.

Missionaries to Mozambique
P,I,A 491 in 75 agencies from 26 countries: USA 125, South Africa 113, Brazil 60, UK 27.

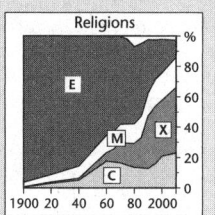

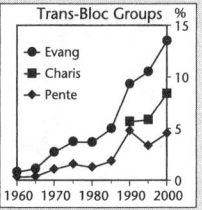

• Answers to Prayer

1 **Peace since 1995 after 30 years of war** and genuine efforts by politicians to maintain that peace.

2 **The fastest church growth** of any Black African country in the 1990s. Hitherto Mozambique had some of the largest unevangelized areas and peoples in the region. The total Christian population more than doubled between 1988 and 2000.

• Challenges for Prayer

1 **Mozambique emerged broken and wounded** from colonialism and three decades of civil war. In 1995 it was reckoned to be the world's poorest nation. The government has worked hard to open up the economy, lay true democratic foundations, grant religious freedom and bind up the wounds of the past. Turn these major challenges it faces into prayer:

M

a) Continuing natural disasters — much of the infrastructure of the more developed south was destroyed in the cyclone and flooding of 2000.

b) The danger of regional disaffection — the more heavily populated north feels neglected.

c) The growing calamity of AIDS with nearly 14% known to be HIV+ and 310,000 AIDS orphans. Medical services are rudimentary for the vast majority.

2 **Mozambique has had religious freedom for the first time in its history**. The Catholic monopoly under Portuguese rule was only breached in the southern third of Mozambique. Protestant ministries were restricted or forbidden. Sporadic but severe persecution of evangelical believers occurred. Under Marxism all Christians suffered. Missionaries were expelled, Christian leaders intimidated and imprisoned, and many churches and institutions seized or destroyed. Discriminatory legislation was passed to limit Christian gatherings to recognized church buildings. Then began the growth. At independence in 1975, Evangelicals were 3.7% of the population. By 2000 this was nearly 12%. The Evangelical Alliance of Mozambique was formed in 1993. Pray that this growth may be maintained and the believers become a wholesome leaven in a society that is morally bankrupt and where life is cheap and short.

3 **Intense suffering created spiritual hunger** and congregations of indigenous Christians mushroomed all over the country. The flooding disasters of 2000 and 2001 stimulated much Christian assistance and churches were planted in refugee camps. Illiteracy, lack of Scriptures, legalism, syncretism and lack of understanding of biblical repentance, faith and the new birth is widespread. Yet the desire for teaching and help, wisely and tactfully given, is immense. Many of the leaders are self-appointed and looking for international links, finances and aid rather than spiritual input. **AIM** in Beira, and many others in Maputo and elsewhere, have developed mobile and TEE training for leaders of these groups. Pray that this massive movement might become Bible-based and mature.

4 **The Catholic Church,** long associated with colonial repression, suffered particularly severely after independence. Huge defections, widespread nominalism and lack of Africanization with a dearth of indigenous clergy led to a big drop in numbers. During the 1990s Catholics began to grow again. Renewal movements among Catholics elsewhere have had little impact here.

5 **Training of church leadership is an urgent priority.** Most congregations are led by men and women with little or no education, and very few by those with theological training of any kind, nor are there funds or adequate facilities to provide it. The government insists that each group provide adequate training for their leaders. Pray for:
a) *Seminaries and Bible colleges*, which have increased in number. The Christian Council of Mozambique run Ricatla Seminary. There are more evangelical seminaries in Maputo — The Evangelical Theological Seminary, also the Union Baptist, Nazarene, and **PAoC** Colleges. The Reformed Seminary is in Tete. The Evangelical **AoG** have two Bible schools. However, there is little training available in the northern half of the country.
b) *Non-formal training* which has proved successful — TEE (United Baptists, **AEF**) and correspondence courses (Emmaus Bible School of the Brethren and Global Literature Lifeline based in Zimbabwe).

6 **Mozambique's unreached peoples** are still numerous and large, but there are few without a witness or an indigenous Christian presence. Much of existing outreach is through Mozambican missionaries and pastors. The challenges:
a) *The Makhuwa.* Some 30-60% are Muslim, 10% Catholic and maybe 10,000 are Evangelicals (**AoG, CoN**, United Baptists and others), but the more Muslim areas towards the coast are less evangelized.
b) *The coastal Swahili-related peoples* have long been Muslim. Only a handful of Mwani believers are known. **SIL** is translating the NT, and **AIM** has a church-planting ministry.
c) *The Makonde in the north-east* are part Muslim, part animist. Only Catholic and Assemblies of God, African churches are known to exist. There were about 30 evangelical congregations in 2000.
d) *The Yao of Niassa Province* along the shores of Lake Malawi are 96% Muslim. Only about 2% are Christian of any kind (mainly Anglican, Catholic and Assemblies of God, African). Both radio (**FEBA**) and the *JESUS* film have made an impact.
e) *The peoples of the Zambezi valley* — especially the Sena, Kunda, Podzo, Nyungwe, Chwabo, Lolo, Kokola, Manyawa, Marenje and Takwane.

7 Sections of the population that are less evangelized:
a) *The cities.* War, famine and poverty have filled Beira and Maputo with refugees. Violence and crime are widespread. AIDS is a major problem.
b) *The Northern Provinces* of Cabo Delgado and Niassa are the least evangelized.
c) *The Muslim population* has grown since independence, but is largely confined to the north and the coastal provinces. The Yao and Swahili-related peoples are Muslim and the Makonde and Makua largely Muslim. Until recently there was little outreach to Muslims and committed workers are still few.
d) *Students.* There are only three University-level institutions with 7,000 students. ABEMO(**IFES**) has unique witness and discipleship opportunities among them.

8 **Expatriate missionaries** were expelled in 1975/76, but since 1982 doors have opened once more. Conditions are often harsh, travel difficult, the cities violent and disease common, so the loss-rate has been high. Pray for perseverance in learning Portuguese and local languages, health, safety and fruitfulness. Much evangelism has been done in short term efforts but few converts become disciples. Mozambique is still a pioneer field and more missionaries are needed for this task. The greatest need is for all levels of leadership training, initiating youth and children's work, aid programmes, involvement in medical needs — especially in AIDS-related ministries. Major mission agencies: **SIL** (40), **YWAM** (39), **AIM** (37), **CCCI** (21), **SIM** (19), **AoG** (17), **IMB-SBC** (13) and SdA (10).

9 **Bible translation and distribution.** The Bible Society has a bookshop and 3 depots and great freedom to operate, but lack of Bibles, foreign currency and means of distribution limit this ministry. Projects for new translations or revisions have also been hampered. The government changed its language policy in 1982 to actively encourage the use of local languages, but a nation-wide policy on orthography is needed or in progress. **SIL** has workers who promote the study of Mozambican languages. Bible translation is needed in at least 10 and possibly 15 languages — especially in Makua, Mwani and Sena. A number of other languages with inadequate New Testaments require new translations. Pray for the 10 translation projects in progress by **SIL** and others, one being the Lomwe Old Testament (**SIM**, **UBS**).

10 Christian help ministries for prayer:

a) ***Literature*** is easily imported but in short supply. Distribution and high costs are major problems, and Christian bookstores are limited in number and in range of stock. People are eager for literature. **CLC** has a bookstore in Maputo, and are initiating Book Aid for importing second-hand Christian books from Brazil. Agencies outside the country have done much to send in good evangelistic literature (All Nations Gospel Publishers, South Africa; Global Literature Lifeline, Zimbabwe; **Open Doors**; **SGM**; Frontline Fellowship) and the gospel broadsheet *CEDO* (**WEC**). **SU** has started work in Mozambique with the aim of providing good Bible reading aids.

b) ***Radio*** has been used of God in church-planting and teaching. There is a Christian FM station in Maputo. Both **TWR** and **FEBA** have studios in the country — **TWR** also using innovative 'container' studios in the north. **TWR**-Swaziland and Johannesburg broadcast 19 hours a week in Portuguese and 7 other languages; **FEBA**-Seychelles a further 16 hours in Portuguese, Makonde, Sena and Swahili.

c) ***The JESUS film*** has been used among refugees and in some areas in Mozambique, but only 5% of the population have seen it in one of the 10 language editions available. A further 12 language versions are in production. Pray for the resources and strategies to make more effective use of it.

d) ***GRN*** have prepared messages in 23 of Mozambique's languages.

e) ***Development programmes*** by Christian agencies are welcomed by the government. ACRIS, a Christian medical association formed in 1991, is taking over administration of some hospitals and clinics and providing Christian medical personnel. **WVI** and others have been supplying basic needs to many. **MAF** and AirServ International have several planes involved in these programmes, but flying conditions are tricky. Pray that these efforts may strengthen believers and stimulate evangelism.

Myanmar

Union of Myanmar

AUGUST 20-21

ASIA

Revised February 2004

GEOGRAPHY
Area 676,577 sq.km. Basin and delta of the Irrawaddy River ringed by a horseshoe of high mountains that isolates the country from India, China and Thailand.

Population		Ann.Gr.	Density
2000	45,611,177	+1.24%	67 per sq. km.
2010	50,902,661	+1.07%	75 per sq. km.
2025	58,120,485	+0.76%	86 per sq. km.

More recent estimates indicate the population in 2000 to be 49 million.

Capital Yangon 5,000,000. Other major city: Mandalay 800,000. **Urbanites** 27%.

PEOPLES
Very diverse ethnically. Official figures downplay the sizes of ethnic minorities.
Sino-Tibetan 89.3%.
Burmese (Bama) 57.5%
Other 19.8%. Karen(16) 4.8 mill.; Chin(8 languages, numerous dialects) 1.2m; Arakanese (Rakhine) 730,000; Kachin(8) 900,000; Taungyo 620,000; Intha 200,000; Kado 180,000; Chaungtha 170,000; Lisu(2) 170,000; Akha 140,000; Rawang 100,000.
Tai 8.5%. Shan (3) 3.2m; Lu-Tai(3) 320,000.
Chinese 3.5%. Large increase in 1990s.
Mon-Khmer 5.7%. Over 13 peoples, the largest: Mon 1.1m; Palaung(5) 600,000; Wa (Vo, Kawa) 1.1m; Khmu 100,000.
Other 5%. Rohingya 1.4m; Indian 750,000; Nepali (Gurkhali) 200,000; Malay 26,000; Moken (Sea Gypsy) 5,000.

Literacy 83%. **Official language** Burmese. **All languages** 107. **Languages with Scriptures** 18Bi 11NT 16por 15w.i.p.

ECONOMY
Rich in natural resources, but ravaged by the greed of its rulers. Few countries have been so effectively plundered and impoverished by its own leaders. The large teak forests are being stripped. The most successful export is opium, producing over 50% of the world's supply from the so-called Golden Triangle in the Lao-Thai border region. **HDI** 0.580; 128th/174. **Public debt** 4% of GNP. **Income/person** $2,610 (8% of USA).

POLITICS
The country has known little peace since the Japanese invasion of World War II, in 1942. Independent from Britain in 1948 as a Federal Union of seven districts and seven ethnic minority states. Insensitivity of the central government to the aspirations of ethnic minorities provoked unrest and bitter ethnic wars in nine areas. Popular demands for democratic rule opened the way for elections in 1990. The opposition party won 85% of the seats, but the military regime refused to hand over power. The secretive military junta, the 'State Peace and Development Council', has turned Myanmar into a prison with widespread human rights abuses and killings, forced labour, rape and imprisonment used as tools of repression. Most of the democratic leaders have been arrested, exiled or killed. A member of ASEAN.

RELIGION
Officially Buddhism is no longer the state religion, but the military regime actively promotes it. Theoretically, there is freedom of religion, but because Christianity is strong among the restive ethnic minorities there is much discrimination against Christians. There have been many cases of enforced conversions to Buddhism and violence against rural Christians. **Persecution index** 30th in the world.

Religions	Population %	Adherents	Ann.Gr.
Buddhist	82.90	37,811,666	+0.9%
Christian	8.70	3,970,000	+3.8%
Muslim	3.80	1,733,225	+1.2%
Chinese	3.00	1,368,335	+9.8%
Traditional ethnic	0.80	364,889	-3.2%
Hindu	0.50	228,056	+1.2%
non-Religious/other	0.30	136,834	+1.2%

Christians	Denom.	Affil.%	,000	Ann.Gr.
Protestant	26	6.02	2,747	+3.6%
Independent	41	1.22	556	+6.2%
Anglican	1	0.12	57	+2.6%
Catholic	1	1.32	600	+2.2%
Marginal	1	0.02	10	+5.2%

Churches	MegaBloc	Cong.	Members	Affiliates
Myanmar Baptist Conv	P	3,750	617,781	1,900,000
Catholic	C	1,096	372,671	600,000
Assemblies of God	P	1,500	110,000	255,000
Churches of Christ	P	1,200	100,000	180,000
Methodist	P	300	60,000	100,000
Lisu Christian	I	583	35,000	75,000
Ch of Prov of M	A	731	27,794	56,700
Seventh-day Adventist	P	173	20,555	50,000
Evangelical Free	P	420	12,000	30,000
Presbyterian	P	256	11,785	29,496
Self Supp Karen Bapt	I	140	14,000	28,000
Believer's Church	I	600	15,625	25,000

M

Christian Brethren	P	110	9,200	23,000
Mara Evangelical	I	96	10,938	17,170
Foursquare Gospel	P	85	6,000	11,000
Jehovah's Witnesses	M	113	2,950	10,178
Full Gospel Assembly	I	27	5,000	9,000
Christian Reformed	P	71	2,800	3,500
Chr & Miss Alliance	P	9	1,989	3,000
Other denoms [50]		4,815	356,000	529,000
Total Christians [69]		16,170	1,811,000	3,970,000

Trans-bloc Groupings	**pop.%**	**,000**	**Ann.Gr.**
Evangelical	5.2	2,355	+4.2%
Charismatic	0.8	350	+6.3%
Pentecostal	0.6	287	+6.7%

Missionaries from Myanmar
P,I,A 3,160 in 40 agencies: 3,100 in Myanmar.

Missionaries to Myanmar
P,I,A 159 in 32 agencies.

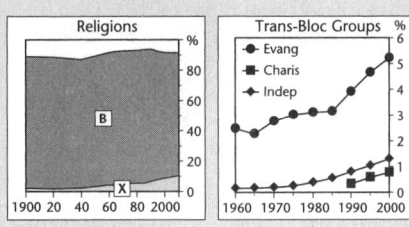

• Answers to Prayer

1 **Despite the isolation and repression of Christians,** there has been considerable growth among some ethnic minorities and a great interest in the gospel among Buddhist monks. There have been examples of outstanding miracles leading to many conversions.

• Challenges for Prayer

1 **Four decades of repressive military rule** have isolated the nation and brought it to destitution. Widespread despair followed the repression of democracy in 1990. The courage of the leader of the main opposition party, Aung San Suu Kyi, was recognized in her being awarded the 1991 Nobel Peace Prize. She has remained under house arrest since 1990. Pray that the international community and the other ASEAN members might speak out and act to bring democracy. Pray for an orderly transfer to a just and democratic government that will rebuild the country with both democratic and religious freedom.

2 **There has been continual warfare since 1942.** Since independence, the central government has sought to crush dissension among ethnic minorities. Massive destruction of property and life has deeply affected the Karen, Shan, Wa and Chin peoples particularly. During the 1990s there were up to 2 million refugees — most within Myanmar, and many in India, Bangladesh and Thailand. Pray for ethnic harmony, effective federalism and peace.

3 **The isolation of the Church in Myanmar has lasted for 30 years.** All Protestant and most Catholic missions were expelled in 1966. Praise God for foundations laid by Adoniram Judson, the famous American Baptist missionary, and those who followed — for on these foundations the Church has grown and become an effective missionary-sending body. Pray for the removal of restrictions on fellowship with Christians from other lands.

4 **The military regime is seeking to marginalize and even eliminate the Church,** yet growth continues. Christianity has been deeply rooted and has grown stronger in adversity. Many Christians are well-educated and are in positions of responsibility all over the country. However, growth slowed during the 1980s because of liberal theology. Growth is now most marked in the newer denominations. The most growth has been among ethnic minorities — the entire northern Chin groups, Lushai Chin, Mara, Matu Chin in southern Chin State and the majority of several Kachin groups (Jingphaw, Rawang), Lisu and Lahu and 40% of the Karen are Christian. Pray that they may continue to evangelize every sub-group in their respective peoples and reach out to other unreached peoples and to the Burmese majority.

5 **Challenges facing the Church in Myanmar:**

a) *Fortitude and faithfulness under persecution.* There is much freedom yet also there are many imposed restrictions — on buildings, proselytizing, job opportunities and importation of literature. There have been many cases of Christians being forced to build Buddhist temples and to renounce their faith.

b) *Liberal theology* in some of the older, ecumenical seminaries is creating a church leadership that scorns evangelicals and the message of new birth. Pray that the Bible may retain its rightful place in the affections of both leaders and church members.

c) *Nominalism* among third- and fourth-generation Christians is widespread. Pray for revival.

d) *Most Christians are from minority groups* which are embroiled in military actions against the central government. Pray that this may not cause bitterness, hatred of other peoples, compromise of their faith, or blunting of a missions vision.

e) *Reconciliation and unity* among Christians is a serious need. The causes of division are various — ethnic, political, passivism or military activism, and doctrinal. Pray that the Myanmar Biblical Christian Fellowship and the Myanmar Evangelical Christian Fellowship may effectively promote unity.

6 **Theological education** is of vital importance. There are over 90 theological institutions in Myanmar. Many are liberal in theology. Many are tribally based and are basic and small in student numbers with few resources. Pray specifically for the 15 member institutions of the evangelical *Myanmar Theological Association*. For special prayer mention: the Evangel Bible College (**AoG**, 60 students), ACTS Bible College (Church on the Rock, 90 students), Hebron (Brethren, 20 students) and Evangelical Bible Seminary — the last with over 120 students from many denominations and impacting the Church in a significant way.

7 **Buddhism is strongly entrenched** among the Burmese majority, the Shan and the Mon, and of deep influence in more animistic peoples. The power of demonic spirits, astrology, superstition and the occult pervades all sections of the community. Only about 5% of Christians have come to Christ out of Buddhism. Pray for significant breakthroughs in every people and demonstrations of the power of Jesus. Pray also for conversions among the 750,000 Buddhist monks — may of whom have shown great interest in Christian radio broadcasts.

8 **The least evangelized peoples:**

a) *The Bama (Burmese) peoples*. There are only about 50,000 Christians among them. It is not easy for tribal believers to witness to them because of the years of mistrust, nor is it easy for the politically dominant Bama to receive the gospel from them without prejudice. Pray for conversions among this staunchly Buddhist people.

b) *The Shan* are Buddhist, related to the Thai and live in the Golden Triangle. They have suffered much in the wars with the military regime. Drugs and AIDS are major scourges. Only 0.6% are Christian, and few have Bibles. The archaic Shan NT is being rewritten.

c) *Other Buddhist minorities* have few Christians — the Palaung (0.2%); Mon (0.9%); Taungyo (0.5%); Lu (0.6%) and numerous other smaller groups.

d) *The more animistic peoples*. Some are less reached, but significant turnings are now taking place among the Southern Chin, Naga, Mru, Rawang, Mahei, Wa and Akha. Pray for the emergence of vital church-planting movements among each of them. Poverty, opium-growing, lack of Christian literature — especially the Scriptures — and inadequate teaching are negatives.

e) *The Chinese*. There were 62 churches and 10,000 believers in 1990 with 2% of their population Christian. The massive influx of Chinese over the Yunnan border from China has reduced this percentage. Mandalay is now 30% Chinese. Many of these Chinese in the north are less reached.

f) *The Chettiyars, an Indian minority*, who originated from the former French enclaves in India, and other Indians from many states in India. Among them are Muslims and Hindus. Very little outreach has been directed towards them.

g) *The Rohingya of Arakan*, Muslim descendants of Arabs, Moors, Moghuls and Bengalis who settled in Arakan 1,000 years ago. The Myanmar military regime has denied them citizenship, and in both 1978 and 1991 over 250,000 were driven from their homes and forced to become refugees in Bangladesh. They have since been permitted to return, but have become marginalized and introverted. There are no known Christians among them.

h) *The Hindus and Nepalis* were long neglected. In 1928 the first church among them was planted and now there are just a few groups of believers.

i) *AIDS victims*. AIDS is a major disaster with over 530,000 infected (2% of the population), and over 43,000 orphans. The causes are girls driven to prostitution on a large scale in Thailand, intravenous drug-taking and large movements of people as forced labourers. Virtually nothing is being done to prevent its spread or meet the overwhelming emotional and spiritual needs of those affected.

9 **The missionary vision of the Church** has led to new peoples opening up to the gospel. There are an estimated 900 or so cross-cultural Myanmarese serving the Lord. Their main sending bodies are the Baptists, **AoG**, Presbyterians, Christian Brethren and Churches of Christ. **GFA** is the largest agency which works with the Believers Church and they have 800 missionaries and 2 missionary training schools with over 270 students. Pray for this vision to be sustained, supported and expanded and then bear much fruit.

10 Christian help ministries for prayer:

a) *There is a shortage of Bibles* and all forms of Christian literature in Burmese and minority languages because of import restrictions. Some Burmese Bibles and NTs are being printed in Myanmar, but funding and supplies are difficult to obtain. The Evangelical Literature Centre (7 bookstores) and **CLC** (1 bookstore in Yangon) are providing critically needed literature through publishing.

b) *Bible translation* is a major challenge. There are teams working on 14 NT translations, but at least a further 14, and possibly up to 54, languages need translation. Most of the work will need to be done by Myanmar translators. Pray for evangelical translators to be raised up to continue existing programmes and for an adequate survey of the remaining unmet need.

c) *Christian radio* has been effective with broadcasting in 17 languages. Major radio agencies and their broadcasting languages: **FEBC** (Akha, Burmese, Jingpo, Chin (4), Karen (2), Lahu, Lisu, Lushai, Palaung, Rawang and Shan) and **TWR** (Burmese, English). Bama listeners are becoming more receptive as a result. Pray for the production of programmes and provision of equipment.

d) *The JESUS film* has been widely shown in film and on television.

e) *GRN* has made recordings available in 149 languages, but importation and distribution problems limit their usefulness.

Namibia
Republic of Namibia

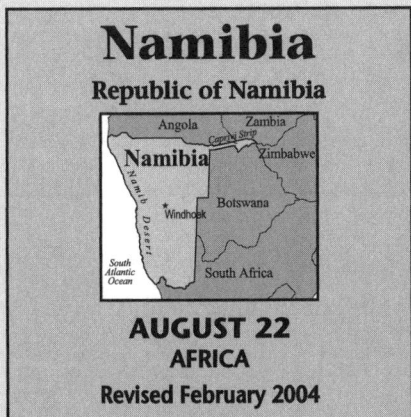

AUGUST 22
AFRICA
Revised February 2004

GEOGRAPHY
Area 823,144 sq.km. Predominantly arid, semi-desert; the driest African land south of the equator.

Population	Ann.Gr.	Density
2000	1,725,868	+2.26%	2 per sq. km.
2010	1,915,827	+0.87%	2 per sq. km.
2025	2,337,592	+1.43%	3 per sq. km.

Most people live on the central plateau and the better-watered northern border regions adjoining Angola.

Capital Windhoek 250,000. **Urbanites** 39%.

PEOPLES
Five major groupings and 28 languages.
Bantu 73.1%. Ovambo 870,000 (half the population in 6 ethnic groups; politically dominant); Kavango 166,000 (Kwangali and Hambukushu); Herero 138,000 (also Dhimba and Himba); Caprivi peoples (3) 80,000; Tswana 8,000.
Khoisan 8.6%. Nama 104,000; San (10) 45,000.
Damara 6.4%. A non-Khoisan people that speaks Nama.
European 4.5%. Afrikaner 60,000; German 13,000; English-speakers 11,000.
Mixed Race 7%. Afrikaans-speaking.
Other 0.4%.

Literacy 76%. **Official language** English, though few speak it, most speaking Afrikaans. **All languages** 28. **Languages with Scriptures** 9Bi 3NT 3por 1w.i.p.

ECONOMY
Mining diamonds, uranium and many other minerals, cattle ranching and fishing are all important. Many still live in deep poverty. Serious droughts afflicted the country during the 1990s. **Unemployment** 30%+. **HDI** 0.638; 115th/174. **Public debt** 20% of GNP. **Income/person** $2,110 (7% of USA), but big disparities between rich and poor.

POLITICS
A German colony 1883-1915. Ruled by South Africa 1915-1990. Independence gained in 1990 after a long, costly war which severely dis-

N

rupted the social and economic fabric of the country. The major party, SWAPO, renounced Marxism and espoused multi-party democracy and a mixed economy. A member of the British Commonwealth.

RELIGION
Secular state with freedom of religion. Despite the high profile of Christian denominations, non-Christian religions are being granted similar opportunities in schools and in the media.

Religions	Population %	Adherents	Ann.Gr.
Christian	79.95	1,379,831	+1.9%
Traditional ethnic	15.00	258,880	+3.2%
non-Religious/other	5.00	86,293	+4.9%
Jewish	0.05	863	-4.4%

Christians	Denom.	Affil. %	,000	Ann.Gr.
Protestant	36	41.43	715	+7.5%
Independent	111	11.60	200	+5.1%
Anglican	1	3.36	58	-3.7%
Catholic	1	15.93	275	+0.4%
Marginal	2	0.15	3	-2.9%
Unaffiliated		7.48	129	n.a.

Churches	MegaBloc	Cong.	Members	Affiliates
Evangelical Lutheran	P	110	208,800	522,000
Catholic	C	144	164,671	275,000
Anglican	A	89	11,600	58,000
Uniting Ref Ch of S.A.	P	133	33,950	53,850
Protestant Unity	I	210	20,958	35,000
Seventh-day Adventist	P	47	10,932	22,000
Ovambo Independent	I	60	9,009	20,000

Rhenish Ch in Namibia	P	14	9,500	19,000
Full Gospel Ch of God	P	45	7,120	14,000
Herero	I	60	5,988	10,000
African Methodist Epis	I	39	3,135	9,500
Baptist Conv. of N	P	49	3,815	8,000
Other Protestant [16]	P	57	4,000	8,000
Evangelical Bible	P	22	4,500	7,500
German Lutheran	P	20	4,000	7,000
United Congregational	P	7	2,163	2,879
Jehovah's Witnesses	M	19	963	2,300
Other denoms [120]		1,260	101,000	178,000
Total Christians [152]		2,385	606,000	1,252,000

Trans-bloc Groupings	pop.%	,000	Ann.Gr.
Evangelical	10.3	179	+11.3%
Charismatic	4.2	72	+2.2%
Pentecostal	1.6	28	+0.5%

Missionaries from Namibia
P,I,A 26 in 4 agencies — mainly in Namibia.

Missionaries to Namibia
P,I,A 259 in 40 agencies from 15 countries: South Africa 132, USA 47, Germany 22.

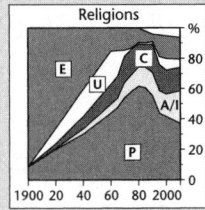

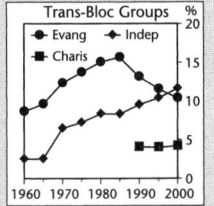

• Answers to Prayer

1 **Stability and some economic progress** marked the post-independence 1990s despite the fears of many for ethnic strife and economic collapse. The scars of the colonial and apartheid past are gradually healing. There was much united prayer by Christians at the time. There is a significant national prayer movement.

• Challenges for Prayer

N

1 **The potential for economic collapse and strife is high** if there is a failure in political leadership. Pray for the government and its leaders.

2 **Namibia for long had the highest percentage of Christians for any country in Africa**. The early labours of German and Finnish Lutheran and then Anglican missionaries gave birth to large denominations. The influence of liberal and then black theology eroded that spiritual heritage, and true discipleship and holy living are now in short supply and nominalism widespread. There is a noticeable turning away from Christianity and a lack of openness to the gospel. Pray for a unity, based on Scripture and bathed in the Spirit, that will bring reconciliation and revival.

3 **The evangelical witness has been strengthened** in recent years through new missionary thrusts by the **NGK**, **SIM** (formerly AEF)/**AIM**, **YWAM**, Baptists and Pentecostals to areas and peoples only superficially touched by the gospel. Charismatic fellowships — both independent and within many denominations — have brought new life and fervour. The Namibia Evangelical Fellowship was formed in 1989 and has over 180 members but has struggled to maintain a significant voice in the religious life of the country. Pray for healthy and effective cooperation among believers in evangelism, deepening the spirituality of the churches and speaking out as a prophetic voice to the nation.

4 **Leadership training.** The major denominational seminary in the country has been much influenced by black and liberation theology to the spiritual impoverishment of students going into the ministry. The result: accelerated nominalization of the churches, lowering of moral standards for leaders and followers, and reliance on occultism rather than the Lord. Pray for the only evangelical diploma and degree level training facility in the country — Namibia Evangelical Theological Seminary in Windhoek (**SIM/AIM**, **NGK**).

5 **African Independent Churches** are strong among the Herero, Basters, Damara and Nama, bringing compromise with the ancestor worship and witchcraft of their forebears and hostility to the gospel. Pray for the tactful ministry of the **NGK**, **AIM** and **SIM** missionaries and Namibian Christians by means of teaching, radio and help ministries which are bringing many leaders to a living faith in Christ.

6 **There are serious social issues** that must be addressed by Christians. The government has not the resources to handle these and the churches have not risen to the challenges of:

a) *Poverty* with large disparities between the rich and poor and over 30% unemployment. Ovamboland in the north is particularly affected. Many flock to the cities seeking work, causing shanty towns to multiply.

b) *AIDS*. This has become a silent and largely ignored calamity with between 20-25% of adults and young people infected and already 67,000 AIDS orphans. **SU**'s *Aid for AIDS* programme is one of the few effective efforts to address the root problems of the epidemic.

c) *The legacy of apartheid and war* — their scars and distortions affect nearly every ethnic group. These require spiritual solutions. Pray for full reconciliation and healing of the past through faith in Christ.

7 **Young people** have become much more materialistic and are rejecting Christianity as irrelevant to their needs. Substance abuse, immorality and the rapid spread of HIV are the result. Christian camps are struggling to attract young people. Pray for innovative and effective ministry by churches and agencies. **YWAM** and **SU** have expanding programmes to them. **IFES** pioneered work in the 1990s with active groups in the university and in polytechnic colleges and expanding in the north. Pray for fruit.

8 **Missionaries in both older and newer missions** need acute sensitivity and understanding as they minister within the new context of independence. Major missions are: **NGK** (66 workers), Finnish Lutheran (47), **YWAM** (36), **SIM/AIM** (28), **IMB-SBC** (16).

9 **The less-evangelized peoples:**

a) *The San* (Bushmen) — much romanticized but in reality a suffering people. Marginalized, generally landless farm labourers or squatters, and often affected by alcoholism. They need spiritual and physical help. The **NGK** has laboured for years, and there were 5 congregations among the Heikum, Kxoe and Kung and 6 pastors in 1993.

b) *The peoples of the Kavango and Caprivi Strip* in the north-east — the Yeyi, Mafue, Subiya and Hambukushu. Many are animists and some are Adventists. **AIM/SIM** have planted a number of churches among the Hambukushu (3 with 150 believers), Luchazi and Lozi.

c) *The Himba* (5,000) and *Dhimba* (15,000) are offshoots of the Herero people in the barren north-east and in south-west Angola. Nearly all are animist and a few Lutheran and Reformed Christians. Bible translation into Dhimba is progressing slowly.

d) *The German- and English-speaking communities* are more influenced by secular humanism. Over 60% of the Germans have no link with a church. Pray for the evangelical churches among them.

10 **Christian help ministries:**

a) *Bible translation*. All the major languages have full Bibles. The Namibia Bible Society is involved in revisions of these, the completion of the Mbukushu Bible and translation into one of the San languages and into Dhimba.

b) *Christian literature* for local languages and away from main centres is scarce. Christian Mobile Literature, **SU** and **YWAM** all have bookstores.

c) *MAF-Canada* operates a flying ministry from Windhoek — mainly to Angola. Pray for its development as a service to the church.

d) **The JESUS film** sound-tracks have been prepared by Media for Christ in 8 Namibian languages and is in preparation in a further three. Pray for lasting results from the showing of this film.

e) **Christian radio.** Programmes on the national network have had a remarkable impact counteracting liberal theology, restoring evangelicalism to mainline churches, and opening up resistant peoples such as the Herero to biblical teaching. Most of the 60 hours of religious programming every week has been evangelical in content, but since 1991 this has been reduced with mainline churches taking control of content. Media for Christ gained permission to start a Christian radio station. Pray for the continued development of this ministry. **TWR-Swaziland** broadcasts in both English and Afrikaans to Namibia.

Nauru

Republic of Nauru

AUGUST 22

PACIFIC

 GEOGRAPHY
Area 21 sq.km. A single coral island once covered with phosphate from fossilized bird droppings 300 km west of Banaba, Kiribati.

Population	Ann.Gr.	Density
2000	11,519	+1.87%	549 per sq. km.
2010	13,790	+1.80%	657 per sq. km.
2025	17,821	+1.69%	849 per sq. km.

Capital Yaren, 560.

PEOPLES
Micronesian 78%. Nauruan 6,000, I-Kiribati 2,000.
Other 22%. Chinese 900; Caucasian 800; Tuvaluan 900.

Literacy 93%. **Official languages** Nauruan, English. **All languages** 3. **Languages with Scriptures** 2Bi.

ECONOMY
Considerable wealth from mining phos-phate, but this has left 80% of the island unusable and reserves of the chemical are now exhausted. The invested profits provide much of the country's income. Now an important offshore banking centre. **Income/person** $10,000 (35% of USA).

 POLITICS
German rule 1888-1914. UN trusteeship administered by Australia and Britain until independence in 1968. Nauruans resisted invitations for resettlement elsewhere in 1964. Nauru became a member of the UN in 1999.

RELIGION
Freedom of religion.

Religions	Population %	Adherents	Ann.Gr.
Christian	90.50	10,425	+1.9%
non-Religious/other	4.90	564	+3.9%
Chinese	3.00	346	-1.0%
Baha'i	1.60	184	+1.9%

Christians	Denom.	Affil.%	,000	Ann.Gr.
Protestant	6	56.03	6	-23.3%
Anglican	1	2.95	0	-1.2%
Catholic	1	27.78	3	+2.0%
Marginal	1	0.28	0	+3.1%
Unaffiliated		3.46	0	n.a.

Churches	MegaBloc	Cong.	Members	Affiliates
Congregational	P	20	1,958	4,700
Catholic	C	2	1,860	3,200
Nauru Independent	P	2	359	600
Anglican	A	3	153	340
Other denominations [5]		5	478	1,186
Total Christians [9]		32	4,808	10,000

Trans-bloc Groupings	pop.%	,000	Ann.Gr.
Evangelical	9.0	1	-3.8%
Charismatic	7.8	1	+4.4%
Pentecostal	5.2	1	+6.0%

• Challenges for Prayer

1 **Offshore banking on the internet** is now a major source of income. This is a euphemism for money laundering for Russian crime syndicates — the sums processed are estimated at more than $US 65 billion. Pray for both the Nauruan and international authorities to courageously tackle this evil that enriches a few criminals and impoverishes millions, bankrupting countries.

2 **The wealth of Nauruans** contrasts markedly with the relative poverty of surrounding island states. Materialism has sapped the people of spiritual concern. Church life is at a low ebb. There are few evangelical believers. This isolated island paradise of materialism, where everything has been free, may end with the exhaustion of the phosphate deposits. There is low life-expectancy because fresh food cannot be grown locally. Pray that these realities may cause a turning to God.

3 **The only clearly evangelical witness** is through the small but growing Pentecostal Nauru Independent Church. The *JESUS* film has been seen by almost the whole population.

4 **The workers attracted to Nauru** by phosphate mining have the instability of impermanence — many live in temporary accommodation and their exploitation is becoming a concern to surrounding Pacific states. Little is being done to evangelize them.

Nepal
Kingdom of Nepal

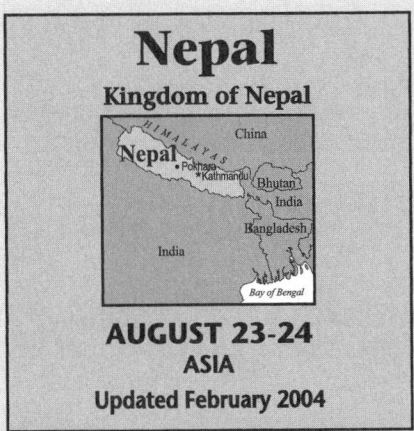

AUGUST 23-24
ASIA
Updated February 2004

GEOGRAPHY
Area 147,181 sq.km. A mountain-ringed Himalayan state between China (Tibet) and India. It contains 8 of the 10 highest mountain peaks in the world.

Population	Ann.Gr.	Density
2000	23,930,490	+2.38%	163 per sq. km.
2010	29,715,459	+2.12%	202 per sq. km.
2025	38,010,174	+1.37%	258 per sq. km.

Capital Kathmandu 1,500,000. The city has doubled in size during the 1990s. **Urbanites** 14%.

PEOPLES
Indo-Aryan 79%. 27 peoples. Mainly south and east. Largest: Nepali 12 mill.; Maithili 2.85m; Bhojpuri 1.79m; Tharu(6) 1.29m; Awadhi 483,000; Urdu 261,000; Hindi 220,000; Rajbansi 110,000.
Tibeto-Burman 17%. 68 peoples, mainly in north and west. Largest groups: Tamang 1.17m; Newari 892,000; Rai(10) 567,000; Magar 558,000; Limbu 328,000; Gurung(4) 294,000; Sherpa 158,000.
Munda-Santal 0.3%. 2 peoples.
Other 3.7%. Bhutan refugees 150,000; Indians, Tibetans.
Caste groups are important in this largely Hindu society. These are often more important sociologically than is eth-

nicity. Some groups: Chhetri 3.8m; Hill Brahman 3.1m; Magar 1.7m; Maki/Lohar 1.2m; Yadav/Ahir 1m; Musalman (Muslim) 850,000; Chamar 263,000.

Literacy 40%. **Official language** Nepali. **All languages** 124. **Languages with Scriptures** 6Bi 11NT 9por 12w.i.p.

ECONOMY
An isolated subsistence economy. The terrain is difficult and in habitable regions there is a high population density with rapid deforestation and ecological damage. The development of roads, agriculture and social projects has been slow. Main foreign exchange earners are tourism, agriculture and Gurkha soldiers serving in foreign armies. Dependent on foreign aid and good relations with India. **HDI** 0.463; 144ᵗʰ/174. **Public debt** 48% of GNP. **Income/person** $220 (0.7% of USA) with 42% living below the poverty line.

POLITICS
Nepal was never ruled by colonial powers. Political isolation from the outside world ended in 1951. In 1962, the King assumed executive power in a government system with no political parties. Massive civil unrest in 1990 brought about extensive liberalization and multi-party elections. The 1990s were characterized by a succession of short-lived coalition governments in a time of difficulty. The Congress Party formed a majority government in 2000. Poverty and official corruption have been factors in provoking Maoist guerrilla warfare in some areas since 1996. The assassination of most of the royal family in 2001 seriously destabilized the country. The 8-year civil war has spread through much of the country bringing economic damage, destruction and 5,000 deaths.

RELIGION
The world's only Hindu Kingdom. Hinduism is recognized as the national religion, but the constitution guarantees some religious freedom for other faiths. People are free to choose their religion but it is illegal to convert others. Any infringing of this is liable to lead to imprisonment for nationals or expulsion of foreigners. Official religion figures of the 1991 census are suspect with

minority religions under-represented. **Persecution Index** 42nd in the world.

Religions	Population %	Adherents	Ann.Gr.
Hindu	74.82	17,904,793	+2.0%
Buddhist	16.00	3,828,878	+2.4%
Muslim	5.00	1,196,525	+4.6%
Christian	1.89	452,286	+16.1%
Other religions	1.70	406,818	+2.4%
non-Religious/other	0.50	119,652	+7.1%
Sikh	0.06	14,358	+6.2%
Baha'i	0.03	7,179	+2.4%

The boundary between Hinduism and Buddhism is not distinct; Buddhists are officially 7.8%, Muslims 3.5%, Christians 0.17%.

Christians	Denom.	Affil.%	,000	Ann.Gr.
Protestant	15	0.59	141	+26.2%
Independent	27	1.22	292	+19.6%
Roman Catholic	1	0.05	12	+19.1%
Marginal	6	0.01	2	+15.6%

Churches	MegaBloc	Cong.	Members	Adherents
Independent Congs	I	600	45,000	90,000
Ntnl Chs Fell of N (NCFN)	I	260	28,000	60,000
Foursquare Gospel	P	600	36,667	55,000
Assemblies of God	P	315	29,000	54,000
Pentecostal Ch of N	I	300	25,000	37,000
Evangelical Chr Fell. of N	I	120	8,333	20,000
Believers Church (GFA)	I	200	8,000	18,000
Agape Fellowship	I	52	6,000	15,000

Catholic	C	30	8,392	12,000
Nepal Bapt Chr Council	P	65	7,500	12,000
Evang Alliance Ch of N	I	40	4,800	12,000
Assemblies (El Shaddai)	P	40	3,500	7,000
Emmanuel Ch Assoc.	I	32	3,400	5,200
Lord's Assemblies	I	13	2,000	5,000
Presbyterian Ch Council	P	19	3,000	5,000
Eastern Nepal Charis.Fell.	I	22	2,200	4,700
Seventh-day Adventist	P	5	785	1,500
Other denoms [37]		331	16,000	33,400
Total Christians [54]		3,044	237,700	446,800

Trans-bloc Groupings	pop.%	,000	Ann.Gr.
Evangelical	1.6	376	+23.6%
Charismatic	1.2	284	+25.3%
Pentecostal	0.7	158	+23.7%

Missionaries from Nepal
P,I,A 746 in 13 agencies to 4 countries: Nepal 710, India 33.

Expatriates to Nepal
P,I,A 717 in 90 agencies from 30 countries: UK 149, USA 125, Germany 48, Korea 47, Australia 32, Norway 30.

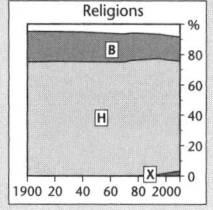

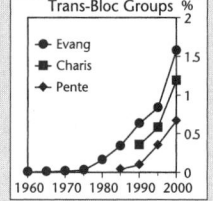

• Answers to Prayer

1 **The opening up of Nepal.** No Christian was officially allowed to live in Nepal before 1960. By 1990 there was a measure of religious freedom to worship, but not to proselytize.

2 **The thrilling growth of the Church.** The first group was formed in 1959 with 29 Christians. By 1985 there were about 50,000 believers. At the climax of persecution in 1990 there were 200,000. By 2000 there were 400,000; some estimate even 500,000 in 3,000 or more congregations! The secret: prayer, willingness to suffer for Jesus, dynamic Nepali initiative in evangelism and church planting, and God's miracle-working power.

3 **There is a church planted** in every one of the 75 districts of Nepal and there are at least some believers in most peoples and caste groups of the country.

4 **Increased unity** after some difficult years during the 1990s. The Nepal Christian Society was formed in 1996 as a coordinating fellowship for Evangelicals.

• Challenges for Prayer

1 **The country needs political stability and continuity of government** after the first tempestuous decade of democracy which culminated in the assassination of the Royal Family. Pray for the King crowned in 2001 - he has neither the stature nor the popularity of the former king. Pray also for peace. Pray for an honest, balanced, fair government that is able to seriously tackle the immense economic problems of the country. Rampant corruption and the poverty of most of the population is fundamental to the present fighting.

2 **Religious freedom** has increased, but is still only partial. Persecution from the authorities was greatly reduced in 1990 with the advent of democracy. All Christian prisoners were released and all pending court cases against over 300 Christians were dismissed. Over the 1990s there have been a number of Christians who have been arrested, imprisoned or even murdered in custody for seeking to preach to Hindus. Increasing Hinduist persecution of Christians in India is impacting official attitudes. Militant Hinduists in Nepal are targeting Christians with virulent propaganda and violence which aims to drive all Christians from the country. Pray for:

a) *Full religious freedom* to be both guaranteed in the constitution and upheld by the authorities.

b) *The thwarting of the designs of the extremists* and for their eyes to be opened to the Lord Jesus.

3 **The Church in Nepal** has flourished under pressure as a remarkable indigenous movement. It has grown in numbers, diversity and maturity, but with growth and greater freedom there are issues which need prayer:

a) *Denominationalism* — many foreign-based denominations as well as indigenous networks of churches have been established. Pray that the Church may be kept from divisions, doctrinal disputes and error. Pray specifically for the Nepal Christian Society (NCS) as it seeks to provide a forum for prayer, sharing, unity and cooperative ministries.

b) *Persecution, though less severe than in the 1980s, is still real.* This is not only from the Hinduist extremist movements but also socially from families and communities and, in some areas, from the Maoist guerrillas. Pray for grace and perseverance for believers and that Christians may be accepted and appreciated for their contribution to the country's well-being. Pray also for efforts by the NCS and others engaged in securing the legal and religious rights of Christians with regard to arbitrary arrests, evangelism, property, discrimination, etc.

c) *Partnership between churches and foreign agencies.* Support in finance and personnel is appreciated, but all too often there has been inadequate local cooperation and communication. Remote control through finance has serious moral and spiritual consequences. Pray for wisdom and sensitivity for all parties involved.

4 **Vision for the future**:

a) *The two HIM-COE conferences of 1996 and 1998* brought together most Nepali Christian leaders and others serving in the Himalayas. These conferences helped to consolidate various visions for church planting and leadership training over the whole region. The Himalayan Ministries partnership was formed linking national and international churches and agencies to reach Nepalis world-wide through prayer, research, outreach and literature.

b) *The Sowers Ministry is a Nepali-founded mission agency,* now headquartered in Hong Kong but with over 100 workers in 8 lands.

Pray that many Nepalis may be challenged, called, equipped and sent out by local churches to Nepal, the Himalayan region, needy North India and beyond.

5 **The first generation of Nepali leaders** laid a good foundation. Pray for:

N

a) *Effective transfer of leadership* to a second generation.

b) *Men and women of vision* who are filled with the Holy Spirit for the task ahead. For many, ministry will be arduous and will provide little to live on.

c) *Leadership training.* For years no formal training was possible. There are now over 13 Bible colleges and seminaries, as well as shorter-term training, provided by various churches and agencies. Most are linked with the Association of Theological Educators, Nepal. GFA has three centres from which 100 Nepali evangelist-missionaries graduate annually.

6 **The social challenges for Christian ministry**. Both Nepali Christians and foreign agencies have done much to minister to the uplift of the nation with short and long-term social services — giving much opportunity for showing Christian values and love in:

a) *Alleviating poverty* — only 15% of the population has access to electricity. Much is done in education, job creation enterprises, water purification, etc., by Christians.

b) *Confronting the continuing evils of caste discrimination* (despite it being illegal), the widespread use of bond slavery and child labour (500,000 economically active under 14 years). Parliament passed the Child Labour Act in March 2000, pray for its widespread implementation.

c) ***Opposing the trafficking of Nepali girls*** for the Indian and Middle East 'sex' industry which is a terrible evil. There are an estimated 250,000 in India (mainly Mumbai) where they are terribly abused; 60-70% are HIV+ and few will reach 25 years. Nepali Christians are seeking to reach and rescue some of these unfortunates in Mumbai.

d) ***Providing health services.*** Over 20% of hospitals and clinics, and nearly all of leprosy control work are Christian-run (**TLM**, **UMN**, **INF**, others). The AIDS pandemic overwhelming the health services. There were 45,000 sufferers in 2000 (an underestimate).

7 **The less reached.** Many peoples and castes are only marginally reached. Pray for:

a) ***The influential high-caste Brahmin and Chhetri*** (Rajput). Pride, idol worship, fear and demonic bondage keep many from openly coming to Christ. Yet in contrast to India, a significant number have done so.

b) ***The Awadhi and Maithili of the Terai lowlands*** on the Indian border. Few of them have heard the gospel and these few have been unresponsive. The Tharu are more animist than Hindu; many little churches are springing up among them.

c) ***The Mountain peoples — almost entirely Tibetan-related.*** Most are lamaistic Buddhists living in isolated mountain communities, such as the Loba people of Mustang. Most are small in number and Christians are few. There are an increasing number of believers among the Sherpa of the Mt. Everest area.

d) ***Tibetan refugees*** — long unreached; now there is a steady trickle of people seeking the Lord and several congregations among them.

e) ***The increased numbers of Muslims.*** Many are Bengali, Kashmiri or Urdu-speaking traders. Only about 20 Muslim-background believers are known. There is no focused outreach to them.

f) ***University students.*** There are 100,000 students in 3 universities on 150 campuses. In 1996 NBCBS(**IFES**) had 25 groups, but most students remain unreached.

8 **Missions have played a remarkable supportive role** in improving health, agriculture and education. Relationships with the government can be delicate, and visa applications are carefully screened. Pray for wisdom and grace for leaders and missionaries, and for the entry of called workers. Pray for radiance of life and continued freedom to share the gospel in all contacts with Nepalis as the medical workers minister in hospitals, dispensaries, leprosy and health programmes, and others in education institutions. The **United Mission to Nepal** is the largest body representing 50 agencies from 20 or more countries. The **International Nepal Fellowship** has 80 workers (from 10 seconding agencies and 12 nations) mainly in the west of Nepal. **Human Development and Community Services** is an indigenous mission agency that is taking on an increasing number of projects in close cooperation with churches and missions. There has been significant input from at least 12 Indian evangelical agencies; **GFA** has placed 152 missionaries around the country.

9 **Nepalis who have migrated** temporarily for work or permanently in large numbers to India, the Himalayan region and beyond, may total 10 million.

a) ***In India,*** Sikkim state is 75% Nepali and Darjeeling District in West Bengal is 60% Nepali. Bhutan is 40% ethnic Nepali. Numerous Nepali churches have come into being; pray for their growth and greater involvement in cross-cultural outreach

b) ***In Bhutan,*** Nepalis have suffered discrimination, and in 1991 many were expelled and now live as refugees in UN camps in south-east Nepal where they are spiritually and economically deprived. There are some churches among them.

c) ***Many Nepalis serve as Gurkha soldiers*** in the British, Brunei and Indian armies. Many others serve as security guards from the Middle East to East Asia. Among them there are some Christian groups. Pray for effective outreach to them.

10 **Other help ministries** for which prayer is requested:

a) ***Bible translation*** is in progress in 12 languages, but practical and spiritual obstacles to their completion are many, one being the low literacy and lack of literacy programmes in local languages. Pray for all who are committed to complete these projects. There are 83 languages without any Scriptures at all and 16 for which there is a definite need for translation.

b) ***The Bible Society's ministry*** has expanded after years of great difficulties. Distribution of Scriptures, especially the New Testament in Nepali, has mushroomed. The International Bible Society has also opened up ministry.

c) Christian literature can now be freely printed and distributed without censorship, though there have been problems with importation. Pray for **The Bible Society** bookshop in Kathmandu, **OM** and **GFA** publishing house and literature distribution teams, and **EHC**'s ambitious house-to-house literature campaigns with many mobilized. The latter has covered all Nepal and has started over again. Pray that these burgeoning literature ministries may enhance spiritual and church growth.

d) Cassette tapes are a useful evangelistic and teaching tool, but players are not widely available. **GRN** has recorded 101 languages and dialects.

e) Bible correspondence courses have long been a key means of outreach, but the programme lacks funds and personnel to continue effectively. The response since 1990 overwhelmed the resources of the three correspondence schools. There were 50,000 students in 1995, leading to many new churches.

f) Christian radio. Some local programmes are broadcast on special Christian occasions. GFA has been an indigenous broadcasting agency for the past 10 years receiving significant response. **TWR** broadcasts 5.5 hrs/week from Russia, and **FEBA** 30 minutes. There are reception and publicity problems which limit the listenership.

g) The JESUS film has been widely used and about 25% of the population have viewed it in 6 languages. The film is being dubbed in a further 17 languages. The Indian-produced film *Daya Sagar*, on the life of Jesus, is popular among non-Christians.

Netherlands
Kingdom of the Netherlands

AUGUST 25
EUROPE
Revised February 2004

GEOGRAPHY
Area 41,785 sq.km. Northwestern Europe occupying the Rhine delta; over 30% is below sea level.

Population		Ann.Gr.	Density*
2000	15,785,699	+0.42%	378 per sq. km.
2010	15,972,738	+0.04%	382 per sq. km.
2025	15,781,965	-0.12%	378 per sq. km.

*Excluding inland water areas.

Capital Amsterdam (administrative capital) 2,050,000; The Hague (seat of government) 450,000. Other major city: Rotterdam 1,175,000 — the world's busiest seaport. **Urbanites** 91%.

PEOPLES
Indigenous 90.1%. Dutch 13.8 million; Frisian 375,000; Roma (Gypsy) 8,000.
Ex-colonial 3.1%. Surinamer 320,000; Antillean 98,000; Maluku (Indonesian) 50,000; Other Indonesian 20,000.

Other 6.8%. Moroccans 240,000; Turks 220,000; EU Citizens 200,000; Kurds 70,000; Chinese 70,000; Somali 30,000; Afghans 27,000; (former) Yugoslav 25,000; Iranians 24,000; Ghanaians 15,000; Cape Verdian 13,000; Tamil 10,000.

Literacy 99%. **Official languages** Dutch (Nederlands), Frisian. English is in wide use. **All languages** 16.

ECONOMY
Strong industrial, agricultural and trading economy. One of the world's leading exporting nations. Member of the EU. Unemployment is low, but a generous social security system supports a large number who are registered unfit for work. **HDI** 0.921; 8ᵗʰ/174. **Public debt** 54% of GNP. **Income/person** $25,940 (82% of USA).

POLITICS
Protestant-led revolt against Spain established Dutch independence in 1568 and dynamized the country to become one of the world's great commercial nations. Stable, democratic, constitutional monarchy.

RELIGION
There is freedom of religion — but also freedom for almost any lifestyle! Anti-discrimination legislation increasingly threatens Christian liberties and absolutes in the name of 'tolerance'.

Religions	Population %	Adherents	Ann.Gr.
Christian	55.93	8,828,941	-0.9%
non-Religious/other	37.98	5,995,408	+2.4%
Muslim	5.40	852,428	+2.0%
Hindu	0.30	47,357	+0.4%
Buddhist	0.20	31,571	+0.4%
Jewish	0.19	29,993	+2.7%

Christians	Denom.	Affil.%	,000	Ann.Gr.
Protestant	72	21.65	3,417	-1.5%
Independent	88	0.83	131	+0.6%
Anglican	1	0.06	9	+0.2%
Catholic	2	32.82	5,181	-1.0%
Orthodox	6	0.07	11	+2.5%
Marginal	41	0.50	79	-0.8%

Churches	MegaBloc	Cong.	Members	Affiliates
Catholic	C	1,700	3,622,740	5,180,518
Netherlands Ref Ch (NHK) *	P	1,700	457,240	2,080,442
Reformed (GK) *	P	847	405,166	676,627
Reformed (Liberated)	P	280	73,865	125,048
Ref. Chs in N & NA	P	156	51,800	98,450
Chr Reformed (CGK)	P	107	44,564	74,739
Jehovah's Witnesses	M	399	31,915	54,000
Netherlands Ref Chs	P	104	18,305	30,021
Mennonite Brotherhood	P	135	13,000	30,000
Indonesian Chs [19]	P	154	13,165	22,380
Reformed Chs in Neth	P	50	9,758	20,644
Baptist Union	P	87	12,202	20,000
Apostolic	P	38	9,500	18,050
Full Gospel Churches	P	38	8,000	15,000
Lutheran *	P	56	7,304	14,900
Free Evang Congregations	P	43	7,000	14,000
Remonstrant Brotherhood	P	98	7,756	12,000
Fell of Pentecostal Chs (AoG)	P	57	6,000	10,500
Salvation Army	P	80	7,156	10,000
Assoc of Free Evang Congs	P	46	7,100	9,581

	Denom.	Affil.%	,000	Ann.Gr.
Bethel Pentecostal	I	43	4,605	9,000
Latter-day Saints (Morm)	M	39	5,594	8,000
Berea Fellowship	I	30	3,000	5,500
Other denoms [169]		1,815	157,000	289,000
Total Christians [210]		8,102	4,983,654	8,828,000

* These three denominations united as the Protestant Church of the Netherlands in 2003.

Trans-bloc Groupings	pop.%	,000	Ann.Gr.
Evangelical	4.5	714	-0.6%
Charismatic	2.5	387	-0.2%
Pentecostal	0.6	99	+0.0%

Missionaries from Netherlands

P,I,A est. 1,530 in 90 agencies of which 1,000+ serve in 120 countries. Note: There has been no survey of Netherlands mission involvement for many years — figures approximate.

Missionaries to Netherlands

P,I,A 296 in 62 agencies from 27 countries: USA 139, UK 36, Canada 23, Korea 20.

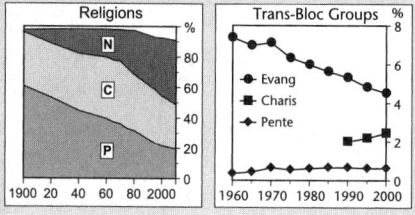

• Challenges for Prayer

1 **The Netherlands has two major claims to fame:**

a) *A glorious history as a Christian nation* — its fight for religious freedom, ministry to refugees and Jews, and a record of extensive involvement in missions to other lands.

b) *A decadent present as a secular society* that has turned its back on its past. There has been a dramatic decline in the number of Christians in this generation and today's openly permissive society is renouncing its heritage. There are few restrictions on drugs, deviant life styles, prostitution, homosexuality and abortion. The Netherlands is the first country to legalize euthanasia and has become a world leader in promoting a New Age world-view with its values. Pray for a revival that restores the nation spiritually. Pray that the government may also be influenced for good.

2 **The historic Protestant Churches** have suffered calamitous losses — from 60% of the population in 1900 to 21% in 2000. By 2015 over half their membership will be over 65 in both the many Calvinist denominations and most of the Free churches. Pray for:

a) *New life* to replace traditions, structural rigidity and increasingly irrelevant theological disputes.

b) *A re-commitment to the Scriptures* instead of free-thinking liberalism and tolerant pluralism.

c) *Restoration of a prophetic message* that is relevant to young people today and addresses the tide of secularism, New Age, the occult, eastern and western cults, rampant immorality and a rising crime rate.

d) *Concern for the salvation of souls* in a climate where dialogue and compromise are prized more than evangelism. The NHK, GK and Lutherans have formed a church union — pray that this not be at the expense of outreach. Many of the churches in this union allow gay marriages.

e) *A new generation of leaders* with spiritual passion for God's glory and Kingdom extension, and also effective ministry preparation.

3 The Roman Catholic Church is likewise declining in members (41% of the population in 1980, 33% in 2000), priests and missionaries every year. The liberal wing is opposed by the hierarchy but has a strong influence in bending the Church into a liberal direction. However, the growing charismatic and evangelical movements within the Church, with a widespread Bible study and home prayer cell network, are positive signs.

4 There are signs of hope in the gloom! Water these tender plants in prayer:

a) *There is growth* in the number and vitality of many independent, charismatic and Pentecostal congregations. Yet the need is for consistent discipleship, disciplined prayer and study of the Word and lives that demonstrate the gospel.

b) *The Evangelisch Werkverband* is a growing evangelical wing in SOW with 300 pastors involved. May this movement be respected, accepted and be catalytic in the whole emerging denomination.

c) *The significant impact of the Evangelical Alliance and Evangelische Omroep* in drawing together a wide spectrum of Evangelicals for fellowship, encouragement and action. Evangelicals are often fragmented and individualistic. Pray for spiritual unity with a drawing together of denominations, institutions, agencies and ethnic groups with a single vision for reaching the nation and the world, and the willingness to financially support this with generosity.

5 Young people's ministry has become harder through indifference and an interest in non-Christian religious experiences. Christianity is perceived as irrelevant, yet many young people are searching for answers in a society that has lost its direction. Pray for:

a) *Parents* to see the need to witness to their children, and bring them to faith in Christ.

b) *Schools* to provide adequate Christian education.

c) *Churches to gain the interest* of young people by addressing their felt needs.

d) *Street evangelism, coffee bars*, camps and outreach to drug addicts through **YWAM**, Agape (**CCCI**) and **YFC**.

e) *University students* who live in a high-pressure ideological battle zone where it is hard to stand for Jesus. Pray for **Navigator** and **IFES** groups on many campuses. About 2,500 students are affiliated to over 40 groups linked with the latter.

f) *A challenge to missions and outreach* that will give young people a cause for which to live and die. The cost of commitment is too high for most. Triennial Europe-wide youth missions conferences hosted in the Netherlands have had a significant impact on young people.

6 Dutch missions, long eclipsed, are gaining new workers and increased interest. The EMA has grown to a membership of approximately 65 agencies. A better understanding of unreached peoples and of the need of the former Communist world and the Middle East has increased recruitment and prayer. Many Dutch missionaries are involved in Bible translation and evangelical aid programmes. Catholic missions once sent out 18,000 missionaries, but this is now reduced to about 3,000.

N

7 The less-reached need prayer as do those who will cross social and cultural barriers to bless them with the gospel of Christ.

a) *Nearly half the population* has been alienated from exposure to the gospel and has no meaningful link with anything Christian. A whole new pattern of ministry needs to be developed. Alpha courses for seekers are proving one fruitful approach.

b) *The highly secularized cities*. Amsterdam has become a byword for godlessness. Over half the population claims no religious affiliation. The large drop-out population and the moral collapse hamper witness to the unconverted. Over 75% of the Arab, Asian and Southern European migrant population lives in Amsterdam, Rotterdam, The Hague and Utrecht. A number of churches and agencies have ministry to these sections of the community, but most such work is on a small scale. Notable are the efforts of international movements such as **YWAM**, Agape (**CCCI**), and **OM**, as well as Dutch agencies. Pray for the turning of the tide of permissiveness in these cities.

c) *Migrant ethnic minorities* are increasing in numbers and by 2015 will comprise 17-18% of the population and speak over 140 languages. Many form an urban underclass with high unemployment, involvement with drugs, and crime. A number of congregations have been formed among the Ghanaians, Indonesians, Antilleans, Chinese and other groups. Pray that these may be spiritually effective and vigorous in outreach to every culture.

*d) **Muslims** will soon be one-tenth of the population, but come from many cultures. Specialized efforts and committed friendship are needed to reach them. Pray for those seeking to reach them, such as SVEOM, *Evangelie en Moslems, Stichting Gave,* Gospel for Guests, **YWAM** in Amsterdam and various churches. Only a few have come to the Lord, and lack of nurture and care means a high casualty rate. Pray specifically for:*

i   The Turks and Kurds among whom are now several groups of believers.

ii   Moroccans — many being Berber Rif and Shilha.

iii Iranians and Afghans.

*e) **The Chinese**, many of whom are Buddhist. There are over 10 churches among them (**COCM**).*

*f) **The Hindus** — mainly Suriname Asians and Sri Lankan Tamil (Christar).*

8 Christian media ministries:

*a) **The Netherlands Bible Society** has an extensive ministry. The Bible is to be found in over 65% of homes, but is not read or studied enough. A new Dutch translation of the Bible is to be published in 2004.*

*b) **Christian TV and radio**. Evangelische Omroep (EO) has had a remarkable ministry for over 30 years, with weekly broadcasts for 18 hours on national TV and 60 hours on radio. EO has the largest young peoples' club in the country. Its programming has generated a large response and following with an extensive counselling ministry and encouragement to many Christian ministries. Pray that its biblical approach may not be compromised by liberal or worldly trends, yet be effective in reaching heart needs with relevant programming and in a vocabulary non-Christians will understand.*

Netherlands Antilles

Dominican Republic, Puerto Rico, St. Martin, St. Eustatius

Netherlands Antilles

Caribbean Sea

Windward Islands

Willemstad

Venezuela

AUGUST 25
LATIN AMERICA

GEOGRAPHY
Area 800 sq.km. Two larger, barren islands, Curaçao and Bonaire off the coast of Venezuela, and two and a half smaller islands in the Leeward islands 800 km to the northeast. St. Maarten is shared with France. In 1986, Aruba withdrew from the Netherlands Antilles as an autonomous territory of the Netherlands.

Population		Ann.Gr.	Density
2000	216,775	+1.11%	271 per sq. km.
2010	236,607	+0.83%	296 per sq. km.
2025	258,459	+0.46%	323 per sq. km.

Curacao 76%; St Maarten 17%; Bonaire 5.4%; St Eustatius 1%, Saba 0.6%.

Capital Willemstad 119,000. **Urbanites** 92%.

PEOPLES
Netherlands citizens 86.9%.
Afro-Caribbean/Creole 86.4%. A blend of African, Amerindian, Dutch, Surinamer and Latin American origin.
Dutch 0.5%.
Foreign 13.1%.
Euro-American 6%. Dutch, Portuguese, US, British.
Latin American 5.6%. Dominican, Colombian, Venezuelan.
Other 2%.

Literacy 95%. **Official language** Dutch. **Common languages** Papiamento (84% of the population) in the southern two islands, English in the northern two and a half islands.

ECONOMY
Well developed; mainstays being oil trans-shipment, tourism and financial services.
Income/person $11,500 (37% of USA).

POLITICS
Integral part of Kingdom of Netherlands with domestic autonomy for each island and parliamentary democratic government. Relationships with the mother country and between the islands is a matter of intense political debate.

RELIGION
Complete freedom of religion.

Religions	Population %	Adherents	Ann.Gr.
Christian	96.09	208,299	+1.1%
non-Religious/other	2.41	5,224	+2.8%
Hindu	0.66	1,431	+1.4%
Muslim	0.31	672	+3.9%
Jewish	0.24	520	+1.1%
Chinese	0.20	434	+1.1%
Buddhist	0.06	130	+1.1%
Baha'i	0.03	65	+0.9%

Christians	Denom.	Affil.%	,000	Ann.Gr.
Protestant	26	9.97	22	+3.3%
Independent	24	2.64	6	+2.3%
Anglican	1	0.92	2	+0.0%
Catholic	1	72.89	158	+1.0%
Marginal	1	1.85	4	-2.3%
Unaffiliated		7.83	17	n.a.

Churches	MegaBloc	Cong.	Members	Affiliates
Catholic	C	37	93,491	158,000
Seventh-day Adventist	P	27	2,460	5,854
Jehovah's Witnesses	M	22	1,600	4,000
Other Pentecostal [15]	I	31	1,850	3,700
Baptist Convention	P	8	1,164	2,600
Methodist	P	3	1,100	2,442
Anglican	A	1	699	2,000

Evangelical	P	14	800	2,000
Assemblies of God	P	15	950	2,000
Other Charismatic [7]	I	14	850	1,700
Ch of God (Cleveland)	P	5	350	680
Other denoms [22]		42	3,803	6,360
Total Christians [53]		219	109,100	191,300

Trans-bloc Groupings	pop.%	,000	Ann.Gr.
Evangelical	7.9	17	+4.6%
Charismatic	7.4	16	+1.8%
Pentecostal	1.3	3	+3.2%

Missionaries from Netherlands Antilles
P,I,A 4 in 4 agencies in 3 countries.

Missionaries to Netherands Antilles
P,I,A 153 in 12 agencies from 10 countries: USA 100, Netherlands 9.

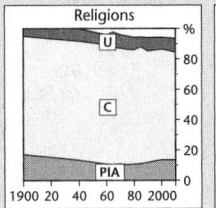

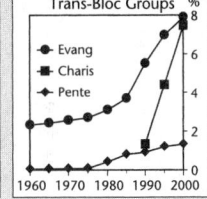

• Challenges for Prayer

1 **Openness to the gospel has not resulted in a great harvest.** Moral laxity, superstition, and the growing marginal sects show how few understand the message of salvation. Catholics are the majority on all islands but St. Eustatius which is predominantly Methodist and Adventist. Major church-planting missions: **TEAM** (14 workers) and **SBC** (6).

2 **Evangelical witness has progressed slowly but steadily.** A vital, growing church in every island is a target for prayer. **TEAM** has concentrated on evangelism and church planting among the Papiamento-speaking majority. These 12 churches are a large part of the evangelical witness, but Pentecostal and Baptist congregations are also growing.

3 **The Papiamento Bible** was finally published in 1997 (**TEAM**). Pray for this Bible to impact the majority of the population who use it. Pray also for literacy programmes and more Christian literature in the language. **TEAM** run a Christian bookstore on Curaçao. The *JESUS* film has been little used.

4 **Christian radio** is a significant ministry which involves most of the Protestant missionary force. **TEAM** concentrates on local Papiamento broadcasts from Radio Victoria. **TWR**, from their powerful station on Bonaire and by satellite, concentrates on Latin America and the world in English (52 hrs), Spanish (33) and Portuguese (26) as well as two Amerindian languages. Pray for the **TWR** missionary community of 54 expatriate workers on Bonaire who maintain the radio ministry, often with little visible encouragement, yet much fruit.

New Caledonia

Territory of New Caledonia and Dependencies

AUGUST 26
PACIFIC

GEOGRAPHY
Area 18,734 sq.km. One large 400 km-long island, the Loyalty Islands, and other smaller coral islands 1,400 km north-east of Australia.

Population		Ann.Gr.	Density
2000	214,029	+2.09%	11 per sq. km.
2010	245,885	+1.26%	13 per sq. km.
2025	285,515	+0.94%	15 per sq. km.

Capital Nouméa 118,000. **Urbanites** 60%.

PEOPLES
Melanesian 52%. Indigenous (Kanak) 93,000 (27 distinct languages). Mixed race 20,000.
Polynesian 14%. Wallisian 16,000; Tahitian 7,000; Futunan 3,600.
Caucasian 28.8%. Caledoche French 54,000 (75% Caledoche, 25% Metropolitan French); Italian 5,600.
Asian 5.2%. Indonesian 8,000; Vietnamese 3,000.

Literacy 92%. **Official language** French. **All languages** 38. **Languages with Scriptures** 4Bi 1NT 4por.

ECONOMY
Rich mineral deposits (40% of the world's nickel reserves and third largest producer) have brought prosperity to the immigrant peoples. The Asian recession of the late '90s slowed growth. **Unemployment** 15%. **Income/person** $15,720 (59% of USA).

POLITICS
French colony in 1883; overseas territory of France since 1946. Exploitation of, and discrimination against, the indigenous peoples provoked an independence movement which led to violence in 1985. Agreement was reached for three regional governments in 1988, leading to a referendum on independence in 1998. This resulted in an agreement for 20 years of local autonomy with partnership between the indigenous Melanesians and immigrants.

RELIGION
Freedom of religion in an increasingly secularized society. Almost the entire non-Melanesian, and most of the Melanesian, population has no meaningful contact with a church.

Religions	Population %	Adherents	Ann.Gr.
Christian	82.80	177,216	+1.5%
non-Religious/other	13.00	27,824	+7.1%
Muslim	3.50	7,491	+1.5%
Baha'i	0.50	1,070	+2.1%
Buddhist	0.20	428	+2.1%

Christians	Denom.	Affil.%	,000	Ann.Gr.
Protestant	3	13.88	30	+1.0%
Independent	5	4.66	10	+2.6%
Catholic	1	51.39	110	+0.7%
Marginal	3	2.73	6	+1.8%
Unaffiliated		10.14	22	n.a.

Churches	MegaBloc		Cong.	Members	Affiliates
Catholic	C	40	52,885	110,000
Evang Chs of NC and LI	P	177	5,747	25,000
Free Evangelical	I	74	1,200	9,000
Jehovah's Witnesses	M	23	1,578	4,200
Assemblies of God	P	26	2,800	4,000
Latter-day Saints (Morm)	M	7	480	1,200
Seventh-day Adventist	P	5	334	700
Other denominations [6]		26	869	1,500
Total Christians [13]		378	65,893	155,600

Trans-bloc Groupings	pop.%	,000	Ann.Gr.
Evangelical	7.5	16	+2.0%
Charismatic	6.8	15	+1.6%
Pentecostal	1.9	4	+2.7%

Missionaries from New Caledonia
P,I,A 3 in 2 agencies.
Missionaries to New Caledonia
P,I,A 17 in 5 agencies.

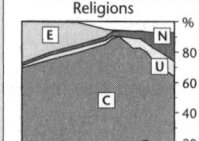

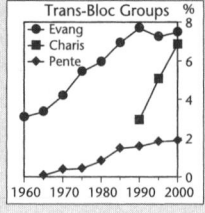

• Challenges for Prayer

1 **The 1998 accord** commits the government to enact legislation to restore rights, respect cultures and draw the marginalized Kanaks into full partnership in economic, legal and political life. The period of transition needs to be a time of healing for the serious mistakes of the past. Pray that this time of change may be positive, peaceful and fair to all.

2 **The Kanak peoples are Christianized** and nearly every village has a church, but the traumatic colonial take-over damaged their self-image and led them to confuse the gospel with Western culture. Christianity is often a veneer over the underlying animism of the past. Even many pastors fail to discern between occultic practices and what the gospel teaches. Pray that a truly biblical yet indigenous Christian witness may be raised up, and the power of the gospel demonstrated over all the power of the evil one.

3 **Many of the Protestant churches are influenced by liberation theology,** though in recent years the Free Evangelical Church has become theologically evangelical, with touches of revival. Pray for the raising up of many godly leaders. There is an interdenominational Bible School which had 50 students in 1999.

4 **Missions.** The first missionary was a Rarotongan from the Cook Islands. Later LMS work was taken over by the PMS. The **AoG** has grown both among the urban Melanesians and the Francophones. Pray for expatriate missions ministry into the churches to be fruitful and blessed of God.

5 **Less reached peoples:**

a) *The 8,000 Muslims of Javanese and Arab descent* retain their religion, but are losing their languages. Little has been done to reach them.

b) *Polynesian Islanders* retain their own culture and language. There are a few evangelical believers among the Wallisians and Futunans; most are traditionally Catholic.

c) *The Caledoche* are descendants of convicts and settlers who arrived in the last century. Most live in and around Nouméa. They are fairly closed to outside influence, and there are very few evangelical believers among them. The **AoG** have won some to Jesus.

d) *The Metropolitan French* are usually only in the country for a few years as bureaucrats or business people. Very few have any interest in or contact with a church during their sojourn.

6 **Bible translation** is still a challenge as Melanesian languages regain their status in the school system. There are 7 languages with an established translation need and 21 others need further survey work. Pray for the ongoing need for research, continuing translation work and the calling and equipping of translation teams. Pray also that the Scriptures may provide solid foundations for the gospel in each ethnic group.

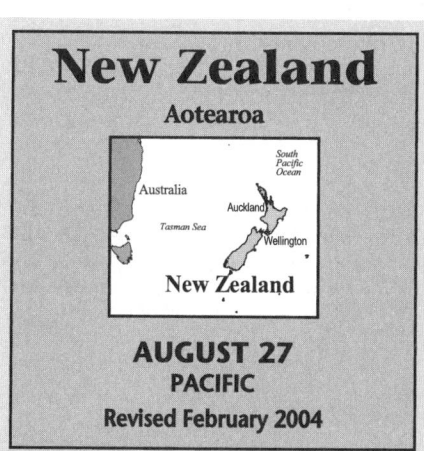

New Zealand
Aotearoa

New Zealand

AUGUST 27
PACIFIC
Revised February 2004

GEOGRAPHY
Area 267,515 sq.km. Two mountainous main islands 1,600 km southeast of Australia.

Population	Ann.Gr.	Density
2000	3,861,905	+1.02%	14 per sq. km.
2010	4,207,078	+0.83%	16 per sq. km.
2025	4,694,964	+0.67%	18 per sq. km.

Nearly 75% of the population live in the North Island.

Capital Wellington 350,000. Other major city: Auckland 1.1 mill. About 30% of the population live in the Auckland area. **Urbanites** 84%.

PEOPLES
Roughly 15% of the population would consider themselves of more than one race.
European 77%.
Polynesian 18.2%. Maori 510,000; Pacific Islanders 193,000 (Samoan, Tongan, Cook Is, Niue, etc.)
Asian 4.3%.
Other 0.5%.

Literacy 99%. **Official languages** English, Maori. **All languages** 17, two of which are indigenous.

N

ECONOMY
Highly efficient export-oriented agricultural industry with timber and tourism also becoming important. Painful and radical restructuring, ending of subsidies and partial dismantling of the welfare state enabled the country to weather the two major international recessions of the 1990s. There is a considerable 'brain drain' to Australia and elsewhere. **HDI** 0.901; 18th/174. **Public debt** 50% of GNP. **Income/person** $15,720 (50% of USA).

POLITICS
The Treaty of Waitangi between the Maori and the British in 1840 granted the latter the right to settle in exchange for guarantees of Maori land and natural resources. The present dispute is concerning the degree of sovereignty the treaty granted the British. Independent of Britain in 1907. A stable parliamentary democracy with the British Monarch as head of state.

RELIGION
Freedom of religion. No established church.

Religions	Population %	Adherents	Ann.Gr.
Christian	61.71	2,383,182	+0.3%
non-Religious	35.00	1,351,667	+1.9%
Buddhist/Chinese	1.13	43,600	+8.7%
Hindu	0.95	36,688	+6.2%
Muslim	0.46	17,765	+4.4%
Other	0.40	15,448	+3.8%
Jewish	0.17	6,565	+5.0%
Baha'i	0.09	3,500	+1.0%
Sikh	0.09	3,476	+3.4%

Christians	Denom.	Affil.%	,000	Ann.Gr.
Protestant	63	20.60	796	-1.6%
Independent	12	1.94	75	+3.9%
Anglican	1	15.54	600	-1.3%
Catholic	1	12.17	470	-0.3%
Orthodox	3	0.22	8	+5.2%
Marginal	18	3.87	150	-0.6%
Unaffiliated		7.37	284	n.a.

Churches	MegaBloc	Cong.	Members	Affiliates
Anglican	A	667	84,034	600,000
Catholic	C	325	315,436	470,000
Presbyterian	P	700	52,821	440,000
Methodist	P	150	16,492	110,000

Latter-day Saints (Morm)	M	188	56,376	84,000
Baptist Union	P	260	23,000	53,000
Ratana	M	96	19,162	32,000
Assemblies of God	P	230	14,535	25,000
Christian Fellowships [4]	I	150	12,000	24,000
Christian Brethren	P	240	12,987	20,000
Jehovah's Witnesses	M	183	15,850	20,000
Salvation Army	P	110	6,400	13,000
Seventh-day Adventist	P	85	10,000	13,000
Apostolic	P	105	5,500	10,000
Orthodox [3]	O	9	5,592	8,500
Ringatu	M	34	5,030	8,400
Elim Pentecostal	P	56	5,035	7,200
Lutheran	P	20	1,800	5,100
Assoc Chs of Christ	P	39	1,717	4,000
Cong Union of NZ	P	8	320	4,000
Reformed Chs of NZ	P	18	2,308	3,300
Other denoms [74]		1,310	86,400	144,300
Total Christians [100]		4,983	752,800	2,098,800

Trans-bloc Groupings	pop.%	,000	Ann.Gr.
Evangelical	22.1	854	-0.8%
Charismatic	9.5	366	+0.6%
Pentecostal	2.5	96	+3.4%

Missionaries from New Zealand
P,I,A 1,836 in 84 agencies, with 1,400 to 114 countries.

Missionaries to New Zealand
P,I,A 326 in 56 agencies from 29 countries.

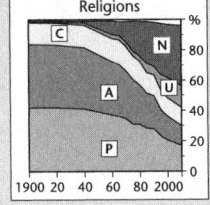

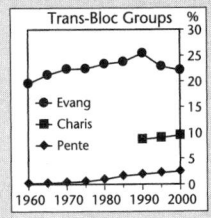

• Answers to Prayer

1 **A moving of the Holy Spirit** in the 1960s brought renewal and widespread change in nearly every denomination. Many new charismatic congregations emerged and mainline denominations became more evangelical — a marked feature in the large Presbyterian Church. Over the 1990s new Pentecostal denominations emerged. Apostolic and Elim churches showed some growth. The Brethren and Reformed churches have reversed their decline.

2 New Zealand is ranked fourth in the world for missionaries sent out per head of Christian population.

• Challenges for Prayer

1 **The rapid secularization of society** has led to declines among Anglicans, Presbyterians, Methodists and, to a lesser extent, Catholics. Those with no religion rose from 1.1% in 1951 to 26% in 1996. Church attendance is declining and in 2000 was 14% of the population, but only 19% of attenders are in their 30s, and 8% in their 20s. There is growing interest in New Age religions, but the Church is criticized as too traditional, so the decline is set to continue unless God intervenes. The Presbyterians are sorely divided over such issues as the practice of homosexuality. Earlier Pentecostal and charismatic growth has slowed and the attrition rate is high. Many Christians pray for a fresh outpouring of the Spirit — pray with them for this.

2 **The lack of meaningful interfacing** between Christians and the secularized majority is giving concern. New initiatives sparked by Willow Creek, use of Alpha courses and special seeker services are helping, as is the Christian schooling network. Pray for relevance, authenticity, vibrancy, and winsomeness in witness for believers. The decline in the welfare state has also given churches more awareness of opportunities to help the poorer sectors of the community with local food banks, budget counselling, etc. Pray that these avenues of community ministry might bear spiritual fruit.

3 **Extensive church planting** during the 1990s yielded mixed results — more churches were planted, but many of these were less viable because conversions did not increase. There has been a greater emphasis on increased cooperation between denominations in planting viable rural churches and starting work among immigrant minorities. Pray for an effective, unified witness that impacts the unconverted.

4 **Young people are deeply affected by the strong secular emphasis** of the state education system and relatively few are active Christians. Pray for the ministry of **SU** in secondary schools; TSCF(**IFES**) and **CCCI** in universities are important. TSCF has a specific ministry to the increasing numbers of international students. There is a popular Christian music festival, Parachute, which has a large following. In a nation of sports-lovers, there are some fine Christian sportsmen and women. Pray for more athletes to become wholesome role-models for young New Zealanders and by their bold witness draw many to the Saviour.

5 **The missions vision of the New Zealand Church** is an example to many other lands, but has faltered in recent years. The Perspectives on the World Christian Movement courses have had significant impact leading to new candidates for Bible School training and then going into missions as a result. Pray for these and their preparation for cross-cultural service. There are 19 residential Protestant Bible schools, of which the largest and best known is the Bible College of New Zealand in Auckland, and some 60 part-time schools. Pray for this missions vision to be nurtured by pastors and embraced by whole congregations.

6 **A Maori cultural revival** and compensation for infringements of the 1840 Treaty have impacted the non-Maori majority. Many Maori resent their cultural dislocation which has put them at a social disadvantage — high unemployment, relative poverty, crime, youth gangs, welfare needs are the result. Syncretistic sects such as Ringatu and Ratana as well as the Mormons have gained large followings. Very few attend evangelical churches. Pray that Maori may find their full cultural blossoming in embracing the fullness of the gospel and pray for a new generation of Maori evangelical leaders to emerge.

7 **New Zealand's increasing diversity of cultures** presents new challenges. Many immigrants find that they have few job opportunities commensurate with their training, and unemployment is high. Increasing numbers of churches are reaching out to new immigrants with English language classes and other practical assistance which has created significant opportunities. Pray for these groups:
a) *Polynesians have immigrated* to NZ seeking employment. Large communities of Samoans, Tongans and Islanders from the NZ-administered Cook, Tokelau and Niue Islands live in the cities. Auckland has the largest Polynesian population of any city in the world, with over 100,000. Many live in poorer areas of South Auckland where poverty and lack of employment are common and crime is high. Many go to church but young people are generally disillusioned with their churches.
b) *Chinese immigrants* have a long history in New Zealand. Recently immigration has increased, mainly from Hong Kong and Taiwan. Although 75% claim to be 'Christian', only 12% of these attend church regularly. There are a growing number of churches with a significant Chinese membership. May they be challenged to daring discipleship and missions.
c) *Indians are increasing in numbers*, especially from Fiji since the 1987 and 2000 coups. There is some outreach to them; a number of them are Christians.
d) *Southeast Asian refugees* and the Japanese community are predominantly Buddhist. Attempts have been made to reach them and there are Japanese congregations in Auckland and Christchurch.
e) *The 4,000 Jews* (400 of these are recent migrants from the former USSR) have one CWI couple and several others seeking to reach them.
f) *Muslim outreach* is being developed, but there has been little lasting fruit to date.

g) ***South Africans and Koreans*** have increased in numbers. Many are active Christians. Koreans have started 60 churches in Auckland alone. Pray for their witness and integration into the wider Christian community.

8 Specialized Christian ministries:

a) ***Radio Rhema*** has a wide coverage and listenership throughout the country. Programmes are also produced for ethnic minorities and young people (Life FM).

b) ***Open Air Campaigners*** has a unique evangelistic and mobilizing ministry among Christians for outreach.

c) ***Alpha Courses*** are in wide use and increasing numbers of people are involved.

d) ***Prison Ministries*** are active in many prisons. Many prisoners have been converted. Pray for them in the difficulties they face following their release.

e) ***The JESUS film*** has been shown in public cinemas as well as being widely available on video. Pray for lasting fruit from the project to distribute a copy of this powerful video to every home in the country.

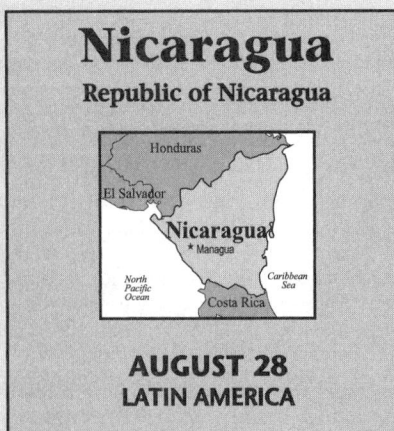

Nicaragua

Republic of Nicaragua

AUGUST 28
LATIN AMERICA

 GEOGRAPHY
Area 127,849 sq.km. The largest of the Central American Republics; poor communications with the sparsely populated eastern half of the country.

Population		Ann.Gr.	Density
2000	5,074,194	+2.77%	40 per sq. km.
2010	6,529,320	+2.40%	51 per sq. km.
2025	8,696,054	+1.69%	68 per sq. km.

Most live on the Pacific coast and adjacent highlands. Central America's most sparsely populated state.

Capital Managua 1,050,000. **Urbanites** 54%.

PEOPLES
Spanish-speaking 86.7%. Ladino (Eurindian) 3.36m; European-origin 700,000; Zambo/Mulatto 253,000. Three Hispanicized Amerindian peoples: Matagalpa 35,000; Monimbo 18,000; Subtiaba 9,000.

English/Creole-speaking 8.3%. On the Caribbean coast. African-origin 420,000; Black Carib (Garifuna)

2,600; Rama 1,100.
Amerindian-speaking 4.7%. Miskitu 266,000 (nearly half Spanish-speaking); Sumu 12,000. **Other** 0.3%. Chinese 10,000, etc.

Literacy 66%. **Official language** Spanish. English-speaking communities on Atlantic coast. **All languages** 7. **Languages with Scriptures** 3Bi 1NT 1w.i.p.

ECONOMY
Many minerals, fertile soil and low population make the country potentially wealthy. The poorest Central American state because of nearly two centuries of dictatorships, civil wars and natural calamities. Sandinista Marxist economic policies and confrontation with the USA in the 1980s led to hyper-inflation and economic collapse. Democratic government in the 1990s has been unable to reduce levels of mismanagement, corruption and exploitation. Recovery is painfully slow and public debt massive. Hurricane Mitch in 1998 further impoverished the country. **HDI** 0.616; 121st/174. **Unemployment** 10-40%. **Public debt** 252% of GNP. **Income/person** $410 (1.3% of USA).

POLITICS
Independent republic since 1838. The brutal and corrupt Somoza dictatorship ended in 1979 after a bitter civil war. The Sandinista government imposed Marxist ideology and economic principles despite much internal resistance and US-supported subversion by the 'Contras' from surrounding lands. The economic failures, human rights abuses and arrogance of the Sandinistas caused them to lose the 1990 and 1996 elections, but the democrats have lost much respect and credibility in their failure to grapple with the many national problems.

RELIGION
Secular state with some abuses of religious freedom under the Sandinista government. Complete religious freedom since 1990.

N

Religions	Population %	Adherents	Ann.Gr.
Christian	90.90	4,612,442	+2.6%
non-Religious/other	9.10	461,752	+4.2%

Christians	Denom.	Affil.%	,000	Ann.Gr.
Protestant	30	11.66	592	+3.9%
Independent	79	6.94	352	+5.1%
Anglican	1	0.16	8	+1.0%
Catholic	1	75.91	3,852	+2.2%
Marginal	3	1.43	72	+6.5%
Doubly affiliated		*-5.22*	*-265*	*n.a.*

Churches	MegaBloc	Cong.	Members	Affiliates
Catholic	C	320	2,000,000	3,852,000
Assemblies of God	P	710	86,862	181,000
Seventh-day Adventist	P	97	44,803	85,000
Moravian	P	200	25,000	76,000
Ch of God (Cleveland)	P	396	25,553	65,000
Apostolic Ch of Faith in J C	I	200	16,000	50,000
Jehovah's Witnesses	M	239	14,410	50,000
Nat'l Baptist Conv	P	152	18,200	40,000
Pente Ch of God Mission	I	211	12,529	40,000
Ch of God of Prophecy	P	350	16,902	34,000
Christian Assemblies	I	98	8,321	25,000
Latter-day Saints (Morm)	M	39	11,640	22,000
Christian Pentecostal	I	130	8,000	22,000
United Pentecostal	P	273	9,000	19,200
Ch of the Nazarene	P	130	9,500	15,000
Brethren in Christ	P	70	2,800	12,000
Fed of Central American	P	75	6,000	10,000
Int'l Baptist	P	50	4,080	8,500
Episcopal	A	63	3,402	8,300
Evang Mennonite	P	83	4,306	6,000
Other denominations [94]		1,709	97,500	255,600
Doubly affiliated			*-132,500*	*-265,000*
Total Christians [114]		5,595	2,292,000	4,611,600

Trans-bloc Groupings	pop.%	,000	Ann.Gr.
Evangelical	16.3	825	+4.2%
Charismatic	17.4	883	+3.2%
Pentecostal	11.0	560	+3.3%

Missionaries from Nicaragua
P,I,A 41 in 9 agencies to 4 countries: 32 in Nicaragua.

Missionaries to Nicaragua
P,I,A 153 in 48 agencies from 14 countries: USA 111, Korea 9, Mexico 8.

• Answers to Prayer

1 **God has used various means to bring about a remarkable turning to Himself**, many involving suffering:

a) ***Natural disasters*** such as volcanic eruptions, earthquakes (Managua levelled in 1972) and hurricanes (Mitch, 1998) have shocked many unbelievers into a living faith.

b) ***The massive upheavals of war***, tyranny and the failure of politicians to bring improvements have helped the disillusioned find hope in God.

c) ***Extensive evangelism*** by mass crusades, 'Evangelism in Depth' programmes and local church outreaches have all added to the Kingdom too.

2 **Evangelicals** grew from 1.8% (28,000 in 320 churches) in 1960 to 13.7% (500,000 in 4,100 churches) in 1990. In 2000, estimates were 21.4% with one million in over 7,000 churches.

• Challenges for Prayer

1 **Nicaragua remains a deeply divided nation.** The traumatic events of 1979-1998 have divided politicians (Sandinista, Contra and democrats), communities (the Hispanic-Mestizo west and Creole-Amerindian east), trade unions, churches and families. Pray the government would gain the authority and respect of all communities to institute the needed structural, sociological and economic changes.

2 **Hurricane Mitch** traumatized the nation with massive destruction of roads, housing and farmland. Over 9,000 perished and 2 million were made homeless. It will take 15 years or more to repair the estimated $15 billion damage caused. International aid quickly dried up after the initial effort, and little has been done to alleviate the massive foreign debt. Pray for emotional healing, wise, long-term economic aid and spiritual fruit. Many national, denominational and interdenominational economic uplift programmes have been launched — CEPAD (The Evangelical Committee for Relief and Development), **AoG**, Verbo Church, etc. Pray also for spiritual needs to be met and churches to multiply.

3 **Rapid growth of Evangelicals** in an impoverished and dysfunctional society has exposed weaknesses and problems. Pray for resolution to:

a) *The deep trauma suffered by so many who are coming to the churches* — bereavement, family break-ups, material losses, etc. About 70% of church members are jobless.

b) *The divisions among the churches* — on Liberation Theology, the work of the Holy Spirit, and interpersonal conflicts.

c) *Involvement in politics.* Evangelicals are now one-fifth of the population, but do not agree on how to be effective and prophetic — inside the present corrupt political system, or outside it?

4 **Ministry challenges for the Church** in the new millennium:

a) *Revival* for the English/Creole and Miskitu churches in the Caribbean eastern provinces. Many are Moravian, Anglican or Catholic and are often traditional and syncretistic. The Miskitu suffered particularly severely at the hands of the Sandinistas.

b) *Vision for outreach.* **Vision 2000** brought together many churches and agencies to plant churches in every town and village. The **AoG**, **CAMI** and Baptists set bold goals and much was achieved, but there remain many pockets of need as well as re-building scattered congregations and their meeting places.

c) *Young people* have grown up in a country ravaged by war and distorted by Marxism. Few healthy two-parent families exist. Not many churches are equipped and committed to effectively meeting their special needs. *Gente Nueva* and *Hosanna*(**IFES**) have groups in 6 universities with effective evangelistic Bible studies.

d) *The Sandinista and 'Contra' soldiers* who are angry, disillusioned and often landless. They need those who can minister love and spiritual healing to them after the bitter war with its many atrocities meted out to opponents and innocent civilians alike.

e) *The Hispanicized Indians.* These are nominally Catholic, and few active evangelical congregations exist among them.

f) *The Garifuna* are still largely animist, but there are some churches among them. The NT is being translated.

5 **Missions vision** is in its early stage of development. Poverty and disasters have slowed progress. **YWAM** is being used of God to stimulate this.

6 **The expatriate missionary force** was greatly reduced in the 1980s. Numbers increased in the 1990s. Pray that attitudes of the past may be rectified and that they might be used of God to strengthen the maturing church. The major task for missionaries is in Bible teaching and leadership training as well as in helping to alleviate the enormous material and social needs. The largest agencies are: Presbyterians (22), Mennonites (15), **IMB-SBC** (13) and **AoG** (8).

7 **Christian support ministries** for prayer:

a) *A Christian hovercraft ministry* along the *Rio Grande de Matagalpa* which links the Atlantic with the highland lakes of Nicaragua and Managua. This could have a significant impact.

b) *Christian radio and TV.* There is one Christian TV station and six radio stations.

c) *The Bible Society* has done much in enabling the translation and distribution of the new Sumu and Miskitu Bibles.

d) *The JESUS film* has been seen by almost the entire population on film and TV.

e) *Development projects* for urban, rural and agriculture by means of credit and training that contributes to socio-economic and spiritual growth.

Niger
Republic of Niger

AUGUST 29
AFRICA

0.298; 173rd/174. **Public debt** 68% of GNP. **Income/person** $200 (0.9% of USA).

POLITICS
For centuries the Tuareg dominated much of the Sahel. French colonial rule 1921-1960. Military regimes with a number of coups. A brief period of democratic rule 1993-96 presaged the democratic government formed in 1999. There has been Tuareg insurgency in the north for some years.

RELIGION
A non-confessional state with considerable freedom of religion and few restrictions on mission work. Islamic fundamentalists are pushing for change and imposition of *shari'a* law. **Persecution index** 68th in the world.

Religion	Population %	Adherents	Ann.Gr.
Muslim	97.59	10,471,507	+3.9%
Traditional ethnic	2.00	214,602	-14.0%
Christian	0.40	42,920	+5.4%
Baha'i	0.01	1,073	n.a.

Christians	Denom.	Affil.%	,000	Ann.Gr.
Protestant	13	0.12	12	+11.9%
Independent	18	0.09	9	+2.2%
Catholic	1	0.18	20	+4.1%
Marginal	1	0.01	1	+4.8%

Churches	MegaBloc	Cong.	Members	Affiliates
Catholic	C	21	9,000	19,600
Evangelical	P	106	2,000	5,000
Union of Evang Prot	P	46	1,125	2,700
Assemblies of God	P	22	1,000	2,000
Evangelical Baptist	P	11	550	1,100
Jehovah's Witnesses	M	7	232	1,000
Salama Evangelical	I	10	300	750
Ev. Christian Assemblies	I	9	300	750
Abundant Life	I	12	360	720
Other denoms [24]		70	5,924	8,765
Total Christians [33]		314	20,791	42,385

Trans-bloc Groupings pop. %		,000	Ann.Gr.
Evangelical	0.1	14	+10.0%
Charismatic	0.1	10	+5.0%
Pentecostal	0.0	2	+13.5%

Missionaries from Niger
P,I,A 45 in 8 agencies, nearly all in Niger.

Missionaries to Niger
P,I,A 343 in 35 agencies from 29 countries: USA 128, Brazil 36, UK 32, Nigeria 21.

GEOGRAPHY
Area 1,186,408 sq.km. Sahara desert in centre and north. Only the southwest and a narrow strip along the Nigerian border in the south are savannah grasslands.

Population		Ann.Gr.	Density
2000	10,730,102	+3.24%	9 per sq. km.
2010	14,485,881	+3.00%	12 per sq. km.
2025	21,495,434	+2.44%	18 per sq. km.

Capital Niamey 1,000,000. **Urbanites** 17%.

PEOPLES
All peoples 36.
Chadic 46.3%. Hausa (6): Tazarawa 2,247,000; Adarawa 968,000; Arewa 924,000; Mauri 376,000; Kurfey 204,000.
Nilo-Saharan 27%. 15 peoples:
Southern Songhai(5): Zarma (Djerma) 1,600,000; Kado 353,000; Dendi 73,000; Kurtey 32,000; Wogo 28,000. Northern Songhai(3): Semi-nomadic Tihishit(2) 30,000 and settled Tasaweq (Bingalli) 9,000. Kanuri(3): Manga 633,000; Mober 61,000; Tumari 14,000. Tubu(2): Daza 93,000; Teda 21,000.
Tuareg 12.2%. Six ethnic groups; three languages: Tamajaq-Tayert 565,000; Tamajaq-Tawellemenet 518,000; Tamajaq-Tahaggart 11,000.
Fulbe (Fula) 10%. The more settled Sokoto 750,000; the largely nomadic Bororo and Wodaabe 225,000.
Arab 2.3%. Shuwa nomads 67,000; Algerians, Lebanese, etc.
Gur 1.3%. Mossi 107,000; Gurma 67,000.
Other 0.9%. Nigerians, Togolese, French.
Literacy 17%. **Official language** French. Language of wider communication Hausa. **All languages** 21. **Languages with Scriptures** 3Bi 5NT 4por 8w.i.p.

ECONOMY
Mining of uranium and other minerals has brought some economic development to this impoverished land, but in the 1980s the Sahel famine, collapse of the uranium market and Nigeria's closure of the common border devastated the economy. Ninety per cent of the population live at bare subsistence level at the best of times. **HDI**

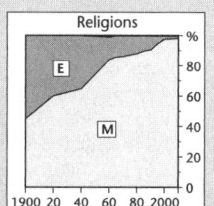

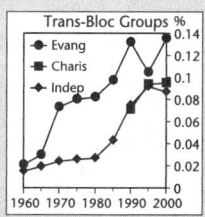

• Answers to Prayer

1 **The firstfruits of conversions** from among the Wodaabe Fulbe and Manga Kanuri Muslims.

2 **Many churches have been planted** through the impact of humanitarian help by Christians through well-digging, leprosy control and health services.

3 **The establishment of an evangelical movement** which is united, visionary and cross-denominational — the Alliance of Evangelical Churches and Missions (AMEEN).

4 **The great increase of churches in Niamey** — from 1 evangelical church in 1975 to over 50 in 2000.

• Challenges for Prayer

1 **This Muslim land is open for the gospel,** and Muslims are more receptive than ever before, yet response has been small and church growth slow. Islam is strong and well-organized. There is an Islamic university 54km from Niamey. Pray that the land may remain open, and that every social, religious and spiritual barrier to the knowledge of the Lord may be removed. The spiritual effects of folk Islam and demonic oppression are a major hindrance to people coming to Christ.

2 **The number of professing Christians** has actually declined since independence — largely because many of the Catholics were French expatriates who have now left the country. Evangelicals have steadily grown but are still a very small minority. There are groups of churches among the Hausa (**SIM**, etc.), Gurma and Zarma (Ev. Baptists), and the beginnings among the Tuareg, Wodaabe and Manga. Pray that there might be a significant increase in those openly confessing Christ and in churches planted.

3 Significant prayer challenges:

a) *Many believers are isolated*, often illiterate and rarely have systematic Bible teaching available.

b) *There are not enough mature leaders* — there have been a number of church splits.

c) *Leadership training* — the EERN (SIM-related) runs two middle-level Bible schools and two basic Bible schools. There are also many small Bible training schools in the country, run by six different denominations. Pray for effective ways to train more leaders and give further training to those in pastoral work.

4 **This pioneer land still needs missionaries** for all parts of the country. The loving ministry of Christian aid missionaries has won credibility for the gospel and increased interest and response from both Muslims and animists. Pray for more labourers. The major mission agencies: **SIM** (154), **WH** (43), **AoG** (38), **IMB-SBC** (16), **SIL** (15), **YWAM** (10), Evangelical Baptists (4). There is a growing contribution from missions from Nigeria (**CAPRO, EMS**). Pray for sensitivity in helping the small, young churches and their leaders to maturity.

N 5 **The least reached of Niger.** Pray for:

a) *The Tuareg*, once rich, but now impoverished and resentful due to drought, famine, changing trade patterns and political changes. The selfless ministry of a partnership of missionaries from **SIM**, the Baptists, Sahara Desert Mission and others has opened the hearts of some, and there are some groups of believers. **SIM** and **SIL** missionaries are translating the Scriptures; the Tamacheq New Testament was published in 1991. **YWAM** and **WH** also have a commitment to reach these people. Tuareg customs and their unique alphabet hint at a possible once-Christian heritage.

b) *The Zarma,* who are Muslim but strongly influenced by traditional practices. Only a few hundred believers are known. Evangelical Baptist missionaries have laboured long but no significant breakthrough has yet come among this resistant people.

c) *The five Kanuri peoples* have a long history of 1,000 years of Islam. Missionaries of **SIM**, **SIL**, **WH**, etc., have recently seen a change. Manga Christians, though still few, are seeing their numbers grow from near zero. Scripture portions are available and more of God's Word is in preparation (**SIL**, **SIM**).

d) *The Fulbe (Fulani)*, both the settled Sokoto and nomadic Wodaabe Fulbe of the west, and the less Islamized nomadic Fulbe across the whole country. **SIM** has 12 workers committed to the Fulbe. There have recently been an increasing number of conversions among the Wodaabe; there were over 60 believers in 1991 and 350 in 2000.

e) *The Songhai* were reached out to by **SIM** in 1989. Two couples are now working among them. A few have been won to Christ and a congregation has been formed.

f) *The Tubu peoples* in the east. **SIL** is working on a translation for the Daza language and five national workers are ministering among them.

6 **There may be over 14 unreached peoples** with no work among them, but investigations are underway for ministry among the Sokoto Fulbe, the Kanuri-Mober (**SIM**). The Kanuri-Tumari, Arabs (**SIM**), Kurfey, Mauri, Tyenga, Dendi, Kurtey, Wogo and the Kado Songhai. Pray that teams may be called and formed for each of these peoples.

7 **Bible translation and distribution.** The Zarma Bible was published in 1991. Pray for an impact to be made; 25% of Niger's population understand Zarma. **SIL** workers are committed to translation programmes in Tamajaq-Tawellemmet, Kanuri-Manga, Kanuri-Tumari, Fulbe (Fulfulde) and Tubu-Daza. There are three definite, and possibly two other, languages into which translation is necessary.

8 **Young people** have been the most responsive, yet little has been done to minister to this key section of the nation. There is a small GBEEN (**IFES**) group in the university and 13 groups in colleges and schools with 70 members. **The Navigators** and **CCCI** also have ministries in Niger. Pray for a deep and lasting impact through campus ministries.

9 Specialist Christian ministries in Niger:

a) *SIM's medical ministry* through the Galmi hospital and also in Danja through leprosy control has successfully opened hearts for the gospel.

b) *The many prostitutes* in the capital are the focus of a significant outreach by **CAPRO**.

c) *Christian literature*. Poverty and illiteracy are severe limitations. There are just two Christian bookstores in the country.

d) *The audio-media ministry* which has been inadequately funded or exploited. **GRN** have prepared messages in 34 languages/dialects of Niger. Cassettes are an important ministry to nomads.

e) *The JESUS film* has been widely viewed in 5 languages; a further 8 are in preparation.

Nigeria

Federal Republic of Nigeria

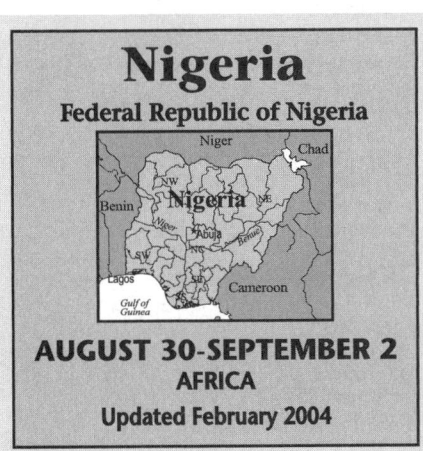

AUGUST 30-SEPTEMBER 2
AFRICA
Updated February 2004

GEOGRAPHY
Area 923,768 sq.km. Mangrove and tropical rain forests in the south, savannah and grasslands in the north. The country is drained by the Niger-Benue river systems.

Population		Ann.Gr.	Density
2000	111,506,095	+2.42%	121 per sq. km.
2010	138,698,398	+2.15%	150 per sq. km.
2025	183,041,179	+1.70%	198 per sq. km.

Africa's most populous nation. Census figures have in the past been manipulated for religious or political advantage by the ruling Muslim elite. The figures of the 1991 census have been widely accepted.

Capital Abuja 500,000. Other major cities: Lagos 5 mill.; Ibadan 1.7m; Kano 1.5m; Port Harcourt 1.2m; Kaduna 1m; Enugu 900,000; Jos 650,000. **Urbanites** 44%. Neglect of agriculture has accelerated urban migration.

PEOPLES
Over 490 ethnic groups. The triangular rivalry between the Hausa/Fulani, Yoruba and Igbo have dominated Nigerian politics since independence.

Guinean 49.5%. Mainly across south and centre. Over 70 peoples, mostly Christian, some Muslim. Yoruba 20.3mill.; Igbo (Ibo) 19.9m; Edo 1.1m; Nupe 1.1m; Ijaw(4) 970,000; Igala 891,000; Idoma(4) 800,000; Igbirra 660,000; Urhobo 608,000; Isekiri 557,000; Isoko 423,000; Gbari 409,000; Esan 357,000; Izi 357,000; Ewe 340,000; Ezaa 322,000.

Hausa-Chadic 20.6%. Mainly in north. Though over 25% of all people speak Hausa, many who embrace Islam switch to Hausa. Over 100 peoples, majority are Muslim. Hausa 23m.

Bantoid peoples 12%. Mainly south-west and centre. Mainly Christian, over 200 peoples, largest: Ibibio 3.6m; Tiv 2.8m; Anaang 1m; Kaje 307,000.

Fulbe (Fulani) 11.1%. Mainly in north; many speaking Hausa, largely Muslim. Total 12.3m in 7 groups.

Kanuri 3.2%. Three peoples; total 3.6m. Muslim.
Sudanic 1.2%. Mainly north-east, mainly ethnic religions. 50 peoples, largest: Mumuye 536,000; Yungur 108,000; Chamba Daka 78,000.
Other 2.4%. Songhai 300,000; Shuwa Arab 250,000.
Literacy 64%. **Official language** English. Hausa is widely used in the north and middle belt, Yoruba in the south-west, Igbo in the south-east and Pidgin English all over the south. **All languages** 470; 96% of the population uses 21 major languages. **Languages with Scriptures** 16Bi 47NT 87por 46w.i.p.

ECONOMY
Rich in agricultural land and mineral resources and large oil reserves. The enormous oil wealth was squandered on prestige projects and embezzled by a series of corrupt rulers. The military dictator Abacha misappropriated an estimated $7 billion during his misrule. It is reckoned that the stolen wealth is about equal to the national debt of $30 billion. Agriculture, transportation, storage systems and the basic economy were neglected. Over 34% of the population live below the poverty line and unemployment is 28%. The new Obasanjo government has instituted stern measures to root out the massive culture of corruption, rectify past errors and diversify the economy. The north is totally dependent on the oil wealth of the south. **HDI** 0.456; 146th/174. **Public debt** 68% of GNP. **Income/person** $280 (0.9% of USA).

POLITICS
Independent from Britain as a federation in 1960. Component states now number 36 with a federal capital area. There are wide differences between the cultures of the feudal and predominantly Muslim north and the entrepreneurial largely Christian south. This and the manipulations of the Muslims to retain political control are the main causes of the turbulent post-independence history of tension, violence, coups and civil war. The sudden death of the brutal Muslim military ruler, Abacha, in 1998 and subsequent democratic elections in 1999, brought Olusegun Obasanjo, a committed Christian, to the Presidency. He wisely and tactfully moved to bring about change while endeavouring to preserve national unity — despite efforts by the former ruling elite and Islamists to frustrate and discredit his administration. In the 2003 election religion became the big issue, but Obasanjo was preferred by 62% of voters. Muslim violence and massacre of Christians continues to destabilize the country.

RELIGION
Constitutionally Nigeria is a secular state with freedom of religion. For nearly 40 years the northern ruling elite gave preferential treatment to Muslims and discriminated against Christians. Little was done to stop persecution of Christians in the north with tragic results of churches burnt and many Christians killed. Since 1999 Muslim state leaders have imposed *shari'a* law in 12 northern states and despite undertakings are imposing *shari'a*

law on Christians as well as causing much resentment among Christians. NOTE: The claims and counter-claims of Muslims, Christians and individual denominations are impossible to verify and are often inflated. Estimates for Muslims vary between 30-50% and for Christians, 40-60%! **Persecution index** 36th in the world (in the north).

Religions	Population %	Adherents	Ann.Gr.
Christian	52.61	58,663,357	+3.5%
Muslim	41.00	45,717,499	+2.7%
Traditional ethnic	5.99	6,679,215	-5.9%
non-Religious/other	0.40	446,024	+8.5%

Traditional religions are nearer 13% of the population, and so both Muslims and Christians are correspondingly lower than the above figures indicate.

Christians	Denom.	Affil.%	,000	Ann.Gr.
Protestant	523	15.84	17,665	+5.0%
Independent	4,200	18.25	20,345	+3.8%
Anglican	1	10.12	11,280	+7.1%
Catholic	1	13.45	15,000	+4.1%
Orthodox	3	0.00	4	+1.9%
Marginal	23	0.95	1,055	+10.2%
Unaffiliated		1.18	1,313	n.a.
Doubly affiliated		*-7.17*	*-8,000*	*n.a.*

Churches	MegaBloc	Cong.	Members	Affiliates
Catholic	C	16,000	8,500,000	15.00m
Anglican	A	9,000	3,000,000	11.280m
Ev Ch of W. Afr (ECWA)	P	6,000	2,500,000	4,600,000
Christ Apostolic	I	6,667	700,000	2,000,000
Assemblies of God	P	7,726	650,000	1,811,400
Baptist Convention	P	6,664	1,040,000	1,800,000
Methodist	P	3,400	680,000	1,700,000
Ch of God Mission Int'l	I	5,333	800,000	1,400,000
Ch of Christ in N (TEKAN)	P	833	250,000	1,400,000
Redeemed Chr Ch of God	I	5,000	563,000	1,250,000
Ch of the Lord (Aladura)	I	1,125	450,000	1,250,000
Ch of Chr/TIV (TEKAN)	P	3,300	210,000	950,000
Apostolic	P	7,432	550,000	900,000
Cherubim & Seraphim [300]	I	4,000	400,000	800,000
Deeper Life Bible	I	6,000	450,000	800,000
Lutheran Ch of Christ	P	1,168	160,000	715,000
Jehovah's Witnesses	M	4,229	226,353	600,000
Evang Ref Ch (TEKAN)	P	280	171,429	600,000
Brethren	P	424	150,000	450,000
Living Faith Ministries	I	800	160,000	400,000
Gospel Faith Mission	I	1,300	150,000	350,000
Seventh-day Adventist	P	622	152,332	305,000
Qua Iboe	P	1,200	160,000	260,000
Presbyterian	P	700	90,000	214,000
Chr Reformed (TEKAN)	P	600	76,000	185,000
Churches of Christ	P	2,000	75,000	150,000
Lutheran	P	350	42,000	90,000
Reformed Ch of Christ	P	300	40,000	85,000
Un Ch of Christ (TEKAN)	P	81	31,650	66,000
Ch of God (Cleveland)	P	156	15,586	30,000
Apostolic Chr Ch (Naz)	P	38	3,810	8,000
Other denoms [4,646]		43,243	6,328,000	13,902,000
Doubly affiliated			*-3,809,524*	*-8,000,000*
Total Christians [4,975]		144,700	24.966m	57.350m

Trans-bloc Groupings pop. %	,000	Ann.Gr.
Evangelical	23.5 26,243	+3.8%
Charismatic	18.2 20,279	+3.5%
Pentecostal	10.9 12,142	+5.0%

Missionaries from Nigeria
P,I,A approx. 3,800 in 150 agencies to 50+ lands: Nigeria 3,100+, Benin 38, USA 30, Côte d'Ivoire 24, Niger 21, Ghana 19, UK 18.

Missionaries to Nigeria
P,I,A 697 in 71 agencies from 22 lands: USA 434, UK 62,

Denmark 34, Canada 32, Korea 25.

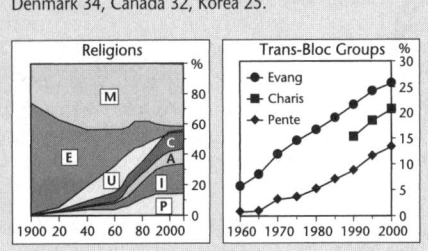

• Answers to Prayer

1 The ending of a largely Muslim political dominance and the election of Obasanjo, a committed Christian believer. Opportunity is given for a new beginning for the country.

2 The spirit of prayer among Christians — stimulated by the political stresses of the recent past and by Muslim persecution in areas where there is a Muslim majority. Some of the largest prayer meetings in history have been in Nigeria (an estimated 3 million in Lagos). This fervent prayer has been behind all the political change and spiritual growth.

3 The dynamic growth of the Church has been spectacular. This has been among Anglicans, Baptists, evangelical groups such as ECWA and TEKAN with interdenominational roots (**SIM**, **SUM/AP**, etc.) and Pentecostal and charismatic denominations (both indigenous and international). A few specifics:

a) *Anglicans* have grown from 900,000 in 1960 to perhaps 11 million in 2000. There have been other, more exaggerated, claims.

b) *SIM*'s work, begun with such cost a century ago, has resulted in a dynamic church, ECWA, with 4.6 million people and 1,400 missionaries serving Christ in Nigeria and abroad.

c) *Evangelicals* have grown from 2.1 million in 1960 (5.7%) to 17.2 million in 1980 (17.2%) and 26 million in 2000 (23.5%).

d) *The Full Gospel Businessmen's Fellowship* with 800 chapters has had a significant impact on the leaders of the political and commercial world.

4 Revival among university students in the 1970s (NIFES) has led to dramatic growth and missions vision through such organizations as Deeper Life Bible Church, Redeemed Christian Church of God, Church of God Mission and many others. The missions vision has blossomed despite economic distress.

• Special Issues for Prayer

NOTE Jan 2003: There has been a steady deterioration of communal cohesion with the continued rise of Islamism and marginalization of Muslims on the centres of power. The following are worthy of much prayer:

1 Shari'a law has been imposed on 12 states. Promises to non-Muslims have not been kept and there has been increased discrimination against Christians, forced closure and destruction of churches and outright persecution in some northern states.

2 Islamism has gained in influence and is exploiting the frustration of Muslim leaders at losing much of their control in national affairs. Any opportunity is taken to use mob violence to disrupt the government and attack Christians. Even in Christian majority areas there have been many Christians killed, churches and property destroyed and rape used against Christian women. The Western press consistently ignores these reports or downplays this as "communal violence".

3 The 2003 presidential elections were made into a contest between Islam and Christianity by the Muslims. The danger is that this may lead to war or division of the country.

• Challenges for Prayer

1 The unity of Nigeria. The combined effects of ancient tribal hatreds, Muslim conquests, British colonial policy in which the North and South were handled differently and the bitter Biafra war of 1967-70 have left deep scars. Pray for healing and reconciliation.

2 **The government needs time,** the support of the people and courage to bring about the painful reconstruction of the country after four decades of being plundered by its leaders. Pray for the right balance between tact and firmness and between revolution and evolution in economic affairs, vested interests and tribalism.

3 **The introduction of** *shari'a* **law** in northern Muslim states is a direct challenge to the federal government and a danger to national stability. Pray with Nigerian Christians for the preservation of national unity, the integrity of the federal constitution and for full religious freedom.

4 **The culture of greed and corruption** runs deep. Nigeria has become infamous for spectacular international scams, international crime and drug-running. Pray that God may raise up many more who fear Him and have the moral integrity and courage to tackle the rottenness manifest in society. Pray that Christian values and lifestyle may affect every area of national life and that Nigeria attain its potential as a light to the world for God.

5 **Massive church growth has its dangers.** Pray against:

a) *Widespread evangelism unaccompanied by follow-up and balanced teaching.* Numerous doctrinal distortions (lack of preaching Christ and salvation by grace alone), an over-emphasis on material prosperity, undue stress on certain spiritual gifts and unethical fundraising are bringing dissension to the Body of Christ.

b) *Divisions.* A profusion of competing denominations and sects has emerged. There are too many one-man ministries with little accountability to the Body of Christ. Pray that the pride, carnality and tribalism underlying this may be replaced with humility, simplicity of lifestyle and holiness.

c) *Second-generation nominalism* in both traditional and younger churches is becoming a big problem. Double standards are widespread, and immorality, membership of secret societies and compromise with the world bring strife and disrepute for the gospel.

d) *Syncretistic Christianity.* Many indigenous groups have sprung up with a desire for God, but with much admixture of unbiblical world-views and practices. Many are open to greater gospel light but are often isolated from, or shunned by, more orthodox churches. A number of large Pentecostal denominations are also showing syncretistic tendencies.

6 **Christian leaders** are under great stress in today's Nigeria — economic and political pressure, but also for those in the north, real dangers from Muslim extremists. Many have an internationally significant ministry. Pray for:

a) *A multiplication of leaders* well versed in the Scriptures, spirit-led, skilled in disciple-making and steeped in the knowledge of God and the power of prayer.

b) *The 160+ seminaries and Bible schools in Nigeria* and a number of missions training schools. There are also a number of TEE courses. Six evangelical seminaries offer postgraduate degrees. Nigeria is a base for the Accreditation Council for Theological Education in Africa (ACTEA) which is a vital instrument for improving theological education all over Africa. The major lack is for more non-denominational Bible schools geared to give biblical training to founders and pastors of independent groups. By 2003 there were 40 missionary training schools in the country.

c) *Mentor leaders to be raised up.* One-man ministries, dictatorial leadership, empire-building and unwillingness to delegate responsibility to the upcoming generation are common weaknesses. The gap between older and younger pastors is often large.

d) *Improved cooperation and fellowship* across denominational boundaries. Pray for evangelical bodies such as the Pentecostal Fellowship of Nigeria and the Nigeria Evangelical Fellowship as well as those representing a wider spectrum — CAN and the Christian Council of Nigeria.

7 **Persecution in Nigeria's northern states** between 1991 and 2003 led to the deaths of thousands of believers, murder of pastors and destruction of hundreds of churches in Kaduna, Gombe, Sokoto, Kano, Bauchi, Plateau, etc. This has united Christians as never before, but also driven them to the Lord in prayer. The level of violence and extremism has increased since 9/11. Pray for:

a) *Forgiveness* for persecutors and deliverance from a spirit of revenge.

b) *Restoration and recovery* for those who have suffered loss, bereavement and rape.

c) *The Christian Association of Nigeria* and its ministry of representing Nigeria's 58 million Christians to the local and federal authorities.

d) *The conversion of Muslims* — both persecutors and those appalled by the behaviour of their co-religionists. There have been many won to Christ over recent years.

8 **Nation-wide interdenominational movements** have been used of God to make a deep impact on specific sections of the community. Of note:

a) *Secondary schools.* **SU** in the south and **FCS** (Fellowship of Christian Students) in the north have had a big impact through a network of groups in many schools. There is considerable opposition and trials in the three northern regions, yet a great harvest is being won. Pray that Christian teachers, advisors and student leaders may be encouraged and strengthened.

b) *Universities and colleges.* NIFES (Nigeria Fellowship of Evangelical Students), the largest member body of **IFES**, has over 35,000 members on 400 campuses with their largest groups in the south, though the growth of denominational campus ministries has somewhat diluted their impact. NIFES asks for prayer for their inductive Bible Study programme and its leaders as students learn to dig out biblical truths and discern error. **FCS** is stronger in the North Central region and has 351 groups involving 145,000 post-secondary students. They have successfully mobilized outreach into secondary and, more recently, into primary schools. Their impact on non-Christians has been significant, with many Muslim students being won to Jesus. Apathy, discouragement and violent cults have all been problems on campuses. Pray that the national executive and campus leaders may give both vision for evangelism and missions, and spiritual depth based on sound teaching to the members. Pray also that Christian graduates may maintain the vision, contribute more actively to the life of local churches, and be willing to go into full-time pastoral or missionary service.

c) *The upper and business class.* The Full Gospel Businessmen's Fellowship, Pan-Africa Christian Women's Alliance, Nigerian Women for Christ, the newly-formed Covenant Keepers (a ministry to men) and others, exert influence in much of the country. Pray that Christians may win many influential people to Christ and that the whole nation may be thereby uplifted.

9 **Signs of visionary advances.** Water these in prayer:

a) *Significant research* by **Calvary Ministries, AoG** and the Nigerian Baptist Convention has focused the attention of churches and agencies on the unreached. Nearly every one of Nigeria's 168 less-reached peoples have been adopted for prayer and outreach. Yet there still lacks a full survey of Nigeria's harvest force and mechanisms for cooperative outreach.

b) *The AD2000 and Beyond Movement* had a significant impact in bringing together denominations and agencies during the 1990s. Bold plans for advance were set and many were mobilized for church growth and for church planting among the unreached. Coordination of, and adequate preparation for, outreaches and ministries are often lacking.

10 **Significant ministry challenges:**

a) *The African Indigenous 'spiritual' churches* have multiplied — especially those related to the Aladura, the Cherubim and Seraphim Church and the Christ Apostolic Church. Some are highly syncretistic, others marginal in theology, and still others of varying degrees of orthodoxy. Pray that their leadership may be rightly helped by other Christians, and biblical theology and practices adopted.

b) *Young people and schools ministry.* Legally, religious education should be given to all in schools. Christian religious knowledge teachers only number about 15,000. They have great opportunity, but limited resources. With help from the International Institute for Christian Studies, government sponsored in-service training and manuals are giving them fresh impetus. **CEF** reaches 50,000 monthly in Good News Clubs. CEM, an indigenous agency, has a significant Christian camping ministry.

c) *The AIDS crisis.* Official estimates for 1999 indicated 5% of the population (2.4m) were carrying the virus. The actual figure may be nearer 7 — 8%. There are an estimated 1.4 million AIDS orphans. **SU**'s Aid for AIDS and 'How to Live God's Way' programmes are impacting youth. Churches need to be mobilized to minister to those affected.

d) *Nigeria's unreached.* Intense research over the 1990s has revealed that 168 peoples are inadequately reached through lack of resident workers, indigenous churches, Bible translation, etc. Of these, 45 have no church and 34 have no known believers. Pray that those agencies and churches that have adopted them for ministry may carry through that commitment to a successful conclusion.

e) ***Nigeria's Muslims.*** Many have become more open to the gospel despite Nigeria's religious tensions. Thousands have come to Christ, but many face death threats, discrimination and ostracism. Pray for wise and effective methods of witness. Powerful Christian literature for Muslims is now being published.

f) ***Refugees.*** Conflicts across West Africa have brought Chadians, Sierra Leonans, Liberians, etc., to Nigeria. Pray that the unconverted may be reached and the believers among them activated and trained for ministry to their compatriots.

g) ***Development ministries for the rural poor.*** Poverty has prompted many Nigerian churches to establish departments of health and rural development. **RURCON** and its local subsidiary, CRUDAN, provide consultation and training. Pray for effective holism in ministry in the Church.

11 **Mission vision.** Nigeria has become one of the major missionary-sending countries of the developing world. The stimulus of Lausanne 1974 and the Nigeria Congress on Evangelization 1975, as well as the founding of the **Nigeria Evangelical Missions Association** (NEMA), and the AD2000 and Beyond Movement in the 1990s, have helped to push this vision. Pray for:

a) ***The ministry of NEMA***, with a membership of over 90 agencies in 2003, in coordinating the missions thrust to the unreached in Nigeria and beyond, and as a forum for sharing skills, resources and vision.

b) ***Denominational agencies with a strong missions programme.*** The **Evangelical Missionary Society** of ECWA has by far the largest number of cross-cultural missionaries (1,400 in 1996). The Deeper Life Bible Church and the Living Faith Church have sent out missionaries to over 45 nations. The **AoG**, Baptists, Churches of Christ in Nigeria (TEKAN) and others also have strong missionary sending programmes. Pray that other denominations may catch the vision.

c) ***Interdenominational agencies*** have multiplied — such as **Calvary Ministries** (300 workers), **Christian Missionary Foundation** (226), His Grace Evangelical Movement (29), Full Stature Missions (24), and others. Pray for the defining and clarifying of long-term goals.

d) ***Missionary support.*** Few congregations really understand their responsibility to support mission agencies by praying, giving and going. Pray for Nigerian support agencies which seek to address this problem and act as a bridge between churches and missionaries on the fields. There are about 600 Nigerian missionaries serving in other lands, mainly in West Africa, where they face difficulties in receiving funds to provide for their material needs and educate their children.

12 **Expatriate missionaries** have steadily declined in numbers as the large and mature Nigerian Church takes on the ministries they once did. Pray for harmonious cooperation between foreign and indigenous agencies and churches. Key ministries for expatriates include Bible teaching and leadership training, teaching Bible knowledge in schools, a wide range of supportive and aid ministries, and training Nigerian missionaries. Pray for the safety, health and effectiveness of the missionary force — each of these factors has become even more of a spiritual battleground in today's Nigeria. Some of the larger agencies are **SIM** (106 workers), **IMB-SBC** (95), **AP** (52), **CRWM** (43), **QIF** (15), **CMS** (16).

13 **Literature is vital for the growth of the Church.** It is avidly sought but in short supply. Pray for:

a) ***Nigerian authors*** who are interested in writing on a wide range of issues in a culturally relevant way, but lack the means and publishing resources.

b) ***Publishing.*** Christian publishers — such as ECWA Productions, TEKAN Publications, Baraka Publications, Calvary Ministries Media Services and **SU** — publish books, magazines, Sunday School materials and Bible-reading notes, but all face frustrating limitations because of the economic situation and need prayer.

c) ***Distribution.*** Although there are well over 300 Christian bookstores in Nigeria, turnover and stock range are severely limited by the price and lack of foreign exchange. Major distribution agencies are the 18 Challenge Bookstores (ECWA), and 30 bookstores affiliated with TEKAN and **SU**.

14 Christian media ministries:

a) ***Bible translation*** remains a major challenge. The Bible Society of Nigeria together with the Nigeria Bible Translation Trust and other denominations and agencies have made much progress since 1966, with Bibles completed in a further 7 languages, NTs in 35 and portions in 56. Of the 379 languages without the Scriptures, projects are under way in 45, but a further 54 have a proven translation need.

b) *Christian radio*. Over 85% of the population has a shortwave radio receiver, and even more have access to FM. Both local and international radio broadcasts are used by Christians. Pray for all unreasonable restrictions to be lifted for local radio. **TWR** broadcasts 3.5 hrs/wk in Hausa, Fulani, Kanuri and Nupe — languages of 4 of Nigeria's largest and least evangelized peoples.

c) *Christian television*. Television is used by many Christian groups, but creative and diverse programming is a great need. **NLFA**, ELWA, Baptist Media and *Muryar Bishara*, all have studios. There is a need for greater cooperation between groups to cut high costs.

d) *The JESUS film* has been used in 19 languages. An amazing 142 other language editions are in production. ECWA and Baptist media have produced other films and filmstrips; pray these tools may be used effectively.

e) *GRN* has recordings in 482 languages and also innovative cassette and record playback machines for ease of use. Pray for recordings in 127 northern languages yet untackled.

f) *Drama*, using traditional themes, is useful in evangelism and teaching. Mount Zion Ministries, Peace Foundation Ministries and others promote this medium.

THE STATES OF NIGERIA

Three main regions emerged as a result of colonial policy. The British retained the pre-colonial Hausa-Fulani Muslim feudal rulers of the north and allowed them to extend their rule over the peoples of the Middle Belt, few of whom were Muslim at that time. The South developed a more western system of government. Between 1967 and 1995 the number of states was increased from 12 to 36, plus a Federal Capital Territory. These states are clustered in 6 political zones: SE, SS, SW, NCentral, NE and NW, but here they are grouped broadly in the 3 major regions of Nigeria.

THE SOUTHERN ZONES

SE

GEOGRAPHY **Area** 29,525 sq.km. 5 states: Abia, Anambra, Ebonyi, Enugu, Imo.

Population 13,500,000.

PEOPLES Major peoples Igbo, Ibibio.

RELIGION Christian 80%; Muslim 5%; Traditional 15%.

SS

GEOGRAPHY **Area** 84,587 sq.km. 6 states: Akwa-Ibom, Bayelsa, Cross River, Delta, Edo, Rivers.

Population 16,300,000.

PEOPLES Major peoples Ijaw, Isekiri, Isoko, Urhobo.

RELIGION Christian 75%; Muslim 5%; Traditional 20%.

SW

GEOGRAPHY **Area** 78,771 sq.km. 6 states: Ekiti, Lagos, Ogun, Ondo, Osun, Oyo.

Population 22,200,000.

PEOPLES Major peoples Yoruba.

RELIGION Christian 70%; Muslim 20%; Traditional 10%.

N

1 Critical issues:

a) *Christian-Muslim relations* have soured since 1995. The *shari'a* law issue and subsequent violence against Christians in northern states created violent backlashes against Muslim minorities in southern cities. Pray for Christian values to prevail.

b) *Oil wealth* derived from the south-east has been spent elsewhere. Local peoples have suffered severe pollution, degradation of the environment and have received little compensation or investment in return. The situation in Ogoni-land has been particularly bad. Pray for justice and the light of Christ to shine into the situation.

2 The SW was pioneered by Anglicans, Methodists and Southern Baptists and the SS and SE by Presbyterians, Catholics, **QIF** and others. Christians are in the great majority. Pentecostal churches are now the predominant influence and the fastest growing — ranging from small groups meeting in homes to mega-churches. Rural areas lack dedicated pastors because of the relative poverty. Pray for sacrificial concern among Christians for the less reached and less privileged areas. Pray also for revival to make the Christians into true disciples of Jesus.

3 The less reached peoples and areas:

a) **The Muslim suburbs** (*sabongari*) in southern towns and cities where Northerners congregate. Very little prayer concern or evangelism has been directed to these difficult areas.

b) **Muslim groups among Southern peoples.** The Yoruba Muslims are influential and make up about 25% of all Yoruba. Muslim missionary efforts and enticements with money and favours have brought pockets of other southern peoples to Islam, including some among the Igbo. Pray for specific outreach to these Muslims.

c) **The Niger Delta (SS).** Many peoples live in these virtually inaccessible swampy, riverine areas largely bypassed by missions. **CMS** and **CMF** have church planting ministry in the area.

d) **Coastal areas:** Ondo, Ogun, Edo and Delta States where the Christian presence is not deeply rooted.

e) **Other needy areas:** the Benin border area (SW) and Cross River State (SS) where ethnic religions and secret societies are strong (ECWA/**SIM**).

THE CENTRAL ZONE
NORTH CENTRAL AND FEDERAL CAPITAL TERRITORY
GEOGRAPHY Area 266,617 sq.km. 7 states: Abuja, Benue, Niger, Kogi, Kwara, Nasarawa, Plateau.
Population 20,800,000.

PEOPLES **Major peoples** No dominant group, but a medley of over 230 languages, most using Hausa as a trade language. Largest: Edo, Esan, Gbari, Idoma, Igala, Igbirra, Nupe, Tiv.
RELIGION Christian 55%; Muslim 30%; Traditional 15%.

1 **Dramatic church growth** over the past 40 years. The New Life for All movement was highly successful in the 1960s and 1970s. Major denominations are ECWA, Anglican, Baptist, the TEKAN family of churches and, more recently, various Pentecostal and charismatic churches. Pray for the spiritual growth of believers and also for the conversion of the younger generation — evangelical nominalism is a major problem. Pray for revival and a vision for cross-cultural outreach — present growth is not revival.

2 **Muslim missionary activity** has intensified in the region. Considerable efforts are made to win over followers of ethnic religions and backsliding Christians. Pray that these attempts may be frustrated by conversions to Christ. Pray that Christians may overcome historic hatreds and personal fears for courageous witnessing to Muslims in love.

3 **Less-reached peoples.** There are still 60 — 70 peoples in the region who have shown only a small response. This is changing with increased Nigerian research and missionary outreach. There are two main areas of particular need:

a) **Plateau State.** Many peoples have turned to the Lord, but some are more resistant, such as the predominantly traditionalist Mada (105,000), and the nominally Catholic/traditionalist Goemai (278,000) and Ingwe (47,000).

b) **Along the Niger River and Benin border** where there are numerous unreached and partially-reached peoples. Pray for the Muslim Nupe, traditionalist Kambari (75,000), Gbari Yamma (40,000), Dukawa (97,000), Busa (45,000) and Kamuku (30,000). Some of the Dukawa and sections of the Kambari are now turning to Islam. Only a handful of Christian workers are attempting to reach them (UMCA, **CMF**, **CM**, CRWM, LCCN, EMS-ECWA).

THE NORTHERN ZONE
NE
GEOGRAPHY Area 272,395 sq.km. 6 states: Adamawa, Bauchi, Borno, Gombe, Katsina, Taraba, Yobe.
Population 15,000,000.
PEOPLES Major peoples Kanuri, Fulani, Bachama.

RELIGION Muslim 50%; Traditional 30%; Christian 20%.

NW
GEOGRAPHY Area 191,873 sq.km. 6 states: Jigawa, Kaduna, Kano, Kebbi, Sokoto, Zamfara.
Population 23,800,000.
PEOPLES Major peoples Hausa, Fulani.
RELIGIONS Muslim 67%; Traditional 20%; Christian 13%.

1 Critical issues:

a) ***The proclamation of shari'a law*** in many northern states (8 by March 2001) has precipitated Nigeria into a constitutional crisis and directly challenged the federal government. Pray for a wise defusing of this explosive situation.

b) ***Shari'a law*** has also led to restrictions on church buildings, banning of Christian religious education in state schools, communal violence, destruction of many churches and loss of life — especially of Christians. Christians have been automatically degraded to become second-class citizens. Pray that Christians may respond with meekness and love and win the right to testify about Christ.

2 **The gospel has made progress since independence** despite considerable opposition from the Muslim rulers. Many smaller non-Muslim peoples are responding to the gospel as have a small, but increasing number of Muslim-majority peoples. Because persecution of Muslim-background believers has often been severe, an underground network of believers is developing. Pray for the protection and growth of this movement.

3 **There is a great need for Nigerian missionaries** to build on the foundations laid by **SIM**, SUM/**AP** missionaries in the past. The Nigerian Church is burdened for this area. Pray for the sending of missionaries who will be well-prepared and effective in such a hostile, dangerous environment.

4 Unreached peoples:

a) ***The Fulani (Fulbe)*** are a strategic people right across Africa and are also black Africa's largest unreached people cluster. Their origins were in Senegal, but their greatest numbers are in Nigeria where 12 million of the 20 million Fulani live. They form both the strongly Muslim ruling class in Nigeria and also the nominally Muslim nomadic cattle grazers over much of Nigeria and the Sahel. Pray that Nigerian and expatriate Christians may catch a vision for their evangelization. Pray that God may give the right strategies for reaching both groups — the nomadic cattle people being a particular challenge. About 93% of Nigerian Fulani are Muslim. There has been a growing response through ECWA-**SIM** and others, and there may now be 5,000 Christians. In 1983 the **Joint Christian Ministry in West Africa** was formed to specifically coordinate evangelism, literature, radio and training ministries for the Fulani. If the gospel gripped this group, all West Africa would be affected! Many of the urban Fulani speak only Hausa and must be reached through this language.

b) ***The Hausa*** are known as Muslims, but maybe 30%, while claiming to be Muslim, actually follow their traditional religions. Among these are the **Maguzawa**, a people with their own distinctive culture, and among them an exciting turning to Christ is happening. The Isawa, a Hausa Muslim sub-group that gives high honour to Jesus, are responding to the gospel. Pray for large numbers of Hausa to be won for Christ in this day of opportunity.

c) ***The Kanuri of Borno State*** are strongly Muslim, and have been so for 1,000 years. There are only a few believers among the 4 million Kanuri after years of witness by TEKAN-SUM/**AP**, **CMF**, **CM** and other Nigerian missions. There are over 70 Nigerian denominations present in Maiduguri, the state capital, but almost all are from southern Borno and other areas of Nigeria. There is no Kanuri church, and though the NT is now published, the key to the hearts of the Kanuri has yet to be found. Pray that the breakthrough may soon come.

d) ***The Gwoza Hills*** (Adamawa and Borno). The area has become a spiritual battleground, with some peoples turning from paganism — some to Islam and others to Christ. Over 23 peoples live in the area. Pray for those in the heart of this battle — such as the Guduf (36,000), Dughwede (42,000) and Marakam (4,000).

e) ***The mountain regions in the east along the Cameroon border in Taraba and Adamawa States***. This is the home of over 50 peoples, some scarcely affected by the modern world and many unreached. Pray especially for pioneer outreach to the Mumuye (500,000), Chamba (150,000), Bata (50,000) and Koma (37,000).

Norway
Kingdom of Norway

SEPTEMBER 3
EUROPE

GEOGRAPHY
Area 323,878 sq.km. A long, mountainous fjord-indented land. One of the four Scandinavian countries. Also included are the Arctic dependencies of Jan Mayen and Svalbard (Spitzbergen) Islands — 62,000 sq.km.

Population	Ann.Gr.	Density
2000	4,461,033	+0.53%	14 per sq. km.
2010	4,643,522	+0.36%	14 per sq. km.
2025	4,812,063	+0.17%	15 per sq. km.

A further 2,600 on Svalbard (Russians 62%, Norwegians 38%).

Capital Oslo 493,973. **Urbanites** 75%.

PEOPLES
Indigenous 90.7%. Norwegian 4 mill.; Saami (Lapp, 5 groups) 24,000; Roma (Gypsy) 3,500. **Foreign-origin** 9.3%.
European 5.4%. Swedish 46,400; Danish 45,000; British 27,000; former Yugoslav 23,000; German 20,000; Finnish 10,000.
Other 3.9%. North American 23,000; Pakistani 21,000; Vietnamese 15,000; Arab 13,000; Turk 10,000; Iranian 9,000; Tamil 9,000; Polish 8,500; Filipino 8,000; Chinese 6,000; Somali 5,200.

Literacy 96%. **Official language** Norwegian (Bokmal and Nynorsk). **All languages** 13. **Languages with Scriptures** 6Bi 1NT.

ECONOMY
Strong and wealthy industrial state with high earnings from oil, mining, fishing and forest products. HDI 0.927; 2ⁿᵈ/174. **Public debt** 24% of GNP. **Income/person** $36,100 (115% of USA).

POLITICS
Independent from Sweden in 1905 as a parliamentary monarchy. The only Scandinavian country to stay out of membership of the EU.

RELIGION
The Lutheran Church is the official State Church, but there is complete freedom for other denominations and religions.

Religions	Population %	Adherents	Ann.Gr.
Christian	93.71	4,180,434	+0.4%
non-Religious/other	5.01	223,498	+2.3%
Muslim	1.04	46,395	+3.5%
Buddhist	0.16	7,138	+3.2%
Baha'i	0.04	1,784	+0.5%
Jewish	0.04	1,784	+6.5%

Christians	Denom.	Affil.%	,000	Ann.Gr.
Protestant	23	89.50	3,992	+0.3%
Independent	38	1.19	53	+5.6%
Anglican	1	0.03	1	-1.6%
Catholic	1	0.87	39	+2.5%
Orthodox	1	0.05	2	+2.8%
Marginal	6	0.56	25	+4.2%
Unaffiliated		5.81	259	n.a.
Doubly affiliated		*-4.30*	*-192*	*n.a.*

Churches	MegaBloc	Cong.	Members	Affiliates
Lutheran	P	1,305	2,800,000	3,832,700
Independent [25]	I	214	29,000	47,500
Pentecostal Movement	P	250	28,571	44,000
Catholic	C	34	28,889	39,000
Evangelical Luth Free	P	97	7,343	21,000
Congregation of Christ	P	40	8,000	20,000
Jehovah's Witnesses	M	188	10,700	19,474
Mission Covenant	P	80	8,500	17,000
Methodist	P	51	5,794	13,500
Baptist	P	65	5,150	10,500
Salvation Army	P	120	7,800	9,000
Free Evang Assemblies	P	80	5,500	9,000
Seventh-day Adventist	P	72	5,100	6,200
Latter-day Saints (Morm)	M	29	2,922	4,500
Other denoms [32]		104	10,200	19,695
Doubly affiliated			*-142,200*	*-192,000*
Total Christians [70]		2,729	2,821,200	3,921,000

Trans-bloc Groupings	pop. %	,000	Ann.Gr.
Evangelical	9.3	416	+2.4%
Charismatic	4.9	219	+1.4%
Pentecostal	1.7	75	+2.6%

Missionaries from Norway
P,I,A 1,060 in 30 agencies to 82 countries: Japan 87, Ethiopia 52, Bolivia 37, Cameroon 32, Nepal 30.

Missionaries to Norway
P,I,A 59 in 17 agencies from 16 countries.

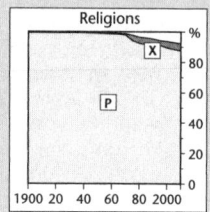

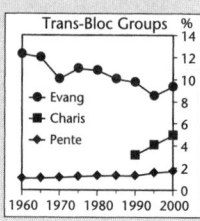

• Answers to Prayer

1 **Norway's large contribution to world evangelization continues.** It is one of the top sending nations in the world.

2 **The 1998 general election** resulted in the new Prime Minister and majority of the Cabinet being committed Christians. Many Christians had prayed and fasted for God to intervene and reverse decades of moral slide. Though that government subsequently fell in 2000, Christians have gained a new faith for change in their country.

• Challenges for Prayer

1 **Norway has a rich spiritual heritage.** The influence of Pietism, prayer and revival movements within the State Church over the past 200 years are still strong. About 90% of Norwegians are church members and 30% would claim a personal relationship to Christ, but only 5-10% are active and regular participants in congregational life.

2 **The Lutheran Church of Norway** is unique in Europe, for although it is the State Church, many of the pastors are theologically evangelical. Out of revival and persecution have sprung up many voluntary organizations within the Church — agencies, prayer houses and fellowships — which have been a source of good in promoting Christian schools, theological education and foreign missions. The State Church has been polarized by the efforts of some bishops to bring in new freedoms for homosexuals within the Church. Pray that this large Church and its leadership may be committed to biblical theology and faith. Pray also for revival once more.

3 **The (non-State) Free Churches are a significant minority** with high levels of member-commitment to congregational life and to missions. Since 1983 the number of new churches planted has increased significantly — both in the older Free Churches, Pentecostals and also many newer independent and charismatic congregations. DAWN conferences have been catalytic for promoting this. In 1998 churches committed themselves to planting 500 new churches by 2003. Pray that the present up-turn in outreach and spiritual life might be strengthened and increased.

4 **Theological training** is largely in the independent and evangelical Lutheran schools of Oslo and Stavanger, ensuring the strength of the evangelical position in the churches, but there are big pressures on them to compromise on the issue of homosexuality. There are also numerous smaller seminaries and Bible schools providing trained workers for Christian ministry in Norway and abroad. Pray that many may be called and equipped.

5 **Young peoples' ministry** has been stimulated by the impact of the new charismatic youth movement *Jesus Revolution* and the older **IFES** movement. Pray for growth and lasting impact in lives and in new and old churches.

6 **More needy areas and peoples** to bring before the throne:

a) *Oslo and the surrounding area* has a lower number of evangelical Christians but this is where over half the population lives. Some of the newer Pentecostal and charismatic churches have seen many born again and set free from alcohol and drugs.

b) *The Saami* live in the far north and are culturally and linguistically very different. Many are still reindeer herders. Most are nominally Lutheran but committed Christians are relatively few.

c) *The Norwegian Humanist Association* is a well-organized body which emulates some Christian traditions. Around 67,000 are involved.

d) *Immigrant minorities* have increased rapidly in the past several decades — major groups needing specialized help being:

   i *Muslims* from North Africa, Turkey, Iran, Pakistan and Somalia. Over 75% are linked to Muslim activities. There are 51 mosques. Most live in the Oslo area.

   ii *Asians* — of special need are the Sri Lankan Tamils, Vietnamese and Chinese.

   iii *Refugees* from Bosnia, Yugoslavia and Albania.

7 **Norway's commitment to world evangelization** has been exemplary. There are an estimated 2,600+ prayer houses (many involved in missions) and 14,000 mission support groups in the country. The Norwegian Mission Council has provided support and fellowship for most of the mission agencies. In 2001 the Norwegian Council for Mission and Evangelism assumed this role. The number of missionaries sent out had declined somewhat, but by 2000 this had stabilized. Saami Christians have started a missionary training college to prepare and send missionaries to reach other Arctic peoples in the fSU. Pray that vision for world evangelization may increase and bear much fruit.

Oman

Sultanate of Oman

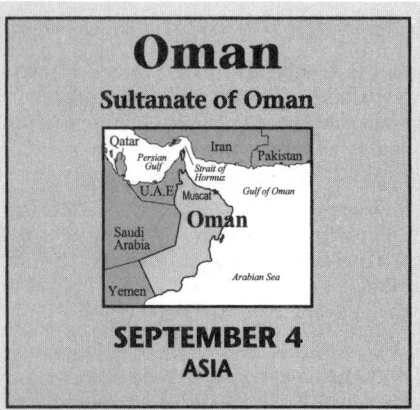

SEPTEMBER 4
ASIA

GEOGRAPHY
Area 300,000 sq.km. A mountainous land on the southeast coast of Arabia and the strategic tip of the Musandam Peninsula that dominates the entrance to the Arabian/Persian Gulf.

Population	Ann.Gr.	Density
2000	2,541,739	+3.35%	8 per sq. km.
2010	3,517,471	+3.28%	12 per sq. km.
2025	5,351,885	+2.55%	18 per sq. km.

Capital Muscat. Muscat urban area pop: 600,000. **Urbanites** 72%.

PEOPLES
About 27% of the population and 65% of the workforce are foreign. Percentages below are estimates.

Arab 67.1%. Mostly Omani, also Gulf State Arab, Saudi Arabian, Egyptian, Jordanian, Palestinian. Also Swahili-speaking groups.
South Asian 21%. Including Indian, Pakistani (Baluch), Bangladeshi, Sri Lankan.
Mahra 5.1%. Two non-Arab indigenous minorities.
Iranian 2.8%.
Other 4%. Filipino, African, European, North American.

Literacy 67.1%. **Official language** Arabic. **All languages** 13. **Languages with Scripture** 2Bi 2por 1w.i.p.

ECONOMY
A latecomer as a Middle Eastern oil producer. Oil revenues finance agricultural and industrial diversification. Oil wealth has been dis-tributed wisely for the improvement of living standards. **Unemployment** 12% among nationals. **HDI** 0.725; 89th/174. **Public debt** 18.6% of GNP. **Income/person** $6,050 (19.2% of USA).

POLITICS
An isolated feudal monarchy until 1970; a benevolent absolute monarchy since then when the Sultan was ousted by his son. No political parties permitted, but there is considerable personal freedom and political stability. One of the most socially progressive nations in the region.

RELIGION
Ibadi Islam is the state religion. Churches and church activities for the expatriate communities are permitted, but proselytising Muslims is forbidden. The Sultan has consistently opposed fanatical Islam since his reign began in 1970.

Religions	Population %	Adherents	Ann.Gr.
Muslim	92.66	2,355,175	+3.1%
Hindu	3.00	76,252	+8.1%
Christian	2.54	64,560	+4.0%
Buddhist	1.20	30,501	+12.1%
non-Religious/other	0.40	10,167	+3.4%
Baha'i	0.20	5,083	+3.4%

Christians	Denom.	Affil.%	,000	Ann.Gr.
Protestant	21	0.24	6	+5.0%
Anglican	1	0.14	4	+1.8%
Catholic	1	1.22	31	+4.4%
Orthodox	3	0.14	4	+5.3%
Unaffiliated		0.80	20	n.a.

Churches	MegaBloc	Cong.	Members	Affiliates
Catholic	C	21	19,872	31,000
Orthodox [3]	O	13	2,632	3,500
Anglican	A	3	1,296	3,500
Mar Thoma	P	7	804	1,850
S. Asian Prot grps [5]	P	8	500	1,000
Pentecostal groups [6]	P	12	600	900
Protestant Ch in Oman	P	4	350	875
Other denoms [8]		22	804	1,370
Total Christians [26]		90	26,858	44,000

Trans-bloc Groupings	pop. %	,000	Ann.Gr.
Evangelical	0.3	9	+5.2%
Charismatic	0.2	4	+5.8%
Pentecostal	0.0	1	+12.4%

• Challenges for Prayer

1 **Rapid social change since 1970 has transformed Oman.** Oil wealth, rising education levels and the opening up to the wider world have broadened the minds of Omanis. The younger generation in particular are outward looking and interested in new ideas. Pray that many may become receptive to spiritual change too. Though slavery was abolished many years ago there still remains a 'spirit of slavery' in attitudes, creating another obstacle to the gospel in the hearts of Omanis.

2 **The unreached.** The entire Muslim majority is a big challenge. There are perhaps a handful of indigenous believers, none professing Christ openly — pray that they may grow and begin to meet with other believers. There are no known believers among the Mahra of Dhofar, the Baluch of the eastern coasts, the rural population or the Swahili speakers.

3 **Almost the entire Christian population is expatriate.** There are four centres where Christians of over 30 denominations or languages meet and where services in many languages are held. There are no restrictions on evangelism among expatriates, and there is a steady stream of conversions among Asians in both the newer and more traditional churches. The churches are very active, conducting home groups, TEE and Alpha courses. Pray for the Christians to live godly lives that clearly display Christ to their unbelieving neighbours, both expatriate and Omani.

4 **Christian professionals and workers.** Pray that they might boldly share the gospel effectively through exemplary lives. The Reformed Church in America has had a good witness here since 1890, when Samuel Zwemer, the famous missionary to Muslims, began his work in Oman. Their hospital, clinics and missionary workers have been incorporated into the government health service. Christians also have a strong presence in the education and business sectors. Pray that by all means the gospel may be proclaimed through a pure lifestyle and fervent witness. Pray that their numbers may be increased through the calling of others. Pray also for perseverance and tenacity.

5 Other means of witness:

a) *The Bible Society* has a good ministry in distributing the Scriptures in many languages to the expatriate communities. They now inhabit a newly built Bible Centre, including a bookshop. Distribution of Christian literature in Arabic requires more innovation — pray for this to happen.

b) *Christian radio broadcasts in Arabic* are clearly heard from **FEBA** radio (17 hours/week) and **TWR** (10 hours/week). There is a sizeable audience, and some have come to the Lord as a result. **SAT-7** is making an impact through satellite television broadcasts.

c) *Almost 2,000 Omanis are studying in the West.* Pray for effective witness to them.

d) *Internet use is accelerating.* Pray that this may prove a good way reach and disciple a new generation of Omanis.

Pakistan
Islamic Republic of Pakistan

SEPTEMBER 5-8
ASIA
Updated February 2004

 GEOGRAPHY
Area 796,095 sq.km, which includes 83,700 sq.km of the third of Kashmir controlled by Pakistan. Arid mountains in the north and west. Sindh desert in southeast. Vast irrigation schemes in the fertile Indus valley.

Population		Ann.Gr.	Density
2000	156,483,155	+2.81%	197 per sq. km.
2010	199,744,986	+2.41%	251 per sq. km.
2025	262,999,723	+1.49%	330 per sq. km.

Several million migrant workers in Persian Gulf and elsewhere.
Capital Islamabad 1.1 mill. Other major cities: Karachi 11.9m (maybe 16m+); Lahore 6.25m; Faisalabad 2.3m; Rawalpindi 2.1m; Multan 1.5m; Gujranwala 1.45m; Hyderabad 1.4m; Peshawar 1,325,000. **Urbanites** 33%.

PEOPLES
Indo-Aryan 78.8%.
Panjabi-related 56.4%. Panjabi 75m; Saraiki 15m; Hindko 5.8m; Dogri 840,000. Northern plains, politically dominant.
Sindhi 11.8%; 18.5m in southeast.
Mohajirs (Urdu-speaking) 7.6%. Indian Muslim immigrants at time of independence. Mainly Karachi and Hyderabad.
Northern peoples 2%. Numerous smaller groups. Largest: Khowari (Chitrali) 370,000; Shina 400,000; Kohistani 260,000; Kashmiri 140,000; Torwali 90,000.
Tribal peoples of Sindh 1%. 14 groups; largest: Koli(4) 288,000; Bagri 276,000; Marwari Bhil (Dhatki, 3) 256,000; Meghwar Bhil 220,000.
Indo-Iranian 18.5%
Pathan 13.1%. Speaking Pushtu (Pashtun), two main groups: Pakhtun (mainly Pakistan) 8.1m; Pashtun (mainly Afghan — many refugees) 12.3m, straddling the Afghan border.
Baluch 4.2%. 6.7m in the west.
Persian 1.2%. Tajik 1,450,000; Dari/Hazara 340,000; Iranian 40,000; Wakhi 25,000; Parsee 7,000.
Dravidian 1.6%. Brahui 2.6m who live among the Baluch.
Tibetan 0.5%. In the far north and Kashmir: Balti-Purik 800,000.
Other 0.6%. Uzbek 640,000; Arab 155,000.
Literacy 38% officially, many estimate it is nearer 25%. **Official language** Urdu, which is becoming widely used by all. **All languages** 69. **Languages with Scriptures** 5Bi 6NT 9por 16w.i.p.

 ECONOMY
Main exports are sports goods, textiles, garments and heroin. Much of the agricultural land and commerce is controlled by a few, very wealthy, families. About 40% of government income is spent on the military and development of nuclear weapons. Other factors besieging the economy include uncontrolled population growth, lack of water and land, the effects of the Afghanistan wars, and a high level of corruption. The infrastructure of the country is being eroded through lack of investment. The extreme Islamist movement is deeply influencing the state such that economic collapse could be hastened. **HDI** 0.508; 138th/174. **Public debt** 36% of GNP. **Income/person** $500 (1.6% of USA).

 POLITICS
Muslim politicians insisted on a separate state resulting in the partition of British-ruled India at independence in 1947. Pakistan's subsequent disastrous history includes four conflicts with India, the loss of Bangladesh, the destabilizing effects of two decades of war in Afghanistan and political upheavals. There has been a series of inept civilian governments and autocratic military dictatorships each as corrupt as its predecessor. Policy has increasingly been dictated by an Islamist extremist minority which has close ties with the Taliban movement in Afghanistan. The civilian government of Nawaz Sharif openly exploited Islamism for political gain, entrenching the Islamist agenda in social, political life and foreign policy (Kashmir, Afghanistan). It was overthrown in a military coup in 1999 led by General Musharraf. The 9/11 crisis forced Musharraf to balance US demands for dealing with the Islamist Taliban and Al Qaeda terror network, and the political power of Islamists who protect them. There is a deep resentment against the 'Christian' West for invading Afghanistan and Iraq.

 RELIGION
An Islamic republic. The government of Nawaz Sharif pursued a policy of Islamization of the legal system, taxation, public life and discrimination against all Muslim and non-Muslim religious minorities despite widespread popular misgivings. *Shari'a* law has been increasingly applied — even to Christians and Hindus — despite its contravention of the constitution. This gives numerous opportunities for the majority Sunni Muslims to oppress and persecute Shi'a Muslims, Ahmaddiya, Hindus and Christians. Despite promises, the military ruler, General Musharraf, has backed away

from regulating the procedure for blasphemy charges in the face of violent threats by Islamists. The level of Islamic terror against Western and Christian targets in Pakistan has greatly increased since 2001. Yet there remains a surprising degree of religious freedom and the government regularly assures minorities of their freedom and opportunities under the law. **Persecution Index** 17th in the world.

Religions	Population %	Adherents	Ann.Gr.
Muslim	96.08	150,349,015	+2.8%
Christian	2.31	3,614,761	+3.7%
Hindu	1.50	2,347,247	+2.8%
Baha'i	0.06	93,890	+6.6%
Other	0.03	46,945	+11.5%
Traditional ethnic	0.02	31,297	-5.2%

The Ahmaddiya are a deviant sect of Islam that is not considered Muslim by the state. However, they are included in the Muslim percentages here.

Christians	Denom.	Affil.%	,000	Ann.Gr.
Protestant	20	1.28	1,997	+5.0%
Independent	29	0.32	502	+4.9%
Catholic	1	0.70	1,100	+2.6%
Marginal	2	0.01	18	+1.4%

Churches		MegaBloc	Cong.	Members	Affiliates
Ch of Pakistan	P	1,856	464,000	1,160,000
Catholic	C	100	540,000	1,100,000
Presbyterian Ch of Pak	P	210	75,000	420,000
Assoc Reformed Presb	P	50	35,971	150,000

Salvation Army	P	650	40,000	57,000
National Methodist	P	214	19,231	55,000
Full Gospel Assemblies	P	60	13,932	45,000
Christian Brethren	P	112	11,000	36,000
Seventh-day Adventist	P	79	5,986	15,000
Ch of God (Cleveland)	P	70	4,519	14,000
Baptist Bible Fellowship	P	50	1,500	2,700
Evang Alliance	P	8	700	2,000
Jehovah's Witnesses	M	10	501	1,700
Other denoms [41]		2,276	368,800	556,000
Total Christians [54]		5,745	1,581,200	3,614,000

Trans-bloc Groupings	pop. %	,000	Ann.Gr.
Evangelical	0.4	616	+6.9%
Charismatic	0.3	447	+5.5%
Pentecostal	0.1	82	+6.0%

Missionaries from Pakistan
P,I,A 174 in 15 agencies; nearly all in Pakistan.

Expatriates to Pakistan
P,I,A 579 in 66 agencies from 23 countries: USA 172, UK 103, Canada 83, Korea 42, Australia 38.

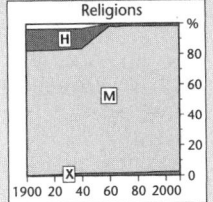

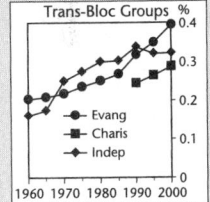

• Challenges for Prayer

1 **After half a century of misrule,** Pakistan needs a government that allows a real democracy to develop and spends its income on economic rather than military development, ends a culture of uncontrolled corruption and gives a fair deal to all its citizens. Pray for the binding of the spirit of lawlessness and violence that has crippled this nation, and for the raising up of leaders of integrity.

2 **Islamism** has severely damaged the economy and social cohesion of society. It has trampled on the constitutional rights of women and minorities, subverted the judicial system and brought fear and violence to this nation. The network of Islamic schools has poisoned the next generation with hatred for India, the West and Christians, and extolled a willingness to die fighting for Islam. Islamist extremists also provided the seed-bed for the Taliban movement that seized control of Afghanistan in 2001, and hosted them and their Al Qaeda allies after their ejection from Afghanistan in 2002. In the 2002 elections Islamists gained control of the key provinces of NWFP and Baluchistan which border on Afghanistan. Pray that this ideology might be so discredited that its influence may be broken.

3 ***Shari'a* law** has only been partially implemented, but its effects for minorities are dire. There is a mandatory death sentence for 'disrespect to the Prophet' and a life sentence for desecration of the Qur'an. The potential for malicious rumours and false charges against Christians has been realized. Innocent people have been sentenced to long terms of imprisonment. Any judge that seeks to dismiss the charges is intimidated and threatened. Pray for the abrogation of discriminatory legislation — specifically, the blasphemy law — implementation of a fair system of justice and a police force that impartially applies the law.

4 **Christian missions have been working in the land since 1833.** Christian standards and institutions have had a deep impact on the country — a fact which Islamists want to ignore. Presbyterians, Anglicans, Methodists and, later, Salvation Army missionaries pioneered the work. There was a great turning to the Lord from among six of the 30 scheduled Hindu castes between 1890 and 1930. This was accompanied by revival in 1904.

Other missions, predominantly evangelical, entered Pakistan around the time of independence. There are few Muslims who would think of becoming Christians. Most despise the humble origins of the church here which first reached the Hindu 'untouchables', or Dalit of the Panjab, or tribal peoples of the Sindh. Pray that these barriers of culture, religion and history may be broken down. Pray for more effective partnering between groups in their ministry.

5 **Christians who come from a Muslim background are particularly under threat** with the implementation of *shari'a* law. There are possibly thousands of secret believers, but only a small, yet increasing number have confessed Christ and identify openly as Christians — for it could lead to their martyrdom. Pray for protection, multiplication, and for good integration into culturally appropriate Christian fellowships. All too often such believers have the double trauma of rejection by their community and then non-acceptance by the Christian community.

6 **The Church has grown** despite many social disadvantages. Many Christians live in deep poverty and on the margins of society but the last two decades have shown a distinct improvement through the emphasis on education with more embarking on professional careers. Pray for:

a) *Revival.* Lack of teaching, poverty and illiteracy have hastened the lowering of spiritual standards, nominalism, corruption and the practice of occultism among those who profess to be Christian. There has been little significant conversion growth for several decades except among the Mawaris and Koli in the Sindh desert.

b) *Spiritual leadership in the churches.* There has been a tragic history of leadership struggles, court cases, factionalism and divisions in some denominations. Pray that they may be models of spirituality and godliness.

c) *Courage to share their faith with non-Christians.* Everything conspires to make Christians fearful, introspective and silent, yet despite the negatives, there is a considerable degree of freedom to openly share the gospel. Only a few have a burden for reaching Muslims. **OM** teams have challenged many believers to become involved in outreach — pray that this challenge may affect whole congregations.

d) *Unity.* **PEACE** is the Pakistan Evangelical Alliance formed to encourage mission and evangelism. Pray that it may also bring about greater unity.

e) *A missionary vision.* Some Pakistani believers have started fellowship groups in a number of Middle Eastern lands, some with an outreach to non-Christians but there is much fragmentation in the work. Pray for those involved in such ministry, which is often at considerable personal risk.

7 **Persecution and intimidation** have increased since 1991 with a large escalation after 2001. Christians are barred from some professions and the most menial tasks are reserved for Christians alone. Their testimony in court is half the value of that of a Muslim. Beatings, imprisonments and murder go unpunished, as well as the destruction of property and churches. Christian girls have been abducted, raped, forced to become Muslim and, even when their abductors are taken to court, charges against them have been dismissed. In 1998 a whole Christian village of 30,000 was razed by a Muslim mob on the basis of a rumour. Extremist Islamic groups have murdered foreign and national believers and specifically targeted Christian institutions and churches. Fear and dismay have gripped the Christian community. Pray that these sufferings may draw Christians close to the Lord and strengthen them in faith and courage so that they may bear a pure testimony to those who oppress them.

8 **Leadership training.** There are 12 Protestant and 6 Catholic theological colleges and Bible schools, the best known being the inter-church/mission theological seminary and United Bible Training Centre at Gujranwala. Pray for this and also the **TEAM**-related Bible Institute in Rawalpindi. Too few prospective leaders respond to the call of God, and lack of finance limits many yet others have emigrated to the West. Pray that a higher proportion of Pakistani Christian leaders may be able to serve in national churches without needing the support of foreign agencies. A number of denominations use TEE courses from the Open Theological Seminary in Lahore which has 900 students in 60 centres. New, innovative ways of training new leaders, despite their poverty and lack of education are needed.

9 **The unreached.** Over 160 ethnic groups and 40 language groups are without viable, indigenous congregations and an effective cross-cultural missions initiative. Few countries present a greater challenge for missions. Pray specifically for the larger groups mentioned in the lists above. Also pray for:

a) **The Baluch and the Brahui.** Some 75% of the world's 4.5m Baluch live in Pakistan. There are only about 10 known Christian Baluch in the world, though there are reports of some groups of believers in Baluchistan. Over 1 million live and work in Karachi. Baluchistan is largely desert and not open for expatriate workers. Pray for the inter-agency fellowship that is reaching out to this strategic and restive people. There are only a few known Christians among the Brahui, who live among them. **FEBA** broadcast every week in both Baluch and Brahui; the *JESUS* film is in both languages.

b) **The Pathan** of the North West Frontier with Afghanistan who are famed for their combativeness and clannishness. They control the lucrative drug and weapons trade in Pakistan and Afghanistan. Over 2m live in Karachi. There are only two known Pushtu-speaking congregations, and a steadily growing number of believers. A handful of expatriate workers are committed to ministry among them (**TEAM**, North West Frontier Fellowship and others operating as NGOs).

c) **The peoples of the far north.** Over 27 smaller people groups live in the mountain valleys of Kashmir, Kohistan, Swat, Dir, Chitral, Gilgit and the Hunza. The Kalash are largely animist, but turning to Islam since 1975. All the other peoples are Muslim — Sunni, Shi'a and Ismaili. Pray especially for the Burusha of the Hunza, the Tibetan-related Balti, the Khowari of Chitral, the Shina, as well as the numerous smaller groups. There is not one known church among any of these peoples and only a handful of Christians. The medical work of the Brethren has been the means of many openings for the gospel.

d) **The Panjabi majority** on the Indus plain. Christians are almost exclusively from the Hindu minorities that were originally at the bottom of the social order. **Christar**, **CBI**, **SIM** and **CMS** have planted growing churches among them. Few Muslims have been reached.

e) **The Sindhi.** **CBI**, FEBI and some other groups are seeking to reach them, but there are less than 50 known believers and no truly Sindhi congregation of believers. **FEBA** broadcasts in both Sindhi and Panjabi. A Sindhi Partnership has been formed linking churches and agencies with ministry to them.

f) **Karachi**, which is a lawless city. It has a huge population (double the official figures). Inter-ethnic conflicts, kidnappings and violent crime are endemic, yet it is a key to reaching the country. There are an estimated 1 million drug addicts in the city, and CMS and others have commenced a ministry to them. The 120,000 Christians in the city are almost entirely Panjabi and Goanese. Pray for outreach and church-planting teams for every ethnic group in the city - especially for the Urdu-speaking Mohajirs, the 500,000 Ismaili Muslims, the 7,000 wealthy Parsees and numerous Afghan refugees.

g) **Afghan refugees.** Their numbers have fallen but there are around 1.8 million in camps and increasingly in the cities. Most are Dari- and Pushtu-speaking, but there are also many Uzbek, Tajik and other groups represented. For years Christian aid organizations provided valuable material and spiritual aid, but the ministry has been greatly reduced due to extremist Muslim pressure, persecution, kidnapping and even murder of Christian workers. Pray for those who continue this thankless task for Jesus' sake, and pray for eternal fruit. There are a number of Afghan believers in Karachi and Islamabad.

h) **The Ahmaddiya.** This is an aggressively missionary-minded Muslim sect but largely driven underground in Pakistan by intense Muslim persecution. Few of the three million Ahmaddiya world-wide have ever come to Christ, but their sufferings are making them more open for the good news.

10 **Young people** are a major subject for prayer since 50% of the population is under 15. Only 25% of children go to school and exploitative child-labour affects 6 to 20 million. Drug abuse is a major problem. Few ministries major on either Christian or non-Christian youth. Good work is being done by **SU**, **CEF**, **CCCI**, Church Foundation Seminars and **YFC**, but the labourers equipped for these specialized ministries are few. Pray for the ministry of **SU** staff workers. Pray for PFES(**IFES**) who have 15 staff workers and an expanding ministry among 1,000 or more Christians in 20 universities and colleges.

11 **Expatriate workers** continue to minister in the country and there are many opportunities for service. Most are serving within existing church structures and institutions, and a minority in pioneer outreach and church planting. Pray for their protection, their fruitfulness and for creative opportunities to reach the numerous unreached peoples and areas. Some major agencies: **Interserve** (83 workers), **TEAM** (58), **CMS** (41), **SIM** (24), **OM** (10).

12 **Pakistanis have emigrated all over the world** in recent years — especially to the Middle East, North America, Britain and Australia. Very few Muslims of Pakistani origin have come to Christ in these lands, and Christians have done relatively little to reach out to them. This is particularly true for the 500,000 living in Britain. Pray that some of these emigrants might gain a burden to return to share the gospel.

13 **Christian help ministries:**

a) *Bible translation.* This is a big challenge with only 7 languages having a NT or Bible. Translation teams are working on 16 languages, and a further three need extensive revision. Research may reveal that up to 55 languages require NT translation teams. Pray for expatriates and nationals to be called and equipped for translation work.

b) *Bible correspondence courses.* These have proved a useful means for teaching Christians and non-Christians and a major factor in Muslims coming to Christ. Pray for the intermission Pakistan Bible Correspondence Institute — with five regional centres and 40 staff with 9-10,000 students actively involved. Also pray for courses run by the Swedish Pentecostals. Pray for the staff and students, and that there may be eternal fruit.

c) *Literature production.* The MIK Christian Publishing House was pioneered by Brethren missionaries. Here a wide range of Christian literature, including **SGM** publications, is translated, edited and published. Pray for vision and faith for writers, staff and readers alike.

d) *Literature distribution.* **The Bible Society** has a vital Bible printing, translating and distribution network. **CLC** has two bookstores and 9 workers. **OM** teams have distributed millions of leaflets and books around the country.

e) *The JESUS film* has been widely shown in 13 languages with possibly 16% of the population having viewed it. A further 12 languages are in preparation. Pray for the protection of projection teams and receptiveness in every community where it is shown.

f) *Christian radio.* The lack of mature, trained Christians in many languages hinders the faster expansion of this vital ministry; yet new broadcasting languages are being added by the 'Radio by 2000' partnership of **TWR, FEBA, HCJB,** etc. **FEBC** broadcast in Urdu, Panjabi, Pushtu, Baluch, Dari, Sindhi, Hindko, Brahui and Siraiki; **TWR** in Urdu. **IBRA** produce the largest number of daily programmes in Pushtu, and broadcast twice weekly in Panjabi and Hindko. For many this is the only way to hear the gospel. Broadcasting hours are limited, however.

g) *Cassettes.* **GRN** have prepared recordings for distribution in 71 languages and dialects.

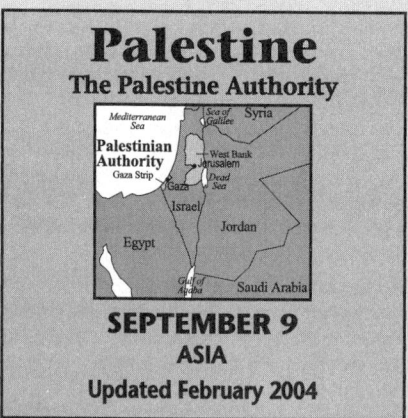

Palestine
The Palestine Authority

SEPTEMBER 9

ASIA

Updated February 2004

Population		Ann.Gr.	Density
2000	3,391,000	+4.0%	543 per sq. km.
2010	4,627,000	+3.2%	683 per sq. km.
2025	7,333,000	+3.1%	1,170 per sq. km.

All Palestinians 5,200,000 — 70% are displaced: 15% internally, 25% in Jordan, 12% in Lebanon, 12% in the Gulf and 6% elsewhere.

Capital Jerusalem is claimed as capital. Other major city: Gaza 1,100,000. **Urbanites** n.a.

 **PEOPLES**
Arabs 92%.
Jews 6%.
Other 2%. Samaritans, Druze, etc.
Literacy 70%. **Official language** Arabic.

ECONOMY
Israel's stranglehold on communications, industry investment, control of water supplies and restrictions on Palestinian labour in Israel have severely reduced living standards and raised unemployment to 40% in 2000 and higher since then. The inefficient, corrupt Palestinian administration intensifies the population's economic plight. Almost complete dependence on foreign aid.

P

GEOGRAPHY
Area 6,243 sq.km comprising two separate parts — the West Bank and the Gaza Strip. The Palestine Authority controls the main towns and scattered enclaves. The rest is made up of 240 Jewish settler enclaves and areas controlled by the Israeli military authorities.

POLITICS

The loss of most of their land in 1948 and the conquest of the remainder by Israel in 1967 dominates the life of Palestinians. International efforts to achieve a compromise settlement of the bitter confrontations between Israelis and Palestinians have all collapsed. The Palestinian Authority was allowed to extend its jurisdiction to most towns and some rural areas, but by 2000 this was only 38% of the West Bank and Gaza. Yasser Arafat is committed to Palestinian statehood. The authoritarian rule of Arafat, passions aroused by the renewal of the intifada conflict in 2000 and the growing power of the Islamist Hamas movement dedicated to the total eradication of Israel, cast doubt on the long-term value of any written agreements. The US-led War on Terror after 9/11 has been a grave setback to all efforts at finding a solution. This war is perceived by many, and successfully portrayed by Islamists, as a war against the Arabs and Islam itself and also a support to the uncompromising stance of Israel. Since 2002 the level of the conflict between the Palestinian factions and the Israeli forces increased with a succession of Palestinian suicide bombings and Israeli military retaliation with the Palestinian Authority humiliated and neutralized.

RELIGION

Arafat's political and economic failures have increased support for the Islamists and brought further pressure on the dwindling and marginalized Christian population. **Persecution index** 61st in the world.

Religions	Population %	Adherents	Ann.Gr.
Muslim	86.56	2,935,590	+4.8%
Jewish	9.50	322,182	+8.7%
Druze/Other	2.00	67,828	+5.0%
Christian	1.94	65,793	-1.7%

Christians	Denom.	Affil.%	,000	Ann.Gr.
Protestant	9	0.11	4	+0.5%
Independents	1	0.01	0	-0.3%
Anglican	1	0.02	1	-7.8%
Catholic	5	1.09	37	-1.6%
Orthodox	8	0.49	17	-4.3%
Marginal	1	0.02	1	+0.8%
Unaffiliated		0.20	7	n.a.

Churches	MegaBloc	Cong.	Members	Affiliates
Catholic [5]	C	28	20,556	37,000
Greek Orthodox	O	11	8,750	14,000
Armenian Apostolic [2]	O	2	400	800
Coptic Orthodox	O	4	444	800
Assemblies of God	P	12	220	780
Episcopal	A	3	333	600
Assoc of Baptist	P	4	240	420
Romanian Orthodox	O	1	231	300
Seventh-day Adventist	P	4	200	250
Chs of Christ/ Chr Ch	P	2	70	170
Church of the Nazarene	P	1	40	130
Chr & Miss Alliance	P	1	43	129
Lutheran	P	2	316	120
Ethiopian Orthodox	O	2	30	39
Other denoms [6]		34	2,400	3,420
Total Christians [25]		111	34,300	59,000

Trans-bloc Groupings	pop.%	,000	Ann.Gr.
Evangelical	0.1	3	-1.3%
Charismatic	0.2	6	-0.9%
Pentecostal	0.0	1	+4.3%

• Challenges for Prayer

1 **Pray for solutions to these major issues:**

a) *An equitable settlement of the land issue*, and the future of the Jewish settlements in the Palestinian areas. Both sides feel they have strong legitimate claims to the land.

b) *A fair apportionment of the water resources* — Israel uses 115% of the land's renewable water and makes little available to the Palestinians.

c) *The future of Jerusalem* — claimed by both sides, each as their exclusive capital.

d) *The unresolved future for the Palestinian exiles* who make up 55% of all Palestinians. Two million live in 61 refugee camps in surrounding lands.

e) *The neutralization of the after-effects of 9/11*, the War on Terror, and distorted Islamist anti-Western propaganda against efforts to find a peaceful solution.

Pray not only for the peace of the land, but that Jewish Israeli and Palestinian Arab may meet the Prince of Peace, through whom alone any meaningful reconciliation can come.

2 **Christian Palestinians** trace their roots back to pre-Islamic times. The antagonisms of the conflict have provoked many to emigrate to Western countries, and their numbers have declined dramatically from around 10% in 1940 to 1.4% in 2000. Many see the Christians as having been the glue for, and a bridge in, society. Pray that Orthodox, Catholic and Protestant Christians alike may stand for and witness to the Truth, and be protected amid rising levels of intimidation by their Muslim neighbours.

3 **Arab Evangelicals** number about 2,000 in 30 churches, of which 20 are on the West Bank. They feel rejected by Jews, Arabs, traditional Christians and even Western Evangelicals and thus isolated. Those from a Muslim background have been specifically targeted by Islamists. The loss of leadership through emigration is serious. Bethlehem Bible College is a key ministry with 80 full- or part-time students. Pray for these brethren to stand steadfast and immovable in the Lord.

4 Areas of special challenge for ministry:

a) *The squalor and hopelessness of Gaza's teeming multitudes*. There is only one evangelical church and few ministering the gospel.

b) *The Islamists* with their bitterness see violence and revenge as their only option.

Panama
Republic of Panama

SEPTEMBER 9
LATIN AMERICA

GEOGRAPHY
Area 77,082 sq.km. The narrowest point of the Central American isthmus, and bisected by the Panama Canal.

Population	Ann.Gr.	Density
2000	2,855,683	+1.65%	37 per sq. km
2010	3,266,131	+1.26%	42 per sq. km
2025	3,779,174	+0.85%	49 per sq. km

Over half the population lives close to the Canal.

Capital Panama City 1,075,000. Other major city: Colón. **Urbanites** 55%.

PEOPLES
Considerable racial intermingling, but a fairly stratified society.

Spanish-speaking 79.2%. Ladino (Mestizo) 1.9 mill.; Afro-Caribbean 270,000; Caucasian 130,000.

Amerindians 8.1%. Speaking 11 languages: Guaymi(3) 123,000; Kuna(2) 48,000; Embera 12,000; Buglere 3,800; Waunana 2,700; Teribe (Naso) 2,200; Bribri 2,000.

Asians 9%. Chinese(3) 150,000; East Indian 96,000; Arab(3) 17,000; Japanese 1,200.

English-speaking 3.7%. West Indian origin 130,000; US citizens, etc.

Literacy 91%. **Official language** Spanish. **All languages** 14. **Languages with Scriptures** 2Bi 4NT 2w.i.p.

ECONOMY
Due to its key geographic location, Panama's economy is service-based, heavily weighted toward banking, commerce and tourism. The hand-over of the canal and military installations by the US has given rise to new construction projects. President Moscoso's administration inherited an economy that is much more structurally sound and liberalized than the one inherited by its predecessor. Since the departure of the American troops and civilian population, the economy has slowed, but there is expectation for better growth in the future. **HDI** 0.791; 49ᵗʰ/174. **Public debt** 61% of GNP. **Income/person** $7,600 (22% of USA).

POLITICS
Republic with a constitutional democracy. With US backing, Panama seceded from Colombia in 1903 and promptly signed a treaty with the US allowing for the construction of a canal and US sovereignty over a strip of land on either side of the structure (the Panama Canal Zone). The US Army Corps of Engineers built the Panama Canal between 1904 and 1914. On 7 September 1977, an agreement was signed for the complete transfer of the Canal from the US to Panama which was accomplished by the end of 1999. With US help, dictator Manuel Noriega was deposed in 1989. The first woman president Mireya Elisa Moscosa Rodriguez, was elected 1 September 1999.

RELIGION
Secular state with religious freedom but also a recognition of Catholicism as the religion of the majority.

Religions	Population %	Adherents	Ann.Gr.
Christian	88.09	2,515,571	+1.6%
Muslim	3.50	99,949	+0.0%
non-Religious/other	3.00	85,670	+3.1%
Buddhist	2.10	59,969	+4.8%
Baha'i	1.27	36,267	+2.0%
Sikh	1.00	28,557	-0.3%
Traditional ethnic	0.50	14,278	-2.0%
Hindu	0.29	8,281	+1.0%
Jewish	0.25	7,000	+3.4%

Christians	Denom.	Affil.%	,000	Ann.Gr.
Protestant	36	15.10	431	+4.4%
Independent	46	4.89	140	+9.8%
Anglican	1	0.82	24	+2.0%
Catholic	1	75.25	2,149	-0.3%
Orthodox	1	0.05	1	+0.0%
Marginal	2	2.14	61	+3.8%
Doubly affiliated		*-10.16*	*-290*	*n.a.*

Churches	MegaBloc	Cong.	Members	Affiliates
Catholic	C	184	1,200,559	2,149,000
Assemblies of God	P	450	60,000	142,000
Foursquare Gospel	P	720	54,102	108,000
Seventh-day Adventist	P	147	35,300	62,000
Ch of God (Cleveland)	P	180	12,275	36,650
Latter-day Saints (Morm)	M	42	17,460	33,000
Jehovah's Witnesses	M	195	9,695	28,000
Episcopal	A	29	7,057	23,500
Baptist Convention	P	96	6,897	16,259
Churches of Christ	P	115	5,000	12,500
New Tribes Mission	P	50	6,000	11,000
Guaymi Ev. Ch Assoc	I	34	5,000	10,000
Methodist [3]	P	8	2,200	7,500
Pentecostal Christian	I	17	3,000	6,000
Ch of the Nazarene	P	37	2,100	3,200
Other denoms [71]		628	52,173	156,924
Doubly affiliated			*-173,653*	*-290,000*
Total Christians [88]		2,932	1,305,165	2,515,500

Trans-bloc Groupings	pop. %	,000	Ann.Gr.
Evangelical	18.2	520	+6.2%
Charismatic	17.5	500	+5.8%
Pentecostal	14.4	412	+6.7%

Missionaries from Panama

P,I,A 85 in 16 agencies to 12 countries: Panama 59, Middle East 8.

Missionaries to Panama

P,I,A 264 in 35 agencies from 15 countries: USA 200, Canada 10.

• Answers to Prayer

1 **Rapid recovery in the 1990s** from the desperate days of Noriega's misrule, corruption and drug-running. There is new hope for the future.

2 **Continued spiritual interest and responsiveness.** Evangelicals have grown from 4.8% of the population (73,000) in 1970 to 18% (520,000) in 2000. This is turning the tide against the moral degeneration of society.

3 **Since 1997 there has been a spreading prayer movement** among pastors seeking God's face for revival. This has led to unprecedented unity and increased cooperation in a wide range of ministries.

• Challenges for Prayer

1 **Panama is a nation of great diversity, and great potential.** Because of its strategic location and the canal, Panama has become a melting pot of many races. The country's motto is 'Panama, Bridge to the World, Heart of the Universe'. Pray that this unique nation may bless the world.

2 **The complete turn-over of the Panama Canal and the US military bases** officially took place on 1 January 2000. Pray for the leaders of the nation as they meet these new challenges and the many problems of the nation. Pray that they might seek God's wisdom in the affairs of the nation and the administration of the canal. Pray for the elimination of corruption on all levels, and for an honest government led by godly principles.

3 **Nominalism** is widespread in the Catholic Church and also in many of the English-speaking churches. The Catholic Church has suffered large losses to Evangelicals, JWs and Mormons, and has not the vitality or the manpower (70% of priests are foreign) to halt the decline. Pray for Holy Spirit-led revival to turn this trend around.

4 **Major challenges facing Evangelicals:**

a) Spiritual unity in vision. Although there has been progress made in recent years, too often local churches are more concerned about larger buildings, denominational loyalty and fame than they are in working together to reach the lost, especially beyond their own local interest.

b) The moral decay which impacts family life. Family conflicts and break-ups are common. Over 72% of births are illegitimate. Domestic violence has become a serious issue because of its increase. Pray that Christians may demonstrate an alternative Biblical model. Sadly commitment is weak due to many factors, — the absence of godly fathers in the family, ungodly authority structures and lack of discipleship in the church. Pray for the Holy Spirit to convict many of sin and lead them to the Saviour.

c) *Effective ministry to young people.* Many are disillusioned by the traditional church and authority structures. While efforts to minister to teenagers and children have increased, dynamic ministries dedicated to their blessing need to emerge. There is an increasing problem with young people forming gangs and taking drugs.

d) *Theological training that encourages holiness of life and spirituality.* There are now 25 or more Bible schools (15 **AoG** with 500 students) and seminaries, as well as four TEE programmes. Pray for more Panamanians to be called into full-time service. Godly, mature leadership is needed to energize the church and combat the widespread activities of cultic groups.

5 **Amerindians** have been responding well to the gospel. The church-planting ministries of numerous denominations and missions have been fruitful. All eight peoples now have viable churches. The Bible translation programme of **SIL** in seven languages is nearing its goal of a NT for each. **SIL** workers have had frustrating delays — pray for the completion of the remaining two NTs. Pray also for the full flowering of a vital and truly indigenous church in each people, and for the work of **NTM** and **GMU** to this end.

6 **Missionary vision.** Panama is slowly developing into a sending nation. The missionary conference, *Latin America 2000,* drew in an attendance of over 5,000. There are already more than 7 Panamanians working full-time in the 10/40 window. **YWAM**, **OM**, **AoG**, SOMEP (Evangelical Panamanian Missionary Society) and CMP (Panamanian Missionary Cooperation) are working to equip, train and mobilize the Church into world missions. Pray for the Church to catch the vision and send out an army of missionaries.

7 **The less-reached sections of the population.** Pray for:

a) *The upper-middle classes.* They remained aloof from the gospel until the mid 1970s. A number of lively charismatic fellowships have been started since then. There are now many professional and business people who follow Christ.

b) *The Chinese.* They are rapidly being assimilated, but many still speak Cantonese and Hakka. Most are nominal Catholics or follow traditional Chinese religions. There are 4 Chinese missionaries ministering to them, and 4 small congregations. The Baptists also have a ministry among them. Some Chinese communities are still unreached.

c) *The South Asians* who are largely Gujarati-speaking. Most are Muslims, some Hindus and others Sikh. There is no known specific outreach to them.

d) *The 7,000 Jews.* There is a Panamanian Christian outreach to them called Messianic Association 'Remnant of Israel'.

8 **University students** are a key challenge. There are 75,000 students in 14 tertiary institutions. The Campus ministry *Minamundo* or CAC (**LAM**, **IFES**) now has 200 students in 16 groups in universities and aims to expand ministry to high schools.

9 **Foreign missionaries.** Over 90% of the mission force is North American. The Panama-Colombia border continues to be a problem area of violence. Both Colombian guerrillas and the drug cartels have increased their activities, putting the lives of the indigenous peoples in danger. Due to the danger and violence, the Darien province has virtually closed to missionary activity. The **NTM** missionaries that were kidnapped near the border in 1993 have yet to be released. The largest agencies: **NTM** (96 workers), **IMB-SBC** (27), **CCCI** (22), **AoG** (16), Christian Churches/Churches of Christ (16), **YWAM** (15), **GMU** (12), Lutheran Church, Missouri Synod (12), **CAMI** (7), **WBT** (7).

10 Christian help ministries for prayer:

a) *Literature.* This is distributed by the Bible Society and a dozen bookstores (one of **CLC**). Poverty, illiteracy and low interest in reading limit the impact. **EHC** has launched a ministry of inspiring churches into widespread Christian literature outreach.

b) *The JESUS film* has been widely shown in 5 main languages. Guaymi and Kuna versions are in preparation.

c) *Radio and television.* There is one Christian TV channel (Channel 24) and 13 radio stations: HOXO, affiliated with **HCJB** Ecuador; one with **TWR** Bonaire; 3 with **AoG**; one sponsored by **LAM**, and others.

Papua New Guinea

Independent State of Papua New Guinea

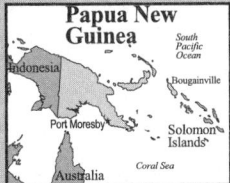

Papua New Guinea
South Pacific Ocean
Indonesia
Bougainville
Port Moresby
Solomon Islands
Australia
Coral Sea

SEPTEMBER 10-11
PACIFIC
Updated February 2004

GEOGRAPHY
Area 462,840 sq.km. Eastern half of New Guinea, the second largest island in the world, plus Bougainville in the Solomon Islands, also many smaller islands in the north and east which make up the nation of Papua New Guinea. The other half of the island (lying just north of Australia) is West Papua (Irian Jaya), part of Indonesia. PNG is a land of high mountains, dense forests, lowland swamps, coral islands, torrential rainfall, many rivers, and beautiful flora and fauna including the bird of paradise — the national emblem.

Population	Ann.Gr.	Density
2000	4,806,640	+2.25%	10 per sq. km.
2010	5,917,105	+2.04%	13 per sq. km.
2025	7,459,895	+1.26%	16 per sq. km.

Capital Port Moresby 380,000. **Urbanites** 17%.

PEOPLES
About 1,000 peoples speaking 816 languages. Ethnically and linguistically the world's most complex nation, whose cultures have been moulded by geography, successive immigrations, sorcery, fear and warfare, and more recently by Christianity, colonialism, World War II and modernization.
Melanesian 99%. Numerous tribal groups, over half of which are less than 1,000 in population. Largest: Enga 235,000; Chimbu(2) 185,000; Melpa 104,000; Huli 91,000; Kamano 90,000; Tolai 89,000; Wahgi 80,000; Sinasina 76,000; Boikin 53,000; Kapau 54,000.
Other 1%. Polynesian, Caucasian, West Papuan refugees 7,000.

Literacy 43%. **Official language** English. National languages Tok Pisin (Melanesian — English Creole) used in centre and north, and increasingly in the south-west, and Motu in south. **All languages** 816. **Languages with Scriptures** 8Bi 150NT 110por 170w.i.p.

ECONOMY
Predominantly subsistence agricultural/fishing economy, supplemented by cash crops (tea, coffee and copra), an expanding mining industry and increasing local manufacture. Many problems (land compensation claims, rugged terrain, earthquakes, aggressive multinational corporations, droughts and war) complicate the wise exploitation and management of the land's rich mineral, timber, fish, oil and gas resources. Recession and endemic corruption in the late 1990s led to reduced foreign investment and lower income from produce. High urban unemployment with considerable anarchy in many areas. **HDI** 0.570; 129th/174. **Public debt** 31% of GNP. **Income/person** $930 (3% of USA).

POLITICS
The north and east parts (called German New Guinea) were under German control until World War I and the south (called British New Guinea) was under British rule until 1901. The latter then came under Australian rule and was called Papua. Australia continued to administer Papua and New Guinea until independence in 1975 when Papua New Guinea became a state within the British Commonwealth. The nation is governed by a democratic parliamentary system and administered on a decentralized basis by 20 provincial governments. There was a costly uprising on Bougainville Island 1988-2000. Economic collapse in 2002 led to new parliamentary elections and a change of government.

RELIGION
Freedom of religion. Almost the entire population has links to a Christian denomination. The old ethnic religions remain a powerful underlying influence.

Religions	Population %	Adherents	Ann.Gr.
Christian	97.28	4,675,899	+2.3%
Traditional ethnic	1.80	86,520	+1.1%
Baha'i	0.70	33,646	+2.2%
non-Religious/other	0.10	4,807	-11.0%
Buddhist	0.07	3,365	-0.4%
Chinese	0.05	2,403	-4.4%

Christians	Denom.	Affil.%	,000	Ann.Gr.
Protestant	56	58.60	2,817	+3.8%
Independent	33	5.60	269	+3.3%
Anglican	1	5.62	270	+2.4%
Catholic	1	28.09	1,350	+0.2%
Marginal	47	2.57	124	+2.0%
Unaffiliated		6.79	326	n.a.
Doubly affiliated		*-9.99*	*-480*	*n.a.*

Churches	MegaBloc	Cong.	Members	Affiliates
Catholic	C	1,815	798,817	1,350,000
United	P	3,500	600,000	1,000,000
Evang Luth Ch of PNG	P	3,000	532,468	820,000
Seventh-day Adventist	P	737	184,428	290,000
Anglican	A	900	108,000	270,000
Foursquare Gospel	P	900	65,000	100,000

P

Gutnius Lutheran	P	560	51,667	93,000
Bethel Pentecostal Tab	I	273	41,000	82,000
Baptist Union (W Highl.)	P	400	35,000	75,000
United Pentecostal	P	317	68,571	72,000
Chr Revival Crusade	I	269	35,000	60,000
Evangelical Ch of PNG	P	210	24,000	56,000
Apostolic	P	290	27,000	38,000
Christian Brethren	P	360	22,000	38,000
Indigenous (NTM)	P	250	19,000	34,000
Assemblies of God	P	137	7,000	26,000
Jehovah's Witnesses	M	52	3,434	15,000
Ch of the Nazarene	P	260	10,000	14,000
Apostolic Christian	P	60	3,000	12,000
Evang Ch of Manus	P	16	2,200	5,500
Latter-day Saints (Morm)	M	28	2,695	4,500
Other denoms [118]		2,147	186,000	374,000
Doubly affiliated			*-267,000*	*-480,000*
Total Christians [139]		16,524	2,559,600	4,349,000

Trans-bloc Groupings pop. %	,000	Ann.Gr.
Evangelical	21.1	1,014	+3.3%
Charismatic	12.4	598	+3.5%
Pentecostal	9.2	442	+3.5%

Missionaries from Papua New Guinea

P,I,A 339 in 17 agencies to 8 countries: PNG 310, Australia 11.

Missionaries to Papua New Guinea

P,I,A 2,221 in 88 agencies from 35 countries: USA 1,228; Australia 260; New Zealand 147; Canada 115; UK 89; Finland 70; Germany 68; Korea 49; Philippines 36.

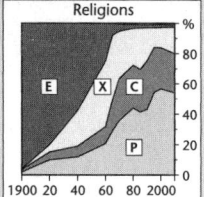

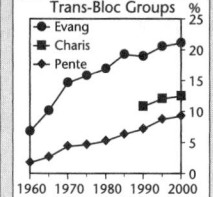

• Answers to Prayer

A national prayer movement for revival was born in 1997 in response to the serious problems of the young nation. Results:

1 **The peace accord in Bougainville in 2000.** An interim government has been set up, disarmament commenced and plans initiated for an ultimate referendum on independence.

2 **The 1998 elections** resulted in many active Christians entering Parliament.

• Challenges for Prayer

1 **The government faces a daunting task** of uniting such a variety of peoples into a single nation. Tribal fighting and revenge killings still occur, especially in the Highlands. The messy war in Bougainville was badly handled. Corruption in government seriously impaired several administrations in the 1990s and led to lawlessness and the economic collapse of 2002. Social dislocation caused by the drift of people to the cities, and unemployment for the educated youth, have led to social problems, including crime and violence. Pray that the leaders of this land may seek righteousness and the guidance of God in the affairs of their nation.

2 **Economic development is a major challenge.** Mining and logging companies have had overly much influence in the capital and the media; serious ecological damage and social unrest have been the result. Over 80% of the population is still isolated and living at subsistence level. Availability and quality of health care is limited. There was much loss of life and property in the 1990s through volcanic eruptions, *El Niño* drought and a tsunami (North Coast). Both local and national governments need wisdom in balancing development with long-term environmental and social stability.

3 **Over the past 120 years the gospel has spread throughout PNG,** first along the coast and then inland, and finally in the past 40 years into the Highlands. Nearly all tribes have been reached. In some there have been mass movements to Christianity. Today over 96% claim to be Christian. Praise God for the presence of an alive, vibrant church today. But ready acceptance of the gospel has resulted in a superficial Christianity of the majority without a radical transformation of basic values and beliefs. True discipling is an urgent need. In some areas there is disillusionment and a turning back to traditional customs, drunkenness, gambling or cargo cults. Pray for revival and deep repentance which will result in true disciples and transformed cultures. Revivals have occurred in many areas (e.g. East and West Sepik, New Britain, North Solomons and Highlands areas) but follow-up discipling in these situations is greatly needed. There is also vigorous growth in Pentecostal and charismatic fellowships in many areas, especially the towns.

4 **The PNG Church faces challenging problems:**

a) *Effective discipling.* Nominalism, syncretism, fear of witchcraft and evil spirits are wide-spread. Notable is the expansion over the 1990s of NTM church-planting to many tribes hitherto superficially evangelized.

b) *Strong tribal ties, ancient animosities and diversity of languages.* These are barriers that hinder fellowship and flow of spiritual blessing.

c) *Lack of Scriptures and illiteracy in many languages.* The results are many — nominalism, slow growth, spiritual apathy and vulnerability to error.

d) *Denominational rivalry.* Rural communities and churches are harmed. Church discipline is hindered, denomination hopping increased and local leadership undermined. There is good cooperation between main denominations at national level. The Melanesian Council of Churches was the first ecumenical body in the world to include the Roman Catholic Church along with Protestants. The main body linking Evangelicals is the Evangelical Alliance.

5 **Leadership training is a priority.** Many small Bible schools are run by churches and missions. There are a number of denominational theological colleges. The well-known interdenominational Christian Leaders' Training College (CLTC), with 120 full-time students and an international faculty, trains leaders for churches from all over PNG and the Solomon Islands. Churches are recognizing the value of TEE as a tool for training the many marginally-literate rural pastors and church workers who have received minimal grounding in the faith. Pray for:

a) *Men and women called of God* to full-time service as pastors, missionaries, etc. The lure of highly paid secular jobs is strong for those with good education.

b) *Bible teachers* who can impart a love of God's Word to students and the desire to apply its truths to their own cultures.

c) *The provision of mature, articulate Christian leaders* who will significantly influence the spiritual life of the nation, and establish the church on biblical foundations.

d) *Specialized urban training programmes* to prepare leaders for urban ministries (CLTC Centres in Port Moresby and Law; Baptist Urban Pastoral Training Centre [BUPTC] in Port Moresby).

e) *The excellent TEE programme* in English run by CLTC to serve PNG and the Pacific, and development of more TEE programmes in Tok Pisin in the country.

6 **There is increasing missionary vision in the country.** The indigenous PNG Missionary Association is being used of God to stimulate mission awareness and prepare and send missionaries overseas. It also coordinates a national prayer movement called Global Prayer Warriors. CLTC runs an annual missions conference called Launch Out. **OM** have a base in PNG and many nationals have already served on the MV *Doulos*. Many denominations have sent or are planning to send overseas missionaries. Many are working cross-culturally within the country. The **NTM** Missionary Training Centre provides a two-year course for prospective PNG missionaries.

7 **Missionaries** both from the South Pacific and the West suffered disease and martyr-dom at the hands of cannibals during the early days of church-planting just over 100 years ago. The large investment of missionary personnel in evangelism, church-planting, health, education and development has significantly changed the land and its people. Many missionaries continue to work in these areas as well as translation, teaching, discipling, leadership training and support work. The larger mission agencies are: **SIL** (686 workers), **NTM** (535), Pentecostal agencies (109), Lutheran agencies (94), **CoN** (64), Baptist agencies (62), Evangelical Bible Mission (55), Pioneers (44), SdA (37), Christian Brethren (34), Liebenzell (32). Pray for:

a) *Good relationships* between expatriate and national workers.

b) *A greater emphasis on relating the gospel* to local cultures in order to see a more indigenous expression of Christianity.

c) *Those committed to strengthening* the church through various ministries.

d) *Those involved in translation* and literacy programmes. A great deal of work is still to be done in these areas.

e) *Those involved in health*, education and community development programmes.

8 **Aircraft of missionary organizations are an essential lifeline** for the work of churches and missions. Many areas are only accessible by air. Flying conditions are some of the worst in the world, with thick forests, high mountains, dense clouds and treacherous weather conditions. Pray for the flying staff of **MAF**-Australia (with 54 workers, 20 planes and a helicopter), of **SIL** (4 planes and 2 helicopters), **NTM** (3 planes and 1 helicopter), and all who service these planes and travel in them. Several aircraft have crashed with loss of life, and **MAF** has suffered one high-jacking! **Helimission** have a ministry with helicopters.

9 **Ministry to young people is one of the most crucial for PNG today.** They are vulnerable in a rapidly changing society, there are few job openings and many urban youth have joined criminal gangs. Yet there are encouragements:
a) **SU** has a good ministry among students in high schools and is seeking to expand through regional workers.
b) **TSCF(IFES)** has 30 groups among the 15,000 tertiary students.
c) **YWAM** has valuable input in youth training and mobilization for evangelism and missions. Camps (especially at Easter) are very significant in youth ministry.
Pray for the many 'graduates' of these ministries, that they may impact their nation for good.

10 **Peoples and areas of special spiritual need.** Few PNG peoples are unevangelized and unoccupied by missions, but there are several groups and areas of special need:
a) *Unreached people groups*. Some tribes are only now being discovered and opened up in isolated parts of the country, e.g. the Star Mountains on the West Papua border, and some Fly and Sepik River valleys and swamps.
b) *Cargo cult followers*. Of the people groups who are affect by cargo cults, some within the groups have turned back to biblical Christianity. Pray for those pockets where cargo cults are still firmly entrenched (e.g. some parts of Manus Island where Liebenzell Mission works, Bougainville and Madang Province).
c) *Squatter settlements*. Increasing numbers of people live in squatter settlements outside towns and cities. They are places of poverty and social unrest.
d) *Prisoners*. They tend to be very open to Christian witness. **Prison Fellowship International** has a well-established ministry which is bringing hope and blessing to many.
e) *Chinese*. The Chinese merchant community are often third- or fourth-generation in PNG, and are still resistant to the gospel.

11 **Translation and literacy** programmes and the provision of appropriate Christian literature are fundamental for acculturalizing the gospel. Pray for this demanding ministry and those committed to its accomplishment. **SIL/WBT**, the **Bible Society** and the indigenous **Bible Translators' Association** are involved in over 170 translation projects and about 160 languages now have a Bible or NT. Translation teams are definitely needed for 135 languages and possibly for a further 466.

12 Christian help ministries for prayer:
a) *Local radio* is a vital link used by churches and Christian workers to exchange news and spread the gospel, and *Kristen Radio* has a modern studio for national and regional Christian broadcasting on the national radio network. EM-TV is now operating throughout the country; Christians have input through the Churches' Council for Media Coordination. **TWR** broadcasts 7hrs/wk in English to PNG.
b) *Christian Radio Missionary Fellowship* (CRMF) serves the churches by providing two-way radio contact for those in isolated areas.
c) *Christian cassettes* are an effective tool for evangelism and teaching, especially for the large numbers of rural illiterates, many of whom speak only their tribal languages. Language Recordings (**GRN**) has produced materials in 651 languages and dialects, and flip charts are effectively used in conjunction with them.
d) *Christian literature*. There are 5 main publishing groups: Christian Books Melanesia (Brethren), Evangelical Brotherhood Church (Swiss Missions), *Kristen Press* (Lutheran), the interdenominational Melanesian Institute and **The Bible Society**. Much excellent material is being produced, and there are Christian bookstores in most towns — including **CLC** with 5 staff, one store and a mail order ministry.
e) *Films and videos*. Several Christian film libraries have been operated over the past years,

and many churches use films regularly. Video is increasingly popular, and **Kristen Komunikaisen** in Lae are planning involvement in this ministry. The *JESUS* film is extensively used in English and Tok Pisin.

BOUGAINVILLE

AREA 9,300 sq.km. The most northerly of the Solomon Islands but arbitrarily linked in colonial times to PNG.

POPULATION 160,000. About 20,000 lost their lives in the fighting during the 1990s. A further 40,000 became refugees.

PEOPLES Approximately 25 Melanesian and Polynesian peoples.

ECONOMY A large copper mine opened in 1972 provided 35% of the national income to the PNG central government but severely damaged the ecology of the islands. The mine was closed in 1989.

POLITICS Local opposition to incorporation in PNG at independence in 1975 led to a war for Bougainville's independence in 1988. After intense fighting, a cease-fire was finalized in 1998. In 2000 negotiations about the future status of Bougainville commenced.

RELIGION Almost entirely Christian. Roman Catholics 80%, United Church 10%, also SdA. Many are nominal with much syncretism.

• Challenges for Prayer

1 **Peace and reconciliation** after 25 years of bitterness and hatred between the PNG government and the Islanders.

2 **The economic and social dislocation** has been immense, though by 2000 nearly all refugees had returned to their homes. Pray that Bougainville might experience recovery at every level — especially the spiritual.

Paraguay
Republic of Paraguay

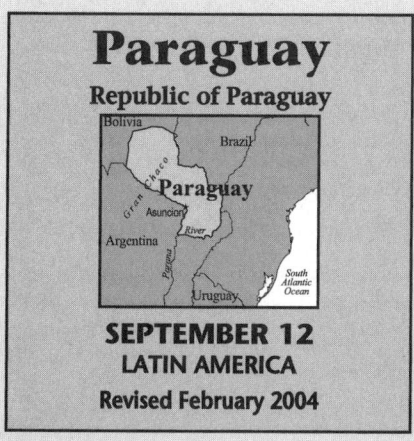

SEPTEMBER 12
LATIN AMERICA
Revised February 2004

Capital Asuncion 1,100,000. Urbanites 55%.

PEOPLES
One of the most homogenous populations of South America.

Spanish/Guaraní-speaking 94%. Of mixed Spanish and Guaraní descent. About 8% speak only Guaraní.

Amerindian peoples 1.4%. Mainly in the sparsely populated Chaco. 18 groups, largest: Chulupé/ Nivacleño 13,000; Lengua 10,000; Pai Tavytera 10,000.

Immigrant minorities 4.6%. German 90,000; Brazilian 50,000; Italian 33,000; Ukrainian 33,000; Japanese 15,000; Chinese 10,000; Korean 10,000; Lebanese 10,000.

Literacy Officially 90%, but much of it minimal. **Official languages** Spanish, Guaraní. The latter is understood by 90% of the population. **All languages** 21. **Languages with Scripture** 5Bi 6NT 5por 6w.i.p.

GEOGRAPHY
Area 406,752 sq.km. Landlocked nation between Brazil, Argentina and Bolivia. The Paraguay River divides the more fertile and developed east from the forests, marshes and ranches of the sparsely populated Gran Chaco.

Population		Ann.Gr.	Density
2000	5,496,453	+2.63%	14 per sq. km
2010	6,980,320	+2.35%	17 per sq. km
2025	9,355,207	+1.77%	23 per sq. km
Estimated national population for 2001 is 6.3 million.			

ECONOMY
Few natural resources besides agriculture and hydro-electric power. Landlocked status and lack of mineral resources hinders development. Large-scale hydro-electric projects are boosting the economy, but the cycle of poverty continues and was worsened by neighbouring Argentina's economic collapse after 2000. **HDI** 0.730; 84th/174. **Unemployment** 9.8%. **Public debt** 14.6% of GNP. **Income/person** $2,000 (6.3% of USA).

P

POLITICS

Independent from Spain in 1811. Devastating wars with surrounding nations in 1864-70 and 1932-35. Corrupt military dictatorship 1954-89. Since then economic and democratic reforms have slowly reintegrated Paraguay into the world's political and trade network.

RELIGION

Complete separation of Church and State and equality before the law of all religious bodies was declared in 1992, but the Catholic Church still wields significant political and social power.

Religions	Population %	Adherents	Ann.Gr.
Christian	97.95	5,383,776	+2.6%
non-Religious	1.00	54,965	+6.0%
Traditional ethnic	0.62	34,078	+2.0%
Buddhist/Chinese	0.23	12,642	+1.3%
Baha'i	0.10	5,496	+4.8%
Jewish	0.05	2,748	-1.1%
Muslim	0.05	2,748	+7.3%

Christians	Denom.	Affil.%	,000	Ann.Gr.
Protestant	67	4.69	258	+3.1%
Independent	26	3.65	201	+8.0%
Anglican	1	0.29	16	+2.7%
Catholic	1	84.98	4,671	+1.8%
Orthodox	3	0.17	10	+1.9%
Marginal	2	0.94	50	+13.5%
Unaffiliated		3.23	177	n.a.

Churches	MegaBloc	Cong.	Members	Affiliates
Catholic	C	350	2,330,000	4,671,000
El Pueblo de Dios	I	200	42,857	150,000
Mennonite groups [12]	P	135	25,000	62,000
Latter-day Saints (Morm)	M	141	21,164	40,000
Assemblies of God	P	70	12,454	37,000
Baptist Convention	P	106	7,981	19,000
Other Pentecostal [13]	P	140	7,000	17,500
Anglican	A	36	6,400	16,000
Congregation of P	I	197	9,850	15,000
Seventh-day Adventist	P	39	7,788	14,000
Ch of God (Cleveland)	P	146	7,618	14,000
Ev Miss Assemb of God	P	35	6,250	13,000
Grace and Glory	P	61	5,500	11,000
Jehovah's Witnesses	M	86	6,883	10,000
Ev Ch of the River Plate (Lut)	P	52	4,192	7,000
Evangelical Lutheran	P	75	5,000	6,200
Assoc of United Christians	P	13	2,000	6,000
Christian Brethren	P	72	2,041	6,000
Slavic Baptist	P	33	3,000	4,500
Other denoms [60]		541	38,000	85,500
Total Christians [102]		2,528	2,551,000	5,205,000

Trans-bloc Groupings	pop. %	,000	Ann.Gr.
Evangelical	4.8	266	+3.8%
Charismatic	4.5	247	+3.7%
Pentecostal	2.4	133	+4.6%

Missionaries from Paraguay

P,I,A 106 in 14 agencies to 13 countries: Chile 46, Paraguay 18, Ecuador 17.

Missionaries to Paraguay

P,I,A 606 in 83 agencies from 25 countries: USA 249, Brazil 85, Korea 78, Germany 46, Canada 32.

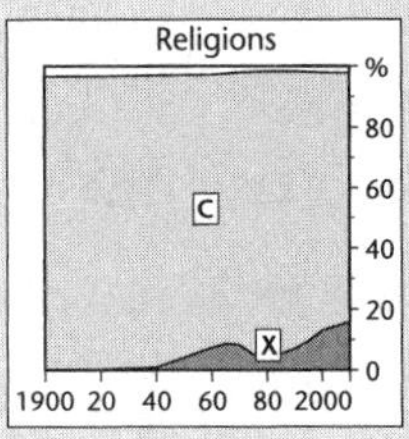

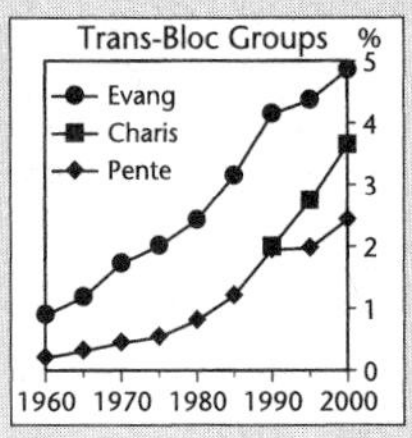

• Challenges for Prayer

1 **Paraguay still suffers the effects of two centuries of tyranny, war and government incompetence.** Occasional internal political strife and a lack of strong moral leadership hinder the country's progress. Paraguay is one of the most corrupt countries in Latin America. Pray that godly men would emerge from this Christianized nation to lead with wisdom and uprightness.

2 **The Roman Catholic Church** has long dominated the spiritual and political life of Paraguay. Although it speaks out against immorality and corruption, there is also much superstitious traditionalism, strong devotion to Mary, and occult-related bondage to many pre-Christian deities and customs. These practices keep millions from liberty in the Lord Jesus and must be broken by prayer. Only a minority of committed Christians are from the Spanish-Guaraní Mestizo majority. Paraguay has never had a true spiritual awakening.

3 **Most of Paraguay's Protestants** are German-speaking Mennonites and Lutherans, Ukrainian Baptists and Pentecostals and Korean Presbyterians. These immigrant communities are often culturally isolated from the mainstream of national life, and therefore lack outward vision. Nominalism is also a common problem — pray that these communities might experience a renewal of spiritual vigour and the birth of a vision for a transformed Paraguay.

4 **Evangelical church growth continued through the 1990s**, with the majority of growth coming through Mennonite, Pentecostal and Independent churches. Most of these groups have entered Paraguay from Brazil and Argentina, and have retained their characteristic zeal and initiative. Unfortunately, there is need for Biblical input on such issues as fellowship with other Christian groups, attitudes towards wealth, and leadership models. Pray that all of these groups might submit their beliefs and practices to Scripture.

5 **Evangelical Christian leaders** increasingly work together to promote large evangelistic crusades and the evangelization of the country. The great needs in prayer are:

a) *Leadership development — an essential ministry.* Bible Colleges for most of the Protestant denominations and an Evangelical University provide improved training for the growing number of theological students.

b) *A lifestyle set by leaders as an example* to their flocks marked by holy living, prayer, right use of Scripture, and bold evangelism.

c) *Unity in the church.* An association of pastors is working to promote united strategies for the country's evangelization and for the care of pastors of small or isolated churches.

d) *The impartation of a missionary vision* to the Church — the formation of a National Committee for Missions (CONAMI) was a solid first step. Pray that Paraguayans may see themselves as responsible for, and capable of, the evangelization of their country.

6 **Work among the Indian minority peoples has been fruitful.** Many have become Christians through the work of **SAMS** among the Chorote, Sanapana, Toba, Angaite and Lengua; **NTM** with the Achés, Angaité, Ayoré, Avá, Chamacoco, Lengua, Manjui; the **Mennonites** among the Lengua and Chulupé; and **Light to the Indians** among the Lengua, Chulupé and Guaraní in the southeast. Various development projects, and the provision of education, the Scriptures and biblical training help many new churches to become viable and self-sufficient. Pray for the young churches as they adapt to the national culture.

7 **Missionary help is needed,** and there is an open door for those who can serve the Paraguayan brethren and strengthen national leadership. The main ministries needing personnel are church planting, leadership training and Bible translation. Rural areas are in need of and responsive to aid and development work, and there are over 400 villages in the interior without any evangelical witness. The largest agencies are **NTM** (75 workers), **AoG** (56), **IMB-SBC** (41), **Light to the Indians** (40), **SAMS** (26) and **SIM** (25).

8 Christian help ministries.

a) *The Bible Society.* Extensive Scripture distribution has had great impact, but this has been blunted by limited functional literacy, particularly among the Amerindians.

b) *Bible translation.* The Guaraní Bible was completed in 1996, as well as two other indigenous New Testaments. Four more translations are in progress. Pray for the safe completion of these projects and accompanying literacy programmes.

c) *GRN has made recordings* in 15 languages or dialects. Pray for their wise use.

d) *Radio is an increasingly influential and fruitful ministry.* HCJB broadcasts 10 hours/week in German and nearly 10 hours/day in Spanish. **TWR**'s national partner translates programmes in Guaraní for airing on local radio. **IBRA** also broadcasts through nine local radio stations.

e) *The JESUS film* is used in German, Guaraní, Plautdietsch and Spanish.

Peru

Republic of Peru

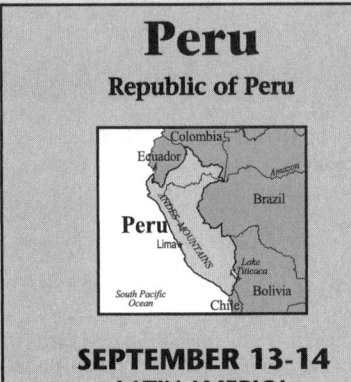

SEPTEMBER 13-14
LATIN AMERICA

 GEOGRAPHY
Area 1,285,216 sq.km. Three main zones — dry coastal plain in the west where most of the cities and industry are located, high Andean plateau which is more agricultural, and Amazon jungles in the east.

Population		Ann.Gr.	Density
2000	25,661,669	+1.75%	20 per sq. km
2010	29,885,322	+1.45%	23 per sq. km
2025	35,518,199	+1.02%	28 per sq. km

Capital Lima 7,350,000. Other major cities: Arequipa 656,000; Trujillo 530,000; Iquitos 275,000. **Urbanites** 71%.

PEOPLES
The mixing of ethnicity, cultures and languages makes a clear breakdown difficult.
Amerindian 54.7%.
  Highland peoples 51.7%. Quechua(33) 13.1m; Aymara 1.2m.
  Lowland peoples 3%. 300,000 speaking over 50 languages.
Mestizo 32%. Mixed race.
White 12%. Mainly of Spanish origin.
Other 1.3%. Japanese 120,000; Chinese 115,000.

Literacy 87%. **Official languages** Spanish, Quechua. **All languages** 92. Spanish-speakers 80.3%. Most Amerindians are Spanish-speaking or bilingual, 10% of Quechua, 30% of Aymara and 40% of lowlanders use their mother tongue in the home. **Languages with Scripture** 25NT 27por 21w.i.p.

ECONOMY
Climatic changes during the 1990s and the devastation of guerrilla insurgency led to the collapse of the fishing and mining industries and reduced the majority of the population to desperate poverty with raging hyper-inflation. Fujimori's government brought about a dramatic turnaround between 1992 and 1997 with inflation tamed and an economic recovery. The Asian recession and *El Niño* weather upheavals were then major setbacks. Over 40% of the population live in extreme poverty. **HDI** 0.739; 80th/174. **Public debt** 32% of GNP. **Income/person** $2,600 (8% of USA).

POLITICS
Fully independent from Spain in 1824. A long history of dictatorships and repressive military rule. Democratic government between 1980 and 1991 was not able to reform the inequalities in society nor deal with the corrupt judiciary and police. Two violent, extremist and Maoist terrorist movements brought the country to its knees in 15 years of guerrilla warfare. Over 30,000 perished through the terrorists or the equally cruel military reactions. Needed repairs to the infrastructure of the country is estimated to ultimately cost $US25 billion. President Fujimori was elected in 1990 and 1995. He won the war against terrorism but became increasingly autocratic. A dubiously managed election to an unconstitutional third term in 2000 was followed a few months later with his resignation in the face of exposed political manipulation. New elections were held in 2001.

RELIGION
Religious freedom is guaranteed in the 1978 constitution, but the Catholic Church as the officially recognized state church receives preferential treatment. The Catholic Church has a decisive influence which is discriminatory against non-Catholics in taxes, property, education and politics.

Religions	Population %	Adherents	Ann.Gr.
Christian	90.06	23,110,900	+1.4%
non-Religious/other	8.32	2,135,051	+5.3%
Traditional ethnic	1.20	307,940	+3.5%
Buddhist	0.31	79,551	+2.4%
Baha'i	0.09	23,096	+1.7%
Jewish	0.02	5,132	+1.7%

It is reckoned that 25% of Peruvians are Christo-pagan, believing more in animism and witchcraft.

Christians	Denom.	Affil.%	,000	Ann.Gr.
Protestant	56	6.58	1,688	+5.5%
Independent	97	3.98	1,020	+8.4%
Anglican	1	0.01	2	-1.0%
Catholic	1	68.97	17,700	-0.4%
Marginal	4	3.27	840	+4.2%
Unaffiliated		15.04	3,860	n.a.
Doubly affiliated		*-7.79%*	*-2,000*	*n.a.*

Churches	MegaBloc	Cong.	Members	Affiliates
Catholic	C	2,380	9.725m	17.70m
Seventh-day Adventist	P	1,153	413,625	550,000
Latter-day Saints (Morm)	M	600	175,824	320,000
IEP- Evang Ch of Peru	P	2,000	100,000	300,000
Israelite Ch of New Cov.	M	200	140,000	280,000
Jehovah's Witnesses	M	720	69,965	240,000
Assemblies of God	P	2,800	150,000	238,000
Ch of the Nazarene	P	1,200	65,000	120,000
Evang Miss. Mvt [2]	I	240	46,000	86,000
Evang Pente Ch of JC	I	850	36,000	85,000
Chr and Miss. Alliance	P	320	27,341	84,675

FAIENAP (Native Ev) [10]	I	480	30,000	70,000
Independent Baptist	P	450	19,000	35,000
Ch of God of Prophecy	P	460	16,500	32,000
U. of Bapts of S.Peru	P	220	11,000	27,500
Pilgrim Evangelical	P	380	10,000	27,000
Methodist	P	110	8,500	24,000
Ch of God (Cleveland)	P	268	10,720	22,000
Evang Ch of NE Peru	P	115	7,500	19,000
Christian Brethren	P	210	11,000	19,000
Evang Presb & Ref	P	220	5,000	16,500
Indig Native American [11]	I	110	5,500	16,500
Emmanuel Revival	I	60	6,000	12,000
Other denoms [117]		5,598	354,756	926,373
Doubly affiliated			*-1,099,000*	*-2,000,000*
Total Christians [160]		21,144	10.346m	19.250m

Trans-bloc Groupings	pop. %	,000	Ann.Gr.
Evangelical	8.7	2,242	+6.9%
Charismatic	6.2	1,589	+6.3%

Pentecostal	3.8	965	+7.9%

Missionaries from Peru
P,I,A 362 in 31 agencies to 28 countries: Peru 265, USA 20, Colombia 12.

Missionaries to Peru
P,I,A 1,003 in 103 agencies from 28 countries: USA 597, UK 75, Brazil 51, Germany 49, Canada 47, Switzerland 41, Korea 27.

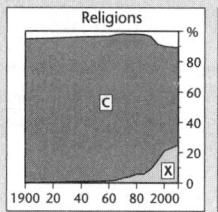

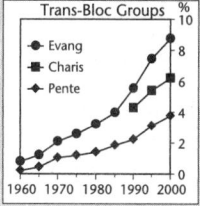

• Answers to Prayer

1 The National Prayer Movement was launched in 1989 in response to Peru's national crisis. The answers:

a) The capture of the terrorist leaders in 1992 and 1993 and the virtual ending of warfare.

b) A massive turning to Christ — especially among the Quechua of the Andes.

2 The growth and maturing of the Church among many of the Amazon Amerindian peoples. The exceptional Bible translation and literacy work of SIL and others played a significant part in this.

• Challenges for Prayer

1 Peru needs an effective democratic government with the courage and strength to deal with the real issues. Pray for the strengthening of:

a) The fragile peace. Major societal change is needed — corruption, racism, religious freedom and an unfair judicial system are endemic. The problem of terrorism has not ended.

b) The tentative economic recovery. Some have benefited, but the majority have not been positively affected. The massive slums ringing Lima are little changed. Over 200,000 rural Peruvians are involved in cultivating narcotics.

2 The Catholic Church is in a crisis. Over 80% of its clergy are foreign. It is polarized between the traditionalists and those who espouse liberation theology. The charismatic movement has had a deep impact, but those touched have often formed autonomous groups or joined evangelical churches. There has been large loss of numbers to indigenous movements and foreign sects, as well as to the Evangelicals. Only 15% of Catholics are regular in church attendance; the great majority are highly syncretistic Christo-pagans. Pre-Hispanic religions are being revived and new religious movements multiplying. Pray for many to come to the light and liberty of the biblical gospel.

3 Evangelical churches have grown dramatically since the first evangelical congregation was started a century ago. Evangelicals were only 0.8% (76,000) in 1960, 2.9% (500,000) in 1980 and 8.7% (2.2m) in 2000. The greatest growth was in the worst times of violence and social breakdown. Persecution between 1980 and 1994 was sometimes severe at the hands of both the terrorists and the army in areas of fighting over the cultivation of narcotics — each regarding Evangelicals as a threat. Over 750 evangelical leaders were martyred and some sentenced to imprisonment on trumped-up charges. Growth has been most marked in the work of **CMA**, IEP(**SIM-LL**), **CoN**, **AoG** and numerous indigenous Pentecostal groups. After peace came, growth slowed. Pray for a new and deeper work of the Holy Spirit to re-ignite the Church.

517

4 **The coming of peace** has highlighted serious issues that need to be addressed by Evangelicals. Pray for:

a) *Unity.* Evangelicals have become a significant source of leadership, stability, social aid and hope since 1980. There are sharp divisions within some denominations over the issue of worship styles and charismatic gifts. There has been too little fellowship between leaders.

b) *Nominalism to be tackled.* This is rapidly becoming a major issue in all evangelical groups. Apathy is widespread. Earlier zeal has waned and church growth has slowed in the late 1990s. JWs, Mormons and an indigenous sect, the Israelitas, have been highly successful in recruiting fringe Evangelicals who have not been discipled. Many congregations need intensive re-evangelization and effective discipling programmes, but lack the resources.

c) *Ministry to victims of war and deprivation.* The war left hundreds of widows, thousands of orphans and hundreds of thousands of traumatized, impoverished people who need material, emotional and spiritual help. Many congregations seek to alleviate the needs — often 70% of members are unemployed. Many Christian ministries (**WVI**, Food for the Hungry, Compassion International, Agape Network, **TEAR Fund**) have also contributed to programmes for both rural and urban slum areas.

d) *Evangelicals to be more prophetic in society.* Political and social influence has grown, but Evangelicals are deeply divided on involvement in political life. Evangelicals who were congress members in the past regime had a poor testimony and lost credibility. Yet there are serious issues to be tackled — religious freedom, societal transformation, the neglected poor, child abuse, etc.

5 **The Quechua and Aymara peoples**, the descendants of the Incas, have begun to emerge from centuries of oppression, cultural deprivation, grinding poverty and isolation. Quechua was recognized as an official language in 1975. The Quechua Church has grown rapidly as Christianity at last becomes indigenized in Scriptures, structures, worship and music. Whole villages have been turning to Christ. Pray for:

a) *Millions of mountain Quechua and Aymara* who are still bound by superstitions of pagan and 'Christian' origin. Many migrated to the cities during the war.

b) *Bible translation* which has been a major factor in the Quechua renaissance and church growth. The Cuzco and Ayacucho languages have the whole Bible and 3 other Quechua languages the NT (**UBS**, **SIL**, IEP, **SBC**); a further 12 languages are being translated. Pray for translation and literacy teams as they make these vital Scriptures available and understandable.

c) *Breaking down centuries of pain*, resentment and prejudice between Quechua and Spanish-speakers and a unity at the Cross of Christ as brethren.

6 **The Lowland Amerindians** have responded to the preaching of missionaries of South American Mission, Swiss Indian Mission, **SIL** and others. The three Lowland provinces of the upper Amazon have the highest percentage of evangelical believers in the country. A network of churches planted by different agencies is developing and growing (FAIENAP) in 13 or more peoples. The problems they face are huge — ecologically insensitive oil and mining companies, terrorism and drug trafficking. Pray that the churches among them may become strong and enable these peoples to withstand the destructive impact of the outside world on their cultures. **SIL** has been involved in the translation of 17 NTs for non-Quechua peoples, and has teams committed to a further 12.

7 **The lack of trained, mature leaders is so critical that further church growth is endangered.** Doctrinal confusion, deficient theology and the multiplication of sects must be answered by clear biblical teaching, but few pastors have the gifts and training. The IEP had 1,300 churches in 1998, but only 80 with pastors having any formal academic training. Immorality, alcohol abuse and sin can often be ignored or practiced by pastors. Many pastors can be legalistic and domineering, inhibiting initiative and stimulating apathy in their followers. Pray for:

a) *A multiplication of godly role-model pastors* who walk with Jesus.

b) *Leadership training.* The SEBAP (**CMA**) and Lima (**LL**, **SIM**, etc.) Seminaries are key for Spanish-speaking countries. At least 20 other Bible schools are preparing workers for the ministry. Poverty and lack of finance seriously limits the number who can receive such training.

c) ***TEE is an essential alternative***, but hampered by lack of teaching personnel and suitable teaching materials. There is also a lack of enthusiasm for such training by those who would most benefit. **SIM** missionaries are involved with 700 TEE students. *Segadores* trains rural pastors and potential missionaries.

d) ***Sunday school teachers and youth leaders***. The majority of congregations provide no special teaching or programmes for young people — a major deficiency that must be rectified.

8 **Vision for the future** has been stimulated by ***Peru Para Cristo*** (**DAWN**) through the challenge of planting a church in each of the 90,000 villages and communities. By 2000 there were over 17,000 evangelical churches. Pray for this vision to be attained, unity in purpose gained, the harvest retained and leadership multiplied to cope with such growth.

9 **Foreign missions** have passed through difficult times, especially those from USA (68% of the missionary force); anti-American press reports, spy scares, and the widespread activities of Mormons and JWs have not helped. The majority of the missionary effort is directed to pioneer work in the eastern jungle, Bible translation and leadership training. Reinforcements are needed. Some larger agencies are: **SIL/WBT** (189 workers), **LL** (72), **IMB-SBC** (63), ABWE (54), BMM (34), **AoG** (28), Swiss Indian Mission (28), **SIM** (27) Mennonites (21), Brethren (21), **CMA** (20), **TEAM** (14), **WT** (10) and EFCA (10).

10 **Challenge areas for ministry:**

a) ***Lima*** is Latin America's fifth-largest city. Over 60% live in slums that ring the city where abject poverty, unemployment and malnutrition are rife. Few have found the key to the evangelization of the sprawling slums of Lima and the nurture of churches in that difficult environment, though the Pentecostals and **SAMS** have made a good beginning. Praise God for the remarkable church growth in Lima through the ministry of **CMA**, **AoG**, Baptists, **SAMS** and **TEAM** over the last 20 years.

b) ***Specific areas with fewer Evangelicals*** are the coastal provinces and the Amazon Lowland Spanish-speaking farmers. There are also pockets of need in the high plateau with unevangelized villages and towns. In the southern Andes areas of Ayacucho, Apurimac and Arequipa there are over 1,000 villages with but 12 small Christian groups.

c) ***Less reached Amerindian tribal peoples***. There are 10 marginally reached peoples with a total population of 4,000 but less than 100 Christians. There are a further 10 peoples — 1,000 with no work or churches.

d) ***The business/professional and upper classes***. They are staunchly traditional Catholics, few having a personal relationship with the Lord Jesus, and are rather isolated from most existing evangelical witness.

e) ***Ethnic minorities***. The 7,000 **Gypsies** (many still speaking Romani and with one congregation of believers), the **Chinese** with several small congregations, and the **Japanese** (many now returning to Japan). Pakistani Muslims (3,000) are established on the southern coast.

f) ***Street children*** have multiplied in Lima especially. Poverty, social breakdown and war have led to many being abused, exploited and forced to work long hours for a pittance.

g) ***AIDS*** is becoming a significant issue with 100,000 carrying the HIV virus. **YFC** is involved in AIDS awareness teaching among young people.

11 **Student ministry** is strategic for Peru's future. There is widespread disillusionment and frustration, and Christian students need great courage to stand out for Jesus. Pray for the ministry of AGEUP(**IFES**) with 5 staff workers and 33 groups in the 50 universities. The 714,000 students have a lower proportion of Evangelicals than any other major section of the population.

12 **Peruvian missions interest is growing,** but lack of knowledge and funds limits that growth. The **CMA**, Baptists and **AoG** have launched missions programmes. There is a post-graduate faculty of Mission at CEMAA in Lima. Indigenous mission agencies have grown — some being AMEN (*Asociación Misionera Evangélica a las Naciónes*), Segadores and IMA (*Impacto Mundial de Avivamento*). **OM** and **YWAM** have become sending agencies. Missionary training programmes have increased in number during the 1990s. Pray for this vision to increase and mature.

13 Christian media.

a) **Radio** has a wide audience, both the local *Radio del Pacifico* (**TEAM**) in Lima, and the large international stations of **HCJB** Ecuador (Spanish and Quechua), and **TWR** Bonaire (Spanish) with thousands of hours of broadcasting per week in Spanish and 100 in 17 Quechua dialects! **TWR** and **HCJB** also use the ALAS satellite.

b) **Christian programmes on local television** are proving important for reaching those living in well-guarded high-rise apartments.

c) **The JESUS film** has been viewed by most of the population either on film or on TV. It is in use in 6 languages and a further 15 languages are in production.

d) **Christian literature.** CLC has a bookstore and mobile ministry. **SIM** have launched a large pastors' mini-library project. **EHC** is in the middle of its second nation-wide coverage with evangelistic literature.

e) **GRN** have made recordings available in 66 of Peru's languages and dialects.

Philippines

Republic of the Philippines

SEPTEMBER 15-17
ASIA
Updated February 2004

 GEOGRAPHY
Area 300,000 sq.km. 80 provinces; 7,250 islands, of which over 700 are inhabited. The largest are Luzon (116,000 sq.km.) in the north and Mindanao (102,000 sq.km.) in the south. Over 75% mountains; prone to devastating typhoons.

Population	Ann.Gr.	Density
2000	75,966,500	+2.13%	253 per sq. km.
2010	90,544,498	+1.65%	302 per sq. km.
2025	108,251,048	+1.12%	361 per sq. km.

Capital Manila 13.2 million. **Other major cities:** Davao 1.15m; Cebu 1.03m. **Urbanites** 58%.

PEOPLES

Malayo-Indonesian Filipinos 94.2%.
Major peoples Tagalog 22.3 mill.; Cebuano 17.7m; Ilocano 7.1m; Hiligaynon (Visaya) 6.9m), Bicol 4.3m; Waray (Samar/Leyte) 2.9m.
Tribal peoples 2.8%. In the more inaccessible mountain areas of: Luzon (46 peoples) 1.3m; Mindanao(43) 700,000; Mindoro(11) 280,000; Palawan(7) 90,000.
Muslim majority peoples 5%. 13 peoples, the largest (in Mindanao): Maranao 1.1m; Magindanao/Ilanun 1.4m; Subanon/Kalibugan

63,000. On the islands south-west of Mindanao: Tausug 600,000; Sama(3) 300,000; Yakan 82,000; Bajau(2) 77,000.
Mixed race 3.5%. Filipino, Spanish, American, Chinese, many speaking Tagalog.
Chinese 2.1%. Urban, extensive involvement in commerce and industry.
Other 0.2%. US citizens, Vietnamese, Arab, Japanese, Korean, South Asian, etc.
Literacy 95%. **Official languages** Filipino (based on Tagalog), English. **All languages** 169. **Languages with Scriptures** 8Bi 52NT 37por 44w.i.p.

ECONOMY
A mixed agricultural and industrial economy. High population growth, widespread corruption, protectionism, social and political unrest, two guerrilla wars and a series of natural disasters have played havoc with the economy, causing widespread poverty and unemployment. The uncontrolled crime wave and series of kidnappings along with the closing of US military bases in 1992 have cut aid and inhibited foreign investment. The Asian economic crisis of 1997 was a further setback. Between 32% and 50% live below the poverty line. Remittances from the millions of Filipinos working abroad are a major source of foreign exchange. **HDI** 0.740; 77th/174. **Public debt** 29% of GNP. **Income/person** $1,200 (4% of USA).

POLITICS
A Spanish colony from 1565 to 1898; hence the Catholic majority and many Spanish customs. Ruled by the USA until independence in 1946. Martial law imposed in 1971 to combat Communist subversion; the country became virtually a one-party republic. Political manipulation, mismanagement and abuse of civil liberties stimulated antipathy to the Marcos regime and led to its downfall in 1986. Democratic rule since then, but none have adequately addressed the need for land reform, for taming the excesses of the military, for limiting the power of the elite and ending the Muslim secessionist and Marxist guerrilla wars. The Philippines is a member of ASEAN. President Estrada's time in office ended in 2001 due to pub-

lic indignation at corruption. The new government has only succeeded in making small improvements and reforms.

RELIGION
Freedom of religion. The Catholic Church wields enormous influence. The Muslim minority in Mindanao seeks to set up an independent Islamic state in the south. **Persecution Index** 51st in the world (in Muslim areas only).

Religions	Population %	Adherents	Ann.Gr.
Christian	93.19	70,793,181	+2.1%
Muslim	5.00	3,798,325	+3.0%
non-Religious/other	1.11	843,228	+2.3%
Traditional ethnic	0.60	455,799	+0.5%
Chinese	0.10	75,967	+2.1%

Christians	Denom.	Affil.%	,000	Ann.Gr.
Protestant	95	6.79	5,161	+5.6%
Independent	355	15.24	11,580	+9.1%
Anglican	1	0.16	118	+1.5%
Catholic	1	67.13	51,000	+0.4%
Marginal	45	8.71	6,618	+1.8%
Doubly affiliated		*-4.88*	*-3,693*	*n.a.*

Churches	MegaBloc	Cong.	Members	Affiliates
Catholic	C	2,600	27.568m	51.00m
Phil. Indep (Aglipayan)	I	10,204	3,571,429	5,500,000
Iglesia ni Cristo	M	8,600	1,500,000	4,100,000
Jesus is Lord Church	I	3,000	1,200,000	2,000,000
Jesus Miracle Crusade	I	2,000	705,882	1,200,000
Seventh-day Adventist	P	4,000	830,000	1,160,000
United Ch of Christ	P	2,800	280,000	950,000
Assemblies of God	P	3,100	122,000	500,000
United Methodist	P	1,300	252,747	460,000
Latter-day Saints (Morm)	M	1,307	300,699	430,000
Jehovah's Witnesses	M	3,486	132,496	407,494
Chr and Miss Alliance	P	2,300	140,383	290,000
Conv of Phil Bapt	P	710	110,000	220,000
Phil Bapt Conv.(SBC)	P	1,784	102,120	200,000

Phil Benevolent Miss	M	1,000	100,000	180,000
Evang Methodist	P	380	68,000	170,000
United Pentecostal	P	2,700	115,000	152,000
Church of God (Clev)	P	501	70,000	130,000
Foursquare Gospel	P	1,180	56,000	120,000
Episcopal	A	570	39,454	118,362
Chr Ch/Ch of Christ	P	1,600	75,000	110,000
Good Shepherd	I	315	50,000	80,000
Assoc of Fund Baptists	P	1,250	49,000	78,000
Alliance of Bible Chr	P	450	20,000	50,000
Cons Bap Assoc	P	300	25,000	48,000
Baptist Bible Fell.	P	1,400	28,000	47,600
Tribal Chs (NTM)	P	170	16,000	40,000
Wesleyan	P	310	19,000	35,000
Baptist General Conf	P	230	15,500	31,000
Other denoms [470]		21,700	2,565,000	4,672,000
Doubly affiliated			*-2,500,000*	*-3,693,000*
Total Christians [499]		**81,227**	**37.628m**	**70.786m**

Trans-bloc Groupings	pop. %	,000	Ann.Gr.
Evangelical	16.7	12,663	+9.4%
Charismatic	14.1	10,749	+9.7%
Pentecostal	2.9	2,211	+11.4%

Missionaries from Philippines
P,I,A 2,829 in 122 agencies to 77 countries: Philippines 1,968; Thailand 138.

Missionaries to Philippines
P,I,A 2,734 in 192 agencies from 35 countries: USA 1,574; Korea 516, Canada 152, UK 108, Papua New Guinea 36.

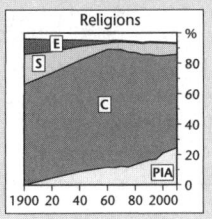

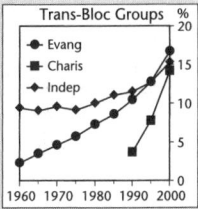

• Answers to Prayer

1 **The dramatic growth in the number of evangelical churches.** At the time of the launch of the 1974 **DAWN** vision of 50,000 churches by 2000, there were only 5,000 evangelical churches. By 1998 this had become 30,000, and by 2000 possibly approaching 40,000. Yet the rapid growth of the 1980s was not maintained in the 1990s. Evangelicals among Protestants and Independents have increased to about 10% of the population.

2 **The effective expansion of nearly all evangelical denominations** — most marked among the Full Gospel groups and indigenous Pentecostal denominations.

3 **Increased spiritual unity.** The **Philippine Council of Evangelical Churches** (PCEC) has established warm fellowship and cooperated in developing common goals for ministry — a change from a decade ago. Many local and regional **Ministerial Fellowships** have been established — enhancing the rate of church growth, but this needs to be extended to all areas. Pray that this unity continues and is strengthened, and that it extends to mainline Protestant denominations.

4 **Over 300,000 Filipino intercessors** have been raised up through **Intercessors for the Philippines**. Each have committed themselves to pray one hour a day for the nation. Stand with these intercessors, asking God to sustain them and to give much fruit.

• Challenges for Prayer

1 The great potential of the Philippines has not yet been realized despite being rich in natural resources and having a well-educated population. Failures by successive governments to deal with the serious economic and social issues (see above) have held back development, and kept half the population in poverty. Pray specifically for:

a) *A government that actively pursues justice and righteousness.* There are key Christians in major posts of leadership — may they decisively influence the nation for good. Pray for the **Fellowship of Christians in Government** which exists to fight corruption and promote biblical standards.

b) *A change in the political culture* that deals with the endemic greed and corruption, ends cronyism, and also initiates long-delayed land reform (70% of farmers are landless) and improves the health and prospects of the poor by investment in the basic infrastructure of the country.

c) *Peace in Mindanao* between the marginalized, resentful Muslim population and the government and local 'Christian' majority. Extreme Islamist factions are unwilling to compromise and claim four provinces, two with Muslim minorities, for an Islamic state. The level of violence and the terrorist atrocities on locals and foreigners increased after 9/11. The Abu Sayyaf terror organization has close links with Al Qaeda and Osama bin Laden. Pray for a fair, workable solution that will end the cycle of violence, kidnappings and suffering. Pray also that the centuries of perceived 'Christian' oppression may end with a freedom and respect for the gospel.

2 The Roman Catholic Church has changed much as the Philippines becomes more multi-denominational. There are very large charismatic movements within the Church — **El Shaddai** embracing anything from 4 to 8 million people and **Couples for Christ** with groups in almost every parish. Yet critical issues remain:

a) *Coming to terms with the loss of its privileged monopoly status* of a century ago. Some seek to preserve the unsatisfactory inequalities of society, some show hostility to Evangelicals because of their success. Pray for new life to course through the Church, its leadership, institutions and parishes. Over 2,000 Filipino Catholic missionaries serve in other lands.

b) *Large numbers of Catholics* are more influenced by animism and witchcraft than by Christianity. They need exposure to the biblical gospel.

c) *The charismatic networks* have large numbers but many are more influenced by superstitions than by the Scriptures, and salvation by works rather than by grace. Yet among them are an increasing number of committed evangelical believers.

3 Filipino Evangelicals have multiplied — but so too have the challenges. Pray for the spiritual health of the Church and a facing up to dangers:

a) *Rapid growth with inadequate discipling.* Damaging splits in denominations, erroneous teachings, syncretistic worldview and superficiality are the result.

b) *Complacency and second-generation nominalism.* The successes of the 1980s were not fully repeated in the 1990s. The hype about growth should be counterbalanced by recognizing spiritual shallowness at the grass roots. Pray for new vision, new direction from God for setting biblical priorities and goals, and renewed momentum for growth in the new millennium.

c) *Poverty in many congregations.* The availability of foreign funds and an expectation that foreigners take charge can lead to passivism and a dependence on man rather than on God. Pray that these believers may be spiritually enriched by a greater dependence on God. Pray for a spirit of generosity for those whose economic situation has improved. Pray also for a loving sensitivity to this on the part of foreign workers and donors who seek to help them.

4 The training and discipling of new leaders is a priority. Praise God for many Filipino leaders with national and international influence. Yet even the 100+ seminaries and Bible colleges and numerous TEE courses have not kept pace with the need. Frequent denominational splits and the proliferation of new groups — often led by those with minimal training and little accountability — have led to doctrinal distortions and moral failures. Many do not see formal training as an asset. Many of those who graduate are reluctant to serve in rural areas where the need and poverty is greater. Hundreds of rural congregations languish without adequate leadership. Many of the better qualified emigrate to the USA.

Pray for such institutions as the Alliance Bible Seminary (**CMA**), Philippine Baptist Theological Seminary (**IMB-SBC**), ATS, FEBIAS (**SEND**), APTS in Baguio (**AoG**), ISOT Asia (**CCCI**). Pray that God may continue to raise up godly, committed leaders.

5 **The Filipino Church is becoming a significant missionary-sending Church.** With over 35,000 evangelical churches and with the Filipino cultural flexibility, use of English and simple life-style, the potential is great. The DAWN goal in 1978 for 2,000 missionaries by 2000 has been exceeded. Of the estimated 2,700 cross-cultural missionaries nearly 900 are serving in other countries. Pray for:

a) *Growth of this vision*, that it be embraced by local churches — with all the supportive implications.

b) *Major Filipino agencies*: **CMA** (309 workers), Free Believers in Christ (197), Philippines Missionary Fellowship (160), Tribes and Nations Outreach (108), RCMH (103), Hosanna (78), Christ to the Orient (76), **AoG** (70), Asian Center for Mission (65), FIFCOP (49), Church of God (42), Philippine Frontline Ministries (38), Victory World Mission (31), Church of the Foursquare Gospel (24). There are also significant numbers of Filipinos serving with international missions: **CCCI** (149), SdA (117), **YWAM** (51), **OM** (48), AsEF (24), **CBI** (23), IT (23), **OMF** (17).

c) *The Philippine Missions Association*. The PMA is a coordinating body for most of the 118 mission agencies based in the country. Pray for effective national and international networking to maximize the impact of the Filipino missions trust.

d) *The PMA goal* — an additional 5,000 missionaries by 2020.

e) *Missionary training*. Praise God for such as Asian Center for Missions (ACTM), Great Commission Missionary Training Center, School of Frontier Missions and Cross-Train, where many Filipinos are prepared for missionary service. The ACTM has trained over 300 in 9 centres and is expanding this training to other Asian countries. Pray for the further development of such programmes.

6 **Expatriate missionaries** are decreasing in numbers (except for the Koreans) as the Philippines Church matures. Praise God for all achieved! Much remains to be done and outside assistance is welcome. Pray for wisdom for expatriates in finding the most appropriate roles for this time, and for discerning input from Filipino leadership regarding this. Pray for harmonious working relationships. The largest mission agencies: **WBT** (284), **NTM** (218), **CCCI** (197), **IMB-SBC** (144), **OMF** (137), **Action International Ministries** (96), AoG (95), **YWAM** (75), **CC/CC** (75), **CMA** (72), **CBI** (69), **SEND** (59), BBF (47), **FEBC** (42), **Christian Brethren** (41), **CoN** (36), EFC (36), **Christar** (32), **OCI** (28).

7 **Metro Manila** is a mega-city of enormous challenge, but also where God is working. Much prayer since 1985 has brought about positive change. Over 15% of the population is linked to an evangelical church but a big proportion comes from outside Metro Manila. Pray specifically for:

a) *The poor*. Over 5,000 migrate to Manila daily. Most start life in the city in one of the 1,000 or more squalid slums — some built on the city's rubbish dumps. These newcomers are more receptive for the gospel, yet most of the churches are in more affluent areas.

b) *Those who minister to the poor*. Many cooperative efforts linking national and international agencies and churches have sprung up, such as the **National Coalition for Urban Transformation** (NCUT) which links denominations to facilitate urban improvement. The **Alliance of Christian Transformational Agencies** and **Mission Ministries Philippines** are inter-agency networks aiming at innovative ministries for the poor. Special mention must be made of the ministries of **Action International Ministries**, **Servants to Asia's Urban Poor** and **IT**. Pray for discernment for effective ministry, eternal fruit and viable churches that impact the city to result.

8 **Special ministry challenges:**

a) *Students*. Over 2 million are studying in 1,360 tertiary colleges and universities. Many agencies are involved — **CCCI** with vision for Christian movements in 118 key campuses nation-wide, IVCF(**IFES**) with 35 staff in ministry on 81 campuses, **Navigators**, **AoG** and others. Pray for effective Evangelical cooperation, multiplication of conversions and the development of a nation-wide student missions movement.

b) *Children* — over a third of the population is under 15. **CEF** has 70 workers with ministry in 25 areas for school children. IVCF(**IFES**) has ministry in 52 high schools.

However, 30% of school age children are unable to attend school, the majority of them working. There are at least 40 Christian groups ministering to them, but the needs are great.

c) **Sex 'trade' workers.** Over 60,000 children and 500,000 women are involved. Many more are victims of trafficking to other countries. Pray for all involved (**YWAM** and others) in rescuing, rehabilitating and discipling these tragic victims of sin.

9 **The major export of the Philippines** is people. Filipinos are rich in skills but work opportunities are few. There are estimated to be over 6.5 million in Asian, Middle Eastern and Western countries as nurses, engineers, seamen, domestic servants, nannies and menial workers. Many have gone to difficult and 'closed' countries to be witnesses for Christ, and some have suffered much for the gospel. Pray for all Christians that they may shine for Him. Pray for the unconverted that they may hear the gospel — especially pray for the 244,000 Filipino seamen scattered around the world (the largest number for any nation).

10 **Less-reached peoples and areas.** Great progress has been made in reaching out to isolated tribal peoples all over the islands. By 1995 the Unreached People Task Force of the PMA identified 13 remaining unreached peoples; 12 are Muslim. There are also a number of unreached animistic peoples which perhaps should have been included but were not researched at that time. Pray for the Church to be stirred up in loving concern for Muslims and led in wise ways of reaching them.

a) **Mindanao** now has a high proportion of Evangelicals but growth has slowed recently and revival is needed. The major challenge is that of Islam. The ongoing war and deep resentment of the Magindanao and Maranao are major obstacles to witness. Yet Christian concern for them has increased. In 1987 there were just a few foreign missionaries. Now there are over 200, mainly Filipinos, seeking to minister to them — sometimes at risk of their lives. There is a steady trickle of conversions and a few churches planted. Pray for these believers who face great pressures. **OMF**, **SEND**, **TEAM**, **SIM** and others have ministry to them.

b) **The Sulu Islands** between Mindanao and Borneo are the home of the Muslim Tausug, Samal, and Yakan peoples. Among the Sama Bajao Sea Gypsies there has been a significant breakthrough with numbers coming to Christ in Davao City, Batangan and Metro Manila.

c) **Palawan.** A long, isolated island that is rapidly developing with many new Tagalog and Muslim immigrants. Among the indigenous Palawan (3 distinct peoples, each of 10,000 and a further 2,000 Muslims), Tagbanwa (40,000) and plains Cuyunon there has been response through the ministry of **NTM**. Much Bible translation work has been done and churches planted. The remaining challenges are to see spiritual fruit among the superficially Muslim Molbog (5,000) on Balabac and surrounding islands and Jama Mapun (15,000) on Cagayan Island.

d) **Luzon.** Praise God for church growth in the north-central mountainous area, where many of its peoples, the Ifugao, Bontok, Kankanay, Kalinga and Isnag have been turning from animism to Christ. Mountain Province is 16.5% Evangelical, Ifugao 24%, Benguet 29%, but the Bicol region remains the neediest — Albay Province 1.7% Evangelical, Camarines Norte 1%, Catanduanes 0.7%. Many small, semi-nomadic hunter-gatherer Dumagat Negrito peoples live on the typhoon-lashed, rugged north and north-east coastal mountains of Luzon. Few have become Christian, and the task of church planting is complex. **NTM** has made a large investment of personnel among these peoples.

e) **Visayas** — the most needy region of the country. The islands of Samar, Cebu and Leyte are all only about 2% Evangelical — far below the national average of 10% (for P,A,I). Response is now good but poverty, despair and a spirit of defeat are widespread. Pray for more church planters and vigorous church growth. The original DAWN vision of 1974 was a church for each of the 42,000 *barangays* (neighbourhoods). There are still 26,000 without a church. Pray that this vision might be realized.

11 **Ethnic minorities:**

a) **The Chinese** number 850,000. Most are wealthy and have been targets of much crime and kidnapping. Many are Catholic but only 3% are evangelical Christians. There are 78 predominantly Chinese evangelical congregations with 18,000 members. Their goals: 500 full-time workers, 30,000 worshipers. Pray that many more may find their true security in Jesus.

b) Panjabis — many are Sikh (30,000), others are Muslim and Hindu. Pray for spiritual breakthroughs among them and that the few believers may multiply. Pray for the few Christian workers among them. (**IMI**).

c) Sri Lankans — the Tamil and Sinhala number 12,000. There are 10 known believers among them.

12 Christian support ministries for prayer:

a) The Philippine Bible Society. The PBS(**UBS**) is extensively involved in translation, production, distribution and promotion of the Bible. A 'centennial of biblical Christianity' edition of the Bible (200,000 copies) was distributed at low cost in Tagalog, Cebuano and English. Pray for the Bible to make deep and lasting impact on lives.

b) Bible translation has been, and continues as, a major ministry involvement of a number of agencies — of special mention is **SIL** and its daughter indigenous offshoot, **The Translators Association of the Philippines**. By 2000 there were 60 NTs or Bibles completed with work in progress in 44 languages. Out of 51 languages without the Scriptures, 3 have a definite need for translation teams.

c) Literature is extensively used by Christians. There are over 44 denominational and non-denominational literature agencies for printing, publishing and distribution. Pray for the work started by **OMF** (publishing house and network of bookstores), **CMA**, **CLC** and others. There are more than 100 Christian bookstores in the country. The use of Bible comic books is proving effective in reaching youth.

d) The ministries of EHC and the Bible League have had significant impact. **EHC** is in the midst of its third nation-wide coverage with evangelistic literature. **The Bible League**'s follow-up Bible Correspondence Courses (1,000 a day completed) and provision of Bibles for discipling have all led to many conversions and hundreds of new churches.

e) Christian television. Extensive use of radio and TV is made by Christians. Few countries are better served. A Christian TV Channel, Zoë Broadcasting, is now operating.

f) Christian radio. **FEBC** Philippines has 20 stations from which over 2,000 hours of programmes a week are broadcast in 40 languages in other lands and 14 Philippines languages. Pray for:

i *The 200 (mainly Filipino) staff,* that they may know the blessing of the Lord in ministries that are often behind the scenes.

ii *The programming studios and programme producers,* smooth running of broadcasting equipment, printing presses, and follow-up ministries.

iii *The spiritual impact on Filipino audiences.* Many local stations are used for smaller language groups.

iv *The fruitfulness of international ministries* to Asian countries and regions more difficult to access — especially China, Siberia, Indo-China and Myanmar.

g) The JESUS film has had an immense impact, 75% of the population having seen it. Of the 79 targeted languages, 25 are completed and 41 in production. Pray for long-term fruit with churches gathered and growing through its use.

h) GRN have prepared messages in 132 of the languages of the nation.

Poland

Republic of Poland

SEPTEMBER 18-19
EUROPE
Updated February 2004

![GEOGRAPHY] **GEOGRAPHY**
Area 312,683 sq.km. Central European plain with Baltic coastline.

Population		Ann.Gr.	Density
2000	38,765,085	+0.08%	124 per sq. km.
2010	39,190,093	+0.12%	125 per sq. km.
2025	39,069,168	-0.13%	125 per sq. km.

Capital Warsaw 2,350,000. Other major cities: Katowice 2.85 mill.; Lodz 1.1m. **Urbanites** 62%.

![PEOPLES] **PEOPLES**
Slavic 99.1%. Polish 37,675,000; Belarusian 220,000; Ukrainian 300,000; Kashubian 180,000; Russian 30,000.
Other 0.9%. German 300,000; Gypsy 30,000.

Literacy 99%. **Official language** Polish. **All languages** 10. **Languages with Scriptures** 4Bi 1NT 3por 2w.i.p.

![ECONOMY] **ECONOMY**
Before 1940 Poland's economy was agricultural. Communist rule emphasized development of heavy industry which not only damaged the economy but also the environment. Reforms in the 1990s have transformed the economy into one of the most robust in Central Europe. **Unemployment** 15%. **HDI** 0.802; 44th/174. **Public debt** 24% of GNP. **Income/person** $3,590 (11.4% of USA).

![POLITICS] **POLITICS**
Poland became a nation in the 11th Century and united with Lithuania in 1569. It was weakened, divided and occupied by many nations since then. One quarter of the population died in World War II. Communist rule was imposed in 1945 but poverty and labour turmoil led to the Solidarity Movement protests and a multi-party democracy in 1989. Poland joined NATO in 1999 and the EU in 2004.

![RELIGION] **RELIGION**
All religions have equal rights before the law, but the Roman Catholic Church exercises its traditional pride of place in Polish society. It has been aggressive since 1989 in attempting to shape a state based on Catholic principles and theology. A low level discrimination of non-Catholic denominations is evident and Evangelicals tend to be categorized as sectarian by the more established denominations.

Religions	Population %	Adherents	Ann.Gr.
Christian	90.29	35,000,995	-0.3%
non-Religious	9.58	3,713,695	+3.9%
Other	0.13	50,396	+0.1%

Christians	Denom.	Affil.%	,000	Ann.Gr.
Protestant	21	0.40	154	+0.2%
Independent	9	0.24	94	-0.5%
Catholic	2	78.11	30,280	-0.6%
Orthodox	4	1.43	553	+0.0%
Marginal	13	0.56	218	+0.8%
Unaffiliated		9.55	3,702	n.a.

Churches	MegaBloc	Cong.	Members	Affiliates
Catholic	C	9,500	19,736,842	30,000,000
Orthodox	O	312	343,750	561,000
Catholic - Eastern Rite	C	84	140,000	280,000
Jehovah's Witnesses	M	1,624	126,635	211,480
Ev Ch of Augsburg Conf	P	284	64,000	87,000
Polish Nat Catholic	I	100	28,571	54,000
Old Catholic Mariavite	I	53	14,286	23,000
Pentecostal Ch of P.	P	180	12,079	19,474
Indep Auton RC Parishes	I	1	6,579	10,000
Chs of Christ	P	65	6,500	8,500
Seventh-day Adventist	P	123	5,542	8,500
Polish Baptist Union	P	64	4,107	6,500
Methodist	P	46	4,500	6,000
Free Evangelical	P	33	2,300	4,600
Reformed Evangelical	P	10	2,500	4,000
Christian Brethren	P	40	1,500	4,000
Other denoms [39]		242	17,400	29,120
Total Christians [55]		12,761	20.517m	31.299m

Trans-bloc Groupings	pop. %	,000	Ann.Gr.
Evangelical	0.2	75	+0.0%
Charismatic	3.9	1,530	-0.6%
Pentecostal	0.1	24	-4.2%

Missionaries from Poland
P,I,A 117 in 11 agencies to 7 countries: Poland 105.
Missionaries to Poland
P,I,A 151 in 42 agencies from 14 countries: USA 100, Canada 14, Switzerland 10.

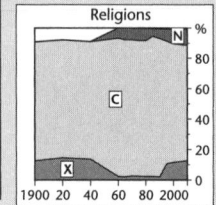

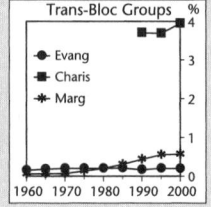

• Challenges for Prayer

1 **Dreams of instant wealth from capitalism** have proved elusive and hollow. Crime, violence and immorality are on the rise — particularly in the younger generation. Pray for the stability, progress and freedom that allows the good news to be preached. Pray that the Polish quest for material advancement might be subordinated to the search for God.

2 **The Catholic Church** was long the custodian of Polish culture and nationalism in the face of Russian imperialism and Soviet Communism. It successfully blocked all efforts by the Communists to deprive it of its independence and foist atheism on the nation. It is theologically conservative with a strong emphasis on the Virgin Mary and the saints. It regained considerable political influence in 1989.

a) *The Catholic Church's* popularity drops with every flex of its political muscles. It is accused of trying to create a repressive religious state. The 1990s marked a rejection of the values of the Church by many Poles. Regular church attendance dropped from 58% in 1989 to 23% in 1999.

b) *Pray that Poland's religious leaders* may know a life of holiness and a close walk with God. Pray that the Church's opposition to the new materialism and godlessness might be sensitive and discerning. While Polish candidates for the priesthood dropped by 30% in the 1990s, the nation still sends out large numbers of priests throughout the world.

c) *The most important pilgrimage destination* for Polish Catholics is the Black Madonna in Cyestochowa. Pray that Christ might become the focus of worship and thanksgiving. Renewal movements such as Oasis/Light of Life had much influence in the 1980s and many came to personal faith in Christ as a result of Bible study groups. Pray that biblical teachings and values might be retained and enhanced.

3 **Evangelical Christians** have long been a very small minority, but much has developed in recent years.

a) *Evangelism and church planting* have increased. A national research project is underway to help determine the needs for strategic church planting and outreach and Christian leaders continue to meet to strategize and cooperate. **SGA** is very active in evangelism in cooperation with local churches, and the Baptists have embarked on an ambitious church planting plan. Pray that this may lead many to Christ.

b) *Evangelical unity has been limited.* Although the 1990s brought both a multiplication and division of denominations, the founding of a national Polish Evangelical Alliance in 1999 was a cause for rejoicing. Pray for its growth. Pray that the Holy Spirit may bring reconciliation, fellowship and unity of vision in Jesus' name. Pray for the ministry of the Polish Ecumenical Council which brings together many Christian groups outside of the Roman Catholic Church.

c) *The multiplication of foreign sects and religions* has brought confusion. Jehovah's Witnesses far outnumber Evangelicals. New Age and paganism have rapidly gained followers. Pray for the defeat of every ideological assault on biblical truth and a demonstration of the power and lordship of Jesus Christ.

4 **Bible training for church leaders,** a much needed ministry, is developing fast. There are about 25 Protestant institutions ranging from seminary level to part-time or correspondence Bible schools — remarkable for a land with so small a Protestant presence! Pray for biblical faithfulness, spiritual power and missions vision to be the hallmark of the ministry of graduates.

5 **Young people and students,** while sceptical of organized religion are receptive to the good news of Jesus. The Christian Students Association (**IFES**), has groups in almost all of the 30 universities. **SU** focuses their ministry on younger students. Summer camps are a major ministry for nearly all evangelical denominations and agencies. Pray for the strategic work of Youth Forum, which is an alliance of Polish Christian youth associations. May this generation which first tasted political freedom also be the first to know *en masse* the freedom found only in Christ!

6 **Thousands of towns and villages remain without an evangelical witness,** often mired in empty tradition. Pray for Polish Evangelicals to catch a vision for the salvation of their countrymen as well as their European neighbours.

7 **Foreign mission agencies had a supportive role in Communist days**. Now many agencies, including BCU, **CBI**, CCCC, **CMA**, **SEND** and others, minister directly. Pray that cultural sensitivity and humble servanthood to the national believers may characterize their ministry in the new Poland. Pray for sustained commitment — many groups entered Poland only to leave plans and projects unfinished as they departed for other, more "fashionable", fields.

8 **The literature ministry continues to grow**. Christian commentaries and books are being translated into Polish and printed in increasing numbers. Areopag, a publishing company, and Logos, a ministry affiliated with **SGM**, are developing indigenous Christian literature ministries. **CLC** are opening Christian bookstores around the country. The Bible Society is publishing a new Bible translation endorsed by both Catholics and Protestants, and plays a vital role in Poland and surrounding lands. Pray that these burgeoning ministries might remain financially viable while blessing many with God's Word.

9 **Teaching English** (TEFL) is a wonderful opportunity to serve as a bridge to the gospel; young people especially are keen to learn. **ECM** and the Baptists, among others, have schools established for this purpose.

10 **Christian radio and television programmes** may be aired on national and local networks. **TWR** broadcast in Polish by local radio (10 hrs/wk) and Astra satellite (3.5 hrs/wk), as do AWR (7 hrs/wk). A **TWR** production team has been established in Poland to develop programmes; pray that these might reach into the hearts of many.

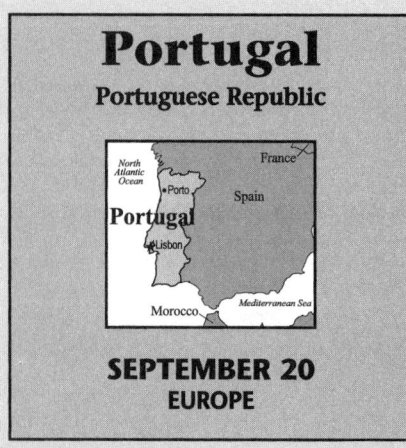

Portugal
Portuguese Republic

SEPTEMBER 20
EUROPE

Indigenous minorities 1.1%. Roma (Gypsy, 3) 80,000; Galician 15,000; Mirandesa 10,000.
EU Citizens 0.5%. British 13,000; Spanish 10,000; German 9,000; French 6,000; Dutch 3,000.
Other 1.4%. Cape Verdian 40,000; North African Arab 28,000; Brazilian 20,000; Angolan 16,000; Guinea-Bissau 13,000, Goanese 8,000.

Literacy 92%. **Official language** Portuguese. There are 190,000,000 Portuguese speakers world-wide. **All languages** 7.

ECONOMY
Impoverished by years of dictatorship and colonial wars. Rapid improvement of living standards since entry into the EU in 1986. Manufacturing and tourism are major components of the GNP. **Unemployment** is only 4%. **HDI** 0.858; 28th/174. **Public debt** 37% of GNP. **Income/person** $11,000 (35% of USA).

GEOGRAPHY
Area 92,389 sq.km occupying 15% of the Iberian Peninsula, which is shared with Spain. Also the Atlantic islands of the Azores (2,247 sq.km, 9 islands) and Madeira (794 sq.km, 2 islands).

Population		Ann.Gr.	Density
2000	9,874,853	+0.04%	107 per sq. km
2010	9,776,944	-0.14%	106 per sq. km
2025	9,348,354	-0.35%	101 per sq. km

Capital Lisbon 2,800,000. Other major city: Porto 1,700,000. **Urbanites** 30%.

PEOPLES
Portuguese 97%. Over 1 million live and work in other European countries.

POLITICS
Independent kingdom from 1143. A republic in 1910. The 1974 revolution ended 48 years of dictatorship whereupon a socialist democracy was instituted. All Portugal's African colonies (Mozambique, Angola, Guinea-Bissau, São Tomé & Príncipe, Cape Verde) were hastily granted independence in 1975. Membership of the EU has brought stability and strengthened democracy.

RELIGION
Freedom of religion since 1974, but with the Roman Catholic Church retaining some privileges. New laws in planning could lead to granting the same privileges to all minority religions.

Religions	Population %	Adherents	Ann.Gr.
Christian	94.39	9,320,874	-0.1%
non-Religious/other	5.00	493,743	+3.1%
Muslim	0.50	49,374	+4.6%
Hindu	0.10	9,875	+2.2%
Jewish	0.01	987	

Christians	Denom.	Affil. %	,000	Ann.Gr.
Protestant	44	1.26	124	+0.5%
Independent	28	2.20	217	+3.3%
Anglican	1	0.03	3	-0.9%
Catholic	1	74.94	7,400	-0.7%
Orthodox	1	0.01	1	-0.9%
Marginal	3	1.22	120	+1.6%
Unaffiliated		14.73	1,454	n.a.

Churches	MegaBloc	Cong.	Members	Affiliates
Catholic	C	4,335	5,248,227	7,400,000
Universal Ch of K of G	I	40	48,000	120,000
Jehovah's Witnesses	M	650	47,206	80,000
Assemblies of God	P	459	40,000	75,000
Manna Christian	I	70	20,000	45,000
Latter-day Saints (Morm)	M	182	20,000	40,000
Seventh-day Adventist	P	85	8,091	18,000
Christian Brethren	P	113	4,100	6,200
Congreg of Christ	I	122	3,653	6,100
Baptist Convention	P	63	4,379	5,824

Lusitanian	I	17	1,320	5,100
Methodist	P	17	1,500	3,500
Presbyterian	P	29	900	2,300
Ch of the Nazarene	P	23	920	1,500
Mennonite Brethren	P	2	40	72
Other denoms [64]		454	31,500	57,500
Total Christians [80]		6,661	5,480,000	7,866,000

Trans-bloc Groupings	pop. %	,000	Ann.Gr.
Evangelical	3.1	307	+2.5%
Charismatic	2.9	290	+2.5%
Pentecostal	2.6	256	+1.5%

Missionaries from Portugal

P,I,A 215 in 26 agencies to 19 countries: Portugal 43, France 19, USA 18.

Missionaries to Portugal

P,I,A 411 in 66 agencies from 15 countries: USA 178, Brazil 103, UK 44, Norway 43, Spain 32.

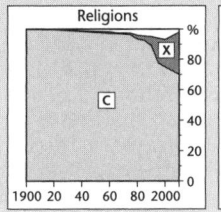

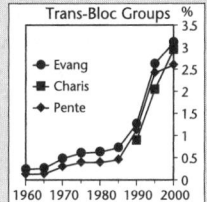

• Answers to Prayer

1 **The 25 years of religious freedom** have resulted in the steady and increased growth of Evangelicals from 55,000 in 1975 to over 307,000 in 2000.

• Challenges for Prayer

1 **Religious and political freedoms** gained in 1975 have transformed the nation, but the ancient heart-bondages remain. The veneration of Mary is a 'Christian' veneer over the old paganism and an estimated 90% of the population consult spiritist mediums and witches. To this are added the new bondages of materialism, self-centredness and alcohol and drug abuse. The teachings of the Jehovah's Witnesses, Mormons and New Age philosophies have gained a wide hearing. Pray for many to be released and for discerning Christian leaders able to effectively expose these false doctrines.

2 **The Roman Catholic Church** is strongly traditional and has much influence, but needs renewal. The north is more loyal to the Church, but in the centre and south the Church is becoming irrelevant to the secularized majority of the population. Pray for a renewing work of the Holy Spirit in which many are opened to the illumination of the Scriptures, freed from traditionalism and introduced to a warm personal relationship with Jesus.

3 **Evangelical growth** has accelerated in the 1990s, especially among Pentecostal and charismatic groups, but is also hampered by weaknesses which constrain that growth.
a) *Serious divisions*. Many denominations have suffered acrimonious splits — especially some Pentecostal denominations. An over-emphasis on prosperity teaching has divided congregations and brought confusion and disillusionment to many.
b) *The need for a united vision*. The Portuguese Evangelical Alliance has gained in stature and influence in recent years. Pray that God may grant wisdom, unity and faith for advance together to Portuguese Evangelicals.
c) *The lack of concern for world evangelization*. The Portuguese Church has a unique role to play because of the wide use of their language. There is too little involvement in missions in many evangelical churches — the exception being the Assemblies of God, the

Mana churches and several individual congregations. **YWAM**'s King's Kids ministry and Discipleship Training Schools are challenging young people for missions.

4 **Many congregations lack full time workers** with adequate theological depth and spiritual maturity. There are nine seminaries, including the Assemblies of God, Portuguese Bible Institute (founded by **GEM**), Presbyterian, Baptist and Bethel Bible Institutes (founded by Brazilian missionaries). The PBI now offers university-level and post-graduate degrees. The PBI, Baptists and ICI (**AoG**) run TEE programmes and Núcleo, a widely used Bible Correspondence Course. Pray that these may contribute to meeting the ministry needs of the churches.

5 **There remain pioneer challenges despite recent church growth.** Pray for:

a) *The seven northern and north-eastern provinces* which are strongly traditional Catholic; relatively few evangelical churches exist. Brethren, Baptists, **AoG**, *Missão Antioqía*, **GEM**, **TEAM** and **ECM** have church-planting programmes in the area.

b) *The four provinces in the south* which are poor, with few people ever going to church. Attendance at mass by people in Beja province is less than 3% of the population. Evangelical churches are few.

c) *The 316 counties*, 69 of which still have no evangelical congregation. In these counties live 800,000 people.

d) *The 4,400 localities*. Only 768 have a resident evangelical witness.

e) *Madeira Island* (273,000) which has only 13 small evangelical churches, and the **Azores** (253,000) with a further 26, most being Assemblies of God and Baptist. Four of the nine islands have no churches.

f) *Ethnic minorities* — there is little specific outreach to the 50,000 or so African and Arab Muslims or to the Hindu Goanese or Macau Chinese.

6 **Young people are often spiritually neglected.**

a) *Drug abuse* is a growing problem — over 50% have experimented with drugs. **Teen Challenge**, **Betel**-Spain and also **TEAM** and **ECM** have ministries of rehabilitation and discipling addicts.

b) *Student work* is still in a pioneer stage. GBUP(**IFES**) has a ministry that is established in eight universities and also in some high schools. **CCCI** and **Navigators** also have a ministry on several campuses.

c) *International students* are a specific focus of **GEM** along with a year-long internship programme for short-term missionary training.

d) **SU** and **CEF** have ministries among school children.

7 **Expatriate missions** have not found Portugal easy for ministry. Pray for perseverance, cultural adaptation and fruitfulness. Quality workers are needed in the many unreached areas for ministry in evangelism, church planting, Bible training and music. Some significant missions: **GEM** (28), **TEAM** (17), **AoG** (15), **Betel**-Spain (11), **CoN** (7), **Word of Life** (7). A growing number of Brazilian missionaries are entering the land (104 in 1998) and finding acceptance once they realize that Portugal is different from Brazil.

8 Christian media ministries:

a) *The Bible Society* has a growing national and international ministry in Bible production and distribution.

b) *Núcleo* which has a vital coordinating ministry for the Body of Christ in research, publishing, printing tracts and distributing cassettes and films.

c) *Ten Christian bookstores*, one run by **CLC**.

d) *CEDO*, a gospel broadsheet ministry of **WEC** sends out 150,000 copies four times a year to 60 countries around the world. The response is good from Mozambique and Angola, and is increasing from Portugal.

e) *Christian radio* is widely used. Local FM and medium-wave stations are used by various denominations and agencies. The Evangelical Alliance produce two TV programmes weekly. The Catholics have a TV station.

f) *The Internet* is a new area for evangelistic ministry which needs to be taken up by Christians with the right skills.

Puerto Rico
Commonwealth of Puerto Rico

North Atlantic Ocean

San Juan

Puerto Rico

Caribbean Sea

SEPTEMBER 21
LATIN AMERICA

GEOGRAPHY
Area 9,104 sq.km. Greater Antilles, between Dominican Republic and the Virgin Islands.

Population	Ann.Gr.	Density
2000	3,868,602	+0.81%	425 per sq. km
2010	4,158,727	+0.68%	457 per sq. km
2025	4,477,962	+0.43%	492 per sq. km

Puerto Ricans in USA now number 3 million.

Capital San Juan 2,550,000. Two-thirds of the population live in the metropolitan area. **Urbanites** 75%.

PEOPLES
Euro-American 74.6%. Spanish-speaking 2.8 mill.; English-speaking 85,000.
Afro-Caribbean 25.2%. Mostly Spanish-speaking; a few French- and English-speaking.
Other 0.2%. Chinese 2,000, Lebanese.
Literacy 90%+. **Official languages** Spanish, English.

ECONOMY
Mountainous and densely populated with few natural resources. A free market economy with manufacturing, trade and tourism the largest sources of income. Nearly 88% of exports are to mainland USA. **Public debt** 62% of GNP. **Income/person** $8,200 (26% of USA).

POLITICS
A Spanish colony for 400 years. Related to the USA after the Spanish-American war of 1898.

RELIGION
Freedom of religion.

Religions	Population %	Adherents	Ann.Gr.
Christian	97.00	3,752,544	+0.8%
non-Religious/other	1.98	76,598	+1.2%
Spiritist	0.70	27,080	+0.8%
Muslim	0.13	5,029	+11.1%
Hindu	0.09	3,482	+3.2%
Jewish	0.07	2,708	+0.8%
Buddhist	0.03	1,161	+0.8%

Christians	Denom.	Affil.%	,000	Ann.Gr.
Protestant	45	15.92	616	+2.5%
Independent	54	13.20	511	+1.8%
Anglican	1	0.32	12	+0.7%
Catholic	1	74.96	2,900	+0.8%
Orthodox	1	0.03	1	+0.0%
Marginal	8	3.02	117	+1.2%
Unaffiliated		0.74	29	n.a.
Doubly affiliated		*-11.19*	*-433*	*n.a.*

Churches		MegaBloc	Cong.	Members	Affiliates
Catholic		C	1,075	1,650,000	2,900,000
Other Pentecostal [30]		I	1,915	229,814	370,000
Pentecostal Ch of God		P	720	100,000	160,000
Assemblies of God		P	280	56,000	100,000
Seventh-day Adventist		P	260	31,524	78,000
Jehovah's Witnesses		M	328	25,778	75,000
Baptist Convention		P	105	35,000	70,000
Defenders of the Faith		I	180	17,500	35,000
Ch of God (Cleveland)		P	235	17,496	29,000
Latter-day Saints (Morm)		M	70	16,084	23,000
United Methodist		P	72	10,000	20,000
Disciples of Christ		P	100	10,778	18,000
Chr & Miss Alliance		P	60	6,500	15,000
Boriquén Presby Synod		P	71	8,300	15,000
Ch of the Nazarene		P	40	2,994	5,000
Other denoms [66]			1,498	130,400	244,000
Doubly affiliated				*-247,429*	*-433,000*
Total Christians [110]			7,009	2,100,700	3,724,000

Trans-bloc Groupings	pop.%	,000	Ann.Gr.
Evangelical	27.6	1,066	+2.3%
Charismatic	25.2	976	+2.1%
Pentecostal	20.0	772	+2.4%

Missionaries from Puerto Rico
P,I,A 190 in 25 agencies to 26 countries: Puerto Rico 64, USA 58, Costa Rica 9, Spain 8, Dominican Republic 8, Panama 8.

Missionaries to Puerto Rico
P,I,A 142 in 33 agencies from 9 countries. USA 130, Germany 3.

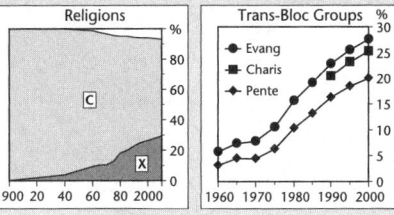

P

• Challenges for Prayer

1 **The long unresolved issue of Puerto Rico's political future** has divided the nation. People are torn between the present political status as a commonwealth linked to the USA, becoming a US state, or complete independence. The use of Vieques Island as a bombing range by the US Navy is a serious source of controversy. Pray for a resolution to these complex conflicts — a political and identity crisis which affects every level of society.

2 **Puerto Rico is traditionally Catholic**, but Evangelicals have grown rapidly from 0.1% in 1900, to 5.7% in 1960 and nearly 30% in 2000 — some claim this may have risen to 45%. Nearly 50% of Evangelicals are Pentecostal or Charismatic. There are numerous small indigenous networks of churches and independent congregations. There is also a large charismatic movement in the Catholic Church. There are many Christian ministries (8 Christian TV channels, many local radio stations, etc.) but not much impact has been made on the life of the nation, which is a complex post-modern society with all its associated problems.

3 **Societal problems cry out for Christian involvement.** The incidence of AIDS, alcoholism, drug addiction, corruption, crime and poverty are some of the highest in the Americas. Pray for humility, repentance, spiritual unity and burden for the lost among Christian leaders.

4 **The Church needs new vision:**

a) *Locally for effective discipling* and a return to the Scriptures. The 1997 DAWN saturation church planting conference was one catalytic beginning.

b) *Globally for effective support* and nurture of missions vision. A new interest in missions is developing in churches after decades of negativism. Pray that this interest may lead to greater impact on the world's unreached. There is much interest in unreached cities in Spain. Over 200 Puerto Ricans serve in indigenous movements such as AMIES International and in international missions such as **YWAM**, **OM** and **WBT**. Pray for the effective training and support of new mission ventures. COMIBAM is bringing together interdenominational (and denominational) mission agencies for fellowship and cooperation for world evangelization.

c) *For students.* ABU(**IFES**) has a growing work with groups on some campuses — pioneering work is needed for other campuses with an inadequate student witness.

5 **Over-population and unemployment** have forced over 3 million Puerto Ricans to emigrate to the USA. About half live in and around New York, where they form the lowest income group. Some live in Hispanic ghettos, where frustration has driven large numbers to violence, drugs and immorality. Pray for all specifically ministering to this community.

Qatar

State of Qatar

SEPTEMBER 22

ASIA

Population		Ann.Gr.	Density
2000	599,065	+1.80%	53 per sq. km.
2010	692,178	+1.37%	61 per sq. km.
2025	778,537	+0.47%	68 per sq. km.

Capital Doha 339,471. **Urbanites** 91%.

PEOPLES
The expatriate community makes up the majority of the population and is very difficult to accurately enumerate. Many Qatari citizens are of foreign extraction.
Arab 50%. Qatari 120,000; Other Arab (Egypt, Palestine, Jordan, Lebanon, etc.) 180,000.
South Asian 23%. Indian (esp. from Kerala) 108,000; Pakistani 100,000, Sri Lankan 18,000.
Persian 16%.
East Asian 7%. Filipino 36,000.
Other 4%. Caucasian 18,000.

GEOGRAPHY
Area 11,400 sq.km. Arabian peninsular state that is almost entirely desert.

Literacy 79%. **Official Language** Arabic. **All languages** 3. **Languages with Scripture** 2Bi.

 ECONOMY
Petroleum products are 81% of exports.

Qatar has some of the world's largest gas reserves. Oil wealth is used to diversify the economy. Qataris live in great wealth, but the Asians constitute an economic lower class. **HDI** 0.814; 41st/174. **Income/person** $16,160 (51% of USA).

POLITICS
Part of Turkish-Ottoman Empire until 1918. Under British protection until independence in 1971. The current Emir ousted his father in a bloodless coup in 1995. His foreign and domestic policies reflect a remarkably open and progressive attitude.

RELIGION
The strict Wahhabi form of Sunni Islam is the state religion. Proselytism of Muslims is forbidden, but expatriate Christians are allowed to practice their faith. **Persecution Index** 23rd in the world.

Religions	Population %	Adherents	Ann.Gr.
Muslim	79.43	475,837	-0.3%
Christian	10.47	62,722	+13.0%
Hindu	7.20	43,133	+17.6%
Buddhist	1.80	10,783	+10.4%
non-Religious/other	0.90	5,391	+2.9%

Baha'i	0.20	1,198	+1.8%

Christians	Denom.	Affil.%	,000	Ann.Gr.
Protestant	18	2.88	17	+17.7%
Independent	5	0.43	3	+23.7%
Anglican	1	0.87	5	+11.6%
Catholic	1	5.01	30	+10.8%
Orthodox	3	0.70	4	+7.0%
Marginal	5	0.58	4	+18.5%

Churches	MegaBloc	Cong.	Members	Affiliates
Catholic	C	14	16,667	30,000
Protestant groups [12]	P	30	5,500	11,000
Anglican	A	4	1,200	5,200
Pentecostal groups [3]	P	18	2,500	5,000
Orthodox [3]	O	8	2,515	4,200
Marginal groups [5]	M	5	2,188	3,500
Independent [5]	I	5	1,625	2,600
Other denoms [3]		20	619	1,250
Total Christians [33]		104	32,814	62,750

Trans-bloc Groupings	pop. %	,000	Ann.Gr.
Evangelical	2.5	15	+17.9%
Charismatic	1.9	11	+18.5%
Pentecostal	0.8	5	+20.1%

• Challenges for Prayer

1 **There were no Qatari believers** before 1985. Several have come to the Lord outside the country, but have suffered much for Him. Pray that they may become the nucleus of a Qatari Church.

2 **Expatriates are drawn from many nations by the high earnings in Qatar** but Christians are restricted in their witness because of the tight control of the authorities. Believers have long met together informally, but in 2000 the Emir granted land for a Christian compound to be built for the purpose of holding services. Pray that this development may foster unity and cooperation between the diverse groups of believers.

3 **Christian impact on society.** Pray that the small groups of believers among Indians, Pakistanis, Egyptians, Filipinos and Westerners may bear fruitful witness to their own communities. Pray also that there may be opportunities to share with non-Christians of all peoples in the country.

Q

Réunion
Department of Réunion

Mozambique
Madagascar
Mauritius
St-Denis
Réunion
Indian Ocean

SEPTEMBER 23
AFRICA

GEOGRAPHY
Area 2,544 sq.km. Rugged, mountainous volcanic Indian Ocean island 700 km east of Madagascar. The largest of the Mascarene Islands which include Mauritius.

Population	Ann.Gr.	Density
2000	699,406	+1.32%	275 per sq. km
2010	777,722	+0.98%	306 per sq. km
2025	879,761	+0.72%	346 per sq. km

Capital Saint-Denis 140,000. **Urbanites** 68%.

PEOPLES
Creole 59.4%. Afro-European, etc.
South Asian 28.2%. Tamil 171,000; Gujarati 18,000; Panjabi 3,000.
European 4.4%. French and Réunionese; also 4,000 military personnel.
Other 8%. Chinese(3) 20,000; East African 14,000; Malagasy 10,000, Comorian 9,000.

Literacy 91%. **Official language** French. Common language French Creole, which is replacing minority languages.

ECONOMY
Dependent on production of sugar and tourism. Rum, vanilla and light industry provide some export earnings. Heavily dependent on French and EU subsidies and aid and also income from the military bases. Exports are 8% of imports. **Unemployment** 40%. **Income/person** $8,880 (13.7% of USA).

R

POLITICS
Uninhabited until French settlement in 1642. Overseas department of France since 1946.

The level of dependency on France means there is little incentive to seek greater autonomy.

RELIGION
Freedom of religion, but Catholicism is culturally dominant. French anti-sect legislation is putting pressure on smaller religious groups and denominations.

Religions	Population %	Adherents	Ann.Gr.
Christian	84.90	593,796	+1.0%
Hindu	6.70	46,860	+1.3%
non-Religious/other	6.18	43,223	+6.3%
Muslim	2.15	15,037	+0.9%
Baha'i	0.07	490	-1.3%

Christians	Denom.	Affil.%	,000	Ann.Gr.
Protestant	10	5.53	39	+3.4%
Independent	5	0.49	3	+8.2%
Catholic	1	84.36	590	+0.6%
Marginal	2	0.91	6	+1.3%
Doubly affiliated		-6.39	-45	n.a.

Churches	MegaBloc	Cong.	Members	Affiliates
Catholic	C	76	329,609	590,000
Assemblies of God	P	160	20,000	32,000
Jehovah's Witnesses	M	30	2,701	8,500
Seventh-day Adventist	P	18	1,238	2,900
Evangelical	P	10	830	1,300
Reformed	P	4	580	900
Other denoms [12]		42	3,601	5,900
Doubly affiliated			-28,000	-44,800
Total Christians [18]		340	330,600	594,000

Trans-bloc Groupings	pop. %	,000	Ann.Gr.
Evangelical	5.2	37	+3.8%
Charismatic	8.3	58	+2.5%
Pentecostal	4.9	34	+3.8%

Missionaries from Réunion
n.a.

Missionaries to Réunion
P,I,A 18 in 8 agencies from 6 countries.

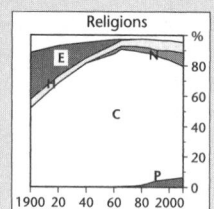
Religions

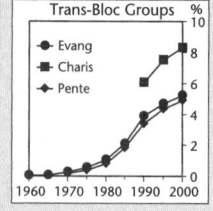
Trans-Bloc Groups
Evang
Charis
Pente

• Answers to Prayer

1 **Praise God for dramatic initial growth** since 1966 when the French Assemblies of God and then from 1970 AEF/**SIM** missionaries arrived. Many churches have helped people to be freed from occult bondage. The March for Jesus contributed to a greater networking together of Reformed, charismatic and evangelical congregations. Pray for growth in grace, numbers and spiritual understanding in these young and enthusiastic churches.

• Challenges for Prayer

1 **The dark legacy of slavery**, which was abolished in 1848, overshadows the present. The Creole population are descendants of those slaves. Poverty, unemployment, alcoholism, dysfunctional families and high illegitimacy have marginalized this large underclass. A deep work of healing and laying to rest the legacy of the past is still far from complete. Pray for the whole population to come to terms with the past — only really possible through faith in Christ.

2 **Although Catholicism is the professed religion** of over 80% of the population, the Malabar religion — a synthesis of Hinduism and African witchcraft — is the real faith of half the population and probably 90% are involved in some way. Since Vatican II, Bible reading has been promoted in the Catholic Church, and there is now a vigorous charismatic renewal movement. Pray for the eyes of many nominal Christians to be opened to their need and to the Saviour.

3 **Mature leadership for the young, growing churches is a priority**. Most leadership training is informal or must be pursued outside the territory.

4 **Young people** need prayer:

a) *Christians in the churches* — that they have high standards of holy living and that spiritual leaders for the **future** might be raised up.

b) *The disadvantaged* — the gap between them and the sophisticated, educated youth is widening. There are many challenges for reaching them effectively.

c) *YWAM* have a good ministry in motivating youth for evangelism and missions. **CEF** have a significant ministry to children through camps and Good News Clubs.

5 **Christian media**. Pray for impact through:

a) *Christian literature and Bible distribution*. There is only one Christian bookstore, nevertheless much literature has been distributed around the island.

b) *Radio.* There are private radio stations run by the Catholics, SDA and **AoG**. There is an encouraging response to **FEBA**'s daily broadcasts in French from Seychelles.

Romania

SEPTEMBER 24-25
EUROPE
Updated February 2004

GEOGRAPHY
Area 237,500 sq.km. Balkan state on the lower Danube River, mostly fertile rolling plains.

Population	Ann.Gr.	Density
2000	22,326,502	-0.36%	94 per sq. km.
2010	21,524,798	-0.38%	91 per sq. km.
2025	19,945,452	-0.58%	84 per sq. km.

Capital Bucharest 2,300,000. **Urbanites** 55%.

PEOPLES
Romanian 85.1%. A Latin people descended from Romans settled in Dacia.
Hungarian 7.1%. Primarily found in Transylvania.
Roma (Gypsy) 5.4%. Government figures admit only 400,000, but could be as high as 2 million.
Turkic 0.8%. Rumelian Turks 145,000; Tatar 22,000.
German 0.5%. Significant losses since 1988 due to emigration.
Other 1.1%. Most Eastern European ethnicities.

Literacy 97%. **Official language** Romanian. **All languages** 14. **Languages with Scriptures** 8Bi 2NT 3por 4w.i.p.

ECONOMY
A land rich in agriculture, minerals and oil but pillaged by a rapacious elite under Communism. Government reluctance and a strangling bureaucracy has slowed economic reform as Romania lags ever further behind other former Communist states. **Unemployment** 45% in 1998. **HDI** 0.752; 68th/174. **Public debt** 25.6% of GNP. **Income/person** $1,410 (4.5% of USA).

R

POLITICS
Communist coup in 1947 with Russian support. One of the Communist bloc's most oppressive and cruel regimes. Revolution of 1989-90 overthrew that regime, but former Communists still play a large role in government. There is a revival of anti-minority nationalism against Hungarians and Gypsies. Romania aspires to EU membership by 2007.

RELIGION
Under Communism, manipulation and control of the churches was oppressive, with severe persecution for those who refused to submit. A proposed bill on religious freedom contained policies as strict as any in the former Soviet Union, but this was withdrawn. Only 15 religious groups are officially recognized — others can only operate as associations. Minority groups find that most persecution comes from the Orthodox Church rather than the government itself.

Religions	Population %	Adherents	Ann.Gr.
Christian	87.85	19,613,832	-0.2%
non-Religious/other	11.08	2,473,776	-1.3%
Muslim	1.00	223,265	-0.4%
Jewish	0.04	8,931	-4.7%
Other	0.03	6,698	-0.4%

Christians	Denom.	Affil.%	,000	Ann.Gr.
Protestant	20	6.38	1,425	+0.4%
Independent	17	0.65	144	+5.3%
Anglican	1	0.00	0	+1.1%
Catholic	3	7.30	1,630	-0.4%
Orthodox	8	77.86	17,383	-2.2%
Marginal	3	0.64	142	+2.1%
Doubly affiliated		-4.98	-1,120	n.a.

The 1992 Census figures were not available at the time of writing in 2000, but upon acquisition, reported as follows: All Orthodox 87%, Catholic 6.1%, Protestant 5.8%, Marginal 0.59%, Muslim 0.25%, Non-Religious/other 0.45%.

Churches	MegaBloc	Cong.	Members	Affiliates
Romanian Orthodox	O	12,420	11.888m	17.00m
Roman Catholic	C	1,200	960,000	1,350,000
Reformed Ch of R	P	777	550,000	725,000
The Lord's Army	O	300	150,000	300,000
Greek Catholic	C	60	167,665	280,000
Pentecostal Chs in R	P	2,335	150,000	250,000
Christian Brethren [2]	P	871	55,657	150,000
Romanian Bapt Union	P	1,510	88,200	115,000
Seventh-day Adventist	P	1,056	71,544	100,000
Unitarian Chs in R	M	175	16,000	80,000
Jehovah's Witnesses	M	527	37,915	60,000
Old Ritual Orthodox	I	93	36,913	55,000
Other Indep [10]	I	400	20,000	40,000
Ev Luth Presb Synod	P	45	16,000	32,000
Ukrainian Orthodox	O	20	23,308	31,000
Gypsy Evang Mvmt	I	100	15,000	30,000
Ev Ch of Augs Conf	P	150	11,810	16,889
Hungar. Bapt Union	P	140	9,078	15,160
Other denoms [23]		267	64,700	95,000
Doubly affiliated			-772,414	-1,120,000
Total Christians [51]		22,446	13.559m	19.605m

Trans-bloc Groupings	pop. %	,000	Ann.Gr.
Evangelical	6.3	1,412	+1.1%
Charismatic	1.8	409	+1.9%
Pentecostal	1.3	297	+1.3%

Missionaries from Romania
P,I,A 115 in 15 agencies to 6 countries: Romania 107.

Missionaries to Romania
P,I,A 453 in 85 agencies from 20 countries: USA 274, Korea 35, Australia 14.

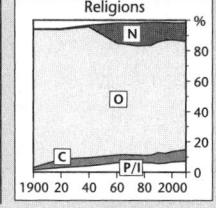

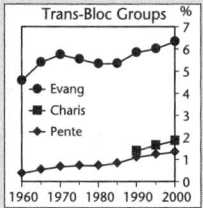

• Answers to Prayer

1 **Romania has Europe's third highest population of Evangelicals,** but the number of evangelical believers has not grown substantially since 1990, though evangelical denominations have grown.

2 **Since 1989, Romania has seen a sustained church planting movement,** with an average of five new church buildings opening every week until 1999. Only a lack of human and material resources prevents this from continuing at such a rate.

• Challenges for Prayer

1 **The burden of a tragic past** lies heavily upon Romania. The moral vacuum left by Ceausescu's Communists has been replaced by every kind of social evil. Substance abuse, prostitution and violent crime are all on the increase. Romania has one of the highest abortion rates in the world. With freedom has come wealth for a few, but grinding poverty for the majority. Many spend most of their income on food. Pray that the nation's leaders might boldly and uprightly address the many problems with wise solutions. Pray that this disastrous legacy might be replaced by one of peace and righteousness.

2 **Religious freedom** is a treasured, but threatened gain. The government, at the urging of some Orthodox leaders, has set tight restrictions for the registration and activity of other religious groups. Some groups in the Orthodox Church, reacting to what they see as Protestant predation of the faithful, are violently opposing evangelistic outreach. Millions of Romanians have grown up as "Christians", but with no meaningful exposure to the gospel — only 2-4% of Orthodox believers take their faith very seriously. Pray that there may be full freedom for the proclamation of the gospel and that there may be respect and trust — in all directions — between the major Christian bodies.

3 **The Lord's Army** is a remarkable, unofficial renewal movement within the Orthodox Church with about 300,000 converted adherents and many more sympathizers. It was severely persecuted in the past by both the Communists and the Orthodox hierarchy. Recently the Orthodox Church decided that the movement should be welcomed in the Church. The Lord's Army has close links with the Evangelical Alliance. Pray these believers may act as leaven in the whole Orthodox Church with its large nominal membership.

4 **The challenges facing the Church.** The church in Romania has developed well in the few years since the fall of Communism. A strong foundation has been laid for leadership and many types of ministry. Still, there are many needs which warrant prayer.

a) *The transition from severe persecution and restrictions, to freedom* of worship and witness has not been easy. Pray for flexibility and vision for the leadership; legalism and isolationism still threaten progress. Church structures can no longer function as in the days when the Church was underground. Pray that spiritual discipline and commitment may not be compromised.

b) *Ethnic divisions infect Christians too.* The poisoned relationships between Romanians and Hungarians and condoning the shameful treatment of Gypsies need an application of the Cross of Christ to heal these breakdowns. Denominational difference have intensified the issue further.

c) *Materialism imported from the West* has damaged spirituality. Westerners displayed a lack of wisdom in Romania by creating division and jealousy with their well-publicized material assistance. The deep spirituality of long-suffering churches was adversely affected as some agencies brought their Western values. Pray that outside assistance might be offered in an attitude of humility and service to the Romanian Church.

d) *Meeting the needs of Christian youth.* Few are able to minister meaningfully to young people.

e) *Nominalism among the German and Hungarian Protestants.* Many of the Lutheran and Reformed Churches need renewal. Most Protestant and evangelical growth is offset by losses in these ethnic groups.

f) *The Evangelical Alliance (EA)* formed in 1991 brings together the main Protestant and Independent bodies. Romanian Evangelicals suffer from a lack of unity and cooperation between denominations and para-church ministries. Pray that effective unity, cooperative evangelism and bold vision be promoted.

g) *A saturation church planting movement* is developing in Romania, as are several prayer movements. Pray that these movements might flourish despite government restrictions intended to thwart them.

5 **Bible training for existing and future leaders is a great need.** The average pastor supervises five churches. Most new churches lack a pastor, and many pastors lack training. This has hindered church growth.

a) *Bible schools and seminaries* have been launched by the Baptists, Pentecostals, Brethren and Presbyterians. The **Romanian Missionary Society** has started a Christian University in Oradea that focuses on training pastors and teachers. There are also modular training courses run by the **SGA.** While hundreds every year are taught in these places of learning, they are not yet enough to fill the needs of the churches. Pray that the schools might be able to train increasing numbers of students. Pray that the quality of teachers, course work and environment may be such that facilitate the formation of godly, visionary, educated Christian workers and leaders for the nation.

b) *BEE (Bible Education by Extension)* was pioneered in Romania and spread to many Communist Bloc countries. The work continues but has now become the basis of extensive development of Bible training in the denominations and is entirely run by Romanians. Pray for the hundreds of evangelical leaders studying part-time in BEE and other TEE courses. An advanced course is also now part of the programme.

6 **After Communism's collapse,** a profusion of agencies, congregations and individuals rushed in to help. Amidst much that was good and worthwhile, many went in with little tact and less wisdom. Short-term aid poured in, but the genuine needs were the establishment of an infrastructure for future work, and long-term workers who would learn the local language and facilitate the church to minister — rather than ministering instead of them. Pray that expatriates called to serve may show sensitivity, humility and an ability to learn from, and work alongside, Romanian Christians. Many Western groups are now working in partnership with Romanian agencies and churches.

7 **The younger generation** is the one which suffers most from the scars of Communism and its after-effects. Christian teachers are being trained so that this generation of children may be discipled. **CCCI**, ASCER/**IFES**, **YFC**, **CEF**, and the SdA all actively work with children and young people. Christian camps (RMS, **Crusaders**) have proved to be a very fruitful ministry. Perhaps the greatest need is that of the hundreds of thousands of orphans and street children — a legacy of Ceausescu's anti-contraception and high birth rate policies. The HIV rate among them is the highest in Europe. Working among them are the **Baptists**, **Samaritans Purse**, **SGA**, **WVI** and many other expatriate and national agencies. Pray that young people may encounter in very real ways the love of Christ, that they might be integrated into the church and used mightily of God to reach their own generation.

8 **The Romanian Church** is awakening to its responsibility to play its part in the Great Commission. It is also beginning to address the great social needs surrounding it. A national interdenominational sending agency was founded in 2000. Romanians can easily access fields which Westerners cannot. However, the economic situation in Romania is a challenge for the churches and those they would send. Pray for the removal of every barrier to the full flowering of an indigenous missions movement.

9 **The church is not evenly spread** throughout the nation. Pray for these less reached portions:

a) ***The Roma (Gypsy) community.*** Many live in ghettos and isolated villages. They are despised and neglected. Hundreds of thousands have fled Romania, only to meet harsh treatment in other European countries. But outreach to Gypsies is on the increase, and large numbers are turning to the Lord. Many Christian Gypsies now have bold vision to reach their own. The recent completion of the Kalderash Bible is a boon to the Gypsy believers.

b) ***The Muslims,*** who are predominantly Turks, Tatars and some Bulgarians. Most live in the southeast province of Constanta. Very little has been done to reach them, and Islamists from Turkey are becoming very active amongst them.

c) ***The south-east regions.*** There are three times more evangelical churches per capita in the north-west than in the south-east. There are 7,000 villages without an evangelical church in the south-east. Pray that believers might be burdened for these less reached areas and bring the light of the gospel to them.

10 **Christian media ministries.**

a) ***Literature.*** For years Romania has depended on free Western-produced Bibles and literature. This has often undermined the local publishers who operate without Western financing. Pray for the Romanian Bible Society, the **CLC** literature distribution base and many others, as they seek to establish a viable, indigenously-funded literature ministry. **SGA** and **RMS** assist in the translation and publication of Christian books and commentaries in Romanian — pray that more locally-written material might become available. Few pastors have a theological library.

b) ***Radio.*** Radio broadcasting is being taken up by evangelical groups, with assistance from agencies such as **RMS** and **HCJB**. But much of their work is met with opposition and legal wrangling; pray for complete freedom to broadcast the gospel. Pray for both local commercial Christian stations and transmissions from abroad (**TWR**) in both Romanian and Roma (Gypsy).

c) ***The JESUS film*** is shown in German, Hungarian, Balkan Romani, Romanian and Romanian sign language. More than half of the country has seen the film, and response to the message of the film is spectacular. Pray for the conservation of new believers in Bible-believing churches.

Russia

Russian Federation

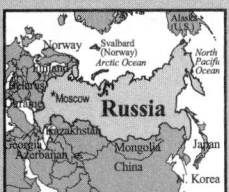

Russia

GEOGRAPHY

Area 17,075,400 sq.km. The world's largest country extending across 11 time zones between the Baltic and the Pacific. The Russian Federation is composed of 89 administrative districts including 21 republics, 49 regions (oblasts), 2 federal cities, 6 ethnic territories, 10 ethnic districts and one autonomous region.

Population		Ann.Gr.	Density
2000	146,933,847	-0.16%	9 per sq. km.
2010	144,418,309	-0.16%	8 per sq. km.
2025	137,932,932	-0.39%	8 per sq. km.

Massive decline — an estimated 30 million loss between 2000 and 2050 is likely. A further 25 million Russians live in 15 other fSU states. Siberia has one of the lowest population densities in the world.

Capital Moscow 13.2mill. **Other major cities:** St. Petersburg 5.55m; Nizhny Novgorod 1.98m; Rostov-on-Don 1.8m; Yekaterinburg 1.58m; Novosibirsk 1.55m; Samara 1.43m; Volgograd 1.4m; Chelyabinsk 1.3m; Omsk 1.2m; Kazan 1.2m; Perm 1.15m; Saratov 1.15m; Ufa 1.1m. **Urbanites** 73%.

PEOPLES

Great diversity made more complex by migrations, intense efforts to Russify minorities and immigration of fSU peoples into the present Russian Federation.

Indo-European 88.7%.
Slav(8) 84.9%. Russian 121m; Ukrainian 1.9m; Belarusian 440,000; Polish 90,000.
Caucasus Peoples 2.6%. Chechen 1.2m; Circassian (Adygey, Cherkess, Kabardi) 620,000; Avar 602,000; Armenian 556,000; Darghin 374,000; Lezhgi 238,000; Ingush 224,000; Georgian 136,000; Lak 122,000; Tabassaran 98,000.
Indo-Iranian 0.6%. Ossetian 400,000; Roma (Gypsy) 180,000.
Other 0.6%. German 580,000; Moldavian 145,000; Greek 85,000.
Turkic-Altaic(38) 8.2%.

Turkic 7.2%. Tatar (Bolgar) 6m; Chuvash 1.8m; Bashkort 1.8m; Kazakh 664,000; Azeri 350,000; Kumyk 290,000; Karachay-Balkar 240,000; Uzbek 130,000.
Altaic 1%. Buryat Mongolian 436,000; Yakut 400,000; Tuvin 215,000; Kalmyk Mongolian 200,000; Altai 83,000; Nogai 77,000; Evenki 32,000.
Finno-Ugric(29) 2.3%. Mordvinian(3) 1.2m; Udmurt 746,000; Mari(3) 736,000; Komi(3) 500,000; Finnish (Karelian, Inkeri) 270,000; Estonian 48,000; Khanti-Mansi 32,000.
Other 0.8%. Jews 470,000 and declining; Koreans 110,000.

Literacy 98%. **Official language** Russian; local languages in autonomous republics. **All languages** 96. **Languages with Scriptures** 3Bi 8NT 40por 80w.i.p.

ECONOMY

Vast natural resources and potentially the world's wealthiest country. Inadequate, crumbling infrastructure and the long-term structural and moral effects of the Marxist centralized command economy have prevented their exploitation for the benefit of the people. Efforts by the government to liberalize the economy and reduce state ownership have only been partially successful due to resistance by political and bureaucratic interest groups. By 1998 over 70% of the GDP was privately generated. Over 60% of the major state industries were taken over by the former Communist managers, many of whom became enormously wealthy. Criminal 'mafia' syndicates seized control of much of the economy (500 banks, 40,000+ businesses and 47 stock exchanges) and milked them for their own benefit with an estimated $300 billion stashed away in foreign banks. The domestic economy, the taxation system and effective trading virtually collapsed. About 30% of the people live on less than US$1.00 a day, 38% live in absolute poverty and 75% are worse off now than under Communism. There has been a significant up-turn economically since 1999 with a more stable government and increased earnings from oil exports. **HDI** 0.747; 71ᵃ/174. **Public debt** 26% of GNP. **Income/person** $2,680 (9% of USA).

POLITICS

Russia has known little but autocracy or tyranny since it became a country in the 8th Century. The Tsarist Empire collapsed in 1917 following the Bolshevik Communist revolution. Russia dominated the USSR from its founding in 1922, and the Communist leadership exploited both the ordinary Russian people, the many ethnic groups and client satellite states it seized or controlled. The resentment of the oppressed hastened the dismemberment of the USSR once central control in Moscow was weakened. A multi-party federal democracy was instituted in 1990 but the subsequent decade was traumatic. The tensions and confrontation between reformers and traditionalists, Westernizers and Slavophiles, Moscow and the restive republics and regions all hindered

R

balanced development. The unexpected election of President Putin in 1999 had much public support and restored authority at the centre to initiate change. Some fear a xenophobic nationalism and an erosion of basic freedoms. A large part of the press and media were once more directly or indirectly controlled by the government by 2001. Putin's power base and control of the reins of power made his re-election in 2004 almost automatic.

RELIGION

Freedom of religion written into the constitution. There is no formal state church, but Orthodoxy's 1,000-year history as part of the culture of Russia gives the Church enormous political influence. The 1997 federal law on freedom of religion was pushed through the Duma (Parliament) at the insistence of the Orthodox hierarchy. It supersedes all local laws, imposes restrictions on and discriminates against minority religions — especially newer arrivals. The legislation is so complex and ambiguous that its application is haphazard. In some areas it has become a pretext for arbitrary restrictions on local and expatriate organizations. **Persecution index** 58th in the world — higher in some Muslim-majority Russian republics.

Religions	Population %	Adherents	Ann.Gr.
Christian	54.07	79,447,131	-0.5%
non-Religious	31.08	45,667,040	-0.8%
Muslim	10.20	14,987,252	+1.3%
Other	2.50	3,673,346	+12.1%
Traditional ethnic	1.10	1,616,272	+5.1%
Buddhist	0.70	1,028,537	+1.3%
Jewish	0.32	470,188	-3.0%
Baha'i	0.03	44,080	+8.3%

Christians	Denom.	Affil. %	,000	Ann.Gr.
Protestant	34	0.65	950	+3.0%
Independent	32	1.47	2,158	+0.2%
Anglican	1	0.00	3	+5.7%

Catholic	1	1.02	1,500	+2.9%
Orthodox	8	41.26	60,624	+0.0%
Marginal	13	0.27	392	+17.4%
Unaffiliated		9.40	13,809	n.a.

Churches	MegaBloc	Cong.	Members	Affiliates
Russian Orthodox (ROC)	O	8,000	39.00m	60.00m
All Old Believers [3]	I	200	1,063,830	1,500,000
Catholic	C	300	974,026	1,500,000
Armenian Apostolic	O	12	239,521	400,000
Jehovah's Witnesses	M	904	107,111	280,000
Fringe Orthodox [8]	I	70	140,541	260,000
Lutheran	P	175	149,701	250,000
Union of Ev Chr Bapt	P	1,200	85,000	243,100
Union of CEF (Pente)	P	1,348	115,000	187,500
Unregis Pentecostal	I	300	46,000	110,000
Seventh-day Adventist	P	520	49,356	110,000
Indep Baptist Congs	P	850	45,000	85,000
Baptist Council (Unreg)	I	144	11,500	23,000
Other denoms [67]		2,244	416,000	678,000
Total Christians [89]		16,267	42.404m	65.627m

Trans-bloc Groupings	pop. %	,000	Ann.Gr.
Evangelical	0.7	1,000	+5.4%
Charismatic	0.3	509	+4.9%
Pentecostal	0.3	416	+2.9%

Missionaries from Russia
P,I,A 382+ in 17 agencies to 12 countries: Russia 355.

Missionaries to Russia
P,I,A 2,200+ in 146 agencies from 35 countries: USA 794, Ukraine 359, Korea 316, Finland 82, Canada 71.

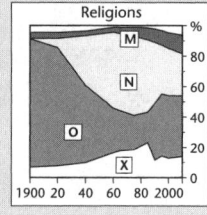

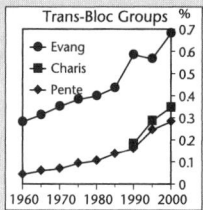

• Answers to Prayer

1 The spectacular collapse of Communism in 1990-1991 with little bloodshed was a direct answer to prayer. The ideology that sought to destroy Christianity and promised to parade the USSR's last Christian on television was defeated by Christians who prayed. Open Doors and others called for a seven-year campaign of prayer for the Soviet Union in 1984 with the specific goal of complete religious liberty and Bibles available for all. Much of this was achieved! Praise God!

2 The break-up of the Soviet Union opened up unprecedented opportunities for evangelism, church-planting, re-establishing a Christian infrastructure, many partnering networks, theological education, Bible translation and distribution. Churches of all kinds doubled from 7,500 to 15,000 in the 1990s. It is reckoned 20% of Russians moved from atheism to some profession of Christianity in that time — including many leading politicians.

3 The Bible is now freely available after years of costly 'smuggling' of God's Word. Between one and two million Bibles are printed and distributed in Russia every year.

4 Radio was a primary propaganda tool for the Communists — Radio Moscow and many local FM stations are now widely used by Christians.

5 **Many hitherto totally unreached peoples** — Muslim, superficially 'Orthodox' pagans and Buddhist — were given the opportunity to hear the gospel for the first time, and in many the first churches were planted.

• Challenges for Prayer

1 **Russia is a proud but despairing nation.** It has been systematically plundered and looted by the very ones who once deceived it with the morally destructive Communist ideology. Democracy appears a farce, economic progress an illusion and capitalism another form of banditry. The hopes of spiritual renewal of the early 1990s have been dashed by the failures of both political and Church leadership. Pray that Christian values of loving, sacrificial service and moral integrity might dispel the corrosive impact and legacy of Communism on both society and the Christian Church.

2 **The government faces a daunting task.** The election of President Putin brought a ray of hope that the catastrophic decline of the 1990s might be reversed. Major issues for prayer:

a) Political wisdom in balancing the need for strong government but with democratic accountability and respect of basic freedoms. A new tyranny is likely to arise if the present system fails.

b) Economic stability. Much must be done to set up the legal framework and financial accountability to successfully privatize industry, make services work and encourage investment. The poverty of the majority and their hopelessness has stimulated crime, drug abuse, alcoholism, family breakdown and suicide to alarming heights. Many ordinary people live for months without wages.

c) Justice. The economic levers of society have fallen into the hands of criminal networks that have crippled business initiative and subverted the bureaucracy. There is no chance of change for the better without confronting these dark forces which make a mockery of legislation that cannot be enforced.

d) Building a multi-cultural nation after centuries of imperial and Communist tyrannies and, at times, ethnic genocide. The Chechen war is one manifestation of the feelings of ethnic minorities having suffered injustice and mistreatment not only in the Caucasus but also the Urals, Siberia and the Arctic. Russification policies deprived minorities of their land and wealth and suppressed their languages and cultures. There is an ardent Russian nationalist movement which jeopardizes any move towards fair multi-culturalism and is virulently anti-Semitic and anti-foreign. Such attitudes threaten the integrity and survival of the Russian Federation. Inflamed nationalism severely hinders the progress of the gospel.

e) Upholding constitutionally guaranteed freedom of religion. An alliance of the Russian Orthodox Church (hostile propaganda and misrepresentation), the Press (biased reporting) and the local and regional authorities (imposing arbitrary restrictions on religious minorities) all threaten it. Such has been the pressure that the 1997 legislation with its punitive restrictions on religious minorities was passed despite its violation of human and constitutional rights. It became a bureaucratic nightmare involving the re-registration of all churches. Non-Orthodox have been made into second-class citizens, or even strangers in their own land. Pray that this legislation may be nullified and repealed, and true religious freedom re-established. Recent positive court cases and presidential recommendations have eased the pressure since 1999, but the battle is far from over.

f) Health. The combined effects of the collapse of funding for health services, the availability of free abortions for birth control and a general sense of communal despair is causing accelerated population decline through family disintegration, alcoholism, TB, AIDS, high infant mortality and emigration. Pray for improved funding, morale to be restored and Christians to play a greater role in health care.

g) A facing up to present and looming ecological disasters. Many thousands of square kilometres have been made uninhabitable by nuclear disasters and weapons testing (Chernobyl 1986, and parts of the Urals, Kazakhstan and the Arctic) and chemical/biological poisonings. The oil industry has massively polluted vast areas.

3 **The Church in Russia has suffered the most severe and sustained persecution** of any nation in recent history. All deaths in the *gulags* (prison camps) between 1920 and 1990 are reckoned at 20 million; a further 16 million perished *en route* to them —

many were Christian. It is reckoned 200,000 Christian leaders were martyred and a further 500,000 imprisoned. There were 100,000 church-owned buildings in 1920 (mainly Orthodox); by 1940 only 1,000 were in use by Christians, the rest being seized or destroyed. Structures and ministries were emasculated or manipulated, leadership cowed into compliance and compromise, Christians discriminated against, their children harassed and denied educational opportunities, and millions consigned to years of imprisonment, exile or psychiatric 'treatment'. Give thanks to God for His protection and for enabling His Church to survive, grow and triumph in the end. Praise God also for many agencies in the West who did so much to maintain links between the persecuted Church and Christians in the free world, and to provide Bibles, literature and practical help. Of special mention: **UBS**, **Open Doors**, **Light in the East** (Germany), **SGA** and Keston Institute in England, Swedish Slavic Mission, Bibles to All (Sweden) and *Avainsanoma* (Finland).

4 **The Russian Orthodox Church (ROC)** survived Communism and remains the one major symbol of Russian identity. Its liturgy and teachings continue to mould Russian culture. Openly professing Orthodox increased from 30 million in 1985 to 60 million in 2000. The Church is using every possible means to regain its exclusive spiritual dominance lost nearly a century ago. Pray for:

a) *An enhancement of the good* — an emphasis on the beauty and greatness of God and on the doctrine of the resurrection of Christ.

b) *An ending of intolerance*. The ROC's claim to be the one true apostolic Church and that all other faiths are invalid or sectarian stimulate attitudes of repression, tyranny and bigotry.

c) *A facing up to compromise under Communism*. Many of today's leaders have been exposed as tools of the atheists. Compromise brought deep divisions that still remain unaddressed years after Communism's demise.

d) *A rooting out of a culture of corruption* in the ROC. While attacking Western materialism the ROC has gained a dubious reputation for bribery, simony (awarding church posts for money), smuggling alcohol and tobacco, tax evasion and money laundering.

e) *True spiritual life*. The ROC claims to speak for all Russians, but only 3% are actively involved and 7% go to church once a month, though 50% claim a nominal allegiance to the Church and may have been baptized. There continues to be a disastrous neglect of the youth of Russia. Passive belief needs to change into a life-changing faith.

f) *Renewal movements within the ROC*. The traditionalists are the more powerful but are out of touch, clinging to a Slavonic Church liturgy which few understand, and grasping for political power. The reformers are often persecuted but are more Bible-focused, open for change and tolerant. Pray that future leaders may come from this more spiritual movement.

g) *Theological education*. This has long been neglected but the 5 Orthodox theological institutions of 1988 had become 51 in 1995. Pray that there may be true spiritual life in these.

5 **The religious freedom of the 1991-1997 period** was a time of euphoria, excitement and interest created by disillusionment with the old system and its leaders. The ideological vacuum was rapidly filled by eager foreign Evangelicals, Western and Eastern sects, the indigenous Vissarion movement and a rise in occultism, parapsychology and even Satanism. Roman Catholics multiplied because of their credible opposition to Communism. Evangelical congregations increased from 2,700 in 1990 to possibly 6,000 in 2000 but the Evangelical percentage increase was far less (0.6% to 0.7%). The expected harvest was not brought in to the churches. Pray for the redressing of these weaknesses:

a) *Inappropriate evangelism*. Huge evangelistic outreaches by foreign evangelists drew many people, glowing reports of 'conversions' gave high profile to the gospel, but long-term results were less encouraging. The long-persecuted churches were culturally isolated, lacked disciplers and could not cope with the new-style aggressive evangelism. Pray for flexibility, adaptability and culturally suitable local church outreach. Today's harsher spiritual climate calls for more effective means to welcome the many who have no understanding of Christian things.

b) *The need for practical holiness and integrity in daily life*. Communism created a society where deceit, fear, low moral and work standards, and unwillingness to make decisions became normal. This spirit affects many Christians too.

c) *Serious divisions*. These were rooted in the efforts of Communists to divide Christians. The bitterness between the formerly registered and unregistered churches (Baptists and

Pentecostals) continues today. The extreme hostility of some Evangelicals against anything Pentecostal or charismatic hinders cooperation and fellowship. This has been further complicated by imported divisions with the arrival of foreign programmes, finances and teachings. There is still no cooperative network to link together all Evangelicals. Pray for unity in the Holy Spirit and a breaking down of all barriers to fellowship.

d) *Emigration of Christians*. This has become an unspoken but crippling problem. The overall economic crisis, despair about the future, relentless Orthodox-instigated propaganda against 'sects' and the increase in crime, provoke any with the means or contacts to emigrate to the West. Many of the evangelical population under Communism were ethnically German — most Mennonites and many Baptists and Lutherans have now emigrated to Germany. They have been followed by many Russian Evangelicals. Many pastors have left; theological students trained abroad rarely return. The loss of leadership and educators is now crippling growth, damaging morale and hindering vision for the future. A new generation of committed leaders of bold faith is needed.

6 **Godly Christian evangelical leaders are too few** — lack of training in the past, lack of funding today and the loss of many through emigration contribute to this lack. Foreigners cannot fill the gap, but can assist in strengthening local churches and their leadership. The needs:

a) *Biblical leadership patterns*. Authoritarian leadership is a legacy of Russia's past as is the lack of theological depth. The results are petty legalisms, unquestioned authority, and theological 'fads'.

b) *Systematic teaching* and expository preaching through the Bible is rare. Pray for the many new theological institutions — most of US or Korean origin. There were 120 known in 1998. Pray also for the **Euro-Asian Accreditation Association** that seeks to ensure common standards in these institutions. Theological education is still too foreign and needs to be rapidly indigenized and address the issues relevant to Russia's unique situation.

c) *TEE is an important training tool*. SEAN launched a nation-wide programme in 1998 which is being embraced by many denominational and interdenominational networks to assist the thousands of pastors and preachers with minimal theological education. **Bible Education by Extension** (BEE) is now one of the largest TEE programmes in the world. The **Learning Alliance** (**MAF**, ASCP, **GEM**, Russian Ministries, etc.) are setting up innovative distance learning programmes. Pray for their successful growth and the development of appropriate teaching materials and methods.

7 **Vision for outreach.** Evangelicals learned to survive under persecution, but this needs to change. There is little indigenous initiative for nation-wide planning — those that exist are often of foreign origin. Pray for a new spirit of faith and expectancy and emergence of goals that enthuse local congregations across the Federation. Pray for:

a) *Church planting*. There is probably a gospel preaching church in Russia for every 30,000 people. Thousands of churches should be planted. **Project 250** (Russian Ministries) is a vision for planting a church for every 5,000 people by 2020. Similar visions are being taken up by many expatriate agencies including the Alliance for Saturation Church Planting (**UWM**, World Witness, **CBI, IMB-SBC, NTM, TEAM, The Bible League**, Global Missions Fellowship and others). Pray that this might become a network of indigenous and foreign workers that impacts the Federation by training and equipping thousands of church planters.

b) *An indigenous trans-denominational vision to emerge*. There needs to be initiative and funding for research, publicity and envisioning Russian believers. Evangelical congregations are unevenly distributed.

c) *Missions vision*. For years, Russian culture and language dominated and those of ethnic minorities was suppressed. Over 18% of the population is non-Russian and speak nearly 100 languages. Pray for a missions vision in the Russian church and ability to bridge the cultural and social barriers Russian missionaries face. Ukrainians have been far more active than Russians in cross-cultural outreach in Russia. Pray for the launching of many more Russian mission agencies.

8 **Expatriate Christians responded in large numbers** to the sudden opening of Russia in 1990. Some estimate over 1,500 missions and church-based agencies launched into ministry — delivering aid, support, preaching, evangelizing and Bible teaching. There were no structures and fellowship mechanisms in the country to coordinate or give guidance to this inrush. Much good was achieved, but also much bad perpetrated — importation of Western and Asian cultural forms or denominational differences, insensitivity to indigenous culture and leadership, unwise use of funds, and ecclesiastical empire-building. Most were short-term, relatively few were committed to long-term immersion in the language and culture. This and the assiduous activities of the Moonies, JWs, Mormons and others provoked an increasing negative reaction from the people. Conditions for foreign workers are now far less favourable, visas hard to obtain and renew. A number have been expelled. There are estimated to be 3,000 or more expatriate Christians serving in Russia. Pray for:

a) *Long-term missionaries* — for good relations with local government authorities, the issue of visas, local acceptance, wise deployment and protection from violence and malicious accusations. Some leading church and government officials hint that missionaries are linked with foreign intelligence agencies.

b) *All expatriates to be culturally sensitive* and respectful of Russian culture and links with Orthodoxy, and supportive of local initiatives, visions and leadership in churches. This was not a strong characteristic of many in the 1990s.

c) *Missionaries and agencies* to be models in networking and cooperative fellowship. There are several inter-agency networks — **Alliance for Social and Cultural Progress** (ASCP), and Association for Spiritual Renewal as well as partnerships focused on the major ethnic minorities for Bible translation, outreach, etc.

9 **Nation-wide ministry challenges** in special need of prayer:

a) *Over 90% of Russians* have no meaningful link with a church — whether Orthodox or not. Evangelical Christianity has not gained a firm foothold in European Russia, unlike in neighbouring Ukraine. In Siberia, Evangelicals have enjoyed more growth. In contrast the Jehovah's Witnesses have seen massive growth — which has its negative impact on Evangelicals.

b) *The rich and influential* are hardly touched by evangelical Christianity, which is seen as linked to ethnic minorities (Germans, Estonians, Ukrainians, etc.) or the poor and marginalized.

c) *Muslims* are becoming more visible and outspoken and radical Islam is increasing in influence. Around 15% of the population are of recognized Muslim ethnic groups — Turkic Central Asians, Caucasus peoples, Kurds, etc., but only 2-3% would be practising Muslims. There is a growing sense of confrontation provoked by the earlier Russian war in Afghanistan and continuing war in Chechnya. Muslims equate Christianity with crude Orthodox Christian attempts at forcible conversions. Pray that historic, social and spiritual barriers to the gospel may be removed.

d) *The 25 million Russians of the 'near abroad'.* The collapse of the USSR left many of them as ethnic minorities in the 15 new states formed — often hated and resented. Their status and future are far from secure. A further 9 million Russians have emigrated back to the Russian Federation — often with very little. Pray that many among them might become receptive to the gospel.

e) *Students and young people.* Over 3.6 million study in 48 universities and 866 higher education institutes. Various international student agencies work with networks of Christian groups on campuses. There are strong influences from both secularism and American culture, but no more than a curiosity about Christianity — few are ready for the demands of discipleship in a highly dysfunctional society and the pervasive suspicions sown by Orthodox propaganda. Pray for strong witnessing groups that impact intellectuals, and effective leadership for them.

f) *Children.* They are at high risk of violence, abuse, neglect and abandonment because of the economic crisis and severe breakdown of family life. Some estimate that there are 1.2 million street children in the cities, 650,000 orphans housed in grim, inadequate orphanages and many in prisons. Many turn to extreme violence and crime. There is a growing concern for churches to become involved in ministry to them. Pray for the emerging umbrella organization **To Russian Children with Love** linking 40 agencies and Russian churches as strategies are developed to meet their needs. **CEF** run training courses for children's evangelists and a BCC with 70,000 children involved.

g) *Alcoholics.* No country has such a severe alcohol abuse problem as Russia. Official estimates are that 40% of men and 7% of women are alcoholics. Anything is stolen and sold for vodka. The effects on family life and society are staggering. Ministry in this area is limited. In 1997 the ASCP launched OPORA — an evangelical body set up to develop ministries for those involved in substance abuse, training for churches, setting up of support groups, training workers, producing literature, etc. Other churches and agencies are beginning to address this serious problem.

h) ***Drug abusers***. Addicts numbered 130,000 in 1990, but by 1998 this had climbed to 3 million. Drug rehabilitation is a major challenge for Christian ministry.

i) ***AIDS victims***. AIDS has grown massively through drug use and promiscuity. In 1997 100,000 were known to be infected. Estimates for 2000 are 800,000, but no one knows the true number because of inadequate healthcare funding. It is feared that by 2010 there will be 500,000 AIDS orphans.

j) ***Prisoners***. Over 1.7 million are behind bars in overcrowded prisons, 20,000 die annually, TB affects 15% and AIDS is spreading rapidly. A Russian ministry, Liberty Through Jesus, reaches out to them. Much more needs to be done.

k) ***New religionists***. Some claim massive followings. The Hare Krishna are found all over the RF. The indigenous messianic *Vissarion* movement claims 10 million followers, mainly in Siberia. The JWs are now 260,000 in number. Parapsychologists, hypnotists, shamanists and Satanists have gained wide publicity and influence. Pray that Christians may be trained and armed with the Truth to combat these and win those ensnared. The **Center for Apologetics Research** seeks to help pastors and churches with training and literature.

l) ***Unreached peoples***. There may be up to 100 ethnic minorities without an indigenous church or where work is still in a pioneer stage. (See below under the different ethnic republics.) Pray for effective partnering and viable strategies to plant churches among them. Several widely dispersed peoples need prayer:

i   *The Jews once numbered over 2 million,* but now are reduced to a quarter of this. Many are emigrating to Israel, but there are important concentrations in European Russian cities. Though most are secularized, some have been open to the gospel and come to Christ — a large proportion of Messianic Jews in Israel are of recent Russian and Ukrainian origin. There are also pockets of Georgian, Tat and Hill Jews in the Caucasus region totalling 14,000 who are still unreached.

ii   *The Roma (Gypsies).* These live scattered over European Russia with many in the Urals. In some areas there has been an awakening and churches have been planted. About 5% of Russian Gypsies are Evangelicals.

iii   *The Chinese.* Illegal immigrants into Siberia and the Russian Far East are increasing and may now number over 1 million. There are 2 Chinese congregations in Moscow.

10   **Christian Support Ministries** for prayer:

a) ***Bible distribution***. The Swedish-founded Bible translation agency **IBT** has had a praiseworthy ministry since 1973 of translating the Scriptures in 50 languages (3Bi, 12NT, 36por) and the Children's Bible in 28. The Bible Society of Russia (BSR) was re-established in 1992 and now has a large depot from which 2 million Bibles and NTs are distributed annually. A long-awaited modern Russian translation of the Bible is underway.

b) ***Bible translation*** is an ongoing challenge. The BSR(**UBS**), **IBT** and **SIL** are working together on 80 translation projects. There are 30 million people who speak languages without a NT. Pray for the personnel, competent native language speakers, finances and freedom to complete this daunting task. Among many of these peoples there may be no more than a handful of believers.

c) ***Christian literature***. There are now several Christian Publishers — MIRT, Bibles for All and Triad being three large ones. Printing, distribution and sales are immense challenges due to Russia's size and economic crisis. Far too little is locally written. Massive free distributions of Western-produced literature has often proved inappropriate, costly and damaging to local initiative. Pray for effective cooperation in literature strategies.

d) ***Newspaper evangelism***. The Christian agency **Good News** (supported by AMG Int., German Evangelical Alliance, **SGA** and others) has bought space in newspapers — with over 3 billion messages distributed by 2000 and netting a letter response of 2 million.

e) ***MAF-USA*** entered Russia in 1992 and from its base in Moscow has developed an unusual service — logistics, warehousing of Christian materials for 70 organizations and supplying literature for **Russian Ministries**, **CoMission II**, distance learning and email/internet services.

f) **The JESUS film** has been extensively shown on TV, film and video and the equivalent of 80% of the population has viewed it in one of 28 languages. A further 10 languages are in preparation.

g) **Christian radio** played an honoured role during Communist rule in evangelism and encouragement of Christians. The influence of Christian agencies such as **TWR, FEBC, HCJB, IBRA,** Russian Christian Radio (Earl Poysti) and others cannot be underestimated. Today these same agencies are free to buy broadcast time on local FM stations in cities across the RF and also transmit internationally from Radio Moscow (**TWR**) and Siberia (**TWR** to India in 28 languages). Praise God for this astonishing reversal! **Radio Theos** has a significant impact from stations in St Petersburg and Moscow. **HCJB** is coordinating a consortium of agencies to set up 24 hours/day Christian broadcasting by satellite to the whole country. Pray for continued freedom to broadcast, for programme producers, for eternal fruit.

h) **Christian TV.** **CBN** claims to have built up a viewership of 25 million and by 1996 had received 15 million responses and linked 750,000 to BCCs.

GEO-ETHNIC ENTITIES OF THE RUSSIAN FEDERATION

The Russian Federation is a complex patchwork of republics, regions, territories and districts. These are grouped below by geo-cultural affinities because of their commonalities. All have suffered severely through Russian imperial conquest, Communist oppression, cultural suppression, crude Russification and imposition of Russian Orthodoxy. Some have survived ethnocide and massive deportations under Stalin. A number of Caucasus and Siberian peoples lost half their populations during that time. Pray that reconciliation between peoples through deep repentance and forgiveness might be achieved and the negatives of the past no longer hinder the spread of the knowledge of the love of Christ.

Please turn the many facts that follow into prayer for the salvation of these many unreached peoples and for the building up of the Body of Christ.

THE ARCTIC PEOPLES OF EUROPE AND SIBERIA

Republic and regional populations Komi 1.18m; Sakha (Yakutia) 1.02m; Karelia 785,000.
Districts Khanty-Mansi 1.33m; Yamalo-Nenets 488,000; Komi-Permyak 157,000; Chukotka 91,000; Nenets

48,000; Taymyr 47,000; Koryat 33,000; Evenki 20,000. The climate is harsh and living conditions extreme. Most of the indigenous peoples are of hunting-gathering and reindeer herding cultures. The Russian communities are mostly involved in the oil industry or mining, and live in the towns.

1 **Karelia** was seized from Finland after World War II; most of the Karelian Finns fled to Finland; 74% of the population is Russian. Pray for adequate leadership for the churches. There are about 15,000 Evangelicals.

2 **Komi and Komi-Permyak** in the north Urals are rich in minerals. The Finno-Ugric Komi number 344,000; most are still pagan. Evangelicals among Russians (mainly) and Komi number about 1,500. They faced increased opposition in the late 1990s. Many areas are without a witness.

3 **The Nenets (35,000) and the Finno-Ugric Khanti (22,000), Mansi (8,000) and Saami (3,000)** are largely shamanists. There are only a handful of committed believers and a few fellowships using their own languages. There is openness to the gospel as long as it is not linked to Russian dominance.

4 **Sakha** has a high degree of autonomy and is potentially wealthy with gold, diamonds and other minerals. Half the population is Russian and the other half the indigenous Turkic Sakha (Yakut — 400,000). Paganism among the Sakha and related Evenki (32,000) has revived. Evangelical work was pioneered by the Ukrainian Light of the Gospel (now Light in the East). InterAct Ministries and other agencies have joined them. In 1987 there were 30 Yakut believers, but in 1999 there were 45 churches or groups in 32 of the 505 towns with 300 active believers.

5 **Chukotka** is the home of the Eskimo-related Chukchi (17,000) and Koryak of the northern Kamchatka Peninsula peoples. A number of Chukchi have come to Christ through Alaskan Eskimo evangelists from across the Bering Strait.

6 **Bible translation** work has begun in all of these Arctic peoples and those of Kamchatka. Mark's Gospel was published in Mansi and Khanti in 2000.

THE NORTH CAUCASUS PEOPLES

Republics Dagestan 2,098,000; Chechnya 1,200,000; Kabardino-Balkariya 790,000; Severnaya Ossetiya-Alaniya (North Ossetiya) 663,000; Adygeya 450,000; Karachayevo-Cherkesiya 436,000; Ingushetiya 300,000.

1 **The North Caucasus region** lies between the Black and Caspian Seas. There are 8 republics (including Abkhazia) and a medley of 50-60 ethnic groups of Caucasus, Turkic and Iranian origin. These restive peoples have long resented Russian domination. The Chechen wars of the 1990s have destabilized the whole region. Pray for wisdom, restraint and moderation to replace present extremes and rhetoric and for a fair political solution — especially in Chechnya, Dagestan, Ingushetiya and Abkhazia.

2 **Islam predominates** in all the indigenous peoples except the Ossetians who are largely nominal Orthodox. The Islamists, with much help from the Muslim world, have wrested the initiative in Chechnya and its war against the Russians. They press for a single Islamist North Caucasus state. Pray that Islamist plans may be thwarted and the whole region experience peace, progress and religious freedom.

3 **The North Caucasus peoples** are some of the least-reached on earth, and certainly live in Europe's least evangelized region. Most of the 50 or so ethnic groups have no churches or Christians and little or nothing of the Scriptures in their languages. Pray for open doors and favourable conditions for Christians to reside and witness. At present Westerners would be prime targets for kidnapping. Pray for the inter-agency partnership that is working to bring blessing in Christ to this region. Pray also for **IBT** and its work of translation of the Bible into 25 languages of the area.

4 **The Cherkess** (Circassian) people (585,000) were divided by Soviet ethnic engineering into three republics — Adygeya, Kabardino-Balkaria and Karachayevo-Cherkess. They speak three dialects, Kabardian, Cherkess and Adyghe. Over 1.5 million live scattered over the Middle East and Eurasia. They were Christian from the 6th to 15th Century when they turned to Islam. In 1993 only 5 Christians were known, but by 1999 this had climbed to 40. These few believers are subject to intimidation. Pray for the small emerging house groups and those Russian and expatriate workers seeking to reach and help them (**IBT**, Light in the East, Bible League). The NT was completed in Adyghe in 1991.

5 **The Turkic Balkar** (80,000) and **Karachay** (169,000) are nominally Muslim and live among the Cherkess. The Russian New Way Mission works among the Balkar and also produces literature in the language. The Karachay can read the Balkar NT. There are only a handful of believers.

6 **Chechyna** has long resisted Russian rule. The wars of the 1990s continue with the Russians controlling the plains in the day and Chechen guerrillas the mountains. This war is part of a wider strategy to form an Islamic Caucasus state. The 950,000 Chechen are almost entirely Muslim and have been radicalized by indigenous Sufism and international Islamists. Over 100,000 Chechen have died and 500,000 are refugees in surrounding states and RF republics. The nation is traumatized, the country devastated and almost all the limited Christian presence eliminated or expelled. Christian aid organizations have withdrawn to work among refugees in North Ossetiya and Ingushetiya (Salvation Army, Russian Ministries, World Concern, **WVI**). Pray that out of this suffering might emerge a Chechen Church — only 10 believers are known.

7 **Dagestan** is 94% Muslim and home to 34 ethnic groups. The largest indigenous groups: Avar 602,000; Darghin 374,000; Lezhgi 238,000; Lak 122,000; Tabassaran 98,000; Nogai 91,000. It is the poorest republic in the RF. The nearby Chechen War has deeply destabilized the republic. There is a rapid rise in extreme Muslim Wahhabite groups (7% of the population) who are violently bent on forming an Islamic republic. All Christian work is under threat and dangerous for Christian workers — kidnapping, intimidation and violence have been commonplace. There are possibly no more than 10 individual believers among the 34 indigenous peoples, though the 1,000-member Hosanna Church in the capital has many Muslim background believers. **IBT** is working on 14 languages (Mark's gospel in 6; The Avar NT for 2005). Tabassaran is reputed to be the world's most complex language.

8 **The Ossetians** live in both Georgia and Severnaya-Ossetiya. The republic is struggling to cope with the disruptions caused by the Chechen war (refugees) and war with the Ingush but there are few Evangelicals and little outreach. There is a revival of paganism.

9 **Abkhazia** is an unrecognized republic of 525,000 people that emerged from the Georgian-Abkhaz war in the early 1990s. There are many fSU peoples in Abkhazia; Abkhazians being only 17% of the population and are almost all nominally Muslim, overlaying Abkhaz paganism. There are very few Evangelicals and virtually none among the Abkhazians. **IBT** is translating the NT.

R | # THE ALTAI-MONGOLIAN PEOPLES
Republics Buryatiya 1,053,000; Khakasiya 586,000; Kalmykiya 319,000; Tuva 309,000; Altay 202,000. | **Districts** Ust-Ordyn Buryat 143,000; Agin Buryat 79,000.
All but the Altay and Khakassians are Buddhist in culture. Buddhism is experiencing a renaissance.

 Kalmykiya lies north-west of the Caspian Sea. There is rapid desertification and impoverishment due to local corruption and mismanagement. Kalmyks are 45% of the republic's population. The Kalmyk are related to the Mongolians and are Europe's only Buddhist people. There is much occult bondage. A Ukrainian mission Light of the Gospel pioneered church planting; other missions followed. There are only 50 believers and several fellowships of Kalmyk. The NT is planned for completion in 2001.

2 **The Buryat people** live north of Mongolia, around Lake Baikal, which contains 20% of the world's fresh water. Half of the 450,000 Buryat live in Buryatiya. They are the largest indigenous ethnic group in Siberia. Lamaistic Buddhism has revived considerably since 1990. An abortive attempt at evangelizing the Buryat by the LMS from England (1817-1830) was ended by Buddhist and Orthodox opposition. Since 1990 a partnership of 26 agencies are working for their evangelization. There are now some believers and small, but growing churches. The NT is being translated.

3 **Tuva** (Uriankhai) lies north-west of Mongolia. The Tuvinians (207,000) are a Turkic people who suffered severely under Communist rule. They are renowned for their unique *khomeii* singing with two voices. Tuva is economically destitute; crime, alcohol abuse, the occult and drugs are major social problems. Lamaistic Buddhism and shamanism are strong. There were no believers in 1990. Since 1997 there has been significant response to the gospel with spiritual strongholds breached. The **AoG** now have 14 churches with over 1,000 believers. The NT is due for completion in 2001. The *JESUS* film was completed in 1997.

4 **Khakasiya** to the north-west of Tuva is 80% Russian. The Khakass people are a small minority. They are Turkic shamanists with very few Christians and little evangelical work. They have requested the Tatar people to send Muslim missionaries. The Evangelical Lutheran Mission was forcibly closed in 1998. Pray that this small people might be evangelized.

THE URAL-VOLGA REPUBLICS

Republics Bashkortostan 4,097,000; Tatarstan 3,760,000; Udmurtia 1,639,000; Chuvashiya 1,361,000; Mordoviya 956,000; Mari-El 766,000.

The South Urals are rich in minerals and agricultural land. The indigenous peoples of three republics (Bashkortostan, Chuvashiya and Tatarstan) are Turkic and descendants of the ancient Bolgar peoples. The other three republics are basically Finno-Ugric. The Chuvash, Udmurt, Mari, Erzya and Mordvin are superficially Orthodox and basically animist and the Tatar and Bashkort (Bashkir) largely Muslim.

1 **Tatarstan** has abundant resources — minerals and farmland. It has a high degree of political autonomy. The Tatar have long been Muslim and are Russia's largest Muslim people (5.7 million) though many are nominal or secular. About 10% of Tatars are nominally Orthodox. Since 1990 Islam has advanced with 500 mosques built by 1996 and an Islamic University founded in 1999.

a) *Legislation passed in 1999* is even more draconian than the 1997 RF laws. The Orthodox and Muslims banded together to prevent other faiths gaining a foothold. The state has the power to liquidate any religion that is not officially registered — and that is very hard to obtain. Pray that religious freedom might be upheld.

b) *There are some evangelical churches or groups*, most Russian-speaking and about 30, mostly small, groups in Kazan, the capital. Tatar believers increased during the 1990s but still only number around 300 — most in Russian-language churches and some in 15 Tatar-speaking fellowships. Increased persecution has brought about closer fellowship among Evangelicals historically divided by language and the charismatic issue. Pray especially for the Tatar Church to be protected — the authorities have harassed them.

c) *Christian literature* in Tatar is increasing. The NT is to be published in 2001 and the OT is being translated.

2 **Bashkortostan** is the home of the **Bashkort** (Bashkir), a Turkic people related to the Tatar.

a) *The Bashkort* became Muslim in the 16th Century, but the old folk religion and occultism remain strongly entrenched. Pray for the binding of the powers that hold them.

b) *There were 12 congregations of Evangelicals* in 1998, but none which used the Bashkort language. By 2001 there were 6 Bashkort-speaking fellowships and 150 known believers. Registration of churches is very difficult and the authorities obstructive. There has been response among university students. Pray for the planting and growth of mature Bashkort churches.

c) *The Bashkort NT* will be adapted from the Tatar NT. Literature in Bashkort is appreciated. Some foreign tentmakers involved in Bible translation were expelled in 1999.

3 **The Chuvash** are predominantly secular/atheist with a nominal Orthodox background. The rise of nationalism has stimulated a return to paganism and a growing interest in Islam. There are a few evangelical churches but most use Russian. A new translation of the NT and Bible is underway but finance is lacking to print what has been prepared for publication.

4 **The Hill and Meadow Mari** are indigenous to Mari El, 700km east of Moscow. They became nominally Orthodox two centuries ago. About 30% are Orthodox, 60% syncretistic/pagan. In the 1990s the local government declared paganism as the official religion. Today there are 35 Orthodox, and about 25 struggling Baptist, Lutheran and Pentecostal churches. The two **Mordvin** peoples of Mordoviya, the Erzya and Moksha, are similar to the Mari, but more strongly Orthodox in culture.

5 **The Udmurt** are 31% of the population of Udmurtiya. The enforced Orthodoxization of the Udmurt bred a hatred and fear of Russians. Since 1990 there has been a revival of paganism. Despite negative propaganda and banning of all missionaries, there are 21 officially registered evangelical churches and others still applying. There are 7,000 active evangelical church members out of a 50,000 strong community. The Udmurt OT is being translated.

Rwanda
Republic of Rwanda

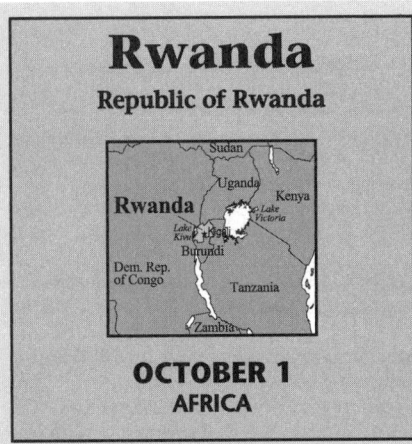

OCTOBER 1
AFRICA

GEOGRAPHY
Area 26,338 sq.km. A fertile, mountainous country similar to its southern neighbour, Burundi.

Population		Ann.Gr.	Density
1990	6,987,000	+2.9%	265 per sq. km.
1995	5,259,000	-5.5%	200 per sq. km.
2000	7,733,127	+8.02%	294 per sq. km.
2010	9,534,549	+2.10%	362 per sq. km.
2025	12,426,835	+1.51%	472 per sq. km.

A massive 25% population loss in 1994-5 through massacres, genocide (nearly 1 million) and flight of refugees (over 1 mill.). Most of the latter have returned.

Capital Kigali 237,782. **Urbanites** 5.4%.

PEOPLES
Hutu (Bantu) 81%. The former serf class.
Tutsi (Nilotic) 18%. The former feudal rulers.
Twa (Pygmy) 0.3%.
Other 0.7%.

Literacy 60%. **Official languages** French, English, kiNyarwanda. The entire population speaks kiNyarwanda.

ECONOMY
Fertile agricultural land with few natural resources. Main sources of foreign exchange are coffee, tea and aid. Over-population and distance from the sea inhibit development. Nearly 40 years of conflict between the Hutu and Tutsi peaked in the terrible events of 1994-5. The economy was severely dislocated and continues to be so with the ongoing Central African War mainly in neighbouring Congo-DRC. There have been recent improvements as the government attempts to restructure and privatize the economy. **HDI** 0.379; 164th/174. **Public debt** 59% of GNP. **Income/person** $210 (0.7% of USA).

POLITICS
A feudal Tutsi monarchy which continued through German colonial occupation (1899-1916) and Belgian Mandate (1916-1962). A Hutu revolt overthrew the Tutsi government in 1959 with many Tutsi killed or driven into exile. A Tutsi invasion from Uganda in 1990 led to conflict, many deaths and the displacement of thousands of people. Hutu extremists seized power in 1994 and put into action the planned genocide of the Tutsi minority and Hutu moderates. In 100 days 800,000 perished. The more disciplined Tutsi-led forces gained control and over a million Hutu fled to surrounding lands. The extremist Interahamwe Hutu militia then spread terror and destruction in the Congo and areas of Rwanda. The transitional government struggles to reduce inter-ethnic hatred and institute a non-racial democracy while protecting the minorities. All international efforts to broker a lasting peace failed to overcome the fears and hatred of extremists.

RELIGION			
There is full freedom of religion.			

Religions	Population %	Adherents	Ann.Gr.
Christian	80.83	6,250,687	+8.0%
Muslim	10.50	811,978	+8.4%
non-Religious/other	4.50	347,991	+8.0%
Traditional ethnic	3.97	307,005	+6.8%
Baha'i	0.20	15,466	+8.0%

Christians	Denom.	Affil.%	,000	Ann.Gr.
Protestant	20	18.76	1,451	+6.5%
Independent	11	0.81	63	+11.6%
Anglican	1	10.59	819	+7.1%
Catholic	1	42.67	3,300	+8.5%
Orthodox	1	0.01	0	+0.0%
Marginal	1	0.26	20	+14.6%
Unaffiliated		7.73	597	n.a.

Churches	MegaBloc	Cong.	Members	Affiliates
Catholic	C	1,133	1,813,187	3,300,000
Anglican	A	2,000	245,961	819,050
Seventh-day Adventist	P	909	342,664	520,000
Pentecostal	P	1,859	139,423	290,000
Presbyterian	P	74	120,000	216,000
Free Methodist	P	200	30,000	130,000
Baptist Union	P	299	36,557	110,000

Assoc des Eg Baptistes	P	126	27,000	59,000
Ch of the Nazarene	P	110	28,000	42,000
Jehovah's Witnesses	M	92	6,828	20,000
Church of God (Clev)	P	79	6,608	13,000
Assemblies of God	P	51	4,892	10,782
Other denoms [23]		682	59,390	123,200
Total Christians [35]		7,614	2,860,510	5,653,000

Trans-bloc Groupings	pop. %	,000	Ann.Gr.
Evangelical	22.8	1,762	+6.9%
Charismatic	9.1	706	+7.2%
Pentecostal	4.3	336	+6.3%

Missionaries from Rwanda
P,I,A 46 in 6 agencies — most in Rwanda.

Missionaries to Rwanda
P,I,A 76 in 23 agencies from 13 countries: USA 33, UK 8, Denmark 7, Korea 6.

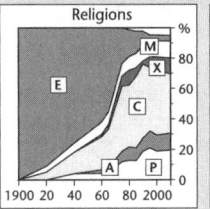

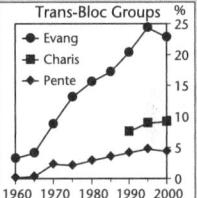

• Challenges for Prayer

1 **The genocide that caused the death of a million men, women and children** stunned the world and traumatized the nation.

a) *Rwanda desperately needs peace and an end to centuries of inter-ethnic hatred*. Pray that the transitional government, the churches and international bodies may succeed in achieving this.

b) *The United Nations as well as Western and African governments all failed* to act in time and with courage to prevent the 1994 calamity. Death, despair and disillusionment prevail. Pray that this dark cloud may be lifted. Conditions were slowly improving by 2000.

c) *The transitional government will end in 2003*. Pray that a fair, stable, non-racial political and social democratic framework may be established by then.

d) *The need for justice*. Many of the most responsible for the genocide are still on the loose. Over 125,000 have been detained because of their possible involvement, with many innocent among the guilty, but the courts are only slowly processing them — at present rates it will take 200 years! Of Rwanda's 719 magistrates in 1994, only 250 survived. Pray for justice to be done, and to be seen to be done in a timely way.

2 **The East African Revival** began in Rwanda in the 1930s. The blessing was lost and the heritage of tribalism which was crucified with Jesus on the cross, forgotten. Many were shocked that a nation nearly 90% 'Christian' could sink to such barbarities. Too few Christians spoke out against the atrocities, and some even connived with the perpetrators. Pray for a deep spirit of repentance, and for revival to sweep through the churches once more. Pray that the Church may be cross-centred, Bible-based, supra-tribal and become truly prophetic and evangelistic. Recent suffering has increased the fervour of many.

3 **Many Christians suffered much.** Thousands of spiritual leaders were murdered. Many leaders despair of being able to cope with the desperate physical, social, psychological and spiritual damage done. Pray for all involved in reconciliation, counselling, discipling and training ministries. Bible schools and seminaries are seeking to regain lost ground in providing leaders for the future. There is a dearth of good Bible study aids. Pray

OCTOBER 1 · RWANDA

that God may raise up men and women of God fitted for Rwanda's hour of need. Pray also for protection for church leaders from extremists who still want to promote tribalism and fuel ethnic hatreds.

4 **Young people** were deeply affected by the events of the 1990s. Pray for:

a) *Ministry to university students* which has had to begin from scratch. All 60 GBU(**IFES**) Bible study leaders lost their lives; most graduates fled. Of the 5,000 university students, 1,000 come to GBU meetings, but follow-up is hard due to lack of resources. **CCCI** also has a significant campus ministry.

b) *Scripture Union* which has a ministry among young people of all churches, thus helping to lessen denominational rivalry. Pray for blessing on the daily Bible-reading notes and extension of this ministry to the churches, for this is often the only systematic Bible training most people get. Pray also for the **SU** programme to develop materials for new converts — few churches have a vision for this.

c) *Other Christian associations* such as **AEE**, **YWAM**, **YFC** and *Moucecore* who are working to help young people overcome their problems and build up their unity as one people.

d) *Orphans from genocide, war and AIDS may number 500,000*. There are over 85,000 child-led families (usually young girls) caring for 300,000. Pray for churches and agencies seeking to alleviate the pain and the poverty of these children and to help initiate income-generating work for them.

5 **Missionaries** have returned since 1994. The demands are enormous with the lack of national Christian workers. Conditions can be emotionally harrowing — especially when engaged in helping those most affected by the war and by AIDS. Pray that their contribution might be invigorating for the Church and uplifting for the people. The largest agencies: Swedish Pentecostal Mission (25 workers), SdA (18), Evangelical Friends (6), **CMS** (Mid-Africa Ministry) (5), **WVI** (5), **AoG** (4), **IMB-SBC** (3).

6 **Ministry challenges** that need intercession:

a) *AIDS has become another nightmare* for this beautiful, but tragic land. In 2000 there were at least 400,000 infected (11% of the population) and 270,000 orphaned due to AIDS. Pray that more might be done by Christians in prevention (**SU** and Aid for AIDS, etc.) and in care for those affected.

b) *The Pgymy Twa* are marginalized. Many are itinerant potters. Some reckon that up to 75% were killed in the genocide. Relatively fewer of this people are Christian.

c) *Muslims* have increased significantly in the 1990s through an aggressive mosque-building programme. Many have been attracted by Muslim claims of the tolerance and peace found in Islam in contrast to the genocidal 'Christians'. Estimates of their percentage vary between 2% and 5%. There is no specific ministry equipped or committed to reach them.

d) *Detainees and prisoners* languishing in over-crowded prisons face a long and hopeless future. Pray for churches seeking to minister to their physical and spiritual needs.

7 **Christian support ministries:**

a) *Christian radio* — **TWR** broadcasts in kiNyarwanda from Johannesburg, South Africa.

b) *The JESUS film* has been viewed by the equivalent of 40% of the population.

R

Samoa

Independent State of Samoa

Samoa

OCTOBER 2
PACIFIC

GEOGRAPHY
Area 2,831 sq.km. Two large volcanic islands, Savai'i and Upolu, and seven small islands covered by lush tropical rainforest.

Population	Ann.Gr.	Density
2000	180,073	+1.44%	64 per sq. km.
2010	216,958	+1.90%	77 per sq. km.
2025	271,417	+1.35%	96 per sq. km.

Over 200,000 Samoans live in American Samoa, USA, New Zealand and Australia.

Capital Apia 40,000. **Urbanites** 21%.

PEOPLES
Indigenous Polynesian 98.3%.
Samoan 15,800; Euronesian 18,000.
Other 1.7%. Other Polynesian, European.

Literacy 99%. **Official languages** Samoan, English. **Languages with Scriptures** 2Bi.

ECONOMY
Agricultural subsistence economy. Imports far exceed exports. Heavily dependent on remittances from Samoans abroad and tourism. Neighbouring American Samoa has a much higher living standard but with more cultural dilution. **HDI** 0.747; 70th/174. **Public debt** 75% of GNP. **Income/person** $1,170 (4% of USA).

POLITICS
German rule 1900-1914, thereafter New Zealand UN trusteeship until independence in 1962. Parliamentary democracy of the elite until 1991, when universal suffrage was introduced.

RELIGION
Constitutional freedom of religion is often not upheld at a local village level.

Religions	Population %	Adherents	Ann.Gr.
Christian	96.90	174,500	+1.4%
Baha'i	2.00	3,600	+2.5%
non-Religious/other	1.10	1,981	+5.6%

Christians	Denom.	*Affil.%	,000	Ann.Gr.
Protestant	15	61.94	112	-0.3%
Independent	5	0.68	1	+25.8%
Anglican	1	0.24	0	+1.4%
Catholic	1	20.82	38	+0.3%
Marginal	6	37.87	68	+4.4%
Doubly affiliated		-24.67	-44	n.a.

*More than 100% due to Mormon baptisms; many remaining in or returning to their original denominations.

Churches	MegaBloc	Cong.	Members	Affiliates
Congregational Chr	P	285	32,000	70,000
Latter-day Saints (Morm)	M	154	46,154	66,000
Catholic	C	27	20,000	37,500
Methodist	P	100	9,000	20,000
Assemblies of God	P	52	6,000	11,550
Seventh-day Adventist	P	17	3,806	5,300
Ch of the Nazarene	P	10	460	750
Christian Brethren	P	6	290	580
Ch. of God (Cleveland)	P	2	138	270
Other denoms [15]		60	3,458	6,940
Doubly affiliated			-26,500	-44,400
Total Christians [24]		713	94,700	174,500

Trans-bloc Groupings	pop.%	,000	Ann.Gr.
Evangelical	4.0	7	+4.0%
Charismatic	9.2	17	+1.9%
Pentecostal	8.0	14	+0.0%

Missionaries from Samoa
P,I,A 72 in 3 agencies to 12 countries: NZ 20+.

Missionaries to Samoa
P,I,A 10 in 5 agencies from 4 countries.

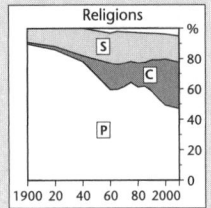

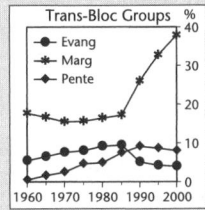

• Challenges for Prayer

1 **Samoans have been Christian for over a century**, and every village has at least one church, but the traditional class structure and pre-Christian cultural standards were not necessarily transformed by the gospel. Pride, political manipulation, formalism, ignorance, denominational rivalry and division, heavy demands for ministerial support, and compromise had already weakened the Church before the challenge presented by the influx of cults, high teenage suicide, and the need to provide a future and a hope for the next generation. Pray for both government and church leaders of Samoa; there are committed Evangelicals among them.

S

2 **The growth of Mormonism** has been both spectacular and relatively unchallenged. Pray for all seeking to enlighten Samoan Christians of Mormonism's errors and to win Mormons to Jesus. Pray for renewal and revival. The whole nation has an obligatory quiet time for prayer and Bible reading at dusk.

3 **The growth of Evangelicals** has been predominantly through the Assemblies of God. They and other evangelical agencies, such as Youth for Christ, have met with opposition, and individual Christians have faced pressure from traditional leaders who also lead mainline churches. Pray for complete freedom for the gospel and for harmony between the newer and the more traditional branches of the Church.

4 **Unity among Evangelicals has long been lacking.** Pray that the Samoan Evangelical Alliance, formed in 1991, may be a means for overcoming the prevailing nominalism, underscore personal commitment to Christ, and further the cause of the gospel.

5 **Samoan missionaries played a major role in evangelizing** the Pacific in the last century. Most Samoans serving abroad today are pastoring Samoan migrant congregations. An exception to this is the contingent of 44 Samoan **YWAM**ers serving around the world. Pray for them and their ongoing influence in their home churches.

San Marino

Most Serene Republic of San Marino

OCTOBER 2
EUROPE

GEOGRAPHY
Area 61 sq.km. A city state in north central Italy near Rimini.

Population	Ann.Gr.	Density
2000	26,514	+1.28%	435 per sq. km.
2010	29,407	+0.96%	482 per sq. km.
2025	32,392	+0.49%	531 per sq. km.

Capital San Marino 2,294.

PEOPLES
Sammarinese 83.1%.
Italian 12%.

Other 4.9%.
Literacy 99%. **Official language** Italian.

POLITICO-ECONOMIC
Independent republic since AD301. In customs union with Italy. Main foreign exchange earners are tourism (3.3 million visitors annually) and postage stamps. **Income/person** $34,330 (109% of USA).

RELIGION
No official religion, though almost the entire population was baptized Catholic. Theoretically there is freedom of religion.

Religions	Population %	Adherents	Ann.Gr.
Christian	92.30	24,472	+1.1%
non-Religious/other	7.00	1,856	+3.4%
Baha'i	0.70	186	+2.8%

Christians	Denom.	Affil.%	,000	Ann.Gr.
Protestant	1	0.04	0	+0.0%
Catholic	1	88.63	24	+0.8%
Marginal	1	1.01	0	+2.6%
Unaffiliated		2.62	0	n.a.

Churches	MegaBloc	Cong.	Members	Affiliates
Catholic	C	12	15,461	23,500
Jehovah's Witnesses	M	2	184	268
Other denoms (1)		0	6	10
Total Christians [3]		14	15,651	23,778

• Challenges for Prayer

1 **The Sammarinese** are Catholic by tradition and culture, but most give only lip service to the Church and are very materialistic. The only non-Catholics are some JWs, a small group of Baha'i and several Waldensian Church families. Pray that they may have a life-changing encounter with the Lord Jesus Christ.

2 **San Marino proclaims itself "Ancient Land of Liberty".** There is freedom to worship, but not to evangelize — any outreach by evangelical believers in the past has resulted in jailing and expulsion from the country. It is also almost impossible for foreigners to reside in the country. There is only one indigenous evangelical believer reported, but no evangelical church exists.

São Tomé & Príncipe

Democratic Republic of São Tomé and Príncipe

OCTOBER 2
AFRICA

GEOGRAPHY
Area 1,001 sq.km. Two larger and several smaller islands in the Gulf of Guinea 200 km west of Gabon.

Population	Ann.Gr.	Density
2000	146,775	+2.06%	147 per sq. km.
2010	175,794	+1.74%	176 per sq. km.
2025	217,146	+1.26%	217 per sq. km.

Capital São Tomé 43,420. **Urbanites** 44%.

PEOPLES
Forro and Angolares 75%. Descendants of African slaves. The Forro are politically dominant, the Angolares more rural. The Moncó live on the island of Príncipe.

Other 25%. Fang from Equatorial Guinea, Mestizo (mixed race), Portuguese and other Europeans. Also many contract labourers from Cape Verde, Angola and Mozambique.

Literacy 74% (in reality closer to 34%). **Official Language** Portuguese, but three Creole dialects and 3 Angolan langauges also spoken. **All languages** 6.

ECONOMY
Subsistence agriculture; cocoa the major export. Oil speculation in the Gulf of Guinea presents new economic opportunities and risks. Unemployment is very high, possibly above 30%. **HDI** 0.609; 123rd/174. **Public debt** 567% of GNP. **Income/person** $290 (0.9% of USA).

POLITICS
Settled by Portuguese in 1493, and became a major slave transhipment centre. Independent from Portugal in 1975 as a Marxist republic. A multi-party democracy was instituted in January 1991, whose tenure was interrupted for one week in 1995 by a bloodless, but farcical, military coup.

RELIGION
Secular state with freedom of religion.

Religions	Population %	Adherents	Ann.Gr.
Christian	92.90	136,354	+2.1%
non-Religious/other	4.70	6,898	+0.8%
Traditional ethnic	2.00	2,936	+2.1%
Muslim	0.30	440	+0.0%
Baha'i	0.10	147	+2.0%

Christians	Denom.	Affil.%	,000	Ann.Gr.
Protestant	6	2.66	4	+1.5%
Independent	5	0.55	1	+9.1%
Catholic	1	83.12	122	+2.1%
Marginal	1	0.61	1	+15.9%
Unaffiliated		5.96	8	n.a.

Churches	MegaBloc	Cong.	Members	Affiliates
Catholic	C	12	74,390	122,000
Seventh-day Adventist	P	6	1,312	2,500
Assemblies of God [4]	P	6	520	1,300
Jehovah's Witnesses	M	6	275	900
Pentecostal groups [4]	I	6	250	500
other Evangelical [4]	P	5	250	500
Deeper Life	I	1	150	300
Other denoms [3]		3	70	100
Total Christians [19]		45	77,217	128,100

Trans-bloc Groupings	pop.%	,000	Ann.Gr.
Evangelical	2.2	3	+4.9%
Charismatic	2.3	3	+3.8%
Pentecostal	1.4	2	+4.5%

Missionaries from São Tomé
P,I,A 20, all in São Tomé.

Missionaries to São Tomé
P,I,A 26 in 6 agencies: Brazil 24.

• Challenges for Prayer

1 **The vast majority of the population is Catholic**, but morals on the islands do not reflect this. Ninety percent of children are born illegitimately — the world's highest rate. Pray that the Church may experience a renewal that challenges people's empty religion.

2 **Evangelical growth has accelerated** since independence — mainly through the work of the Portuguese Assemblies of God and more recently through Brazilian (**YWAM**) and Nigerian (Deeper Life) missionaries as well as a number of Pentecostal and other denominations in the late 1990s. Pray that these missionaries might have a great evangelistic and church planting impact on these islands. Pray for the development of locally-led congregations with effectively trained Christian leaders. Pray also for local support for national workers and for the launching of an interdenominational training centre.

3 **Less-reached sections of the population** are the Príncipe islanders, the rural Angolares and the contract labourers, with each group having its own distinct Creole dialect. Pray for their salvation.

Saudi Arabia

Kingdom of Saudi Arabia

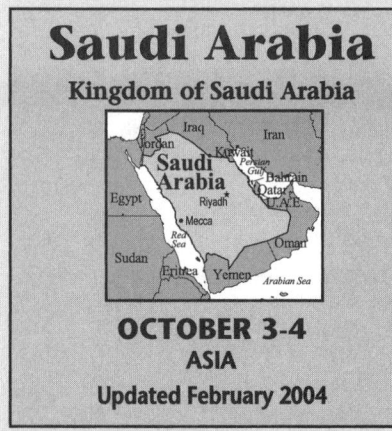

OCTOBER 3-4
ASIA
Updated February 2004

GEOGRAPHY
Area 2,240,000 sq.km. The major part of the Arabian Peninsula; 95% desert but containing 25% of the world's known oil reserves.

Population		Ann.Gr.	Density
2000	21,606,691	+3.43%	10 per sq. km.
2010	28,778,495	+2.80%	13 per sq. km.
2025	39,964,965	+1.87%	18 per sq. km.

Capital Riyadh 3.35 mill. Other major cities: Jiddah 2.1m; Mecca 920,000. **Urbanites** 80%.

PEOPLES
With the presence of such a large number of foreigners, all figures are estimates.
Arab 83.8%.
  Saudi Arab 72.9%.
  Foreign Arab 10.9%. Egyptian 1.2m; Yemeni 500,000; Palestinian 300,000; Jordanian 200,000.
Asian 14.2%. Indian 1m; Pakistani 800,000; Filipino 600,000; Bangladeshi 200,000; Iranian 150,000; Sri Lankan 150,000.
African 1.4%. Nigerian, Sudanese, Somali.
Other 0.6%. American, British, French, Italian.

Literacy 62.8%. **Official language** Arabic. **All languages** 5.

ECONOMY
Enormous oil wealth produces two-thirds of government revenue and is used to improve services and communications, develop industries and finance Islamic expansion around the world. The combined effects of eighteen consecutive years of budget deficits, spectacular corruption of the large royal family and the heavy cost of the 1991 Gulf War (at least US$50 billion) have enforced a measure of austerity since 1990. A major economic overhaul is overdue. **HDI** 0.740; 78th/174. **Income/person** $7,150 (22.7% of USA).

POLITICS
Absolute monarchy and a semi-feudal state with administration, diplomacy and commerce tightly controlled by the large royal family. Since 1991 there has been pressure from democrats to liberalize the country and from hard-line Islamists to exert more control. The 9/11 attack on the USA led to major changes. Saudi Arabia is seen as both the provider of much of the finance and manpower for Islamist terror networks and also its leadership as one of the primary 'hate' targets of Al Qa'eda led by Osama bin Ladin. After the US-led invasion of Iraq in 2003 all US military bases in the country were moved elsewhere — this was a major original stimulus for the formation of Al Qaeda.

RELIGION
An Islamic state committed to the role of the custodian of Islam and its holiest sites. The majority of Saudis are Wahhabi Sunnis. Religions other than Islam are prohibited even for expatriate Christian gatherings. Uncontrolled and distorted anti-Western preaching in mosques has been a major factor in giving support to Islamist *jihad* against non-Muslims. All non-Muslim figures are estimates. **Persecution index** 1st in the world.

Religions	Population %	Adherents	Ann.Gr.
Muslim	92.83	20,057,491	+3.2%
Christian	4.54	980,944	+4.3%
non-Religious/other	1.40	302,494	+8.5%
Hindu	0.60	129,640	+28.8%
Buddhist/Chinese	0.42	90,748	+2.9%
Sikh	0.19	41,053	+5.8%
Baha'i	0.02	4,321	+3.4%

Christians	Denom.	Affil.%	,000	Ann.Gr.
Protestant	21	0.67	144	+5.9%
Independent	30	0.54	117	+7.9%
Anglican	1	0.01	2	+0.0%
Catholic	3	1.83	395	+1.9%
Orthodox	4	0.55	119	+8.3%
Marginal	4	0.14	30	+8.5%
Unaffiliated		0.80	173	n.a.

Churches	MegaBloc	Cong.	Members	Affiliates
Catholic [3]	C		276,224	395,000
Protestant [20]	P	128	25,600	128,000
Orthodox [4]	O		83,217	119,000
Independent [30]	I		73,125	117,000
Marginal groups [4]	M		18,750	30,000
Other denoms [2]			8,200	18,000
Total Christians [63]			485,116	807,000

Trans-bloc Groupings	pop.%	,000	Ann.Gr.
Evangelical	0.9	188	+6.8%
Pentecostal & Charismatic	0.4	88	+7.1%

• Challenges for Prayer

1 **Saudi Arabia** once had a large Christian population. They were expelled when Islam gained control 1,300 years ago. It is now one of the least evangelized nations on earth. No Christian workers are permitted and all Christian 'propaganda' banned. No Christian is permitted to set foot in Islam's holiest city, Mecca. Pray that soon this land may have many Christians praising the Lamb that was slain.

2 **The world's 1.2 billion Muslims are required to pray towards Mecca five times daily.** Every year over two million make the *Hajj* or pilgrimage to the city. This is the culmination of many people's religious lives. Pray that the eyes of many may be opened to see the emptiness and bondage under which they live, and embrace the freedom that is in Christ. Praise God that a small but growing number are doing just that — even in Saudi Arabia!

3 **Saudi Arabia has the world's worst record on religious freedom and human rights.** This was achieved through a corrupt judicial system, arrogant religious police (*mutawwa*), and the corroboration of the government. This record is regularly condemned by Christian and secular international bodies promoting freedom of conscience. Pray for an easing of tight controls, and for freedom of religious expression.

4 **Saudi society is straining at the seams.** The ailing and aged rulers walk the tightrope between those pushing for liberalization and those demanding stricter Islamization. The economy is sagging and there is a growing gap between rich and poor. The venality and greed of the leadership provide fertile soil for Al Qa'eda Islamism to grow. Since 2001 suicide bombings and acts of terror are destabilizing the country. Saudi women have an average of seven children, but the youth find few employment opportunities. Pray that these tensions might expose the true nature of Islam and cause many to seek the truth and peace found only in Christ.

5 **A massive Islamic missionary effort** is coordinated by the Muslim World League in Mecca. Billions of dollars are spent every year to propagate Islam around the world —aid to countries considered sympathetic, building mosques, sending missionaries, literature, radio, etc. Huge funding has been provided to Islamist groups that support violent *jihad*. The Saudi government denies Christians the liberty to share their faith, yet demands this liberty for Muslims living elsewhere. Some of the world's largest printing presses are in Saudi and churn out 28 million Qurans annually for worldwide distribution.

6 **Although Saudi Arabia signed the U.N. Charter,** which guarantees freedom of religion, Saudis who confess Christ face the death penalty if discovered. Still, a substantial number are secretly seeking and finding Him. All converts discovered in the past have been executed. Pray for the preservation and multiplication of believers, and the legalization of Christian worship. Pray that Saudi believers may be able to meet together in safety and have access to God's Word.

7 **Life is difficult for expatriates.** Often pressured to leave home to make money here, they lose their personal and religious freedom. Many of these foreigners have little access to the gospel, although there are many Christians among them. Pray for a witness to flourish amongst these groups.

8 **Christian expatriates** live under strict surveillance. Secret gatherings are hunted down and leaders subjected to beatings, imprisonment, expulsion, and even execution. This is particularly so for Asian Christians who have often been the most effective witnesses and whose governments have the least international clout. There are perhaps only 50,000 practising believers, although many more would join them were the risks not so great. Pray for encouragement and strength for the believing community. There are few opportunities to interact with Saudis, and very few expatriates speak Arabic. Pray that other Arabs might gain a burden to reach Saudis.

9 **Witnessing by other means:**

a) ***Saudis abroad.*** Students, businessmen and tourists visit the West, where they can be reached. Many prefer to travel during the summer months and the month of fasting!

b) ***Christian radio.*** Over 146 hours of broadcasting weekly in Arabic are available through **FEBA**, High Adventure, **TWR**, **IBRA** and **HCJB**(WRMF). Many listen secretly and there are isolated radio converts in some regions.

c) ***Christian literature and video cassettes.*** These are banned, and are therefore in great demand. Many copies of the Scriptures and the ***JESUS*** video are in surreptitious circulation.

d) ***Satellite television.*** Almost every home has a television and over 50% have satellite dishes. In such an environment, Christian television such as SAT-7, The Bible Channel and CBN can be greatly used to bring Saudis to Jesus.

Senegal
Republic of Senegal

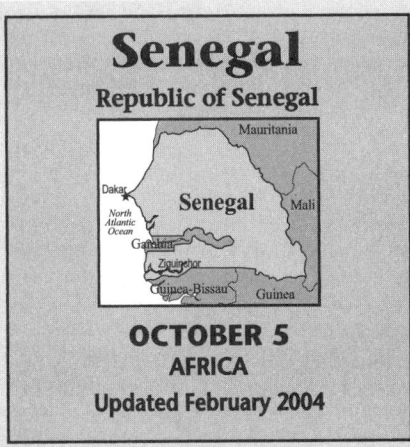

OCTOBER 5
AFRICA
Updated February 2004

GEOGRAPHY
Area 196,722 sq.km. Mainland Africa's most westerly state — arid and with few natural resources.

Population		Ann.Gr.	Density
2000	9,481,161	+2.62%	48 per sq. km.
2010	12,166,453	+2.48%	62 per sq. km.
2025	16,742,579	+1.94%	85 per sq. km.

The majority of the population live on the southern coast and around the capital.

Capital Dakar 2,350,000. **Urbanites** 43%.

PEOPLES
Over 52 ethnic groups in three main linguistic families; only the largest are listed.
West Atlantic 88.7%.
Wolof(2) 42.5%. Wolof 3.7mill.; Lebu 130,000.
Fulbe (Fula, Pulaar)(5) 24.3%. Fulacunda 950,000; Tukulor 910,000; Fulbe Jeeri 350,000; Futa Jalon 100,000.
Serer(9) 14.8%. Sine 1.2m; Safi 48,000; Non 30,000.
Bak 5.3%. Jola (14) 430,000; Balanta 62,000.
Other(9) 1.8%. Manjak 80,000; Bainuk 22,000; Mankanya 20,000; Konyagi 14,000.
Mande(8) 8.4%. Mandinka 310,000; Malinke 210,000; Soninke 135,000; Bambara 105,000; Jahanka

23,000; Susu 16,000.
Arab-Berber 0.6%. Maure 20,000, greatly reduced from 300,000 in 1989; Lebanese 20,000.
Other 2.3%. Cape Verdian 58,000; French, other African.

Literacy 33%. **Official language** French. Language of wider communication Wolof; spoken as first language by 44% of population. **All languages** 39. **Languages with Scriptures** 3Bi 3NT 6por 19w.i.p.

ECONOMY
Subsistence agricultural economy. Main exports are peanuts, fish and phosphates. Considerable improvement during the 1990s but slowed by erratic rainfall and the Casamance unrest. Unjust EU food subsidies undercut local agricultural production with EU imports. **HDI** 0.426; 153ʳᵈ/174. **Public debt** 65% of GNP. **Income/person** $530 (1.7% of USA).

POLITICS
Independent from France in 1960. A multi-party democracy with a peaceful transfer of power to the former opposition in 2000. The separatist conflict in the SW Casamance province has caused disruption and distress with 60,000 local people becoming refugees.

RELIGION
Secular state with freedom of religion despite the large Muslim majority. Three Muslim Sufi brotherhoods, the Mouride, Tidjane and Qadiri, have great influence in political and economic life. In 2003 the Muslim President proposed to make Senegal 100% Muslim and impose *shari'a* law.

Religions	Population %	Adherents	Ann.Gr.
Muslim	92.07	8,729,305	+2.6%
Christian	4.76	451,303	+2.3%
Traditional ethnic	2.97	281,590	+2.3%
Baha'i	0.20	18,962	+8.7%

Christians	Denom.	Affil.%	,000	Ann.Gr.
Protestant	20	0.10	9	+1.8%
Independent	6	0.15	14	+2.9%
Catholic	1	4.48	425	+2.3%
Marginal	1	0.02	2	+1.0%

Churches	MegaBloc	Cong.	Members	Affiliates
Catholic	C	100	247,093	425,000
Lutheran (Finnish)	P	56	1,976	3,300
Jehovah's Witnesses	M	21	863	2,100
Assemblies of God	P	49	950	1,250
Baptist (CBI)	P	12	150	600
Evangelical (WEC)	P	12	150	400
Baptist Convention	P	7	175	400
Other denoms [21]		94	7,475	17,812
Total Christians [28]		351	258,832	451,000

Trans-bloc Groupings	pop.%	,000	Ann.Gr.
Evangelical	0.1	7	+1.6%
Charismatic	0.2	16	+2.2%
Pentecostal	0.0	1	+0.6%

Missionaries from Senegal
P,I,A 44 in 7 agencies to 3 countries: Senegal 40.

Missionaries to Senegal
P,I,A 482 in 45 agencies from 28 countries: USA 232, UK 48, Finland 31, Brazil 28, Canada 24, Switzerland 23.

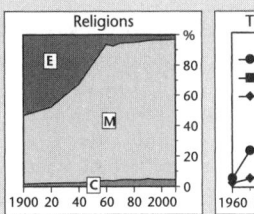

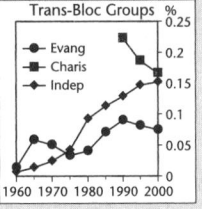

• Challenges for Prayer

1 **Islam grew from about 45% of the population in 1900 to over 92% in 2000**. It is the religion of almost all the Wolof, Fulbe and Mande peoples. Praise God for religious freedom; tolerance for other religions has long been a source of pride. However since 2001 the level of Islamist extremism has markedly increased. There have been attacks on Christian churches and strong moves to create an Islamic state. Pray for the thwarting of extremist plans and pray for safety of Christians and the preservation of freedom of religion.

2 **The three Muslim Sufi brotherhoods are well-organized**, wealthy and politically powerful; over 85% of all Muslims belong to one of them. The Mouride Brotherhood is virtually a state within a state based in their capital, Touba, and with a global economic empire in Europe and North America based on the peddling trade. Pray for a significant breakthrough for the gospel with key leaders meeting with the Lord Jesus Christ.

3 **The Casamance in the south has been troubled by a guerrilla war** — the local Jola feeling disenfranchized and marginalized in the Wolof-dominated capital, Dakar. Pray that there might be the political will to reach a just settlement for all involved. Christian and economic activity has been disrupted for a decade.

4 **Christians are confined to sections of the Serer, Jola and Cape Verdian peoples.** There are also some congregations among smaller ethnic groups in the south. Their influence is disproportionately great through their input into health services and education. Sadly most are nominally Catholic and from a non-Muslim background. Their lifestyle often does no credit to the cause of Christ, for few know real freedom in Christ and victory over the powers of darkness. Muslims refer to Christians as 'those who drink' rather than those who follow Christ.

5 **Evangelical believers are few,** the rate of growth slow, and only among the Serer (FLM, **AoG**), Bassari (AoG), Balanta (**WEC**, AoG, **NTM**), and Jola (WEC, **IMB-SBC**) has there been any significant church planting. Believers are scattered, often poorly taught and under constant pressures from Muslim or animistic relatives to conform. The lack of believing girls tempts many young men to marry unbelievers or to immorality. Only now are stable congregations emerging after years of work. Pray for a strong church with a backbone of Christian families to be planted in each ethnic group.

6 **Christian leaders are few,** but an increasing number of young men are completing theological training at various levels. There are probably no more than 100 full-time national Christian workers. *Institut Evangélique de Dakar* (IED) is a cooperative effort with **CBI**, **UWM**, **MTW**, **Brethren** and two local churches. There are three other Bible schools in the country and **YWAM** runs a biennial six-month discipleship course. Pray that many more men of God may be raised up who can pastor believers and lead them out in effective evangelism.

7 **Missions in Senegal have struggled for years without much fruit in the adult population**, but among young people results have been more encouraging. WEC entered the Casamance in the south in 1936 among the Fulbe, in the 1950s to the Jola and Balanta, and later the predominantly Muslim Senegal River Valley in the north. Other pioneer missions have followed, and there are now 25 church-planting missions serving in the country. The largest are **NTM** (69 workers), **WEC** (53), **YWAM** (34), **IMB-SBC** (33), Finnish Lutherans (29), **UWM** (23), AoG (11). Pray for more long-term church planters called of God to serve in this needy but open land. Pray also for encouragement among the missionary teams; most are young, inexperienced and short on leadership in a difficult, unresponsive field. **SIL** (58), serving as an NGO, has an important presence in Senegal providing help in literacy, linguistic research and Bible translation in many language groups.

8 Major areas of the country are still very much pioneer situations.

a) *Dakar is the home of a quarter of the population of Senegal.* Every ethnic group is represented. In 1990 there were 15 evangelical groups but by 1996 this had reached 33 (27% Wolof-speaking, 14% Serer, 11% Jola and 20% foreign). Dakar is the mission base for most agencies, but only a few missionaries are actually committed to church planting. Pray for this city to become a source of gospel light for the whole country.

b) *The Senegal River Valley in the north and northeast is a major development zone.* Only a few missionaries are working on this strategic frontier with closed Mauritania, among the Tukulor, Maure, Wolof, Fulbe and Soninke (WEC, Lutherans, IMB-SBC, YWAM and others). There are some small groups of believers but no viable church in the entire area, and up-river only a handful of missionaries.

c) *The central and eastern areas of Senegal are sparsely populated and unevangelized,* as is the territory along the frontier of inland Gambia. There is an AoG church in Tambacounda, but the members are mostly Bassaris who have migrated there from another area seeking employment.

d) *Young people.* Many have flocked to the cities in search of education and employment. Their commitment to conservative Islam is not so great, and YWAM, Gideons and some churches are seeking to reach them. IMB-SBC, UWM and others have a youth work in Dakar. The small **IFES** group in Dakar is fervent, but most of the members are non-Senegalese. Recent political unrest and student dissatisfaction have restricted evangelistic outreach. Pray for an impact for God to be made on children and young people.

9 Unreached peoples. Pray for the planting of strong churches among the:

a) *Wolof.* Despite much effort by, and increasing cooperation among, the missionaries of AoG, CBI, IMB-SBC, Brethren, WEC, **SIM** and others, results have been meagre. There are possibly only about 100 believers and the beginnings of a few congregations. Pray that the advent of the Wolof New Testament, Jesus film and the patient friendship evangelism of Christian workers may break down the barriers preventing this proud people from seeking Jesus. Pray also for the breaking of the underlying spiritism which binds many and for the birth of a truly indigenous Wolof Church with its own hymnody and worship style.

b) *Serer.* Strongly fetishist until the 20th Century, now many are becoming Muslim or Catholic, and a good number Protestant — FLM, AoG, CBI, IMB-SBC and SIM have seen an encouraging response. Bible translation in three Serer languges (Ndut, Non, Safi) is underway (SIL, NTM, etc.)

c) *Fulbe.* Largely a pastoral people, some are nomadic. Almost all are at least nominally Muslim. The Lutherans work among the northern Fulbe and WEC in the Casamance. In the latter area are two small congregations. The Fulacunda NT was published in 2000 (WEC).

d) *Tukulor.* Muslim for 900 years, and considering themselves as the defenders of that faith. It is a miracle that there are 15-20 believers (WEC, Lutherans, YWAM). The Tukulor NT was published in 1998.

e) *Jola,* speaking 14 major dialects and languages. Islam is more prevalent in the north of their area but all are bound by fetishism. There are now six Jola-led congregations and seven or more new, growing groups (WEC, CAPRO, IMB-SBC and others). The Kwatay NT was published in 2000. Pray for the failure of the new cycle of 30-year fetishist initiation ceremonies starting in this decade.

f) *Maures.* All are Muslim, with only a few known believers. The majority live in inaccessible Mauritania, though many can be reached in the Senegal River Valley (WEC). There is a weekly local church radio programme in the Hassaniya language.

g) *Muslim Mande peoples.* Those still totally unreached are: Mandinka, Jahanka, Bambara, Kassonke and Susu. Beginnings have been made among the Soninke (Pioneers, WEC, Korean Methodists) but results have yet to be seen.

h) ***The smaller peoples on the southern border*** who are animistic or nominally Muslim. NTM has a major thrust to evangelize the Balanta-Ganja, Manjak, Budik, Bainuk, Badjaranke, Malinke and Jalonke, with plans also to reach the Mankanya. Some work has been done among the Konyagi (AoG), but the fetishist Mankanya, Bayot, Bainuk and Ganja are unreached. The work has been disrupted by the Casamance unrest.

10 **Bible translation.** Much was achieved in the 1980s and '90s. Six long-awaited New Testaments were published, namely Wolof (CBI, Brethren), Serer (Finnish Lutheran), Mandinka (WEC, Gambia), Tukulor (SIL), Fulacunda (WEC) and Bassari (AoG). Pray for a wide dissemination and deep impact on readers. Work on 19 other New Testaments is in hand; pray especially for work on several Jola languages (WEC, SIL). The Wolof OT is being translated and there are plans for translating the OT into Tukulor and Fulacunda.

11 **Specialist Christian ministries** for prayer:

a) ***Literature.*** Several agencies are seeking to publish and distribute affordable French Christian literature (SBIS, **SU**, etc.). Reading rooms have been a major outreach tool to Muslims in many urban centres. Pray for meaningful conversations with enquirers. Pray for the publication and distribution of effective Christian literature.

b) ***The JESUS film*** has been widely used all over the country in 10 languages. A further 8 languages are in preparation.

c) ***Cassette tape ministries.*** GRN has recordings available in 33 languages. Scripture on tape has been particularly effective for the Wolof and Serer.

d) ***Christian radio programmes*** can be broadcast on national and local stations. Pray that churches and missions may make full use of this medium (IMB-SBC, WEC, Brethren). **HCJB** broadcast 15 minutes in Wolof 5 days/week.

Seychelles
Republic of Seychelles

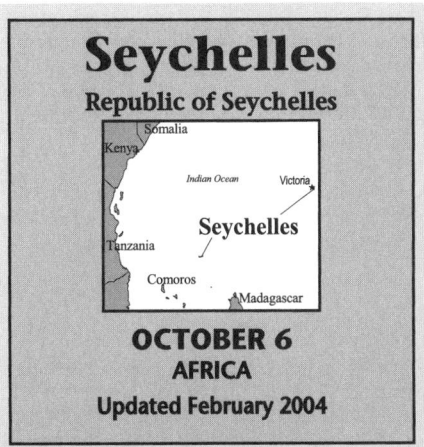

OCTOBER 6
AFRICA
Updated February 2004

GEOGRAPHY
Area 453 sq.km. A group of 92 granite and coral islands spread across 400,000 sq.km of the Indian Ocean, 1,600 km east of Kenya.

Population	Ann.Gr.	Density
2000	77,435	+1.07%	171 per sq. km.
2010	85,582	+0.99%	189 per sq. km.
2025	97,962	+0.86%	216 per sq. km.

Capital Victoria 25,000. **Urbanites** 65%.

PEOPLES
Creole 89.1%. Predominantly of African, European and some Asian origin.
Asian 6.3%. Tamil, Hindi and Gujarati 3,000; Chinese 1,000.

African 3.1%. Malagasy, Réunionese, Swahili, Guinean.
European 1.5%. British, French.
Literacy 84%. **Official languages** French and English. **All languages** 3. **Languages with Scriptures** 2Bi 1NT.

ECONOMY
Tourism and fishing are important to an economy where the value of imported goods is nearly triple that of exports. Economic diversification has helped overcome over-dependence on those two sectors. **HDI** 0.755; 66th/174. **Public debt** 24.5% of GNP. **Income/person** $6,910 (23% of USA).

POLITICS
French colony 1756-1814, then British-ruled until independence in 1976. The coup of 1977 resulted in a one-party socialist government. The collapse of Communism elsewhere and the choking off of foreign aid finally brought about a multi-party election in 1992 — wherein the dictator became the president. A new constitution was recently approved by referendum.

RELIGION
Religious freedom. Catholics and Anglicans were vocally opposed to single-party rule.

Religions	Population %	Adherents	Ann.Gr.
Christian	96.89	75,027	+1.1%
non-Religious	2.00	1,549	+2.1%
Hindu	0.50	387	-0.9%
Baha'i	0.40	310	+2.1%
Muslim	0.21	163	-0.7%

Christians	Denom.	Affil.%	,000	Ann.Gr.
Protestant	5	2.83	2	+3.2%
Independent	2	0.10	0	+7.5%
Anglican	1	7.36	6	+1.5%
Catholic	1	90.40	70	+1.9%
Marginal	1	0.58	0	+12.9%
Doubly affiliated		*-4.27*	*-3*	*n.a.*

Churches	MegaBloc	Cong.	Members	Affiliates
Catholic	C	17	41,420	70,000
Anglican	A	12	2,167	5,700
Evangelical	P	2	487	750
Pentecostal	P	2	400	700
Seventh-day Adventist	P	4	352	588
Jehovah's Witnesses	M	3	213	450
Other denoms [4]		6	90	230
Doubly affiliated			*-1,800*	*-3,400*
Total Christians [10]		46	43,330	75,000

Trans-bloc Groupings	pop.%	,000	Ann.Gr.
Evangelical	5.3	4	+1.7%
Charismatic	7.1	5	+1.9%
Pentecostal	1.0	1	+1.6%

Missionaries to Seychelles

P,I,A 18 in 5 agencies from 5 countries: UK 12, Barbados 2, Brazil 2, Canada 2.

C 60. M 4.

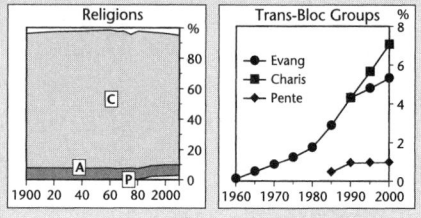

• Challenges for Prayer

1 The vast majority of Seychellois claim to be Christian, but the faith of many is tainted by immorality, superstition and nominalism. *Gris-gris*, African-based spiritism based on black magic and herbalism, permeates the lives of Christians. Too many believers lack a personal relationship with Christ, depending instead on the rites of baptism and confirmation. Pray that the Holy Spirit may bring new life evidenced by repentance and sustained fruit.

2 The arrival of FEBA missionaries in 1971 gave openings for an evangelical witness to be established. Subsequently, **AIM** and **PAoC** missionaries and indigenous Christians were able to help in establishing new evangelical and Pentecostal congregations. At the same time, the evangelical witness in the Anglican Church grew strongly. Praise God for these developments. Pray for spiritual life to be maintained and deepened and for the provision of Seychellois leaders for the congregations.

3 Evangelical missionary work, restricted in the past to technical and help ministries, now enjoys wider opportunities. **AIM** missionaries run the Christian Resource Centre as a means of helping in leadership development for the churches. Pray for committed workers to be called to serve the Seychellois Church.

4 Less reached peoples:

a) *The outer and less-populated islands* are isolated and have had little challenge to a personal commitment to Christ.

b) *The youth* need spiritual attention aimed at their particular needs. Pray for effective ministries to be developed to win them for the Lord

5 FEBA celebrated 30 years of radio broadcasting on Mahé in 2000. The strategically-placed islands enabled, at its height, 290 hours of broadcasting per month in 25 languages to South Asia, 160 hours/month in 11 languages to Africa and 210 hours/month in 17 languages to Muslim countries of West and South Asia. Changing patterns of radio broadcasting with a shift to local radio stations and the government demand to move its transmitter to a new site led to the closure of the ministry in 2003. Continue to pray for this ministry.

a) *The preparation of programmes* in more languages in receiving areas. By 2003 FEBA was preparing broadcasts in 60 languages and to 40 countries.

b) *Continued broadcasting* from local radio stations in Africa and Asia.

c) *Effective means of reaching Muslims.* There has been a growing response from Muslims in the Middle East and Hindus in India.

d) *For effective follow-up of listeners' letters.*

e) *The development of broadcasting* in more languages throughout Africa and Asia.

Sierra Leone
Republic of Sierra Leone

OCTOBER 7
AFRICA
Updated February 2004

GEOGRAPHY
Area 71,740 sq.km. Small coastal state between Guinea and Liberia.

Population		Ann.Gr.	Density
2000	4,854,383	+3.00%	68 per sq. km.
2010	6,017,780	+2.15%	84 per sq. km.
2025	8,085,454	+1.86%	113 per sq. km.

Capital Freetown 1,175,000; the city is swollen with refugees. **Urbanites** 37%.

PEOPLES
West Atlantic(11) 45.3%. Temne 1.3mill.; Limba 380,000; Sherbro(3) 200,000; Fulbe (Fula) 190,000; Kissi 120,000; Krim 20,000; Gola 10,000.
Mande(8) 43.8%. Mende 1.4m; Kuranko 225,000; Kono 176,000; Loko 138,000; Susu 127,000; Maninka 113,000; Yalunka 40,000.
Kwa(3) 1.3%. Bassa 27,000; Kru 10,000.
Krio (Creole) 8.6%. Descendants of released slaves and detribalized urbanites.
Other 1%. Guineans, Liberians, South Asians 5,000; Lebanese 1,500.

Literacy 31%. **Official language** English. Trade language Krio (Creole) spoken by 10% of the populations as first language and 90% as second. **All languages** 23. **Languages with Scriptures** 1Bi 9NT 4por 7w.i.p.

ECONOMY
Rich in natural resources — diamonds, gold, titanium, iron ore, etc. Despite gross mismanagement and corruption, some prosperity until 1991. The descent of the country into anarchy caused the economy to collapse. The control of the diamond fields by rebels ensures the continuance of the conflict. It became one of the poorest and most desperate countries on earth. A slow economic recovery since the ending of the civil war in 2002. **HDI** 0.254; 174th/174. **Public debt** 117% of GNP. **Income/person** $160 (0.5% of USA).

POLITICS
Founded as a home for freed slaves in 1797. Independent from Britain in 1961. The onset of the Liberian civil war in 1990 triggered the collapse of the government. A series of military coups and guerrilla wars ensued in efforts to control the lucrative diamond fields in the south-eastern part of the country. Only through intervention by Nigeria, the Organization of African States (OAS), UN and the British was conquest by the rebel forces prevented. The British also enabled the ending of the civil war in 2002. An uneasy peace has since prevailed and the new government has set up a Truth and Reconciliation Commission to help this traumatized nation come to terms with its tragic recent past.

RELIGION
Freedom of religion. Islam has steadily increased in influence, but the pervasive power of ethnic religions, the occult, secret societies and Freemasonry underlie the present chaos.

Religions	Population %	Adherents	Ann.Gr.
Muslim	70.00	3,398,068	+4.5%
Traditional ethnic	18.24	885,439	-1.8%
Christian	11.72	568,934	+2.9%
Hindu	0.04	1,942	-5.0%

Christians	Denom.	Affil.%	,000	Ann.Gr.
Protestant	27	5.40	262	+6.1%
Independent	58	2.68	130	+2.1%
Anglican	1	0.54	26	+0.4%
Catholic	1	2.99	145	+1.3%
Orthodox	1	0.00	0	-8.0%
Marginal	2	0.11	5	+2.2%

Churches		MegaBloc	Cong.	Members	Affiliates
Catholic		C	40	84,302	145,000
United Methodist		P	230	90,000	110,000
Wesleyan		P	180	11,000	28,000
Anglican		A	54	13,542	26,000
United Brethren in Christ		P	54	6,200	20,000
Seventh-day Adventist		P	51	11,597	17,000
National Pentecostal		I	25	6,587	11,000
Baptist Convention		P	67	6,728	9,000
Assemblies of God		P	30	1,200	6,500
Ch of God of Prophecy		P	12	1,342	4,000
West Africa Methodist		P	17	2,116	4,000
Apostolic		P	10	3,000	4,000
Missionary		P	45	1,500	3,000
Jehovah's Witnesses		M	20	806	2,500
Other denoms [77]			1,100	97,000	178,000
Total Christians [91]			1,939	336,811	569,000

Trans-bloc Groupings	pop.%	,000	Ann.Gr.
Evangelical	3.2	155	+2.9%
Charismatic	3.3	161	+2.8%
Pentecostal	1.2	57	+3.7%

S

Missionaries from Sierra Leone		

Missionaries from Sierra Leone
P,I,A Unknown; an estimated 40.

Missionaries to Sierra Leone
P,I,A Unknown; an estimated 78.

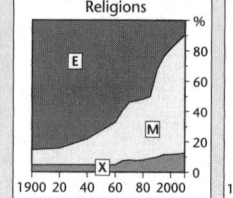

Religions

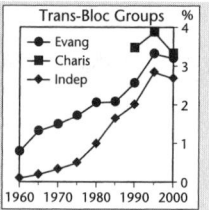

Trans-Bloc Groups

• Answers to Prayer

1 A prayer and reconciliation conference in 2000 drew together 1,200 Christian leaders from nearly all denominations. This represented over 80% of all leaders. There was deep contrition over national sins and the failures of the Church to confront witchcraft, immorality and secret societies within and outside the churches. May this new beginning result in the healing and transformation of the land.

2 The ending in 2002 of the ten-year series of Civil Wars which devastated the country and its people.

• Challenges for Prayer

1 Sierra Leone became infamous for the barbaric maiming of innocent victims as an instrument for terror and control. Thousands of men, women and children and even babies, have had limbs cruelly amputated. Over 100,000 have been slain. Over 70% of girls and women who fell into the hands of rebels were raped. Thousands of children have been kidnapped, made into child-soldiers, drugged and forced to kill even their own relatives. Nearly the whole population has had experience of being refugees. Pray that all the instigators who unleashed such terror might be brought to justice and even to repentance and faith in Christ. Pray for all efforts by Sierra Leonean and expatriate Christians to roll back the emotional, economic and health damage.

2 The new government has a great responsibility, and few resources to enable change for the better. The process will take decades. Pray that this government might be honest, accountable to the people and might establish peace, initiate an effective process of national reconciliation and build up the shattered economy. Pray that committed Christians may be a vital part of the new leadership.

3 Sierra Leone was the first West African country to be evangelized. The first Protestant Church was started among freed slaves in Freetown in 1785. Yet after over 200 years of effort, under 12% of the country claims to be Christian. Very few denominations have grown significantly in the past 40 years or made a lasting impact on the country. Pray for revival, a spirit of prayer and unity, a strong desire to live for Jesus alone and commitment to holistic outreach to their traumatized fellow-countrymen.

4 The unchallenged power of the occult lies behind all the greed and cruelty, and also the powerlessness of the Church. Many Christians have compromised in this area; nominalism and sin are the result. Pray that these powers may be bound, the influence of secret societies broken and that covenants made with demonic powers may be renounced.

5 Restoration ministries are the great need as the nation and Church struggle to rebuild. Nearly every Christian ministry suffered loss of property and personnel, and many institutions had to shut down. Pray for:

a) *The Evangelical Fellowship of Sierra Leone* which has become a focal point for cooperation, vision and ministry for many agencies and denominations. It spearheaded vital research on the unreached in the 1990s and is now heavily committed to coordinating various restoration ministries.

b) *New vision for compassionate outreach.* Freetown is chock full of refugees from all over the country who are living in squalor.

c) *Few churches are equipped* to cope with the millions of traumatized and impoverished people. Pray for the Holy Spirit to gift and empower many to minister in this area and enable victims to become effective disciples. Pray also for humanitarian aid agencies who seek to alleviate the suffering (**WVI**, **TEAR Fund**, and others).

d) **Child victims of war.** Over 6,000 children were forced to become soldier killers. All are deeply affected psychologically. Many thousands of children lost limbs, homes and families. Pray for all seeking to rehabilitate them. A number of international agencies are seeking to work with Sierra Leoneans in this exacting ministry (**WEC**-Rainbows of Hope).

e) **AIDS** has become a rapidly growing threat. In 2000 over 70,000 were known to be infected and a further 56,000 children orphaned.

6 **Young peoples' ministry** has never been more crucial and needs to be expanded. SU and YFC have had an impact on the more educated. SLEFES(**IFES**) has had 29 groups in tertiary institutions but many have been closed down. Pray that Christian graduates may decisively impact the nation.

7 **The lack of spiritual and biblically trained leadership** has become even more critical. The ministries of the Catholic, Anglican and Methodist Seminaries and the evangelical **AoG** and Sierra Leone Bible Colleges have all been hampered. It is reckoned that 70% of all pastors have had no formal theological training. Pray for the full resumption of training and the calling of workers for the harvest. The **AoG** run the ICI-TEE system but this too has been affected.

8 **The challenge of the unfinished task.** The pride and superiority shown by the Krio 'Christian' population and the continued growth of Islam limited church growth in the tribal hinterland. During the 20th Century Islam grew from 10% to maybe 80% of the population. Nearly every tribe has, to a great extent, been Islamized yet in most there is a growing Christian minority. Pray for renewed vision among Evangelicals for effective outreach to:

a) *The partially evangelized Temne, Mende, Yalunka, Kuranko* and *Loko*. Only the Kono of all the tribal peoples are over 10% Christian.

b) *The Muslim Fulbe, Susu, Malinke* and *Vai* and the more traditional *North Kissi, Klao* and *Bom* remain without significant outreach or response.

Pray also that the research work of YWAM and the EFSL begun in the 1990s might be resumed, completed and used to mobilize prayer and strategic outreach.

9 **Expatriate missions** have ministered for two centuries, but Sierra Leone remains a pioneer field. Missions have had to withdraw most or all of their personnel. Pray for the right strategies for resumption of ministries and for excellent partnering relationships with local Christians and churches. Many workers will be needed for rehabilitation ministries, leadership training and Bible translation. Major agencies involved in ministry: The Missionary Church, Lutheran Bible Translators, Wesleyan Church, United Brethren, United Methodist, **AoG**, **YWAM**.

10 Christian support ministries:

a) **Bible translation** is a continuing need and work is in hand in 7 languages, mainly through the ministry of Lutheran Bible Translators. The Kono NT and other projects have been delayed due to the evacuation of expatriate translators. Pray for resumption and completion of this task.

b) **Christian radio.** The gap left by the destruction of Radio ELWA (**SIM**, Liberia) in 1990 has yet to be filled. Pray that regular radio ministry may once more be launched. **TWR** broadcasts in English 5.5 hours daily from South Africa.

c) **Christian literature.** CLC has a strategic and well-used bookstore in Freetown. Pray for the ministry of the written page. Pray also for the granting of permits to import literature — these are often hard to obtain, and there are severe shortages of stock; literature and Bibles are prohibitively expensive as a result. The EMA-CLC Book Aid project importing second-hand Christian books is a spiritual lifeline.

d) **The JESUS film** is in use in 9 languages with a further 5 in preparation. It has been seen by almost the entire population.

Singapore
Republic of Singapore

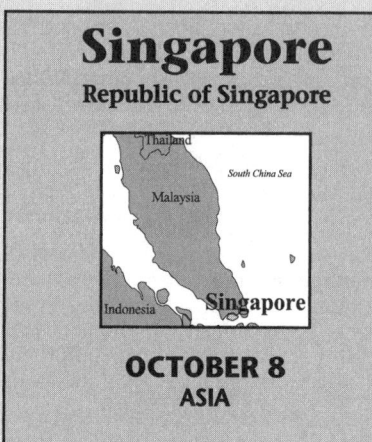

Thailand
South China Sea
Malaysia
Indonesia
Singapore

OCTOBER 8
ASIA

GEOGRAPHY
Area 648 sq.km. One larger and many smaller islands off the southern tip of Peninsular Malaysia, and strategically located for communications and trade.

Population	Ann.Gr.	Density
2000	3,566,614	+1.44%	5,734 per sq.
2010	3,885,328	+0.69%	6,247 per sq.
2025	4,167,756	+0.37%	6,701 per sq.

Capital City state. **Urbanites** 100%. Singapore is Asia's cleanest and greenest city.

PEOPLES
Multi-racial and multi-lingual society.
Chinese 77%. Language origin: Hokkien 1mill.; Teochew 530,000; Cantonese 420,000; Hakka 170,000; Hainanese 170,000; and others.
Malay 14.1%. Both of Malay and Indonesian origin.
Indian 7.6%. 95% speak English. Ethnic origin: Tamil 130,000; Malayali 16,000; Panjabi 16,000; Bengali 14,000; Sindhi 6,000; Hindi 6,000. Also 35,000 Indian migrant labourers.
Other 1.3%. Filipino 60,000; Thai 35,000; Japanese 20,000; Sri Lankan 12,000; Indonesian 12,000; Korean 3,000; Jews 300.

Literacy 90%. **Official languages** Mandarin (Chinese), English, Malay, and Tamil Indian. English is the primary language for education. **All languages** 24.

ECONOMY
Post-independence growth to become one of the world's wealthiest and most efficient trading and financial centres. **HDI** 0.888; 22nd/174. **Public debt** None. **Income/person** $32,810 (105% of USA).

POLITICS
British rule 1824-1959. Autonomy 1959-63. Part of the Malaysian Federation 1963-65. Independent as a parliamentary democracy in 1965. The strong, paternalistic government of Prime Minister Lee and his successor Goh Chok Tong, have provided direction and stability for spectacular economic growth. The government has wide-ranging powers to limit dissent. While not always applied, legislation is in place which restricts freedom of expression and the press.

RELIGION
Freedom of religion, but concerns to maintain ethnic and religious harmony are expressed in legislation limiting public proclamation of religious belief. All religions are enjoined not to be involved in politics.

Religions	Population %	Adherents	Ann.Gr.
Buddhist	42.50	1,515,811	+4.4%
Muslim	14.90	531,425	+1.2%
non-Religious/other	14.80	531,000	+1.9%
Christian	14.60	520,726	+2.9%
Chinese religions	8.50	303,162	-10.0%
Hindu	4.00	142,665	+2.2%
Sikh	0.50	17,833	+1.4%
Baha'i	0.10	3,567	+1.4%

Christians	Denom.	Affil.%	,000	Ann.Gr.
Protestant	23	5.01	179	+3.4%
Independent	29	2.49	89	+7.1%
Anglican	1	1.18	42	+4.0%
Catholic	1	4.21	150	+2.6%
Orthodox	2	0.06	2	+0.0%
Marginal	6	0.20	7	+3.5%
Unaffiliated		1.45	52	n.a.

Churches	MegaBloc	Cong.	Members	Affiliates
Catholic	C	37	104,895	150,000
Methodist	P	43	30,000	56,000
Independent Congs [10]	I	117	22,000	48,000
Anglican	A	57	18,000	42,000
Assemblies of God	P	46	13,877	41,060
Bible Presbyterian [3]	P	30	7,500	19,000
Baptist Convention	P	31	6,761	17,000
Christian Brethren	P	22	6,500	13,000
Presbyterian	P	43	6,800	13,000
Faith Community Bapt	P	10	5,000	11,000
City Harvest	P	3	6,875	11,000
Other Independent	I	25	3,000	5,700
Trinity Christian Centre	I	5	3,125	5,000
Lutheran [2]	P	7	2,400	4,500
Seventh-day Adventist	P	6	2,240	4,000
CNEC Churches	P	10	1,500	3,500
Evangelical Free	P	10	1,100	3,200
Other denoms [35]		93	12,400	22,000
Total Christians [64]		595	254,000	469,000

Trans-bloc Groupings	pop.%	,000	Ann.Gr.
Evangelical	7.8	277	+4.6%
Charismatic	5.0	178	+5.0%
Pentecostal	1.4	48	+2.0%

Missionaries from Singapore
P,I,A 715 in 43 agencies to 47 countries: Singapore 329.
Missionaries to Singapore
P,I,A 336 in 70 agencies from 22 countries: USA 173, Korea 60, New Zealand 22.

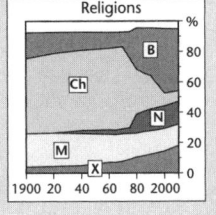

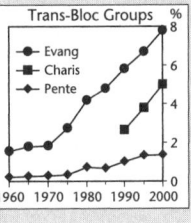

• Answers to Prayer

1 The growth of the Church in Singapore since 1970 has been high. In 1970, affiliated Christians were 6.8% of the population, but by 2000 this had become 13.1%. Over the same period Evangelicals grew from 1.8% to 7.8% with the greatest growth among Methodists, charismatic churches and several Pentecostal denominations.

2 The responsiveness of the educated. Rapid social change, economic development and widespread use of English have been contributing factors. The population is nearly 15% Christian, but among university students it is 33.5% and it is even higher among medical students. Christians have an influence in society larger than their national percentage.

3 The revitalizing of traditional denominations. Methodists, Presbyterians and others are largely evangelical. The Anglican Church is strongly evangelical and charismatic. Many churches have moved over to, or started out as, 'cell churches' whose influence has spread to many countries.

4 Singapore has become a key Christian base and mission-sending country. About 457 cross-cultural missionaries are serving the Lord — almost one missionary to each Protestant/Independent/Anglican church — one of the best ratios in the world.

• Challenges for Prayer

1 Church growth peaked in the 1980s and early 1990s but has since slowed. Goals for growth by 2000 were not attained and young people are becoming less responsive. Pray for a new faith, vision and dynamism to characterize the Church in the new millennium.

2 Major challenges facing the Church:

a) *Coping with affluence* — while maintaining a spiritual cutting edge, and using wealth effectively for God's Kingdom. Many young Christians become inactive once they marry and become enmeshed in the materialistic rat-race.

b) *Handling restrictive government legislation limiting outreach*. Christians need sensitivity in Singapore's multi-faith context, but also boldness to stand firm when fundamental issues of freedom of religion are challenged.

c) *Maintenance of adequate family life and witness* in high-rise flats and full employment.

d) *Unity among churches*. The Love Singapore Movement has been a means of drawing churches together. There is great expectation of a significant harvest of people into the Kingdom from 2001 onwards. The Union of Chinese-speaking Christian Churches of Singapore brings together the Chinese-speaking congregations.

e) *Mobilization*. Creative ways of releasing more long-term workers must be found. Compulsory military service for men, career concerns in a competitive society and cultural perceptions about overseas service are obstacles.

3 Bible training in the 16 seminaries, Bible schools and missions training schools is becoming a key ministry for Christians all over Asia. Worthy of particular mention are the **Singapore Bible College**, Trinity Theological College, Theological Centre for Asia, Tung Ling Bible School and the specifically missions-preparation institutions of **YWAM**, Asian Cross-Cultural Training Institute, Discipleship Training Centre and Bethany School of Missions. **The Haggai Institute** has provided stimulating short-term courses for pastors and Christian workers from all over the world, especially Asia and Africa. Some churches run their own theological training programmes. Pray that graduates of these may have the endurance and faith for long-term service at home and abroad.

4 **Young people** have been the most responsive segment of the population but there is a growing problem with alienated youth from dysfunctional backgrounds. Many youth ministries such as **Eagles Evangelism**, **Youth for Christ**, the Boys' Brigade and others have a decisive impact. Among undergraduates, over 34% are involved with FES(**IFES**), **CCCI** and **Navigators** groups. Pray for continued relevance, freshness and spiritual power in ministry to the rising generation of youth. Pray also that all those discipled might be well integrated into local churches.

5 **The blossoming of missions vision in Singapore** is cause for much praise. The seminal impact of **OM** and its ship ministry was a significant factor. **The Singapore Centre for Evangelism and Missions** has played a catalytic role in unifying and mobilizing the Singaporean missions enterprise. A large minority of churches have active missions programmes. Singaporean missionaries overseas increased from 140 in 1988 to an estimated 386 in 2000. About half of all congregations send their missionaries direct to the field. Many others serve with international missions such as **YWAM** (49), **OMF** (34), **CCCI** (33), **WEC** (30), **OM** (32), **WBT** (27), **Navigators** (18) and **SIM** (16). Pray specifically for:

a) *A higher proportion of long-term missionaries* sent to unreached peoples — short-term missions are popular but inadequate.

b) *Better relationships between churches and sending agencies.* The long-term impact of congregations sending missionaries direct has often not been strategically significant.

c) *Churches to adopt an unreached people.* Over 60 have done so and are committing significant resources into this vision.

6 **Singapore's less-reached peoples:**

a) *The Malay population.* All are considered Muslim by birth, and for years the community was economically isolated. Christians of other ethnic groups are hesitant to evangelize for fear of upsetting inter-communal relationships. Less than 100 active Christian Malays are known. Pray for the removal of all psychological, political and spiritual barriers to the gospel. Drug addiction is a major problem among Malay young people.

b) *The Indian population* is 55% Hindu 25.6% Muslim, 5% Sikh and 12% Christian. There is very little outreach to the Muslims or the Gujarati, Sindhi, Hindi and Bengali-speaking communities with origins in North India. The Christian community has many lively churches, but is only keeping pace with population growth. Pray that the many linguistic and religious barriers within the Indian population may be lowered.

c) *Migrant workers* have greatly increased. Some Singaporean churches reach out to Filipinos, Thai, Burmese and Japanese. There is a Foreign Christian Workers' Fellowship — pray for the right strategies for evangelism, follow-up and integration of converts into local and home churches. There are lively churches among Filipinos, Koreans and Indonesians. The challenge is outreach to the migrant Indians (0.5% Christian), Bangladeshis and Sri Lankans.

d) *Drug addicts* — a growing problem, with an estimated 15,000 addicts. Twelve Christian groups are involved in drug rehabilitation programmes. Teen Challenge has a notable ministry among them.

7 **Singapore is a strategic and stable base** for Christian ministries and outreach with its dynamic missions-minded Church and unrivalled facilities. Most expatriate missionaries based in Singapore are involved in international ministry. Various key international organizations have their headquarters there — World Evangelical Fellowship (WEF), Evangelical Fellowship for Asia, **YFC**, **OMF**, etc. Many others have important hubs of ministry — notably the **UBS**, **SU**, ASeF, **Navigators**, **IMB-SBC**, **TLM**, **OM**, **SIM**, **WEC**, **SIL**/WBT, **YWAM**, etc. Pray that Singapore may be a means of blessing the many less-evangelized nations and peoples around it.

8 **There is a plethora of Christian support ministries** having national or international impact with involvement in:

a) *Literature.* There are nearly 60 Christian bookstores (7 of **SU**) and over 8 publishers of books, magazines and tracts.

b) *Radio.* Both **FEBC** and **TWR** have offices here; the latter broadcasting 10.5 hrs/wk to Singapore from Guam.

Slovakia

OCTOBER 9
EUROPE
Updated June 2004

GEOGRAPHY
Area 49,035 sq.km. Central European state once the eastern 40% of Czechoslovakia.

Population	Ann.Gr.	Density
2000	5,387,191	+0.12%	110 per sq. km.
2010	5,456,375	+0.11%	111 per sq. km.
2025	5,392,691	-0.19%	110 per sq. km.

Capital Bratislava 452,053. **Urbanites** 57%.

PEOPLES
Slavic 80.7%. Slovak 4,256,000; Czech 59,000; Ruthenian 16,000; Ukrainian 16,000.
Other 19.3%. Hungarian 571,000; Roma (Gypsy) 453,000.

Literacy 96%. **Official Language** Slovak. **All Languages** 9. **Languages with Scripture** 5Bi 1NT 1por 1 w.i.p.

ECONOMY
The transition from Communism to market capitalism has not been easy for Slovakia. High dependence on archaic heavy industry, and a ragged privatization scheme exacerbated the economic problems. Strong economic growth in the 1990s was not enough to lower the unemployment rate of 14%. **HDI** 0.813; 42ⁿᵈ/174. **Public debt** 23% of GDP. **Income/person** $3,410 (12% of USA).

POLITICS
Part of Czechoslovakia until Slovakia's separation from the Czech Republic in 1993. Multiparty republic, currently led by a broad coalition government that replaced the former nationalistic ex-Communist leadership in 1998. Slovakia became a member of the EU in 2004.

RELIGION
The constitution provides for freedom of religion, and the government respects this in practice.

Religions	Population %	Adherents	Ann.Gr.
Christian	82.94	4,468,136	-0.7%
non-Religious/other	17.00	915,822	+4.8%
Other	0.03	1,616	+8.6%
Muslim	0.02	1,077	+15.0%
Jewish	0.01	539	+0.1%

Christians	Denom.	Affil. %	,000	Ann.Gr.
Protestant	15	8.59	463	+1.1%
Independent	4	0.06	3	+4.8%
Catholic	2	62.41	3,362	-1.5%
Orthodox	1	0.41	22	-11.3%
Marginal	2	0.45	24	+0.8%
Unaffiliated		11.03	594	n.a.

Churches	MegaBloc	Cong.	Members	Affiliates
Catholic	C	1,350	2,000,000	3,200,000
Ev Ch of Augs Conf (Luth)	P	329	152,381	320,000
Greek Catholic	C	108	100,000	162,000
Reformed	P	327	92,308	120,000
Jehovah's Witnesses	M	183	12,416	24,000
Orthodox	O	12	14,667	22,000
Apostolic (AoG)	P	25	1,650	5,050
Other Protestant [6]	P	35	2,450	4,900
Seventh-day Adventist	P	43	2,145	4,600
Baptist Union	P	17	2,014	3,600
Ch of the Brethren	P	35	1,250	2,200
Christian Fellowship	I	11	700	1,600
Evangelical Methodist	P	5	320	1,500
Christian Assemblies	P	27	400	800
Other denoms [5]		10	1,118	2,000
Total Christians [24]		2,517	1,584,000	3,874,000

Trans-bloc Groupings	pop.%	,000	Ann.Gr.
Evangelical	1.5	79	+1.3%
Charismatic	1.7	93	+0.6%
Pentecostal	0.1	5	+15.2%

Missionaries from Slovakia
P,I,A 7 in 3 agencies; Slovakia 6.

Missionaries to Slovakia
P,I,A 131 in 29 agencies from 12 countries: USA 96, UK 9, Germany 7.

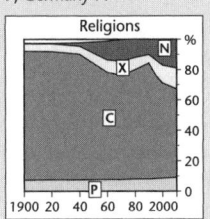
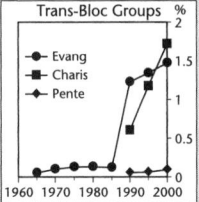

• Challenges for Prayer

1 **Slovakia, as a nation, needs a sense of direction** after the years of foreign rule, Communist economics and the 'velvet divorce' from the Czech Republic. Pray that as the economy picks up and becomes more linked with the EU, materialism and falling moral standards may not dull the present search for meaning and reality evident in many.

2 **Slovakia has a strong Christian heritage**, but the Catholic and mainline Protestant churches (Lutheran and Reformed) are more traditional and the majority of congregations are declining in numbers and attendance. The Lutheran Church holds an annual youth conference which draws a considerable number of young people. Pray against a spirit of passivity and even cynicism and pray for a revelation of God's glory so that many become enthused for the Kingdom in these denominations.

3 **Evangelical denominations are few and small.** They suffer from a minority complex. Some congregations are growing but others are merely in survival mode. There needs to be a clear understanding and experience of the gospel within each congregation so that its truths are communicated to listeners hardened by centuries of Church history. Pray for a clear expounding of God's Word that results in obedience to His authority among young and old alike.

4 **Vision for the future is still limited.** The Alliance of Evangelical Churches is promoting a vision for church planting. There are at present about 250 evangelical congregations in the country, but for every community to have a congregation there would need to be nearly 6,000 churches planted. Pray that such a vision might be adopted and implemented in an effective church planting programme.

5 **Training for leaders and believers alike is essential.** The Slovak Evangelical Alliance is sponsoring a church planters' training programme to educate and train laity — nearly 100 have finished this course already. There is a good Bible School attached to the university in Banska Bystrica for preparing pastors, evangelists, Christian teachers for schools, etc. Pray that many godly leaders may be formed through this programme, and bring the good news to Slovakia and beyond.

6 **There is much room for growth in missions** — both sending and receiving. There are several agencies with missionaries in the country (Churches of Christ 19; **CCCI** 14; **ABWE** 12, LCMS 7, **GEM** 4), but more workers and trainers are needed. **OM** conducts Love Europe campaigns on a short-term basis. The Apostolic Church has formed the first Slovak foreign missions sending body. Pray that the mission agencies and local churches would cooperate to the best effect, working together with joy and humility. Ask the Lord to burden Slovaks with a desire for world evangelization.

7 Less reached peoples:

a) *Hungarians make up more than 10% of the population.* There have been tensions between Slovaks and Hungarians over the issue of minority rights and language use. Pray for fair and just solutions. Most Hungarians are Catholic, but with some Reformed congregations and a few evangelical groups. Pray that Hungarian Christians may be mobilized to reach their kin in Slovakia.

b) *The Roma (Gypsies)* have a very different culture and worldview. They are often disliked and mistrusted. Attempts have been made to help them but they are suspicious and resistant to change. Pray for understanding as to how to help them most effectively and for love that will overcome the barriers and stereotypes that hinder spiritual ministry. There are some ministries committed to reach them.

8 Special ministries:

a) *Youth work* is an exciting area and many youth congresses and prayer meetings occur yearly. **SIET** is a network of national youth organizations with an excellent track record for cooperation between denominations. Pray against the attacks of the evil one to bring disunity. Pray that God may raise up a new generation of holy, faith-filled believers through these movements.

b) *The JESUS film* is completed for every language in Slovakia, except for some of the Roma dialects. Pray for wisdom and fruitfulness for the **CCCI** teams showing the film across the country.

c) *Christian literature.* Only recently has specifically Slovak evangelical literature been published — most books being in Czech. Pray for wisdom in selection of book titles and the best language in which to publish.

d) *Radio.* **TWR** has a broadcast centre in Bratislava, and transmits 7.5 hrs/wk in Slovak, 7 hrs/wk in Hungarian, as well as in English and Czech. The lack of gospel radio in Roma languages needs to be addressed.

Slovenia

Republic of Slovenia

OCTOBER 9
EUROPE
Updated February 2004

of skirmishes with the Serbian/Yugoslav army. Became a member of the EU in 2004.

RELIGION
Freedom of religion, but with the Catholic Church having an influential role.

Religions	Population %	Adherents	Ann.Gr.
Christian	85.16	1,690,900	-0.4%
non-Religious/other	13.29	263,900	+2.7%
Muslim	1.55	30,776	-0.7%

Christians	Denom.	Affil.%	,000	Ann.Gr.
Protestant	6	1.11	22	+0.6%
Independent	1	0.08	2	-0.6%
Catholic	1	81.59	1,620	-0.4%
Orthodox	3	2.22	44	-1.3%
Marginal	2	0.16	3	+2.9%

Churches	MegaBloc	Cong.	Members	Affiliates
Catholic	C	1,000	1,117,241	1,620,000
Orthodox [3]	O	6	27,500	44,000
Lutheran	P	30	7,600	19,000
Jehovah's Witnesses	M	30	1,866	3,050
Pentecostal	P	16	700	1,521
Seventh-day Adventist	P	13	498	700
Reformed	P	3	200	400
Baptist	P	4	150	330
Latter-day Saints (Morm)	M	3	125	200
Other denoms [2]		5	900	1,700
Total Christians [13]		1,110	1,156,800	1,690,900

Trans-bloc Groupings	pop.%	,000	Ann.Gr.
Evangelical	0.2	3	+3.9%
Charismatic	1.1	21	+0.1%
Pentecostal	0.1	2	+6.1%

Missionaries from Slovenia
P,I,A 3 known — all in Slovenia.

Missionaries to Slovenia
P,I,A 46 in 10 agencies from 6 countries: USA 34, Australia 7.

GEOGRAPHY
Area 20,256 sq.km. Alpine state adjoining Italy and Austria.

Population		Ann.Gr.		Density
2000	1,985,557	-0.04%		98 per sq. km.
2010	1,950,573	-0.24%		96 per sq. km.
2025	1,817,953	-0.58%		90 per sq. km.

Capital Ljubljana 269,621. **Urbanites** 51%.

PEOPLES
Slav 96.4%. Slovene 1.8 mill.; Croat 56,000; Serb 42,000, Bosnian 30,000.
Other 3.6%. German/Austrian 40,000; Hungarian 11,000; Italian/Friulian 10,000.

Literacy 99%. **Official languages** Slovene, Hungarian, Italian. **All languages** 6. **Languages with Scriptures** 3Bi 1NT.

ECONOMY
The most prosperous of the former Yugoslav republics. While the transition to a market economy was painful, the benefits are now being reaped. The bulk of trade has shifted from former Yugoslav Republics to Central and Western Europe. **HDI** 0.845; 33rd/174. **Public debt** 10.6% of GNP. **Income/person** $9,840 (31% of USA).

POLITICS
Dominated for centuries by Austria. Part of Yugoslav federation in 1918 until independence and democracy established in 1991 after 10 days

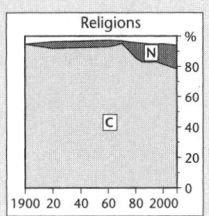

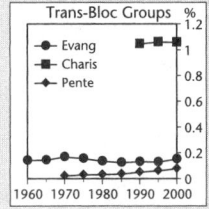

• Challenges for Prayer

1 **Slovenia has a strong Catholic tradition.** However, the three main Christian groups (Catholic, Orthodox, Lutheran) have little spiritual vitality. Widespread atheism and increasing rates of suicide and abortion challenge the Church's role in society. Pray that the many nominal Christians in the mainline churches might be awakened and come to personal faith in Christ.

2 **Bible distribution** is a major task. The Slovenian Bible Society has completed a new translation into Slovene; all major Christian groups cooperated in this project. The Society aims to distribute the Bible throughout Slovenia via schools and secular bookshops. There is only one evangelical bookshop in the country. **EHC** has managed to distribute

Christian literature to about 80% of all households in Slovenia. Pray that the new Bible and EHC literature might touch the hearts of Slovenians.

3 **Slovenia has had a Protestant witness** since the Reformation, but there are still very few evangelical churches. Even these few lack teaching and leadership training, although the Pentecostals have a small Bible School. Church planting teams consisting of both foreign and local believers are needed for most towns. Other Christian ministries include:

a) *Student work.* **CCCI** (18 workers), **Navigators** (6) and **IFES** (2) are all pioneering student witness in Ljubljiana and elsewhere.

b) *Radio.* **TWR** broadcasts and **IBRA** prepare one hour a week in Slovene. Catholic radio programmes are also broadcast on former army frequencies.

c) *The JESUS film* is available in Slovene and German.

Solomon Islands

OCTOBER 10
PACIFIC
Updated February 2004

GEOGRAPHY
Area 27,556 sq.km. Six of the 7 major volcanic islands of the Solomon Islands, also numerous smaller coral atolls. Bougainville Island is, at present, part of Papua New Guinea. The major islands are Guadalcanal, Choiseul, New Georgia, Santa Isobel, Malaita and San Cristobal.

Population		Ann.Gr.	Density
2000	443,643	+3.19%	16 per sq. km.
2010	587,925	+2.74%	21 per sq. km.
2025	816,561	+1.92%	30 per sq. km.

Capital Honiara 52,000 on Guadalcanal Island. **Urbanites** 18%.

PEOPLES
Over 90 ethnic groups.
Melanesian 90.7%. Speaking 60 languages; largest: Kwaraae 39,000, Toambaita 34,000; Areare 20,000; Kwaio 19,500; Lau 19,000.
Polynesian 3.7%. Speaking 6 languages — mainly on outlying coral atolls.
Other 5.6%. Vanuatu 9,000; I-kiribati 6,700; English-speaking 3,600; Chinese 3,000.

Literacy 54%, the lowest literacy rate in the Pacific.
Official language English. Trade language

Solomons Pidgin, spoken by half the population. **All languages** 66, but up to 120 if distinct dialects included. **Languages with Scriptures** 2Bi 10NT 7por 17w.i.p.

ECONOMY
Over 90% of the population depend on subsistence agriculture and fishing. Rich mineral resources remain to be exploited. Fishing and forestry are the main export earners. The two years of ethnic conflict severely damaged the economy, and the health and education services, with exports almost halved since mid-2000 and little early prospect of recovery. **HDI** 0.623; 118th/174. **Public debt** 26% of GNP. **Income/person** $900 (3% of USA).

POLITICS
Independent from Britain in 1978 as a parliamentary monarchy. Ethnic tensions between peoples of Guadalcanal and immigrants from Malaita erupted in violence in 1998 and a coup in 2000 with a virtual collapse of effective government. Intervention by Australian and New Zealand forces has brought some stability and breathing space to begin the political and economic restructuring of the country.

RELIGION
Freedom of religion but with a strongly Christian emphasis.

Religions	Population %	Adherents	Ann.Gr.
Christian	96.18	426,696	+3.2%
Cargo Cults	1.92	8,518	+3.4%
Traditional ethnic	1.50	6,655	+1.9%
Baha'i	0.40	1,775	+3.2%

Christians	Denom.	Affil. %	,000	Ann.Gr.
Protestant	12	41.60	185	+3.0%
Independent	7	5.00	22	+4.1%
Anglican	1	35.16	156	+1.9%
Catholic	1	16.91	75	+0.9%
Marginal	2	1.26	6	+2.0%
Unaffiliated		1.40	6	n.a.
Doubly affiliated		*-5.18*	*-23*	*n.a.*

Churches	MegaBloc	Cong.	Members	Affiliates
Ch of Melanesia	A	1,182	70,909	156,000
South Seas Evangelical	P	600	63,400	85,000
Catholic	C	174	43,605	75,000
United Ch in PNG/SI	P	300	29,940	50,000
Seventh-day Adventist	P	159	27,491	43,000
Christian Fellowship	I	79	6,347	10,600
Jehovah's Witnesses	M	39	1,582	5,500
Chr Outreach Centre	I	50	2,500	5,000
Assemblies of God	P	19	693	2,100
Other denoms [14]		68	4,712	11,150
Doubly affiliated			*-11,500*	*-23,000*
Total Christians [23]		2,670	239,700	420,300

Trans-bloc Groupings	pop.%	,000	Ann.Gr.
Evangelical	34.6	153	+3.4%
Charismatic	19.1	85	+3.6%
Pentecostal	3.2	14	+2.6%

Missionaries from Solomon Islands
P,I,A est. 44 in 5 agencies.

Missionaries to Solomon Islands
P,I,A est. 66 in 12 agencies.

• Answers to Prayer

1 The Solomons have had a history of revivals — in SSE churches in 1935 and 1970, then in nearly all denominations in 1982 onwards. People in all parts of the country came to the Lord and enthusiastically became involved in churches, house groups, prayer meetings and outreach. Evangelical and charismatic believers have grown much in all denominations. The result is a waning of syncretistic 'cargo cults' and the indigenization of the gospel to local cultures.

• Challenges for Prayer

1 The tragic conflict of 1998-2001 left the country with no effective government, a severely damaged economy and infrastructure. Pray that all ethnic tension, vengefulness and bitterness may be dispelled and reconciliation sought. Pray for a government to be raised up that can deal with anarchy, criminality and ethnic conflict and then restore the nation's stability and progress.

2 The revival is history now. Pray that its quickening effects might restore the damaged spiritual life of the country in the wake of the violence and give strength, vigour and spiritual power to a new generation of Christians.

3 Inadequate training of pastors is the biggest bottleneck for the Church's growth in maturity and expansion. There have been some damaging cases of clerical misdemeanors which have brought discredit to the Lord. Pray for the six SSEC Bible Schools, the Anglican Theological College, and also TEE programmes. Pray also for a greater global missions vision.

4 The ministry of expatriate mission agencies is winding down as the Church matures, and was severely disrupted in the civil unrest. Most missionaries are involved in Bible teaching, translation or specialist ministries. The largest agencies: **CCCI** (8 workers), **Pioneers** (SSEM) and **YWAM** (7 each). CCCI have their Pacific HQ in Honiara as well as their New Life Training Center.

5 Unreached peoples. The land has been so exposed to the gospel that only pockets of resistant animists on Guadalcanal and Malaita hold out against the gospel. Yet the continued influence of syncretistic or almost pagan 'cargo cults', which have prompted an exodus from churches in the past, shows the need for a personal appropriation of the gospel by each generation.

6 Youth ministries. These are important with the rapid population growth and large numbers of third- and fourth-generation Christians. Drug abuse is becoming a serious problem. **SU** has vital groups in many of the high schools. **CEF** has 5 workers among children. The poverty and social breakdown since 1998 has deeply affected the schooling system.

7 **Christian support ministries for prayer:**

a) ***Bible translation.*** National believers are taking the initiative, and this long-underestimated ministry is now receiving the attention it deserves. Pray for the 17 translation projects by UBS and **SIL** (20 workers); 20 more languages may still need to be tackled. The major need is for the completion of the Bible in Pidgin (the trade language). Only 10 of the 66 languages have the New Testament.

b) ***The JESUS film*** has been viewed by over half the population in English. Two local language editions are in preparation.

c) ***GRN*** has gospel messages available in 85 languages and dialects — a good resource in a nation with so many small language groups.

d) ***Christian hospitals*** are significant for the country. The Solomons have one of the highest incidences of malaria in the world.

Somalia
Soomaaliya

OCTOBER 11
AFRICA

GEOGRAPHY
Area 637,000 sq.km. The arid Horn of Africa east of Ethiopia and Kenya.

Population	Ann.Gr.	Density
2000	10,097,177	+4.25%	16 per sq. km.
2010	14,130,792	+3.17%	22 per sq. km.
2025	21,211,280	+2.51%	33 per sq. km.

These population figures are broad estimates and likely to be too high. A further one million are refugees in Africa, Yemen, Europe and North America.

Capital Mogadishu 900,000; Somaliland: Hargeisa 350,000; Puntland: Garoowe. **Urbanites** 37%.

PEOPLES
Somali 97.4%. Complex hierarchy of clans based on paternal descent.
Northern Somali 77%. Four major clan families: Dir, Daarood, Hawiye, Isxaaq. Numerous clans and subclans; largely semi-nomadic.
Southern Somali 20.4%. More despised; some mixed with Bantu ex-slaves, largely agricultural. Main clan families: Digil, Rahanwiin (Maay-speaking) 650,000; Garre 50,000; Jiddu 44,000; Tunni 43,000; Dabarre 38,000 — all related to Somali.
Bantu 1.6%. Wagosha-Mushungulu 85,000; Benadiri-Bajuni Swahili 40,000.

Other 1%. Oromo 50,000; Arab 30,000; Eyle Khoisan (Bushmen).

Literacy 24%, but in decline. **Official languages** Somali, Arabic (few speak it). **All languages** 14. **Languages with Scriptures** 6Bi.

ECONOMY
Subsistence pastoral economy — largely camel or cattle herding; some agriculture in south and north-west. Economy in ruins in Somalia, and controlled by warlords trading in narcotics, arms and food aid. Majority of population totally dependent on food aid and remittances from relatives abroad. No formal economy exists. Some recovery and reconstruction in Somaliland.

POLITICS
United as a single country in 1960 soon after the British (in north) and Italians (in south) granted independence to their respective fiefs. Cold war rivalries provided Somalia with ample weapons — first from the USSR, then from the USA — for disastrous wars against Ethiopia and clan fighting. These brought the country to destitution. The corrupt and repressive dictatorship of Siyaad Barre ended in a bloody civil war in 1991 but with no viable alternative government emerging. The country slid into clan warfare with warlords vying for power. Most of the fighting has been in Mogadishu and the agricultural lands in the south, which induced terrible famine. UN intervention in 1992 was a disaster and resulted in humiliating withdrawal in 1995. Anarchy has reigned since then with no national government. In late 2000 a transitional national government was formed in Mogadishu. Somaliland in the north-west declared its independence from Somalia in 1991 but remains unrecognized internationally. Puntland in the northeast has set up its own autonomous government.

RELIGION
Islam is the official religion. Islamists gained influence in both the south and Somaliland and seek to enforce *shari'a* law. There were many Ethiopian Orthodox refugees in Somalia during the 1970s and '80s. **Persecution index** 25th in the world.

Religions	Population %	Adherents	Ann.Gr.
Muslim	99.95	10,092,128	+4.2%
Christian	0.05	5,049	+4.2%

Christians	Denom.	Affil.%	,000	Ann.Gr.
Protestant	1	0.00	0	n.a.
Independent	1	0.00	0	n.a.
Anglican	1	0.00	0	n.a.
Catholic	1	0.00	0	n.a.
Orthodox	1	0.03	4	-2.6%
Unaffiliated		0.01	1	n.a.

Churches	MegaBloc	Cong.	Members	Affiliates
Ethiopian Orthodox	O		1,400	3,500
Catholic	C		116	200
Other denoms [3]		0	79	165
Total Christians [5]		0	1,595	3,865

• Challenges for Prayer

1 **Somalia is the most lawless country in the world**. In contrast, the unrecognized Somaliland has a good measure of stability and peace. After 10 years of violence and anarchy, Somalis are desperate for peace and restoration of civil order. Tentative efforts to form a government are ignored or derided by some of the warlords. Pray that all factions may agree on the formation of a national government and that future rulers might learn from the past, govern the nation for the good of its people, respect human rights and also grant true religious freedom.

2 **Islam has failed the people**. Two powerful competing Sufi brotherhoods have contributed to present troubles. The evident greed, intolerance and lack of love have discredited Islam. Some are seeking solutions in radical Islam. Many Islamist teachers have flooded into Somaliland and Puntland where there is more stability. Pray that Islamist plans may be thwarted and a new religious tyranny prevented.

3 **National recovery is the need**, but the population is traumatized by suffering, death, famine and the savagery of the fighting. Over 300,000 have died. Over 25% of all children under five perished. Pray for:
a) *Wise administration of aid*. The UN and the many NGOs involved in the 1990s unwittingly became the suppliers and sustainers of the war — the militias helped themselves to weapons, supplies and equipment. Pray for protection and effective ministry for aid workers — many of whom are Christians.
b) *Refugees* and ministry to them in Kenya (500,000). There is need for ministry to the refugees in Ethiopia (200,000), Yemen (60,000), the Gulf and the West also.

4 **The work of missions** has been limited, dangerous and hedged with restrictions, and in 1974 was forced to cease. Swedish Lutherans won a few hundred to Christ in the south between 1898 and 1935. Mennonites and **SIM** (1953-74) also saw a few hundred turn to the Lord. Pray for workers for the Somali to be called, prepared and ready for the opening of these defiantly closed doors.

5 **The Somali Church** has been driven underground. A number of believers have been martyred, others have been publicly named as targets for execution. In 1991 there were about 500 Somali Catholics and several hundred Evangelicals — most being secret believers and nearly all in the south; with few in Somaliland. Some have since fled the anarchy, taking refuge in Kenya, Ethiopia, Yemen and elsewhere. Globally there may now be 2,000 Somali Christians. Pray for their protection, growth in the faith and boldness to witness when opportunities arise. Pray also for Somali Christian families to be raised up — the great majority of Christians are men.

6 **Strong prejudices** against Christianity need to be broken down. These are:
a) *Muslim association of Christianity with oppression* — may refugees and recipients of help from Christians be touched and respond.
b) *Perceived incompatibility of Christianity with nomadism* — 60% of Somalis are semi-nomadic.

7 **About 3.5 million Somalis live in surrounding lands**. Ethiopia (approx. 2.8m); Kenya (511,000); Djibouti (192,000). **SIM**, **SBC**, Life Ministries, **CBIM** and others have a ministry to Somalis in Kenya, and **RSTI** in Djibouti. Pray for Christian aid workers and

S

their tactful witness. Pray that all these ministries may have an impact on Somalia itself and that viable Somali churches may be planted.

8 **Christian specialist ministries:**

a) *The Somali Bible* was published in 1977. Distribution is only possible in refugee camps and among Somalis outside Somalia. Pray for the wide dissemination of the Scriptures.

b) *Bible translation* is definitely needed for the Maay Somali, whose language is somewhat divergent.

c) *Christian radio* has been a major means of lessening anti-gospel prejudice and aiding the conversion of Somalis. Pray for the work of Somali Voice of New Life (CNC-**SIM**) based in Nairobi and broadcasts of **FEBA** (30 min/day) and **TWR** (15 min/day). It is a constant struggle to maintain, and a challenge to expand, this service.

d) *Follow-up Bible correspondence courses* are run by CNC — with a thousand or more active students in 13 countries. The collapse of postal services in Somalia has hindered any meaningful follow-up ministry.

South Africa

Republic of South Africa

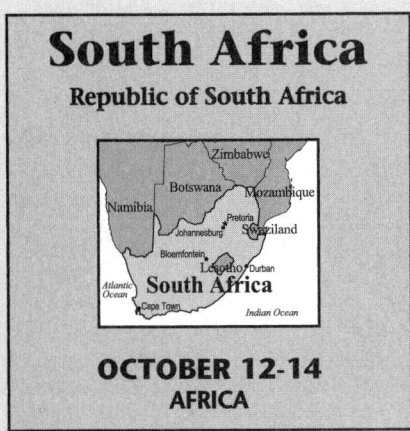

OCTOBER 12-14
AFRICA

Sotho 25% in 3 groups: Tswana 3.3m; Pedi (N. Sotho) 3.7m; Sotho 3.1m.
Other 7.4%. Tsonga 1.7m; Venda 890,000.
Caucasian 10.9%; declining through emigration and lower birth rate. Afrikaner 2.4m; English-speaking 1.4m; Portuguese 500,000; Greek 70,000; German 40,000.
Coloured (mixed race) 8.9%. 90% live in the northern and Western Cape. Cape Malays are considered part of this community.
Asian 2.6%. Over 75% in KwaZulu Natal. South Asians 1.1m; Chinese 40,000.
Other 0.9%. Migrant labour and illegal immigrants.
Literacy 82%. Functional literacy is much lower at around 62%. **National languages** 11 — all the major ethnic languages. English and Afrikaans are the main languages in higher education. **All languages** 32. **Languages with Scriptures** 19Bi 1NT 1w.i.p.

GEOGRAPHY
Area 1,218,363 sq.km. A republic with nine provinces at the southernmost point of Africa. Relatively well-watered in the east; arid with increasing desertification towards the west coast.

Population		Ann.Gr.	Density
2000	40,376,579	+1.51%	33 per sq. km.
2010	42,514,924	+0.32%	35 per sq. km.
2025	46,015,286	+0.64%	38 per sq. km.

Nearly one million not born in South Africa. Estimates for illegal immigrants from other African countries range from 4 million to 12 million.

Capital Cape Town (legislative) 2.6 million. Pretoria (administrative) 1.7m; Bloemfontein (judicial) 325,000. Other major cities: Johannesburg/Rand 5.6m; Durban 2.8m; Port Elizabeth 1.2m; Vereeniging 1.2m. These figures are likely to be low due to the massive population of migrants living in informal housing. **Urbanites** 54%.

PEOPLES

African 76.7%. Majority in 7 provinces:
Nguni 44.3% in five groups: Zulu 9.1m; Xhosa 7.1m; Swazi 1m; Ndebele(2) 565,000.

ECONOMY
The richest and most industrialized country in Africa (25% of Africa's GNP, 40% of its industrial output). The world's biggest exporter of non-petroleum minerals — especially gold, platinum, chrome, diamonds and coal. Well diversified, industrial economy. Lack of oil, water and an erratic rainfall hinder growth. The post-apartheid government promised to stimulate development, initiate affirmative action to further African economic progress and open up the economy. The economy has not grown sufficiently to improve employment, housing, education and give hope for the future to the impoverished majority. The burgeoning AIDS calamity is damaging growth. **Unemployment** 25% (38% for youth and may be much higher). **HDI** 0.695; 101st/174. Public debt 9% of GNP. **Income/person** $3,210 (10% of USA) — but big disparities between wealthy and poor.

POLITICS
The Union of South Africa was formed in 1910. A white minority parliamentary republic was created in 1961. The infamous 'apartheid' system politically and economically marginalized non-whites and brought untold pain and suffering

to the majority. A worsening economic climate, increasing political isolation, a deteriorating security situation and the ending of the Cold War all triggered rapid changes in the 1980s. The last laws undergirding apartheid were repealed in 1991 and the country's first free national democratic elections took place in 1994. Nelson Mandela's government worked hard to set up a free, non-racial government and constitution, and initiate the long healing process with commendable successes. Much disillusionment has set in due to the slow rate of change, limited economic growth and increasing crime and corruption.

RELIGION
Freedom of religion. A strong push to give all religions equal say has given high profile to the ethnic African religions, Islam, Hinduism, humanism and the interfaith movement at the expense of Christianity.

Religions	Population %	Adherents	Ann.Gr.
Christian	73.52	29,684,861	+1.2%
Traditional ethnic	15.00	6,056,487	+0.8%
non-Religious/other	8.08	3,262,428	+6.5%
Muslim	1.45	585,460	+2.8%
Hindu	1.25	504,707	+0.4%
Baha'i	0.50	201,883	+1.5%
Jewish	0.17	68,640	+1.5%
Buddhist/Chinese	0.03	12,113	+10.1%

Christians	Denom.	Affil.%	,000	Ann.Gr.
Protestant	185	21.06	8,502	-0.3%
Independent	4,589	37.99	15,339	+2.6%
Anglican	2	3.96	1,600	-4.8%
Catholic	1	8.35	3,372	+2.4%
Orthodox	4	0.12	48	+6.3%
Marginal	12	0.54	218	+1.0%
Unaffiliated		1.50	605	n.a.

Churches	MegaBloc	Cong.	Members	Affiliates
Zion Christian [3]	I	4,800	2,100,000	4,200,000
Catholic	C	902	2,107,807	3,372,492
Ch of Prov of SA (Ang)	A	1,200	389,610	1,500,000
Methodist	P	4,500	462,379	1,462,379
Dutch Reformed (NGK)	P	1,164	900,000	1,227,621
Uniting Ref Ch in SA	P	734	650,000	1,205,943
Apost. Faith Miss (AFM)	P	2,200	500,000	1,000,000
Assemblies of God	I	2,000	320,000	1,000,000
Evang Luth Ch in S.A.	P	1,693	460,478	769,000
12 Apostles Ch in Christ	I	3,196	361,111	650,000
Full Gospel Ch of God	P	1,247	263,469	400,000
Presbyterian Ch of Afr.	I	300	100,000	350,000
New Apostolic	I	1,598	230,393	345,589
Dutch Reformed (NHK)	P	325	169,000	300,000
Int'l Fell of Chr Chs	I	362	180,000	300,000
United Congregational	P	345	183,846	270,253
Pentecostal Protestant	P	700	110,000	160,000
Jehovah's Witnesses	M	1,331	67,069	155,000
Presbyterian Ch of SA	I	266	79,000	150,000
Seventh-day Adventist	P	576	58,291	140,000
Baptist Union of S.A. [2]	P	423	49,402	112,402
Reformed (GK)	P	286	75,000	101,159
Moravian [2]	P	55	31,400	100,200
Ch of England in SA	A	160	10,481	100,000
Reformed Presbyterian	P	102	42,400	90,000
Africa Evangelical	P	214	18,402	60,000
Baptist Convention	P	130	32,800	55,000
Pentecostal Holiness	P	525	35,645	49,900
Salvation Army	P	145	16,556	45,000
Ch of the Nazarene	P	481	27,000	37,162
Evangelical Bible [3]	P	260	22,000	35,000
Zulu Congregational	I	44	15,000	23,000
Other denoms [4,760]		8,284	4,074,086	9,332,000
Total Christians [4,800]		40,548	14.143m	29.080m

Trans-bloc Groupings	pop.%	,000	Ann.Gr.
Evangelical	19.3	7,774	+2.1%
Charismatic	24.4	9,862	+2.1%
Pentecostal	8.4	3,384	+2.5%

Missionaries from South Africa
P,I,A 2,622 in 126 agencies of which 1,494 are in 100 other countries.

Missionaries to South Africa
P,I,A 1,258 in 140 agencies from 40 countries: USA 538, Germany 139, UK 136, Korea 54, Canada 52.

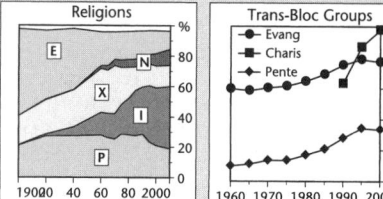

• Answers to Prayer

1 **Transition from white rule and apartheid to a non-racial democracy** was achieved relatively peacefully rather than the feared bloodbath. The courage of F.W. de Klerk, the magnanimity of Nelson Mandela and the prayers of God's people were key components in this.

2 **The institution of a functioning democracy** and two successful general elections in 1994 and 1999.

3 **Strenuous efforts by local churches to roll back the centuries** of discrimination, oppression and pain have borne fruit. The Truth and Reconciliation Commission under Archbishop Desmond Tutu was one means to begin addressing the wrongs of the past. There is a great distance to go, but praise God for what has been achieved.

4 The massive growth of global vision and multiplication of South African mission involvement by all communities after the ending of South Africa's diplomatic isolation in 1993. Innovative strategies for sending and support have been developed. In 1993 there were 650 South Africans serving abroad. That number had reached 1,870 in 1999.

5 The multiplication of Christian ministries to help the disadvantaged — slum-dwellers, unemployed, the victims of rape, crime and AIDS, etc., has been a remarkable testimony.

• Challenges for Prayer

1 The need for stable government. The euphoria of the 'New' South Africa has worn off. Pray for all in leadership that wise decisions, fair laws and economic betterment may be the hallmark. There are too many African examples of demagoguery, decline, corruption and cronyism for there to be any complacency. There are many committed Christians at every level in society.

2 The need for ongoing healing and reconciliation. The legacy of contempt, mistrust, fear, injustice, violence, intimidation and deep hurt has scarred the soul of the nation. Pray for a healthy balance between non-racialism and affirmative action (favouring the previously disadvantaged) in education, the economy, employment and leadership.

3 The need for economic betterment. There are extremes of wealth and poverty with the attendant evils of corruption, crime. Tangible improvements are needed to head off a future explosion. Pray that the available resources may be best used for the good of all.

4 The need for effective policing and administration of justice. The escalating crime wave has shocked the nation (200,000 murders in the 1990s), limited foreign investment and restrained the flow of tourists. The major growth industry is security. Violent robberies, car-hijacking and rape are commonplace. The country has a murder rate over seven times that of the USA and few crimes end up with convictions. The police force is discouraged, under-trained and under-equipped to cope. Pray that both this epidemic and underlying malaise might be healed. Pray for Christian ministries among children at risk, jobless young people, prisoners and to the police force, to bear much fruit.

5 AIDS has become the primary cause of death. Daily 1,200 victims are buried. There were 420,000 AIDS orphans in 2000. Over 20% of the adult population and a third of all teachers are infected. The economy is increasingly affected through loss of skills and time off work. The age expectancy of the population has fallen rapidly and medical services cannot cope. Pray that this terrible pandemic might be tamed and that Christians might be used of God in caring for the victims and raising moral and family standards to prevent its spread. There are dozens of Christian agencies and NGOs, as well as many churches, active in this field.

6 Biblical Christianity continues to thrive and has grown in influence despite the post-Christian moral slide in society.

a) *There has been much enthusiasm, multiplied prayer networks* and vigorous outreach in evangelism, missions and social concern. There is a bewildering variety of Christian agencies springing up to minister to needy sections of society. The **Caring for the Poor and Needy Network** mobilizes churches for prayer and to initiate ministries with the poor.

b) *Pentecostal denominations* have flourished among all communities growing from 400,000 in 1960 to 1.1 million in 1980, and then to 3.5 million in 2000. Notable has been the ministry of the **AoG** (Back to God), Apostolic Faith Mission, Full Gospel Church of God and others.

c) *Charismatic networks* have multiplied among all population groups and had a significant impact with a wide range of ministries and mission outreach. Over one million Christians are linked to such as the Rhema Churches and the Hatfield Christian Church network.

d) *Mainline denominations* have, in parts, been transformed by new vision, structures and outreach. The cell church movement has had significant impact. The NGK (DRC) has many mega-churches, much increase in missions output and renewal in many congregations.

e) *The massive growth of African Independent/Indigenous Churches* to 32% of the African population — 10 million people linked to possibly 4,500 to 6,000 church groups (many being of one congregation only) which range from evangelical/Pentecostal to highly syncretistic.

7 **Challenges for South African Christians.** Pray for:

a) ***Adaptability*** in the face of rapid social change. South Africa has become a pluralist society and Christians are no longer tied to the power structures. Denominations and congregations that cannot adapt are losing people — many traditional and even evangelical denominations are in decline.

b) ***A prophetic voice*** for the Church in a society that no longer holds to moral absolutes, and where the post-Christian worldview holds centre stage in the media and has pushed through legalization of abortion, pornography, prostitution and gambling. Homosexuality is actively promoted.

c) ***Deep reconciliation***. Evangelicals were reluctant to challenge the evils of apartheid. There still remain divisions and unfinished business. A number of denominations, including the NGK, AFM, Full Gospel and Baptists have gone through painful periods of dealing with the past. There has been the formation of a united evangelical voice in the launch of The Evangelical Alliance of South Africa in 1995. There is, however, a long way to go before trust and understanding are built, and meaningful cooperation developed across cultural barriers. Pray that the whole Church may be able to lay the sad past to rest and envision the future together.

d) ***Revival*** in mainline denominations. Whilst there is much spiritual life, there is also much traditionalism, nominalism and 'churchianity' in the Dutch Reformed family of churches, Anglicans, Methodists and others.

8 **The training of Christian leaders** is a multi-faceted challenge. Much is being done, but much remains to be done.

a) ***There are 49 theological, degree-awarding*** university faculties and seminaries and 50 or more residential Bible Colleges with over 6,000 students (14% foreign) and over 1,000 lecturers. Finances to support this abundance is a challenge to churches, students and the institutions themselves. Since 1997 there has been a decline in numbers because of this. Many larger, newer churches have also set up their own Bible training programmes.

b) ***Distance learning, or TEE,*** is a cost-effective alternative, but to many Africans who need it most, it is seen as a second-class option. In 1999 nearly 22,000 were involved in TEE programmes provided by about 28 different centres.

c) ***The numerous African Independent Churches (AICs) are often pastored by those with little education***. Many of these churches are more influenced by African customs and world-view, and can be highly syncretistic. Yet these leaders can be very open to appropriate, sensitively applied, teaching and brought to a more biblical understanding. Increasing numbers of Christian educators are concentrating on providing this needful but often frustrating ministry. Pray that this extraordinary and significant movement may retain the best of African culture yet become biblical and accountable to the wider Body of Christ.

9 **Ministry challenges** for the Church in South Africa:

a) ***AIDS victims***. This horrendous pandemic is silently destroying swathes of society. Only Christians have a meaningful message of eternal hope and the moral foundation to prevent its spread. Pray for Christians involved in caring for victims, orphans and bereaved and in challenging young people to change their lifestyle.

b) ***Urbanites***. The dismantling of apartheid legislation ended decades of enforced rural poverty among Africans. Millions moved to the cities and over a fifth of all Africans live in 'informal' housing or in vast squatter camps and slums even though the government has done much to improve the housing situation. It is a challenge for churches to find building sites for urban congregations. Many Africans live in huge suburbs that became household names around the world — Soweto and Alexandra (Johannesburg), Kwa Mashu (Durban), Gugulethu (Cape Town), Sharpeville, etc. Pray for:

i *The churches, believers and their witness* in a society full of social stress, where tribal and family authority has broken down, and where political, ethnic and criminal violence is commonplace. Rape, teenage pregnancies and murder are perpetrated unchecked, and AIDS is a scourge. Pray that they may be protected, given grace to stand for Jesus and be lights for Him in these very places.

ii *Evangelistic outreach* through churches and agencies (Assemblies of God, African Enterprise, Dorothea Mission, Africa for Christ Evangelistic Association, Gospel Ambassadors for Christ, etc.). The major new challenge is the evangelization of the new squatter settlements which leads to church planting. Much is being done locally, and church growth in them is fast.

c) *Young people and children* — over 45% of the population is under 20. Youth ministry is vital for South Africa's future spiritual health.

i *There are over 25 agencies with specific ministry to young people.* The great challenge is meeting the needs of the many poor, without opportunities or education and who become a fertile recruiting area for violence and crime.

ii *Children of school age* are ministered to by over 10 major agencies — **SU** with 106 full-time staff, **CEF** with 50 workers and many others. The big growth area is coping with the rapidly increasing number of AIDS orphans and victims of sexual abuse.

iii *University students.* SCO(**IFES**) has ministry on 130 campuses with over 8,000 students involved and also a ministry in many secondary schools. **CCCI** has over 130 workers — many in campus ministry. There are, however, over 600,000 students in tertiary education.

d) *Muslims* are only 1.4% of the population (600,000), but exercise an influence far greater than their numbers with many holding high office in the government. Most are of the South Asian and Cape Malay communities, but there are now over 40,000 Africans who have become Muslim in recent years. Very few Muslims have ever openly become followers of the Lord Jesus, so pray for ministries among:

i *Cape Malays* (240,000), who mainly live around Cape Town and are part of the Afrikaans-speaking coloured community. They are descended from political prisoners and slaves brought by the Dutch to the Cape centuries ago. They cling strongly to their religion and culture. There is a cooperative fellowship of agencies seeking to witness and disciple them (Life Challenge/**SIM**, **WEC**, and others). There has been some fruit but pressures on these believers can be intense.

ii *Asians* (250,000), mainly in the Durban area of KwaZulu-Natal. Most are of Gujarati, Urdu and other Indian ethnic groups. Nearly 23% of the South Asian community is Muslim. Ministry among them is low-key and fruit hand-picked. Full Gospel Churches, Baptists, **SIM** and Jesus to the Muslims are all involved in this outreach.

iii *Pray for Muslim background believer (MBB) churches to emerge.* Pray also that the small, but violent Islamist PAGAD movement might be neutralized — a vigorous campaign by them against drug rings in Cape Town degenerated into a violent guerrilla movement that has murdered, maimed and bombed themselves into newspaper headlines.

e) *Hindus* are 50% of the Asian population. There has been a steady flow of Hindu people to Christ and now 19% of the Asian population is Christian. There are still many who need the freedom there is in Christ. Demonization is a major problem. The work of the Full Gospel Church of God, Apostolic Faith Mission, **NGK**, **AEF/SIM**, Church of England in South Africa and the Baptists has been fruitful with some large and lively churches. The great potential for these believers to go out as missionaries is beginning to be realized.

f) *The Chinese* are of three types — long-term residents, immigrants from Taiwan in the 1980s and the present legal and illegal immigration from mainland China. A number of churches and missions (**SIM** included) have ministry among them. The biggest challenge is reaching the mainlanders who are proving more responsive.

g) *The Portuguese* and *Greek* communities are largely Catholic or Orthodox. There are some Portuguese evangelical congregations, but the Greeks are more neglected.

h) *The Jews* live largely in Gauteng and in Cape Town. There is a small, but growing number of Messianic Jews (**CWI**, **JfJ**).

i) *Mine workers* are drawn from all over rural South Africa and surrounding nations. Many men live separated from their families for long periods of time. At any one time 400,000 are living on large mine compounds of the Free State, Gauteng and the Northern Province. Various missions and agencies seek to minister to them.

j) *Illegal immigrants* have streamed over South Africa's borders — especially from Mozambique, Malawi, Angola, Congo, Burundi, Rwanda and even Nigeria. Their numbers may be very large indeed but no one really knows. Pray that these people may be adequately helped spiritually — whether Christian or not.

10 **Missions vision** has flourished since 1991 and the ending of South Africa's 30-year diplomatic isolation. South Africa's commitment in the past was notable with internationally known agencies such as **NGK**(DRC) which had a major outreach for many years to a number of African nations, **AEF** (now SIM), **IHCF** with a world-wide ministry to and through medical workers, Africa Evangelistic Band, **Dorothea Mission** and more recently **African Enterprise**. The **NGK** has renewed its commitment to missions and has done much for neighbouring territories. Local AFM and charismatic churches have developed many new mission initiatives. **OM** and **YWAM** have done much in training and sending out young people into ministry. Pray for:

a) *The continued growth and health of the missions movement.* The **Love Southern Africa** vision, the local expression of the AD2000 and Beyond Movement, was a catalyst to the new missions thrust that has aroused many congregations to action for world evangelization and resulted in a multiplication of short-term teams and long-term workers. **Love Southern Africa** has been taken over by the Mission Mobilizers Network.

b) *Good cooperation between churches, Bible colleges and mission agencies.* In 2000 the **World Evangelization Network of South Africa** (WENSA) was formed as a hub of 25 networks linking agencies and denominations. Mission agencies need to adapt to the growing direct involvement of local congregations in missions.

c) *Strategic development of vision.* The World Mission Centre has developed **Gateway Strategy Networks** with congregation 'hubs' that focus on specific unreached peoples or regions and to which other congregations relate and team up for information dissemination and in praying for, supporting and sending missionaries. By 1999 there were 7 regional and 17 national hubs in existence. Pray for the widest possible involvement of South Africa's 40,000 or so evangelical congregations.

d) *South African missionaries around the world.* Over 40% are in other African countries and 20% in 10/40 Window countries. Adequate support is a constant problem because of the national economic difficulties and the many demands on ministry in South Africa. This is especially true for missionaries from the Coloured, Asian and African communities. New and relevant ways of doing mission need to be sought to draw these population groups into cross-cultural mission. The devaluation of the Rand, the local currency, has not helped in supporting foreign missions.

e) *The emergence of missionary outreach from the Black churches.* There is great potential, but obstacles for its realization are enormous, and the relatively few missionaries from this community have a hard task to convince the church leadership of the validity of missions, let alone raising missionary support. The **Mission Mobilizers Network** has a strong burden to facilitate this vision, and WENSA is contributing to this.

11 **Expatriate missions.** Mission work began among indigenous peoples in 1799. Nearly every major denomination in Europe and North America has played a part in their evangelization. Despite tragic mistakes, heroic efforts have yielded much fruit. The missionary force has reduced in numbers as mature churches have emerged, and most existing ministries are in church development, leadership training, youth, literature and radio ministries. Pray for fruitful ministries for them in times of great difficulty and discouragement.

12 **Christian help ministries.** The scope and scale of specialized Christian ministries is impressive. The giving needed to sustain them is prodigious! Pray specifically for:

a) *Bible production and distribution.* Nearly every language has the entire Bible. Massive numbers are sold or distributed annually by **The Bible Society**. Pray for increased reading of the Scriptures and for lasting, formative impact on lives.

b) *Christian literature* is available in abundance. There are 42 Christian publishers and 216 Christian bookstores. Of note are All Nations Gospel Publishers with a world-wide distribution of evangelistic tracts and booklets.

c) *Christian broadcasting* has a large following. Pray specifically for:

i *Religious programming* aired on radio and television by the **South Africa Broadcasting Corporation**. Air time is awarded broadly in proportion to the percentages of the national religions. Pray that the biblical and evangelical content may be maintained and not restricted.

ii *Local community FM radio stations.* These have multiplied and many are specifically Christian. Results have been good. Pray that licences might continue to be issued — the government has shown some reluctance to do so. From South Africa this vision has spread to many other countries in Africa under the umbrella of **Radio Africa Network.**

iii *International Christian broadcasters.* **FEBC** has increased its ministry in the country. **TWR** has a major input with stations in Johannesburg and nearby Swaziland; they broadcast 243 hrs/wk in 8 national languages. A further 125 hrs/wk are broadcast in 4 languages by satellite.

iv *The 23+ Christian radio and television agencies* based in South Africa and the programmes they produce.

d) **The JESUS film** is widely used in 18 languages and a high proportion of the population has seen it.

e) **MAF** has a base in South Africa; its main ministry is flying teams for ministry to surrounding countries.

Spain
Kingdom of Spain

OCTOBER 15-16
EUROPE
Revised February 2004

GEOGRAPHY
Area 504,783 sq.km. The major part of the Iberian peninsula and Balearic Islands in the Mediterranean. Also included are the Canary Islands off north-west Africa and the enclaves of Ceuta and Mellila on the North African coast.

Population		Ann.Gr.	Density
2000	39,759,775	+0.03%	79 per sq. km.
2010	39,223,193	-0.19%	78 per sq. km.
2025	36,798,293	-0.52%	73 per sq. km.

Capital Madrid 5 mill. Other major cities: Barcelona 4.2m; Valencia 1,375,000; Sevilla 1.05m; Bilbao 1m. **Urbanites** 78%.

PEOPLES

Indigenous 98%.
Spanish 90.3%. Major languages: Castilian 29m; Catalan 6.7m; Galician 3m; Asturian 450,000; Extremaduran 200,000; Aragonese 30,000.
Basque 5.7%. Euskera is the primary language of 42% of the 1.1m Basques in the Basque Autonomous Region. All Basques 2.2m.
Other 2%. Roma (Gypsy) 600,000+.
Foreign 2%. North African/Arab 450,000; Latin American 160,000; EU citizens 100,000; Chinese 30,000; Iranian 15,000.

Literacy 97%. **Official language** Castilian. Catalan, Galician and Basque are the official languages in the respective autonomous regions. Spanish is the first language of 340 million people; the world's third most widely-used language. **All languages** 14. **Languages with Scriptures** 4Bi 1NT 3por 4w.i.p.

ECONOMY
The mightiest economic power in the world in the 16th Century followed by three centuries of decline and economic stagnation until entry into the EU in 1986. Integration into Europe has transformed the country into a modern, confident, industrial power with rapidly rising living standards. Main sources of income are tourism and industry. **HDI** 0.894; 21st/174. **Public debt** 55% of GNP. **Income/person** $14,490 (46% of USA).

POLITICS
Spain's tumultuous past moulds the present. The Muslim Moorish occupation lasted 700 years, ending in 1492. The world-wide Spanish empire lasted for three centuries. The last two centuries have been marked by instability, civil wars and dictatorships; the latter under General Franco lasted from 1939 to 1975. Constitutional monarchy with an effective multi-party democracy. Wide powers have been given to 17 autonomous communities as a means of preserving national unity. The left-wing Basque ETA terrorist campaign for full Basque independence has plagued Spain and divided the Basque community since 1961.

RELIGION
During Franco's dictatorship, Catholicism was the state religion. Non-Catholics, especially Evangelicals, were subject to discrimination and even persecution. The 1978 constitution guaranteed equality of rights for all ideologies and religions, though Catholicism remains the official religion. Equality for Evangelicals, Muslims and Jews was only established in 1992. There are still evidences of covert discrimination against religious minorities. Over 30% of the population, though baptized Catholic, no longer claim any link with Catholicism and a further 40-50% are inactive.

Religions	Population %	Adherents	Ann.Gr.
Christian	67.77	26,945,200	-2.7%
non-Religious/other	30.89	12,281,794	+8.1%
Muslim	1.20	477,117	+3.7%
Jewish	0.13	51,688	+5.4%
Buddhist	0.01	3,976	n.a.

Note: Denominational figures have been revised downwards from those used in the 1993 edition of **Operation World**.

Christians	Denom.	Affil.%	,000	Ann.Gr.
Protestant	130	0.42	169	+2.1%
Independent	50	0.05	19	+2.9%
Anglican	1	0.07	29	+2.9%
Catholic	3	66.70	26,519	-2.9%
Orthodox	1	0.01	4	+4.6%
Marginal	8	0.52	206	-0.1%
Unaffiliated		0.63	250	n.a.
Doubly affiliated		*-0.63*	*-250*	*n.a.*

Churches	MegaBloc	Cong.	Members	Adherents
Catholic	C	21,500	8,705,714	33.51m
Jehovah's Witnesses	M	1,313	102,853	156,000
Filadelfia Evang	P	613	30,000	60,000
Latter-day Saints (Morm)	M	180	24,476	35,000
Christian Brethren	P	140	11,000	18,000
Baptist Union	P	73	8,365	14,000
Seventh-day Adventist	P	68	6,945	13,000
Spanish Evangelical	P	40	2,700	10,000
Assemblies of God	P	140	6,000	8,500
Fed of Spanish Pente	P	65	2,800	4,060
Other denoms [182]		884	48,000	110,000
Disaffiliated	*C*		*-3,500,000*	*-7,000,000*
Doubly affiliated			*-182,000*	*-250,000*
Total Christians [192]		25,016	5.266m	26.696m

Trans-bloc Groupings	pop.%	,000	Ann.Gr.
Evangelical	0.4	174	+2.3%
Charismatic	1.1	447	-0.7%
Pentecostal	0.2	97	+3.2%

Missionaries from Spain
P,I,A 416 in 43 agencies. Spain 129; Argentina 38, Italy 17, Mexico 14, all Middle East 29, Portugal 32.

Missionaries to Spain
P,I,A 1,266 in 182 agencies from 38 countries: USA 499, UK 149, Brazil 60, Germany 55, Canada 52, Mexico 37, Korea 25.

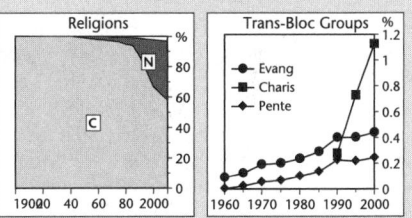

• Answers to Prayer

1 **The transformation of Spain since 1974 is astonishing** — from dictatorship to liberty, poverty to wealth, isolation to integration into Europe and religious discrimination to rampant secularism.

2 **The people movement among Spain's despised, marginalized Roma (Gypsies) since 1966.** The Filadelfia movement has become the largest evangelical body in the country.

3 **Evangelicals have grown in numbers** from a paltry 3- 4,000 adult believers in 1900, to 20,000 in 1970, to an estimated small, but significant 96,000 in 2000. There were 300 evangelical congregations in 1970, but 2,000 by 2000 as well as the Filadelfia Roma churches. Churches in Madrid have grown from 18 to 189 over that period.

• Challenges for Prayer

1 **The Inquisition is a dark shadow lying over Spain.** In the name of Christ, the Catholic Church burned at the stake hundreds of thousands of innocent Spanish Jews, Moors and Protestants in the 16th Century. This weapon of repression was then used throughout the Americas against the indigenous population. The Church became associated with bigotry and tyranny, and also was tainted by association with the Franco dictatorship. Pray that this stain on the Spanish nation may be fully repented of and renounced and the shame on Christianity diminished.

2 **The Catholic Church** is in serious crisis. Its loss of numbers and influence and the widespread mistrust of it as an institution has had a demoralizing effect. Few applicants for the priesthood has caused the average age of priests to rise to 57. There were 23,000 seminarians in 1960 but less than 2,000 in 1999. The charismatic movement has grown, but is small with about 30-35,000 active members in 650 groups. Yet the centuries of control and instruction have inoculated most people against considering a more biblical Christianity. Pray that the legacy of bondage and blindness may be removed.

3 **There is a spiritual vacuum** which is being filled by:

a) *Secularism and materialism.* There has not been the longed-for turning to a personal relationship to Christ as religious freedom has increased.

b) *Foreign cults.* There are more Jehovah's Witnesses than Evangelicals, and Mormon numbers have rapidly increased — in contrast to a painfully slow Evangelical growth.

c) *The occult.* Mediums, witchcraft, astrology, parapsychology and Satanism have a high profile.

d) *Drugs.* There are reckoned to be 300,000 addicted to heroin and cocaine, a major factor in the AIDS epidemic. In 2000 there were estimated to be 120,000 carrying the HIV virus (0.6% of the population)), and AIDS victims are more numerous than in any other European country. RETO, REMAR (Pentecostal) and **Betel** (**WEC**-related) have had success in rehabilitating drug addicts in centres in many parts of the country. RETO has 50 rehabilitation centres and ministry in 10 countries, REMAR has communities in 165 Spanish towns and works in 57 countries. The Betel converts have planted 10 churches and have extended their ministry to over 10 other countries.

e) *Gambling.* This is a major obsession, with 11% of private-sector spending misused at great social cost to families.

Pray for spiritual power, love and wisdom for all seeking to minister to these people bound by Satan's wiles.

4 **The growth of Evangelicals has been steady**, but not as fast as expected. The 6,000 Protestant church members in 1932 had increased to 20,000 in 1963, 36,000 in 1980 and 96,000 in 2000, yet they are very unevenly distributed. Most churches are concentrated in Catalonia (especially Barcelona), Andalucia and, to a lesser extent, the areas around Madrid. A third of these are Roma who are culturally isolated. Pray for:

a) *Revival.* Spain has never experienced an outpouring of the Holy Spirit in revival.

b) *Freedom from the effects of being a despised and rejected minority* in order to make full use of today's freedom and equality by vigorous outreach.

c) *Spanish evangelical churches to lose their 'foreign-ness'.* Many missionaries have unwittingly imported their national and doctrinal idiosyncrasies and tried to control the churches they planted, stunting indigenous expression and leadership.

d) *Greater cooperation between denominations in fellowship and evangelism.* There is an individualistic independence and mistrust of others that has long inhibited cooperation. FEREDE has become a key network hub for evangelical denominations to give focus in ministry and to speak for Evangelicals to the government.

5 **Vision for the future** has been lacking because of the fragmented world of Evangelicals. Pray for effective, culturally appropriate methods of outreach and for nation-wide evangelistic strategies to be developed. The effective use of orchestras and musical performances in public and on television by Evangelicals has been one notable avenue used since 1995. Women Aglow in Spain has grown steadily since 1975 — many women have come to Christ and joined evangelical churches. Pray also for the growth of missions vision. The *Llamada* conferences every three years and the ministry of **OM**, **WEC**, **WH** and Latin American missions have inspired young people to go to the Middle East and Africa, in spite of the shortage of sending structures and supportive churches. Pray for the vision to mature. Pray also for the growth and development of Spanish mission agencies.

6 **Leadership training.** The small size of the evangelical community and the high level of unemployment make it difficult for small congregations to support full-time workers or for Christians to commit themselves to the work of the Lord. In 1990 there were about 1,350 pastoral workers — but only a minority working full-time in the ministry. Many young people have been enthused for Christian service and missions through the ministry of **OM** and **YWAM**. There are 15 seminaries and Bible schools — one of each initiated by **GEM**. **TEAM**, in partnership with World Link Ministries, has launched an extension seminary specifically to train church planters which has proved unusually successful. **TEAM**, **OMS**, **AoG**(ICI), the Baptist Union and **Open Bible Standard Mission**(INSTE) run TEE programmes. Pray that from this input there might be a good supply of godly men and women to further the gospel in Spain and beyond.

7 There has been a considerable increase in missionaries and agencies since 1975, yet unoccupied areas are numerous. Two-thirds of the missionary force is concentrated in Madrid or around Barcelona. Proliferation of agencies and lack of coordination are issues for concern. Pray for:

a) *Missionaries* to be called to less evangelized areas, such as Castilla Leon, parts of Andalucía, the northern provinces of Galicia, Asturias, Cantabria and the Basque country.

b) *Good relations between expatriate and national workers.* Missionaries and nationals are about equal in number, but most missionaries have the financial freedom to work full-time, which many of the nationals cannot do. The potential for pain in relationships is obvious.

c) *Missionaries to be able to integrate fully into Spanish culture and life.* Many new missionaries remain aloof and need pastoral care and encouragement to adapt and become effective church planters. There is much pioneer evangelism, but little fruit in churches planted.

Some larger missions are: **AoG** (81), **WEC** (52), **YWAM** (50), **IMB-SBC** (45), Christian Brethren (42), **ECM** (41), **OM** (34), **TEAM** (33), Finnish Free Mission (30), **GEM** (27), **OMS** (24), **GMU** (23), **CAMI** (21), ABWE (18), **WH** (18), WT (16), **SEND** (14), **UFM** (13).

 The need of Spain is enormous:

a) *Over 13 million* live in towns, villages and districts where there is no evangelical church.

b) *Of the 17 regions*, three have less than 20 Protestant churches — Cantabria (14), Lo Rioja (8) and Navarra (10). Galicia is less than 0.2%, and Extremadura 0.1%, evangelical.

c) *Of the 52 provinces*, 28 have fewer than 1,000 evangelical believers.

d) *The one million students* are largely unevangelized. In 1967 there were but 12 known evangelical students in universities. In 2000 there were over 500 linked with **IFES** groups served by 9 staff workers. There are 15 university towns without an evangelical student witness. Pray for the consolidation of existing work and expansion to other campuses and to secondary schools.

The less evangelized minorities:

a) *The Basques* — an ancient and proud people without a single Euskera-speaking Protestant church. The ETA movement has terrorized and polarized society in the Basque region. The 100 evangelical churches in the four provinces where Basques live (Guipúzcoa, Vizcaya, Alava and Navarra) are Spanish-speaking. There are about 50 scattered Basque evangelical believers who find it difficult to worship or witness in their own language. Only the beginnings of evangelistic and literature ministries have been made. The differing dialects in an already difficult language complicate the task. There is an almost complete lack of evangelistic and teaching materials available — and at a time when Euskera is widely used in the education system. Pray for those involved in ministry — **AoG**, **CAMI**, Baptists, **YWAM** and **WEC**. Pray that the centuries-old suspicions, fears and reserve of the Basque people may be broken down.

b) *The Muslims* number around 450,000. The Moors ruled much of Spain for 700 years and Muslims long to win back what they lost. Saudi Arabia funded the building of Europe's largest mosque in Madrid. South Spain is a key base area for 16 agencies committed to evangelizing North Africa. Pray for the Malaga Media Centre (**Avant-GMU**) and the Ibero-American Institute of Islamic Studies (PMI and others). Pray for effective partnering in ministry to Muslims.

c) *There is a large inflow of North and West Africans* in southern Spain. Many make the hazardous crossing of the Straits of Gibraltar; over 3,000 drowned in the 1990s attempting this. There may be 250,000 illegal immigrants in southern Spain; they are often exploited and abused.

d) *Chinese* numbers have increased. **COCM** has planted one Church of 200 believers in Barcelona.

10 **The Canary Islands** form an archipelago of seven larger islands off Africa's north-west coast. Among the 1,630,000 inhabitants are but 3,600 believers in 75 small churches and fellowships — most being on the two larger islands and over half being

Assemblies of God. There is need for more evangelism on the smaller islands of Lanzarote, Fuerteventura, Gomera, La Palma and Hierro and for more teaching for the scattered groups of believers.

11 **Ceuta** (65,000) and **Melilla** (57,000) are two city enclaves on Morocco's north coast. Nearly 40% of the population is Muslim, half speaking Cherja, a Berber language. There are 2 small evangelical churches (one Arabic- and one Spanish-speaking) in Ceuta plus a REMAR and a Betel Centre, and one church in Melilla. Pray for these cities to be effective means of bringing the gospel to North Africa.

12 **Christian help ministries**. Pray for the effectiveness of these ministries:

a) *Christian literature* has been a major factor in church growth, yet the Spanish are poor readers, making literature work expensive and bookstores hard to finance. Pray for the 21 bookstores; **CLC** has 4 centres and a distribution network serving evangelical bookstores throughout Spain. Christian books are both imported and published in Spain, but too few are written by and for Spaniards.

b) *Pocket Testament League* has impacted Spain through literature, well-publicized research and promotion of missions vision.

c) *Christian radio*. By 1997 there were 25 local radio stations run by Evangelicals, 17 of them by Radio Amistad (**CoG**). For several years the authorities have singled out evangelical stations for closure and 10 were shut down in 1999. Pray that this discriminatory process may be halted. REMAR has 3 radio stations. **TWR** broadcasts in Spanish from Monte Carlo.

d) *Christian TV*. A Christian channel has been launched in Madrid, and nation-wide

Sri Lanka

Democratic Socialist Republic of Sri Lanka

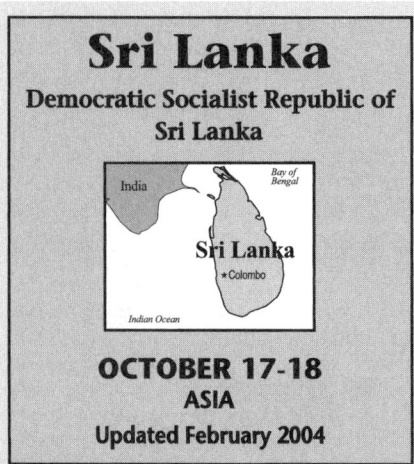

OCTOBER 17-18
ASIA
Updated February 2004

GEOGRAPHY
Area 65,610 sq.km. Large island 80 km. south-east of India.

Population	Ann.Gr.	Density
2000	18,827,054	+0.99%	287 per sq. km.
2010	20,869,505	+1.04%	318 per sq. km.
2025	23,546,757	+0.67%	359 per sq. km.

There are over 1,500,000 Sri Lankans in other lands.

Capital Colombo (administrative) 2,400,000; Sri Jayewardenepura Kotte (legislative) 150,000. Other major city: Jaffna 700,000. **Urbanites** 22%.

PEOPLES
Sinhala 74.6%. An Aryan people; largely Buddhist and 4% Christian. Many castes — unusual for

Buddhist societies.
Tamil 17%. Declining through war and flight of over 700,000 from the country. Approximately 80% Hindu, 20% Christian.
Lanka Tamil 2,170,000. Resident for over 1,000 years in Jaffna in the north and on the east coast.
Estate Tamil 1,030,000. Migrant labourers arriving in 19th and 20th Centuries and working mainly in highland tea plantations.
Moor 7.6%. Arab-Tamil descent.
Burgher 0.4%. Euro-Asian parentage. Many have emigrated to Australia. Most live around Colombo.
Other 0.4%. Malay 47,000; Veddah 700 (the original inhabitants; most speak Sinhala).
Literacy 90%. **Official languages** Sinhala and Tamil, with English as the link language. **All languages** 7. **Languages with Scriptures** 3Bi.

ECONOMY
Largest export earnings are from tea, textiles and foreign employment. Increasing industrialization since 1977. The 17-year war has slowed and distorted what would have been a healthy economy. Foreign investment and tourism are greatly reduced and much of the national infrastructure is damaged. High unemployment — especially among Tamil — has caused many to seek work elsewhere. **HDI** 0.721; 90th/174. **Public debt** 45% of GNP. **Income/person** $800 (2.5% of USA).

POLITICS
Independence in 1948 as a parliamentary democracy after 450 years of successive colonial administrations by the Portuguese, Dutch and British. Attempts to Sinhalize national life in 1956 and the attendant discrimination against eth-

nic and religious minorities provoked increasing communal violence and efforts by extremists to fight for an independent Tamil state in the north and east. A bitter civil war broke out in 1983, but all efforts to settle the conflict by local politicians and an aborted three-year Indian military intervention (1987-89) failed because of the intransigence of the extremists on both sides. The Tamil LTTE built up a formidable guerrilla army with liberal Tamil expatriate funding that intimidated and terrorised Tamil moderates, assassinated two Presidents (including Rajiv Gandhi of India) and attempted to assassinate the incumbent, Chandrika Kumaratunge, in 1999. Politics is increasingly violent and democratic processes are being eroded which serves to increase support for the Marxists who caused much death and havoc in an uprising in 1987-89. Norwegian mediation led to a cease-fire between the Tamil LTTE and Sri Lanka government in 2002, but tortuous negotiations may yet founder on the deep divisions between the hawks (led by the President) and doves (led by the Prime Minister). A loose federal structure is the most likely way ahead for restoration of peace.

RELIGION

Buddhism is the state religion and, as such, is protected and promoted. Although freedom for other religions is assured, there has been a steady erosion of that freedom with discrimination against minority religions in taxation, employment and education and, since 1988, a rising anti-Christian feeling. Christianity is perceived as foreign and a colonial imposition (sadly a partial truth under Portuguese and Dutch rule) and Evangelicals as purportedly using financial inducements to poor Buddhists for unethical conversions. By 2004 there were moves afoot by extremist Buddhists to force the government to pass draconian laws forbidding conversion. The Supreme Court has also ruled that freedom to worship does NOT include freedom to propagate one's faith and in so doing outlaws evangelism.

Religions	Population %	Adherents	Ann.Gr.
Buddhist	71.93	13,542,300	+1.1%
Hindu	12.00	2,259,246	-0.6%
Muslim	8.00	1,506,164	+1.2%
Christian	7.62	1,434,622	+2.0%
non-Religious/other	0.20	37,654	+1.0%

Sikh	0.15	28,241	-0.3%
Baha'i	0.10	18,827	+1.0%

Christians	Denom.	Affil.%	,000	Ann.Gr.
Protestant	20	0.87	164	+3.9%
Independent	41	0.58	109	+20.1%
Anglican	1	0.29	54	+0.7%
Catholic	1	5.58	1,050	+1.2%
Marginal	2	0.04	8	+2.4%
Unaffiliated		0.26	50	n.a.

Churches	MegaBloc	Cong.	Members	Affiliates
Catholic	C	330	586,592	1,050,000
Assemblies of God	P	70	10,000	77,000
Ch of Ceylon	A	146	34,000	53,900
Methodist	P	143	17,049	28,471
Believers Church (GFA)	I	200	9,000	18,000
Ch of South India	P	68	5,000	15,165
Foursquare Gospel	P	298	6,187	15,000
Gethsemane Gospel	I	39	7,500	11,232
Calvary	I	60	4,000	8,150
Fell of Free Chs	I	18	3,060	8,000
Jehovah's Witnesses	M	69	3,171	8,000
Ceylon Pentecostal Mis	I	53	4,192	7,000
Seventh-day Adventist	P	28	3,252	6,500
Salvation Army	P	39	2,900	3,979
Margaya Fellowship	I	20	1,700	3,500
Baptist Union	P	25	2,200	3,000
Gospel Ministries	I	39	1,007	2,750
Other denoms [48]		381	37,000	65,700
Total Christians [65]		2,026	738,000	1,385,000

Trans-bloc Groupings	pop.%	,000	Ann.Gr.
Evangelical	1.3	236	+11.4%
Charismatic	1.6	305	+6.7%
Pentecostal	0.9	161	+6.3%

Missionaries from Sri Lanka
P,I,A 717 in 18 agencies to 5 countries: Sri Lanka 712.

Missionaries to Sri Lanka
P,I,A 145 in 39 agencies from 17 countries: USA 45, Korea 43, UK 21.

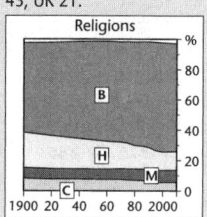

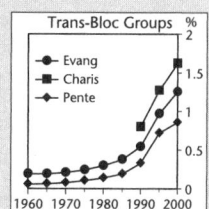

• Answers to Prayer

1 **Revival and strong evangelical growth since 1980** — all during the most harrowing warfare and militant opposition from the majority religion and despite a high rate of Christian emigration. In 1980 Evangelicals numbered around 50,000 (0.36%) but by 2000 were nearly 240,000 (1.25%). These successes lie behind Buddhist pressures to legislate against evangelism.

2 **The multiplication of churches** through the committed ministry of many humble Sri Lankan missionary evangelists. In the years 1970-79 only 26 new churches were planted, from 1980-84 there were 153, and then between 1990-97, over 330.

3 The raising up of world-class **Christian leaders**, evangelists, Bible teachers and Christian apologists who impact the nation and beyond.

• Challenges for Prayer

1 Claimed by some to be the site of the Garden of Eden, Sri Lanka is now an island of tears. The ugly conflict between the Sinhala and Tamil has brought great suffering with an estimated 100,000 killed, 800,000 Sri Lankans (mainly Tamil) have emigrated or fled to India and the West, and between 700,000 and 1.5 million displaced in Sri Lanka. Pray specifically for:

a) *The neutralization of the power and influence of Buddhist Sinhala extremists*. It was their efforts to marginalize and suppress the Tamils that led to the present war. The cruelty and corruption of the armed forces have done great damage to the moral fibre of the nation.

b) *The ending of the Tamil LTTE violence* whose ruthlessness and use of child soldiers and young suicide bombers have shocked the world and spread terror across much of the country.

c) *For honest, fair government* for this multi-religious, multi-ethnic country. The bitterly divided Sinhala political scene prevents moves towards peace.

d) *For the cease-fire to be maintained until an equitable agreement is reached.* Pray for willingness for both sides to negotiate an equitable peace that gives respect to the major communities and protects their civil, economic and religious rights.

e) *For the binding of unleashed demonic powers*. The reality of the spirit world and associated idolatry underlie the present evils in Sri Lanka.

2 Buddhists have long prided themselves on their non-violent religion and tolerance. The bigotry and violence of Buddhist extremists against both Hindu Tamil and Christians has shattered that image. There is widespread disillusionment in both Buddhism and Hinduism that has caused many to consider the claims of Christ despite the social disadvantages and threat of persecution. Pray for increased numbers to find peace in Him.

3 Traditional, mainline Churches declined from 21% of the population in 1722 to 7% in 1990 and that decline continues. The causes — nominalism, inability to lay aside foreign worship patterns, use of European languages and theological liberalism that led to syncretism, and little outreach. Rampant Buddhism steadily whittled away their flocks. Added to this was the large-scale emigration of Tamil Christians over the past 20 years. Praise God for growing evangelical movements in the Anglican, Methodist and Baptist Churches. Pray for:

a) *A return to Biblical theology and holiness in the major seminaries and in the congregations*. Liberal theology has emphasized dialogue, compromise and social engineering rather than evangelism, confrontation of error and personal faith in Christ. This has also led the present Catholic and Anglican leaders to support the Buddhist and Hindu desires for strict anti-conversion laws being considered in 2004 and in so doing, siding them against Evangelicals.

b) *Cultural adaptation* to make worship, hymnology, language and structures relevant and welcoming to non-Christians.

c) *A vision for evangelism and outreach* to non-Christians whatever the cost. Large areas of the country are without a gospel witness; nearly all Christians are concentrated in the Colombo and Jaffna urban regions; few live in the rural areas. Many trained workers emigrate, and few are willing to work in the less-privileged rural areas.

S4 Evangelicals have reversed the Christian decline with a surge of spiritual life and vision. The revival has deepened faith, raised expectancy, hastened indigenization, prepared many for persecution and stimulated vigorous outreach. There are many new Christians from the Buddhist and Hindu communities. Pray for:

a) *The ongoing outreach of Pentecostal, charismatic and other evangelical groups*. Particularly successful have been the efforts of the **AoG** and the Foursquare Church. Evangelistic campaigns by Reinhard Bonnke and others have stimulated nation-wide interest.

b) *The growing Sri Lanka missions movement*. Notable are the efforts of pioneer workers of YFC, Margaya Mission, Gospel Ministries, Lanka Village Ministries (LBC Alumni) as well as newer and older denominations. The 420 rural churches in 1983 had grown to over 1,200 by 2000.

c) *Increased unity*. The Church as a whole is deeply divided — especially ethnically in the Catholic Church, and theologically among Protestants — which hinders progress and presenting a united front to those that oppose them. *The National Christian Evangelical Alliance* has proved a blessing in bringing a wide spectrum of Evangelicals together for dynamic action in discipling the nation for Christ. An emerging goal is to see the number of evangelical congregations tripled by 2005.

d) *Effective correction of weaknesses* — too much individualism and fragmentation among newer evangelical groups, too little national coordination of ministry, under-discipled converts and inadequate indigenization of every facet of church life.

e) *The Church as a catalyst for national reconciliation*. There is no other national structure that could meaningfully bring together the bitterly divided ethnic communities.

5 **Evangelicals have done much to improve theological education** over the past three decades — Lanka Bible College (LBC) in Kandy, the Colombo Theological Seminary, the Bible Schools of **AoG**, Foursquare, Calvary Theological Seminary, **GFA** and others have been training a growing number of effective Christian workers. LBC launched a degree programme to train teachers of Christianity for schools. A number run extension and TEE courses. Pray for the development and increased spiritual impact of these institutions.

6 **Persecution increased** in the 1990s in the wake of effective evangelical outreach. At a national level Buddhist extremists seek to curtail foreign funding, limit church building and criminalize 'unethical' conversions, and at a local level hinder Christian activities. In the 1990s over 35 churches were destroyed, hundreds of Christians assaulted and some even martyred. Among the Tamil there has also been persecution from the LTTE and Hindu extremists. Since 2002 the level of violence and persecution of Christians has significantly increased. This has been especially severe for small village congregations of believers and a number of churches have been destroyed and congregations scattered. Pray for Christians to be exemplary witnesses in these afflictions.

7 **Missionary work** has been restricted by the authorities. New visas have been extremely hard to obtain. Pray for a change — the needs are so numerous that the resources of the Sri Lankan Church are inadequate for covering all the needs in evangelism, church planting and other ministries. **TWR** has 20 workers, but most are deployed in their international broadcasting ministry. **CCCI** has 73 national and expatriate workers. Other missions such as the Salvation Army, Methodists, Swedish Free Mission, **AoG**, **BMS**, **IMB-SBC** and SdA have just a handful of workers each. Pray in a new generation of missionaries able to culturally identify with Sri Lanka's present need.

Special ministry challenges:

a) *The Lanka Tamil community*, once relatively prosperous but now impoverished, vengeful and fearful, needs prayer. Large numbers have had to flee the enforced recruitment of their children by the Tamil Tigers (LTTE) and the violence of war. Most abhor the violence but have no way to stand against it. Pray for those ministering to the refugees in India (300,000+), Europe/N America (300,000+) and also within Sri Lanka. Pray for the conversion of LTTE leaders and guerrillas.

b) *The Estate Tamils* have long been a despised and marginalized community, but possibly up to 20% are professing Christians. Since 1980 over 10,000 have come to Christ through the Free Churches Fellowship, **AoG** and the Smyrna Church. They are leaderless and divided. Recently the LTTE have sought to embroil this community in the war. Pray for the effective discipling of believers.

c) *Young people.* Youth programmes are limited and most young people have little meaningful contact with the gospel. Of special note for prayer are these ministries:

i *The dynamic ministry* of **YFC** and also **CCCI** among urban youth.

ii *The work of FOCUS*(**IFES**) among students. The South Asia office of **IFES** is located in Sri Lanka. **CCCI** has a ministry among students.

iii *Children in crisis* — the war, together with the tourist industry have led to an infamous child-porn and paedophile 'industry'. Over 30,000 children are believed to be enmeshed. Several Christian ministries are involved in meeting their needs.

iv *Children of war* — many Tamil children have been brainwashed into becoming killing machines. Many thousands will need intensive help to recover from this trauma.

d) **The villages** present a challenge. Throughout the land are rural communities that have never heard the gospel. There are 36,000 villages in Sri Lanka, but only 1,200 have Protestant Christian groups. Many areas are devoid of any witness. The ravaged villages of the north and east are particularly needy. **AsEF** and others are ministering to them.

e) **The urban slums** are little evangelized. Most Christians are among the more prosperous. A few churches and groups are taking up this challenge.

9 Unreached peoples of Sri Lanka:

a) **The Moors** are generally traders, bureaucrats and farmers. Until recently there were few converts out of Islam, but through one indigenous ministry over 100 Muslims have believed in Christ. The **AoG** has a good ministry among economically depressed Muslims in Colombo.

b) **The Malays** are syncretistic Muslims, and potentially more open. Pray for a specific ministry to them.

c) **Other unreached social groups**: the educated Buddhists, coastal-belt fishing communities, the Tamil and Sinhala refugees, villages being set up under the 'Village Re-awakening' programme, and the Tamil and Sinhala militants who continue to polarize the country. There is also a resurgence of the radical Marxist party, the JVP.

d) **Tribal groups**: the Rodhiya (7,000), Gypsies (1,000) and Veddah. Kithu Sevana Ministries (**YFC**) has a work among the Rodhiya.

10 Christian media ministries:

a) **Literature**. This is in great demand. Literacy is high, but good, inexpensive and culturally relevant literature is not being printed and distributed in sufficient quantities to make use of the opportunity. The main publishers — Pragna Publishers, the Bible Society, Gospel Ministries, **YFC**, Lanka Bible College (theological books and study materials), **SGM** (Scripture portions) — have published much, but too few committed colporteurs are available. There is a dearth of good pre-evangelism literature for Buddhists and Muslims. **New Life League** has a printing press in Colombo which is much used for printing gospel literature. **EHC** is in the process of a third nation-wide gospel literature distribution programme (7 million distributed so far with 230,000 responses). **CLC** has recently established three Christian bookstores with a growing distribution ministry.

b) **The JESUS film** has been fairly widely shown with the equivalent of 41% of the population viewing it. This ministry is much affected by both the war and opposition by religious extremists — pray for the film teams often in dangerous situations. National TV now broadcasts the Indian production 'Jesus Calls' in three languages weekly — a miracle!!

c) **Radio**. Sri Lanka is thinly covered by international broadcasters — **FEBA** Seychelles broadcasts 9 hrs/wk in Tamil and 3.5 hrs in Sinhala. However, **TWR**'s ministry from Sri Lanka to India and Bangladesh on medium-wave is highly successful. There are large audiences for 13 languages and 44 hrs/wk of broadcasting. **Back to the Bible** prepares widely heard programming in English, Sinhala and Tamil.

S

St. Helena

British Overseas Territory of St. Helena

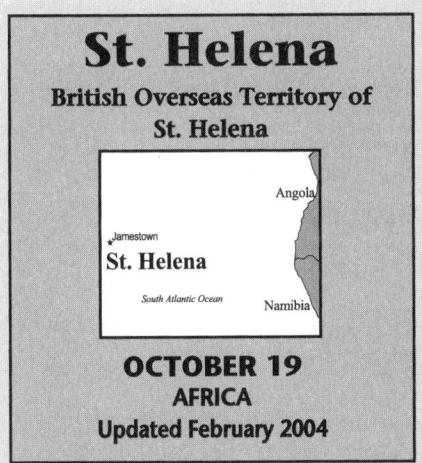

St. Helena

South Atlantic Ocean

Jamestown

Angola

Namibia

OCTOBER 19
AFRICA
Updated February 2004

 GEOGRAPHY
Area 412 sq.km. St. Helena (122 sq.km.) 2,000 km west of Angola in the south Atlantic. Two dependencies: Ascension Island (90 sq.km.) 600 km. to the northwest, and Tristan da Cunha (100 sq.km.) 1,200 km. to the south. There are also several uninhabited islands.

Population		Ann.Gr	Density
2000	6,293	+0.84%	15 per sq. km.
2010	6,841	+0.84%	17 per sq. km.
2025	7,756	+0.84%	19 per sq. km.

St. Helena 83%; Ascension 11%; Tristan 5% of population.
Capital Jamestown 864.

PEOPLES
St. Helenan 93%. Predominantly British but also Chinese, African, Malay.
Expatriate 7%. British and US administrative, scientific and military personnel — mainly on Ascension Island.
Literacy 98%. **Official language** English.

 ECONOMY
Heavily dependent on income from communications and military installations on Ascension. There is a growing fishing industry.

 POLITICS
British overseas territory. All St. Helenans will become full British citizens by 2010.

RELIGION
There is religious freedom.

Religions	Population %	Adherents	Ann.Gr.
Christian	95.70	6,022	+0.8%
non-Religious/other	4.00	252	+3.6%
Baha'i	0.30	19	-4.6%

Christians	Denom.	Affil.%	,000	Ann.Gr.
Protestant	3	5.59	0	+0.9%
Independent	1	1.08	0	+2.9%
Anglican	1	82.42	5	+0.8%
Catholic	1	1.27	0	-7.5%
Marginal	2	6.67	0	+3.1%

Churches	MegaBloc	Cong.	Members	Affiliates
Anglican	A	16	3,990	5,100
Jehovah's Witnesses	M	3	197	300
Baptist	P	1	68	136
Seventh-day Adventist	P	1	78	111
Salvation Army	P	1	68	105
Catholic	C	2	52	80
Other denoms [2]		2	121	188
Total Christians [8]		26	4,574	6,020

Trans-bloc Groupings	pop.%	,000	Ann.Gr.
Evangelical	5.2	0	+1.2%
Charismatic	1.1	0	+2.9%

Missionaries to St. Helena
P,I,A 6 in 3 agencies. **C** 1.

• Challenges for Prayer

1 **The Christian community** is increasingly materialistic and nominal with church attendance in rapid decline. Most are indifferent to the gospel. The JWs and The Way International have, conversely, grown. Pray for revival for a weakened Church and a spiritual awakening that will result in the evangelization of this generation of Islanders.

2 **Evangelical Christians** are largely linked with the Baptist Church and the Salvation Army and tend to be of the older generation. Few young people are active Christians and many move away seeking better employment opportunities. There is no evangelical witness on Ascension or Tristan.

3 **A large proportion of the working population** lives and works on the communications and military bases of **Ascension** and the **Falklands Islands** because of the lack of employment opportunities. Pray both for the evangelization of these transient communities and for a restoration of strong Christian family units, the latter being adversely affected by the unstable patterns of the society.

St. Kitts-Nevis
Federation of St. Kitts & Nevis

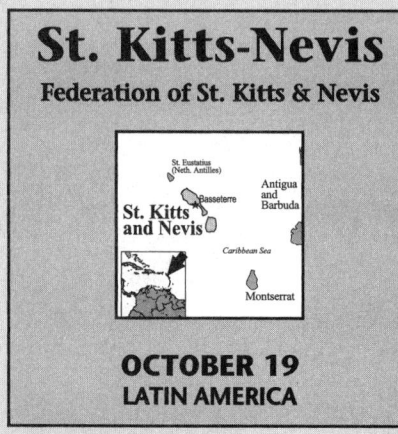

OCTOBER 19

LATIN AMERICA

GEOGRAPHY
Area 269 sq.km. Two volcanic islands in the Caribbean Leeward Islands. St. Kitts 176 sq.km; Nevis 93 sq.km.

Population	Ann.Gr.	Density
2000	38,473	-0.78%	143 per sq.km.
2010	36,321	-0.51%	135 per sq.km.
2025	35,052	-0.10%	130 per sq.km.

Capital Basseterre 15,000. **Urbanites** 43%.

PEOPLES
Afro-Caribbean 95%.
South Asian 3%.
Other 2%.

Literacy 88%. **Language** English.

ECONOMY
Nevis was once the richest Caribbean island, producing 85% of the British Empire's sugar. The collapse of the world sugar price forced the federation into diversification. Tourism is now important. **HDI** 0.781; 51ˢᵗ/174. **National debt** 23% of GNP. **Income/person** $6,260 (20% of USA).

POLITICS
Independent from Britain 1983 as a federal parliamentary democracy. Nevis now has internal self-rule, but almost seceded from the Federation in 1998.

RELIGION
Complete religious freedom.

Religions	Population %	Adherents	Ann.Gr.
Christian	95.58	36,772	-0.8%
non-Religious/other	4.00	1,539	+0.8%
Baha'i	0.42	162	-0.2%

Christians	Denom.	Affil.%	,000	Ann.Gr.
Protestants	26	55.79	21	-1.5%
Anglicans	1	25.99	10	-0.2%
Roman Catholics	1	6.50	2	-1.5%
Marginal Christians	7	2.47	1	-2.9%
Unaffiliated		4.83	2	n.a.

Churches	MegaBloc	Cong.	Members	Affiliates
Anglican	A	10	5,000	10,000
Methodist	P	28	4,750	9,500
Moravian	P	3	848	2,800
Catholic	C	10	1,786	2,500
Ch of God Prophecy	P	12	650	1,750
Seventh-day Adventist	P	10	1,062	1,700
Baptist Convention	P	5	800	1,120
Wesleyan	P	19	650	950
Ch of God (Cleveland)	P	4	272	800
Chr Brethren	P	12	280	450
Ch of God (Anderson)	P	4	250	400
Other denoms [24]		20	1,500	2,950
Total Christians [35]		137	17,860	34,920

Trans-bloc Groupings	pop.%	,000	Ann.Gr.
Evangelical	22.9	9	-2.2%
Charismatic	10.5	4	-2.3%
Pentecostal	7.7	3	-2.5%

• Challenges for Prayer

1 **St. Kitts** has gained an unhappy reputation for drug-trafficking and money laundering. In contrast, Nevis is off the beaten track with over 70% of the population being churchgoers. Pray that both islands may gain a reputation for godliness and spirituality.

2 **The profusion of denominations**, outreach ministries and Christian radio programmes gain limited response from the unconverted. Pray for revival, changed lives and vision for reaching the wider world. There are no known missionaries from these islands.

St. Lucia

State of St. Lucia

Martinique

St. Lucia
Castries

Caribbean Sea
Saint Vincent

North Atlantic Ocean

OCTOBER 19
LATIN AMERICA

GEOGRAPHY
Area 617 sq.km. Windward Islands, between Martinique and St. Vincent. One of the most beautiful islands in the Caribbean.

Population	Ann.Gr.	Density
2000	154,366	+1.39%	250 per sq. km.
2010	175,541	+1.26%	285 per sq. km.
2025	208,093	+1.08%	337 per sq. km.

Capital Castries 15,000. **Urbanites** 48%.

PEOPLES
Afro-Caribbean 90.5%.
Mixed race 5.5%.
South Asian 3.2%.
Euro-American 0.8%.
Literacy 82%. **Official language** English but 80% speak French Creole (Kweyol).

ECONOMY
Tourism is important. Agriculture going through painful diversification from dependence on banana and sugar growing. **HDI** 0.737; 81ˢᵗ/174. **Public debt** 22% of GNP. **Income/person** $3,510 (11% of USA).

POLITICS
Seven times under French, and seven times under British rule. Independent from Britain in 1979. A stable parliamentary democracy.

RELIGION

Freedom of religion.

Religions	Population %	Adherents	Ann.Gr.
Christian	96.10	148,346	+1.4%
Spiritist	1.70	2,624	+2.6%
Hindu	0.90	1,389	+1.4%
Muslim	0.50	772	+1.4%
Other	0.40	617	+1.4%
Baha'i	0.20	309	+1.4%
non-Religious	0.20	309	+1.4%

Christians	Denom.	Affil.%	,000	Ann.Gr.
Protestant	27	18.40	28	+1.8%
Independent	6	1.68	3	+19.4%
Anglican	1	2.40	4	+1.1%
Catholic	1	72.55	112	+0.6%
Marginal	5	1.67	3	+1.4%
Unaffiliated		2.30	4	n.a.
Doubly affiliated		*-2.92*	*-4*	*n.a.*

Churches	MegaBloc	Cong.	Members	Affiliates
Catholic	C	24	59,259	112,000
Seventh-day Adventist	P	32	7,584	12,665
Anglican	A	2	1,850	3,700
Pentecostal Assemblies	P	18	1,796	3,000
Apostolic Faith	P	5	1,000	2,500
Baptist Churches [3]	P	20	950	1,900
Jehovah's Witnesses	M	9	721	1,500
Evang Ch of W Indies	P	10	600	1,200
Other denoms [31]		95	3,671	6,315
Doubly affiliated			*-2,400*	*-4,500*
Total Christians [41]		215	77,431	144,780

Trans-bloc Groupings	pop.%	,000	Ann.Gr.
Evangelical	12.3	19	+4.2%
Charismatic	6.5	10	+6.7%
Pentecostal	6.3	10	+6.9%

Missionaries from St. Lucia
P,I,A 14 in 4 agencies to 7 countries: St. Lucia 3, Albania 2.

Missionaries to St. Lucia
P,I,A 12 in 5 agencies from 4 countries: USA 11, Canada 2.

• Challenges for Prayer

1 **The large nominal Christian population** needs liberation from the deadening blanket of religion without life in a society where 80% of all children are born out of wedlock. Pray for a spiritual awakening among them.

2 **The number of churches alive in the Spirit** have multiplied — but so have divisions. Pray for unity among believers. **UFM** has entered with a church-supportive ministry in discipleship and equipping pastors for effective service. Pray for this.

3 **The upper strata of society** are less influenced by vital Christianity and materialism is becoming a major block to spiritual life as the economy improves. **IFES** has pioneered a work in secondary schools with encouraging results and plans to launch ISCF groups in 90% of secondary and tertiary schools and colleges. Pray that Bible-believing Christians may influence every level of society for good and for God.

4 **The majority of St. Lucians and Dominicans speak a French Creole.** A **WBT** team is facilitating translation of the New Testament for them. **CLC** has a Christian bookstore in Castries. Pray that the Word of God may thereby become more precious, understood and applied in daily life.

St. Pierre & Miquelon

Territorial Collectivity of St. Pierre and Miquelon

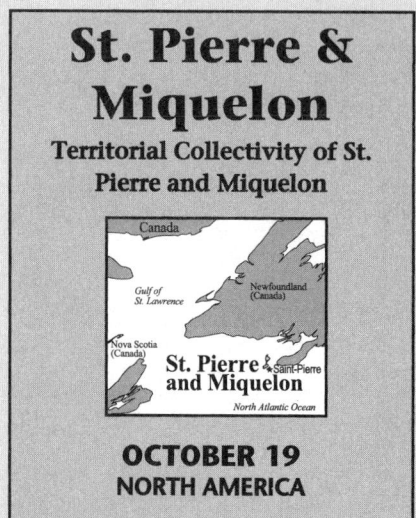

St. Pierre & Saint-Pierre and Miquelon

North Atlantic Ocean

OCTOBER 19
NORTH AMERICA

GEOGRAPHY
Area 242 sq.km. Eight rocky islands at the mouth of Canada's St. Lawrence River, and 25km south of Newfoundland.

Population	Ann.Gr.	Density
2000	6,567	+0.28%	27 per sq. km.
2010	6,778	+0.33%	28 per sq. km.
2025	7,171	+0.40%	30 per sq. km.

Capital St Pierre 5,500. **Urbanites** 83%.

PEOPLES
French of predominantly Breton and Basque origin.

Literacy 99%. **Official language** French.

ECONOMY
The collapse of the cod-fishing industry has made the islands heavily dependent on French economic aid. **Unemployment** 11%. **Income/person** $11,000 (39% of USA).

POLITICS
An overseas department of France; the last vestige of France's once vast North American possessions.

RELIGION
Freedom of religion.

Religions	Population %	Adherents	Ann.Gr.
Christian	97.69	6,415	+0.1%
Other	2.31	152	+9.2%

Christians	Denom.	Affil.%	,000	Ann.Gr.
Protestant	2	0.61	0	+2.5%
Catholic	1	96.70	6	+0.1%
Marginal	1	0.38	0	+4.0%

Churches		MegaBloc	Cong.	Members	Affiliates
Catholic		C	3	3,994	6,340
Jehovah's Witnesses		M	1	10	25
Other denominations [3]			2	28	52
Total Christians [5]			6	4,032	6,400

Trans-bloc Groupings	pop.%	,000	Ann.Gr.
Evangelical	0.4	0	+0.0%
Pentecostal & Charismatic	1.2	0	+0.0%

Missionaries to St Pierre and Miquelon
P,I,A 2 in 1 agency. **C** 17.

• Challenges for Prayer

1 **These isolated islands and their people have long been Catholic.** Traditions are strong and change has been hard in the large economic and social upheavals affecting the islanders. Pray for many to come to a vital, personal faith in the Lord Jesus.

2 **The first active evangelical congregation** was formed in 1998. Pray for this small congregation of Baptists, that they may live lives that commend the gospel. The French **AoG** have also started a work.

S

St. Vincent

St. Vincent and the Grenadines

OCTOBER 19
LATIN AMERICA

GEOGRAPHY
Area 389 sq.km. Windward Islands; located between St. Lucia and Grenada. One larger island and a chain of 16 smaller islands and islets to the south.

Population	Ann.Gr.	Density
2000	113,954	+0.72%	293 per sq. km.
2010	121,403	+0.61%	312 per sq. km.
2025	130,781	+0.44%	336 per sq. km.

Capital Kingstown 15,908. **Urbanites** 25%.

PEOPLES
Afro-Caribbean 84.5%. Many of mixed background.
East Indian 5.5%.
Carib 2%; with much African intermarriage.
Euro-American 3.5%, many Portuguese.
Other 4.5%.

Literacy 96%. **Languages** English (official) and Creole.

ECONOMY
Economic reliance on a single crop, the banana, is being alleviated somewhat by growth in tourism. Poverty is common due to chronic underemployment (41%) and unemployment (30%+). **HDI** 0.744; 75th/174. **Public debt** 43.6% of GNP. **Income/person** $2,420 (7.7% of USA).

 POLITICS
Independent from Britain as a parliamentary democracy in 1979. A member of the Commonwealth.

RELIGION
There is complete freedom of religion.

Religions	Population %	Adherents	Ann.Gr.
Christian	92.20	105,066	+0.6%
Traditional ethnic	2.00	2,279	+0.7%
Hindu	2.00	2,279	+0.7%
Other	1.50	1,709	+4.5%
Muslim	1.00	1,140	+0.7%
non-Religious	1.00	1,140	+2.9%
Baha'i	0.30	342	+0.7%

Christians	Denom.	Affil.%	,000	Ann.Gr.
Protestant	36	63.74	73	+5.5%
Independent	4	12.59	14	+2.4%
Anglican	1	16.67	19	-8.7%
Catholic	1	8.78	10	+0.0%
Marginal	2	0.82	1	+1.3%
Unaffiliated		10.66	12	n.a.
Doubly affiliated		*-21.06*	*-24*	*n.a.*

Churches	MegaBloc	Cong.	Members	Affiliates
Anglican	A	23	3,800	19,000
Methodist [3]	P	20	6,100	16,100
Seventh-day Adventist	P	30	9,403	15,000
Spiritual Baptist	I	78	7,784	13,000
Catholic	C	19	5,291	10,000
Ch of God Cleveland [3]	P	34	3,700	6,400
Baptist [3]	P	28	1,700	3,700
Christian Brethren [2]	P	23	1,300	2,850
Jehovah's Witnesses	M	7	307	630
Other denoms [32]		104	16,000	30,200
Doubly affiliated			*-14,371*	*-24,000*
Total Christians [48]		366	41,000	92,900

Trans-bloc Groupings	pop.%	,000	Ann.Gr.
Evangelical	24.4	28	+3.3%
Charismatic	30.5	35	+4.1%
Pentecostal	28.9	33	+4.4%

Missionaries from St. Vincent
P,I,A 8 in 4 agencies.

Missionaries to St. Vincent
P,I,A 23 in 8 agencies. C 6.

• Answers to Prayer

1 **Through the ministries of the Evangelical Association and DAWN**, cooperation between the various evangelical churches has improved in recent years.

• Challenges for Prayer

1 **St. Vincent is a religious country**, but most are not related to God through a personal faith in Jesus Christ. There is a crisis of holiness, lack of spiritual fruit and growing apathy, especially relating to missions. Pray for revival and the restoration of a Biblically-based, Spirit-led Church.

2 **There is a general lack of Biblical leadership** in the churches, especially in the area of Bible teaching. Pray for the encouragement of such through the three Bible School extension programmes (**AoG**, Church of God, **WT**).

Sudan

Republic of Sudan

OCTOBER 20-21
AFRICA
Updated February 2004

GEOGRAPHY
Area 2,503,890 sq.km. Africa's largest country. Desert in north, merging into grasslands and mountains in the centre and tropical bush in the south. Straddling the Nile Rivers. Nuba Mountains in the centre.

Population	Ann.Gr.	Density
2000	29,489,719	+2.07%	12 per sq. km.
2010	36,256,579	+2.05%	14 per sq. km.
2025	46,264,179	+1.38%	18 per sq. km.

Over 2 million deaths through war, genocide and famine since 1983. Almost the entire southern population has been displaced during the course of the war, with over 5 million affected. A further 500,000 refugees have fled to surrounding lands.

Capital Khartoum 10,000,000. The three-city agglomeration of Khartoum, Omdurman and Khartoum North are surrounded by millions living in shanty towns. **Urbanites** 25% officially, but closer to 50% in reality.

PEOPLES
Over 244 ethnic groups.
Arab 45.2%. Predominantly in the north. The Arab population is intermingled with numerous indigenous peoples. Many distinct peoples of the north and centre have become Arabized. Specific categories (with overlap): Sudanese 3.7m; Egyptian 360,000. Badawi (largely nomadic tribes and clans, 62) 11.7m - 29 of these peoples are of non-Arab origin (Nubian, Kordofan and Darfur); Baggara cattle herders 4m; Kababish speakers 2.1m; Shukriya 165,000.
Non-Arab 54.8%. Largely in the centre and south.
Nilotic 24.4%. 90 peoples, largest: Dinka(6) 1.7m; Nuer(2) 1.33m; Bari 378,000; Lotuko 274,000; Shilluk 259,000; Toposa 140,000; Didinga 111,000; Lwo 91,000.
Sudanic 12.9%. 92 peoples. Nubian 751,000; Fur 717,000; Zande 517,000; Daju(2) 182,000; Masalit 164,000; Mondari 110,000; Moru 103,000; Murle 89,000; Tama 44,000; Midob 43,000.
Nuba Mountain peoples 6.5%. 44 peoples, most small in numbers: Moro 187,000; Kadugli 156,000;

Koalib 61,000; Krongo 39,000.
Cushitic 5%. Beja 1.5m; Ethiopians/Eritreans 100,000+.
Other 6%. 15 peoples. Hausa 489,000; Berti 200,000; Zaghawa 146,000; Fulbe 133,000.

Literacy 46%; functional literacy nearer 33%. **Official language** Arabic. **All languages** 132. **Languages with Scriptures** 7Bi 15NT 12por 19w.i.p.

ECONOMY
Enormous agricultural and mineral resources but largely unexploited because of war and decay of the communications network. The cost of war and diplomatic isolation have impoverished all, but the genocide and use of famine as a weapon of war has devastated the south. There have been massive famines during the 1990s. In the late 1990s oil income became substantial - much being used for weaponry. **HDI** 0.475; 142nd/174. **Public debt** 95% of GNP. **Income/person** $290 (0.9% of USA).

POLITICS
Joint Egyptian and British control 1899-1956. After independence northern efforts to Islamize and Arabize the south led to civil war. Bitter fighting between Arab northerners and non-Arab southerners 1955-72. After 12 years of uneasy peace, and a degree of autonomy for the south, fighting broke out again in 1983 after renewed attempts to enforce Islam in the south. An extremist Islamist coup in 1989 led to increased fighting between Muslims and southerners in the Nuba Mountains and the southern provinces. Oil income and aid from Iran, Malaysia and Indonesia enabled the beleaguered and diplomatically isolated regime to continue the war despite huge losses and a stalemate. For a time Sudan offered refuge to Islamist extremists. War weariness and strong pressure from Western governments after 9/11 pushed both sides together for peace talks, which by Feb 2004 had led to some possibility of a peace agreement, sharing of oil wealth and a federal solution for the moment.

RELIGION
The constitution offers some religious freedom, but in practice those freedoms are arbitrarily abused. Declared an Islamic Republic in 1983 in contravention of the 1972 peace accord with the southerners. The threatened application of *shari'a* law on non-Muslims and Muslims alike was a direct cause of intensified civil war. Crude attempts to Islamize non-Muslims continue to be made. All schools in the north, including those run by Christians, have been turned into Qur'anic schools to the dismay of the 2 million Christians in the north. Yet despite discrimination, bulldozing of churches and persecution of individuals, there is considerable freedom for Christian ministries. **Persecution index** 5th in the world.

Religions	Population %	Adherents	Ann.Gr.
Muslim	65.00	19,168,317	+1.8%
Christian	23.19	6,838,666	+5.5%
Traditional ethnic	10.61	3,128,859	-2.3%
non-Religious/other	1.20	353,877	+2.9%

Christians	Denom.	Affil.%	,000	Ann.Gr.
Protestant	15	2.90	855	+6.8%
Independent	28	0.33	97	+19.4%
Anglican	1	7.14	2,106	+7.0%
Catholic	1	11.87	3,500	+4.7%
Orthodox	4	0.95	280	+2.3%
Marginal	1	0.00	1	+4.6%

Churches	MegaBloc	Cong.	Members	Affiliates
Catholic	C	140	2,034,884	3,500,000
Episcopal	A	2,100	632,432	2,106,000
Presbyterian	P	600	130,000	450,000
Sudan Church of Christ	P	560	80,000	190,000
Africa Inland	P	50	11,994	80,000
Sudan Interior	P	130	20,000	30,000
Assemblies of God	P	50	7,000	20,000
Sudan Pentecostal	I	65	5,200	18,200

Trinity Presby Ch of S	I	306	7,266	16,474
Other denoms [41]		336	221,885	428,094
Total Christians [50]		4,337	3,150,661	6,838,768

Trans-bloc Groupings	pop.%	,000	Ann.Gr.
Evangelical	10.3	3,051	+7.0%
Charismatic	5.5	1,634	+6.6%
Pentecostal	0.1	38	+8.1%

Missionaries from Sudan
PAI 65 in 5 agencies to 7 countries: Sudan 50, Ethiopia 4.

Missionaries to Sudan
PAI 260 in 30 agencies from 20 countries: USA 89, UK 55, Sweden 22, Germany 16. C 418.

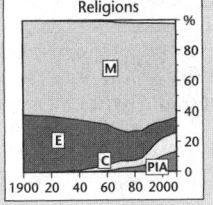

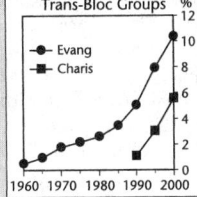

• Answers to Prayer

1 **Due to the long and terrible warfare,** Christians have spread all around the country, leading to a multiplication of congregations in areas with many unreached peoples.

2 **The massive growth of Christianity** in the southern peoples from 5% in 1960 to perhaps 70% in 2000. The major breakthroughs among the Bor Dinka in 1995 with collective renunciation of the old ethnic religions and wholehearted commitment to Christ. There have been similar turnings among other peoples.

3 **Intense prayer in 2002 for a lasting peace agreement** has brought both warring factions to virtual agreement.

• Challenges for Prayer

1 **Sudan's civil war** was one of the world's longest conflicts in the 20th Century. Pray for lasting peace and formation of a viable multi-cultural, multi-religious society. Wrongs have been done - the British colonial rulers (they brought peace, honest administration and an end to slavery, but were short-sighted in handling the south), atrocities of both northerners and southerners and the bitter divisions among the southerners themselves. Pray for repentance, restitution and rebuilding of communal life.

2 **Sudan's leaders proudly boast that they are the leaders of the Islamic Revolution in Africa.** In fact, an Islamist Arab minority has used this as a tool to strengthen their personal control of the economy and political power. The tragic cost is 2 million dead, millions traumatized, an economy devastated and a country divided. Pray for the disarming of the spiritual powers that have held the land in centuries of bondage and that a fair and durable peace be established. There was once a strong Christian presence in northern Sudan, and for nearly a millennium the majority of the population were Christians. Muslims invaded and defeated the Christians at the end of the 13th Century and gradually Islamized the area by the 15th Century - a process now being extended to the non-Muslim south.

3 **The human tragedy of Sudan** was ignored until it was revealed that the Islamic government had sanctioned the re-institution of slavery. Many southerners have suffered from slave raiders. An estimated 60,000 - 200,000 are now chattel slaves. The controversial buying back of slaves by Western NGOs is probably helping to perpetuate this evil. Pray that this wicked practice may be ended, and pray that world leaders may prevail upon the government to change its policy and seek the welfare of all Sudan's peoples.

4 **The Church has grown in the midst of suffering.** Catholics, Episcopalians and the Church of Christ in Sudan (fruit of **SUM-AP** ministry in the Nuba Mountains) have seen significant turnings to Christ. Massive population movements have broken down barriers of customs and languages to bring many to Christ from hitherto unreached peoples. For many, becoming a Christian is an expression of opposition to Islam, and so nominalism is still a problem, but for many others it is a genuine work of the Holy Spirit. The Episcopal and Presbyterian Churches have experienced revival, and there have been significant people movements among the Nuer (Presbyterian), Mabaan, Uduk (Sudan Interior Church), Dinka and Moru (Episcopal), Toposa, Acholi (Africa Inland Church) and some of the Nuba tribes (Sudanese Church of Christ). Pray that Christians may demonstrate a love and concern for others that transcends ethnic and racial divisions - especially to their Muslim neighbours.

5 **There has been persecution of the Church** over much of the past 50 years, but much more since 1985. Deliberate attempts to eliminate a viable Christian presence have been extreme, and have included bombing of Sunday church services, destruction of hospitals, schools, churches and Christian villages, massacres, killing of pastors and leaders and a food-for-conversion policy for refugees banished to desert areas around Khartoum. Slavery has been re-instituted with slave raiding and trading. Persecution has been especially severe in the Nuba Mountains. Whole areas have been laid waste and lands seized and given to Arabs. Pray that Christians may bear good witness to their persecutors in these sufferings and become spiritually strong as a result. Pray also that the sufferings of Christians might become widely known and that peace, justice and religious freedom be firmly established.

6 **The pressing needs of the Church:**

a) *Commitment to Jesus to increase* despite aching needs and terrible suffering.
b) *Unity that transcends tribal boundaries and battle lines.* The Sudan Council of Churches in the north and the New Sudan Council of Churches in the south need to be able to prepare for peace and unite all Christians. There have been ethnic and political divisions that have divided the Church. The NSCC was able to mediate peace between the Nuer and Dinka in 1999. Pray that Christians may be delivered from bitterness and hatred and find unity at the cross.
c) *Recovery* — many churches, villages and towns in the south were destroyed and rebuilt several times. Education and health services barely functioned for two decades. There are few with the skills and education to lead reconstruction programmes. A large proportion of the non-Arab population has gone through traumatic experiences.
d) *The provision of physical needs.* Some agencies went to great lengths and risked danger in bringing food, medicines, Bibles, etc. to the centre and south of the country despite the threats of the government. Of special note is the work of Open Doors, Voice of the Martyrs, Frontline Fellowship, Christian Solidarity International, Samaritan's Purse and WVI. Pray for the safety of workers and effective use of limited resources. Pray also for the re-opening of the country for Christian ministry to these needs.
e) *Vision for the future.* By 1998 there were over 5,000 churches. '**Cush for Christ 2000**' is a saturation church planting project with goals to plant 25,000 churches and to reach every people by 2010.

7 **Sudanese Christian leaders** have achieved so much against all the odds. Many have lost their lives in serving Jesus. Few have had opportunity for formal theological education. The few theological institutions function under considerable difficulty. Pray for leadership, as there are too many young converts for the pastoral care and teaching available. A number of Bible schools function but with many disruptions. Pray for the AIC Bible School, the Anglican Seminary, the SIC/**SIM** and SCOC/SUM-**AP** Gideon Theological College now based in Omdurman, and a Pentecostal Bible school in Juba. The Bishop Gwynne College in W. Equatoria and the Christian Liberty Academy — the first Christian high school in the South — have been restored (Frontline Fellowship). Pray for the provision of adequate facilities, staff and Sudanese leaders. Many Sudanese are studying in other lands.

8 **Ministry challenges for the Church:**

a) *Muslim majority.* The population in the north is largely Sunni Muslim, though among them are 300,000 or more Coptic Christians and maybe 2 million southern Christians displaced by war. Sufi religious orders are strong - especially Ansar, followers of the famous Mahdi. A small but increasing number have become Christians - disillusioned by Islam and attracted to Jesus. There are probably some thousands of these. There are reports of whole villages turning to Christ. Pray that their numbers may increase. There is a remarkable openness among many.

b) Khartoum may now have 13 million inhabitants. Vast shanty towns of displaced Nuba Mountain and southerner populations have sprung up. Poverty and deprivation are widespread and Christians are often subjected to harassment, destruction of church buildings and discriminatory taxes and laws. In 1997 there were officially only 171 churches, but unofficially many smaller groups also exist. Most use Arabic in services. Many congregations are introspective and in 'survival mode'. Pray that they may impact the Muslims around them and that many more churches be planted.

c) The Nuba Mountain peoples, an island of non-Muslims in a sea of Islam. Whole tribes have turned to Christ (Episcopal Church, Sudanese Church of Christ); a few others have become Muslim. There are still a number of unreached groups, but 60% of the population has fled the area. Government policy has sought to eliminate the Nuba by destruction of their villages, murder and their relocation as slave labour.

d) The SPLA, the southern army, had a bad record for atrocities, but since front-line-trained chaplains were appointed a large number of soldiers have become believers. Pray for the maturing and growth of this movement to Christ and its wholesome impact on their lifestyle.

e) Children and young people. There are few southern children who have had opportunity for education. Many are traumatized. There are many street children in Khartoum, an estimated 30,000 of them homeless (**SIM**). **CMS** helps the Christians with an 'Under Tree School' programme. Many young men and even children are press-ganged to become soldiers by both sides in the conflict.

9 **Less-evangelized peoples** are many in the west, east and north of Sudan. There are also some peoples in the Nuba Mountains and in the south which are still largely unreached. Pray especially for:

a) Darfur Province in the west which was Christian a millennium ago. It is now one of the least evangelized areas on earth. There are no known believers among the indigenous peoples - the Fur, Masalit, Zaghawa, Daju, Tama, Bideyat, Midob, Fulbe and Hausa.

b) The Beja on the Red Sea Coast were famed as the 'Fuzzie Wuzzies'. They were once Christian. Now only 4 believers are known. There is a limited outreach to them.

c) The Nubians of the Nile valley are an ancient people with great kingdoms who were Christian for 1,000 years. Relentless Muslim pressure led to their Islamization 600 years ago. There are only a handful of believers today. Several Christian agencies have ministry to them.

d) The nomadic and semi-nomadic Baggara tribes in the central belt of the country are numerous, but few have had much exposure to the gospel, and little has been done to reach them. They speak 3 to 4 major Arabic dialects, but many are of non-Arab origin.

10 **Missionary activity on the part of expatriates has steadily decreased,** and few expatriate Christian workers remain. In 1964 missionaries were expelled from the south, and limited ministry had been permitted in the Khartoum area (**SIM**, **CMS**) and among Ethiopian refugees. The **ACROSS** programme run by **SIM**, **AIM**, SUM-**AP**, **TEAR Fund** and others carried on a vital range of help ministries between 1972 and 1988 before the enforced closure of its ministry. Since then only a low-profile spiritual ministry and aid programme has been permitted in Khartoum and a few outlying areas. The rate of expulsions and refusals of visas has been stepped up since 1990. Pray for:

a) The few Christian agencies still able to carry on in the north.

b) Input to the south where the Khartoum regime is not in control; these ministries are largely based in Kenya.

c) The reopening of the land so that aid may be given to help the Church repair the immense emotional and physical damage to lives and property, and to train a new generation of leaders.

d) The calling and preparation of indigenous and expatriate workers to evangelize the many peoples of the north who have never had the opportunity to hear the gospel.

e) The health and protection of missionaries serving in dangerous areas.

11 Christian help ministries:

a) *The Bible Society* has done much to supervise translation work and distribute Scriptures from their Khartoum depot.

b) *Bible translation* - still a major need. Of the 81 languages without Scriptures, there are at least 18 with a definite need. Pray for the many Sudanese Christians involved in planning for, or actually translating the Scriptures in 73 languages. Expatriates seek to help, encourage and train for the task. Pray for the rapid completion of these NTs and Bibles despite the many obstacles.

c) *Christian literature* is in short supply. Importation into the north is difficult but not impossible. Pray for all involved in bringing Scriptures, hymn books, etc., to remote and war-zone areas (Frontline Fellowship, Open Doors, etc.). **OM** have a remarkable literature ministry including an annual book exhibition on the Nile in Khartoum. Pray that the great hunger for Christian and educational reading materials might be met.

d) *The JESUS film* has been extensively used and maybe half of the northern population has seen it. Pray for lasting impact on individuals and communities, and for safety for film teams.

e) *Christian radio*. Impact is diminished by lack of batteries or hand-winding radios. **FEBA** broadcasts 4 times/week in Nuer and Dinka, and is wanting to start programmes in Beja. Both **TWR** and **FEBA** broadcast daily in Arabic.

f) *GRN* has produced recordings in 120 languages and dialects.

Suriname

Republic of Suriname

OCTOBER 22
LATIN AMERICA

GEOGRAPHY
Area 163,820 sq.km. Northeast coast of South America between Guyana and French Guiana.

Population	Ann.Gr.	Density
2000	417,130	+0.39%	3 per sq. km.
2010	452,074	+1.13%	3 per sq. km.
2025	524,642	+0.86%	3 per sq. km.

Many Surinamers migrated to the Netherlands around the time of independence.

Capital Paramaribo 210,000. **Urbanites** 54%.

PEOPLES
Startling ethnic diversity — a legacy of colonial importation of indentured labour.

Asians 51%. East Indian (mostly originating from Bihar) 140,000; Indonesian (mainly Javanese) 67,000; Chinese 13,000; Hmong (refugees from Laos) 2,000.
Afro-Caribbean 41%. Creole 140,000; Bush Negro (Saramaccan, Aukaan, Kwinti) 40,000.
Amerindian 7%, in 6 ethnic groups.
Other 1%. Dutch 1,000; Guyanese, Portuguese.

Literacy 93%. **Official language** Dutch. **Trade language** Sranang Tongo (Taki-taki). **All languages** 16. **Languages with Scriptures** 4Bi 4NT 4por 4w.i.p.

ECONOMY
Bauxite, aluminium, rice, forest products and eco-tourism are the main sources of foreign exchange. The 20-year post-independence instability brought severe decline. Suriname is heavily dependent on aid and remittances from emigrant Surinamers. HDI 0.757; 64th/174. **Public debt** 40% of GNP. **Income/person** $1,000 (4% of USA).

POLITICS
Independent from the Netherlands in 1975. A leftist military coup in 1980 with Cuban and Libyan help brought instability, repression and suffering to the country. A succession of coups, uprisings and abortive elections followed. An internationally supervised election in 1991 and a peace agreement in 1994 with rebels in the east restored the country to democratic government and peace. There has subsequently been a series of unstable coalition governments, but the former military dictator still exercises much influence.

RELIGION			
There is full freedom of religion.			

Religions	Population %	Adherents	Ann.Gr.
Christian	46.85	195,425	+0.8%
Hindu	27.00	112,625	+0.1%
Muslim	19.40	80,923	+0.2%
non-Religious/other	2.80	11,680	+0.4%
Traditional ethnic	2.60	10,845	-1.8%
Baha'i	1.20	5,006	+0.4%
Chinese	0.10	417	+0.4%
Jewish	0.05	209	-3.1%

Christians	Denom.	Affil.%	,000	Ann.Gr.
Protestant	21	18.84	79	+1.8%
Independent	9	0.88	4	+13.2%
Anglican	1	0.19	1	-0.5%
Catholic	1	22.53	94	+0.6%
Marginal	2	1.42	6	+2.3%
Unaffiliated		2.99	12	n.a.

Churches	MegaBloc	Cong.	Members	Affiliates
Catholic	C	30	48,958	94,000
Moravian	P	55	37,956	52,000
Reformed Ch of Suriname	P	8	3,799	6,800
Jehovah's Witnesses	M	35	1,978	5,500
Evang Lutheran	P	7	2,198	4,000
Seventh-day Adventist	P	14	2,915	4,000

Evang Ch of W Indies	P	16	1,300	2,800
Other Indep Charis [5]	I	8	952	2,000
Church of the Nazarene	P	11	1,100	1,500
United Baptist	P	9	220	620
Wesleyan	P	30	300	600
Chr and Miss Alliance	P	2	244	549
Assemblies of God	P	6	200	475
Other denoms [17]		47	4,300	8,100
Total Christians [34]		278	106,400	183,000

Trans-bloc Groupings	pop.%	,000	Ann.Gr.
Evangelical	4.1	17	+5.5%
Charismatic	3.3	14	+5.9%
Pentecostal	0.7	3	+8.1%

Missionaries from Suriname
P,I,A 8 in 6 agencies: Suriname 5.

Missionaries to Suriname
P,I,A 156 in 28 agencies from 9 countries: USA 102, Netherlands 29.

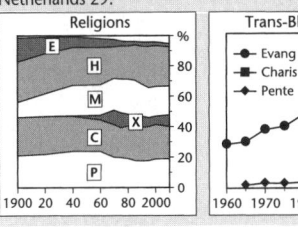

• Challenges for Prayer

1 **Suriname's post-independence experience was disastrous.** Pray for continued peace, godly leaders, stable government, economic improvement, and, above all, for spiritual awakening. The young nation is compartmentalized by race and religion, and the potential for further conflict remains.

2 **Nearly half the population professes to be Christian**, but few know much of a personal faith in Christ and Christian belief is often mixed with spiritism. Both the Moravian and Catholic Churches have large followings. In the Moravian Church are some evangelical leaders, revival prayer groups and also spiritual awakening among young people. Pray for revival to sweep through the traditionalism of the majority of Christians.

3 **The evangelical witness** has grown significantly from a very small percentage in 1960 through a variety of Pentecostal and charismatic movements in nearly every culture. Pray for the continuance of increasing trans-denominational cooperation in Bible-related ministries, the March for Jesus and in outreach.

4 **Christian leaders** with a warm personal faith and biblical message are few. Pray for the three small Bible schools (two Pentecostal and one Baptist), and also for the ministry of Christian leaders in re-laying biblical foundations and standards in a nation that has lost its way morally and ethically in the confusion after independence.

5 **Most of the six Amerindian peoples are now at least nominally Christian.** WT has seen people movements among the Wayana, Akurio and Trio. The coastal Carib and Arawak are more needy. Pray for stability, maturity and indigeneity to be maintained in the tribal churches, the pressures to conform to the missionary and the coastal cultures are overwhelming. Some have reverted to indigenous customs. Pray for the service of two **MAF** planes that make the ministry of **WT** practicable.

6 **Missions** and their ministries have resumed after years of disruption. The major ministry challenges are for more effective discipling of new leaders, Bible translation (5 NTs are being translated — mainly through the 38 **SIL/WBT** workers in Suriname) and pioneer outreach to non-Christian peoples. Other larger agencies include: **WT** (15), **Christar** (9), **SBC** (8).

7 **Less-reached peoples:**

a) *The Javanese* are predominantly Muslim — but nominally so. Through the work of the Indonesian Missionary Fellowship **Christar**, **CMA** and others, at least 10 churches have been planted. The vision is for a church for every Javanese community. The Suriname Javanese NT was published in 2000.

b) *The Indian community* has shown little response to the gospel. The ministry of **Christar**, **CMA** and **WT** has led to the planting of five congregations largely made up of former Hindus. The Pentecostals have had significant success in church planting. The Muslim community is unreached. Pray for barriers of occultism, prejudice and misunderstanding to be broken down.

c) *Chinese* are responding to the ministry of two Chinese **CMA** missionary couples, and there are two growing congregations with a cross-cultural missions vision for Suriname and French Guiana.

d) *Bush Negroes* are descendants of escaped slaves who formed their own distinctive communities. Six groups and languages have developed. Many of these communities were decimated and scattered in reprisals for local uprisings against the military regime. Bible translation work is in progress in Aukaans and the NT completed in Saramaccan. Witchcraft and fear of spirits is widespread, but there are some strong Christians among them (**WT** and **Baptists**). Many communities are only superficially evangelized. Pray for decisive breakthroughs in these peoples bound by the occult.

e) *The Laotian Hmong* live in several villages. **CMA** missionaries have planted several congregations among them, but the lack of Hmong pastors limits the work.

8 **Specialist Christian ministries** for prayer:

a) *The Suriname Bible Society* (UBS) has played a key role in not only Bible translation and distribution, but also in producing a daily 20-minute TV programme, promoting ministry for families, AIDS issues, etc. Bible distribution has increased since independence.

b) *Bible translation* continues through the ministry of **The Bible Society** and **SIL**. Seven translation projects are being tackled.

c) *Student ministry*. JSS(**IFES**) has expanded ministry since the 1980s. There are Christian groups in 18 of the 20 tertiary institutions.

d) *The JESUS film* has been extensively used in film showings and on TV in the 4 major languages.

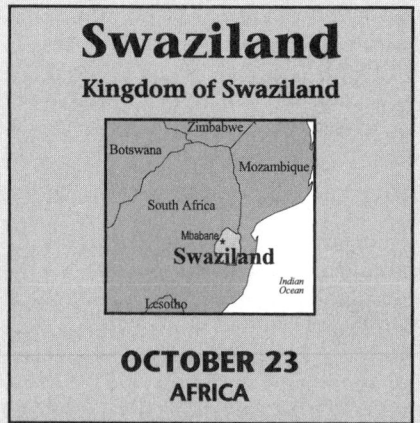

Swaziland
Kingdom of Swaziland

OCTOBER 23
AFRICA

Population		Ann.Gr.	Density
2000	1,007,895	+2.93%	58 per sq. km.
2010	1,310,450	+2.55%	75 per sq. km.
2025	1,784,790	+1.82%	103 per sq. km.

Capital Mbabane 80,000. Other major city: Manzini 100,000. **Urbanites** 38%.

PEOPLES

Bantu 96.7%.
 Nguni 92.7%. Swati (Swazi), Zulu 30,000.
 Other 4%. Tsonga 30,000; Mozambican refugees.
 Other 3.3%. European 20,000; Eurafrican 11,000; South Asian 1,500.

Literacy 67%. **Official languages** siSwati, English. **All languages** 4. **Languages with Scriptures** 3Bi 1NT.

ECONOMY
 Mostly pastoral and agricultural, but also some mineral production. Main exports: sugar, citrus, timber, paper pulp. Some manufacturing. Not highly populated in some areas. Part of

GEOGRAPHY
 Area 17,364 sq.km. Small, fertile, well-watered, landlocked enclave between Mozambique and South Africa.

Southern African Customs Union and Rand Monetary Area. AIDS is beginning to seriously affect the economy with an incidence of over 25%. **HDI** 0.644; 113th/174. **Public debt** 14% of GNP. **Income/person** $1,520 (5% of USA).

 POLITICS
A British protectorate 1899-1968. An absolute monarchy with democratic government suspended in 1973 pending agreement on a new, but much-disputed constitution. All political parties are banned. The dispute between the entrenched traditionalists and the frustrated progressives desiring democratic reforms is a deeply divisive issue yet to be resolved.

RELIGION

Religions	Population %	Adherents	Ann.Gr.
Christian	82.70	833,529	+3.2%
Traditional ethnic	14.70	148,161	+1.2%
non-Religious/other	1.00	10,079	+2.9%
Muslim	0.95	9,575	+4.0%
Baha'i	0.50	5,039	+5.1%
Hindu	0.15	1,512	+1.6%

Christians	Denom.	Affil.%	,000	Ann.Gr.
Protestant	33	11.52	116	+0.6%
Independent	83	61.04	615	+5.2%
Anglican	1	0.76	8	-8.5%
Catholic	1	4.74	48	+2.1%
Marginal	2	0.59	6	+1.1%
Unaffiliated		3.95	40	n.a.

Churches	MegaBloc	Cong.	Members	Affiliates
All Indig AICS [70]	I	4,640	232,000	580,000
Catholic	C	100	26,264	47,800
Ch of the Nazarene	P	115	9,500	22,000
Assemblies of God	P	61	8,000	16,000
Methodist	P	106	4,500	13,000
Evangelical	P	85	5,300	12,000
Kukhanyokuaha	I	25	4,300	8,600
Free Evang Assembly	I	80	4,000	8,000
Anglican	A	77	3,850	7,700
Africa Evangelical	P	36	3,000	7,500
Jehovah's Witnesses	M	63	2,029	5,000
Swedish Free	P	30	2,667	4,000
Other denoms [40]			570	33,000	62,000
Total Christians [121]		5,988	338,000	794,000

Trans-bloc Groupings	pop.%	,000	Ann.Gr.
Evangelical	29.4	297	+3.7%
Charismatic	52.3	527	+5.0%
Pentecostal	4.3	44	+3.9%

Missionaries from Swaziland
P,I,A 29 in 6 agencies to 4 countries: Swaziland 19, Mozambique 8.

Missionaries to Swaziland
P,I,A 145 in 30 agencies from 14 countries: USA 83, South Africa 24, Norway 11. **C** 263. **M** 30.

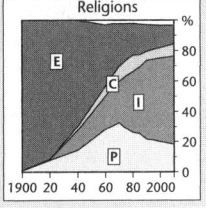

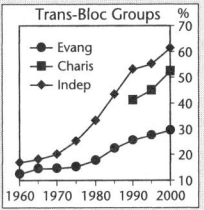

• Answers to Prayer

1 **Faithful sowing of the gospel** for 150 years has led to a strong evangelical community comprising nearly 30% of the population. Church attendance is a high 27% of the population.

2 **The Swaziland Evangelism Task (SET) conference** in 1995 was a watershed for the country. A saturation church-planting vision with goals was launched. This was the first time the Council of Swazi Churches (mainline denominations), the Swaziland Conference of Churches (Evangelicals) and League of African Independent Churches had related and fellowshipped together.

• Challenges for Prayer

1 **The unresolved constitutional issue is a source of potential conflict.** Pray for the wide acceptance of a constitution that both respects human rights and tradition and also respects the honoured place of the king and democratic freedoms.

2 **Few African countries have retained such strong ties with pre-colonial political and cultural society**. This leads to a clash between the claims of the past and those of biblical Christianity resulting in much compromise among Christians. The many evangelical churches have made little headway over the past decades and are generally stagnating. Pray for revival, holy living, a clear evangelical message proclaimed and greater unity among Christian leaders. Pray also that the strong hold of witchcraft and ancestor worship, as well as the spirit of polygamy and immorality, might be broken within the churches and nation. It is the men who are most bound — over 70% of church members are women.

3 The Church faces many challenges:

a) *Nominalism has become a major problem.* The churches are not holding their young people. They reject the spiritual weakness and compromise of their elders.

b) *The African Independent Churches* have gained a following of over half the population — especially among men. They range from an evangelical theological position to a high degree of compromise with polygamy, witchcraft, ancestor veneration and appeasement sacrifices. The 'Ethiopian' churches broke away early from the mission-planted churches and tend to be oriented to the Old Testament. The large 'Zionist' movement has a strong emphasis on both pentecostal gifts and traditional customs. Pray that these many congregations may be increasingly moulded by the Scriptures. Pray that other churches may be more welcoming to them and also learn from their often more effective integration of Christianity and Swazi culture.

c) *Christian unity.* Denominational rivalry has long characterized the Church. Pray that the SET goals may further enhance the new spirit of togetherness.

d) *Quality Christian leadership is in short supply.* The multiplicity of small congregations means that most pastors are poorly trained and paid, and are therefore part-time in ministry. Few congregations are confident to confront either traditionalists or intellectuals, and so have little impact on the unchurched. Pray for changes in attitudes, patterns of giving, and the level of commitment among leaders and led alike. There are seven Bible schools or seminaries in Swaziland.

4 Vision for the future.

a) *Several good examples of growth* are evident in the **CoN**, **AoG** and more recently launched, Deeper Life Bible Church from Nigeria as well as the indigenous Christian Family Centre, International Tabernacle and Faith Christian Fellowship. Pray that other evangelical groups may reverse decades of stagnation or decline.

b) *The SET vision* in 1995 was to double the number of churches in Swaziland by 2015 and increase average congregation size from 52 to 74.

5 Ministry challenges facing the Church:

a) *Coping with the increasingly devastating consequences of the AIDS pandemic.* For too long the churches have ignored the growing crisis.

b) *Youth ministry.* The large levels of youth unemployment bodes ill for future social stability — over 60% of youth are under 20 and by 2006 there may be 115,000 AIDS orphans.

c) *The Muslims,* though few, have made a big effort to increase their numbers and build mosques. The churches are ill-equipped to respond.

6 Most Protestant missions and missionaries are evangelical, the largest agencies being **CoN** (23 workers), InterAct (Sweden, 5), **IMB-SBC** (4). The majority are heavily committed to institutional programmes and to radio ministry, and only a minority are in direct church development. Pray for a happy and close relationship between expatriates and national believers — there has been a history of breakdowns and divisions.

7 Christian media ministries:

a) *The Bible Society* published the full Swati Bible in 1998 after years of linguistic domination of the related Zulu. Pray for its impact on Church life and Christian holiness.

b) *Christian literature* in Swati is limited. **CLC** and Church of the Nazarene both have a bookstore in Manzini.

c) *National Christian radio.* The SCC Media Centre produces 18 hours of Christian programming weekly for broadcasting on national radio.

d) *International Christian radio.* **TWR** has 5 short-wave, 1 medium wave and 2 FM transmitters reaching a potential 400 million people in 53 languages in Africa and south-west Asia. Pray for provision of programming in each language — especially those with few believers or in war zones.

Sweden

Kingdom of Sweden

OCTOBER 24
EUROPE
Revised February 2004

GEOGRAPHY
Area 449,964 sq.km. The largest of the Scandinavian countries, a land of mountains and forests. Only 10% of the land is cultivated.

Population		Ann.Gr.	Density
2000	8,910,214	+0.25%	20 per sq. km.
2010	9,039,070	+0.08%	20 per sq. km.
2025	9,096,927	-0.01%	20 per sq. km.

Capital Stockholm 1,650,000. Other major cities: Göteborg 460,000, Malmö 250,000. **Urbanites** 84%.

PEOPLES
Indigenous 88.8%. Swedish 7,860,000; Meankieli (Finnish) 50,000; Saami (Lapp, 5) 16,000; Roma (Gypsy) 5,000.
Non-indigenous 11.2%.
   Nordic 3.6%. Finnish 223,000; Norwegian 50,000; Danish 45,000; Estonian 11,000.
   Other foreign 7.6%. Former Yugoslavia 148,000; Iranian 52,000; Latin American 50,000; Iraqi 46,000; Turk 36,000; Kurd 35,000; Somali 16,000; Chinese 8,000.

Literacy 99%. **Official language** Swedish. **All languages** 11. **Languages with Scriptures** 4Bi 1NT 3por 4w.i.p.

ECONOMY
Highly developed industry and information technology. The extensive social welfare system requires high taxation lowering international competitiveness. **HDI** 0.923; 6th/174. **Public debt** 32% of GNP. **Income/person** $26,210 (83% of USA).

POLITICS
Parliamentary government with a constitutional monarchy. The 185 years of strict neutrality and the past 60 years of almost uninterrupted social democracy as a welfare state has moulded Swedish society. A member of the EU.

RELIGION
Complete freedom of religion. The Church of Sweden (Lutheran) was the State Church until 2000. It still has an important role because of its size and history. There are 21 denominations and religious groups that are given some state funding.

Religions	Population %	Adherents	Ann.Gr.
Christian	54.65	4,869,432	-1.0%
non-Religious	41.82	3,726,251	+1.8%
Muslim	3.10	276,217	+4.7%
Jewish	0.18	16,000	-0.8%
Other	0.14	12,474	-1.1%
Hindu	0.06	5,000	+4.0%
Buddhist	0.04	4,000	+0.2%
Baha'i	0.01	900	+0.2%

The official Christian figure is 89% but an estimated 2-3 million Swedes no longer claim to be Christian or believe in God.

Christians	Denom.	Affil.%	,000	Ann.Gr.
Protestant	34	59.41	5,293	-0.6%
Independent	10	0.49	44	+1.9%
Anglican	1	0.03	3	+0.0%
Catholic	1	1.77	158	-0.8%
Orthodox	14	1.11	99	+0.2%
Marginal	8	0.60	53	-1.3%
Doubly affiliated		*-8.76*	*-780*	*n.a.*

Churches	MegaBloc	Cong.	Members	Affiliates
Ch of Sweden (Luth)	P	2,543	2,900,000	7,505,930
Catholic	C	40	123,000	158,000
Pentecostal Movement	P	489	90,815	147,000
Swedish Miss Covenant	P	840	67,000	145,000
InterAct	P	344	29,000	50,000
Estonian Lutheran	P	9	11,500	49,500
Swedish Evang Mission	P	515	18,000	45,000
Finnish Lutheran	P	16	16,000	40,000
Jehovah's Witnesses	M	344	23,559	39,000
Baptist Union	P	337	18,553	36,000
Syrian Orthodox	O	40	18,182	28,000
Salvation Army	P	175	7,300	23,000
Swedish Alliance Miss	P	234	12,800	23,000
Serbian Orthodox	O	8	11,500	23,000
Greek Orthodox	O	4	11,184	17,000
Latter-day Saints (Morm)	M	52	5,444	9,200
Methodist	P	67	5,177	9,000
Finnish Orthodox	O	1	1,400	2,500
Other denoms [50]		345	54,000	100,000
Doubly affiliated			*-570,000*	*-780,000*
Disaffiliated	P		*-2,000,000*	*-2,800,000*
Total Christians [68]		6,400	856,000	4,850,000

Many Swedes have both membership in the Church of Sweden and in other denominations or fellowships.

Trans-bloc Groupings	pop.%	,000	Ann.Gr.
Evangelical	4.9	438	+1.4%
Charismatic	2.4	214	+2.9%
Pentecostal	1.8	163	-0.2%

Missionaries from Sweden
P,I,A 1,106 in 49 agencies to 100 countries: Tanzania 158, Ethiopia 40.

Missionaries to Sweden
P,I,A 104 in 24 agencies: USA 28, Canada 22.

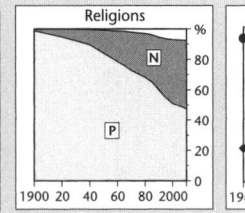

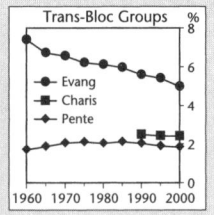

• Challenges for Prayer

1 The 19ᵗʰ Century was notable for revivals, a vigorous free church movement and great commitment to missions. The 20ᵗʰ Century was the opposite with rapid secularization and emergence of one of the most permissive societies in Europe. Government legislation reflects this. Pray for a reversal of these trends, a national awakening and the re-evangelization of Sweden.

2 The Church of Sweden is no longer the State Church, but its size, political influence and social impact is large. There are many serious problems, among them a widespread rejection of the Bible as the literal Word of God or as the Church's final authority. Many forms of liberal theology are vigorously promoted — feminism (with inclusive language in referring to God), homosexualism (making homosexual 'weddings' an equally viable option), relativism and universalism. There is an evangelical minority, but all conservative views are marginalized. Pray that this Church might be shaken out of error and become a source of life in the Spirit.

3 The spiritual need of Sweden has steadily grown over the 20ᵗʰ Century. In 1900, 99% of the population professed to be Christian. By 2000, 78% had been baptized as infants, less than 48% believed there is a God and only 5% regularly went to church. Over half the population has no real knowledge of the Christian faith. The decline has affected nearly every denomination whether Lutheran, Baptist, Methodist or Pentecostal. Pray that a new surge of life and vision may galvanize discouraged saints and stimulate faith that God can give growth in Sweden. Pray that congregations may also become more relevant and effective in the Sweden of today with its secularized, postmodern and New Age worldviews. Pray for courage to witness in a society where promoting absolutes is labelled 'intolerance'.

4 There are encouragements — water these in prayer:

a) *There is some growth in the newer charismatic networks.* InterAct (formed out of a union between the Örebro Mission, the Holiness Union and the Free Baptists) has new vision and plans for growth and outreach.

b) *The Pentecostal Movement* broadcasts on 100 radio stations and runs a successful drug rehabilitation programme.

c) *The Pentecostals, InterAct and the Alliance Mission* jointly own a Christian daily newspaper that has a significant readership.

d) *Credo,* the IFES-linked student ministry, has grown through some innovative outreach; there were groups on 18 campuses in 2000.

e) *The Alpha Course movement* is growing and in 2000 there were 261 of these evangelistic and discipling groups functioning — both in the Church of Sweden and in other denominations.

5 Theological training is a key prayer target. There are two main theological faculties at the universities, where many pastors are trained. This education is affected by the humanistic influence of the universities in general. However, the Johannelund Seminary is conservative evangelical with 130 students; many graduates become Lutheran pastors. The Free Churches run 4 theological schools with one- to four-year courses, including InterAct, Pentecostal, Swedish Mission Covenant Church/Baptist Union, Methodist and Alliance. There are also many short-term Bible courses offered by most denominations. Besides these, there are independent Bible Schools that run mostly one year courses. Over 150 young people are trained annually in short-term courses held by YWAM. OM also has done much to motivate young people for evangelism and missionary service.

6 **Missionary outreach from Sweden** has been outstanding. The contribution of the Lutheran Church and all the Free Churches in over 100 countries has been used of God. Yet both numbers of missionaries and levels of interest have decreased markedly, with the Swedish Missionary Council Member statistics dropping from 927 missionaries in 1997 (the data used in this book) to 715 in 2000. Pray for a quickening of this vision among young people for short-term and, even more, for long-term work. Pray for the notable work of the **Institute of Bible Translation** in Stockholm with the vision to provide a translation of the NT in every non-Slavic language of the fSU.

7 **Ministry challenges in Sweden:**

a) ***Youth***. A whole generation of young people is growing up — a generation who have no meaningful exposure to the gospel. Few churches and agencies are equipped to handle this challenge.

b) ***The Saami peoples*** of Lapland in the north speak five languages. All are nominally Christian. Bible translation is in progress in 2 of the languages and one other was published in 2000. Pray that there might be an authentic Saami expression of the Church.

c) ***There are rural and urban areas*** with few evangelical churches; the latter are unevenly distributed due to localized revivals in the past.

d) ***The Balkan Wars of the 1990s***, with the horrendous ethnic hatreds and 'cleansing', led to a flood of up to 300,000 Albanian, Croatian, Bosnian and Serb refugees into Sweden. Some have since returned home, but many of these tragic, distressed people remain.

e) ***Political and religious refugees***, first from the Communist Bloc, but increasingly from the Middle East and Africa have been given a refuge in Sweden. They are more open to the gospel, but workers among them are few.

f) ***Muslims*** have grown from a handful in 1960 to around 300,000 in 2000. Many are from the former Yugoslavia, Turkey (Turks and Kurds), Iran and North Africa. Pray for the calling of workers to minister to them and for the provision of the outreach tools needed.

g) ***The Chinese*** number around 7,000. **COCM** has been used of God to plant three churches among them. A newer challenge is the number of Mainland Chinese students coming to Sweden.

Switzerland
Swiss Confederation

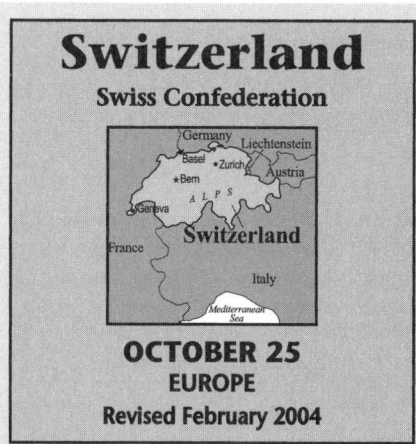

OCTOBER 25
EUROPE
Revised February 2004

GEOGRAPHY
Area 41,293 sq.km. Mountainous land; 26% agriculturally unproductive. The Swiss Alps are one of the greatest tourist attractions in the world.

Population	Ann.Gr.	Density
2000	7,385,708	+0.67%	179 per sq. km.
2010	7,602,762	+0.18%	184 per sq. km.
2025	7,586,992	-0.10%	184 per sq. km.

Capital Bern (admin) 327,000. Lausanne (judicial) 289,000. Other major cities: Zürich 984,000; Basel 631,000; Geneva 515,000. **Urbanites** 68%.

PEOPLES
Indigenous 78%. Swiss German 4 mill.; Romande French 1.2m; Italian 250,000; Rheto-Roman 50,000; Roma (Gypsy) 23,000.
Foreign residents 22%. Italian 360,000; former Yugoslav and Albanian 350,000; Portuguese 130,000; German/Austrian 120,000; Spanish 105,000; Turk/Kurd 80,000; French 54,000; Tamil 40,000; Other Asian (Chinese, Vietnamese, etc.) 45,000.

Literacy 99%. **Official languages** German, French, Italian, Rheto-Roman. **Languages with Scriptures** 4Bi 3NT 3por 1w.i.p.

ECONOMY
A strong and wealthy industrial state. Both tourism and banking are important foreign exchange earners. Recovering from a recession in the 1990s. Surrounded by the EU, but hitherto has rejected joining it. Living costs are high. **HDI** 0.914; 12th/174. **Public debt** 36% of GNP. **Income/person** $43,060 (137% of USA) — one of the world's highest.

POLITICS
Confederation founded in 1291 and federal state in 1848. Federal democratic govern-

ment with the constituent 20 cantons and 6 half-cantons retaining a high degree of autonomy. A strong policy of non-involvement in world politics and strict neutrality — so is not even a member of the UN despite hosting the offices of many UN and other international bodies.

RELIGION
The federal constitution guarantees religious freedom, but relationships between cantonal governments and the churches are decided locally. The post-Reformation confrontations between Catholics and Protestants helped determine the majority religion of each canton.

Religions	Population %	Adherents	Ann.Gr.
Christian	86.56	6,393,069	+0.4%
non-Religious/other	8.20	605,628	+1.9%
Muslim	3.10	228,957	+3.5%
Other	1.80	132,943	+7.4%
Jewish	0.24	17,726	-1.7%
Baha'i	0.10	7,386	+0.7%

Christians	Denom.	Affil.%	,000	Ann.Gr.
Protestant	94	40.84	3,016	+0.1%
Independent	67	1.21	89	+3.7%
Anglican	1	0.18	13	+0.5%
Catholic	2	44.16	3,261	+0.5%
Orthodox	10	1.11	82	+1.8%
Marginal	31	1.28	95	-0.6%
Doubly affiliated		-2.22	-163	n.a.

Churches	MegaBloc	Cong.	Members	Affiliates
Catholic	C	1,590	1,630,000	3,260,000
Fed.of Swiss Prot Chs [20]	P	1,078	2,159,091	2,850,000
New Apostolic	I	235	24,000	36,500
Jehovah's Witnesses	M	300	18,077	29,500
Fell of Pente Free Chs [20]	P	250	15,000	25,000
Exclusive Brethren [3]	P	220	8,784	19,500

Old Catholic	I	47	13,300	19,000
Methodist	P	170	9,000	14,000
Fell of Free Evang Congs	P	93	7,600	12,000
St Chrischona Pilgrim Miss.	P	100	6,100	10,000
Salvation Army	P	90	5,974	9,200
Evangelical Fell (EGW)	P	23	4,450	8,450
Seventh-day Adventist	P	57	4,080	8,160
Latter-day Saints (Morm)	M	37	5,035	7,200
Union of Free Miss Congs	P	70	4,000	5,500
Evang Assem of Fr-sp Sw	P	41	3,500	4,500
Mennonite	P	14	2,300	4,000
Baptist Fellowship	P	15	1,400	2,400
Other denoms [148]		1,119	141,300	231,700
Doubly affiliated			-114,000	-163,000

Total Christians [206]		5,549	3,949,000	6,393,000

Trans-bloc Groupings	pop.%	,000	Ann.Gr.
Evangelical	4.1	306	+0.8%
Charismatic	3.5	259	+1.0%
Pentecostal	0.6	45	-1.0%

Missionaries from Switzerland
P,I,A 1,481 in 90 agencies to 113 countries: Brazil 55, France 50, Burkina Faso 50, Cameroon 48, Guinea 42, Peru 39, Bolivia 32, Japan 26, Kenya 24, Senegal 23, Chad 22.

Missionaries to Switzerland
P,I,A 556 in 44 agencies from over 30 countries: USA 70, Germany 26, UK 41, Korea 21. C 1,200. M 200.

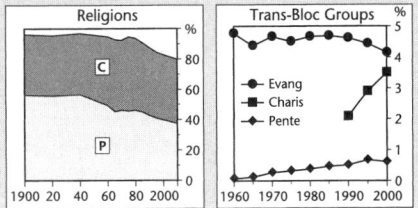

• Answers to Prayer

1 The development of a trans-denominational vision for saturation church planting in the nation, of which *FocuSuisse* is a part.

2 A strong, growing prayer movement which is raising expectancy for revival — 3 national 40-day fasts have been held, and the 24-7 prayer movement is gaining momentum among young people.

3 Continued Swiss commitment to world evangelization despite the relatively small community of Evangelicals.

• Challenges for Prayer

1 The great reformers, Calvin and Zwingli, expounded the truths of Scripture in this land, but few today have any interest or understanding of what real Christianity is. Wealth, comfort, indifference and a vague religiosity have become the norm. The socio-politico upheavals towards the end of the 20th Century stirred an uncertainty and identity crisis in the hearts of many, but it is the occult and eastern religions that the younger generation are exploring. Many baptised as children no longer retain any church link, and enrolled membership of Protestants and Catholics has halved in 30 years. Pray that the Swiss may find the true way in Jesus Christ, and that the nation might be stirred again by the Holy Spirit.

2 **The falling away of the Swiss from the churches is gaining momentum.** Lack of clergy in the Catholic Church and widespread espousal of liberal and neo-orthodox ideas in many of the Cantonal Reformed Churches have sapped the spirituality of many congregations. This is only partially offset by the growth of Pentecostal, charismatic and evangelical Free churches. Pray that:

a) *Prayerful men and women of God* in both the leadership and the congregations may be used to bring revival to the whole Swiss nation.

b) *There may be a deeper level of unity* in prayer and vision among evangelical leaders across the denominations. The Evangelical Alliance and Federation of Free Churches have been cooperating well since 2000.

c) *Congregational outreach* may increase through personal evangelism, home Bible studies and cell/house church planting. Pray that true believers in both the Cantonal and Free Churches may be more effectively motivated and activated for outreach.

3 **Renewed vision** is being generated.

a) *The Swiss Evangelical Alliance*, Free Churches and other agencies are working on a renewed vision for the evangelization of Switzerland. Research in 1998 revealed many hundreds of towns and villages without a resident evangelical congregation. Pray for the doubling of the number of congregations. In 1998 there were 1,078 Reformed parishes and 1,186 Free churches, and over the period 1997-1999 60 new churches were planted and 10 closed.

b) *Denominational goals.* The Fellowship of Pentecostal Free Churches aimed to double the number of Francophone congregations in the 1990s. The national Federation of Free Evangelical Churches set a similar goal for the country and is growing at 6% a year. The International Christian Fellowship has grown through multiplying cell churches. Pray for the full achievement of these goals in the coming decade 2000 -2010.

c) *There is a nation-wide initiative of outreach* using Alpha courses. Pray for this and other innovative methods of reaching the unchurched, and for open hearts and changed lives.

4 **In the Catholic cantons,** predominantly in the south and centre of the country, the small evangelical witness is growing; centuries-old prejudices and religious polarizations are breaking down. Pray that many may find a personal relationship with Jesus and come to assurance of salvation, and that a living fellowship of believers may come into being in every community.

5 **Young people** are being lost to the churches, which has serious implications for the future. Pray for:

a) *Outreach through agencies* such as **CCCI, OM, YWAM,** BESJ (*Jungschar*) and the Cevi.

b) *Specific ministries to young people:*

  i *SU* in schools and with a good camp ministry.

  ii *CEF* to children; they have an international training centre at Kilchzimmer.

  iii *IFES* with 50 Francophone groups (GBU) and many German-speaking (VBG). For most students, life has no meaning; suicides are many and drug abuse too common.

c) *The ICF Church in Zürich* has grown, triggering a wave of new youth congregations being launched — pray for the spiritual development of this movement.

6 **Bible training** is provided by a number of institutions. From them, graduates have gone out for Christian service all over the world. Remember the:

a) *German-speaking seminaries*: STH Basel, TDS Aarau, TSC St. Chrischona, TS Bienenberg, BS Beatenberg and *Institut für Gemeindebau und Weltmission* (IGW).

b) *French-speaking Bible schools*: Emmaus, *Institut Biblique de Genève,* IBETO (Pentecostal) and **YWAM.**

Pray that these may retain their spiritual cutting edge, and become a means of blessing and revival in Switzerland. The number of students is in sharp decline in all but IGW. Pray that these institutions might be both flexible and relevant for today's generation and that many might be called and equipped for service.

7 The *Arbeitsgemeinschaft Evangelischer Missionen* (AEM) was formed in 1972 to strengthen and coordinate missionary vision and outreach — especially in the Free Churches. There are 45 member agencies representing over 1,000 missionaries. The *Fédéra-*

tion des Missions Évangéliques Francophones (**FMEF**) has the same vision for the French-speaking Protestant churches in Switzerland and France. The ***Communauté de Travail des Églises Chrétiennes de Suisse*** links together eight denominational missions. Pray for a greater awareness and sense of responsbility in Swiss churches for world evangelization, and support of the commendably large missionary force.

8 **Peoples and areas where the evangelical witness is small:**

a) ***Cantons***. The German-speaking cantons of Luzern, Zug, Schwyz and Uri, the largely Francophone Valais and Fribourg and the Italian-speaking Ticino are culturally Catholic with few evangelical groups.

b) ***The 30 or more foreign communities***. Switzerland has the highest proportion of foreign residents of any major state in Europe. The major cities are becoming internationalized — Geneva is 35% non-Swiss. There are a number of agencies and churches committed to minister to them — most are linked to the ***Arbeitsgemeinschaft für Ausländermission*** of the **AEM**. There are now evangelical congregations, or groups within multicultural churches, among 28 ethnic groups — Italian (16 congregations), Spanish (11), Croat (10), Tamil (9), Hungarian (9), Yugoslav (9), Vietnamese (8), Turkish (6), etc.

9 **Local radio and TV stations** are well used by several Swiss Christian agencies, and have great potential for reaching the population. The Christian broadcast ***Fenster zum Sonntag*** has an audience of nearly 70,000 weekly. Pray for more openness on national radio and television. **TWR** broadcasts in German, French and Italian through the Astra satellite, and from Albania in German.

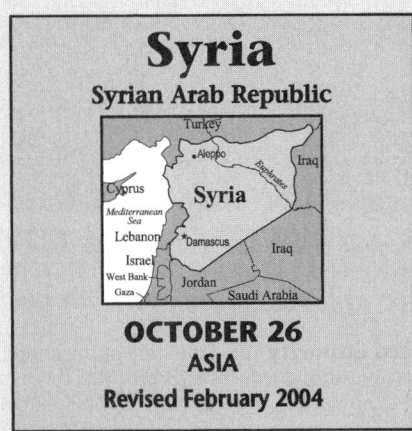

Syria
Syrian Arab Republic

OCTOBER 26
ASIA
Revised February 2004

GEOGRAPHY
Area 185,180 sq.km. Fertile plain on Mediterranean coast; 60% desert in centre and east but crossed by Euphrates River.

Population		Ann.Gr.	Density
2000	16,124,618	+2.57%	87 per sq. km.
2010	20,464,138	+2.33%	111 per sq. km.
2025	26,291,810	+1.38%	142 per sq. km.

Capital Damascus 2,550,000. Other major city: Aleppo 1.9mill. **Urbanites** 52%.

PEOPLES
Arab 92%. Bedouin 1,300,000; Palestinian 550,000.
Other 8%. Kurd 800,000; Armenian 150,000; Turk/Turkmen 150,000; Assyrian 50,000; Iranian 50,000; Ossetian 50,000; Circassian (Adygey) 25,000; Dom Gypsy 10,000.

Literacy 71%. **Official language** Arabic. **All languages** 17. **Languages with Scripture** 4Bi 2NT 1por 4w.i.p.

ECONOMY
Oil and agriculture are important. Heavy military spending in decades of confrontation with Israel have hampered development. Poor economic infrastructure and growing vulnerability to regional water shortages increase the possibility of future economic downturns. **HDI** 0.663; 111th/174. **Public debt** 98% of GNP. **Income/person** $1,120 (3.6% of USA).

POLITICS
Independent from France in 1946. Continuous upheavals until the coup in 1970. Relative internal stability under an Alawite minority, military-civilian socialist government. Since 1973, Syria has sought to gain political dominance in war-torn Lebanon and still exerts a strong influence over its small neighbour. Longstanding President Assad's iron grip on power was finally loosened by his death in 2000. Bashar, his son and heir has inherited the mantle of leadership. The 2003 US-led invasion of Iraq placed great pressure on Syria which may lead to significant changes in its political future.

RELIGION
Prior to 1973 Islam was the religion of the state. Since then it has been a secular state with Islam recognized as the religion of the majority, and all other minorities accorded definite rights and privileges, with a measure of religious freedom.

Religions	Population %	Adherents	Ann.Gr.
Muslim	90.32	14,563,755	+2.7%
Christian	5.12	825,580	+0.7%
non-Religious	2.90	467,614	+2.6%
Other (Druze, etc.)	1.55	249,932	+3.0%
Baha'i	0.10	16,125	+2.6%
Jewish	0.01	1,612	-10.7%

Christians	Denom.	Affil.%	,000	Ann.Gr.
Protestant	15	0.16	26	+0.0%
Independent	1	0.03	5	+2.1%
Anglican	1	0.02	4	+3.0%
Catholic	6	1.80	290	+0.7%
Orthodox	6	3.10	500	+0.7%
Marginal	6	0.01	1	+1.2%

Churches	MegaBloc	Cong.	Members	Affiliates
Catholic [6]	C	226	162,000	290,000
Greek Orthodox	O	150	135,000	242,000
Armenian Apostolic	O	23	64,835	118,000
Syrian Orthodox	O	25	50,279	90,000
Assyrian Ch of the East	O	26	26,374	48,000
Union of Ev Armenian	P	24	6,044	11,000

Nat Ev Synod of L & S	P	46	4,790	8,000
Anglican	A	2	2,156	3,600
Nat'l Evang Alliance	P	19	1,050	1,750
Other denoms [23]		48	6,500	12,600
Total Christians [37]		**589**	**459,000**	**825,000**

Trans-bloc Groupings	pop.%	,000	Ann.Gr.
Evangelical	0.1	17	+1.2%
Pentecostal & Charismatic	0.0	3	+2.2%

Missionaries from Syria
P,I,A 7 in 2 agencies.

Expatriates to Syria
P,I,A 19 in 7 agencies.

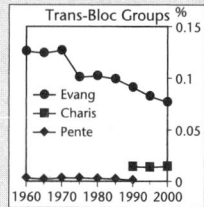

• Challenges for Prayer

1 **The Alawite minority regime** has retained power by crushing all political dissent. The country has been involved in wars and confrontations with surrounding states for the last 50 years. Pray for both political and religious freedom.

2 **Christian minorities are respected and tolerated** and have freedom to worship and witness within their own community, but all activities that could threaten the government or communal harmony are watched. Evangelicals currently enjoy good standing, so they are hesitant to jeopardize this by witnessing too forthrightly. Pray that they might discern how best to share Christ.

3 **The Muslim majority has a false conception of what a true Christian is.** Pray that they may be enlightened by contacts with believers who have a holy lifestyle and radiant witness. Many Muslims are in daily contact with Christians, as are Syrian soldiers based in Lebanon.

4 **Syrian Christians have been a respected minority** since the time of the church in Antioch (Acts 13). The Orthodox and Catholics survived the rule of the Byzantines, Muslim Arabs, Crusaders, and Ottomans. Most Christians are Arab, but there is also a large Armenian community. Christians are influential in the cities, professions, politics and the armed forces, but their percentage of the population is shrinking due to a high rate of emigration to the Americas and Africa. Pray that believers may rediscover the zeal of the church of Antioch, and experience spiritual renewal. Pray that they may move past tolerating, fearing or even despising their Muslim neighbours and adopt an attitude of warm-hearted love.

5 **The Protestant witness is small**, but churches are slowly growing. The majority of Protestant converts come out of the Orthodox and Catholic churches. There is an evangelical presence in most cities, but rarely in smaller towns. Lack of full-time workers and leadership development opportunities inhibit growth, but TEE is a helpful means for giving training. Pray for more TEE tutors. Pray also for the Lord to infuse the church with zeal for the lost and give Christians godly discernment in their witness.

6 **Conversions out of Islam are few, but increasing.** Spiritual bondages, social barriers and religious prejudices must be broken down before some will take the decisive step. For those who do, pray for perseverance in persecution, acceptance into fellowship by other believers and growth to maturity. Most churches in Syria are not yet ready to evangelize Muslims, let alone receive converts from Islam. There are signs of positive results from Bible Correspondence Courses and student outreach.

7 **Unreached peoples** to pray for:

a) *The Sunni Arab majority*, very few of whom have heard the gospel.

b) *The Alawites* who are a rural community, but very influential in the army and government. Their beliefs differ much from orthodox Islam. Little specific effort has been directed to them.

c) *The Druze* in the far south who are a secretive offshoot of Islam. They have been largely unresponsive, but there are a handful of converts.

d) *The Kurds* of the north and northwest who might be more receptive. Some are Orthodox Christian, others are Yezidis and Shi'a, but most are Sunni Muslim.

e) *The Bedouin, Circassian, Turkmen and Gypsy minorities* who are solidly Muslim with no known Christians.

8 **Foreign Christian workers are few, but some reside in the country.** Pray for a more open door to this needy land. Pray for the ministry of Christian professionals living in the country.

9 **Christian media.**

a) *Literature is freely available*, and there is a brisk sale of Bibles from the two Bible Society bookrooms. This organisation has become well known through the annual book fair. Many secular bookstores also regularly request shipments of the Scriptures for sale. Pray for the powerful impact of God's Word on all who read it.

b) *The JESUS film* is widely circulated on video cassette in Arabic. It is also available in Circassian, Iraqi Arabic, Western Armenian, Assyrian, Standard Kurmanji and Syriac. Pray for many non-Christians to follow Him as a result.

c) *Radio/Television.* Many Muslims listen to Christian radio. **TWR** broadcasts 11.5 hrs/wk in Arabic. Programmes aimed at Kurds in Turkey are heard by Syrian Kurds also. **SAT-7** has a valuable ministry in beaming Christian TV programmes to those with satellite dishes. Aleppo has more viewers of **SAT-7** than any other Arab city.

Tajikistan
Republic of Tajikistan

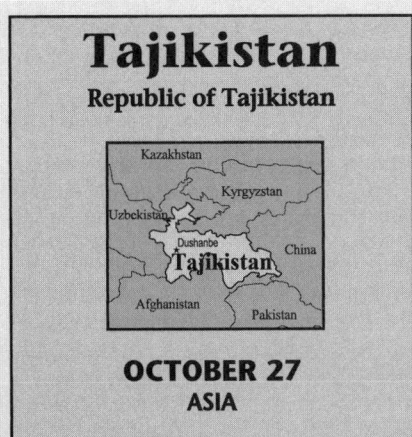

OCTOBER 27
ASIA

Population		Ann.Gr.	Density
2000	6,188,201	+1.48%	43 per sq. km.
2010	7,133,677	+1.58%	50 per sq. km.
2025	8,856,904	+1.27%	62 per sq. km.

Capital Dushanbe 582,400. **Urbanites** 28%.

PEOPLES
Civil war caused the exodus of the majority of non-indigenous peoples and a great loss of ethnic diversity.
Indo-European 72.2%.
Iranian 69.2%. Tajik 4.1mill; Pamir peoples (6) 78,000; Persian 50,000.
Slav 2.6%. Russian 136,000; Ukrainian 19,000. Other 0.4%.
Turkic/Altaic 27.2%. Uzbek 1.55mill; Kyrgyz 62,000; Tatar 35,000; Turkmen 19,000.
Other 0.6%.

Literacy 98%. **Official language** Tajik. **All indigenous languages** 10. **Languages with Scripture** 2Bi 3 w.i.p.

GEOGRAPHY
Area 143,100 sq.km. The southernmost republic of the former USSR bordering on Afghanistan, China, Uzbekistan and Kyrgyzstan. The Pamir and Tien-Shan Mountains are 93% of the surface area.

ECONOMY
Rich in minerals, coal, oil and hydroelectric power, thus far little used. The Soviet collapse and ensuing civil war have damaged

much of the economic infrastructure and reduced most of the population to poverty. The cost of the damage is estimated at eighteen times the GNP. Racketeers have muscled in on much of the nation's legitimate economy as well as illegal arms and drugs flowing from Afghanistan. **HDI** 0.665; 108th/174. **Public debt** 33.3% of GNP. **Income/person** $300 (1% of USA) the poorest of the former USSR republics.

POLITICS
The northern portion of the Persian Empire until the 12th Century. Russian colonial rule from the mid-19th Century. In 1929, Stalin abitrarily defined the borders of the Central Asian republics, deliberately creating large ethnic minorities in each to discourage ethnically-motivated insurgency against Moscow. After the Soviet collapse, civil war broke out, pitting ex-Communists against Islamists and secular democrats. With massive Russian support the former prevailed, although a 1997 peace accord was signed by all factions. Multi-party elections in 2000, albeit flawed, were a step forward.

RELIGION
Religious freedom is guaranteed, but fear of radical Islam provides the government with an excuse to watch all religious activity closely. Proselytism is not forbidden, but any activity causing religious tension is quashed.

Religions	Population %	Adherents	Ann.Gr.
Muslim	89.50	5,538,440	+1.8%
non-Religious	9.09	562,507	-0.7%
Christian	1.38	85,397	-4.0%
Other	0.03	1,857	-12.5%

Christians	Denom.	Affil.%	,000	Ann.Gr.
Protestant	5	0.06	4	+11.1%
Independent	3	0.00	0	+15.0%
Catholic	1	0.11	6	-6.3%
Orthodox	5	1.20	74	-4.2%
Marginal	1	0.01	1	+30.9%

Churches	MegaBloc	Cong.	Members	Affiliates
Russian Orthodox	O	16	49,000	70,000
Catholic	C	3	3,892	6,500
Baptist	P	20	500	1,000
Pentecostal	P	7	350	875
Seventh-day Adventist	P	6	583	874
Korean Pentecostal	P	4	225	750
Jehovah's Witnesses	M	6	250	673
Lutheran	P	2	299	500
Other denoms [7]		3	3,050	4,700
Total Christians [15]		67	58,100	85,900

Trans-bloc Groupings	pop.%	,000	Ann.Gr.
Evangelical	0.1	3	+15.3%
Charismatic	0.0	2	+12.2%
Pentecostal	0.0	2	+11.4%

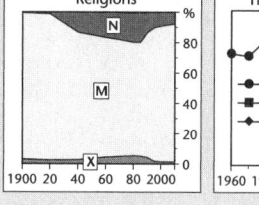
Religions

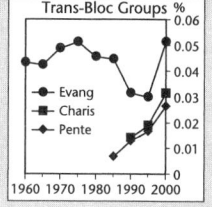
Trans-Bloc Groups %

• Answers to Prayer

1 **In 1992 there were only 2 or 3 Tajik believers,** in 2000 there were several hundred worldwide.

2 **The tragedies of the civil war** have opened people's hearts to the loving witness of Christians and response is encouraging.

• Challenges for Prayer

1 **The civil war ended** with the signing of a peace accord in 1997, but not before terrible damage was inflicted on the country. Over fifty thousand were killed and as many as one million were displaced. Poverty and extreme hardship is now common. Those under government care, such as prisoners, the aged, and orphans are most at risk. Pray that the peace might take root — sporadic violence continues — and allow the government to address the economic and social issues which keep people in poverty. Pray for stability that might enable Christians to offer physical and spiritual help.

2 **The Christian Church** is largely composed of ethnic Europeans, but has been drastically reduced by emigration. During the civil war, those fleeing were almost entirely non-Tajik, and represented much of the country's skilled labour. Pray that the remaining believers might see their unique opportunity to be witnesses to Tajiks and other unreached peoples. Pray for the establishment of a strong multi-ethnic Christian witness in each city which can then reach out to rural areas.

3 **Although 90 percent of citizens profess to be Muslims,** only a fraction regularly practice Islamic ritual. Most are more influenced by superstition and Zoroastrian beliefs. Nevertheless, the number of functioning mosques grew in a decade from 18 to 4,000. Islamists have significantly increased their strength in society since the 1997 peace accord granted them participation in the government. Tajikistan's proximity to Iran and Afghanistan makes it all the more vulnerable to Islamism. Pray for extremism to be restrained, and that Muslims might have unprecedented opportunities to discover Christ.

4 **Expatriate involvement.** Tajikistan, with its great social and spiritual needs, is open for sensitive Christian ministry. There is a network of agencies concerned for Tajikistan, but the civil war discouraged expatriate workers from entering until recently. Pray that the current freedoms for Christians and Christian workers might continue, despite opposition from both anti-religionists and Islamists. Several ministries are now being used of God: relief, development and aid distribution; English, computer and health education; prison ministry and other means. Pray for the calling and entry of more long-term personnel. Pray for ethnically related Iranians to become witnesses. They could have a unique role to play in winning Tajiks to Jesus.

5 **Tajiks number 10 to 11 million in Central Asia.** For nearly a thousand years, there was no significant outreach to Tajiks. Now, in addition to the hundreds of believers in Tajikistan, there are a further 1,000+ in neighbouring countries like Afghanistan, Pakistan and Uzbekistan. Pray for this growth to increase, and pray for the establishment of an indigenous Tajik Church free from undue Russian or Western influences. Pray also for good cooperation among all concerned for the Tajiks.

6 **The unreached.** Indigenous peoples with little opportunity to hear the gospel:

a) *Uzbeks.* The Uzbeks lost much in the war, and gained little from the new peace arrangements. They number 1.55 million, yet are neglected by the missions rightly focusing on Tajiks. Pray for Christian workers specifically called to witness to Uzbeks in Tajikistan.

b) *The mountain peoples of the Pamirs* in the east — there are no known Pamiri Christians. In that region live six Muslim peoples of the Ismaili sect — the Ishkashimi, Roshani, Bartangi, Shughni, Wakhi and Yazgulyam, who have never been reached.

c) *The 133 other ethnicities* in Tajikistan, the vast majority of whom have no specific Christian outreach.

7 Christian media ministries.

a) *The whole Bible in Tajik* (Cyrillic Script) was completed in 1992 (**IBT**). Thousands of New Testaments, Gospels, and tracts are being brought into the country; pray for their effective distribution. **GRN** has materials in seven languages.

b) *The JESUS film* is available in Dari, Farsi, Russian, Tajik and Uzbek and has been shown on national television. The video is in high demand in several languages.

c) *Christian radio.* **HCJB** and **TWR** both broadcast in Tajik fi hour/week. Various agencies broadcast in Uzbek a total of three hours/week. There are several more programmes in Farsi and Dari that can be understood, but too few people have short-wave radios to benefit from any of these.

T

Tanzania

Republic of Tanzania

OCTOBER 28-29
AFRICA

GEOGRAPHY
Area 945,037 sq.km. Comprising mainland Tanganyika and the offshore islands of Zanzibar and Pemba (2,460 sq.km.).

Population		Ann.Gr.	Density
2000	33,517,014	+2.29%	35 per sq. km.
2010	42,235,298	+2.33%	45 per sq. km.
2025	57,918,322	+1.98%	61 per sq. km.

Capital Dar-es-Salaam 3,000,000. Growth from 700,000 in 1990. Capital designate: Dodoma 250,000. **Urbanites** 25%.

PEOPLES
Indigenous ethnic groups 160+. Widespread promotion and use of Swahili has obscured some tribal divisions.
Bantu peoples 92.4%. 125 peoples, largest: Sukuma 3.2 mill.; Chagga(3) 1.56m; Gogo 1.37m; Haya 1.37m; Nyamwezi 1.2m; Makonde 1.14m; Ha 990,000; Hehe 860,000; Ruguru 692,000; Swahili-Shirazi 672,000; Bena 670,000; Kami 670,000; Shambala 664,000; Zaramo 627,000; Nyakyusa 550,000; Makhuwa 550,000; Yao 492,000; Mwera 469,000; Zigula 460,000; Hutu 440,000; Asu 431,000; Rangi 300,000.
Nilotic 2.9%. 8 peoples: Maasai(4) 526,000; Luo 280,000; Tatooga/Barabaig 200,000.
Cushitic 2%. 7 peoples: Iraqw 462,000; Somali 50,000.
Khoisan 0.4%. 7 peoples: Sandawe 80,000; the original San (Bushmen) inhabitants of central and southern Africa.
Other 2.3%. South Asian (predominantly Gujarati) 360,000; Arab 200,000; Chinese 15,000.
Refugees. Mainly Burundi and Rwanda Hutu. Also Somalis, Congolese, etc.

Literacy 68%. **Official languages** Swahili, English; 2% speak only Swahili and no local African language. **All languages** 135. **Languages with Scriptures** 17Bi 17NT 15por 10w.i.p.

ECONOMY
Agricultural subsistence economy yet with much potential for development. The disas-

trous experimentation with socialism after independence led to nationalization of many businesses and collectivization of rural communities. The results were a bloated bureaucracy, deterioration of industry and the infrastructure, serious reduction in living standards and drying up of international investment. During the 1990s the economy opened up resulting in steady improvement, but the reliance on foreign aid hampers entrepreneurial initiative. AIDS has become a serious problem. **HDI** 0.421; 156th/174. **Public debt** 92% of GNP. **Income/person** $210 (0.7% of USA).

POLITICS
Tanganyika gained independence from Britain in 1961, Zanzibar in 1963. The two countries united as a one-party federal socialist republic in 1964, though Zanzibar has retained a considerable degree of autonomy. The one-party system ended in 1992 and a multi-party democracy was instituted. For 35 years Tanzania has been an 'island of peace' in a troubled region. There are recurring differences between the Mainland and Zanzibar which threaten the bonds between them.

RELIGION
There is religious freedom, and equal rights and opportunities for both Muslims and Christians to worship and propagate their faiths.

Religions	Population %	Adherents	Ann.Gr.
Christian	51.42	17,234,449	+3.9%
Muslim	31.80	10,658,410	+2.4%
Traditional ethnic	15.15	5,077,828	-2.5%
Hindu	0.90	301,653	+4.7%
Baha'i	0.40	134,068	+2.3%
non-Religious/other	0.30	100,551	+2.3%
Sikh	0.03	10,055	+2.3%

Christians	Denom.	Affil.%	,000	Ann.Gr.
Protestant	46	16.86	5,650	+3.6%
Independent	41	2.23	749	+2.8%
Anglican	1	7.91	2,650	+10.6%
Catholic	1	24.76	8,300	+2.4%
Orthodox	1	0.04	13	+2.1%
Marginal	2	0.07	23	+5.2%
Unaffiliated		3.73	1,249	n.a.
Doubly affiliated		*-4.18*	*-1,400*	*n.a.*

Churches	MegaBloc	Cong.	Members	Affiliates
Catholic	C	800	4,486,486	8,300,000
Anglican	A	8,000	1,086,066	2,650,000
Evangelical Lutheran	P	6,500	1,000,000	2,500,000
Pentecostal Chs Assoc.	P	1,600	320,000	650,000
Africa Inland	P	500	180,000	540,000
Seventh-day Adventist	P	964	207,893	460,000
Assemblies of God	P	1,689	300,000	450,000
New Apostolic	I	1,125	225,000	450,000
Moravian	P	380	280,000	430,000
Baptist Convention	P	1,238	97,955	190,000
Mennonite [2]	P	340	43,000	95,000
Ch of God (Cleveland)	P	325	30,000	70,000
Pentecostal Holiness	P	100	33,000	65,000
Pentecostal AoG	P	800	33,000	55,000

Full Gospel Bible Fell	I	30	16,000	35,000
Foursquare Gospel	P	250	15,000	28,000
Jehovah's Witnesses	M	188	8,408	23,000
Pente Evang Fell (Elim)	P	160	7,000	16,000
Christian Brethren	P	95	3,500	9,000
Free Methodist	P	4	1,000	2,000
Other denoms [71]		2,005	149,500	367,000
Doubly affiliated			-583,000	-1,400,000
Total Christians [92]		27,100	7.940m	15.985m

Trans-bloc Groupings	pop.%	,000	Ann.Gr.
Evangelical	17.0	5,699	+6.4%
Charismatic	12.8	4,298	+4.8%
Pentecostal	4.7	1,576	4.4%

Missionaries from Tanzania
P,I,A 232 in 21 agencies, mainly within country.

Missionaries to Tanzania
P,I,A 1,272 in 110 agencies: USA 375, Germany 169, UK 117, Finland 80, Korea 78.

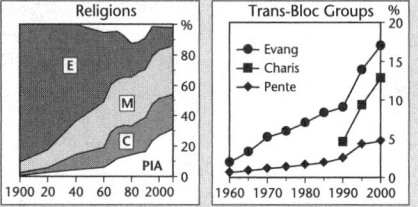

• Answers to Prayer

1 **Peaceful change** from the well-intentioned but disastrous socialist experiment to a more free, democratic society in 1992-1995.

2 **The dramatic growth of Evangelicals** in both Lutheran, Anglican and many Pentecostal denominations in the 1990s from 2.3 million (9.3%) in 1990 to 5.7 million (17.2%) in 2000, and the overall growth of Christians from 34% to 48%.

3 **The move of the Holy spirit in many denominations** resulting in vigorous outreach, bold faith and vision for advance. Many Muslims have been coming to Christ.

• Challenges for Prayer

1 **The delicate inter-communal balance and political stability of the country cannot be taken for granted.** The Muslim community is increasingly polarized between moderates and Islamists; the latter pressing for political influence and privileges and resentful of the perceived advantages enjoyed by Christians. Pray that the government may be wise and even-handed, and that communal harmony and religious freedom may be maintained in both the mainland and Zanzibar.

2 **The growth of the mainline Churches has been good but patchy.** Revival movements in both the Lutheran and Anglican Churches have brought life to traditional congregations; most of the bishops are Evangelicals. However, there are problems that limit growth in numbers and spirituality.
a) *There are extensive areas where the churches have stagnated* and where many potentially open villages are unreached. There are too few evangelists and church planters.
b) *Western cultural forms* combined with African worship patterns of singing, choirs and collections leave little time for biblical teaching.
c) *There is a critical lack of trained, mature leaders*. Many pastors have to care for 20 or more congregations.
d) *AIDS continues its frightening growth* and rapidly rising death rate. It has now afflicted over 1.3 million (8.1% of the population) and left 1.1 million orphaned children. The social fabric and economic structure of the country is being deeply affected. Pray for church teaching programmes aimed at slowing the spread of the disease, and for counselling clinics and care structures for victims.

3 **The Pentecostal movement** has flourished with many denominations growing. A wide range of evangelistic literature, media and social ministries have impacted the nation. Most are international; indigenous movements have been less influential than in other African countries. Pray for continued growth, increased maturity and unity across the evangelical spectrum — essential in the face of rising Muslim militancy.

4 **Leadership training** needs to be given top priority in the churches. Training facilities and funding are limited. Pray for the 15 or so Bible schools and seminaries in the country. Many need upgrading to higher levels to prepare leaders for an increasingly literate population. More use is being made of short-term residential training courses, **TEE** and also cassette Bible schools for training local leaders.

5 **Vision for the future** has rapidly developed during the 1990s with national conferences focusing on reaching the least evangelized.

a) ***Excellent research on Tanzania's peoples*** through Pioneer Bible Translators and others has shown the need. Over 100 peoples have many Christians, 11 have 10-25% Christian, 9 have 5-10% and 29 have less than 5% — many of these still unreached and with no church.

b) ***National congresses*** have been used of God to challenge the churches to work together and also send out missionaries. There are some serving cross-culturally in Zanzibar and on the coast. AIC has opened a missionary training college.

c) ***The AIC*** (daughter church of **AIM**) has set the goal of doubling their church population in the decade before their centenary year, 2008.

6 **Ministry among young people** has been particularly encouraging, but they face challenges of low employment prospects and increasing exposure to Western influences.

a) ***Schools are obliged to provide religious education***, but there are 53 schools for every qualified RE teacher. Christian teachers can and do have a big impact. Pray for church programmes to equip teachers for this key role.

b) ***Scripture Union*** has had a major impact, but leadership and vision is the need. Pray for a fresh anointing of the Spirit and a new cutting edge. **SU**'s 'Aid for AIDS' programme, encouraging young people to be morally pure, is a key ministry.

c) ***TAFES(IFES) groups*** in universities and colleges are large and evangelistic. Many students are being converted, including Muslims. Lack of staff workers is a hindrance to better national coverage and coordination of outreach and discipling. Pray for the 35 groups and five staff workers.

7 **The unfinished task in Tanzania**. Great growth among Christians must not obscure the real needs. The coast, Zanzibar and many of the peoples in the southern provinces are largely or almost entirely Muslim. Increased conversions from among Muslims still leave the great majority unreached. Pray specifically for:

a) ***Zanzibar*** which is famous for its cloves, but infamous as an Arab base for its centuries-long African slave trade.

i *On the two main islands,* Zanzibar (450,000) and Pemba (330,000) are three distinct indigenous ethnic groups. Almost all are Muslim, though there are a few believers. Many others are spiritually seeking, but held back by fear.

ii *Areas of special need:* Zanzibar Town, the east coast and the small Tumbatu Island are strongholds and spiritual oppression is intense.

iii *Christians* have increased in numbers, boldness and unity during the 1990s. There are more than 10 congregations on Zanzibar Island and 4 on Pemba. Pray for their preservation and effectiveness as witnesses.

b) ***The Muslim peoples of the coastal regions*** live under the curse of the historic slave trade. Most have few Christians — in some very few. Major challenges by region: **Tanga**: Digo (88,000), Dhaiso (29,000) and Somali. **Pwani/Dar-es-Salaam**: Zigula (no known church), Kami, Rufiji (75,000), Ngendereko (110,000). **Lindi**: Machinga (36,000), Ndonde (15,000), Ngindo (220,000). Pray that Christians from other ethnic groups among them may be used of God to bless them with the gospel.

c) ***The Inland peoples*** yet to be effectively reached: the Datooga and Barabaig (200,000), are largely animist and the Rangi and Chasi (40,000) are Muslim.

d) ***The peoples on the Mozambique border***. The Brethren from Germany have worked and prayed for a breakthrough among the Islamized Makonde and Yao, and are only now starting to see the beginnings of a harvest.

e) ***The South Asian community*** speaks a range of Indian languages, predominantly Gujarati, but also Hindi and Panjabi speakers are present. Most are Hindu or Muslim. There are relatively few Christians among them.

8 **Missionaries** continue to play a vital role with a wide range of ministries in outreach, church support, training and specialist ministries. Increasingly, nationals are replacing expatriates and the number of missionaries is falling. Major mission agencies are Lutherans (340, mainly Scandinavian and German), **AIM** (95), Anglicans (88 in **CMS** and Crosslinks), **SBC** (86), Swedish Free Mission (75), and **Brethren** (73, from Germany and Britain).

Christian support ministries:

a) *Bible translation* is now being tackled in earnest. It had been assumed that the widespread use of Swahili would have diminished the need. The three main agencies involved are **The Bible Society**, **SIL** and Pioneer Bible Translators. The latter have been used of God in mobilizing the Church for the unreached. There are 10 translation programmes under way, but a further 45 of a possible 79 languages definitely need translation teams.

b) *Christian literature* is vital for an increasingly literate nation, yet the poverty and difficulty of obtaining foreign currency to buy supplies hamper printing and distribution on a larger scale. Pray for more Tanzanians with the gifts and calling to write appropriate Christian articles and books. Pray also for the **Central Tanganyika Press** (Anglican), **Africa Inland Press**, *Kanisa la Biblia* **Publishers** (Bible commentaries and theological books), the extensive publishing and printing ministry of the Pentecostal Churches Association and for effective distribution of their products. **SU**, the Bible Society, the AIC and **CLC** have thriving Christian bookstores. The **Gideons** are active in placing New Testaments in schools.

c) *Missionary flying* is an essential service ministry to the Church and mission agencies because of the lack of good roads. **MAF**-Europe has its biggest operation in Tanzania — 10 aircraft (including one float plane on Lake Victoria) based at Dodoma and 7 satellite bases with 20 expatriate and 49 national workers. They are involved in moving Christian workers and maintaining medical programmes and outreach to the Maasai, Iraqw and Barabaig. Evangelism and the showing of the *JESUS* film at airstrips is one evangelistic spin-off! **MAF** have also developed ministry in e-mail support which is well used in rural areas.

d) *Christian radio* has greatly expanded. The Lutherans, Pentecostal Churches Association/**IBRA** and **TWR** have recording studios. **IBRA** has a daily listenership of over 5 million in Swahili and a good letter response. **FEBA** uses 16 local stations and its shortwave station in the Seychelles for daily programmes in Swahili (10 hrs/wk), Makonde and Yao. **TWR** broadcasts from Swaziland and Johannesburg, South Africa in English (28 hrs/wk), Swahili (14) and Yao (2). In 1993 Christians took on one of the three national TV channels. Pray for lasting fruit in lives to result.

e) *The JESUS film* is being widely used in 15 languages and a further 27 are in preparation.

f) *GRN* have recordings in 82 languages. Cassettes are widely used for evangelism, Scripture reading and teaching.

Thailand
Kingdom of Thailand

OCTOBER 30-31
ASIA
Revised February 2004

T

GEOGRAPHY
Area 513,115 sq.km. A fertile and well-watered land bordering on Myanmar, Laos, Cambodia and Malaysia.

Population		Ann.Gr.	Density
2000	61,399,249	+0.93%	120 per sq. km.
2010	66,510,844	+0.78%	130 per sq. km.
2025	72,716,978	+0.49%	142 per sq. km.

Capital Bangkok 10 mill. Other major cities: Chiengmai 1m; Khorat 235,000. **Urbanites** 34%.

PEOPLES

Thai 80.4%.
Thai 79.9%. Four main peoples: Central 21.5m; Isan (Lao-Thai) 16.3m; Northern 6.5m; Southern 4.8m.
Tai 0.5%. 9 peoples, largest: Lao Phuan 97,000; Lu 83,000; Phuthai 62,000; Shan 60,000; Nyaw 55,000.
Chinese 10.5%. Most now Thai-speaking. They control 85% of the Thai economy.
Malay 3.8%. Most in the far south.
Mon-Khmer 3.4%. 20 peoples, largest: Khmer (Cambodian) 1.2m; Kui 217,000; So 58,000.
Tibeto-Burman 1.1%. 15 peoples, largest: Karen(6) 540,000; Lahu(2) 32,000.
Meo-Yao 0.2%. 4 peoples, largest: Meo (Hmong, 3) 76,000; Yao 37,000.
Other 0.6%. South Asians 200,000; Vietnamese 104,000; Westerners, Koreans, Japanese.

Literacy 94%. **Official language** Thai. **All languages** 75. **Languages with Scriptures** 15Bi 9NT 11por 27w.i.p.

ECONOMY

Fertile agricultural land — exporting rice, sugar, rubber. Rapid industrialization has led to a strong electronic and garment industry. Endemic corruption at every level of society has hastened deforestation, slowed taming of drug trafficking from the 'Golden Triangle' in the far northwest of the country and helped precipitate the Asian economic crash in the late 1990s. **HDI** 0.753; 67th/174. **Public debt** 13% of GNP. **Income/person** $2,740 (9% of USA).

POLITICS

A kingdom since the 13th Century, and never ruled by a Western power. Constitutional monarchy, with the popular king having a strong unifying and stabilizing role. The powerful army dominated politics and commercial life for 60 years. Corrupt, selfish practices of army leaders spread corruption to all levels of society and served to protect crime, prostitution, drug-dealing and arms rackets. The army's violent suppression of pro-democracy demonstrations in 1992 led to its humiliation. Successive civilian governments have paid lip-service to purging corruption from society, but in practice little has changed. Grass-roots and media pressure may force through some of the desired reforms.

RELIGION

Freedom of religion is guaranteed in the constitution, which was modified in 1998 to loosen ties between the State and Buddhism and increase harmony between religious communities.

Religions	Population %	Adherents	Ann.Gr.
Buddhist	92.34	56,696,067	+0.6%
Muslim	5.24	3,217,321	+2.1%
Christian	1.62	994,668	+4.7%
Chinese	0.40	246,000	-1.4%
Other	0.40	245,000	+6.9%

Christians	Denom.	Affil.%	,000	Ann.Gr.
Protestant	48	0.47	290	+3.4%
Independent	28	0.43	266	+7.3%
Anglican	1	0.00	0	-0.7%
Catholic	1	0.42	255	+0.6%
Marginal	3	0.02	12	+4.7%
Unaffiliated		0.28	171	n.a.

Churches	MegaBloc	Cong.	Members	Affiliates
Catholic	C	350	137,838	255,000
Ch of Christ in T (CCT)	P	481	50,000	69,000
Karen Baptist Conv	P	88	16,730	30,000
Chr Chs/Chs of Chr	P	140	12,500	22,000
Seventh-day Adventist	P	37	10,924	20,974
Lahu Baptist Conv	P	108	8,130	20,325
Hope of God Intl	I	500	10,000	18,000
Chs Related To OMF	P	229	8,000	16,000
Finnish Free Mission	P	63	6,000	15,000
Full Gospel Ch Found.	P	32	5,000	10,000
Thai Bapt Chs Assoc	P	48	3,771	8,372
Latter-day Saints (Morm)	M	35	4,216	7,800
Gospel Church of T	P	112	4,004	7,195
Evang Covenant	P	330	3,400	7,140
Full Gospel Fell Ch	P	39	3,600	7,000
Chr Fellowship (AoG)	P	89	4,000	6,500
Jehovah's Witnesses	M	52	1,827	4,348
Bonds of Fellowship	P	95	1,600	4,000
Other denoms [63]		1,859	124,300	295,600
Total Christians [81]		4,687	416,000	824,000

Trans-bloc Groupings	pop.%	,000	Ann.Gr.
Evangelical	0.7	437	+6.4%
Charismatic	0.6	345	+6.8%
Pentecostal	0.1	70	+9.3%

Missionaries from Thailand
P,I,A 884 in 24 agencies to 6 countries: Thailand 875.

Missionaries to Thailand
P,I,A 1,500 in 130 agencies from 33 countries: USA 617, Korea 188, Philippines 138, Australia 70, Canada 68, Germany 67, Finland 65, UK 58. **C** 400. **M** 100.

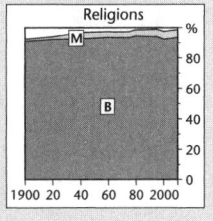

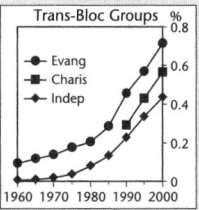

• Answers to Prayer

1 **Rising interest and more church growth in the 1990s** could signify an impending breakthrough. There is expectancy and even excitement that after little growth for a century the harvest is beginning to be gathered. In 1900 Christians were 0.6% of the population; in 1985 this had only risen to 0.9% but in 2000 this reached 1.6%.

2 **Christian radio, the *JESUS* film, drama** and a growing prayer movement are all giving a new level of spiritual response.

• Challenges for Prayer

1 **Thailand means *Land of the Free*** because it successfully retained its freedom when surrounding countries were colonized by Western powers. It is believed that a special guardian angel, *Phra Sayam Devadhiraj*, protected the land, and a golden image of this spirit being was made. It has been worshipped ever since. The land is in bondage to a complex web of culture, spirit appeasement, occult practices and Buddhism, with a social cohesiveness out of which few have dared to come. For many Thai, their nationality and religion are inextricably linked. Pray for the spiritual breakthrough so that in the Lord Jesus the Thai may be free indeed.

2 **The rottenness at the core of Thai society** can only be fully excised and cleansed through a turning to God. Corrupt military, government and police leaders have protected the large sex trade, drug networks, crime syndicates and ecological degradation of the country. The sex 'industry' contributes 14% to the GDP of the country. The informal economy is larger than the official economy. Pray that honest, just leaders may be raised up who will also lay legal and social frameworks that will limit corruption.

3 **The growth of the Church has been disappointing.** After four centuries of Catholic and 175 years of Protestant work, Thai Christians are only 1.6% of the population. The Catholic Church's percentage has scarcely increased in 40 years. Only in the 1980s did Protestants begin to do any better. Much of the growth has been among the Thai-speaking Chinese in cities and the marginalized tribal peoples. Pray for:

a) *The Church of Christ in Thailand*, the largest Protestant denomination (within which many denominational missions serve). Nominalism and theological compromise are problems, with marginal growth since 1960.

b) *The Evangelical Fellowship of Thailand*. This links the majority of evangelical bodies in fellowship. In 1992 there were over 1,200 congregations, 56 national ministries and 53 expatriate organizations linked with the EFT.

c) *High standards of holiness in church life*. Church leaders need to squarely face up to syncretism, a high rate of backsliding, misuse of church funds and a tolerant condoning of sin resulting in failure to discipline leaders who err.

d) *A true indigenization of the Thai Church*. Thai music, hymnody, art forms, worship patterns and architecture need to be encouraged and developed under the Holy Spirit's guidance.

e) *Ethnic Chinese churches* have multiplied, especially in Bangkok, and Chinese Christians are a significant minority in the Church. The dynamism and financial clout of this community, if fully activated, could be a significant force for evangelization. There are too few ethnic Chinese full-time workers.

f) *Revival*. Increased wealth is leading to a complacency and materialism that deadens passion for God and concern for evangelism.

g) *New spiritual vitality and vision*. Many congregations are poor, rural and often illiterate.

4 **The lack of Thai leadership** in the churches is a contributory factor to the slow growth, failures of rural churches and lack of vision. In 1995 there were only 400 pastors in evangelical churches — about a quarter of the number of missionaries. Pray for more to be called and kept in pastoral ministry. There are about 20 Bible schools and seminaries and a further 7 TEE programmes operating in the country. Many graduates do not go into full-time church-planting or pastoral work. Pray for the **Bangkok Bible College** (initiated by **CMA** and **OMF**, with 140 graduates), **Phayao Bible College** (**OMF** with 200 students and 1,000 graduates) and many denominational Bible colleges. Praise God for fine evangelical leaders in churches, but those with integrity and who are adequately trained and mature are few. Deference given to older pastors inhibits the development of younger workers.

5 **Missions** have considerable freedom for ministry despite a quota system which somewhat restricts the number of visas. Major involvement in the past was institutional; medical work and schools playing an important role in winning the first converts and planting the first churches in many parts of the land. The major emphasis is now on urban and rural evangelism, church planting and Bible teaching. Pray for:

a) *The calling, entry and preparation of new workers* to this exacting field. There are good opportunities for sharing the gospel through teaching English and ministry in schools.

b) *Safety*. Disease, road accidents and insurgency have led to the loss of a number of missionaries.

c) *Effective partnership* with Thai believers in strategic outreach.

d) *The major agencies*. **OMF** has 163 missionaries in five fields (among tribal peoples in the north, Thai in the centre, south and Bangkok). Other major agencies: **NTM** (90 in tribal work), **CCCI** (74), **IMB-SBC** (73), **AoG** (53), **WEC** (51 in the northwest and

Bangkok), **CMA** (50), **YWAM** (41 in refugee work and evangelism), Tribes and Nations Outreach (37), SdA (34), Finnish Free Mission (34).

Sectors of the population with special ministry needs:

a) *Bangkok*, one of Asia's most influential cities, and known as the city of angels and city of sin. Over 2 million derive their income from the sex 'industry'. Most of the country's 100,000 male and 700,000 female prostitutes cater to the lusts of Thai and foreign 'tourists'. Crime, drugs and alcohol abuse are widespread. AIDS has become a major scourge — some estimate that 40 — 80% of prostitutes end up with the disease. Pray for Thai and expatriate Christians seeking to win people from sin to Christ in this traffic-clogged, polluted city (Servants to Asia's Urban Poor, **AoG**, **IMB-SBC**, **WEC** and others). There are only an estimated 40,000 evangelical believers in the city.

b) *Children in crisis*. Many girls are kidnapped or sold at a very young age into prostitution — which includes terrible abuse and, in all likelihood, an early death. Many come from Thai ethnic minorities and the surrounding nations. It is estimated that 20% of all Thai girls between 11 and 17 become involved. There are over 35,000 homeless street children. There are over 5 million children involved in child labour. Pray for all involved in reaching out and seeking to rescue these tragic little ones.

c) *AIDS victims*. The official figure in 1999 was 755,000 with HIV; the true figure may be nearer 2 million and rising fast, despite vigorous action by the government. The churches need to wake up to this crisis and minister life to the suffering and the bereaved.

d) *Of the 73 provinces* 14 had fewer than 1,000 Christians of any type in 1992, and three had less than 100 (Phangnga, Ranong and Angtong); four had no evangelical congregations. The situation in 2000 had only marginally improved.

e) *The middle and upper classes*, wealthy and educated, but showing little response to the gospel. By contrast, interest in the occult and necromancy is reported to be strong.

f) *Students*. Witness to them is small but growing. Twelve Christian hostels for students, run by six agencies, have proved valuable for discipling students and initiating Christian campus groups. **YFC**, TCS(**IFES**), **CCCI** and an indigenous movement called *Yuwakrit* have seen conversions and growth of groups on campuses. The vast majority of the 1.2 million students remain unevangelized.

g) *Buddhist monks* number over 300,000. The monastic institution has been discredited by high-profile scandals. Pray for Christian outreach to them — many are genuinely seeking peace.

h) *Refugees* — hundreds of thousands from Laos, Cambodia and Vietnam found refuge in Thailand during the Vietnam War. Only the Hmong from Laos are still a major challenge, most of the refugees having been resettled elsewhere or returned home. There are possibly 1 million more recent arrivals from Myanmar, whose military government wages a brutal war against the ethnic minorities — especially the Karen.

Of the 2.5 million Muslims, 90% are Malay. Nearly all live in the five southern-most provinces, where there has been political tension and guerrilla activity by Communists (until 1992) and also by Muslim separatists. This is the only major Malay community in Asia open for evangelism, yet after years of hard work only about 100 have turned to Christ. The upsurge in Islam in Malaysia to the south is affecting the Thai Malays and complicating outreach. Many seekers are held back by fear. Pray for the local believers and missionary team, and for their outreach through postal evangelism, radio and literature. The Jawi Malay New Testament is being distributed to Malays, as well as a new BCC in Thai and Malay especially written to help Malay Muslims.

The tribal peoples, largely marginalized through lack of personal documentation and ignorance of the Thai language, have begun to respond in significant numbers. This follows years of hard work by Baptists and **WEC** among the Karen, and **OMF** among eight tribes in the north. The younger work of **NTM** in 12 tribes around the country is beginning to see results in tribal churches planted. Many workers are needed to win and disciple tribal peoples. Pray for:

a) *The multiplying, but scattered congregations* among the northern Hmong, Lahu, Lisu, Akha and Karen peoples. Lack of leaders and second-generation nominalism are problems. The Buddhist Shan and Taoist/animist Yao have been less responsive.

b) **The Kui, Khmu and Khmer** peoples in the east who are unreached. **CMA** works in the area, but there are insufficient workers to concentrate on them, especially the newly responsive Northern Khmer. The Kui New Testament was recently published (**CMA**) and there are now four churches and about 150 Kui believers. The Mennonites have commenced work among the Khmu.

c) **The Golden Triangle.** Opium poppies are the only lucrative cash crop for most of the northern tribes. Cultivation is an acute temptation for Christians and a formidable barrier to repentance for non-believers. The narcotics trade breeds insecurity and violence. Pray for believers and missionaries in sensitive areas.

d) **A Tribal Discipleship Center**, run by **AO,** is providing some workers for the harvest.

9 **Christian Help Ministries** are well developed in Thailand and bearing fruit.

a) **Bible translation** is still a major target for prayer. Work is in progress in 27 languages — main agencies being Thailand Bible Society, **IBS, SIL, NTM** and **OMF**. Of 29 languages without Scriptures, 10 definitely need translation programmes. There are four different versions of the Thai Bible in circulation.

b) **Christian radio** has been very effective. Many Thai stations daily air Christian programmes. **FEBC**, Full Gospel Mass Communications and Voice of Peace Studio prepare a wide range of programmes. Response from **FEBC**'s 22 half-hour programmes a day has been gratifying — 2,500 letters a month; 100 are referred to churches every month and 6,000 are doing BCCs. Response has been from both Buddhists and Muslims.

c) **Christian literature** is increasing. Over 1,000 Thai books have been published. There is increasing cooperation between publishers (such as **CLC**, **OMF** [Kanok] and **CMA**). There are more than 20 Christian bookstores in the land, 3 of which are run by **CLC**.

d) **The JESUS film** has been viewed by an equivalent of a third of the population in 17 languages; a further 15 are in preparation.

e) **Cassette ministries** were first developed in Thailand. The **Voice of Peace Studio** pioneered the use of evangelistic and teaching cassettes, which are most effective in rural areas. **GRN** have produced materials in 64 languages and have a key base in Chiengmai.

Timor Leste

East Timor

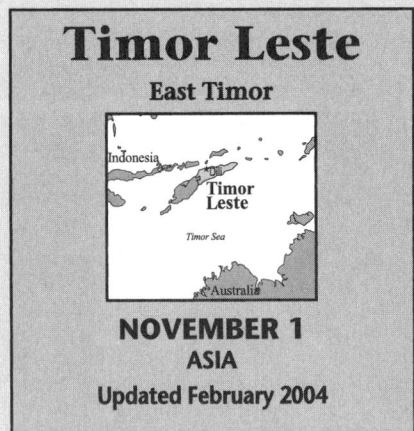

NOVEMBER 1

ASIA

Updated February 2004

GEOGRAPHY
Area 14,874 sq.km. Eastern half of Timor and the Ocussi-Ambenu enclave in Indonesian West Timor and Atauro Island.

Population		Ann.Gr.	Density
2000	884,541	+1.68%	59 per sq. km.
2010	1,015,062	+1.35%	68 per sq. km.
2025	1,185,000	+0.79%	80 per sq. km.

At the beginning of 2001 there were still over 100,000 refugees from Timor Leste; most held in camps in West Timor and elsewhere.

Capital Dili, an estimated 40,000 in 2001; much of the city was destroyed in 1999.

PEOPLES
Approximate percentages for 1998 in brackets.
Timorese 96.1% [78%].
  Indo-Malay 79%; 9 peoples. Largest: Tetun (Tetum) 370,000; Mamba 96,000; Kemak 60,000; Ambenu 60,000; Galoli 60,000; Tukudete 50,000.
  Papuan 17.1%; 6 peoples. Largest: Makasae 70,000; Bunak 50,000; Dagoda (Fatukulu) 30,000.
Indonesian 2% [20%]. Most fled with the ending of Indonesian occupation.
Other 1.9%. Chinese 4,000; UN forces and officials.
Literacy low. **Official language** Portuguese (10% understand it), Tetun is understood by 50%, and most understand Indonesian. **All languages** 17. **Languages with Scriptures** 2Bi 1por 1w.i.p.

ECONOMY
Ignored by the Portuguese, much developed by the Indonesian military but more as a source for the enrichment of the elite, then destroyed in vengeance after the vote for independence in 1999. The new nation must re-build from nothing. Potential in agriculture, sandalwood, minerals and also oil and gas. The majority live in deep poverty. An agreement with Australia over exploitation of oil and gas in the Timor Sea could yield important revenue.

<table>
<tr><td colspan="2">POLITICS</td><td>Religions</td><td>Population %</td><td>Adherents</td><td>Ann.Gr.</td></tr>
</table>

POLITICS

Portuguese rule from 1511 to 1974 followed by a precipitate hand-over to ill-prepared Timorese. In the ensuing civil war, Indonesian invasion and suppression, famines, lack of health facilities and economic distress, possibly 200,000 people died and population growth was stunted. The Indonesian occupation and Timorese resistance made a mockery of claims that integration of East Timor into Indonesia was voluntary. International pressure led to a referendum on independence in 1999. Heavily armed militia supported by the army systematically looted and destroyed much of the country's infrastructure, buildings and economy before the UN intervened. Approximately 75% of the population became refugees. The UN-led administration handed over to a Timorese government in 2001, but it will take decades for the battered nation to be able to stand on its own.

RELIGION

Catholicism was the state religion and the religion of the elite until 1975. It became the only viable and organized Timorese social structure after 1999. There is concern that non-Catholic religious minorities could be subject to discrimination.

Religions	Population %	Adherents	Ann.Gr.
Christian	89.16	788,657	+2.5%
Traditional ethnic	8.22	72,709	+4.7%
Muslim	2.10	18,575	-17.6%
Chinese	0.30	2,654	-14.2%
Hindu	0.20	1,769	-6.2%
Baha'i	0.02	177	-11.5%

Christians	Denom.	Affil.%	,000	Ann.Gr.
Protestant	2	3.96	35	-3.1%
Independent	2	0.11	1	+7.4%
Catholic	1	85.09	753	+3.0%

Churches	MegaBloc	Cong.	Members	Affiliates
Catholic	C	55	442,800	752,700
Assemblies of God	P	60	12,000	18,000
IPTL — Reformed Ch of T	P	50	10,000	17,000
Other denoms [2]		5	500	1,000
Total Christians [5]		170	465,265	788,700

Trans-bloc Groupings	pop.%	,000	Ann.Gr.
Evangelical	2.5	22	+4.3%
Charismatic	2.8	25	+5.8%
Pentecostal	2.0	18	+6.7%

Missionaries to Timor Leste:
P,I,A 50 in 5 agencies from 6 countries.

• Challenges for Prayer

1 **Timor's birth as a nation was traumatic.** The vindictive destruction of life and property and the forcible abduction of many Timorese by the departing Indonesian military and their Timorese allies have left a legacy of hatred and trauma that will take decades to heal. Pray that Christians might contribute effectively to the spiritual, moral and economic recovery and health of the Timorese people.

2 **Timor's future is uncertain.** The UN Temporary Administration had an overwhelming task of defending the country and laying the basic structures for administration and economic survival, but the visibly high living standards of the 7,000 UN military and civilians, and lack of cultural sensitivity created resentment. Pray for all seeking the welfare of Timor, and pray for the new indigenous government to further national unity despite ancient ethnic and recent political divisions.

3 **The Catholic Church** grew fast as a visible symbol of national resistance to the Indonesians, but the deep occultism of the ethnic religions remains strong. Protestants have been viewed with suspicion as originating from Indonesia. Pray that there may be both religious and also spiritual freedom for Timorese.

4 **Only in recent years have Protestant churches gained a foothold.** The Assemblies of God was started in the 1960s by Alorese Indonesians and has grown strongly on Atauro Island and in Dili. The IPTL (GKTT) was started by Indonesian immigrants and many Timorese joined — but rarely with true conversion. Nominalism and lack of understanding of the gospel characterize the majority. About half its membership fled to Indonesia in 1999. There is great need for biblically trained and spiritually active pastors. Pray that this latter Church may experience new life, find purpose and become a blessing. Pray that evangelical churches may be planted in every people and area of Timor. **Christian Vision** has a three-year plan for evangelism and church planting for the whole country in association with the **AoG**.

5 Specific ministry challenges:

a) Traumatized children and young people — many have lost all, including parents. Droves roam the streets; youth unemployment runs at 80%. Pray for effective holistic ministry and discipleship ministries to be established to help them and also the churches in the process.

b) ***Almost all Timor's peoples are still unreached.*** Only among the Tetun have there been significant conversions to Christ. Only Tetun has anything of the Scriptures (the NT) but at least 7 and maybe up to 13 languages need their own translations. Pray for pioneer church planters and translators to be sent to them.

6 **Foreign missions.** Many NGOs have entered to give help at different levels. Pray for effective strategies that empower the effectiveness of the churches. The great need is for long-term involvement in the life and cultures of the people and for effective discipling and modelling ministries. Significant missions: **Christian Vision** (30), **WEC** (10), **YWAM** (6) and Baptists (4).

Togo
Togolese Republic

NOVEMBER 2
AFRICA

 **GEOGRAPHY**
Area 56,785 sq.km. The Atlantic coastline is only 56 km long but the little land stretches 540 km northwards to the Sahel. Wedged between Ghana and Benin.

Population	Ann.Gr.	Density
2000	4,629,218	+2.66%	82 per sq. km.
2010	5,953,281	+2.55%	105 per sq. km.
2025	8,482,467	+2.19%	149 per sq. km.

Capital Lomé 700,000. **Urbanites** 31%.

PEOPLES
Over 78 ethnic groups in 2 major language families.
Kwa 53.4%. Mainly in the southern half of Togo; largest: Ewe 1,050,000; Wachi 570,000; Mina 327,000; Ife-Yoruba(3) 166,000; Aja 142,000; Akposo 121,000; Anufo (Chakossi) 53,000; Akebu 52,000; Fon 46,000; Mahi 30,000.
Gur 42.4%. Mainly in the north; largest: Kabiye (Kabré) 730,000; Kotokoli (Tem) 300,000; Moba (Bimoba) 243,000; Nawdm (Losso) 187,000; Lama (Lamba) 177,000; Gurma 154,000; Ntcham 150,000; Konkomba 67,000; Akaselem (Chamba) 45,000; Ngangam 44,000; Taberma (Somba) 26,000; Mossi 25,000.
Foreign 2.2%. Ghanaian, Beninese, Nigerian, French, Lebanese.
Other 2%. Fulbe 64,000; Hausa 13,000; Bisa 10,000.

Literacy 52%. **Official language** French. **All languages** 43. Only two indigenous languages used in education system: Ewe/Mina and Kabiye. **Languages with Scriptures** 6Bi 7NT 3por 12w.i.p.

ECONOMY
Subsistence agriculture involves 80% of the population. Main exports are phosphates, cotton, cocoa. Economic growth lags behind population growth because of endemic corruption and a large, inefficient state sector. Much foreign aid has been suspended because of lack of fiscal discipline and a poor human rights record. **HDI** 0.469; 143rd/174. **Public debt** 81% of GNP. **Income/person** $300 (1.1% of USA).

POLITICS
German colony 1884-1914. Independent from France in 1960. One-party military-civilian regime in power since 1967. Pressure internally and externally to open up the country to multi-party democracy led to a national conference in 1991 in which Eyadema, the President, was stripped of his powers and a transitional government installed. A referendum in 1992 confirmed a multi-party constitution, but its provisions were eroded in a contest of power between Eyadema and the transitional government. This degenerated into anarchy and virtual civil war between the southern and central peoples. Eyadema, a Kabiye from the north, maintains a facade of democracy, but personally controls the military, the justice system and all political processes.

RELIGION

A period of intense anti-Christian rhetoric in the 1970s cooled to an official indifference. In 1978, 20 religious groups were banned, only Muslims, Catholics and five Protestant churches were legally permitted to function. In 1990 nearly all restrictions were lifted, and there has been considerable religious freedom since.

Religions	Population %	Adherents	Ann.Gr.
Christian	50.66	2,345,162	+4.1%
Traditional ethnic	24.34	1,126,752	-0.8%
Muslim	24.00	1,111,012	+3.5%
non-Religious/other	1.00	46,292	+7.3%

Christians	Denom.	Affil.%	,000	Ann.Gr.
Protestant	20	12.33	571	+10.9%
Independent	53	5.43	251	+9.5%
Catholic	1	24.84	1,150	+3.8%
Marginal	1	0.86	40	+6.4%
Unaffiliated		7.20	333	n.a.

Churches	MegaBloc	Cong.	Members	Affiliates
Catholic	C	140	631,868	1,150,000
Evang Presbyterian	P	516	117,000	300,000
Assemblies of God	P	680	110,000	150,000
Methodist	P	70	22,000	45,000
Jehovah's Witnesses	M	162	11,011	40,000
Baptist Convention	P	260	15,010	38,000
New Apostolic	I	81	16,111	29,000
Ch of Pentecost	I	170	8,500	22,000
Evangelical Baptist	P	40	2,600	6,000
Lutheran	P	35	1,700	6,000
Team Togo	P	12	350	600
Other denoms [64]		1,989	133,113	226,000
Total Christians [75]		4,155	1,069,000	2,012,000

Trans-bloc Groupings	pop.%	,000	Ann.Gr.
Evangelical	9.0	417	+13.8%
Charismatic	7.8	362	+14.4%
Pentecostal	3.8	174	+19.9%

Missionaries from Togo
P,I,A 97 in 13 agencies to 8 countries: Togo 81.

Missionaries to Togo
P,I,A 256 in 28 agencies from 27 countries: USA 138, France 24, Nigeria 19, Ghana 17.

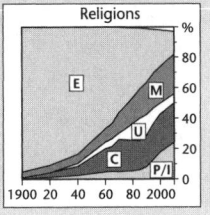

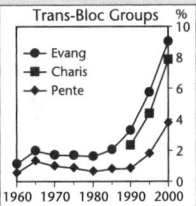

• Answers to Prayer

1 **Regaining religious freedom in 1990** has given a decade of more rapid church growth and reaching of many peoples for the first time. Evangelicals have grown from 17,000 in 1960 to nearly 400,000 in 2000.

2 **The Assemblies of God set the goal of 300 churches and 36,000 members by 2000.** They exceeded this with 110,000 members by the beginning of 2001.

• Challenges for Prayer

1 **The government of Eyadema** has been maintained by manipulation of elections, widespread human rights abuses and crushing of any dissension through fear and poverty. The southern peoples have been politically marginalized. Pray that those in leadership might have a change of heart or be replaced by those who fear God, respect the constitution and treat every section of society fairly.

2 **The Church in Togo stagnated between 1960 and 1990.** The long established Evangelical Presbyterian Church became theologically liberal and nominal and remained confined to the Ewe, while the Methodists remained among the Mina. The Catholics likewise only grew slowly. During the 1980s newer evangelical groups began to grow — the **AoG** (once mainly in the north and now predominantly in the south), the Baptists (**IMB-SBC** and ABWE in the south) and the Missouri Synod Lutherans among the Moba in the north have all seen encouraging results. Many new denominations from outside Togo commenced work in the '90s and all denominations began to grow rapidly. Pray for the establishment of strong, indigenous congregations and denominations with visionary leadership.

3 **Leaders for the young churches are few,** and training facilities in Togo limited. Pray for appropriate vernacular and French Bible Schools and TEE programmes to be launched. The Baptist School of Theology and **AoG** Advanced School of Theology in Lomé serve Francophone countries all over West Africa. There are several recently-started Bible schools. Pray for many more Spirit-filled Togolese leaders to be raised up for the multiplying churches.

4 **The whole body of Christ in Togo is beginning to unite in common vision** for reaching every part of their land — and beyond. Pray for barriers of mistrust and denominationalism to be broken down and for a Great Commission movement to be firmly established. A national survey of the unfinished task was under way by 2001 on behalf of many evangelical churches and agencies with the help of **SIL**. Pray for its successful conclusion and results that lead to church planting among these peoples.

5 **The strongly entrenched powers of darkness have scarcely been challenged** through intercessory prayer and confrontation with the power of the gospel. The two major forces to be tackled:

a) *The idolatry and strong secret societies* of the Ewe, Fon and other tribes with intense opposition to the gospel. Christians cannot grow in their faith until they have fully repented and renounced the works of darkness.

b) *The growing strength of Islam*. Muslims dominate in trading, taxi services, and in national education throughout Togo. There is a steady stream of conversions to Islam throughout the country, yet there are few Christian workers focused on Muslim evangelism in the eight Muslim peoples or the high concentrations of Muslims in urban areas — a total of 1,100,000.

6 **The less-evangelized peoples of Togo**. Togo and Benin have long had the highest percentage of unevangelized traditionalists in Africa. In 1990, 15 peoples had evangelical congregations in their cultures, 25 had none. Many of these unreached peoples now have congregations or groups of believers, but in most, only a beginning has been made. The major challenges:

a) *The eight majority-Muslim peoples* — the Kotokoli (**SIM**, **IMB-SBC** and now 50 believers), Anufo (**YWAM**, 200 believers), Akaselem (**AoG**, handful of believers), Bago (9,000), Akpe (4,000) and Anii (1,000) as well as the more dispersed Hausa and Fulbe (Baptists).

b) *The northern traditional peoples* — the Nawdm (**AoG**, Baptist, Deeper Life), Konkomba (Ghana workers), Taberma (**AoG**, Baptist, Church of Pentecost), Sola, Lokpa, Mossi (AoG), Bisa. Pray for these pioneering efforts to see breakthroughs for the gospel.

c) *The south-central traditional peoples* — the Akebu, Anyanga, Adele, Delo and Kpessi.

d) *The southern coastal area* which is poorly researched. There are likely to be many unmet needs among the Fon, Mahi and others.

Many of these peoples could be best reached by Ghanaian and Benin believers who are of the same language group.

7 **Ministries to young people and children developed rapidly** in the greater freedoms of the 1990s.

a) *Schools and the university* — **CCCI** and GBUST(**IFES**) have campus ministries with a growing number of students involved. The latter had 33 groups with 700 members in 1998. **SU** has a good ministry in high schools — but many schools have not yet a witness. Pray for the development of mature believers and groups.

b) *Churches are generally ill-equipped* to address the needs of children or young people. Pray for more with vision and gifting to change this situation.

c) *There is a significant evil trade in children* who are 'exported' to other lands for the sex industry. Pray that this may be ended.

8 **Evangelical missions have been few**, but have increased in number during the '90s. Church planters, disciplers and leadership trainers are needed. The largest missions are **YWAM** (64), ABWE (46), **IMB-SBC** (38), **AoG** and Ministry of Jesus (22).

9 **Bible translation remains a major ministry challenge**. Pray especially for the completion of the whole Bible in Kabiye — one of the two indigenous languages used in schools. There are at least six and possibly a further 12 languages into which the NT should be translated. Work is in progress in 17 languages, 10 of which are in the hands of the 37 **SIL** workers. Pray that there might be adequate teaming up of translators with evangelical church planters.

10 **Christian media ministries** for prayer are:

a) *Christian literature* is in great demand. Pray for the ministry of both the well-used **CLC** bookstore and of **The Bible Society** in distributing Scripture. The latter has a successful

'Faith Comes by Hearing' programme of cassette tapes of Bible readings for pre-literates which has enhanced desires both for literacy and for the printed Scriptures.

b) ***GRN*** have produced materials in 32 languages.

c) ***EHC*** has launched an ongoing nation-wide coverage. After 800,000 booklets had been distributed response was so significant that 349 Christ groups were started by 1999.

d) ***Christian radio*** — local stations broadcast Christian programmes; there is also one well-acclaimed Christian radio station in Lomé. A national Christian television channel opened in 2001.

e) ***The JESUS film*** has been shown extensively in film and on TV in seven languages. A further nine language versions are in preparation.

Tonga
Kingdom of Tonga

South Pacific Ocean

Tonga

Nuku'alofa

NOVEMBER 3
PACIFIC

GEOGRAPHY
Area 747 sq.km. Archipelago of 171 coral and volcanic islands 600 km east of Fiji, 36 being inhabited.

Population		Ann.Gr.	Density
2000	98,546	+0.28%	132 per sq. km.
2010	101,251	+0.27%	136 per sq. km.
2025	105,126	+0.24%	141 per sq. km.

Much emigration to Australia and New Zealand where 50,000 Tongans live.

Capital Nuku'alofa 32,000. **Urbanites** 43%. A considerable migration to the capital from outer islands.

PEOPLES
Polynesian 98.3%. Tongans speaking three related languages.

Other 1.7%. English-speaking 600; Other Pacific Islanders 500; Chinese 250.

Literacy 100%. **Official language** Tongan. **All languages** 5. **Languages with Scriptures** 3Bi.

ECONOMY
Subsistence agriculture and some tourism. The value of imports is four times larger than exports (mainly to Japan). Remittances from Tongans abroad and aid bridge the difference. **Pub-** **lic debt** 34% of GNP. **Income/person** $1,790 (6% of USA).

POLITICS
British Protected State 1900-1970. Constitutional monarchy with the king and nobles having the predominant influence. Since 1990 there has been a growing movement to curb the power of the aristocracy and make the constitution more democratic.

RELIGION
Though avowedly Christian, there is freedom for all religions. The Free Wesleyan Church enjoys a privileged position with the king as titular head.

Religions	Population %	Adherents	Ann.Gr.
Christian	95.17	94,000	+0.2%
Baha'i	2.40	2,365	+1.1%
non-Religious/other	2.30	2,267	+1.2%
Buddhist	0.11	108	+0.2%
Hindu	0.02	20	+1.0%

Christians		Denom.	Affil.%,000	Ann.Gr.
Protestant	7	40.93	40	-0.1%
Independent	5	19.73	19	+0.0%
Anglican	1	0.57	1	-0.2%
Catholic	1	14.21	14	+0.3%
Marginal	2	40.77	40	+0.5%
Doubly affiliated		*-21.01*	*-21*	*n.a.*

The high doubly affiliated figure is largely due to Mormon claims for those who still retain membership of other denominations.

Churches	MegaBloc	Cong.	Members	Affiliates
Latter-day Saints (Morm)	M	162	16,000	40,000
Free Wesleyan	P	190	8,964	32,000
Catholic	C	13	8,140	14,000
Free Church of Tonga	I	80	6,294	9,000
Ch of Tonga	I	40	3,593	6,000
Seventh-day Adventist	P	14	1,600	5,400
Tokailolo Fellowship	I	10	1,500	3,000
Assemblies of God	P	15	1,100	2,200
Other denoms [9]		28	1,619	2,916
Doubly affiliated			*-12,575*	*-21,000*
Total Christians [17]		552	36,235	94,000

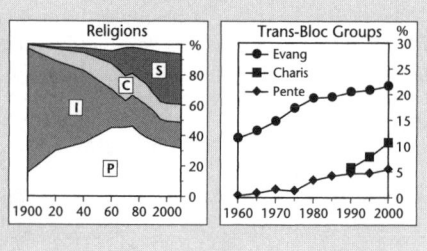

Trans-bloc Groupings	pop.%	,000	Ann.Gr.
Evangelical	21.6	21	+0.4%
Charismatic	10.5	10	+1.5%
Pentecostal	5.4	5	+2.9%

Missionaries from Tonga
P,I,A 44 in 5 agencies to 9 countries: Tonga 15, S. Asia 8, Taiwan 3.

Missionaries to Tonga
P,I,A 25 in 7 agencies from 10 countries: NZ 7, UK 4, USA 4. C 40. M 250.

• Answers to Prayer

1 **For two centuries Tonga has been a Christian kingdom**. In 1995, the king, a committed Christian, publicly re-dedicated the nation to God — the first king in three generations to do this.

2 The Jesus March of 1995 included almost half the country's population.

3 The indicators of hope for spiritual change:

a) *The rapid growth* of evangelical, charismatic and Pentecostal groups within and outside the mainline denominations.

b) *The impact of SU*, with a group in nearly every village and through whom many have been converted.

• Challenges for Prayer

1 The Tongan Church has had a glorious history of missionary outreach, but for decades the vision has languished. Over the last ten years there has been renewed interest with evangelical Christians forming a group to promote a missions vision. YWAM's University of the Nations has a branch in Tonga with a specific burden to encourage this. Pray that good intentions may become Kingdom-advancing action.

2 The 20ᵗʰ Century has been one of spiritual decline. There has been a sad history of bitter schisms within Methodism. Politics and Church are intimately intertwined. Doctrinal extremes and personalities have played their part in dividing denominations. Pray for humility and godliness to characterize leadership and pray for revival.

3 Tonga has the world's highest national percentage of Mormons — but probably half of those baptized as Mormons would not consider themselves such (hence the large doubly affiliated figure). The country's largest employers are Mormons. Pray for the error of this sect to be exposed as such, and for many to find freedom in Christ.

4 The less-reached. The growing Chinese community is the only unreached people group, some immigrating from Hong Kong and China.

5 Support ministries. Pray for the lasting impact of:

a) *The JESUS film* which has been widely used in Tongan and English.

b) *The Christian TV station*.

c) *Christian literature*. Both **The Bible Society** and **SU** distribute Bibles and other Christian materials widely.

T

Trinidad & Tobago

Republic of Trinidad and Tobago

Map showing North Atlantic Ocean, Caribbean Sea, Martinique, St. Lucia, St. Vincent, Barbados, Grenada, Port of Spain, Tobago, Trinidad and Tobago, Venezuela

Tobago

NOVEMBER 3

LATIN AMERICA

GEOGRAPHY
Area 5,124 sq.km. Two islands off the coast of Venezuela.

Population	Ann.Gr.	Density
2000	1,294,958	+0.51%	253 per sq. km.
2010	1,374,007	+0.66%	268 per sq. km.
2025	1,493,418	+0.45%	291 per sq. km.

Capital Port of Spain 300,000. **Urbanites** 72%.

PEOPLES
Afro-Trinidadian 40%. A further 18% of mixed race.
Indo-Trinidadian 40.3%.
Euro-Trinidadian 0.6%.
Other 1.1%. Chinese 6,000; US citizens 2,700; Lebanese 1,000.
Literacy 98%. **Official language** English.

ECONOMY
Oil is very important, providing half of export earnings. Unwise central planning and profligate spending of oil wealth in the late 1970s led to recession. Recovery began in 1994 with a freer market economy. The only Caribbean island with a strong industrial base. **HDI** 0.797; 46th/174. **Public debt** 28% of GNP. **Income/person** $4,250 (14% of USA).

POLITICS
Independent of Britain in 1962 as a parliamentary democracy. Prolonged economic recession in the 1980s provoked political and ethnic tensions culminating in an abortive coup by militant black Muslims in 1990. Politics have been polarized racially, but with the election of the first Indian-origin Prime Minister in 1995 the racial issue has become less pronounced.

RELIGION
There is religious freedom for all.

Religions	Population %	Adherents	Ann.Gr.
Christian	71.21	922,140	+1.2%
Hindu	19.00	246,042	-1.5%
Muslim	5.70	73,813	+0.2%
non-Religious/other	1.44	18,647	-1.5%
Baha'i	0.95	12,302	+1.6%
Sikh	0.80	10,360	-1.8%
Traditional ethnic	0.40	5,180	+0.5%
Chinese	0.40	5,180	-0.5%
Buddhist	0.10	1,295	+0.5%

Christians	Denom.	Affil.%	,000	Ann.Gr.
Protestant	57	21.23	275	+2.5%
Independent	33	3.96	51	+8.3%
Anglican	1	12.51	162	+0.4%
Catholic	1	30.89	400	+0.2%
Orthodox	3	0.56	7	+0.0%
Marginal	10	2.06	27	+1.9%

Churches	MegaBloc	Cong.	Members	Affiliates
Catholic	C	68	228,571	400,000
Anglican	A	88	30,798	162,000
Seventh-day Adventist	P	136	53,534	100,000
Presbyterian	P	105	13,986	40,000
Pentecostal Assemblies	P	180	17,000	32,300
Jehovah's Witnesses	M	91	8,010	17,800
Ch of God (Cleveland)	P	68	9,295	16,000
Foursquare Gospel	P	30	7,000	11,000
Methodist	P	27	4,300	10,750
Baptist Convention	P	58	4,559	9,100
Open Bible Standard	P	75	5,500	8,800
Baptist Union	P	21	3,200	6,400
Ch of the Nazarene	P	26	4,200	6,000
Assoc of Evang Bap	P	12	900	2,142
Chr Brethren	P	31	700	1,400
Other denoms [90]		557	53,500	98,400
Total Christians [105]		1,573	445,000	922,000

Trans-bloc Groupings	pop.%	,000	Ann.Gr.
Evangelical	15.2	197	+3.8%
Charismatic	10.9	141	+3.9%
Pentecostal	8.6	111	+4.6%

Missionaries from Trinidad
P,I,A 42 in 10 agencies to 10 countries: Trinidad 23.
Missionaries to Trinidad
P,I,A 97 in 22 agencies from 9 countries: USA 79.

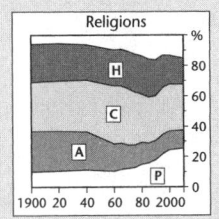

Religions chart (H, C, A, P) 1900–2000

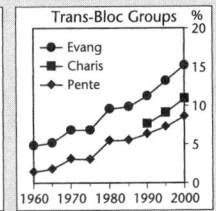

Trans-Bloc Groups chart: Evang, Charis, Pente 1960–2000

• Challenges for Prayer

1 **Inter-ethnic harmony** has been hindered by political parties aligned according to race and the activities of several extremist minorities among Muslims, Hindus and some 'Christians'. Pray that the government may be impartial and fair to all ethnic groups.

2 **The Church is one of the only structures** that has bridges to every Trinidadian community. Most of the Afro-, Euro-Trinidadian and Chinese, and over 20% of the Indian population, are professing Christians.

3 **The Christian Church is very fragmented** — between traditional and newer denominations and a growing multiplicity of Indian and Black-led charismatic and Pentecostal ministries. There is little cohesion with common spiritual goals, outreach or missions involvement. There is a lack of national vision and purpose and many 'Christian' families are dysfunctional. Pray for revival to enliven and empower the Church.

4 **Religious instruction in public schools** presents an exciting opportunity for the gospel. Many Trinidad Christians are engaged in this ministry. Pray for the young people of all races. **YFC**, **CEF** and **IFES** have work among students. Little is done in the churches to disciple children.

5 **A cross-cultural vision** is lacking in most churches. Pray for a greater awareness of local and world needs, and for effective training to be given in cross-cultural outreach. Only a handful of Trinidadians have gone overseas as missionaries — mostly with **OM**, **YWAM** and **WBT**.

6 **The South Asian** community largely originated from North India. It is the largest non-Christian community in the Caribbean. Many Hindus and some Muslims have turned to Christ and over 20% of the South Asian population is Christian today. The Presbyterians, **WT** and **TEAM** have planted strong churches and there are also many Pentecostal and charismatic congregations with largely Indian believers. The special challenge is the need of the Indian Muslim community.

7 **Christian media ministries:**

a) *Christian literature.* **CLC** operates three bookstores that are widely appreciated and extensively used. Pray for the 13 workers.

b) *Christian radio and TV programmes* broadcast on the national network. **TWR** and other Christian agencies also broadcast radio programmes from outside the country and have a large audience. Pray for the production of programmes that are relevant and spiritually effective.

Tunisia

Republic of Tunisia

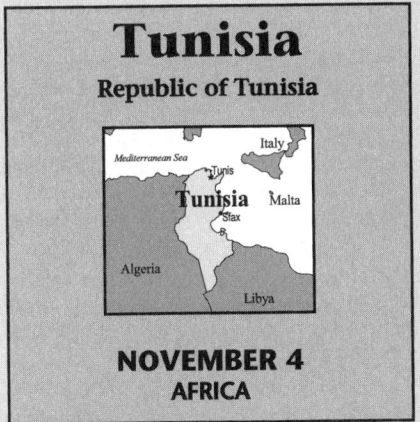

NOVEMBER 4

AFRICA

20%. **HDI** 0.695; 102nd/174. **Public debt** 48.5% of GNP. **Income/person** $2,110 (6.7% of USA).

POLITICS
Independent from France in 1956. A republic with strong presidential government and a virtual single party state. The repression of fundamentalist Muslims has been severe, with frequent serious human rights abuses. Multi-party elections were held in 1999, but the President received 99.4% of the vote.

RELIGION
Islam is the state religion. The government has maintained a secular tone and only a minority actively practice their faith. Politicised Islam has been met with little tolerance by the state. Not favourable to any form of Christian proselytism, but tolerance shown to foreign religious minorities. **Persecution index** 13th in the world.

GEOGRAPHY
Area 154,530 sq.km. Mountainous and agricultural in the north, Sahara desert in the south. The site of notable civilizations: Carthaginian, Berber Christian and Arab Islamic.

Population		Ann.Gr.	Density
2000	9,585,611	+1.40%	62 per sq. km.
2010	10,928,892	+1.29%	71 per sq. km.
2025	12,843,081	+0.94%	83 per sq. km.

Capital Tunis 1,900,000. Other major city: Sfax 900,000. **Urbanites** 63%.

PEOPLES
Arab 96.5-98.5%. Mixed Berber and Arab descent makes it difficult to ascertain actual ethnic division. A small number from other Arab countries.
Berber 1-3%.
Other 0.5%. French, Italian, Jewish.

Literacy 67%. **Official language** Arabic. French is widely used. **All languages** 7. **Languages with Scriptures** 2Bi 2por.

ECONOMY
Sustained development since independence. Textiles, tourism, olive oil and phosphates are the major foreign currency earners. **Unemployment**

Religions	Population %	Adherents	Ann.Gr.
Muslim	99.66	9,553,020	+1.4%
Christian	0.22	21,088	+0.5%
non-Religious/other	0.10	9,586	+1.4%
Jewish	0.02	1,917	-6.5%

Christians	Denom.	Affil. %	,000	Ann.Gr.
Protestant	3	0.00	0	+2.9%
Independent	1	0.00	0	+11.0%
Anglican	1	0.00	0	-2.5%
Catholic	1	0.21	20	+0.0%
Orthodox	2	0.00	0	+0.7%
Marginal	1	0.00	0	+0.0%

Churches	MegaBloc	Cong.	Members	Affiliates
Catholic	C	14	11,628	20,000
Indigenous believers	I	2	100	200
Other denoms [7]		5	352	562
Total Christians [9]		21	12,000	20,800

Nearly all Christians are non-Tunisians.

Trans-bloc Groupings	pop.%	,000	Ann.Gr.
Evangelical	0.0	0	+7.4%
Pentecostal & Charismatic	0.0	0	+9.6%

• Challenges for Prayer

1 In earlier centuries the Christian Church was widespread, producing such leaders as Tertullian and Cyprian. Schism, heresy, a failure to put roots deep in the local culture or translate the Bible into local languages, foreign invasions and finally Islam, brought about its demise. There are about 200 committed indigenous believers today; but about half that number meet together regularly for worship. Pray that a living, growing Church might become a reality again in this land.

2 Tunisia is the one of the most progressive and open societies in the Arab world. While the outward trappings of Islam are obvious, most people are more committed to secular dreams of wealth. Pray that the emptiness of religious posturing, spiritual apathy, and materialism might be exposed and replaced with spiritual hunger for Jesus.

3 A century of missionary involvement produced little fruit, but signs of a change are evident. A concerted prayer movement for Tunisia in 1999 coincided with significant (for such a small church) numbers of people turning to Christ. Pray that the centuries-old barriers to the gospel might be demolished through continued intercession, and that these first fruits might become a great harvest of souls.

4 **There are a number of new believers** and new church groups that have come into being over the past few years. Pray for their continued growth and discipleship. However, the Church is still a tiny proportion of the total population. Some are isolated, fearful, with very limited opportunities for fellowship and discipling. To some, emigration is an easy option; pray that God may give them a vision of the Church He wants to build through them. Pray for lasting commitment to Jesus, as few Tunisian believers have stood in the faith for more than 10 years. Amongst the increasing numbers of new believers, pray for safety, encouragement, integration into the Body and boldness — many have a vision for evangelism.

5 **Leadership** is gradually developing for the several small groups of indigenous believers. Pray that anointed leaders may be raised up for this time, and that the right means for their theological and spiritual development might be discerned. Pray for unity and cooperation — historically a problem, but now an issue being actively addressed.

6 **The Christian population** is overwhelmingly nominal, expatriate and predominantly Catholic, and is now one-fifteenth of its size in 1956. There are two functioning Protestant denominations — Anglican and French Reformed. Pray that committed expatriate Christians may discover quality opportunities to share their faith, encourage seekers and disciple young believers. Pray also for sensitivity and a persevering, servant spirit in situations that require sensitivity and wisdom. Pray for others to be called of God into this ministry.

7 Specific unreached areas and peoples:

a) ***The young people are disillusioned*** with the existing situation and many are negative about their own land; most are completely apathetic about spiritual things.

b) ***The southern part of the country*** is a spiritual desert. Sfax is a needy city, but there is a witness there.

c) ***The Berber communities*** maintain some of their distinctives even though they have largely lost their languages. Their ancestors were Christian. The island of Djerba with 65,000 people, mostly Berber, is a specific challenge with its unique culture and with very few known Christians. There are also two Jewish settlements.

d) ***Kairouan*** is seen by some as the fourth most holy city in Islam — many go there for pilgrimages, healing and help. Pray that in their search they might find Jesus.

8 Reaching Tunisians by other means.

a) ***The hundreds of thousands of Tunisians in Europe.*** Mostly in France, but also several thousand in Germany and in Belgium, they are being reached by a number of agencies, but more could be done. Pray for openness and spiritual receptivity.

b) ***Christian radio*** has a growing impact. **TWR** broadcasts 18.5 hrs/wk in Arabic from Cyprus and Monte Carlo. **HCJB** (7 hrs/wk) and **FEBA** (5 hrs/wk) also broadcast in Arabic. Many listen, and meaningful response and follow-through with BCCs has been increasing. **GMU** in Spain and **AWM** in France are also involved in radio programming and BCC ministry in Arabic.

c) ***Scripture translation*** into Tunisian Arabic is in progress — an essential task if the gospel is to be clearly heard and understood.

d) ***Some Christian literature*** is now openly sold but is not widely available. Pray that the Bible and Christian books might become more widely distributed though bookshops, and Christian literature made available throughout the land.

e) ***The JESUS film*** is available in two translations — Standard Arabic and Tunisian Arabic. Pray for the wide dissemination of this film and the development of a wider ministry of Christian cassettes and videos in Tunisian Arabic.

Turkey
Republic of Turkey

NOVEMBER 5-7
ASIA
Revised February 2004

ECONOMY

Tourism, agriculture and industry are all important to the economy; rapid development in 1980s. It is self-sufficient in agriculture. Remittances from the 3 million Turks working in Western Europe are a significant source of foreign exchange. Inflation in the 1990s, again in 2001 and the devastating 1999 earthquake have slowed growth. Massive development of both the Tigris and Euphrates river basins in the east. The economy needs to be modernized in preparation for possible entry into the EU. Turkey has the world's 17th largest economy. It is, at the same time, one of Europe's poorer nations yet the richest and most developed of the six Turkic nations of west and central Asia. **HDI** 0.728; 86th/174. **Public debt** 24% of GNP. **Income/person** $3,130 (10% of USA).

GEOGRAPHY

Area 779,452 sq.km. Straddles two continents; 3% in Europe (Thrace), 97% in Asia (Anatolia). Also controls the Bosphorus Strait and the Dardanelles, vital sea links between the Black Sea and the Mediterranean. Its strategic position has made the area of prime importance throughout history.

Population		Ann.Gr.	Density
2000	66,590,940	+1.68%	85 per sq. km.
2010	76,054,450	+1.24%	98 per sq. km.
2025	87,869,200	+0.86%	113 per sq. km.

Capital Ankara 3.25 million. Other major cities: Istanbul 10.1m; Izmir 2.4m; Bursa 1.3m; Adana 1.1m. **Urbanites** 65%.

PEOPLES

Strong pressures on ethnic minorities to adopt Turkish culture and language make it hard to obtain objective figures.

Turks 76–80%. A Central Asian people that conquered and largely absorbed the indigenous peoples of the land from the 11th Century onward. Though ethnically diverse, Turks have a fairly homogeneous culture. Distinctive sub-groups: Azeri 680,000 in the east; Koruk (Gagauz) 665,000; Crimean Tatar 400,000.

Kurds 14–20%. (The Kurds claim 21-25%). An Indo-Iranian people in southeast Anatolia, probably related to the ancient Medes. Many Kurds use Turkish as their primary language. Main language groups: Kurmanji 5–9m; Dimli (Zaza) 1.15m.

Arabs 1.8%. In south Anatolia adjoining Syria.

Muslim minorities 1.8%. Gypsy (Turkish, Arlije, Domari) 590,000; Kabardian (Circassian) 550,000; Laz 137,000; Bulgarian Pomak 300,000; Albanian 91,000; Bosnian 90,000; Abkhazian 39,000.

Refugees 1.3%. Iranians 560,000; Bulgarian Turks 200,000; Central Asians 90,000.

Non-Muslim minorities 0.2%. Armenian 45,000; Jews 8,000; Assyrian 2,000; Greek 4,000. Rapid decline through emigration. Note religious graph. There were 1.75m Armenians and 1.5m Greeks in Turkey in 1900.

Literacy 82%. **Official language** Turkish. **All languages** 36. **Languages with Scriptures** 7Bi 5NT 5por 13w.i.p.

POLITICS

The Turkish Ottoman Empire once stretched across North Africa, Arabia, Western Asia and Southeast Europe. Its demise and final fragmentation in World War I led to revolution, the birth of modern Turkey and the formation of a republic in 1923 by the much revered Atatürk. Periods of social disorder and military rule led to a return to democratic government in 1983, with the military still retaining considerable influence. Turkey is a member of NATO, but is in dispute with fellow NATO member, Greece, for long-standing historic reasons and over territorial rights in the Aegean Sea and the division of Cyprus. Suppression of the large Kurdish minority moderated during the 1990s. The long, bitter war with Kurdish separatists caused 30,000 deaths and the ravaging of the southeast, but after 1999 its intensity was considerably reduced. Turkey's economic links with Europe, cultural links with Central Asia and proximity to conflicts in Iraq, the Balkans and the Caucasus have enhanced its strategic importance. There are tensions between Turkey and nearly all its neighbours.

RELIGION

Turkey's Ottoman Empire was for centuries the guardian of all the holy places of Islam and its chief protagonist. Since the sweeping reforms of the 1920s, Turkey has officially been a secular state. In recent years Islam has become politically more important. The constitutional guarantee of religious freedom has not been fully upheld; instances of discrimination and harassment of religious minorities are many, but there has been a distinct improvement since 2000. **Persecution index** 39th in the world.

Religions	Population %	Adherents	Ann.Gr.
Muslim	99.64	66,351,213	+1.7%
Christian	0.32	213,091	+3.7%
Jewish	0.04	26,636	+1.7%

Sunni Muslims 72-80%, Alevi 17-25%, mainly, but not only, among Kurds. Shi'a among Azeri and Iranians. There are also Yezidis among the Kurds.

Christians	Denom.	Affil.%	,000	Ann.Gr.
Protestant	6	0.03	19	+2.7%
Independent	4	0.02	14	+10.7%
Anglican	1	0.00	2	+0.1%
Catholic	2	0.05	30	+2.0%
Orthodox	10	0.21	138	+4.9%
Marginal	4	0.01	5	+3.1%

Churches	MegaBloc	Cong.	Members	Affiliates
Armenian Orthodox	O	19	25,749	43,000
All Foreign Protestants	P	51	5,594	16,000
Catholic	C	50	9,281	15,500
Catholic Eastern Rite	C	56	8,982	15,000
Greek Orthodox	O	5	2,098	3,000
Turkish Indig. believers	I	34	2,000	3,000
Jehovah's Witnesses	M	23	1,559	2,600

All Minority Indig. Prots	P	8	600	1,500
Other denoms [19]		43	58,400	112,700
Total Christians [27]		289	114,300	213,000

Trans-bloc Groupings	pop.%	,000	Ann.Gr.
Evangelical	0.0	20	+8.4%
Charismatic	0.0	11	+7.1%

• Answers to Prayer

1 **The emergence of a small, but significant Turkish Evangelical Church.** Turkish believers probably numbered about 10 in 1960. This had risen to about 2,000 in 34 fellowships by 2000 and 76 fellowships with 3,000 by 2003.

2 **The legal recognition of the existence of a Turkish Protestant Church** and the official establishment of several Protestant congregations.

3 **The increasing openness** on the part of the authorities to recognize Turkey as a multi-cultural, multi-religious country.

• Challenges for Prayer

1 **Turkey remains the largest unreached nation in the world.** For over 1,000 years it was a bastion of Christianity, but it became a strong propagator of Islam. The Christian population has declined from 22% to 0.32% since 1900 — most of these Christians being non-Turkish. Few of the 66 million Muslims have ever heard the gospel.

2 **Turkey is a nation torn in opposite directions.** It straddles Europe and Asia; some strive to bring the country into the EU, others to strengthen ties with Muslim states to the south and east. The constitution, judiciary and army are secular and uphold religious freedom, but many politicians, the police and the growing Islamist movement are hostile to anything Christian. Pray that all attempts to restrict religious freedom may be frustrated, and that ambiguities in the law may be clarified — it is the latter that open the way for mis-treatment of Christians.

3 **The many critical issues facing the nation** need political leadership of high calibre for their resolution. The military needs to serve the government rather than manipulate it. Serious failings in human rights need to be addressed and a solution found to the Kurdish issue. Raging inflation and an archaic economic system need to be courageously tackled. A harsh application of Atatürk's strong secularism is feeding a rising Islamist movement and needs to be rethought.

4 **The barriers of prejudice and hatred of the gospel can appear insurmountable.** Pray for the following to be broken down:
a) Historical. Turkey's long association with Islam and more than a millennium of bitter wars with 'Christian' Europe make conversion appear almost an act of treachery.
b) Cultural. To be a Turk is to be a Muslim, even if only nominally so. Family pressure, police intimidation and threats from Muslim extremists keep many from coming to Christ, and force others to remain secret believers.
c) Fixed attitudes. A deep-seated resistance in the general public to anything Christian makes any form of witnessing difficult. A radical change in public attitudes and press coverage of Christians must be prayed for.
d) Biased understandings. Evangelical Christians are lumped together with Armenian terrorists and Jehovah's Witnesses. Sensational articles in the Press and biased television

programmes spread untruths about Christians, further inflaming public opinion. Muslim misconceptions about Christian doctrine present another major barrier.

e) **The legacy of violent past suppression of Christian minorities**. The turbulence and political instability before and after World War I brought about widespread violence and forced deportation for many Armenians. Armenian nationalists, urged on by Russian agents, fought for a separate homeland. The horrific Turkish response resulted in the virtual elimination of Armenians through expulsions or massacres. Some estimate 1.5 million died. Pray that the cloud of prejudice and darkness might be lifted and many might find joy and peace in the forgiveness offered by the Lord Jesus.

5 **The ancient churches** survived until the beginning of the 20th Century, but since then have been decimated by massacres (Armenians), severe persecution (Assyrians) and emigration (Greeks, etc.). Pray for the remnant that survives — for re-kindling of faith and for a work of the Holy Spirit. Their numbers have been reduced to an estimated 138,000 in 12 different traditions.

6 **The Turkish Church** has at last become a visible reality, but still only constitutes 0.003% of the ethnic Turkish population. Pray for:

a) **The Turkish Protestant Christian Council**. This links all the evangelical fellowships and their leaders. Denominationalism has not been an issue — but could be. Pray that the Turkish leaders may be discerning and wise in developing the appropriate structures, teaching, hymnody, worship patterns and fellowship levels.

b) **Strong, united fellowships**. Close family ties and the security it confers mean that family rejection after conversion can be traumatic. Fellowships need to become surrogate families. Backsliding has been common, compromise in marrying non-Christians frequent, and relationship breakdowns between believers disheartening.

c) **Avoidance of internal dangers** — doctrinal extremes, legalism, personality clashes, disunity.

d) **Courage in persecution**. Social ostracism, harassment by police, arbitrary arrests, and disruptions of church services on spurious pretexts have all occurred — bringing some insecurity, fear and uncertainty. The courts usually throw out any charges made against Christians, but inevitably this is stressful.

e) **Perseverance**. Emigration is often a way to escape persecution, find a good paying job or find a foreign marriage partner.

f) **Legal recognition of the Protestant Church as a whole**. This has yet to be gained, but a number of individual congregations have been legally recognized thus enabling them to build or buy property.

7 Vision for the future is developing.

a) **In 2000 goals were set** by the Church that by 2005 there be a congregation in 50 of Turkey's 80 provinces (15 had a congregation in 2000) and 10,000 Turkish evangelical believers. Pray that this may be achieved.

b) **Bible training for leaders**. There are now two small Bible schools — Hall of Tyrannus near Ephesus and Bithynia Bible Institute in Istanbul, with several others being planned. A TEE programme is in operation.

8 **Kurds** are a majority in 16 provinces in east and south-east Turkey; 500,000 annually leave for other areas in Turkey and Europe. Pray for:

a) **A complete end to the hostilities** between the army and Kurdish separatists and a fair resolution to the causes. Over 30,000 have been killed, thousands of villages razed and millions displaced and impoverished.

b) **Cultural rehabilitation of the Kurds**. Vigorous suppression of their culture and language has moderated. Kurdish newspapers are now allowed and even the *JESUS* film in Kurmanji has been legalized.

c) **The Muslim Alevi and Yezidi sects** (the latter based on Zoroastrianism and the occult) many of whom are Kurds. Their nominal Islamic practice and high respect for Jesus give unique witness opportunities. New literature and music cassettes are being developed specifically for them.

d) **The emergence of a Kurdish expression of the Church**. There may be 300 Kurdish believers world-wide, but no fellowships exist in Turkey, though there are a number of Kurdish believers in Turkish-speaking fellowships. Pray for all those seeking openings for reaching them, translation of the Scriptures (all main Kurdish languages are being worked on), use of the *JESUS* film and other Kurdish literature.

9 Other specific unreached peoples and areas abound. Pray for:

a) *A living, growing fellowship of believers* in each of the 80 provinces — 56 of them have no Christian workers or groups. Especially needing prayer are the turbulent eastern Anatolian provinces (largely Kurdish) and the Black Sea coast (many Laz).

b) *University students.* There are 1.4 million students in 817 universities and colleges, but there is very little specific campus ministry apart from Izmir, though a number of students have come to the Lord.

c) *Children.* They are difficult to reach. The problem of street children is growing in Istanbul and Izmir. A Turkish children's Bible was published recently. Camp ministry has been effective (Kuçak).

d) *The ethnic Muslim minorities and Central Asian refugee communities* listed under **Peoples** above. None of these peoples have been evangelized; many live in their own communities, though use of their languages is declining.

e) *Iranian refugees* who have fled the violence and Islamic extremism of the 1979 Revolution. Over 560,000 still remain in Turkey — many in Istanbul, while many others have moved on to Western countries. There has been a response to the gospel in Istanbul and Ankara and small Persian-speaking congregations have been established with possibly 50 believers in 2000.

10 Missionary work began in 1821, but was soon directed to the more receptive non-Muslim minorities in the hope of reaching the majority through them. Since 1960 renewed prayer and effort is slowly yielding fruit among Muslims. All expatriates have long lived under the threat of police harassment and expulsion from the country, but earlier expulsions were quashed and declared illegal in three court cases in 1992. Pray for:

a) *Those called*, equipped and gifted for tentmaking ministries in this land where vital opportunities to share one's faith are hard to find.

b) *Opportunities* for ministry that will enable the whole country to be exposed to the gospel. Most expatriates are engaged in teaching, study, business, or on tourist visas. Few have ever lived in eastern Anatolia, the Black Sea coast or the interior provinces.

c) *The right relationship* with indigenous believers — too many foreigners in an area can stifle the development of mature leadership.

d) *The 50 or so agencies*, with around 400 expatriates, from over 20 countries with a specific burden and calling to minister to Turks, and for the continuance of fruitful cooperation among them.

11 Other means of witness are bearing fruit and need prayerful support:

a) *Bible translation.* Both Turkish NT translations published in 1988/89 have been well received and widely sold or distributed. **The Bible Society** is overseeing the completion of the entire Bible for 2001.

b) *The Bible Society has a well-visited bookstore* in Istanbul and is able to distribute Bibles and Christian literature to colporteurs and secular bookstores. Newspaper advertisements in 2000 generated an unprecedented response.

c) *Christian literature.* There are now seven Turkish Christian publishing houses that handle Bibles, over 100 book titles and two magazines. Literature is often well received but distributors are sometimes threatened by Islamic extremists. There is a great need for Turkish Christian authors.

d) *Postal evangelism* in innovative ways — pen pals, broadsheets, offers of BCCs, etc., — has generated increased response. **Good News Ministries** oversee a large BCC programme with follow-up.

e) *Christian radio.* The breakdown of regulatory controls has opened the way for a 24-hour Christian FM station in Istanbul. International broadcasters also have significant input. **TWR**, partnering with **IBRA**, broadcast 10 hrs/wk from Central Asia and Russia. There are plans for Christian television by satellite.

12 **Ministry to Turks outside Turkey:**

*a) **The 3 million Turks and Kurds in Western Europe**.* Migrant labourers in Germany (2.1m), Netherlands (290,000), France (350,000), UK (200,000), Austria (100,000), Belgium (95,000), Switzerland (50,000) and Sweden (37,000) are far more accessible to Christian workers but are also more conservative. A number of churches and international agencies are seeking to evangelize them, but local hostility to migrant workers impedes this outreach. Among such are **OM**, **WEC**, **Turkish World Outreach** and *Orientdienst*. There are possibly 100 converted Turks as a result of this ministry. There is also a work among the 95,000 Turks in Australia. Pray for the multiplication of Turkish and Kurdish Christian groups in these areas and for them to make an impact on their homelands.

*b) **Turks in the Balkans**.* There are opportunities for ministry among Turkish minorities in Bulgaria (1.1m), Macedonia/Serbia (250,000), Romania (150,000) and Greece (140,000). The opening up of Bulgaria and Bulgarian Turks to the gospel may be of great significance for the Church in Turkey. Over 12,000 Turks and Turkish-speaking Gypsies in the Balkans have come to Jesus through a people movement since the late 1980s. Pray for ministry directed to teaching and mobilizing these believers.

Turkmenistan

NOVEMBER 8
ASIA

GEOGRAPHY
Area 488,100 sq.km. Two populated strips of irrigated land on its northern and southern borders separated by the barren Kara-Kum Desert. Only 1% of the country is irrigated arable land; 80% is desert.

Population	Ann.Gr.	Density
2000	4,459,293	+1.80%	9 per sq. km.
2010	5,218,906	+1.54%	11 per sq. km.
2025	6,286,522	+1.20%	13 per sq. km.

Capital Ashgabat 490,000. **Urbanites** 45%.

PEOPLES
Numerous ethnic minorities from all over the former USSR, but many are emigrating.
Turkic/Altaic 90.6%. Turkmen 3,500,000; Uzbek 410,000; Kazakh 90,000; Azerbaijani 50,000; Tatar 35,000.
Indo-European 9.3%.
Slav 5.5%. Russian 245,000; Ukrainian 20,000.
Iranian 2.4%. Baluch 34,000; Persian 12,000.
Other 1.4%. Armenian 30,000; Lezhgin 11,000.
Other 0.1%.

Literacy 98%. **Official language** Turkmen using Latin script as in Turkey since 1994; previously Cyrillic script. **All languages** 2. **Languages with Scriptures** 1Bi 1por 1w.i.p.

ECONOMY
Famed for its carpets, horses, camels and desert, but oil and gas production are the major sources of wealth, followed by production of cotton. The country is almost entirely dependent on water from the Amu Darya River, which is already over-used and heavily polluted. The economy is bankrupt, centralized, corrupt under the personal control of the President. It has some of the largest unexploited gas and oil fields in the world, but is a prisoner to its geographical position as a land-locked state far from the sea, surrounded by the politically sensitive Caucasus, Iran, Afghanistan and Russia. Turkey is the more favoured model for the economy and trade links are being developed with it. **HDI** 0.712; 96th/174. **Public debt** 41% of GNP. **Income/person** $640 (2% of USA) officially, but in practice, half of this.

POLITICS
Nomadic tribal past; only united as a country under Russian Tsarist rule in 1881. A Soviet Republic until independence in 1992. The former Communist leader Saparmurat Niyazov transformed himself into a nationalist dictator, the Turkmenbashi. He controls the army, police, the justice system, the economy and the press, and in 2000 had himself declared President-for-life. Any opposition is ruthlessly crushed, but the oil-hungry West does not protest.

RELIGION
Constitutionally there is freedom of religion. In practice this is limited to Sunni Islam or Russian Orthodox — all other forms of Islam or minority religions are subject to severe repression.

and harassment. Islam has never been strong and was severely repressed under Communism but now is gradually gaining in influence and strength. The government leans more to a Turkish form of Islam. **Persecution Index** 15th in the world.

Religions	Population %	Adherents	Ann.Gr.
Muslim	91.84	4,095,415	+3.4%
non-Religious/other	5.47	243,923	-12.8%
Christian	2.66	118,617	-1.3%
Jewish	0.03	1,338	-3.9%

Christians	Denom.	Affil.%	,000	Ann.Gr.
Protestant	3	0.01	0	+8.1%
Independent	1	0.01	0	+22.6%
Orthodox	3	2.53	113	-1.6%
Marginal	1	0.11	5	+10.8%

Churches	MegaBloc	Cong.	Members	Affiliates
Russian Orthodox	O	6	60,000	90,000
Armenian Apostolic	O	3	13,990	20,000
Jehovah's Witnesses	M	15	1,500	5,000

Turkmen Union	I	30	300	500
Seventh Day Adventist	P	2	100	187
Baptist	P	2	60	130
Other denoms [2]		3	2,200	3,150
Total Christians [8]		61	78,150	119,000

Trans-bloc Groupings	pop.%	,000	Ann.Gr.
Evangelical	0.0	1	+14.2%
Charismatic	0.0	0	+12.0%
Pentecostal	0.0	0	+1.3%

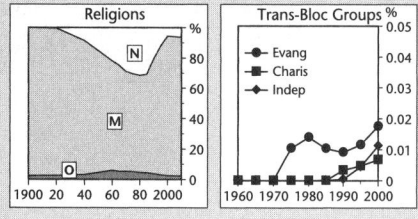

• Challenges for Prayer

1 **The President has built up a personality cult** around himself which resembles Stalin and the Muslim caliphs of past centuries. He has built palaces and memorials to himself all over the country whilst his subjects suffer in dire poverty. He calls himself the 'King of kings'. Pray for a change of heart like Nebuchadnezzar (Daniel 4:28-37) or a change of government to one that respects constitutionally promised human rights and religious freedoms.

2 **Ethnic Turkmen Christians** are few but have increased in 10 years from one or two to possibly 500-600. Most Christians are Russians, Ukrainians and Armenians; and among them are a few hundred evangelical believers. They have been brought to a greater unity and stronger faith through persecution and the Church continues to grow despite the threat to their lives, homes and jobs. Pray for these believers to stand firm in their faith, and to win others to Christ.

3 **Hostility against any evangelical Christian activity or even presence, has increased** since 1997. Nearly all foreign Christians have been expelled. Several national pastors have been exiled, beaten up, heavily fined and imprisoned. Congregations have been intimidated and forbidden to meet. Pray for a softening of the attitude of the authorities, for courage for Christians in the country to stand firm and for Christians outside to pray and speak up against these actions.

4 **There is an international network of Christians concerned** for the evangelization of this land. Pray for Turkmenistan to open up for sharing the good news.

5 Witness by other means:

a) *The Turkmen NT* was published in 1994 and work continues on completing the OT. Pray for the importation, distribution and impact on readers. There are also a number of Christian book titles available in Turkmen.

b) *Christian radio* programmes commenced in 2001. Pray for all involved in producing and airing these programmes.

c) *The JESUS film*, video and audio tapes are available in Turkmen and it is occasionally shown on national TV. Pray for lasting impact on those who have seen it and that they would pass on the video from family to family.

6 **The diaspora.** The Turkmen people live in many surrounding lands: Iraq (1.3 mill.), Iran (1m), Afghanistan (521,000), Uzbekistan (156,000), Syria (150,000), Pakistan (100,000), Russia (40,000) and Tajikistan (19,000). Nearly every one of these communities remains almost completely unevangelized.

Turks & Caicos Islands

NOVEMBER 8
LATIN AMERICA

GEOGRAPHY
Area 500 sq.km. An archipelago of 30 coral islands at the southeastern end of the Bahamas.

Population	Ann.Gr.	Density
2000	16,760	+3.65%	34 per sq. km.
2010	23,068	+3.11%	46 per sq. km.
2025	33,769	+2.31%	68 per sq. km.

Capital Cockburn Town 5,300. **Urbanites** 45%.

PEOPLES
Afro-Caribbean 95% (estimated). Includes a rapidly growing and undocumented number of Haitians.
Euro-American 5%.

ECONOMY
Tourism, offshore financial services, and fishing are the main sources of income. The islands have a history of being used as a transhipment point for illegal drugs and a laundering location for the profits. **Unemployment** 10%. **Income/person** $7,700 (24% of USA).

POLITICS
A territory of the United Kingdom with considerable local autonomy until 1986, when direct rule was imposed for some years as a result of drug-related corruption in the government. The political treatment of the drug-trafficking issue remains important and volatile but is being seriously addressed.

RELIGION
Complete freedom of religion. Catholic numbers are possibly significantly larger than indicated due to the presence of Haitian immigrants.

Religions	Population %	Adherents	Ann.Gr.
Christian	93.18	15,617	+3.7%
non-Religious	4.22	707	+3.0%
Spiritist	2.60	436	+3.7%

Christians	Denom.	Affil.%	,000	Ann.Gr.
Protestant	6	52.07	9	+2.8%
Anglican	1	11.93	2	+2.2%
Catholic	1	26.85	4	+8.4%
Marginal	1	2.33	0	+2.1%

Churches	MegaBloc	Cong.	Members	Affiliates
Catholic	C	3	3,147	4,500
Baptist Union	P	12	500	3,900
Anglican	A	7	741	2,000
Methodist	P	4	460	1,350
Ch of God of Prophecy	P	10	230	770
NT Ch of God (Clev)	P	3	308	684
Other denoms [3]		13	1,300	2,400
Total Christians [9]		52	6,700	15,600

Trans-bloc Groupings	pop.%	,000	Ann.Gr.
Evangelical	34.3	6	+3.0%
Charismatic	12.4	2	+3.6%
Pentecostal	8.7	1	+3.7%

Missionaries to and from Turks & Caicos
n.a.

• Challenges for Prayer

1 **Christian values in society are being challenged** by offshore finance dealing with its frequent money laundering, tourism with its increasing licentiousness and by illegal drug trafficking. Pray that the churches might address this through holy living and genuine faith.

2 **The inflow of immigrants.** Most are illegal and from Haiti. They are poised to outnumber natives, or "Belongers". Pray that believers might meet these newcomers with biblical love and share with them the gospel.

Tuvalu

State of Tuvalu

South Pacific Ocean

Tuvalu

Fongafale★

NOVEMBER 8
PACIFIC

GEOGRAPHY
Area 24 sq.km. Nine low coral atolls in the central Pacific, eight of which are inhabited.

Population	Ann.Gr.	Density
2000	11,719	+2.73%	488 per sq. km.
2010	15,022	+2.44%	626 per sq. km.
2025	20,674	+2.01%	861 per sq. km.

Capital Funafuti 4,000. **Urbanites** 46%.

PEOPLES
Polynesian 91.2%. Tuvaluan.
Micronesian 7.2%.
Other 1.6%. Chinese, European, etc.
Literacy 95%. **Official languages** Tuvalu, English.
Languages with Scriptures 1 Bi.

ECONOMY
Main sources of income are from fishing licences, internet hosting (with the 'tv' domain name), postage stamps, an international trust fund and remittances from Tuvaluans who live outside the country. **Public debt** 86% of GNP. **Income/person** $650 (2.7% of USA).

POLITICS
Independent from Britain in 1978 as a parliamentary monarchy. Once known as the Ellice Islands.

RELIGION
Strongly Protestant; other religions not granted freedom until 1964.

Religions	Population %	Adherents	Ann.Gr.
Christian	98.00	11,485	+2.7%
Baha'i	1.00	117	+3.7%
non-Religious/other	1.00	117	+5.0%

Christians	Denom.	Affil.%	,000	Ann.Gr.
Protestant	4	90.62	11	+2.5%
Catholic	1	1.71	0	+6.0%
Marginal	1	1.62	0	+2.6%
Unaffiliated		4.05	0	n.a.

Churches	MegaBloc	Cong.	Members	Affiliates
Tuvalu	P	14	4,080	10,200
Seventh-day Adventist	P	1	145	260
Catholic	C	1	120	200
Jehovah's Witnesses	M	3	45	190
Pentecostal groups [2]	P	4	104	160
Total Christians [6]		23	4,500	11,000

Trans-bloc Groupings	pop.%	,000	Ann.Gr.
Evangelical	5.1	1	+3.0%
Charismatic	1.4	0	+5.6%
Pentecostal	1.4	0	+5.6%

Missionaries from Tuvalu
n.a.

Missionaries to Tuvalu
P,I,A n.a. **C** 1.

• Challenges for Prayer

1 **Tuvalu may be the first nation to disappear as a result of global warming** and the rise in ocean levels. Pray that the uncertainty of the future may bring spiritual earnestness.

2 **Tuvalu was first evangelized by Cook Island missionaries**. The Congregational Church is effectively the established church; nominalism and tradition are brakes on spiritual life and fervour. The work of **AoG** and Church of God of Prophecy are the only distinctly evangelical ministries on the islands. Pray for spiritual life for all groups.

T

Uganda

Republic of Uganda

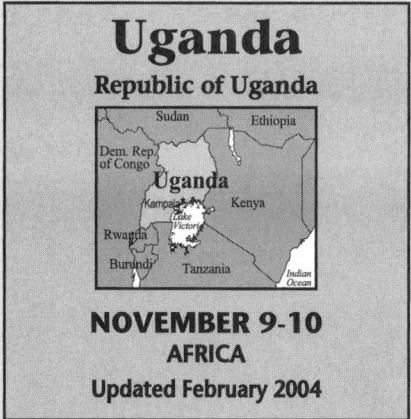

NOVEMBER 9-10
AFRICA
Updated February 2004

 GEOGRAPHY
Area 241,040 sq.km. Much of the land is fertile and well-watered. The climate is temperate in the highlands. Long known as the 'Pearl of Africa'.

Population		Ann.Gr.	Density
2000	21,778,450	+2.84%	90 per sq. km.
2010	29,830,737	+3.13%	124 per sq. km.
2025	44,435,310	+2.43%	184 per sq. km.

No one knows the numbers who perished during Amin's dictatorship and the subsequent civil wars, famines and tribal killings. Estimates vary from 800,000 to 2 million. The impact of AIDS has been devastating and slowed population growth.
Capital Kampala 1.2 mill. Other major city: Entebbe 50,000. **Urbanites** 13%.

 **PEOPLES**

Over 56 ethnic groups; four major divisions.
Bantu 64.8%. 26 peoples, largest: Ganda 3m; Nkole 1.91m; Kiga 1.63m; Soga 1.61m; Hutu 1.18m; Masabu (Gisu) 880,000; Nyoro 580,000; Tooro 570,000; Tutsi 522,000; Konjo 424,000.
Nilotic 27.9%. 18 peoples, largest: Teso 1.17m; Lango 1.14m; Acholi 874,000; Alur 459,000; Karamojong 391,000.
Sudanic 5.4%. 8 peoples: Lugbara(2) 1.14m; Madi(2) 226,000.
Other 1.9%. Congolese, Rwandan, Kenyan, Sudanese, etc.

Literacy 62%. **Official language** English. **All languages** 46. **Languages with Scriptures** 15Bi 5NT 4por 9w.i.p.

 ECONOMY
Fertile with good soil and three annual growing seasons. The main export crop is coffee. The healthy economy of the 1960s was damaged by the expulsion of the Asian business community in 1972 then virtually destroyed by tyranny and wars. There has been a slow, but steady improvement since 1992, but continued warfare in the north and west and the ravages of AIDS and disease keep the majority of the population in deep poverty. **HDI** 0.404; 158ᵗʰ/174. **Public debt** 48% of GNP. **Income/person** $330 (1% of USA).

 POLITICS
Independent from Britain in 1962. An attempt to delicately balance the political powers of the southern Bantu kingdoms and northern Nilotic peoples ended in 1967, when the northerner Milton Obote took complete control, favouring his own tribe, the Lango. Anarchy increased until Idi Amin seized power in 1971. The crazed dictatorship of Amin brutalized the country as the army pillaged and murdered with impunity. Amin's invasion of north-west Tanzania in 1978 provoked a vigorous response, and in 1979 Tanzanian and Ugandan exile troops deposed the military regime, restoring Obote to power. Continued inter-tribal warfare and government incompetence racked the country. Yoweri Museveni gained power in 1986 and has gradually brought a measure of stability unknown for 25 years. A 'no party' democracy was constituted. The Rwanda-Burundi wars and subsequent Central African War involved Uganda in military adventures in Congo, Sudan and Rwanda and against the so-called Lord's Resistance Army (LRA) in north-west Uganda. Since 2002 peace has gradually come in all the conflicts but for that of the LRA.

RELIGION
Under Amin there were restrictions and intense persecution of Christians. For a time the Muslim minority was favoured. There is now freedom of religion.

Religions	Population %	Adherents	Ann.Gr.
Christian	88.65	19,306,596	+2.9%
Muslim	6.00	1,306,707	+2.8%
Traditional ethnic	4.15	903,806	+1.5%
non-Religious/other	0.60	130,671	+6.7%
Baha'i	0.40	87,114	-1.7%
Hindu	0.20	43,557	+2.8%

Most Muslims live in the northwest, but some are sprinkled all over the country. No group has a Muslim majority, but there are large minorities among the Kakwa, Madi and Woga. The majority of traditional religionists are of four or five north-eastern peoples — the Karamojong, Pokot, etc.

Christians	Denom.	Affil.%	,000	Ann.Gr.
Protestant	39	6.39	1,391	+7.1%
Independent	24	2.67	581	+2.9%
Anglican	1	39.40	8,580	+3.0%
Catholic	1	41.92	9,130	+3.0%
Orthodox	2	0.14	30	+1.4%
Marginal	2	0.04	9	+4.0%
Doubly affiliated		*-1.91*	*-416*	*n.a.*

Churches	MegaBloc	Cong.	Members	Affiliates
Catholic	C	432	5,217,143	9,130,000
Ch of Uganda	A	13,000	3,747,000	8,580,000
Pentecostal AoG	P	2,400	192,000	480,000
New Apostolic	I	625	125,000	250,000

Seventh-day Adventist	P	651	106,119	190,000
Elim Pentecostal Fell	P	667	80,000	177,600
Ch of the Redeemed	P	620	62,000	124,000
Ch of God (Cleveland)	P	500	70,000	120,000
Deliverance	P	220	33,000	66,000
Baptist Ch of U	P	785	32,700	60,000
Other Indigenous [7]	I	65	26,000	52,000
Ch of God (Anderson)	P	420	25,000	45,000
Full Gospel	P	39	11,818	39,000
Jehovah's Witnesses	M	34	2,370	7,000
Reformed Presbyterian	P	12	3,000	5,000
Latter-day Saints (Morm)	M	2	1,000	2,000
Other denoms [48]		1,744	213,900	393,500
Doubly affiliated			-182,000	-416,000
Total Christians [70]		22,216	9.766m	19.305m

Trans-bloc Groupings	pop.%	,000	Ann.Gr.
Evangelical	46.3	10,079	+3.6%
Charismatic	19.5	4,251	+4.1%
Pentecostal	6.0	1,299	+6.9%

Missionaries from Uganda
P,I,A 773 in 19 agencies to 9 countries: Uganda 730, Zimbabwe 9.

Missionaries to Uganda
P,I,A 552 in 93 agencies from 25 countries: USA 200, UK 96, Korea 59, Germany 49. C 1,400. O 10. M 50.

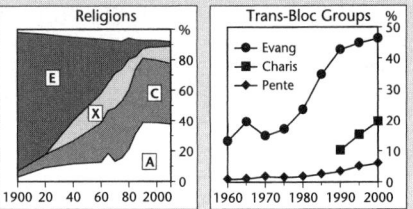

• Answers to Prayer

1 Uganda is the first country in the world with a massive AIDS problem to halve and even reduce the numbers of the afflicted from possibly 25% in 1992 to possibly 8-10% in 2000 and around 5% in 2004. Both government and churches faced up to the terrible calamity and have successfully worked to achieve this reduction.

2 The East African Revival brought new life and fervency to the large Church of Uganda and other smaller denominations for 30 years after its beginnings in 1936. Its characteristics were the centrality of Christ expressed in repentance, brokenness and walking in the light. Internal divisions and the awful years of persecution and suffering between 1967 and 1986 damped the fires of revival.

3 Renewed revival from 1986 onwards — widespread prayer movements, the amazing growth of the Pentecostal Assemblies and a revival movement in the Catholic Church in 1995 are manifestations of this. Renewal in the latter has led to gospel preaching, healings and the burning of fetishes.

• Challenges for Prayer

1 The devastation of the Amin and Obote years with unrestrained terror, murder, tribal warfare and corruption destroyed much of the economic and social fabric of the nation and hastened the spread of AIDS. Peace negotiations in progress in 2003-2004 might at last succeed. Pray for lasting solutions in the series of wars in Sudan, Rwanda and Congo in which Uganda has also been embroiled.

2 The LRA, a blasphemous terrorist militia that has been waging a campaign of terror amongst the predominantly Christian populations of Northern Uganda and Southern Sudan for the past 17 years. The characteristics of the LRA are unimaginable barbarity and widespread use of kidnapped child soldiers. The leader of the LRA was a spirit medium but was killed in Jan 2004. Pray that the LRA may be destroyed as an organization.

3 The Church though in part being revived and growing, needs prayer for:

a) *Loving unity in Christ*. Reconciliation is needed between tribes, between Protestant and Catholic, revived and non-revived, charismatic and non-charismatic.

b) *Continued renewal*. While most of the population claims to be Christian, widespread polygamy, a culture of promiscuity and paying mere lip-service to God, belies this.

c) *Training of a new generation of leaders*. Uganda Christian University (formerly Bishop Tucker Theological College) once strongly evangelical, has some liberal teachers on the faculty. There are several Pentecostal Bible schools and a Baptist Seminary. **YWAM** provides short-term training in their Discipleship Training School. Pray for the preparation of spiritual, godly leaders.

4 **Major ministry challenges for the Ugandan Church:**

a) ***The AIDS disaster.*** Though the infection rate is falling, the devastation for families and communities is great. Maybe three million are living with the disease. There are nearly two million orphans of AIDS and war. Much is being done by churches and agencies in AIDS support (CMS, **YWAM**), caring for orphans (Watoto Childcare Ministries caring for over 1,000 — **PAoC**/Pentecostal Assemblies) and preventive ministry in promoting Christian values — chastity outside marriage and faithfulness within it (**SU** — Aid for AIDS). Pray for these.

b) ***Young people's*** ministry — vital for rebuilding the country in the wake of the devastation of war and AIDS. Pray for the extensive ministry of **SU** in schools and for FOCUS (**IFES**) in Makarere University (where the Christian Union has a membership of 500 among the 9,000 students) and ministry on 64 other campuses. Life Ministry (**CCCI**) on the university campus, disciples faculty and students and challenges those with the maturity for involvement in world missions. Pray also for effective youth programmes in churches — not a priority in the past.

c) ***Children in crisis.*** The large number of orphans and the increased levels of poverty deprive many of care, finance for education and hope. Pray especially for:

  i   *Abducted children.* The Lord's Resistance Army has abducted over 10,000 children as child-soldiers or sex-slaves; 70% of their 'army' is made up of drugged, brainwashed children. Pray for all seeking to rehabilitate those who are physically freed (**WVI**, others).

  ii *Street children*, who have multiplied in Kampala (**AIM**, others).

d) ***Refugees*** are housed in many camps — over 100,000 Sudanese in the north, many Congolese in the west and Rwandans in the south-west. There are also Ugandan refugees forced into camps in the LRA-affected areas in the north-west. This is an immense extra burden for the country. Pray for all who seek to minister to them. **MAF**'s role in flying help to them is important.

5 **Missions vision in the Ugandan Church.** The large number of committed Christians and the experience of both revival and suffering give Ugandans a unique basis to share the gospel elsewhere. A growing number are serving abroad — most short-term (Life Ministries). A number of Ugandan cross-cultural ministries have been formed — **UEMA** (Uganda Evangelical Mission Agency), **Agape United Mission** and **Here is Life** — the latter for ministry among Muslims in the north-west.

6 **Expatriate missionaries are appreciated.** Most had to leave the country during Amin's dictatorship. Uganda's economic and social condition makes for many opportunities for expatriate Christian ministry. The dominance of Western agencies belongs to the past, so pray for a close fellowship between expatriates and Ugandan believers and the calling of those eager to serve the Church in reconstruction, development, Bible training and other ministries. Some of the larger missions: **MAF** (63 workers), **CMS**-MAM (62), **IMB**-SBC (28), Pentecostals (22), Diguna (19), **YWAM** (10 and 58 nationals), **TEAR Fund** (8), **CCCI** (2 and 66 nationals).

7 **The remaining unreached** are still in need of pioneer workers. Pray for:

a) ***Muslims*** who are a minority in many peoples. The Kakwa (100,000 — 13%), Madi in the north-west and Soga (15%) in the south-west have significant numbers of Muslims. There has been a rise in Islamist extremism. Arab states have poured large sums of money into education. The Muslim University in Kampala is one part of their strategy. Relatively little has been done to sensitively reach out specifically to them, and converts have been few and persecuted.

b) ***The northeast peoples*** — the Karamojong, Pokot (67,000) and Jie (75,000), who are only partially-reached nomadic peoples. In the last few years many Karamojong have turned to the Lord after years of vicious tribal warfare and severe cattle disease. The big challenge is to plant viable congregations that fit the style of a semi-nomadic people with a growing culture of violence and gun-bearing.

8 **Christian support ministries:**

a) ***The Bible Society*** has done much to promote new Bible translations and publish Bibles. Sales have gone down because of poverty. In the 1980s average annual sales were 200,000. This was reduced to 50,000 in 1998. All Christian literature ministries are similarly crippled. Pray for the provision of the Scriptures. There are 13 languages remaining without God's Word — 4 definitely needing a translation. **SIL** is now assisting in this ministry.

b) **MAF's flying programme** has been a blessing to many — with a float plane to the isolated island communities in Lake Victoria, and other planes serving Christian ministries to churches, refugees, in health and vaccination programmes, etc. The dangerous roads make this a vital ministry.

c) **The JESUS film**. Forty languages are targeted, 19 have been completed and a further 16 are in preparation.

d) **Christian radio and TV programmes** are aired on the national network and are widely appreciated. Pray for effective programming and lasting fruit.

Ukraine

NOVEMBER 11-12
EUROPE

early 1990s. The nation is finally beginning to climb out of its post-Communist economic disaster, but not without cost. Living standards have generally declined, corruption is rampant, debts to the World Bank/IMF are massive and energy payments to Russia are in arrears. **HDI** 0.721; 91ˢᵗ/174. **Public debt** 13% of GNP. **Income/person** $1,040 (3.3% of USA).

POLITICS
For centuries Ukraine was dominated and fought over by a succession of powers. Independence was declared in 1991, but many want to revive closer associations with Russia — an issue that will long remain central to Ukrainian politics. When the Communist Party was banned, its leaders metamorphosed into nationalists, but the old state apparatus and bureaucracy was transplanted into the multi-party democratic system. The failure thus far of democratic mechanisms to achieve economic reform has caused many to remember nostalgically the Communist era.

GEOGRAPHY
Area 603,700 sq.km. A flat, fertile, forested plain with few natural boundaries.

Population		Ann.Gr.	Density
2000	50,455,980	-0.38%	84 per sq. km.
2010	48,723,593	-0.33%	81 per sq. km.
2025	45,687,963	-0.50%	76 per sq. km.

Capital Kyiv (Kiev) 3.35 mill. Other major cities: Donets'k 2.15m; Kharkiv 2.0m; Dnipropetrovs'k 1.6m; Odessa 1.13m. **Urbanites** 68%.

PEOPLES
Widespread inter-marriage of Ukrainians and Russians blurs ethnic divisions.
Indo-European 97.7%.
Slav 96.1%. Ukrainian 34.5m; Russian 13.2m; Belarusian 420,000; Bulgarian 222,000; Polish 210,000.
Other 1.6%. Moldavian/Romanian 445,000; Greek 95,000; German 55,000; Armenian 52,000; Roma (Gypsy) 47,000; Georgian 24,000.
Turkic/Altaic 1.2%. Crimean Tatar 300,000; Tatar 95,000.
Other 1.1%. Jews 410,000; Hungarian 176,000.

Literacy 99%. **Official language** Ukrainian, but Russian widely spoken. **All languages** 8. **Languages with Scriptures** 3Bi 1NT 1por 1wip.

ECONOMY
Rich in natural resources. Reserves of coal, iron ore, oil and natural gas. Agricultural production is one of the world's highest. Reform packages have halted the hyper-inflation of the

RELIGION
The Church was severely persecuted under Communism. Freedom of religion since 1990, but there are somewhat restrictive conditions for non-traditional groups. **Persecution index** 78ᵗʰ in the world.

Religions	Population %	Adherents	Ann.Gr.
Christian	88.12	44,461,810	+0.9%
non-Religious	10.56	5,328,151	-8.0%
Jewish	0.75	378,420	-3.9%
Muslim	0.45	227,052	-0.8%
Other	0.12	60,547	+14.0%

Christians	Denom.	Affil.%	,000	Ann.Gr.
Protestant	41	3.00	1,511	+2.6%
Independent	16	1.21	611	+3.0%
Catholic	2	11.79	5,950	+1.8%
Orthodox	6	62.71	31,640	+0.7%
Marginal	4	0.51	259	+15.1%
Unaffiliated		8.90	4,490	n.a.

Churches	MegaBloc	Cong.	Members	Affiliates
Ukrainian Orthodox [2]	O	7,900	21.379m	31.00m
Eastern-rite Catholic	C	3,200	3,496,503	5,000,000
Latin-rite Catholic	C	500	620,000	950,000
Autocephalous Orth [3]	O	1,200	389,610	600,000
Old Believers	I	72	284,431	475,000
Ev Chr & Baptists [3]	P	2,236	127,000	380,000

Evangelical Pente Union	P	1,200	120,000	370,000
Jehovah's Witnesses	M	800	113,000	252,000
Unregis. Pentecostal	P	530	130,000	250,000
Seventh-day Adventist [2]	P	713	59,263	136,000
Reformed	P	95	19,500	130,000
Indep Pente Union [5]	P	239	30,000	100,000
Charismatic groups [6]	I	300	29,940	50,000
Lutheran	P	30	25,974	40,000
Unregistered Baptist	P	90	9,200	24,000
Church of God (Clev)	P	26	5,784	12,000
Latter-day Saints (Morm)	M	60	3,000	7,000
Other denoms [35]		329	117,800	195,600
Total Christians [67]		19,520	26.960m	39.972m

Trans-bloc Groupings	pop.%	,000	Ann.Gr.
Evangelical	2.7	1,358	+3.3%
Charismatic	1.7	854	+3.7%
Pentecostal	1.6	787	+3.8%

Missionaries from Ukraine
P,I,A 906 in 16 agencies to 10 countries: Ukraine 530, Russia 359.

Missionaries to Ukraine
P,I,A 463 in 70 agencies from 22 countries: USA 340, Canada 19, South Africa 17, Germany 12, Australia 11.

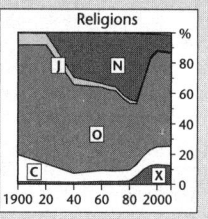

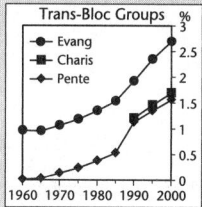

• Answers to Prayer

1 **Praise the Lord for the rich Christian heritage** of Ukraine. This was the Bible belt of the Soviet sphere, with half of the former USSR's Baptists and Pentecostals. Since independence evangelical churches have nearly doubled, despite difficult conditions. Pray that these congregations might continue to multiply and mature.

2 **Praise God for the emergence of many dynamic and visionary Ukrainian mission agencies** who minister both at home and all over the former Soviet Union.

• Challenges for Prayer

1 **The aftermaths of both independence and the Chernobyl disaster** still have tragic impact on Ukrainians. Poverty, rather than riches, has been the outcome of freedom for many. Strict reform measures combined with rampant corruption is only likely to intensify the problem. The vacuum left by Communism's demise has often been filled with violent crime, breakdown in family structures and sexual immorality. In addition, radiation pollution from Chernobyl still affects huge swathes of the country. The consequent weakening of immune systems, combined with a rapidly spreading AIDS virus could do incalculable damage to an already shrinking population. Pray that amidst the darkness, many would seek the Light.

2 **Ukraine is a key state,** a spiritual bridge between east and west, Orthodox and Catholic. Kyiv was where Slavic Christianity was born 1,000 years ago. Most Ukrainians are of the Ukrainian Orthodox Church. Many others are of the Greek or Uniate Catholic Church, which follows the Orthodox liturgy and structure but accepts the leadership of the Pope. The Orthodox Church is torn by strife as factions proclaim loyalty to competing patriarchs based in Kyiv and Moscow. The Autocephalous Orthodox Church (until recently banned, and still not formally registered) condemns them both for compliance with the Communists, but is itself beset with schisms. All these groups compete for the reclamation of buildings seized by the Communists. Much superstition and superficiality exist, but there is also a spiritual minority with a love for the Scriptures. Pray that spiritual life and renewal rather than power-politics may govern structures and relationships within these large bodies.

3 **Ukraine has a strong Christian heritage,** but suffering under Communism was severe. Evangelical Christians have emerged stronger and more numerous from 130 years of unrelenting persecution in which millions of Christians were killed. Pray that full freedom of religion for all groups may be enshrined in the constitution, practised by the state, and fully utilised by believers. Pray that the church might adjust to a new context, and meet its challenges boldly. Among these are:

a) ***The need for full restoration and reconciliation.*** The era of Communist persecution is over but the scars of intimidation, manipulation and betrayal are not entirely healed.

Orthodox, Catholic and Protestant Churches all face this. Pray for firmness, fairness and forgiveness in handling all who compromised. Pray that those who did not bend might now demonstrate flexibility in church structure, and in enabling congregations to be outward looking rather than insular.

b) *Lack of unity*. Communist subterfuge brought division and chaos between registered and unregistered congregations of nearly all denominations. Since 1990, disputes have come into the open. These issues have been recognised by Ukrainian Christians and are being addressed. Pray for removal of prejudice, mistrust, personality clashes, and structures that prevent fellowship and promote competition — especially in tapping Western funds and aid.

c) *The lack of resources* for maximising the present harvest. Most evangelical denominations are growing rapidly, hampered only by an inability to erect buildings and train leaders. Due to the economic situation church buildings, discipleship materials, disciplers and basic equipment are in short supply. Pray that the kingdom of God's growth would not be stunted by simple financial needs.

d) *Religious freedom is somewhat threatened* by the entrenched religious hierarchy and by government actions taken to limit the expansion of cults and sects. Registering churches or missions can be a very difficult and delicate process. Pray for wisdom and the right combination of discretion and boldness on the part of Christian workers.

4 **Good, spiritual, theological training is a great need**. Many have benefited from theological education since 1989, but with many more churches beginning or waiting for pastors, the need is as urgent as ever. Thousands of students have been trained in dozens of seminaries, Bible schools and institutes. Over 10,000 have taken the Life in Christ Correspondence Course. Resources are the greatest challenge to Christian educators — the lack of trained teachers is overshadowed by the lack of textbooks, facilities and funding for the students themselves. Western agencies are proving invaluable in this area, particularly **SGA**, but also Calvary Chapel Mission to the Ukraine, **GEM** and Baptist and Pentecostal groups. Pray for wise, helpful co-labouring with expatriate partners to raise up many trained Christian leaders for Ukraine and all the former USSR. Pray also for openings and support in ministry for those who graduate.

5 **Expatriate agencies**. Some such as Light in the East, **SGA** and many others faithfully served the persecuted church before 1989 and continue to do so. Hundreds of others have flocked in to the country since then, but all too often with great insensitivity to the local situation, a lack of long-term commitment and unhealthy attitudes about money and "sponsorship". Pray for more long-term workers who will learn the language and culture to better serve the Ukrainian Church in Bible teaching and in modelling a Christian life style in family and ministry. The most effective missions are often those who facilitate the growing Ukrainian mission effort through consultation and troubleshooting.

6 **Indigenous agencies**. There are now hundreds of Ukrainian agencies working in evangelism, literature, with prisoners, in summer camps and schools, and especially in much needed humanitarian work such as hospitals, orphanages and soup kitchens. Pentecostals and Baptists minister in many ways both in Ukraine and by sending missionaries to other former Soviet states, as do Missionary Brotherhood (LITE) and Light of the Gospel Mission. Pray for the burgeoning Ukrainian missionary movement — may the Lord prosper their work and may Western groups truly serve them selflessly.

7 **Outreach challenges:**

a) *Students.* CoMission, CCX(**IFES**), **CCCI** and others have developed campus ministries, and student groups are multiplying. CCX has groups meeting in 15 different cities, and most student missions have a healthy mix of expatriate and national workers. Summer camps (often held in former Communist Youth facilities) have proved fruitful. Pray that the right strategies and structures might help to evangelize this post-Soviet generation.

b) *Crimea.* This highly russified region differs from the rest of Ukraine, with continuing Communist sentiment and interest in reunification with Russia. Yet over 250,000 exiled Crimean Tatars have been welcomed back from Stalin-era exile in Central Asia. There are only a handful of Tatar Christians, and very few evangelical churches in the whole region. There are several Slavic and Western missions seeking to reach them. Openness increased after public apologies by Christians for their ill treatment and exile. The New

Testament is being translated. Pray a Tatar Church into being.

c) Ukrainian Jews. Many have emigrated to Israel and the West and the population continues to drop by 10% annually. Chosen People Ministries have seen fruit in outreach to them. There are dozens of Messianic synagogues, and a Messianic Bible school.

d) The eastern part of the country has much less of an evangelical presence than the western part, and is in more need of missionaries. There are still 20,000 villages and towns without an evangelical church in Ukraine.

e) Cults, in particular Jehovah's Witnesses, Mormons and eastern mystical groups, are gaining many converts. Pagan revival movements such as RUNVira and the Perunists also pose a challenge. Churches must realise that they are competing with these groups for the souls of Ukrainians. There are two apologetics and research centres whose goal is to promote greater discernment among Christians and encourage outreach to cult followers.

8 **Christian media ministries** for prayer:

a) Bible ministries. The Ukrainian Bible Society (**UBS**) was restarted in 1991. Many realise the need of the Bible for restoration of moral and absolute values in society. The **UBS** has a unique and strategic ministry in that it is welcomed in the Orthodox and Catholic Churches. There are far more opportunities than there is finance — pray for the Lord's limitless provision to be released.

b) Literature. There is a great need for Christian literature in Ukrainian. Russian literature is much more plentiful and Ukrainian therefore ignored by publishers. **EHC** has distributed over 6 million pieces of literature through the Ukrainian churches.

c) Radio and television. These are open for Christian programmes. **CBN** have a major television network based in Kyiv. **HCJB** (with CMAssociates), **FEBC** and **TWR** all broadcast several hours a week in Ukrainian with good repsonse. Even more hours are broadcast in Russian. One hour a week is broadcast in Tatar on shortwave. There is also a need for Christian television programmes.

d) The JESUS film is shown in Hungarian, Romanian, Russian and Ukrainian.

United Arab Emirates

NOVEMBER 13
ASIA

GEOGRAPHY
Area 77,700 sq.km of desert and mountains on the Arabian Gulf and the Gulf of Oman. Seven emirates: Abu Dhabi, Dubai, Sharjah, Ras al Khaimah, Ajman, Umm al Qaiwain and Fujairah.

Population	Ann.Gr.	Density
2000	2,441,436	+2.01%	31 per sq. km.
2010	2,851,247	+1.46%	37 per sq. km.
2025	3,283,949	+0.71%	42 per sq. km.

Capital Abu Dhabi 398,695. **Other major city:** Dubai 669,181. Urbanites 84%.

PEOPLES
All figures are estimates. The massive presence of expatriate workers – often illegal – makes accurate figures difficult to obtain.
Arab 32%. Emirati 18%. Other Arab 14%. Egyptians, Jordanians, Palestinians, Yemenis.
South Asian 59%. Indian, Pakistani, Bangladeshi, Sri Lankan.
Other 9%. Filipino, Iranian, European, East Asian.
Literacy 79.2%. **Official language** Arabic. **All indignous languages** 8. **Languages with Scripture** 4Bi 1por 1w.i.p.

ECONOMY
Breathtaking advance from poverty to fabulous wealth in one generation. Massive development and diversification schemes funded by oil wealth have boosted tourism, trade and finance. Abu Dhabi has enormous oil reserves. Dubai's are much smaller. The other 5 emirates have little or no oil. Dubai is an important commercial, information technology and industrial centre. The UAE's great economic dilemma is its complete dependence on cheap foreign labour. **HDI** 0.812; 43rd/174. **Income/person** $18,290 (61% of USA).

POLITICS
The British-protected Trucial States became an independent confederation of monarchies in 1971. No political parties or elections are permitted. The Emir of Abu Dhabi is President of the Supreme Council which rules the country.

RELIGION
Islam is the religion of state, with a Sunni majority and a small Shi'a minority. There is freedom to worship and witness within the expatriate communities, but no outreach to the indigenous population is officially permitted. Limited non-Muslim religious expression is permitted. Religious figures are estimates. **Persecution Index** 36th in world.

Religions	Population %	Adherents	Ann.Gr.
Muslim	65.45	1,597,920	+1.5%
Hindu	17.00	415,044	+3.3%
Christian	9.25	225,833	+2.5%
Buddhist	4.00	97,657	+2.5%
Other	2.50	61,036	+3.7%
non-Religious	1.30	31,739	+4.5%
Baha'i	0.50	12,207	+6.7%

Christians	Denom.	Affil.%	,000	Ann.Gr.
Protestant	28	0.50	12	+3.4%
Independent	6	0.08	2	+3.7%
Anglican	1	0.36	9	+7.7%
Catholic	1	5.32	130	+2.5%
Orthodox	7	2.99	73	+1.9%

Churches	MegaBloc	Cong.	Members	Affiliates
Catholic	C	7	90,909	130,000
Orthodox groups [6]	O	7	13,400	67,000
Protestant groups [28]	P	47	5,111	12,200
Anglican	A	9	2,613	8,700
Armenian Apostolic	O	2	3,593	6,000
Independent groups [6]	I	6	945	1,890
Total Christians [43]		78	116,600	225,800

Trans-bloc Groupings	pop.%	,000	Ann.Gr.
Evangelical	0.8	19	+3.8%
Charismatic	0.3	8	+3.9%

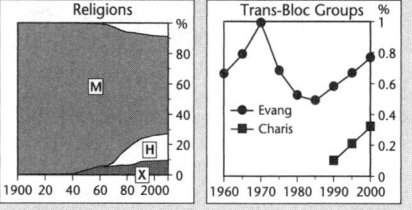

• Challenges for Prayer

1 **Radical changes of the last generation** have made UAE citizens more cosmopolitan and open to new ideas, yet the rise of extreme Islamism has led to increased restrictions. Many are in daily contact with Christians, but few believers have opportunity to openly share their faith because of the possible results — arrests are not unusual. Pray for courage, wisdom and an atmosphere in which the gospel can be shared freely.

2 **Expatriate Christians** have relative freedom for discreet witness and worship as the nation becomes more open and international. Several parcels of land have been granted recently for the development of Christian compounds. Pray for the many English, Arabic, Urdu, Filipino and Indian language worship groups and congregations. Many believers have a vision for evangelising their own ethnic group and beyond, but they need training. There are several TEE programmes active in UAE for training leaders — pray for this vital work. Pray also for the strategic partnerships which labour and intercede specifically for the Gulf states.

3 **There are limited medical facilities** in which expatriates are involved. These are dependent on good relationships with the authorities. Pray for the provision of godly staff willing to serve in them.

4 **The unreached:**

a) The indigenous Arab population. Both urban educated and rural illiterate have had little exposure to the gospel. There are some Gulf Arab believers. Their faith exposes them to persecution and possibly even death — pray for their encouragement and for steadfastness. Discipleship for these believers and opportunity for fellowship are great needs. Some are enrolled in Arabic language BCCs.

b) Many expatriate communities. The Iranian (Persian, Kurd, Baluch), Pakistani (Panjabi, Pushtun and Baluch), Somali and Sudanese communities here have no known groups of believers among them.

c) Women are less marginalized here than in some Arab countries, but they are nevertheless socially isolated from much potential contact with believers. Pray for fellowship and strength for those who secretly believe.

5 **Media available for outreach.** Signs indicate that there are many who are eager to learn about the gospel in private and who enthusiastically digest Christian material and programmes. Pray that many might come to accept Jesus as Saviour and grow as disciples, despite the obvious lack of church structures for these private believers.

a) ***Radio and television.*** **FEBA** Seychelles and **TWR** Cyprus have Arabic broadcasts which reach the UAE, and Christian television programmes, via **SAT-7** satellite, are available weekly on Friday afternoons. The latter are increasingly effective. Pray for increased broadcasting and widespread awareness of the broadcast times.

b) ***The JESUS film*** had been translated into most of the languages present in the Emirates, including Arabic.

c) ***Video tapes are widely*** used but the distribution of Christian tapes is difficult.

d) ***Christian literature*** distribution is limited by the fact that it must be done discreetly.

United Kingdom
United Kingdom of Great Britain and Northern Ireland

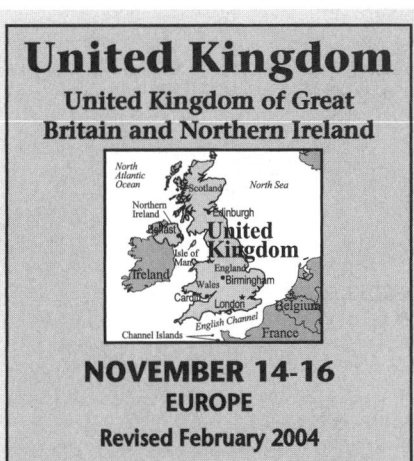

NOVEMBER 14-16
EUROPE
Revised February 2004

GEOGRAPHY
Area 244,110 sq.km. Two main islands: Britain and the north-east of Ireland. A union of four countries: England 130,400 sq.km, Scotland 78,800 sq.km, Wales 20,800 sq.km and Northern Ireland 14,100 sq.km. Also three small autonomous states which are dependencies of the British Crown: Isle of Man 588 sq.km (in the Irish Sea), Channel Islands 194 sq.km (Guernsey, Jersey).

Population	Ann.Gr.	Density
2000	58,830,160	+0.18%	241 per sq. km.
2010	59,331,486	+0.06%	243 per sq. km.
2025	59,960,856	+0.04%	246 per sq. km.

England 83.5%, Scotland 8.7% (93,000 speaking Gaelic), Wales 5% (600,000 speaking Welsh), Northern Ireland 2.8%.

Capital London 11.8 mill. Other major city conurbations: Birmingham/West Midlands 2.3m; Manchester 2.25m; Leeds/Bradford 2.1m; Glasgow 1.85m; Liverpool 1.42m; Sheffield 1.28m; Newcastle 1.1m. **Urbanites** 90%.

PEOPLES
Anglo-Saxon/Celtic 89.3%. English 43.6m; Scots 4.7m; Irish 3m (including 1.4m Irish Republic residents living in the UK), Welsh 1.12m.

Asian 4%. Largest groups: Panjabi 471,000; Bengali 400,000; Urdu-speaking 400,000; Chinese 250,000; Kashmiri 117,000; Tamil 90,000; Japanese 55,000.
European 2.1%. Greek 230,000; Italian 200,000; German 200,000; Polish 135,000.
Afro-Caribbean 1.7%. Caribbean origin; majority British-born.
Middle Eastern 0.8%. Arab 170,000; Turk 150,000; Iranian 100,000; Kurd 35,000.
African 0.5%. Nigerian, Ghanaian, Somali, etc.
Other 1.6%. Jews 305,000; Roma/Irish Travellers (Gypsy) 200,000; British Commonwealth citizens 250,000; US citizens 180,000.

Literacy 98%. **Official language** English; in Wales both English and Welsh. English has become the primary language of 288 million in the world, as well as the major language of international communication for over 900 million. **All languages** 15 indigenous, over 200 immigrant languages. **Indigenous languages with Scriptures** 7Bi 2NT. There have been more translations of the Scriptures into English than into any other language.

ECONOMY
The world's first industrialized economy — now increasingly a service economy. Post-WWII decline through poor management, low investment, labour unrest and high levels of public ownership was reversed in the mid-1980s with large-scale re-vamping of obsolete economic structures. One of the more reluctant members of the EU, and resistant to entry into Euro monetary system. **HDI** 0.918; 10th/174. **Public debt** 33% of GNP. **Income/person** $20,870 (67% of USA).

POLITICS
Parliamentary, constitutional monarchy. The UK was formed in 1801 as a Union of Great Britain and Ireland. Southern Ireland formally seceded from the Union in 1921. The British Empire, once covering / of the world, has become 60 independent states, most being members of the British Commonwealth. Since 1945 the transition from a world power to a European state linked to its own continent has not been easy. The centuries-long conflict between the Irish and British (over sovereignty of Northern Ireland) still defies

full resolution. After three decades of guerrilla war waged by the Irish Republican Army (IRA, opposed to British rule) and 'Loyalist' paramilitary groups, a political settlement was agreed in 1998 toward the cessation of all hostilities and the decommissioning of weapons. An uneasy peace prevails in Northern Ireland.

RELIGION

There is full religious freedom. The Church of England (Anglican) is recognized as the Established Church in England, and the Church of Scotland (Presbyterian) in Scotland. The Sovereign is recognized as the titular head of the Church of England. The disestablishment of the Church is increasingly being advocated.

Religions	Population %	Adherents	Ann.Gr.
Christian	67.63	39,786,837	-0.6%
non-Religious/other	28.00	16,472,445	+1.9%
Muslim	2.00	1,176,603	+1.2%
Hindu	0.84	494,173	+1.2%
Sikh	0.68	400,045	+2.4%
Jewish	0.52	305,917	-0.6%
Buddhist	0.28	164,724	+5.1%
Baha'i	0.05	29,415	+0.2%

Christians	Denom.	Affil.%	,000	Ann.Gr.
Protestant	90	7.58	4,457	-0.8%
Independent	261	1.50	885	+3.0%
Anglican	4	43.30	25,475	-0.3%
Catholic	1	9.69	5,700	+0.1%
Orthodox	19	0.63	370	+3.4%
Marginal	36	2.28	1,344	+0.5%
Unaffiliated		2.64	1,556	n.a.

Churches	MegaBloc	Cong.	Members	Affiliates
Church of England	A	16,110	1,280,000	24.40m
Catholic	C	4,270	1,722,000	5,700,000
Church of Scotland (Presby)	P	1,533	614,980	1,200,000
All Methodist [6]	P	6,636	366,820	1,100,000
Church of Ireland (Ang)	A	457	160,800	640,000
Baptist Union of GB	P	1,971	142,058	550,000
Newer (House) Chs [30]	I	1,928	135,200	405,600
All Orthodox [19]	O	161	207,930	370,000

Church in Wales (Ang)	A	1,500	86,700	350,000
Presby. Ch in Ireland	P	600	214,745	285,000
Jehovah's Witnesses	M	1,478	146,640	270,000
Latter-day Saints (Morm)	M	480	120,130	185,000
Elim Pentecostal	P	613	69,320	145,000
United Reformed	P	1,700	87,250	138,000
Assemblies of God	P	664	61,150	135,753
Congregational [5]	P	1,089	66,163	120,000
Christian Brethren	P	1,340	61,225	120,000
Scottish Episcopal	A	312	48,900	85,000
Salvation Army	P	770	51,180	62,000
Baptist Union of Wales	P	500	20,650	60,000
Afro-Carib. Pente [140]	I	400	29,000	58,000
Presby. Ch of Wales	P	1,013	45,400	53,870
FIEC (Fell of Indep. Ev.)	P	421	36,960	53,000
African Indigenous [20]	I	396	14,000	42,000
Gypsy Evang Mvt	I	175	26,000	40,000
Baptist U. of Scotland	P	175	15,410	38,525
Friends (Quakers)	P	511	18,615	30,000
Other denoms [171]		6,800	605,952	1,594,000
Total Christians [412]		54,003	6.455m	38.231m

Trans-bloc Groupings	pop.%	,000	Ann.Gr.
Evangelical	8.5	4,997	+0.3%
Charismatic	3.8	2,252	+1.1%
Pentecostal	0.9	550	+1.5%

Missionaries from UK
P,I,A 10,654 in 183 agencies to 198 countries: Kenya 225, Brazil 212, France 211, Zambia 184, Spain 175, South Africa 165, Tanzania 153, Pakistan 151, Nepal 148, Congo 120, Zimbabwe 115, Philippines 109, Uganda 103.

Missionaries to UK
P,I,A 1,604 in 170 agencies from 54 countries: USA 898, Korea 123, Canada 79, South Africa 78, Brazil 52.

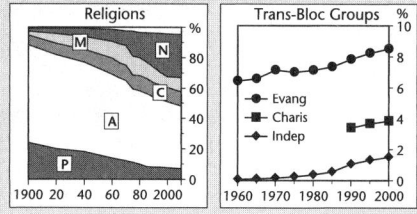

UNITED KINGDOM — GENERAL

• Answers to Prayer

1 **The cease-fire in the Northern Ireland 'Troubles'** has largely been maintained since 1998.

2 **Evangelical Christians are basically maintaining numbers,** despite considerable church decline, and are becoming more prominent in mainline denominations. Some newer movements and innovative post-modern culture churches are growing.

U 3 **Some ethnic minorities** have been more receptive with considerable growth in African-initiated churches, multi-ethnic churches and also over 6,000 'Travellers' (Roma/Gypsy) coming to Christ in the past few years (Gypsy Evangelical Movement).

• Challenges for Prayer

1 **Britain needs to regain a sense of purpose and direction for the 21ˢᵗ Century.** The nation is torn between its European geography and its Atlanticist culture. Pray that political leadership may have the moral integrity and courage to give the correct lead. Membership of the EU and differing views on the degree of federalism desirable and its impact on national life is a matter for intense public concern and debate.

2 **A sense that all is not well pervades the country.** The 'freedoms' of the 1960s led to social disaster and hastened spiritual decline. Many are discouraged about the future and cynical about the seeming impotence of politicians to deal with the malaise. The gay rights movement, though representing a small minority, has seized the initiative in many areas of public life and in government legislation. Spiritual need is highlighted by increasing violence in the cities, the high divorce, suicide and illegitimacy rates, and drug abuse. Paralleling this is the growing number of younger people who have no contact with or knowledge of Christianity. Without a radical change, disaster looms. Pray for national repentance and restoration to the spiritual vigour that once made Britain's Christians a blessing to the world.

3 **A national awakening is needed.** There has been one every century in the last 800 years — the last was in 1859-69. The Judeo-Christian heritage has been so eroded by post-modernist worldviews that public opinion is no longer Christian. Christians have been marginalized in the media, public life, government legislation and school curricula. Religious pluralization has sapped the confidence of many Christians to testify boldly and even believe that Jesus is the *only* way to the Father. The steep decline in numbers of the Methodists, Anglicans, United Reformed, Brethren and other denominations continues and the Baptists and newer (house) churches have plateaued. Pray that Christians might become passionate for God's honour, burdened to pray for revival and be freed from a deadening negativism and materialism that pervades the life of the churches.

4 **Tolerance is the 'in' word.** The influx of non-Christian religions has affected the worldview of the population. The spokesmen for Islam, Buddhism, Hinduism, etc., push for legislation that will favour their religions, and demand freedoms they would never grant Christians in their lands of origin. Astrology, the occult, reincarnation, old world paganism (Druid/Wicca) and even Satanism have become popular, with a massive increase in literature promoting their ends. The mission field has come to the UK — and many non-Western Christians perceive the UK itself as a mission field. Pray that UK Christians may recover a confidence in the 'intolerant' gospel and a passion for sharing it with the majority who have little concept of its content.

5 **The future of the Church of England is crucial for the country** and is the 'mother' Church for the world's 80 million Anglicans. This composite body is an umbrella under which Anglo-Catholics, liberals and Evangelicals co-exist and where, tragically, equivocation on homosexuality and the basic tenets of the Christian faith are condoned. Fragmentation of the Church over such issues as ordination of women, ecumenism and dis-establishment is possible. Yet Evangelicalism is a growing force and gaining centre stage: 27% of bishops, 53% of clergy, 60% of ordinands and 40% of church-goers espouse its cause. The 1998 Lambeth Conference of the Anglican Communion was a resounding setback for liberalism as the non-Western majority strongly affirmed biblical values. The charismatic movement has also contributed to an extensive renewal movement in the Church. Pray that Church leadership might regain a prophetic role and speak with clear biblical authority to a nation that is morally and spiritually adrift.

6 **There are signs of hope** — water these tender plants with prayer:

a) ***Traumatic social change*** and the devastating consequences of violence, family breakdown and fear for the future have brought a new openness to consider spiritual solutions.

b) ***Renewal movements***. Many pastors and congregations experienced charismatic renewal between the 1960s-'80s. This also gave rise to a new family of churches. The house church movement, or Newer Churches, grew fast and have become a significant spiritual force in the nation, deeply affecting church structures and fellowship patterns, and have enlivened worship across the denominational spectrum. Their growth slowed in the 1990s. Nation-wide, these changes have been stimulated by major trans-denominational gatherings such as Greenbelt and Spring Harvest.

c) **New younger generation movements** are emerging with radically new approaches — Internet café gatherings, WEB prayer and culturally appropriate worship styles, such as Tribal Generation, flowing from the Church of England, and also others spontaneously springing up in different parts of the country.

d) **The Alpha Course phenomenon** has spread across the country to nearly every denomination and across the world as one of the most successful outreach programmes run by churches in the UK today. These user-friendly introductory courses explain Christianity in a relaxed and informal environment. About 6,400 congregations were using the Alpha courses in 1998 with over 650,000 individuals having completed one.

e) **Christian leaders** from across the denominational spectrum are meeting regularly for prayer together in many cities and towns. This is leading to cooperative efforts in ministry.

7 **Evangelical Christianity** has grown slowly in percentage of the population, of church-goers and as a proportion of active membership in mainline denominations, but there are definite challenges:

a) **To maintain and increase unity** in fellowship and vision. **The Evangelical Alliance** has done much to encourage this and give credibility to Evangelicals in national life. The EA represents 1.3 million Evangelicals, 30 denominations and 800 agencies.

b) **A widespread loss of confidence** and certainty about models for church life and outreach. There were a number of initiatives in the 1990s which fizzled out or did not halt the overall malaise and decline.

c) **A common cynicism about the future** and the state of the Kingdom of God in the world which cripples enthusiasm for missions locally or overseas. Pray for restoration of vision and faith in God's ability to change Britain once more.

8 **Christian leadership** is under intense pressure — church members are more demanding, less committed, giving less and often more interested in self-fulfilment than sacrificial service. There is a lack of effective Bible teachers and expositors. Pray for effective discipling and training of a new generation of leaders in both congregational and more formal theological training. There were 59 residential denominational colleges and 25 interdenominational colleges with a total of 7,150 students in 1999. Pray that these may not only impart a theological education, but also spirituality and world vision.

9 **Young people** are more spiritually open, but increasingly come from dysfunctional families, a history of drug abuse and promiscuous lifestyles. They need intense, loving help to become effective disciples. Pray for:

a) **Religious education teachers** in schools. RE is a core subject by law but is often ignored, resisted or even opposed by school authorities and students. Pray for Christians involved in this ministry and for meaningful ways of making the message of the gospel come alive.

b) **Commitment** to Jesus and His will, to the discipline of Bible study and to the church. Few have come from a background of church life.

c) **Effective discipling of children.** Sunday School is a fading institution and viable alternative models are lacking.

d) **Youth movements.** Covenanters, Crusaders, **SU** and British YFC have long had significant impact. Newer movements such as Soul Survivor and Oasis are proving innovative and effective.

e) **Missions vision** — few young people have much exposure to a vision for the world. The ministries of **OM**, **World Horizons**, **YWAM** and Worldwide Message Tribe are seeking to redress this with short-term training and exposure.

10 **Students** are exposed to great pressures in the secular education system. A largely godless and materialistic younger generation is being formed by it. Relatively few secondary schools have a live, outgoing witness from staff or student groups. Pray for:

a) **The SU and Christian Union groups** in schools — for their growth and multiplication, and for Christian teachers to be used of God to help launch such groups.

b) **The Campus Christian groups** among the 900,000 full-time students in colleges and universities. Their growth and diversity is encouraging, the main ones being Agapé (**CCCI**), **Navigators**, Fusion and UCCF(**IFES**). The oldest and most widespread is the work of

UCCF with Christian Unions in nearly 600 colleges and universities, yet a further 300 have no permanent group. Pray for mature, stable leadership, effective support and advice from the 45 travelling secretaries, and establishment of a viable witness in every college. The student population is one of the more receptive segments of society.

c) **Overseas students.** About 400,000 overseas students are granted visas every year — 80,000 to do university degrees. Outreach to them is varied but too limited, and many return home without ever hearing the gospel. UCCF(**IFES**), International Student Christian Services with 40 staff in 18 cities, In Contact Ministries, and others have ministry to them.

11 **Britain's contribution to world evangelization** in the last 200 years is unique. Interest has waned and many congregations have never even sent out their own missionary. In 2000 there was only one Protestant missionary overseas for every 6 churches. There is a widespread conviction that either the job has been done or that efforts should be concentrated on Britain's need. Pray for:

a) **A renewed commitment** by local congregations to world evangelization, to pray out their members to the areas of greatest need, and to care adequately for those who go.

b) **An increase in recruitment** for missions; pray that the growth in short-term involvement may lead to increased long-term recruitment and support.

c) **The coordinating role of Global Connections** (EMA) in promoting vision and cooperation among mission agencies and in local churches for world evangelization.

12 **The growing non-Anglo-Saxon minority** has become a significant part of UK urban life in the past 50 years. Many cities have large minority communities and in some they have become the majority. Some communities such as the Afro-Caribbean and Chinese have a higher proportion of active Christians than the indigenous population. Others come from countries where the gospel is little known and entry of missionaries impeded. Cultural distance, racial discrimination and even open hostility have antagonized many against 'Christianity'. Pray for:

a) **Local congregations** in multi-ethnic areas to open their doors, homes and hearts to this mission field on their doorstep, and to find effective ways of making friendships, meeting needs and winning some for the Lord.

b) **Specialist cross-cultural workers** to be called both for training churches and ministering to specific ethnic groups. Unique ministries already involved: **South Asian Concern, OM** (Turning Point), **YWAM, In Contact Ministries**, and also missionaries linked with **Interserve, ECM, MECO, BCMS Crosslinks, WEC, IMI, IT, RSTI** as well as non-Western mission agencies.

c) **Better coordination of effort and research of the need.** South Asia Concern has completed a detailed survey of the 1.5 million South Asians. Many ethnic minority communities are completely unreached due to lack of information to mobilize a ministry to reach them.

d) **Effective use of literature and other media.** Some **CLC** bookstores stock minority language literature. **WEC**'s 'SOON' broadsheet ministry in English, French, Fulbe and Swahili reaches many. **In Contact Ministries** specializes in literature on Islamics and in ethnic minority languages.

13 **Specific ethnic minority groups** that need intercession:

a) **Caribbean and African peoples.** There are over 200 denominations; 20% of the population is church-going. In the past, these churches have been somewhat isolated from the mainstream of evangelical Christianity. The African Caribbean Evangelical Alliance (ACEA) is committed to creating an equitable partnership through their programmes of networking and community building. Pray that ACEA may be able to continue giving a sense of unity to these churches and help them to combat the growing social and economic problems faced by the black community in general.

b) **South Asians.** An increasing number of people are coming to Christ from the Hindu and Sikh communities, but few from among Muslims; about 4% of all South Asians are Christian. The greatest need is among the Panjabi, Kashmiri, Bangladeshi and Pathan communities.

c) **Middle Eastern peoples.** Outreach is largely localized and sporadic. Many wealthy **Arabs** come to the UK as tourists, businessmen and students; some have come to faith. There are several Christian fellowships for Arabs and a few for the **Turks, Kurds** and **Iranians**.

There is also a Bible Training School (**ELAM Ministries**) for preparing Iranians for ministry. The **Yemenis** and 50,000 **Moroccans** are unreached.

d) Muslims now officially number over 1.2 million, but the actual number is probably much higher. About fi from Pakistan,/from the Middle East and a further/from India and Bangladesh. Large-scale illegal immigration, and an increasingly strident radical Islam of a minority that seeks to alter British society in favour of Islam, have helped to alienate Muslims from the indigenous majority. Muslims see the conversion of England to Islam as a key strategy for winning Europe. London has become a hub for extreme, militant Islamist organizations. Pray for a breakdown of cultural and social barriers on both sides and for opportunities to be created for sharing the gospel.

e) Chinese. They have mainly come from Hong Kong and Vietnam, but increasingly from Mainland China as illegal immigrants and students. The Chinese Overseas Christian Mission (**COCM**) has a successful church planting and student ministry. There are around 70 Chinese churches and about 7% of Chinese are Christian.

f) The Jewish community. This is slowly declining through assimilation (80% have no religious commitment to Judaism) and marriage. Many are disillusioned by the rigid legalism and internal squabbling of communal leaders. Many of the believers integrate into Gentile churches, though there are also eight fellowships of Messianic Jews and possibly about 2,000 believers altogether. Pray for the ministry of CMJ, **MT**, **CWI** and **Jews for Jesus**. There is increasing opposition to such ministry both from Jewish anti-missionary groups and from liberal Christian circles.

14 Christian media ministries:

a) Christian literature and Bibles. Few nations have such an extensive range of Christian literature, Bible versions and the facilities to acquire them. **The Gideons International** distributed 20 million NTs and Bibles in their first 40 years of ministry. In 2000 there were 506 Christian bookstores carrying an average of 3,600 titles! There are over 100 Christian publishers publishing 4,400 new titles annually. **The Bible Societies** not only have a ministry of Bible translation, publication and distribution in Britain and around the world, but also a wide range of catalytic ministries to stimulate Christian growth. **BookAid** has a remarkable ministry of exporting one million surplus and second-hand Christian books annually to poorer countries. Pray for these ministries and for Christians to become more avid readers.

b) Christian broadcasting. The 1990 Broadcasting Act opened unprecedented opportunities for Christians to own radio stations, satellite and cable TV stations. Pray for wisdom and balance in the face of opportunities. Many Christians are active in secular broadcasting as well as religious programming on national radio and television — over 6 million view *Songs of Praise* every week. Pray for positive impact. All efforts at ending the BBC's monopoly on (increasingly multi-faith) national, terrestrial religious broadcasting have failed — pray for change.

ENGLAND

GEOGRAPHY

Area 130,400 sq.km.

Population 49,100,000; 377 people/sq.km.

Capital London 11.8 million. Other major cities: Birmingham/West Midlands 2.27m; Manchester 2.25m; Leeds-Bradford 2.1m; Sheffield 1.28m; Newcastle-Tyneside 1.1m; Liverpool-Merseyside 1.42m; Nottingham 686,000; Coventry 676,000; Bristol 660,000.

• Challenges for Prayer

1 **England is the most secular of the four countries that comprise the UK.** The steady decline in belief and church attendance is of deep concern. About 62% of the population has belief in God, 38% that Jesus is the Son of God, 23% that the Bible is the unique Word of God, 16% visit a church during the course of a year and 11% at least once a month. Nominalism and notional Christianity are enormous challenges. A nodding acquaintance with the structures and trappings of Christianity and basking in the afterglow of Christian influence anaesthetize the majority. Pray that the Holy Spirit may break down the barriers and bring a sense of the holiness of God.

2 **London is one of the world's hub cities** for finance, travel, politics, etc. The spiritual life of London — or lack of it — impacts the world. It is also the destination of a high proportion of the inflow of migrants over the past 50 years. Pray for:

a) *Inner-city church planting.* Relatively few successful models exist — a few are the Ichthus Fellowship with growing congregations in southeast London, the International Christian Centre (Nigerian-led) in east London and multi-ethnic Kensington Temple in central London. Pray for the city to be effectively evangelized.

b) *Ethnic minorities* are increasingly becoming the majority in many London boroughs. Over 50% of church-goers in London are non-indigenous. London is the home of nearly all the UK Bangladeshis (the largest concentration in the world outside their homeland), Kurds and Turks and these constitute some of its least reached peoples.

3 **England's inner cities** have become physical and spiritual wastelands, riddled with drugs and crime. Dying congregations, closed churches and churches converted into Muslim mosques, Hindu temples or Sikh *godwaras* are commonplace. Pray that God may raise up an army of workers with effective ways of meeting the many needs of these multi-lingual, multi-cultural areas.

NORTHERN IRELAND

GEOGRAPHY

Area 14,100 sq.km.

Population 1,663,000; 118 people/sq.km.

Capital Belfast 704,000.

POLITICS

The problems of Northern Ireland are but a continuation of the centuries-old tension between the Celtic Irish and Anglo-Saxon Scots-English. It is a historical coincidence that the former are Catholic and the latter largely Protestant. The partition of Ireland between the 26 counties of the South and 6 counties of Ulster in the north did not solve the problem, for an indigenous and dissatisfied minority of Catholics who remained in Ulster under the British Crown still aspired to an all-Ireland republic while the majority of the people adhered strongly to the British link. The civil rights campaign by the disadvantaged Catholic Irish in the late 1960s degenerated into civil violence waged by extremist IRA and 'Loyalist' factions. The impact on social, economic and political life in the Province and the UK has been large, resulting in over 3,600 deaths. The 1998 political agreement led to a cease-fire, Ireland-wide consultative structures and a power-sharing government in Belfast.

• Challenges for Prayer

1 **A measure of peace has returned to Northern Ireland** but the mistrust and resentment for the past remain and the stashed weapons are not yet decommissioned. Pray for real heart changes that lead to repentance and forgiveness for past history, and reconciliation between both communities. Pray for the local, Irish Republic and British politicians who must work together in seeking a lasting solution.

2 **Northern Ireland's conflict** has given opponents of Christianity opportunity to dismissively claim that 'religions cause wars'. Pray that the grounds for this may be removed. Pray that both Catholics and Protestants may continue to be the instigators of reconciliation and leaders in godliness, prayer and commitment to the Lord Jesus.

3 **The Northern Irish are a church-going people** — the great majority, both Protestant and Catholic, are regular in church attendance and the decline elsewhere in the British Isles is less evident here. The Catholic percentage is slowly increasing (34.9% in 1961, 38.4% in 1991) and that of the largest Protestant body, the Presbyterians, decreasing (29% and 21.4% respectively). Within a   radius of Belfast is one of the highest concentrations of evangelical churches in the world. Most Protestant denominations are strongly evangelical in faith. Pray that this may be accompanied by personal faith in Christ, commitment to prayer, involvement in outreach and dedication to missions.

4 **The missionary burden of Northern Ireland churches** is higher than elsewhere in the UK. Pray that this generosity in giving of money and personnel for world evangelization may continue!

SCOTLAND

GEOGRAPHY
Area 78,800 sq.km.
Population 5,128,000; 65 people/sq.km.
Capital Edinburgh 648,000. Other major cities: Glasgow 1,851,000; Aberdeen 217,000.

POLITICS
In 1998 Scotland once more had its own parliament after nearly 300 years of representation only in London. A strong minority continue to press for full independence within the EU.

• Challenges for Prayer

1 **Revivals** in past centuries and the localized revivals of the northeast coast in 1925 and Lewis in the Hebrides in the 1950s need to be repeated on a national scale.

2 **Scotland has sent out great men and women to bless the world** such as David Livingstone, Robert Moffatt, Mary Slessor and Eric Liddell. May this tradition continue!

3 **The Church of Scotland** is Presbyterian in structure and is the established Church. There are stirrings of new life, with a rapid increase in the numbers of evangelical theological students and ministers, which is changing the Church. However, nominalism is widespread, liberal theology still dominant and Freemasonry influential. The general decline in membership and church attendance has not been halted. Pray for this Church to return to its biblical roots and the faith of its early martyrs.

4 **Church growth** has been evident among Catholics, Baptists, Pentecostals and especially the newer churches. Pray for the effective re-evangelization of Scotland. Strathclyde, which includes Glasgow and is Scotland's most densely populated area, has the lowest percentage of Protestants. The Aberdeen area has the highest percentage of non-church-goers.

WALES

GEOGRAPHY
Area 20,800 sq.km.
Population 2,921,000; 140 people/sq.km.
Capital Cardiff 655,000 (including the Rhondda Valley).

POLITICS
Wales has had a national assembly since 1998, but for the nationalists, this falls far short of their dream of Welsh independence.

• Challenges for Prayer

1 **Wales is known as the land of revivals.** From early in the 18th Century, Wales experienced a consistent series of revivals. The last of these occurred in 1904. The decline in church attendance and closure of churches since then has been higher than any other part of the UK. Pray that revival may come again — many groups in Wales are praying for this!

2 **Economic changes have had a profound impact.** The decline of the coal and slate industries has led to much depopulation and depression in industrialized areas. Coupled with an acceptance of a social gospel, this has led to empty chapels and a spiritually hardened population. Pray for the many small evangelical fellowships that are seeking to maintain their witness in these hard and unreceptive areas.

3 **Wales** struggles to preserve its own language and culture. About 17% of the population is fluent in Welsh and 34% use it regularly, but the decline in Welsh-speaking congregations has been even worse. Pray that the Holy Spirit might breathe upon the Welsh culture and revive congregations to again becoming a blessing to the world.

United States of America

GEOGRAPHY
Area 9,529,063 sq.km. The world's third largest nation in area and population.

Population		Ann.Gr.	Density
2000	278,357,141	+0.84%	29 per sq. km.
2010	297,988,958	+0.66%	31 per sq. km.
2025	325,572,586	+0.53%	34 per sq. km.

Immigration rates are high with 42 million foreign-born and approx. 3,000 legal immigrants arriving daily.

Capital Washington DC 745,000. Other major cities: New York 20.2 mill.; Los Angeles 16m; Chicago 8.8m; Washington-Baltimore 7.3m; San Francisco 6.85m; Philadelphia 6.05m; Boston 5.65m; Detroit 5.4m; Dallas 4.9m; Houston 4.6m; Atlanta 3.9m; Miami 3.7m; Seattle 3.55m; Phoenix 3.1m; Cleveland 2.95m; Minneapolis 2.9m; San Diego 2.75m; St. Louis 2.6m; Denver 2.5m; Pittsburgh 2.4m; Tampa 2.3m; Portland 2.25m; Cincinnati 2m; and 48 other mega cities. **Urbanites** 76%.

PEOPLES
A nation of immigrants with the greatest ethnic-origin diversity of any nation in history.
Euro-American 70.7%. Descendants of English settlers, then British and Irish and then from all Europe. Also Cubans, Puerto Ricans, etc., from Latin America. Estimates for the Roma (Gypsy) vary between 1.1 and 2.5 million.
Afro-American 12.4%. Most of their forebears came to the Americas as slaves. Increasing immigration from Caribbean, Haiti (800,000), Somalia (100,000) and Latin America.
Latin Mestizo 7%. Mixed race (Hispanics of all racial types are 12.6%).
Asian 4.5%. Predominantly in western USA and Hawaii. Largest communities: Filipino 3.3m; Korean 2.1m; South Asian 2.1m; Chinese 1.9m; Japanese 1.2m; Vietnamese 1.2m; Cambodian 210,000; Lao 164,000; Meo(Hmong) 100,000.
Middle Eastern 4.3%. Jews 5.6m — of which 500,000 originate from the fSU; Arab 3.2m; Iranian 2m;

Turk 100,000; Afghan 60,000.
Native American 0.9%. Amerindian(266) 1.9m; Inuit (Eskimo) 60,000 in Alaska; Aleut 2,000 in the Alaskan Aleutian Islands.
Polynesian 0.2%. Hawaiian 340,000; Samoan 95,000.
Literacy 96% (functional literacy 85%). **Official language** English. The growing Spanish-speaking Hispanic population is 11.2% of the population and numbers 34 million. **All indigenous languages** 176, of which 77 are close to extinction. Numerous languages and dialects still used by immigrants from all continents. About 13% of the population use a language other than English in the home. **Indigenous languages with Scriptures** 6Bi 11NT 39por 25w.i.p.

ECONOMY
The most powerful, diverse and technologically advanced economy in the world. Rich in agricultural and natural resources, yet 35 million live below the poverty line. A free-market economy with great flexibility. Part of NAFTA, the North American Free Trade area. Strong importer from other lands and a large adverse trade balance — so any US economic downturn has global repercussions. **HDI** 0.927; 3rd/174. **Public debt** 66% of GNP. **Income/person** $31,380.

POLITICS
Independent from Britain in 1776 as a federal republic. The number of states increased from the original 13 to 50 as the nation expanded westwards across the continent and the Pacific Ocean. The strong democratic tradition, emphasis on private initiative and civil liberties have helped to make the nation a world leader. The USA emerged from World War II as the leading industrial and military power in the world — but for 40 years was in cold-war confrontation with the USSR. Military defeat in the Vietnam War was a trauma from which the USA slowly recovered in the 1980s, but still deeply affects foreign policy. The evaporation of the threat from the USSR with its collapse in 1991 left the USA as the only global superpower, but uncertain in its application of that power toward a more peaceful world. The multiplication of localized ethnic wars, and increased danger from well-armed but small terrorist forces demand a watchful vigilance from the USA.
NOTE Jan 2004: This prediction was tragically realized on 11 Sept 2001. See below for additional information.

RELIGION
Freedom of religion is written into the constitution. No state in the world has been so strongly influenced by biblical Christianity. The principle of the separation of Church and State has been misused by liberal and anti-Christian minorities to limit the public exercise of religion and to promote permissive legislation. The Religious Freedom Act of 1998 was passed to empower the President to act against nations reported as persecuting religious minorities.

Religions	Population %	Adherents	Ann.Gr.
Christian	84.53	235,295,291	+0.7%
non-Religious	9.40	26,165,571	+1.5%
Jewish	2.00	5,567,143	-0.1%
Muslim	1.49	4,147,521	+1.7%
Buddhist	0.90	2,505,214	+3.2%
Other religions	0.52	1,447,457	+2.5%
Traditional ethnic	0.40	1,113,429	+1.9%
Hindu	0.38	1,057,757	+2.5%
Baha'i	0.26	723,729	+0.8%
Sikh	0.07	194,850	+0.8%
Chinese	0.05	139,179	+5.4%

Christians	Denom.	Affil.%	,000	Ann.Gr.
Protestant	670	24.29	67,611	-0.1%
Independent	2,409	24.32	67,686	+2.2%
Anglican	1	0.86	2,400	-1.1%
Catholic	1	20.84	58,000	-0.8%
Orthodox	68	2.08	5,780	+0.8%
Marginal	358	3.77	10,485	+0.5%
Unaffiliated		15.62	43,479	n.a.
Doubly affiliated		*-7.24*	*-21,150*	*n.a.*

Churches	MegaBloc	Cong.	Members	Affiliates
Catholic	C	23,000	40.00m	58.00m
Southern Baptist Conv	P	40,870	15.73m	20.00m
Charis netwks [1860]	I	101,716	11.20m	16.00m
United Methodist	P	36,000	8.40m	10.50m
Nat Bap Conv of USA	I	33,000	8.50m	9.60m
Ch of God in Christ	I	17,000	2.10m	7.00m
Latter-day Saints(Morm)	M	11,300	3.60m	5.20m
Evang Luth Ch in A	P	10,900	3.84m	5.19m
African Meth Epis	I	8,200	2.80m	4.00m
Nat Bapt Conv of A	I	12,336	3.10m	4.00m
Presbyterian Ch (USA)	P	11,000	2.70m	3.64m
Nat Miss Bapt Conv	I	1,100	2.70m	3.20m
Full Gosp networks [45]	I	8,529	1.71m	2.90m
Assemblies of God	P	12,727	1.51m	2.60m
Luth Ch-Missouri Syn	P	6,220	1.95m	2.60m
Episcopal Ch in USA	A	5,400	1.45m	2.40m
Amer Bapt Chs in USA	P	5,837	1.52m	2.30m
Jehovah's Witnesses	M	11,275	0.98m	2.20m
Orthodox Ch in Amer	O	600	0.96m	2.20m
Gr Orth AD of N&S A	O	540	1.60m	2.00m
United Ch of Christ	P	6,000	1.50m	1.88m
Chs of Christ (non-inst)	P	14,500	1.17m	1.80m

Chr Chs/Chs of Christ	P	5,600	1.15m	1.25m
Full Gosp Bapt Ch Fell	I	6,000	0.60m	1.25m
Prosperity Chs [15]	I	6,857	0.86m	1.20m
Seventh-day Adventist	P	4,406	0.84m	1.12m
Ch of the Nazarene	P	5,120	630,000	945,000
Ch of God (Cleveland)	P	6,500	680,000	900,000
Amer Baptist Assoc	P	1,860	280,000	800,000
Christian Ch (Disciples)	P	3,800	540,000	800,000
Willow Creek Assoc	I	3,000	280,000	700,000
Calvary Chapels Int'l	I	1,000	380,000	550,000
Korean Presb Ch of A	I	1,700	204,000	510,000
Chr and Miss Alliance	P	1,975	146,000	340,000
Reformed Ch in Amer	P	956	189,338	312,802
Presbyterian C in A (PCA)	P	1,400	250,000	300,000
Pentecostal Holiness	P	1,700	190,000	300,000
Evang Free	P	1,300	140,000	280,000
Conserv Baptist Assoc	P	1,030	192,000	274,560
Assoc of Int Gospel Ass.	I	470	220,000	265,000
Assoc of Vineyard	I	600	140,000	196,000
Salvation Army	P	1,270	80,000	140,000
Christian Brethren	P	850	60,000	105,000
Other denoms [1,554]		112,775	19.54m	30.21m
Doubly affiliated			*-12.59m*	*-20.15m*
Total Christians [3,514]		548,219	134.00m	191.80m

Trans-bloc Groupings	pop.%	,000	Ann.Gr.
Evangelical	32.5	90,446	+2.0%
Charismatic	24.7	68,634	+1.7%
Pentecostal	12.3	34,197	+2.6%

Missionaries from USA

P,I,A 60,200 in 631 agencies to 220 countries.
C 6,000. M 200,000, mainly Mormon short-termers.

Missionaries to USA

P,I,A 1,873 in 139 agencies from 115 countries: Peru 415, Brazil 384, Philippines 289, Mexico 283, Japan 247, Kenya 201.

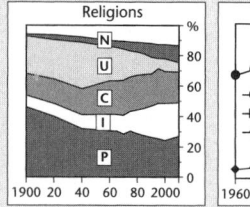

Religions

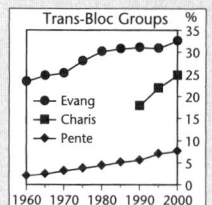

Trans-Bloc Groups

• Answers to Prayer

1 **Prayer networks, and numbers involved, increased significantly in the 1990s** through many channels — Mission America with the Lighthouses of Prayer, increased prayer by students before schools for their schools, prayer walking, Pray World of CCCI, Lydia Fellowship and increased involvement in global prayer initiatives.

2 **The post-WWII rise of Evangelicals** from the wings of national life to centre-stage. The crucial issue — will this influence be rightly exercised in the 21st Century? The national percentage of Evangelicals has only increased from an estimated 29% to 32%, but their impact on national life is very significant.

3 **The massive growth of the newer Pentecostal** and, even more, the Charismatic networks across the spectrum of Christian megablocs and denominations from 10% of the population in 1970 to around 25% in 2000. There have been localized revivals such as that in the Brownsville Assemblies of God in Pensacola, Florida in 1995, with thousands repenting and many being touched by the Holy Spirit.

4 The impact of Billy Graham; arguably *the* Evangelical of the 20th Century. God gave him grace to remain humble and true to his high calling as an evangelist. He has preached the gospel to more people and witnessed to more leaders than any person who has ever lived. His greatest contribution to the Kingdom has been his unwavering support for world evangelization through such great conferences as Berlin 1966, Lausanne 1974 and the series of Amsterdam Evangelists' Conferences in the 1980s and 2000. These became, under God, catalytic for the astonishing growth of Christianity in Africa, Latin America and Asia.

5 The nation-wide impact of newer movements:

a) *Promise Keepers* in providing a spiritual dynamism to Christian men confused about their role in society.

b) *Renewal among Catholics* — over 30% testify to being born again through faith in Christ.

c) *The New Culture churches* with radically different, but culturally appropriate worship patterns for Generation X and Y youth.

d) *The rapid growth of Evangelicalism* in mainline denominations such as the United Methodists and others, which has eroded the power-base of theologically liberal leaders and their espousal of such contra-biblical issues as homosexuality and extreme feminism.

e) *A strong movement against the evils of society* — drug abuse, promiscuity and pornography, permissive legislation, abortion and crime. These are what the media (especially films) portray, giving a distorted image of the USA to the world. Pray for the multiplicity of networks and bodies that have sprung up to confront the wrongs of society and that they may retain biblical balance and political objectivity.

• Challenges for Prayer

1 The USA's role in the world during the 1990s was unique as the sole super-power. Every policy choice in economics, politics and use of the armed forces has global reverberations. The US President wields awesome power. Pray for the President, his choice of leadership team, the Congress and Senate and their legislation so that decisions may be wisely made and well balanced between often conflicting domestic and international requirements. There is a real danger of US military dominance leading to a political and cultural insensitivity that isolates the country at a time when global consensus in major political, military, ecological and economic issues has never been more crucial.

Special Note Jan 2004: The impact of the September 11, 2001 terrorist attack.

The Islamist movement, Al Qaeda, developed into a sophisticated worldwide terror network during the 1990s. It launched carefully planned attacks on US/Western and Israeli targets, the worst being the series of attacks on the New York World Trade Center and the Pentagon on Sept 11, or 9/11. This was the first direct military attack on the mainland USA in nearly two centuries, and shocked the country and projected it into a long-term War on Terror. The outworkings of these events are still being realized with significant changes nationally and globally. Here are a few comments and prayer items:

a) *The impact on the national psyche was massive.* The anger, frustration and loss of a sense of security ran deep. The economy was pushed towards recession, tourism and air travel declined and great changes in government and its security services initiated. Pray that the response of the government as well as individuals might be wise, measured, strategic and fitting for a nation that is seen to be Christian. Pray for a wise handling of issues of concern to Islam and to Muslims.

b) *The impact on the world is equally large.* The first major result was the war in 2002 against the terror base that Taliban-ruled Afghanistan had become in hosting the leadership of Al Qaeda. Second has been a global move in the 'War on Terror' against any likely terrorist entity — in the Philippines, Indonesia, the Middle East, Europe and elsewhere. Third was the invasion of Iraq in 2003 to rid the world of a dictatorship that potentially had the capability of being a terror base and source of dangerous weaponry. Pray that the military and economic power of the USA may be wisely and justly used. The perceived uncritical US support of Israel in its conflict with Palestinians and the apparent tendency to act unilaterally in its own interests is a significant hindrance to effective prosecution of the War on Terror.

2 Globalization of the modern world is largely driven by US technology, media and culture. There are positives — the Internet communications revolution,

widespread use of English, information availability that empowers people and exposes tyrannies, economic development, etc. There are the downsides, too — an insensitive cultural imperialism, imposition of a post-Protestant American individualism without its biblical constraints, a glorified perception of recently gained human rights, freedom and democracy that could generate anarchy and moral collapse. Pray for the restraint of greed and evil and the enhancement of the good in this revolution now taking place.

3 **The Pilgrim Fathers** were determined to establish a land in which they were free to exercise their Christian faith. On that foundation has developed one of the largest and most dynamic Christian movements in history. In the USA are 19% of the Protestants in the world, 21.5% of the Evangelicals and 35% of all the world's foreign missionaries. Evangelistic vitality, generosity and vision have been major factors in the surge of gospel progress. Pray that this may be maintained.

4 **The spiritual heritage of the USA is being eroded** by an unholy alliance of humanists, New Agers and homosexuals. They exploit the provisions of the constitution and their control of the media to disparage and mock Christians and dismantle all they can of anything Christian in public life. Freedom of religion is becoming freedom from religion. They aim to replace 'intolerant' Christian absolutes with their permissive culture. There is scant tolerance for expression of religious values. Pray for a national re-awakening and commitment to that heritage — its loss would impoverish the world.

5 **Christianity is not impacting the nation as it should.** The USA needs revival, yet the word 'revival' has been debased to mean slick mass evangelism and theatrics. The need of the hour is a true revival with conviction of sin, repentance and an outpouring of the Holy Spirit. These are some of the prayer challenges for the 21st Century Church:

a) *The need for biblical holiness* in a time when Christians display little difference in values and lifestyle to non-Christians. Superficiality and materialism are more characteristic than dedication and passion for Jesus and doing His will. The succession of high-profile failures of televangelists, Christian leaders in the church and in politics and the high rate of divorce among church-goers all underline the need. Pray that Christians may repent of carnality, be revived and help to change rather than mimic culture.

b) *A deep commitment to the authority and veracity of the Bible*. Effective expository preaching and solid teaching on the basic doctrines of the faith are not widely evident. The prevailing tolerant pluralism has brought widespread loss of certainty about the Bible and a creeping universalism which cripples vision for evangelism and missions.

c) *Spiritual unity*. The Church in the USA is seriously divided on several key issues and needs prayer. A number of Christians in mainline denominations tilt towards the politically-correct left in supporting pro-choice (abortions) a feminist agenda and gay marriages. Many Catholics, Orthodox and most conservative Protestants would oppose these. Numerous Bible-believing denominations wage war over issues such as eschatology, gifts of the Spirit, definitions of biblical inerrancy, length of the days of creation, etc., while issues of world evangelization are sidelined. Pray for repentance, a seeking after God's priorities and that, through love and grace, a sensitive and balanced handling of divisive areas might be found.

d) *Christian withdrawal from, or involvement in, public life* is an ongoing unresolved tension. The public school system has deep failings — not least the elimination of anything Christian or religious. Massive networks of Christian-run school systems have emerged. Some would consider this separation as a retreat. A spectrum of evangelical groups are working for social change in the USA which include such as Mission America, **WVI**, Prison Fellowship, Promise Keepers and Christian Community Development Association, Evangelicals for Social Action, Concerned Women of America, the Christian Coalition, etc. Efforts by the Moral Majority and the Religious Right to influence the political world have not been entirely successful. Pray for balance, wisdom and long-term involvement of Christians as salt and light in society.

e) *A crisis of leadership* and church structures demand a revolutionary re-think. Common expectations are for a pastor to be a media star at the apex of a pyramid with a performing leadership and spectator laity. Pray for the wider development of a servant leadership that enables the led to be active as biblical apostles, prophets, evangelists, pastors and teachers in a participatory fellowship structure.

f) *Leadership training possibilities abound*. The variety and number of theological training possibilities defies full analysis! There are 644 recognized institutions that award theological degrees. The American Association of Bible Colleges includes 89 accredited evangelical colleges. Pray for a deeper level of commitment to Christian service and especially to world evangelization among professors and students alike. Pray also for flexibility and innovation in leadership training which is fitted for the times in which we live.

6 **Young people** present one of the major areas of spiritual battle today. The bitter fruits of humanistic philosophies are now being harvested in disorientation, spiritual vulnerability, moral decay, rejection of authority, widespread drug abuse and mindless violence. God raised up such organizations as **OM**, **YWAM**, **CCCI**, Teen Challenge and others to combat this confusion and make a mighty impact on the world. Now God is also raising up a new generation of movements for this century — pray for such as Youth Quake and Teen Mania. Pray for the youth. The next generation could be America's most traumatized ever if there is not a decisive work of God's Spirit.

7 **Student ministries** have flourished in recent years. The impact of the complementary ministries of IVCF(**IFES**), **Navigators**, **CCCI** and others has led to effective discipleship and outreach on campuses. The large Urbana conferences of IVCF have challenged many students with the needs of a lost world. The ministries of **Navigators** and **CCCI** have diversified into a wide range of activities in the USA and around the world.

8 **The 35 million-strong Afro-American community** has suffered immensely due to its origins in slavery and subsequent racial discrimination. The civil rights movement achieved much in changing structures and attitudes, but for many the cycle of unemployment, poverty, family instability and crime is unbroken. Pray for:

a) ***Young people*** — especially in the decaying inner cities — many of those in their 20s are in prison. Drug abuse and AIDS are rampant, and murder is the major cause of death for 15- to 34-year-olds.

b) ***Black Muslims*** whose numbers have grown rapidly to over 2.2 million — most from a Christian background. A small but vocal minority belong to Black nationalist groups and to the Nation of Islam organization. The majority are becoming increasingly orthodox in their Islamic faith — yet nearly all are true seekers after God. Pray for effective and loving outreach to them.

c) ***The Afro-American churches***. Many of the largest and most vigorous evangelical churches are Black, but they are isolated from the mainstream of white American evangelical Christianity and also from much meaningful involvement in missions. Pray for a unity of believers that transcends race, and pray for a moving of the Spirit of God in many churches with little spiritual life. Some of these have been deeply impacted by the charismatic movement.

d) ***Greater missions vision among the Christians***. The Destiny Movement (with conferences in 1987 and 1992) is helping to redress this, but most churches lack the structure and practical experience to become effective sending churches.

9 **Church growth among ethnic minorities** is the growing edge of US Evangelicalism today. This is an urban phenomenon — ethnic minorities comprise a majority in 50 US cities. There are an estimated 125 ethnic communities that maintain their cultural cohesion — very few without growing churches. In 20 years Hispanic Protestants have increased from 6% to 26% of the community, with around 10,000 Spanish-speaking congregations in 1998. Networks of congregations have sprung up among Koreans (3,000 churches), Chinese, Filipinos, Arabs and even Iranians. Pray for:

a) ***The effective evangelization and discipling of every ethnic minority***, both new immigrants and those largely integrated into US life, and development of vision and outreach to evangelize their lands of origin through radio, literature and personal evangelism. The major challenge is to mobilize Christians who originate from the Middle East, and from South, Central and East Asia for this.

b) ***The growth and maturation of these churches*** — in language use and in keeping the balance between cultural integrity and integration into US life — especially as second- and third-generation numbers increase. Pray for the provision of wise and forward-looking leaders. Generally lacking sufficient numbers of local pastors, there is a danger that the gaps be filled by those drawn from their more needy lands of origin.

c) ***Effective strategies and cooperation between Anglo-American and ethnic minority churches and agencies*** to ensure these minorities are discipled in what is a highly fragmented ministry. The **SBC** has 250,000 believers in 4,600 congregations and 87 languages; 40% of new **AoG** churches are among ethnic minorities; **CMA**, **CoG** (Cleveland) and others have vigorous church-planting ministries among them too.

d) *Growth of missions vision.* Notable in this is the **Korean World Missions Council** — an interdenominational association linking over 600 North American Korean churches, and sending out an increasing number of missionaries. Pray that this vision may be emulated by other ethnic minority churches.

10 **Native Americans**, or the First Nations, have suffered intensely in their encounter with centuries of European immigrants. They have lost almost all their lands, their self-respect and much of their culture, and they still face prejudice and insensitivity to their plight. Poverty, disease, alcoholism, child abuse and unemployment are common among those on reservations and among the 50% or so who have migrated to the cities. There is a vigorous movement across the country to revive indigenous cultures; this is successfully demanding the honouring of treaties protecting Indian lands and rights that have rarely been kept by the government in the past. Pray for:

a) *Vitalization of Christianity among native Americans.* A profusion of missionary efforts over the centuries has yielded meagre fruit. In the early 1980s there were 2,500 congregations and 320,000 Christians of all kinds, but syncretistic indigenous sects and cults as well as reversions to pre-Christian beliefs are still widespread. Only about 17% of the total population is affiliated with a Christian church. The largest group, the Navajo (200,000), have begun to respond after years of indifference and a very low percentage of believers — now 7.3% of the population.

b) *Bible translation,* which has regained importance as local languages are revived. Over 50 languages are in common use, and **SIL** and others have teams working in 27.

c) *The evangelization of every reservation.* Of the 550 reservations, 54 were surveyed in 1979 and only 20% had a church led by a native American. In the 1990s change came; the Holy Spirit raised up indigenous leaders and new organizations, such as Wiconi International and On Eagles' Wings, as a means to indigenize the gospel and promote reconciliation.

d) *The indigenous peoples of Alaska* who have retained their identity far more than those in mainland USA. Over 16 missions and churches have ministry among them (**SEND**, **Interact Ministries** [formerly Arctic Missions] and **GMU**). The harshness of the climate, geographical isolation and economic stresses complicate the work of bringing churches to maturity. Many of the Aleut and Eskimo are traditionally Orthodox Christians, a legacy of the time when Russia ruled Alaska. Over 71% of the 65,000 indigenous people profess to be Christian.

11 **The less-reached.** The variety and effort expended to evangelize the majority of US residents who do not regularly go to church means that few are unreached, but there are some groups which need input from missions agencies.

a) *The 5.4 million Jews* are an influential but declining minority, even with the recent immigration of 70,000 fSU Jews. It is the largest concentration of Jews in the world. New York is estimated to be 10% Jewish. A growing receptivity and response to the gospel has been evident since 1970, and more Jews are being won to Christ in the USA than anywhere else since New Testament times. There are estimated to be between 30,000 and 100,000 Messianic Jews. Of these, about 15-20,000 have retained their cultural distinctives and meet in Messianic congregations. An estimated 600-1,100 come to Christ each year. There are more than 48 agencies and 325 full-time workers committed to Jewish evangelism — one of the most dynamic and innovative is **Jews for Jesus**. Pray for the maturation of the work after the euphoria of the 1970s.

b) *The sects* pose a challenge. Most of the more aggressively missionary sects such as Christian Science, Mormonism, Jehovah's Witnesses and Scientology originated in the USA. There are reckoned to be 2,500 such sects and exotic cults. Specific efforts to reach such people must be made. Some successes have been seen among both Mormons and Jehovah's Witnesses.

c) *International students* number over 600,000 and come from over 180 countries; 56% from Asia (China 50,000; Taiwan 37,000; South Asia 44,000); 30% are Muslim. Many come from lands unreceptive to missions and with few Christians. Over 37 agencies and many congregations are involved in ministry to them, with remarkable response. The Association of Christian Ministries to Internationals is an umbrella body linking ministries such as **ISI** (with 163 staff), IVCF(**IFES**), **CCCI**, **Navigators** and others. Pray for conversions and discipleship that will enable these students to be effective witnesses as they return home.

d) **Muslims** have steadily increased through immigration and conversion of Afro-Americans. Some reckon the above figure of 4.15 million is too low and may be nearer 6 - 8 million with more than 1,500 mosques. It is claimed that there are 25,000 conversions to Islam annually in the USA. Of special mention:

i   *Arabs.* Many are Muslim but the majority are Christian. The small minority of Islamists among them have gained notoriety for the community.

ii   *Iranians* may now number 2 million with 500,000 in California alone. Disillusionment with Islam has caused some to become Christians — Iranian Christian Fellowships are coming into being.

iii   *Somalis, Afghans, Bosnians,* etc., are all significantly growing refugee communities.

e) **South Asians** are mostly techno-migrants (computer programmers, etc.), and one of the most wealthy ethnic communities in the USA. Nearly all are Muslim, Hindu or Sikh and come from sections of Indian society least exposed to the gospel; few are Christian.

f) **The US prison population** is very large with 1.8 million in jail. No other democratic nation has such a high incarceration rate. Nearly half the prison population is Afro-American. Approximately 400,000 were sentenced for drug-related offences. Pray for ministries such as Prison Fellowship International which seek to minister to them, win them to Christ and rehabilitate them in society.

12 **The US contribution to world evangelization is unique.** Many of the 20th Century gospel advances were pioneered and generously supported by US churches. The number, variety and commitment of US missionaries and agencies have impacted every nation on earth. Over 70,000 US evangelical missionaries were serving Jesus in 2000. Major umbrella bodies for Evangelical agencies are **EFMA** and **IFMA** and, for the more charismatic agencies, **AIMS**. **ACMC** (Advancing Churches in Missions Commitment) acts as a coordinating support structure for local church missions programmes. The largest denominational agencies: **IMB-SBC** (4,570), **AoG** (1,583), **Christian Chs/Chs of Christ** (1,162), Chs of Christ (1,014), **ABWE** (761), **BMM** (612). The largest interdenominational agencies: **WBT/SIL** (2,932), **YWAM** (1,832), **NTM** (1,524), **CCCI** (973), **TEAM** (643) and **SIM** (571). Pray for:

a) **Local churches** to make the Great Commission central to their church life. Only a fraction do — an estimated 400,000 evangelical churches were supporting 70,000 missionaries in 2000; nearly 6 churches for one missionary.

b) **Effective partnership between local churches and mission agencies.** For this, agencies need to adapt their way of operating. Many mission-minded congregations have become impatient with past methods. Many are sending missionaries direct to fields — not always a strategic success.

c) **Viable long-term strategies** that impact the least reached — especially in the 10/40 Window nations and peoples. The huge growth in short-term missions, while positive in many respects, can be to the detriment of long-term impact and fruit.

d) **The impact of 9/11 on recruitment** for missions has been significant, with far fewer willing to go long-term to serve the Lord in other lands. The War on Terror has also complicated and compromised the impact of US missionaries in many lands. Pray for both these negatives to be nullified and the depth and quality of US mission input enhanced.

13 **Christian media ministries.** There is such a profusion, only brief mention for prayer is made here for:

a) **Christian literature.** In the 1980s there were massive increases in sales of Christian literature through the 5,000 Christian bookstores and through secular outlets (16% of all books sold are religious), but the subject matter was more often for the 'fad' market. Pray for a more discerning and book-loving Christian public.

b) **Christian radio and television** which have developed dramatically since 1961. The National Religious Broadcasters links together 1,400 Christian broadcasting bodies which produce 75% of all religious programmes in the USA. There are over 1,100 Christian radio stations and over 350 Christian TV stations in the USA. Pray for:

i   *Wise and sensitive use of these powerful media.* The credibility of all such ministries was damaged by the distorted, fraudulent and immoral lifestyles of certain televangelists and their lack of accountability to the Body of Christ.

ii   *A balance in use of funds* for what is a very expensive ministry.

iii   *Programming that uplifts the Lord Jesus* rather than personalities, products or organizations and that promotes morality, family cohesion and biblical holiness.

Uruguay
Oriental Republic of Uruguay

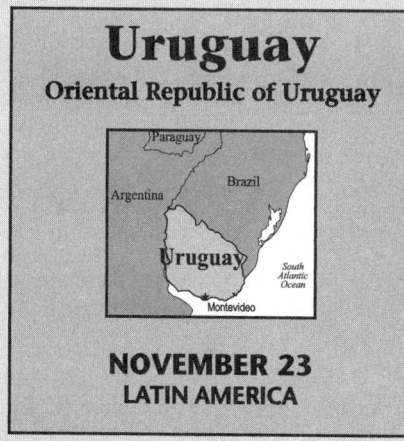

NOVEMBER 23
LATIN AMERICA

GEOGRAPHY
Area 176,215 sq.km. Located between Brazil and Argentina on the east bank of the River Plate estuary.

Population	Ann.Gr.	Density
2000	3,337,058	+0.73%	19 per sq. km.
2010	3,565,821	+0.63%	20 per sq. km.
2025	3,906,674	+0.59%	22 per sq. km.

Capital Montevideo 1,900,000. **Urbanites** 90%.

PEOPLES
The Charrua Amerindians, the indigenous people, were forcibly absorbed by the Spanish settlers.
Spanish-speaking 93.1%. Majority of Spanish origin. Italian origin 25%. Mixed race 7%.
Other 6.9%. Italian 75,000; Jews 55,000; Brazilian 32,000; German 28,000; Russian 15,000.

Literacy 97.5%. **Official language** Spanish.

ECONOMY
Changing from agriculture to industry, services and tourism. A high standard of living for Latin America, but the cost of its extensive welfare system is high. These costs necessitate restructuring, including privatization and inflation reduction. It is a member of MERCOSUR, the South American free trade body. **Unemployment** 11%. **HDI** 0.826; 40th/174. **Public debt** 22.6% of GNP. **Income/person** $6,130 (19.5% of USA).

POLITICS
Independent from Spain in 1828. A long and largely unbroken tradition of democracy and civil liberties, was overturned between 1973 and 1985. Democratically elected governments have ruled since the end of the military regime in 1985.

RELIGION
Separation of church and state in 1918, with no legal preference given to any religion. The most secular state in South America.

Religions	Population %	Adherents	Ann.Gr.
Christian	60.20	2,008,909	+0.3%
non-Religious	24.64	822,251	-0.8%
Spiritist	12.86	429,146	+6.7%
Jewish	1.80	60,067	+0.7%
Other	0.50	16,685	+5.3%

Christians	Denom.	Affil.%	,000	Ann.Gr.
Protestant	30	3.05	101	+0.8%
Independent	29	3.35	112	+5.3%
Anglican	1	0.04	1	+1.6%
Catholic	2	49.59	1,655	-0.1%
Orthodox	6	1.02	34	+1.9%
Marginal	7	3.15	105	+3.0%

Churches		MegaBloc	Cong.	Members	Affiliates
Catholic		C	230	1,807,914	2,513,000
Latter-day Saints (Morm)		M	153	52,000	78,000
New Apostolic		I	170	25,564	34,000
Jehovah's Witnesses		M	135	10,422	22,000
Assemblies of God (USA)		P	129	9,340	18,680
Chr is the Answer Tabern		I	23	8,000	17,600
Waldensian		P	25	3,165	13,685
Baptist Convention		P	60	4,554	11,000
Mision Vida		I	50	4,000	8,800
Seventh-day Adventist		P	45	4,079	8,158
Ch of God (Cleveland)		P	42	3,120	7,800
Assemb. of God (Finland)		P	79	3,116	7,790
Ch of the Nazarene		P	25	1,450	4,500
Other denoms [62]			825	58,000	121,300
Disaffiliated		*C*		*-617,300*	*-858,000*
Total Christians [75]			**1,991**	**1,377,400**	**2,008,300**

Trans-bloc Groupings	pop.%	,000	Ann.Gr.
Evangelical	4.5	151	+4.6%
Charismatic	4.6	154	+4.2%
Pentecostal	2.7	92	+4.7%

Missionaries from Uruguay
P,I,A 82 in 14 agencies to 12 countries: Uruguay 44, Bolivia 4, Brazil 3, Chile 3.

Missionaries to Uruguay
P,I,A 232 in 48 agencies from 19 countries: USA 128, Brazil 30, Argentina 16, Canada 14, UK 11.

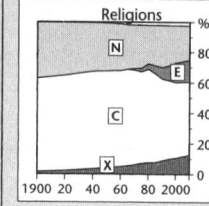

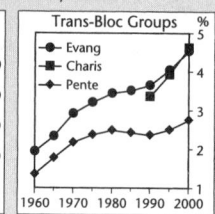

• Answers to Prayer

1 **There is rising hope among Evangelicals.** The last 10-15 years have been ones of heightened expectations, increasing fruitfulness, and unprecedented cooperation. The Evangelical Alliance is aiming to double the number of congregations between 1998 and 2005.

• Challenges for Prayer

1 **Uruguayan society has been characterized by secularism** and hope in man for over 100 years. During the 1970s disillusionment set in, and by the '90s the manifest failure of secularism created a search for the transcendent. While Roman Catholicism may lay claim to 50% of the population, only 40,000 (1.2%) attend Mass. The majority of those affiliated with the Catholic Church are, in practice, non-religious.

2 **Lack of knowledge of God has given opening to a spirit of error.** Brazilian spiritists, once banned, could possibly number a million, many of them members of the Catholic Church. The largest non-Catholic religious bodies are sects such as the Mormons, Jehovah's Witnesses and the New Apostolic Church. New Age thinking has filled the vacuum among the agnostic middle-class and intelligentsia. The Unification Church (Moonies) are also influencing the country through capital investment. Pray for these deceptions to be exposed and the demonic powers behind them defeated.

3 **Evangelical churches** have struggled throughout the past century to make an impact on Uruguayan society, and large-scale efforts garnered only meagre fruit in converts. However, since 1986 the growth of some Pentecostal groups and Baptists has accelerated. Pray for this awakening to continue and that all evangelical churches may find ways to take advantage of this new spiritual interest.

4 **Unity has been one of the fruits of this recent awakening.** While prayer for further unity and fellowship is still needed, churches are working together on an unprecedented scale. Through the ministry of **DAWN**, Evangelical Alliance members launched Cooperacion 2000 — a goal of 2000 new congregations by the year 2005. Many feel as if Uruguay is on the cusp of revival. Pray as well for the 20 or so seminaries or Bible schools. A large increase in congregations will create a demand for godly, well-trained pastors. Some schools have been negatively impacted in the past by liberal theology.

5 **Missions vision** has been limited but is experiencing a flowering of interest. At least two Uruguayan mission agencies have been formed (***Avance*** and ***Desafio Mundial***). There are active international bodies such as **OM, YWAM,** the Baptists and **AoG**. The Uruguayan COMIBAM sponsored a Congress on Missions in 2000, which has increased an awareness in churches of the needs of unreached peoples.

6 **The discouraging days of meagre fruit in pioneer evangelism** are over, but expatriate workers called to serve alongside the Uruguayan church are much needed. Larger missions: **IMB-SBC** (39 workers), **AoG** (34), **BMW** (12), Churches of Christ (12), and the Christian Brethren (10). Church planters from Latin American countries are also having success.

7 **The less-reached:**

a) *The Jews are concentrated in Montevideo.* JAMI has a small witness among them. There is an openness to the gospel.

b) *The Chinese and Japanese communities*. There is no church among them.

c) *The Palestinians living* in several border towns. *Desafio Mundial* is focusing on them.

d) *The upper middle class* living along Montevideo's coast are probably the largest unevangelized group in the country. Baptist and Pentecostal missionaries are working among them.

e) *The poor* are a growing segment of society with 40% of children now being born into poverty as the middle class shrinks. **SAMS** runs a shelter for the homeless in Montevideo. Pray that churches would mobilise to reach this needy group.

8 **Christian support ministries.**

a) *Literature*. A vital Christian ministry in this highly literate land. **CLC** has a ministry through its bookstore and a country-wide bookmobile ministry. **IMB-SBC** and the Bible Society have an extensive literature and Bible distribution ministry. Pray that the written Word may make a lasting impact.

b) *Radio and TV*. Uruguay is one of the few Latin American countries with a very low evangelical presence on radio (only Cuba is worse). **TWR** broadcasts from Montevideo to Uruguay, Argentina and Paraguay. Despite rising costs, there is significant Christian presence in television, with programmes available terrestrially and on cable.

Uzbekistan

Republic of Uzbekistan

NOVEMBER 24-25
ASIA

 POLITICS

Samarkand was the 14th Century capital of Tamerlane's vast Mongol/Turkic empire. Uzbekistan's key position ensures its ongoing political importance in Central Asia. Russian colonial rule 1868-1917. Independent as a democratic republic in 1991. A multiparty republic in name only, where Islamist parties are banned, others shackled, and an autocratic President is in control as firmly as in Communist times. Tokens of ethnic and Islamic culture were adopted as cover for a policy of no change. No freedom of speech or press.

RELIGION

A secular state which promotes a moderate form of Islam. The growing Islamist movement has been vigorously quashed with Christians also affected by government legislation and actions. Christians among ethnic minorities have had more freedom, but Uzbek Christians have received harsh treatment. Proselytizing of Muslims is illegal and switching religions discouraged. **Persecution index** 22nd in the world.

Religions	Population %	Adherents	Ann.Gr.
Muslim	83.50	20,305,406	+3.2%
non-Religious	14.52	3,530,952	-5.0%
Christian	1.28	311,268	-3.3%
Buddhist	0.30	72,954	+1.6%
Traditional ethnic	0.20	48,636	+1.6%
Jewish	0.20	48,636	-9.2%

Almost all the Christians are of ethnic minorities — mainly Russian and Korean.

Christians	Denom.	Affil.%	,000	Ann.Gr.
Protestant	30	0.31	75	+5.4%
Independent	2	0.04	10	+8.6%
Catholic	3	0.09	21	-4.2%
Orthodox	2	0.78	190	-6.5%
Marginal	1	0.01	2	+5.9%
Unaffiliated		0.05	13	n.a.

Churches	MegaBloc	Cong.	Members	Affiliates
Russian Orthodox	O		110,390	170,000
Catholic [3]	C	17	12,575	21,000
Regis. Pentecostal [3]	P	17	4,300	14,320
Charismatic groups	I	15	3,000	9,000
Unregis. Pentecostal	P	30	2,700	9,000
Baptist Union	P	37	3,800	8,000
Korean Presbyterian	P	30	3,600	7,920
Full Gospel	P	15	3,000	7,500
Korean Baptist	P	25	2,600	5,200
Jehovah's Witnesses	M	12	960	2,400
Other denoms [24]		90	27,400	43,700
Total Christians [38]		288	174,350	298,000

GEOGRAPHY

Area 447,400 sq.km. Fertile, irrigated mountain valleys in the east, notably the Ferghana Valley. Desert and Aral Sea in the west.

Population	Ann.Gr.	Density
2000	24,317,851	+1.58%	54 per sq. km.
2010	28,170,066	+1.39%	63 per sq. km.
2025	33,354,778	+1.14%	75 per sq. km.

Capital Tashkent 2,350,000. Other major city: Samarkand 370,000. **Urbanites** 39%.

PEOPLES

Every ethnic group but one of the former USSR is represented in Uzbekistan.
Turkic/Altaic 88.6%. Uzbek 18.5 mill. (some are actually ethnic Tajik); Kazakh 1m.; Tatar 600,000; Karakalpak 540,000; Crimean Tatar 241,000; Kyrgyz 224,000; Turkmen 156,000; Meskhetian 136,000; Azeri 56,000; Uighur 46,000; Bashkir 35,000.
Indo-European 9%. Massive emigration.
  Slav 2.9%. Russian 625,000; Ukrainian 50,000; Belarusian 20,000.
  Iranian 5.5%. Tajik 1.33m; Persian 30,000.
  Other 0.6%. Armenian 58,000; German 12,000.
All other 2.4%. Korean 320,000; Jew 40,000; Mordvinian 15,000.

Literacy 97%. **Official language** Uzbek. **All indigenous languages** 7. **Languages with Scriptures** 1Bi 2NT 1por 2w.i.p.

ECONOMY

Self sufficient with export capacity in both oil and natural gas, and with significant mineral deposits. Lack of water is a critical limiting factor for growth. The world's third largest cotton producer — but only with costly irrigation. Much of the flawed Marxist command structure remains. Uzbekistan has become the primary transhipment nation for the huge drug trade from Afghanistan to Russia and on to Europe. **HDI** 0.720; 92nd/174. **Public debt**

Trans-bloc Groupings	pop.%	,000	Ann.Gr.
Evangelical	0.3	64	+6.4%
Charismatic	0.2	42	+8.0%
Pentecostal	0.1	31	+7.9%

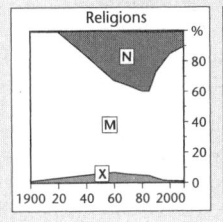

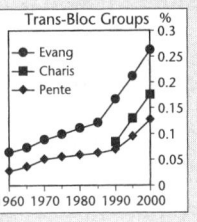

• Challenges for Prayer

1 **Independence has not brought freedom,** but instead, the nation is an arena of warring value systems. The term Uzbek means 'master of himself', but many are seeking to enslave the Uzbeks with their ideologies: radical Islamism (especially in the fertile Ferghana valley), occultism, and several sects. Pray that Uzbeks might find freedom by serving the Lord their Creator and true Master.

2 **Uzbekistan is strategically vital** — whither goes Uzbekistan, so goes Central Asia. There is an intensifying contest between the current regime ('democratic' with leftover Soviet ideology) and Islamism (of the *Wahhabi* sect). But the people are disillusioned — the economy is crumbling under Soviet style control, and corruption within the government is resistant to change and reform. Pray that the nation's leaders may govern uprightly and for regional stability despite attempts by some to exploit and destabilize.

3 **Ecological disasters which Communism left unchecked must be faced.** Lack of water and its misuse in agricultural over-irrigation have created poor soil conditions. This has also hastened the rapid disappearance of the Aral Sea with frightening impact on the environment. Pray that impending crises may cause many to seek God.

4 **Tashkent is the Islamic capital of Central Asia.** Popular local Muslim leaders have influence on the other Muslim-majority republics. Islam is considered an integral part of Uzbek cultural identity rather than just a religion, but this is changing. After independence Muslim missionaries worked hard to rebuild mosques, distribute *Qur'ans* and increase commitment to Islam. The government has since curtailed or stopped their activities. Various Muslim countries poured in funding as they competed for influence. Pray for the release of the people from cultural pressure to be Islamic in a way that will lead to many conversions and integration into Christian fellowships.

5 **Christians are largely of immigrant minorities,** most of whom are now leaving the country. By 2000 the Russian population was reduced to a quarter of its 1985 size. Evangelical churches are growing amongst those who remain — Baptist, Pentecostal and especially Korean denominations. Their situation is not easy. Pray for:

a) ***Freedom for church construction and evangelistic outreach.*** The authorities have obstructed both the registration of Uzbek national churches and attempts to evangelize Uzbeks, in an effort to keep peace with the most strident of the Muslims. Yet the Russians and Koreans have considerable freedom to reach their own people, and are doing so.

b) ***The bridging of the cultural divide*** between Uzbeks, Russians and Koreans. The differences, history, past insensitivity and fears for the future all make outreach to most Uzbeks hard. Pray that Russian and Korean Christians might have a heart for outreach to Uzbeks in culturally sensitive ways.

c) ***The local Christian leaders.*** There is a high level of mistrust and suspicion between different denominations, ethnicities and regions, and very little unity even among leaders. Pray for humility, teachability and reconciliation between Christian leaders. Expatriate Christian cooperation has been excellent. May this be an example to nationals.

6 **Praise God for Uzbek believers** — now numbering 1,000+ attached to about 65 unregistered fellowships with a few thousand more unaffiliated. Most believers are in Tashkent despite 61% of Uzbeks living in rural areas. But much prayer is still needed for:

a) ***The discipling and mentoring of new believers.*** There are many more Uzbek Christians than those associated with churches. Too many fall away when difficulties intensify. Pray that they might be integrated quickly into the spreading home groups, or into fellowships where they can grow.

b) ***Local believers who are accused by society*** of being bought by Western money. Pray that God may keep believers from the love of money and that foreign workers may be sensitive to the disparity in lifestyles between themselves and locals.

c) ***Recognition by the government.*** No Uzbek church has been allowed to officially register yet. Pray for the groups that have been trying to register that they may have freedom to practice their faith, and protection as they do.

d) ***Indigenous leadership to be raised up.*** Bible training for this infant church is urgently needed, as is spiritual maturity and godliness.

e) ***Authenticity.*** Ask the Lord to raise up culturally appropriate Uzbek Christian literature, music, worship styles and fellowship structures.

7 **Uzbekistan is one of the world's worst violators of religious liberty.** Dynamic and evangelism-oriented churches, especially Uzbek churches, are particularly targeted. Official registration eases this problem, but the government has made this almost impossible to achieve. Evangelism or missionary activity can earn three years in prison; organizing an unregistered group, five years. Some Christians have been imprisoned, but they are winning many converts while in prison. Pray for Christians who are under pressure to betray fellow believers ot the authorities. Pray too for those persecuted and in prison, that God may give them strength and boldness.

8 **Expatriate Christians** serving the Lord in Uzbekistan have increased in number. Several agencies are concerned for this spiritually needy land. Pray for effective, fruitful cooperation, provision for safety, health, physical needs and language proficiency.

9 **The unreached.** Only a small fraction of the Muslim majority has ever had the opportunity to believe. Pray specifically for the:

a) ***Karakalpaks,*** who live south of the Aral Sea and who suffer most in health because of environmental degradation — 66% have hepatitis, typhoid or throat cancer. They are proving responsive, as hundreds have become Christians in the last few years. Pray for a strong church to develop among this people and for the completion of the New Testament in their language; only the Gospels are translated.

b) ***Tajiks***, who comprise a majority in both Samarkand and Bukhara. There is only a handful of Christians among them.

c) ***Other Central Asian peoples.*** There are few, if any, Christians among the Kazakhs, Tatars, Crimean Tatars, Kyrgyz, Turkmen and Azeris. They are often neglected here as outreach to them is focused on their home countries.

10 Christian media ministries.

a) ***Bible translation and distribution*** is an ongoing task. Pray for the translation of the OT, and a more understandable revision of the NT in Uzbek. Pray for the government-recognized Uzbek Bible Society, that it may play a key role in distributing the Bible and printing additional Christian literature.

b) ***Christian literature in Uzbek*** is desperately needed, but its production or importation is virtually banned by the government. Pray for mother-tongue writers, poets and hymnologists to be raised up and their works printed.

c) ***Christian radio*** is limited: in programming hours (2 hours/week by **FEBC**, **HCJB** and **TWR** in Uzbek, also a little in Tajik, Kazakh, Kyrgyz); in listeners; and in response. Pray for effective ways of communicating the Good News by this medium.

d) ***The JESUS film*** in Uzbek was banned from public showing after vocal opposition. Yet it is fairly popular and widely accepted. It is available in Uzbek, Tajik, Kazakh, Russian and several other languages spoken here. Increasing numbers of Christian films are available. Pray for their circulation and use. Believers are working towards a video studio where they can produce Christian videos to help evangelize younger Uzbeks.

Vanuatu

Republic of Vanuatu

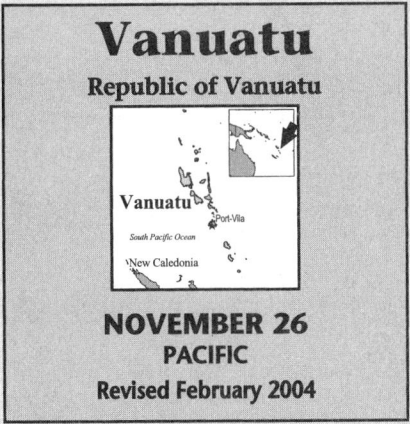

NOVEMBER 26
PACIFIC
Revised February 2004

GEOGRAPHY
 Area 12,190 sq.km. Twelve larger and 70 smaller islands southeast of the Solomon Islands in the SW Pacific. Formerly New Hebrides.

Population	Ann.Gr.	Density
2000	190,417	+2.44%	16 per sq. km.
2010	239,668	+2.28%	20 per sq. km.
2025	319,146	+1.70%	26 per sq. km.

Capital Vila 31,800 on Efate Island. **Urbanites** 20%.

PEOPLES
 **Ni-Vanuatu** 98.6%. Melanesian(102) 182,000; Polynesian(3) 4,000.
Caucasian 1%, mainly English- and French-speaking.
Other Pacific Islanders 0.4%. Wallisians, Fijians, Tongans, I-Kiribati, etc.

Literacy 53%. **Official languages** Bislama (Pidgin English), English, French. **All languages** 109, but only 36 local languages are spoken by more than 1,000 people. **Languages with Scriptures** 4Bi 5NT 29por 15w.i.p.

ECONOMY
Over 80% of the population is involved in subsistence agriculture. Main exports are copra, beef, timber, cocoa. Vanuatu is becoming a noted tax haven and tourist destination. **HDI** 0.627; 116th/174. **Public debt** 16% of GNP. **Income/person** $1,290 (4% of USA).

POLITICS
Bizarre Anglo-French Condominium 1914-1980 with duplicated administration, police and education. Independent in 1980 as a parliamentary republic but politics still affected by the impact of dual colonialism with tensions between Francophone and Anglophone political parties. Recent years have been politically stable.

 RELIGION
There is religious freedom.

Religions	Population %	Adherents	Ann.Gr.
Christian	91.14	173,546	+2.7%
Traditional ethnic	3.00	5,713	-3.3%
Cargo cults	2.70	5,141	+0.3%
Baha'i	2.60	4,951	+4.1%
non-Religious/other	0.50	952	+2.4%
Chinese/Buddhist	0.06	114	-7.6%

Christians	Denom.	Affil.%	,000	Ann.Gr.
Protestant	7	55.72	106	+3.6%
Independent	5	1.88	4	+7.2%
Anglican	1	16.02	30	+2.1%
Catholic	1	14.70	28	+1.5%
Marginal	8	3.41	6	+2.8%
Unaffiliated		1.87	4	n.a.
Doubly affiliated		*-2.47*	*-5*	*n.a.*

Churches		MegaBloc	Cong.	Members	Affiliates
Presbyterian		P	400	40,000	57,000
Ch of Melanesia		A	203	21,329	30,500
Catholic		C	18	17,000	28,000
Assemblies of God		P	77	12,001	20,000
Seventh-day Adventist		P	47	13,253	19,000
Chs of Christ		P	63	3,150	6,300
Apostolic		P	31	1,400	2,800
Free Evangelical		I	20	1,184	1,800
Latter-day Saints (Morm)		M	4	420	600
Other denoms [13]			91	3,650	8,700
Doubly affiliated				*-2,350*	*-4,700*
Total Christians [22]			954	111,000	170,000

Trans-bloc Groupings pop.%		,000	Ann.Gr.
Evangelical	31.7	60	+4.5%
Charismatic	14.2	27	+8.8%
Pentecostal	12.4	24	+10.1%

Missionaries from Vanuatu
P,I,A 7 in 3 agencies to 5 countries.

Missionaries to Vanuatu
P,I,A 34 in 8 agencies from 5 countries: USA 14, Australia 12.

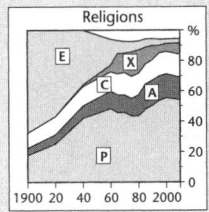

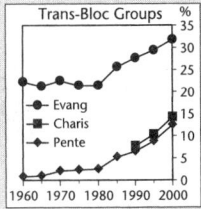

• Answers to Prayer

1 **There have recently been significant turnings to Christ** from the John Frum cargo cultists. (These cults emerged as a result of World War II and a belief that ship- and plane-loads of supplies would come from 'John from' America.) The trigger for these conversions was the ministry of a **YWAM** mercy ship.

2 The whole Bible in Bislama was published in 1998 after 30 years of work. Pray for its effective use.

• Challenges for Prayer

1 Vanuatu's motto is "In God we stand". Pray that the leaders of this complex little nation may be an example in doing so. Christians played a major role in the attainment of independence and in subsequent governments.

2 The Protestant church is numerically strong — mainly Anglicans in the north and Presbyterians in the centre and south. Some islands have been touched by revival and the **AoG** has grown rapidly; however, in other islands spiritual life is at a low ebb, few having heard a clear gospel presentation. Pray for the training of leaders in the **AoG**, Church of Christ, Anglican, Apostolic and two Presbyterian Bible colleges. Pray for Spirit-filled leaders who know how to apply Scripture to life.

3 Missionary martyrs in evangelizing these islands have been many. Today the Church welcomes missionaries in a supportive role for teaching the Word; the largest agencies are **SIL** (12 workers), Australian Churches of Christ (10), and US **AoG** (2). Pioneer work is also still needed for a number of smaller, superficially evangelized peoples, especially in Bible translation and literacy work.

4 The spiritual challenges for Christians:

a) There are pockets of traditional ethnic religion on Tanna, Aniwa, Santo, Vao and other islands.
b) There are many who still follow 'custom' or have been led astray by cargo cults.
c) How to counteract increased Mormon missionary activity.
d) Muslim missionaries are active in setting up mosques and offering free schooling.

Pray for decisive demonstrations of God's power and of holy-living Christians that will win the rising generation of Ni-Vanuatu.

5 Bible translation, vernacular literacy and training Ni-Vanuatu are major ongoing tasks. At least 20, and probably more, languages require NT translations or revisions. UBS and SIL are involved in 13 projects. Pray for wisdom as to which of the small language groups warrant the effort, and for Bible translation/literacy teams of expatriates and people from Vanuatu.

6 Christian media:

a) GRN have increased their range of recordings to 63 language. Pray that this medium may be well-used in this polyglot nation.
b) The JESUS film is being widely shown in Bislama.
c) EHC have seen good response since 1986 to their nation-wide literature distribution campaign.

Venezuela
Bolivarian Republic of Venezuela

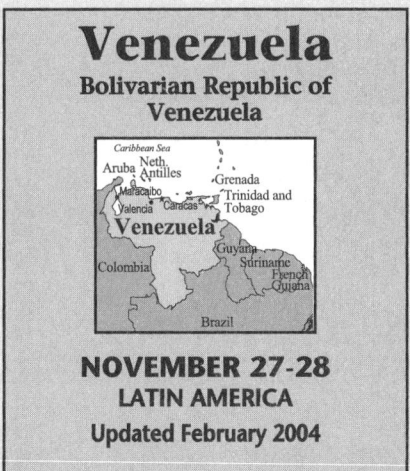

NOVEMBER 27-28
LATIN AMERICA
Updated February 2004

GEOGRAPHY
Area 912,050 sq.km. About 80% of the population lives along the Caribbean coastal belt in the north; the centre and south are grasslands and tropical forest.

Population		Ann.Gr.	Density
2000	24,169,722	+2.04%	27 per sq. km.
2010	28,715,855	+1.64%	31 per sq. km.
2025	34,775,110	+1.11%	38 per sq. km.

Capital Caracas 4,200,000. Other major cities: Maracaibo 1.8 mill.; Valencia 1.48m; Maracay 1,075,000. **Urbanites** 87%.

PEOPLES
Venezuelans 87.2%. Mixed Spanish, indigenous and African background. No census has been taken which classified the population according to ethnicity. Roughly 61% Mestizo, 16% European, 10% African.
Foreigners 11.3%. From 80 different ethnicities.
Amerindians 1.5%. 27 peoples including Yanomami, Guajiro, Maquiritare, Panare and Motilone.

Literacy 90.9%. **Official language** Spanish. **All indigenous languages** 40. **Languages with Scriptures** 1Bi 13NT 7por 14w.i.p.

ECONOMY
One of the world's largest oil producers. About 33% of the GDP and 80% of export earnings come from oil. Falling oil prices in the 1980s, unwise government spending, a bloated civil sector and widespread corruption by the rich elite combined to impoverish fl of the population. A declining tourist sector and natural disasters ($20 billion damage in 1999) conspire against economic diversification and stability. Betweeen 2000 and 2003 economic decline was marked due to civil unrest and the downturn in Latin America. **Unemployment** 27%. **HDI** 0.792; 48ᵗʰ/174. **Public debt** 33.6% of GNP. **Income/person** $3,480 (11% of USA).

POLITICS
Independent from Spain as part of Gran Colombia in 1821; and as a separate state in 1830. A succession of revolutions and harsh dictatorships ended in 1958. Stable democracy for decades until economic stress and disillusionment with corrupt government provoked a number of civilian riots and political coup attempts led by an army colonel who was elected president in 1998 on a platform of anti-corruption and economic reform. Since then government (including the constitution) has been trimmed, empowering the authoritarian-style President. A new constitution and restructured national assembly was approved in a referendum in 2000. The erratic populist policies of President Chavez brought economic decline and a serious polarization in society. Civil unrest and possible coups are a threat. A recall referendum on continued rule by Chavez in August 2004 resulted favourably for Chavez and his supporters.

RELIGION
Religious freedom is still guaranteed in the constitution. The Catholic Church regained official recognition in 1964 after years of strained Church-State relations, and has a strong influence which sometimes causes difficulties for foreign missions — especially in reaching the indigenous Amerindians.

Religions	Population %	Adherents	Ann.Gr.
Christian	94.65	22,876,642	+2.0%
Spiritist	1.60	386,716	+4.8%
non-Religious	1.50	362,546	+0.7%
Traditional ethnic	0.90	217,527	-0.1%
Baha'i	0.60	145,018	+2.0%
Muslim	0.35	84,594	+2.0%
Jewish	0.20	48,339	+2.0%
Buddhist/Chinese	0.20	48,340	+2.0%

Christians	Denom.	Affil.%	,000	Ann.Gr.
Protestant	58	4.99	1,206	+11.3%
Independent	107	6.18	1,495	+12.2%
Anglican	1	0.00	1	+0.0%
Catholic	2	92.22	22,290	+3.8%
Orthodox	6	0.11	26	+2.0%
Marginal	6	1.49	361	+4.3%
Doubly affiliated		-10.36	-2,503	n.a.

Churches		MegaBloc	Cong.	Members	Affiliates
Catholic		C	1,100	12.245m	22.285m
Assemblies of God		P	1,500	180,000	410,000
Jehovah's Witnesses		M	1,185	84,958	260,000
Seventh-day Adventist [2]		P	345	86,076	215,000
Light of the World		I	3,000	105,000	210,000
United Pentecostal		P	489	114,407	135,000
Latter-day Saints (Morm)		M	112	44,500	89,000
Baptist Convention		P	322	27,370	78,000
Kingdom of God (UCKG)		I	50	25,000	67,500
Other Protestant [23]		P	287	25,000	62,500
FIELPV (Pentecostal)		I	210	26,670	60,000

Indig Venez Ch of Apure	I	520	25,500	51,000
Assoc of Ev Chs of the E	P	123	11,685	45,000
OVICE (TEAM)	P	275	22,000	45,000
Church of the Cross	P	27	10,497	35,000
Evangelical Free	P	90	8,550	20,000
Other denoms [140]		4,948	550,294	1,311,000
Doubly affiliated			*-1,195,000*	*-2,503,000*
Total Christians [179]		14,583	12.397m	22.876m

Trans-bloc Groupings	pop.%	,000	Ann.Gr.
Evangelical	10.1	2,439	+12.3%
Charismatic	9.0	2,174	+12.1%
Pentecostal	5.8	1,393	+13.9%

Missionaries from Venezuela
P,I,A 265+ in 26 agencies to 21 countries: Venezuela 200, Colombia 13.

Missionaries to Venezuela
P,I,A 840 in 61 agencies from 21 countries: USA 639, Canada 68, Brazil 57. C est. 5,000. O 10. M 100.

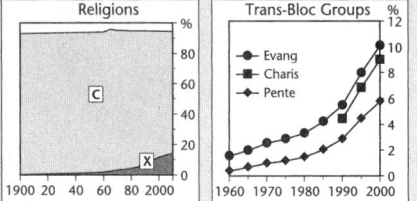

• Answers to Prayer

1 Praise the Lord for tremendous evangelical growth in the last decade. Evangelical believers grew from 1 million in 1990 to around 2.5 million in 2000. There are on average two new evangelical churches planted every day.

2 The burgeoning church is not content to rest on its laurels. Evangelicals aim to plant 15,000 more new churches by 2015, and are working hard to instil missions vision into these young congregations. Research under the auspices of the Evangelical Council of Venezuela and DAWN is resulting in manuals being published for every state facilitating cooperation, vision and church planting.

• Challenges for Prayer

1 On a social level, Venezuela is struggling. Poverty is widespread, living standards are plummeting (60% of urbanites live in slums) and crime is soaring out of control. The use of Venezuela as a drug trafficking conduit increases — the long border with Colombia is impossible to adequately patrol, despite the government's efforts. Pray that just and honourable leadership would be raised up to oppose systemic evil in this nation. Pray for a government determined and upright in its efforts to relieve poverty and combat lawlessness.

2 The religious climate of the country is increasingly opposed to Christ:

a) Venezuela is not at all the Catholic bastion that it seems. The majority of Catholics are nominal — only 20% attend mass — making Venezuela one of the least churchgoing nations in all Latin America. A secular materialist mindset is prevalent in public life. The Catholic hierarchy often seems more concerned with guarding its privileged position and opposing evangelical work than tending to its needy flock.

b) Spiritism is dangerously strong. Up to 85% of the population are involved to a lesser or greater extent in some form of spiritist practice. There are thousands of occult and spiritist shops where witch doctors and their ilk are frequented by rich and poor alike. Television programmes and advertisements promoting this are growing in number.

c) All manner of spiritual forces draw Venezuelans away from Christ. New Age spirituality is increasing, especially among the educated and rich. Satanists actively seek to destroy the Church. Caracas is the site of Latin America's largest mosque. Jehovah's Witnesses and Mormons claim huge numbers and are growing rapidly. Pray that the powers blinding Venezuelans to the truth might be bound, and that the exalted Christ might be revealed to all, drawing many to faith in Him.

3 Venezuela's evangelical breakthrough only really began in the 1980s, but has accelerated since then. Early Protestant growth was slow, but most indigenous Pentecostal and missions-planted churches (especially those linked with the work of the **AoG** and the Brazilian neo-Pentecostal groups) are growing at 10% a year or higher. The evangelical Church is also politically active, speaking out against threats to religious freedom, missions and evangelism.

4 **Challenges facing the churches.** The need is for:

a) *True discipleship.* Many new Christians come from tragic or dysfunctional backgrounds and need much help and spiritual guidance.

b) *Commitment in a society ensnared by materialism and poverty.* Relatively few are willing to commit themselves for full-time ministry, and the loss-rate of pastors going back into secular employment is high.

c) *Unity.* Divisions still hold back effective cooperation in many areas, though levels of cooperation are higher than they ever have been through the work of Amanacer/**DAWN** and others.

d) *Theological orthodoxy.* Spiritual error has crept into many churches, particularly some Pentecostal groups, through prosperity teaching, legalism, or unbiblical practices instituted by misguided leaders.

e) *Missions vision.* Churches are being presented with, and are accepting, the challenge of missions. Both international and indigenous agencies (such as *Operacion Timoteo)* are promoting the vision to send workers to Latin America and beyond, with a strong emphasis on the 10/40 Window countries. Meetings in 1999 by national Evangelicals addressed the need to create wider prayer and training networks. There are missions training schools set up by Foursquare, **YWAM**, **AoG**, **NTM**, Horizontes and Kairos (the latter two of Brazilian origin). Their goal is to send 2,000 missionaries by 2002. Pray for the Lord to prosper this young but growing missions movement.

5 **Leadership training is essential** if present growth rates are to be maintained, urban areas evangelized, and theological error avoided. Of the three seminaries, one was started by **TEAM/**Evangelical Free Church and one by the Baptists. The third is the **Evangelical Seminary of Caracas** which serves both mainline and Pentecostal churches and is developing an MA programme. There are also a number of Bible Institutes and Schools run by many different denominations. The **AoG** has 15 training institutions. Modular and correspondence course training is growing.

6 **The evangelization of some 27 Amerindian tribal peoples** by Evangelicals has been met with opposition and slander by an assorted group of anthropologists, leftist politicians and some Catholic priests. Laws to ban new work and limit existing work among tribal peoples were very nearly passed, but vocal opposition by evangelical groups stopped this. The work of **NTM** (in eight peoples, including the Yanomami) and **TEAM** (in a further six) is at stake. The indigenous peoples themselves were not adequately consulted regarding this bill, but their land and health is threatened by illegal gold prospectors and expanding cattle ranches. Pray for:

a) *The defeat of all attempts* to prevent Amerindian people from having a chance to hear the gospel — few still live in their old traditional ways that some would "protect".

b) *The opening up of the few remaining unevangelized tribes* for evangelical missionaries — Venezuelans of **AoG** and ADIEL (Evangelical Free Church) have well-established tribal works; other Venezuelans are also taking up this challenge.

c) *The continued ingathering* among the Guajiro, Maquiritare, Yanomami, Panare, Motilone, etc., into culturally-appropriate churches. Most of the larger tribes have significant and growing churches.

d) *Bible translation work,* which continues in 14 languages. Between 2-7 more languages may need translation. Pray for the impact of God's Word to be such that these peoples may be spiritually mature enough to cope with the inevitable encroachment of Venezuelan culture and all the trappings of civilisation.

e) *MAF,* which is serving missionaries living in isolated jungle areas.

7 **The work of Protestant missions** has not been easy. Obtaining visas is often a battle in faith. The opposition of the Catholic Church early in the century as well as in the 1990s made mission work difficult, and generated strong anti-foreign sentiment. Pray for more missionaries for urban church planting and Bible teaching ministries, and for close and harmonious cooperation between expatriates and national workers. The largest missions: **NTM** (168 workers), **TEAM** (103), **SBC** (76), Evangelical Free Church Mission (40), **AoG** (56), **LCMS** (27).

8 **The needier sections of society:**

a) *The upper and middle classes* are under-evangelized, but influenced by other religious groups. A number of missions and churches are concentrating efforts to reach these important groups.

b) *Caracas*, the capital, is less evangelized than the Amerindian tribes. Thirty percent of Caraceños were victimised by crime in 1999, but only about 1% are evangelical Christians. Over one million live in the *ranchos* (slums), and entire areas are controlled by gangs or drug barons. Churches and missions (**TEAM**, **CMA**, Lutherans) are mobilising to reach the cities in this most urbanised of Latin American countries.

c) *Students* have been neglected. There are only 10-15 Christian student groups (**CCC**, **MUEVE/IFES**) for 100 universities. More needs to be done to evangelise and disciple this key sector of society.

d) *Prisoners'* lives consist of overcrowded jails, deplorable conditions, frequent killings and riots, and a justice system where the accused spend on average 3½ years awaiting sentence. **VOCEP** and others share Christ in these dangerous places, and significant numbers are coming to faith. Pray for the safety of believing prisoners, for their spiritual growth, and their integration into society and the Church upon release.

e) *Victims of the floods and landslides of 2000.* As many as 50,000 lost their lives, and about 400,000 were rendered homeless and dependent on aid and relief. Evangelical groups cooperated to channel aid to the needy. Their loving witness provided a wonderful testimony; pray that further ministry and fruit might follow.

9 **The unreached minorities:**

a) *The growing Arab* community (100,000+) has become prominent in commerce. Most are Syrians and Lebanese. Some are Orthodox and Maronite Catholics, but many are Shi'a and Sunni Muslims. No direct effort to evangelize them has been made, although some ministries (**WEC**) have a vision for outreach. There are also growing numbers of Iranians and Turks.

b) *The Chinese* are increasing in number and are mainly Cantonese-speaking. There are now seven congregations of believers for the 50,000 strong community. Several missions have a ministry among them (Canadian Chinese, **CMA** and **WEC**).

c) *Other immigrant groups*, such as Italians and Portuguese, have no evangelical believers nor anyone specifically seeking to reach them. There is one Messianic Jewish assembly.

10 **Christian literature is in demand.** Economic conditions adversely affect costs of production and distribution. Both **TEAM** and the Baptists founded publishing houses which are now run by Venezuelans. There is a great need for national authors — whose writings are better received than translated works. **CLC** has a growing wholesale and retail distribution network with six centres. But only three small Christian bookshops exist in Caracas. The Bible Societies are working hard to get Scriptures into the more remote and tribal areas.

11 **Christian radio** is a strategic ministry. There are over 10 evangelical radio stations. **TWR** Bonaire has a wide audience, and many have been won to Christ and edified. Venezuelan believers are starting commercial Christian FM, AM and television stations. Pray that needed permits may be granted and resources gathered to produce quality programmes.

V

Vietnam
Socialist Republic of Vietnam

NOVEMBER 29-30
ASIA

GEOGRAPHY
Area 331,653 sq.km. Long, narrow country occupying the entire eastern and southern coastline of Indochina.

Population		Ann.Gr.	Density
2000	79,831,650	+1.57%	241 per sq. km.
2010	90,764,274	+1.25%	274 per sq. km.
2025	108,037,101	+1.05%	326 per sq. km.

Capital Hanoi 3,500,000. Other major city: Ho Chi Minh City (Saigon) 6.5 mill. **Urbanites** 21%.

PEOPLES
Vietnamese 86.9%. Predominantly coastal people; large cultural differences between northern and southern Vietnamese.
Mon-Khmer 4.1%. 45 ethno-linguistic groups. Largest: Muong 1.14m; Khmer (Cambodian) 1.1m; Bana 170,000; Sedang 120,000; Hre 117,000; Koho 115,000.
Thai-Dai 4.8%. 14 ethno-linguistic groups. Largest: Tay(7) 1.48m; Thai(3) 1.29m; Nung 877,000; San Chay 142,000.
Hmong/Mien 1.6%. 10 groups. Hmong(7) 693,000; Yao(3) 589,000.
Sino-Tibetan 1.6%. 9 groups. Han Chinese 1.12m; San Diu 118,000.
Malayo-Polynesian 1%. 8 groups. Jarai 301,000; Ede 242,000; Cham 123,000.
Literacy 94%. **Official language** Vietnamese. **All indigenous languages** 87. **Languages with Scriptures** 4Bi 11NT 18por 9w.i.p.

ECONOMY
Decades of war and application of Marxist theory depressed the economy and led to high inflation in the 1980s. Reforms in the 1990s brought significant but uneven progress. Urbanites fare better in the new market economy but there is much rural poverty. Vietnam is the world's 2nd largest rice exporter. **Unemployment** 10.3%. **HDI** 0.664; 110th/174. **Public debt** 78.5% of GNP. **Income/person** $310 (1% of USA).

POLITICS
Communist republic declared in North

Vietnam in 1945. There was continuous warfare between 1941 and 1985, under the Japanese, and then against the French, South Vietnam, USA and all surrounding lands. North Vietnam finally conquered the South in 1975, and ruled Cambodia between 1978-85. The Communist party still controls all government policy and activity, although 47% of Party members said they would consider another form of government. Capitalist market economics is proving a serious challenge for the Communists.

RELIGION
Constitutional guarantees of religious freedom are meaningless; actual government policy is to control all religious movements, including Buddhism. Persecution of Christians continues to be harsh, and particularly severe for unregistered and ethnic minority churches. **Persecution index** 6th in the world.

Religions	Population %	Adherents	Ann.Gr.
Buddhist	54.14	43,220,855	+1.5%
non-Religious	21.80	17,403,300	+1.8%
Christian	8.16	6,514,263	+2.5%
Traditional ethnic	8.10	6,466,364	+1.8%
Cao Dai/Hoa Hao	5.60	4,470,572	+0.2%
Chinese	1.10	878,148	-0.2%
Muslim	0.70	558,822	+1.6%
Baha'i	0.40	319,327	-2.9%

Christians	Denom.	Affil.%	,000	Ann.Gr.
Protestant	8	0.89	711	+6.0%
Independent	29	0.57	454	+7.4%
Anglican	1	0.00	4	+3.1%
Catholic	1	6.46	5,155	+1.6%
Marginal	2	0.04	29	+11.3%
Unaffiliated		0.20	160	n.a.

Churches	MegaBloc	Cong.	Members	Affiliates
Catholic	C	1,969	3,347,403	5,155,000
Evangelical	P	316	546,100	640,000
Unreg. house chs [19]	I	1,200	80,000	200,000
Montagnard	I	781	39,039	130,000
Indig. marginals [7]	M	541	54,054	120,000
United Protestant	P	105	10,500	21,000
Assemblies of God	P	281	10,000	20,000
Other denoms [12]		425	38,263	66,550
Total Christians [43]		5,618	4,125,359	6,352,550

Trans-bloc Groupings	pop.%	,000	Ann.Gr.
Evangelical	1.4	1,104	+6.2%
Charismatic	0.7	580	+4.5%
Pentecostal	0.0	26	+2.8%

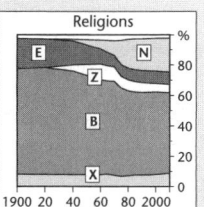

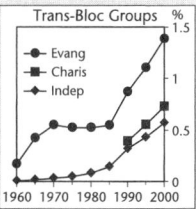

• Answers to Prayer

1 **A growing, witnessing Church is emerging** from years of persecution. A large-scale and sustained turning to God is taking place, in both registered and unregistered churches, and especially among the mountain tribal peoples of central and southern Vietnam. Praise God for preservation and growth. As in China, Communism failed to stamp out the witness, but rather strengthened and spread the flame of the Spirit!

• Challenges for Prayer

1 **One of the few Communist nations in the 21ˢᵗ Century**, Vietnam faces new challenges. Repression of all types of freedom continues, but at the same time, social ills are on the rise. Drug addiction, AIDS, prostitution and exploitation of children are all too common. There are two abortions for every live birth, one of the world's highest rates. Pray that the ideological and moral darkness over this nation might be banished by the light of the gospel.

2 **All open missionary work ceased in 1975.** CMA laboured for 64 years (for 50 years as the only Protestant mission). Other agencies arrived in the 1950s, notably **WEC, SBC, UWM** and **SIL**. In 1974 there were 280 missionaries in the land. The years of sowing are reaping an abundant harvest, and these organizations and others (**AO, YWAM, AoG**) are poised to enter Vietnam once believers' prayers pry open this closed nation.

3 **Vietnam remains one of the worst persecutors of Christians.** Seeing the role of Christianity in the demise of Communism elsewhere, the regime has attempted to either control or wipe out believers. Government efforts have intensified as churches respond to persecution with growth and outreach. Registration implies compromise; failure to register churches is illegal — forcing most believers underground. Pray for:

a) *Those in prison for their faith.* At any time there are probably dozens of Christian leaders imprisoned. Most pastors have had times of imprisonment in grim conditions. Pray for Christians in prison — many prisoners have come to faith through such witness.

b) *Registered churches.* Pray that they may withstand unrelenting government pressures to compromise and conform to strict regulations. The Church in the north has suffered much longer, and the authorities there are more strict. Meetings are only permitted in the few remaining recognized church buildings, the majority have been closed or destroyed. Open evangelism and itinerant ministry is forbidden and contact with foreign Christians restricted. Yet these churches, especially EVCN/**CMA**, have grown.

c) *Unregistered churches.* These are harassed by the police, with meetings frequently broken up and leaders arrested. Yet the courage and tenacity of these believers under pressure rarely fails and growth continues. There are tensions between leaders of registered and unregistered churches.

d) *The Montagnard churches* among the Ede, Jarai, Koho, Mnong, Stieng and others. They have suffered particularly savage persecution — churches razed, congregations scattered, Christians killed. Yet people movements to Christ are still reported. Maintaining adequate fellowship is hard where meetings are illegal and few of their languages have Scriptures. This lack has led to schisms and false teaching in some areas.

4 **Leaders are the key to Vietnamese church.** As numbers increase, so does false teaching and error. Opportunities for training are simply not there. The Catholics have reopened several seminaries, all monitored by the government. There are informal study programmes and unofficial Bible schools in Hanoi, Ho Chi Minh City, Danang and elsewhere. Expatriates often quietly enter the country to do leadership training seminars, but their low profile limits the impact. Pray for the importation of more study materials and theological books. Pray that the Spirit may guide believers into all truth.

5 **The Vietnamese diaspora** was birthed through tragedy as many perished in their flight from the Communists. Two million are settled around the globe, where they are more accessible to ministry. Pray for workers with a heart to reach them. Many thousands are returning to their homeland, amongst them many who became Christians while abroad. Pray that they may endure persecution and not fall away, but rather minister to their countrymen who have not yet heard the words of life.

6 **The country is gradually opening up.** Most of the population was born after the war, and are more interested in capital gain and the outside world than Communist propaganda. They are proving responsive to the gospel. The desperate need for economic development is giving opportunities for tentmakers in business and in teaching English. Christian NGOs who propose legitimate aid projects are increasingly invited to work here. Pray that Vietnam may fully open to missionaries, and that many committed and prepared workers may respond.

7 **The less-reached.** Present church growth is not even — many sections of the community and numerous ethnic groups remain scarcely touched by the gospel.

a) *The northern Vietnamese.* As a result of the longer Communist presence, they are much less evangelized than their southern brethren.

b) *The Muslim Cham and Buddhist Khmer* of the Mekong Delta; only a handful have believed. **FEBC** broadcasts in both Cham and Khmer. Resources are available in Khmer — the Bible, the *JESUS* film, radio — the need is for people who will take them to the Khmer.

c) *The northern minorities* have been beyond the reach of missionaries for 50 years because of war and Communism. Most are Buddhist or animist, many without any known believers. Pray especially for the Giay, Hani, San Chay, Tho and Puoc, the largest groups with no known believers. Christian radio is a key ministry, but only some have programmes in their language. The Hmong church has grown to over 100,000 believers largely through **FEBC** radio. The government has begun jamming broadcasts to them to prevent further growth.

d) *Communist officials and government leaders.* The ideal Communist state for which they fought and suffered is proving a grim failure. Disillusionment is widespread.

e) *The Cao Dai and Hoa Hao religionists* strongly resisted Communism. Together they may number as many as 4.5 million but these religions are declining. Christians must be aware of their unique cultures and beliefs and reach them in a relevant way.

8 Bible and literature ministries:

a) *Vietnamese Bibles were finally printed locally* in 1995. There are now over 35,000 Bibles and 65,000 NTs printed and distributed throughout the country — primarily through state-approved churches. While this is an encouraging development, it is not nearly enough for the great need. Pray that it might increase.

b) *Bible translation* is an ongoing task. Many ethnic minorities lack the Word in their languages — 45 have a definite translation need, with possibly a further 22 that might do so. Pray for the completion of this huge task. A long-needed modern translation of the Vietnamese Bible is now available.

c) *Christian literature* is in great demand, but strictly monitored. Recently 80,000 gospel portions and 120,000 Bible comics were produced locally with permission. Pray for the provision of more literature for evangelism, follow-up and teaching.

9 Media ministries:

a) *The JESUS film and video* is available in Akha, Cantonese, Hmong, Khmer, Lahu and Vietnamese. Lack of freedom and equipment limit their use, but 500 video cassettes were recently legally imported.

b) *GRN have prepared recordings* in 60 languages of Vietnam. Pray that these recordings, as well as cassette players, may be circulated throughout the country.

c) *Christian radio programmes* of **FEBC** have been remarkable in their scope and impact. Vital for believers, they are widely heard despite shortages of batteries and radios and in the face of persecution of listeners if discovered. **FEBC** broadcasts 24 hrs/wk in Vietnamese and one or two programmes/week in 21 other minority languages. **TWR** adds 10 hrs/wk in Vietnamese.

Virgin Islands of the USA

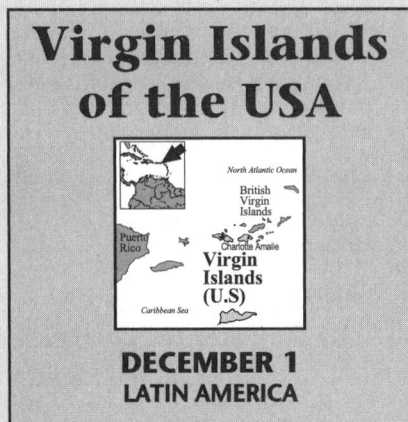

North Atlantic Ocean
British Virgin Islands
Puerto Rico
Charlotte Amalie
Virgin Islands (U.S)
Caribbean Sea

DECEMBER 1
LATIN AMERICA

POLITICS
Danish colony until 1917, when purchased by the USA. A self-governing unincorporated US territory.

RELIGION
Freedom of religion as in USA.

Religions	Population %	Adherents	Ann.Gr.
Christian	96.90	90,072	-0.9%
non-Religious/other	2.20	2,045	+2.1%
Baha'i	0.60	558	-0.8%
Jewish	0.30	279	-0.8%

Christians	Denom.	Affil.%	,000	Ann.Gr.
Protestant	37	34.48	32	-0.3%
Independent	27	12.90	12	-0.6%
Anglican	1	14.85	14	-0.3%
Catholic	1	31.20	29	-1.3%
Marginal	7	2.37	2	-1.2%
Unaffiliated		8.65	8	n.a.
Doubly affiliated		*-7.53*	*-7*	*n.a.*

Churches	MegaBloc	Cong.	Members	Affiliates
Catholic	C	6	16,571	29,000
Episcopal	A	9	6,900	13,800
Seventh-day Adventist	P	13	6,500	8,100
Moravian	P	8	2,100	4,500
Methodist	P	8	2,100	3,800
Independent Baptist	P	5	2,200	2,800
Spanish-speaking [6]	I	38	1,900	2,600
Lutheran	P	7	1,450	2,320
Assemblies of God	P	5	1,350	2,254
Ch of God (Cleveland)	P	7	869	1,700
Ch of God of Prophecy	P	5	800	1,500
Jehovah's Witnesses	M	9	628	1,500
Other denoms [57]		104	8,906	15,170
Doubly affiliated			*-4,192*	*-7,000*
Total Christians [75]		224	48,100	82,000

Trans-bloc Groupings	pop.%	,000	Ann.Gr.
Evangelical	25.8	24	+0.0%
Charismatic	18.7	17	+0.2%
Pentecostal	11.5	11	+0.9%

Missionaries from Virgin Islands
P,I,A None known.

Missionaries from Virgin Islands
P,I,A 40 in 6 agencies from 8 countries: USA 28.

GEOGRAPHY
Area 352 sq.km. In the Leeward Islands lying between Puerto Rico and British Virgin Islands. Three larger and 50 smaller islands.

Population	Ann.Gr.	Density
2000	92,954	-0.85%	264 per sq. km.
2010	87,198	-0.57%	248 per sq. km.
2025	83,559	-0.14%	237 per sq. km.

Rapid growth in the 1970s and '80s through immigration from other Caribbean islands, but decline since then.

Capital Charlotte Amalie 35,000. **Urbanites** 47%.

PEOPLES

English-speaking 83.7%
Afro-Caribbean 69.4%, Euro-American 12.5%, Other 1.8%.
Hispanic-speaking 16.3%.
Afro-Caribbean 10.3%, Euro-American 2.3%, Other 3.7%.

Literacy 90%. **Official language** English, but Spanish widely spoken.

ECONOMY
Tourism is the mainstay of the economy, with over one million visitors a year. A growing industry base, with the ninth largest oil refinery in the world. About half the working population is poor and foreign, creating tensions in society.

• Challenges for Prayer

1 **Tourism and the inflow of wealth** have played havoc with the moral and social fabric of society. Pray that the gospel might impact society, personal lifestyles and family life.

2 **The Christian Church** has become very nominal, lacking in vitality and vision. The Moravians had a glorious past, but they and all churches need revival. The Catholic Church has grown through immigration of Puerto Ricans and also through charismatic renewal. Some evangelical groups have grown (**CoN**, **AoG**, several Church of God denominations and Baptists). The great need is revival.

3 **Specific outreach is needed** for the many tourists, the Hispanic immigrants, the Rastafarians and those involved in the crime 'industry'. Pray that local churches and their leaders may work together in evangelism and in vision for the future.

Wallis and Futuna Islands

French Territory of Wallis and Futuna

Wallis and Futuna

DECEMBER 1
PACIFIC

Literacy 95%. **Official language** French. **All languages** 2. **Languages with Scriptures** 1Bi 1por 1w.i.p.

ECONOMY
Based on export of labour and coconuts.

POLITICS
An overseas territory of France.

RELIGION
Roman Catholicism is the only recognized religion. Virtually a Catholic theocracy. Almost the entire population is church-going.

Religions	Population %	Adherents	Ann.Gr.
Christian	97.76	14,192	+0.5%
non-Religious/other	1.50	218	+4.8%
Baha'i	0.74	107	+2.7%

Christians	Denom.	Affil.%	,000	Ann.Gr.
Protestant	2	0.55	0	+7.5%
Catholic	1	96.49	14	+0.1%
Marginal	1	0.72	0	+11.4%

Churches	MegaBloc	Cong.	Members	Affiliates
Catholic	C	5	8,000	14,000
Other denominations [3]		3	85	185
Total Christians [4]		8	8,085	14,200

Trans-bloc Groupings	pop.%	,000	Ann.Gr.
Evangelical	0.6	0	+7.5%
Charismatic	0.2	0	+13.3%
Pentecostal	0.2	0	+13.3%

Missionaries to and from Wallis and Futuna
n.a.

GEOGRAPHY
Area 274 sq.km. Three groups of coral islands 300 km west of Samoa.

Population	Ann.Gr.	Density
2000	14,517	+0.60%	53 per sq. km.
2010	15,529	+0.70%	57 per sq. km.
2025	17,500	+0.85%	64 per sq. km.

A further 10,000 work in New Caledonia.

Capital Mata-Utu 700.

PEOPLES
Polynesian 96.7%. Wallisian (Ovean) 9,000; Futunan 5,000.
Other 3.3%. French 400.

• Challenges for Prayer

1 **The Catholic Church and Polynesian culture** and social structures have become so interwoven that adherence to Christianity is often more outward than through a living, personal faith. Pray for first-hand faith for these two island peoples.

2 **Until 1985 this territory was one of the few countries of the world without a congregation of evangelical believers**. There is now a small evangelical group on Futuna and also a little Assemblies of God congregation.

3 **Many islanders have migrated to New Caledonia and Vanuatu seeking work**. Pray that some may be won to a personal commitment to Christ there, and thereby bring blessing to their homeland.

4 **Bible translation is a need**. The OT and NT in Wallisian are being translated, but Futunan only has portions.

Yemen
Republic of Yemen

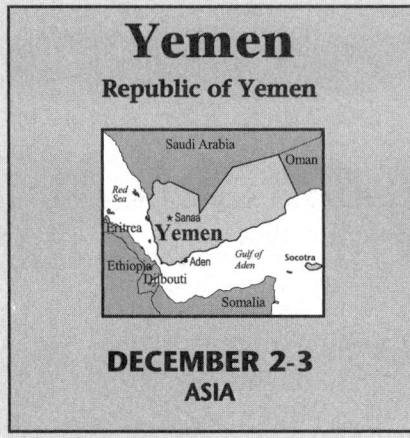

DECEMBER 2-3
ASIA

GEOGRAPHY
Area 531,869 sq.km. Mountainous south and south-western portion of the Arabian Peninsula and also the Indian Ocean island of Socotra.

Population	Ann.Gr.	Density
2000	18,112,066	+3.81%	34 per sq. km.
2010	25,366,187	+3.32%	48 per sq. km.
2025	38,985,203	+2.66%	73 per sq. km.

Capital Sana'a 1,400,000. Other major city: Aden 630,000. **Urbanites** 24%.

PEOPLES
Arab 95%. Over 1,700 clans and tribes. Also: Sudanese 300,000; Omani 120,000; Iraqi 70,000. **Immigrant and Refugee communities** 4.3%. Somali 670,000; South Asian 76,000; Ethiopian 8,000; Eritrean 8,000.
Other 0.7%. Mahri 80,000; Soqotri 40,000.

Literacy 43% (only 23% for women). **Official language** Arabic. **All languages** 7. **Languages with Scriptures** 2Bi 2por.

ECONOMY
Agricultural and pastoral economy — the only part of the Arabian Peninsula with a significant rainfall. Oil provides 95% of foreign earnings. The expulsion of over 1 million Yemeni workers from Saudi Arabia in the 1990 Gulf War was a major blow to the economy. The poorest state in the Middle East. **HDI** 0.449; 148th/174. **Public debt** 93% of GNP. **Income/person** $380 (1.2% of USA).

POLITICS
A turbulent history of wars and conquests. The North was part of the Ottoman Empire until 1918 and then an isolated feudal theocracy until the 1962 Egyptian-engineered republican revolution. Aden (the South) was ruled by Britain until independence in 1967. A Marxist coup ousted the traditional rulers and imposed a leftist regime. The two countries united in 1990 with the north as the dominant partner. A southern secessionist revolt in 1994 led to a northern victory. A strong presidential government with a measure of democracy.

RELIGION
Islam is the official religion and the legal system is based on *shari'a* law. Sunni Islam 62% (in centre and south), Zaidi Shi'a 37% (in north-east), Ismaili 0.9%. Only freedom of religion for non-Muslims. **Persecution index** 5th in the world.

Religions	Population %	Adherents	Ann.Gr.
Muslim	99.94	18,099,388	+3.8%
Christian	0.05	9,056	+0.1%
Jewish	0.01	1,000	+3.0%

Christians	Denom.	Affil.%	,000	Ann.Gr.
Protestant	1	0.00	0	+3.3%
Independent	2	0.00	1	+2.4%
Anglican	2	0.00	0	+15.5%
Catholic	1	0.03	6	+0.7%
Orthodox	2	0.02	3	+2.1%
Marginal	0	0.00	0	

Churches	MegaBloc	Cong.	Members	Affiliates
Catholic	C	4	1,100	5,500
Orthodox [2]	O		1,000	3,000
Anglican	A	4	120	200
Other denoms [4]		4	774	1,244
Total Christians [8]		12	2,994	9,944

Trans-bloc Groupings	pop.%	,000	Ann.Gr.
Evangelical	0.0	1	+5.5%
Charismatic	0.0	1	+4.0%
Pentecostal	0.0	0	+2.7%

• Challenges for Prayer

1 **Yemen has been deeply impacted by wars** over the last 4 decades — 3 civil wars, conflict with neighbouring states and also the effects of the Gulf War, Somalia's collapse into anarchy and the Ethiopian/Eritrean war. The treasured right of Yemenis to bear arms has fuelled tribal rivalries, while widespread corruption provokes kidnappings, crime and sabotage as forms of protest. There are over 50 million firearms in the country. Pray that the government may rule fairly and bring about national unity and peace.

2 **Yemen was once famous for frankincense and myrrh**, but now the growing of the narcotic *qat* has become the mainstay for rural Yemen. Over 80% of the adult population chew it and much of the agricultural land and irrigation water is committed to its cultivation. Nearly 40% of the national economy is involved in *qat*. The negative effects on productivity, social and family life are immense. Corruption in high places prevents developmental programmes from being effective. Less than half the population have access to any health services and nearly half of all children suffer from malnutrition.

3 **Christianity was strong by 400AD,** but was almost completely wiped out by the Muslim conquest in the 7th Century. The Queen of Sheba reigned in Yemen and sought wisdom from Solomon three millennia ago. May the modern people of Sheba seek after the wisdom from God as is promised in Isaiah 60:6.

4 **It is illegal for non-Muslims to proselytize and for Muslims to become Christians**. Yet through radio broadcasts, tactful faith-sharing and the Lord's intervention maybe 100 or so Yemenis have trusted in Christ. For Yemenis it is dangerous to openly become a believer in Jesus because of the many social pressures brought to bear on those who do. Pray that pressures may ease to give Yemenis the freedom to come to Christ and to meet for fellowship. Pray for the conversion of their families, for it is from them that the worst persecution comes.

5 **Most Christians are expatriates.** Many are Ethiopian refugees, among whom are several thriving evangelical congregations. Others are Westerners and South and East Asians in secular jobs or serving with some humanitarian NGOs that are permitted to minister in the country. A church in Aden has been restored to the Christians for worship and wider community service. Pray that expatriate believers may maintain their spiritual growth in the face of many attacks from the enemy of souls through discouragement, sickness, isolation from the wider Christian family, and constant threats to their presence in the land. A number have been kidnapped for brief periods in recent years.

6 **There are a widening range of opportunities for expatriates to serve the Lord** in business, education, health and development programmes. However corruption, official extortion, unrest, archaic laws and poor infrastructure drain time and resources. Pray for Asian, Western and other Christians to respond to God's call to this land and for them to have good opportunity to live and testify for Christ.

7 **Yemen is one of the world's least evangelized countries.** Pray for salvation to come to:
a) ***The Northern tribes*** — including the people of Sana'a, the capital, and the peoples of the northern mountains and north-eastern deserts. Many are semi-nomadic.
b) ***The Central Yemenis***, the key cities being Taiz and Ibb.
c) ***The Tihama Arabs*** of the coastal plains. Many Gulf War returnees were settled in this region. The key city is Hodeida.
d) ***The Southern Yemenis*** of the cosmopolitan city of Aden and those of the Hadhramaut area (both Arab and Mahri).
e) ***The Soqotri islanders***, who were nominally Christians until the 17th Century. There are no known Christians on this isolated Indian Ocean island.
f) ***Yemeni women*** — their lot is harsh, their opportunities for education and a life outside the home limited. How will they hear about Jesus and learn to live for Him?
g) ***The South Asians*** — many are traders and artisans in Aden. Most are Muslim or Hindu, some are Catholic Christians; also the 1,000 or so remaining Yemeni Jews.
h) ***The Somalis***, many of whom are Yemeni residents, others refugees. A few have come to faith but most remain unevangelized.

8 **Christian media** for prayer:
a) ***Bible translation*** — there is need for Yemeni Arabic, Soqotri and Mahri Bibles.
b) ***Bible and literature distribution*** — this is not easy, but tactfully possible — many desire an opportunity to read the Bible.
c) ***The JESUS film***. — now available in several key languages, but opportunities to show the film or distribute the video are limited. Audio cassettes of Christian music, Scriptures, etc., are available.
d) ***Christian Radio***. Broadcasts by **FEBA**-Seychelles (15 hrs/wk) and **TWR**-Cyprus (9 hrs/wk) in Arabic are clearly received. Many are regular listeners, and this has raised interest levels. Pray for lasting fruit and living fellowships of believers to result. **FEBA** also broadcasts 3.5 hrs/wk in Somali. Pray that **SAT-7** may also be available. Many homes have satellite dishes, but only some can access existing broadcasts.

Yugoslavia

Serbia and Montenegro

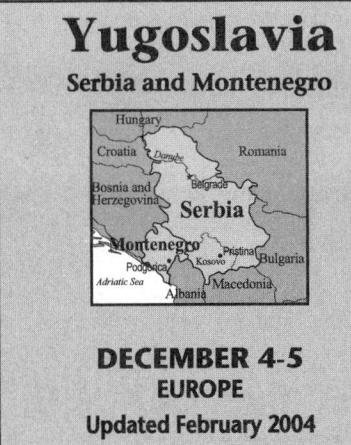

DECEMBER 4-5
EUROPE
Updated February 2004

GEOGRAPHY
Area 102,173 sq.km. Balkan state comprising two republics, Serbia and Montenegro. Serbia has one autonomous province, Vojvodina, in the north and a special region, Kosovo, in the south.

Population		Ann.Gr.	Density
2000	10,640,150	+0.14%	104 per sq. km.
2010	10,762,337	+0.15%	105 per sq. km.
2025	10,844,276	+0.01%	106 per sq. km.

Montenegro has only 6% of the population.

Capital Belgrade 1,750,000. Belgrade has been destroyed and rebuilt 40 times in its history. **Urbanites** 51%.

PEOPLES
Slav 74.5%. Serbian 6.6 mill.; Montenegrin 530,000; Bosnian 344,000; Croat 114,000; Slovak 68,000; Macedonian 48,000.
Albanian 16.5%
Other 9%. Hungarian 350,000; Roma (Gypsy) 300,000; Romanian 42,000; Vlach 18,000; Turk 12,000.

Literacy 93%. **Official language** Serbian. **All languages** 14. **Languages with Scriptures** 5Bi 3NT 2por.

ECONOMY
Poor and impoverished by 45 years of Communism followed by 13 years of self-seeking despotism. The break-up of the larger Yugoslav entity in 1991 and ensuing Balkan wars led to UN trade sanctions and ultimately to NATO military intervention in Kosovo with heavy bombing of its infrastructure and further reductions in living standards. Reconstruction will take time and much foreign investment. **HDI** & **Public debt** n.a. **Income/person** $1,900 (6% of USA).

POLITICS
The division of the Roman empire nearly 1,700 years ago created a major cultural and religious fault-line between the Catholic northwest and the Byzantine southeast of that region. Successive ethnic and imperial conquests further helped to make the Balkans a byword for ethnic hatreds and political intrigue. Yugoslavia developed from fragments of the Austro-Hungarian and Ottoman Turkish empires between 1878 and 1921. Ethnic nationalisms in the country helped trigger World War I and provoke genocidal civil war during World War II. Communism imposed by President Tito in 1945 suppressed deep ethnic hatred between Serb and Croat, and Serb and Albanian. Tito's death in 1980 exposed the nation's festering wounds and loosened the ties between the constituent republics of which Serbia was the dominant member. The break-up of Yugoslavia began with the secession of Slovenia then Croatia in 1991, followed by Bosnia and Macedonia in 1992. The Serbian military opposed the break-up, leading to years of warfare against Croatia and then in multi-cultural Bosnia by attempts to link all Serbian enclaves in Bosnia and Croatia to the Serbian Republic. The remaining two republics have an uneasy and unequal relationship within the reduced federation. The manipulative despotism, nationalism and greed of President Milosevic and his henchmen were major contributory factors to the violence and 'ethnic cleansing' since 1991. Repression of Albanians in the Kosovo region led to warfare and NATO's takeover of Kosovo in 1999 with installation of an interim government in 2000. Though still nominally part of Serbia, the growth of extremism among Albanians in the region makes compromise and lasting resolution unlikely. The popular protests of 2000 forced Milosevic out of office. There is a gradual emergence of democratic government and normalized relationships with the rest of the world. In 2002 the country was renamed to The Federal Republic of Serbia and Montenegro in recognition of the separate entity of the latter.

RELIGION
Strong links between ethnicity and religion have exacerbated tensions in the Balkans for centuries. Both republics are predominantly Orthodox. Constitutionally there is freedom of religion, but with preferential treatment accorded to the Orthodox Church. Since 2000, the Orthodox have sought to re-establish the pre-Communist State-Church relationship and also push for discriminatory legislation against non-Orthodox minorities.

Religions	Population %	Adherents	Ann.Gr.
Christian	67.87	7,221,470	+0.8%
Muslim	16.20	1,723,704	+0.6%
non-Religious/other	15.90	1,691,784	-2.7%
Jewish	0.03	3,192	+0.1%

Christians	Denom.	Affil.%	,000	Ann.Gr.
Protestant	58	1.05	111	+0.0%
Independent	10	1.10	117	+4.7%
Anglican	1	0.00	0	-1.3%
Catholic	2	5.12	545	+1.4%
Orthodox	11	54.36	5,784	+0.0%
Marginal	1	0.06	6	+2.8%
Unaffiliated		6.18	657	n.a.

Christians	Denom.	Affil.%	,000	Ann.Gr.
Church of God	P	17	500	900
Christian Brethren	P	13	450	693
Other denoms [65]		432	118,900	222,400
Total Christians [83]		3,555	4,418,700	6,564,000

Trans-bloc Groupings	pop.%	,000	Ann.Gr.
Evangelical	1.4	151	+4.1%
Charismatic	1.2	130	+3.3%
Pentecostal	0.9	93	+1.0%

Churches	MegaBloc	Cong.	Members	Affiliates
Serbian Orthodox	O	1,783	3,655,172	5,300,000
Catholic	C	176	344,828	500,000
Montenegrin Orth [2]	O	341	132,500	265,000
Church of the Spirit [2]	I	92	41,500	83,000
Slovak Ev Chr (Luth)	P	51	32,867	47,000
Catholic (Byzantine)	C	50	31,034	45,000
Bulgarian Orthodox	O	30	20,000	35,000
Reformed	P	39	12,000	17,000
Gypsy Evang. Mvt.	I	160	8,500	17,000
Seventh-day Adventist	P	171	6,959	10,000
Evangelical (Pente)	P	65	6,200	9,000
Jehovah's Witnesses	M	52	4,026	6,000
Baptist	P	55	1,780	3,500
Methodist	P	28	1,437	2,400

Missionaries from Yugoslavia
P,I,A 29 in 8 agencies to 5 countries.

Missionaries to Yugoslavia
P,I,A 52 in 17 agencies from 9 countries: USA 32, Sweden 6, Korea 4.

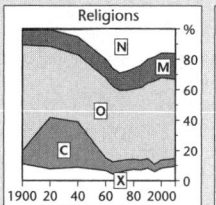

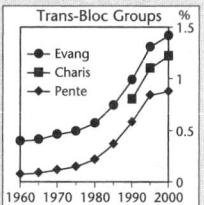

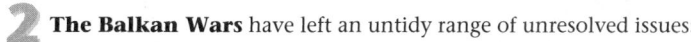

• Challenges for Prayer

1 **Serbian nationalism,** based on centuries of resentment of their victimization at the hands of other nations (Turks, Austrians, Germans, Croats, etc.), has wreaked havoc in the Balkans since 1991. The 'ethnic cleansings' of Catholic Croats, and Bosnian and Albanian Muslims have left a bitter legacy of hatred and revenge atrocities. Pray for deep repentance, forgiveness on all sides and a re-building of trust and cooperation for a better future. Pray for national leaders to be raised up who are free from the shackles of the past.

2 **The Balkan Wars** have left an untidy range of unresolved issues:

a) *The Bosnian Republic* partitioned between Serbs, Croats and Bosnians.
b) *The future of Kosovo* and its angry Albanian majority bent on seizing areas in surrounding states which have Albanian populations.
c) *The several million displaced people* whose homes and lands were destroyed and expropriated with little likelihood of return.
d) *The need for justice* and for perpetrators of atrocities to be apprehended and sentenced.

These issues will haunt Europe for decades to come if there are no effective political, economic and, above all, spiritual solutions. International bodies such as the UN and NATO are compromised and objective arbitration hard to achieve. The indigenous religions — Orthodoxy, Catholicism and Islam — are part of the problem. Pray that the tiny evangelical community might prove a catalyst for good — it is the only body which has been able to retain multi-cultural fellowships.

3 **Democracy in both republics is fragile** and democratic institutions need to be strengthened. The growing influence of the Serbian Orthodox Church could limit this and religious freedoms be eroded. Pray for new life within this ancient Church and also that it may turn its back on its totalitarian instincts and support true religious freedom.

4 **Protestantism** has had a long history among the Hungarian and Slovak minorities in Vojvodina, but little impact on Serbs or Albanians. All Protestants number little over 110,000. There is much nominalism in the Lutheran and Reformed congregations, and revival is needed to free them from formalism and to enable effective witness.

5 **Evangelical believers among Serbs** number only a few thousand. Most Evangelicals are Hungarian and Slovak in Vojvodina and increasingly among the Roma (Gypsy). Evangelical congregations are few, small and scattered outside Vojvodina. The sufferings of the 1990s and outreach by Evangelicals to Serbian refugees from Croatia, Bosnia and Kosovo have won appreciation and open hearts. Some congregations doubled in size in 1999 through conversions among refugees. Some Baptist and Pentecostal churches were damaged during the Kosovo War because of their perceived links with the West. Pray for continued growth in commitment, outreach and numbers.

6 **Crucial issues** for Evangelicals to deal with:

a) *Unity*. The **Evangelical Alliance** seeks to bring together Evangelicals, but some denominations and agencies remain aloof and do not participate.

b) *Leadership training* is limited and poverty hinders the flow of people into ministry. There is one Bible school, the KES, an interdenominational school with links to the Christian Brethren and the Baptists.

c) *Cooperation in outreach and church planting*. The churches can be as 'balkanized' as the politics of their region — hindering effective outreach to the many unevangelized areas. The Baptists and Pentecostals have set up the **Jericho Project** with the vision to plant 20 churches in 4 cities.

7 **Outreach challenges.** Serbia has one of the lowest percentages of Evangelicals in Europe. Specifically for prayer:

a) *Many areas in the centre and south* have very few believers such as the Valjevo area in the centre-west with 2 million people and one small Pentecostal Church.

b) *Students*. EUS(**IFES**) has groups on most campuses in Belgrade, Nis and Novi Sad with 200 students involved. There is a burden to pioneer other areas for student witness.

c) *War refugees* are scattered all over Europe and the Balkans — possibly 3 million have been, or are, refugees — inevitably traumatized, but also open to change.

8 **Montenegro** is a mountainous republic on the coast of the Adriatic Sea. It is fiercely jealous of its tradition of independence and has been resentful of its ties with delinquent Serbia. It is deeply divided on the issue of complete independence. Issues for prayer:

a) *Its political future* — may wisdom prevail on the issue of independence.

b) *Its spiritual renewal* — nominally Orthodox; very few Evangelicals. There are 5 small groups with 300 believers and several missionaries working among Montenegrins.

9 **Kosovo's future** is gloomy and uncertain. Serbs regard Kosovo as the cradle of their culture and religion, but they were driven out by the victorious Ottoman Turks in 1389. Kosovo became part of Serbia after World War I but the Albanian Muslims there multiplied to become over 90% of the population by 1995. The Kosovo crisis was precipitated by Serbian suppression of Albanian culture and Kosovan autonomy. Albanian resistance led to Serbian 'ethnic cleansing' in 1998-99 through murder, rape, pillage and eviction of much of the Albanian population. In turn, this pushed Western nations to intervene and eject Serbian military forces in 1999.

a) *A fair and just peace*. The international NATO military force, KFOR, has sought to lay foundations for future development but is increasingly occupied in keeping apart the diminishing Serb and Roma minorities from the angry Albanian majority. By 2001 the Serb population had been reduced from nearly 10% to 2%. The future for ethnic minorities and the peace-keeping effort in 2001 is bleak; further bloodshed is possible in Kosovo and adjoining Albanian-majority areas of Montenegro, Serbia itself and Macedonia. Pray for moderation and wisdom among leaders of all communities, and for the right political direction for Kosovo to be found. Albanian extremism could mire the whole area in conflict for many years to come.

b) *The Kosovo war* saw over 10,000 Albanians killed and turned 80% of the population into refugees. Their rapid return and massive aid from foreign governments and over 300 NGOs turned Kosovo into a huge building site. Pray for effective coordination and cooperation to maximise the benefits and minimise the negatives (crime, economic distortions, dependency).

c) *The Kosovar Albanian* population is almost entirely Muslim, but there are some Christians. Catholics number about 4,000 and before the war 4 small, disunited evangelical congregations existed in Pristina, the capital, with several groups elsewhere. The impact of the war, efforts of expatriate Christian aid agencies and loving Christian help to refugees in Albania led to rapid multiplication of evangelical groups to 45 by August 2000. Pray that these new believers may grow in grace, and become mature and effective witnesses to Muslims.

10 **Christian mission agencies** have found it hard to establish long-term ministry in Serbia and Kosovo. Pray that openings may increase and long-term workers be called, and that every part of the country (or countries, should Kosovo and Montenegro become independent) be reached. Pray for an effective transition from short-term aid and rehabilitation ministries to long-term community development and discipling by those who are able to learn the cultures and languages. Significant agencies involved are: **YWAM**, **GEM**, **IMB-SBC**, Macedonia Mission, etc.

11 **Many Yugoslavs** moved to other parts of Europe as war or economic refugees. Funds they remit home are the main source of income for much of the population. Pray for effective outreach to Serbians, Albanians and others in Germany, Austria, Switzerland, Sweden, France and elsewhere.

12 Christian media ministries:

a) *Bible and Christian literature* ministries have been hampered by the disruptions and wars. Pray for wise development of such ministries as peace returns so that local initiatives are not crippled by free, but less appropriate, literature from abroad. **The Bible Society** reports great demand for the Scriptures. There is one Christian bookstore in Belgrade.

b) *Christian radio ministries*. Christian radio programming is prepared by KES in Serbian and by **ECM** in Albanian for broadcasting locally and through **TWR** transmitters in Albania. **TWR** broadcasts 8 hrs/wk in Serbian.

Zambia
Republic of Zambia

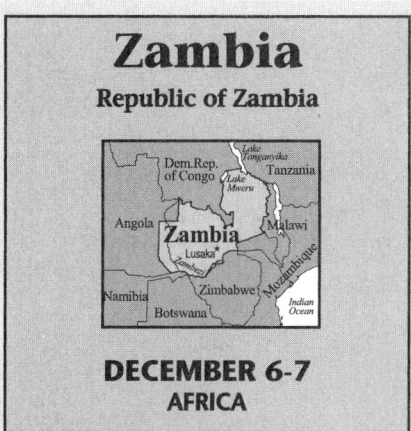

DECEMBER 6-7
AFRICA

GEOGRAPHY
Area 752,614 sq.km. Landlocked, forested Central African country.

Population		Ann.Gr.	Density
2000	9,168,700	+2.27%	12 per sq. km.
2010	11,426,935	+2.39%	15 per sq. km.
2025	15,616,246	+1.85%	21 per sq. km.

Capital Lusaka 1,695,000. Other major cities: Ndola 500,000; Kitwe 446,000. **Urbanites** 22%.

PEOPLES
85 ethnic groups.
Bantu 98%. Bemba-related 3.3 mill.; Nyanja-related 1.6m; Tonga(5) 1.38m; Lozi-related 750,000; Tumbuka 392,000; Lala-Bisa 371,000; Kaonde 248,000; Lunda 222,000; Lamba 214,000; Luvale 205,000; Lenje 171,000.
Khoisan (Bushmen). Under 1,000 in 4 groups, in the west.

Foreign-origin 2%. South Asian 27,000 (mainly Gujarati); European 25,000; Refugees — many Congolese and Angolans fleeing war in their homelands.

Literacy 78% (declining; functional literacy under 25%). **Official language** English. **Trade language** Bemba and Nyanja spoken by large minorities of the population. **All languages** 41. **Languages with Scriptures** 15Bi 8NT 3por 3w.i.p.

ECONOMY
Copper mining and refining has long been the major source of foreign exchange. Post-independence prosperity was squandered by heavy-handed socialism, neglect of agriculture and widespread corruption. The collapse of world copper prices, instability and meddling in wars in surrounding nations further pushed the nation into virtual bankruptcy. The Chiluba government has only partially reformed the economy but done little to stem corruption. The AIDS catastrophe has devastated the population and brought health services to the point of collapse. **HDI** 0.431; 151st/174. **Public debt** 148% of GNP. **Income/person** $370 (1% of USA).

POLITICS
Independent from Britain in 1964. One-party democracy under President Kaunda's leadership until 1991. Growing corruption, economic collapse and a revulsion against one party regimes prompted multi-party elections. The Chiluba government began well in freeing up the economy, allowing press freedom and outlawing abortion, pornography and prostitution. However, it has not maintained democratic freedoms nor improved the quality of life for most Zambians. There is widespread disillusionment.

Z

RELIGION

Kaunda's socialist humanism was government policy. Chiluba, as an active Christian, declared Zambia a Christian country in 1991 but with full religious freedom for all faiths. This was written into the constitution in 1996.

Religions	Population %	Adherents	Ann.Gr.
Christian	85.04	7,797,062	+2.8%
Traditional ethnic	12.62	1,157,090	-1.1%
Muslim	1.40	128,362	+3.0%
Baha'i	0.40	36,675	+3.3%
non-Religious/other	0.40	36,675	+2.3%
Hindu	0.14	12,836	+2.3%

Christians	Denom.	Affil.%	,000	Ann.Gr.
Protestant	49	35.51	3,256	+8.2%
Independent	160	14.55	1,334	+2.2%
Anglican	1	2.40	220	+5.3%
Catholic	1	33.48	3,070	+2.8%
Orthodox	3	0.06	6	+0.1%
Marginal	7	4.86	446	+2.2%
Unaffiliated		4.00	365	n.a.
Doubly affiliated		*-9.82*	*-900*	*n.a.*

Churches	MegaBloc	Cong.	Members	Affiliates
Catholic	C	265	1,784,884	3,070,000
United	P	1,200	250,000	1,000,000
New Apostolic	I	800	320,000	800,000
Reformed Church in Z	P	145	290,000	500,000
Seventh-day Adventist	P	1,078	309,200	420,000
Jehovah's Witnesses	M	2,089	107,233	380,000
Ch of God (Cleveland)	P	490	170,000	300,000
Anglican	A	967	88,000	220,000
Pentecostal AoG	P	330	54,300	154,800
Chr Brethren	P	1,107	60,000	120,000

Baptist Union	P	360	41,500	103,750
Baptist Convention	P	699	41,940	100,000
African Methodist Episc	I	212	18,000	90,000
Pentecostal Holiness	P	400	44,000	73,480
Ch of God (Anderson)	P	600	27,200	68,000
Evang Church in Z	P	800	45,000	60,000
Apostolic Faith Mission	P	340	17,000	34,000
Ch of the Nazarene	P	70	14,000	25,000
N.Baptist Assoc of Z	P	260	9,000	22,000
Brethren in Christ	P	248	14,120	18,000
Other denoms [201]		4,243	360,800	773,000
Doubly affiliated			*-409,000*	*-900,000*
Total Christians [221]		16,703	3,657,000	7,432,000

Trans-bloc Groupings	pop.%	,000	Ann.Gr.
Evangelical	25.0	2,291	+9.0%
Charismatic	18.9	1,730	+4.9%
Pentecostal	10.2	936	+7.2%

Missionaries from Zambia
P,I,A 228 in 22 agencies to 18 countries: Zambia 182.

Missionaries to Zambia
P,I,A 566 in 66 agencies from 24 countries: USA 210, UK 102, South Africa 48, Germany 35, Canada 34, New Zealand 27, Australia 25.

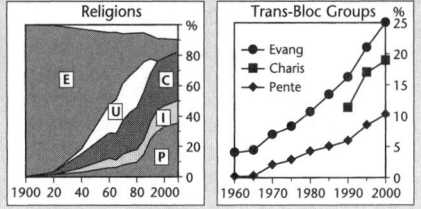

• Answers to Prayer

1 **The growth of the Church** during the 1980s accelerated in the 1990s, helped by President Chiluba's public Christian confession and the opening up of public institutions and media to the gospel. Evangelicals were 515,000 (9%) in 1980, 800,000 (12.6%) in 1990 and 2.2 million (25%) in 2000.

• Challenges for Prayer

1 **President Chiluba** openly dedicated Zambia to God as a Christian nation at his inauguration in 1991. The outworkings in public life have been disappointing, with many in the government becoming ostentatiously wealthy while half the population live in dire poverty. Pray for hearts, worldviews and structures to be moulded by God's Word, for democracy not to be discredited and for Christianity not to be debased or even rejected through such failures.

2 **The widespread poverty and lack of economic progress could lead to unrest or worse.** Pray that the government may tackle the massive problems with honesty and courage. The foreign debt burden is one of the world's highest, and the economic impact of the AIDS pandemic one of the world's worst.

3 **The massive growth of Protestant and Independent churches** has been encouraging. The Spirit of God has moved through the country with many coming to personal faith in Christ — in urban areas, among educated young people and increasingly in rural areas. The United Church (fruit of the work of LMS, Paris Evangelical Missionary

Society, Church of Scotland and Methodist Missionary Society) has a growing evangelical witness and is bringing new life and outreach in once formal congregations. The economic crisis, poverty, unemployment and the AIDS pandemic have all prompted a search after God that multiplied conversions in the 1990s. Yet there are dangers:

a) **Superficiality** and lack of real understanding of the grace as well as the radical demands of the gospel. Many are still bound by fear of witchcraft.

b) **Lack of indigeneity**. There is need for a true African expression of Christian lifestyle, theology and worship patterns.

c) **Too much multiplication of churches by acrimonious divisions**. This is especially true of the burgeoning Pentecostal and charismatic networks.

4 **Rural churches vary widely in spiritual quality and vigour.** Pray for:

a) **The many thriving evangelical congregations in the northwest** among the Luvale, Chokwe, Lunda and others (**Brethren**), Kaonde, Mbwela and Nkoya (**SIM**) and Lamba (Baptist). The area has a high concentration of evangelical believers, but they need a greater vision for cross-cultural outreach to other areas of the land.

b) **The fruitful work of the Brethren in Christ and Churches of Christ** among the Tonga peoples in the south; but some areas are only partially evangelized.

c) **The Reformed Church among the Nyanja** peoples in the east, which is theologically evangelical and now growing fast.

d) **The Lozi and southwestern peoples and the Bemba and northern peoples**, who have few evangelical congregations. Many have become nominally Christian, but because of unclear teaching, large numbers have been swept into sectarian or syncretistic indigenous churches. Pray for churches to be planted in these spiritually needy areas.

e) **The PAoC**, Pentecostal Holiness Church, **SIM**, **Brethren** and Churches of Christ who have all commenced work in the less evangelized northeast.

5 The Evangelical Fellowship of Zambia (EFZ) has become an important focal point of fellowship and cooperative efforts for denominations and agencies. Pray that God may give united vision to Christian leaders as they tackle the daunting problems facing Zambia. In 1998 a new national initiative was launched through the inspiration of the AD2000 and Beyond Movement for outreach within, and missions outside, Zambia.

6 The AIDS crisis is overwhelming the health services (80% in hospitals have AIDS), the pastoral work of churches (many funerals) and family life. Pray specifically for:

a) **All seeking to bring about real change** in sexual behaviour, attitudes to victims and heart attitudes in order to check the spread of the disease. **The Bible Society** with **Jesus Cares Ministry**, **Advocates for Change** and SU's **Aid for AIDS** programmes are some such. Some estimate that half the present population will die of AIDS.

b) **Medical workers** who have to face the daily challenge of so many needing help but who lack resources. Mission hospitals have again become important. It is reckoned that 20-25% of the population has HIV. In prisons, over 50% are infected.

c) **Children**. Zambia probably has the highest level of AIDS orphans (650,000+) in the world. Over 90,000 live on the streets of the cities. Extended families are too overstretched to care for them all.

7 Leadership training. This is a priority in a land where nominalism and syncretism are common. The EFZ has sponsored the Theological College of Central Africa in Ndola — the first evangelical, degree-awarding theological institution in Central Africa. The TCCA, Justo Mwale Theological College, Apostolic and Pentecostal Bible Schools are full to capacity. There are a total of 18 Bible schools. Pray for spiritually and educationally qualified leaders to be prepared through these institutions. TEE is widely used, but has only been partially effective. Lay training is a must, as most church planting has been done by lay people.

8 Young people. SU has had a significant impact in the secondary schools, with large, lively groups in most of them. Many missionaries and Zambian believers have an extensive ministry in teaching the Scriptures in government schools. ZAFES(**IFES**) has three staff workers and groups in almost every post-secondary institution.

9 Missions. There is an open door, but the emphasis is on working within the structure of the national churches, or in preparing Zambians for leadership. The largest are: **Brethren** (133), **SIM** (74), **IMB-SBC** (25), Liebenzell Mission (22), Christian Chs/Chs of

Christ (20), SdA (19), Brethren in Christ (13). Pray for wisdom, tact and humility as they seek to help the Zambian Church. There are many opportunities for service: Bible teaching in schools, medical work, leadership training and the use of technical skills such as in radio and literature production and distribution.

10 **The less reached:**

a) *The many smaller peoples in the southwest* are minimally reached — the Subiya, the 4 Khoisan groups, etc.

b) *The urban satellite towns* of Lusaka, the Copperbelt and Kabwe are spiritually needy. Many are squalid shanty settlements. Pray for the work of **DM** and others in evangelizing these areas where sin is rife.

c) *The Indian Gujarati* community is both Hindu and Muslim, but few are Christian. South African **SIM** and Asian missionaries from Tanzania are working among them.

d) *Muslims* are active in propagating their religion and making liberal use of funds to entice non-Muslims into their sphere of influence. Pray for effective outreach to Muslims. Few Zambian Christians are equipped for this.

11 **Christian specialist ministries:**

a) *Bible translation and distribution.* **The Bible Society** has a key role in a number of OT and three NT translation projects.

b) *Christian literature.* There are 16 Christian bookstores, but the quantity, range and local applicability of available literature are limited. Lack of foreign exchange, local supplies and authors are big limitations.

c) *Christian radio and television* ministries have expanded rapidly. There is now a Christian FM station in Lusaka and a Christian TV channel. The major issue is quality. There are too many frothy Western TV shows whose performance techniques are copied by local preachers.

Zimbabwe
Republic of Zimbabwe

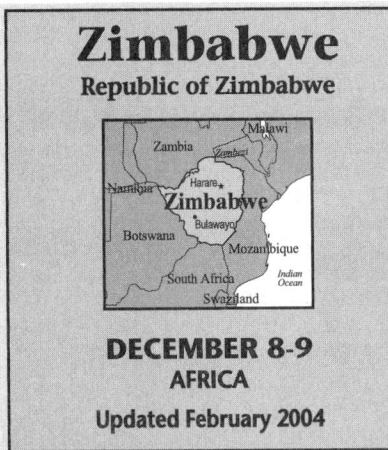

DECEMBER 8-9
AFRICA
Updated February 2004

GEOGRAPHY **Area** 390,759 sq.km. Landlocked state in south-central Africa.

Population	Ann.Gr.	Density
2000	11,669,029	+1.43%	30 per sq. km.
2010	12,863,136	+0.99%	33 per sq. km.
2025	15,092,435	+1.07%	39 per sq. km.

These UN-projected figures do not allow enough for the death rate due to AIDS nor for the possible 2-3 million who have fled to other countries — especially South Africa. The 2025 population may be around 9 million.

Capital Harare 2,300,000. Other major cities: Bulawayo 800,000, Gweru 130,000, Mutare 124,000. **Urbanites** 27%.

PEOPLES Over 42 peoples.
Indigenous 90.9%.
Shona 70.5%. 9 major peoples speaking related dialects and numbering 8.2 mill.
Nguni 14%. Ndebele 1.55m; Kalanga 196,000 (a Shona group being absorbed by Ndebele).
Other 6.4%. Tswana-Sotho 210,000; Shangaan-Tsonga 143,000; Tonga 137,000; Kunda 134,000; Venda 114,000.
Non-indigenous 9.1%.
African 7.9%. Many work as farm labourers. Chewa 575,000; Lozi 130,000; Sena 105,000; Yao 46,000.
Other 1.2%. European 90,000; Coloured 60,000; South Asian 25,000.

Literacy 85%. **Official language** English. **Trade languages** Shona is widely spoken, Ndebele in the west. **All languages** 19. **Languages with Scriptures** 11Bi 2NT 3por 4w.i.p.

ECONOMY Rich in agricultural land and minerals. One of Africa's most successful economies in the 1980s but being dismantled in the 1990s by the corruption, military adventurism and oppression of the government and ruling political party. Decline has been accelerated by periodic droughts, the impact of AIDS and the 1999-2004 seizure and plundering of many of the white-owned farms on which the economy and urban population depend. Since 2000, Mugabe had overseen the forcible expropriation of over 80% of privately owned farmland. By 2004 unemployment had risen above 70% with a high proportion of the population destitute and facing severe famine conditions. Zimbabwe has the world's most rapidly shrinking economy. Inflation runs at an annual rate of over 500%. **HDI** 0.560; 130th/174. **Public debt** 38% of GNP (2001). **Income/person** $720 (2% of USA) (2001).

POLITICS

The Rhodesian declaration of independence from Britain by the white minority in 1965 led to intense guerrilla warfare and eventually independence as Zimbabwe in 1980. The ruling party, ZANU-PF, has so mismanaged the economy that the increasingly unpopular President Mugabe has only been able to retain power by intimidating all who speak against his misrule. Thuggery, murder and destruction have become common. After losing a referendum in early 2000 and only winning the election in mid-2000 by massive intimidation and election fraud, the country has become a dictatorship. The sending of troops in 1998 to support the Kabila regime in Congo was economically disastrous for the nation, but enriched army and political elites. Since 2001 the press has been muzzled, foreign journalists expelled and virtually any sign of dissent savagely repressed.

RELIGION

There is freedom of religion despite post-independence attempts to impose Marxism-Leninism.

Religions	Population %	Adherents	Ann.Gr.
Christian	71.71	8,367,861	+2.3%
Traditional ethnic	26.00	3,033,948	-0.8%
non-Religious/other	1.20	140,028	+3.2%
Muslim	1.00	116,690	+2.7%
Jewish	0.09	10,502	-0.7%

Christians	Denom.	Affil.%	,000	Ann.Gr.
Protestant	53	17.55	2,048	+3.1%
Independent	268	36.44	4,252	+2.4%
Anglican	1	2.74	320	+2.7%
Catholic	1	8.74	1,020	-0.1%

Orthodox	1	0.02	2	-1.0%
Marginal	12	1.14	133	+3.0%
Unaffiliated		13.65	1,592	n.a.
Doubly affiliated		*-8.57*	*-1,000*	*n.a.*

Churches	MegaBloc	Cong.	Members	Affiliates
Zim. Assemb of God, Af.	I	4,000	800,000	1,600,000
Catholic	C	90	539,683	1,020,000
Afr. Apos Ch J Marange	I	500	364,000	910,000
Zion Christian	I	1,389	166,667	500,000
Seventh-day Adventist	P	552	288,380	481,600
Apostolic Faith Mission	P	1,150	110,000	366,300
Anglican	A	674	128,000	320,000
United Methodist (USA)	P	750	73,000	125,000
Methodist (UK)	P	857	60,000	120,000
Chr Chs/Chs of Christ	P	333	75,000	120,000
Baptist Convention	P	590	49,590	110,675
Salvation Army	P	778	70,000	110,000
Evangelical Lutheran	P	235	45,045	100,000
AoG — Back to God	I	550	50,000	95,000
Reformed Ch in Z [3]	P	43	36,000	90,000
Chs of Christ	P	200	23,000	65,780
Jehovah's Witnesses	M	856	27,000	65,521
Brethren in Christ	P	283	24,820	34,000
Ch of Christ (USA)	P	240	9,000	25,000
Other denoms [331]		8,678	703,569	1,696,000
Doubly affiliated			*-500,000*	*-1,000,000*
Total Christians [352]		**22,748**	**3,142,700**	**6,954,900**

Trans-bloc Groupings	pop.%	,000	Ann.Gr.
Evangelical	25.3	2,951	+2.7%
Charismatic	38.3	4,474	+2.6%
Pentecostal	19.7	2,304	+2.9%

Missionaries from Zimbabwe
P,I,A 250 of which about 50 are in 16 foreign countries.

Missionaries to Zimbabwe
P,I,A 500 in 80 agencies from 26 countries: USA 259, UK 93, South Africa 47, Canada 25.

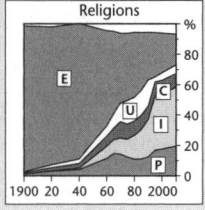

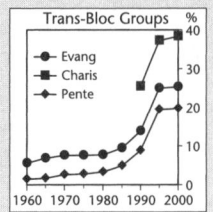

• Answers to Prayer

1 The great freedom since independence to preach the gospel in public, on the media, in schools and prisons despite the worsening political climate.

2 Target 2000, the multi-denominational vision for saturation church planting, set the goal of doubling the number of churches from 10,000 in 1992 to 20,000 in 2000 — the goal was reached!

3 Strong church growth in the 1980s accelerated in the '90s with the number of Evangelicals rising from 1.3 million to 3 million. This growth has been across the spectrum of evangelical and mainline Protestant denominations but especially marked in the indigenous Zimbabwe Assemblies of God Africa (ZAOGA) and a number of younger ministries such as Faith Ministries, Glad Tidings Fellowship and the Alliance Church.

Z

• Challenges for Prayer

1 **Zimbabwe needs a government that will serve the nation** rather than those who govern. Pray for early, non-violent change and for this land to be brought back from the brink of a social and economic abyss. Malnutrition, food shortages and unemployment are growing rapidly and the country is becoming a time bomb. Famine is worst where voters elected opponents to Mugabe; the ruling party controls much of the food supply available. Zimbabwe was once a primary source of food to surrounding nations, but now 50% of the population is dependent on foreign aid.

2 **The AIDS calamity in Zimbabwe is one of the world's worst cases.** A combination of government neglect, lack of healthcare resources, promiscuity and social reluctance to face up to the drastic measures required are the root causes. Over 35% of all adults carried the virus by 2004, but because of the breakdown of the health services the rate is likely to be higher. The number of orphans had risen to over 1 million. Life expectancy has plummeted to 34 for men and 33 for women. Pray for:

a) A radical change in hearts and attitudes to sex and to AIDS itself.

b) Effective government, NGO and church action to stop the spread of the infection.

c) Specific programmes run by Christian agencies to address the issue. Pray that all churches might face up to the moral, spiritual and economic implications of the pandemic for their ministry.

3 **The land issue** needs resolution. Under white rule much of the best land was tamed for agriculture by white settlers. The 4,500 farms became the source of 90% of agricultural exports and most of the marketed food of Zimbabwe and provided employment and homes for up to 2 million people. The need of land for the growing African population has long been a hot issue, but one inadequately addressed by the government. The state-sponsored anarchy in occupation of 4,000 farms by 'war veterans' has caused the eviction of possibly a million farm workers. Pray for the rule of law to be reinstated and an equitable solution found.

4 **The Church has grown**, but so have the challenges. Pray for:

a) A multiplication of mature leaders. Praise the Lord for godly men and women in leadership today, but their numbers must increase to cope with the rapid growth.

b) The Bible schools and seminaries. In 1992 there were 22 such institutions. There are an increasing number of church-based and TEE programmes being set up. Pray for effective teaching and discipling of those called to serve the Lord.

c) Spiritual unity. The **Evangelical Fellowship of Zimbabwe** links together over 160 churches and organizations, the **Pentecostal Fellowship of Zimbabwe** has brought together ten denominations and *Fambidzano* links other African Independent Churches for fellowship and theological instruction. **Target 2000** helped to unite many denominations in a common goal for saturation church planting.

d) A prophetic voice for the Church. Politics has been left to the politicians. Christians are divided on how to cope with the burgeoning political crisis, and often remain silent when a clear moral stand is required. Some denominational leaders are little more than government stooges supporting the dictatorship.

e) A clear stand against witchcraft and demonic powers or veneration of ancestors in the guise of nationalism. Pray that Christians may not compromise, but know power in the name of Jesus to both protect and deliver from fear and bondage.

5 **Vision for the 21ˢᵗ Century**. The **Target 2000** vision was a great boost to the Church, but new initiatives and visions are now needed for the coming decade. Pray that the Lord might reveal His will in this. Missions vision is relatively small, with only about 50 missionaries sent out by 3 million Evangelicals. Pray that the Lord might envision the Church for training, sending and supporting hundreds of workers. Zimbabwean missionaries have had significant impact on Mozambique.

6 **Young people** brought up on the idealistic visions of independence have been disillusioned by empty political slogans, the greed of the powerful and the dearth of jobs. They have become the most receptive section of the population, half of which is under 15 years of age. Pray for the ministries of:

a) **FOCUS(IFES)**, which is responsible for Christian Unions among the 40,000 students in universities and colleges; in nearly all of these there are lively, growing groups. Pray that Christian graduates may become key leaders in the nation.

b) **Scripture Union**, which has had a decisive impact on the educated by their work in the secondary schools. The number of these increased from 250 in 1980 to 1,535 in 1995, and there are large, active, outgoing Christian groups in most of them. The camp ministry has been especially fruitful. A smaller work in the primary schools is getting under way — pray that it may grow through an extensive programme of weekend camps. Pray for more Christian teachers to be raised up to nurture this work in their spare time.

c) **The highly effective Aid for AIDS** programme of **Scripture Union** which was pioneered in Zimbabwe and has spread to many African countries. In this programme, young people challenge other young people to purity in sexual relationships, and to a personal relationship with Jesus as the one way to stop the spread of the disease.

7 **The less-evangelized.** Zimbabwe has been extensively evangelized, but areas of need remain:

a) **The rural areas.** In many districts churches are few and full-time workers even fewer. Pray for the calling of pastors and evangelists willing to serve in rural areas. Pray also for evangelistic outreaches and suitable literature distribution specifically to these areas. Especially effective have been teams showing the **JESUS** film and **Operation Foxfire** teams of **AE**.

b) **The burgeoning cities**, swollen with hundreds of thousands of rural migrants looking for non-existent jobs. Squatter settlements are multiplying and crime is on the increase. Outreach to the unemployed is a major challenge.

c) **Less-reached peoples.** There are congregations in every indigenous people, but relatively fewer among the Tonga, Nambya and Dombe of the Hwange-Kariba area in the north-west (where the **AoG** have made a significant impact with many new churches planted in the 1990s), the Kunda in the northeast, and the Ndau (**SIM**) in the east. The Kalanga and Ndebele have been exposed to the gospel for 130 years, but have been less responsive than the Shona peoples.

d) **Farming areas.** Nearly 2 million labourers and their dependants used to live on 4,500 commercial farms, many owned by whites. This number has been halved; the refugees are crowding into urban slums and are destitute. Over half these labourers are from Malawi and Mozambique. The CCAP(NGK), Salvation Army and others maintain an extensive ministry to these communities — especially to the Malawian Chewa-Nyanja speakers — but many farm communities are without an evangelical congregation of believers.

e) **Muslims.** They are a small minority but wield disproportionate influence on the country through foreign aid 'with strings', mosque-building and scholarships in Muslim universities. Most are Yao from Malawi, many are Gujarati in the main towns, and some are of the indigenous Shona-speaking Remba. Little Christian outreach has been made to win them, and churches are ill-equipped to do so.

8 **The expatriate mission force has steadily been reduced in numbers** because of government unwillingness to give visas for 'preachers of the gospel'. Though the need for missionaries is reduced, there are still a wide range of ministries where input is helpful. The mature church in Zimbabwe can cover most of the ministries. **MAF** has two planes based in Harare for serving the Church. Major agencies are: Chr Ch/Chs of Christ (91), **YWAM** (45), SdA (36), **TEAM** (29), **IMB-SBC** (23), **NGK** (20), **Christian Brethren** (15), **SIM** (15), Brethren in Christ (10).

9 **Christian literature** has become a major ministry in Zimbabwe and beyond — especially Mozambique. Pray for:

a) **Scripture distribution. The Bible Society** has a large Scripture printing and distribution programme. The government ruling for compulsory religious education in schools has led to a massive distribution of Bibles, NTs and Scripture portions. In June 1985 a new start was made to revise the Shona Bible; a reliable revision is long overdue. **SGM**'s Scripture booklets have been widely used in comforting and challenging those impacted by AIDS.

b) **Gospel Literature Lifeline** which has developed a successful tract and follow-up literature ministry with correspondence courses. Much of their distribution is in Mozambique.

c) ***The Christian bookstores*** in most major centres. The shortage of foreign exchange and lack of variety of good, locally-produced materials limits stock and impact.

d) ***CAVA*** (Christian Audio Visual Action) which is, at present, the only major publisher of literature in Shona to counteract the renewed challenge offered by traditional animistic religion. Audio-visual materials are also produced.

10 Christian electronic media:

a) ***Radio and TV programmes*** are broadcast on the national networks. International broadcasts are also received from **TWR** Swaziland in English (33 hrs/wk), Shona (17), Ndebele (7) and Tswana (5). There is a large audience.

b) ***The JESUS film*** has been extensively used in 10 languages for church planting. A further 6 languages of Zimbabwe are in preparation.

Z

Special Ministries

DECEMBER 10-31

• AUDIO CASSETTE TAPE MINISTRIES •

The arrival of inexpensive cassette tape recorders has made it possible to distribute Christian recordings widely to both believers and unbelievers. This has become a valuable tool for evangelism, teaching and the encouragement of believers. Numerous local and international agencies have been founded for the production and distribution of cassette tapes. Pray for:

1 **Skilled labourers** who can handle expensive recording equipment, maintain cassette playback machines and effectively distribute the tapes. Pray for more mission agencies to grasp the significance of this ministry and exploit its potential.

2 **Evangelism through cassettes.** Global Recordings Network (**GRN**) pioneered the use of simple messages on gramophone records for evangelizing minority peoples and isolated groups. These messages are now produced on tapes which are often the only means available to communicate the gospel in the heart language of the people. This is a vital tool for evangelism among unreached peoples. Pray for:

a) *An increase in the numbers and availability* of recorded messages. By 1999 **GRN** had recorded the gospel in its 5,000th language. Thousands more dialects, mostly in Africa, South Asia, China and the South Pacific, could be recorded to great benefit.

b) *Field recordists* — both from **GRN** centres as well as mission and church workers committed to multiply the ministry in producing both evangelistic and teaching tapes. The work is often arduous and difficult, requiring extensive travel and living in challenging conditions. Pray for the right language helpers, preparation of texts, recording and production of tapes. Pray for the protection of delicate equipment handled in situations of geographical and climatic extremes.

c) *Global Recordings Network* — an association of national agencies in some 30 countries (see some names and addresses in Appendix 3). Pray for the strategic development of the vision for reaching every tongue with the gospel by means of recorded messages.

d) *Hand-cranked players.* Thousands of villages in Africa and Asia are without electricity. Pray for the increased production and placement of these cassette players that don't need electricity or batteries.

e) *Field distributors.* They have a key role in all the complexities of strategic placement of cassettes, teaching effective use of tapes, care of machinery and follow-up teaching. More workers are required.

3 **Teaching and church growth through tapes.** In many spiritually hard areas of the world, the few Christians are isolated and have little opportunity to learn new hymns and choruses or receive adequate teaching. Messages on tape can fill that void. Pray for the provision of equipment, batteries and relevant messages. Much useful material is generated for this through tapes prepared for Christian radio programmes. Many TEE courses make extensive use of tapes for teaching purposes.

4 **Bible tapes.** Many new translations of the Scriptures are first circulated on tape with great blessing (Audio Scripture Ministries, Hosanna, IMB, Lutheran Bible Translators, UBS, WBT). This is particularly useful for the world's 2 billion non-readers, for those who have no written Scriptures and for areas where there is a real threat that political events may prevent the printing and distribution of the Word of God.

5 **Effective use of new technology.** Various Christian agencies are developing innovative new technologies for communicating the gospel, such as Galcom in Canada with cheap miniature solar-panel radios and cassette players. Pray that such innovations may multiply opportunities for the least-reached to respond to the gospel.

• CHRISTIAN RADIO •

This has been demonstrated to be one of the most useful aids for world evangelization but its full potential has yet to be realized. Radio has been a key component in the worldwide spread of the gospel, especially in many closed lands. In the same way that radio played a key role in the church's rebirth in former Soviet countries, it is making a unique and vital contribution in many restricted access nations including the Muslim world and east Asia. Formerly closed nations such as Russia and Albania now host sites for international Christian radio broadcasts. In countries like China and Vietnam, large networks of house churches have sprung up through the ministry of Christian radio.

• Challenges for Prayer

1 **Christian radio agencies.** There are dozens of evangelical agencies involved in international and local broadcasting outside of North America. The volume and variety of broadcasting is now huge: in the year 2000 international Christian broadcasting by these agencies attained 5,500 hours/week in 565 languages. Some larger agencies are: **HCJB** World Radio (nearly 1,000 workers and employees in over 90 countries); **TWR** (1,000 workers and employees in over 30 countries); **FEBC** (900 workers and employees in 20 countries); **FEBA** (statistics not available) and **IBRA** (Sweden, with 1,000 workers and employees in 110 countries). These agencies are frequently mentioned throughout this book.

2 **The World by Radio vision.** This was launched by four radio agencies (**TWR, FEBA/FEBC, HCJB** and **SIM**) in 1985 as World by 2000, and was joined later by Back to the Bible Broadcasts, Galcom, **IBRA** Radio and Words of Hope. They committed themselves to work together to provide Christian broadcasts understandable by everyone in the world by the year 2000. Of the total of 372 mega-languages in this category, the original 93 languages with broadcasts in 1985 had increased to 208 in 2000. The planning, research, funding, locating and training of native-language speakers for programmes (in many of these languages there may be few, if any, Christians), studio facilities and all the complexities of maintaining and expanding this ministry need to be covered in prayer.

3 **Good reception in target areas.** Although much broadcasting is now done over medium-wave and FM stations, significant numbers of broadcasts are still delivered via short-wave. The short-wave radio bands are increasingly crowded and interference is a common problem. Good frequency management and powerful transmitters are needed to deliver clear signals. Less-than-daily broadcasts in the minority languages of closed countries are hard to publicize in order to build up a committed audience.

4 **The listeners.** There are 2.5 billion radio receivers in the world and, potentially, most of the world's population could have access to a set. Pray for spiritual fruit in souls saved, Christians strengthened, churches planted and believers discipled.

5 **Follow-up.** Stations and programming agencies have a large staff to handle several million letters, faxes, and e-mails sent in by listeners annually. Pray for the protection of senders and letters in the post — in many restricted access countries there is heavy censorship and only a small proportion of the letters get through. Pray for personal letters, literature and Bible Correspondence Courses sent out in return. Pray for new converts to be linked up with groups of other believers. A successful programme format has been church planting via radio. Many new churches have been planted through radio in a variety of countries.

6 **The ICRE project** (International Communication Research for Evangelism) initiated by **FEBC**. ICRE's main effort has been to provide affordable quality broadcast research for international broadcasters. Its emphasis is now shifting to facilitating Christian broadcasters to initiate and apply research studies in their own countries.

• CHRISTIAN TELEVISION •

Like radio, Christian television has the potential to be a profoundly strategic tool for the spreading of the gospel, but, as yet, has been under-utilized by believers. Nevertheless, there are several encouragements:

1 **More people watch television,** both terrestrial and satellite, than ever before. The opportunities to witness to non-Christians and to train and encourage believers through this medium is virtually unlimited. Unfortunately, apart from all too frequently unedifying material from televangelists, there is little overt Christian presence in television.

2 **Television is one of the few methods** whereby the gospel can permeate the restrictive Arab nations. In many of these countries, a majority of households can receive satellite television, often despite widespread poverty. Responses to previous Christian programmes indicate large and receptive audiences.

3 **Christian programmes,** especially for children, have proved highly successful in the former Soviet countries. In many cases, this is the first exposure of these Eastern Europeans to the gospel.

• Challenges for Prayer

1 **The unbelieving West has used television** as its main vehicle to export values of hedonism, greed and immorality to the rest of the world. This has led to grave misconceptions of Christian values in the non-Christian, non-Western world who often equate 'the West' with 'Christian'. Pray that believers may work through the medium of television to bring salt and light to the world so that non-Christians everywhere can hear the good news and the 'strong man's' goods may be plundered.

2 **Freedom of the airwaves.** The entertainment industry in general derides any honest sharing of the gospel as proselytizing, recruiting or manipulating people. The widespread pluralism and lack of ethical absolutes cause Evangelicals to be denied reasonable access and their message to be diluted or denied air-time. Pray for more Christians to actively minister redemption into the secular television industry.

3 **National initiatives.** Christian radio is increasingly broadcasting indigenously written and produced programmes which more capably speak to the hearts of listeners — pray for television to follow suit. This will require national believers with calling and gifting, and the provision of training and equipment.

4 **Pray for these specific ministries:**

a) *The Christian Broadcasting Network* (**CBN**) airs evangelistic television programmes in 155 nations. Over 135 million watched **CBN** programmes in 2000. **CBN** has production teams in 10 countries, producing original material in over 10 languages. Two of the most successful shows worldwide have been the long-running *The 700 Club* and the children's animated series *Superbook*.

b) *SAT-7 is a satellite television channel* that arose as the fruit of a grassroots Christian media movement in the Middle East, broadcasting daily since 2000. Its threefold goal is to sustain and encourage Christian communities in the Middle East, to provide its whole audience with a culturally appropriate presentation of Christianity in their own language, and to provide a balanced Christian worldview which complements public education and information channels available in the Arab world. The presentation of Christianity as a Middle Eastern religion is a vital part of **SAT-7**'s strategic ministry.

c) *The Bible Channel (TBC) aims to plant house churches* and equip church leaders to be effective throughout the Arab world and in the 10/40 Window. **TBC** focuses on Bible teaching programmes broadcast by satellite for discipling the whole Arab Church in the Middle East and North Africa, both the ancient confessions and the newer groups.

• THE JESUS FILM •

The *JESUS* **Film Project**®, a ministry of Campus Crusade for Christ International, wants to present the *JESUS* film to everyone in the world in a language that they can understand. This literal portrayal of the life of Jesus according to the Gospel of Luke has become one of the most powerful evangelistic tools of recent times and the most translated film in history. By 2001 the number of individual viewings had reached more than 4 billion, with enormous response. Campus Crusade estimates 128 million people have indicated a decision to place their faith in Jesus Christ.

• Challenges for Prayer

1 **Mission agency and denomination partnerships** — these number more than 1,200. Pray that they may be creative in the use of the *JESUS* film and work together with local churches to reach target areas.

2 **Film teams.** When 2001 began, 2,885 teams were on the field in 106 countries with an outlay of $1 million monthly. Pray for film team safety.

3 **Follow-up.** Failure to plan for this can dissipate the impact of the film. Pray for many churches to be planted using this tool.

4 **Public showings** in cinemas, theatres, outdoor venues and on television. Millions see the film this way all around the world. Audiences in former communist countries have been spectacular. Pray for continued opportunities to show the film on national television networks — especially at Christmas and Easter. Pray also for communications centres, set up to help those who trust Christ for salvation.

5 **Videocassettes of the film.** These have become an outstanding tool for home evangelism in repressive situations. Response has been beyond expectations! In many lands the film is banned but thousands of videocassettes circulate quietly. Pray that this tool may help to open difficult lands for the gospel.

6 **Audio-dramatic version of the film.** This audio drama, based on the script of the *JESUS* film and entitled "The Story of Jesus," dramatically presents the story for listening audiences. Pray that audiocassettes and radio broadcasts will reach into areas inaccessible by video and television.

7 **DVDs of the film.** The digital versatile disc format contains the full-length feature film and eight language channels — English, Spanish, French, Portuguese, Korean, Japanese, Chinese (Mandarin), and Arabic — making it possible for approximately 50% of the world's population to view the *JESUS* film in a language they understand. Locally, this tool can be used as a video duplication master and will not deteriorate with use. Pray for the development of regional versions and new distribution and duplication strategies.

• THE INTERNET •

The Internet is changing the way the world communicates. This powerful tool has great significance for evangelism. Web growth in countries like India and China is amazing — it is no longer just for rich Western nations. Users in China were projected to grow from 10 million in 2000 to 100 million in 2003. Much of South America and Asia has rapidly become a 'wired' community. Internet evangelism operates in several main ways:

• Evangelistic web pages which anyone in the world can access.

• One-on-one personal interaction by email or in a 'chat room'.

• 'Streamed' instant sound or video — increasingly effective as access speeds increase.

The Web also helps Christian workers and organizations to network and share information in ways and at speeds which were never previously possible. An urgent prayer request can now travel the world within minutes and be replicated thousands of times.

• Challenges for Prayer

1 **More evangelistic sites.** Although many Christian organizations and churches use the Web to communicate with their own constituencies, there are relatively few websites specifically designed for non-Christian readers. Pray for more Christians to realise the Web's potential for cutting-edge outreach.

2 **English is still the largest language on the Internet,** but others are growing fast. Hundreds of millions of people use English as their first language, and many more read it well enough to access English web pages. But billions do not, and sadly, in most languages there are very few evangelistic websites — pray for more. Chinese, Japanese and Arabic are big needs.

3 **Empowerment at home.** Online evangelism is not just for Christian organizations. One person can touch the world from home — young, retired, disabled, or shy. The Web is a great leveller.

4 **The Middle East.** There is relatively free Internet access throughout the Middle East (except Saudi Arabia). This allows Muslims to consider the claims of Christ in a non-threatening, anonymous way. Pray for more specialist web ministries to Muslims.

5 **Pornography.** It is impossible to completely stop online pornography at its source; pray for Christians and others fighting this problem, both at organizational and personal levels.

6 **Finance.** One reason that relatively few Christian organizations produce websites is that, unlike literature or video, there is no 'product' to sell and therefore no way to recoup production expenses. Pray that Christians may realise the potential of the Web and support evangelistic web ministries with their giving. Campus Crusade [www.ccci.org] and WEC's SOON website [www.soon.org.uk] are groups effectively using online evangelism.

7 **There are many strategies for online evangelism.** WEC has produced a detailed Web Evangelism Guide to explain these concepts [www.web-evangelism.com]. There is a need to translate it into other languages.

8 **Discipling.** As with radio ministry, follow-up of distant converts is a problem. However, the Web allows easy two-way email discipling and counselling. There is much online material for new Christians. There is a growing international, cyberspace community of believers, which is of great help to those who are isolated.

9 **Mobile 'wireless' access to the Web.** One billion people may have Web access through mobile cell phones and handheld devices by 2003. Pray for new evangelistic strategies for this medium.

10 **Chat rooms.** Millions of people access online 'chat' daily. Sensitive witness by Christians in chat rooms is bearing fruit. Two websites focused on this type of outreach are [www.web-evangelism.com/chat] and [www.e-vangelism.org.uk]. Pray for more Christians to take up this ministry.

• BIBLE SOCIETIES AND BIBLE TRANSLATION •

Of the world's 7,148 languages, at least 2,000 still have a need for New Testament translation work and over 2,000 need to be surveyed to ascertain their need. The provision of God's Word in the mother tongue of each people of the world is fundamental to world evangelization. Many agencies are committed to various aspects of making the Scriptures available to all. Most of these are members of the Forum of Bible Agencies, formed in 1992 to link together the efforts of Bible translation and distribution agencies. This Forum has become increasingly important and strategic in the last 8 years. Special mention must be made of the United Bible Societies (UBS), who are strongly committed to the Forum.

• Challenges for Prayer

1 **The national Bible Society members** — in 2000 there were 137 societies working in more than 200 countries and territories. Pray for their staff with their specialized skills for the many tasks. Pray for their walk with God, for guidance in what translation and printing projects to tackle and for relations with other Christian bodies.

2 **Translation and revision work.** UBS staff workers give much encouragement and advice to missionaries and nationals in new language, and modern speech, translation programmes. Much wisdom is needed in the many problems that arise. The UBS was involved in 672 translation projects in 1999, 462 of them being first-time translations.

3 **The printing of the Scriptures.** This presents many problems — in some areas it is high costs, in others it is the lack of facilities or materials. The price of Bibles to the public is reduced through subsidies. Pray for the provision of large sums of money which are needed. The UBS budget for 2000 was $53 million. A major fundraising initiative — "Opportunity 21" — seeks to increase this figure in the years 2001-2004.

4 **Importation and distribution.** Much trouble and effort is expended on importing paper, machinery and completed Bibles. War, political crises and unsympathetic or hostile governments make for long and difficult negotiations. Pray for those involved. Sometimes the UBS depot or bookstore is the only source of Christian literature and Bibles in a country. In others a vast network of churches, shops and local distributors moves out millions of portions of the Scriptures. In 1999 worldwide distribution was 24 million Bibles, 26 million New Testaments and 577 million portions of the Scriptures. What a spiritual impact this could have!

Other specialized agencies to mention for prayer:

5 **Wycliffe Bible Translators/SIL** has a remarkable record in single-minded dedication to the completion of translating the New and Old Testaments into the languages of the world. By 1999, WBT translators had completed 500 New Testaments and were involved in a further 1,100+ projects. Their staff numbers 6,000. However, this number masks the thousands of nationals and other partners that are also involved in the task. In 1999, WBT adopted a new vision, together with their partners worldwide, to start a Bible translation project in every language that needs one by 2025. This means working in new ways, training others and funding national teams to accomplish a task that would normally take 150 years. As WBT serves and equips the Church to do this, pray that the necessary funds and personnel might be released.

6 **Other Bible translation ministries** also work towards these same goals. Amongst them are numbered the Sweden-based Institute for Bible Translation, who focus on the peoples of the former Soviet Union, Pioneer Bible Translators and Lutheran Bible Translators.

7 **Scripture Gift Mission** (SGM International) is a Christian charity producing free Bible resources for people all around the world. SGM works in partnership with Christians and Christian agencies who share these booklets and leaflets with others on a one-to-one basis. SGM has given away 22 million pieces of literature to people in 190 countries in 450 languages through 35 centres worldwide.

8 **The Bible League** provides Scriptures and trains people to use them for discipling seekers into church membership. In 2000 18.5 million Scriptures were provided. These Scriptures were used to disciple 1.7 million people in Bible study, leading 181,090 people to join local churches. In addition, 2,731 new churches were planted in 2000 through the ministry of The Bible League. The Bible League is also one of the leading providers of Scriptures to the Persecuted Church.

9 **Gideons International** currently operate in 175 countries and freely distribute Bibles and New Testaments in hotels, schools, hospitals, prisons and other places to which the public has access. Each week over 1 million copies are personally presented or placed. Countless lives have been transformed, comforted and blessed through the Scriptures placed by Gideons.

10 **The Pocket Testament League** has a ministry of distributing Gospels and New Testaments in 100 or more countries in many languages. These are compiled in a manner to facilitate soul-winning and discipleship.

• CHRISTIAN LITERATURE •

1 **Despite the advent of the electronic age,** book production is increasing faster than ever before, and books remain a key tool for communication — both secular and Christian. Crash course literacy programmes in many parts of the world create an immense desire for any literature among new literates — what an opportunity! Literature also still plays a huge part in sharing the gospel in countries closed to conventional missionary work.

2 **The surfeit of Christian literature** in English, Spanish and German contrasts with the dearth in most other languages. Much of what is available is translated from English, but is an inadequate substitute for locally written materials. Pray for mature Christian writers to be raised up all over the world to write in their heart languages.

3 **Evangelistic literature.**

a) *EHC has a global vision to distribute the gospel message* to every home, systematically, town by town, village by village, until every nation is impacted by the gospel. An estimated 52,000 homes are reached daily using a volunteer force of 3,600. **EHC** has active work in 100 nations, and has distributed 2,012 billion pieces of gospel literature, resulting in an estimated 26 million decisions which are then followed up with discipleship material. Pray for the global direction of this ministry which has launched a campaign to see every home in every nation reached by the end of 2010.

b) *Gospel broadsheets* (single-sheet evangelistic newspapers) *have grown dramatically*. **WEC** is deeply involved in this ministry with an annual production of 6 million. Unlike tracts, broadsheets are regular papers in magazine style distributed worldwide by mail. Current languages for WEC's *SOON* broadsheet include: English, French, German, Portuguese and Swahili, with similar papers in Nepali, Italian and Russian/English operated by related groups. An edition for Fulbe speakers is in the pipeline. Most versions share these characteristics: testimonies, contextualised feature articles, offers of BCC or follow-up material, direct mail to interested individuals as well as bulk supply to Christians for evangelistic distribution. The concept could operate in many other languages — contact **SOON** for details [www.soon.org.uk].

4 **Supply of Christian literature** is hindered in the places of greatest need because of poverty, difficulty of distribution, cost of printing, using expensive materials from the West and rampant inflation. Pray for adequate funding mechanisms in Eastern Europe, Africa and poorer parts of Asia so that indigenous publishing and printing operations can become viable. Well-intentioned Western subsidizing of their own material often undermines efforts to establish indigenous literature ministries. Pray also for BookAid, an innovative method of donating second-hand Christian books to poor countries for sale and for the support of indigenous literature agencies. CLC are also working with Western publishers to make good quality, new books available at more reasonable prices in the developing world.

5 **Literature missionaries are too few.** Pray for the calling of those with the right qualities and qualifications for this ministry – in journalism, printing, publishing, writing, distribution, etc. Few Bible schools give adequate attention to the training of literature missionaries.

6 **Distribution is made through various methods** — Christian bookstores, street selling, bookmobiles, internet selling, etc. Pray for opportunities for personal witnessing and counselling in this distribution work and that the material will have an impact on people's lives. Unique in its global vision and approach is CLC with its 178 Christian bookstores in 54 countries. They urgently need more quality workers.

• THEOLOGICAL EDUCATION BY EXTENSION (TEE) •

TEE is one of the most significant missiological breakthroughs of recent decades. The Western pattern of residential seminaries and Bible colleges for training Christian workers was proving too costly, slow, sometimes inappropriate and not necessarily training those best fitted for the ministry in the rapidly growing Church in other parts of the world.

TEE started in Latin America as a means of training pastors while in the ministry. It has rapidly spread round the world and diversified into distant learning courses at all levels from basic to degree-earning, often supplemented by travelling lecturers, cassettes, videos, Internet connectivity and a wide range of relevant biblical, pastoral and social concern courses. There are hundreds of evangelical TEE centres training tens of thousands of students around the world.

• Challenges for Prayer

1 **Development of TEE at a global level** — through international coordination, sharing of materials, standardization of qualifications and integration of TEE into national theological education systems. In some countries TEE has lost credibility and effectiveness because of this lack. Pray for key international TEE agencies, some listed below.

2 **Provision of trained course writers and coordinators** to make TEE effective at a local level. Adaptability to different levels of education of TEE students and flexibility in travel arrangements can make this a demanding ministry as tutors seek to encourage and help their students.

3 **TEE students** who often live in less than ideal study situations — poverty, hard manual work in the day, lack of study facilities and ongoing demands for ministry. Pray for motivation, discipline, openness to the instruction of the Holy Spirit and, ultimately, more fruitful ministry.

4 **Specific TEE institutions**. Each of these are listed because of their unique contribution to the advancement of TEE and widespread acceptance of the quality of the ministry.
a) **TAFTEE** (India), 28 Netaji Road, Bangalore 520-005, India. Nearly 8,000 students. <taftee@blr.vsnl.net.in>
b) **SEAN International**, The Pound, Whitestone, Exeter, Devon EX4 2HP, England. Materials used worldwide. <SEAN_UK@compuserve.com>
c) **LOGOI**, 14540 SW 136 Street, Suite 200, Miami, FL 33186, USA. Over 45,000 graduates. Mainly Latin America. <logoi@logoi.org>
d) **LOGOS**, Potsdamerstr. 115, 4800 Bielefeld 17, Germany. Russia/Central Europe. <info@logos-international.de>
e) **ACTEA**, PO Box 49, Machakos, Kenya. Linked with the African Evangelical Alliance. <ACTEA@maf.org>
f) **BEE International**. P.O. Box 25520, Colorado Springs, CO 80936-5520 USA <info@beeinternational.org>

• BIBLE CORRESPONDENCE COURSES (BCCs) •

This ministry has grown and become one of the most effective means for following up contacts from literature distribution and Christian radio programmes. The relative ease in using the post in sensitive areas of the world and the emphasis on studying the Word of God has had a great impact on BCC students — some being converted and others being strengthened in their Christian life. This has proved itself to be probably the best single means for winning Muslims.

1 **There are reckoned to be over 300 centres sending out evangelical BCCs.** Pray for workers involved in preparation of materials and helping the students through the post.

2 **Pray for the publicizing of BCCs** through tracts, radio programmes or through other students in lands where there are few believers and doors are closed to missionaries.

3 **Pray for effective personal follow-up of students** by local Christians and for their integration into Christian fellowships.

• RELIEF AND DEVELOPMENT •

The gap between rich and poor, the magnitude of suffering and the number of disasters affecting many areas appears to increase by the year. The ubiquitous television camera vividly portrays suffering caused by wars, famines, natural disasters and man's cruelty to man. Consider the following:

1 **Population growth** of about 80 million annually is straining food, water and fuel resources globally.

2 **The selfishness of rich trading nations** and the continuing impact of loans and debt servicing on poorer nations is denying them the chance to develop their economies to viability. Most aid does not achieve this and some, such as the dumping of food-surpluses can even cause long-term damage to local agriculture. The globalization of market economics has yet to be shown to benefit the poor.

3 **The difference of income/person** between "north" and "south" over the last century has increased from 2:1 to 80:1. Inevitably this fuels the flow of refugees, adds to the impact of natural disasters and increases the likelihood of conflicts.

4 **The impact of the AIDS pandemic,** the revival of resistant strains of malaria, tuberculosis and other diseases as well as the effects of environmental pollution will steadily degrade world health — especially in the poorer countries — and reduce the ability to survive economically.

A compassionate and sacrificial Christian response to human suffering is needed. Pray for:

5 **Wise use of funds given generously by Christians** to aid programmes. There are many risks associated with this work — the need for sustainability and economic feasibility, the expenses of both the aid and the infrastructure to support it, and dealing with less than upright governments all combine to demand great wisdom and discernment. The issue of dependency will always be a sensitive one that needs to be addressed from the perspective of both the donors and those whom the development is meant to benefit.

6 **Those who administer aid and resettlement programmes.** Many agencies have sprung up to channel the giving of Evangelicals — there are over 100 such in North America. Some of the better known are WVI, TEAR Fund, World Relief and MAP International, but there are many others from all over the world. Pray for the provision of the right personnel, a balance between addressing physical and spiritual needs, and for evangelism and church planting to be furthered. Praise the Lord that where care and tact have been exercised and a loving Christian testimony shared, there has been a harvest of souls in a number of countries.

7 **The right balance in giving.** Christian donors need to be guided by the Lord rather than by their emotional response to physical suffering. The famine of the Word of God is still a more serious problem than that of food in Africa today. The giving by Christians to the victims of famine and disaster in Africa and elsewhere is commendable, but it must be matched by a similar generosity to address the great spiritual needs of the churches.

An adequate Christian involvement in development to deal with the causes of suffering is also needed. Pray for:

8 **Development projects** run by Christian agencies and churches. Many agencies have been specifically set up to fund and initiate such schemes. Pray that all projects selected may be those most beneficial to local communities and that local staff and appropriate technology might be found which can continue and expand projects locally without constant foreign input.

9 **Christian workers.** Honest, humble, dedicated expatriate and national workers who have both the technical expertise and who exhibit the love of Christ are in great demand. Pray for many to be called and equipped for development ministries and for their labours to win opportunities to share the gospel. Agriculture, development of effective markets for local products, provision of clean water, literacy campaigns, preventive medicine, etc., are all key areas of need in many parts of the world.

10 **The planting and strengthening of local churches** through these projects. Christian-based development ministries should facilitate the gospel being shared with those helped and result in churches being planted. Where churches already exist, pray that such projects might enable believers to raise the finances to support local ministries and missionary work/workers.

11 **The HIV/AIDS crisis threatens** to undermine development in many parts of the world. Pray that churches will get involved in teaching and demonstrating a different lifestyle, training about AIDS, caring for both those who are suffering and for orphans.

• MEDICAL MISSION WORK •

This has been a central component to Christian ministry on the mission field for many years. Appalling suffering and total lack of medical facilities in many countries impelled pioneer missionaries to expend much labour and money in developing clinics, hospitals, leprosaria, etc. This ministry needs prayer in these days of change, for:

1 **Adaptability.** Governments demand higher standards, and in some lands, are taking over all non-government health services. Medical missionary work must constantly be assessed for usefulness in changing circumstances. The present trend is for fewer, but better equipped and staffed, mission hospitals, more community-based health services and an emphasis on preventive medicine.

2 **Supply of funds and personnel** — that mission boards and national churches responsible may know how to apportion both for the benefit of those most in need. Pray that cross-cultural medical workers may be sensitive in serving the people to whom they are called and in training national staff to carry on the work.

3 **Usefulness in winning people to the Lord.** The primary aim of medical missionary work can sometimes be forgotten in the busyness of a large institution, yet many can be and are won by this means. Pray for the right balance between addressing medical and spiritual needs.

4 **The opening of doors to the gospel.** In many lands this is one of the few means for entry and witness — for example, in China, Yemen, Afghanistan and Bhutan. Pray that the witness of these medical missionaries, albeit tactful, may lead to conversions and the planting of viable churches.

5 **Leprosy work.** This will probably long remain a ministry in which Christians have significant input, especially with Jesus' specific command to heal those with leprosy.

About 4 million people suffer from, or are at risk of, leprosy with more than 700,000 new cases of leprosy detected each year. Pray for the work of The Leprosy Mission, American Leprosy Mission and others, in seeking to minister in the name of Jesus Christ to the physical, mental, social and spiritual needs of individuals and communities disadvantaged by leprosy; working with them to uphold human dignity and eradicate leprosy. Pray for conversions and that new believers may reintegrate into their communities as witnessing Christians, thus becoming the means of starting new congregations.

6 **The AIDS pandemic.** This has become a terrible threat to whole nations — especially in central and southern Africa, India, and southeast Asia. AIDS is likely to become the new frontier in medical missions and in the ministry of local churches in the future. A range of new skills and spiritual gifts will be needed to cope with the stress and demands of ministry to the sick and bereaved. In Africa, by far the worst-stricken continent, organizations such as Scripture Union, the Salvation Army, and Christian Action Against AIDS (ACCS) are ministering though AIDS prevention education and care for AIDS victims.

7 **Health field workers.** Because more people pass through the hospitals of the world than through its churches, Healthcare Christian Fellowship International seeks to win to Christ, and to train, those in health services to implement Christ's Great Commission within the healthcare field. Pray for:

a) *The conversion to Christ* of health field workers.
b) *The witness of Christian* healthcare workers to be both wise and bold to patients and colleagues.
c) *Christian health workers serving in hazardous circumstances.* In countries where churches are closed and Christianity suppressed, hospitals and health care centres remain open — hence the strategic value of this work.
d) *HCFI staff workers who are reaching out to over 100 countries.* Pray for additional staff. Pray also for the major HCFI training ministry in South Africa and the Philippines and for HCFI centres in Europe, Africa, Asia, North and South America.

8 **Exposure of deceptive forms of alternative 'medicine'.** Increasing infiltration of New Age, false religions and humanistic influences in the health field need to be exposed and thwarted.

• MISSIONARY AVIATION •

What an essential means for evangelism and church growth the missionary aviation ministry has become! In many areas access is difficult by any other means. In 1984 there were about 476 aircraft in 48 lands used to transport Christian workers, supplies, hospital patients and aid. A more recent survey has not been made, but this number has not changed much. Without this service, ministries would be slowed or stopped. Some 90 mission agencies have their own aircraft, but other agencies exist solely for the purpose of serving churches and missions.

• Challenges for Prayer

1 **The staff.** There are well over 1,000 missionary pilots, mechanics and support personnel. Their exacting ministry demands high technical ability and efficiency. They also can have a vital spiritual ministry for which they have many unique opportunities. Pray for the provision of workers technically and spiritually equipped for this ministry.

2 **Mission Aviation Fellowship** is unique and deserving of special prayer as the pioneer in this field of ministry and the largest agency, with four branches operating 152 aircraft in over 32 countries, flying over 57,000 hours per year.

3 Other significant flying agencies:

a) *Jungle Aviation and Radio Service* (JAARS) is a vital component of **WBT/SIL**'s Bible translation ministry in 11 lands. JAARS operates 47 aircraft.
b) *Other agencies with a large flying programme* are **AIM**-Air in Kenya (6 aircraft in 5 countries), Wings of the Morning (US Methodist — Democratic Republic of Congo),

Tribal Air (**NTM** — 28 aircraft in 9 countries), and **HeliMission**, which uses helicopters to transport workers and supplies to places where even aeroplanes cannot reach.

4 **The supply of all needs.** Although the overall savings in time and finance are enormous, this type of ministry is costly for both the operators and the users.

5 **Safety.** The record has been good, but there have been a number of tragic accidents. Pilots must often operate from primitive airstrips in wild terrain and dangerous climatic conditions. Pray against distractions — a single mistake by a mechanic or pilot can have tragic consequences.

• MARITIME MINISTRY •

The rapid development of a significant variety of ships with a mobile Christian ministry has proved one of the major means the Holy Spirit has used to spread missions vision, cross-pollinate evangelistic methods, bring spiritual life and renewal in churches and give a unique discipling ministry to young Christians in lands where little of such depth is available.

• Challenges for Prayer

1 OM's **ship ministry** through the MV DOULOS (the oldest ocean-going passenger vessel still in service today) and MV LOGOS II has an average of 500 personnel at any one time. Major ministries include literature distribution, encouraging and equipping local churches, sharing the good news, discipleship training and intercultural exposure.

2 **YWAM's Mercy Ships** MV Anastasis and the smaller MV Good Samaritan have an average of 600 personnel involved in discipling, Christian aid and mobile medical work.

3 **The Pacific Ocean fleet of small vessels.** Thousands of isolated island communities spread over the vastness of the Pacific need encouragement, renewal in lifeless churches and new vision. God is raising up a variety of ministries:
a) *Daystar III*, based in New Zealand, with an extensive ministry of Bible and Christian literature distribution.
b) *The Korean Hannah Mission's* vessel **MV** *Hannah*, with 30 crew and personnel involved in evangelism, church planting, training in missions and discipleship in Asia and the Pacific.
c) *Boat Ministry, Singapore* using ferro-concrete yachts for the islands of Indonesia.
d) *YWAM prayer flotillas* for the Pacific, based in New Zealand.

4 **The inland waters flotilla.** Many missions are expanding this type of ministry:
a) *On the Amazon in South America* (**UFM**, Brazilian Bible Society, Costa Rican Amazonian Mission with three launches reaching 19 tribes and **SIM** in Bolivia).
b) *BEM* on Belgian canals and **GMU** in southwest France.
c) *Hellenic Missionary Union* boat *Morning Star* in the Greek islands.

5 **Provision of funds** for these expensive yet strategic ministries. Costs have risen dramatically in past years.

6 **Provision of technically qualified crew and staff** without whom ships may not sail. This is a constant need.

7 **The spiritual health, growth and safety** of all involved in this demanding ministry. People from many nations have to live and witness together. The loss of the original MV LOGOS near Cape Horn in 1988 highlights the potential for danger.

8 **The ministry of the ships to stimulate world vision,** local evangelism and holy living in ports of call.

9 **Seamen's missions around the world.** There are an estimated 10 million seafarers and fishermen — increasingly non-Western and non-Christian — who have little exposure to the gospel. Mission to Seafarers, Korea Harbour Evangelism and several other organizations have workers in many lands and in hundreds of ports, serving the spiritual and practical needs of seafarers.

• CHRISTIAN TENTMAKERS •

Since the time of Paul, the "original" Christian tentmaker, it has often been expedient or essential to use a secular skill or profession as a platform for sharing the gospel (Acts 18:3). Great movements of people seeking employment or education opportunities since 1950 have enabled Christians to use the same means to evangelize nations, peoples and strata of society otherwise closed to full-time Christian workers. In many nations this is the major and often the *only* way of gaining access to a country.

1 **Hundreds of thousands of Western, Middle Eastern, Asian and African Christians** have moved abroad to seek education opportunities or employment — as doctors, nurses, paramedics, computer consultants, lecturers, teachers, engineers, agriculturalists, house servants, road sweepers, etc. Most have done it for personal reasons. Pray that they may be stirred to witness to non-Christians as they encounter the great spiritual needs, especially of the indigenous communities.

2 **Pray for the specific calling of Christians** with the necessary gifts and training to serve in "closed" lands, especially the Muslim heartlands, the Communist lands of Asia and the former Soviet Union.

3 **Adequate cultural and spiritual preparation** is hard to obtain while retaining the necessary professional expertise, yet it is essential. This special type of ministry needs solid screening of candidates and preparation — pray for these. Pray also that sending churches might affirm and encourage those whom God is calling into this strategic ministry. **Tentmakers International Exchange** [www.csonline.net/tie/] is one organization which puts prospective workers in touch with appropriate sending and training agencies.

4 **These tentmakers often go to areas where the authorities or the people are hostile to Christianity.** Fellowship and pastoral care are vital ingredients in their ability to survive spiritually and be fruitful, but are often hard to provide. Pray especially for those living in lonely, pressurized situations where every action can be carefully monitored. Pray for their protection as they challenge the entrenched powers of darkness. Asian Christians working in the Middle East have been effective tentmakers, but a large number have suffered as a result, some paying with their lives.

5 **Strategic deployment and fruitful service** is a major area of weakness. Too often the long hours of work, isolation and lack of an effective strategy for church planting mean little long-term fruit. Pray that the work of Christian tentmakers may be integrated into ministry networks (local church, mission or inter-agency) which provide continuity in contacts, direction in ministry and result in churches being planted. These networks have been well used by God in most "closed" countries to facilitate vision, teamwork and strategy. Many mission agencies have adapted their structures to facilitate tentmaking and provide the necessary accountability and continuity.

6 **Holy boldness tempered by discernment and tact** are needed where active proselytization is forbidden so that there may be conversions, and fellowships of believers might be established.

7 **The appropriate division of time** is essential to fruitful tentmaking ministry. Employment that gives opportunity both for doing the job in a way that glorifies Christ, and for friendship evangelism, is not easy to procure.

8 **Pray for the granting of long-term visas for tentmakers.** Quarterly trips out of the country to renew short-term visas can be draining and discouraging.

9 **Pray for the conversion of prominent citizens** of these countries through the witness of tentmakers. This could totally change the attitudes of governments and open the doors for wider Christian ministry.

• SHORT-TERM WORKERS (STWs) •

The number of people, both young and old, serving the Lord cross-culturally for periods of a few weeks to two years has grown exponentially in the past three decades. In our shrinking world, more young people travel abroad than ever before. In the case of believers, it is often in the context of short-term missions. It is impossible to assess how many believers all over the world give time during any one year to missionary work, but it almost certainly outnumbers the world's entire full-time missionary force! Tens of thousands of young people go out every year. They mostly come from Western nations, but now almost every nation has had at least one believer involved with short-term missions. The largest groups facilitating this are **YWAM, OM, CCCI,** and TEEN Missions. The workers serve in as many capacities as there are needs.

• Challenges for Prayer

1 **A genuine calling from God.** Inexperience, immaturity, or lack of cross-cultural exposure can make the experience traumatic. Unsuitable and/or unprepared STWs can divert long-term Christian leaders from their ministry, unintentionally offend those they are trying to reach, and slow the advance of the gospel rather than extend it.

2 **Spiritual growth.** The transformed spiritual life of the individual is often the greatest permanent result of short-term ministry. Pray for sufficient pastoral care and fellowship, appropriate in-service teaching and training, but also fruitfulness while ministering.

3 **Protection.** Our world is more dangerous than in past decades; wars, kidnappings, resurgent diseases and spiritual attacks from the enemy must be opposed through prayer.

4 **Long-term ministry** after the short-term experience. Pray that the brief exposure may have a positive influence in bringing many STWs into long-term cross-cultural ministry or into passionate missions advocacy at home. Many long-term sending agencies are developing short-term programmes with this in mind.

• STUDENT MINISTRIES •

The tertiary students of the world constitute one of the most strategic mission fields:

1 **Worldwide there are over 50 million students** in 46,000 universities and colleges. Many will be in leadership roles in 20 years' time.

2 **The percentage of evangelical students** in several countries is generally lower than in the general population. This is true in Latin America, China and many European countries. Whole student cultures remain scarcely influenced by biblical Christianity.

3 **The student world** has radically changed over the past decade. Tertiary institutions are decreasingly incubators for radical causes and increasingly places of self-seeking hedonism, or often in poorer nations, mere survival. Christian ministry must address needs generated by this culture shift.

• Challenges for Prayer

Many agencies have been raised up to reach students. A few key ones are mentioned below, though some have diversified into ministries that have outgrown the student arm of the work.

1 **International Fellowship of Evangelical Students (IFES)** has become a worldwide fellowship of autonomous national movements in universities, with a wide variety of local names. The emphasis of this ministry is evangelism, Bible study groups, literature and missions. This vital field needs much prayer:

a) For the extension of the evangelical witness to universities where none exists. Areas of special need: Latin America, the Muslim world, Francophone Africa, Central and Eastern Europe.

b) **For the right leadership** in the rapidly changing population of the student world —
adult advisers, travelling secretaries and student leaders.

c) **For Christian students and their growth in the Lord** and that from their number some
may go into full-time service for the Lord.

2 **The Navigators,** with their unique personal discipleship emphasis, have made a deep
impact on many. Of the 105 countries where their 3,800 staff minister, 43 have active
collegiate ministries and 13 have ministries to teens or high schoolers. Around one-third of
their field staff are engaged in such ministries. In the USA alone, they have 425 staff in their
collegiate entity, concentrated on 70 campuses.

3 **Agencies specializing in ministry among international students,** such as
IFES, ISI (USA) and **ISCS** (UK) have developed effective outreach to some of the nearly
one million international students in English-speaking nations. In other language areas the
coverage is poorer — especially in Francophone universities. A large number of overseas students have been wonderfully converted in the West and could become a decisive factor for
the spread of the gospel when they return home. Many come from lands closed to the
gospel but, sadly, the majority are repelled by the coldness and lack of concern of "Christians" and return home disillusioned.

4 **Agencies focusing on placing Christian faculty in secular universities** outside of North America give believing academics opportunities to teach their disciplines
from Christian perspectives and to impact students. Pray that these ministries, such as the
International Institute for Christian Studies, might be able to place Christians in posts
where they might share the Truth with many searching students.

5 **Campus Crusade** began and continues as a campus ministry, but the ministry has
broadened out into a multi-dimensional thrust for world evangelization. (See section
on 'The *JESUS* film'.) Over 22,000 workers serve in 186 countries. Pray for their evangelistic, discipling and mobilizing ministry among students.

6 **Student missions conferences** have been used for many years to inspire students
with a vision for the world. Some of the more significant are the triennial Urbana conferences of IVF(IFES) in the USA and the triennial TEMA conferences for European young
people in the Netherlands. Other significant conferences are developing in size and sophistication in Nigeria, Korea and Latin America. Pray that these may be the source of many
becoming committed to world evangelization.

• MINISTRY TO CHILDREN •

The importance of ministry to children and young people cannot be overestimated. They
are the potential Church of tomorrow. Consider the following:

1 **Approximately 4 billion children will be born between 2000 and 2025.** Of
these, 90% will be born in the developing world.

2 **There are 1,510 million children under 15 in less developed countries.**
(Nearly half of Africa south of the Sahara is under 15.) Over 35% of these will grow up
illiterate, most will be poor, and 40% in Asia and 26% in Africa will be malnourished.

3 **There are an estimated 100 million children** who live all or the majority of their
lives on the street.

• Challenges for Prayer

1 **The preservation of the family.** This is under threat worldwide.

a) **In the West**, stable two-parent families are becoming the exception and few children
have any contact with the gospel. The legacy of rejection, spiritual ignorance and deprivation of real love is beginning to bear bitter fruit in delinquency, crime and social
dislocation. Pray for Christian families as they seek to bring up their children in the fear
of the Lord when all around them society is disintegrating and hostile.

b) ***In poor countries*** parents can often do little for their children because they are caught in a cycle of poverty, disease, illiteracy and instability. Debt encourages slave or child labour, poverty and social breakdown and prevents education — 47% of children in sub-Saharan Africa and 34% of children in Asia do not attend school.

2 The children themselves.

a) ***Non-Christian children.*** In few countries (primarily the West) is there a wide range of evangelistic and discipling ministries for children. They are often ignored or treated as if adults in many parts of the world. Children in special need of prayer are:

i *An estimated 100 million indentured or slave children* sold to settle debts — 10 million of these are child prostitutes. As of 2000 there were 300,000 children in over 60 countries involved in armed conflict.

ii *The estimated 100 million street children* in the world with no or minimal family contacts — many in Latin America.

iii *Child-refugees* had risen from 7 million in 1992 to 10 million (those under 18) out of the world's 21.5 million refugees by 2000.

iv *Children affected by AIDS.* During 1998 more than 8,500 children and young people were infected each day. Nearly 8 million African children have been orphaned and at least one million are infected. Six young people are infected with the AIDS virus every minute.

v *The 120 million blind or deaf children* — most of whom will never receive special help.

b) ***Non-Christian children of Christians.*** Numerous children do not follow in the faith of their parents. Many churches do not provide child-specific spiritual care and nurture. Too few Christians are trained to reach out to the children of church members and few churches see the need. Pray for the development of good teachers and materials for successful ministry among such children. **CEF** has a notable record in providing this.

c) ***Christian children.*** They are the best evangelists of their peers. Pray for many in schools with a non-Christian and often hostile environment. Pray for international agencies with specific discipling ministries among children such as **YFC, SU,** Boys' Brigade and Crusaders.

3 Literature for children — a big need in many countries. Only in a few languages is there a wide variety of good literature for this age group.

4 Bible camp ministries. These have been much used of God and have possibly been one of the more fruitful ways of evangelizing and teaching young people. Many churches and agencies run such camps, but there are rarely enough spiritual leaders for this ministry.

5 Missionary children (MKs). The witness of Christian families on the mission field is a significant aspect of witness and teaching by example for many cultures. Yet the personal and educational needs of children is a major factor in terminating or suspending the cross-cultural ministry of their parents at their peak of usefulness.

a) ***MKs grow up bi-cultural or even tri-cultural****,* but often without a sense of belonging to any culture. This enriches some and embitters others. Pray that parents might have great wisdom in keeping ministry and family in balance and give the children a sense of privilege in their enriching experiences. Pray that parents and children might be a united team for the spread of the gospel.

b) ***Education is always a costly challenge*** — in parental time if home schooling is pursued, in separation, much travel and emotional stress if the only option is boarding school away from home, or in finances if secular international schooling is used. Pray for wise decisions for each child as to the option used. Pray for MK schools in various parts of the world and for the provision of funds and missionary staff. Pray that home churches may understand this crucial issue as an integral part of missionary support.

c) ***The growing non-English-speaking missionary force*** is having to face the challenge of the danger that their children may lose contact with their home culture. They often face enormous emotional and educational problems when they return to their home countries. This problem is particularly acute for non-Western children in Western-based mission schools.

d) ***Missionary children need fulfilling careers*** — pray that MKs may find a deep and satisfying relationship with Jesus and then careers enriched by their childhood experiences. Pray that many may become active servants of God.

• OUTREACH TO SECTS OR CULTS •

The worldwide growth and spread of missionary cults of western and eastern origin has been a striking phenomenon in the 20ᵗʰ Century, and is continuing into the 21ˢᵗ. This has accompanied a global pluralization of religions. The religion graphs throughout this book vividly show that the relative simplicity of 1900 has given way to a growing medley of beliefs in 2000. Note the following developments:

1 **Jehovah's Witnesses** have grown worldwide from 916,000 members in 1960 to 6,036,000 in 2000. There are over 14.5 million affiliates today. Many give sacrificial hours in door-to-door work to proclaim a false message in almost every nation and in 400 languages. In some nations — such as Austria, Poland and Spain — Jehovah's Witnesses out-number Evangelicals, and splinter groups abound.

2 **The Mormons** (The Church of Jesus Christ of Latter Day Saints) have similarly grown from 1.4 million adherents in 1960 to 11 million in 2000. The short-term missionary work of the Mormons puts evangelical churches to shame. Many parts of Polynesia are rapidly becoming majority Mormon, and growth in Latin America is remarkable. Mormon missionaries numbered about 60,000 in 2000, working in 150 nations.

3 **Hindu-Buddhist groups** have made remarkable inroads among young people in the West — some *gurus* gaining large followings. Many lives have been damaged by aberrant practices — use of drugs, promiscuous sex and exposure to demonic influences. The *Hare Krishna* (ISKON) movement has rapidly gained a large following in former Soviet states since the ending of Communist rule.

4 **New Age beliefs** have swept through modern cultures in the West and East. In the West a worldview shift to acceptance of eastern mysticism, reincarnation and "self" awareness together with renewed interest in old Western paganism and occultism poses a serious challenge to Christianity and the whole basis on which Western society has been founded. A large minority of churchgoers would accept some New Age premises.

5 **New religious movements** that mix Christian concepts and terminology with indigenous non-Christian beliefs and practices have gained followings of tens of millions — **Christo-paganism** in Latin America, **indigenous syncretistic churches** in Africa (with millions of followers), new movements in China, etc.

• Challenges for Prayer

The following are particular areas of need. Pray for:

1 **Those who have been led astray** into quasi-Christian movements — often through ignorance and the failure of born-again Christians to reach them first. Praise God for thousands who have left such cults and found liberty in Christ.

2 **The removal of bias in Western media towards New Age and Eastern religious concepts** and against biblical Christianity. Pray that Christians may be well-taught and discerning concerning these errors.

3 **Truth to fill the spiritual vacuum in the former atheistic states,** such as the former Soviet Union. This is being filled not only by true Christians but also by numerous eastern and western sects. Pray for the truth to be proclaimed so that all can see what is erroneous.

4 **The preparation of suitable literature and videos** in major languages to help Christians understand and evangelize cultists, and to warn potential cultists. The need for apologetic literature in Eurasia is particularly acute. The organizations below can provide help.

5 Specific organizations needing prayer and offering help:

a) ***The Centers for Apologetics Research*** (Pseudo-Christian, eastern and indigenous sects).
P.O. Box 1196, San Juan Capistrano, CA 92693 USA.
[www.apolresearch.org/eng/intro_eng.php3]

b) ***Christian Research Institute International*** (Pseudo-Christian sects).
CRI International P.O. Box 7000 Rancho Santa Margarita, CA 92688-7000 USA.
Canada: CRI Canada 56051 Airways P.O., Calgary, Alberta T2E 8K5.
[www.equip.org]

c) ***Institute for Religious Research*** (Pseudo-Christian sects).
1340 Monroe Ave. NW, Grand Rapids, MI 49505-4604 USA.
[www.irr.org]

d) ***MacGregor Ministries*** (Pseudo-Christian Sects, New Age).
Box 454 Metaline Falls WA 99153 USA. *Canada:* Box 294 Nelson B.C. V1L 5P9.
[www.macgregorministries.org]

e) ***Reachout Trust*** (Pseudo-Christian Sects, New Age, Occult).
24 Ormond Road, Richmond, Surrey, TW10 6TH UK.
[www.reachouttrust.org]

f) ***Free Minds, Inc.*** (formerly Bethel Ministries — Jehovah's Witnesses).
PO Box 3818, Manhattan Beach, CA 90266 USA.
[www.freeminds.org]

g) ***Concerned Christians and Former Mormons*** (Mormons).
PO Box 18, Mesa, Arizona 85211 USA.
[www.concernedchristians.org]

h) ***Utah Lighthouse Ministry*** (Mormons).
P.O. Box 1884, Salt Lake City, UT 84110 USA.
[www.utlm.org]

i) ***Watchman Fellowship*** (JWs).
Box 13340 Arlington, Texas 76094 USA.
[www.watchman.org]

• URBAN EVANGELIZATION •

For the first time in history, half of the world's population lives in or near a city. By AD2000 there were 20 cities of over 10 million, 60 over 4 million and 402 over one million. The majority of these cities are in the non-Western world and are non-Christian. The great surge of missions outreach in the late 20th Century largely passed by the burgeoning urban population of the non-Western world. Christianity is being marginalized in many, if not most, of the world's largest cities. This will be one of the biggest challenges for missions in the 21st Century when, by its close, 90% of people will be living in urban areas.

• Challenges for Prayer

This major shift in population from rural to urban necessitates a radical shift in thinking and strategy among churches and missions reaching out to the unreached. Pray for:

1 **Appropriate strategies for evangelizing** the major non-Christian cities of the world. The racial, ethnic, linguistic, social and religious complexities of modern cities make an all-out effort essential to reach each cultural unit of these cities. Pray that urban missions advocacy and conferences focusing on urban evangelism may lead to effective cooperation among churches and agencies, without which the task will be impossible to achieve.

2 **The urban poor, the biggest single challenge**. Vast slums and squatter camps are mushrooming throughout Latin America, Africa and many parts of Asia. Appalling conditions and squalor make any Christian ministry difficult and complex. Wisdom is needed in knowing how to combine evangelism and social betterment without creating dependency or churches filled with those seeking escape from the system. Pray for the countless urban poor and for God's guidance as to how to work most effectively amongst them.

3 **The decaying inner cities of the West.** In the midst of affluence many cities have a rotten core. Unemployment, poverty, drug abuse, crime and despair are widespread. Most Christians and churches have migrated to the more comfortable suburbs, leaving these areas with little Christian presence. In many cases, inner cities have become the home of immigrant ethnic minorities who need to be reached with the love of Christ. Pray for bodies such as the Salvation Army, Association of Rescue Missions (USA), Ichthus (UK), Betel (WEC, global) and many others with commitment to these needy peoples.

4 **Christians' preconception of missions** needs to shift from a 19th Century rural, tribal image to a modern, urban one. The Church, and its sending structures in particular, must be advocates of urban mission more than ever. Pioneer work in concrete jungles and vast squatter settlements must be shown to be just as valid as pioneering in rural areas.

5 **The mobilization of a trained and efficient work force.** Christian workers, in general, fear the cities, especially the less comfortable slums and inner cities, and are uncertain as to know how to handle the high costs, complexities and tensions of city ministry. God is raising up new agencies specifically to reach the urban poor such as Servants to Asia's Urban Poor and the Urban Leadership Foundation.

6 **The essential and effective use of all modern methods of communication.** Hundreds of millions need to be confronted with the claims of Christ as quickly and effectively as possible. No one medium can achieve this, but a combination of all in a concerted effort could decisively change the spiritual climate of a city.

• INTERNATIONAL COOPERATION FOR WORLD EVANGELIZATION •

The growth and expansion of the Church world-wide has built up such momentum, and grown in complexity, that close cooperation at every level has become essential. No longer is the missions movement Western, but global, and the potential for disastrous confrontations and relationship breakdowns grows greater. There are different levels of cooperative ministry:

1 **Global**. The spiritual unity of the body of Christ in all its cultural and theological diversity must be maintained. For this Christ prayed. So must we. May that spiritual unity be evident in every place.

2 **Structural**. The Church has three biblical and interdependent functional structures. These are for:
Fellowship — local congregations.
Discipling — training, BCCs, theological institutions, Bible colleges, etc.
Witness — apostolic teams, agencies, missions, etc.
Church history is a long account of failures or breakdowns between these equally vital components of the Church. Pray for:
a) *Supportive appreciation*, meaningful accountability and fellowship in cooperation between local churches, agencies and theological training institutions.
b) *Effective sharing* of resources, personnel and vision between these structures. Too many churches, agencies and theological schools 'go it alone' in seeking to fulfil the Great Commission to the detriment of the wider body of Christ.
c) *Helpful caring and enabling for missionaries* — at every stage of their preparation for, involvement in and changing direction of ministry.

3 **Organizational**. Through the two millennia there have been major conferences that have wrestled with intense theological, structural and relational issues. Few, until recent decades, have convened solely for the fulfilment of the Great Commission. In most major denominational, confessional, evangelical, charismatic or Pentecostal conferences world evangelization has rarely been the major focus — it should be. Pray for any such that God's heart for a lost world might be central.

4 **Interdenominational.** Since the Congress in 1966 in Berlin, great global conferences of Evangelicals have boosted cooperation, enhanced vision and energized action networks; major ones being linked with WEF, Lausanne (LCWE, 1974, 1980, 1989), AD2000 and Beyond (1995,1997), Amsterdam (Billy Graham Evangelistic Association 1983, 1986, 2000). The remarkable impact of these will reverberate into the future. Others will follow, but pray that:

a) *All such conferences or congresses* be according to the leading of the Holy Spirit and with the right leaders and attenders involved. The effort and expense is prodigious. They need to contribute to the goal of world evangelization.

b) *There might be an effective outgrowth* from the AD2000 and Beyond Movement. The latter's great successes in the 1990s in focus on the least reached and networking of active agencies and churches needs to be maintained. The **Great Commission Roundtable** is emerging as a likely coordinating point for this. The hype of the year 2000 has passed but the task has yet to be completed.

5 **Local and Regional.** A characteristic of the 1990s was the multiplication of partnerships linking ministries focused on specific areas, people clusters and ministries in the less evangelized parts of the world. A special focus of Interdev and others has been the 160 or so people clusters. During the 1990s the number of such partnerships increased from 6 in 1990 to 78 in 2000. Pray for the growth and maturing of those now in existence and also for at least 85 other such partnerships which are in various stages of development — from a dreaming to just about being launched. These partnerships have increased cooperation, reduced duplication of effort and provided a forum for fellowship, vision and conflict resolution. Many must operate quietly and sensitively because of the hostile environment in which the outreach is carried out.

• OPERATION WORLD •

Response to the previous five editions of *Operation World* has been encouraging. Many have faithfully prayed through the book and we regularly receive letters which testify to God's guidance for ministry or call to missionary work through this book. Areas and peoples hitherto unevangelized have been prayed open, entered and churches planted.

We estimate that approximately 2 million copies of all earlier editions have been distributed — over 80% in English, but also in French, German, Korean, Portuguese, Spanish, Russian, Czech, etc. We are grateful and humbled by reports that these have had a major input into the development of world missions vision in the non-Western world.

• Challenges for Prayer

1 **The sixth English edition.** This may be the largest print-run ever. Pray that bold distribution plans to get the book into the hands of Christians might be realized. Pray for opportunities to provide subsidized editions for countries with economic problems.

2 **The revised volumes of** *You Can Change the World* **and** *You Too Can Change the World*, the children's version of *Operation World*, are to be released as a single volume entitled *Window on the World*. Each of the original volumes has been well received with a combined circulation of approximately 100,000. The first volume has been translated into more than 20 languages. Many wonderful letters have been received from both children and parents alike telling how the book has challenged and stimulated children to pray for the world, and of how God is calling them to serve as missionaries when the time is right. Pray that the new, combined edition may continue this and restore missions to the heart of children's and young people's ministries in local churches.

3 **Other language editions of both** *Operation World* **and** *Window on the World.* Plans are being made for publication into 10 or more languages. Pray that these editions may be used of God to give missions vision to growing churches around the world and further enhance the development of the global missions movement, especially in Latin America, Africa and Asia.

4 The CD edition of *Operation World* to become a valuable information, research and motivation tool for those with access to computers.

5 A possible 'translation' to be done for young people/youth. Discussions centre upon an edition to be available electronically via a website. Pray that these discussions will result in a culturally-relevant version for young people aged between 15 and 25 which challenges toward active involvement in missions both at home and abroad.

6 Any future editions of *Operation World.* The mantle is shifting from one long-time author to an as-yet unspecified team. Please pray that the right individuals be brought together with the vision, motivation and perseverance to see a future edition written. It is not a job for the faint-hearted!

7 The army of helpers and informants around the world who have contributed to all previous volumes. Pray that their ministries might be blessed, for trust to be built up between them and a future *Operation World* team and that the vital flow of information will continue, enabling future editions to be made possible.

• THE LORD'S RETURN •

The last prayer in the Bible is "Come, Lord Jesus" (Revelation 22:20). Peter tells us that we should be "looking for and hastening the coming of the day of God" (2 Peter 3:12). How better can we do it than by praying for the fulfilment of Genesis 12:3, Revelation 7:9-10 and Matthew 24:14? Pray for:

1 The speediest possible evangelization of the world — of every unreached people group, area, city and nation.

2 The Great Commission to be restored to its rightful centrality in the ministry of the Church worldwide.

3 Your part in achieving this. What is God's will for your life? In the coming year are you willing to do whatever He commands regarding the needs of the world? Is it possible God is calling you to a specific ministry in praying, supporting, or going to the ends of the earth for your Master?

4 Your local church's part. Pray that your fellowship may grow in missionary zeal and commitment in the coming year.

• APPENDIX 1 •
LEADERS OF THE WORLD'S NATIONS

Political changes in the world today are so rapid that the names of leaders have not been included in the text for individual countries. This would date the information too fast! Since the original May 2001 *Operation World* listing there have been 76 changes. Yet these leaders need prayer as the Scriptures exhort us (1 Samuel 12:23, 1 Timothy 2:1-4).

This list comprises the most important decision-makers in the country in Jan 2004 and not necessarily the titular head of state, who often plays a more ceremonial role. Usually this has meant one leader, but in a few countries we have given two. The family of surname is capitalized.

The following websites provide lists of leaders which are frequently updated:

1. <www.rulers.org> which lists heads of state and heads of government for all countries and territories. It is updated almost daily, and gives a daily report on government changes around the world.

2. <www.cia.gov/cia/publications/chiefs> is maintained by the USA CIA. Its country list is not so complete, but its layout is simpler and all cabinet ministers are also given. It is updated monthly.

The final column is left blank. Any leadership change can be entered there.

STATE OR TERRITORY	TITLE	NAME	CHANGES
State or Territory	Title	Name	Changes
Afghanistan	President	Hamid KARZAI	
Albania	President	Alfred MOISIU	
	Prime Minister	Fatos NANO	
Algeria	President	Abdelaziz BOUTEFLIKA	
American Samoa	Governor (Acting)	Togliola TULAFONO	
Andorra	Chief Executive	Marc Forné MOLNÉ	
Angola	President	José Eduardo DOS SANTOS	
Anguilla	Chief Minister	Osbourne FLEMING	
Antigua And Barbuda	Prime Minister	Lester BIRD	
Argentina	President	Nestor KIRCHNER	
Armenia	President	Robert KOCHARIAN	
	Prime Minister	Andranik MARKARYAN	
Aruba	Prime Minister	Nelson O. ODUBER	
Australia	Prime Minister	John HOWARD	
Austria	Chancellor	Wolfgang SCHÜSSEL	
Azerbaijan	President	Ilham ALIYEV	
Bahamas	Prime Minister	Perry CHRISTIE	
Bahrain	Amir	HAMAD bin Issa Al KHALIFAH	
Bangladesh	Prime Minister	Khaleda ZIA (f)	
Barbados	Prime Minister	Owen ARTHUR	
Belarus	President	Aleksandr LUKASHENKO	
Belgium	Prime Minister	Guy VERHOFSTADT	
Belize	Prime Minister	Said MUSA	
Benin	President	Mathieu KÉRÉKOU	
Bermuda	Premier	Alex SCOTT	
Bhutan	King	Jigme Singye WANGCHUK	
Bolivia	President	Carlos MESA	
Bosnia	Chairman of the Presidency	Dragan COVIC	
Botswana	President	Festus Gontebanye MOGAE	
Brazil	President	Luis Inácio LULA da Silva	
British Indian Ocean Terr.	Commissioner	John WHITE	
British Virgin Islands	Chief Minister	Orlando SMITH	
Brunei	Sultan and Prime Minister	Muda HASSANAL BOLKIAH Muʿizzadin Waddaulah	
Bulgaria	President	Georgi PURVANOV	
	Chairman of the Council of Ministers	Simeon SAKSCOBURGGOTSKI	

State or Territory	Title	Name	Changes
Burkina Faso	President and Head of State	Blaise COMPAORÉ	
Burundi	President	Domitien NDAYIZEYE	
Cambodia	King	Norodom SIHANOUK	
	Prime Minister	Samdech HUN SEN	
Cameroon	President	Paul BIYA	
Canada	Prime Minister	Paul MARTIN	
Cape Verde	President	Pedro PIRES	
Cayman Islands	Governor	Bruce DINWIDDY	
Central African Republic	President	François BOZIZÉ	
Chad	President	Idriss DÉBY	
Chile	President	Ricardo LAGOS Escobar	
China, Hong Kong	Chief Executive	TUNG Chee-hwa	
China, Macau	Chief Executive	Edmund HO Hau Wah	
China, People's Republic	President and Gen. Secty. of the Communist Party	HU Jintao	
	Premier	WEN Jiabao	
China, Taiwan	President	CHEN Shui-bian	
China, Tibet	Dalai Lama	Tenzin GYATSO (usually simply 'The Dalai Lama')	
Christmas Island	Administrator	Bill TAYLOR	
Cocos (Keeling) Islands	Administrator	Bill TAYLOR	
Colombia	President	Andrés PASTRANA Arango	
Comoros	President and Head of State	AZZALI Assoumani	
Congo (Brazzaville)	President	Denis SASSOU-NGUESSO	
Congo-DRC	President	Joseph KABILA	
Cook Islands	Prime Minister	Terepai MAOATE	
Costa Rica	President	Miguel Ángel RODRÍGUEZ Echeverría	
Côte d'Ivoire	President	Laurent GBAGBO	
	Prime Minister	Affi N'GUESSAN	
Croatia	President	Stjepan MESIC	
Cuba	President	Fidel CASTRO Ruz	
Cyprus	President	Tassos PAPADOPOULOS	
	Prime Minister (N Cyprus)	Dervis EROGLU	
Czech Republic	President	Václav KLAUS	
	Prime Minister	Vladimír SPIDLA	
Denmark	Prime Minister	Anders Fogh RASMUSSEN	
Djibouti	President	Ismail Omar GUELLEH	
Dominica	Prime Minister designate	Roosevelt SKERRIT	
Dominican Republic	President	Rafael Hipólito MEJÍA Dominguez	
Ecuador	President	Lucio GUTIÉRREZ	
Egypt	President	Mohammed Hosni MUBARAK	
El Salvador	President	Francisco FLORES Perez	
Equatorial Guinea	President	Teodoro OBIANG NGUEMA MBASOGO	
Eritrea	President	Isaias AFWERKI	
Estonia	President	Arnold RÜÜTEL	
Ethiopia	President	Girma WOLDE-GIORGIS	
	Prime Minister	Zenawi MELES	
Faeroe Islands	Prime Minister	Anfinn KALLSBERG	
Falkland Islands	Governor	Howard PEARCE	
Fiji	Prime Minister	Laisenia QARASE	
	President	Ratu Josefa ILOILO	
Finland	Prime Minister	Matti VANHANEN	
France	President	Jacques CHIRAC	
	Prime Minister	Jean-Pierre RAFFARIN	
French Guiana	Prefect	Ange MANCINI	
French Polynesia	President of the Territorial Government	Gaston FLOSSE	
Gabon	President	Omar BONGO	
Gambia, The	President	Yahya JAMMEH	
Georgia	President	Mikhail SAAKASHVILI	
Germany	Chancellor	Gerhard SCHRÖDER	
Ghana	President	John KUFUOR	

APPENDIX 1

State or Territory	Title	Name	Changes
Gibraltar	Chief Minister	Peter CARAUNA	
Greece	Prime Minister	Kostandinos SIMITIS	
Greenland	Prime Minister	Hans ENOKSEN	
Grenada	Prime Minister	Keith MITCHELL	
Guadeloupe	Prefect	Dominique VIAN	
Guam	Governor	Felix CAMACHO	
Guatemala	President	Alfonso Antonio PORTILLO Cabrera	
Guinea	President	Lansana CONTÉ	
Guinea-Bissau	President (interim)	Henrique ROSA	
Guyana	President	Bharrat JAGDEO	
Haiti	President	Jean-Bertrand ARISTIDE	
Holy See (Vatican City)	Pope	JOHN PAUL II (Karol Joseph WOJTYLA)	
Honduras	President	Ricardo MADURO	
Hungary	Prime Minister	Péter MEDGYESSY	
Iceland	Prime Minister	Davíd ODDSON	
India	President	A.P.J. Abdul KALAM	
	Prime Minister	Manmohan SINGH	
Indonesia	President	Megawati SUKARNOPUTRI (f)	
Iran	Supreme Leader	Ayatollah Ali Hoseini-KHAMENEI	
	President	(Ali) Mohammad KHATAMI-Ardakani	
Iraq	President of the Governing Council	Adnan PACHACHI	
Ireland	Prime Minister	Bertie AHERN	
Isle Of Man	Chief Minister	Richard CORKILL	
Israel	Prime Minister	Ariel SHARON	
Italy	Prime Minister	Silvio BERLUSCONI	
Jamaica	Prime Minister	Percival James PATTERSON	
Japan	Prime Minister	Junichiro KOIZUMI	
Jordan	King	ABDALLAH bin Al Hussein	
Kazakhstan	President	Nursultan NAZARBAYEV	
Kenya	President	Mwai KIBAKI	
Kiribati	President	Anote TONG	
Korea, North	Chairman and General Secretary	KIM Jong Il	
Korea, South	President	ROH Moo Hyun	
Kuwait	Prime Minister	Sheikh JABIR Al Ahmad Al Jabir Al SABAH	
Kyrgyzstan	President	Askar AKAEV	
Laos	Chairman of the Council of Ministers	Boungnang VORACHITH	
Latvia	President	Vaira VIKE-FREIBERGA (f)	
Lebanon	President	Émile LAHOUD	
	Prime Minister	Rafiq Al HARIRI	
Lesotho	Prime Minister	Pakalitha MOSISILI	
Liberia	Chairman of the National Transitional Government	Gyude BRYANT	
Libya	Revolutionary Leader	Muammar Abu Minyar Al QADDAFI	
Liechtenstein	Head of Government	Otmar HASLER	
Lithuania	President	Rolandas PAKSAS	
Luxembourg	Prime Minister	Jean-Claude JUNCKER	
Macedonia	President	Boris TRAJKOVSKI	
Madagascar	President	Marc RAVALOMANANA	
Malawi	President	Bakili MULUZI	
Malaysia	Prime Minister	Datuk Seri Abdullah Ahmad BADAWI	
Maldives	President	Maumoon Abdul GAYOOM	
Mali	President	Amadou Toumani TOURÉ	
Malta	Prime Minister	Eddie FENECH ADAMI	
Marshall Islands	President	Kessai H. NOTE	
Martinique	Prefect	Michael CADOT	
Mauritania	President	Maaouya Ould Sidi Ahmad TAYA	
Mauritius	Prime Minister	Paul BÉRENGER	
Mayotte	Prefect	Jean-Jacques BROT	

State or Territory	Title	Name	Changes
Mexico	President	Vicente FOX Quesada	
Micronesia, Federated States	President	Joseph J. URUSEMAL	
Moldova	Prime Minister	Vasile TARLEV	
Monaco	Prince	RAINER III	
Mongolia	President	Natsagiyn BAGABANDI	
Montserrat	Chief Minister	John OSBORNE	
Morocco	King	MOHAMED VI (Sidi MUHAMMED)	
Mozambique	President	Joaquim Alberto CHISSANO	
Myanmar	Chairman of the State Peace and Development Council	THAN SHWE	
Namibia	President	Hifikepunye POHAMBA	
Nauru	President	René HARRIS	
Nepal	King	Gyanendra Bir Bikram Shah DEVA	
	Prime Minister	Surya Bahadur THAPA	
Netherlands	Prime Minister	Jan Peter BALKENENDE	
Netherlands Antilles	Prime Minister	Mirna LOUISA-GODETT (f)	
New Caledonia	President of the Territorial Congress	Pierre FROGIER	
New Zealand	Prime Minister	Helen CLARK (f)	
Nicaragua	President	Enrique BOLAÑOS	
Niger	President	TANDJA Mamadou	
Nigeria	President	Olusegun OBASANJO	
Niue	Premier	Young VIVIAN	
Norfolk Island	Chief Minister	Geoffrey Robert GARDNER	
Northern Mariana Islands	Governor	Juan N. BABAUTA	
Norway	Prime Minister	Kjell Magne BONDEVIK	
Oman	Sultan and Prime Minister	QABOOS bin Said Al Said	
Pakistan	Chief Executive	General Pervez MUSHARRAF	
Palau	President	Tommy REMENGESAU, Jr.	
Palestine Authority	President	Yasir ARAFAT	
Panama	President	Mireya Elisa MOSCOSO (f)	
Papua New Guinea	Prime Minister	Sir Michael SOMARE	
Paraguay	President	Nicanor DUARTE Frutos	
Peru	President	Alejandro TOLEDO	
Philippines	President	Gloria MACAPAGAL-ARROYO (f)	
Pitcairn Island	Island Magistrate and Chairman of the Island Council	Richard FELL	
Poland	President	Aleksander KWASNIEWSKI	
	Prime Minister	Leszek MILLER	
Portugal	President	Jorge Fernando Branco de SAMPIAO	
	Prime Minister	José Manuel DURÃO Barroso	
Puerto Rico	Governor	Sila María CALDERÓN (f)	
Qatar	Amir	HAMAD bin Khalifa Al THANI	
Réunion	Prefect	Gonthier FRIEDERICI	
Romania	President	Ion ILIESCU	
	Prime Minister	Adrian NASTASE	
Russia	President	Vladimir Vladimirovich PUTIN	
Rwanda	President	Paul KAGAME	
Samoa	Prime Minister	Sailele Malielegaoi TUILA'EPA	
San Marino	Secretary of State for Foreign and Political Affairs	Giovanni LONFERNINI & Valeria CIAVATTA (f)	
São Tomé and Príncipe	President	Fradique DE MENEZES	
Saudi Arabia	King and Prime Minister	FAHD bin Abd Al Aziz Al SAUD	
Senegal	President	Abdoulaye WADE	
	Prime Minister	Mame Madior BOYE	
Seychelles	President & Prime Minister	France-Albert RENÉ	
Sierra Leone	President	Ahmad Tejan KABBAH	
Singapore	Prime Minister	GOH Chok Tong	
Slovakia	Prime Minister	Mikuláš DZURINDA	

State or Territory	Title	Name	Changes
Slovenia	Prime Minister	Anton ROP	
Solomon Islands	Prime Minister	Sir Allan KEMAKEZA	
Somalia	President	ABDIQASIM Salad Hassan	
Somaliland	President	Dahir Riyale KAHIN	
South Africa	President	Thabo Mvuyelwa MBEKI	
Spain	King	JUAN CARLOS I	
	President of the Government	José María AZNAR	
Sri Lanka	President	Chandrika Bandaranaike KUMARATUNGA	
	Prime Minister	Ranil WICKREMASINGHE	
St Helena	Governor	David HOLLAMBY	
St Kitts-Nevis	Prime Minister	Denzil DOUGLAS	
St Lucia	Prime Minister	Kenny D. ANTHONY	
St Pierre & Miquelon	Prefect	Claude VALLEIX	
St Vincent	Prime Minister	Ralph GONSALVES	
Sudan	President	Omar Hassan Ahmad Al BASHIR	
Suriname	President	Ronald VENETIAAN	
Svalbard	Governor	Morten RUUD	
Swaziland	King	MSWATI III (Makhosetive)	
	Prime Minister	Themba DLAMINI	
Sweden	Prime Minister	Göran PERSSON	
Switzerland	President	Joseph DEISS	
Syria	President	Bashir ASSAD	
Tajikistan	President	Imomali RAHMONOV	
Tanzania	President	Benjamin William MKAPA	
Thailand	King	BHUMIBOL Adulyadej (RAMA IX)	
	Prime Minister	THAKSIN Shinawatra	
Timor Leste	President	Xanama GUSMÃO	
	Prime Minister	Mari Bin Amude ALKATIRI	
Togo	President	Gnassingbe EYADEMA	
Tokelau Islands	Administrator	Neil WALTER	
Tonga	King	Taufa'ahau TUPOU IV	
Trinidad & Tobago	Prime Minister	Patrick MANNING	
Tunisia	President	Zine Al Abidine BEN ALI	
Turkey	President	Ahmet Necdet SEZER	
	Prime Minister	Recep Tayyip ERDOGAN	
Turkmenistan	President	Saparmurat NIYAZOV	
Turks & Caicos Islands	Chief Minister	Michael MISICK	
Tuvalu	Prime Minister	Saufatu SOPOANGA	
Uganda	President	Yoweri MUSEVENI	
Ukraine	President	Leonid KUCHMA	
	Prime Minister	Victor YUSHCHENKO	
United Arab Emirates	Prime Minister	Sheikh MAKTUM ibn Rashid Al MAKTUM	
United Kingdom of	Queen	Elizabeth II	
Great Britain & N.I.	Prime Minister	Tony BLAIR	
United States Of America	President	George W. BUSH	
Uruguay	President	Jorge BATLLE	
Uzbekistan	President	Islam KARIMOV	
Vanuatu	Prime Minister	Edward NATAPEI	
Venezuela	President	Hugo CHÁVEZ	
Vietnam	Prime Minister	Phan Van KHAI	
	General Secretary of the Communist Party	Le Kha PHIEU	
Virgin Islands (USA)	Governor	Charles TURNBULL	
Wallis and Futuna Islands	High Administrator	Christian JOB	
Western Sahara	Prime Minister (SADR)	Abdelkader Taleb OUMAR	
Yemen	President	Ali Abdullah SALEH	
Yugoslavia (Serbia & Montenegro)	President	Vojislav KOSTUNICA	
Zambia	President	Levy MWANAWASA	
Zimbabwe	President	Robert MUGABE	

• APPENDIX 2 •
FURTHER PRAYER INFORMATION

The information in *Operation World* gives a general overview of the world and the growth of the Kingdom of the Lord Jesus Christ, but for more effective prayer you need to receive regular material containing more detail and updated information. To enable this, we have indicated many agencies in bold type abbreviations throughout the book. Our prayer is that you may make use of the contact details of these agencies and publishers of printed and electronic information. Every Christian with a heart for the evangelization of the world ought to subscribe to several publications. Why not write to some of the addresses in the pages that follow, or visit some of the websites included here?

These lists are not complete, but representative, and deemed helpful for a worldwide readership. Most of those listed below have asked to be included, but we could not include all who asked to be. Both denominational and interdenominational agencies have been listed, but the emphasis has been more on the latter because of the broader interest to the majority of readers.

A • PUBLICATIONS
Providing Worldwide Prayer Information in English

Here follows a brief list of publications which are wholly or partially given to the provision of such information.

UNITED STATES OF AMERICA

Brigada Today
Expansion Team, 3700 Hopewell Rd, Louisville, KY 40299

www.brigada.org
wide range, missions-specific

Christianity Today
PO Box 37060, Boone, IA 50037-0060

www.ChristianityToday.com
section on global news

Compass Direct
PO Box 27250, Santa Ana, CA 92799

www.compassdirect.org
info on persecuted Church

Church Around the World
Tyndale House Publishers,
PO Box 80, Wheaton, IL 60189-0080

www.tyndale.com
brief but global church news

DAWN Report
DAWN Ministries,
5775 N. Union Blvd., Colorado Springs, CO 80918

www.dawnministries.org
church planting/church growth

Evangelical Missions Quarterly
Evangelical Missions Information Service,
PO Box 794, Wheaton, IL 60189

www.wheaton.edu/bgc/emis
missions articles and news

FrontierScan
U.S. Center for World Mission,
1605 E. Elizabeth St., Pasadena, CA 91104

www.uscwm.org
unreached peoples

Global Prayer Digest
U.S. Center for World Mission,
1605 E. Elizabeth St., Pasadena, CA 91104

www.uscwm.org
unreached peoples

International Bulletin of Missionary Research
Overseas Ministries Study Center,
490 Prospect St., New Haven, CT 06511

www.OMSC.org
articles, missiology

International Journal of Frontier Missions
7665 Wenda Way, El Paso, TX 79915

<philothea@earthlink.net>
articles, missiology

Mission Frontiers
U.S. Center for World Mission,
1605 E. Elizabeth St., Pasadena, CA 91104

www.uscwm.org
mission news and articles

Moody Magazine
820 N. LaSalle Blvd., Chicago, IL 60611

n.a.
global news

Network-News
Network for Strategic Missions,
1732 South Park Court, Chesapeake, VA 23320

www.strategicnetwork.org
large missions knowledge base

WEF Religious Liberty Commission
World Evangelical Alliance,
PO Box 511194, Milwaukee, WI 53203

www.worldevangelical.org
the persecuted Church

World Christian
World in Need Press,
PO Box 1525, Oak Park, IL 30304

<WINPress7@aol.com>
pioneer missions

World Christian News & Books
YWAM International,
PO Box 26479, Colorado Springs, CO 80936

www.ywam.org
wide range of news

World Pulse
Evangelical Missions Information Service,
PO Box 794, Wheaton, IL 60189

www.wheaton.edu/bgc/emis
world mission news

UNITED KINGDOM

FFM Prayer Bulletin
Fellowship of Faith for the Muslims,
PO Box 5864, Basildon, Essex, SS13 3FF

<admin@f-f-m.org.uk>
emphasis on Muslims

Frontier
Keston Institute, 4 Park Town, Oxford, OX2 6SH

www.keston.org
the persecuted Church

World Report
United Bible Societies World Service Center,
7th Flr, Reading Bridge House, Reading, RG1 8PG

www.biblesociety.org
Bible translation, distribution

OTHER WESTERN NATIONS

FFM Prayer Bulletin
Fellowship of Faith for the Muslims,
PO Box 65214, Toronto, ON M4K 3Z2, Canada

www.ffmna.org
emphasis on Muslims

Friday Fax
<fridayfax@dawneurope.net>

www.dawnministries.org
news from around the world

IDEA
idea e.V, Steinbühlstr. 3, 35578 Wetzlar, Germany

www.idea.de
global information

Intercessors Network
<Intercessors.Network@Telia.com>
Storskiftesgatan 87, S-58334 Linkoping, Sweden

prayer information

ASIA

Asian Report
Asian Outreach, GPO Box 3448, Hong Kong

n.a.
news on Asian missions

Berita NECF — Malaysia
National Evangelical Christian Fellowship of Malaysia,
32 Jalan SS2/103, 47300 Petaling Jaya, Selangor, Malaysia

www.necf.org.my
world and S.E. Asian news

AFRICA

Missions Update – Nigeria
Christian Missionary Foundation,
UIPO Box 9890, Ibadan, Oyo State, Nigeria

www.cmfmissions.org
African missions

• APPENDIX 2 •
B • WEBSITES

The advent of the media age has made information remarkably more accessible to the public, but the sheer volume of it can be intimidating. The following list is not intended to be comprehensive and is only an infinitesimal representation of the available material — the *Operation World* CD has a much longer list of similar sites. We have tried to include both secular and Christian websites for those countries with multiple entries.

AREA	TITLE	ADDRESS
World	*WorldSkip.com*	www.worldskip.com
World	*CIA World Factbook 2000*	www.odci.gov/cia/publications/factbook
World	Geographia	www.interknowledge.com
World	*Countries of the World*	www.infoplease.com/countries.html
World	*Library of Congress Country Studies*	lcweb2.loc.gov/frd/cs/cshome.html
Africa	*NewAfrica.com*	www.newafrica.com
Africa	*North-Africa.com*	www.north-africa.com
Africa	*Africa South of the Sahara — Selected Internet Resources*	www-sul.stanford.edu/depts/ssrg/africa
Africa	*Index on Africa*	www.afrika.no/index
Asia	*ArabNet*	www.arab.net
Asia	*About Asia (on the OMF Website)*	www.omf.org.uk
Asia	*Gulf/2000 Project*	gulf2000.columbia.edu
Europe/Asia (fSU)	*East-West Church and Ministry Report*	www.samford.edu/groups/global/ewcmreport
Latin America	*LANIC Latin American Network Information Center*	www.lanic.utexas.edu/las.html
Latin America	*LatinWorld*	www.latinworld.com
Latin America	*Intervizion*	www.intervizion.net
Pacific	*Pacific Studies WWW Virtual Library* coombs.anu.edu.au/WWWVL-PacificStudies.html	
Pacific	*CocoNET Wireless - Pacific Islands News and Information*	www.uq.edu.au/coconet
Afghanistan	*Afghanistan Online*	www.afghan-web.com
Albania	*Albanian Home Page*	www.albanian.com/main
Albania	*Alb-Info Albanian Guide*	www.albinfo.com
Algeria	*Permanent Mission of Algeria to the UN*	www.algeria-un.org/nspage.html
Algeria	*AlgeriaInfo.com*	www.algeriainfo.com
American Samoa	*Amerika Samoa*	www.ipacific.com/samoa
Andorra	*Centre Nacional D'Informatica*	www.andorra.ad
Andorra	*Andorra On Line*	www.andorraonline.ad
Angola	*Angola — Official Website*	www.angola.org
Angola	*Republic of Angola Home Page*	zhenghe.tripod.com/a/angola/
Anguilla	*Anguilla Information Page*	www.offshore.com.ai/anguilla
Antigua	*Antigua and Barbuda Guide*	www.antiguanice.com
Antigua	*Antigua Today!*	www.antiguatoday.com
Argentina	*El Sur del Sur*	www.surdelsur.com
Argentina	*Logos Internet*	www.logos.com.ar
Armenia	*Embassy of the Republic of Armenia*	www.armeniaemb.org
Armenia	*Armenian Research Center*	www.umd.umich.edu/dept/armenian
Aruba	*Aruba On-Line*	www.arubatourism.com
Australia	*Australia: Beyond the Fatal Shore*	www.pbs.org/wnet/australia
Australia	*Down Under Christian Internet Directory*	www.ozemail.com.au/~phopwood
Austria	*Austrian Press and Information Service*	www.austria.org
Austria	*Austria Cafe*	www.austria-cafe.com
Azerbaijan	*A to Z of Azerbaijan*	www.azerb.com
Azerbaijan	*Republic of Azerbaijan*	www.president.az/azerbaijan/
Bahamas	*What's On — Bahamas*	www.whatsonbahamas.com
Bahrain	*Bahrain This Month*	www.bahrainthismonth.com

Bahrain	Bahrain — Blue Chip Country	www.bpmb.com
Bangladesh	Homeview Bangladesh	www.homeviewbangladesh.com
Bangladesh	Open Doors' Country Profile on Bangladesh	www.gospelcom.net/od/banglapro.htm
Barbados	Global Barbados	www.globalbarbados.com
Belarus	Data Web-Server	www.data.minsk.by
Belarus	WWW Belarus	www.belarus.net
Belgium	Webwatch	www.webwatch.be
Belgium	ERTSite	www.ping.be/erts
Belize	Government of Belize	www.belize.gov.bz
Belize	BelizeSearch.com	www.belizesearch.com
Benin	Government Website	planben.intnet.bj
Benin	Index on Africa — Benin	www.afrika.no/index/Country_pages/Benin
Bermuda	Bermuda Online	www.bermuda-online.org
Bhutan	Home Page of the Bhutan Website	www.bhutan-info.org
Bhutan	Kingdom of Bhutan	www.kingdomofbhutan.com
Bolivia	Bolivian — Index of Pages About Bolivia	www.bolivian.com
Bolivia	Bolivianet	www.bolivianet.com
Bosnia	Embassy of Bosnia and Herzegovina	www.bosnianembassy.org
Bosnia	Bosnia HomePage at Cal Tech	www.cco.caltech.edu/~bosnia
Botswana	IBIS	www.info.bw
Botswana	Botswana Online	www.botswana-online.com
Brazil	Infobrasil	www.infobrasil.org
Brazil	Brasil 2010	www.brasil2010.org
Brazil	Brasil-Brazil	www.brasil-brazil.com.br
British Virgin Islands	British Virgin Islands' Home Page	www.britishvirginislands.com
Brunei	His Majesty the Sultan of Brunei Web Site	www.bruneisultan.com
Brunei	BruNet Homepage	www.brunet.bn
Bulgaria	Bulgaria Online	www.online.bg
Bulgaria	Wonderland Bulgaria	www.omda.bg
Burkina Faso	Welcome to Burkina Faso	www.primature.gov.bf
Burundi	Burundi Home	www.burundi.gov.bi
Cambodia	angkor.com	www.angkor.com
Cambodia	Cambodian Information Center	www.cambodia.org
Cameroon	Home Page of the Republic of Cameroon	www.compufix.demon.co.uk/camweb
Cameroon	Postcards from Cameroon	www.geocities.com/TheTropics/Shores/4051
Canada	Evangelical Fellowship of Canada	www.efc-canada.com
Canada	Canada Christian Central	www.cccentral.com
Canada	canada.com	www.canada.com/home
Cape Verde	Cabo Verde Reference Page	users.erols.com/kauberdi
Cayman Islands	Cayman Islands	www.cayman-islands.com
CAR	Navel of Africa	www.venus.dti.ne.jp/~tee/
Chad	Africa South of the Sahara: Chad www-sul.stanford.edu/depts/ssrg/africa/chad.html	
Channel Islands	Channel Islands Intro Page	user.itl.net/~glen/Clintro.html
Chile	Government of Chile Home Page	www.gobiernodechile.cl
Chile	Chile Online	www.chile-online.com
China, PRC	Chinese Christian Internet Mission	www.ccim.org
China, PRC	Inside China Today	www.insidechina.com
China, PRC	China Source	www.chsource.org
China, Hong Kong	Hong Kong Internet Directory	www.internet-directory.com
China, Macau	Macao SAR of the People's Republic of China	www.macau.gov.mo
China, Taiwan	Taiwan Mission Quarterly	www.members.aol.com/taimission
China, Taiwan	Republic of China at a Glance	www.gio.gov.tw/info/nation
Colombia	Qué Hubo!	www.quehubo.com
Colombia	Indexcol	www.indexcol.com
Comoros	Comoro Islands' Home Page	www.ksu.edu/sasw/comoros/comoros.html
Congo	CongoWeb	www.congoweb.net
Congo, DRC	Congo-Pages	www.congo-pages.org
Costa Rica	Costa Rica Internet Directory	www.arweb.com/cr

Costa Rica	Costa Rica YellowWeb	www.yellowweb.co.cr
Côte d'Ivoire	Cote d'Ivoire Page	
	www.sas.upenn.edu/African_Studies/Country_Specific/Cote.html	
Croatia	Croatia Net	www.croatia.net
Cuba	Cuban Culture	www.cubanculture.com
Cuba	Open Doors' Country Profile on Cuba	www.gospelcom.net/od/cubapro.htm
Cyprus	Eureka! The Indexer of Cyprus	www.kypros.org/Eureka
Cyprus	Cyprus Home Page	www.kypros.org/Cyprus/root.html
Czech Republic	Orientation Czech Republic	www.cz.orientation.com
Czech Republic	Czech Info Center	www.muselik.com/czech/frame.html
Denmark	Denmark — an In-Depth Description of Denmark	www.um.dk/english/danmark
Denmark	Introduction: Denmark — the Basic Facts	www.lysator.liu.se/nordic/scn
Djibouti	STID — Djibouti Telecoms	www.intnet.dj
Dominica	Virtual Dominica	www.delphis.dm/home.htm
Dominican Republic	Dominican Republic Homepage	pegasus.cc.ucf.edu/~jtorres/domrep
Dominican Republic	Dominican Republic One	www.dr1.com
Ecuador	Ecuaworld	www.ecuaworld.com
Egypt	History of Christianity in Egypt	www.interoz.com/egypt/chiste0.htm
Egypt	Guardian's Egypt	www.guardians.net/egypt
El Salvador	Terra — El Salvador	www.terra.com.sv
El Salvador	Republica El Salvador	www.sv
Equatorial Guinea	Equatorial Guinea Page	
	www.sas.upenn.edu/African_Studies/Country_Specific/Eq_Guinea.html	
Eritrea	Eritrean Network Information Center	www.eritrea.org
Estonia	Estonia Country Guide	www.ciesin.ee/ESTCG
Estonia	Estonia-Wide Web	www.ee/www/welcome.html
Ethiopia	Cyber Ethiopia	www.cyberethiopia.com
Ethiopia	Ethiopian News	www.ethio.com
Falklands	Falkland Islands News Network	www.sartma.com
Fiji	Fiji Government Official Site	www.fiji.gov.fj
Fiji	Fiji Online	www.fiji-online.com.fj
Finland	Virtual Finland	virtual.finland.fi
Finland	Finland	www.siba.fi/finland.html
France	Francegate.com	www.francegate.com
French Polynesia	French Polynesia	www.polynesianislands.com/fp
Gabon	Gabon Interactif!	www.gabon-net.com
Gabon	Gabon Central	www.wadou.com/gabon
Gambia	Official Web Site of the Republic of Gambia	www.gambia.com
Gambia	Gambia News	www.gambianews.com
Gaza Strip	Gaza Strip Links	www.middlebury.edu/~gferguso/gaza.html
Georgia	GeREs — Georgian Resources on the Internet	www.nplg.gov.ge/geres
Georgia	Georgia Net	www.georgia.net.ge
Germany	Evangelical Alliance of Germany	www.ead.de
Germany	Sharelook	www.sharelook.de
Germany	ChrisNet	www.chrisnet.de
Ghana	Ghana Forum	www.ghanaforum.com
Gibraltar	Gibraltar Magazine Online	www.gibraltar.gi/gibmag
Greece	Hellenism Network	www.hellenism.net
Greece	Greekiosk	www.greekiosk.com
Greenland	Expo 2000 — Greenland	www.visitgreenland2000.gl
Greenland	Greenland Guide	www.greenland-guide.dk
Grenada	Grenada Explorer	www.grenadaexplorer.com
Guadeloupe	Consul-General of Guadeloupe	www.cg971.com
Guam	Official Guam Website	ns.gov.gu
Guatemala	Guatemala, the Quetzal's Land	www.serve.com/Mario_Villalta/guatengl.htm
Guatemala	Guatemalan Web Page Directory	mars.cropsoil.uga.edu/trop-ag/guatem.htm
Guinea	webGuinée	www.guinee.net

Guinea	FAQ about Republic of Guinea	
	www.boubah.com/Guineenews/GuineaFAQ.html	
Guinea-Bissau	Guinea-Bissau Page	
	www.sas.upenn.edu/African_Studies/Country_Specific/G_Bissau.html	
Guyana	Guyana News & Information	www.guyana.org
Guyana	Guyana Guide and News	www.guyanaguide.com
Haiti	Haiti Global Village	www.haitiglobalvillage.com
Haiti	Windows on Haiti	www.windowsonhaiti.com
Holy See	Vatican Facts	www.vaticanfacts.com
Honduras	Honduras Net	www.honduras.net
Honduras	Hondirectorio	www.hondirectorio.com
Hungary	Center for Culture and Communication	www.c3.hu
Hungary	The Hungary Page	www.hungary.org/users/hipcat
Iceland	Go Iceland	www.goiceland.org
Iceland	Millenium Celebration in Iceland	www.kristni.is
India	India Christian.com	www.indiachristian.com
India	India-Web	www.india-web.com
India	India Gospel Network	www.indiagospel.net
Indonesia	Indonesian Homepage	indonesia.elga.net.id
Indonesia	Muara Informasi Kristen	www.pesta.org
Iran	Open Doors' Country Profile on Iran	www.gospelcom.net/od/iranpro.htm
Iran	Iran Culture and Information Center	www.iranvision.com
Iran	CyberIran.com	www.cyberiran.com
Iraq	IraqNet	www.iraq.net
Iraq	Iraq4ever	www.welcome.to/iraq4ever
Ireland	Ireland Now	www.ireland-now.com
Ireland	Ireland's Portal	www.irelandsportal.com
Israel	SABRAnet	www.sabranet.com
Israel	Virtual Jerusalem	www.virtualjerusalem.com
Italy	Italian Ministries	www.csnet.it/femi
Italy	Windows on Italy	www.mi.cnr.it/WOI/woiindex.html
Jamaica	Jamaica Netlink.com	www.jamaica-netlink.com
Jamaica	Discover Jamaica	www.discoverjamaica.com
Japan	Mission Japan	www.missionjapan.org/e_index.html
Japan	All About Japan (LIFE Ministries)	www.lifejapan.org
Japan	Japan Information Network	www.jinjapan.org
Japan	Mission Japan Dot Com	www.missionjapan.com
Jordan	Baladna	www.baladna.com.jo
Kazakhstan	Kazakhstan Online	www.welcome.to/Kazakhstan
Kazakhstan	Welcome to Kazakhstan	www.kz/Firsteng3.htm
Kenya	Kenyalogy	www.kenyalogy.com
Kenya	Tim's and Laura Beth's Kenya Page	www.blissites.com/kenya
Kenya	Kenyaweb	www.kenyaweb.com
Kiribati	Kribati	www.trussel.com/f_kir.htm
Korea, North	DPRK — Democratic People's Republic of Korea	www.kimsoft.com/dprk.htm
Korea, North	Korean Central News Agency	www.kcna.co.jp
Korea, South	Korean Christian Internet Resources	member.aol.com/kcirkcir/index.htm
Korea, South	Korea History, Culture, Language	myhome.hananet.net/~mjssj
Korea, South	KOIS — Korean Information Service	www.kois.go.kr
Kuwait	Web Pages In and About Kuwait	www.kuwait.net
Kyrgyzstan	Kyrgyzstan: Business and Tourist Directory	www.geocities.com/TheTropics/Shores/7432
Kyrgyzstan	Kyrgyzstan	
	www.coyneair.com/useful_links/kyrgyzstan.htm	
Laos	Laos Infosite	www.ocf.berkeley.edu/~kongsab
Laos	Open Doors' Country Profile on Laos	www.gospelcom.net/od/laospro.htm
Latvia	Guide to Latvia	www.latnet.lv/guide2Latvia
Latvia	Virtual Latvia	www.vernet.lv/VT
Lebanon	Lebnet's Resource Center	www.lebnet.org

Lebanon	*Lebanon-Online*	www.lebanon-online.com.lb
Lesotho	*Lesotho Page*	
	www.sas.upenn.edu/African_Studies/Country_Specific/Lesotho.html	
Liberia	*Liberian Connection*	www.liberian-connection.com
Libya	*Libyana*	www.libyana.org
Libya	*Libya Resources on the Internet*	geocities.com/LibyaPage
Liechtenstein	*Liechtenstein Links*	
	www.cc.gatech.edu/gvu/people/Phd/Benjamin.Watson/links/liechtenstein.html	
Lithuania	*Lituanica.com — Lithuanian Web Directory*	www.lituanica.com
Lithuania	*Lithuanian Home Page*	neris.mii.lt
Luxembourg	*LuXPoint*	www.luxpoint.lu
Luxembourg	*Luxweb*	www.luxweb.lu
Macedonia	*Macedonian Cultural & Information Centre*	www.macedonia.co.uk
Macedonia	*Macedonia FAQ*	faq.macedonia.org
Madagascar	*Madagasikara: the Rainbow Island*	archive.dstc.edu.au/AU/staff/andry/Mada.html
Madagascar	*Madagascar — Up Close and Personal*	www.anthrotech.com/madagascar
Malawi	*Malawi*	
	www-sul.stanford.edu/depts/ssrg/africa/malawi.html	
Malaysia	*National Evangelical Christian Fellowship*	www.unityonline.com/necf
Malaysia	*Malaysian Christian Guide*	www.christian.com.my
Malaysia	*Malaysia Homepage*	www.mymalaysia.net.my
Maldives	*inMaldives.com*	www.inmaldives.com
Mali	*Mali*	
	www-sul.stanford.edu/depts/ssrg/africa/mali.html	
Malta	*Search Malta*	www.million1.com
Malta	*Malta Network Resources*	www.maltanetworkresources.com
Marshall Islands	*Bikini Atoll*	www.bikiniatoll.com
Martinique	*Martinique.org*	www.martinique.org
Mauritania	*Mauritania — Government Official Site*	www.mauritania.mr
Mauritius	*Ile-Maurice.com*	www.ile-maurice.com
Mauritius	*Mauritius Island On-Line*	www.maurinet.com
Mexico	*Open Doors' Country Profile on Mexico*	www.gospelcom.net/od/mexicpro.htm
Mexico	*Mexico Online*	www.mexicool.com
Micronesia	*Micronesia Center*	www.micronesia-center.com
Micronesia	*Federated States of Micronesia*	www.fm
Moldova	*Moldavian Web Directory*	www.inter.net.md
Monaco	*Brigitte's Pages — History of Monaco*	www.worldroots.com/brigitte/monaco.htm
Mongolia	*Mongolia Online*	www.mol.mn
Mongolia	*Oyunbilig's Great Mongol Home Page*	www.mongols.com
Montserrat	*Montserrat — the Emerald Isle*	www.ms
Morocco	*Welcome to Morocco*	www.mincom.gov.ma
Morocco	*House of Morocco*	www.maroc.net
Mozambique	*Mozambique*	
	www-sul.stanford.edu/depts/ssrg/africa/moz.html	
Mozambique	*Mozambique Home Page*	www.mozambique.mz
Myanmar	*Golden Land Myanmar*	www.myanmar.com
Myanmar	*Myanmar — Land of Pagodas*	triton.ori.u-tokyo.ac.jp/~moe/myanmar.html
Namibia	*M-web Namibia*	www.iwwn.com.na/iwwn
Namibia	*Namibia Ministry of Environment and Tourism Home Page*	www.iwwn.com.na/namtour
Nepal	*Window to Nepal*	www.cybermesa.com/~rotto
Nepal	*Nepal Pride*	www.nepalpride.homestead.com
Netherlands	*One Way — Christelijk Trefpunt*	www.oneway.nl
Netherlands	*Favoriet.nl*	www.favoriet.nl
Netherlands Antilles	*Netherlands Antilles*	www.gov.an
New Caledonia	*New Caledonia Home Page*	www.new-caledonia.com/eng.htm
New Zealand	*NewZealand.com*	www.newzealand.com
New Zealand	*Centre for Mission Direction*	www.cmd.org.nz
New Zealand	*Vision Net*	www.vision-nz.co.nz

APPENDIX 2   726

Nicaragua	*Nicaragua's TravelNet*	www.centralamerica.com/nicaragua
Nicaragua	*Experience Nicaragua*	library.thinkquest.org/17749
Niger	*Focus on Niger*	www.txdirect.net/users/jmayer/fon.html
Nigeria	*Nigerian Nation*	www.aghadiuno.atfreeweb.com
Nigeria	*Nigeria.com*	www.nigeria.com
Niue	*Niue — Rock of Polynesia*	www.niueisland.com
Norway	*Info Norway*	
	www.geocities.com/Yosemite/1145/norway.html	
Norway	*Norwegian Scenery.com*	www.norwegian-scenery.com
Oman	Sultanate of Oman Home Page	members.tripod.com/~omanpage
Oman	*Julands Omani Oasis*	www.geocities.com/Heartland/Acres/2692
Pakistan	*Adil Najam's Tour-de-Pakistan*	www.mit.edu/people/anajam/pakistan.html
Pakistan	*ePakistan.com*	www.epakistan.com
Palestine Authority	*Complete Guide to Palestine's Websites*	www.birzeit.edu/links
Palestine Authority	*Palestine-Net*	www.palestine-net.com
Panama	*PanamaInfo*	www.panamainfo.com
Panama	*Focus on Panama*	www.coralys.com/panama
Papua New Guinea	Papua New Guinea Net Search	www.pngnetsearch.com
Papua New Guinea	P*apua New Guinea Online*	www.niugini.com
Paraguay	*Absolutely Unofficial Homepage of Paraguay*	www.eskimo.com/~krautm
Peru	*Peru 2000*	www.intinet.com/peru2000
Peru	*Open Doors' Country Profile on Peru*	www.gospelcom.net/od/perupro.htm
Philippines	*Philippines by Rochelle*	members.aol.com/atinyrock
Philippines	*Yehey*	www.yehey.com
Poland	*Poland Online*	www.polandonline.com
Poland	*Polish World*	www.polishworld.com
Portugal	*Top 5% Portugal*	www.ip.pt/top5/main.html
Portugal	*A Collection of Home Pages About Portugal*	www.well.com/user/ideamen/portugal.html
Puerto Rico	*Welcome to Puerto Rico!*	welcome.topuertorico.org
Puerto Rico	*Wepa! Search Puerto Rico!*	www.wepa.com
Qatar	*Qatar Info Magazine*	www.qatar-info.com
Qatar	*Ministry of Foreign Affairs — Qatar*	www.mofa.gov.qa
Romania	*RomaniaByNET*	www.romaniabynet.com
Romania	*Romanian Voice*	www.romanianvoice.com
Russia	*Russia Religion News*	www.stetson.edu/~psteeves/relnews
Russia	*Russia Alive!*	www.alincom.com/russ
Russia	*Russia Intercessory Prayer Network*	www.ripnet.org
Rwanda	*Rwanda Information Exchange*	www.rwanda.net
Sahara	*ARSO — Association for the Referendum of*	www.arso.org
	Western Sahara	
Samoa	*Pacific Encounters*	www.merriewood.com/pacific
Samoa	*Planet Samoa*	www.planet-samoa.com
San Marino	*Republic of San Marino*	www.inthenet.sm/homepage.htm
Sâo Tomé	*Welcome to Sâo Tomé e Príncipe*	www.sao-tome.com
Sâo Tomé	*Sâo Tomé e Príncipe Homepage*	www.stome.com
Saudi Arabia	*Open Doors' Country Profile on Saudi Arabia*	www.gospelcom.net/od/saudipro.htm
Saudi Arabia	*Saudi Arabia Internet Pages*	www.saudi-pages.com
Saudi Arabia	*Saudi Arabia Information Resource*	www.saudinf.com
Senegal	*Senegal Online*	www.senegal-online.com
Senegal	*Earth2000.com — the Resource for*	www.earth2000.com
	Everything Senegalese	
Seychelles	*Worldskip — Seychelles*	www.worldskip.com/seychelles
Sierra Leone	*Sierra Leone Community*	home5.swipnet.se/~w-59204
Sierra Leone	*Sierra Leone Web*	www.sierra-leone.org
Singapore	*Antioch*	www.antioch.com.sg
Singapore	*Singapore Christians' Directory*	web.singnet.com.sg/~timotan/christ.htm
Slovakia	*Slovakia.org*	www.slovakia.org
Slovakia	*Slovakia Document Store*	slovakia.eunet.sk

Slovenia	Internet Resources on Slovenia	www.ssees.ac.uk/slovenia.htm
Slovenia	Slovenia Tourist Information	www.slovenia-tourism.si
Solomon Islands	Solomon Islands Home Page	www.solomons.com
Somalia	ACG Somalia Page	ww.abyssiniacybergateway.net/somaliaSomalia
	Links to Somalia Information	
	www.antro.uu.se/staff/bernhela//Somalia.html	
South Africa	Christians in South Africa	www.christians.co.za
South Africa	South Africa — An Overview	www.gov.za/sa_overview
Spain	Sí Spain	www.sispain.org
Spain	Alianza Evangélica Española	www.lander.es/~aee
Sri Lanka	Open Doors' Country Profile on Sri Lanka	www.gospelcom.net/od/srilanpro.htm
Sri Lanka	Lanka Online	lankaonline.com
St. Helena	St-Helena-Island.net	www.st-helena-island.net
St. Lucia	Saint Lucia — A Guided Tour	geoffray.schmitt.free.fr
St. Pierre & Miquelon	St. Pierre and Miquelon	www.st-pierre-et-miquelon.com
St. Vincent	Welcome to St. Vincent and the Grenadines	www.vincy.com
Sudan	Sudan 101	www.sudan101.com
Sudan	Sudan Net	www.sudan.net
Suriname	Home Page for Suriname	www.sr.net/srnet/InfoSurinam
Suriname	Surinam.net	www.surinam.net
Svalbard	Svalbard Pages	www.svalbard.com
Swaziland	Swazi.com	www.realnet.co.sz
Swaziland	Swaziland Page	www.pitt.edu/~tgsst10/swaziland.E.html
Sweden	Swedish Information Smorgasbord	www.sverigeturism.se/smorgasbord
Sweden	Swedish Christian Link Collection	www.makarios.nu/sv
Switzerland	Swiss Evangelical Alliance	www.each.ch
Switzerland	Open Directory Project Switzerland	www.dmoz.ch
Syria	Syria — The Cradle of Civilizations	www.syria.arabicnet.com
Syria	Café-Syria	www.cafe-syria.com
Tajikistan	Travel Tajikistan	www.traveltajikistan.com
Tajikistan	Tajikistan Update	www.angelfire.com/sd/tajikistanupdate
Tanzania	INCORE Guide — Conflict & Ethnicity in Tanzania	
	www.incore.ulst.ac.uk/cds/countries/tanzania.html	
Tanzania	Official Website of Tanzania	www.tanzania-online.gov.uk
	High Commission London	
Thailand	Amazing Thailand	www.thaifile.com
Thailand	Thai Worship Network	www.universalontime.com/worship
Timor Leste	East Timor Internet Resources	www.uc.pt/timor/netret.htm
Togo	Togo Contact	www.refer.org/togo_ct/accueil.htm
Togo	Republic of Togo Official Home Page	www.afrika.com/togo
Tonga	Planet Tonga	www.planet-tonga.com
Trinidad & Tobago	Trinbago.com	www.trinbago.com
Tunisia	Pagetunisie — Home of the Tunisian Expatriate	www.pagetunisie.com
Tunisia	Tunisia Online	www.tunisiaonline.com
Turkey	Türkiye on the Web — A Cultural Warehouse	www.columbia.edu/~sss31/Turkiye
Turkey	All About Turkey	www.balsoy.com/Turkiye
Turkmenistan	Turkmenistan Information Center	www.turkmenistan.com
Turkmenistan	Guide to Turkmenistan	www.icctm.org/turk_noframe.html
Turks & Caicos Is	Turks & Caicos Islands Gateway	www.turksandcaicos.tc
Tuvalu	Tuvalu Online	members.nbci.com/tuvaluonline/index.htm
Uganda	Uganda	www.uganda.co.ug
Uganda	Uganda Online National Information Center	www.nic.ug
Ukraine	Ukrainian Language, Culture, and Travel Page	pages.prodigy.net/l.hodges/ukraine.htm
Ukraine	InfoUkes	www.infoukes.com
United Arab Emirates	UAE Forever	www.uaeforever.com
United Arab Emirates	United Arab Emirates Internet Pages	www.uae-pages.com
United Kingdom	Kingdom Search	www.kingdomsearch.co.uk
United Kingdom	UK Christian Handbook	www.ukchristianhandbook.org.uk
United Kingdom	Great British Pages	www.great-british-pages.co.uk

United Kingdom	Evangelical Alliance UK	www.eauk.org
United States	Goshen.net	www.goshen.net
United States	Ethnic Harvest	www.ethnicharvest.org
United States	National Association of Evangelicals — USA	www.nae.net
United States	Crosswalk	www.crosswalk.com
Uruguay	República Oriental del Uruguay	www.presidencia.gub.uy
Uzbekistan	Freenet Uzbekistan	www.freenet.uz
Uzbekistan	Open Doors' Country Profile on Uzbekistan	www.gospelcom.net/od/uzbekpro.htm
Vanuatu	Vanuatu Online	www.vanuatu.net.vu
Venezuela	Venezuela Online	www.venezuelaonline.com/new
Venezuela	Auyantepui — Venezuela en la Web	www.auyantepui.com
Vietnam	Vietnam Culture and Information	www.vnnews.com/coci
Vietnam	Open Doors' Country Profile on Vietnam	www.gospelcom.net/od/vietpro.htm
Virgin Is of the USA	About the USVI	www.antillesresorts.com/
Yemen	Arabia Online	www.yemen-online.com
Yemen	Republic of Yemen — Ministry of Information	www.yemeninfo.gov.ye
Yugoslavia	Kosovo for Christiana	www.uea.ac.uk/~f709762/kosovo/kosovo.htm
Yugoslavia	Yugoslavia Today	www.centraleurope.com/yugoslaviatoday
Yugoslavia	Federal Republic of Yugoslavia	www.gov.yu
Zambia	Zambia Online	www.zambia.co.zm
Zambia	Zamnet	www.zamnet.zm
Zimbabwe	Zimbabwe — NewAfrica.com	www.newafrica.com/zimbabwe
Zimbabwe	ZimWEB	www.mother.com/~zimweb
Geography	World Missions Atlas Project	www.worldmap.org
Languages	Ethnologue: Languages of the World	www.sil.org/ethnologue
Languages	Human Languages Page	www.june29.com/HLP
Missions	Christian Missions Home Page (SIM)	www.sim.org
Missions	Mission Frontiers	www.missionfrontiers.org
Missions	MIssion Review	www.missionreview.com
MIssions	Network for Strategic Missions	www.strategicnetwork.org
Missiology	Lausanne Occasional Papers	www.gospelcom.net/lcwe/LOP
News	Religion Today	www.religiontoday.com
Peoples	UNPO — Unrepresented Nations and Peoples Organization	www.unpo.org
Peoples	Joshua Project	www.joshuaproject.net
Peoples	PeopleTeamss	www.peopleteams.org
Peoples	Unreached Peoples Prayer Profiles	www.bethany.com/profiles/home.html
Peoples	Nomadic Peoples Network www.globalconnections.co.uk/groups_details.asp?ID=16	
Persecution	International Day of Prayer for the Persecuted Ch	www.persecutedchurch.org
Persecution	Open Doors International	www.gospelcom.net/od
Persecution	Voice of the Martyrs	www.vom.org
Persecution	Compass Direct	www.compassdirect.org
Persecution	Barnabas Fund	http://www.barnabasfund.org/
Persecution	Forum18	http://www.forum18.org/
Persecution	World Evangelical Alliance - Religious Freedom Commission http://www.WorldEvangelical.org/rlc.html	
Religions	World Religions Index	www.wri.leaderu.com
Religions	The Religious Movements Homepage	www.religiousmovements.org
Religions	Internet Sacred Text Archive	www.sacred-texts.com/index.htm

• APPENDIX 2 •
C • PRAYER NETWORKS

Visit these websites to link up with other intercessors. This is only a selection of those networks known to us – there are undoubtedly several more. They cover a wide range of focuses and theological perspectives.

NAME	WEBSITE/EMAIL ADDRESS	FOCUS
24-7 Prayer	www.24-7prayer.com	Youth specific; global 24 hour a day prayer
Charisma News Email	www.charismanews.com	
Generals of Intercession	www.generals.org <generals@generals.org>	Spiritual Warfare
Global Harvest Ministries	www.globalharvest.org <info@globalharvest.org>	40/70 Window/ Spiritual Warfare
International House of Prayer	www.ihopkc.com/default2.htm <info@ihopkc.com>	24 Hour a Day Intercessory Worship
Joel News International	www.joelnews.org <mvdwoude@xs4all.nl>	
National Pastor's Prayer Network	www.nppn.org <Updates@nppn.org>	Pastor's prayer groups; global
National Prayer	www.nationalprayer.org <natlpray@aol.com>	USA and World
NUPSA	www.nupsa.co.za <nupsa@global.co.za>	Africa
Pray! magazine (Navigators)	www.navpress.com/praymag.asp	
PrayerWave Asia	PrayerWaveAsia@pacific.net.sg	
PrayWORLD (CCCI)	www.prayworld.org	Global
U.S. Prayer Center	www.usprayercenter.org <usprayercenter@cs.com>	Discipling the nations in prayer
WEF's Religious Liberty E-mail Conference	www.WorldEvangelical.org	

• APPENDIX 3 •
MISSION AGENCIES

Selected agency details are given in this Appendix. Two categories are given – Interdenominational Inter-mission agencies and also 113 specific mission agencies. The final section of this Appendix gives some information on the number of workers and major fields of these agencies. There is more information on several thousand agencies on the CD version.

A • INTERDENOMINATIONAL INTER-MISSION AGENCIES

Significant national, regional and international evangelical bodies are given below as representative of the many in existence. Most are in English-speaking countries, but a small number of non-English-speaking bodies are also given. Many provide regular prayer information. Where known, both their addresses and website/email details are given.

Global

GCR	**Great Commission Roundtable**	www.gcroundtable.net
	800 W. Chestnut, Monrovia, CA 91016, USA	
LCWE	**Lausanne Committee for World Evangelism**	www.gospelcom.net/lcwe
	PO Box 661029, Arcadia, CA 91066, USA	
WEA	**World Evangelical Alliance (formerly WEF)**	www.worldevangelical.org
	PO Box WEF, Wheaton, IL 60189, USA	

Africa

AEA	**Association of Evangelicals of Africa**	www.worldevangelical.org
	PO Box 49332, Nairobi, Kenya	

Asia

EFA	**Evangelical Fellowship of Asia**	www.worldevangelical.org
	Victoria Chambers 2nd Flr., 4-1-826 J N Rd, Hyderabad, Andrhra Pradesh 500001, India	

Australia

AEA	**Australian Evangelical Alliance**	
www.evangelicalalliance.org.au		
	PO Box 175, Box Hill VIC 3128	

Brazil

AMTB	*Associação de Missões Transculturais Brasileiras*	www.infobrasil.org/amtb
	Caixa Postal 6101, 70749-970 Brasília-DF	
COMIBAM	**Brazilian Association of Missions**	
	Caixa Postal 21468, 04620-970 São Paulo, SP	

Caribbean

EAC	**Evangelical Association of the Caribbean**	www.worldevangelical.org
	41 Elizabeth Park (2), Worthing W9, Barbados	

Europe

EEA	**European Evangelical Alliance**	http://www.europeanea.org/
	European Evangelical Alliance, 186 Kennington Park Road London, SE11 4BT, United Kingdom	
TEMA	**The European Missionary Association**	www.mission.org
	Eendrachtstr. 33, 3784 KA Terschuur, The Netherlands	

Germany

AEM	*Arbeitsgemeinschaft Evangelikaler Missionen*	www.aem.de
	Hindenburgstr. 36, 70825 Korntal	

Hong Kong

HKACM	Hong Kong Association of Christian Missions	www.hkacm.org.hk
	PO Box 71728, Kowloon CPO	

India

CONS	Council on National Service	<hbi@vsnl.com>
	86-89 Medavakkam Tank Road, Kilpauk, Tamil Nadu — 600 010	
EFI	Evangelical Fellowship of India	<efiindia@del2.vsnl.net.in>
	803/92 Deepali, Nehru Place, New Delhi – 110 019	
IMA	India Missions Association	www.imamissions.org
	48 First Main Road, East Shenoy Nagar, Chennai – 600 030	
AICC	All India Christian Council	www.indianchristians.org
	79/B Flr. 1&2 Street No.8, West Marredpally, Secunderabad – 500 026	

Netherlands

EZA	*Evangelische Alliante*	www.eanl.nl
	Hoofdstr. 51a, 3971 KB, Driebergen	

Nigeria

NEMA	Nigeria Evangelical Missions Association	www.urbanonramps.com/nema/
	PO Box 5878, Jos	www.NigeriaMissions.org

Pacific

EFSP	Evangelical Fellowship of the South Pacific	www.worldevangelical.org
	PO Box 2311, Mansfield DC, QLD 4122, Australia	

Philippines

ACM	Asian Center for Missions
	4th Flr, Sagittarius Bldg., H.V. dela Costa St.,
	Salcedo Village Makati 1227
PCEC	Philippine Council of Evangelical Churches, Inc.
	62 Molave St., Project 3, Quezon City

Singapore

EFS	Evangelical Fellowship of Singapore
	490 Upper Bukit Timah Road, Sing. 678093
SCEM	Singapore Centre for Evangelism and Mission
	Raffles CPO Box 1052, Sing. 911736

South Africa

TEASA	The Evangelical Alliance of South Africa
	PO Box 1751, Johannesburg 2000
WENSA	World Evangelisation Network — South Africa
	PO Box 30221, Sunnyside 0132

United Kingdom

GC	Global Connections	www.globalconnections.co.uk
	186 Kennington Park Road, London, SE11 4BT	

United States

AAPC	Adopt-A-People Clearinghouse	www.aapc.net
	PO Box 63600, Colorado Springs, CO 80962-3600	
ACMC	Advancing Churches in Missions Commitment	www.acmc.org
	4201 N. Peachtree Road, Suite 300, Atlanta, GA 30341	
AIMS	Association of International Mission Services	
	PO Box 64534, Virginia Beach, VA 23464	
EFMA	Evangelical Fellowship of Mission Agencies	
	4201 N. Peachtree Rd. #300, Atlanta, GA 30341-1207	
IFMA	Interdenominational Foreign Mission Association	www.ifmamissions.org
	PO Box 398, Wheaton, IL 60189-0398	
MARC-WV	Missions Advanced Research & Communications Center	www.wvi.org

• APPENDIX 3 •
B • MISSION AGENCIES

Bold type abbreviations of mission agencies are given below, together with contact addresses (292 of them) and websites.

We have carefully selected 113 evangelical mission agencies with the size, range of ministries or uniqueness, that are representative of the nearly 3,000 agencies that are listed in our database. These 113 agencies had nearly 109,000 workers in 2000/01, which is over half of all P, I and A missionaries we could identify.

Please refer to the last section of Appendix 3 for the worker statistics and major fields/ministries of these agencies.

We have grouped together similar missions from different countries even if there is no direct organizational link; for instance AoG, ISI, Brethren, GRN.

ABMS **(Global interAction) Australian Baptist Missionary Society**
    Aust.   PO Box 273, Hawthorn, VIC 3122   www.globalinteraction.org.au

ABWE **Association of Baptists for World Evangelism**   www.abwe.org
    USA   PO Box 8585, Harrisburg, PA 17105

AE **African Enterprise, Inc.**
    S.Afr.   Box 13140, Cascades 3202   www.africanenterprise.org.za
    UK   Victoria House, Victoria Rd.,
        Buckhurst Hill, IG9 5EX
    USA   Box 727, Monrovia, CA 91017   www.africanenterprise.org

AEF **Asia Evangelistic Fellowship**
    Sing.   # 68 Lorong 16 Geylang, Association
        Building #05-07, Sing. 398889
    Aust.   PO Box 122, Epping, NSW 1710   www.aefi.org.au
    India   Romm 10 Bhavana, 422 V.S.Marg,
        Phabhadevi, Mumbai, India 400025

AFM **Anglican Frontier Missions**   www.AFM-25.org
    USA   PO Box 18038, Richmond, VA 23226

AIM **AIM International**
    Aust.   PO Box 744, Castle Hill, NSW 1765
    Canada 1641 Victoria Park Ave., Scarborough,   www.aimcanada.org
        ON M1R 1P8
    S.Afr.   Box 109, Plumstead 7800
    UK   Halifax Place, Nottingham NG1 1QN   www.aimeurope.net
    USA   PO Box 178, Pearl River, NY 10965   www.aim-us.org

AM **Antioch Mission (Brazil)**
    Brazil   Missão Antioquia, Caixa. Postal 275,
        Sao Roque — SP, BRAZIL CEP. 18.130

AoG **Assemblies of God**
    USA   1445 N. Boonville Avenue,   www.ag.org
        Springfield, MO 65802
    Aust.   PO Box 336, Mitcham, VIC 3132
    NZ   PO Box 74-138, Auckland   www.agnz.org
    UK   Hook Place, Burgess Hill   www.aog.world.ministries.org.uk
        West Sussex, RH15 8RF

AOI **Asian Outreach International**
    HK   Int'l HQ, GPO Box 3448   www.asianoutreach.org
    Aust.   PO Box 167, Seacliff Park, SA 5049
    Canada PO Box 1422, Peterborough, ON K9J 7H6   www.asianoutreach.ca
    NZ   PO Box 2160, Tauranga, 3000   www.asianoutreach.org.nz
    Sing.   Robinson Road, PO Box 3568   www.antioch.com.sg/mission

| | **UK** | PO Box 789, Sutton Coldfield, West Midlands, B74 2XJ |
| | **USA** | 305 NE 192nd Avenue, Vancouver, WA 98684S |

AP   **Action Partners**
Aust. PO Box 6532, Baulkham Hills, NSW 2153
UK   Bawtry Hall, Bawtry, Doncaster,   www.actionpartners.org.uk
        South Yorkshire, DN10 6JH

AWM **Arab World Ministries**   www.awm.org
UK   PO Box 51, Loughborough, LE11 0ZQ
Canada PO Box 3398, Cambridge, ON N3H 4T3
USA   PO Box 96, Upper Darby, PA 19082

BBF   **Baptist Bible Fellowship International**   www.bbfimissions.com
USA   PO Box 191, Springfield, MO 65801

BCWM **Brethren in Christ World Missions**
USA   PO Box 390, Grantham, PA 17027   www.bic-church.org/wm
Canada 2619 Niagara Parkway, Fort Erie, ON L2A 5M4

BEM   **Belgian Evangelical Mission**   www.b-e-m.org
Belg. Bld Lambermont 158, B-1030 Brussels

BFM   **Bethany Fellowship Missions**   www.bethfel.org
USA   6820 Auto Club Road, Suite D, Bloomington, MN 55438

BMM **Baptist Mid-Missions**   www.bmm.org
USA   7749 Webster Road, Cleveland, OH 44130-8011

BMS   **BMS World Mission**   www.bms.org.uk
UK   PO Box 49, 129 Broadway, Didcot, OX11 8XA

C   **Crosslinks**   www.crosslinks.org
UK   251 Lewisham Way, London, SE4 1XF

Ch   **Christar** (previously **International Missions, Inc.**)
Canada Box 20164, St. Catharines, ON L2M 7W7 www.intermissions.org
USA   PO Box 14866, Reading, PA 19612-4866 www.christar.org

CAMI **CAM International**   www.caminternational.org
USA   8625 La Prada Dr., Dallas, TX 75228

CB   **Christian Brethren Assemblies**
Aust. Australian Missionary Tidings (CMML), PO Box 125, Eastwood, NSW 2122
Canada MSC, 509-3950 14th Avenue, Markham, www.msc.on.ca
        ON L3R 0A9
NZ   Missionary Services New Zealand, PO Box 744, Palmerston North
UK   Echoes of Service, 1 Widcombe Crescent, www.echoes.org.uk
        Bath, Avon, BA2 6AQ
USA   CMML, Inc., PO Box 13, Spring Lake, NJ 07762-0013

CBI   **CB International**   www.cbi.org
USA   1501 W. Mineral Ave, Littleton, CO 80120

CBIM **Canadian Baptist International Ministries** www.cbmin.org
Canada 7185 Millcreek Drive, Mississauga, ON L5N 5R4

CBM **Christian Blind Mission International**
Canada PO Box 800, Stouffville, ON L4A 7Z9   www.cbmi-can.org
USA   PO Box 19000, Greenville, SC 29602   www.cbmi-usa.org

CCCI **Campus Crusade for Christ International**
USA   100 Lake Hart Drive, Orlando, FL 32832   www.ccci.org
Canada PO Box 300, Stn. A, Vancouver, BC V6C 2X3   www.crusade.org
UK   Agapé Ministries Ltd., Fairgate House,   www.agape.org.uk
               Kings Rd, Tyseley, Birmingham, B11 2AA

CEF **Child Evangelism Fellowship**
USA   PO Box 348, Warrenton, MO 63383   www.cefinc.org
Canada PO Box 165, Winnipeg, MB R3C 2G9   www.cefcanada.org
Switz.   Kilchzimmer, CH-4438 Langenbruck   www.cefinc.org/europe
UK   64 Osborne Road, Levenshulme,
               Manchester, M19 2DY

CLC **CLC International**
UK   291 Abbeydale Road, Sheffield, S7 2LE   www.clc.org.uk
Aust.   PO Box 213, Bungalow, Cairns, QLD 4870   www.clci.com.au
USA   PO Box 1449, Fort Washington, PA 19034   www.clcusa.org

CM **Calvary Ministries (CAPRO)**
Nigeria PO Box 22104, Ibadan

CMA **Christian & Missionary Alliance**
USA   PO Box 35000, Colorado Springs, CO 80935   www.cmalliance.org
Aust.   PO Box 336, Curtin, ACT 2605
Canada PO Box 7900, Willowdale, ON M2K 2R6   www.cmacan.org
UK   10 Alpha Avenue, Garsington,
               Oxford, OX44 9BQ

CMF **Christian Missionary Foundation**   www.cmfmissions.org
Nigeria UIPO Box 9890, Ibadan, Oyo State

CMJ **Church's Ministry among Jewish People**   www.cmj.org.uk
UK   30c Clarence Road, St. Albans, AL1 4JJ

CMS **Church Mission Society**
UK   Partnership House, 157 Waterloo Road,   www.cms-uk.org
               London, SE1 8UU
Aust.   93 Bathurst Street, Sydney, NSW 2000
NZ   CMS and SAMS,   www.nzcms.org.nz
               167 Wairakei Rd, Christchurch, 8005

COCM **Chinese Overseas Christian Mission**   www.cocm.org.uk
UK   PO Box 5240, Brinklow, Milton Keynes,
               MK6 2YY

CoGWM **Church of God World Missions**   www.cogwm.org
USA   P.O.Box 8016, Cleveland, TN 37320

CoN **Church of the Nazarene**   www.nazarene.org/wm
USA   6401 The Paseo, Kansas City, MO 64131

CRWM **Christian Reformed World Missions**   www.crwm.org
USA   2850 Kalamazoo Avenue, SE.,
               Grand Rapids, MI 49560

CWI **Christian Witness to Israel**
UK   166 Main Rd, Sundridge, Sevenoaks   www.cwi.org.uk
               TN14 6EL
NZ   PO Box 6455, Auckland

DAWN Dawn Ministries www.dawnministries.org
USA 5775 North Union Blvd.,
Colorado Springs, CO 80918

DM Dorothea Mission
S.Afr. PO Box 911-024, Rosslyn 0200

ECM European Christian Mission www.ecmi.org
UK 50 Billing Road, Northampton, NN1 5DH
Aust./NZ PO Box 15, Croydon, NSW 2132, Australia
Canada 1077 56th Street, Suite 226, Delta, BC V4L 2A2
USA PO Box 1006, Point Roberts, WA 98281

EF Elim Fellowship www.frontiernet.net/~elim/
USA PO Box 57A, Lima, NY 14485

EHC Every Home for Christ
USA PO Box 35950, Colorado Springs, CO 80935

ELAM Elam Ministries
UK Grenville, Grenville Rd., Shackleford,
Godalming, GU8 6AX

EMS Evangelical Missionary Society of West Africa (ECWA)
Nigeria PO Box 63, Jos, Plateau State

F Frontiers www.frontiers.org
USA 325 N. Stapley Drive, Mesa, AZ 85203
Switz. PO Box 351, 9424 Rheineck, CH-9424
UK PO Box 600, Hemel Hempstead, HP3 9UG

FEBA Feba www.feba.org.uk
UK Ivy Arch Road, Worthing, BN14 8BX
S.Afr. PO Box 21768, Helderkruin 1733

FEBC Far East Broadcasting Company www.febc.org
Aust. PO Box 183, Caringbah, NSW 1495
NZ PO Box 4140, Hamilton, 2032
USA PO Box 1, La Mirada, CA 90637

FFM Fellowship of Faith for Muslims
UK PO Box 5864, Basildon, Essex, SS13 3FF
Canada PO Box 65214, Toronto, ON M4K 3Z2 www.ffmna.org

FMPB Friends Missionary Prayer Band
India 110 Baracah Road, Kilpauk, Chennai 600010

GEM Greater Europe Mission www.gemission.org
USA 18950 Base Camp Rd, Monument, CO 80132
Canada 100 Ontario Street, Oshawa, ON L1G 4Z1

GFA Gospel for Asia www.gfa.org
USA 1800 Golden Trail Court, Carrollton, TX 75010

GMU Avant Ministries (formerly Gospel Missionary Union) www.avantministries.org
USA 10000 N. Oak Trafficway, Kansas City,
MO 64155
Canada 2121 Henderson Highway, Winnipeg, MB R2G 1P8

GRN Global Recordings Network www.gospelrecordings.com
Aust. Language Recordings Inc., Private Mail Bag 19,
Castle Hill, NSW 1765
Canada Language Recordings Int'l, 120 Lancing Dr.,
Unit #6, Hamilton, ON L8W 3A1
India GR Associates, 7/4 Commissariat Rd, Bangalore 560025

Kenya Language Recordings Int'l, PO Box 21244, Nairobi
Nigeria GR Nigeria, PMB 2201 Jos, Plateau State
Phil. GR, PO Box 40, Valenzuela City, Phil. 1469
Sing. GR, PO Box 512, Serangoon Central, Sing. 9155
S.Afr. Good News Media, PO Box 269,   www.bmedia.co.za/gnm
Wellington 7654
UK Language Recordings UK, PO Box 197,
High Wycombe, HP14 3YY
USA GR USA, 41823 Enterprise Circle N. Temecula, CA 92590

HCJB   **HCJB World Radio**   www.hcjb.org
UK   131 Grattan Road, Bradford, BD1 2HS
USA   PO Box 39800, Colorado Springs, CO 80949

I   **Interserve**   www.interserve.org
UK   325 Kennington Road, London, SE11 4QH
Aust.   PO Box 231, Bayswater, VIC 3153
Canada 10 Huntingdale Blvd., Scarborough, ON M1W 2S5
NZ   PO Box 10-244, Auckland, 1030
USA   PO Box 418, Upper Darby, PA 19082

IA   **InterAct — Nybygget-Kristen samverkan**
Sweden Olaig 4, Box 1624, 701 16 Örebro

IBRA   **International Broadcasting Association**   www.ibra.org
Sweden PO Box 4033, SE-141 04, Huddinge

IBT   **Institute for Bible Translation**   www.IBTnet.org
Sweden Box 20100, S-104 60 Stockholm
UK   PO Box 6481, Colchester, Essex, CO4 3AF

IEM   **Indian Evangelical Mission**
India   38 Langford Rd, Bangalore — 560025

IET   **Indian Evangelical Team**   www.pgv.com
India   126 Andheri Modh, Mehrauli,
New Delhi 110030

IFES   **International Fellowship of Evangelical Students**
UK   321 Banbury Rd., Oxford, OX2 7JZ   www.ifesworld.org
NZ   PO Box 9672, Wellington, 6031   www.surf.to/tscf
Aust.   PO Box 684, Kingsford, NSW 2032   www.afes.org.au
USA   PO Box 7895, Madison, WI 53707   www.gospelcom.net/iv

IMI   **International Missions, Inc. (**See **Ch.)**

INF   **International Nepal Fellowship**   www.inf.org.np
Aust.   PO Box 602, Wahroonga, NSW 2076
NZ   PO Box 91731, AMSC Auckland
UK   69 Wentworth Road, Harborne,   www.inf.org.uk
Birmingham, W Midlands, B17 9SS

ISI   **International Students Incorporated**
USA   PO Box C, Colorado Springs, CO 80901   www.isionline.org
UK   Friends International, 3 Crescent Stables,   www.friendsinternational.org.uk
139 Upper Richmond Rd, London, SW15 2TN

IT   **International Teams**   www.iteams.org
Canada 1 Union St., Elmira, ON N3B 3J9
USA   411 W. River Rd., Elgin, IL 60123

JEB   **Japan Evangelistic Band (**See **JCL)**

JCL	**Japan Christian Link**	www.jclglobal.org

JCL   **Japan Christian Link**   www.jclglobal.org
Aust.   Suite 316 Robina Town Centre,
        Robina, QLD 4230
Germ.   Goertzallee 105, Berlin 12207
UK   PO Box 68, Sevenoaks, Kent, TN13 2ZY
USA   PO Box 33201, Seattle, WA 98133
Japan   JEB, 32-15, 6 Chome, Shioya Cho,
        Tarumi Ku, Kobe 655-0872, Hyogo-ken

JFJ   **Jews for Jesus**   www.jewsforjesus.org
USA   60 Haight Street, San Francisco, CA 94102

LAM   **Latin America Mission**   www.lam.org
Canada 3075 Ridgeway Drive, Unit #14,
        Mississauga, ON L5L 5M6
USA   PO Box 52-7900, 5465 NW 36th Street,
        Miami, FL 33152-7900

LCMS   **Lutheran Church Missouri Synod Board for Missions**
USA   1333 S. Kirkwood Road, St. Louis,   www.lcms.org
        MO 63122-7295

LL   **Latin Link**   www.latinlink.org
UK   175 Tower Bridge Road, London, SE1 2AB

LM   **Liebenzell Mission**
Germ.   Postfach 1240, 75375 Bad Liebenzell   www.liebenzell.org
Canada R.R. #1, Moffat, ON L0P 1J0   www.liebenzell.ca
USA   PO Box 66, Schooley's Mtn., NJ 07870

MAF   **Mission Aviation Fellowship**
Aust.   PO Box 211, Box Hill, VIC 3128
Canada PO Box 368, Guelph, ON N1H 6K5
S. Afr.   PO Box 1688, Edenvale, 1610
UK   Henwood, Ashford, Kent, TN24 8DH   www.maf-uk.org
USA   PO Box 3202, Redlands, CA 92373-0998   www.maf.org

MECO   **Middle East Christian Outreach**   www.gospelcom.net/meco
Aust.   PO Box 1286, Burwood, NSW 1805
Canada PO Box 23555, Brampton, ON L6V 4J4
UK   22 Culverden Park Road, Tunbridge Wells, Kent, TN4 9RA
USA   PO Box 531151, Indianapolis, IN 46253-1151

MT   **The Messianic Testimony**
UK   93 Axe St., Barking, Essex, IG11 7LZ   www.charitynet.org/
S.Afr.   PO Box 23749, Claremont, Cape 7735

MTW   **Mission to the World**
USA   1600 North Brown Road, Lawrenceville, GA 30043

N   **Navigators**
Aust.   GPO Box 4636TT, Melbourne, VIC 3001   www.navigators.org.au
Canada Box 27070, London, ON N5X 3X5   www.navigators.ca
NZ   PO Box 5344, Papanui, Christchurch 8030
USA   PO Box 6000, Colorado Springs, CO 80934   www.navigators.org
UK   Adyar House, 32 Carlton Crescent,
        Southampton, SO15 2EW

NGK   **Nederduitse Gereformeerde Kerk**
S.Afr.   Box 19, Bloemfontein 9300

NTM   **New Tribes Mission**
Aust.   Box 84, Rooty Hill, NSW 2766
Canada PO Box 707, Durham, ON N0G 1R0   www.ntmc.ca

	UK	Derby Rd, Matlock Bath, Matlock, Derbyshire, DE4 3PY	www.ntm.org.uk
	USA	1000 E. First Street, Sanford, FL 32771	www.ntm.org
	Phil.	PO Box M-038, Mandaluyong City 1550	

OAC **Open Air Campaigners**
| | UK | 30 Garth Twenty, Killingworth,
Newcastle upon Tyne, NE12 6LN | www.oacgb.org.uk |
| | USA | PO Box 2542, Stuart, FL 34995 | www.oaci.org |

OCI **OC International** www.oci.org
	Sing.	Bras Basah, PO Box 0311, Sing. 911811
	USA	PO Box 36900, Colorado Springs, CO 80936
	Africa	PO Box 76037, Nairobi, Kenya, East Africa
	Lat. Am.	PO Box 260877, Pembroke Pines, FL 33026, USA

OD **Open Doors With Brother Andrew**
	Neth.	PO Box 47, Harderwijk 3840 AA
	S.Afr.	Box 990099, Kibler Park, Johannesburg 2053
	UK	PO Box 6, Witney, Oxon, OX8 7SP
	USA	PO Box 27001, Santa Ana, CA 92799 www.opendoorsusa.org

OM **Operation Mobilization**
	Aust.	PO Box 32, Box Hill, VIC 3128	www.om.org.au
	Canada	212 West Street, Port Colbourne, ON L3K 4E3	www.omcanada.org/
	Sing.	68 Lorong 16 Geylang, #03-06 Association Building, Sing. 398889	www.omsingapore.com
	S.Afr.	Private Bag X03, Lynnwood Ridge 0040	www.omsa.org.za
	UK	The Quinta, Weston Rhyn, Oswestry, Shropshire, SY10 7LT	www.uk.om.org
	USA	PO Box 444, Tyrone, GA 30290	www.usa.om.org

OMF **OMF International**
	Sing.	Int'l HQ, 2 Cluny Road, Sing. 259570	www.omf.org
	Aust.	PO Box 849, Epping, NSW 1710	www.au.omf.org
	Canada	5759 Coopers Avenue, Mississauga, ON L4Z 1R9	www.omf.ca
	NZ	PO Box 10-159, Auckland 1030	www.nz.omf.org
	S.Afr.	PO Box 41, Kenilworth 7745	www.za.omf.org
	UK	Station Approach, Borough Green, Sevenoaks, TN15 6BG	www.omf.org.uk
	USA	10 W Dry Creek Circle, Littleton, CO 80120	www.us.omf.org

OMS **OMS International** www.omsinternational.org
	Aust.	PO Box 897, Ringwood, VIC 3134
	Canada	PO Box 10, Burlington, ON L7R 3Y3
	NZ	PO Box 962, Hamilton
	S.Afr.	PO Box 560, Florida Hills 1716
	UK	1 Sandileigh Avenue, Didsbury, Manchester, M20 3LN
	USA	941 Fry Road, Greenwood, IN 46142-6599

P **Pioneers** www.pioneers.org
| | USA | 12343 Narcoossee Road, Orlando, FL 32827 |

PAoC **Pentecostal Assemblies of Canada** www.paoc.org
| | Canada | 6745 Century Avenue, Mississauga,
ON L5N 6P7 |

PI **Partners International**
| | USA | 1313 N. Atlantic Street, Ste 4000,
Spokane, WA 99201 www.partnersintl.org |

| | UK | Bawtry Hall, Bawtry, Doncaster, DN10 6JH | www.worldshare.org.uk |

PMF **Philippine Missionary Fellowship**
Phil. PO Box 3284, Manila

QIF **Qua Iboe Fellowship** web.ukonline.co.uk/qua.iboe
UK 14 Glencregagh Court, Belfast, BT6 0PA

RSTI **Red Sea Team International**
Aust. GPO 3302, Sydney, NSW 2001
UK PO Box 19929, London, N3 1WW www.rsmt.u-net.com
USA PO Box 2047, Lexington, SC 29071

SA **Salvation Army**
UK Int'l HQ, 101 Queen Victoria Street, www.salvationarmy.org
London, EC4P 4EP
Aust. PO Box 4256, Manuka, ACT 2603
Canada 2 Overlea Blvd, Toronto, ON M4H 1P4 www.salvationarmy.ca
NZ PO Box 6015, Wellington 6001
USA PO Box 269, Alexandria, VA 22313 www.salvationarmyusa.org

SAMS **South American Mission Society** www.samsgb.org
UK Allen Gardiner House, Pembury Road,
Tunbridge Wells, Kent, TN2 3QU

SAO **SAO Cambodia** www.sao-cambodia.org
UK Bawtry Hall, Bawtry, Doncaster, DN10 6JH

SAT **SAT-7** www.sat7.org
Cyprus PO Box 26760, CY-1647 Nicosia
USA PO Box 113, Wayne, PA 19087-0113
UK PO Box 1214, Bristol, BS99 2RS

SBC **Southern Baptist Convention — International Mission Board**
USA PO Box 6767, Richmond, VA 23233 www.imb.org

SEND **SEND International** www.send.org
Canada RR 3, Komoka, ON N0L 1R0
USA PO Box 513, Farmington, MI 48332

SGA **Slavic Gospel Association**
Aust. PO Box 396, Noble Park, VIC 3174
UK 37a The Goffs, Eastbourne, BN21 1HF
USA 6151 Commonwealth Dr., www.sga.org
Loves Park, IL 61111

SGM **Scripture Gift Mission International**
UK 3 Eccleston St., London, SW1W 9LZ members.aol.com/sgmint
Aust. PO Box 688, Castle Hill, NSW 1765
Canada #32 — 300 Steelcase Road West, www.sgmcanada.org
Markham, ON L3R 2W2
India Post Box 5316, 18/1 Infantry Road
Bangalore 560 001
NZ PO Box 10274, Auckland 3
S.Afr. PO Box 591025, Kengray, www.sgm.org.za
2100, Johannesburg
USA PO Box 410280, Melbourne, FL 32941 www.sgm.org

SIL see WBT

SIM	**SIM International**	www.sim.org
	USA PO Box 7900, Charlotte, NC 28241	
	Aust. Locked Bag 2, Taren Point, NSW 2229	
	Canada 10 Huntingdale Blvd., Scarborough, ON M1W 2S5	
	NZ PO Box 38588 Howick, Auckland 1730	
	Sing. 116 Lavender St., Pek Chuan Bldg. # 04-09, Sing. 338730	
	S.Afr. Private Bag X1, Clareinch 7740, Cape Town	
	UK Wetheringsett Manor, Wetheringsett, Stowmarket, IP14 5QX	

SU **Scripture Union**
> **UK** 207-209 Queensway, Bletchley, Milton Keynes, MK2 2EB — www.scriptureunion.org.uk
> **USA** 150 Strafford Ave. Ste 215, Wayne, PA 19087 — www.scriptureunion.org
> **Africa** PO Box 52443, Nairobi, Kenya

SUM **SUM Fellowship (**See **AP)**

TBL **The Bible League** — www.bibleleague.org
> **USA** 16801 Van Dam Rd., South Holland, IL 60473

TEAM **TEAM (The Evangelical Alliance Mission)**
> **Canada** PO Box 56030, Calgary, AB T2E 8K5 — www.teamcanada.org
> **USA** PO Box 969, Wheaton, IL 60189 — www.teamworld.org

TEAR **Tearfund** — www.tearfund.org
> **UK** 100 Church Road, Teddington, TW11 8QE

TLM **The Leprosy Mission**
> **UK** 80 Windmill Road, Brentford, TW8 0QH — www.leprosymission.org
> **Aust.** PO Box 293, Box Hill, VIC 3128
> **Canada** 75 The Donway W., Ste 1410, North York, ON M3C 2E9 — www.tlmcanada.org

TWR **Trans World Radio** — www.twr.org
> **UK** 11 St. James Gardens, Swansea, SA1 6DY
> **USA** PO Box 8700, Cary, NC 27512-8700

UBS **United Bible Society** — www.biblesociety.org
> **UK** 7th Flr., Reading Bridge House, Reading, RG1 8PJ

UFM **UFM Worldwide**
> **UK** 47a Fleet Street, Swindon, SN1 1RE — www.ufm.org.uk
> **USA** PO Box 306, Bala Cynwyd, PA 19004 — www.ufm.org

UWM **United World Mission** — www.uwm.org
> **USA** PO Box 668767, Charlotte, NC 28266-8687

WBT **Wycliffe Bible Translators**
> **Aust.** 70 Graham Road, Kangaroo Ground, VIC 3097 — www.wycliffe.org.au
> **Canada** 4316 10 St. NE, Calgary, AB T2E 6K3 — www.wycliffe.ca
> **NZ** PO Box 13347, Onehunga, Auckland 1132 — www.wycliffe.org/WBT-NZ/
> **S.Afr.** PO Box 548, Kempton Park 1620
> **UK** Horsleys Green, High Wycombe, HP14 3XL — www.wycliffe.org.uk
> **USA** PO Box 628200, Orlando, FL 32862 — www.wycliffe.org

WEC	**WEC International**	www.wec-int.org

WEC   **WEC International**   www.wec-int.org
  UK   Int'l HQ, Bulstrode, Oxford Road,
         Gerrards Cross, SL9 8SZ
  Aust.   48 Woodside Avenue, Strathfield, NSW 2135
  Canada 37 Aberdeen Avenue, Hamilton, ON L8P 2N6
  HK   PO Box 73261, Kowloon Central Post Office, Kowloon
  NZ   PO Box 27-264, Mt Roskill, Auckland, 1030
  Sing.   PO Box 142, Sing. 915805
  USA   PO Box 1707, Fort Washington, PA 19034

WGM   **World Gospel Mission**   www.wgm.org
  USA   PO Box 948, Marion, IN 46952

WH   **World Horizons**   www.worldhorizons.org
  UK   Centre for the Nations, North Dock, Llanelli,
         Carmarthenshire, Wales, SA15 2LF
  USA   PO Box 17721, Richmond, VA 23226
  Sing.   PO Box 0653, Sing. 914406

WT   **World Team**   www.worldteam.org
  USA   1431 Stuckert Road, Warrington, PA 18976

WVI   **World Vision International**
  Aust.   Box 399-C, Melbourne, VIC 3001   www.worldvision.com.au
  Canada 6630 Turner Valley Road, Mississauga,   www.worldvision.ca
         ON L5N 2S4
  UK   599 Avebury Blvd., Milton Keynes, MK9 3PG
  NZ   Private Bag 92 078, Auckland, 1020   www.worldvision.org.nz
  USA   800 W. Chestnut Ave., Monrovia,   www.wvi.org
         CA 91016-3198

YFC   **Youth for Christ International**
  Sing.   10 Lorong 27A Geylang House,   www.youthnet.org.sg
         #03-01 Emmanuel House, Sing. 388107
  Aust.   PO Box 629, Box Hill, VIC 3128   www.auslife.com.au
  Canada 2540-5 Avenue, NW Calgary, AB T2N 0T5   www.yfccanada.com
  France 4 Rue de la Croix, 68520 Burnhaupt-le-Bas   www.jpcfrance.com
  UK   PO Box 5254, Halesowen,   www.yfc.co.uk
         W. Midlands, B63 3DG
  USA   7670 S. Vaughn Ct., Englewood, CO 80110   www.yfc.org

YWAM   **Youth With A Mission**   www.ywam.org
  Kenya E Africa Office: PO Box 59443, Nairobi
  Neth.   Europe Office: Jeugd Met Een Opdracht,
         Centrum's Heerenhof, Zwarteweg 10,
         8181 PD Heerde
  NZ   Pacific Office: PO Box 13580, Auckland, 1132
  Sing.   SE Asia Office: Geylang PO Box 25, Sing. 913801
  S.Afr.   S Africa Area Office: PO Box 589, Hluhluwe 3960
  Thai.   Mercy Ministries: GPO Box 177, Bangkok 10501
  UK   Frontier Missions: FM Int'l Coordination Office,
         Highfield Oval, Harpenden, Herts, AL5 4BX
  USA   Mercy Ships: PO Box 2020, Lindale, TX 75771
         King's Kids Int'l: 75-5851 Kuakini Hwy,
           Kailua-Kona, HI 96740
         N America Office: 7085 Battlecreek Rd. SE,
         Salem, OR 97301

• APPENDIX 3 •

C • MISSION AGENCY STATISTICS

The global statistics are given followed by their largest non-confidential fields. Please note that the statistics in this Appendix are largely 2001 figures, whereas those used in the main body of the text may be from earlier years.

Agency	No. of Workers	from Countries	to Fields
ABMS	107	4	12
Thailand (19), Central Asia (17), Malawi (15), SE Asia (15), Australia (12), PNG (12)			
ABWE	850	3	46
USA (100), Peru (54), Portugal (47), Philippines (46), S Africa (46), Chile (30)			
AE	91	13	13
Zimbabwe (21), S Africa (12), Uganda (12), Kenya (7), Rwanda (7), USA (6), Ghana (5)			
AEF	267	14	12
Mainly Asia (257)			
AFM	25	1	4
Asia (8), World (8), S Asia (5), Mid. East (4)			
AIM	900	23	25
Kenya (354), USA (115), Tanzania (112), Mozambique (38), Uganda (37), UK (32)			
AM	100	3	20
Bolivia (18), Brazil (16), S Africa (10), UK (7), Asia (6), Spain (5), Ukraine (4)			
AoG	3,546	58	153
USA (170), Brazil (158), Philippines (147), Asia (137), Mexico (105), PNG (101)			
AOI	363	26	23
Mainly Asia (301)			
AP	208	10	15
Unspecified (63), Nigeria (54), Cameroon (19), UK (19), Chad (16), N Africa (10)			
AWM	327	20	28
Middle East (97), France (60), N Africa (46), USA (37), UK (33)			
BBF	905	1	79
Mexico (73), USA (68), Philippines (54), UK (46), Kenya (42), Brazil (38)			
BCWM	79	3	12
Zimbabwe (33), USA (9), Zambia (9), Venezuela (8), Colombia (4), Mexico (4)			
BEM	93	11	1
Belgium (93)			

Agency	No. of Workers	from Countries	to Fields
BFM	168	14	22
Asia (37), Brazil (34), USA (19), Mexico (18), Paraguay (10), France (8), Japan (6)			
BMM	1,065	2	44
USA (449), Brazil (155), Peru (40), Australia (28), Côte d'Ivoire (28), Ecuador (26)			
BMS	207	1	28
Brazil (41), Asia (31), Albania (19), SE Asia (13), France (10), Belgium (9)			
C	101	6	16
Tanzania (35), Kenya (12), France (8), UK (8), Zimbabwe (8), Uganda (7)			
Ch	313	9	26
Asia (57), USA (52), Middle East (42), W Asia (35), E Asia (27), Philippines (24)			
CAMI	241	10	11
Mexico (67), Guatemala (61), USA (26), Spain (21), Costa Rica (19)			
CB	1,429	20	97
France (219), Zambia (127), Asia (70), Mexico (47), Brazil (45), Italy (43)			
CBI	630	1	46
USA (82), Côte d'Ivoire (64), Philippines (49), Brazil (31), Japan (22)			
CBIM	95	1	20
Canada (22), Bolivia (10), Kenya (8), Brazil (7), Asia (6), Belgium (6)			
CBM	129	17	42
Kenya (11), USA (11), Tanzania (10), Bosnia (9), Uganda (9)			
CCCI	15,218	118	135
E Asia (3,224), Asia (2,953), SE Asia (1,186), South Korea (789), Middle East (312)			
CEF	1,192	18	54
USA (774), Asia (71), Canada (55), Germany (51), S Africa (51), Switzerland (19)			
CLC	547	55	55
UK (73), Colombia (41), Asia (40), Chile (36), France (30), Venezuela (24)			

Agency	No. of Workers	from Countries	to Fields
CM	198	6	17
	Nigeria (92), Côte d'Ivoire (19), Southern Africa (13), Togo (12), Benin (8)		
CMA	1,652	13	61
	Philippines (326), USA (120), SE Asia (116), Australia (91), Peru (81)		
CMF	294	13	15
	Nigeria (123), Africa (66), Benin (42), Côte d'Ivoire (17), Gambia (8), Kenya (5)		
CMJ	40	6	2
	Mainly Israel		
CMS	458	11	52
	Asia (56), Australia (52), Tanzania (49), Uganda (33), Kenya (29), UK (24)		
COCM	44	2	4
	UK (39), Holland (2), Romania (2), China, Hong Kong (1)		
CoGWM	307	12	55
	USA (63), Philippines (37), Kenya (17), Ecuador (11), Europe (8), Brazil (7)		
CoN	562	7	69
	PNG (53), S Africa (42), Philippines (33), Guatemala (30), Switzerland (27)		
CRWM	244	3	23
	Nigeria (36), Philippines (33), Dominican Republic (25), Asia (23), Japan (22)		
CWI	34	8	9
	UK (14), Israel (9), Australia (2), Bulgaria (2), New Zealand (2), France (1)		
DAWN	11	6	6
	World (3), Africa (2), Asia (2), S Africa (2), Europe (1), Latin America (1)		
DM	92	10	9
	S Africa (36), Zimbabwe (26), Malawi (8), Zambia (8), Namibia (5), Germany (3)		
ECM	248	16	22
	Spain (45), Austria (32), Italy (25), Albania (18), Australia (18), France (17)		
EF	148	2	30
	USA (31), Kenya (17), Mexico (16), Asia (12), Tanzania (11), Niger (8)		
EHC	723	68	69
	Asia (374), Vanuatu (32), PNG (26), Fiji (22), Micronesia, Fed. States (19)		
ELAM	n/a		
EMS	1,423	2	6
	Nigeria (1400), Chad (8), Ghana (8), Niger (3), Benin (2), UK (2)		
F	692	33	63
	Middle East (190), Asia (171), SE Asia (43), N Africa (45), USA (36)		
FEBA	n/a		
FEBC	138	10	12
	USA (56), Philippines (39), Canada (12), Northern Marianas Is. (10)		
FFM	n/a		
FMPB	880	1	1
	India (880)		
GEM	351	4	27
	Belgium (41), France (37), USA (35), Rep. of Ireland (33), Spain (27)		
GFA	12,565	11	11
	India (10,795), SE Asia (1,050), Asia (564), USA (71), Middle East (62)		
GMU	520	21	30
	USA (82), Ecuador (59), Bolivia (45), Europe (36), Brazil (30), Spain (28)		
GRN	290	25	34
	USA (66), Australia (43), Asia (34), UK (13), Mexico (6), Nigeria (6)		
HCJB	356	14	11
	Ecuador (222), USA (102), UK (12), New Zealand (5), Australia (2)		
I	525	14	19
	Asia (285), Middle East (89), E Asia (19), USA (15), Canada (10)		
IA	150	1	30
	CAR (28), SE Asia (15), Asia (12), Brazil (10), E Asia (10), France (10),		
IBRA	n/a		
IBT	n/a		
IEM	472	1	6
	Mainly India		
IET	1,996	2	3
	Mainly India		
IFES	1,374	57	124
	Asia (206), Canada (120), South Korea (89), SE Asia (83), Chile (54)		
INF	133	16	
	Many seconded from other agencies eg. Tearfund, BMS World Mission, Interserve, WEC International.		
ISI	230	2	2
	USA (80), UK (50)		

Agency	No. of Workers	from Countries	to Fields
IT	386	17	34
	USA (62), Austria (48), Canada (29), UK (28), France (25), Philippines (21)		
JCL	16	5	3
	Japan (10), UK (4), Germany (2)		
JFJ	64	2	6
	USA (56), S Africa (4), Europe (2), Israel (1), UK (1)		
LAM	238	9	16
	Mexico (81), Costa Rica (65), USA (25), Colombia (21), Venezuela (12)		
LCMS	406	1	37
	E Asia (74), USA (57), Europe (33), Japan (31), Venezuela (27), Nigeria (24)		
LL	158	11	15
	Peru (41), Bolivia (24), Ecuador (22), UK (19), Argentina (17), Brazil (16)		
LM	221	11	23
	PNG (32), Japan (27), Zambia (22), Micronesia, Fed. States (20), France (14)		
MAF	923	20	41
	USA (165), SE Asia (93), PNG (84), Kenya (74), Tanzania (69), Australia (63)		
MECO	87	11	13
	Mainly Middle East (68)		
MT	24	4	8
	UK (12), France (4), Israel (2), Middle East (2), Hungary (1), Ukraine (1)		
MTW	459	2	40
	Mexico (58), Japan (38), France (36), Ukraine (36), S Africa (35), Peru (31)		
N	4,089	66	104
	USA (1800), Asia (407), Europe (164), South Korea (143), UK (104)		
NGK	395	2	34
	S Africa (106), Namibia (71), Mozambique (43), Malawi (24), Zimbabwe (20)		
NTM	3,073	32	31
	PNG (547), USA (513), Brazil (369), Philippines (226), Venezuela (181)		
OAC	202	19	20
	USA (89), UK (23), New Zealand (22), Australia (19), Asia (14), Canada (8)		
OCI	313	20	27
	USA (59), Philippines (32), Guatemala (26), SE Asia (25), Brazil (22)		
OD	71	9	8
	USA (34), Australia (8), Brazil (7), France (5), Asia (4), Canada (4)		
OM	2,977	79	61
	Asia (618), On Ships (451), UK (317), Middle East (225), USA (123), Germany (109)		
OMF	1,245	23	32
	SE Asia (402), E Asia (201), Japan (137), Philippines (125), UK (48), Asia (41)		
OMS	538	9	26
	USA (118), Europe (94), E Asia (49), Ecuador (36), Mexico (22), Colombia (21)		
P	843	27	50
	Asia (175), SE Asia (143), E Asia (79), PNG (53), Europe (39), Ghana (29), Togo (25)		
PAoC	179	2	30
	Canada (22), Kenya (18), Asia (17), Brazil (17), SE Asia (12), Malawi (9)		
PI	50	3	7
	Mainly USA (34)		
PMF	269	1	3
	Mainly Philippines (265)		
QIF	28	2	4
	Nigeria (16), Burkina Faso (5), UK (5), Chad (2)		
RSTI	98	7	11
	Middle East (36), Djibouti (17), Mali (11), UK (11), Canada (4)		
SA	513+	18+	69+
	Unspecified (79), Europe (34), Australia (27), Canada (20), Zimbabwe (18)		
SAMS	229	6	19
	UK (53), Paraguay (20), Argentina (19), Chile (18), USA (14), Brazil (14)		
SAO	18	5	2
	Mainly Cambodia (16)		
SAT	70	8	6
	Middle East (59), USA (8), UK (2)		
SBC	5,034	6	97
	Asia (1904), Latin America (1264), Africa (845), Europe (549), USA (472)		
SEND	512	9	24
	USA (131), E Asia (67), Japan (64), Philippines (50), Ukraine (44), Spain (27)		
SGA	44	3	3
	Mainly USA (42)		

Agency	No. of Workers	from Countries	to Fields
SGM	138	28	27
	UK (34), Asia (21), Brazil (6), Philippines (6), Singapore (6), Poland (5)		
SIM	1,693	26	54
	USA (209), Ethiopia (160), Niger (133), Nigeria (112), S Africa (108)		
SU	720+ worldwide		
	Africa (535+), Americas (77+), UK & Rep. of Ireland (108+)		
TBL	Total Personnel Worldwide: 390		
TEAM	862	23	40
	Japan (101), Venezuela (89), USA (83), France (43), Asia (42), Middle East (42)		
TEAR	73	17	29
	Burundi (7), Asia (5), Honduras (5), Kenya (4), N Africa (4), Yugoslavia (4)		
TLM	203	18	24
	Asia (46), S Africa (36), UK (30), Australia (15), Canada (9)		
TWR	409	11	23
	Netherlands Antilles (102), USA (85), Guam (31), Austria (26), Swaziland (25)		
UBS	n/a		
UFM	515	7	34
	Brazil (127), Haiti (41), France (31), SE Asia (30), USA (26), Germany (25)		

Agency	No. of Workers	from Countries	to Fields
UWM	212	6	29
	USA (57), Europe (19), Bolivia (16), E Europe (12), Hungary (11), Belgium (10)		
WBT	7,031	35	78
	USA (1,014), PNG (686), Asia (382), Philippines (284), Mexico (235), Peru (221)		
WEC	1,925	53	65
	UK (182), Australia (88), C Asia (70), Senegal (66), USA (62), Côte d'Ivoire (61)		
WGM	289	3	18
	USA (85), Kenya (59), Bolivia (34), Honduras (29), Mexico (15), Tanzania (14)		
WH	530	31	30
	Brazil (105), UK (61), Middle East (57), Niger (55), Spain (29), France (28), Asia (25)		
WT	418	6	27
	USA (63), Cameroon (36), Canada (36), Philippines (32), SE Asia (31), Haiti (20)		
WVI	1,559	7	41
	USA (691), Canada (318), Australia (244), Philippines (148), SE Asia (40)		
YFC	n/a		
YWAM	11,808	132	144
	USA (2,814), Brazil (1,068), Asia (666), UK (556), Australia (518), South Korea (508), Netherlands (196), Canada (194), New Zealand (192), SE Asia (162), Switzerland (162)		

• APPENDIX 4 •
THE WORLD'S MISSIONARY FORCE

These tables give an analysis of foreign and indigenous Protestant, Independent and Anglican missionaries received and sent for each country of the world. We were not able to obtain adequate statistics for other megablocs, so these have been omitted from these tables. The vast majority of missionaries in these tables are Evangelicals. We have only totalled the numbers of missionaries identified – possibly the true number of P,I and A missionaries serving may be 10-20% higher than figures given for some countries. The complete listing of numbers of missionaries sent and received, by mission agencies, and numbers to and from each country is to be found on the *Operation World* CD. There are now Christian missionaries sent and received by nearly every country in the world – a real globalization of the missionary force!

Explanation of columns

Column 1 - **Countries grouped by continent.** Some countries impose restrictions on mission activity, and any data relevant to these countries is included in the "Confidential" supplementary line for Africa and Asia and "n.a." inserted in the statistics line.

Missionaries TO country — relating to countries which receive missionaries.

Column 2 - The number of **mission agencies** identified as having a ministry in the country.

Column 3 - **Foreign missionaries.** These include expatriate workers and their spouses (if not indigenous), furloughing missionaries assigned to these countries and also STWs (the latter are not separately enumerated in this table, but this detail is given on the CD).

Column 4 - **National missionaries.** All missionaries working within their own home country. This includes field missionaries and also those in a supportive role, but with missionary status.

Column 5 - **The total number of national and foreign missionaries** serving in a country.

Column 6 - **Ratio of the number of people in the country for every missionary.** This is a rather simplistic, but useful way of assessing the density of missionaries and, by comparison with the Christian population of the country, a measure of the need for further missionary input.

Missionaries FROM country — relating to countries which send missionaries.

Column 7 - **The number of agencies with an indigenous base** in the country. International agencies will have multiple entries in the countries, but the continental totals include such agencies once only.

Column 8 - **The total number of national missionaries** – in their own and in other lands.

Column 9 - **The number of national missionaries serving in other lands.**

Column 10 - **The percentage of cross-cultural workers** as a percentage of the total.

Column 11 - **Ratio of churches for each missionary.** This is an indication of how many churches are needed, on average, to send one missionary. This is a useful guide to the level of interest in missions in the country.

Global table of Protestant, Independent and Anglican missionaries

World by Continents	Missionaries TO country					Missionaries FROM country				
	Agencies	Total Foreign Miss.	Total National Miss.	All Miss.	Pop: Miss. Ratio	Agencies	Total National Miss.	In Other Cntries	% Cross Cultural	P,I,A Ch:Miss. Ratio
Africa	620	17737	9320	27057	28977	395	12442	3126	72.6	48.4
Asia	875	29305	55680	84985	43434	601	69203	13607	59.2	11.3
Europe	564	16197	6901	23098	31596	413	22897	16077	83.4	6.2
Latin America	539	16980	6574	23554	22040	346	10192	3837	69.1	30.3
N. America	151	3008	20368	23376	13246	672	71088	50720	80.7	7.2
Pacific	183	4124	3135	7184	4231	132	9452	3526	72.1	6.1
World	**2932**	**97732**	**104271**	**201928**	**30032**	**2559**	**201928**	**97732**	**71.1**	**11.8**

Country (Africa)	Agencies	Missionaries TO country			Pop: Miss. Ratio	Missionaries FROM country				P,I,A Ch:Miss. Ratio
		Total Foreign Miss.	Total National Miss.	All Miss.		Agencies	Total National Miss.	In Other Cntries	% Cross Cultural	
Algeria	n.a.									
Angola	26	151	33	184	69990	5	38	5	73.7	241.9
Benin	32	230	80	310	19666	9	86	6	41.9	34.5
Botswana	54	276	3	279	5814	3	5	2	40.0	663.8
Burkina Faso	37	387	29	416	28694	9	50	21	50.0	70.9
Burundi	12	50	36	86	77849	3		0	8.3	278.3
Cameroon	52	582	69	651	23172	11	94	27	59.6	140.9
Cape Verde	10	41	5	46	9298	2	8	3	37.5	17.6
CAR	23	154	39	193	18732	4	41	2	29.3	136.9
Chad	36	285	85	370	20678	10	94	9	58.5	48.6
Comoros	n.a.									
Congo	22	121	27	148	19888	4	30	3	16.7	85.9
Congo-DRC	69	652	377	1029	50199	34	416	40	100.0	144.7
Côte d'Ivoire	71	983	151	1134	13039	11	201	50	93.0	41.5
Djibouti	5	33	0	33	19322	0				
Egypt	n.a.									
Equat. Guinea	23	70	12	82	5520	3		0	16.7	23.5
Eritrea	10	33	23	56	68757	2	24	1	100.0	8.2
Ethiopia	62	687	592	1279	48917	15	610	18	73.4	33.6
Gabon	14	98	17	115	10662	4	27	10	37.0	23.7
Gambia	20	123	6	129	10119	3	8	2	75.0	10.3
Ghana	68	416	576	992	20375	52	702	126	77.8	41.8
Guinea	36	357	27	384	19350	5	30	3	13.3	28.2
Guinea-Bissau	29	175	24	199	6096	4	27	3	33.3	4.9
Kenya	173	2254	616	2870	10481	54	686	70	67.1	103.6
Lesotho	32	116	43	159	13538	8	45	2	26.7	146.4
Liberia	37	168	196	364	8665	9	376	180	95.2	11.7
Libya	n.a.									
Madagascar	36	233	77	310	51425	12	99	22	58.6	163.3
Malawi	66	482	71	553	19756	15	92	21	58.7	241.3
Mali	41	414	155	569	19743	8	157	2	79.0	6.0
Mauritania	n.a.									
Mauritius	7	22	1	23	50283	5	7	6	100.0	49.7
Mayotte	3	11	0	11	9238					
Morocco	n.a.									
Mozambique	80	517	36	553	35589	9	39	3	38.5	629.8
Namibia	40	256	26	282	6120	5	31	5	32.3	70.9
Niger	39	371	30	401	26758	10	50	20	64.0	5.7
Nigeria	62	631	2903	3534	31552	66	3351	448	82.3	39.4
Réunion	7	16	0	16	43713	1	1	1	100.0	230.0
Rwanda	24	71	45	116	66665	7	47	2	8.5	135.9
São Tomé	5	24	20	44	3336	3		0	100.0	1.0
Senegal	47	511	39	550	17238	6	43	4	32.6	5.3
Seychelles	3	17	0	17	4555	1	1	1	100.0	26.0
Sierra Leone	23	59	50	109	44536	11	57	7	26.3	32.7
Somalia	n.a.									
South Africa	135	1261	1083	2344	17226	133	2548	1465	79.4	14.9
St Helena	3	6	0	6	1049					
Sudan	29	241	30	271	108818	5	62	33	29.0	67.6
Swaziland	30	133	19	152	6631	6	29	10	82.8	200.2
Tanzania	108	1248	221	1469	22816	21	230	9	72.2	113.5
Togo	27	243	84	327	14157	13	97	13	48.5	39.7
Tunisia	n.a.									
Uganda	78	538	739	1277	17054	20	775	36	44.5	28.1
Zambia	64	594	267	861	10649	27	312	45	78.5	46.0
Zimbabwe	69	480	216	696	16766	25	335	119	57.3	62.2
Other Africa	0	399	0	399	0	0	221	221	16.3	0.0
Confidential*	0	95	413	508	9	29	192	50	60.9	0.0
Africa Total	**620**	**17737**	**9320**	**27057**	**28977**	**395**	**12442**	**3126**	**72.6**	**48.4**

*NOTE: Some statistics for North Africa are subsumed under 'Middle East' which is included in the Asia section.

APPENDIX 4

Country (Asia)	Missionaries TO country					Missionaries FROM country				
	Agencies	Total Foreign Miss.	Total National Miss.	All Miss.	Pop: Miss. Ratio	Agencies	Total National Miss.	In Other Cntries	% Cross Cultural	P,I,A Ch:Miss. Ratio
Afghanistan	n.a.									
Armenia	11	36	0	36	97766					
Azerbaijan	n.a.									
Bahrain	n.a.									
Bangladesh	65	389	529	918	140692	13	536	7	3.4	4.9
Bhutan	n.a.									
Brunei	1	2	0	2	164040	1	1	1	100.0	39.0
Cambodia	60	422	102	524	21312	8	108	6	19.4	4.8
China, HK	90	637	220	857	8127	31	653	433	64.3	2.1
China, Macau	21	105	55	160	2784	2	55	0	0.0	1.4
China, PR	n.a.									
China, Taiwan	128	891	246	1137	19702	21	300	54	42.7	13.2
Georgia	6	22	8	30	165585	3	18	10	61.1	10.6
India	174	1310	40713	42023	24122	233	41064	352	51.7	7.2
Indonesia	111	1663	1753	3416	62351	38	1573	62	26.8	24.9
Iran	n.a.									
Iraq	n.a.									
Israel	63	277	21	298	17187	7	27	6	37.0	4.4
Japan	240	3461	222	3683	34405	56	449	228	70.2	21.4
Jordan	n.a.									
Kazakhstan	n.a.									
Korea, N	n.a.									
Korea, S	43	407	1636	2043	22929	140	12279	10646	91.6	4.2
Kuwait	n.a.									
Kyrgyzstan	n.a.									
Laos	n.a.									
Lebanon	28	128	57	185	17739	9	78	21	85.9	2.2
Malaysia	48	273	258	531	41891	27	394	136	50.0	12.2
Maldives	n.a.									
Mongolia	57	381	65	446	5969	6	67	2	19.4	2.6
Myanmar	31	159	3104	3263	13978	45	3151	47	62.0	4.9
Nepal	87	730	923	1653	14477	16	957	34	62.8	3.1
Oman	n.a.									
Pakistan	63	487	151	638	245271	17	180	29	52.8	31.0
Palestine	n.a.									
Philippines	193	2718	2333	5051	15040	123	3188	856	67.3	18.8
Qatar	n.a.									
Saudi Arabia	n.a.									
Singapore	66	330	373	703	5073	39	773	407	55.5	0.7
Sri Lanka	35	125	678	803	23446	20	684	6	56.7	2.5
Syria	6	16	0	16	1007789	2	5	5	60.0	25.8
Tajikistan	n.a.									
Thailand	132	1513	864	2377	25831	21	873	9	19.1	4.9
Timor Leste	4	42	0	42	21061					
Turkey	n.a.									
Turkmenistan	n.a.									
UAE	n.a.									
Uzbekistan	n.a.									
Vietnam	n.a.									
Yemen	n.a.									
Other Asia	200	9154	100	9254	0	0	371	100	36.7	0.0
Confidential	0	3627	1269	4896	0	67	1419	150	66.2	0.0
Asia Total	**875**	**29305**	**55680**	**84985**	**43434**	**601**	**69203**	**13607**	**59.2**	**11.3**

Country (Europe)	Agencies	Total Foreign Miss.	Total National Miss.	All Miss.	Pop: Miss. Ratio	Agencies	Total National Miss.	In Other Cntries Miss.	% Cross Cultural	P,I,A Ch:Miss. Ratio
		Missionaries TO country				**Missionaries FROM country**				
Albania	74	425	66	491	6341	8	66	0	4.5	2.4
Andorra			0	0						
Austria	66	511	21	532	15433	16	63	43	74.6	8.8
Belarus	16	69	14	83	123327	6	15	1	40.0	92.0
Belgium	55	414	33	447	22732	17	80	47	83.8	10.4
Bosnia	22	155	1	156	25460	1	1	0	0.0	60.0
Bulgaria	31	137	79	216	38079	8	92	13	26.1	19.3
Channel Is	1	2	0	2	76449					
Croatia	27	103	23	126	35497	7	29	6	41.4	9.3
Cyprus	25	131	6	137	5734	3	6	0	83.3	7.8
Czech Rep.	48	236	14	250	40977	7	23	9	39.1	56.4
Denmark	21	74	55	129	41033	30	472	417	91.7	5.6
Estonia	17	100	9	109	12809	10	24	15	62.5	19.5
Faeroe Is	1	1	10	11	3886	12	75	65	84.0	1.3
Finland	12	39	189	228	22701	35	1449	1260	87.9	1.5
France	149	1539	207	1746	33837	54	547	340	72.8	6.8
Germany	143	1537	746	2283	36014	136	3953	3228	88.0	6.5
Gibraltar	5	11	0	11	2280					
Greece	36	141	35	176	60482	12	32	4	50.0	13.3
Holy See	0	0	0	0						
Hungary	68	470	102	572	17545	14	127	25	29.9	24.5
Iceland	8	20	21	41	6853	7	54	33	63.0	5.9
Ireland	47	325	33	358	10420	17	94	61	79.8	10.6
Isle of Man	0	0	0	0						
Italy	89	543	161	704	81389	21	203	42	40.9	16.2
Latvia	15	72	36	108	21820	5	40	4	17.5	14.5
Liechtenstein	0	0	0	0						
Lithuania	15	60	16	76	48293	6	18	2	44.4	15.3
Luxembourg	5	18	0	18	23923	5	5	5	80.0	7.2
Macedonia	11	59	13	72	28105	2	19	6	94.7	3.3
Malta	4	11	0	11	35322					
Moldova	20	76	13	89	49219	4	25	12	52.0	26.0
Monaco	2	14	0	14	2400					
Netherlands	58	286	505	791	19957	72	1341	837	71.7	4.3
Norway	15	60	189	249	17916	29	1045	856	84.7	2.4
Poland	43	168	112	280	138447	15	126	14	16.7	9.7
Portugal	71	410	33	443	22291	28	231	198	91.3	6.4
Romania	88	436	111	547	40816	14	123	12	9.8	62.6
Russia	150	2216	368	2584	56863	18	396	28	64.4	16.9
San Marino	0	0	0	0						
Slovakia	28	143	11	154	34982	6	15	4	80.0	57.4
Slovenia	11	49	3	52	38184	1	3	0	0.0	23.7
Spain	176	1266	141	1407	28259	40	419	281	77.3	4.7
Svalbard	0	0	0	0						
Sweden	25	104	76	180	49501	46	1126	1050	93.2	5.2
Switzerland	40	240	341	581	12712	89	1404	1063	86.3	2.4
Ukraine	77	572	537	1109	45497	14	914	377	82.8	6.4
UK	171	1681	2498	4179	14078	166	8164	5666	88.3	5.6
Yugoslavia	20	62	26	88	120911	10	31	6	38.7	32.6
Other Europe	0	1211	47	1258	0	0	47	47	100.0	0.0
Europe	**564**	**16197**	**6901**	**23098**	**31596**	**413**	**22897**	**16077**	**83.4**	**6.2**

Country (Latin Amer)	Total Agencies	Total Foreign Miss.	Total National Miss.	All Miss.	Pop: Miss. Ratio	Agencies	Total National Miss.	In Other Cntries Miss.	% Cross Cultural	P,I,A Ch:Miss. Ratio
Anguilla	1	2	0	2	4155	0				
Antigua	5	19	4	23	2937	2	4	0	25.0	27.3
Argentina	94	744	154	898	41233	41	492	338	82.7	31.6
Aruba	1	2	0	2	51374	1	1	1	100.0	67.0
Bahamas	13	50	0	50	6131	1	2	2	100.0	455.0
Barbados	5	38	12	50	5409	6	23	11	47.8	18.9
Belize	30	128	15	143	1683	4	17	2	41.2	35.6
Bolivia	96	1020	95	1115	7470	16	107	12	59.8	72.3
Brazil	201	2981	3985	6966	24421	139	5801	1912	71.4	14.5
British Virgin Is	1	2	0	2	10683	0				
Cayman Is	5	17	0	17	2257	2	3	3	100.0	21.3
Chile	67	624	173	797	19086	17	251	78	34.7	78.2
Colombia	80	818	207	1025	41289	32	286	79	76.6	44.2
Costa Rica	70	437	119	556	7236	29	324	205	75.9	9.8
Cuba	11	25	22	47	238312	5	27	5	18.5	177.4
Dominica	11	26	4	30	2357	2	4	0	25.0	28.5
Dominican R.	45	282	55	337	25209	9	72	17	40.3	53.8
Ecuador	90	1084	120	1204	10503	22	148	28	41.9	22.6
El Salvador	30	138	74	212	29604	17	206	132	73.8	39.8
Falkland Is	2	7	0	7	322	0				
French Guiana	6	13	2	15	12088	2	4	2	100.0	13.0
Grenada	8	20	2	22	4260	2	3	1	100.0	64.3
Guadeloupe	2	8	1	9	50632	1	1	0	100.0	160.0
Guatemala	71	666	166	832	13684	32	264	98	62.5	83.3
Guyana	21	80	18	98	8789	7	21	3	57.1	83.0
Haiti	79	452	13	465	17682	7	19	6	36.8	423.0
Honduras	71	428	58	486	13345	20	121	63	70.2	71.9
Jamaica	38	192	44	236	10943	13	62	18	32.3	83.2
Martinique	1	1	4	5	79072	3	5	1	40.0	40.4
Mexico	196	2267	428	2695	36691	51	641	215	64.4	76.1
Montserrat	0	0	0	0		1	1	1	100.0	13.0
Neth. Antilles	12	146	2	148	1465	4	4	2	50.0	40.0
Nicaragua	47	154	34	188	26990	11	43	9	76.7	116.1
Panama	32	248	59	307	9302	18	91	32	51.6	27.6
Paraguay	78	707	25	732	7509	16	113	88	83.2	17.2
Peru	107	1071	268	1339	19165	33	366	98	73.0	47.1
Puerto Rico	31	136	64	200	19343	27	186	122	66.1	29.5
St Kitts-Nevis	1	2	0	2	19237	1	1	1	100.0	120.0
St Lucia	5	12	3	15	10291	3	13	10	76.9	13.5
St Vincent	6	23	5	28	4070	5	10	5	50.0	33.7
Suriname	28	144	7	151	2762	6	8	1	75.0	26.4
Trinidad	22	93	23	116	11163	9	36	13	36.1	37.6
Turks & Caicos	0	0	0	0		0				
Uruguay	52	258	45	303	11013	12	67	22	43.3	21.2
Venezuela	64	831	142	973	24840	25	221	79	62.9	54.8
Virgin Is, US	6	38	0	38	2446					
Other Lat Amer.	0	546	122	668	0	0	123	122	99.2	0.0
Latin America	**539**	**16980**	**6574**	**23554**	**22040**	**346**	**10192**	**3837**	**69.1**	**30.3**

Country (North Amer)	Total Agencies	Total Foreign Miss.	Total National Miss.	All Miss.	Pop: Miss. Ratio	Agencies	Total National Miss.	In Other Cntries Miss.	% Cross Cultural	P,I,A Ch:Miss. Ratio
Bermuda	5	9	0	9	7177	1	2	2	100.0	63.0
Canada	59	450	2664	3114	10002	161	7001	4337	80.8	2.7
Greenland	9	31	1	32	1755	1	1	0	0.0	109.0
St Pierre & M.	1	2	0	2	3284	0				
USA	126	2516	17703	20219	13767	632	64084	46381	80.7	7.6
N. America	**151**	**3008**	**20368**	**23376**	**13246**	**672**	**71088**	**50720**	**80.7**	**7.2**

APPENDIX 4

Country (Pacific)	Agencies	Total Foreign Miss.	Total National Miss.	All Miss.	Pop: Miss. Ratio	Agencies	Total National Miss.	In Other Cntries	% Cross Cultural	P,I,A Ch:Miss. Ratio
Amer. Samoa	4	8	0	8	8511					
Australia	99	810	2155	2965	6367	90	4167	2019	70.0	3.3
Christmas Is		0	0	0		0				
Cocos Is		0	0	0						
Cook Is	3	4	1	5	3904	2	7	6	85.7	14.0
Fiji	32	148	59	207	3946	8	102	43	47.1	21.1
Fr. Polynesia	5	26	4	30	7835	2	6	2	33.3	23.7
Guam	20	193	0	193	868	1	1	1	100.0	126.0
Johnston Is		0	0	0		0				
Kiribati	1	1	0	1	83387	0				
Marshall Is	4	17	0	17	3778	0				
Micronesia	14	57	24	81	1465	6	29	5	17.2	8.1
Nauru		0	0	0		0				
New Caledonia	5	17	0	17	12590	2	3	3	100.0	101.0
New Zealand	52	332	419	751	5142	81	1694	1275	81.1	2.4
Niue		0	0	0		1	2	2	100.0	10.0
Norfolk Island		0	0	0		0				
N Mariana Is	15	74	0	74	1059	0				
Palau	5	11	0	11	1766	1	6	6	100.0	4.3
PNG	84	2207	349	2556	1881	18	383	34	71.0	37.3
Pitcairn Is		0	0	0		0				
Samoa	6	11	0	11	16370	3	67	67	100.0	7.8
Solomon Is	13	72	39	111	3997	5	44	5	84.1	55.8
Tokelau Is		0	0	0		0				
Tonga	7	25	13	38	2593	5	44	31	70.5	8.5
Tuvalu		0	0	0		0				
Vanuatu	9	36	72	108	1763	4	78	6	7.7	11.4
Wallis&Futuna		0	0	0		0				
Other Pacific		0	0	0		0	21	21	100.0	0.0
Pacific Total	**183**	**4124**	**3135**	**7184**	**4231**	**132**	**6654**	**3526**	**72.1**	**0.0**
Other (World)	0	10381	2293	12674	0	0	9452	6839	56.0	0.0
World Total	**2932**	**97732**	**104271**	**201928**	**30032**	**2559**	**201928**	**97732**	**71.1**	**11.8**

The global totals show 201,928 missionaries sent and received.

Of these 104,196 are serving within their own country and 58,357 within a near culture.

There are 97,732 missionaries serving in a country other than their own.

• APPENDIX 5 •
ABBREVIATIONS

$	USA dollars
A	Anglican (in Christian megabloc table)
AIC	Africa Inland Church (AIM-related)
AICs	African Independent Churches
AIDS	Acquired Immune Deficiency Syndrome
AME	African Methodist Episcopal Church
Amer.	American
AMG	AMG Int. (formerly American Mission to Greeks)
Ang.	Anglican
Ann.Gr.	Annual growth
Apos.	Apostolic
ASEAN	Assoc. of South East Asian Nations
Assoc.	Association/Associated
BBF	Baptist Bible Fellowship International
BCC	Bible Correspondence Course(s)
BCMS	Bible Churchman's Missionary Society; now Crosslinks
Bi	Bible
Breth	Brethren
C	Catholic (Christian megabloc)
CAPRO	See Calvary Ministries (CM, Nigeria)
Cath.	Catholic
CCAP	Church of Central Africa, Presbyterian (Malawi, C. Africa)
CFAN	Christ For All Nations
Ch	Church
Ch. of S.	Ch. of Scotland
Charis	Charismatic
Chr	Christian
Chr Chs/ Chs of Chr.	Christian Churches/Churches of Christ
CIM	China Inland Mission; now OMF
CMJ	Church Mission to the Jews (Anglican)
CNEC	Christian Nationals Evangelism Commission, see Partners International
CNI	Church of North India
COMIBAM	Congreso Misionero Ibero Americano
Comm.	Community
cong.	congregation
Cons.	Conservative
CSI	Church of South India
DAWN	Discipling A Whole Nation Movement
DRC	Dutch Reformed Church (South Africa, Netherlands)
ECWA	Evangelical Church of West Africa (SIM-related)
Eg	Eglise (French = Church)
EHC	Every Home for Christ (formerly Every Home Crusade)
EKD	Evangelische Kirche in Deutschland (Germany)
EU	European Union

Ev/Evang	Evangelical
Fell.	Fellowship
FFM	Finnish Free Mission (Pentecostal), also Fellowship of Faith for Muslims
FGBMFI	Full Gospel Business Men's Fellowship International
FLM	Finnish Lutheran Mission
frat	fraternal
fSU	former Soviet Union
GDP	Gross Domestic Product (excluding imports and exports)
GDR	German Democratic Republic (East Germany)
GNP	Gross National Product (including imports and exports)
Gr	Greek
grps/gps	groups
HCJB	Radio Voice of the Andes (formerly WRMF, Ecuador)
HDI	Human Development Index
HIV	Human Immune Virus (AIDS)
HIV+	carrying the virus leading to AIDS
HMU	Hellenic Missionary Union
Hol.	Holiness
HQ(s)	Headquarter(s)
hrs/wk	hours per week
I	Independent/indigenous (in Christian megabloc table)
ICFG	International Church of the Foursquare Gospel
ICI	International Correspondence Institute (AoG)
IEP	Iglesia Evangélica Peruana (SIM-related)
IMS	Indian Missionary Society
Ind.	Independent
Intl./Int'l	International
ISCF	International Student Christian Fellowship
JPL	Joshua Project List
JW/JWs	Jehovah's Witnesses
KAR	Kurdish Autonomous Region (Iraq)
LMS	London Missionary Society (UK)
m/mill.	million
M	Marginal (Christian megabloc), also Muslims (Religion charts)
MB	Mission Biblique (France/Switzerland)
MBBs	Muslim-Background Believers
Mercosur	Latin American Southern Cone Free Trade Association
Miss	Mission/missionary
MKs	Missionaries' children
Morm	Mormon
Mvmt/Mvt	Movement
Nat/Natl	National
NATO	North Atlantic Treaty Organization

NGK	Nederduits Gereformeerde Kerk (Dutch Reformed Church, S. Africa)	stw/STW	Short-term worker
NGO	Non-Governmental Organization	Tab	Tabernacle
NLFA	New Life For All	TEE	Theological Education by Extension
NMS	National Missionary Society (India)	TESOL	Teaching English as a Second Language
NT	New Testament	TSPM	Three Self Patriotic Movement (China)
NZ	New Zealand		
O	Orthodox (Christian megabloc)	UCCF	Universities and Colleges Christian Fellowship (IFES)
OAS	Organization of African States		
P	Protestant (Christian megabloc)	UK	United Kingdom of Great Britain and Northern Ireland
Pent/Pente	Pentecostal		
PFI	Prison Fellowship International	unreg	unregistered
PHC	Pentecostal Holiness Church	Un	Union/United
por	portion (of Bible)	UN	United Nations
PRC	People's Republic of China	WCE	World Christian Encyclopedia
Prosp	Prosperity	w.i.p.	work in progress (Scripture translation)
Prot	Protestant		
RB2000	Radio by 2000, formerly World by 2000	X	Christians (generic) used in graphs
RC	Roman Catholic	xcul	Missionaries working cross-culturally (in homeland or abroad)
Rep	Republic		
SAM	South American Mission (formerly South American Indian Mission)	YMCA	Young Men's Christian Association
SCM	Student Christian Movement		
SdA	Seventh-day Adventist Church		
SIB	Sidang Injil Borneo (Malaysia, OMF-related)		
sq.km	square kilometres		

• APPENDIX 6 •
DEFINITIONS

10/40 Window The area of the world between latitudes 10° and 40° north of the equator covering North Africa, Middle East and Asia. The window has in view most of the world's areas of greatest physical and spiritual need, most of the world's least-reached peoples and most of the governments that oppose Christianity. See map on p. 17.

adherent A follower of a particular religion, church or philosophy. This is the broadest possible category of such followers and includes professing and affiliated adults and also their children (practising and non-practising) who may reside in a given area or country. As it refers to those who, if not under coercion, would claim to have a religion even if their adherence is only nominal, it is the only figure that can be used to adequately compare the relative numbers of followers of different religions and Christian traditions. This is the term used in the Religions table.

adult members Adult church members over 12 — 18 years of age (depending on the denomination) who are communicants or full members. Adult members are given in the second column of statistics in the denominational tables.

affiliated Christians All who are considered as belonging to organized churches. This includes full members, their children and other occasional attenders considered as part of the church community. These figures represent the whole Christian community or inclusive membership. Affiliated Christians are given in the 3rd column of the Christian megabloc tables as a percentage of the total population and in the 5th column of statistics in the denominational tables as a rounded number.

Affinity Bloc A major grouping of peoples with a broad range of affinities such as geography, culture, language, history. Examples: Arab, Turkic, Malay. There are 11 such in the 10/40 Window area.

Ahmaddiya An Islamic revivalist movement which originated in Pakistan, but has now spread to Africa and other continents. It is not considered truly Islamic by orthodox Muslims.

Alpha course Informal gatherings, usually in homes, for introducing the gospel to non-Christians. Started in the UK but spread to many countries during the 1990s.

animism Belief that inanimate objects are inhabited by spirits which must be appeased/placated to avert harm.

born-again believers Those who by grace and through faith in the atoning work of Christ have been regenerated by the Holy Spirit. However, in common usage it often includes those who claim an evangelical conversion experience.

cargo cults Melanesian Pacific syncretistic religious movements that sprang up during World War II synthesizing ethnic beliefs and western materialism.

Charismatics Those who testify to a renewing experience of the Holy Spirit and present exercise of the gifts of the Spirit such as glossalalia, healing, prophecy and miracles. The Charismatic renewal or "Second Wave" Pentecostalism has generally remained within mainline denominations. There is a further "Third Wave" renewal movement with many characteristics of the Second Wave but with less open identification with Pentecostalism or the Charismatic Movement. Second and Third Wave Charismatics are counted as a single entity in this book. In our global survey of denominations we have assessed percentages of affiliated Charismatic Christians for each of the 33,000 denominations in the world for 1990 and 2000 only. The assessment largely excludes those no longer actively associated with Charismatic renewal.

Christian Any who profess to be Christians. The term embraces all traditions and confessions of Christianity. It is no indicator of the degree of commitment or theological orthodoxy.

Church (with capital C). A particular denomination, or the universal visible Church at a national or worldwide level.

church (with a small c). A local fellowship of believers. The word is commonly used to mean a church building or church service, but here this usage has largely been avoided. The starting of churches is termed church planting.

creative-access nation A country which limits or forbids the entry of Christian missionaries and for which alternative legal means of entry are required to enable Christians to live for Christ.

cross-cultural missionaries Full-time Christian workers sent by their churches to work among peoples of a different culture, either within their own nations or abroad.

denomination Any association or network of local congregations linked together, formally or informally, within any given country. Note that international denominations are counted multiple times according to the number of countries in which they have an established presence.

disaffiliated Christians Those who have repudiated their church membership. Appears in both the denomination and Christian megabloc tables as a negative figure and in italics.

doubly affiliated Christians Those who maintain links with two or more denominations at the same time. This appears as an italicized negative figure in both the denomination and the Christian megabloc tables.

ethnic religions A generic term covering a range of informal religions based on ethnicity, i.e. ancestor worship, animism, fetishism, shamanism, spiritism, etc. In the Religions tables it is listed as 'Traditional ethnic'.

ethnocultural A people with commonalities of culture, history, customs and a self identity which may be a sub-division of, or transcend, language or ethnicity, i.e. caste groups in India.

ethnolinguistic people An ethnic or racial group speaking its own language. A people distinguished by its self-identity with traditions of common descent, history, customs and language. In this book a trans-national people is counted multiple times according to the number of countries where it has maintained its own ethnolinguistic identity and culture.

evangelicals (with a small 'e'). A term not used in Operation World. Now used by the 2001 World Christian Encyclopedia to signify all those likely to be interested in the fulfilment of the Great Commission. This category is so broad that we felt it was not a category we could employ here with profit. It is synonymous with the term 'Great Commission Christian' which is also not used in this book.

Evangelicals All who generally emphasize the following:

1 The Lord Jesus Christ as the sole source of salvation through faith in Him.

2 Personal faith and conversion with regeneration by the Holy Spirit.

3 A recognition of the inspired Word of God as the only basis for faith and Christian living.

4 Commitment to biblical witness, evangelism and mission that brings others to faith in Christ.

Evangelicals are largely Protestant, Independent or Anglican, but some are Catholic or Orthodox. It is one of the trans-megabloc groupings in this book.

Note: The definition of Evangelicals and the statistics relating to them are so fundamental to the contents of this book that it is important for the reader to understand the implications. It enables a measurement of the size and spectacular numerical growth of evangelical Christians over the last few decades.

The noun "Evangelical" is capitalized since it represents a body of Christians with a fairly clearly defined theology (as also Orthodox and Catholic bodies, etc.). Evangelicals are here defined as:

1 All affiliated Christians (church members, their children, etc.) of denominations that are evangelical in theology as defined above.

2 The proportion of the affiliated Christians in other denominations (that are not wholly evangelical in theology) who would hold evangelical views.

3 The proportion of affiliated Christians in denominations in non-Western nations (where doctrinal positions are less well defined) that would be regarded as Evangelicals by those in the above categories.

This is a theological and not an experiential definition. It does not mean that all Evangelicals as defined above are actually born-again. In many nations only 10-40% of Evangelicals so defined may have had a valid conversion and also regularly attend church services. However, it does show how many people align themselves with churches where the gospel is being proclaimed.

evangelism The activity of Christians spreading the gospel.

evangelization The process of proclaiming the gospel globally or regionally.

evangelized The state of having had the gospel communicated and offered in such a way that the hearer becomes aware of the claims of Christ, and the need to obey and follow Him. Possibly over 2 billion have been exposed to the gospel but are not linked with any Christian church.

evangelized non-Christian world Non-Christians who have been, or are likely to be, exposed to the gospel. The equivalent of World B.

fetishist One who attributes magical powers to inanimate objects and depends on amulets, charms, etc., for protection or aggression. Mainly Africa and the Americas.

First Wave Charismatics are members of classical Pentecostal denominations.

foreign missionary A full-time Christian worker serving in a country other than his or her own.

godwara A Sikh place of worship.

Great Commission The final series of commands of the Lord Jesus Christ before His Ascension for His followers to evangelize, baptize, disciple and teach all the peoples of the world.

harvest force The entire body of Christians potentially or actively engaged in Great Commission activity.

home missionary (or domestic missionary). A full-time Christian worker serving as a missionary (usually cross-culturally) in his or her own country.

Independents One of the 6 major Christian megablocs used in this book. This category includes many of the more recent break-aways from denominations in other megablocs, indigenous denominations not started by foreign missionaries and post-denominational networks.

Liberation theology Christian theology redefined on the basis of sociological, and often Marxist, presuppositions of oppression, thereby motivating the poor to claim equal participation in society.

Marginal One of the 6 Christian megablocs as defined in this book comprising marginal or fringe Christian groups. See next item.

marginal groups A general term used in this book to describe all semi-Christian or fringe groups, sects and cults that accept certain Christian features and parts of the Scriptures, together with supplementary revelations claimed to be divine. Most claim that they alone have the "truth". Many readers may understandably question the validity of including these groups as Christian. However, we consistently classify a person's religion according to his or her self-assessment. All of these groups claim allegiance to Christ even if their theological understanding of His person, deity, atoning work or resurrection may be defective. See prayer items for ministry to these groups given for December 27.

Megabloc One of the 6 major groupings of Christian denominations as used in this book. Frequently abbreviated as follows: Protestant P, Independent I, Anglican A, Catholic C (sometimes R), Orthodox O, Marginal M.

missionary One who is sent with a message. This word of Latin derivation has the same basic meaning as the wider use of the term "apostle" in the New Testament. The Christian missionary is one commissioned by a local church to evangelize, plant churches and disciple people away from his home area and often among people of a different race, culture or language. Modern usage varies widely with strong regional preferences:

1 *The stricter North American usage* — all sent to evangelize, plant churches or minister outside their homelands.

2 *The wider European and Latin American usage* — all sent to evangelize, plant churches or minister cross-culturally whether in other lands or in their homelands.

3 *The even broader African and Asian usage,* which is closer to the biblical concept indicated above and which encompasses all those sent to evangelize, plant churches and minister away from their home areas whether cross-culturally or not and whether in their own countries or abroad. However, such breadth in the use of "missionary" makes it harder for the researcher to specify the cultural or geographical distance a Christian worker must cover in order to be properly categorized as a missionary (as contrasted with an evangelist). It is especially helpful in such a case to be able to identify the sub-division of missionaries working within their own or a near culture.

In this book we have sought to synthesize differing perspectives in dividing all missionaries of each country and region into the three categories of foreign, cross-cultural and home/domestic. Most, but not all, foreign missionaries are cross-cultural, for many are actually working within expatriate communities of their own culture.

non-Western world The countries of Latin America, Africa and Asia. Rarely have we used the synonymous terms Third World or Two-Thirds World which can be seen as negative or patronizing and which are becoming obsolete since the collapse of the Communist Second World.

Pentecostals Those affiliated to specifically Pentecostal denominations committed to a Pentecostal theology usually including a post-conversion experience of a baptism in the Spirit, present exercise of the gifts of the Spirit and speaking in tongues.

people cluster A grouping of peoples with commonalities of a shared identity, language, culture, history and often a common name. Usually trans-national.

people group A significantly large sociological grouping of individuals who perceive themselves to have a common affinity with one another. From the viewpoint of evangelization, this is the largest possible group within which the gospel can be spread without encountering barriers of understanding or acceptance. There are basically three types:

1 *Ethnolinguistic people group,* which defines a person's identity and primary loyalty according to language and/or ethnicity. This is the category that has been emphasized in this book. We have

reserved the word people rather than people group for this type. Cross-cultural church-planting teams of missionaries are needed for peoples in this category. Of the estimated 12,000 ethno-linguistic peoples, probably over 9,000 already have at least one or two viable indigenous churches within their culture.

2 *Sociological people group* — a grouping defined by its long-term relation to the rest of society, such as by migration or traditional occupation or class, but not having a self-contained culture or identity as an ethnic group. In most cases local church outreach is required — either to plant daughter churches or to incorporate converts into multi-social congregations. There are probably hundreds of thousands of such people groups.

3 *Incidental people groups* — casual associations of individuals which may be temporary and usually the result of circumstances rather than personal choice. Examples of such groups are high-rise flat dwellers, drug addicts, occupational groupings, commuters, etc. These groupings present unique problems and opportunities for evangelism, but only rarely will it be appropriate for specific churches to be planted for the sole benefit of such groups.

people movement A movement of a large number of non-Christians in a particular people into the Church. This is frequently a group decision. It presents a wonderful opportunity to win and disciple many for the Lord by leading them into a personal faith in the Lord Jesus Christ. Failure to do so can soon lead to nominalism or syncretism.

polytheism Belief in many gods.

post-charismatics Those once involved but no longer active in Charismatic renewal.

professing A claim of allegiance to a religious belief — whether known to, or listed in the records of, an organized religion. Professing Christians usually number more than affiliated Christians. Where the difference is significant a figure for unaffiliated Christians is added to the megabloc table in the country section. Professing = (affiliated + unaffiliated) - doubly affiliated.

reached/unreached A term that is widely used today to describe people groups and areas that have or have not responded to the preaching of the gospel. The use of the term has been continued in this book despite the faultiness of the terminology. Strictly, it should be a measure of the exposure of a people group to the gospel and not a measure of the response.

renewal A quickening or enlivening in personal commitment to Christ in the churches. Charismatic renewal in the historic denomina-tions is an example. See above under Charismatics.

restricted-access nations States that limit or prevent Christian ministry by expatriates as missionaries. Alternatively they are called creative-access nations, where expatriates must seek secular avenues of entry — business, medical work, teaching, as house servants and other means. Most countries in this category have been Communist or Muslim, but today are predominantly Muslim.

revival The restoring to life of believers and churches which have previously experienced the regenerating power of the Holy Spirit but have become cold, worldly and ineffective. Often wrongly used of evangelistic campaigns, revival really signifies a sovereign act of God as an answer to prayer in bringing about a religious awakening and outpouring of the Spirit on His people.

Second Wave Charismatics Christians who have experienced renewal within mainline non-Pentecostal denominations.

shamanism Traditional ethnic religious belief centred on a hierarchy of healers and soothsayers. A term used primarily in Asia.

shari'a The Islamic body of law based on the Qur'an and tradition (hadith).

Shi'a Muslims Followers of Ali, the cousin of Mohammed. The second largest branch of Islam. Strong in Iran, Central and South Asia.

short-term worker (STW) A missionary serving for a period of 6 months to 2 years only.

Sunni Muslims Followers of the main branch of Islam.

syncretism The attempt to synthesize elements of different religious systems into a single body of belief and practice. Baha'i, for instance, is a synthesis of Islamic, Christian and other religious tenets. Some African Indigenous Churches have sought to synthesize elements of Christianity with pre-Christian traditional beliefs.

Third Wave Charismatics Christians in newer charismatic denominations or post-denominational networks.

Traditional ethnic A generic term used in the Religions table to cover all the informal and ethnic religions in a country.

trans-bloc grouping A term used to cover Evangelicals, Charismatics and Pentecostals in this book. Each of these are found in some or most of the 6 Christian megablocs.

unaffiliated Christians Those who profess to be Christians but who are not known to any church.

Universalism The belief that ultimately all people will be saved irrespective of religious belief or lack of it while on earth. The underlying premises are that many have an implicit awareness of a supernatural being to which they respond by doing good to others and that a loving God could not consign people to eternal punishment for sin — non-biblical teaching rejected by nearly all Evangelicals.

unreached people An ethnolinguistic people among whom there is no viable indigenous community of believing Christians with adequate numbers and resources to evangelize their own people without outside (cross-cultural) assistance. Other researchers have adopted the terms "hidden people" or "frontier people group".

Wahhabi A conservative, fundamentalist Muslim sect. Largely in Saudi Arabia, Gulf States and Central Asia.

Western World The countries of Europe, North America and Australasia.

World A Nations and peoples in the least evangelized world. Those nations and peoples that are less than 50% evangelized as defined in the World Evangelization Database compiled by Dr David Barrett and team.

World B Nations and peoples in the evangelized non-Christian world. Defined as those nations and peoples that are more than 50% evangelized but less than 60% Christian (including all major Christian groups).

World C Nations and peoples in the Christian world. Defined as those nations and peoples that are more than 60% professing Christian. This includes all nominal and affiliated Christians of all ecclesiological traditions and not only Protestants.

Yezidi A syncretistic religion in Iraq, Turkey and the Caucasus based on Zoroastrian, Jewish, Nestorian, Christian and Muslim beliefs. Largely among Kurds.

• APPENDIX 7 •
OPERATION WORLD DATABASE

The entire database is being made available with the publication of the book. The CD will give more details about its contents.

Development of the Database

We developed the database in 1984 in preparation for the 1986 edition of *Operation World*. A major contributory factor was the publication of the *World Christian Encyclopedia* (WCE) in 1982. This volume, together with a wide-ranging search for denominational and religious data, enabled us to compile tables for denominations, religions and countries. We have updated these tables for each five year period since 1960.

In 1990 we also added a fourth set of tables on mission agencies covering mission details, sending bases and fields.

We have not developed tables for peoples or languages, but have relied on the Wycliffe Ethnologue and on the WCE database (published for the first time in the 2001 edition of the Encyclopedia). Our input into both these databases has been considerable.

The database contains the following:

1. Denominations Approximately 33,000 denominations are covered (6,335 records for individual denominations and a further 742 records, each of which refers to undocumented denominations which we have further grouped together). This contains over one million discrete pieces of information! The period covered is 1960-2000.

2. Religions with 3,648 records covering 16 major religions and the period 1900-2025.

3. Missions with information on 1,200 agencies, 3,393 bases and 16,000 fields of ministry.

4. Countries with geographical economic and social information from multiple sources.

The development of the programming was ably done by Kathy Lannon of Global Mapping for the 1986 edition, followed by Marko Jauhiainen for the 1993 edition and rewritten by Maurice Manktelow in Delphi software for the present edition. It is this latter software that is provided as an access tool on the CD with some adjustments to make it suitable for this medium. A further programme, developed by Jonathan Manktelow, generated the graphs. This programme is included on the CD and is also commercially available [www.grapl.com].

Methodology of the Database

The statistics in *Operation World* are an important supportive framework for the main thrust of the book. We see the statistics as part of our accountability to God and to our readers. We have therefore followed a number of fundamental principles:

1. Verifiable data. All information is sourced. Much has had to be by extrapolation, interpolation and derivation in religions and denominations. Where this has been done, it is clearly indicated. Where data provided has proved inconsistent or had to be adjusted to fit new population estimates, the source has been modified by a following '*' or '%'. For this reason we are happy to publish the information on the CD.

2. The 100% rule. All data components must add up to the whole - all peoples in a country must equal the population of the country; all denominations must add up to the total of affiliated Christians, etc. We have therefore had to devise mechanisms for adding missing data or subtracting over-counted or doubly counted populations. For instance:

a) *Many Chinese and Japanese* follow both Buddhism and their ethnic religions such as Taoism or Shintoism.

b) *Many Latin Americans were baptized as Catholics* but are now active Pentecostals. The Catholic Church still counts such as Catholic.

3. Making all statistics compatible so that realistic totals may be derived. For example:

a) *Denominational data* is often incompatible - some denominations define 'members' as active adult baptized members, others as the whole Christian community or affiliates. Sometimes a denomination changes its definition from one year to the next. We therefore used a ratio system to relate congregation size, adult membership affiliates, and, where known, attendance figures. The ratios were derived uniquely for each denomination based on past statistics, growth patterns, family sizes, age structures, etc. All these ratios are accessible to the user of the CD.

b) Missions data. Some agencies only include the husband, but not the wife. We include both, and had to make upward estimates for some statistics which we were given.

c) Religions data is often distorted by power and politics - overcounting of Hindus in India, inflated statistics for Muslims in Nigeria, Malaysia, Indonesia, etc., Catholic claims based on broad percentage estimates in Latin America and Europe, and so on. We have had to modify some statistics to adhere to our 100% rule.

4. Major focus on the Evangelical/ Charismatic streams of Christianity from which comes the majority of the users of this book. There are few objective statistics. We therefore had to make percentage estimates for each denomination based on:

a) Firm local data or estimates

b) The theological position of the denomination. All denominations considered theologically conservative evangelical were entered as 100% Evangelical (See definitions in Appendix 6). All denominations considered charismatic or Pentecostal were entered as 100% charismatic.

c) General developments within pluralistic denominations, e.g. the (Presbyterian) Church of Scotland becoming more evangelical, the African Methodist Episcopal Church becoming more charismatic. An evangelical percentage was entered for 1960 and 2000 and a charismatic percentage for 1990 and 2000. Intermediate years were proportionately derived.

5. Compatibility with the World Christian Encyclopedia. There are only two extant global statistical surveys of Christianity - the WCE and OW. Many readers may never see a copy of the WCE, but we felt it important to point out the issues raised below. Over the years, the authors of the two volumes have sought to collaborate as far as possible in sharing information, standardizing categories, agreeing on definitions and trying to come to convergence in key concepts. The two volumes serve

very different readerships and have different goals. Here are listed some of the convergences and divergences.

a) The convergences:
i *Both volumes published in 2001* use the UN continental divisions. So, totals for continents are comparable. The 1993 OW classification of the world into 8 cultural-religious regions, though preferable, was unique to OW 1993, making it difficult to compare regions with other published data.

ii *Both volumes used the same UN world population figures* issued in 1998.

iii *The 6 megablocs of Christianity* were hammered out in much discussion as we wrestled to cope with post-denominationalism and the growing phenomenon of independency in Christianity. This led to a re-adjustment of our megabloc and denomination codes to align with the WCE.

iv *Sharing of data and information* from both OW and WCE research was extensive between 1990 and 1998. The pressures of publication and the sheer volume of information reduced this flow in the last several years.

b) The divergences:
i *The Christian megablocs* - WCE and Operation World have used slightly different criteria in assigning post 1945 denominations to the 'I' category. OW was more cautious. In this edition of OW, Protestants tend to be more numerous and Independents less than in the WCE because of this.

ii *Denominational data.* The WCE largely used data of 1990-1995 (much, incidentally, taken from the 1993 OW database). This was then extrapolated to 2000. A high proportion of OW data is from the period 1998-2000.

iii *Definition of Evangelicals.* This is, perhaps, the most significant difference between WCE and OW 2001. OW has largely continued using the same definition for Evangelicals and used the same methodology as in past editions. The new WCE has used a radically different measure of Evangelicals (related to historic denominations with links to the Reformation) and of 'evangelicals' (Great Commission Christians) in all megablocs. In the preparation of OW we believed it important to maintain continuity for the sake of our large readership. We also felt the categorization too arbitrary and difficult to determine statistically in a way in which we could make the methodology transparent. It is therefore important to note that there is no longer any comparison between the figures for Evangelicals in the respective volumes.

iv *Handling of Charismatic renewal.* At best, any figures are reasonable estimates for most denominations. We were more cautious in OW and tended to use figures for active participants. WCE was broader and also did more intensive research into this, but the results were only available shortly before the publication of OW 2001. Over all, the high degree of similarity in the global and continental summaries, despite methodological differences is a gratifying relief!

6. To give enhanced value with the publication of the CD version. The volume of information is so large, that even this 800+ page book cannot do more than present a summary for data and information. The CD has much fuller information. The deficiencies of the book:

a) Limited listings of denominations and agencies.

b) No sources given.

c) Broad generalizations - the problem of copyright prevents us from sharing raw textual information.

d) Inability to manipulate the data.

We trust that the CD version will be a good stimulus for further research and development.

• APPENDIX 8 •
STATISTICAL SOURCES

A complete bibliography is impossible to provide here! Only some of the more significant sources can be given.

Primary sources

1. Personal correspondence. For the production of this edition we have sent out or received approximately 50,000 emails, personal letters and questionnaires for information and checking of data and the text. We have preferred nationals to expatriates, but often the latter have been in a better position to respond.

2. Personal conversations around the world in many providential times of fellowship with key informants.

3. Numerous surveys and documents as well as circulars and reports produced by individuals and mission agencies. Much of the more significant information gathered has been collated in chronologically-ordered country or subject files in our Research Office.

4. Wide-ranging searches on the Internet.

Secondary sources

1. General

Encyclopedia Britannica Book of the Year 1998, 1999, 2000. ISBN 0-85299-7592-9.
The World Factbooks, CIA, USA 1989-2000.
World Population Data Sheets 1990-2000, Population Reference Bureau. [www.prb.org/prb/]

2. Religions

National Censuses where available.
National Christian Handbooks (Europe), MARC Europe 1990-2000.
Encyclopedia Britannica Book of the Year, 2000, 2001.
World Christianity Series 1979-1991. MARC/World Vision, USA.
World Christian Encyclopedia, Barrett, David B. and Johnson, Todd, Eds. (Oxford University Press 1982, 2001) ISBN 0 19 572435 6.
World Christian Handbooks 1962, 1967. World Dominion Press, London, UK. Website [www.adherents.com]

3. Statistics for specific items (where supplementary to the above).

a) Area
The above.

b) Population
Government Censuses, where available.

c) Peoples
World Evangelization Database 1992, Dr David Barrett and Todd Johnson.
Joshua Project List Database 2000, AD2000 and Beyond Movement, Dan Scribner.

d) Literacy
The above.

e) Languages
Ethnologue 11th, 12th and 13th Editions, Barbara F. Grimes, Ed. (WBT/SIL 1992/1996/2001)
ISBN 1 55671 026-7. [www.sil.org]

f) **Bible Translation**
   Ethnologue 1992, 1996, 2001.
   World Translations Progress Reports, UBS (1992-1999).

g) **Economic data**
   The above.

h) **Urban statistics**
   World Christian Encyclopedia, Barrett and Johnson, 2001.
   Various websites.

i) **Denominations**
   Denominational statistics, handbooks and responses to questionnaires.
   World Christian Encyclopedia, Barrett and Johnson, 2001.
   National surveys, handbooks, etc., from numerous countries, notably DAWN/Satura-
   tion church-planting surveys and Cliff Holland, PROLADES, Costa Rica for Latin
   America.
   Church growth books, Wm. Carey Library, etc.
   World Christianity Series, 1979-1991, MARC/World Vision, USA.

j) **Missions**
   North American Protestant Ministries Overseas, MARC 1998.
   Mission Handbook (US and Canadian Christian Ministries Overseas) ed. John Siew-
   ert and Dotsey Welliver, EMIS, Billy Graham Center, USA, 2001. ISBN 0 961
   7751-5-7
   UK Christian Handbook 2000/01, Peter Brierley, Ed. MARC Europe, ISBN 1 85321 133 8.
   From Every People, Larry Pate, MARC 1989, ISBN 971-511-162-9.
   The Last Age of Missions, Lawrence E. Keyes, Wm. Carey Library, 1983. ISBN 087808
   4355.
   Christian Handbooks (Europe), P. Brierley, MARC Europe 1985-1992.
   Guida delle Missioni Catholiche, 1989, Vatican, Rome.
   Numerous surveys. In a number of countries (Australia, Germany, Netherlands, New
   Zealand) we had to conduct a national survey by post because no such survey had
   been carried out in recent years.
   Questionnaires were sent out to many hundreds of mission agencies — for those listed
   in Appendices 2 and 3 this was done twice — 1997 and 2001.
   Mission journals and publications.

• APPENDIX 9 •
OTHER *OPERATION WORLD* RESOURCES

Operation World CD

NEW! The CD is available separately from the book. This contains text, databases and graphics of *Operation World.* See page xvii for more details.

Available from your Christian bookstore or:
Gabriel Resources, PO Box 1047, Waynesboro, GA 30830, USA
<info@omlit.om.org>
Paternoster UK, PO Box 300, Kingston Broadway, Carlisle, CA3 0QS
www.paternoster-publishing.com

Operation World

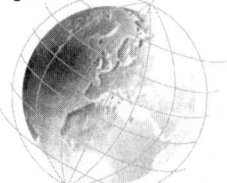

CD-ROM

Window on the World
by Daphne Spraggett with Jill Johnstone
The best-selling books *You Can Change the World* Vols 1+2 written for children and families have been completely revised and provided with stunning graphics in a single volume with the title *Window on the World.* Specifically designed for use in the family for prayer and with information covering many countries and peoples of the world.

Available from your Christian bookstore or:
Gabriel Resources or:
Paternoster UK

Window on **the World**

Daphne Spraggett with Jill Johnstone

When we pray God works

One Hundred Days
by Glenn Myers
NEW! Around the world in 100 Days of Prayer. Extracts from *Operation World* in a CD-sized book.

Available from your Christian bookstore and **Paternoster Publishing.**

Operation World Desk Calendar
Newly designed — Spiral desktop Prayer Calendar highlighting key points and concerns for each day.

Available from your Christian bookstore or:
Gabriel Resources, PO Box 1047, Waynesboro, GA 30830, USA
<info@omlit.om.org>
Paternoster UK, PO Box 300, Kingston Broadway, Carlisle, CA3 0QS
www.paternoster-publishing.com

Operation World

Prayer Calendar

When We Pray God Works

Patrick Johnstone & Jason Mandryk

Operation World Website
www.operationworld.org

The official website for *Operation World,* containing news, stories, answers to prayer and web-specific features to enhance the book. Will also include facilities to submit new information for upcoming revisions.

Other language versions

Printed:
German, Chinese, Korean, Spanish, Portuguese and probably other languages.
Contact **Paternoster Publishing** for details, or for how to arrange translations into other languages.

Operation World Wall Map
Newly designed *Operation World* map of the world and
Operation World Inflatable Globe
Both available from your Christian bookstore or:
Gabriel Resources or **Paternoster Publishing**

The Church Is Bigger Than You Think
by Patrick Johnstone
An essential companion to *Operation World*
This book handles the theological background to *Operation World* - written to encourage and challenge local churches, mission agencies and theological trainers to work together as the Church for world evangelization.

A revised edition is planned for 2006.

Available from your Christian bookstore or:
Christian Focus Publications, Geanies House,
Fearn, Tain IV20 1TW, UK
www.christianfocus.com

Overhead Transparencies
Hundreds of overhead transparencies have been designed over the years and are available in either transparency or electronic formats. Many new OHTs containing the graphics used in *The Church Is Bigger Than You Think* and in this edition of *Operation World* are available. Visit the website for more details.

Futher enquiries to:
International Research Office, WEC International,
Bulstrode, Oxford Road, Gerrards Cross, Bucks SL9 8SZ, UK
www.operationworld.org

Global Mapping International, 15435 Gleneagle Drive
Suite 100, Colorado Springs, CO 80921, USA
www.gmi.org

Missions in the Third Millennium
21 Key Trends for the 21st Century
by Stan Guthrie
An overview of World Missions. This is a well-written, incisive analysis of the world and missions today!

Available from your Christian bookstore and
Paternoster Publishing.

PEOPLES INDEX

In the text of this book, there are hundreds of references to just some of the many thousands of peoples in the world. With the increased awareness of the Church to the missiological significance of ethnic groups, it was felt that mention of these groups in *Operation World* should be documented. This index is extensive, but not comprehensive. Many peoples are known by a variety of names. All the variations mentioned in the text are indexed here; refer to the main text to see how these names interrelate.

Note Feb 2004: In revising parts of the text in this reprint, some of the page numbers may no longer be correct. The page number could, in such cases, be one integer higher.

A

Aari 243, 246-247
Abkhazian 267-268, 548, 633
Aborigine 59, 83-85
Abron 274
Abu Charib 152
Abung 345
Aceh 43, 338, 344
Achés 515
Achi 287
Acholi 598, 641
Adamawa (Pygmy) 140, 149, 195, 494, 495
Adamawa Fulani 140
Adarawa 485
Adare 243
Adele 626
Adi 319-320, 326, 332, 334
Adi Andhra 319, 326
Adi Dharmi 332
Adi Dravida 326, 334
Adi Galong 319
Adi Minyong 319
Adivasi 309
Adygey 361, 375, 377, 539, 610
Afar 16, 27, 224-226, 240-247
Afghan . 15, 47, 61-63, 258, 269, 309, 322, 352, 476, 500, 503, 657, 662
Afrikaner 465, 576
Afro-Caribbean . . . 74-75, 91, 98, 104, 109, 125, 143, 148, 205, 207, 216, 226-227, 259, 283-287, 298, 302, 368, 432, 454, 476, 506, 531, 592-595, 600, 639, 649, 653, 678
Afro-Indian 189
Agew 243
Agni 208, 212
Ahanta 274
Ahir . . . 309, 315, 319, 321, 324-328, 331, 334-336, 469
Ainu 370, 374
Aja 106-107, 624
Ajuran 382
Akan 208, 274
Akaselem 624, 626
Akebu 624, 626
Akha 180, 395, 462-465, 621, 677
Akpe 626
Akposo 624

Aku 265-266
Akurio 601
Akwaio 296-297
Akwapim 274
Akyem 274
Alambadi Kurichchan 326
Alawite 610-612
Albanian . . . 16, 51-55, 63-66, 85-86, 224, 269, 273, 279, 281, 361, 364, 367, 414-415, 607, 633, 682-685
Aleut 657, 662
Algerian 23, 66-69, 455
Alor 623
Alsatian 254
Altai 539
Altaic 15-16, 159, 172-176, 267, 377, 392, 447, 539, 612, 637, 644, 666
Alur 197, 641
Ambenu 348, 622
Amdo Tibetan 169, 176, 178
Amer 240
American . . . 124, 148, 214, 236, 269, 279, 282, 302, 438, 444-446, 476, 496, 498, 506, 508, 520, 544, 556, 591, 629, 649, 657-663
Amerindian . . . 14, 31-38, 75-76, 104, 111-114, 119, 122-124, 155, 189-192, 205, 207, 226, 230-231, 236, 238, 259-260, 287, 289, 296-297, 302-303, 438-440, 476-477, 482-483, 506, 508, 513-519, 600-601, 657, 664, 671, 673
Amhara 243-246
Ami 169
Amis 186, 188
Anaang 488
Andhra Coastal Muslim 319
Andorran 70-71
Angaité 515
Angkola 344-345
Angolan 117, 195, 528, 555, 685
Angolares 555-556
Anii 107, 626
Ansari 321, 335
Antambahoaka 418
Antankarana 418
Antillean 82, 254, 256, 259-260, 433, 473, 475
Anuak 244, 247

Anufo 624, 626
Anyanga 626
Anyi 274
Apatani 319
Arab . . 15-16, 20, 26-27, 38-39, 43, 46-47,
    67-68, 75-76, 86-89, 92-93, 119, 131,
    134, 140-143, 149-154, 189, 193, 197,
    199, 207, 214-218, 224, 226, 230, 233-
    236, 240-243, 254, 269, 273, 279, 281,
    284, 297, 302, 304, 338, 352, 355-357,
    361-364, 375-380, 383, 390-391, 399-
    402, 408-409, 416, 428, 431, 434-435,
    438, 455, 457, 464, 475, 479, 485-488,
    496, 498, 500, 504-506, 520, 528, 530,
    532, 556-558, 574, 582, 586, 596-599,
    610-612, 615, 617, 631, 633, 643, 647-
    649, 653, 657, 661-662, 674, 680-681,
    695; Baggara, 140, 152, 596, 599;
    Bedouin, 66, 233, 235, 355, 357, 361,
    376, 408, 435, 610, 612; Emirati, 647;
    Marsh, 355, 357; Shuwa, 27, 140, 142,
    149-154, 485, 488
Aragonese 582
Arakanese 94, 462
Arakh 327
Arawak 104, 228, 260, 296-299, 601
Arawak Taino 228
Areare 572
Arecuna 296
Arewa 485
Arleng 320
Arlije 633
Armenian 79-81, 89-90, 127-128, 217-
    218, 233, 254-255, 267, 279-280, 302,
    352-357, 363, 375, 378, 390, 399-401,
    505, 539-540, 610-612, 633-638, 644,
    648, 666
Arora 309, 315, 324
Arumun 63
Arunthathiar 319
Ashanti 274
Ashenkazi 16
Ashkun 62
Asian-Caribbean 284
Assamese . . 16, 97, 110, 310, 320, 329-330
Assangori 152, 154
Assyrian 79, 217, 267, 352-358, 399,
    610-612, 633, 635
Asturian 582
Asu 615
Attie 212
Auca. See Waorani
Aukaan 600
Australian Aborigine 59, 83
Austrian . . . 87-88, 269, 410, 571, 607, 683
Austronesian 159, 169
Avá 515
Avar 89-91, 539, 548
Awadhi 335, 469, 472
Ayi 165, 180
Ayizo 106
Aymara . 34, 76, 78, 111-114, 155, 516, 518
Ayoré 515

Ayoreo 111
Azande 197
Azari 352
Azerbaijani. See Azeri
Azeri . . . 16, 79, 89-91, 267, 269, 352, 355,
    377, 539, 633, 637, 666
Aztec 438

B

Babinga 264
Badaga 310, 334
Badawi 596
Badhai 335
Badjaranke 561
Badyara 295
Baga 290, 292
Bagdi 309, 336
Baggara. See Arab
Bagirmi 149, 152, 154
Bago 626
Bagri 327, 500
Baheng 171
Bahna 309
Bahraini 92
Bai 178, 180
Bai Ma 178
Baiga 327
Baihong 180
Bainuk 558, 561
Bairwa 333
Bajau 350, 425-426, 520, 524
Bajun 383
Bajuni 574
Bak 558
Baka 140
Bakgalagadi 118
Bakhtiari 352, 354
Balabac 524
Balai 327, 333
Balanta 26, 293-295, 558-561
Bali 16, 338, 346-348
Baliem Dani 351
Balkar 539, 548
Balmiki 309, 322, 324, 332, 335-336
Balti 325, 500, 503
Baluch . . 16, 47, 61-63, 352, 355, 498-504,
    637, 648
Bama 462-465
Bambara 27, 133-134, 208-211, 257,
    428-430, 434-435, 558, 560
Bamiléké 140, 142
Bana 675
Banda 149, 151, 419
Bandi 405
Bangi 195
Bangla 94, 97
Bangladeshi 94-97, 126, 316, 370, 408,
    422, 427, 498, 556, 647, 653
Bangni 319
Bania. .319-320, 323-324, 327-328, 333, 335
Banjar 338, 348, 425
Banjara 309, 315, 319, 326

Banka 430
Banten 346
Bantu 20, 28, 71, 117-118, 140, 149,
195, 197, 238, 262, 380, 403, 419, 458,
465, 488, 550, 574, 602, 615, 641, 685
Banyumasan 346
Baonuo 171
Baoulé 208-212
Bara 418
Barabaig 615-618
Barbadian 98
Barhai 309, 335
Bari 596
Bariba 106-108
Barma 152, 154
Barman 320
Bartangi 614
Bashkir 549, 666
Bashkort 16, 539, 549
Basketo 243
Basor 327
Basque . 51, 55, 254, 257, 438, 582, 585, 594
Bassa 140, 405, 563
Bassossi 140
Baster 467
Bata 151, 495
Batak 48, 338-339, 344-345
Batanga 238, 240
Batin 345
Bauri 336
Bawean 346
Bawn 95
Bayaka 140
Bayot 295, 561
Beafada 26, 293, 295
Bedar 326
Bedia 321
Bedouin. See Arab
Beja 16, 27, 233, 240-241, 530, 596,
599-600; Beni, 240; Beni Amer, 240; Hed-
erab, 240
Belarusian 55, 99, 100-101, 242, 377,
397, 411, 526, 539, 644, 666
Belime 107
Belu Tetun 348
Bena 615
Benadiri 574
Bench 243, 246-247
Benga 238, 240
Bengali . . . 1, 16, 94-97, 249, 310, 320-322,
330, 335-337, 464, 472, 566, 568, 649
Bengkulu 344-345
Benguet 524
Beni 240
Beni Amer 240
Berber . . . 16, 20, 22, 26, 66-69, 233, 235,
254, 257, 273, 408, 428, 434-435, 455-
457, 476, 558, 586, 631-632; Ghadames,
408; Jalo, 408; Jofra, 408; Kabyle, 22, 26,
66-69, 254, 257; Riff, 254; Shawiya, 26,
66, 68, 254; Siwa, 233, 235; Zuara, 408
Bertha 244
Berti 596

Bete 140
Bété 208, 210, 212
Betsimisaraka 418
Bhambi 309
Bhangi . . 309, 323-324, 327-328, 332-336
Bharia Bhumia 327
Bharwad 323
Bhathudi 332
Bhattra 327
Bhil 16, 309-310, 315, 323, 327-329,
333, 500; Marawi, 310, 333, 337
Bhil Mina 309
Bhilala 333
Bhoi 327, 335
Bhojpuri 321, 335, 337, 436-438, 469
Bhoksa 335
Bhotia 324, 333-335
Bhuiya 309, 321, 332
Bhumihar 309, 315, 321
Bhumij 321, 332, 336
Bhutanese 16, 111
Biao Mien 170-171
Bicol 520, 524
Bidan 434
Bideyat-Zaghawa 152, 599
Bidoun 390-391
Bihari 16, 94, 97, 249, 321
Bijago 293-295
Bilen 240, 241
Bima 347
Bimoba 274, 277, 624
Bingalli 485
Binjhia 327
Bioko 238
Bira 201
Birifor 131, 210, 274, 277
Bisa 197, 210, 624, 626, 685
Bisaya 425-426
Bissa 131, 134
Black Bobo 131
Black Moor 434
Bobo . . . . 131-132, 428-429; Red, 131
Bodi 246
Bodo 309, 320
Bofi 151
Bogol 173
Boikin 509
Boko 106-107
Bokoto 151
Bolgar 539, 549
Bolivian 76, 112-114
Bolon 131-132
Bom 565
Bomu 134, 428
Bonan 169, 176
Boni 382
Bontok 524
Borana 246, 380, 382
Boro 309
Bororo 485
Boruca 207
Bosnian . 16, 55, 85, 115-116, 212-213, 269,
273, 414, 571, 607, 633, 662, 682-683

Bosnian Muslim 115, 273
Bouyei 171
Boya 319, 334
Bozo 27, 428-430
Brahmin 309, 315, 319-328, 331-336
Brahui . 16, 61-63, 352, 355, 500, 502, 504
Brao 137
Brazilian . . 36, 121-124, 185, 259, 260, 513,
   528, 530, 555, 664-665, 672-673, 704
Breton 254, 594
Bribri 205, 207, 506
British . . 33, 57, 83, 92, 104, 124, 140, 143,
   148, 155, 170, 217, 248-249, 269, 278-
   279, 296, 302, 359-360, 380, 410, 422,
   431, 450, 476, 480, 496, 528, 556, 561,
   591, 637, 649-657
Brong 274
Bru 395
Brukpa 325
Budik 561
Buduma 152
Bugi 16, 338, 348-349, 425
Buglere 506
Bulang 180
Bulgarian 52, 127-130, 273, 281, 447-
   449, 538, 633, 637, 644, 683
Bulli 131
Bulsa 132, 274, 277
Bumi 246
Bumiputera 422
Bunak 622
Bunun 169, 186
Bunuo 171
Burba 106-107
Burgher 586
Burkinabé 131-134, 208
Burmese 16, 47, 94, 462-465, 568
Burundian 199
Buryat 174, 451, 539, 548-549
Busa 494
Busansi 274
Bushmen. See San, Khoisan
Bwa 428
Bwamu 132

C

Cabe 107
Cabécar 205, 207
Caboverdian 147-148, 293, 473, 528,
   558-559
Caboverdian Creole 147
Cai 171
Cakchiquel 287
Calabrian 364, 367
Calderon 230, 232
Caledoche French 478-479
Cambodian . . 83, 137-139, 254, 257, 618,
   657, 675
Canadian 132, 143-148, 674
Canari 230
Cantonese . . 159, 170, 181, 184, 251, 422,
   508, 566, 674, 677

Cape Malay 576, 580
Carib . . 104, 190, 226-227, 260, 289, 296-
   297, 302, 482, 595, 601, 650
Carolinian 443-446
Catalan 70, 254, 582
Catio 189
Caucasian 69, 89, 205, 267, 468, 478,
   506, 509, 532, 576, 669
Cayapa 230
Cebuano 520, 525
Celtic 51, 83, 85, 359-361, 649, 655
Central Tibetans 179
Chadian 16, 27, 151, 154-155, 491
Chadic 27, 140, 152, 485, 488
Chagga 615
Chagos Islander 437
Chakkliyan 334
Chakma 94-97, 320, 330, 335
Chakossi 624
Cham 65, 137, 139, 675, 677
Chamacoco 515
Chamar . . 309, 315, 321-328, 332-336, 469
Chamba 488, 495, 624
Chamba Daka 488
Chami 192
Chamorro 15, 286, 445, 446
Chamus 382
Changana 458
Changpa 325
Changping Iu Mien 171
Channan 326, 334
Chari-Bagirmi 152, 154
Charrua 664
Chasi 617
Chaudhri 323
Chaungtha 462
Chechen . . . 267-268, 375, 377, 539, 541,
   547-548
Chenchu 319
Cherkess 539, 548
Cheruman 326
Chettiyar 464
Chewa 419-421, 458, 688, 691
Chhetri 469, 472
Chilean 76, 155, 157-158
Chimborazo 230, 232
Chimbu 509
Chin 47, 94, 310, 329-330, 462-465
Chinese 1, 2, 9, 14-16, 33, 36, 38, 41-44, 46-
   47, 51, 57-59, 69, 76, 78, 82, 83-87, 91,
   98, 101, 104-105, 112, 119, 122, 126-
   127, 137, 139, 143-144, 146, 159-190,
   205, 207, 214, 216, 219, 226-232, 236,
   250-251, 254-259, 260-262, 286-289,
   296, 302, 304, 338-340, 344-348, 361-
   364, 368, 370, 373, 385-389, 392-397,
   416, 422-426, 432, 436-438, 443-446,
   451, 453, 462, 464, 468, 473-477, 480-
   482, 496-497, 506-509, 512-521, 524,
   530-531, 534, 545, 556, 561, 566-567,
   572, 576, 577, 580, 582, 585, 591, 600-
   602, 605, 607, 615, 618-623, 627-630,
   640, 649, 653-654, 657-658, 661, 665,

669, 671, 674, 675, 696, 697
Chiquitano 111
Chiriguano 76, 78, 114
Chitrali 500
Chokwe 71, 197, 687
Chong 137
Chonyi 383
Chopi 458
Chorote 515
Chorti 289, 302
Chotra Bansi 309
Chrame 178
Chuan Miao 178
Chuhra 324, 332
Chukchi 547
Chukotka 547
Chulupé 513, 515
Chuuk 286, 443-444
Chuvash 539, 549-550
Chwabo 458, 460
Circassian . . 355, 361, 375, 539, 548, 610,
  612, 633
Colombian 9, 190-192, 476, 508
Coloured 576, 581, 688
Comorian 28, 193-194, 416, 418, 534
Congolese . . . 101-103, 134, 196-202, 615,
  641, 643, 685
Coreguaje 192
Corsican 254
Creole . . 82, 147, 238, 259-260, 265, 293,
  436, 476, 483-484, 534-535, 561, 563,
  600; Caboverdian, 147; French, 227, 284,
  432, 534, 593; Guianese, 260; Por-
  tuguese, 147, 293, 295
Crimean Tatar. . 127, 633, 644, 646, 666,
  668
Croat 85-86, 115-116, 212-213, 269,
  304, 367, 571, 607, 610, 682-683
Cuban 72, 148, 215-216, 600, 657
Cuiba 192
Cun 171
Cutchi 380, 383
Cuyunon 524
Cypriot 217-219, 279
Czech . . . 49, 127, 219, 220-221, 273, 569,
  570, 712

D

Daarood 574
Daasenach 246-247, 382
Daba 140
Dabarre 574
Dagaaba 274
Dagaari 131-132, 276
Dagba 149
Dagoda 622
Dagomba 274, 277
Dahalo 382
Dai . . . 14, 16, 47, 152, 160, 180, 675, 677
Dairi 344
Daju 27, 152, 596, 599
Dalit 44, 309, 312-313, 315, 319-324,

327-333, 336, 501
Damara 465, 467
Dan 170
Danakil 224
Dane 32, 223-224, 246-247, 269, 282,
  307-308, 397, 496, 605, 678
Dani 350-351
Darfur 27, 596, 599
Darghin 539, 548
Dari 61, 63, 352, 500, 503-504, 614
Dassa 107
Datooga 617
Daur 172-173
Daw 395
Dawa 246
Dayak . . 338, 345, 348, 426; Sea, 126-127,
  348, 426
Daza 27, 152, 485, 487
Deccani 16, 319, 326, 328
Dega 274
Deli 338, 344-345
Delo 626
Dendi 106-107, 485, 487
Deng 179
Deori 320
Desano 192
Devadasi 326
Dhaiso 617
Dhangar 323, 326
Dhanka 323
Dhanuk 321, 324, 335
Dhimba 465, 467
Dhobi 309, 315, 319, 321, 335-336
Dhodia 323
Dhor 323
Dida 208, 210
Didinga 596
Digil 574
Digo 383, 617
Dimasa 320
Dime 246
Dimli 633
Dinka 596-600
Dir 503, 574
Dire 246
Ditammari 106-107
Djerma 485
Doghosie 131-132
Dogon 27, 131-134, 428-430
Dogra 325
Dogri 324, 500
Dohoi 348
Dom 309, 325, 336, 610
Domari 633
Dombe 691
Dong 159, 169, 171
Dongxiang 160, 165, 169
Dorobo 382
Dosadh 321
Dravidian 47, 249, 309-310, 427, 500
Drukpa 110-111
Druze 361, 363, 399-402, 504-505,
  611-612

Duala 140
Dubla 323
Dughwede 495
Dukawa 494
Dum 325
Dumagat 524
Dungan 377, 392, 394
Dusadh 309
Dusun 425
Dutch 33, 82, 101, 104, 117-118, 269,
    344, 473-476, 528, 580, 587, 600
Duun 428, 430
Dyan 131
Dyerma 107
Dzalakha 110
Dzongkha 110

E

E 170
East Bank Jordanian 375
Easter Islanders 155, 158
Eastern Khampa 178
Eastern Lipo 165, 180
Ebore 246
Ede 675-676
Edo 487, 493-494
Egyptian 92, 233-236, 363, 375-377,
    390-391, 399, 408, 498, 533, 556, 596,
    647, 680
Ejagham 140
Elgeyo 380
Embera 189, 506
Embu 380
Emerillon 260
Emirati 647
Ende 347
Enga 509
Enger Yugur 169
Enim 345
Enshi Miao 178
Epena 192
Ergong 178
Eritrean 233, 241, 596
Erzya 549-550
Esan 487, 494
Eshira 262
Eskimo. See Inuit
Estate Tamil 586, 589
Estonian 242-243, 539, 544, 605
Ethiopian 15, 224-225, 233, 240-241,
    244-247, 281, 296, 361, 363, 369, 505,
    574-575, 596, 599, 604, 680, 681
Eton 140
Eurafrican 189, 296, 298, 602
Eurindian 189, 482
Euro-American 32-33, 74-75, 91, 125,
    226-227, 230, 236, 283, 298, 368, 438,
    454, 476, 531, 593, 595, 639, 657, 678
Euronesian 203, 553
Evenki 174, 451, 453, 539, 547
Ewe 274, 277, 487, 624-626
Ewondo 140

Extremaduran 582
Eyle 574
Ezaa 487

F

Faeroese 247-248, 282
Falasha 16, 243, 361, 363
Fali 140, 142
Falkland Islander 249
Fang 140, 238, 240, 262, 264, 555
Fante 274
Farsi 92, 352, 612, 614
Fatukulu 622
Felupe 293, 295
Fijian 58-59, 249-252, 669
Filipino . . 15, 48, 69, 83, 92, 126-127, 143,
    181, 184, 186, 218, 286, 361, 364, 370,
    374, 376, 390, 408, 422, 425-426, 443-
    447, 496, 498, 520-525, 532-533, 556,
    566, 568, 647-648, 657, 661
Finnish 119, 184, 188, 242, 246, 252-
    254, 363, 382, 466-467, 496, 539,547,
    559-561, 585, 605, 619, 621
Flemish 101-104, 254
Fon 106-108, 624, 626
Forro 555
Frafra 131, 274, 277
French . . . 66, 70, 101, 106, 140, 143, 145,
    149, 155, 194-195, 208, 224, 254-259,
    262, 269, 284, 364, 413, 416, 428, 432,
    434, 450, 455, 478, 485, 528, 534, 556,
    558, 561, 607, 624, 631, 679; Canadian
    145
Frisian 269, 473
Friulian 212, 364, 367, 571
Fula 107, 428, 485, 558, 563
Fulacunda 292, 558-561
Fulani 27, 107, 143, 263, 486-488,
    492-495
Fulanke 428, 430
Fulbe 16, 27, 106-107, 131-132, 140-
    143, 149-152, 155, 210, 254, 263-266,
    274, 277, 290-293, 295, 428-430, 434-
    435, 485-488, 492-495, 558-560, 563,
    565, 596, 599, 624, 626, 699
Fungom 140
Futunan 478, 679

G

Ga Mong 171
Gabbra 382
Gabonese 262-264
Gabri 152
Gadaboursi 224
Gadaria 335
Gaddi 324-325
Gagauz 127, 447-449, 633
Gagou 210
Galician 528, 582
Galoli 622
Galong 319
Gamit 323, 328

Gan 159, 174, 334
Gana 428, 430
Ganda 327, 641
Gangakula 326
Ganja 561
Garasia 323, 333
Garhwali 336
Garia 309
Garifuna 104-105, 287, 289, 302-303,
482, 484
Garo 94-95, 310-311, 330
Garre 574
Gauda 331
Gawwada 243
Gayo 344
Gban 210
Gbari 487, 494
Gbari Yamma 494
Gbaya 140, 149-152
Ge 171
Gedeo 243
Gelao 180
Gen 106, 144, 387
Georgian . . . 79, 89, 90, 91, 267, 268, 269,
539, 545, 548, 644
German 45, 101, 104, 119, 143, 155,
212, 219, 230, 254, 269-273, 279, 304,
364, 367, 377, 379, 392-393, 397, 410,
413, 438, 450, 465-467, 496, 513, 526,
528, 535, 537, 539, 543, 544, 571, 576,
607, 644, 649, 664, 666, 683; Low, 111
Germanic 51, 102, 252, 410
Ghadames 408
Ghagar 233
Ghanaian . . . 208, 266, 275-277, 473, 475,
624, 626, 649
Gheg 63, 66
Ghirath 324
Ghorbati 352
Giay 180, 677
Gibraltarian 278
Gidar 140, 142
Gilaki 352, 355
Gimira 243
Gio 405, 406
Giriama 383
Gisu 641
Giziga 140, 142
Glaro 210
Goanese 322, 503, 528, 530
Goemai 494
Goffa 243
Gogo 615
Gola 405, 407, 563
Golla 334
Golog 176
Gond . . 16, 309-310, 315, 319, 321, 327-332
Gondaru 326
Gonja 274-277
Goran 63, 65, 152
Gorontalo 349
Gouin 131
Gouro 208-212

Gowari 328
Gowli 319, 326
Grebo 405, 407
Greek 51, 55, 63-65, 79, 85, 111, 127,
140, 217-219, 224, 226, 267, 269, 273,
279-281, 361-364, 367, 431, 539, 576,
580, 633-645, 649, 704
Greenlander 223, 282
Grenadian 284
Grusi 27, 131
Gtsang 179
Gua 274
Guahibo 189
Guajiro 189, 671, 673
Guamanian 286-287
Guang 274
Guarani 78, 111, 123
Guarayu 111
Guatemalan 104
Guaymi 205, 207, 506, 508
Gude 142
Guduf 495
Guéré 208, 210
Guianese 260
Guinean 208, 291-293, 487, 561, 563
Gujar 309, 315, 324-325, 333
Gujarati . 16, 183, 249, 310, 322-324, 328,
337, 380, 383, 416, 418, 421, 508, 534,
561, 568, 580, 615, 617, 685, 688, 691
Guji 246
Gujjar 324-325
Gulai 152
Gumuz 244, 247
Gun 106, 107
Gundi 149
Guopu 171
Gur . . 16, 27, 131, 208, 274, 428, 485, 624
Gurage 243, 247
Gurenne 131-134, 274
Gurkha 183, 469, 472
Gurkhali 462
Gurma 27, 106, 108, 131-134, 485-486, 624
Gurmantche 107
Gurung 16, 110, 333, 469
Guyanese 296, 297, 600
Gypsy 16, 38, 51, 63, 66, 86, 115-116,
127-130, 158, 189, 212, 219, 233, 254-
255, 273, 279, 281, 304, 307, 315, 352,
355, 357, 361, 397, 414, 438, 447, 449,
462, 473, 496, 519, 524, 526, 528, 535-
539, 545, 569-570, 582, 583, 590, 605,
607, 610, 612, 633, 637, 644, 649, 650,
657, 682-683; Arlije, 633; Banjara, 309,
315, 319, 326; Dom 309, 325, 336, 610;
Domari, 633; Ghargar, 233; Ghorbati,
352; Halebi, 233; Lombadi, 315; Nawar,
352; Roma, 38, 51-53, 55, 63, 65, 130,
158, 244, 254-256, 273, 279, 281, 304,
307, 315, 414-415, 447, 473, 496, 528,
535, 539, 545, 569-570, 582-584, 605,
607, 644, 649-650, 657, 682-684; Romani
127, 130, 279, 364, 519, 538; Sea, 462,
524; Xoraxai, 66

H

Ha 615
Haavu 197
Hadiyya 243, 247
Hainanese 159, 171, 425, 566
Haitian . . 91, 216, 227-229, 259-260, 298,
  300, 639
Hajong 94, 320, 330
Hakka . . . 16, 159, 170-171, 181, 186, 188-
  189, 422, 425, 436, 508, 566
Halam 335
Halba 327, 328
Halebi 233
Halh 451
Han Chinese . . 47, 159, 165-166, 168-181,
  186-187, 675
Hani 180, 677
Haoni 180
Harari 243, 246
Haratine 434-435
Harijan 309
Hassaniya 16, 434-435, 455-458, 560
Hausa 16, 27, 66, 107, 140, 142, 151-
  152, 195, 210, 263, 485-495, 596, 599,
  624, 626
Hawiye 574
Haya 615
Hazara 16, 61-62, 352, 500
Hedareb 240
Hehe 615
Heikum 467
Herero 71, 73, 117-119, 465-468
Hezhen 173
Hiligaynon 520
Hill 545
Hill Brahman 469
Himba 465, 467
Hindi . . . 94, 110, 249, 322-337, 469, 561,
  566, 568, 617
Hindko 500, 504
Hispanic . . 32, 76, 91, 148, 214, 216, 227,
  439, 483, 517, 532, 657, 661, 678
Hjua 395
Hkauri 180
Hmong 47, 159, 169-173, 178, 180,
  254, 257-260, 395-397, 600, 602, 618,
  621, 657, 675, 677. See also Miao
Hmong Daw 395
Hmong Hjua 395
Hmong-Mien 159, 170-173, 178, 180,
  395, 397, 675
Hmu 171
Hokkien 188, 422, 566
Hoklo 186, 188
Holaya 326
Honduran 104
Hor 321
Hre 675
Hui 16, 47, 159-160, 165, 168-181, 184, 189
Huitoto 192
Huizhou 159, 168
Hukwe 71
Huli 509
Hunanese 159
Hunde 201
Hungarian 53, 86, 212, 304-307, 535-
  538, 569-571, 610, 644, 647, 682-683
Hutu 22, 134-135, 199, 550, 615, 641

I

Iban 126-127, 348, 426
Ibibio 488, 493
Ibo 487
Icelandic 307-308
Idiga 319
Idoma 487, 494
Ife 106-107, 624
Ifugao 524
Igala 487, 494
Igbirra 487, 494
Igbo 140, 487-488, 493-494
Ignaciano 111
Ijaw 487, 493
Ilanun 425, 520
Ilavar 309
Ilocano 520
Imazighen 20, 26, 66, 68, 455
Inca 112, 518
Indian 14, 16, 58, 74, 83, 92-93, 104,
  110-111, 114, 125-126, 181, 189, 191,
  226, 230, 232, 249-251, 283, 287, 296,
  309-338, 368, 390-391, 422-428, 436-
  441, 462, 464, 471-473, 481, 498, 500,
  506, 515, 518-519, 532, 556, 566, 568,
  580, 587, 590, 595, 600, 602, 617, 629-
  630, 647-648, 661-662, 688; Amerindian,
  14, 31-38, 75-76, 104, 111-114, 119,
  122-124, 155, 189-192, 205, 207, 226,
  230-231, 236, 238, 259-260, 287, 289,
  296-297, 302-303, 438-440, 476-477,
  482-483, 506, 508, 513-601, 657, 664,
  671, 673; Carib, 104, 190, 227, 289, 296-
  297, 302, 482, 595, 601, 650; East, 105,
  508; West, 254, 284, 506
Indonesian 33, 48, 83, 85, 171, 181,
  184, 338-351, 416, 422-426, 473-475,
  478, 520, 566, 568, 600, 602, 622, 623
Inga 192
Ingush 539, 548
Ingwe 494
Inkeri 539
Intha 462
Inuit 143, 146, 282, 547, 657, 662
Iranian . . 15-16, 47, 61, 63, 83, 86-93, 207,
  218, 223-224, 258, 267, 269, 273, 279,
  309, 322, 352-355, 370, 374, 390-391,
  473, 476, 496, 498, 500, 539, 547, 556,
  582, 605, 610, 612, 614, 633, 636-637,
  647-649, 653, 657, 661-662, 666, 674
Iraqw 615, 618
Irish 83, 359, 360-361, 649, 655, 657
Irish Traveller 649
Irular 334

Isan 618
Isawa 495
Isekiri 487, 493
Ishilhayn 455
Isnag 524
Isoko 487, 493
Israeli . . 8, 43, 361-363, 399, 401, 504-505
Issa 224
Issaq 224
Istrian 212
Isxaaq 574
Italian 9, 76, 85, 101, 119, 143, 155,
    212-213, 240, 244, 254, 257, 269, 273,
    278, 364-367, 410, 413, 431, 438, 450,
    478, 513, 554, 556, 571, 574, 607, 610,
    631, 649, 664, 674, 699
Iu Mien . . . . 170-173; Changping, 171
Ivoirian 208-212
Ixil 287, 289
Izi 487

J

Jabarti 241
Jacaltec 289
Jahanka 558, 560
Jain 15, 310, 316, 323-329, 333, 335,
    380, 383
Jakanke 290, 292
Jakun 424
Jalia 320, 336
Jalon 292, 558
Jalonke 561
Jama Mapun 524
Jamaican 9, 227, 368-369
Jamatia 335
Jambi 344, 345
Japanese . . . 1, 9, 16, 33, 38, 46-47, 76, 83,
    111, 119, 122, 137, 166, 172, 181, 186,
    205, 286, 338, 370-374, 387-388, 438,
    443-446, 462, 481, 506, 513, 516, 519,
    520, 566, 568, 618, 649, 657, 665, 675,
    696-697
Jarai 137, 139, 675-676
Jat 309, 315, 324, 332-335
Jatapu 319
Jaunsari 335
Javanese. See Jawa
Jawa 38, 48, 259, 338-340, 345-348,
    425, 479, 600, 602
Jawa Tengger 346
Jebala 455
Jeeri 558
Jew . . . 2, 15-16, 21, 32-33, 38, 41, 45, 48,
    51, 55, 58, 64, 76-79, 82-93, 100-105,
    109, 112, 115, 120, 127-130, 144, 148,
    156, 158, 182, 190, 198, 205, 212, 214,
    217-220, 223, 228, 230, 237, 242-243,
    250-257, 267-273, 278-279, 302-306,
    352-354, 359-365, 368, 377, 392, 397-
    400, 411-413, 439, 447-450, 455-456,
    466, 473-474, 477, 480-481, 496, 504-
    508, 514, 516, 529, 531, 536, 539-540,
    545, 566, 569, 577, 580-583, 601, 605,
    608, 611, 631-633, 638, 644, 646, 649-
    650, 654, 657-658, 662-666, 671, 674,
    678-682, 689; Ukrainian, 363, 646
Jiarong 178
Jiddu 574
Jie 643
Jin 159, 177
Jing 170
Jingpo 165, 180-181, 465
Jofra 408
Jogi 333-336
Jola 26, 265-266, 293, 558-561
Jotoni 430
Jula . . 27, 131-134, 208-212, 274, 428, 430
Julaha 324

K

Kaanba 131
Kaba 149, 152
Kababish speakers 596
Kabardi 539
Kabardian 548, 633
Kabiye 108, 624, 626
Kabré 624
Kabyle 22, 26, 66-69, 254, 257
Kachari 320
Kachhi 327, 335
Kachin 462-463
Kadazan 425-426
Kado 152, 165, 180, 462, 485, 487
Kadugli 596
Kaficho 247
Kahar 321, 335
Kaibartta 320, 335, 336
Kaje 488
Kaka 140, 149
Kakwa 641, 643
Kalal 319, 326
Kalanga 117-119, 688, 691
Kalash 503
Kalibugan 520
Kalinga 524
Kallan 334
Kalmyk 539, 548
Kalwar 309
Kamano 509
Kamba 380
Kambaata 243, 247
Kambari 494
Kamboh 332
Kami 615, 617
Kamma 309
Kammalan 334
Kamuku 494
Kanak 478-479
Kanakkam 326
Kanaura 324
Kandra 331
Kandu 321
Kanet 324
Kanjobal 287

Kankanay 524
Kannada 310, 322, 326, 328, 334
Kanu 321
Kanuri . . . 16, 27, 140, 142, 152, 155, 485-488, 492-495
Kaonde 685, 687
Kapau 509
Kapingamarangian 443
Kapsiki 140, 142
Kara 151, 637
Karaboro 131
Karachay 539, 548
Karamojong 641, 643
Karbi 320
Kare 149
Karelian 539, 547
Karen 47, 462-465, 618-621
Karo 246, 339, 344
Kasena 131, 274-277
Kashmiri . 310, 325-326, 472, 500, 649, 653
Kashubian 526
Kasonke 428, 430
Kassonke 27, 560
Katang 395
Kathodi 328
Kati 62
Kattunayakan 334
Kaur 345
Kavango 465, 467
Kawa 180, 462
Kawar 327
Kayan 126, 348, 426
Kayastha 309, 335-336
Kazakh 16, 160, 165, 176, 179, 377-379, 392, 451, 453, 539, 637, 666, 668
Kebumtamp 110
Kedayan 126, 426
Keffa 243
Kekchi 236, 287, 289
Kelabit 127
Kemak 622
Kensiu 424
Kenyah 126, 348, 426
Kera 152
Ketchi 104
Kewat 327, 335
Khakas 173
Khakass 549
Khalkha 174, 451
Khambu 333
Khampa Tibetan 176-179
Khandait 331
Khanti 539, 547
Kharia 320-321, 331
Kharwar 321
Khas 333
Khasi 47, 94-95, 309, 330
Khmer . . . 16, 47, 137-139, 159, 180, 395, 424, 462, 618, 621, 675, 677
Khmu 395-397, 462, 621
Khoisan . . 20, 71, 117, 380, 382, 465, 467, 574, 615, 685, 688
Khond 309, 331

Khorasani 352, 355
Khowari 500, 503
Khyang 97
Kiga 641
Kikuyu 380
Kimoso 416
Kipsigis 380
Kiput 126
Kirabi 110
Kisan 331
Kissi . . 290-293, 405, 563, 565; North, 565
Kituba 197
Klao 405, 565
Ko 131
Koalib 596
Kochin 361
Kohistani 500
Koho 675-676
Koiri 309, 321
Kokna 323, 328
Kokola 460
Kol 327, 331, 335
Kolho 332
Koli . 309, 323-324, 327, 328, 335, 500, 502
Koli Mahadev 309, 323, 328
Kolowar 328
Komering 345
Komi 539, 547
Komo 244
Komono 131-132
Komso 247
Konda Dhora 319, 334
Konda Reddi 334
Kongo 71, 74, 195, 197
Konjo 641
Konkani 310, 322, 326, 328
Konkomba 274-277, 624, 626
Kono 27, 290, 563, 565
Konso 243
Konyagi 558, 561
Konyanke 290
Koorete 247
Kordofan 596
Korean . . 15, 33, 43-44, 46-47, 69, 76, 92, 114, 119, 122, 155, 159, 165, 174, 175, 266, 286-287, 370-373, 377-379, 382, 385-393, 408, 435, 445-446, 451, 482, 513-514, 520, 523, 539, 543, 560, 566, 568, 613, 618, 657-658, 661, 666-667, 696, 704, 712
Kori 309, 336
Korku 327-329
Korono 332
Koruk 633
Koryak 547
Kosovar 63-65, 684
Kosraean 443
Kota 262, 264
Koti 458
Kotoko . . 106, 140, 142, 152, 274, 624, 626
Kouya 210
Koya 319, 332
Koyaka 208

Kpelle 290-293, 405, 407
Kpessi 626
Krahn 405-407
Kravet 137, 139
Krim 563
Krio 563, 565
Krongo 596
Kru 208, 405, 563
Krumen 210
Kuba 201
Kuchi 62
Kui 137, 310, 331, 618, 621
Kuki 47, 310, 329, 330
Kukna 323
Kulango 208, 212, 274, 276
Kulon 346
Kumhar 327, 333, 335
Kumyk 539
Kuna 506, 508
Kunama 240-241
Kunbi 309, 319, 323, 328
Kunda 460, 688, 691
Kundu 140
Kung 71, 467
Kuranko 290, 563, 565
Kuravan 326
Kurd 8, 16, 43, 47, 79-83, 86, 88-92,
    101, 104, 254, 267, 269, 273, 352-358,
    375, 377, 392, 399, 473, 476, 544, 605,
    607, 610, 612, 633-637, 648-649, 653,
    655; Kurmanji 81, 91, 355, 358, 612, 633,
    635; Luri, 352-355; Sorani, 355, 358;
    Yazidi, 355
Kurfey 485, 487
Kuria 380
Kurmanji . . 81, 91, 355, 358, 612, 633, 635
Kurmi 309, 315, 321, 327, 335
Kurtey 485, 487
Kuruba 309, 326, 334
Kuruma 131
Kuruman 334
Kusale 131
Kusasi 274, 277
Kushwaha 321
Kuwaiti 375, 390-391
Kwa 140, 274, 563, 579, 624
Kwadi 71
Kwahu 274
Kwaio 572
Kwangali 73-74, 465
Kwanyama 74
Kwaraae 572
Kwinti 600
Kwongsai 425
Kxoe 467
Kyrgyz . . 16, 160, 165, 179, 392-394, 612,
    666, 668

L

Labbai 334
Ladakhi 325
Ladin 364, 367

Ladino 33, 104, 236, 302, 482, 506
Lagoon peoples 208
Lagou 171
Lahu 180-181, 397, 463, 465, 618, 621, 677
Lak 539, 548
Lalung 320
Laluo 180
Lama 624
Lamaholot 347
Lamba 106, 624, 685, 687
Lambada 309
Lambya 419, 421
Lami 180
Lampung 344-345
Lampung Abung 345
Lampung Peminggir 345
Lampung Pubian 345
Landoma 290
Langbassi 151
Lango 641
Lanka Tamil 318, 586, 589
Lao 16, 137, 254, 257, 395-397, 462,
    618, 657
Laotian 259, 396, 602
Lapp 252, 496, 605
Lashi 180
Latin/Romance 51, 102
Latvian 397-399
Lau 572
Lawa 180
Laz 269, 633, 636
Lebanese .76, 146, 192, 208, 210, 227, 254,
    259, 262, 290, 368, 390, 399, 400-405,
    485, 513, 531, 558, 563, 624, 629, 674
Lebu 558
Lega 197, 201
Lele 152, 290
Lematang 345
Lembak 345
Lenca 236, 302-303
Lendu 197
Lengua 513, 515
Lenje 685
Lepcha 110, 333-334
Leyte 520, 524
Lezhgi 89-91, 539, 548, 637
Lhasa Tibetans 179
Lhoba 179
Li 171
Liberian 266, 405-408, 491, 563
Liechtensteiner 410
Ligbi 274, 277
Ligurian 364, 450
Limba 563
Limbu 110, 469
Limbum 140
Lingala 195, 197, 202
Lingao 171
Lingayat 309, 326, 328
Lio 347
Lipo . . . . 165, 180; Eastern, 165, 180
Lisu 165, 180-181, 462-465, 621
Lithuanian 55, 397, 411-412

Loba 110, 472
Lobi 27, 131, 208, 212
Lobiri 132
Lodha 327, 335-336
Lohar 321, 324, 335, 469
Loko 563, 565
Lokpa 106-107, 626
Lolo 460
Loma 405
Lombard 364
Lomwe 419, 421, 458, 461
Lor 346
Losso 624
Lotuko 596
Low German 111
Lozi 117, 467, 685-688
Lu 395, 462, 464, 618
Luba 197
Luchazi 71, 74, 467
Lugbara 197, 641
Lunda 71, 685, 687
Luo 380, 615
Luoluopo 180
Luri 352-355
Lushai 330, 463, 465
Luto 151
Luvale 71, 685, 687
Luxembourgers 413
Luyia 380
Luzon 520, 524
Lwo 596
Lyele 131-132

M

Maasai 380, 382, 615, 618
Maay 574, 576
Maba 27, 152, 154
Mabaan 598
Macanese 184-185
Macedonian 55, 63, 65, 85, 127, 280,
414-415, 682
Machinga 617
Macushi 296-297
Mada 494
Madan 355, 357
Madi 641, 643
Madiga 309, 319, 326
Madura 16, 48, 338, 345-348
Mafi 140
Mafue 467
Mag 335
Magar 469
Magindanao 520, 524
Maguzawa 27, 495
Magyar 304
Mahadev 309, 323, 328
Mahafaly 418
Mahali 336
Mahar 309, 315, 327-329
Mahei 464
Mahi 624, 626
Mahili 95

Mahishya 331, 335-336
Mahisyada 309
Mahli 321
Mahongwe 264
Mahou 208, 210
Mahra 498-499
Mahratta 309, 315, 323, 326, 328
Mahyavanshi 323
Maithili 321, 469, 472
Majang 247
Majingai 152
Makaa 140
Makasae 622
Makassar 338, 349, 351
Makhuwa 193, 458-461, 615
Maki 469
Makian 350
Makonde 28, 458-461, 615-618
Makwe 458
Mala 309, 319
Mala Sale 319
Malabar Muslim 326-327, 535
Malagasy . . 15, 48, 193-194, 225, 416-418,
534, 561
Malakote 382
Malawian 419
Malay 15-16, 43, 48, 83, 85, 126-127,
137, 171-172, 184-186, 189, 338, 344-
345, 348, 350, 422-426, 462, 566, 568,
576, 580, 586, 590-591, 618, 621-622;
Cape, 576, 580
Malayali . . 92, 326, 334, 337, 391, 422, 566
Malayarayan 326
Malaysian 126, 370, 424-426, 566
Maldivian 427-428
Male 247
Maleku 205, 207
Mali (Ethiopia) 246
Mali (India) 327, 328, 333
Malian 27, 208, 428
Malinke . 16, 208, 210, 254, 257, 274, 290,
292, 428-430, 558, 561, 565
Maltese 85, 278, 431-432
Malto 321
Maluku 339, 341, 345, 349-350, 473
Mam 274-277, 287, 289
Mamba 622
Mamprusi 274-277
Mamsani 352
Manchu 160, 168, 172-177, 451
Manchurian 16
Mandailing 344, 345
Mandara 140, 142
Mandarin 159, 186-189, 566, 696
Mande 26, 131, 208, 265, 274, 290,
293, 405, 428, 558-560, 563; South, 208
Mandingo . . . 27, 265, 293, 295, 405-407.
See also Mandinka
Mandinka 265-266, 293, 558-561
Mandja 149
Mandyak 26
Manga 485-487
Mangarevan 261-262

Mangbetu 197
Manggarai 347
Mangkong 395
Mangrik 325
Maninka 293, 428, 430, 563
Manipuri 310, 329
Manjak 558, 561
Manjako 265-266, 293-295
Manjui 515
Mankanya 293, 295, 558, 561
Mano 290, 405, 406
Mansi 539, 547
Mansoanka 295
Manya 290-292, 407
Manyawa 460
Manyika 458
Mao 159, 161, 173, 329
Maori 59, 203, 479-481
Mappila 309, 326-327
Mapuche 76, 155-158
Mapudungun-speaker 155-158
Mapun 425, 524
Maquiritare 671, 673
Mara 463
Marakam 495
Marakwet 380
Maranao 520, 524
Marathi 16, 310, 322-323, 326-328
Maravan 334
Maravi 419, 458
Marba 152
Marenje 458, 460
Mari 539, 549-550
Marka 131, 430
Maron 259-260
Maronite 144, 217, 219, 400-401, 674
Marquesan 261-262
Marsh Arab 355, 357
Marshallese 444-445
Maru 180-181
Masa 140
Masabu 641
Masalit 27, 152, 596, 599
Mashi 73
Masmaje 152
Massa 152
Mataco 76, 111
Matagalpa 482, 484
Matang 328
Maure 265, 428, 430, 558, 560
Maures 20, 560
Mauri 485, 487
Mauritanian 434-435
Mauritian 437
Mawari 310, 333, 337, 502
Maxi 106
Mayan . 34-35, 104-105, 287-289, 438, 442
Mazanderani 16, 352
Mazhabi 332
Mbai 151-152
Mbangwe 264
Mbanza 195
Mbati 149

Mberi 262
Mbete 195
Mbo 140
Mbororo Fulbe 140, 149, 151, 155
Mboshi 195
Mbukushu 73, 117-118, 467
Mbum 140, 142, 149
Mbunda 71
Mbundu 71
Mbwela 71, 73, 687
Meankieli 605
Mede 633
Megh 325
Meghwal 323, 333
Meitei 329
Meitei Pangal 329
Mekitelyu 205, 207
Melanau 426
Melanesian . . . 57, 249, 478-479, 509-513,
    572, 669
Melayu . . . . . 344-345, 350. See also Malay
Melpa 509
Mende 407, 563, 565
Mentawai 344
Meo 47
Merina 416, 418
Mestizo . . . 14, 33, 76, 104, 111, 119, 155,
    189, 205, 230, 236, 302, 438, 483, 506,
    514, 516, 555, 657, 671
Métis 143
Mhali 321, 336
Miao . . . . 165, 168-173, 178-181, 395. See
    also Hmong
Micronesian . . 58, 286, 287, 443-447, 468,
    640
Midob 596, 599
Mien159, 170-173, 178, 180, 395, 397, 675
Mijikenda 380, 383
Mikea 416
Mikifore 290
Mikir 320, 330
Millet 52, 128-129
Mimi 152
Min Bei 159, 169
Min Dong 159, 169
Min Nan 159, 169
Mina 107, 309, 327, 333, 624-625
Minahasa 339, 345, 349
Minangkabau . 16, 338, 344-345, 351, 425
Mindanao 426, 520-524
Mindoro 520
Mingrel 269
Mingrelian 267
Minianka 428-429
Minnan 181, 186
Minyong 319
Mirandesa 528
Miri 320
Mishmi 320
Mising 320
Miskitu 302-303, 482, 484
Mixteco 438
Mizo 310, 314, 320, 329-330

Mjuniang 171
Mnong 137, 139, 676
Mo 274, 361
Moba 624-625
Mober 485, 487
Mofu 142
Mogh 94, 97
Mohajir 500, 503
Moken 462
Molbog 425, 524
Moldavian 447, 539, 644
Mon . . . 47, 137, 159, 180, 395, 424, 462,
464, 618, 675
Mona 210
Monba 179
Moncó 555
Mondari 596
Monégasque 450
Mongo 197
Mongolian 16, 62, 89, 159-160, 166-
169, 172-176, 179, 451-453, 539, 666
Mongour 176
Monimbo 482
Mon-Khmer 47, 137, 159, 180, 395,
424, 462, 618, 675
Monpa 319
Montagnard 47
Montenegrin 55, 682-683
Monzombo 195
Moor . . . 428, 434-435, 464, 583-586, 590;
Black, 434; White, 434-435
Moore 131-134
Mordvin 539, 549, 550, 666
Moro 596
Moroccan . . . 66, 104, 278-279, 364, 455-
457, 473, 476, 654
Mortlockese 443
Moru 596, 598
Mossi 27, 107, 131-133, 208, 274,
276, 430, 485, 624, 626
Mosuo 178
Motilone 671, 673
Mozambican 419, 460, 461, 602
Mozhihei 173
Mru 94, 97, 464
Muchi 95
Mulao 170-171
Mulao Jia 171
Mulatto . . . 33, 119, 189, 214, 298, 300, 482
Mum 140
Mumuye 488, 495
Munda . . 95, 309-310, 320-321, 331, 336-
337, 469
Mundang 140, 152
Munnur 319
Munyoyaya 382
Muong 675
Murao 335
Murle 244, 247, 596
Mursi 246-247
Murut 126-127, 425-426
Musahar 321
Musalman 469

Musgum 140
Mushungulu 574
Mutrasi 319
Mwani 458-461
Mwera 615
Mzab 66-68

N

Naba 27, 152, 154
Nadar 326, 334
Nadia 323
Nafaanra 274
Naga 309-310, 320, 329-331, 464
Nago 107
Nagot 106, 107
Nahuatl 438
Nai 309, 319, 327
Naikda 309
Nair 326, 334
Nalu 26, 293, 295
Naluo 180
Nama 465, 467
Namasudra 95, 309, 320, 335-336
Nambya 691
Nancere 152
Nandi 197, 380
Nanerge 131
Nanjingren 171
Nankana 274, 276
Nankani 277
Nanumba 277
Nara 240-241
Naso 506
Nasu 165, 171, 180
Nateni 106
Nath 335-336
Nathembo 458
Natimba 107
Native American 32, 517, 657, 661
Native Canadian 143
Nau Buddh 327-328
Navajo 661
Nawar 352
Nawdm 624, 626
Nawuri 277
Naxi 180
Nayar 309, 326, 334
Nchumburu 277
Ndau 458, 691
Ndebele 117, 576, 688, 691-692
Ndonde 617
Neapolitan 364, 366
Negrito 524
Nenet 547
Nepali 110-111, 126, 181, 183, 310,
316, 322, 324, 330, 333, 336, 462, 469-
472, 699
Newar 16
Ngada 347
Ngaju 348
Ngala 197
Ngalops 110

Ngam 152
Ngambai 152
Ngangam 624
Ngankala 73
Ngbaka 149, 195, 197
Ngemba 140
Ngendereko 617
Ngindo 617
Ngonde 419, 421
Ngoni 419
Ngumba 238, 240
Ngumbi 238
Nguni 576, 602, 688
Nia 48, 339, 344
Nicaraguan 148
Nicobari 337
Nigerian . . 22, 25, 106-107, 265-266, 292,
    485-495, 555-556, 624, 649, 655
Nilotic 197, 380, 550, 596, 615, 641
Nissi 319
Nisu 180
Nivacleño 513
Njebi 197, 262
Njemps 382
Nkole 641
Nkom 140
Nkoya 687
Nkundu 197
Nobiin 233
Nocte 319
Nogai 539, 548
Non 558, 560
North African 67, 104, 257, 259
North Kissi 565
Nosu 171, 178, 180
Nso 140
Nsongo 71
Ntcham 624
Nu 180
Nuba mountain peoples 596-599
Nubian 16, 27, 233, 235, 596, 599
Nuer 244, 596, 598, 600
Nukuoro 443
Nuna 131-132
Nung 170, 675
Nunu 170-171
Nupe 487, 492, 494
Nuristani 61-62
Nyakusa 419
Nyamwezi 615
Nyaneka 71, 73
Nyanga 201
Nyanja 419, 421, 458, 685, 687, 691
Nyaw 618
Nyemba 71
Nyoro 641
Nyungwe 458, 460
Nzakara 149
Nzebi 196
Nzema 274

O

Occitan 254
Ogan 345
Oirat 176, 451
Okinawan 370
Olot 173
Omani 224, 498-499, 680
Omotic 243
Orang Asli 424-425
Oraon 94-95, 309-310, 321, 327, 331,
    336-337
Oriya 310, 327, 331-332, 337
Orma 382
Oromo 16, 243-247, 380, 382, 574;
    Aari, 243, 246, 247; Borana, 246, 380,
    382; Guji, 246
Oroqen 174
Osing 346
Ossetian 267-269, 539, 547-548, 610
Otavalo 230
Otomi 438
Ouaddai-Fur 27, 152, 154, 596, 599
Ovambo 71, 465-466
Ovimbundu 71
Oyapi 260

P

Pacific Islander . . . 48, 444-445, 479, 627, 669
Paez 189
Pagalu 238
Pahari 110, 324-325
Pai Tavytera 513
Paite 329
Paiwan 169, 186
Pajadinka 295
Pakhtun 500
Pakistani 61, 63, 92, 143, 181-184,
    214, 269, 370, 374-375, 390, 393, 408,
    422, 427, 496-503, 519, 532-533, 556,
    647-648
Palaung 462-465
Palawan 520, 524
Palestinian 8, 39, 42, 76, 92, 146, 233,
    361, 375-376, 390-391, 399, 402, 498,
    504-505, 556, 610, 647, 665
Palikur 260
Pallan 334
Palyu 170
Pamiri 612, 614
Pan 331
Pana 430
Pande 196
Pandit 325
Panika 327
Paniyan 326
Panjabi 183, 249, 251, 310, 322, 324,
    332-337, 380, 383, 422, 425, 436, 438,
    524, 534, 566, 617, 648-649, 653
Pankhu 95
Papel 26, 293-295
Papuan 351

Paraguayan 76, 515
Paraiyan 326, 334
Paraja 332
Pardhan 328
Pardhi 328
Parja 331
Parsee 15, 48, 61-62, 310, 316, 323,
   329, 354, 383, 500, 503
Pashtun 61-62, 500
Pasi 309, 315, 321, 323, 335
Pasisir Kulon 346
Pasisir Lor 346
Patamona 296-297
Pataree 63, 65
Patelia 323
Pathan . . . 16, 47, 309, 327-328, 335, 500,
   502, 653
Paundra 336
Pawi 330
Pedi 117, 576
Peminggir 345
Pendalunga 346
Penghu Islander 189
Persian 16, 43, 47-48, 61-63, 79, 89,
   323, 352-357, 399, 498, 500, 532, 613,
   636-637, 648, 666
Peruvian 35, 516-519
Phende 197
Phuan 395, 618
Phunoi 395
Phutai 395
Phuthai 618
Piedmontese 364
Pila 106
Pingdi 170
Pinghua 170
Pipil 236
Pocomam 236, 287, 289
Pocomchi 287, 289
Pod 309, 336
Podzo 458, 460
Pohnpeian 443
Poi 330
Pokomo 383
Pokot 380, 382, 641, 643
Pol 196, 320
Polish 85, 219, 221, 254, 269, 304, 377, 397,
   411-412, 496, 526-528, 539, 644, 649
Poluo 180
Polynesian 57-58, 69, 155, 158, 186,
   203-204, 249, 261, 384, 443, 478-481,
   509, 513, 553, 572, 627, 640, 657, 669,
   675, 679
Pomak 129-130, 281, 633
Pontian Greek 279
Portuguese . . . 70, 119, 185, 254, 257, 269,
   278, 296, 322, 368, 413, 458, 476, 528-
   530, 555, 576, 580, 586, 595, 607, 622,
   674
Provençal 254
Pubian 345
Puerto Rican 531-532, 657, 678
Puku 238

Pulaar 27, 434, 558
Punan 426
Punjabi . . 310, 324, 500, 503-504. See also
   Panjabi
Punu 196-197, 262
Puoc 677
Putonghua 159, 166-181
Puxian 169
Puyi 16
Pygmy 16, 20, 28, 71, 134, 140, 142,
   149, 151, 195-201, 262, 264, 550;
   Babinga, 264; Kimoso, 416; Mikea, 416
Pyuma 186

Q

Qashqai 352, 354
Qatari 532-533
Qiang 178
Quechua 34-35, 76, 78, 111-114, 155,
   192, 230, 516-520
Quiche 287, 289
Quichua . . . . . . 230-232. See also Quechua

R

Rabari 309
Rabha 320, 330
Rabha Koch 330
Rahanwiin 574
Rajasthani 310, 333
Rajbangsi 94
Rajbanshi 309
Rajbansi 336, 469
Rajbongsi 320
Rajput . . 309, 315, 321-327, 332-336, 472
Rakhine 462
Ralte 330
Rama 482
Rangi 615, 617
Rapa Nui 155, 158
Rarotongan 479
Rashaida 240
Rathawa 323
Rathia 324
Rawang 180, 462-465
Rayalseema Muslim 319
Reang 330
Red Bobo 131
Reddi 319, 334
Rejang 345
Rendille 380, 382
Réunionese . . 193, 194, 254, 416, 534, 561
Riang 335
Riau 48, 338, 344-345
Riff 254, 455, 476
Rodhiya 590
Rohingya 94, 97, 462, 464
Roma (Gypsy) 38, 51-55, 63, 65, 130,
   158, 244, 254-256, 273, 279, 281, 304,
   307, 315, 414-415, 447, 473, 496, 528,
   535, 539, 545, 569-570, 582-584, 605,
   607, 644, 649-650, 657, 682-684 See also
   Gypsy

Romande French 607
Romani . . . . 127, 130, 279, 364, 519, 538.
  See also Roma, Gypsy
Romanian . . . 65, 130, 252, 269, 273, 304-
  307, 361-364, 447-449, 505, 535-538,
  644, 647, 682
Ronga 458
Rongmahbrogpa Amdo 169
Roshani 614
Rotuman 249
Rtahu Amdo 178
Rufiji 617
Ruguru 615
Rukai 186
Rumelian Turk 115, 129, 535
Runga 149-154
Russian 9, 45, 55, 79, 89-90, 99, 127,
  159, 179, 205, 217-218, 242-243, 252,
  254, 267-268, 304, 361, 363, 377-379,
  385, 387, 392-393, 397, 411-412, 438,
  447-448, 451, 453, 468, 496, 526-527,
  536, 539-550, 612-614, 635,-638, 644,
  647, 664-667, 699, 712
Ruthenian 304, 569
Rwandan 134, 195, 198-199, 550-552, 641
Ryukyuan 370

S

Saami 547, 605, 607
Sabaot 380, 382
Sadgaola 336
Sadgope 336
Safi 558, 560
Saharan 21, 23, 27-28, 140, 152, 154,
  408, 428, 485, 708; Western, 66
Sahariya 327, 333
Saho 27, 240-241
Saini 332
Sakalava 418
Sakha 547
Salar 165, 176, 179
Salasaca 230, 232
Saliba 192
Sama 425, 520, 524
Saman 173
Samar 520, 524
Samaritan 361, 598, 704
Sambla 131
Samburu 380, 382
Same 252
Sami 496-498
Sammarinese 554
Samo 131-132
Samoan 69, 203-204, 249, 479, 481,
  553-554, 657
Samon 309, 315
San 73, 117-119, 382, 465, 467, 574,
  615, 685
San Chay 675, 677
San Diu 675
Sanapana 515
Sandawe 615

Sanghir 339, 349
Sangla 110
Sango 149-152, 155, 202
Sani 180
Santal 94-97, 110-111, 232, 309-310,
  320-321, 331-332, 336, 469
Sanye 382
Saora 319, 327, 336
Sara 149, 152
Saragh Yugur 169
Saraguro 230, 232
Saraiki 500
Sarakole 293, 295, 428
Saramaccan 600, 602
Sardinian 364
Sasak 16, 338, 347
Saudi 42, 44, 61, 92, 151, 224, 266,
  376, 393, 498, 556-558, 585
Saur 327
Savara 331
Sawu 348
Sayyid 328
Scots 359, 649, 655
Sea Gypsy 462, 524
Sedang 675
Sediq 186
Seeku 131
Segeju 383
Seke 238
Semai 424-425
Semendo 345
Sena 419, 421, 458-461, 688
Senari 131
Senegalese 265, 560
Senoi 424
Senufo . . . 27, 131-132, 208, 212, 428-429
Sephardim 16, 361
Serb . . 53, 55, 65, 85-86, 115-116, 127, 212-
  213, 304, 307, 414, 571, 605, 682-685
Serer 26, 265, 558-561
Seychellois 562
Shahseven 352
Shaikh 309, 328, 330, 333-336
Shan 462-465, 618, 621
Shangaan 688
Shaozhou 170
Sharchagpakha 110
Shawiya 26, 66, 68, 254
She 169
Shengzha Nosu 178
Sherbro 563
Sherpa 469, 472
Shi 197
ShiBushi 194
Shilha 26, 66, 68, 455, 476
Shilluk 596
Shina 500, 503
Shona 117, 458, 688, 691-692
Shuar 230, 232
Shui 171
Shuixi Nosu 171
Shukriya 596
Shuwa Arab 27, 140, 142, 149-154, 485, 488

Sicijuubi 131
Sicilian 364-367
Sidamo 243, 247
Sierra Leonean 265, 405, 564
Sikh . . 2, 15, 32, 33, 41, 51, 58, 61-62, 83,
144, 146, 249-251, 310, 316, 324-327,
332-335, 380, 383, 422, 425, 470, 480,
506, 524, 556, 566, 568, 587, 615, 629,
650, 653, 655, 658, 662
Sikka 347
Sikkim Bhotia 333
Sikkimese 334
Silpkar 335
Simalungun 339, 344
Simeulue 344
Sinasina 509
Sindhi . . . 16, 183, 310, 315, 322-323, 333,
500, 503-504, 566, 568
Sine 558
Sinhala 525, 586-588, 590
Sisaala 131-132, 274-277
Siwa 233, 235
Siyal 332
Slav 51, 99-101, 115, 127, 212, 219,
242, 267, 279, 377, 379, 392, 397-398,
411, 414, 447, 514, 526, 539, 542, 569,
571, 607, 612, 637, 644-646, 666, 682
Slovak . . 212, 219-221, 304, 569-570, 682-
683
Slovene 86, 571-572
Slovenian 364, 571
Soga 641, 643
Sogwo Arig 176
Sokoto 485-487, 490, 494
Sola 107, 626
Solar 347
Solor 347
Somali 16, 22, 27, 223-226, 243-246,
252, 380, 383, 473, 496, 556, 574-576,
605, 615, 617, 648-649, 662, 680-681
Somba 106, 624
Somray 137
Sonar 309, 315, 319, 328
Songe 197
Songhai . . . 16, 27, 66, 131-132, 211, 428-
430, 485-488
Soninke . . 16, 27, 132, 134, 210, 254, 257,
265, 428-430, 434-435, 558, 560
Soqotri 680-681
Sorani 355, 358
Sorb 269
Sotho 403, 404, 576, 688
Souss 455
South African 22, 117, 403-404, 420,
482, 576-582, 688
South Asian . . 15-16, 33, 38, 47, 57, 74-75,
92, 94, 98, 104-105, 117, 125, 134, 143,
146, 181, 183, 197, 207, 214, 226, 278-
279, 283, 285, 296, 354, 361, 368, 380,
419, 458, 498, 506, 508, 520, 532, 534,
563, 576, 580, 592-595, 600, 602, 615-
618, 630, 647, 653, 657, 662, 680-681,
685, 688

Southeast Asian 47, 481
Spanish . . . 70, 76, 85, 101, 119, 155, 254,
257, 269, 273, 278, 438, 455, 514, 516,
528, 582-586, 607, 610, 664, 671
Sri Lankan 218, 376, 422, 427, 476, 497-498,
525, 532, 556, 566, 568, 586-589, 647
St. Lucian 593
Stieng 137, 139, 676
Suay 395
Subanon 520
Subia 117-118
Subiya 467, 688
Subtiaba 482
Sudanese . . . 151, 233, 235, 246, 408, 556,
596-600, 641, 643, 648, 680
Sudanic . . 20, 27, 140, 149, 152, 197, 240,
243, 488, 596, 641
Sukuma 615
Sulung 320
Sumbawa 347
Sumerian 357
Sumo 302-303
Sumu 482, 484
Sunda 16, 48, 338, 345-348
Sunni Arab 355-357, 612
Sunri 336
Suodi 178
Suri 247
Surinamer 473, 476, 600
Susu . . . 290, 292-295, 558, 560, 563, 565
Swahili . . 193-197, 201, 380, 383, 458-461,
498-499, 561, 574, 615, 618, 653, 699
Swati 602, 604
Swazi 458, 576, 602-604
Swedish 114, 196, 246, 252-253, 307, 496,
504, 542, 545, 552, 575, 589, 603-607,
617
Swiss 114, 142-143, 154, 272, 292,
410, 450, 512, 518-519, 607, 608-610;
German, 607
Sylheti 94, 97
Syrian . . . 76, 192, 226, 284, 309-311, 355-
356, 399-400, 432, 610-612, 674

T

Tabassaran 539, 548
Taberma 624, 626
Tabwa 197
Tacana 111
Tadava 334
Tagal 426
Tagalog 520, 524-525
Tagba 131
Tagbanwa 524
Tagin 319-320
Taguana 208
Tahaggart 485
Tahitian 261-262, 478
Tai 159, 170-173, 177, 180-181, 186,
395-396, 462, 618
Tai/Dai 180
Taita 380

Taiwanese 16, 186-188
Tajik . . 16, 61-63, 159, 165, 179, 352, 377,
    392, 394, 500, 503, 612-614, 666, 668
Takistani 352
Takwane 460
Talysh 89-91, 352
Tama 27, 152, 154, 596, 599
Tamajaq 485, 487
Tamasheq 26
Tamazight 66, 455, 457
Tamiang 344
Tamil 43, 92, 249, 254, 269, 284, 310,
    316-319, 326, 334, 337, 421-422, 425,
    432, 436, 438, 473, 476, 496-497, 525,
    534, 561, 566, 586-590, 607, 610, 649;
    Estate, 586, 589; Lanka, 318, 586, 589
Tampuan 137, 139
Tangam 320
Tanti 321
Tanu 319
Tarifit 455-456
Taroko 186
Tarra 246
Tasaweq 485
Tashilhayt 455, 456
Tat 89-91, 352, 545
Tatar 16, 89, 101, 127, 165, 242, 377,
    392, 397, 411-412, 535, 538-539, 549,
    612, 633, 637, 644-647, 666-668
Tati 336
Tatooga 615
Tatwa 321, 336
Taungyo 462, 464
Tausug 425, 520, 524
Tavara 458
Tawellemenet 485
Tayal 186, 188
Tayert 485
Tazarawa 485
Teda 27, 152, 408, 485
Téén 210
Teke 195-196, 262, 264
Telaga 309, 319, 334
Teli 309, 321, 324, 327-328, 331, 335
Tem 106, 108, 624
Temate 350
Temier 424
Temne 563, 565
Temuan 424-425
Tengger 346
Teochew 422, 425, 566
Teribe 506
Teso 380, 641
Tetela 197
Tetun (Tetum) 348, 622, 624
Tewe 458
Teymur 352
Thado 329
Thai 16, 47, 126-127, 137-138, 170,
    184, 186, 370, 374, 422, 462, 464, 566,
    568, 618-622, 675
Thakur 328
Thandan 326

Tharu 335, 469, 472
Tho 170, 677
Thori 333
Tibetan 16, 42, 44, 47, 110, 160, 169,
    171, 173, 176-180, 310, 316, 322-325,
    333-334, 395, 462, 469, 472, 500, 503,
    675; Amdo, 169, 176, 178; Central, 179;
    Khampa, 176-179; Lhasa, 179
Tidore 350
Tiefo 131
Tigon 140
Tigray 243-247
Tigre 16, 240-241
Tigrinya 240-241
Tihishit 485
Timor . . 39, 43, 338-341, 345-348, 622-624
Tipera 94, 309
Tiv 488, 494
Tiwa 320
Toambaita 572
Toba 76-78, 344, 515
Tofin 106
Togolese 485, 624-625
Tol 303
Tolai 509
Toma 290-293
Tongan 69, 203, 249, 479, 481, 627-
    628, 669
Tooro 641
Toposa 596, 598
Toraja 338-339, 345, 349
Torbish 415
Torgut 179
Torwali 500
Tosk 63, 66
Toura 210
Trinidadian 629-630
Trinitario 111
Trio 601
Tripura 330, 335
Tripuri 94, 310, 335
Tsaangi 196
Tsakhur 89-91
Tsangi 264
Tsimane 111
Tsonga 458, 576, 602, 688
Tswa 458
Tswana 117-119, 465, 576, 688, 692
Tu ....
    176
Tuamotuan 261-262
Tuareg . . 16, 20, 26, 66, 68, 131-132, 210,
    254, 428-430, 485-486
Tubu 485, 487
Tucano 192
Tugen 380
Tuikuk 335
Tujia 168, 173
Tukudete 622
Tukulor . 265, 428, 430, 434-435, 558-561
Tumari 485, 487
Tumbuka 419, 421, 685
Tunisian 631, 632

INDEX • PEOPLES

Tunni 574
Tupuri 140, 152
Turk . . . 16, 29, 47, 55, 80, 83, 86-89, 104,
   115, 127-130, 217, 219, 223-224, 233,
   252, 254, 269, 273, 279, 281, 302, 355,
   414, 449, 473, 476, 496, 535, 538, 605,
   607, 610, 633-639, 649, 653, 655, 657,
   674, 682-684; Rumelian . . 115, 129, 535
Turka 131
Turkana 380, 382
Turkic . . 1, 15-16, 47, 51, 61, 89, 127-128,
   159, 172, 174, 176, 179, 267, 352-355,
   358, 377, 392-393, 447, 451, 535, 539,
   544, 547-549, 612, 633, 637, 644, 666
Turkish 65, 79, 85, 89, 101, 115-116,
   127-130, 217-219, 258, 269, 279-280,
   375, 377, 393, 410, 415, 533, 610, 633-
   638, 682
Turkmen . . 16, 61-63, 352, 355, 610, 612,
   637-638, 666, 668
Turkoman 352, 357-358
Tushu 171
Tusian 131
Tutsi 22, 134-135, 197, 550, 641
Tutung 126
Tuva 179, 548-549
Tuvaluan 384, 468, 640
Tuvinian 451, 539, 549
Twa 134-135, 550, 552
Tyenga 487
Tyrolese 364, 367
Tzotzil 438
Tzutujil 287

U
Udi 89-90
Udmurt 539, 549-550
Uduk 247, 598
Ukrainian . . . 45, 79, 89, 99, 143-144, 242,
   267, 273, 361, 363, 377-379, 392-393,
   397, 411, 447, 449, 513-514, 526, 536,
   539, 543-548, 569, 612, 637-638, 644-
   647, 666
Ulithian 443
Upsantec 289
Urdu 1, 94, 297, 310, 316-328, 333-
   336, 391, 436-438, 469, 472, 500,
   503-504, 580, 648-649, 653
Urhobo 487, 493
Uriankhai 451, 453, 549
Uruguayan 665
US citizen See American
Utsat 171-172
Uyghur . . . 16, 160, 165-166, 179-180, 377,
   379, 392, 666
Uzbek 16, 61-63, 165, 179, 377-378,
   392, 394, 500, 503, 539, 612, 614, 637,
   666-668

V
Vaddar 328, 334
Vai 405, 407, 565

Vaisya 319, 333, 335
Vakkaliga 309, 326
Vania 309
Vanniyan 334
Vanniyar 309
Varli 323, 328
Veddah 586, 590
Venda 576, 688
Venetian 213, 364
Venezuelan 476, 671-674
Vettuvan 326
Viet 395
Vietnamese 16, 47, 83, 85, 137, 139,
   159, 254, 257, 395, 397, 432, 478, 496-
   497, 520, 607, 610, 618, 657, 675-677
Vige 131
Visaya 520
Viswakarma 309, 319, 326, 334
Vlach 63, 65, 115-116, 279, 281, 682
Vo 462

W
Wa 47, 165, 180-181, 462-464
Waci 106
Wagosha 574
Wahgi 509
Waigeli 62
Waiwai 296-297
Wakhi 500, 614
Wala 274
Wali 277
Wallisian 478, 679
Walloon 101-102
Wan 210
Wancho 319-320
Waorani 230, 232
Wapishana 296, 297
Waray 520
Wasa 274
Wassulunke . . . 27, 210, 290-292, 428, 430
Wata 246
Waunana 506
Wayana 260, 601
Welsh 649, 656
Wend 269
West Atlantic 26, 131, 140, 149, 290,
   293, 405, 428, 558, 563
West Indian 254, 284, 506
Western Khampa. See Tibetan
Western Lipo 180
Western Saharan . . . . 66. See Saharan
Western Xibe 179
White Moor 434-435
Wichi 76, 78
Widekum 140
Wobe 208
Wodaabe 485-486
Woga 641
Wogo 485, 487
Wolaytta 243, 247
Woleaian 443
Wolio 425

Wolof 16, 26, 210, 254, 257, 265-266, 430, 434-435, 558-561
Woni 180
Wu 159, 177, 181
Wunai 173
Wusa Nasu 171

X

Xhosa 403, 576
Xiandao 180
Xiang 159, 173
Xibe 175, 179
Xoraxai (Gypsy) 66
Xweda 106

Y

Yacouba 208, 212
Yadau 319
Yadav . . . 321, 324-328, 331, 335-336, 469
Yadava 309, 315
Yaka 71, 149, 195, 240
Yakan 520, 524
Yakuba 208, 210, 212
Yakut . . . . 539, 547. See also Sakha
Yalunka 27, 290, 563, 565
Yami 186, 188
Yana 131
Yanghuang 171
Yanomami 123, 671, 673
Yao (Africa) . . 28, 419-421, 458, 615, 617, 688, 691
Yao (Asia) 170-173, 180, 618, 621, 675
Yaouré 210
Yapese 443
Yazgulyam 614
Yazidi 355
Yemeni . 224, 226, 556, 647, 654, 680-681

Yemsa 243
Yenadi 319, 334
Yerukala 319
Yeyi 117-119, 467
Yi 171, 178, 180
Yom 106, 233
Yombe 197
Yoruba . . 106, 108, 487-488, 493-494, 624
Younuo 171
Yucatec 104, 438
Yueh 159, 181
Yugoslav 53, 88, 116, 254, 473, 496, 571, 607, 610, 682
Yungur 488
Yuracare 111

Z

Zaghawa 152, 408, 596, 599
Zambian 419, 685-688
Zambo 482
Zande 149-152, 596
Zanskar 325
Zanzibarian 28
Zaomin Yao 170
Zapoteco 438
Zaramo 28, 615
Zarma 27, 485-487
Zaza 633
Zenati 233
Zerma 16
Zhuang . . . . . 160, 166, 170-171; Northern 170
Zigula 615, 617
Zimbabwean 117, 690
Zombo 189
Zuara 408
Zulu 403, 458, 576-577, 602, 604

PLACES INDEX

This index lists references to geographical places mentioned in the text. Included are states and provinces, cities, seas, lakes and rivers, and mountains. Countries are not included here. *Note Feb 2004*: In revising parts of the text in this reprint, some of the page numbers may no longer be correct. The page number could, in such cases, be one integer higher.

A

Aarau 609
Aberdeen 656
Abia 493
Abidjan 23, 208-212
Abkhazia 547-548
Abu Dhabi 647
Abuja 487, 494
Accra 274
Aceh 43, 338, 344
Adamawa 140, 494-495
Adana 633
Addis Ababa 243, 245, 247
Adelaide 83
Aden 680-681
Adygeya 547-548
Aegean Sea 279, 633
Agana 286
Agin Buryat 548
Agra 335
Aguascalientes 441
Ahmadabad 323
Aizawl 330
Ajman 647
Åland Islands 252
Alaska 657, 662
Alava 585
Albay Province 524
Aleppo 610, 612
Aleutian Islands 657
Alexandra 579
Algiers 66
Allahabad 335
Almaty 377, 378
Almolonga 289
Alofi 203
Alor 338, 347
Alsace 255, 256
Altay 548
Amazon 122-123, 230, 516-519, 704
Ambon 340, 345, 350
Amman 375, 377
Amritsar 332
Amsterdam 473-476, 659, 712
Amu Darya River 8, 43, 637
Amur River 8, 43
Anambra 493
Anatolia 633, 636
Andaman Islands 337
Angtong 621
Anhui 168
Anjouan 193
Ankara 633, 636

Annobon Island 238, 240
Anshan 175
Anshun 171
Antananarivo 416
Antilles, Greater 531
Antioch 611
Antwerp 101, 104
Apia 553
Apurimac 519
Arabian Sea 323, 337, 352
Arakan 464
Aral Sea 44, 377, 666-668
Arequipa 516, 519
Argatala 335
Asansol 336
Ashgabat 637
Asmara 240, 241
Assam 320, 330
Astana 377
Asturias 585
Asuncion 513
Atauro Island 622-623
Athens 279-281
Atlanta 657
Atlas Mts 66, 68, 455
Auckland 205, 479-482
Austral 261
Avarua 203
Ayacucho 518-519
Ayodhya 336
Azores 528, 530

B

Baden-Württemberg 271
Baghdad 355, 357
Baikal, Lake 549
Bairiki 384
Baja California 441
Baku 89-91
Balearic Islands 582
Bali 342, 346
Balkans . . . 8, 51-55, 63-64, 115, 127, 212-
213, 279, 281, 305, 535, 538, 607, 633,
637, 682-684
Baluchistan 502
Bamako 428, 430
Bandar Seri Begawan 126
Bandung 338, 345
Bangalore 326, 700
Bangka-Belitung 344
Bangkok 44, 618-621
Bangui 149-152
Banjul 265-266

Baotou 174
Barcelona 582-585
Barranquilla 189
Baruch 323
Basel 348, 422, 426, 607, 609
Bashkortostan 54, 549
Basra 357
Basseterre 592
Basse-Terre 284
Bastar 328
Batangan 524
Bathinda 332
Bauchi 490, 494
Bavaria 272
Bawean 346
Bayan-Olgiy 453
Bayelsa 493
Beatenberg 609
Beijing 159-161, 164, 168, 172, 177-
    178, 182
Beira 458, 460
Beirut 399, 402
Beja Province 530
Bekaa Valley 402
Belem 119
Belfast 655
Belgrade 682-685
Bellavista prison 190
Belmopan 104
Belo Horizonte 119
Bengkulu 344-345
Benguela 71
Benue 494
Benxi 175
Berlin 51, 269-272, 659, 712
Bern 607
Bessarabia 448
Bethlehem 386, 505
Bhopal 327-328
Bhubaneshwar 331
Biafra 489
Bicol 520, 524
Bienenberg 609
Bihar 318-322, 331, 337, 600
Bilaspur 325
Bilbao 582
Biltine 154
Bioko 238
Birmingham 649, 654
Bishkek 392-394
Bissau 293, 294
Bithynia 635
Black Sea 267, 633, 636
Blantyre 419, 421
Bloemfontein 576
Bogotà 192
Bologna 367
Bombay 309, 328
Bonaire . . 79, 82, 124, 192, 476, 477, 508,
    520, 674
Bongolo 265
Bonn 269
Borneo 126, 348, 422, 425, 426, 524

Borno 494-495
Bosphorus Strait 633
Boston 657
Bougainville 58, 509-513, 572
Brabant 103
Bradford 649
Brahmaputra River 43, 94, 320
Brasilia 119
Bratislava 569, 570
Brazzaville 195-196
Brisbane 83
Bristol 654
Brittany 257
Bromo . . . . Mt., 346
Brussels 101, 103
Bucharest 535
Budapest 304, 307
Buenos Aires 76-79
Bujumbura 134, 136
Bukavu 202
Bukhara 668
Bulawayo 688
Burgenland 88
Bursa 633
Buryatiya 548-549

C

Cabo Delgado 460
Cagayan Island 524
Cairo 233-236
Calabria 365
Calais 257
Calcutta 315, 336-337
Cali 189, 192
Calicut 326
Camarines Norte 524
Campeche 440
Campinas 119
Canary Islands 20, 582, 585
Canberra 83
Cantabria 585
Canton 170
Cape Town 576, 579-580
Caprivi Strip 465, 467
Caracas 671-674
Carchi 232
Caroline Archipelago 443
Casablanca 455
Casamance 265, 558-561
Caspian Sea 89, 352, 547-548
Castries 593
Catanduanes 524
Caucasus . . . 8, 16, 53, 55, 79, 89-90, 267,
    539, 541, 544-548, 633, 637
Cayenne 259
Cebu 520, 524
Celebes 349
Cenderawasih Bay 351
Ceuta 20, 457, 582, 586
Chagos Archipelago 124, 436, 437
Champagne-Ardennes 257
Chandigarh 324, 332, 337

Changchun 159, 175
Changde 173
Changsha 173
Channel Islands 49, 649
Chaozhou 170
Chari River 154
Charleroi 103
Charlotte Amalie 678
Chechnya 53-54, 544-547
Chelyabinsk 539
Chengdu 159, 178
Chennai 315, 317, 334
Chernobyl 99-100, 541, 645
Chhattisgarh 318
Chiapas 440
Chicago 657
Chiengmai 618, 622
Chifeng 174
Chisinau 447
Chittagong 94, 96
Choiseul 572
Chongqing 168-169
Christmas Island 57, 83
Chuuk 286, 443-444
Chuvashiya 549
Cincinnati 657
Cleveland 657
Cochin 326
Cocos Islands 57, 83
Coimbatore 334
Colima 441
Cologne 269
Colombo 586-590
Colón 506
Conakry 290-292
Constanta 538
Constantine 66
Copenhagen 223
Copperbelt, The 688
Cordoba 76
Corfu 281
Corsica 257
Cotonou 106, 108
Coventry 654
Crete 281
Crimea 646
Cubatao 119
Curacao 476
Curitiba 119
Cuttack 331
Cyclades Islands 281
Cyestochowa 527

D

Dacia 535
Dadra 337
Dagestan 54, 547-548
Dakar 558-560
Dalap-Uliga-Darrit 444
Dalian 175
Dallas 657
Dalmatia 213

Daman 337
Damascus 610
Danang 676
Dandong 175
Danja 487
Danube River 86, 212, 304, 535
Dardanelles 633
Dar-es-Salaam 615, 617
Darfur 27, 596, 599
Darien 508
Darjeeling 472
Darkhan 451
Datong 177
Davao 520, 524
Debar 415
Delhi 309, 315, 322, 324
Denver 657
Detroit 657
Dhaka 94-97
Dharamsala 316, 325
Dharavi 328
Dhofar 499
Diego Garcia 124, 436
Dili 622-623
Dir 503, 574
Dispur 320
Diu 337, 675
Djerba 632
Dodecanese Islands 281
Dodoma 615, 618
Doha 532
Douala 140
Dubai 647
Dublin 359-361
Durango 441
Durban 576, 579-580
Dushanbe 612
Düsseldorf 269
Dzaoudzi 194

E

East Timor ... 39, 338, 340, 347, 622, 623
Easter Island 155, 158
Ebonyi 493
Echeng 173
Edinburgh 656
Edo 487, 493, 494
Eifel 272
Eire 359
Ekiti 493
Ellice Islands 640
Emilia-Romagna 367
England .. 55, 256, 542, 649, 651, 654, 655
Entebbe 641
Enugu 487, 493
Ephesus 635
Erdenet 451
Essen 269
Euphrates River 43, 355, 610, 633
Evenki 174, 451, 453, 539, 547
Everest, Mt 179, 472
Extremadura 585

F

Faeroe Islands 49, 223, 247-248, 282
Falkland Islands 35, 77, 248-249, 591
Faridabad 324
Faridkot 332
Fergana Valley 392, 394, 666-667
Fes 455
Flanders 103
Flores 347
Fly River 512
Fortaleza 119
Frankfurt 269
Fribourg 610
Fuerteventura 586
Fujairah 647
Fukuoka 370
Fuling 168, 169
Fushun 175
Fuxian 175
Fuzhou 169, 174

G

Gaberone 117-119
Gajapati 331
Galapagos Islands 230, 232
Galicia 585
Galmi 487
Gambier 261
Ganges River ... 43, 94, 315, 321, 335-336
Gangtok 333
Gansu 159, 165, 169, 179
Garoowe 574
Gaza Strip 361, 504-505
Geneva 607, 610
Genoa 364
Gilbert 384
Gilgit 503
Gjirokaster 65
Glasgow 649, 656
Goa 322
Gobi Desert 169, 451
Goiania 119
Golan Heights 361, 363
Golden Triangle . 9, 44, 462, 464, 619-622
Goma 202
Gombe 490, 494
Gomera 586
Gongzhuling 175
Göteborg 605
Gran Chaco 513
Greater Antilles 531
Guadalajara 438
Guadalcanal 572-573
Guam 57, 167, 286-287, 445, 568
Guanajuato 441
Guangzhou 159, 170
Guantánamo 214
Guatemala City 287
Guayaquil 230, 232
Guera Mts 154
Guernsey 649
Gugulethu 579
Guigang 170
Guipúzcoa 585
Guiyang 171
Guizhou 159, 171
Gujarat 323-324, 331, 337
Gujranwala 500, 502
Gweru 688
Gwoza Hills 495

H

Hadhramaut 681
Hague, The 473, 475
Haicheng 175
Haikou 171
Hainan 159
Halmahera 338-339, 350
Hamburg 269
Hamipur 325
Handan 172
Hangzhou 181
Hanoi 675-676
Hanover 269
Harare 688, 691
Harari 243, 246
Harbin 159, 172
Hargeisa 574
Haryana 315-316, 324, 332, 337
Havana 214-215
Hayastan 79
Hebrides 656
Hefei 168
Heilongjiang 159, 175
Helsinki 252, 254
Henan 172
Heze 177
Hierro 586
Himachal Pradesh 315-316, 324
Hiroshima 370
Hispaniola 227, 298
Ho Chi Minh City 675-676
Hohhot 174
Hokkaido 370
Honiara 572, 573
Honshu 370
Houston 657
Huaide 174
Huainan 172
Huambo 71
Hunan 173
Hunza 503
Huzhou 168
Hwange-Kariba 691
Hyderabad 319, 500

I

Ibadan 487
Iberian Peninsula 528, 582
Iles des Saintes 284
Imo 493
Imphal 329
Indore 327

Indus Valley 43, 500, 503
Ingushetiya 547-548
Inner Mongolia 159
Ionian Sea 279, 281
Iquitos 516
Irbil 355
Ireland, Northern 53, 359-360, 649-650, 655
Irian Jaya 350, 509
Isfahan 352, 354
Islamabad 500, 503
Isle of Man 49, 649
Istanbul 280, 633-636
Istria 213
Itanagar 319
Izmir 633, 636

J

Jabalpur 327
Jaffna 586, 588
Jaipur 333
Jakarta 48, 338-341, 345
Jalisco 441
Jambi 344-345
Jammu 325
Jamshedpur 321
Jan Mayen 496
Java 48, 338-346, 426
Jersey 649
Jerusalem . . 8, 43, 181, 361, 385, 504-505
Jharkhand 318, 321
Jiamusi 172
Jiangxi 174
Jiddah 556
Jigawa 494
Jilin 159, 175
Jinan 159, 177
Jingmen 173
Johannesburg . . . 211, 461, 552, 576, 579, 582, 618
Johnston Island 57, 286
Jordan . . . . River 8, 43, 375, 504,
Jos 487
Juba 598

K

Kabardino-Balkariya 547
Kabul 61-62
Kabwe 688
Kaduna 487, 490, 494
Kairouan 632
Kalahari Desert 117
Kalimantan . . 43, 48, 338-339, 342-343, 348
Kalmykiya 548
Kamchatka Peninsula 547
Kampala 641, 643
Kandhamal 331
Kandy 589
Kano 487, 490, 494
Kanpur 335
Kaohsiung 186
Kapuas River 348
Karachayevo-Cherkesiya 547

Karachi 500-503
Karelia 547
Karnataka 316, 326
Kashmir . . 43, 309, 315, 324-326, 500, 503
Katerini 280
Kathmandu 469, 473
Katowice 526
Katsina 494
Kavango 465, 467
Kayes 430
Kazan 539, 549
Kebbi 494
Kerala 314, 327, 532
Khakasiya 548-549
Khanty-Mansi 547
Kharkiv 644
Khartoum 596, 598-600
Khorat 618
Kigali 550
Kindu 202
Kinnaur 325
Kinshasa 197, 200-202
Kitakyushu 370
Kitwe 685
Kogi 494
Kohima 330
Kohistan 503
Kolkata 315, 336-337
Köln 269
Komi 539, 547
Komi-Permyak 547
Koror 446
Koryat 547
Kosovo 52-54, 63-65, 269, 414-415, 682-685
Kosrae 443
Koutiala 430
Kowloon 181
Kuala Lumpur 422
Kullu Valley 325
Kumasi 274, 276
Kunming 180
Kurdish Autonomous Region 355, 357
Kuwait 39, 356, 375, 390-391
Kwa Mashu 579
Kwangju 386
Kwara 494
KwaZulu-Natal 20, 580
Kyiv 644-647
Kyushu 370

L

La Désirade 284
La Palma 586
La Paz 111
Laayoune 457
Ladakh 325-326
Lae 513
Lagos 487, 489, 493
Lahore 500, 502
Lahul 325
Laiwu 177

Lakshadweep 337, 428
Lampung 344-345
Lanzarote 585
Lanzhou 169
Lausanne 492, 607, 659, 712
Law 181-182, 363, 511
Leeds 649
Leeward Islands 74, 125, 454, 476, 592, 678
Lefkosa 219
Lefkosia 217
Leiyang 173
Leon 438, 585
Leshan 178
Lewis 656
Leyte 520, 524
Lhasa 179
Lianyuan 173
Liaoning 159, 175
Libreville 262-263
Liège 103
Liling 177
Lille 254
Lilongwe 419, 421
Lima 516-520
Limousin 257
Lindi 617
Line 384
Linyi 177
Lisbon 528
Liupanshui 171
Liuzhou 170
Liverpool 649
Ljubljiana 571-572
Lo Rioja 585
Lodz 526
Loire Valley 257
Loja 232
Lombardy 367
Lomblin 347
Lombok 346-347
Lomé 624-627
London 649, 654-656
Los Angeles 657
Loyalty Islands 478
Luanda 71, 73
Lubango 73
Lubumbashi 197
Lucknow 335
Ludhiana 332-333
Lusaka 685, 688
Luxembourg 49, 103, 413-414
Luzern 610
Luzon 520, 524
Lyon 254

M

Macau . . . 39, 159-160, 170, 184-185, 530
Madang 512
Madeira 528, 530
Madhya Pradesh 315, 328
Madrid 582-586
Madura 16, 48, 338, 345-346, 348

Madurai 334
Maharashtra 315-316, 329
Mahé 562
Majuro 444
Makarere 643
Malabo 238
Malaga 585
Malaita 572-573
Male 247, 427
Malmö 605
Maluku 339, 341, 345, 349-350, 473
Malvinas Islands 35, 76-77, 248-249
Mamoudzou 194
Manado 341, 349
Managua 482-484
Manama 92-93
Manaus 119
Manchester 649, 654
Manchuria 159, 172, 175
Mandalay 462, 464
Manila 139, 317, 520, 523, 524
Manipur 329
Mannheim 269
Manus Island 510, 512
Maputo 458-461
Maracaibo 671
Maracay 671
Mariana Islands 57, 286-287, 443-446
Marianas Archipelago 286
Marie Galante 284-285
Mari-El 549
Marquesas 261
Marrakech 455
Marseille 254, 257
Marshall Islands 57, 443-445
Mascarene islands 534
Maseru 403
Mashhad 352
Matagalpa, River 482, 484
Matana 135
Mata-Utu 679
Matsu 186
Maun 119
Mayotte 19, 21, 193-194
Mbuji-Mayi 197
Mecca 556-557
Medan 338
Medellín 189, 192
Meerut 335
Mekong River 43, 137, 677
Melanesia 57, 59, 512, 572, 669
Melbourne 83-85
Melilla 20, 586
Mellila 457, 582
Mexico City 1, 33, 438, 441
Miami 657, 700
Mianyang 178
Michoacán 441
Micronesia 57-58, 443
Midway 286
Milan 364, 367
Mindanao 426, 520-524
Minsk 99, 101

Mizoram 311, 330
Mogadishu 574
Mombasa 380, 383
Monrovia 405, 407
Monte Carlo 66, 259, 450, 586, 632
Montenegro 53, 63-66, 682-685
Monterrey 438
Montevideo 664-665
Montreal 143
Mordoviya 549-550
Moroni 193
Moscow 402, 409, 539-540, 545-546,
    550, 613, 645
Mostar 116
Mosul 355
Mukden 175
Multan 500
Mumbai 44, 309, 315-317, 328, 471
München 269
Munich 269
Musandam Peninsula 498
Muscat 498
Mustang 472
Mutare 688
Mwali 193
Mweya 135

N

Nagaland 311, 319, 331
Nagar Havali 337
Nagorno-Karabakh 79, 81, 89-90
Nagoya 370
Nagpur 328
Nairobi 380-383, 576
Nakhichevan 89
Nampula 458
Namur 103
Nanchang 174
Nancy 257
Nanjing 163, 166, 174
Nanning 170
Nantes 257
Naples 364-365
Nasarawa 494
Nashik 328
Natal 576
Nauru 57-58, 384, 468-469
Navarra 585
Nayarit 441
Ndola 685, 687
Neijiang 178
Nenets 547
Nevis 592
New Britain 510
New Georgia 572
New Territories 181
New York 1, 364, 532, 657, 662
Newcastle 649
Niamey 485-486
Niassa 460
Nicobar Islands 337
Nicosia 217

Nile River . . 8, 27, 233, 235, 596, 599, 600
Ningbo 181
Ningxia 159-160, 165
Nis 684
Nizhny Novgorod 539
Njazidja 193
Norfolk Islands 57, 83
North Caucasus 547
Northern Ireland 53, 359-360, 649-650, 655
Nottingham 654
Nouakchott 434
Nouméa 478-479
Novi Sad 684
Nunavut 146
Nurnberg 269
Nusa Tenggara 342
Nuuk 282
Nyankunde 202
Nzwani 193

O

Odessa 644
Ogoni-land 493
Ogun 493-494
Okavango Swamp 118
Okayama 370
Olmos 77
Omdurman 596, 598
Omsk 539
Ondo 493-494
Oradea 537
Oran 66
Orchid Island 188
Orissa 320-331
Oromia 246
Osaka 370
Osh 392
Osijek 213
Oslo 496-497
Ossetia, North 547-548
Osun 493
Ottawa 143
Ouaddai 154
Ouagadougou 131, 133
Ovamboland 467
Oxus River 8, 43
Oyo 493

P

Padova 367
Pago Pago 69
Palau 57, 236, 286, 446-447
Palawan 520, 524
Palembang 338
Palermo 364
Palestine 233, 361, 364, 375, 504, 532
Palikir 443
Pamir mountains 612
Panama City 506
Papeete 261-262
Papua . . . 43, 57-59, 87, 102, 338-339, 342-
    343, 350-351, 509-510, 521-572

Paris 254, 257-258, 433
Patagonia 248
Patna 321
Pegalu Island 238
Peking 159
Pemba 615, 617
Penghu Archipelago 186, 189
Perm 539
Perth 83, 86
Peshawar 500
Phangnga 621
Philadelphia 657
Phnom Penh 137-138
Phoenicia 399
Phoenix 384, 657
Picardy 257
Pingxiang 172, 174
Pittsburgh 657
Plate, River 514, 664
Plateau 176, 494
Plymouth 454
Pohnpei 286, 443
Pointe Noire 195
Polynesia 48, 57, 59, 261, 709
Pondicherry 337
Pontianak 348
Port Elizabeth 576
Port Louis 436
Port Moresby 509, 511
Port of Spain 629
Port Stanley 248
Port-au-Prince 298
Portland 657
Porto 119, 528
Porto Alegre 119
Porto-Novo 106
Prague 219-221
Praia 147
Pretoria 46, 576
Príncipe 528, 555-556
Puebla 438
Puerto Rico 29, 229, 531-532, 678
Pune 314, 328
Punjab 311, 324, 332, 337, 500-501
Puntland 20, 574-575
Pusan 386
Puyang 172
Pwani 617
Pyongyang 385

Q

Qingdao 159, 177
Qinghai 165, 179
Qinzhou 170
Qiqihar 172
Qom 352
Qomolangma, Mt 179
Quebec 32, 37, 143-145
Quemoy 186
Quito 230, 232
Qujing 180

R

Rabat 455
Rajasthan 315, 333
Ranchi 321
Rand 576, 581, 603
Ranong 621
Ras al Khaimah 647
Rawaki 384
Rawalpindi 500, 502
Recife 119
Reykjavik 307
Rhondda Valley 656
Riau 48, 338, 344-345
Riga 397-398
Rio de Janeiro 119, 122
Rio Muni 238
Rivers 493
Riyadh 556
Rizhau 177
Rome 26, 301, 364, 367
Rosario 76
Rota 445
Rotterdam 473, 475
Ruhr 269
Rupnagar 332

S

Saba 476
Sabah 422, 426
Sahara Desert 8, 26, 428, 455, 486
Saigon 675
Saint-Denis 534
Saipan 445-446
Sakha 547
Salamat 154
Salvador 119
Samar 520, 524
Samara 539
Samarkand 666, 668
San Cristobal 572
San Diego 657
San Francisco 657
San Jose 205
San Juan 531, 710
San Justo 76
San Marino 49, 554
San Salvador 236
Sanghir Island 349
Sangrur 332
Santa Cruz 111
Santa Fé de Bogotà 189
Santa Isobel 572
Santiago 155-158
Santos 119
São Paulo 1, 33-34, 119, 122
São Tomé 528, 555
Sapporo 370
Sarajevo 115-116
Saratov 539
Sarawak 126, 422
Sardinia 364, 367

Saurashtra 323
Sawu Island 348
Saxony 271
Schwyz 610
Scotland . . 247, 363, 420, 649-650, 656, 687
Seattle 657
Semarang 338, 345
Sendai 370
Senegal River Valley 435, 559-560
Seoul 386, 388-389
Sepik 510, 512
Seram 350
Serbia 53-54, 63, 115, 127, 212, 637,
682-685
Severnaya Ossetiya-Alaniya 547
Sevilla 582
Sfax 631-632
Shaanxi 177
Shaba 199
Shandong 177
Shanghai 159, 174, 177, 181
Shantou 170
Shanxi 177-178
Sharjah 647
Sharpeville 579
Sheba 681
Sheffield 649, 654
Shenyang 159, 175
Shenzhen 170
Shijiazhuang 172
Shikoku 370
Shillong 330
Shimla 324
Shiraz 352, 354
Siberia 9, 15, 42, 47, 49, 55, 160, 172,
175, 287, 525, 539, 541, 544-546, 549
Sichuan 168, 178-179
Sicily 364-365
Sidon 402
Siegerland 271
Sikkim 333-334, 472
Sinai Desert 233
Sinaloa 441
Sindh 500-502
Skopje 414-415
Society 261
Sofia 127, 129
Sokoto 485-487, 490, 494
Solomons 510, 572-574
Somaliland 20, 574-575
Sonora 441
Soufrière, Mt 454
South Georgia 248
South Sandwich Islands 248
South Urals 549
Soweto 579
Spiti 325
Spitzbergen 496
Sri Jayewardenepura Kotte 586
Srinagar 325
St Barthélemy 284, 285
St Eustatius 476
St Kitts 29, 592

St Louis 657
St Maarten 476
St Martin 284-285
St Petersburg 546
St Pierre 31-32, 594
Star Mts 512
Stavanger 497
Stockholm 605, 607
Strathclyde 656
Stuttgart 269
Sucre 111
Suez Canal 233
Suining 178
Suixian 168
Suizhou 173
Sulawesi 339-343, 346, 349, 426
Sulu Islands 524
Sumatra 48, 338-346, 422, 425
Sumba 339, 347
Sumbawa 347
Sunda Islands . . 16, 48, 338, 345-346, 348
Sundergarh 331
Surabaya 338, 345
Surat 323
Suva 249
Suzhow 168
Svalbard 49, 496
Swat 503
Sydney 83-85

T

Tabasco 440
Tabriz 352
Taegu 386
Taejon 386
Tahiti 261
Taian 175
Taipei 186
Taiyuan 177
Taklamakan Desert 179
Talaud Island 349
Tallinn 242
Tamale 274
Tambacounda 560
Tamil Nadu 316, 337
Tampa 657
Tanga 617
Tanganyika 134, 615, 618
Tangshan 172
Tanjungkarang 338
Taraba 494, 495
Tarawa 384
Tashkent 666-667
Tatarstan 54, 549
Taymyr 547
Tegucigalpa 302
Tehran 352, 354
Tel Aviv 361
Temate 350
Tete 460
Thessaloniki 279-281
Thimpu 110

Thrace 633
Tianjin 159
Tianshui 169
Tibesti Mts 154
Tibet 6, 15, 43, 47, 179, 324-325,
333-334, 469
Ticino 610
Tidore 350
Tien Shan Mts 392
Tienanmen Sq., ... 160
Tien-Shan Mts 612
Tigris River 43, 355, 633
Tigris-Euphrates basin 8
Tijuana 438
Timor Leste ... 39, 338, 340, 347, 622-623
Tindouf 66, 457
Tinian 445
Tirana 63-64, 88
Tokyo 1, 41, 370-373
Toluca 438
Toronto 143-146, 300
Torreon 438
Torshavn 247
Touba 559
Trans-Dniester 448
Transnistria 448
Transylvania 307, 535
Trentino 367
Tripoli 402, 408
Tripura 330, 335
Trivandrum 326
Trujillo 516
Tuamotu 261
Tumbatu Island 617
Tunis 631
Turin 364-367
Tuva 179, 548-549
Tyrol 88

U

Udmurtia 549
Ufa 539
Ujung Pandang 338
Ulaanbaatar 451
Ulsan 386
Ulster 655
Umbria 367
Umm al Qaiwain 647
Union Territories 309, 337
Upolu 553
Urals 55, 541, 545, 547
Urgel 70
Uri 610
Uriankhai 451, 453, 549
Urumqi 179-180
Ust-Ordyn Buryat 548
Utrecht 475
Uttar Pradesh 315, 318, 336
Uttaranchal 318

V

Vadodara 323
Vaduz 410
Valais 610
Valencia 582, 671
Valetta 431
Valjevo 684
Vancouver 143, 146, 316
Varanasi 315, 335-336
Vatican City 301
Veneto 367
Venice 367
Vereeniging 576
Vicenza 367
Victoria (Seychelles) 561
Victoria, Lake 618, 644
Vienna 86, 88
Vijayawada 319
Vila 669
Vilnius 411-412
Virgin Islands 29, 125, 454, 531, 678
Visakhapatanam 319
Visayas 524
Vizcaya 585
Vojvodina 307, 682-683
Volgograd 539
Volta, Lake 274-277
Voralberg 88

W

Wafangdian 175
Wake Island 286
Wales 55, 649-650, 656
Wallonia 103
Warsaw 526
Washington DC 657
Weifang 177
Wellington 479
West Bank 361, 363, 375, 504-505
West Bengal 472
West Midlands 649, 654
West Papua 338, 509, 512
West Timor .. 338, 340-341, 347-348, 622
Western Sahara ... 8, 20, 23, 66, 455, 457
Willemstad 476
Windhoek 465, 467
Wuhan 159, 173
Württemberg 271
Wuxi 174

X

Xian 176
Xiangxiang 173
Xiantao 173
Xining 176
Xintai 172
Xuzhou 174

Y

Yakutia 547
Yamalo-Nenets 547
Yamoussoukro 208
Yangcheng 177
Yangtze River 162, 168, 173, 178
Yaounde 140
Yap 443
Yellow River 172, 175, 176
Yellow Sea 175, 177
Yerevan 79, 81
Yinchuan 175
Yobe 494
Yokohama 1
Yueyang 173
Yulin 170
Yunnan 159, 178, 180, 464

Z

Zacatecas 441
Zagorjé 213
Zagreb 212
Zambezi River 419, 458, 460
Zamfara 494
Zanzibar 615-617
Zaozhuang 177
Zhanjiang 170
Zhengzhou 172
Zhongshan 170
Zibo 177
Zigong 178
Zomba 421
Zug 610
Zürich 607, 609